Research on Fuzzy Logic and Mathematics with Applications II

Research on Fuzzy Logic and Mathematics with Applications II

Guest Editor

Saeid Jafari

MDPI

Basel • Beijing • Wuhan • Barcelona • Belgrade • Novi Sad • Cluj • Manchester

Guest Editor
Saeid Jafari
Mathematics and Philosophy Department
College of Vestsjaelland South
Slagelse
Denmark

Editorial Office
MDPI AG
Grosspeteranlage 5
4052 Basel, Switzerland

This is a reprint of the Special Issue, published open access by the journal *Symmetry* (ISSN 2073-8994), freely accessible at: https://www.mdpi.com/journal/symmetry/special_issues/Research_Fuzzy_Logic_Mathematics_Applications_2.

For citation purposes, cite each article independently as indicated on the article page online and as indicated below:

Lastname, A.A.; Lastname, B.B. Article Title. *Journal Name* **Year**, *Volume Number*, Page Range.

ISBN 978-3-7258-5331-1 (Hbk)
ISBN 978-3-7258-5332-8 (PDF)
https://doi.org/10.3390/books978-3-7258-5332-8

Contents

About the Editor

Saeid Jafari

My name is Saeid Jafari and I am a Professor of Mathematics at the College of Vestsjaelland South, as well as Director of the Mathematical and Physical Science Foundation (www.topositus.com). My research interests include topology, fuzzy, neutrosophic and digital topologies, graph theory and functional analysis, fractional differential equations, differential geometry, symplectic geometry, mathematical aspects of particle physics, the Philosophy of Science and the philosophical aspects of quantum field theory. These areas form the foundation of the various projects and research endeavors I regularly undertake, and I have published many research papers and book chapters on these topics.

symmetry

MDPI

Editorial

Research on Fuzzy Logic and Mathematics with Applications II

Saeid Jafari

College of Vestsjaelland South & Mathematical and Physical Science Foundation, 4200 Slagelse, Denmark; saeidjafari@topositus.com

Preface

The notion of a non-rigid fuzzy set was introduced by Lotfi A. Zadeh [1] in 1965. In order to analyze the imprecision, fuzzy sets are promising since they have no fixed extension, and also the laws of consistency and the excluded middle do not work. It is well known that in daily life and also in scientific thinking, we time and again encounter concepts which are ambulant, mobile, flexible, and dialectical. The problem of how to formalize such non-rigid concepts emerged. Tackling this problem gave rise to the concept of the fuzzy set, which adds to the classical two-valued logic an infinite-valued logic to take care of non-rigid objects and reflects the concepts (with non-fixed extension) of the objective reality, i.e., an infinite value of truth lying in the interval from 1 to 0. Zadeh is also the founder of fuzzy logic [2–4]. Since the advent of the notion of the fuzzy set, Zadeh and other researchers have used this important set and established a great deal of interesting research in fuzzy logic, fuzzy topology, fuzzy arithmetics, etc. This Special Issue deals with fuzzy logic and mathematics, with applications in decision making, data mining, graph theory, risk assessment, information theory, and other engineering applications.

In this present issue, there are 22 research articles: "Research on Fuzzy Logic and Mathematics with Applications II" of the MDPI *Symmetry* journal. In what follows, we will provide a brief account of their results and findings.

In Contribution 1, "Bipolar Spherical Fuzzy Soft Topology with Applications to Multi-Criteria Group Decision-Making in Building Risk Assessment", Adem Yolcu presents a bipolar spherical fuzzy soft set as well as a bipolar spherical fuzzy soft topology. In this respect, the author introduces several new, useful, and important notions, such as a bipolar spherical fuzzy soft intersection, a bipolar spherical fuzzy soft null set, a spherical fuzzy soft absolute set, and other operations on bipolar spherical fuzzy soft sets, including the bipolar spherical fuzzy soft open set, the bipolar spherical fuzzy soft closes set, etc. Furthermore, the author sets forth a group decision-making algorithm based on the TOPSIS (Technique of Order Preference by Similarity to an Ideal Solution) approach to problem solving along with a numerical example to justify the applicability of the suggested approach.

In Contribution 2, "Some Properties of Cubic Fuzzy Graphs with an Applications", the authors Xiaolong Shi, Maryam Akhoundi, Ali Asghar Talebi, and Seyed Hossein Sadati introduce the notion of the Wiener index in a cubic fuzzy graph as a cubic fuzzy number. They also offer some properties in this regard. They discuss a comparison between a connectivity index and the Wiener index, changes in the Wiener index by deleting a node or an edge, and determining the Wiener index in some specific cubic fuzzy graphs. Moreover, they utilize the concepts of the saturated cubic fuzzy cycle to determine the Wiener index. They provide an application of the Wiener index to investigate the properties of some monomer molecules.

In Contribution 3, "Prioritized Aggregation Operators for Intuitionistic Fuzzy Information Based on Aczel–Alsina T-Norm and T-Conorm and Their Applications in Group Decision-Making", the authors Mehwish Sarfraz, Kifayat Ullah, Maria Akram, Dragan Pamucar, and Darko Božanić focus on proposing prioritized aggregation operators (AOs) for intuitionistic fuzzy (IF) information. More specifically, they propose IF-prioritized Aczel–Alsina averaging (IFPAAA) and IF-prioritized Aczel–Alsina geometric (IFPAAG) operators and present the fact that these AOs fulfill the basic features of aggregation. Moreover, they also study some results related to these AOs. The authors not only give an application used in an MADM (multi-attribute decision-making) problem but also provide a comparison of the proposed AOs with other well-known AOs to show the significance of the IFPAAA and IFPAAG operators.

In Contribution 4, "Novel Complex Pythagorean Fuzzy Sets under Aczel–Alsina Operators and Their Application in Multi-Attribute Decision Making", Huanhuan Jin, Abrar Hussain, Kifayat Ullah, and Aqib Javed offer a detailed explanation of the notion of the Aczel–Alsina t-norm and t-conorm under the system of complex Pythagorean fuzzy sets. They obtain some basic operational laws of the Aczel–Alsina t-norm and t-conorm. They discuss some aggregation operators of complex Pythagorean fuzzy sets, and in order to solve an MADM (multi-attribute decision making) technique, the authors construct an example. Further, through a comparison between the results of the AOs and the new ones, they show the preferences of the proposed AOs established in this article.

In Contribution 5, "Confidence Levels-Based Cubic Fermatean Fuzzy Aggregation Operators and Their Application to MCDM Problems", the authors Harish Garg, Muhammad Rahim, Fazli Amin, Saeid Jafari, and Ibrahim M. Hezam focus largely on the utilization of cubic Fermatean fuzzy set features to resolve two kinds of problems: knowledge of rating domains and the performance of rating objects (called confidence levels). The authors introduce information aggregation operators with confidence degrees to cope with the ambiguous information of the aggregated arguments. They propose two AOs, i.e. the confidence cubic Fermatean fuzzy weighted averaging operator and the confidence cubic Fermatean fuzzy weighted geometric operator, using them as a framework to create an MCDM (multi-criteria decision-making) process supported by an example showing how effective and applicable it is.

In Contribution 6, "A Novel GDMD-PROMETHEE Algorithm Based on the Maximizing Deviation Method and Social Media Data Mining for Large Group Decision Making", Juxiang Wang, Si Li, and Xiangyu Zhou propose not only a new generalized probabilistic hybrid distance measure method based on Hamming distance but also an extended GDMD-PROMETHEE large-scale multi-attribute group decision-making method. The latter is based on the former. These are proposed due to the complexity of emergency-handling decision making and the asymmetry of user evaluation information. They calculate the objective weight of decision makers and also the comprehensive weights of the attributes. They provide a realization of the distance measures and information fusion of probabilistic linguistic term sets under a cumulative prospect theory and the ranking results of the emergency-handling plans based on the extended GDMD-PROMETHEE algorithm. In this respect, they provide and discuss a case study of the explosion-accident-handling decision making of Shanghai "6.18" Petrochemical to show the advantages of their algorithm with respect to the traditional ones.

In Contribution 7, "Fermatean Fuzzy CODAS Approach with Topology and Its Application to Sustainable Supplier Selection", Hafiz Muhammad Athar Farid, Mohamed Bouye, Muhammad Riaz, and Nimra Jamil establish the new notion of Fermatean fuzzy topology based on the class of Fermatean fuzzy sets. It is worth mentioning that a Fermatean fuzzy set (FFS) is a reliable method for representing uncertainty in "multi-criteria decision-making" (MCDM). The authors introduced and studied several new and important notions in the context of FFT. Moreover, they proposed a technique based on a Fermatean fuzzy "combinative distance-based assessment" to deal with multiple challenges in sustainable supply chain management. Among others, they develop an application to show the benefit of the suggested supplier selection approach.

In Contribution 8, "Multiple-Attribute Decision Making Based on Intuitionistic Hesitant Fuzzy Connection Set Environment", Wajid Ali, Tanzeela Shaheen, Iftikhar Ul Haq, Hamza Ghazanfar Toor, Faraz Akram, Saeid Jafari, Md. Zia Uddin, and Mohammad Mehedi Hassan propose the suitability of combining the intuitionistic hesitant fuzzy set (IHFS) and set pair analysis (SPA) theories in multi-attribute decision making (MADM) and present a hybrid model named intuitionistic hesitant fuzzy connection number set (IHCS). They also pinpoint the benefits of their proposed work and provide a graphical interpretation to show the consistency and efficiency of their approach.

In Contribution 9, "Application of the Double Fuzzy Sawi Transform for Solving a Telegraph Equation", Atanaska Tencheva Georgieva and Albena Pavlova offered a new double fuzzy transform called the double fuzzy Sawi transform and presented some basic properties of both the single fuzzy Sawi transform and the double fuzzy Sawi transform. They also obtained the exact solution of a non-homogeneous linear fuzzy telegraph equation under a generalized Hukuhara partial differentiability. They exhibited with examples, utilizing the symmetric triangular fuzzy numbers, the validity and superiority of the double fuzzy Sawi transform in solving the fuzzy linear telegraph equation.

In Contribution 10, "Cosine Similarity Measures of (m, n)-Rung Orthopair Fuzzy Sets and Their Applications in Plant Leaf Disease Classification", Arpan Singh Rajput, Shailja Shukla, and Samajh Singh Thakur study ten similarity measures that employ cosine and cotangent functions for comparing (m, n)-rung orthopair fuzzy sets. They used the proposed weighted similarity measures for real-world problems in building-material analysis. Further, they performed a comparative analysis between the proposed measures, demonstrating the efficiency of them with respect to the existing ones.

In Contribution 11, "Choquet Integral-Based Aczel–Alsina Aggregation Operators for Interval-Valued Intuitionistic Fuzzy Information and Their Application to Human Activity Recognition", Harish Garg, Tehreem, Gia Nhu Nguyen, Tmader Alballa, and Hamiden Abd El-Wahed Khalifa investigate the problem of human activity recognition (HAR). In this respect, they use the proposed theory of Aczel and Alsina—the Aczel–Alsina norms—and the derived theory of Choquet. They demonstrate not only some characteristics and features of the presented techniques but also utilizing these techniques to evaluate the HAR multiattribute decision-making complications. By applying a functional model for HAR problems, they demonstrate a two-folded goal: to justify the evaluated approaches and also their efficiency.

In Contribution 12, "Fuzzy Soft Sets and Decision Making in Ideal Nutrition", Abdelfattah A. El-Atik, Radwan Abu-Gdairi, Arafa A. Nasef, Saeid Jafari, and Mohammed Badr apply the fuzzy set theory with respect to the selection of a burning problem for the nutrition of students in decision making. They show the supremacy and effectiveness of their approach compared with other approaches.

In Contribution 13, "Multi-Attribute Group Decision Making Based on Spherical Fuzzy Zagreb Energy", Gang Fang, Uzma Ahmad, Sobia Ikhlaq, and Leila Asgharsharghi expand the notion of fuzzy Zagreb indices of the fuzzy graph to the spherical fuzzy Zagreb indices of the spherical fuzzy graph (SFG) to better handle some real-world problems. By using examples, they define the spherical fuzzy Zagreb matrix of SFG and Zagreb energy of SFG. They develop several lower and upper bounds of the spherical Zagreb energy of SFG and offer an application of SFG by computing the Zagreb energy in a decision-making problem.

In Contribution 14, "Baire Category Soft Sets and Their Symmetric Local Properties", Zanyar A. Ameen and Mesfer H. Alqahtani focus on the study of soft sets of the first and second Baire categories. They establish the main properties of soft sets. They introduce some types of soft points, where soft sets are of the first or second category. They present several interesting, useful, and important results.

In Contribution 15, "Fuzzy Logic and Its Application in the Assessment of Information Security Risk of Industrial Internet of Things", Seyit Kerimkhulle, Zhulduz Dildebayeva, Akylbek Tokhmetov, Akzhibek Amirova, Jamalbek Tussupov, Ulzhan Makhazhanova, Alibek Adalbek, Roman Taberkhan, Alma Zakirova, and Alua Salykbayeva concentrate on the issue of information security in the Industrial Internet of Things (IIoT) environment. They perform an information security risk assessment in the IIoT. Indeed, the authors analyze the information security threats for IIoT systems and set forth a proposed method. They provide examples of calculating the information security risk assessment in the IIoT environment based on this method and state that their proposed approach can be used as a foundation for creating expert decision support systems for designing IIoT systems.

In Contribution 16, "A Novel Concept of Level Graph in Interval-Valued Fuzzy Graphs with Application", Yongsheng Rao, Siran Lei, Ali Asghar Talebi, and Masomeh Mojahedfar study the level graph of an interval-valued fuzzy graph (IVFG), since many practical problems can be modeled and solved using the IVFG. In this regard, they investigate four operations: the Cartesian product, composition, union, and join. Moreover, they offer an application of the IVFG in order to spot the most effective person in a hospital information system.

In Contribution 17, "Bipolar Fuzzy Supra Topology via (Q-) Neighborhood and Its Application in Data Mining Process", Banu Pazar Varol and Hami Malkoç investigate the neighborhood structures in bipolar fuzzy supra-topological space and exhibit the usefulness and applicability of bipolar fuzzy supra-topology to the medical diagnosis problem. They introduce some new and useful notions, and the obtained results are interesting. Moreover, the characterization of bipolar fuzzy supra-topological space in terms of quasi-neighborhoods is also given.

In Contribution 18, "An Introduction to Single-Valued Neutrosophic Primal Theory", Fahad Alsharari, Hanan Alohali, Yaser Saber, and Florentin Smarandachenn investigate the interconnection among the single-valued neutrosophic grill, single-valued neutrosophic primal, and their stratification. By introducing the notion of a single-valued neutrosophic primal, they create a broader framework than the fuzzy primal and intuitionistic fuzzy primal. They also offer, among others, a new notion of the single-valued neutrosophic primal topology and obtain several interesting and important results.

In Contribution 19, "A Novel Neutrosophic Likert Scale Analysis of Perceptions of Organizational Distributive Justice via a Score Function: A Complete Statistical Study and Symmetry Evidence Using Real-Life Survey Data", Seher Bodur, Selçuk Topal, Hacı Gürkan, and Seyyed Ahmad Edalatpanah introduce a new area of research in social science and use ten questions measuring distributive justice on classical Likert and neutrosophic Likert scales consisting of two subdimensions—distributive and procedural justice. The provided a comparison between the neutrosophic scale and the traditional Likert scale. They also discuss the symmetric and non-symmetric properties of statistical analysis in addition to general symmetric and non-symmetry properties. The authors believe that the new notion of neutrosophic Likert scale and the survay approach have som advantages what concerns collecting detailed and sensitive information on many topics, such as economics, health and etc.

In Contribution 20, "On Neutrosophic Fuzzy Metric Space and Its Topological Properties", Samriddhi Ghosh, Sonam, Ramakant Bhardwaj, and Satyendra Narayan introduce and study a generalized metric space called neutrosophic fuzzy metric space. They obtained several new and important properties and establish counterparts of well-known theorems, such as the Uniform Convergence Theorem and the Baire Category Theorem, in the context of the neutrosophic fuzzy metric space.

In Contribution 21, "A New Fuzzy Bayesian Inference Approach for Risk Assessments", Jintao Xu, Yang Sui, Tao Yu, Rui Ding, Tao Dai, and Mengyan Zheng propose a new fuzzy Bayesian network (BN) inference approach for risk assessments since they realized that BN cannot deal with the uncertain, fuzzy, random, and conflicting information from experts' knowledge in the process of conducting a risk assessment. They obtain some BN inference results, which they analyze by utilizing the proposed algorithm, and two common BN inference algorithms, which the authors establish in the paper. Moreover, they validate the effectiveness of the proposed approach.

In Contribution 22, "Research on Heave Compensation System Based on Switched Reluctance Motor", Juan Chen, Lai Jiang, and Xiaoping Zhang offer a composite control strategy based on a switched-reluctance motor (SRM)-driven active heave compensation device to live up to the requirements of the marine work platform for real-time control, time-varying speed, and the time-varying torque control of the motor-driven active heave compensation device. They use a model prediction trajectory algorithm to predict the compensation displacement obtained using the dynamic model and consider some other necessary matters. Moreover, they verify the system feasibility by setting different wave parameters.

Conflicts of Interest: The author declares no conflicts of interest.

List of Contributions:

1. Yolcu, A. Bipolar Spherical Fuzzy Soft Topology with Applications to Multi-Criteria Group Decision-Making in Buildings Risk Assessment. *Symmetry* **2022**, *14*, 2362.
2. Shi, X.; Akhoundi, M.; Talebi, A.A.; Sadati, S. H. Some Properties of Cubic Fuzzy Graphs with an Application. *Symmetry* **2022**, *14*, 2623.
3. Sarfraz, M.; Ullah, K.; Akram, M.; Pamcur, D.; Božanić, D. Prioritized Aggregation Operators for Intuitionistic Fuzzy Information Based on Aczel–Alsina T-Norm and T-Conorm and Their Applications in Group Decision-Making. *Symmetry* **2022**, *14*, 2655.
4. Jin, H.; Hussain, A.; Ullah, K.; Javed, A. Novel Complex Pythagorean Fuzzy Sets under Aczel–Alsina Operators and Their Application in Multi-Attribute Decision Making. *Symmetry* **2023**, *15*, 68.
5. Garg, H.; Rahim, M.; Amin, F.; Jafari, S.; Hazem, I.M. Confidence Levels-Based Cubic Fermatean Fuzzy Aggregation Operators and Their Application to MCDM Problems. *Symmetry* **2023**, *15*, 260.
6. Wang, J.; Li, S.; Zhou, X. A Novel GDMD-PROMETHEE Algorithm Based on the Maximizing Deviation Method and Social Media Data Mining for Large Group Decision Making. *Symmetry* **2023**, *15*, 387.
7. Frid, H. M. A.; Bouye M.; Riaz, M.; Jamil, N. Fermatean Fuzzy CODAS Approach with Topology and Its Application to Sustainable Supplier Selection. *Symmetry* **2023**, *15*, 433.
8. Ali, W.; Shaheen, T.; Ul Haq, I.; Toor, H. G.; Akram, F.; Jafari, S.; Zia Uddin, Md., Hassan, M.M. Multiple-Attribute Decision Making Based on Intuitionistic Hesitant Fuzzy Connection Set Environment. *Symmetry* **2023**, *15*, 778.

9. Georgieva, A.T.; Pavlova, A. Application of the Double Fuzzy Sawi Transform for Solving a Telegraph Equation. *Symmetry* **2023**, *15*, 854.
10. Rajput, A.S.; Shukla, S.; Thakur, S.S. Cosine Similarity Measures of (m, n)-Rung Orthopair Fuzzy Sets and Their Applications in Plant Leaf Disease Classification. *Symmetry* **2023**, *15*, 1385.
11. Garg, H.; Tahreem.; Nguyen, G.N.; Alballa, T.; Abd El-Wahed Khalifa, H. Choquet Integral-Based Aczel–Alsina Aggregation Operators for Interval-Valued Intuitionistic Fuzzy Information and Their Application to Human Activity Recognition. *Symmetry* **2023**, *15*, 1438.
12. El-Atik, A.A.; Abu-Gdairi, R.; Nasef, A.A.; Jafari, S.; Badr, M. Fuzzy Soft Sets and Decision Making in Ideal Nutrition. *Symmetry* **2023**, *15*, 1523.
13. Fang, G.; Ahmad, U.; Ikhlaq, S.; Asgharsharghi, L. Multi-Attribute Group Decision Making Based on Spherical Fuzzy Zagreb Energy. *Symmetry* **2023**, *15*, 1536.
14. Ameen, Z.A.; Alqahtani, M.H. Baire Category Soft Sets and Their Symmetric Local Properties. *Symmetry* **2023**, *15*, 1810.
15. Kerimkhulle, S.; Dildebayeva, Z.; Tokhmetov, A.; Amirova, A.; Tussupov, J.; Makhazhanova, U.; Adalbek, A.; Taberkhan, R.; Zakirova, A.; Salybayeva, A. Fuzzy Logic and Its Application in the Assessment of Information Security Risk of Industrial Internet of Things. *Symmetry* **2023**, *15*, 1958.
16. Rao, Y.; Lei, S.; Talebi, A.A.; Mojahedfar, M. A Novel Concept of Level Graph in Interval-Valued Fuzzy Graphs with Application. *Symmetry* **2023**, *15*, 2106.
17. Varol, B.P.; Malkoç, H. Bipolar Fuzzy Supra Topology via (Q-) Neighborhood and Its Application in Data Mining Process. *Symmetry* **2024**, *16*, 216.
18. Alsharari, F.; Alohali, H.; Saber, Y.; Smarandache, F. An Introduction to Single-Valued Neutrosophic Primal Theory. *Symmetry* **2024**, *16*, 402.
19. Bodur, S.; Topal, S. Gürken, H.; Edalatpanah, S. A. A Novel Neutrosophic Likert Scale Analysis of Perceptions of Organizational Distributive Justice via a Score Function: A Complete Statistical Study and Symmetry Evidence Using Real-Life Survey Data. *Symmetry* **2024**, *16*, 598.
20. Ghosh, S.; Sonam.; Bhardwaj, R.; Narayan, S. On Neutrosophic Fuzzy Metric Space and Its Topological Properties. *Symmetry* **2024**, *16*, 613.
21. Xu, J.; Sui, Y.; Yu, T.; Ding, R.; Dai, T.; Zheng, M. A New Fuzzy Bayesian Inference Approach for Risk Assessments. *Symmetry* **2024**, *16*, 786.
22. Chen, J.; Jiang, L.; Zhang, X. Research on Heave Compensation System Based on Switched Reluctance Motor. *Symmetry* **2024**, *16*, 1256.

References

1. Zadeh, L.A. Fuzzy Sets. *Inf. Control* **1965**, *8*, 338–353. [CrossRef]
2. Zadeh, L.A. Outline of new approach to the Analysis of Complex Systems and Decision. *Processes* **1973**, *1*, 28–44. [CrossRef]
3. Zadeh, L.A. Fuzzy algorithms. *Inf. Control* **1968**, *12*, 94–102. [CrossRef]
4. Zadeh, L.A. Making computers think like people. *IEEE Spectr.* **1984**, *8*, 26–32. [CrossRef]

symmetry

MDPI

Article

Research on Heave Compensation System Based on Switched Reluctance Motor

Juan Chen [1,2,*], Lai Jiang [1] and Xiaoping Zhang [1]

[1] School of Information and Electrical Engineering, Hunan University of Science and Technology, Xiangtan 411201, China; 20020401007@mail.hnust.edu.cn (L.J.); xpzhang@hnust.edu.cn (X.Z.)
[2] Key Laboratory of Metallogenic Prediction of Nonferrous Metals and Geological Environment Monitoring, Central South University, Ministry of Education, Changsha 410083, China
* Correspondence: chenjuan@hnust.edu.cn; Tel.: +86-18684882476

Abstract: Aiming at the requirements of the marine work platform for real-time control, time-varying speed and the time-varying torque control of the motor-driven active heave compensation device, this paper introduces a composite control strategy based on the switched reluctance motor (SRM)-driven active heave compensation device. As for the compensation error caused by the time lag in the real-time system, the model prediction trajectory algorithm is used to predict the compensation displacement obtained using the dynamic model. The next time, the control parameters are then provided for the SRM control system in advance to reduce the compensation error. The SRM control strategy selects a double closed-loop compound control strategy of Back Propagation (BP) fuzzy neural network Proportion Integration Differentiation (PID) control. Its outer speed loop uses a fuzzy controller to quickly track a wide range of speed changes. The torque inner loop uses BP neural network adaptive PID control. This helps to reduce torque ripple and to ensure that the electromagnetic torque output of the SRM remains stable. Finally, the system feasibility is verified by setting different wave parameters. The simulation results show that the simulation conditions can reach 97.5% and 96.4% under the 3 and 4 wave levels, respectively. The simulation effect is satisfying, which verifies the feasibility of the proposed scheme.

Keywords: active heave compensation (AHC); SRM; model prediction trajectory generation; fuzzy control; BP neural network; adaptive PID control

1. Introduction

The heave compensation device is a tool used to assist the stable operation of underwater workload. It is of great significance when the development of marine resources means facing the deep sea [1]. In order to overcome the influence of strong nonlinear interference such as sea wind and waves on the normal operation of heave compensation equipment, the active heave compensation drive device often works in the operating conditions of frequent braking, acceleration and deceleration and reciprocating operation. SRM has the advantages of a small starting current, a large starting torque, a simple structure, high efficiency, strong fault tolerance and a wide speed-regulation range, which is suitable for the active heave compensation drive system of ocean winches. The symmetry of the stator and rotor position design of SRM reduces the estimated response time of the stator and rotor position, and improves the dynamic response performance of the motor when different phase currents are switched during operation.

However, in the heave compensation system, the motor is in the operation state of time-varying speed, time-varying torque, and the torque ripple phenomenon is remarkable. The research on SRM mainly focuses on this. Several researchers have proposed different control strategies. Sun et al. designed a nonsingular terminal sliding mode controller for direct torque control [2]. This method achieves SRM high-quality tracking at high speed. An innovative fuzzy controller model is proposed in [3]. The torque pulsation control effect of a sliding mode controller with improved reaching law is compared with that of a new fuzzy controller. It is verified that the fuzzy control model significantly improves the torque performance and reduces the torque fluctuation. Rajendran A et al. designed fuzzy and PI controllers for switched reluctance motor, and compared and analyzed their performance characteristics under such parameters as torque, current, stator current and speed of switched reluctance motor, and verified the control performance of fuzzy and PI controllers [4]. Jing et al. designed a fuzzy indirect instant torque controller to suppress torque ripple. Through comparison and analysis with the traditional proportional differential indirect instant torque controller, the effectiveness of the fuzzy indirect instant torque controller in suppressing torque ripple was verified [5]. Senthil et al. proposed a hybrid observer (HO) method for observing high and low motor speeds, respectively. The adaptive neural fuzzy interference system (ANFIS) and Fuzzy-PID are used to estimate the sensorless velocity error and position error of 6/4 pole SRM, and good results are obtained [6]. In order to suppress the torque pulsation of the switched reluctance motor and improve the effective torque, Akar et al. added a fuzzy logic controller (FLC) to the design of the speed loop of the SRM, which has obvious effects on current control and phase current square sum control [7]. Hence, the fuzzy-PID method is proved to be effective in suppressing torque ripple.

Considering the complexity of the operating environment, as well as the system's high hysteresis, time variability, and nonlinear difficulties, many researchers integrate the Deep Learning algorithm and PID to increase controller performance. Zhang et al. suggested a triple network model to improve the complex dynamic features of PID controllers in the process of temperature object control. The model may output three PID parameters. This model features the single output properties of a TS-type fuzzy neural network, and its algorithm performance outperforms traditional PID, BP neural network PID, and conventional fuzzy neural network PID approaches [8]. In order to more accurately describe the motion state of the vehicle during driving, Jiang et al. designed an adaptive neural network controller to control the body motion state of the suspension, such as acceleration (BA), sprung mass displacement (SMD), unsprung mass displacement (UMD) and dynamic wheel load (DWL) during movement. Compared with the traditional PID control strategy, the adaptive neural network control strategy has better control performance [9]. In order to realize active control and vibration energy collection, Liu et al. designed a PID controller electromagnetic energy regeneration suspension system based on a BP neural network algorithm. Through simulation analysis, the dynamic performance of the vehicle and the energy recovery rate of the vehicle were improved under the condition that the road performance and speed conditions of the system were changed [10]. In order to reduce the impact of vibration on commercial vehicles during driving, Ma et al. proposed a negative stiffness control strategy. In the process of air pressure search, an adaptive fuzzy neural network was used to train the air pressure data, and the optimal air pressure of the air spring under different working conditions was obtained to achieve negative stiffness control [11].

In the process of heave compensation, the electromagnetic torque of SRM changes with the change in speed. The electromagnetic torque is related to the speed, speed change and load torque in the actual operation process [12]. The heave compensation system is a complex and variable nonlinear system [13,14]; the parameters collected by the sensor are processed and the control signal provided to the braking mechanism lags. This gives the motor a wide range of changes in the speed, and its load torque will also change due to the rotation of the motor runner. The PID controller has its advantages in robustness, simplicity and predictability [15,16], but while it is generally suitable for a linear system, in a nonlinear system PID controller, the structure design, anti-interference ability and parameter tuning will encounter challenges. A BP fuzzy neural network PID controller combined with the learning ability of a neural network and adaptive performance can adapt to a complex nonlinear system.

Therefore, this paper uses a fuzzy controller to follow the given speed signal, while the BP neural network PID controller is used in the torque inner loop to ensure the optimal output of the control signal. According to the fact that the motion trajectory of the mother ship is continuous and high-order differentiable in the heave compensation process, the trajectory change in the next control cycle is obtained using the method of model prediction trajectory generation. This paper presents a heave compensation system based on composite control SRM.

The remainder of this paper is organized as follows. In Section 2, the dynamic model of AHC is analyzed, and the specific algorithm of compensation displacement and model prediction trajectory generation is discussed. Section 3 introduces the SRM and details the calculation of the variation law of electromagnetic torque of SRM during heave compensation, which has a reference value for analyzing the variation of torque in the simulation results. In Section 4, the SRM control system is designed. The simulation results are analyzed in Section 5. Finally, conclusions are drawn in Section 6.

2. AHC Model

In this paper, AHC is principally composed of an SRM module, transmission module, control module and sensor module. Its structure is shown in Figure 1. The SRM module consists of SRM and a switch power device, which consists of the accountable power output of the AHC system. The transmission module consists of a drum and a winch, which might properly transmit the power output from the SRM to the cable. The control module is the core of the total system used for sensor data processing, providing correct control signals for the switch power device through algorithms. The sensor is divided into two components. The first component records the system parameters, such as the angle sensor of the SRM used for the feedback of SRM control and the accumulator of the winch used for the supplement of ship heave displacement. The second component consists of the collection of ocean parameters, such as the activity of ocean wave height, the activity of ship heave speed, etc. The total system cooperates to understand the compensation result of AHC.

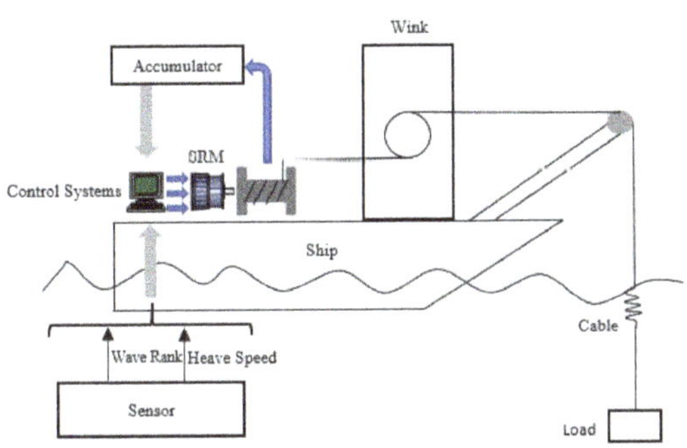

Figure 1. Structure of the active heave compensation system.

2.1. Dynamics Equation of the System

In this paper, the models of the heave compensation system include the marine working system and underwater working load. In order to study the dynamic characteristics between them, a simplified model based on system dynamic change is used. The assumptions for the institution of the system model are as follows: (1) The dynamic changes in the system square measure are analyzed within the one-dimensional direction. Since the ship motion changes within the three-dimensional space, the analysis has remodeled the three-dimensional space and transformed the one-dimensional cable's length change, which is analyzed in Section 2.2. (2) While the heave compensation system works, the cable deformation due to the influence of tension is consistent with the deformation caused by still water. (3) An order of magnitude differences exists between the ship mass and the load mass.

According to the restrictions, the dynamic equilibrium equation of heave compensation system is given by the following [17]:

$$\begin{cases} M_1\ddot{x}_1 + C_{x1}\dot{x}_1 = F_{M1} - M_1 g + K(x_1 - x_2 - r\theta) \\ M_2\ddot{x}_2 + C_{x2}\dot{x}_2 = F_{M2} + K(x_1 - x_2 - r\theta) - M_2 g \end{cases} \quad (1)$$

where M_1 and M_2 are, respectively, the mass of the mother ship and load, x_1 and x_2 are, respectively, the heave displacement of the mother ship and load, C_{x1} and C_{x2} are, respectively, the resistance coefficient of the mother ship subjected to sea water on the sea surface and the resistance coefficient of the loaded carrier water, F_{M1} and F_{M2} are, respectively, the buoyancy of the mother ship and load, K represents the elastic coefficient of the cable and $r\theta$ denotes the tension provided by the compensation system, where r is the runner radius and θ is the rotation angle.

2.2. Mathematical Model of Heave Motion

Under the influence of sea wind and waves, the offshore platform working in waves will produce six degrees of freedom oscillations; heave, sway, surge, yaw, pitch and roll. Among them, the three degrees of freedom of heave, roll and pitch are the main factors causing load fluctuation, while the other three degrees of freedom will be attenuated due to ship attitude control, which can be ignored for calculation simplification

In order to ease the measurement of the attitude change in the hull, the motion monitoring unit (MRU) of the offshore working platform is generally installed on the central axis of the mother ship. The relative position between the winch and MRU will not change when the crane of the heave compensation system is working. Therefore, the change in relative position between the hull and the load can be calculated and analyzed as follows.

The attitude decomposition of a ship show in Figure 2. The three-dimensional coordinate origin $o(0,0,0)$ is set to the position of MRU when it is static, while the winch initial coordinate position is $P(0, Lcos\xi, Lsin\xi)$. The coordinate position of the workload is $Y(x_Y, y_Y, z_Y)$, where L, θ, β and ξ are the absolute distance between the origin and the winch, the forward inclination angle of the mother ship, the heeling angle of the mother ship and the internal angle of the winch relative to the origin, respectively. The three-dimensional motion trajectory p of the winch in the heave motion is given by the following:

$$\begin{cases} x_P = L\cos\xi\sin\beta \\ y_P = L\cos(\theta+\xi) \\ z_P = D_H + L\sin(\theta+\xi) - L\sin\xi(1-\cos\beta) \end{cases} \quad (2)$$

where D_H is the heave displacement change in the mother ship.

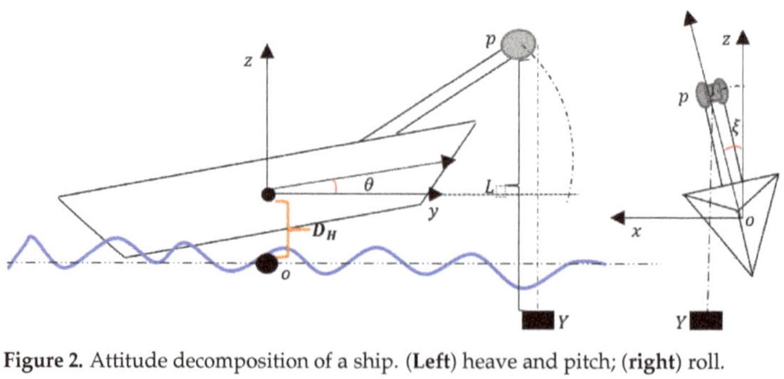

Figure 2. Attitude decomposition of a ship. (**Left**) heave and pitch; (**right**) roll.

Using Equation (2), the distance change between the winch and the working load can be calculated as follows:

$$X_c = \sqrt{(x_P - x_Y)^2 + (y_P - y_Y)^2 + (z_P - z_Y)^2} \tag{3}$$

Generally, due to the mechanical balance, the fluctuation of the underwater working load will only have a displacement change in the vertical direction, which should be eliminated by the heave compensation system. Therefore, in Equation (3), X_c can be used to simplify the calculation, while $x_Y$andy_Y are set to zero. By substituting Equation (2) into Equation (3), the change law of cable length can be computed as follows:

$$\Delta X_c = L_{\text{int}} - X_c \tag{4}$$

$$V_{Cable} = \frac{d\Delta X_c}{dt} \tag{5}$$

where L_{int} is the distance between the winch and the load at the beginning, and V_{Cable} is the change rate of the cable.

2.3. Estimation of the Resulting Vertical Motion

In the heave compensation movement, the winch is mounted on the mothership when full. The track of the winch changes within the three-dimensional system with the influence of the ocean waves on the mothership, inflicting load instability. Consequently, AHC is required to make up for this displacement. The most intuitive expression of displacement compensation is the change in cable length during heave compensation. The three-dimensional coordinate change in the winch can be transformed into the cable length change in the one-dimensional coordinate, using Equations (4) and (5). Continuous and high-order derivable input reference trajectory is required for the prediction of heave displacement trajectory. It can be easily demonstrated that the change in the cable length in Equation (4) meets this requirement. For the next moment, the trajectory prediction is based on the displacement at the sampling time, and the high-order derivative is based on the displacement trend at the sampling point. As shown in Equation (6), the prediction model can be calculated as a matrix, expressed in Equation (7).

$$\begin{aligned}
y(k) &= a_1\dot{y}(k-1) + a_2\ddot{y}(k-1) + \cdots \\
&\quad + a_M \Delta y^{(M)}(K-1), \\
y(k+1) &= a_1\dot{y}(k) + a_2\ddot{y}(k) + \cdots \\
&\quad + a_M y^{(M)}(K) \\
&\quad \cdots, \\
y(k+P) &= a_1\dot{y}(k+P-1) + a_2\ddot{y}(k+P-1) \\
&\quad + \cdots + a_M y^{(M)}(K+P-1) \\
&= \sum_{i=1}^{M} a_i \cdot y^{(i)}(K+P-1)
\end{aligned} \tag{6}$$

According to the principle of predictive control, the output expression is given by the following:

$$\hat{Y}_o = A \cdot Y_o + u \tag{7}$$

such that

$$A = \begin{bmatrix} a_1 & a_2 & \cdots & a_M \end{bmatrix} = \begin{bmatrix} \frac{T}{1!} & \frac{T^2}{2!} & \cdots & \frac{T^M}{M!} \end{bmatrix};$$

$$\hat{Y}_o = \begin{bmatrix} \hat{Y}_o(K) \\ \hat{Y}_o(K+1) \\ \cdots \\ \hat{Y}_o(K+P) \end{bmatrix};$$

$$u = \begin{bmatrix} u(K) \\ u(K+1) \\ \cdots \\ u(K+P-1) \end{bmatrix}; Y_o = \begin{bmatrix} \dot{y}(k-1) & \ddot{y}(k-1) & \cdots & y^{(M)}(K-1) \\ \dot{y}(k) & \ddot{y}(k) & \cdots & y^{(M)}(K) \\ \cdots & \cdots & \cdots & \cdots \\ \dot{y}(k+P-1) & \ddot{y}(k+P-1) & \cdots & y^{(M)}(K+P-1) \end{bmatrix}$$

where $K, K+1, \cdots K+P$ are prediction steps.

The selection of prediction steps should be based on the control cycle selection. As for the track prediction generation described in this paper, the derivation to fourth order can meet the accuracy requirements through simulation tests. In the case where more accuracy is needed, it can be achieved by solving higher order derivatives. However, this will challenge the data computing ability of the control chip.

Two methods exist for solving optimal problems in predictive control. The first method consists of ensuring a fast performance, while the second one ensures a smooth output. In this paper, the first method is used for trajectory tracking. According to the objective function in Equation (8), the weight Q, which guarantees fast performance, should take precedence over the coefficient weight R which guarantees a smooth output.

$$J = \frac{1}{2}\sum_{i=0}^{P} [Y_o(K+i) - \omega(K+i)]^2 \cdot Q + \sum_{j=0}^{M} [u(k+j-1)]^2 \cdot R \tag{8}$$

where ω is the track reference value.

In the SRM AHC system, the power output of the motor, as well as the speed and speed change rate limits, are the constraints of the prediction trajectory, expressed as follows:

$$\begin{aligned} -\delta(K)\cdot n_N &\leq \tfrac{d}{dt}\hat{Y}_o(K) \leq \delta(K)\cdot n_N \\ -\delta(K)\cdot a_N &\leq \tfrac{d^2}{dt^2}\hat{Y}_o(K) \leq \delta(K)\cdot a_N \\ -\delta(K)\cdot j_N &\leq [\hat{Y}_o(K)]''' \leq \delta(K)\cdot j_N \end{aligned} \tag{9}$$

where n_N, a_N, j_N is the rated value of the motor and $\delta(K)$ is the constraint factor, such that $\delta(K) \in [0.95, 1]$.

An additional constraint on the full system life within the operation of the motor exists. This is that the form of the predicted trajectory should be adjacent to the actual trajectory at the previous time, and its high-order derivative cannot be continuously zero. If there is a jump within the reference input such as speed or acceleration, it will directly lead to drastic changes in the phase current of the motor, leading to a power output disorder, which results in irreversible motor damage.

3. SRM Mathematical Model and Reference Torque Calculation

3.1. SRM Mathematical Model

The coupling between the stator coils of the SRM is very weak and the mutual inductance between the two phases can be ignored. Therefore, the voltage balance equation can be established for single-phase windings:

$$\frac{di_K}{dt} = \frac{1}{L}\left(U_K - R_K i_K + i_K \frac{dL_K}{d\theta_m}\omega\right) \tag{10}$$

where U_K is the terminal voltage of phase K winding, R_K denotes phase K winding resistance, i_K represents the phase K winding current, θ_m is the motor angle and ω is a mechanical angular speed.

$$\frac{d\omega}{dt} = \frac{1}{J}(T_e - D\omega - T_L) \tag{11}$$

where T_e is the electromagnetic torque of the motor, J denotes the moment of inertia, D represents the friction coefficient, T_L is the load torque and $\frac{d\omega}{dt}$ is the angular acceleration.

3.2. Variation of Torque

Equation (12) shows that the SRM's rotational balance equation consists of four parts; the electromagnetic torque T_e, load torque T_L, friction torque $D\omega$ inertial torque $J\frac{d\omega}{dt}$, and angular acceleration of the motor a, where the direction of the inertial torque is opposite to the angular acceleration of the motor. In the process of heave compensation, SRM has four operating states, as shown in Figure 3. According to the symmetry of each phase of the motor, the flux characteristics obtained by each phase winding at the same angle are the same. When rotating counterclockwise, the commutation sequence of SRM is A $\rightarrow$ B $\rightarrow$ C. The difference between braking and driving is that when driving, the rotator angle is $0^\circ \sim 45^\circ$, while when braking, the rotator angle is $45^\circ \sim 90^\circ$. When rotating clockwise, the commutation sequence is C $\rightarrow$ B $\rightarrow$ A. The driving angle is $45^\circ \sim 90^\circ$ and the braking angle is $0^\circ \sim 45^\circ$.

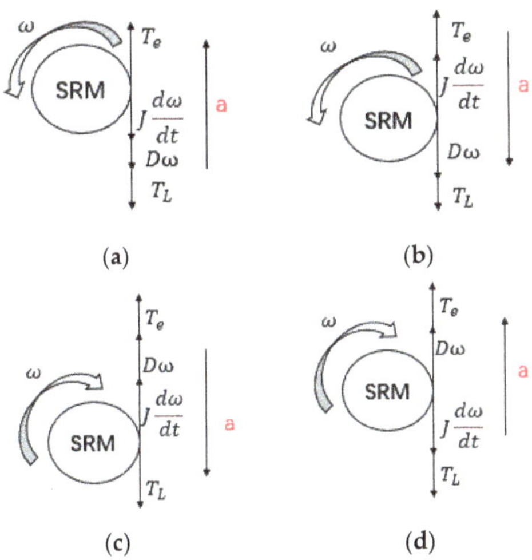

Figure 3. Rotation balance diagram for the four operation modes of SRM. (**a**) Counterclockwise drive. (**b**) Counterclockwise braking. (**c**) Clockwise drive. (**d**) Clockwise braking.

Equation (11) shows that for SRM, a direct conversion relationship between the torque and the speed exists. In addition, the load torque is a potential energy load torque in the heave compensation system. Its direction will not change, while its size will change with the rotation of the winch, following a change rule given by the following:

$$T_L = (M_2 g + M_2 r \frac{d\omega}{dt}) r \tag{12}$$

The variation law of the electromagnetic torque under each operating state of SRM can be obtained using Equations (11) and (12) as follows:

$$\begin{cases} \text{Counterclockwise drive}: & T_e = T_L + J\frac{d\omega}{dt} - D\omega \\ \text{Counterclockwise braking}: & T_e = T_L + J\frac{d\omega}{dt} + D\omega \\ \text{Clockwise drive}: & T_e = T_L - J\frac{d\omega}{dt} + D\omega \\ \text{Clockwise braking}: & T_e = T_L - J\frac{d\omega}{dt} - D\omega \end{cases} \tag{13}$$

$$\begin{cases} T_e = G_O r - \sqrt{(\frac{\xi \mu H \delta^2}{2r})^2 + (\frac{D \mu H \delta}{2r})^2} \sin(\delta t + \varphi) \\ T_e = G_O r - \sqrt{(\frac{\xi \mu H \delta^2}{2r})^2 + (\frac{D \mu H \delta}{2r})^2} \sin(\delta t - \varphi) \\ T_e = G_O r + \sqrt{(\frac{\sigma \mu H \delta^2}{2r})^2 + (\frac{D \mu H \delta}{2r})^2} \sin(\delta t + \psi) \\ T_e = G_O r + \sqrt{(\frac{\sigma \mu H \delta^2}{2r})^2 + (\frac{D \mu H \delta}{2r})^2} \sin(\delta t - \psi) \end{cases} \tag{14}$$

where $\xi = (J + mr^2)$, $\delta = \frac{2\pi}{T}$, $\varphi = arctan(\frac{\xi\delta}{D})$, $\sigma = (J - mr^2)$ and $\psi = arctan(\frac{\sigma\delta}{D})$.

Considering the simulation modeling, it is also necessary to establish the relationship between the drum angle and the electromagnetic torque, replace Equation (12) into Equation (14), and perform the Laplace transformation in order to obtain the transfer function of the drum angle to the electromagnetic torque of SRM:

$$\begin{cases} \frac{\theta_{(s)}}{T_{e(s)}} = \frac{1}{(mr^2 - J)s^2 - Ds} \\ \frac{\theta_{(s)}}{T_{e(s)}} = \frac{1}{(mr^2 + J)s^2 - Ds} \\ \frac{\theta_{(s)}}{T_{e(s)}} = \frac{1}{(mr^2 + J)s^2 + Ds} \\ \frac{\theta_{(s)}}{T_{e(s)}} = \frac{1}{(mr^2 - J)s^2 + Ds} \end{cases} \tag{15}$$

4. Design of the SRM Control System

In this paper, the given speed signal of SRM is time-varying when completing the heave compensation task, and a control strategy of the raPID response and an automatic adjustment of control parameters is needed. Moreover, the electrical characteristics of SRM have a strong nonlinearity, while the classical control strategy is not applicable. Consequently, this paper introduces the compound control strategy of fuzzy control and BP neural network adaptive PID control. $u(t)$ is the control output, K_P denotes the PID control gain, K_I represents the PID integral time constant and K_D is the PID differential time constant. T_{ref} is the reference torque, T is the actual torque and $e(t)$ is the error between them. n^*_{ref} is reference speed, n_T is the actual speed. $y(t)$ is platform heave displacement, $y_0(t)$ is load heave displacement. The structure diagram of the control system is shown in Figure 4.

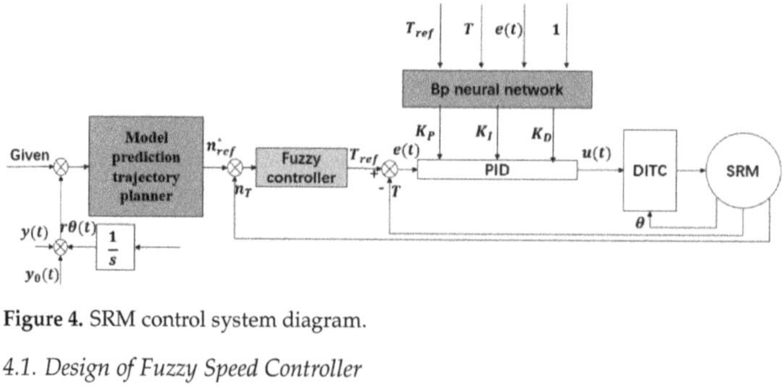

Figure 4. SRM control system diagram.

4.1. Design of Fuzzy Speed Controller

Heave compensation devices are mostly used on the ship for ocean resource acquisition and exploration. The volume of heave compensation devices should not be too large. Therefore, the size of the working motor is also limited. During the motor operation, the given potential transmitted from the heave displacement to the speed will continuously change in a large range.

The maximum output torque of the SRM is limited due to current limitation. Due to the strong nonlinear electrical characteristics of SRM, when the SRM is changing speed and being disturbed, the reluctance of the motor will change when the center line of the salient pole of the rotor and the salient pole of the stator is aligned or staggered. This is because of the symmetry characteristic of the double salient poles of the stator and rotor of the SRM, resulting in a large torque ripple caused by a series of pulse torque superposition which will affect the response speed of SRM. Therefore, in this paper, the control parameters are changed by fuzzy parameter adjustment to suppress the torque ripple and optimize the operation state of SRM. Compared with the traditional PID control, fuzzy control has strong advantages in terms of tracking signals with a large range of changes, based on an expert system. Therefore, according to the characteristics of large-scale variation of the motor speed in the heave compensation system, the fuzzy controller is used in the speed loop control, introduced as follows.

The fuzzy controller adjusts the control parameters based on the expert system, while the control system determines the change law of control quantity through membership degree. The input of the fuzzy system is generally two. The input error ($E_{fuzzy}(t)$ and the deviation of input error $\left(EC_{fuzzy}(t)\right)$ are calculated as follows: $E_{fuzzy}(t) = \left(n^*_{ref} - n_T\right)K_e$, $EC_{fuzzy}(t) = \frac{d\left(n^*_{ref} - n_T\right)}{dt}K_{ec}$. Their membership degree is computed as

$$y^e_{fuzzy}(E_{fuzzy}(t)) = \frac{\sum\limits_{j=1}^{n} E_{fuzzy}(t)M_j(E_{fuzzy}(t))}{\sum\limits_{j=1}^{n} M_j(E_{fuzzy}(t))} \tag{16}$$

$$y^{ec}_{fuzzy}(EC_{fuzzy}(t)) = \frac{\sum\limits_{i=1}^{m} EC_{fuzzy}(t)M_i(EC_{fuzzy}(t))}{\sum\limits_{i=1}^{m} M_i(EC_{fuzzy}(t))} \tag{17}$$

$$U_{fuzzy}(t) = U_{ij}(y^e_{fuzzy}(E_{fuzzy}(t)), y^{ec}_{fuzzy}(EC_{fuzzy}(t))) \tag{18}$$

$$T^*_{ref} = K_u U_{fuzzy}(t) \tag{19}$$

where $M_j\left(E_{fuzzy}(t)\right)$ and $M_i\left(EC_{fuzzy}(t)\right)$ are, respectively, the membership functions of $E_{fuzzy}(t)$ and $EC_{fuzzy}(t)$, calculated using the area center of gravity method.

Equation (18) denotes the output expression of fuzzy control, where $\boldsymbol{U_{ij}}(\boldsymbol{x1}, \boldsymbol{x2})$ is the conversion function from the fuzzy to real number. Equation (19) represents the reference torque calculation. The greatest advantage of fuzzy control is that it can subjectively set the change law of the controller, and the quantization factor can also be modified according to the experimental results, in order to achieve the optimal effect.

The fuzzy controller takes the error between the given speed and the actual speed of SRM and the change rate of the error as the input, and the reference torque as the output. Its structure is shown in Figure 5; the structure adopts the mode of double input and single output, where the input is the error E, the variation of the error EC, the output U, and the quantization factor α. The fuzzy rule table can be changed online by selecting different factors according to the requirements of system control.

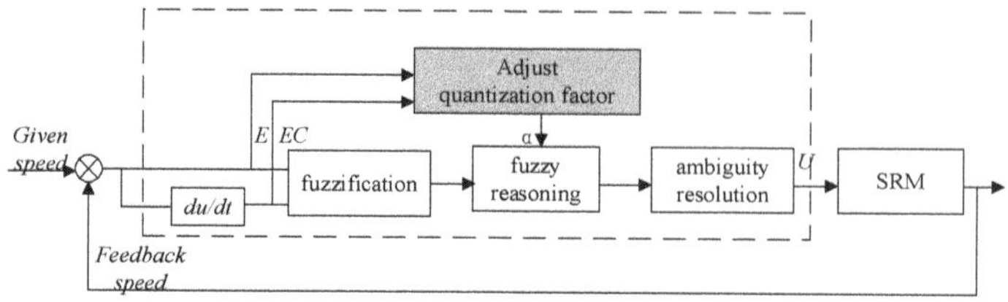

Figure 5. Fuzzy control flow.

According to the motor control principle, when the input speed is greater than the given speed, the expected torque decreases. On the contrary, the torque is expected to increase. Based on the definition of fuzzy control input and output control rules, the control rules are digitized and tabulated in Table 1.

Table 1. Fuzzy control rule.

U		E						
		NL	**NM**	**NS**	**ZE**	**PS**	**PM**	**PL**
EC	NL	NL	NL	NL	NL	NM	NS	ZE
	NM	NL	NL	NL	NM	NS	ZE	PS
	NS	NL	NL	NM	NS	ZE	PS	PM
	ZE	NL	NM	NS	ZE	PS	PM	PL
	PS	NL	NS	ZE	PS	PM	PL	PL
	PM	NL	ZE	PS	PM	PL	PL	PL
	PL	ZE	PS	PM	PL	PL	PL	PL

4.2. Design of BP Neural Network Adaptive PID Controller

One of the most challenging tasks in achieving PID controller stability is designing the three parameters of the controller, which have traditionally been adjusted by experiment and experience and have been extensively studied in the literature, but are mostly used for linear systems [18], and designing an optimal PID controller for nonlinear systems with complex multi-variable characteristics has always been a challenge. The reason is that the nonlinearity, strong coupling and uncertainty of complex multi-variable nonlinear systems make optimizing PID controller parameters difficult [19,20]. The author has solved H∞ control for nonlinear systems and achieved good results. However, if the PID controller adjusts the controller parameters through feedback, the H∞ control may not be accurately satisfied when the feedback gain cannot be guaranteed as small as possible. In practical application, it is complicated to design a PID controller which can solve the H∞ control problem and adapt to the characteristics of a nonlinear system.

In the control of a torque inner loop, because the electrical characteristics of SRM are nonlinear, and the given input in this application is also a time-varying signal, the traditional PID control using fixed PID parameters cannot lead to satisfactory results. The PID parameters are continuously adjusted during the operation of the system in order to make it converge towards the optimal control output. The performance of the whole SRM AHC can then be improved. A BP neural network adaptive PID control is used in the torque inner loop control in order to adjust the PID parameters in real time. The BP neural network has a three-layer structure, as shown in Figure 5. The output layer has four nodes corresponding to the system operation state. The hidden layer has six nodes, while the output layer is composed of three nodes, whose output corresponds to K_P, K_I and K_D, which are the three PID adjustable parameters.

The input vector is given by $x = \left[T_{ref}(k), T(k), e(k), 1 \right]$, where $T_{ref}(k)$ is the reference torque, $T(k)$ is the actual torque and $e(k)$ is the error between them. The input and output of the hidden layer are expressed as follows:

$$\begin{cases} IN_j^{(2)}(k) = \sum\limits_{j=1}^{P} w_{ij}^{(2)}(k) x_j^{(1)}(k) \\ OUT_j^{(2)}(k) = f[IN_i^{(2)}(k)], \quad j = 1, 2 \ldots 6 \end{cases} \tag{20}$$

where $IN_i^{(2)}$ is the hidden layer input, $OUT_i^{(2)}$ is the hidden layer output, $w_{ij}^{(2)}(k)$ denotes the weight of the corresponding hidden layer node, $f[\cdot]$ represents the activation function and $f[\cdot] = \tanh x$.

The input and output of the output layer are given by the following:

$$\begin{cases} IN_l^{(3)}(k) = \sum\limits_{j=1}^{L} w_{jl}^{(3)}(k) OH_i^{(2)}(k) \\ OUT_l^{(3)}(k) = g[IN_l^{(3)}(k)], \quad l = 1, 2, 3 \end{cases} \tag{21}$$

where $IN_l^{(3)}$ is the input of the output layer, $OUT_l^{(3)}$ is the output of the output layer, [out] in the output vector $OUT_1^{(3)}$ is equal to K_P, $OUT_2^{(3)}$ is equal to K_I, $OUT_3^{(3)}$ is equal to K_D, $w_{ji}^{(3)}(k)$ represents the weight of the output layer node and $g[\cdot]$ denotes the activation function of the output layer such that $g[\cdot] = \frac{1}{2}[1 + \tanh x]$.

The performance index function is a quadratic function expressed as follows:

$$J = \frac{1}{2}[T_{ref}^*(k) - T(k)]^2 \tag{22}$$

The steepest descent method is used to update the weight and search according to the negative gradient direction of the weight. The weight Equation (23) of the output layer and the weight Equation (24) of the hidden layer are then obtained:

$$\begin{cases} \Delta w_{jl}^{(3)}(k) = A_{jl}(k) \delta_l^{(3)} x_j^{(1)}(k) + \alpha \Delta w_{jl}^{(3)}(k-1) \\ \delta_l^{(3)} = e(k) \frac{\partial \hat{y}(k)}{\partial u(k)} \frac{\partial u(k)}{\partial OUT_l^{(3)}(k)} g'[IN_l^{(3)}(k)] \end{cases} \tag{23}$$

$$\begin{cases} \Delta w_{ij}^{(2)}(k) = A_{ij}(k) \delta_i^{(2)} x_j^{(1)}(k) + \alpha \Delta w_{ij}^{(2)}(k-1) \\ \delta_i^{(2)} = f'[OUT_j^{(2)}(k)] \sum\limits_{i=1}^{3} \delta_i^{(3)} w_{jl}^{(3)}(k) \end{cases} \tag{24}$$

where $g'[\cdot] = g(x)[1 - g(x)]$ and $f'[\cdot] = [1 - f^2(x)]/2$.

The PID parameters obtained by the BP neural network adaptive algorithm generate the control quantity $u_{(k)}$ using the incremental digital PID control law of Equation (25).

$$u(k) = u(k-1) + \begin{bmatrix} e(k) & -e(k-1) & 0 \\ e(k) & 0 & 0 \\ e(k) & -2e(k-1) & e(k-2) \end{bmatrix} \begin{bmatrix} K_P \\ K_I \\ K_D \end{bmatrix} \tag{25}$$

where $u_{(t)}$ is the control output, $e_{(t)}$ is the error between the actual torque and the given torque, K_P denotes the PID control gain, K_I represents the PID integral time constant and K_D is the PID differential time constant.

5. Results

In this section, the model prediction trajectory algorithm and SRM AHC are simulated. For the model prediction trajectory algorithm, the compensation displacement change obtained in Section 2.2 is used as the input signal, while the predicted displacement change, velocity and error curve between the predicted value and the actual value are, respectively, shown. Practically, the prediction time is set according to the control period of the controller. In this section, in order to make the predicted value different from the input value, the predicted time is set to 0.1 s. The simulation of SRM AHC is used to evaluate the effect of different levels of waves, and to compare the compensation displacement curve with the actual displacement curve. It also shows the compensation error, SRM speed change and torque change curve.

5.1. Fuzzy Controller Performance

The simulation speed is set at 150 r/min and SRM's rated power is 60 kw. The specific parameters of the motor are given in Table 2.

Table 2. The specific parameters of the motor.

Parameters	Value
Stator/rotor poles	6/4
Rated current (A)	260
Resistance of stator (Ω)	0.05
Moment of inertia (kg·m·m)	0.05
Damping coefficient (N·m·s)	0.02
Load torque TL (N·m)	10

As show in Figure 6, due to the large error at startup, the input error E mostly affects the control; PID control has the fastest speed response, but the overshoot is large and the stable speed is slow. Fuzzy-PID control has the fastest speed rise and its performance is stable. The system's dynamic and steady-state quality have substantially improved as a result of fuzzy algorithm optimization; it now has a fast response, minimal overshoot and high steady-state accuracy.

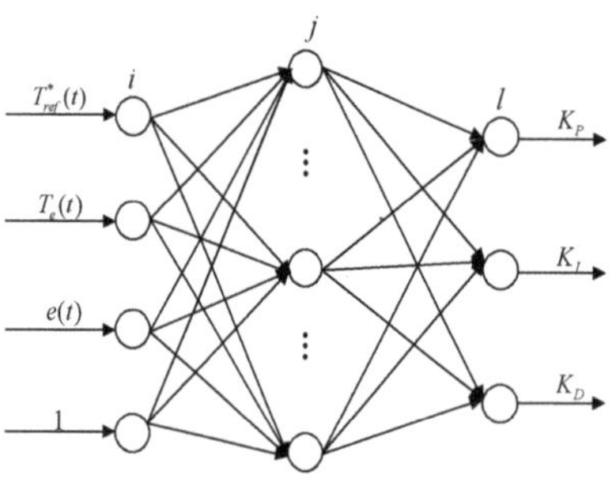

Figure 6. Controller model for the BP neural network adaptive PID.

Figure 7 shows the curves of the speed, torque and current changes in the SRM system using Fuzzy-PID and PID control strategies under normal conditions. From Figure 7a, it can be seen that the rise times of Fuzzy-PID and PID are 0.08 and 0.15, respectively. In the steady state, the torque ripple is about 8.1% and 14% in Figure 7b. The PID produces serious torque ripple in the start-up stage of SRM. From the current change in Figure 7c. It can be seen that the SRM system using the PID control strategy in the start-up stage will enable the phase current to reach the rated value in multiple commutation cycles; the phase current is about 28% in the steady state. For the SRM system using the Fuzzy-PID control strategy in Figure 7d, the torque change in the start-up stage is more optimized than PID control strategies and the phase current is about 10% in the steady state. From the current change in Figure 7e. It can be seen that in the SRM system using the PID control strategy, the flux is about 30% in the steady state. For the SRM system using the Fuzzy-PID control strategy in Figure 7f, the flux change in the start-up stage is more optimized than the PID control strategies and the flux is about 18% in the steady state. According to the speed, torque, current and flux characteristics of SRM, the Fuzzy-PID is more reasonable and improves the working efficiency of the SRM system.

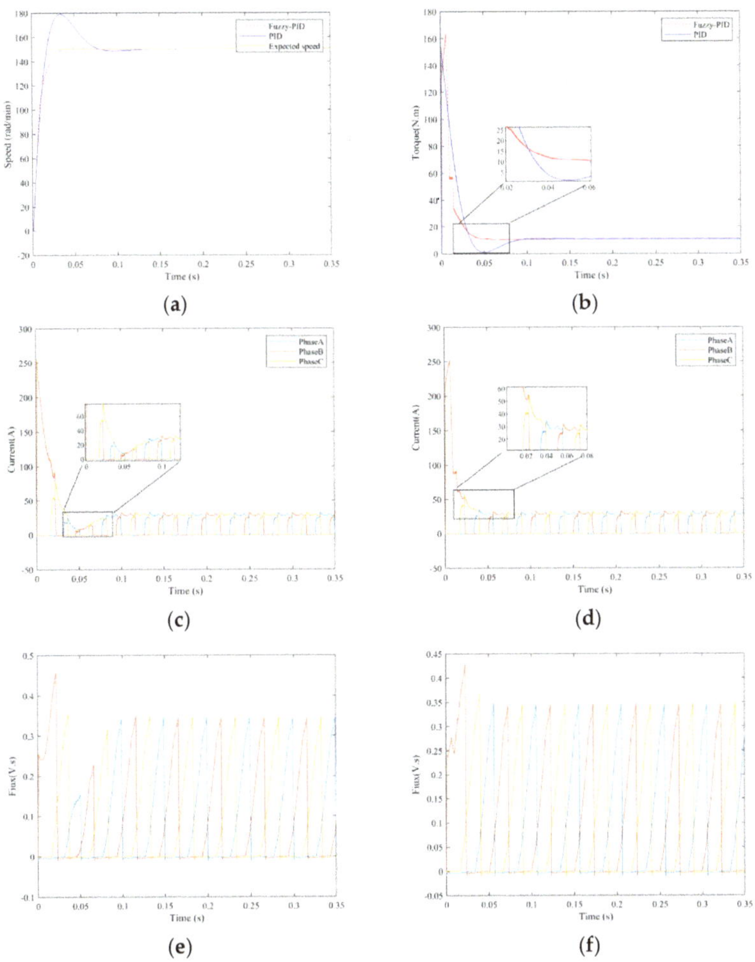

Figure 7. Speed, torque, current and flux comparison of the Fuzzy-PID and PID controllers' performance. (**a**) Speed. (**b**) Torque. (**c**) Current PID. (**d**) Current Fuzzy-PID. (**e**) Fiux PID. (**f**) Fiux Fuzzy-PID.

5.2. Results of the Model Prediction Trajectory

The model prediction trajectory algorithm predicts the change in the displacement trajectory in the $T+1$ control period, based on the displacement in the T sampling period and the high-order derivative of the displacement trend. In this control strategy, the sampling period has a high multiple time relationship with the control period. If the fourth derivative needs to be calculated, the control period should be at least eight times the sampling period. Theoretically, the prediction accuracy is higher with the increase in the derivative order. However, it does not have a high cost performance due to the limitation of the control system.

Figure 8 shows the simulation results of the model prediction trajectory provided by the input signal of Equation (4). In Figure 8a, the red solid line is the actual displacement track, while the blue dotted line is the predicted track. It can be seen that the actual displacement trajectory is similar to the predicted trajectory height. According to the local enlarged graph, the difference between the two curves is only 0.1 s in phase, which is in line with the actual parameter design. It can be seen from the error curve in Figure 8b that when the model prediction trajectory algorithm is running, the error reaches the limit amplitude when there is no sampling information at the starting moment. With the increase in the simulation time, the error is reduced to the normal level. It can also be observed from the simulation results that the model prediction trajectory generator has the characteristics of fast prediction. It can predict the state parameters in the next time with a high precision, as long as the parameters are collected in a certain time.

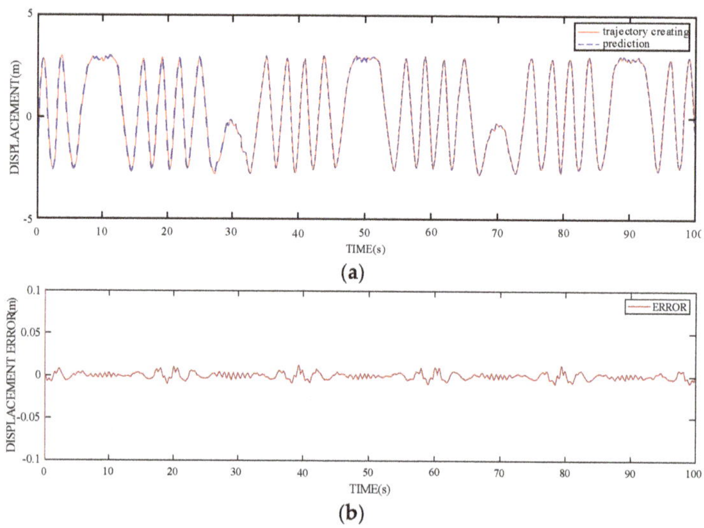

Figure 8. Simulation results of the model prediction trajectory. (**a**) Comparison between the model predicted trajectory and actual displacement trajectory. (**b**) Error curve.

5.3. Results of SRM AHC

The SRM AHC system introduced in this paper is simulated in MATLAB/Simulink, and its feasibility is verified using different wave level parameters. The length of the umbilical cable is 1400 m, and the effective wave height is 1 m and 1.5 m, respectively, under the wave period of 5 s. In the simulation system, the ship heave motion signal uses the analog signal of Section 2.2. It uses the model of Section 2.3 for predicting the trajectory in order to generate early prediction and reduce the compensation error caused by time delay factors. In the simulation, level 3 waves and level 4 waves are set for feasibility verification.

Figures 9 and 10 show the simulation results of SRM AHC under level 3 and level 4 waves, respectively. The curves in Figure 9a represent the actual heave compensation displacement, the SRM AHC displacement and the error. It can be seen that the compensation displacement curve of SRM AHC mainly coincides with the actual heave displacement change curve. In order to verify the heave compensation degree, $\boldsymbol{R}$ is defined as the curve fitting degree coefficient, computed as follows:

$$R = \frac{\sum_{i=1}^{n} (y_i - \hat{y})^2}{\sum_{i=1}^{n} (Y_i - \hat{Y})^2} \times 100\% \quad (26)$$

where y_i is the compensation displacement value, $\hat{y}$ denotes the average value of compensation displacement, Y_i represents the actual displacement value and $\hat{Y}$ is the average of the actual displacement.

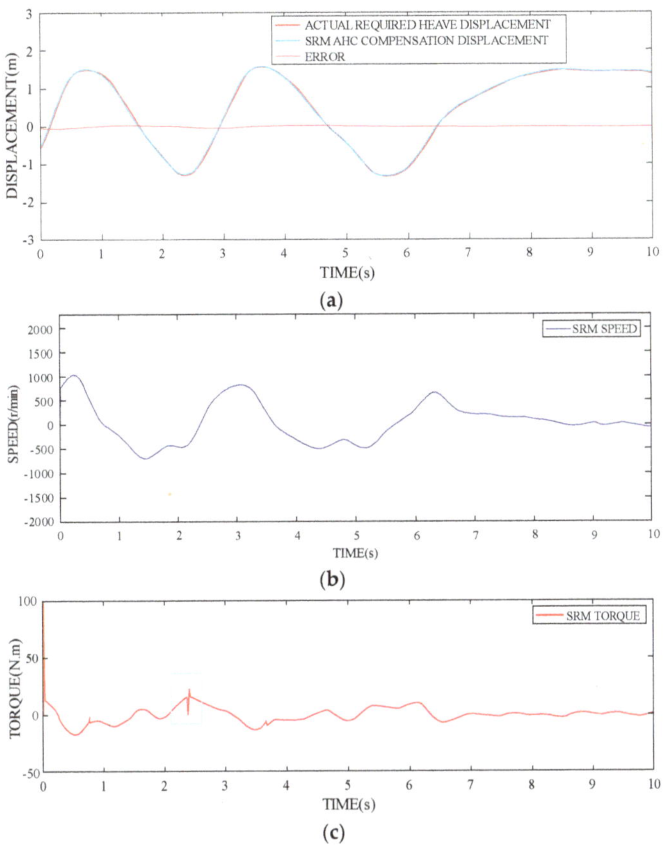

Figure 9. Simulation results of SRM AHC under level 3 waves. (**a**) Comparison between actual required heave compensation displacement curve and SRM AHC displacement curve and error. (**b**) Speed change in SRM AHC. (**c**) Torque change in SRM AHC.

The judgment of fitting quality is performed through R. More precisely, when R approaches 100%, the fitting degree is better.

It can be seen from Figures 9a and 10a that the fitting coefficients of the SRM AHC displacement curve and actual displacement curve reach 97.5% and 96.4%, respectively. Figures 9b and 10b show the speed change in SRM AHC during heave compensation. It can be seen that the speed change is continuous, and the higher the wave level, the larger the speed change range. Therefore, in order to protect the motor from exceeding the rated speed, the proposed SRM AHC can only perform under the sea conditions of a certain level.

Figures 9c and 10c show the variation law of the electromagnetic torque of SRM during heave compensation. In the start-up phase of SRM AHC, in order to make the motor speed track the actual required speed, the start-up electromagnetic torque is very large. When the speed is tracked, the change law of the electromagnetic torque begins to be related to the derivative of the SRM speed change. The torque ripple in the small blue frame appears in the electromagnetic torque change diagram, because the SRM speed is exactly zero when heave compensation is carried out. However, the load torque and speed change rate are not zero. According to the torque balance formula during SRM operation in Equation (11), when the speed is zero, but the load torque and speed change rate are not zero, SRM needs to generate electromagnetic torque for torque balancing. Therefore, torque ripple is generated. When the speed change rate is greater, the peak value of torque ripple is greater, which verifies the reason of torque ripple. For SRM AHC, since the occurrence moment is the zero-speed moment of SRM, and the time of torque ripple is very short, the influence on SRM speed can be ignored. The heave displacement is the integral expression of SRM speed, which has no influence from the simulation results of speed change and compensation displacement change.

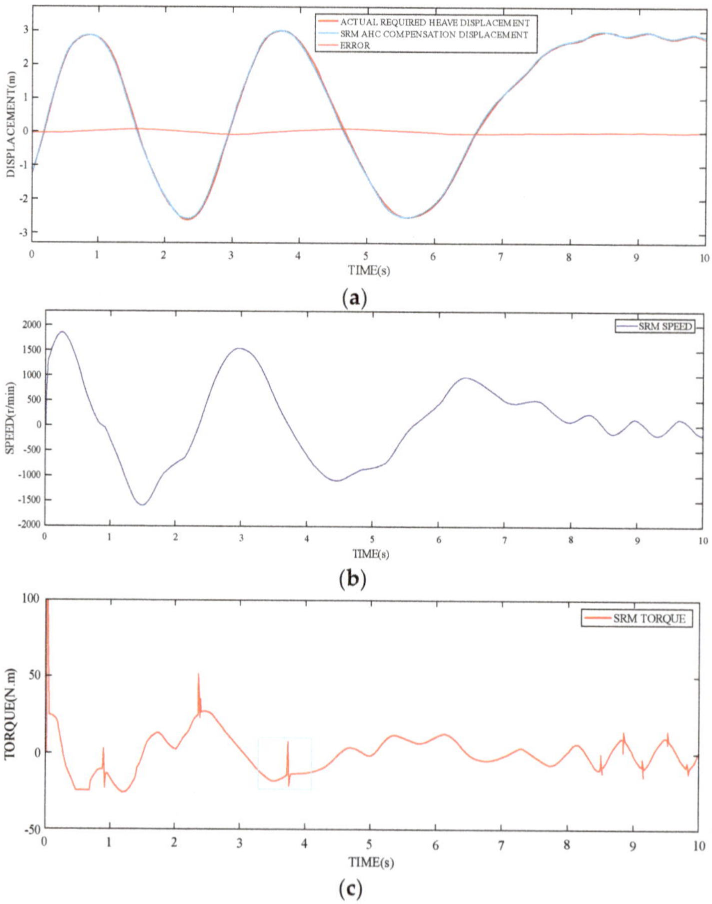

Figure 10. Simulation results of SRM AHC under level 4 waves. (**a**) Comparison between actual required heave compensation displacement curve and SRM AHC displacement curve and error. (**b**) Speed change in SRM AHC. (**c**) Torque change in SRM AHC.

6. Conclusions

This paper proposes a SRM AHC system which uses the model prediction trajectory generation algorithm to generate the heave displacement trajectory of the next control cycle and to reduce the compensation error caused by the time-delay between the sensor and the actuator in the heave compensation process. Because heave compensation has a time-varying speed and a time-varying torque for the motor system, the control strategy of fuzzy and BP neural network adaptive PID control is used for SRM control. The strong robustness of the fuzzy control and the strong learning ability of the neural network can track the time-varying given signal. Finally, the system was simulated on MATLAB/Simulink in order to verify the efficiency and feasibility of the SRM AHC scheme. This paper provides methods for the marine work platform for the real-time control, time-varying speed and time-varying torque control of the motor-driven active heave compensation device, and the method helps to reduce torque ripple to ensure that the electromagnetic torque output of the SRM remains stable. In the future, we will consider the simulation of actual sea conditions, wind and wave interference to improve the control effect of the heave compensation system.

Author Contributions: J.C.: Writing—review and editing, methodology, formal analysis, funding acquisition; L.J.: software, original-draft writing, investigation; X.Z.: methodology; Investigation. All authors have read and agreed to the published version of the manuscript.

Funding: This research was funded by National Natural Science Foundation of China (Grant No. 52204210), Natural Science Foundation of Hunan Province, China (Grant No. 2023JJ30242), Open Research Fund Program of Key Laboratory of Metallogenic Prediction of Nonferrous Metals and Geological Environment Monitoring (Central South University), Ministry of Education (Grant No. 2022YSJS08) and Research Foundation of Education Bureau of Hunan Province, China (Grant No. 21B0452).

Data Availability Statement: The datasets used and/or analyzed during the current study available from the corresponding author on reasonable request.

Acknowledgments: The authors would like to express their gratitude to the referees for their valuable comments and suggestions in improving writing this paper.

Conflicts of Interest: The authors declare no conflicts of interest.

References

1. Zhao, F.; Zhong, Y.; Fu, Z. Active and passive heave compensation system based on feedback linearization sliding mode variable structure control. *Ocean Eng.* **2024**, *305*, 117962. [CrossRef]
2. Sun, X.; Feng, L.; Zhu, Z.; Lei, G.; Diao, K.; Guo, Y.; Zhu, J. Optimal design of terminal sliding mode controller for direct torque control of SRMs. *IEEE Trans. Transp. Electrif.* **2021**, *8*, 1445–1453. [CrossRef]
3. Kudiyarasan, S.; Sthalasayanam, N.; Karunakaran, V. Minimization of torque pulsations by using a novel fuzzy controller in SRM drives for EV applications. *Heliyon* **2023**, *9*, 3. [CrossRef] [PubMed]
4. Rajendran, A.; Karthik, B. Design and analysis of fuzzy and PI controllers for switched reluctance motor drive. *Mater. Today Proc.* **2021**, *37*, 1608–1612. [CrossRef]
5. Jing, B.; Dang, X.; Liu, Z.; Long, S. Torque ripple suppression of switched reluctance motor based on fuzzy indirect instant torque control. *IEEE Access* **2022**, *10*, 75472–75481. [CrossRef]
6. Murugan, L.S.; Maruthupandi, P. Sensorless speed control of 6/4-pole switched reluctance motor with ANFIS and fuzzy-PID-based hybrid observer. *Electr. Eng.* **2020**, *102*, 831–844. [CrossRef]
7. Akar, O. Control Techniques of the Modified Stator and Rotor Pole Shape in a 6/4 Switched Reluctance Motor: Effects on Torque Ripple Minimization. In *Electric Power Components and Systems*; Taylor & Francis: Abingdon, UK, 2024; pp. 1–12. [CrossRef]
8. Hao, Z.H.; Yapei, T.; Yuxiang, G.; Jun, T.; Tianci, H. PID Temperature Control Algorithm Based on Multiple Fuzzy Neural Networks. *J. Xihua Univ. Nat. Sci. Ed.* **2023**, *42*, 58–65. [CrossRef]
9. Jiang, X.; Cheng, T. Design of a BP neural network PID controller for an air suspension system by considering the stiffness of rubber bellows. *Alex. Eng. J.* **2023**, *74*, 65–78. [CrossRef]
10. Liu, J.; Li, X.; Zhang, X.; Chen, X. Modeling and Simulation of Energy-Regenerative Active Suspension Based on BP Neural Network PID Control. *Shock Vib.* **2019**, *2019*, 4609754. [CrossRef]
11. Ma, Z.; Xu, X.; Xie, J.; Jiang, X.; Wang, F. Negative Stiffness Control of Quasi-Zero Stiffness Air Suspension via Data-Driven Approach with Adaptive Fuzzy Neural Network Method. *Int. J. Fuzzy Syst.* **2022**, *24*, 3715–3730. [CrossRef]
12. Xie, T.; Huang, L.; Guo, Y.; Ou, Y. Modeling and simulation analysis of active heave compensation control system for electric-driven marine winch under excitation of irregular waves. *Meas. Control* **2023**, *56*, 1004–1015. [CrossRef]

13. Xu, J.; Wang, Y.; Ma, J.; Zhan, Y. Cascade control of active heave compensation nonlinear system for marine crane. *J. Mar. Sci. Eng.* **2023**, *11*, 1092. [CrossRef]
14. Woodacre, J.K.; Bauer, R.J.; Irani, R.A. A review of vertical motion heave compensation systems. *Ocean Eng.* **2015**, *104*, 140–154. [CrossRef]
15. Apkarian, P.; Bompart, V.; Noll, D. Non-smooth structured control design with application to PID loop-shaping of a process. *Int. J. Robust Nonlinear Control IFAC-Affil. J.* **2007**, *17*, 1320–1342. [CrossRef]
16. Apkarian, P.; Noll, D. The H∞ control problem is solved. *Aerosp. Lab* **2017**, *13*, 1–11. [CrossRef]
17. Zhao, Y.; Li, C.; Deng, Y. Modeling and simulation analysis on the control system of marine shipborne electric driven winch. *Comput. Simul.* **2016**, *33*, 244–249.
18. Zhao, C.; Guo, L. PID controller design for second order nonlinear uncertain systems. *Sci. China Inf. Sci.* **2017**, *60*, 022201. [CrossRef]
19. Zeng, G.Q.; Xie, X.Q.; Chen, M.R.; Weng, J. Adaptive population extremal optimization-based PID neural network for multivariable nonlinear control systems. *Swarm Evol. Comput.* **2019**, *44*, 320–334. [CrossRef]
20. Ma, X.; Zhou, J.; Zhang, X.; Zhou, Q. Development of a robotic catheter manipulation system based on BP neural network PID controller. *Appl. Bionics Biomech.* **2020**, *2020*, 8870106. [CrossRef]

symmetry

MDPI

Article

A New Fuzzy Bayesian Inference Approach for Risk Assessments

Jintao Xu [1,2,3], Yang Sui [1,2,*], Tao Yu [1,2,*], Rui Ding [1], Tao Dai [1,2] and Mengyan Zheng [1,2]

1 School of Nuclear Science and Technology, University of South China, Hengyang 421001, China; xujt27@mail2.sysu.edu.cn (J.X.)
2 Hunan Engineering & Technology Research Center for Virtual Nuclear Reactor, University of South China, Hengyang 421001, China
3 Sino-French Institute of Nuclear Engineering and Technology, Sun Yat-sen University, Zhuhai 519082, China
* Correspondence: suiyang@usc.edu.cn (Y.S.); yutao@usc.edu.cn (T.Y.)

Abstract: Bayesian network (BN) inference is an important statistical tool with additive symmetry. However, BN inference cannot deal with the uncertain, fuzzy, random, and conflicting information from experts' knowledge in the process of conducting a risk assessment. To tackle this issue, a new fuzzy BN inference approach for risk assessments was proposed based on cloud model (CM), interval type-2 fuzzy set (IT2 FS), interval type-2 fuzzy logic system (IT2 FLS), modified Dempster–Shafer (D-S) evidence theory (ET), and Latin hypercube sampling (LHS) methods along the following lines. Firstly, CM was integrated into IT2 FS, and CM-based IT2 FS (CM-IT2 FS) was defined in the IT2 FLS. Secondly, modified D-S ET was utilized to determine the CM-IT2 FS-based a priori probabilities, and the CM-IT2 FS-based BN model was established. Thirdly, the CM-IT2 FS-based a priori probabilities were reduced to the CM-IT1 FS-based ones using a type reducer in the IT2 FLS, LHS was applied to propose a new fuzzy BN inference algorithm, and then, the new algorithm was used in a typical case to perform the fuzzy BN positive inference for risk prediction and the fuzzy BN reverse inference for risk sensitivity analysis. Finally, the BN inference results were analyzed using the proposed algorithm and the two common BN inference algorithms, and the effectiveness of the proposed approach was validated. It can be concluded that the proposed approach was both accurate and promising.

Keywords: Bayesian network inference; risk assessment; information fusion; experts' knowledge

1. Introduction

Risk assessment is most beneficial for a complex system [1]. The aim of a risk assessment is to quantify the uncertain risks and to determine the probabilities of risk occurrence events and their impact on project objectives [2]. Therefore, assessing the risk of a complex system using a scientific tool is crucial.

The Bayesian network (BN) method is an advanced artificial intelligence tool [3]. BN inference is the procedure of combining the a priori probability and conditional probability, which can be obtained either using experts' knowledge or by data analysis [4], to calculate the updated probability of nodes [5,6]. It has characteristics with additive symmetry. The advantage of BN inference is that it can comprehensively utilize a priori and posteriori probabilities, and thus, it exhibits higher estimation accuracy and robustness [7]. BN inference includes BN positive inference and BN reverse inference. BN positive inference can be used to predict the occurrence probability for leaf nodes, which is a type of system failure, and BN reverse inference can be used to analyze the system sensitivity in the BN model [8]. BN inference has been explored as a potential valuable technique to conduct the risk assessment [9]. Recently, BN inference has been extensively employed for risk assessments in many complex systems that include nuclear power plants (NPPs) [10–12], petrochemical plants [13–16], construction projects [17–20], hazardous material transportation [21–24], etc. However, BN inference uses crisp probabilities; thus, it is challenging to deal with the uncertain information from experts' knowledge [25,26].

The type-2 fuzzy set (FS) (T2 FS) method, an extension of the type-1 FS (T1 FS) method, was first proposed by Zadeh in 1975 [27]. Based on the T2 FS, the type-2 fuzzy logic system (T2 FLS) was proposed by Karnik et al. in 1999 [28]. T2 FLS can be useful in dealing with highly uncertain information [29]. The reason for this is that the membership degree of T2 FS is a fuzzy value in the interval [0, 1] compared to that of T1 FS, which has a crisp value [30]; however, the computational complexity of T2 FLS is quite high [31]. As a restricted class of T2 FLS, interval T2 FLS (IT2 FLS) was proposed to avert the significant computational requirement that was mainly created by its type reducer [32]. Many researchers have recently been applying IT2 FLS to deal with the uncertain information from experts' knowledge for risk assessments [33–35]. Nonetheless, it is challenging to use IT2 FLS to deal with the fuzzy and random information from experts' knowledge [36].

The cloud model (CM) method based on the probability statistics theory and the traditional fuzzy set [37] provides a scientific way to solve the aforementioned challenging task. CM can be utilized to achieve the bidirectional conversion between qualitative linguistics and quantitative value and to characterize the fuzziness and randomness for a research object using digital characteristics [38]. CM is often used to deal with fuzzy and random information in risk assessments [39–41]. Consequently, to deal with the uncertain, fuzzy, and random information from experts' knowledge, CM should be integrated into interval T2 FS (IT2 FS) to define the CM-based IT2 FS (CM-IT2 FS) in the IT2 FLS. Unfortunately, this is still a gap in the current research.

Since experts provide risk assessment judgements based on their own professional knowledge, conflicting information is generated [42]. Thus, the CM-IT2 FS-based conflicting information should be fused. Currently, the Dempster–Shafer (D-S) evidence theory (ET) [43], which uses the information fusion rule to fuse conflicting information [44], can only be applied to fuse the T1 FS-based conflicting information, and this T1 FS-based conflicting information includes triangular fuzzy numbers [45], trapezoidal fuzzy numbers [46], interval-valued fuzzy sets [47], intuitionistic fuzzy sets [48], etc. Therefore, the D-S ET has to be modified to fuse the CM-IT2 FS-based conflicting information.

Considering that BN inference for risk assessments was to be improved by CM, IT2 FS, IT2 FLS, and modified D-S ET, the conventional BN inference algorithm is no longer suitable. Thus, an applicable BN inference algorithm should be defined. Presently, the Monte Carlo sampling (MCS) method and the variational inference (VI) method are the two main methods used to define the fuzzy BN inference algorithms in the T1FSs environment [49], in which MCS is used to randomly generate the samples through distribution functions of input random variables and VI is used to transform complicated inference issues into high-dimensional optimized ones. However, they are inefficient for large samples [50,51].

The Latin hypercube sampling (LHS) method, a stratified random sampling technique [52], has attracted interest from academics. LHS can divide the range of cumulative distribution function (CDF) of each variable into equal probability intervals and randomly generate a sampling value for each interval [53,54]. The above process ensures that all the sampling values can cover the sampling intervals [55]. Evidently, LHS can produce a higher number of stable and precise results than MCS with the same sampling number [56]. However, it is difficult to apply LHS to propose a fuzzy BN inference algorithm in the CM-IT2 FS environment. One reason for this may be that there is no one-to-one mapping relationship between each variable and its CDF for the CM-IT2 FS. To obtain this one-to-one mapping relationship, the fused CM-IT2 FS-based conflicting information should be reduced to the CM-IT2 FS-based information. Fortunately, IT2 FLS can reduce the IT2 FS-based information to the IT1 FS-based information using a type reducer [57], and this provides a potential solution to overcome the above difficulty.

The above literature shows that there is still a research gap pertaining to the fuzzy BN inference for risk assessments with respect to the uncertain, fuzzy, random, and conflicting information from experts' knowledge. Therefore, the innovative purpose of this study is to propose a new fuzzy BN inference approach for risk assessment by studying the following problems: (1) how to integrate CM into IT2 FS in order to define the CM-IT2 FS in the IT2 FLS; (2) how to utilize modified D-S ET to determine the CM-IT2 FS-based a priori probabilities in order to establish the CM-IT2 FS-based BN model; (3) how to apply LHS to propose a new fuzzy BN inference algorithm on the basis of the CM-IT1 FS-based a priori probabilities obtained by reducing the CM-IT2 FS-based ones using a type reducer in the IT2 FLS; and (4) how to conduct the fuzzy BN positive and reverse inferences for risk assessments using the proposed algorithm.

Three original contributions of this study can be summarized as follows:

(1) The CM-IT2 FS was defined in the IT2 FLS through Definitions 1 to 6, and the uncertain, fuzzy, and random information from experts' knowledge was dealt with accordingly.
(2) The CM-IT2 FS-based conflicting information from experts' knowledge was dealt with and fused using modified D-S ET, as shown in Equations (8)–(10), and then, the CM-IT2 FS-based BN model was established.
(3) A new fuzzy BN inference algorithm was proposed using LHS, as shown in Definition 13, and the risk prediction and risk sensitivity analysis were conducted by the proposed algorithm for a typical case.

This paper is outlined as follows. Section 2 introduces the preliminaries. Section 3 presents the proposed approach. Section 4 describes the case study. Section 5 validates and discusses the availability of the proposed approach. Section 6 concludes our study.

2. Preliminaries

2.1. CM-IT2 FS in the IT2 FLS

Definition 1 [58]. *IT2 FLS is composed of a fuzzifier, a rule, an inference engine, a type reducer, and a defuzzifier. The fuzzifier is responsible for converting the expert judgement information, which is qualitative linguistics, into a form of IT1 FS. The rule is used to perform the fuzzy operation. The inference engine provides a mapping from the IT1 FS to the IT2 FS. The type reducer converts the IT2 FS into the IT1 FS. The defuzzifier produces the crisp output. The general architecture of IT2 FLS is shown in Figure 1.*

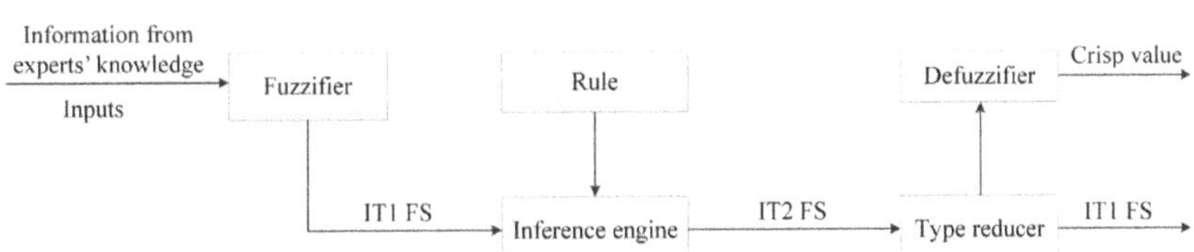

Figure 1. General architecture of IT2 FLS.

Definition 2 [59]. *B is a qualitative linguistic set in the domain; x is assumed to be a random number that obeys a normal distribution with $x \in B$.* The membership degree *$\mu(x)$ of x is a random number with a stable inclination and $\mu(x) \in [0,1]$.*

Definition 3. *In the CM-IT2 FS, $\tilde{\tilde{r}}_{ij}$ represents the CM-IT2 FS-based membership degree of the i-th assessment index subordinating to the j-th risk level, and it can be defined as follows.*

$$\tilde{\tilde{r}} = (\tilde{r}^L, \tilde{r}^U) = \begin{pmatrix} (r_1^L, r_2^L, r_3^L, r_4^L; H_1(r^L), H_2(r^L)), \\ (r_1^U, r_2^U, r_3^U, r_4^U; H_1(r^U), H_2(r^U)) \end{pmatrix} \quad (1)$$

where $\tilde{r}^L$ and $\tilde{r}^U$ are T1FSs, and they represent the lower and the upper membership degree functions of CM-IT2 FS, respectively; r_1^L, r_2^L, r_3^L, r_4^L, r_1^U, r_2^U, r_3^U, and r_4^U represent the reference points for $\tilde{\tilde{r}}$; $H_1(r^L)$ and $H_2(r^L)$, the upper and lower limits for the lower membership degree function, respectively; and $H_1(r^U)$ and $H_2(r^U)$ represent the upper and lower bounds for the upper membership degree function, respectively.

Definition 4. *In the CM-IT2 FS,* $\tilde{\tilde{R}}_i$ *represents the CM-IT2 FS-based membership degree set of the i-th assessment index subordinating to all risk levels, and it is defined as follows:*

$$\tilde{\tilde{R}}_i = \left\{\tilde{\tilde{r}}_{i1}, \cdots, \tilde{\tilde{r}}_{ij}, \cdots, \tilde{\tilde{r}}_{iJ}\right\} = \left\{(\tilde{r}_L^{i1}, \tilde{r}_U^{i1}), \cdots, (\tilde{r}_L^{ij}, \tilde{r}_U^{ij}), \cdots, (\tilde{r}_L^{iJ}, \tilde{r}_U^{iJ})\right\} \tag{2}$$

where $j = 1, 2, \cdots, 5$.

2.2. CM-IT2 FS-Based BN Model

Definition 5 [60,61]. *BN is a directed acyclic graph, which is composed of nodes and arrows. The nodes represent the random variables. The arrows, which connect parent nodes and their child nodes, represent the conditional dependencies between different variables. The occurrence probability of root node is called the a priori probability. The probability of non-root node is called the conditional probability. Each node codifies a conditional probability distribution. The probability distribution of random variables is called the joint probability distribution, and can be defined as follows:*

$$P(X_1, \cdots, X_i, \cdots, X_n) = \prod_{i=1}^{n} P(X_i | pa(X_i)) \tag{3}$$

where $X_1, \cdots, X_i, \cdots, X_n$ *are the random variable set;* $pa(X_i)$ *is the parent node; and* $P(X_i|pa(X_i))$ *is the conditional probability.*

Definition 6 [62]. *If a set* $\Theta = \{u_1, \cdots, u_i, \cdots, u_n\}$ is a non-empty finite one with n mutually exclusive elements included, Θ is the framework of discernment. The power set of Θ is denoted by $PS(\Theta)$. A set function m: $PS(\Theta) \to [0,1]$ *is regarded as an evidence source if it satisfies the following conditions:*

$$\begin{cases} \sum\limits_{u_i \subseteq PS(\Theta)} m(u_i) = 1 \\ m() = 0 \end{cases} \tag{4}$$

where $m(u_i)$ *represents the occurrence probability of* u_i.

Definition 7. *The CM-IT2 FS-based membership degree set in Definition 6 is defined as a basic belief assignment in the D-S ET using Equation (5).*

$$\tilde{\tilde{m}}(x_i) = \tilde{\tilde{R}}_i \tag{5}$$

Definition 8 [63]. *The traditional information fusion rule is defined to fuse the conflicting information from experts' knowledge using Equations (6) and (7).*

$$K = \sum_{i=1}^{n} \prod_{e=1}^{z} m_e(x_i) \tag{6}$$

$$m^*(x_i) = \begin{cases} 0, & x_i = \varnothing \\ \frac{\sum\limits_{i=1}^{n} \prod\limits_{e=1}^{z} m_e(x_i)}{1-K}, & x_i \neq \varnothing \end{cases} \tag{7}$$

where K denotes a measure of conflict as the coefficient; $m_e(x_i)$ *represents the basic belief assignment of the i-th assessment index by e-th expert; and* $m^*(x_i)$ *is the fused evidence.*

Definition 9 [64]. *The modified information fusion rule is utilized to fuse the conflicting information from experts' knowledge using Equations (8)–(10), and the D-S ET is modified. In Equations (8)–(10), there is a high degree of conflict in the obtained evidence when* $K \geq 0.95$, *and no conflict in the evidence is observed when* $0 \leq K < 0.95$.

$$\tilde{m}^L(x_i) = \begin{cases} \frac{1}{1-K^L}\prod_{e=1}^{z} m_e^L(x_i), & K^L < 0.95 \\ K^L\frac{1}{z}\sum_{e=1}^{z} m_e^L(x_i) + \prod_{e=1}^{z} m_e^L(x_i), & K^L \geq 0.95 \end{cases} \tag{8}$$

$$\tilde{m}^U(x_i) = \begin{cases} \frac{1}{1-K^U}\prod_{e=1}^{z} m_e^U(x_i), & K^U < 0.95 \\ K^U\frac{1}{z}\sum_{e=1}^{z} m_e^U(x_i) + \prod_{e=1}^{z} m_e^U(x_i), & K^U \geq 0.95 \end{cases} \tag{9}$$

$$\tilde{\tilde{m}}^*(x_i) = (\tilde{m}^L(x_i), \tilde{m}^U(x_i)) \tag{10}$$

where K^L and K^U are coefficients of lower and upper bounds for $m(x_i)$, respectively; $\tilde{m}^L(x_i)$ and $\tilde{m}^U(x_i)$ are lower and upper membership degree functions for $m(x_i)$, respectively; and $\tilde{\tilde{m}}^*(x_i)$ is the fused information.

Definition 10. *The fused conflicting information is defined as the CM-IT2 FS-based a priori probability using Equation (11). Based on this, the CM-IT2 FS-based BN model is established.*

$$\tilde{\tilde{P}}(X_i) = \tilde{\tilde{m}}^*(x_i) \tag{11}$$

2.3. New Fuzzy BN Inference Algorithm

Definition 11 [65]. *The CM-IT2 FS-based a priori probability is reduced to the CM-IT1 FS-based one using Equations (12)–(14) in the type reducer of the IT2 FLS.*

$$r_i^L = \frac{(r_{i4}^L - r_{i1}^L) + (H_1(r_i^L) \times r_{i2}^L - r_{i1}^L) + (H_2(r_i^L) \times r_{i3}^L - r_{i1}^L)}{4} + r_{i1}^L \tag{12}$$

$$r_i^U = \frac{(r_{i4}^U - r_{i1}^U) + (H_1(r_i^U) \times r_{i2}^U - r_{i1}^U) + (H_2(r_i^U) \times r_{i3}^U - r_{i1}^U)}{4} + r_{i1}^U \tag{13}$$

$$\tilde{P}(X_i) = (r_i^L, r_i^U) \tag{14}$$

Definition 12. *The fuzzy probability of occurrence for leaf node T is defined using Equation (15) after determining the CM-IT1 FS-based a priori probabilities and conditional probabilities. The updated fuzzy a priori probability, called fuzzy posteriori probability, is defined using Equation (16). The fuzzy sensitivity performance measure (SPM), which denotes the sensitivity degree of root nodes, is defined using Equation (17).*

$$\tilde{P}(T) \cong \sum_{i=1}^{n} \tilde{P}(X_i) \otimes P(T|X_i) \tag{15}$$

$$\tilde{P}(X_i|T) \cong \tilde{P}(X_i) \otimes P(T|X_i) \oslash \tilde{P}(T) \tag{16}$$

$$S\tilde{P}M(X_i, T) \cong \sum_{j=I}^{V} (\tilde{P}(T|X_{ij} = 1) \ominus \tilde{P}(T)) \oslash \tilde{P}(T) \tag{17}$$

where $\tilde{P}(T)$ is the fuzzy occurrence probability; $\tilde{P}(X_i)$ is the fuzzy a priori probability; $P(T|X_i)$ is the conditional probability; $\tilde{P}(X_i|T)$ is the fuzzy posteriori probability; $S\tilde{P}M(X_i, T)$ is the fuzzy SPM; and $\tilde{P}(T|X_{ij} = 1)$ is the updated fuzzy occurrence probability.

Definition 13. *A new fuzzy BN inference algorithm is proposed using LHS. The proposed algorithm is as follows Algorithm 1:*

Algorithm 1: A new fuzzy BN inference algorithm

1: **Set batch number**: s samples for a variable generated in a loop.
2: **for** each one of all variables
3: Initialize the samples number as zero.
4: Define an interval [0, 1] in the samples space, then partition the interval into s equally sized segments,
5: Randomly sample s samples from the interval [0, 1], and record each as ξ_{ki}.
6: Generate a random value γ_{ki} by using $\gamma_{ki} = \frac{k-1+\xi_{ki}}{s}$, then shuffle s random values (sampling values).
7: Employ $F(\gamma_i) = P\{X_i \leq \gamma_i\}$ to compute the CDF for s random values.
8: Generate s a priori probability samples by using $P_k(X_i) = F^{-1}(\gamma_{ki})$.
9: If s a priori probability samples have been generated, save into the matrix, or return to 3
10: **Define** a row in the matrix as a set of a priori probability samples.
11: Initiate the parameters and structure in the CM-IT2 FS-based BN model.
12: Assign a priori probability samples to the root node, and calculate the fuzzy occurrence probability using Equation (15).
13: Calculate fuzzy posteriori probability using Equation (16).
14: Calculate fuzzy SPM using Equation (17).
15: If all batches of samples have been calculated, output the results, or return to 12.
16: End

3. Proposal of a New Fuzzy BN Inference Approach

In this study, CM, IT2 FS, IT2 FLS, modified D-S ET, and LHS were applied to introduce a new fuzzy BN inference approach for risk assessments. Figure 2 illustrates its theoretical framework, comprising three stages and twelve relevant steps.

3.1. *Stage 1: Define the CM-IT2 FS in the IT2 FLS*

At stage 1, the CM-IT2 FS was defined in the IT2 FLS, which included five steps.

3.1.1. Create the Index System

The index system is the basis to assess the studied risk.

3.1.2. Obtain the Qualitative Linguistics for Each Assessment Index

It is assumed that the qualitative risk assessment standard is composed of five risk levels, including level 1 (very low risk), level 2 (low risk), level 3 (medium risk), level 4 (high risk), and level 5 (very high risk). The senior experts on risk assessments were invited to provide their qualitative linguistics for each assessment index according to the risk assessment procedure.

3.1.3. Transform the Qualitative Linguistics into the Quantitative Cloud Characteristics

The golden section method [66], as shown in Table 1, was applied to transform the qualitative linguistics into the quantitative cloud characteristics for each assessment index. Then, the CM-based membership degree set of each assessment index subordinating to five risk levels $\mu_i = \{\mu_{i1}, \mu_{i2}, \mu_{i3}, \mu_{i4}, \mu_{i5}\}$ was obtained, where $\mu_{ij} = (Ex_{ij}, En_{ij}, He_{ij})$ and $j = 1,2,3,4,5$.

Table 1. Golden section method.

Qualitative Linguistics	Quantitative Cloud Characteristics		
	Ex	*En*	*He*
Level 1	X_{max}	En_0	$He_0/0.382$
Level 2	$Ex_0 + (X_{max} + X_{min})/2$	$0.382 \times (X_{max} + X_{min})/6$	$He_0/0.618$
Level 3	$(X_{max} + X_{min})/2$	$0.618En_0$	He_0

Table 1. *Cont.*

Qualitative Linguistics	Quantitative Cloud Characteristics		
	Ex	*En*	*He*
Level 4	$Ex_0 - (X_{max} + X_{min})/2$	$0.382 \times (X_{max} - X_{min})/6$	$He_0/0.618$
Level 5	X_{min}	$En_0/0.618$	$He_0/0.382$

Notes: *Ex* (expectation value), *En* (entropy value), and *He* (hyper-entropy value) are three digital characteristics of CM; X_{max} and X_{min} represent the upper and lower bounds for the given qualitative linguistics, respectively; X_{max} is taken from Table 2, and X_{min} takes a value of 0; and Ex_0, En_0, and He_0 are the quantitative cloud characteristics for the middle cloud, taking values of 0.5, 0.103, and 0.005, respectively.

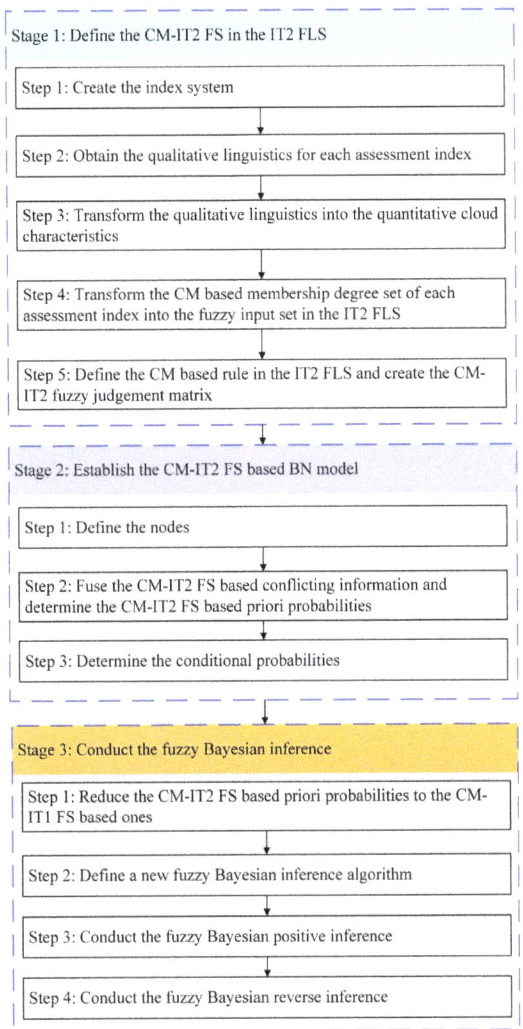

Figure 2. Theoretical framework of the proposed approach.

Table 2. Value of Xmax in Table 1.

Qualitative Linguistics	X_{max}	Qualitative Linguistics	X_{max}	Qualitative Linguistics	X_{max}
Level 1	0.9	Level 2	0.7	Level 3	0.5
Level 4	0.3	Level 5	0.1		

3.1.4. Transform the CM-Based Membership Degree Set of Each Assessment Index into the Fuzzy Input Set in the IT2 FLS

The fuzzifier in the IT2 FLS and Equations (18)–(20) [67] was used to transform the CM-based membership degree set of each assessment index for the CM-IT1 FS-based membership degree set $\widetilde{\mu}_i$, and $\widetilde{\mu}_i = \{\widetilde{\mu}_{i1}, \widetilde{\mu}_{i2}, \widetilde{\mu}_{i3}, \widetilde{\mu}_{i4}, \widetilde{\mu}_{i5}\}$. The $\widetilde{\mu}_i$ was inputted into the IT2 FLS as the fuzzy input set.

$$\mu_{ij}^L = Ex_{ij} - 3En_{ij} \tag{18}$$

$$\mu_{ij}^U = 1 - Ex_{ij} - 3En_{ij} \tag{19}$$

$$\widetilde{\mu}_{ij} = (\mu_{ij}^L, \mu_{ij}^U) \tag{20}$$

3.1.5. Define the CM-Based Rule in the IT2 FLS and Create the CM-IT2 Fuzzy Judgement Matrix

The CM-based rule in the IT2 FLS was defined using Equations (21) and (22). The $\widetilde{\mu}_i$ was iterated twice by the defined rule and inference engine in the IT2 FLS. Afterwards, the $\widetilde{\mu}_i$ was transformed as the CM-IT2 FS-based membership degree set $\widetilde{\widetilde{R}}_i$, and $\widetilde{\widetilde{R}}_i = \left\{\widetilde{\widetilde{r}}_{i1}, \widetilde{\widetilde{r}}_{i2}, \widetilde{\widetilde{r}}_{i3}, \widetilde{\widetilde{r}}_{i4}, \widetilde{\widetilde{r}}_{i5}\right\}$. Then, the CM-IT2 fuzzy judgement matrix $\widetilde{\widetilde{W}}$ for n assessment indexes from one expert's knowledge was created using Equation (23), as follows:

$$\widetilde{r}_{ij}^U = (\widetilde{\mu}_{ij})^{\alpha} \tag{21}$$

$$\widetilde{r}_{ij}^L = (\widetilde{\mu}_{ij})^{\frac{1}{\alpha}} \tag{22}$$

where α is the cut set, and it takes a value of 2.

$$\widetilde{\widetilde{W}} = \begin{bmatrix} \widetilde{\widetilde{r}}_{11} & \widetilde{\widetilde{r}}_{12} & \widetilde{\widetilde{r}}_{13} & \widetilde{\widetilde{r}}_{14} & \widetilde{\widetilde{r}}_{15} \\ \vdots & \vdots & \vdots & \vdots & \vdots \\ \widetilde{\widetilde{r}}_{i1} & \widetilde{\widetilde{r}}_{i2} & \widetilde{\widetilde{r}}_{i3} & \widetilde{\widetilde{r}}_{i4} & \widetilde{\widetilde{r}}_{i5} \\ \vdots & \vdots & \vdots & \vdots & \vdots \\ \widetilde{\widetilde{r}}_{n1} & \widetilde{\widetilde{r}}_{n2} & \widetilde{\widetilde{r}}_{n3} & \widetilde{\widetilde{r}}_{n4} & \widetilde{\widetilde{r}}_{n5} \end{bmatrix} \tag{23}$$

Through steps in Sections 3.1.2–3.1.5 in stage 1, the CM-IT2 FS was defined in the IT2 FLS.

3.2. *Stage 2: Establish the CM-IT2 FS-Based BN Model*

At stage 2, the CM-IT2 FS-based BN model was established, and it included three steps.

3.2.1. Define the Nodes

The studied risk was defined as leaf nodes, and its causes were defined as middle nodes and root nodes, according to the analysis results.

3.2.2. Fuse the CM-IT2 FS-Based Conflicting Information and Determine the CM-IT2 FS-Based a Priori Probabilities

The CM-IT2 FS-based membership degree set in $\widetilde{\widetilde{W}}$ was defined as a basic belief assignment using Equation (5). Afterwards, the evidence matrix $\widetilde{\widetilde{M}}$ was created, as shown in Equation (24). Then, the CM-IT2 FS-based conflicting information was fused using

Equations (8)–(10), and the CM-IT2 FS-based a priori probabilities of root nodes were determined using Equation (11).

$$\tilde{\tilde{M}} = \begin{bmatrix} \tilde{\tilde{m}}_1(x_1) & \cdots & \tilde{\tilde{m}}_e(x_1) & \cdots & \tilde{\tilde{m}}_z(x_1) \\ \vdots & \ddots & \vdots & \ddots & \vdots \\ \tilde{\tilde{m}}_1(x_i) & \cdots & \tilde{\tilde{m}}_e(x_i) & \cdots & \tilde{\tilde{m}}_z(x_i) \\ \vdots & \ddots & \vdots & \ddots & \vdots \\ \tilde{\tilde{m}}_1(x_n) & \cdots & \tilde{\tilde{m}}_e(x_n) & \cdots & \tilde{\tilde{m}}_z(x_n) \end{bmatrix} \tag{24}$$

3.2.3. Determine the Conditional Probabilities

Conditional probabilities of non-root nodes were determined based on the data analysis of the risk accident to be studied and the engineering experiences and knowledge from experts.

Through Sections 3.2.1–3.2.3 in stage 2, the CM-IT2 FS-based BN model was established.

3.3. *Stage 3: Conduct the Fuzzy BN Inference*

At stage 3, the new fuzzy BN inference was conducted, and it included four steps.

3.3.1. Reduce the CM-IT2 FS-Based a Priori Probabilities to the CM-IT1 FS-Based Ones

The CM-IT2 FS-based a priori probabilities were reduced to the CM-IT1 FS-based ones using a type reducer in the IT2 FLS and Equations (12)–(14).

3.3.2. Propose a New Fuzzy BN Inference Algorithm

A new fuzzy BN inference algorithm was proposed using LHS, as shown in Definition 13.

3.3.3. Conduct the Fuzzy BN Positive Inference

The fuzzy BN positive inference was conducted using the proposed fuzzy BN inference algorithm (**Algorithm 1**) to calculate the fuzzy occurrence probability of the risk to be studied so as to take scientific decisions to prevent the risk of accidents.

3.3.4. Conduct the Fuzzy BN Reverse Inference

The fuzzy BN reverse inference was conducted using the proposed fuzzy BN inference algorithm (**Algorithm 1**) to analyze the risk sensitivity in order to recognize the key risk factors. In reality, the risk management process should be enhanced according to the fuzzy SPM.

4. Case Study

A complex system, which was the NPP in Xudabo Nuclear Power Co., Ltd. (XNPCL), was selected as the case study. It adopts the VVER-1200 technology and is being constructed, at present, in Northeast China.

The deep foundation excavation engineering (DFEE) was selected as the research object in XNPCL. The DFEE has the characteristics of large investments, long engineering cycles, complicated techniques, and unpredictable risk factors [68]. Therefore, it is necessary to conduct the DFEE risk assessment for the NPP construction project.

The DFEE risk assessment was conducted by using the three stages presented in Section 3. Firstly, 10 experts with more than 10 years of experience in risk assessments for NPP construction projects were invited as the senior experts. Then, they conducted the on-site inspection and accessed the relevant information and data. Furthermore, they provided their qualitative linguistics according to the DFEE risk assessment procedure. Finally, the qualitative linguistics was converted into the quantitative value for the DFEE risk prediction and the DFEE risk sensitivity analysis.

4.1. Stage 1: Define the CM-IT2 FS in the IT2 FLS

4.1.1. Create the Index System

The index system of the assessed DFEE risk was created on the basis of the DFEE risk assessment procedure in XNPCL, and it is shown in Table 3.

Table 3. Index system.

Index	Sub-Index
Bracing system instability (U_1)	Bracing overall system instability (R_{11}) Bracing system break (R_{12}) Kick damage (R_{13})
Soil deformation (U_2)	Soil landslide (R_{21}) Soil permeation (R_{22}) Foundation surge (R_{23})
Mechanical injury (U_3)	Mechanical collapse (R_{31}) Unsafety behavior (R_{32})

4.1.2. Obtain the Qualitative Linguistics for Each Assessment Index

The qualitative linguistics for each assessment index was provided by senior experts based on the DFEE risk assessment procedure.

4.1.3. Transform the Qualitative Linguistics into the Quantitative Cloud Characteristics

The qualitative linguistics was transformed into quantitative cloud characteristics for each assessment index, and then, the CM-based membership degree set of each assessment index subordinating to five risk levels was obtained through Section 3.1.3. Taking the qualitative linguistics for the assessment index R_{11} from the first expert as an example, its CM-based membership degree set was as follows: $\mu_1 = \{(0.7, 0.103, 0.013), (0.85, 0.045, 0.008), (0.35, 0.309, 0.005), (0.15, 0.045, 0.008), (0, 0.809, 0.013)\}$.

4.1.4. Transform the CM-Based Membership Degree Set of Each Assessment Index into the Fuzzy Input Set in the IT2 FLS

The CM-based membership degree set of each assessment index was transformed into the CM-IT1 FS-based set $\widetilde{\mu}_i$, and the $\widetilde{\mu}_i$ was inputted into the IT2 FLS as the fuzzy input set through Section 3.1.4. Taking the CM-based membership degree set in Example 1 as an example, its corresponding fuzzy input set was as follows: $\widetilde{\mu}_1 = \{(0.156, 0.500), (0.010, 0.591), (0.156, 0.500), (0.259, 0.359), (0.156, 0.500)\}$.

4.1.5. Define the CM-Based Rule in the IT2 FLS and Create the CM-IT2 Fuzzy Judgement Matrix

The CM-based rule in the IT2 FLS was defined, and then, the CM-IT2 fuzzy judgement matrix $\widetilde{\widetilde{R}}$ for eight assessment indexes from one expert was created through Section 3.1.5. Taking the CM-IT2 fuzzy judgement matrix $\widetilde{\widetilde{W}}$ for eight assessment indexes from the first expert as an example, the following matrix was established:

$$\widetilde{\widetilde{W}} = \begin{bmatrix} \begin{pmatrix} (0.0000, 0.0100, 0.0100, 0.3162; 0.9, 0.9), \\ (0.1220, 0.5910, 0.5910, 0.8768; 1.0, 1.0) \end{pmatrix} & \cdots & \begin{pmatrix} (0.0625, 0.0500, 0.0500, 0.8409; 0.9, 0.9), \\ (0.0000, 0.0010, 0.0010, 0.3162; 1.0, 1.0) \end{pmatrix} \\ \vdots & \ddots & \vdots \\ \begin{pmatrix} (0.0006, 0.1562, 0.1562, 0.6287; 0.9, 0.9), \\ (0.0625, 0.5000, 0.5000, 0.8409; 1.0, 1.0) \end{pmatrix} & \cdots & \begin{pmatrix} (0.0625, 0.5000, 0.5000, 0.8409; 0.9, 0.9), \\ (0.0005, 0.1562, 0.1562, 0.6287; 1.0, 1.0) \end{pmatrix} \end{bmatrix}$$

4.2. Stage 2: Establish the CM-IT2 FS-Based BN Model

4.2.1. Determine the Nodes

The DFEE risk for the construction project in XNPCL was defined as leaf nodes, and indexes and sub-indexes in Table 3 were defined as middle nodes and root nodes, respectively.

4.2.2. Fuse the CM-IT2 FS-Based Conflicting Information and Determine the CM-IT2 FS-Based a Priori Probabilities

The evidence matrix $\tilde{\tilde{M}}$ was created, the CM-IT2 FS-based conflicting information was fused, and the CM-IT2 FS-based a priori probabilities of root nodes were determined through the Section 3.2.2, and the results are shown as follows:

$$\tilde{\tilde{M}} = \begin{bmatrix} \begin{pmatrix} (0.0000, 0.0100, 0.0100, 0.3162; 0.9, 0.9), \\ (0.1220, 0.5910, 0.5910, 0.8768; 1.0, 1.0) \end{pmatrix} & & \begin{pmatrix} (0.0167, 0.3590, 0.3590, 0.7741; 0.9, 0.9), \\ (0.0045, 0.2590, 0.2590, 0.7134; 1.0, 1.0) \end{pmatrix} \\ \begin{pmatrix} (0.0006, 0.1562, 0.1562, 0.6287; 0.9, 0.9), \\ (0.0625, 0.5000, 0.5000, 0.8409; 1.0, 1.0) \end{pmatrix} & & \begin{pmatrix} (0.0060, 0.1562, 0.1562, 0.6287; 0.9, 0.9), \\ (0.0625, 0.5000, 0.5000, 0.8409; 1.0, 1.0) \end{pmatrix} \\ \begin{pmatrix} (0.0167, 0.3590, 0.3590, 0.7741; 0.9, 0.9), \\ (0.0045, 0.2590, 0.2590, 0.7134; 1.0, 1.0) \end{pmatrix} & \cdots & \begin{pmatrix} (0.0000, 0.0100, 0.0100, 0.3162; 0.9, 0.9), \\ (0.1220, 0.5910, 0.5910, 0.8768; 1.0, 1.0) \end{pmatrix} \\ \begin{pmatrix} (0.0625, 0.5000, 0.5000, 0.8409; 0.9, 0.9), \\ (0.1562, 0.1562, 0.1562, 0.6287; 1.0, 1.0) \end{pmatrix} & & \begin{pmatrix} (0.0006, 0.1562, 0.1562, 0.6287; 0.9, 0.9), \\ (0.0625, 0.5000, 0.5000, 0.8409; 1.0, 1.0) \end{pmatrix} \\ \begin{pmatrix} (0.0625, 0.5000, 0.5000, 0.8409; 0.9, 0.9), \\ (0.0000, 0.0100, 0.0100, 0.3262; 1.0, 1.0) \end{pmatrix} & & \begin{pmatrix} (0.0166, 0.3590, 0.3590, 0.7741; 0.9, 0.9), \\ (0.0045, 0.2590, 0.2590, 0.7164; 1.0, 1.0) \end{pmatrix} \\ \vdots & \ddots & \vdots \\ \begin{pmatrix} (0.0006, 0.1562, 0.1562, 0.6287; 0.9, 0.9), \\ (0.0625, 0.5000, 0.5000, 0.8409; 1.0, 1.0) \end{pmatrix} & & \begin{pmatrix} (0.0167, 0.3590, 0.3590, 0.7741; 0.9, 0.9), \\ (0.0045, 0.2590, 0.2590, 0.7134; 1.0, 1.0) \end{pmatrix} \\ \begin{pmatrix} (0.0000, 0.0100, 0.0100, 0.3162; 0.9, 0.9), \\ (0.1220, 0.5910, 0.5910, 0.8768; 1.0, 1.0) \end{pmatrix} & & \begin{pmatrix} (0.0060, 0.1562, 0.1562, 0.6287; 0.9, 0.9), \\ (0.0625, 0.5000, 0.5000, 0.8409; 1.0, 1.0) \end{pmatrix} \\ \begin{pmatrix} (0.0006, 0.1562, 0.1562, 0.6287; 0.9, 0.9), \\ (0.0625, 0.5000, 0.5000, 0.8409; 1.0, 1.0) \end{pmatrix} & \cdots & \begin{pmatrix} (0.0000, 0.0100, 0.0100, 0.3162; 0.9, 0.9), \\ (0.1220, 0.5910, 0.5910, 0.8768; 1.0, 1.0) \end{pmatrix} \\ \begin{pmatrix} (0.0167, 0.3590, 0.3590, 0.7741; 0.9, 0.9), \\ (0.0045, 0.2590, 0.2590, 0.7134; 1.0, 1.0) \end{pmatrix} & & \begin{pmatrix} (0.0006, 0.1562, 0.1562, 0.6287; 0.9, 0.9), \\ (0.0625, 0.5000, 0.5000, 0.8409; 1.0, 1.0) \end{pmatrix} \\ \begin{pmatrix} (0.0625, 0.5000, 0.5000, 0.8409; 0.9, 0.9), \\ (0.0006, 0.1562, 0.1562, 0.6287; 1.0, 1.0) \end{pmatrix} & & \begin{pmatrix} (0.0166, 0.3590, 0.3590, 0.7741; 0.9, 0.9), \\ (0.0045, 0.2590, 0.2590, 0.7164; 1.0, 1.0) \end{pmatrix} \end{bmatrix}$$

Taking the assessment index R_{11} as an example, its CM-IT2 FS-based a priori probability is shown in Table 4.

Table 4. CM-IT2 FS-based a priori probability.

Index	Risk Level	A Priori Probability
R_{11}	Level 1	((0.0000, 0.1439, 0.1439, 0.5148; 0.9, 0.9), (0.0006, 0.4732, 0.4732, 0.8214; 1.0, 1.0))
	Level 2	((0.0000, 0.1269, 0.1269, 0.5649; 0.9, 0.9), (0.2214, 0.5184, 0.5184, 0.8501; 1.0, 1.0))
	Level 3	((0.0000, 0.2137, 0.2137, 0.6063; 0.9, 0.9), (0.0000, 0.4068, 0.4068, 0.7878; 1.0, 1.0))
	Level 4	((0.0000, 0.1229, 0.1229, 0.2548; 0.9, 0.9), (0.0000, 0.0933, 0.0933, 0.2360; 1.0, 1.0))
	Level 5	((0.0325, 0.1526, 0.1526, 0.2747; 0.9, 0.9), (0.0000, 0.0380, 0.0380, 0.1655; 1.0, 1.0))

4.2.3. Determine the Conditional Probabilities

The conditional probabilities of non-root nodes were determined through Section 3.2.3. Some conditional probabilities are shown in Table 5.

Table 5. Some conditional probabilities.

R_{11}	R_{12}	R_{13}	$P(U_1 \mid R_{11}, R_{12}, R_{13})$	R_{11}	R_{12}	R_{13}	$P(U_1 \mid R_{11}, R_{12}, R_{13})$
Level 1	Level 1	Level 1	(1, 0, 0, 0, 0)	Level 1	Level 2	Level 1	(0.6, 0.4, 0, 0, 0)
		Level 2	(0.6, 0.4, 0, 0, 0)			Level 2	(0.4, 0.6, 0, 0, 0)

Table 5. *Cont.*

R_{11}	R_{12}	R_{13}	P (U_1 | R_{11}, R_{12}, R_{13})	R_{11}	R_{12}	R_{13}	P (U_1 | R_{11}, R_{12}, R_{13})
		Level 3	(0.4, 0.3, 0.3, 0, 0)			Level 3	(0.3, 0.4, 0.3, 0, 0)
		Level 4	(0.4, 0.2, 0.2, 0.2, 0)			Level 4	(0.3, 0.2, 0.3, 0.2, 0)
		Level 5	(0.4, 0.15, 0.15, 0.15, 0.15)			Level 5	(0.2, 0.3, 0.15, 0.15, 0.2)

Through the above Sections 4.2.1–4.2.3, the CM-IT2 FS-based BN model, as shown in Figure 3, was created.

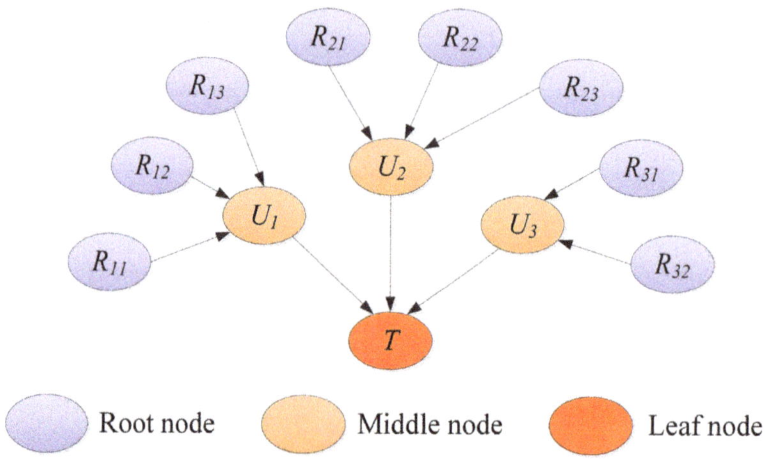

Figure 3. CM-IT2 FS-based BN model.

4.3. *Stage 3: Conduct the fuzzy BN Inference*

4.3.1. Reduce the CM-IT2 FS-Based a Priori Probabilities to the CM-IT1-FS-Based Ones

The CM-IT2 FS-based a priori probabilities were reduced to the CM-IT1 FS-based ones through Section 3.3.1. Taking the assessment index R_{11} as an example, its CM-IT1 FS-based a priori probability is shown in Table 6.

Table 6. CM-IT1 FS-based a priori probability.

Index	Risk Level	A Priori Probability
R_{11}	Level 1	(0.1935, 0.4186)
	Level 2	(0.1983, 0.5565)
	Level 3	(0.2477, 0.3800)
	Level 4	(0.1010, 0.1190)
	Level 5	(0.0585, 0.1455)

4.3.2. Propose a New Fuzzy BN Inference Algorithm

The proposed new fuzzy BN inference algorithm from LHS is shown in Definition 13. The sampling number was set as 1000.

4.3.3. Conduct the Fuzzy BN Positive Inference

The fuzzy occurrence probability of the DFEE risk was calculated using the proposed fuzzy BN inference algorithm (**Algorithm 1**), and Figure 4 shows the risk prediction result. The prediction result indicates that the DFEE risk was assessed as low risk (level 2).

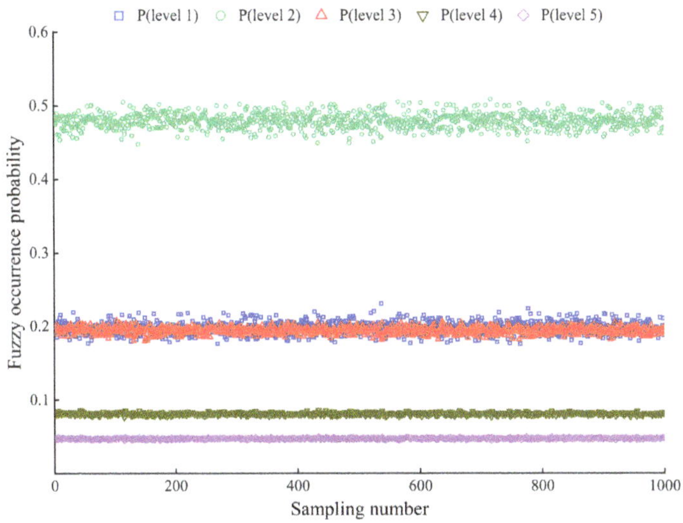

Figure 4. Fuzzy occurrence probability of the DFEE risk.

4.3.4. Conduct the Fuzzy BN Reverse Inference

The fuzzy SPM was calculated using the proposed fuzzy BN inference algorithm (**Algorithm 1**), and Figure 5 shows the boxplot of the fuzzy SPM of the assessment index R_{11}.

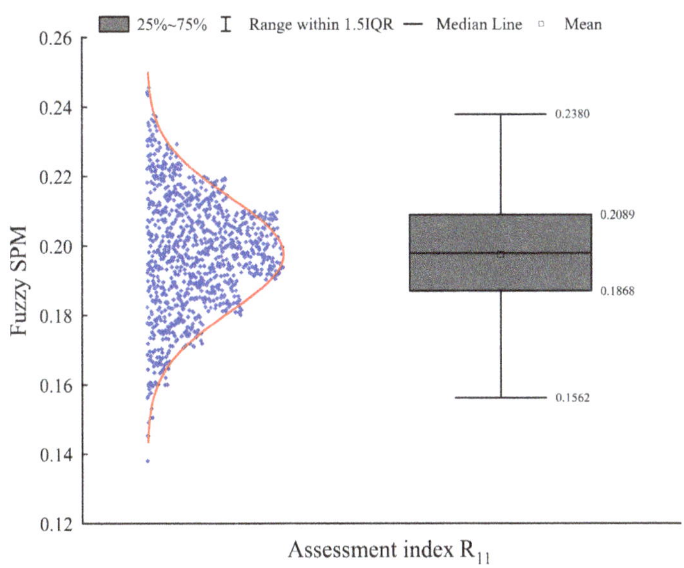

Figure 5. Boxplot of fuzzy SPM.

As shown in Figure 5, the scatter plots of the fuzzy SPM for the assessment index R_{11} followed a normal distribution. The sampling numbers near the upper margin (0.2380) and the lower margin (0.1562) were quite small. The sampling numbers from the upper quartile (0.2089) to the lower quartile (0.1868) were large. The length from the upper quartile to the lower quartile was short. The above analysis indicated that the fuzzy SPM for the assessment index R_{11} was ideal.

5. Validation and Discussion

For the sake of validating the availability of the proposed fuzzy BN inference approach for risk assessments, we conducted the following two tasks.

5.1. The BN Positive Inference Results Were Analyzed

The CM-IT2 FS-based, CM-IT1 FS-based, and traditional CM-crisp value-based a priori probabilities were compared and analyzed. Taking the assessment index R_{11} as an example, its coefficient K was 0.9986, and this indicates that the information from experts' knowledge was highly conflicting. Modified D-S ET was utilized to fuse the above three kinds of a priori probabilities, and the fusion results are shown in Table 7.

Table 7. Comparison of fusion results.

Risk Level	CM-IT2 FS-Based a Priori Probability	CM-IT1 FS-Based a Priori Probability	CM-crisp Value-Based a Priori Probability
Level 1	((0.0000, 0.1439, 0.1439, 0.5148; 0.9, 0.9), (0.0006, 0.4732, 0.4732, 0.8214; 1.0, 1.0))	(0.2935, 0.4186)	0.2954
Level 2	((0.0000, 0.1269, 0.1269, 0.5649; 0.9, 0.9), (0.2214, 0.5184, 0.5184, 0.8501; 1.0, 1.0))	(0.2983, 0.5565)	0.3581
Level 3	((0.0000, 0.2137, 0.2137, 0.6063; 0.9, 0.9), (0.0000, 0.4068, 0.4068, 0.7878; 1.0, 1.0))	(0.1477, 0.3800)	0.2595
Level 4	((0.0000, 0.1229, 0.1229, 0.2548; 0.9, 0.9), (0.0000, 0.0933, 0.0933, 0.2360; 1.0, 1.0))	(0.0010, 0.1190)	0.045
Level 5	((0.0325, 0.1526, 0.1526, 0.2747; 0.9, 0.9), (0.0000, 0.0380, 0.0380, 0.1655; 1.0, 1.0))	(0.0585, 0.1455)	0.042

Then, the BN positive inference was conducted, and the DFEE risk prediction results are shown in Figure 6. For high risks, the ranking of the obtained occurrence probabilities was as follows: proposed fuzzy BN inference algorithm (14.67%) > CM-IT1 FS-based fuzzy BN inference algorithm (10.39%) > traditional CM-crisp value-based BN inference algorithm (6.82%).

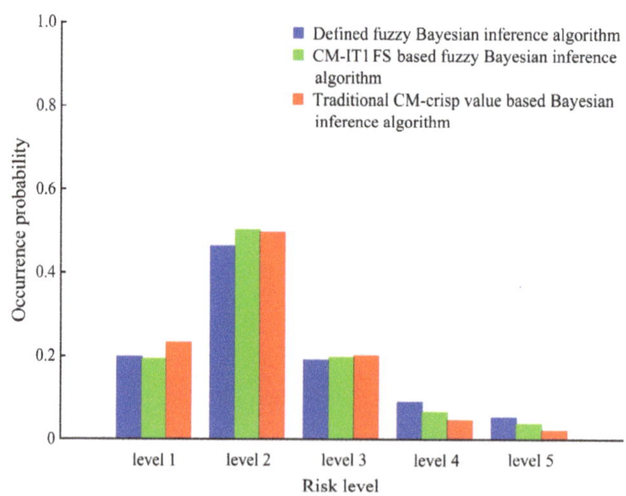

Figure 6. DFEE risk prediction results. Note: Occurrence probabilities were obtained using the proposed fuzzy BN inference algorithm and the CM-IT1 FS based fuzzy BN inference algorithm, and they are the mean values of the sampling values.

The reasons for the above ranking were as follows. Most a priori probabilities obtained using the CM-IT1 FS-based fuzzy BN inference algorithm and the traditional BN inference algorithm were assigned to low and medium risks (levels 1, 2, and 3), but high risks (levels 4 and 5) were underestimated. When the realistic DFEE risk is high, the risk prediction result obtained using the proposed fuzzy BN inference algorithm can truly reflect the actual situation. This is of great help for decisionmakers to take timely corrective actions to avoid the risk of accidents.

5.2. The BN Reverse Inference Results Were Analyzed

The BN reverse inference was conducted. The SPMs for each root node were calculated; the results are shown in Table 8, and the rankings of SPMs for each root node are shown in Table 9. In Tables 8 and 9, SPM_1 and SPM_2 represent the obtained mean values of fuzzy SPMs using the proposed fuzzy BN inference algorithm and the CM-IT1 FS-based fuzzy BN inference algorithm, respectively, and SPM_3 represents the obtained SPM using the traditional CM-crisp value-based BN inference algorithm.

Table 8. SPM calculation results.

Root Node	SPM_1	SPM_2	SPM_3	Root Node	SPM_1	SPM_2	SPM_3
R_{11}	0.1975	0.2656	0.5843	R_{22}	0.1937	0.2623	0.3567
R_{12}	0.2560	0.3228	0.5945	R_{23}	0.1323	0.1774	0.3398
R_{13}	0.1321	0.1772	0.4817	R_{31}	0.0092	0.0188	0.4571
R_{21}	0.2557	0.3223	1.2607	R_{32}	0.2280	0.3195	0.5364

Table 9. SPM rankings.

Root Node	SPM_1	SPM_2	SPM_3	Root Node	SPM_1	SPM_2	SPM_3
R_{11}	4	4	3	R_{22}	5	5	7
R_{12}	1	1	2	R_{23}	6	6	8
R_{13}	7	7	5	R_{31}	8	8	6
R_{21}	2	2	1	R_{32}	3	3	4

As shown in Table 8, the order of SPM was $SPM_3 > SPM_2 > SPM_1$. As shown in Table 9, four risk factors containing R_{12}, R_{21}, R_{32}, and R_{11} had a great impact on the occurrence of the DFEE accidents.

The reasons for the above results were as follows: When compared with the CM-IT1 FS-based a priori probability and the CM-crisp value-based a priori probability, the CM-IT2 FS-based a priori probability had a wider range of values because it expressed more uncertain, fuzzy, random, and conflicting information. The comparative result is shown in Table 7. When calculating the fuzzy SPM of root node X_i using the proposed fuzzy BN inference algorithm, we assumed that the a priori probability of X_i subordinating to the j-th level was 1, and the a priori probabilities subordinating to the other four risk levels were 0, and this would change its fuzzy a priori probability. Meanwhile, in the process of random sampling for fuzzy a priori probabilities of other root nodes, it would produce some difference among sampling values and CM-crisp value-based a priori probabilities. This process compensated for the changing value of fuzzy a priori probability of root node X_i to some extent, which caused little change in the fuzzy occurrence probability of leaf nodes, making SPM_1 smaller than SPM_1 and SPM_3.

6. Conclusions

In our study, a new fuzzy BN inference approach for risk assessments was proposed on the basis of CM, IT2 FS, IT2 FLS, D-S ET, and LHS methods. The DFEE risk prediction and DFEE risk sensitivity analysis were conducted using the proposed fuzzy BN inference algorithm. The DFEE risk prediction result indicated that the DFEE risk was assessed as low risk, however, attention should be paid to the potential high risks. The DFEE risk sensitivity analysis result indicated that four risk factors had a great impact on the occurrence of DFEE accidents, and this provided the clear direction for XNPCL to continuously improve the DFEE risk management process.

However, our study has the following two limitations: One is that we only analyzed the DFEE risk for the NPP construction project. The other is that we only used the proposed approach for a typical case. Therefore, in a future study, we will expand the studied risk to other risks, which include work at height, temporary electricity, occupational health, etc., to propose a universal fuzzy BN inference approach for safety-related risk assessments, and then we will use the proposed approach in other projects.

Author Contributions: Conceptualization, J.X.; methodology, R.D.; software, T.D.; validation, M.Z.; formal analysis, R.D. and M.Z.; resources, T.Y.; data curation, Y.S.; writing—original draft preparation, J.X.; writing—review and editing, Y.S.; visualization, T.D.; supervision, T.Y.; project administration, Y.S.; funding acquisition, Y.S. All authors have read and agreed to the published version of the manuscript.

Funding: This research was funded by the National Natural Science Foundation of China, grant number 52174189 and 11805094, and the Natural Science Foundation of Hunan Province, grant number 2023JJ10035.

Data Availability Statement: Data are contained within the article.

Conflicts of Interest: The authors declare no conflicts of interest.

References

1. Peet, W.; Ryan, R. Risk Management in a Network Operation—Understanding Complex Systems. In *Owning the Future: Integrated Risk Management in Practice*; Centre for Advanced Engineering: Christchurch, New Zealand, 1998; pp. 255–274.
2. Yang, Y.; Wang, J.; Wang, G.; Chen, Y.W. Research and Development Project Risk Assessment Using a Belief Rule-Based System with Random Subspaces. *Knowl.-Based Syst.* **2019**, *178*, 51–60. [CrossRef]
3. Sun, B.; Zhou, Y.; Wang, J.; Zhang, W. A New PC-PSO algorithm for Bayesian Network Structure Learning with Structure Priors. *Expert Syst. Appl.* **2021**, *184*, 115237. [CrossRef]
4. Akhavan, M.; Sebt, M.V.; Ameli, M. Risk Assessment Modeling for Knowledge Based and Startup Projects Based on Feasibility Studies: A Bayesian Network Approach. *Knowl.-Based Syst.* **2021**, *222*, 106992. [CrossRef]
5. Zarei, E.; Azadeh, A.; Khakzad, N.; Aliabadi, M.M.; Mohammadfam, I. Dynamic Safety Assessment of Natural Gas Stations Using Bayesian Network. *J. Hazard. Mater.* **2017**, *321*, 830–840. [CrossRef]
6. Zhang, G.H.; Chen, W.; Jiao, Y.Y.; Wang, H.; Wang, C.T. A Failure Probability Evaluation Method for Collapse of Drill-and-Blast Tunnels Based on Multistate Fuzzy Bayesian Network. *Eng. Geol.* **2020**, *276*, 105752. [CrossRef]
7. Li, K.; Fang, L.; Lu, T. Bayesian Panel Smooth Transition Model with Spatial Correlation. *PLoS ONE* **2019**, *14*, e0211467. [CrossRef] [PubMed]
8. Yu, J.; Wu, S.; Yu, Y.; Chen, H.; Fan, H.; Liu, J.; Ge, S. Process System Failure Evaluation Method Based on a Noisy-OR Gate Intuitionistic Fuzzy Bayesian Network in an Uncertain Environment. *Process Saf. Environ. Prot.* **2021**, *150*, 281–297.
9. Dong, Y.; Wang, T. Risk Evaluation of Registered Specifications and Internal Release Limits Using a Bayesian Approach. In Proceedings of the Pharmaceutical Statistics: MBSW 39, Muncie, IN, USA, 16–18 May 2016; Liu, R., Tsong, Y., Eds.; Springer International Publishing: Cham, Switzerland, 2019; pp. 89–99.
10. Kim, J.; Shah, A.U.A.; Kang, H.G. Dynamic Risk Assessment with Bayesian Network and Clustering Analysis. *Reliab. Eng. Syst. Saf.* **2020**, *201*, 106959. [CrossRef]
11. Lee, C.J.; Lee, K.J. Application of Bayesian Network to the Probabilistic Risk Assessment of Nuclear Waste Disposal. *Reliab. Eng. Syst. Saf.* **2006**, *91*, 515–532. [CrossRef]
12. Tolo, S.; Patelli, E.; Beer, M. Bayesian Network Approach for Risk Assessment of a Spent Nuclear Fuel Pond. In *Vulnerability, Uncertainty, and Risk*; American Society of Civil Engineers (ASCE): Reston, VA, USA, 2014; pp. 598–607.
13. Barua, S.; Gao, X.; Pasman, H.; Mannan, M.S. Bayesian Network Based Dynamic Operational Risk Assessment. *J. Loss Prev. Process Ind.* **2016**, *41*, 399–410. [CrossRef]
14. Khakzad, N. Application of Dynamic Bayesian Network to Risk Analysis of Domino Effects in Chemical Infrastructures. *Reliab. Eng. Syst. Saf.* **2015**, *138*, 263–272. [CrossRef]
15. Zhang, J.; Cai, B.; Mulenga, K.; Liu, Y.; Xie, M. Bayesian Network-Based Risk Analysis Methodology: A Case of Atmospheric and Vacuum Distillation Unit. *Process Saf. Environ. Prot.* **2018**, *117*, 660–674. [CrossRef]
16. Lu, Y.; Wang, T.; Liu, T. Bayesian Network-Based Risk Analysis of Chemical Plant Explosion Accidents. *Int. J. Environ. Res. Public Health* **2020**, *17*, 5364. [CrossRef]
17. Chen, T.T.; Leu, S. Sen Fall Risk Assessment of Cantilever Bridge Projects Using Bayesian Network. *Saf. Sci.* **2014**, *70*, 161–171. [CrossRef]

18. Namazian, A.; Haji Yakhchali, S. Modified Bayesian Network–Based Risk Analysis of Construction Projects: Case Study of South Pars Gas Field Development Projects. *ASCE-ASME J. Risk Uncertain. Eng. Syst. Part A Civ. Eng.* **2018**, *4*, 05018003. [CrossRef]
19. Wang, Z.Z.; Chen, C. Fuzzy Comprehensive Bayesian Network-Based Safety Risk Assessment for Metro Construction Projects. *Tunn. Undergr. Space Technol.* **2017**, *70*, 330–342. [CrossRef]
20. Zhang, L.; Wu, X.; Skibniewski, M.J.; Zhong, J.; Lu, Y. Bayesian-Network-Based Safety Risk Analysis in Construction Projects. *Reliab. Eng. Syst. Saf.* **2014**, *131*, 29–39. [CrossRef]
21. Huang, W.; Zhang, Y.; Kou, X.; Yin, D.; Mi, R.; Li, L. Railway Dangerous Goods Transportation System Risk Analysis: An Interpretive Structural Modeling and Bayesian Network Combining Approach. *Reliab. Eng. Syst. Saf.* **2020**, *204*, 107220. [CrossRef]
22. Khan, R.U.; Yin, J.; Mustafa, F.S.; Anning, N. Risk Assessment for Berthing of Hazardous Cargo Vessels Using Bayesian Networks. *Ocean Coast. Manag.* **2021**, *210*, 105673. [CrossRef]
23. Zarei, E.; Gholamizadeh, K.; Khan, F.; Khakzad, N. A Dynamic Domino Effect Risk Analysis Model for Rail Transport of Hazardous Material. *J. Loss Prev. Process Ind.* **2022**, *74*, 104666. [CrossRef]
24. Zhao, L.; Wang, X.; Qian, Y. Analysis of Factors That Influence Hazardous Material Transportation Accidents Based on Bayesian Networks: A Case Study in China. *Saf. Sci.* **2012**, *50*, 1049–1055. [CrossRef]
25. Ferdous, R.; Khan, F.; Sadiq, R.; Amyotte, P.; Veitch, B. Handling and Updating Uncertain Information in Bow-Tie Analysis. *J. Loss Prev. Process Ind.* **2012**, *25*, 8–19. [CrossRef]
26. Tolo, S.; Patelli, E.; Beer, M. Robust Vulnerability Analysis of Nuclear Facilities Subject to External Hazards. *Stoch. Environ. Res. Risk Assess.* **2017**, *31*, 2733–2756. [CrossRef]
27. Hidalgo, D.; Melin, P.; Castillo, O. An Optimization Method for Designing Type-2 Fuzzy Inference Systems Based on the Footprint of Uncertainty Using Genetic Algorithms. *Expert Syst. Appl.* **2012**, *39*, 4590–4598. [CrossRef]
28. Wang, L.X. A New Look at Type-2 Fuzzy Sets and Type-2 Fuzzy Logic Systems. *IEEE Trans. Fuzzy Syst.* **2017**, *25*, 693–706. [CrossRef]
29. Melin, P.; Castillo, O. A Review on the Applications of Type-2 Fuzzy Logic in Classification and Pattern Recognition. *Expert Syst. Appl.* **2013**, *40*, 5413–5423. [CrossRef]
30. Leal-Ramírez, C.; Castillo, O.; Melin, P.; Rodríguez-Díaz, A. Simulation of the Bird Age-Structured Population Growth Based on an Interval Type-2 Fuzzy Cellular Structure. *Inf. Sci.* **2011**, *181*, 519–535. [CrossRef]
31. Li, Y.; Sun, Y.; Hua, J.; Li, L. Indirect Adaptive Type-2 Fuzzy Impulsive Control of Nonlinear Systems. *IEEE Trans. Fuzzy Syst.* **2015**, *23*, 1084–1099. [CrossRef]
32. Khosravi, A.; Nahavandi, S.; Creighton, D. Short Term Load Forecasting Using Interval Type-2 Fuzzy Logic Systems. In Proceedings of the 2011 IEEE International Conference on Fuzzy Systems (FUZZ-IEEE 2011), Taipei, China, 27–30 June 2011; pp. 502–508.
33. Bahrebar, S.; Blaabjerg, F.; Wang, H.; Vafamand, N.; Khooban, M.H.; Rastayesh, S.; Zhou, D. A Novel Type-2 Fuzzy Logic for Improved Risk Analysis of Proton Exchange Membrane Fuel Cells in Marine Power Systems Application. *Energies* **2018**, *11*, 721. [CrossRef]
34. Jana, D.K.; Pramanik, S.; Sahoo, P.; Mukherjee, A. Interval Type-2 Fuzzy Logic and Its Application to Occupational Safety Risk Performance in Industries. *Soft Comput.* **2019**, *23*, 557–567. [CrossRef]
35. Macura, D.; Laketić, M.; Pamučar, D.; Marinković, D. Risk Analysis Model with Interval Type-2 Fuzzy FMEA—Case Study of Railway Infrastructure Projects in the Republic of Serbia. *Acta Polytech. Hung.* **2022**, *19*, 103–118. [CrossRef]
36. Li, X.; Ran, Y.; Zhang, G.; He, Y. A Failure Mode and Risk Assessment Method Based on Cloud Model. *J. Intell. Manuf.* **2020**, *31*, 1339–1352. [CrossRef]
37. Gong, X.; Yu, C.; Min, L. A Cloud Theory-Based Multi-Objective Portfolio Selection Model with Variable Risk Appetite. *Expert Syst. Appl.* **2021**, *176*, 114911. [CrossRef]
38. Yang, X.; Xu, Z.; Xu, J. Large-Scale Group Delphi Method with Heterogeneous Decision Information and Dynamic Weights. *Expert Syst. Appl.* **2023**, *213*, 118782. [CrossRef]
39. Guo, Y.; Meng, X.; Meng, T.; Wang, D.; Liu, S. A Novel Method of Risk Assessment Based on Cloud Inference for Natural Gas Pipelines. *J. Nat. Gas Sci. Eng.* **2016**, *30*, 421–429. [CrossRef]
40. Wu, Y.; Hu, M.; Liao, M.; Liu, F.; Xu, C. Risk Assessment of Renewable Energy-Based Island Microgrid Using the HFLTS-Cloud Model Method. *J. Clean. Prod.* **2021**, *284*, 125362. [CrossRef]
41. Yu, J.; Chen, H.; Wu, S.; Fan, H. A Novel Risk Matrix Approach Based on Cloud Model for Risk Assessment under Uncertainty. *IEEE Access* **2021**, *9*, 27884–27896.
42. Liu, J.; Gong, B. Analysis of Uncertainty Multi-attribute Group Decision Making Process Based on D-S Evidence Theory. *J. Comput.* **2011**, *6*, 711–717. [CrossRef]
43. Zhang, W.; Ji, X.; Yang, Y.; Chen, J.; Gao, Z.; Qiu, X. Data Fusion Method Based on Improved D-S Evidence Theory. In Proceedings of the 2018 IEEE International Conference on Big Data and Smart Computing (BigComp), Shanghai, China, 15–17 January 2018; pp. 760–766.
44. Dou, Z.; Xu, X.; Lin, Y.; Zhou, R. Application of D-S Evidence Fusion Method in the Fault Detection of Temperature Sensor. *Math. Probl. Eng.* **2014**, *2014*, 395057. [CrossRef]
45. Gong, Y.; Su, X.; Qian, H.; Yang, N. Research on Fault Diagnosis Methods for the Reactor Coolant System of Nuclear Power Plant Based on D-S Evidence Theory. *Ann. Nucl. Energy* **2018**, *112*, 395–399. [CrossRef]

46. Liu, H.; Ma, Z.; Deng, X.; Jiang, W. A New Method to Air Target Threat Evaluation Based on Dempster-Shafer Evidence Theory. In Proceedings of the 2018 Chinese Control And Decision Conference (CCDC), Shenyang, China, 9–11 June 2018; pp. 2504–2508.
47. Pan, Y.; Zhang, L.; Li, Z.W.; Ding, L. Improved Fuzzy Bayesian Network-Based Risk Analysis with Interval-Valued Fuzzy Sets and D-S Evidence Theory. *IEEE Trans. Fuzzy Syst.* **2020**, *28*, 2063–2077. [CrossRef]
48. Guo, J. A Risk Assessment Approach for Failure Mode and Effects Analysis Based on Intuitionistic Fuzzy Sets and Evidence Theory. *J. Intell. Fuzzy Syst.* **2016**, *30*, 869–881. [CrossRef]
49. Zhang, J.; Liu, M.; Dong, M. Variational Bayesian Inference for Interval Regression with An Asymmetric Laplace Distribution. *Neurocomputing* **2019**, *323*, 214–230. [CrossRef]
50. Hajian, M.; Rosehart, W.D.; Zareipour, H. Probabilistic Power Flow by Monte Carlo Simulation with Latin Supercube Sampling. *IEEE Trans. Power Syst.* **2013**, *28*, 1550–1559. [CrossRef]
51. Hoffman, M.D.; Blei, D.M.; Wang, C.; Paisley, J. StochasticVariational Inference. *J. Mach. Learn. Res.* **2013**, *14*, 1303–1347.
52. Shields, M.D.; Zhang, J. The Generalization of Latin Hypercube Sampling. *Reliab. Eng. Syst. Saf.* **2016**, *148*, 96–108. [CrossRef]
53. Banyay, G.A.; Shields, M.D.; Brigham, J.C. Efficient Global Sensitivity Analysis of Structural Vibration for a Nuclear Reactor System Subject to Nonstationary Loading. *Nucl. Eng. Des.* **2020**, *361*, 110544. [CrossRef]
54. Su, L.; Li, X.L.; Jiang, Y.P. Comparison of Methodologies for Seismic Fragility Analysis of Unreinforced Masonry Buildings Considering Epistemic Uncertainty. *Eng. Struct.* **2020**, *205*, 110059. [CrossRef]
55. Banyay, G.A.; Shields, M.D.; Brigham, J.C. Efficient Global Sensitivity Analysis for Flow-Induced Vibration of a Nuclear Reactor Assembly Using Kriging Surrogates. *Nucl. Eng. Des.* **2019**, *341*, 1–15. [CrossRef]
56. Shu, Z.; Jirutitijaroen, P. Latin Hypercube Sampling Techniques for Power Systems Reliability Analysis with Renewable Energy Sources. *IEEE Trans. Power Syst.* **2011**, *26*, 2066–2073.
57. Zhang, Z.; Wang, T.; Chen, Y.; Lan, J. Design of Type-2 Fuzzy Logic Systems Based on Improved Ant Colony Optimization. *Int. J. Control Autom. Syst.* **2019**, *17*, 536–544. [CrossRef]
58. Sanchez, M.A.; Castillo, O.; Castro, J.R. Generalized Type-2 Fuzzy Systems for Controlling a Mobile Robot and a Performance Comparison with Interval Type-2 and Type-1 Fuzzy Systems. *Expert Syst. Appl.* **2015**, *42*, 5904–5914. [CrossRef]
59. Liao, L.; Guo, W.W. Incorporating Utility and Cloud Theories for Owner Evaluation in Tendering. *Expert Syst. Appl.* **2012**, *39*, 5894–5899. [CrossRef]
60. Tolo, S.; Patelli, E.; Beer, M. An Open Toolbox for the Reduction, Inference Computation and Sensitivity Analysis of Credal Networks. *Adv. Eng. Softw.* **2018**, *115*, 126–148. [CrossRef]
61. Khakzad, N. System Safety Assessment under Epistemic Uncertainty: Using Imprecise Probabilities in Bayesian Network. *Saf. Sci.* **2019**, *116*, 149–160. [CrossRef]
62. Bisht, K.; Kumar, A. A Portfolio Construction Model Based on Sector Analysis Using Dempster-Shafer Evidence Theory and Granger Causal Network: An Application to National Stock Exchange of India. *Expert Syst. Appl.* **2023**, *215*, 119434. [CrossRef]
63. Luo, H.; Yang, S.L.; Hu, X.J.; Hu, X.X. Agent Oriented Intelligent Fault Diagnosis System Using Evidence Theory. *Expert Syst. Appl.* **2012**, *39*, 2524–2531. [CrossRef]
64. Xu, J.; Ding, R.; Li, M.; Dai, T.; Zheng, M.; Yu, T.; Sui, Y. A New Bayesian Network Model for Risk Assessment Based on Cloud Model, Interval Type-2 Fuzzy Sets and Improved D-S Evidence Theory. *Inf. Sci.* **2022**, *618*, 336–355. [CrossRef]
65. Wu, Z.; Yang, C.; Zheng, R. Developing a Holistic Fuzzy Hierarchy-Cloud Assessment Model for the Connection Risk of Renewable Energy Microgrid. *Energy* **2022**, *245*, 123235. [CrossRef]
66. Xu, J.; Zhai, J. Research on the Evaluation of Green Innovation Capability of Manufacturing Enterprises in Innovation Network. *Sustainability* **2020**, *12*, 807. [CrossRef]
67. Huang, G.; Xiao, L. Failure Mode and Effect Analysis: An Interval-Valued Intuitionistic Fuzzy Cloud Theory-Based Method. *Appl. Soft Comput.* **2021**, *98*, 106834. [CrossRef]
68. Zhou, H.; Zhang, H. Risk Assessment Methodology for A Deep Doundation Pit Construction Project in Shanghai, China. *J. Constr. Eng. Manag.* **2011**, *137*, 1185–1194. [CrossRef]

symmetry

MDPI

Article

On Neutrosophic Fuzzy Metric Space and Its Topological Properties

Samriddhi Ghosh [1], Sonam [1], Ramakant Bhardwaj [1] and Satyendra Narayan [2,*]

[1] Department of Mathematics, Amity University Kolkata, Newtown, Kolkata 700135, West Bengal, India; samriddhi.ghosh3@s.amity.edu (S.G.); smotla@kol.amity.edu (S.); rbhardwaj@kol.amity.edu (R.B.)
[2] Department of Applied Computing, Sheridan Institute of Technology, Oakville, ON L6H 2L1, Canada
* Correspondence: satyendra.narayan@sheridancollege.ca or narayan.satyendra@gmail.com

Abstract: The present research introduces a novel concept termed "neutrosophic fuzzy metric space", which extends the traditional metric space framework by incorporating the notion of neutrosophic fuzzy sets. A thorough investigation of various structural and topological properties within this newly proposed generalization of metric space has been conducted. Additionally, counterparts of well-known theorems such as the Uniform Convergence Theorem and the Baire Category Theorem have been established for this generalized metric space. Through rigorous analysis, a detailed understanding of its fundamental characteristics has been attained, illuminating its potential applications and theoretical significance.

Keywords: fuzzy sets; neutrosophic sets; neutrosophic fuzzy sets; neutrosophic metric space; neutrosophic fuzzy metric space

1. Introduction

Fuzzy set theory is a mathematical framework that deals with sets whose elements have degrees of membership. This departure from traditional set theory, where an element either belongs or does not belong to a set, allows for more nuanced and flexible modelling, particularly in situations where boundaries between categories are ambiguous or uncertain. Zadeh's [1] seminal paper, "Fuzzy Sets", published in 1965, laid the foundation for this field of study. This whole new field of study has influenced many other scientific fields since that time. Numerous advancements have emerged subsequent to Zadeh's introduction of fuzzy sets in 1965. For instance, Atanassov [2] introduced intuitionistic fuzzy sets, Smarandache [3] proposed neutrosophic sets, and in 2023, Al-Shami and Mhemdi [4] introduced orthopair fuzzy sets. These foundational contributions paved the way for the development of various related concepts, including the introduction of fuzzy metric spaces by Kramosil and Michálek [5] in 1975 and its modification by George and Veeramani [6] in 1994 , intuitionistic fuzzy topological spaces by Coker [7] in 1997, and intuitionistic fuzzy metric spaces by Park [8] in 2004.

The introduction of all these concepts and ideologies has impacted many other research works by several mathematicians, such as: in 1984, Kaleva and Seikkala [9] defined fuzzy metric space as a distance between two points and expressed it as a positive fuzzy number; in 2006, Smarandache [10] gave the notion of neutrosophic sets as a generalization of intuitionistic fuzzy sets; Salama and Alblowi [11] in 2012 extended the concepts of fuzzy topological space and intuitionistic fuzzy topological space to the case of neutrosophic sets; Ejegwa [12], in 2014, introduced some algebraic operations such as modal operator, and normalization to intuitionistic fuzzy sets; and Majumdar [13] conducted an exploration into the practical applications of neutrosophic sets within decision-making contexts. Apart from these, several researchers delved into various generalizations of fuzzy metric space such as intuitionistic fuzzy metric space, soft fuzzy metric space, fuzzy soft metric space, orthogonal fuzzy metric space, bipolar fuzzy metric space, etc. [14–24]. Furthermore,

Broumi [25] introduced several novel concepts related to neutrosophic sets, including refined neutrosophic sets, bipolar neutrosophic sets, neutrosophic hesitant sets, multi-valued neutrosophic sets, rough neutrosophic sets, and rough bipolar neutrosophic sets. Additionally, Jeyaraman [26] applied multi-criteria decision-making (MCDM) techniques in conjunction with neutrosophic sets to address a real-life problem involving wind turbines.

In 2020, Kirisci and Şimşek [27] introduced the notion of neutrosophic metric spaces. Further, several fixed-point results have been established in this generalization [28] with some generalizations of neutrosophic fuzzy metric space were introduced by researchers such as orthogonal neutrosophic metric spaces by Ishtiaq et al. [29], neutrosophic 2-metric spaces by Asghar et al. [30], orthogonal neutrosophic 2-metric spaces by Janardhanan et al. [31], neutrosophic pentagonal metric spaces by Mani et al. [32], neutrosophic b-metric space [33], etc. Further, Das et al. [34] introduced the conception of neutrosophic fuzzy sets. It is quite noticeable how the concept of fuzzy sets has been used to establish the concept of fuzzy metric space. In a similar way, the ideology of neutrosophic sets has been used to define the conception of neutrosophic metric space. Keeping these in mind, the primary objective of this research is to elucidate the conceptual framework of neutrosophic fuzzy metric space. The concept of neutrosophic fuzzy sets has been utilised for this purpose, in a similar manner as described above.

The motivation behind introducing neutrosophic fuzzy metric spaces (NFMS) lies in their ability to model uncertainty and indeterminacy in real-world phenomena more accurately than traditional fuzzy or crisp sets. Neutrosophic sets allow for the representation of elements with three components, truth, indeterminacy, and falsehood, providing a more nuanced description of uncertainty. An example that highlights the need for NFMS could be in the field of medical diagnosis. Consider a scenario where a patient presents symptoms that are not clearly indicative of a single disease. Traditional fuzzy sets could represent the likelihood of the patient having a certain disease on a continuum between 0 and 1. However, this approach might not adequately capture the uncertainty associated with the diagnosis, especially if the symptoms are ambiguous or conflicting. In contrast, neutrosophic sets can represent the uncertainty more comprehensively by explicitly accounting for the degree of truth, indeterminacy, and falsehood associated with each symptom and potential diagnosis. NFMS can then be used to define a metric space where the distance between two diagnoses reflects not only their similarity but also the degree of uncertainty or indeterminacy associated with each.

By introducing NFMS, we provide a mathematical framework that aligns more closely with the complex and uncertain nature of real-world phenomena, such as medical diagnosis, decision making under uncertainty, or pattern recognition in ambiguous data sets. This motivates the development of NFMS theory to enhance our ability to model, analyze, and make decisions in uncertain environments more effectively.

The following describes the structure of the paper. Some characteristics and fundamental ideas of neutrosophic fuzzy sets and neutrosophic metric spaces are provided in Section 2. Section 3 introduces the conception of neutrosophic fuzzy metric space, followed by examples of neutrosophic fuzzy metric space. The topological characteristics of the established generalization of metric space have been demonstrated in this section. In this section, we have also presented various results describing distinct properties of the established neutrosophic fuzzy metric space, such as the Hausdorff property, compactness, completeness, and nowhere denseness. Section 4 of this work contains the conclusion. Further, this study can be extended to investigate neutrosophic fuzzy metric space in connection with other concepts such as best proximity point results, optimization theory, approximation theory, etc. Moreover, concepts like soft sets, soft equality, soft lattices, etc., can be connected to the established theory and results [35,36].

2. Preliminaries

In this section, we provide some fundamentally useful definitions for establishing the main results. Here, $]0^-, 1^+[$ is a non-standard unit interval, where the non-standard finite numbers $(1^+) = 1 + \varepsilon$, where "1" is its standard part and ε its non-standard part, and $(0^-) = 0 - \varepsilon$, where "0" is its standard part and ε its non-standard part. Here, 0 and 1 are analogously non-standard numbers infinitely small but less than 0 or infinitely small but greater than 1, respectively, and belong to the non-standard unit interval $]0^-, 1^+[$.

Definition 1 ([1]). *With respect to a universal set X, a fuzzy set F is characterised by the expression* $F = \{< a, \mu_F(a) >: 0 \le \mu_F(a) \le 1, a \in X\}$. *Here,* $\mu_F(a)$ *signifies the membership grade of a in F.*

Definition 2 ([27]). *A neutrosophic set* $\mathbf{N}$ *with respect to a universal set X is declared as* $\mathbf{N} = \{< a, (T_{\mathbf{N}}(a), I_{\mathbf{N}}(a), F_{\mathbf{N}}(a)) >: a \in X,\ T_{\mathbf{N}}(a), I_{\mathbf{N}}(a), F_{\mathbf{N}}(a) \in]0^-, 1^+[\}$. *Here,* $T_{\mathbf{N}}(a), I_{\mathbf{N}}(a)$, *and* $F_{\mathbf{N}}(a)$ *denote the truth, indeterminacy, and falsity membership grades of a in* $\mathbf{N}$, *respectively, and* $]0^-, 1^+[$ *a non-standard unit interval.*

Definition 3 ([34]). *A neutrosophic fuzzy set B in a universal set X is defined as*

$$B = \{< x, (\mu_B(x), T_B(x,\mu), I_B(x,\mu), F(x,\mu)) >: x \in X, \mu_B(x) \in [0,1],$$
$$T_B(x,\mu), I_B(x,\mu),\ F(x,\mu) \in]0^-, 1^+[\}$$

In this context, each membership grade $\mu_B(x)$ *is expressed by a truth, indeterminacy, and falsity membership grade denoted by* $T_B(x,\mu), I_B(x,\mu)$ *and* $F(x,\mu)$, *respectively, and* $]0^-, 1^+[$ *a non-standard unit interval.*

Definition 4 ([6,27]). *A function* $\star : [0,1] \times [0,1] \to [0,1]$ *is said to be a continuous t-norm (TN) if the following conditions hold* $\forall\ t,s,j,k \in [0,1]$:

1. $t \star 1 = t$;
2. $t \le s$ *and* $j \le k$ *implies* $t \star j \le s \star k$;
3. *continuity of* $\star$;
4. *commutativity and associativity of* $\star$.

Definition 5 ([6,27]). *A function* $\diamond : [0,1] \times [0,1] \to [0,1]$ *is said to be a continuous t-conorm (TC) if the following conditions hold* $\forall\ t,s,j,k \in [0,1]$:

1. $t \diamond 0 = t$;
2. $t \le s$ *and* $j \le k$ *implies* $t \diamond j \le s \diamond k$;
3. *Continuity of* $\diamond$;
4. *Commutativity and associativity of* $\diamond$.

Definition 6 ([27]). *A 6-tuple* $(G, A, M, R, \star, \diamond)$ *is known as a Neutrophic Metric Space (NMS) if G is a non-empty arbitary set,* $\star$ *represents a continuous t-norm,* $\diamond$ *denotes a continuous t-conorm, and A, M, and R are three fuzzy sets defined on* $G^2 \times (0, \infty)$, *subject to the following conditions for all* $p, q, r \in G$ *and* $s, t > 0$:

1. $0 \le A(p,q,t) \le 1,\ 0 \le M(p,q,t) \le 1,\ 0 \le R(p,q,t) \le 1$;
2. $A(p,q,t) + M(p,q,t) + R(p,q,t) \le 3$;
3. $A(p,q,t) = A(q,p,t)$;
4. $A(p,q,t) = 1$ *if* $p = q$;
5. $\lim_{t\to\infty} A(p,q,t) = 1$;
6. $A(p,q,t) \star A(q,r,s) \le A(p,r,t+s)$;
7. *Continuity of* $A(p,q,.) : \mathbb{R}^+ \cup 0 \to (0,1]$;
8. $M(p,q,t) = M(q,p,t)$;
9. $M(p,q,t) = 0$ *if* $p = q$;
10. $\lim_{t\to\infty} M(p,q,t) = 0$;
11. $M(p,q,t) \diamond M(q,r,s) \ge M(p,r,t+s)$;
12. *Continuity of* $M(p,q,.) : \mathbb{R}^+ \cup 0 \to (0,1]$;
13. $R(p,q,t) = R(q,p,t)$;
14. $R(p,q,t) = 0$ *if* $p = q$;
15. $\lim_{t\to\infty} R(p,q,t) = 0$;
16. $R(p,q,t) \diamond R(q,r,s) \ge R(p,r,t+s)$;

17. *Continuity of* $R(p,q,.) : \mathbb{R}^+ \cup 0 \to (0,1]$;
18. *For* $t \leq 0$, $A(p,q,t) = 0$, $M(p,q,t) = 1$ *and* $R(p,q,t) = 1$.

In this context, $A(x,y,t)$ *represents the degree of nearness,* $M(x,y,t)$ *stands for the degree of neutralness, and* $R(x,y,t)$ *denotes the degree of non-nearness between* x *and* y *with respect to* t*, respectively.*

3. Neutrosophic Fuzzy Metric Space and Its Topological Properties

This section introduces the concept of neutrosophic fuzzy metric space and explores various topological characteristics of it. Firstly, we present the definition of a neutrosophic fuzzy metric space.

Definition 7. *A 7-tuple* $(G, S, A, M, R, \star, \diamond)$ *is known as a Neutrophic Fuzzy Metric Space (NFMS) if* G *is an arbitary set,* $\star$ *is a continuous t-norm,* $\diamond$ *is a continuous t-conorm, and* S, A, M*, and* R *are fuzzy sets on* $G^2 \times (0,\infty)$ *satisfying the following conditions:*
$\forall\, p,q,r \in G$ *and* $t,s > 0$,

1. $0 \leq S(p,q,t) \leq 1,\ 0 \leq A(p,q,t) \leq 1,\ 0 \leq M(p,q,t) \leq 1,\ 0 \leq R(p,q,t) \leq 1$;
2. $S(p,q,t) + A(p,q,t) + M(p,q,t) + R(p,q,t) \leq 4$;
3. $S(p,q,t) = S(q,p,t)$;
4. $S(p,q,t) = 1$ *if* $p = q$;
5. $\lim_{t\to\infty} S(p,q,t) = 1$;
6. $S(p,q,t) \star S(q,r,s) \leq S(p,r,t+s)$;
7. $S(p,q,.) : \mathbb{R}^+ \cup \{0\} \to (0,1]$ *is continuous;*
8. $A(p,q,t) = A(q,p,t)$;
9. $A(p,q,t) = 1$ *if* $p = q$;
10. $\lim_{t\to\infty} A(p,q,t) = 1$;
11. $A(p,q,t) \star A(q,r,s) \leq A(p,r,t+s)$;
12. $A(p,q,.) : \mathbb{R}^+ \cup \{0\} \to (0,1]$ *is continuous;*
13. $M(p,q,t) = M(q,p,t)$;
14. $M(p,q,t) = 0$ *if* $p = q$
15. $\lim_{t\to\infty} M(p,q,t) = 0$;
16. $M(p,q,t) \diamond M(q,r,s) \geq M(p,r,t+s)$;
17. $M(p,q,.) : \mathbb{R}^+ \cup \{0\} \to (0,1]$ *is continuous;*
18. $R(p,q,t) = R(q,p,t)$;
19. $R(p,q,t) = 0$ *if* $p = q$;
20. $\lim_{t\to\infty} R(p,q,t) = 0$;
21. $R(p,q,t) \diamond R(q,r,s) \geq R(p,r,t+s)$;
22. $R(p,q,.) : \mathbb{R}^+ \cup \{0\} \to (0,1]$ *is continuous;*
23. *For* $t \leq 0$, $S(p,q,t) = 0$, $A(p,q,t) = 0$, $M(p,q,t) = 1$ *and* $R(p,q,t) = 1$.

In this context, $S(x,y,t)$ *represents the certainity that distance between* x *and* y *is less than* t*,* $A(x,y,t)$ *represents the degree of nearness,* $M(x,y,t)$ *stadns for the degree of neutralness, and* $R(x,y,t)$ *denotes the degree of non-nearness between* x *and* y *with respect to* t*, respectively.*

Example 1. *Let* (G,d) *be a metric space where* $G = (-\infty,\infty)$ *and* $d(x,y) = |x-y|$*. Define the t-norm and t-conorm,* $\star$ *and* $\diamond$ *as* $x \star y = \min\{x,y\}$ *and* $x \diamond y = \max\{x,y\}$*. And let the fuzzy sets* S, A, M, R *on* $G^2 \times (0,\infty)$ *be defined as:*

$$S(x,y,t) = \frac{t+d(x,y)}{t+2d(x,y)}, A(x,y,t) = \frac{t}{t+d(x,y)}, M(x,y,t) = \frac{d(x,y)}{t+d(x,y)}, R(x,y,t) = \frac{d(x,y)}{t}$$

Note that,
(1) $0 \leq S(x,y,t) \leq 1$,
(2) Since $d(x,y) = d(y,x)$*, we have* $S(x,y,t) = S(y,x,t)$,
(3) $S(x,y,t) = 1$ *if* $x = y$*, and*
(4) $\lim_{t\to\infty} \frac{t+d(x,y)}{t+2d(x,y)} = 1$*, for all* $x,y \in G$ *and* $t > 0$.

(5) $S(x,y,t) \star S(y,z,s) \leq S(x,z,t+s)$, *for all* $x,y,z \in G$, $s,t > 0$.
Similarlly, all the conditions for A, M, *and* R *can be verified. Therefore,* $(G,S,A,M,R,\star,\diamond)$ *is an NFMS induced by a metric* d, *called the standard neutrosophic fuzzy metric.*

Example 2. *Take* $G = [2.5, 3.4]$, $\star$ *be a TN and* $\diamond$ *be a TC defined as* $p \star q = \min\{0, p+q-1\}$ *and* $p \diamond q = p+q-pq$. *Also,* $\forall\ p,q \in G$, $s \in (0,\infty)$, *we define:*

$$S(p,q,s) = 1 - \frac{|p-q|}{2t}$$

$$A(p,q,s) = \frac{s^3 - |p-q|}{s^3}$$

$$M(p,q,s) = \begin{cases} (q-p)/(q+s) & \text{if } p \leq q \\ (p-q)/(p+s) & \text{if } q \leq p \end{cases}$$

$$R(p,q,s) = \begin{cases} (q^2-p^2)/(q^2+s^2) & \text{if } p \leq q \\ (p^2-q^2)/(p^2+s^2) & \text{if } q \leq p \end{cases}$$

Note that,
(1) $0 \leq S(p,q,s), A(p,q,s), M(p,q,s), R(p,q,s) \leq 1$,
(2) Since $|p-q| = |q-p|$, *we have* $S(p,q,s) = S(q,p,s), A(p,q,s) = A(q,p,s)$, $M(p,q,s) = M(q,p,s), R(p,q,s) = R(q,p,s)$,
(3) $S(p,q,s) = A(p,q,s) = 1,\ M(q,p,s) = R(p,q,s) = 0$, *if* $p = q$,
(4) $\lim_{t\to\infty} 1 - \frac{|p-q|}{2t} = 1, \lim_{t\to\infty} \frac{s^3-|p-q|}{s^3} = 1, \lim_{t\to\infty} M(q,p,s) = 0$, $\lim_{t\to\infty} R(p,q,s) = 0$, *for all* $x,y \in G$ *and* $t > 0$.
(5) $S(p,q,s) \star S(q,r,s) \leq S(p,r,t+s),\ A(p,q,s) \star A(q,r,s) \leq A(p,r,t+s)$ $M(p,q,s) \diamond M(q,r,s) \geq M(p,r,t+s),\ R(p,q,s) \diamond R(q,r,s) \geq R(p,r,t+s)$, *for all* $x,y,z \in G$, $s,t > 0$.
Therefore, $(G,S,A,M,R,\star,\diamond)$ *forms an NFMS.*
Remark 1. *The 7-tuple* $(G,S,A,M,R,\star,\diamond)$ *defined in above Example 1 would not be a NFMS if t-norm* $p \star q = \min\{0, p+q-1\}$ *and t-conorm* $p \diamond q = p+q-pq$.

Definition 8. *Consider* $(G,S,A,M,R,\star,\diamond)$ *as an NFMS. For* $\varepsilon \in (0,1)$, $t \in \mathbb{R}^+$, *and* $p \in G$, *denote the set:*

$$O(p,\varepsilon,t) = \{b \in G : S(p,q,t) > 1-\varepsilon,\ A(p,q,t) > 1-\varepsilon,\ M(p,q,t) < \varepsilon,\ R(p,q,t) < \varepsilon\}$$

as an open ball (OB), where p *serves as the center and* ε *as the radius with respect to* t.

Definition 9. *Consider* $(G,S,A,M,R,\star,\diamond)$ *as an NFMS. A subset* H *of* G *is said to be an open set if for each* $p \in H$, *there exists an open ball* $O(p,\varepsilon,t)$ *such that* $O(p,\varepsilon,t) \subset H$.

Theorem 1. *Each OB,* $O(p,\varepsilon,t)$ *within an NFMS constitutes an open set (OS).*

Proof. We consider an open ball $O(p,\varepsilon,t)$ and choose $q \in O(p,\varepsilon,t)$. Then, $S(p,q,t) > 1-\varepsilon,\ A(p,q,t) > 1-\varepsilon,\ M(p,q,t) < \varepsilon,\ R(p,q,t) < \varepsilon$.
There exists $t_0 \in (0,t)$ such that,
$S(p,q,t_0) > 1-\varepsilon,\ A(p,q,t_0) > 1-\varepsilon,\ M(p,q,t_0) < \varepsilon,\ R(p,q,t_0) < \varepsilon$. [Since, $S(p,q,t) > 1-\varepsilon$]
Taking $\varepsilon_0 = S(p,q,t_0)$, $\exists\ \varrho \in (0,1)$ for $\varepsilon_0 > 1-\varepsilon$, so that $\varepsilon_0 > 1-\varrho > 1-\varepsilon$.
For any given ε_0 and ϱ so that $\varepsilon_0 > 1-\varrho$. Then, $\exists\ \varepsilon_1, \varepsilon_2, \varepsilon_3, \varepsilon_4 \in (0,1)$ s.t,
$\varepsilon_0 \star \varepsilon_1 > 1-\varrho,\ \varepsilon_0 \star \varepsilon_2 > 1-\varrho,\ (1-\varepsilon_0) \diamond (1-\varepsilon_3) \leq \varrho,\ (1-\varepsilon_0) \diamond (1-\varepsilon_4) \leq \varrho$.
Choosing $\varepsilon_5 = \max\{\varepsilon_1, \varepsilon_2, \varepsilon_3, \varepsilon_4\}$ and considering the open ball $O(q, 1-\varepsilon_5, t-t_0)$, our motive is to show that $O(q, 1-\varepsilon_5, t-t_0) \subset O(p,\varepsilon,t)$.
Now taking $r \in O(q, 1-\varepsilon_5, t-t_0)$ we get,
$S(q,r,t-t_0) > \varepsilon_5,\ A(q,r,t-t_0) > \varepsilon_5,\ M(q,r,t-t_0) < \varepsilon_5,\ R(q,r,t-t_0) < \varepsilon_5$.

Also,
$S(p,r,t) > S(p,q,t_0) \star S(q,r,t-t_0) \geq \varepsilon_0 \star \varepsilon_5 \geq \varepsilon_0 \star \varepsilon_1 \geq 1-\varrho > 1-\varepsilon$,
$A(p,r,t) > A(p,q,t_0) \star A(p,r,t-t_0) \geq \varepsilon_0 \star \varepsilon_5 \geq \varepsilon_0 \star \varepsilon_2 \geq 1-\varrho > 1-\varepsilon$,
$M(p,r,t) > M(p,q,t_0) \diamond M(q,r,t-t_0) \leq (1-\varepsilon_0) \diamond (1-\varepsilon_5) \leq (1-\varepsilon_0) \diamond (1-\varepsilon_3) \leq \varrho < \varepsilon$,
$R(p,r,t) > R(p,q,t_0) \diamond R(q,r,t-t_0) \leq (1-\varepsilon_0) \diamond (1-\varepsilon_5) \leq (1-\varepsilon_0) \diamond (1-\varepsilon_4) \leq \varrho < \varepsilon$.
Hence, $r \in O(p,\varepsilon,t)$ and $O(q, 1-\varepsilon_5, t-t_0) \subset O(p,\varepsilon,t)$. □

Remark 2. *From Definition 9 and Theorem 1, it can be said that,*

$$\tau_N = \{H \subset G : \exists\, t > 0 \text{ and } 0 < \varepsilon < 1 \text{ such that } O(p,\varepsilon,t) \subset H, \forall\, p \in H\}$$

is a topology on G. In this case every neutrosophic fuzzy metric $N = (S,A,M,R)$ on G produces a topology τ_N on G which has a base as the family of open sets $\{O(p,\varepsilon,t) : p \in N, \varepsilon \in (0,1), \text{ and } t > 0\}$.

Theorem 2. *Let $(G,S,A,M,R,\star,\diamond)$ be an NFMS. Then,*
(i) ϕ and G are open sets in $(G,S,A,M,R,\star,\diamond)$.
(ii) The union of any finite, countable, or uncountable family of open sets is open.
(iii) The intersection of a finite family of open sets is open.

Proof. (i) As an empty set contains no points, the necessity that each point in ϕ is the centre of an open ball contained in it is satisfied automatically.

The whole space G is open since every open ball centred at any of its points is contained in G.
(ii) Let $\{M_\alpha : \alpha \in \Lambda\}$ be a family of open sets and $H = \cup_{\alpha\in\Lambda} M_\alpha$. If $H = \phi$ then it is open [by (i)]. So let $H \neq \phi$. Taking $x \in H$, it can be said that $x \in M_\alpha$ for some $\alpha \in \Lambda$. Since M_α is open, $\exists\, r > 0$ such that $O(x,r,t) \subseteq M_\alpha \subseteq H$ (where $t > 0$). Thus, for each $x \in H \,\exists\, r > 0$ such that $O(x,r,t) \subseteq H$. Implies that H is open.
(iii) Let $\{M_i : 1 \leq i \leq n\}$ be a finite family of open sets in G, and let $M = \cap_{i=1}^n M_i$. If M is empty, then it is open. (by (i)).
Suppose $M \neq \phi$, and $x \in M$. Then, $x \in M_j$, $j = 1,2,...,n$. Since M_j is open, $\exists\, r_j > 0$ such that $O(x,r_j,t) \subseteq M_j$ where $t > 0$ and $j = 1,2,...,n$.
Let $r = min\{r_1, r_2, ..., r_n\}$. Then $r > 0$ and $O(x,r,t) \subseteq O(x,r_j,t)$ where $t > 0$ and $j = 1,2,...,n$. Therefore, $O(x,r,t)$ centred at x satisfies

$$O(x,r,t) \subseteq \cap_{j=1}^n O(x,r_j,t) \subseteq M$$

This completes the proof. □

Theorem 3. *A subset X in a NFMS $(G,S,A,M,R,\star,\diamond)$ is open if it is the union of all open balls contained in X.*

Proof. Let X be open. If $X = \phi$, then there are no open balls contained in it. Thus, the union of all open balls contained in X is the union of an empty class, which is empty and therefore equal to X.
Now if $X \neq \phi$, then since X is open, each of its points is the centre of an open ball entirely contained in X. So X is the union of all open balls contained in it. The converse follows from Theorem 3.1 and Theorem 3.3. □

Definition 10. *Let A be a subset of an NFMS $(G,S,A,M,R,\star,\diamond)$. A point $x \in G$ is an interior point of A if $\exists\, O(x,r,t) \subseteq A$ for some $r,t > 0$. That is, $x \in O(x,r,t) \subseteq A$.*

Theorem 4. *Let A be a subset of an NFMS $(G,S,A,M,R,\star,\diamond)$. Then,*
(i) $Int(A)$ is an open subset of A that contains every open subset of A.
(ii) A is open if $A = Int(A)$.

Proof. Let $x \in Int(A)$ be arbitary. Then, by Definition 3.4, $\exists\, O(x,r,t) \subseteq A$ for some $r,t > 0$. But since $O(x,r,t)$ is an open set [by Theorem 3.1], each point of it is the centre of an open ball contained in $O(x,r,t)$ and consequently also in A. Therefore, each point of $O(x,r,t)$ is an interior point of A. That is, $O(x,r,t) \subseteq Int(A)$. Thus, x is the centre of an open ball contained in $Int(A)$. Since $x \in Int(A)$ is arbitary, it can be said that each $x \in Int(A)$ has the property of being the centre of an open ball contained in $Int(A)$. Hence, $Int(A)$ is open. Now it is to be shown that $Int(A)$ contains every open subset $X \subseteq A$. Let $x \in X$. Since X is open, $\exists\, O(x,r,t) \subseteq X \subseteq A$. So $x \in Int(A)$. This shows that $x \in X \implies x \in Int(A)$. In other words, $X \subseteq Int(A)$.
(ii) is immediate after (i). □

Definition 11. *Let $(G,S,A,M,R,\star,\diamond)$ be an NFMS and let $C(G)$ be the collection of all non empty compact subsets of G. Consider $P,Q \in C(G)$ and $t > 0$.*
Define $H_{\mathfrak{A}}, H_{\mathfrak{B}}, H_{\mathfrak{C}}$ and $H_{\mathfrak{D}} : C(G) \times C(G) \times (0,\infty) \to (0,\infty)$ as follows:

$$H_{\mathfrak{A}}(P,Q,t) = \min\left\{ \inf_{w\in P} \mathfrak{A}(w,Q,t), \inf_{k\in Q} \mathfrak{A}(P,k,t) \right\},$$

$$H_{\mathfrak{B}}(P,Q,t) = \min\left\{ \inf_{w\in P} \mathfrak{B}(w,Q,t), \inf_{k\in Q} \mathfrak{B}(P,k,t) \right\},$$

$$H_{\mathfrak{C}}(P,Q,t) = \max\left\{ \sup_{w\in P} \mathfrak{C}(w,Q,t), \sup_{k\in Q} \mathfrak{C}(P,k,t) \right\},$$

$$H_{\mathfrak{D}}(P,Q,t) = \max\left\{ \sup_{w\in P} \mathfrak{D}(w,Q,t), \sup_{k\in Q} \mathfrak{D}(P,k,t) \right\}.$$

The 6-tuple $(H_{\mathfrak{A}}, H_{\mathfrak{B}}, H_{\mathfrak{C}}, H_{\mathfrak{D}}, \star, \diamond)$ is called Hausdorff NFMS, or shortly HNFMS.

Theorem 5. *Every NFMS possesses the property of being Hausdorff.*

Proof. We consider $(G,S,A,M,R,\star,\diamond)$ as an NFMS. Let $p,q \in G$ be different. Then, $S(p,q,t),\ A(p,q,t),\ M(p,q,t),\ R(p,q,t) \in (0,1)$.
Take $\varepsilon_1 = S(p,q,t), \varepsilon_2 = A(p,q,t), \varepsilon_3 = M(p,q,t), \epsilon_4 = R(p,q,t)$
and $\varepsilon = \max\{\varepsilon_1, \varepsilon_2, 1-\varepsilon_3, 1-\varepsilon_4\}$.
Now, taking $\varepsilon_0 \in (\varepsilon,1), \exists\, \varepsilon_5,\ \varepsilon_6,\ \varepsilon_7,\ \varepsilon_8$ such that,
$\varepsilon_5 \star \varepsilon_5 \geq \varepsilon_0, \varepsilon_6 \star \varepsilon_6 \geq \varepsilon_0, (1-\varepsilon_7) \diamond (1-\varepsilon_7) \leq 1-\varepsilon_0$ and $(1-\varepsilon_8) \diamond (1-\varepsilon_8) \leq 1-\varepsilon_0$.
Taking $\varepsilon_9 = \max\{\varepsilon_5, \varepsilon_6, \varepsilon_7, \varepsilon_8\}$ if we consider the open balls $O(p, 1-\varepsilon_9, \frac{t}{2})$ and $O(q, 1-\varepsilon_9, \frac{t}{2})$. Then, it is clear that, $O(p,1-\varepsilon_9,\frac{t}{2}) \cap O(q,1-\varepsilon_9,\frac{t}{2}) = \emptyset$.
Now, if we choose a point $r \in O(p,1-\varepsilon_9,\frac{t}{2}) \cap O(q,1-\varepsilon_9,\frac{t}{2})$ then,

$$\varepsilon_1 = S(p,q,t) \geq S(p,r,\tfrac{t}{2}) \star S(r,q,\tfrac{t}{2}) \geq \varepsilon_9 \star \varepsilon_9 \geq \varepsilon_5 \star \varepsilon_5 \geq \varepsilon_0 > \varepsilon_1.$$
$$\varepsilon_2 = A(p,q,t) \geq A(p,r,\tfrac{t}{2}) \star A(r,q,\tfrac{t}{2}) \geq \varepsilon_9 \star \varepsilon_9 \geq \varepsilon_6 \star \varepsilon_6 \geq \varepsilon_0 > \varepsilon_2.$$
$$\varepsilon_3 = M(p,q,t) \leq M(p,r,\tfrac{t}{2}) \diamond M(r,q,\tfrac{t}{2}) \leq (1-\varepsilon_9) \diamond (1-\varepsilon_9) \leq (1-\varepsilon_7) \diamond (1-\varepsilon_7) \leq 1-\varepsilon_0 < \varepsilon_3.$$
$$\varepsilon_4 = R(p,q,t) \leq R(p,r,\tfrac{t}{2}) \diamond R(r,q,\tfrac{t}{2}) \leq (1-\varepsilon_9) \diamond (1-\varepsilon_9) \leq (1-\varepsilon_8) \diamond (1-\varepsilon_8) \leq 1-\varepsilon_0 < \varepsilon_4,$$

which shows a contradiction. Therefore, every NFMS is Hausdorff. □

Definition 12. *We consider $(G,S,A,M,R,\star,\diamond)$ as an NFMS. A set $W \subset G$ is known as nuetrosophic bounded (NB) if, there remains a positive real number t and ε in $(0,1)$ satisfying, $S(p,q,t) > 1-\varepsilon,\ A(p,q,t) > 1-\varepsilon,\ M(p,q,t) < \varepsilon$ and $R(p,q,t) < \varepsilon\ \forall p,q \in W$.*

Definition 13. *Let an NFMS $(G,S,A,M,R,\star,\diamond)$ be given, then*

(1) Consider C_N as an assembly of open sets and $W \subseteq \cup_{U\in C_N} U$. Then, the assembly C_N is said to be an open cover(OC) of W.
(2) A subspace W of G is compact, if every open cover of W has a finite subcover.

(3) A subspace W of G is said to be sequentially compact if each sequence in W possesses a convergent subsequence in W.

Theorem 6. *In an NFMS, every compact subset is neutrosophic bounded.*

Proof. We consider $(G, S, A, M, R, \star, \diamond)$ as an NFMS, and W be a compact subset of G. Also consider an open cover $\{O(p, \varepsilon, t) : p \in W\}$ of W where $t > 0$ and $0 < \varepsilon < 1$. W being a compact set, there exists $p_1, p_2, ..., p_n \in W$ in such a way that $W \subseteq \cup_{k=1}^{n} O(p_k, \varepsilon, t)$. Further, for $p, q \in W$ there remains some $k, m \in \{1, 2, 3, ..., n\}$ such that $p \in O(p_k, \varepsilon, t)$ and $q \in O(p_m, \varepsilon, t)$. Then, we can write
$S(p, p_k, t) > 1 - \varepsilon,\ A(p, p_k, t) > 1 - \varepsilon,\ M(p, p_k, t) < \epsilon,\ R(p, p_k, t) < \varepsilon$ and
$S(q, p_m, t) > 1 - \varepsilon,\ A(q, p_m, t) > 1 - \varepsilon,\ M(q, p_m, t) < \varepsilon,\ R(q, p_m, t) < \varepsilon$
Now, take $\alpha = \min\{S(p_k, p_m, t) : 1 \leq k, m \leq n\}$, $\beta = \min\{A(p_k, p_m, t) : 1 \leq k, m \leq n\}$
$\gamma = \max\{M(p_k, p_m, t) : 1 \leq k, m \leq n\}$, $\delta = \max\{R(p_k, p_m, t) : 1 \leq k, m \leq n\}$.
Then, $\alpha, \beta, \gamma, \delta > 0$. From here, we can have some $\varrho_1,\ \varrho_2,\ \varrho_3,\ \varrho_4 \in (0, 1)$ satisfying,

$$S(p, q, 3t) \geq S(p, p_k, t) \star S(p_k, p_m, t) \star S(p_m, q, t) \geq (1 - \varepsilon) \star (1 - \varepsilon) \star \alpha > 1 - \varrho_1,$$
$$A(p, q, 3t) \geq A(p, p_k, t) \star A(p_k, p_m, t) \star A(p_m, q, t) \geq (1 - \varepsilon) \star (1 - \varepsilon) \star \beta > 1 - \varrho_2,$$
$$M(p, q, 3t) \leq M(p, p_k, t) \diamond M(p_k, p_m, t) \diamond M(p_m, q, t) \leq \varepsilon \diamond \varepsilon \diamond \gamma < \varrho_3$$
$$R(p, q, 3t) \leq R(p, p_k, t) \diamond R(p_k, p_m, t) \diamond R(p_m, q, t) \leq \varepsilon \diamond \varepsilon \diamond \delta < \varrho_4$$

Taking $\varrho = \max\{\varrho_1,\ \varrho_2,\ \varrho_3,\ \varrho_4\}$ and $t_0 = 3t$, we have $S(p, q, t_0) > 1 - \varrho,\ A(p, q, t_0) > 1 - \varrho,\ M(p, q, t_0) < \varrho,\ R(p, q, t_0) < \varrho\ \forall\ p, q \in W$. Therefore, the set W is Neutrosophic bounded. □

If $(G, S, A, M, R, \star, \diamond)$ is a NFMS produced by a metric d on G and $W \subset G$, then W is Neutrosophic bounded if it is bounded. As a result with Theorems 5 and 6 it can be written that:

Corollary 1. *In an NFMS, each compact set is both closed set and bounded set.*

Theorem 7. *We consider $(G, S, A, M, R, \star, \diamond)$ as an NFMS and τ_N to be the topology on G produced by the FM, then $\{p_m\} \to p \in G$ if and only if,*

$$S(p_m, p, s) \to 1, A(p_m, p, s) \to 1,\ M(p_m, p, s) \to 0,\ R(p_m, p, s) \to 0, \text{ as } m \to \infty.$$

Proof. We consider $s > 0$. Suppose $p_m \to p$. For any given $\varepsilon \in (0, 1)$, there remains $N \in \mathbb{N}$ such that,

$$p_m \in O(p, \varepsilon, s)\ \forall\ m \geq N.$$

Thus, $1 - S(p_m, p, s) < \varepsilon,\ 1 - A(p_m, p, s) < \varepsilon,\ M(p_m, p, s) < \varepsilon,\ R(p_m, p, s) < \varepsilon$.
In these cases, we express it as follows:

$$S(p_m, p, s) \to 1,\ A(p_m, p, s) \to 1,\ M(p_m, p, s) \to 0,\ R(p_m, p, s) \to 0, \text{ as } m \to \infty.$$

Conversely, suppose $S(p_m, p, s) \to 1, A(p_m, p, s) \to 1,\ M(p_m, p, s) \to 0,\ R(p_m, p, s) \to 0$, as $m \to \infty$, for each $s > 0$. Then for any $\varepsilon \in (0, 1)$, there exists $N \in \mathbb{N}$ so that $1 - S(p_m, p, s) < \varepsilon,\ 1 - A(p_m, p, s) < \varepsilon,\ M(p_m, p, s) < \varepsilon,\ R(p_m, p, s) < \varepsilon\ \forall\ N \in \mathbb{N}$. By this, we obtain $S(p_m, p, s) > 1 - \varepsilon,\ A(p_m, p, s) > 1 - \varepsilon,\ M(p_m, p, s) < \varepsilon,\ R(p_m, p, s) < \varepsilon\ \forall\ N \in \mathbb{N}$. Thus, $p_m \in O(p, \varepsilon, s)\ \forall\ m \geq N$. Hence the proof. □

Definition 14. *We consider $(G, S, A, M, R, \star, \diamond)$ as an NFMS. Any sequence $\{p_n\}$ in G is said to be a Cauchy sequence if for any positive real numbers ε and t, there subsists $N \in \mathbb{N}$ so that, the following conditions hold:*

$$S(p_n, p_m, t) > 1 - \varepsilon,\ A(p_n, p_m, t) > 1 - \varepsilon,\ M(p_n, p_m, t) < \varepsilon,\ R(p_n, p_m, t) < \varepsilon,$$

for all $n, m \geq N$.

Moreover, $(G, S, A, M, R, \star, \diamond)$ *is said to be a complete NFMS if each Cauchy sequence converges with respect to the topology* τ_N *in G.*

Theorem 8. *We consider* $(G, S, A, M, R, \star, \diamond)$ *as an NFMS. Under the assumption that each Cauchy sequence of G possesses a converging subsequence, the NFMS* $(G, S, A, M, R, \star, \diamond)$ *is considered complete.*

Proof. We consider $\{p_n\}$ as a Cauchy sequence in G and assume a subsequence $\{p_{i_n}\}$ of $\{p_n\}$ coverges to a point $p \in G$. We complete the proof by showing $p_n \to p$. Let $t > 0$ and $0 < \nu < 1$. Taking $\varepsilon \in (0,1)$ so that $(1-\varepsilon) \star (1-\varepsilon) \geq 1-\nu, \epsilon \diamond \epsilon \leq \nu$. By the Cauchyness of $\{a_n\}$, there exists $N \in \mathbb{N}$ so that $\forall\, m, n \geq N$,

$$S(p_m, p_n, \frac{t}{2}) > 1-\varepsilon,\ A(p_m, p_n, \frac{t}{2}) > 1-\varepsilon,\ M(p_m, p_n, \frac{t}{2}) < \varepsilon,\ R(p_m, p_n, \frac{t}{2}) < \varepsilon.$$

Since $p_n \to p$, there remains $i \in \mathbb{N}$ satisfying $S(p_i, p, \frac{t}{2}) > 1-\varepsilon,\ A(p_i, p, \frac{t}{2}) > 1-\varepsilon,\ M(p_i, p, \frac{t}{2}) < \varepsilon,\ R(p_i, p, \frac{t}{2}) < \varepsilon, \forall\, i > N$. Then, for $n \geq N$,

$$\begin{aligned}
S(p_n, p, t) &\geq S(p_n, p_i, \tfrac{t}{2}) \star S(p_i, p, \tfrac{t}{2}) > (1-\varepsilon) \star (1-\varepsilon) \geq 1-\nu, \\
A(p_n, p, t) &\geq A(p_n, p_i, \tfrac{t}{2}) \star A(p_i, p, \tfrac{t}{2}) > (1-\varepsilon) \star (1-\varepsilon) \geq 1-\nu, \\
M(p_n, p, t) &\leq M(p_n, p_i, \tfrac{t}{2}) \diamond M(p_i, p, \tfrac{t}{2}) > \varepsilon \diamond \varepsilon \leq \nu, \\
R(p_n, p, t) &\leq R(p_n, p_i, \tfrac{t}{2}) \diamond R(p_i, p, \tfrac{t}{2}) > \varepsilon \diamond \varepsilon \leq \nu,
\end{aligned}$$

Thus, we have $a_n \to a$. Therefore, NFMS $(G, S, A, M, R, \star, \diamond)$ is complete. □

Theorem 9. *Consider* $(G, S, A, M, R, \star, \diamond)$ *as an NFMS and W be a subset of G with the subspace NFM* $(S_W, A_W, M_W, R_W) = (S|_{W^2\times\infty}, A|_{W^2\times\infty}, M|_{W^2\times\infty}, R|_{W^2\times\infty})$. *Then* $(W, S_W, A_W, M_W, R_W, \star, \diamond)$ *is complete if and only if* $W \subset G$ *is closed.*

Proof. Let $W \subset G$ is closed. Suppose $\{p_n\}$ be Cauchy in $(W, S_W, A_W, M_W, R_W, \star, \diamond)$. Since $\{p_n\}$ is Cauchy in G, there exists $p \in G$ such that $p_n \to p$. It is clear that, $p \in \overline{W} = W$ and so $\{p_n\}$ converges in W.

In contrary, let $(W, S_W, A_W, M_W, R_W, \star, \diamond)$ be complete. Also, suppose W is open. If we choose a point $p \in \overline{W}/W$, then there exists $\{p_n\}$ of points belonging to W converging to p and thus, $\{p_n\}$ is Cauchy. This gives, for $n, m \geq N$, each $\nu \in (0,1)$ and $t > 0$, $\exists\, N \in \mathbb{N}$ satisfying

$$S(p_n, p_m, t) > 1-\nu,\ A(p_n, p_m, t) > 1-\nu,\ M(p_n, p_m, t) < \nu,\ R(p_n, p_m, t) < \nu.$$

Now, since $\{p_n\}$ is in W, we can write $S(p_n, p_m, t) = S_W(p_n, p_m, t),\ A(p_n, p_m, t) = A_W(p_n, p_m, t),\ M(p_n, p_m, t) = M_W(p_n, p_m, t),\ R(p_n, p_m, t) = R_W(p_n, p_m, t)$. Therefore, $\{p_n\}$ is Cauchy in W. Since $(G, S, A, M, R, \star, \diamond)$ is complete, $\exists\, q \in W$ such that $p_n \to q$. Hence, $\exists\, n \in \mathbb{N}$ such that $S_W(q, p_n, t) > 1-\nu,\ A_W(q, p_n, t) > 1-\nu,\ M_W(q, p_n, t) < \nu,\ R_W(q, p_n, t) < \nu$ for all $n \geq N$, each $\nu \in (0,1)$ and $t > 0$. Since $\{p_n\}$ is in W and $q \in W$, we can write $S(q, p_n, t) = S_W(q, p_n, t),\ A(q, p_n, t) = A_W(q, p_n, t),\ M(q, p_n, t) = M_W(q, p_n, t),\ R(q, p_n, t) = R_W(q, p_n, t)$. This concludes that $\{p_n\}$ converges both to p and q in $(G, S, A, M, R, \star, \diamond)$. Since $q \in W$ and $p \notin W$, this implies $p \neq q$. This contradiction leads to the desired result. □

Lemma 1. *Let* $(G, S, A, M, R, \star, \diamond)$ *be a NFMS. If* $t > 0$ *and* $0 < \varepsilon_1, \varepsilon_2 < 1$ *satisfy* $(1-\varepsilon_2) \star (1-\varepsilon_2) \geq (1-\varepsilon_1)$, $\varepsilon_2 \diamond \varepsilon_2 \leq \varepsilon_1$, *then* $\overline{O(p, \varepsilon_2, \frac{t}{2})} \subset O(p, \varepsilon_1, t)$.

Proof. We take $q \in \overline{O(p, \varepsilon_2, \frac{t}{2})}$ and $O(q, \varepsilon_2, \frac{t}{2})$ be an open ball with radius ε_2 and centered at q. Since $O(p, \varepsilon_2, \frac{t}{2}) \cap O(q, \varepsilon_2, \frac{t}{2}) \neq \emptyset$, $\exists\, r \in O(p, \varepsilon_2, \frac{t}{2}) \cap O(q, \varepsilon_2, \frac{t}{2})$. Then we obtain,

$$S(p, q, t) \geq S(p, r, \tfrac{t}{2}) \star S(q, r, \tfrac{t}{2}) > (1-\varepsilon_2) \star (1-\varepsilon_2) \geq 1-\varepsilon_1,$$

$$A(p,q,t) \geq A(p,r,\tfrac{t}{2}) \star A(q,r,\tfrac{t}{2}) > (1-\varepsilon_2) \star (1-\varepsilon_2) \geq 1-\varepsilon_1,$$
$$M(p,q,t) \leq M(p,r,\tfrac{t}{2}) \star M(q,r,\tfrac{t}{2}) < \varepsilon_2 \star \varepsilon_2 \leq \varepsilon_1,$$
$$R(p,q,t) \leq R(p,r,\tfrac{t}{2}) \star R(q,r,\tfrac{t}{2}) < \varepsilon_2 \star \varepsilon_2 \leq \varepsilon_1.$$

Hence, $q \in O(p,\varepsilon_1,t)$ and thus $\overline{O(p,\varepsilon_2,\frac{t}{2})} \subset O(p,\varepsilon_1,t)$. □

Theorem 10. *For an NFMS $(G,S,A,M,R,\star,\diamond)$, a subset $W \subset G$ is nowhere dense if and only if each non-empty OS in G consists of an OB such that the closure of the OB and W are disjoint.*

Proof. We consider $\psi \neq \emptyset$, $\psi \subset G$ as open. Then, there exists a non-empty OS Δ such that $\Delta \subset \psi$, $\Delta \cap \overline{W} \neq \emptyset$. If we take $p \in \Delta$, then $\exists\, 0 < \varepsilon_1 < 1$ and $t \in \mathbb{R}^+$ such that $O(p,\varepsilon_1,t) \subset \Delta$. Now, choose $0 < \varepsilon_2 < 1$ such that $(1-\varepsilon_2) \star (1-\varepsilon_2) \geq 1-\varepsilon_1$ and $\varepsilon_2 \diamond \varepsilon_2 \leq \varepsilon_1$. By Lemma 1, we obtain $\overline{O(p,\varepsilon_2,\frac{t}{2})} \subset O(p,\varepsilon_1,t)$. In this scenario, we can assert that $O(p,\varepsilon_2,\frac{t}{2}) \subset \psi$ and $\overline{O(p,\varepsilon_2,\frac{t}{2})} \cap W = \emptyset$.

On the contrary, presume that W is not nowhere dense. Hence, $int(\overline{W}) \neq \emptyset$, indicating the existence of an OS $\psi \neq \phi$ such that $\psi \subset \overline{W}$. Assume $O(p,\varepsilon_1,t)$ as an OB, so as $O(p,\varepsilon_1,t) \subset \psi$. Consequently, $\overline{O(p,\varepsilon_2,t)} \cap W \neq \emptyset$, contradicts the assumption. □

Now, we present the Baire Category Theorem in NFMS.

Theorem 11. *In a complete NFMS, the intersection of countably many dense open sets is dense.*

Proof. Consider a sequence of dense open subsets $\{\psi_n : n \in \mathbb{N}\}$ in a complete NFMS $(G,S,A,M,R,\star,\diamond)$. Then, it is to be proved that the intersection $\bigcap_{n\in\mathbb{N}} \psi_n$ is dense within G. Consider Δ as a non-empty open set of G. As $\psi_1 \in G$ is dense, $\Delta \cap \psi_1 \neq \emptyset$. Let $p_1 \in \Delta \cap \psi_1$. Now, $\Delta \cap \psi_1$ being open, $\exists\, \varepsilon_1 \in (0,1)$, $t_1 > 0$ so that $O(p_1,\varepsilon_1,t_1) \subset \Delta \cap \psi_1$. Choose $\varepsilon_1^* < \varepsilon_1$ and $t_1^* = \min\{t_1,1\}$ such that $\overline{O(p_1,\varepsilon_1^*,t_1^*)} \subset \Delta \cap \psi_1$. As $\psi_2 \in G$ is dense, $O(p_1,\varepsilon_1^*,t_1^*) \cap \psi_2 \neq \emptyset$. Choose $p_2 \in O(p_1,\varepsilon_1^*,t_1^*) \cap \psi_2$. As $O(p_1,\varepsilon_1^*,t_1^*) \cap \psi_2$ is open, $\exists\, \varepsilon_2 \in (0,1/2)$ and $t_2 > 0$ so that $O(p_2,\varepsilon_2,t_2) \subset O(p_1,\varepsilon_1^*,t_1^*) \cap \psi_2$. Choose $\varepsilon_2^* < \varepsilon_2$ and $t_2^* = \min\{t_2,1/2\}$ so that $\overline{O(p_2,\varepsilon_2^*,t_2^*)} \subset O(p_1,\varepsilon_1^*,t_2^*) \cap \psi_2$. By proceeding in this manner, we establish a sequence $\{p_n\}$ in G along with another sequence $\{t_n^*\}$ where $t_n^* \in (0,1/n)$, and

$$\overline{O(p_n,\varepsilon_n^*,t_n^*)} \subset O(p_{n-1},\varepsilon_{n-1}^*,t_{n-1}^*) \cap \psi_n$$

Next, we demonstrate that $\{p_n\}$ is Cauchy. For any t, $v > 0$, we select $N \in \mathbb{N}$ such that $\frac{1}{N} < t$ and $\frac{1}{N} < v$. Thus, for $n \geq N$ and $m \geq n$, we have

$$S(p_n,p_m,t) \geq S(p_n,p_m,1/n) \geq 1-\tfrac{1}{n} > 1-v,$$
$$A(p_n,p_m,t) \geq A(p_n,p_m,1/n) \geq 1-\tfrac{1}{n} > 1-v,$$
$$M(p_n,p_m,t) \leq M(p_n,p_m,1/n) \leq \tfrac{1}{n} \leq v,$$
$$R(p_n,p_m,t) \leq R(p_n,p_m,1/n) \leq \tfrac{1}{n} \leq v.$$

This shows that $\{p_n\}$ is Cauchy. G being complete, there exists $p \in G$ so that $\{p_n\} \to p$. As $a_k \in O(p_n,\varepsilon_n^*,t_n^*)\ \forall\, k \geq n$, we obtain $p \in \overline{O(p_n,\varepsilon_n^*,t_n^*)}$. Hence, it can be written that $a \in \overline{O(a_n,\varepsilon_n^*,t_n^*)} \subset O(a_{n-1},\varepsilon_{n-1}^*,t_{n-1}^*) \cap \psi_n, \forall\, n$. Then, $\Delta \cap (\cap_{n\in\mathbb{N}}\psi_n) \neq \emptyset$. Then $\cap_{n\in\mathbb{N}}\psi_n$ is dense in G. □

Definition 15. *Consider an NFMS $(G,S,A,M,R,\star,\diamond)$. We define a collection $(\mathfrak{D}_m)$, where $m \in \mathbb{N}$, to possess neutrosophic diameter zero (NDZ) if for every $\varepsilon \in (0,1)$ and $t \in \mathbb{R}^+$, there exists $N \in \mathbb{N}$ such that $S(p,q,t) > 1-\varepsilon$, $A(p,q,t) > 1-\varepsilon$, $M(p,q,t) < \varepsilon$, and $R(p,q,t) < \varepsilon$ hold for all $p,q \in \mathfrak{D}_N$.*

Theorem 12. *The NFMS $(G,S,A,M,R,\star,\diamond)$ is complete if and only if each sequence $(\mathfrak{D}_m)_{m\in\mathbb{N}}$ of nested non-empty closed sets, each possessing NDZ, has a nonempty intersection.*

Proof. Assuming the given condition is satisfied, i.e., every sequence $(\mathfrak{D}_m)_{m\in\mathbb{N}}$ of nested nonempty closed sets, each possessing NDZ, has a nonempty intersection. It remains to be demonstrated that $(G,S,A,M,R,\star,\diamond)$ is complete. Consider the Cauchy sequence $\{p_m\} \in G$. Define $\mu_m = a_k : k \geq m$ and $\mathfrak{D}_m = \overline{\mu_m}$. It can then be asserted that $(\mathfrak{D}_m)$

possesses NDZ. Given $0 < \varrho < 1$ and $t > 0$, choose $\varepsilon \in (0,1)$ such that $(1-\varepsilon) \star (1-\varepsilon) \star (1-\varepsilon) > 1-\varrho$ and $\varepsilon \diamond \varepsilon \diamond \varepsilon < \varrho$. As $\{p_m\}$ is Cauchy, there exists a natural number N satisfying

$$S(p_m, q_n, \frac{t}{3}) > 1-\varepsilon,\ A(p_m, q_n, \frac{t}{3}) > 1-\varepsilon,\ M(a_n, a_m, \frac{t}{3}) < \varepsilon,\ R(p_m, q_n, \frac{t}{3}) < \varepsilon,\ \forall\, m,n \geq N.$$

So, we obtain $S(p,q,\frac{t}{3}) > 1-\epsilon$, $A(p,q,\frac{t}{3}) > 1-\epsilon$, $M(p,q,\frac{t}{3}) < \epsilon$, $R(p,q,\frac{t}{3}) < \varepsilon$, $\forall\, m,n \geq \mu_{\mathcal{N}}$ [where $\mu_{\mathcal{N}} = (S,A,M,R)$, the NFM on G].

Select $p, q \in \mathfrak{D}_N$. Then, sequences $\{p_m^*\}$ and $\{q_m^*\}$ exist such that $p_m^* \to p$ and $q_m^* \to q$. Hence, for sufficiently large m, $p_m^* \in O(p,\varepsilon,\frac{t}{3})$ and $q_m^* \in O(q,\varepsilon,\frac{t}{3})$. Consequently, we obtain

$$\begin{gathered}
S(p,q,t) \geq S(p,p_m^*,\tfrac{t}{3}) \star S(p_m^*,q_m^*,\tfrac{t}{3}) \star S(q_m^*,q,\tfrac{t}{3}) > (1-\varepsilon) \star (1-\varepsilon) \star (1-\varepsilon) > 1-\varrho,\\
A(p,q,t) \geq A(p,p_m^*,\tfrac{t}{3}) \star A(p_m^*,q_m^*,\tfrac{t}{3}) \star A(q_m^*,q,\tfrac{t}{3}) > (1-\varepsilon) \star (1-\varepsilon) \star (1-\varepsilon) > 1-\varrho,\\
M(p,q,t) \leq M(p,p_m^*,\tfrac{t}{3}) \diamond M(p_m^*,q_m^*,\tfrac{t}{3}) \diamond M(q_m^*,q,\tfrac{t}{3}) < \varepsilon \diamond \varepsilon \diamond \varepsilon < \varrho,\\
R(p,q,t) \leq R(p,p_m^*,\tfrac{t}{3}) \diamond R(p_m^*,q_m^*,\tfrac{t}{3}) \diamond R(q_m^*,q,\tfrac{t}{3}) < \varepsilon \diamond \varepsilon \diamond \varepsilon < \varrho.
\end{gathered}$$

Therefore, $S(p,q,t) > 1-\varrho$, $A(p,q,t) > 1-\varrho$, $M(p,q,t) < \varrho$, $R(p,q,t) < \varrho$ ($\forall\, p,q \in \mathfrak{D}_N$). This implies that $(\mathfrak{D}_N)$ possesses NDZ, hence, by the assumption, $\bigcap_{m\in\mathbb{N}} \mathfrak{D}_m$ is non-empty. Let $p \in \cap_{m\in\mathbb{N}}\mathfrak{D}_m$. Then, for ε in $(0,1)$ and t, a positive real number, $\exists\, N_1 \in \mathbb{N}$ such that $S(p_m,p,t) > 1-\varepsilon$, $A(p_m,p,t) > 1-\varepsilon$, $M(p_m,p,t) < \varepsilon$, $R(p_m,p,t) < \varepsilon$ ($\forall\, n \geq N_1$). That is, $S(p_m,p,t) \to 1$, $A(p_m,p,t) \to 1$, $M(p_m,p,t) \to 0$, $R(p_m,p,t) \to 0$ for each $t > 0$ as $m \to \infty$. Hence, $p_m \to p$, which means $(G,S,A,M,R,\star,\diamond)$ is complete.

Conversely, assume $(G,S,A,M,R,\star,\diamond)$ is complete. Consider a nested sequence $(\mathfrak{D}_m)_{m\in\mathbb{N}}$ of nonempty closed sets having NDZ. For each $m \in \mathbb{N}$, let p_m be a point in $\mathfrak{D}_m$. Our aim is to demonstrate that $\{p_m\}$ is a Cauchy sequence. Since $(\mathfrak{D}_m)$ possesses NDZ, for $t \in \mathbb{R}^+$ and $\varepsilon \in (0,1)$, there exists $N \in \mathbb{N}$ such that $S(p,q,t) > 1-\varepsilon$, $A(p,q,t) > 1-\varepsilon$, $M(p,q,t) < \varepsilon$, $R(p,q,t) < \varepsilon$ hold for all $p,q \in \mathfrak{D}_N$. Due to the fact that $(\mathfrak{D}_m)$ is nested, it can be written that $S(p_m,p_n,t) > 1-\varepsilon$, $A(p_m,p_n,t) > 1-\varepsilon$, $M(p_m,p_n,t) < \varepsilon$, $R(p_m,p_n,t) < \varepsilon$, $\forall\, m,n \geq N$. Thus, $\{p_m\}$ forms a Cauchy sequence. As $(G,S,A,M,R,\star,\diamond)$ is complete, $\{p_m\}$ converges to some $p \in G$. This implies that $p \in \overline{\mathfrak{D}_m} = \mathfrak{D}_m$, for all m, and therefore, p belongs to $\bigcap_{m\in\mathbb{N}} \mathfrak{D}_m$. □

Theorem 13. *Every separable NFMS possesses second countability.*

Proof. Let $(G,S,A,M,R,\star,\diamond)$ be separable. Consider $W = \{p_j : j \in \mathbb{N}\}, W \subset G$ as countable dense. Define a collection $\mathfrak{B} = \{O(p_k,1/m,1/m) : k,m \in \mathbb{N}\}$. It is evident that $\mathfrak{B}$ is countable. Our objective is to demonstrate that $\mathfrak{B}$ serves as a basis for the assembly of all OS within G. Take ψ as an open set in G containing p. Then, $\exists\, t \in \mathbb{R}^+$, $\varepsilon \in (0,1)$ s.t $O(p,\varepsilon,t) \subset \psi$. Due to this fact, $\varepsilon \in (0,1)$, $\exists\, 0 < \varrho < 1$ s.t $(1-\varrho) \star (1-\varrho) > 1-\varepsilon$ and $\varrho \diamond \varrho < \varepsilon$. Chosse $t \in \mathbb{N}$ so that $1/t < \min\{\varrho, t/2\}$. As $W \subset G$ is dense, $\exists\, p_k \in G$ such that $p \in O(p,1/t,1/t)$. If $q \in O(p_k,1/t,1/t)$, we can write

$$\begin{gathered}
S(p,q,t) \geq S(p,p_k,t/2) \star S(q,p_k,t/2) \geq S(p,p_k,1/t) \star S(q,p_k,1/t) \geq\\
(1-1/t) \star (1-1/t) \geq (1-\varrho) \star (1-\varrho) > 1-\varepsilon,\\
A(p,q,t) \geq A(p,p_k,t/2) \star A(q,p_k,t/2) \geq A(p,p_k,1/t) \star A(q,p_k,1/t) \geq\\
(1-1/t) \star (1-1/t) \geq (1-\varrho) \star (1-\varrho) > 1-\varepsilon,\\
M(p,q,t) \leq M(p,p_k,t/2) \diamond M(q,p_k,t/2) \leq M(p,p_k,1/t) \diamond M(q,p_k,1/t) \leq 1/t \diamond 1/t \leq\\
\varrho \diamond \varrho < \varepsilon,\\
R(p,q,t) \leq R(p,p_k,t/2) \diamond R(q,p_k,t/2) \leq R(p,p_k,1/t) \diamond R(q,p_k,1/t) \leq 1/t \diamond 1/t \leq\\
\varrho \diamond \varrho < \varepsilon.
\end{gathered}$$

Then $q \in O(p,\varepsilon,t) \subset \psi$, thus $\mathfrak{B}$ forms a basis. □

Remark 3. *It is worth noting that second countability implies separability, and second countability is an inherited property. Hence, it follows that every subspace of a separable NFMS is also separable.*

Definition 16. *Consider a set $W \neq \emptyset$ and a NFMS $(G, S, A, M, R, \star, \diamond)$. We say that the sequence of functions $(\mathfrak{f}_m) : W \to G$ uniformly converges to a function $\mathfrak{f} : W \to G$ if corresponding to any $t > 0$, $0 < \varepsilon < 1$, there remains a natural number N satisfying*

$$S(\mathfrak{f}_n(p), \mathfrak{f}(p), t) > 1 - \varepsilon,\ A(\mathfrak{f}_m(p), \mathfrak{f}(p), t) > 1 - \varepsilon,\ M(\mathfrak{f}_m(p), \mathfrak{f}(p), t) < \varepsilon,\ R(\mathfrak{f}_m(p), \mathfrak{f}(p), t) < \varepsilon,$$

for all $n \geq N$ and $p \in W$.

Now we present uniform convergence theorem for NFMS.

Theorem 14. *Let W be a topological space, $(G, S, A, M, R, \star, \diamond)$ be a NFMS, and $\mathfrak{f}_n : W \to G$ be a sequence of continuous functions. If $(\mathfrak{f}_n)$ converges uniformly to $f : W \to G$ then $\mathfrak{f}$ is considered continuous.*

Proof. Assume μ as an OS in G, $p_0 \in \mathfrak{f}^{-1}(\mu)$. Since μ is open, $\exists\, t \in \mathbb{R}^+$, $\varepsilon \in (0,1)$ so that $O(\mathfrak{f}(p_0), \mathfrak{f}(p), t) \subset \mu$. Since $\varepsilon \in (0,1)$, we select $\varrho \in (0,1)$ such that $(1-\varrho) \star (1-\varrho) \star (1-\varrho) > 1 - \varepsilon$ and $\varrho \diamond \varrho \diamond \varrho < \varepsilon$. Given that (f_n) is uniformly convergent to $\mathfrak{f}$,for any $t > 0$ and $0 < \varrho < 1\ \exists\ N \in \mathbb{N}$ so that $S(\mathfrak{f}_n(p), \mathfrak{f}(p), \frac{t}{3}) > 1 - \varrho$, $A(\mathfrak{f}_n(p), \mathfrak{f}(p), \frac{t}{3}) > 1 - \varrho$, $M(\mathfrak{f}_n(p), \mathfrak{f}(p), \frac{t}{3}) < \varrho$, $R(\mathfrak{f}_n(p), \mathfrak{f}(p), \frac{t}{3}) < \varrho$ for all $n \geq N$, $p \in G$. Since $\mathfrak{f}_n$ are continuous, we have for each n that there remains δ, a neighborhood of p_0, so as $\mathfrak{f}_n(\delta) \subset O(\mathfrak{f}_n(p_0), \varrho, \frac{t}{3})$. Therefore, $S(\mathfrak{f}_n(p), \mathfrak{f}_n(p_0), \frac{t}{3}) > 1 - \varrho$, $A(\mathfrak{f}_n(p), \mathfrak{f}_n(p_0), \frac{t}{3}) > 1 - \varrho$, $M(\mathfrak{f}_n(p), \mathfrak{f}_n(p_0), \frac{t}{3}) < \varrho$, $R(\mathfrak{f}_n(p), \mathfrak{f}_n(p_0), \frac{t}{3}) < \varrho\ \forall\ p \in \delta$. Now,

$$\begin{aligned}
S(\mathfrak{f}(p), \mathfrak{f}(p_0), t) &\geq S(\mathfrak{f}(p), \mathfrak{f}_n(p), t/3) \star S(\mathfrak{f}_n(p), \mathfrak{f}_n(p_0), t/3) \star S(\mathfrak{f}_n(p_0), \mathfrak{f}(p_0), t/3) \geq \\
&\quad (1-\varrho) \star (1-\varrho) \star (1-\varrho) > 1 - \varepsilon, \\
A(\mathfrak{f}(p), \mathfrak{f}(p_0), t) &\geq A(\mathfrak{f}(p), \mathfrak{f}_n(p), t/3) \star A(\mathfrak{f}_n(p), \mathfrak{f}_n(p_0), t/3) \star A(\mathfrak{f}_n(p_0), \mathfrak{f}(p_0), t/3) \geq \\
&\quad (1-\varrho) \star (1-\varrho) \star (1-\varrho) > 1 - \varepsilon, \\
M(\mathfrak{f}(p), \mathfrak{f}(p_0), t) &\leq M(\mathfrak{f}(p), \mathfrak{f}_n(p), t/3) \diamond M(\mathfrak{f}_n(p), \mathfrak{f}_n(p_0), t/3) \diamond M(\mathfrak{f}_n(p_0), \mathfrak{f}(p_0), t/3) \leq \\
&\quad \varrho \diamond \varrho \diamond \varrho < \varepsilon, \\
R(\mathfrak{f}(p), \mathfrak{f}(p_0), t) &\leq R(\mathfrak{f}(p), \mathfrak{f}_n(p), t/3) \diamond R(\mathfrak{f}_n(p), \mathfrak{f}_n(p_0), t/3) \diamond R(\mathfrak{f}_n(p_0), \mathfrak{f}(p_0), t/3) \leq \\
&\quad \varrho \diamond \varrho \diamond \varrho < \varepsilon.
\end{aligned}$$

Implies that $\mathfrak{f}(p) \in O(\mathfrak{f}(p_0), \varepsilon, t) \subset \mu\ \forall\ p \in \delta$. Therefore, $\mathfrak{f}(\delta) \subset \mu$ and thus, $\mathfrak{f}$ is continuous. □

4. Conclusions

This study presents an exploration into the realm of neutrosophic fuzzy metric spaces, introducing an innovative extension of traditional metric spaces tailored to accommodate the intricacies of real-world phenomena characterized by uncertainty and imprecision. The motivation behind this work stems from the recognition of the limitations of classical metric spaces in capturing the nuances inherent in complex systems modelled by neutrosophic fuzzy sets. By introducing and investigating the properties of neutrosophic fuzzy metric spaces, we aim to provide a robust theoretical framework capable of addressing these challenges. Our examination of the structural and topological aspects of neutrosophic fuzzy metric spaces has yielded valuable insights into their fundamental characteristics. Through rigorous analysis, we have elucidated key properties such as completeness, continuity, and convergence within this novel framework. Moreover, the establishment of counterparts to well-known theorems such as the Uniform Convergence Theorem and the Baire Category Theorem underscores the theoretical richness and depth of neutrosophic fuzzy metric spaces.

The inspiration for the introduction of Neutrosophic Fuzzy Metric Spaces draws from the pioneering work of M. Kirisci in 2020, where the concept was first proposed and its topological properties were established. This framework offers a versatile framework wherein fixed points for various types of mappings can be determined, presenting applications across diverse domains such as boundary value problems, nonlinear differential and integral equations, optimization theory, variational inequality, and complementarity problems.

Furthermore, NFMS equips us with essential tools to tackle challenges in mathematical analysis and game theory effectively.

Looking ahead, several avenues for future research and application emerge from our findings. Firstly, further exploration of the properties and structures of neutrosophic fuzzy metric spaces promises to deepen our understanding of their mathematical underpinnings. Investigations into additional properties, such as compactness and connectedness, could uncover new insights and lead to the development of more sophisticated mathematical tools and techniques. Additionally, establishing connections between neutrosophic fuzzy metric spaces and other areas of mathematics, such as functional analysis and differential equations, holds the potential to broaden the scope of their applicability and facilitate interdisciplinary collaborations. Beyond the realm of pure mathematics, neutrosophic fuzzy metric spaces offer a powerful framework for modelling and analyzing uncertain and imprecise data, making them particularly relevant in fields such as computer science, engineering, and decision making. Future applications could include the development of robust algorithms for data analysis, optimization techniques for complex systems, and decision support systems for uncertain environments. By bridging the gap between theoretical advancements and real-world challenges, we aim to contribute to the advancement of knowledge and the development of innovative solutions to complex problems.

Author Contributions: Conceptualization, S.G., S., R.B., and S.N.; methodology, S.G., S. and R.B.; validation, S.G., S., R.B., and S.N.; formal analysis, S.G., S., R.B., and S.N.; investigation, S.G., S., R.B., and S.N.; writing—original draft preparation, S.G., S.; writing—review and editing, S., R.B.; visualization and supervision, S.G., S., R.B. and S.N. All authors have read and agreed to the published of the manuscript.

Funding: This research received no external funding.

Data Availability Statement: No data was used for the research described in the article.

Acknowledgments: Authors are thankful to the editors and reviewers for their insightful remarks and suggestions.

Conflicts of Interest: The authors declare no conflicts of interest.

References

1. Zadeh, L.A. Fuzzy sets. *Inf. Control.* **1965**, *8*, 338–353. [CrossRef]
2. Atanassov, K. Intuitionistic fuzzy sets. *Int. J. Bioautomation* **2016**, *20*, 1.
3. Smarandache, F. *A Unifying Field in Logics: Neutrosophic Logic*; Philosophy, American Research Press: New York, NY, USA, 1999; pp. 1–141.
4. Al-shami, T.M.; Mhemdi, A. Generalized frame for orthopair fuzzy sets:(m, n)-fuzzy sets and their applications to multi-criteria decision-making methods. *Information* **2023**, *14*, 56. [CrossRef]
5. Kramosil, I.; Michálek, J. Fuzzy metrics and statistical metric spaces. *Kybernetika* **1975**, *11*, 336–344.
6. George, A.; Veeramani, P. On some results in fuzzy metric spaces. *Fuzzy Sets Syst.* **1994**, *64*, 395–399. [CrossRef]
7. Çoker, D. An introduction to intuitionistic fuzzy topological spaces. *Fuzzy Sets Syst.* **1997**, *88*, 81–89. [CrossRef]
8. Park, J.H. Intuitionistic fuzzy metric spaces. *Chaos Solitons Fractals* **2004**, *22*, 1039–1046. [CrossRef]
9. Kaleva, O.; Seikkala, S. On fuzzy metric spaces. *Fuzzy Sets Syst.* **1984**, *12*, 215–229. [CrossRef]
10. Smarandache, F. Neutrosophic set-a generalization of the intuitionistic fuzzy set. In Proceedings of the IEEE International Conference on Granular Computing, Atlanta, GA, USA, 10–12 May 2006.
11. Salama, A.A.; Alblowi, S.A. Neutrosophic set and neutrosophic topological spaces. *IOSR J. Math.* **2012**, *3*, 31–35. [CrossRef]
12. Ejegwa, P.A.; Akowe, S.O.; Otene, P.M.; Ikyule, J.M. An overview on intuitionistic fuzzy sets. *Int. J. Sci. Technol. Res* **2014**, *3*, 142–145.
13. Majumdar, P. Neutrosophic sets and its applications to decision making. In *Computational Intelligence for Big Data Analysis: Frontier Advances and Applications*; Springer International Publishing: Cham, Switzerland, 2015; pp. 97–115.
14. Alaca, C.; Turkoglu, D.; Yildiz, C. Fixed points in intuitionistic fuzzy metric spaces. *Chaos Solitons Fractals* **2006**, *29*, 1073–1078. [CrossRef]
15. Nădăban, S. Fuzzy b-metric spaces. *Int. J. Comput. Commun. Control.* **2016**, *11*, 273–281. [CrossRef]
16. Sonam; Bhardwaj, R.; Narayan, S. Fixed point results in soft fuzzy metric spaces. *Mathematics* **2023**, *11*, 3189. [CrossRef]
17. Sonam. Some fixed point results in soft fuzzy metric spaces via altering soft distance. *Adv. Math. Sci. Appl.* **2024**, *33*, 189–200.
18. Gregori, V.; Miñana, J.J.; Miravet, D. Fuzzy partial metric spaces. *Int. J. Gen. Syst.* **2019**, *48*, 260–279. [CrossRef]

19. Gregori, V.; Romaguera, S. Fuzzy quasi-metric spaces. *Appl. Gen. Topol.* **2004**, *5*, 129–136. [CrossRef]
20. Sonam; Rathore, V.; Pal, A.; Bhardwaj, R.; Narayan, S. Fixed-Point Results for Mappings Satisfying Implicit Relation in Orthogonal Fuzzy Metric Spaces. *Adv. Fuzzy Syst.* **2023**, *2023*, 5037401. [CrossRef]
21. Zararsız, Z.; Riaz, M. Bipolar fuzzy metric spaces with application. *Comput. Appl. Math.* **2022**, *41*, 49. [CrossRef]
22. Vetro, C. Fixed points in weak non-Archimedean fuzzy metric spaces. *Fuzzy Sets Syst.* **2011**,*162*, 84–90. [CrossRef]
23. Sonam; Chauhan, C.S.; Bharadwaj, R.; Narayan, S. Fixed point results in soft rectangular b-metric space. *Nonlinear Funct. Anal. Appl.* **2023**, *28*, 753–774.
24. Sonam; Bhardwaj, R. Existence and Uniqueness of Solutions of Nonlinear Integral Equations through Results in Fuzzy Bipolar Metric Spaces. *J. Nonlinear Model. Anal.* 2024, *in press*.
25. Broumi, S.; Bakali, A.; Talea, M.; Smarandache, F.; Uluçay, V.; Sahin, M.; Dey, A.; Dhar, M.; Tan, R.P.; Bahnasse, A.; et al. Neutrosophic sets: An overview. In *On Neutrosophic Theory and Applications II*; Pons, Ed.; EU: Brussels, Belgium, 2018; pp. 403–434. ISBN 978-1-59973-559-7
26. Jeyaraman, M.; Jeyanthi, V.; Mangayarkkarasi, A.N.; Smarandache, F. Some new structures in neutrosophic metric spaces. *Neutrosophic Sets Syst.* **2021**, *42*, 49–64.
27. Kirişci, M.; Şimşek, N. Neutrosophic metric spaces. *Math. Sci.* **2020**, *14*, 241–248. [CrossRef]
28. Sowndrarajan, S.; Jeyaraman, M.; Smarandache, F. Fixed point results for contraction theorems in neutrosophic metric spaces. *Neutrosophic Sets Syst.* **2020**, *36*, 308–318.
29. Ishtiaq, U.; Javed, K.; Uddin, F.; Sen, M.D.L.; Ahmed, K.; Ali, M.U. Fixed point results in orthogonal neutrosophic metric spaces. *Complexity* **2021**, *2021*, 2809657. [CrossRef]
30. Asghar, A.; Hussain, A.; Ahmad, K.; Ishtiaq, U.; Sulami, H.A.; Hussain, N. On neutrosophic 2-metric spaces with application. *J. Funct. Spaces* **2023**, *2023*, 9057107. [CrossRef]
31. Janardhanan, G.; Mani, G.; Ege, O.; Varadharajan, V.; George, R. Orthogonal neutrosophic 2-metric spaces. *J. Inequalities Appl.* **2023**, *2023*, 112. [CrossRef]
32. Mani, G.; Subbarayan, P.; Mitrović, Z.D.; Aloqaily, A.; Mlaiki, N. Solving Some Integral and Fractional Differential Equations via Neutrosophic Pentagonal Metric Space. *Axioms* **2023**, *2*, 758. [CrossRef]
33. Saeed, M.; Ishtiaq, U.; Kattan, D.A.; Ahmad, K.; Sessa, S. New Fixed Point Results in Neutrosophic b-Metric Spaces with Application. *Int. J. Anal. Appl.* **2023**, *21*, 73. [CrossRef]
34. Das, S.; Roy, B.K.; Kar, M.B.; Kar, S.; Pamučar, D. Neutrosophic fuzzy set and its application in decision making. *J. Ambient. Intell. Humaniz. Comput.* **2020**, *11*, 5017–5029. [CrossRef]
35. Abbas, M.; Ali, B.; Romaguera, S. On Generalized Soft Equality and Soft Lattice Structure. *Filomat* **2014**, *28*, 1191–1203. [CrossRef]
36. Ali, B.; Saleem, N.; Sundus, N.; Khaleeq, S.; Saeed, M.; George, R. A Contribution to the Theory of Soft Sets via Generalized Relaxed Operations. *Mathematics* **2022**, *10*, 2636. [CrossRef]

symmetry

Article

A Novel Neutrosophic Likert Scale Analysis of Perceptions of Organizational Distributive Justice via a Score Function: A Complete Statistical Study and Symmetry Evidence Using Real-Life Survey Data

Seher Bodur [1], Selçuk Topal [2,*], Hacı Gürkan [3] and Seyyed Ahmad Edalatpanah [4]

[1] Department of Statistics, Bitlis Eren University, Bitlis 13000, Türkiye; skorkmaz@beu.edu.tr
[2] Department of Mathematics, Gebze Technical University, Kocaeli 41000, Türkiye
[3] Vocational School of Hizan, Bitlis Eren University, Bitlis 13000, Türkiye; hgurkan@beu.edu.tr
[4] Department of Applied Mathematics, Ayandegan Institute of Higher Education, Tonekabon 46818-5361, Iran
* Correspondence: stopal@gtu.edu.tr

Abstract: In this study, ten questions measuring distributive justice on classical Likert and neutrosophic Likert scales consisting of two subdimensions—distributive and procedural justice—were used. Participants responded to the same questions for both the classical Likert and neutrosophic Likert scales within a single survey, with the neutrosophic method applied, for the first time, to the questions included in the scale. The neutrosophic scale responses were answered in percentages to resemble natural language, and the answers received for each question were reduced to the range [−1, 1] to grade the agreement approach through a score function used in neutrosophic decision-making theory. In this study, the neutrosophic scale, a scaling method with strong theoretical foundations, was compared with the traditional Likert scale. The results of the statistical analyses (exploratory factor analysis, reliability analysis, neural network analysis, correlation analysis, paired samples *t*-test, and one-way and two-way ANOVAs) and evaluations of the scales were compared to measure organizational justice within a single study. In this article, the symmetric and non-symmetric properties of statistical analysis that are specific to this paper in addition to general symmetric and non-symmetry properties are discussed. These symmetric and non-symmetric features are conceptualized according to the features on which each statistical analysis focuses. Finally, although this study presents a new area of research in the social sciences, we believe that the neutrosophic Likert scale and survey approach will contribute to collecting detailed and sensitive information on many topics, such as economics, health, audience perceptions, advertising responses, and product, market, and service purchase research, through the use of score functions.

Keywords: ANOVA; fuzzy scale; Likert scale; neural network; neutrosophic Likert scale; organizational justice; score function; symmetry; non-symmetry

1. Introduction

Because of the large number of concepts and topics in this study, we have divided this section into the following subsections for readability: organizational justice, Likert scale, neutrosophy and neutrosophic set, neutrosophic Likert scale, and score function. As for the general organization of the study, we follow a descriptive and instructive path by keeping this section broad, shedding light on qualitative and quantitative research.

1.1. Organizational Justice

The theory of organizational justice concerns the extent to which employees perceive that justice occurs in work-related issues [1]. Equity theory suggests that perceptions of fairness arise from an individual's comparison of his or her contributions with subsequent rewards or consequences [2]. Employees want to believe that they are compensated as a result of their performance, a reward which they desire.

The concept of social justice is very helpful in understanding behavioral characteristics. It has been discovered that assessments of the suitability of group processes and results have an impact on both individual and systemic elements, including overall performance, organizational commitment, cooperative behavior, outcome satisfaction, and faith in authority [3]. Three different aspects of justice—interactional, distributive, and procedural—have been used to conceive organizational justice in the published literature. The concept of interactional justice pertains to how employees view the fairness and quality of their interactions with decision-makers, including how well they are treated and whether that treatment is with dignity and respect [4].

Distributive justice, on the other hand, refers to the fairness of decision-making outcomes [5,6], whereas procedural justice concerns workers' perceptions related to the decision-making procedures used to determine the distribution of the outcomes [2,6,7]. According to Colquitt, Greenberg, and Zapata-Phelan, scientific interest in organizational justice can be divided into four main waves of research and theory development, and the period from 1950 to 1970 can be referred to as the distributive justice wave [8,9]. In an organizational setting, perceptions of distributive injustice have been associated with poorer performance, decreased commitment, and increased withdrawal [10,11].

1.2. Likert Scale

The popular psychometric Likert scale, used in the social sciences to measure respondents' attitudes with survey questions, was first proposed by the American social psychologist Likert in 1932. This scale asks participants to indicate their levels of agreement through questions. For example, for a 5-point Likert scale, agreement levels are evaluated by the integer values 1 (strongly disagree) to 5 (strongly agree), and the results are obtained by taking the sum or average of each participant's scores [12].

Likert scales are widely used because they are easy to administer, score, and understand. Additionally, researchers can collect large amounts of effective and inexpensive data in less time and conduct analyses using easy mathematical calculations. Moreover, it is a suitable method for making statistical inferences with good reliability, producing appropriate results.

Although the Likert scale is useful, it also has several disadvantages, such as uncertainty regarding whether responses and measured data should be on an ordinal or interval level. It is assumed that the Likert method has the characteristics of an interval scale [12]. However, many argue that the Likert scale is ordinal [13,14]. An interval scale dictates that there must be an equal interval between any two consecutive scales. For example, for a 5-point Likert scale, each level of agreement is expressed as follows: 1 = "strongly disagree"; 2 = "disagree"; 3 = "neutral"; 4 = "agree"; and 5 = "strongly agree". Here, although the emotional intensity between "strongly disagree" and "disagree" is considered to be equivalent to the emotional intensity between other consecutive categories, participants may not understand the distances between two points of the scale as equal [15]. In this case, this scale will fail to measure actual responses.

When responding to a question on a Likert-type scale, participants must transform their feelings and thoughts into a linguistic expression that is coded with natural numbers and characterized by a ranking order, which can result in information loss, uncertainty, and inaccuracy [16]. Furthermore, the fact that participants' replies may be influenced by earlier questions and their tendency to avoid selecting extreme possibilities on the scale both pose issues.

Because of the difficulties and uncertainties mentioned above, it was thought that the Likert scale may not be the best scale to measure the level of importance among various attributes. Therefore, this has led many researchers to propose different types of scales. In one study, to obtain superior measurements, a neutrosophic approach based on fuzzy set theory was used as an alternative to the Likert scale. Between November and December

2022, a survey was conducted among 1160 young clinical nurses from five hospitals in China's Henan province to investigate the effect of organizational justice on young nurses' turnover intention. The organizational justice scale, turnover intention scale, organizational climate scale, and emotional labor scale were used. The organizational justice scale was scored on a 5-point Likert scale (1 = "strongly disagree"; 2 = "disagree"; 3 = "undecided"; 4 = "agree"; and 5 = "strongly agree"). It was concluded that organizational justice had a significant effect on turnover intentions among the young nurses through the chain mediation of organizational climate and emotional labor [17].

In addition, a survey was conducted with 400 employees to investigate the relationship and impact of organizational justice on employee creativity through the mediating role of leadership styles for academics and staff at Dhofar University in Oman. All items were rated on a 5-point Likert scale. Organizational justice was discussed along the following four dimensions: distributive, procedural, interpersonal, and informational. The results revealed that organizational justice had a positive and significant impact on the distributive, interpersonal, and informational dimensions of employee creativity, whereas procedural justice had a negative and significant impact on employee creativity [18]. Aiming to examine the relationship between organizational justice (procedural, distributive, informational, and interpersonal justice) and organizational citizenship behavior, a survey was administered to 121 faculty members working in ten private universities in Bangladesh. The participants were required to respond to all items using a 5-point Likert scale, ranging from 1 ("strongly disagree") to 5 ("strongly agree"). The study also provided the necessary guidelines on ways organizations can increase citizenship behavior, with an emphasis on fairness and inclusion in the workplace [19].

To develop a strategy to improve the working conditions of nurses in Japan, a survey was administered to nurses using a 5-point Likert scale (1 = "strongly disagree"; 2 = "disagree"; 3 = "undecided"; 4 = "agree"; and 5 = "strongly agree") using three scales: ease of work and organizational justice; organizational citizenship behavior; and job satisfaction. A significant positive correlation between interactional justice and job satisfaction was reported fairly consistently [20]. To determine the effects of organizational support and organizational justice, a survey was applied to trainees in Basque cuisine during the 2022–2023 academic year. In the study, a 7-point Likert-type scale was used. It was concluded that organizational support and organizational justice structures positively affected the happiness parameter at work [21].

In another study, a survey was administered to employees in various sectors in China, including manufacturing, construction, finance, information technology services, and wholesale and retail sectors, to examine the effects of information justice on employees' retention of information through organizational identification and to investigate how justice sensitivity moderates these effects. In this context, informational justice, justice sensitivity, organizational identity, and information hiding scales were used. All items forming the scale were evaluated using a 5-point Likert scale [22]. To show the importance of organizational justice and citizenship behavior in employees' compliance behaviors toward ISPs (information security policies), a survey was conducted on IS users in public and private banks in Ethiopia. A 5-point Likert scale ranging from 1 ("strongly disagree") to 5 ("strongly agree") was used for all measurements in the study. Additionally, an empirical determination was made regarding the mediating role of organizational citizenship behavior between the dimensions of organizational justice and willingness to comply with ISPs [23].

To understand the antecedents of organizational justice, the authors of a previous study conducted a national survey of library employees and compared the predictive power of perceived organizational support, job autonomy, job feedback, and job stress. Organizational justice consisted of four subdimensions: distributive justice (four items), procedural justice (seven items), interpersonal justice (four items), and informational justice (five items). Responses were received from the participants to each statement on a 5-point Likert scale (1 = "strongly disagree"; 2 = "disagree"; 3 = "undecided"; 4 = "agree"; and

5 = "strongly agree"). As a result, they found that providing meaningful and timely work feedback, as well as strengthening perceptions of institutional support and autonomy, can be effective in increasing librarians' overall perceptions of fairness [24]. A survey was conducted to determine the impact on the innovative work behavior of employees operating in the Chinese telecommunication industry. Distributive, procedural, and interactional justice items, representing three subdimensions of organizational justice, were included in a 5-point Likert scale (1 = "strongly disagree"; 2 = "disagree"; 3 = "undecided"; 4 = "agree"; 5 = "strongly agree"). The study concluded that organizational justice has a significant and positive effect on employees' innovative work behaviors and knowledge sharing [25].

The "Fair Learning Environment Scale", which was developed by Özer and Demirtaş (2010) [26] and Lizzio, Wilson, and Hadaway (2007) [27], was used in a Turkish validity and reliability study. The Kaiser–Meyer–Olkin (KMO) value of the scale was determined to be 0.83 by Özer and Demirtaş (2010) [26], and the internal consistency coefficient was determined to be 0.87 for the total scale. A scale with ten questions measuring distributive justice, which consisted of two subdimensions, distributive and procedural, was used.

In the study, several one-sample *t*-tests were conducted, confirming their significant influence on the effectiveness of industrial parks in Iran. The Kruskal–Wallis statistical test was used to prioritize the factors. Furthermore, the Weighted Aggregates Sum Product Assessment (WASPAS), a multi-criteria decision-making method, was employed to rank 15 industrial parks in the Khorasan province of Iran based on the identified factors. It was concluded that the infrastructure facilities factor has the highest priority in influencing the effectiveness of industrial parks [28]. In order to evaluate the efficiency of academic disciplines, a prioritization scale was introduced to rank evaluation factors. Undergraduate programs at Yazd University in Iran were prioritized based on specific factors. These key factors were subsequently weighted and ranked utilizing pairwise comparison (PC) and Analytic Hierarchy Process (AHP) methods. The study findings indicated that the employment rate, the vision of Yazd Province, and the entrance exam scores of incoming students were the most significant factors [29].

This study aimed to explore and prioritize the barriers to tourism growth in rural India by collecting qualitative and quantitative responses from 16 tourism and hospitality management experts from central India. To achieve this goal, interpretive structural modeling (ISM) and decision-making trial and evaluation laboratory (DEMATEL), which are multi-criteria decision-making (MCDM) methods, were integrated [30]. A questionnaire was conducted using a fuzzy Likert scale to evaluate the viewpoints of 24 chicken meat store managers in Arak city. Fuzzy set theory and fuzzy decision-making techniques were employed to rank the six suppliers under investigation. Following the analysis, it was concluded that Dorsa Chicken Company (Supplier 6) exhibited the highest performance, while Fakhrar Company (Supplier 2) demonstrated the lowest performance [31]. In this study, a hybrid fuzzy multi-criteria decision-making approach was employed in the Tehran construction industry, comprising two stages. Initially, the enhanced fuzzy Delphi method was utilized to refine the identified factors, followed by the application of the cybernetic parsimonious fuzzy analytic hierarchy process to prioritize these factors. The study identified "on-site sorting, reuse, and recycling of waste materials", "various procurement models", and "effective implementation of waste management regulations and plans" as the most critical factors [32]. This study aimed to explore distance education alternatives and assess their impact on students' academic performance and attendance. To determine the most suitable options, the study combined the results of the weighted sum method (WSM), weighted product method (WPM), and analytical hierarchy process (AHP), which are widely used multi-criteria decision-making (MCDM) techniques. The findings indicated that a participatory learning environment enhances students' attention, fosters meaningful learning experiences, facilitates high levels of student achievement, and cultivates higher-order critical thinking skills [33].

In this research, the factors determining turnover intention, organizational justice and nursing core competencies of nurses working in tertiary and general hospitals in

South Korea were examined. Organizational justice was assessed using the Justice Scale and nursing core competence was assessed using the Korean Nursing Core Competency Scale. Data collected using online questionnaires were evaluated by multiple regression analysis. They concluded that the way organizational justice type influences turnover intention varies according to clinical experience [34]. In another study, cluster, factor, and item network analyses were used to determine the optimal mathematical design of the Bean Counter Profiling Scale. In addition, a hierarchical clustering analysis using the uncontrolled fuzzy c-means method, an exploratory factor analysis, and item network analysis methods were also applied. A six-element structural architecture of the 68 items of the Bean Counter Profiling Scale was revealed as a result of all statistical techniques used [35].

This study explored the impact of transactional and transformational leadership, along with factors derived from equity theory and goal-setting theory, such as distributive justice and goal clarity, on organizational citizenship behavior (OCB). The research utilized survey data collected from 4133 public employees across central and local governments in Korea, which were analyzed using ordinary least squares regression models. As a result, a negative relationship was observed between distributive justice and OCB, while a positive relationship was observed between goal clarity and OCB [36]. This research examined the effects of COVID-19 layoffs on global hospitality giants like Airbnb. The crisis had underscored issues such as organizational justice, employee satisfaction, and management trust. Throughout the research process, detailed interviews were conducted with laid-off employees, revealing that even during the crisis, empathetic and proactive practices maintained laid-off employees' perceptions of justice. Furthermore, it was emphasized that negative effects can be mitigated through careful practices, highlighting the importance of organizational justice during times of crisis [37].

1.3. Neutrosophy and Neutrosophic Set

Neutrosophy [38] is a philosophical and mathematical framework developed by Florentin Smarandache in the late 20th century. It deals with problems and concepts that involve indeterminacy, ambiguity, and contradictions. Neutrosophic logic extends classical, fuzzy, and intuitionistic fuzzy logic, representing indeterminate, contradictory, and ambiguous information. In classical logic, statements are either true or false, whereas in neutrosophic logic, statements can be true, false, and indeterminate simultaneously. This allows for a more nuanced and flexible approach to reasoning.

Neutrosophic set theory extends the classical, fuzzy, and intuitionistic fuzzy set theories to include sets with indeterminate or uncertain elements. An element in classical set theory is either a member of a set or not. Within the framework of neutrosophic set theory, an element can have varying degrees of membership in a set or have no degree of membership in the set.

The classical theory of probability is extended by neutrophilic probability to handle unpredictable and uncertain occurrences, and events have clearly defined probabilities between 0 and 1. Events in neutrosophic probability can be correlated with degrees of truth, falsehood, and indeterminacy, enabling a more thorough representation of uncertainty. Neutrosophy has found applications in various fields, including artificial intelligence [39], decision-making [40–42], information fusion [43], and risk analysis [44], in which handling uncertainty and ambiguity is essential. It provides a formal framework for dealing with situations in which classical logic and probability theory may need to be revised because of contradictory or indeterminate information. The membership of elements in a set is interpreted in binary terms according to a binary case. In fuzzy set theory, introduced by Zadeh [45], a gradual assessment of the membership of elements in a set is permitted by a membership function that takes values in the real unit interval [0, 1]. Classical binary sets are usually called crisp sets in fuzzy set theory, which is a generalization of the classical set theory.

Intuitionistic fuzzy sets are those whose elements have degrees of membership and nonmembership. The intuitionistic fuzzy set was introduced by Atanassov [46] as an extension of the notion of the fuzzy set, which itself extends the classical notion of a set. Elegant generalizations of intuitionistic fuzzy sets, classical sets, fuzzy sets, dialetheist sets, paradoxist sets, tautological sets, and intuitionistic fuzzy sets based on neutrosophy are provided using neutrosophic set theory [38]. When an element x(T,I,F) has a degree of T ∈ [0, 1], it is true in the set; when it has a degree of I ∈ [0, 1], it is indeterminate; and when it has a degree of F ∈ [0, 1], it is false. Next, we present basic definitions and concepts concerning single-valued neutrosophic sets, fuzzy sets, and intuitionistic fuzzy sets.

Definition 1 ([45]). *A fuzzy set X in U is a set of ordered pairs, defined as* $X = \{(x,\ \mu_X(x))|x \in U\}$, *where* $\mu_X : U \to [0,\ 1]$ *is termed the membership function of X, and* $\mu_X(x)$ *is the degree of membership of the element x in X given a universal set U and a generic element, represented by x.*

Definition 2 ([46]). *An intuitionistic fuzzy set X exists over a discourse-level world. The representation of U is given by* $X = \{(x,\ \mu_X(x),\ \nu_X(x))|x \in U\}$, *where the terms "membership function of X" and "non-membership function of X" for x in X are, respectively,* $\mu_X : U \to [0,\ 1]$ *and* $\nu_X : U \to [0,\ 1]$. *The formula for determining the degree of nonmembership of an element, x, in X is* $\mu_X(x) + \nu_X(x) \leq 1$. *The hesitation degree of an element x is defined by* $\pi_X(x) = 1 - (\mu_X(x) + \nu_X(x))$.

Definition 3 ([38,47]). *Let U be a discourse universe.* $N = \{(x,\ T(x),\ I(x),\ F(x)) : x \in U\}$ *is a neutrosophic set, denoted by a truth-membership function,* $TN : U$ ß$] - 0,\ 1 + [$*; an indeterminacy-membership function,* $IN : U$ ß$] - 0,\ 1 + [$*; and a falsity-membership function,* $FN : U$ ß$] - 0,\ 1 + [$.

Definition 4 ([47]). *Let U be a discourse universe. A single-valued neutrosophic set is defined as* $N = \{(x,\ T(x),\ I(x),\ F(x)) : x \in U\}$, *which is identified by a truth-membership function,* $T_N : U \to [0,\ 1]$*; indeterminacy-membership function,* $I_N : U \to [0,\ 1]$*; and falsity-membership function,* $F_N : U \to [0,\ 1]$, *with* $0 \leq T_N(x) + I_N(x) + F_N(x) \leq 3$.

1.4. Neutrosophy in Social Sciences

Neutrosophic sociology (or neutrosociology) is defined, by Smarandache [48], as the study of sociology using neutrosophic scientific methods. The questionnaire is regarded as a highly important instrument in a survey [49] measuring the opinions of social groupings. Although it has been established that fuzzy replies to survey questions are more suitable than crisp responses, there may be indeterminacy; thus, fuzzy processing may not precisely capture the notion that a responder wishes to communicate, owing to doubts, confusion, and hazy thinking, etc. Modeling such a scenario using neutrosophic sets offers responders a wider variety of possible replies, making it more relevant.

In this study, we present a method for developing single-valued neutrosophic sets from questionnaires applied to social groups. The study in [50] defined, illustrated, and proposed neutrosophic statistical approaches for use in the social sciences. Often, data presented in social sciences research have discrepancies owing to mistakes, conflicting information and sources of knowledge, lack of impartiality, and other causes. As a result, the authors state that, in some circumstances, data in the form of intervals may be required.

1.5. Neutrosophic Score Function

Martinez et al. [49] used a score function ($s :\ [0,\ 1] \to [0,\ 3],\ s(a) = 2 + T - I - F$) to measure neutrosophic values and compare them with each other in a social sciences-based approach. However, we focus on interpreting the measurement of the effects of group decision-making on social choices, and this score function was not used in a study employing a Likert-type scale. The score function was used for the first time with a Likert scale [49], showing that it can be used safely in the social sciences. The function $s(a) = (1 + T - 2I - F)/2$, found in [51], was used in this study; we evaluated it to be appropriate for taking into account the negative, neutral, and positive effects by spreading the score values to the $[-1, 1]$ range in keeping with the nature of neutrosophic research.

1.6. Neutrosophic Likert Scale

A neutrosophic Likert scale was applied for the first time in [52]. Classical satisfaction with life-scale Likert questions were transformed to numerical values between 0 and 100, as it was expected that participants would be able to respond with the following options: "I agree with this statement (...)", "I am neutral (or undetermined) about this statement (...)", and "I disagree with this statement (...)". The results of the study show that the neutrosophic scale is reliable, which also supports the reliability of the classical scale because the Cronbach's alpha constant was at an acceptable level for the three dimensions.

In the current study, transformations were performed within a framework of direct percentages to achieve an effect closer to natural language. There is a connection between fuzzy sets and neutrosophic Likert scales in the way they handle imprecision and uncertainty. Neutrosophic sets and, thus, neutrosophic Likert scales enable an even broader representation that incorporates indeterminacy as a core component, whereas fuzzy sets enable the representation and manipulation of data that are not exactly specified. For survey responses in which participants' opinions not only vary across a spectrum (as accommodated by fuzzy sets) but also may include a degree of indecision or neutrality that is difficult to capture using traditional fuzzy logic or crisp Likert scales, neutrosophic Likert scales are, therefore, particularly well suited.

1.7. Correlation Analysis

Correlation analysis is a basic statistical method used to measure the strength and direction of a relationship between two variables, and it is widely used in various fields, including the social sciences, economics, biology, and finance. Pearson correlation and Spearman correlation are two common methods used to measure the strength and direction of an association between two variables.

The Pearson correlation coefficient (r) measures the linear relationship between two continuous variables, and it assumes that the variables are normally distributed and have a linear relationship.

The Spearman correlation coefficient measures the strength and direction of an association between two variables, but it does not require the variables to be linearly related. Spearman correlation is appropriate when relationships among variables are nonlinear or the data are ordinal or non-normally distributed.

Both Pearson and Spearman correlation coefficients range from -1 to 1, where values closer to 1 or -1 indicate a stronger relationship between the variables, whereas values closer to 0 indicate a weaker relationship.

1.8. Paired Samples t-Test

The paired samples *t*-test, also known as the dependent samples *t*-test, is a statistical method used to compare the means of two related samples. Each observation in one sample is paired with an observation in the other sample. The paired samples *t*-test, like most statistical procedures, uses the null hypothesis and alternative hypothesis. The null hypothesis states that there is no difference between the mean values of the two paired data sets. The alternative hypothesis states that there is a statistically significant difference between the mean values of the two paired data sets.

1.9. ANOVA

ANOVA, or analysis of variance, is a statistical method used to analyze the differences among group means in a sample. It assesses whether the means of two or more groups are statistically significantly different from each other. ANOVA is a powerful tool for understanding group differences and identifying factors that contribute to variability. There are several types of ANOVA, including the following.

One-way ANOVA is a statistical test used to determine whether any statistically significant differences exist among the means of three or more independent groups.

Two-way ANOVA is an extension of the one-way ANOVA and is used in the case of two independent variables (i.e., factors) to study the interaction effect between them on a continuous dependent variable. It allows for examining whether the effect of one independent variable on the dependent variable is contingent on the level of another independent variable, as well as the main effects of each independent variable.

In summary, ANOVA is a versatile statistical method used to compare means across different groups or conditions, and the specific type of ANOVA chosen depends on the design of the study and the number of independent variables involved.

2. Data and Likert Questionnaires

The questionnaires were designed and implemented using Google Forms, which is an effective data collection tool. In the data collection step, the number of participants determined for inclusion in the survey was 119, according to G*Power 3.1.9.4 software. Additionally, a 10-question survey was administered to 126 university students, 10 of whom were selected to aid in determining the attitude of the 5-point Likert scale (1 = "strongly disagree", . . ., 5 = "strongly agree"), as shown in Table 1.

Table 1. Likert scale questions (answers must be filled in as a check mark for a single option).

Questions	Strongly Disagree	Disagree	Neither Agree Nor Disagree	Agree	Strongly Agree
Staff at this school care about students' opinions.	☑	☐	☐	☐	☐
Students' opinions and needs are taken into consideration when making decisions.	☐	☐	☐	☐	☑
Students' rights are important to university staff.	☑	☐	☐	☐	☐
Staff at the university ask students for their ideas on how things could be improved.	☐	☑	☐	☐	☐
When staff make a mistake, they apologize to students.	☐	☐	☑	☐	☐
Staff listen to students' concerns and problems.	☐	☐	☐	☐	☑
Rules and procedures are applied consistently and fairly to all students.	☐	☐	☐	☑	☐
Students' suggestions are ignored or not taken seriously.	☐	☐	☑	☐	☐
Students are evaluated according to clear and objective criteria.	☐	☐	☐	☐	☑
Assessment methods give students a fair opportunity to demonstrate their mastery.	☐	☐	☐	☐	☑

The participants completed the survey by marking only one of these five agreement values. The research data can be accessed from the following link: https://osf.io/xd4t7 (accessed on 28 January 2024).

The neutrosophic scale (a: degree of agreement; b: degree of indeterminacy; c: degree of disagreement) was applied toward measuring organizational justice. These selected questions are shown in Table 2. Survey participants (the same participants previously surveyed, as shown in Table 1) selected a, b, c, and one percentile value each. According to the single-valued neutrosophic set approach, the sum of the percentiles (% values) of a + b + c was between 0 and 300; then, we took one percent of these percentage values and mapped them to the closed interval [0, 1].

Table 2. Neutrosophic scale questions (answers are to be filled out as percentages).

Questions	Agreement Degree	Indeterminacy Degree (Neither Agree Nor Disagree)	Disagreement Degree
Staff at this school care about students' opinions.	50	50	50
Students' opinions and needs are taken into consideration when making decisions.	10	20	30
Students' rights are important to university staff.	100	30	0
Staff at the university ask students for their ideas on how things could be improved.	0	5	75
When staff make a mistake, they apologize to students.	50	30	20
Staff listen to students' concerns and problems.	90	40	45
Rules and procedures are applied consistently and fairly to all students.	30	0	45
Students' suggestions are ignored or not taken seriously.	60	45	40
Students are evaluated according to clear and objective criteria.	30	70	100
Assessment methods give students a fair opportunity to demonstrate their mastery.	50	50	25

Table 3 shows the profile information of the survey participants.

Table 3. Profile information of the survey respondents (N = 126).

Variables	Categories	Number of Cases	Percentage (%)
Gender	Female	82	65.08
	Male	44	34.92
Age	18–21	45	35.71
	22–24	47	37.30
	25–30	24	19.05
	31–40	5	3.97
	41+	5	3.97
Faculty	Vocational School of Hizan	39	30.95
	Vocational School of Health Services	19	15.08
	School of Physical Education and Sports	10	7.94
	Vocational School of Tatvan	8	6.35
	Faculty of Science and Letters	18	14.29
	Faculty of Fine Arts	4	3.17
	Faculty of Health Sciences	7	5.55
	Vocational School of Güroymak	5	3.97
	Faculty of Islamic Sciences	16	12.70
Marital status	Married	9	92.86
	Single	117	7.14

The answers provided by the participants using the Likert and neutrosophic scales are presented in the tables below (Tables 4–7).

Table 4. Responses given by the participants on a Likert scale.

	Q1	Q2	Q3	Q4	Q5	Q6	Q7	Q8	Q9	Q10
Strongly disagree	10	14	10	12	19	15	19	24	12	10
Disagree	14	24	23	28	20	12	18	31	23	18
Neither agree nor disagree	34	17	21	26	27	26	22	23	22	32
Agree	38	43	43	37	39	45	40	38	55	48
Strongly agree	30	28	29	23	21	28	27	10	14	18

Table 5. Participants' answers on a neutrosophic scale.

	Q1	Q2	Q3	Q4	Q5	Q6	Q7	Q8	Q9	Q10
Disagree	15	15	15	18	19	19	13	22	14	17
Neither agree nor disagree	68	65	64	67	62	53	64	73	66	57
Agree	43	46	47	41	45	54	49	31	46	52

Table 6. Likert scale responses to all questions.

	All Questions
Strongly disagree	12
Disagree	21
Neither agree nor disagree	28
Agree	41
Strongly agree	24

Table 7. Neutrosophic scale answers to all questions.

	All Questions
Disagree	9
Neither agree nor disagree	76
Agree	41

Agree and strongly agree, measured on a 1-point Likert scale, ultimately indicate agreement and are selected at a much higher rate than that of agree neutrosophically. Disagree and strongly disagree, measured on a 2-point Likert scale, ultimately represent disagreement and are selected at a much higher rate than that of disagree neutrosophically. Examining the undecided answers used in both scales, it can be seen that the number of undecideds measured using the neutrosophic scale (76) was much higher than the Likert scale (28). In this situation, some of those who answered "agree" strongly agree, and some are close to undecided; some who answered "disagree" strongly disagree, and some are close to undecided. However, a single option does not provide clarity in decision-making and, on the other hand, the answers received are neutrosophic. This can be explained by the fact that it provides a clearer result by expressing freer thinking and the weight of each option.

3. Statistical Analysis

Data analyses were performed with SPSS 26.0 (IBM Corp., Armonk, NY, USA) and MATLAB R2015a software, and an alpha level of 0.05 was considered statistically significant. Exploratory factor analysis (EFA) is a statistical technique widely used to identify the underlying structure of a set of variables and to reduce the complexity of data by identifying meaningful dimensions. An exploratory factor analysis was conducted to reveal the structure of the factors of the Likert and neutrosophic scales for measuring organizational justice. Two tests were applied to the suitability of the scales for an exploratory factor analysis. Firstly, the Kaiser–Meyer–Olkin (KMO) values were calculated as 0.936 and

0.928, respectively; values greater than 0.60 are considered adequate for exploratory factor analysis. Secondly, the results of the Bartlett's test for the Likert scale and neutrosophic scale were $x^2 = 1019.885$ ($p < 0.05$) and $x^2 = 840.290$ ($p < 0.05$), respectively. The findings indicate that the correlations among the items are large enough for an exploratory factor analysis.

As a result of the exploratory factor analysis, it was determined that the Likert scale and the neutrosophic scale, both consisting of 10 items, explained 65.277% and 61.287% of the total variance, respectively. Accordingly, it was concluded that the Likert scale and the neutrosophic scale were valid, suggesting that a single component (a unidimensional construct) was sufficient for both scales, as shown in Figures 1 and 2.

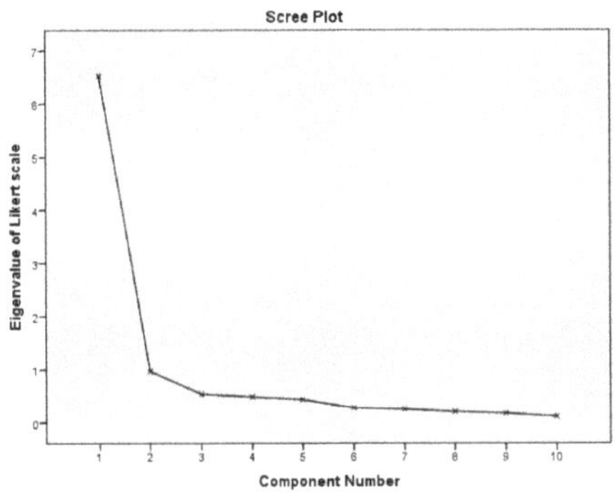

Figure 1. The scree plot of Likert scale by factor analysis.

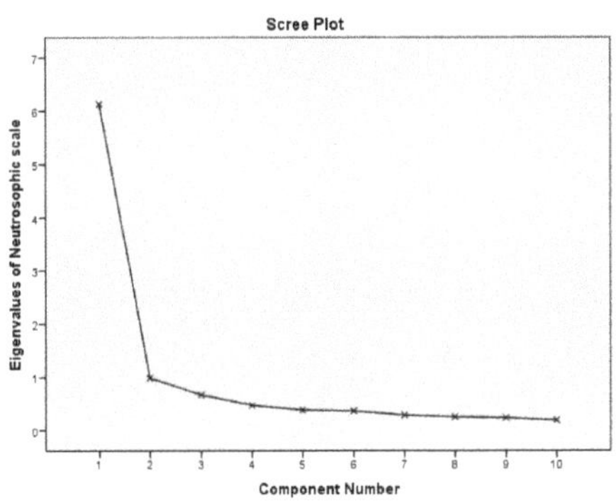

Figure 2. The scree plot of neutrosophic scale by factor analysis.

The descriptive statistics of 126 participants calculated to measure organizational justice using both scales are presented in Table 8.

In terms of descriptive statistics, because the Likert scale took values in the range [1, 5] separately and once, the mean was 33.024, and because the neutrosophic scale took values in the range [−1, 1], the mean was 1.977. Furthermore, the Likert scale's variance was 98.311, whereas the neutrosophic scale's variance was 13.632, showing that the neutrosophic scale's arithmetic mean and standard deviation were smaller. The two scales' standard errors of skewness and kurtosis were the same. Skewness and kurtosis are statistical measures that describe the shape of a distribution. The fact that the standard errors of skewness and kurtosis of the two different scales were the same indicates that the variability in the estimated skewness and kurtosis values is consistent among them.

Table 8. Descriptive statistics.

	Likert Scale	Neutrosophic Scale
Mean	33.024	1.977
Median	36.000	1.200
Mode	46.000	−3.680
Std. deviation	9.915	3.692
Variance	98.311	13.632
Skewness	−0.475	0.037
Std. error of skewness	0.216	0.216
Kurtosis	−0.701	−0.593
Std. error of kurtosis	0.428	0.428
Range	37.000	17.165
Minimum	11.000	−7.710
Maximum	48.000	9.455

Table 9 shows that the data measured using the Likert scale and those measured with the neutrosophic scale have a distribution that differs from normal at a 0.05 level of statistical significance. Additionally, according to the results of the Kolmogorov–Smirnov normality test, the Likert scale and the neutrosophic scale are not suitable for a normal distribution. However, especially in studies in the social sciences, skewness and kurtosis values can be useful in making statistical inferences about the underlying distributions of the data in scales. Skewness and kurtosis values of ±1.0 are considered excellent for most psychometric purposes [53]. In this case, because the skewness and kurtosis values of both scales were ±1.0, a parametric analysis was performed, accepting that they were suitable for a normal distribution.

Table 9. Normal distribution testing using the Kolmogorov–Smirnov test.

	Kolmogorov–Smirnov		
	Statistic	**Df**	**Sig.**
Likert scale	0.126	126	0.000
Neutrosophic scale	0.109	126	0.001

Cronbach's alpha was applied to determine the reliability of the scales [54]. Examining the results (Table 10), the scores obtained with the neutrosophic scale are also highly reliable, as with the Likert scale.

Table 10. Cronbach's alpha coefficient.

Cronbach's Alpha Constant	Variables
0.924	SCORE1, SCORE2, SCORE3, SCORE4, SCORE5, SCORE6, SCORE7, SCORE8, SCORE9, SCORE10
0.894	VAR1a, VAR2a, VAR3a, VAR4a, VAR5a, VAR6a, VAR7a, VAR8a, VAR9a, VAR10a
0.922	VAR1b, VAR2b, VAR3b, VAR4b, VAR5b, VAR6b, VAR7b, VAR8b, VAR9b, VAR10b
0.900	VAR1c, VAR2c, VAR3c, VAR4c, VAR5c, VAR6c, VAR7c, VAR8c, VAR9c, VAR10c
0.933	VAR1, VAR2, VAR3, VAR4, VAR5, VAR6, VAR7, VAR8, VAR9, VAR10

According to the results of the neural network analysis of the two scales in Table 11, Score1 made the least contribution to the classical variable at 16.2%, while Score8 contributed the most at 100.0%.

Table 11. Independent variable importance.

	Importance	Normalized Importance
Score1	0.026	16.2%
Score2	0.077	47.6%
Score3	0.078	48.2%
Score4	0.096	59.7%
Score5	0.113	70.3%
Score6	0.037	23.1%
Score7	0.123	76.2%
Score8	0.161	100.0%
Score9	0.134	83.4%
Score10	0.155	96.2%

According to the Spearman's rho correlation coefficient in Table 12, there is a significant positive correlation between the Likert scale and neutrosophic scale in general, depending on the agree option (except for question 8). On the other hand, because the eighth question is reverse-coded, there is a negative relationship between the Likert scale and neutrosophic scale in terms of the agree option.

Table 12. Correlation among classical items, neutrosophic items, and scores.

		VAR1a	**VAR1b**	**VAR1c**	**Score1**
VAR1	Correlation Coefficient	0.542 **	0.131	−0.069	0.132
	p	0.000	0.144	0.442	0.139
	N	126	126	126	126
		VAR2a	**VAR2b**	**VAR2c**	**Score2**
VAR2	Correlation Coefficient	0.626 **	0.131	−0.161	0.229 **
	p	0.000	0.144	0.072	0.010
	N	126	126	126	126
		VAR3a	**VAR3b**	**VAR3c**	**Score3**
VAR3	Correlation Coefficient	0.540 **	0.021	−0.219 *	0.268 **
	p	0.000	0.817	0.014	0.002
	N	126	126	126	126
		VAR4a	**VAR4b**	**VAR4c**	**Score4**
VAR4	Correlation Coefficient	0.649 **	0.047	−0.296 **	0.280 **
	p	0.000	0.597	0.001	0.001
	N	126	126	126	126
		VAR5a	**VAR5b**	**VAR5c**	**Score5**
VAR5	Correlation Coefficient	0.599 **	−0.024	−0.232 **	0.282 **
	p	0.000	0.789	0.009	0.001
	N	126	126	126	126
		VAR6a	**VAR6b**	**VAR6c**	**Score6**
VAR6	Correlation Coefficient	0.423 **	−0.033	−0.187 *	0.165
	p	0.000	0.717	0.036	0.064
	N	126	126	126	126

Table 12. *Cont.*

		VAR7a	**VAR7b**	**VAR7c**	**Score7**
VAR7	Correlation Coefficient	0.517 **	−0.120	−0.308 **	0.347 **
	p	0.000	0.182	0.000	0.000
	N	126	126	126	126
		VAR8a	**VAR8b**	**VAR8c**	**Score8**
VAR8	Correlation Coefficient	−0.299 **	−0.244 **	0.334 **	−0.047
	p	0.001	0.006	0.000	0.605
	N	126	126	126	126
		VAR9a	**VAR9b**	**VAR9c**	**Score9**
VAR9	Correlation Coefficient	0.334 **	0.021	−0.252 **	0.215 *
	p	0.000	0.812	0.004	0.016
	N	126	126	126	126
		VAR10a	**VAR10b**	**VAR10c**	**Score10**
VAR10	Correlation Coefficient	0.590 **	0.027	−0.153	0.260 **
	p	0.000	0.764	0.088	0.003
	N	126	126	126	126

** Correlation is significant at the 0.01 level. * Correlation is significant at the 0.05 level.

According to the Likert scale, the mean value of the students' perceptions of fairness in the learning environment was found to be 3.302, and this mean value is considered as mid-level. Therefore, it can be concluded that the students mostly preferred to agree. Analyzing the questions as neutrosophic, it is supported by the positive correlation obtained that they give higher scores to the agree option. Likewise, the positive correlation of the scores obtained with the neutrosophic scale supports this outcome.

According to Table 13, there is a mid-level positive ($r = 0.302$) and statistically significant ($p < 0.05$) relationship between the Likert scale and neutrosophic scale.

Table 13. Correlation between neutrosophic scale and Likert scale.

		Likert Scale
Neutrosophic scale	Pearson Correlation (r)	0.302
	p	0.001
	N	126

A paired samples *t*-test was conducted to evaluate whether a statistically significant difference existed between the mean Likert scale and neutrosophic scale. That is, this test was used to examine the means of two different methods on the same survey group. As can be seen in Table 14, the results of the paired samples *t*-test were significant, $t(125) = 36.763$, $p < 0.05$, indicating that there was a significant difference in the Likert scale ($M = 33.024$, $SD = 9.915$, $n = 126$) compared to the neutrosophic scale ($M = 1.977$, $SD = 3.692$, $n = 126$). According to Cohen's rules, the effect size was very large [54]. The mean difference was 31.047, with the 95% confidence interval for the difference between the means of 29.376 and 32.718. The null hypothesis was rejected.

Table 14. Paired samples *t*-test results for the Likert and neutrosophic scales.

		Mean	SD	T	Df	*p*	d
Pair 1	Likert scale–Neutrosophic scale	31.047	9.480	36.763	125	0.000	3.275

d = Effect size.

The attitude toward organizational justice, as measured using the Likert scale and neutrosophic scale, is shown in Table 15 (Table 7 in [55]).

Table 15. Population mean and standard deviation of attitudes toward organizational justice measured using the Likert scale and neutrosophic scale.

Item	Likert Scale		Neutrosophic Scale	
	μ	σ	μ	σ
Staff at this school care about students' opinions.	3.508	1.198	0.187	0.45
Students' opinions and needs are taken into consideration when making decisions.	3.373	1.319	160	0.437
Students' rights are important to university staff.	3.46	1.25	0.236	0.477
Staff at the university ask students for their ideas on how things could be improved.	3.246	1.257	0.148	0.476
When staff make a mistake, they apologize to students.	3.183	1.311	0.193	0.517
Staff listen to students' concerns and problems.	3.468	1.269	0.278	0.515
Rules and procedures are applied consistently and fairly to all students.	3.302	1.358	0.217	0.499
Students' suggestions are ignored or not taken seriously.	2.833	1.27	0.074	0.448
Students are evaluated according to clear and objective criteria.	3.286	1.172	0.229	0.477
Assessment methods give students a fair opportunity to demonstrate their mastery.	3.365	1.136	0.255	0.49

In Table 15, the arithmetic mean (μ) and standard deviation (σ) are presented for the Likert and neutrosophic scales. The arithmetic mean is the most commonly used measure of central tendency. Measures of central tendency are the values around which data tend to cluster in the distribution of a data group and which summarize the data group. The measure of the central tendency does not provide information about the distribution of the data. In this case, measures of dispersion were used.

The most commonly used measure of dispersion is the standard deviation, which measures the variation, or dispersion, of a data set, and a low standard deviation denotes that the data points tend to be close to the mean, whereas a high standard deviation denotes that the data span a wide interval of values. In this case, for the neutrosophic scale, it tended to spread in a narrower interval and close to the mean.

As can be seen in Table 16, A nine (faculty type) X five (age) one-way ANOVA was applied to investigate the single effect. The effect of faculty type on the Likert scale was not statistically significant ($F = 0.744$, $p > 0.05$). On the other hand, the effect of age group on the Likert scale was found to be statistically significant ($F = 2.674$, $p < 0.05$). The difference between the averages of students in the 18–21 age group and the averages of students in the 25–30 age group was found to be statistically significant ($p < 0.05$). At the same time, a significant difference was found between the averages of students in the 22–24 age group and the 25–30 age group. The Likert scale score of students in the 25–30 age group ($M = 38.08$) is higher than that of students in the 18–21 ($M = 31.02$) and 22–24 age groups ($M = 31.80$).

Table 16. One-way ANOVA results for the Likert and neutrosophic scales.

Scale	Effect	Mean Square	F	Significance Level
Likert scale	Faculty	74.340	0.744	0.653
	Age	249.510	2.674	0.035
Neutrosophic scale	Faculty	19.558	1.479	0.172
	Age	17.817	1.320	0.266

The effect of faculty type (F = 1.479, $p > 0.05$) and age group (F = 1.320, $p > 0.05$) on the neutrosophic scale was not found to be statistically significant.

As can be seen in Table 17, Nine (faculty type) X two (gender), nine (faculty type) X five (age), and two (gender) X five (age) two-way ANOVAs were conducted to investigate the single effects and interaction effects of faculty and gender, faculty and age, and gender and age. The individual effects of faculty type (F = 1.231, $p > 0.05$) and gender (F = 2.370, $p > 0.05$) on the Likert scale were statistically insignificant. At the same time, the interaction effect of faculty type and gender on the Likert scale was insignificant (F = 1.623, $p > 0.05$). The single effect of both faculty type (F = 1.135, $p > 0.05$) and gender (F = 0.475, $p > 0.05$) on the neutrosophic scale was statistically insignificant. In addition, the neutrosophic scale did not differ according to the interaction effect of the faculty type and gender (F = 0.515, $p > 0.05$).

Table 17. Two-way ANOVA results for the Likert and neutrosophic scales.

Scale	Single and Interaction Effect	Mean Square	F	Significance Level
Likert scale	Faculty	115.199	1.231	0.288
	Gender	221.773	2.370	0.127
	Faculty X Gender	151.888	1.623	0.136
Neutrosophic scale	Faculty	15.492	1.135	0.346
	Gender	6.489	0.475	0.492
	Faculty X Gender	7.030	0.515	0.821
Likert scale	Faculty	103.403	1.109	0.364
	Age	121.605	1.304	0.274
	Faculty X Age	103.998	1.116	0.350
Neutrosophic scale	Faculty	28.286	2.263	0.029
	Age	20.610	1.649	0.168
	Faculty X Age	16.653	1.332	0.186
Likert scale	Gender	28.130	0.306	0.581
	Age	240.887	2.624	0.038
	Gender X Age	144.901	1.579	0.185
Neutrosophic scale	Gender	10.940	0.836	0.362
	Age	15.716	1.201	0.314
	Gender X Age	28.538	2.181	0.075

The single effect of the faculty type (F = 1.109, $p > 0.05$) and age group (F = 1.304, $p > 0.05$) did not significantly affect the Likert scale. Moreover, the effect of the Likert scale did not differ according to the interaction of the faculty type and age group (F = 1.116, $p > 0.05$). The individual effect of the faculty type on the neutrosophic scale was statistically significant (F = 2.263, $p < 0.05$). The difference between the average of the students in the vocational school of health services and the students in the physical education and sports school was found to be statistically significant ($p < 0.05$). At the same time, the difference between the averages of the students in the vocational school of health services and the students in the Faculty of Islamic Sciences was found to be significant ($p < 0.05$). The neutrosophic scale score of the students in the vocational school of health services (M = 3.38) was higher than the students in both the School of Physical Education and Sports (M = 0.38) and the Faculty of Islamic Sciences (M = 0.99). The effect of age group alone

(F = 1.649, $p > 0.05$) and the interaction of the faculty type and age group (F = 1.332, $p > 0.05$) on the neutrosophic scale were statistically insignificant.

The individual effect of male and female students on the Likert scale was statistically insignificant (F = 0.306, $p > 0.05$). The individual effect of the age group on the Likert scale was statistically significant (F = 2.624, $p < 0.05$). A statistically significant difference was found between the averages of students in the 18–21 age group and those in the 25–30 age group ($p < 0.05$). At the same time, the difference between students in the 22–24 age group and 25–30 age group was found to be statistically significant ($p < 0.05$). Although students in the 25–30 age group had the highest Likert scale scores, the students in the 18–21 age group had the lowest Likert scale scores. The effect of the interaction was statistically insignificant (F = 1.579, $p > 0.05$). The single effect of gender (F = 0.836, $p > 0.05$) and age group (F = 1.201, $p > 0.05$) was statistically insignificant on the neutrosophic scale. At the same time, the effect of the interaction was found to be insignificant (F = 2.181, $p > 0.05$).

In general, when viewed both in Likert and neutrosophic terms, although the effect of demographic variables on perceived distributive justice varied individually according to age and faculty type, no effect of the variables together was found. The results show that the perception of distributive justice increased as age increased. Older people have more realistic expectations based on their life experiences, and as age decreases, expectations increase. As a result of rising expectations, the perceived level of distributive justice decreases. The difference in the perceptions of distributive justice according to faculty types can be explained by the different environments offered by the faculties.

4. Conclusions

The issue of scale is extremely important in the production of information in social sciences research, because scale involves measuring the quality or quantity of entities. Scale development and the validation of measurements still require challenging efforts. Social scientists have developed a number of valid scales, especially in the field of education. These scales are designed to contribute to the measurement of abstract concepts.

In this work, each item of a Likert-type scale was converted into a neutrosophic scale, and responses were received for both scales in a single survey. These classical and neutrosophic Likert scales provided evidence of the answers to ten questions. Although a Likert scale does not fully meet the desires of participants in terms of answer options, the desired answer can be expressed more clearly as a percentage with the neutrosophic scale. When a comparison of the data quality was made, the arithmetic mean and standard deviation for the neutrosophic scale were lower than those for the Likert scale. Therefore, it was concluded that the neutrosophic scale is more suitable for analysis using statistical inferences. Most importantly, both scales are normally distributed, indicating that inferential statistics are appropriate for the analysis, which are extremely important for inferring, drawing conclusions, and making decisions about a population on the basis of the information obtained from the sample.

In this study, item 8 was included by reversing the Likert scale. This can be considered a disadvantage of the Likert scale, because the item's reversal and negative value may confuse participants and cause internal consistency. The neutrosophic scale may be preferred because it was found to be easier to understand and answer by the participants. For example, for the question "The staff at this school care about students' opinions", the participant can choose a level between "agree" and "strongly agree" on a Likert scale. However, if the participant wants to answer closer to "strongly agree", the Likert scale cannot accommodate this exact answer. The desired answer can be expressed more clearly with percentages on the neutrosophic scale.

Additionally, although Likert's method includes a number of lexical scale terms, the neutrosophic approach uses only three lexical scale terms (agree, neutral, and disagree). Therefore, it is easier to find equivalents for "agree", "neutral", and "disagree" in different languages, which can reduce problems of incompatibility in the literal meaning. Moreover, although the Likert scale contains options indicating the decision direction, the percentages of answers are still not clear. With the neutrosophic scale, individuals can express their choices more freely and, thus, more precisely numerically. Although individuals respond according to the most dominant side of the Likert scale, they do not indicate the ratio to other options. However, individuals who choose the same option have different feelings and thoughts compared to the other options. While we do not have a chance to measure this with the Likert scale, clearer results can be obtained with a neutrosophic scale by allowing individuals to express their opinions on a subject with positive, negative, and indecision rates at the same time.

As a result of the exploratory factor analysis performed on both scales, it was seen that they had a one-dimensional factor. Moreover, it was determined that the neutrosophic scale had high reliability, like the Likert scale.

The "Fair Learning Environment Questionnaire", used in a validity and reliability study conducted by Özer and Demirtaş [26] and developed by Lizzio, Wilson, and Hadaway [27] for the Turkish version of the Fairness Perception Regarding the Learning Environment, was used. The Kaiser–Meyer–Olkin (KMO) value of the scale was determined to be 0.83 by Özer and Demirtaş [26], and the internal consistency coefficient was determined to be 0.87 for the total scale.

Another factor taken into account in this study is whether there was a significant difference with the two scales according to the faculty of the participants. The results show that participants were able to evaluate similarly using the two methods, regardless of the faculty in which they studied. Additionally, the effects of faculty and gender on the scales, both individually and in interaction, were examined. It was concluded that neither the individual effect nor the interaction of the participants' faculty and gender created a significant difference with the two scales. The individual effect of faculty type on the neutrosophic scale was statistically significant, and this situation can be explained by the different environments provided by the faculties. It can be said that different practices and conditions affect students' perception of distributive justice. The individual effect of faculty type on the Likert scale was statistically insignificant. It can be said that the difference obtained with the neutrosophic scale arises from the students' ability to express their thoughts other than their standard common answers.

When both the marginal effect and the interaction effect of faculty and gender were examined for the two scales, it was concluded that neither the individual effect nor the interaction of the participants' faculty and gender led to a significant difference. The individual effect of age group on the Likert scale was found to be statistically significant. The results show that the perception of distributive justice increases as age increases, and it can be said that older people have more realistic expectations based on their life experiences, and as age decreases, expectations increase. In addition, the perceived level of distributive justice decreases as a result of rising expectations.

Paired samples t-test has an invariance feature. That is, even if the order of measurements is changed, the result of the paired samples t-test does not change as long as the matching between measurements is maintained. This property makes the paired samples t-test a robust method for comparing two groups or conditions of interest.

In general, the symmetric properties of the analyses used in this study are as follows.

In a correlation analysis, symmetry (Table 18) means that the relationship between two variables is reciprocal and remains balanced regardless of which variable is perceived as the predictor or outcome. Spearman's rho correlation coefficient indicates the direction and degree of the monotonic relationship between two variables (Table 12). In this case, we observed symmetrical structures. Similarly, the Pearson correlation coefficient measures the linear relationship between two variables and assumes symmetry because $Corr(X,Y) = Corr(Y,X)$. The linear relationship between the Likert and neutrosophic scales had a symmetrical structure, as tested by Pearson correlation (Tables 13 and 18).

Table 18. Tabulation and explanation of symmetric and non-symmetric concepts.

	Likert Scale		Neutrosophic Scale	
	General	**Specific**	**General**	**Specific**
Exploratory factor analysis (Here, symmetric refers to number of factor of two scales)				
Symmetric	☐	☑	☐	☑
Non-symmetric	☑	☐	☑	☐
Correlation analysis (this symmetric feature is explained in the conclusion)				
Symmetric	☑	☑	☑	☑
Non-symmetric	☐	☐	☐	☐
One-way ANOVA and two-way ANOVA (Generally speaking, it is non-symmetric regarding group means; specifically, it is non-symmetric regarding the significance of the test)				
Symmetric	☐	☐	☐	☐
Non-symmetric	☑	☑	☑	☑

In one-way and two-way ANOVA, symmetry (Table 18) concerns the equality of variances and homogeneity of group means at different levels of independent variables. An assumption of variance equality in an ANOVA suggests that the variances of the groups are equal. The homogeneity of group averages means that the groups have similar central tendencies. If there is equality of variance in an ANOVA but the group means are not homogeneous, this means that the groups have different variances but may have the same central tendencies. In this case, it may not be appropriate to address the issue of symmetry. Symmetry is when the data distribution is in some way balanced. When the group means of the data set are not homogeneous, it is possible to make an assessment of whether the data distribution is symmetrical, but it cannot be directly related to the ANOVA results. Symmetry may depend on the distribution of the data set and differences between groups, and ANOVA results do not provide specific information on this issue. Therefore, the information on the equality of variance and homogeneity of group means obtained from ANOVA results can be used to understand the distribution of the data set and differences between groups, but it is not sufficient to make a specific judgment about symmetry.

On the other hand, while correlation coefficients are used to understand the nature of the relationship between two variables, ANOVA is used to compare the means of more than one group, so naturally the symmetry concepts between the two concepts and analyses are different from each other.

In addition, as a result of exploratory factor analysis, it was determined that both scales could be reduced to a single factor and had a symmetrical structure. In addition, according to the one-way ANOVA results, it was proven that the faculty type was not statistically significant in terms of Likert and neutrosophic scales and showed non-symmetrical features. Similarly, in the two-way ANOVA analysis, the individual and interaction effects of faculty and gender variables were not statistically significant for both scales, indicating a non-symmetrical structure.

In possible future study, we plan to use machine learning models to predict demographic data, such as age, education, marital status, and sex, from the answers provided to questions in the classical Likert and neutrosophic Likert scales. Another possible future study direction can involve the help of the newly developed RANCOM method, which focuses on making weighted judgments about the evaluations of experts in different fields who evaluate neutrosophic Likert scale data [56].

Author Contributions: Conceptualization, S.T. and S.B.; Funding acquisition, S.B.; Investigation, S.B. and S.T.; Methodology, S.B. and S.T.; Resources, S.T., H.G. and S.A.E.; Software, S.B. and H.G.; Supervision, S.T. and S.A.E.; Validation, S.B., S.T., H.G. and S.A.E.; Visualization, S.A.E.; Writing—

original draft, S.B., S.T. and H.G.; Writing—review and editing, S.B., S.T., H.G. and S.A.E. All authors have read and agreed to the published version of the manuscript.

Funding: This research did not receive a specific grant from any funding agency in the public, commercial, or not-for-profit sectors.

Data Availability Statement: The data sets generated and/or analyzed in this study are available via an OpenScienceFramework repository (https://osf.io/xd4t7) (accessed on 28 January 2024).

Acknowledgments: We would like to thank the handling editor and the anonymous reviewers for their careful reading and helpful remarks.

Conflicts of Interest: The authors have no competing interests to declare that are relevant to the contents of this article.

References

1. Greenberg, J. Employee theft as a reaction to underpayment inequity: The hidden cost of pay cuts. In *Occupational Crime*; Routledge: London, UK, 2018; pp. 99–106.
2. Adams, J. Stacy. Inequity in social exchange. In *Advances in Experimental Social Psychology*; Academic Press: Cambridge, MA, USA, 1965; Volume 2, pp. 267–299.
3. Colquitt, J.A.; Conlon, D.E.; Wesson, M.J.; Porter, C.O.; Ng, K.Y. Justice at the millennium: A meta-analytic review of 25 years of organizational justice research. *J. Appl. Psychol.* **2001**, *86*, 425. [CrossRef] [PubMed]
4. Ramamoorthy, N.; Patrick, C.F. Individualism/collectivism, perceived task interdependence and teamwork attitudes among Irish blue-collar employees: A test of the main and moderating effects? *Hum. Relat.* **2004**, *57*, 347–366. [CrossRef]
5. Colquitt, J.A.; Zapata-Phelan, C.P.; Roberson, Q.M. Justice in teams: A review of fairness effects in collective contexts. *Res. Pers. Hum. Resour. Manag.* **2005**, *24*, 53–94.
6. Greenberg, J. Organizational justice: Yesterday, today, and tomorrow. *J. Manag.* **1990**, *16*, 399–432. [CrossRef]
7. Cropanzano, R.; Schminke, M. Using social justice to build effective work groups. In *Groups at Work*; Psychology Press: London, UK, 2014; pp. 143–171.
8. McMillan-Capehart, A.; Richard, O. Organisational justice and perceived fairness of hiring decisions related to race and gender: Affirmative action reactions. *Equal Oppor. Int.* **2005**, *24*, 44–57. [CrossRef]
9. Colquitt, J.A.; Greenberg, J.; Zapata-Phelan, C.P. What is organizational justice? A historical overview. In *Handbook of Organizational Justice*; Psychology Press: London, UK, 2013; pp. 3–56.
10. Schwarzwald, J.; Koslowsky, M.; Shalit, B. A field study of employees' attitudes and behaviors after promotion decisions. *J. Appl. Psychol.* **1992**, *77*, 511. [CrossRef]
11. Pfeffer, J.; Langton, N. The effect of wage dispersion on satisfaction, productivity, and working collaboratively: Evidence from college and university faculty. *Adm. Sci. Q.* **1993**, *38*, 382–407. [CrossRef]
12. Likert, R. A technique for the measurement of attitudes. *Arch. Psychol.* **1932**, *22*, 140.
13. Hodge, D.R.; Gillespie, D. Phrase completions: An alternative to. *Soc. Work Res.* **2003**, *27*, 45. [CrossRef]
14. Pett, M.A. *Nonparametric Statistics for Health Care Research: Statistics for Small Samples and Unusual Distributions*; Sage Publications: New York, NY, USA, 2015.
15. Crask, M.R.; Fox, R.J. An exploration of the interval properties of 3 commonly used marketing-research scales-a magnitude estimation approach. *J. Mark. Res. Soc.* **1987**, *29*, 317–339.
16. Disegna, M.; D'Urso, P.; Massari, R. Analysing cluster evolution using repeated cross-sectional ordinal data. *Tour. Manag.* **2018**, *69*, 524–536. [CrossRef]
17. Su, Y.; Jiang, Z.; Meng, R.; Lu, G.; Chen, C. The effect of organizational justice on young nurses' turnover intention: The mediating roles of organizational climate and emotional labour. *Nurse Educ. Pract.* **2023**, *72*, 103723. [CrossRef] [PubMed]
18. Jaboob, M.; Awain, A.M.S.B.; Al-Ansi, A.M. Sustaining employees' creativity through the organizational justice: The mediating role of leadership styles. *Soc. Sci. Humanit. Open* **2023**, *8*, 100693.
19. Rahman, M.H.A.; Karim, D.N. Organizational justice and organizational citizenship behavior: The mediating role of work engagement. *Heliyon* **2022**, *8*, e09450. [CrossRef] [PubMed]
20. Shimamura, M.; Fukutake, M.; Namba, M.; Ogino, T. The relationship among factors of organizational justice, organizational citizenship behavior, job satisfaction, and ease of work among Japanese nurses. *Appl. Nurs. Res.* **2021**, *61*, 151479. [CrossRef] [PubMed]
21. Ravina-Ripoll, R.; Balderas-Cejudo, A.; Nunez-Barriopedro, E.; Galvan-Vela, E. Are chefs happiness providers? Exploring the impact of organisational support, intrapreneurship and interactional justice from the perspective of happiness management. *Int. J. Gastron. Food Sci.* **2023**, *34*, 100818. [CrossRef]
22. Xu, G.; Huang, Y.; Huang, S.S. Informational justice and employee knowledge hiding behaviours: Mediation of organizational identification and moderation of justice sensitivity. *Heliyon* **2023**, *9*, e14697. [CrossRef] [PubMed]
23. Aebissa, B.; Dhillon, G.; Meshesha, M. The direct and indirect effect of organizational justice on employee intention to comply with information security policy: The case of ethiopian banks. *Comput. Secur.* **2023**, *130*, 103248. [CrossRef]

24. Matteson, M.L.; Ming, Y.; Silva, D.E. The relationship between work conditions and perceptions of organizational justice among library employees. *Libr. Inf. Sci. Res.* **2021**, *43*, 101093. [CrossRef]
25. Akram, T.; Lei, S.; Haider, M.J.; Hussain, S.T. The impact of organizational justice on employee innovative work behavior: Mediating role of knowledge sharing. *J. Innov. Knowl.* **2020**, *5*, 117–129. [CrossRef]
26. Özer, N.; Demirtaş, H. Students' perceptions regarding the fairness of learning environment in faculty of education. *Egit. Arastirmalari-Eurasian J. Educ. Res.* **2010**, *38*, 126–145.
27. Lizzio, A.; Wilson, K.; Hadaway, V. University students' perceptions of a fair learning environment: A social justice perspective. *Assess. Eval. High. Educ.* **2007**, *32*, 195–213. [CrossRef]
28. Moghimi, F.; Baradaran, V.; Hosseinian, A.H. Identifying the influential factors on the effectiveness of industrial parks and using an MCDM method to rank them: Case study of Iran. *J. Facil. Manag.* **2023**, *21*, 816–844. [CrossRef]
29. Kianypoor, H.; Nosrati Malekjahan, A.; Kashan, A.H. An MCDM Approach for Prioritization of Faculties and Disciplines in Educational Institutions: A Real Case Study. In *International Conference on Information Science and Applications*; Springer Nature: Singapore, 2023; pp. 459–481.
30. Jena, R.K.; Dwivedi, Y. Prioritizing the barriers to tourism growth in rural India: An integrated multi-criteria decision making (MCDM) approach. *J. Tour. Futures* **2023**, *9*, 393–416. [CrossRef]
31. Etebari, A.; Arab, R.; Amirkhan, M. Evaluation of Performance of Chicken Meat Suppliers Using Fuzzy-MCDM Method (Case Study: Arak City-Iran). *Int. J. Math. Model. Comput.* **2023**. [CrossRef]
32. Kabirifar, K.; Ashour, M.; Yazdani, M.; Mahdiyar, A.; Malekjafarian, M. Cybernetic-parsimonious MCDM modeling with application to the adoption of Circular Economy in waste management. *Appl. Soft Comput.* **2023**, *139*, 110186. [CrossRef]
33. Alshamsi, A.M.; El-Kassabi, H.; Serhani, M.A.; Bouhaddioui, C. A multi-criteria decision-making (MCDM) approach for data-driven distance learning recommendations. *Educ. Inf. Technol.* **2023**, *28*, 10421–10458. [CrossRef] [PubMed]
34. Choi, H.; Shin, S. The factors that affect turnover intention according to clinical experience: A focus on organizational justice and nursing core competency. *Int. J. Environ. Res. Public Health* **2022**, *19*, 3515. [CrossRef] [PubMed]
35. Rad, D.; Cuc, L.D.; Lile, R.; Balas, V.E.; Barna, C.; Pantea, M.F.; Bâtcă-Dumitru, G.C.; Szentesi, S.G.; Rad, G.A. Cognitive Systems Engineering Approach Using Unsupervised Fuzzy C-Means Technique, Exploratory Factor Analysis and Network Analysis—A Preliminary Statistical Investigation of the Bean Counter Profiling Scale Robustness. *Int. J. Environ. Res. Public Health* **2022**, *19*, 12821. [CrossRef]
36. Ha, T.S.; Moon, K.K. Distributive Justice, Goal Clarity, and Organizational Citizenship Behavior: The Moderating Role of Transactional and Transformational Leadership. *Sustainability* **2023**, *15*, 7403. [CrossRef]
37. Lee, S.; Hong, S.; Shin, W.Y.; Lee, B.G. The Experiences of Layoff Survivors: Navigating Organizational Justice in Times of Crisis. *Sustainability* **2023**, *15*, 16717. [CrossRef]
38. Smarandache, F. A unifying field in logics: Neutrosophic logic. In *Philosophy*; American Research Press: Champaign, IL, USA, 1999; pp. 1–141.
39. Elhassouny, A.; Idbrahim, S.; Smarandache, F. Machine learning in neutrosophic environment: A survey. *Infin. Study* **2019**, *28*, 58–68.
40. Jha, S.; Kumar, R.; Son, L.H.; Chatterjee, J.M.; Khari, M.; Yadav, N.; Smarandache, F. Neutrosophic soft set decision making for stock trending analysis. *Evol. Syst.* **2019**, *10*, 621–627. [CrossRef]
41. Liu, P.; Liu, X. The neutrosophic number generalized weighted power averaging operator and its application in multiple attribute group decision making. *Int. J. Mach. Learn. Cybern.* **2018**, *9*, 347–358. [CrossRef]
42. Abdel-Basset, M.; Saleh, M.; Gamal, A.; Smarandache, F. An approach of topsis technique for developing supplier selection with group decision making under type-2 neutrosophic number. *Appl. Soft Comput.* **2019**, *77*, 438–452. [CrossRef]
43. Bhattacharya, S. Neutrosophic information fusion applied to the options market. *Invest. Manag. Financ. Innov.* **2005**, *2*, 139–145.
44. Chang, K.H. A Novel Risk Ranking Method Based on the Single Valued Neutrosophic Set. 2022. Available online: https://books.google.com.au/books?hl=zh-TW&lr=&id=-cpAEAAAQBAJ&oi=fnd&pg=PA1&dq=Chang,+K.H.+A+Novel+Risk+Ranking+Method+Based+on+the+Single+Valued+Neutrosophic+Set;&ots=sgMxyS3Obl&sig=Nlb1wWaw8u0Ts-enhJVtr9kGxRI&redir_esc=y#v=onepage&q=Chang,%20K.H.%20A%20Novel%20Risk%20Ranking%20Method%20Based%20on%20the%20Single%20Valued%20Neutrosophic%20Set;&f=false (accessed on 22 February 2024).
45. Zadeh, L.A. Fuzzy sets. *Inf. Control* **1965**, *8*, 338–353. [CrossRef]
46. Atanassov, K. Intuitionistic fuzzy sets. In Proceedings of the VII ITKR's Session, Sofia, Bulgaria, 20–23 June 1983.
47. Wang, H.; Smarandache, F.; Zhang, Y.; Sunderraman, R. Single Valued Neutrosophic Sets. *Rev. Air Force Acad.* **2012**.
48. Smarandache, F. Introduction to Neutrosophic Sociology (Neutrosociology). 2019. Available online: https://digitalrepository.unm.edu/math_fsp/28 (accessed on 22 February 2024).
49. Martínez, C.R.; Hidalgo, G.A.; Matos, M.A.; Smarandache, F. Neutrosophy for Survey Analysis in Social Sciences. *Neutrosophic Sets Syst.* **2020**, *37*, 1.
50. Jarr'ın, A.A.A.; Tamayo, D.S.P.; Giler, S.A.M.; Zambrano, J.C.A.; Fernandez, D.M.M. Neutrosophic statistics applied in social science. *Neutrosophic Sets Syst.* **2021**, *44*, 1–9.
51. Şahin, R. Multi-criteria neutrosophic decision making method based on score and accuracy functions under neutrosophic environment. *Appl. Math. Inf. Sci.* **2011**, *5*.

52. Duran, V.; Topal, S.; Smarandache, F. An application of neutrosophic logic in the confirmatory data analysis of the satisfaction with life scale. *J. Fuzzy Ext. Appl.* **2021**, *239*, 262–282.
53. Hair, J.F.; Black, W.C.; Babin, B.J.; Anderson, R.E. *Multivariate Data Analysis*; Pearson Education, Ltd.: London, UK, 2013.
54. Cohen, J. *Statistical Power Analysis for the Behavioral Sciences*, 2nd ed.; Lawrence Erlbaum Associates: Hillsdale, NJ, USA, 1998.
55. Vonglao, P. Application of fuzzy logic to improve the Likert scale to measure latent variables. *Kasetsart J. Soc. Sci. Sci.* **2017**, *38*, 337–344. [CrossRef]
56. Więckowski, J.; Kizielewicz, B.; Shekhovtsov, A.; Sałabun, W. RANCOM: A novel approach to identifying criteria relevance based on inaccuracy expert judgments. *Eng. Appl. Artif. Intell. Sci.* **2023**, *122*, 106114. [CrossRef]

symmetry

MDPI

Article

An Introduction to Single-Valued Neutrosophic Primal Theory

Fahad Alsharari [1,†], Hanan Alohali [2,†], Yaser Saber [3,*,†] and Florentin Smarandache [4,†]

1 Department of Mathematics, College of Science, Jouf University, Sakaka 72311, Saudi Arabia; f.alsharari@ju.edu.sa
2 Department of Mathematics, College of Science, King Saud University, P.O. Box 2455, Riyadh 11451, Saudi Arabia; halohali@ksu.edu.sa
3 Department of Mathematics, College of Science Al-Zulfi, Majmaah University, P.O. Box 66, Al-Majmaah 11952, Saudi Arabia
4 Department of Mathematics, University of New Mexico, Gallup, NM 87301, USA; smarand@unm.edu
* Correspondence: y.sber@mu.edu.sa
† These authors contributed equally to this work.

Abstract: This article explores the interconnections among the single-valued neutrosophic grill, single-valued neutrosophic primal and their stratification, uncovering their fundamental characteristics and correlated findings. By introducing the notion of a single-valued neutrosophic primal, a broader framework including the fuzzy primal and intuitionistic fuzzy primal is established. Additionally, the concept of a single-valued neutrosophic open local function for a single-valued neutrosophic topological space is presented. We introduce an operator based on a single-valued neutrosophic primal, illustrating that the single-valued neutrosophic primal topology is finer than the single-valued neutrosophic topology. Lastly, the concept of single-valued neutrosophic open compatibility between the single-valued neutrosophic primal and single-valued neutrosophic topologies is introduced, along with the establishment of several equivalent conditions related to this notion.

Keywords: single-valued neutrosophic primal; single-valued neutrosophic primal topology; single-valued neutrosophic open compatibility

1. Introduction

Topology, a highly versatile field of mathematics [1], finds extensive application across both the scientific and social science domains, prompting the emergence of numerous innovative concepts within its standard frameworks. Kuratowski [2] examined the notion of ideals derived from filters, which can be seen as dual to filters. The notion of the fuzzy grill was given by [3]. Chattopadhyay and Thron [4] utilized grills to establish various topics, including closure spaces, while Thron [5] defined proximity structures within grills. Roy et al. [6] introduced novel definitions related to grills, with Roy and Mukherjee [7–9] subsequently exploring diverse topological properties associated with grills. Numerous applications stemming from these studies are documented in various works [10–16]. Given the dual nature of primal concerning grills, we draw inspiration from Janković and Hamlett [17] to introduce a new topology based on ideal structures.

The concept of neutrosophic sets, introduced as a generalization of intuitionistic fuzzy sets, was initially proposed in [18]. Salama et al. [19] and Wang et al. [20] have extensively investigated neutrosophic sets and their single-valued neutrosophic, abbreviated as *svn*, counterparts. Numerous applications stemming from these studies are documented in various works [21–24]. Stratified single-valued soft topogenous structures have been studied by Alsharari et al. [25].

Saber et al. have conducted extensive research on single-valued neutrosophic soft uniform spaces, single-valued neutrosophic ideals, abbreviated as *svnis*, and the connectedness and stratification of single-valued neutrosophic topological spaces expanded with an ideal [26–28]. The neutrosophic compound orthogonal neural network (NCONN), for the first time, contained the NsN weight values, *NsN* input and output, and hidden layer neutrosophic neuron functions; to approximate neutrosophic functions, *NsN* data have been studied by Ye et al. [29]. Shao et al. [30] introduced the concept of the probabilistic single-valued (interval) neutrosophic hesitant fuzzy set, extensively investigating the operational relations of *PINHFS* and the comparison method of probabilistic interval neutrosophic hesitant fuzzy numbers (*PINHFNs*). Rıdvan et al. [31] examined the notion of the neutrosophic subsethood measure for single-valued neutrosophic sets. The neutrosophic fuzzy set and its application in decision-making was defined by Das et al. [32].

The objective of this paper is to explore the inter-relations between the single-valued neutrosophic grill (*svn-grill*) and single-valued neutrosophic primal (*svn-primal*), along with their stratification, while showcasing some of their inherent properties. Additionally, we investigate the quantum behaviors within a novel structure denoted as $\Xi^{\star}_{r}(\mathcal{T}^{\tau\pi\sigma}, \mathcal{P}^{\tau\pi\sigma})$, as defined in Definition 11. Furthermore, we introduce and analyze both the *svn primal* and its associated topology. We also derive several preservation properties and characterizations regarding svn-primal open compatibility.

2. Preliminaries

This section presents the fundamental definitions and results necessary for our study. Initially, we define a neutrosophic set (for short, *n-set*) and a single-valued neutrosophic set (for short, *svn-set*). For a more comprehensive understanding of *n-set* theory and *svn-set* theory, readers are directed to [18,20,33]. Conventionally, $\xi^{\pounds}$ denotes the family encompassing all *svn-sets*, defined on £. Here, $\xi = [0,1]$, $\xi_0 = (0,1]$ and for any $\alpha \in \xi$ and $z \in \pounds$, $\overline{\alpha}(z) = \alpha$.

We begin with the definition of a neutrosophic set as follows:

Definition 1 ([18]). *Let £ be a non-empty set. An n-set on £ is defined as*

$$\Xi = \{\langle z, \tau_{\Xi}(z), \pi_{\Xi}(z), \sigma_{\Xi}(z)\rangle \mid x \in \pounds, \tau_{\Xi}(z), \pi_{\Xi}(Z), \sigma_{\Xi}(z) \in]^{-}0, 1^{+}\lfloor\},$$

representing the degree of membership where ($\tau_{\Xi}(z)$), the degree of indeterminacy ($\pi_{\Xi}(z)$) and degree of nonmembership ($\sigma_{\Xi}(z)$); $\forall$ $z \in \pounds$ to the set Ξ.

We now discuss the concept of the *svn-set*, which is a more specific type of neutrosophic set.

Definition 2 ([20]). *Let £ be a space of points (objects) with a generic element in £ denoted by z. Then Ξ is called an svn-set in £ if Ξ has the form $\Xi = \{\langle z, \tau_{\Xi}(z), \pi_{\Xi}(z), \sigma_{\Xi}(z)\rangle \mid x \in \pounds\}$ where $\tau_{\Xi}, \pi_{\Xi}, \sigma_{\Xi} : \pounds \to \xi = [0,1]$. In this case, σ_{Ξ}, π_{Ξ} and τ_{Ξ} are called the falsity membership function, indeterminancy membership function and truth membership function, respectively.*

An svn-set *Ξ on £ is named as a null* svn-set *(for short, $\overline{0}$), if $\tau_{\Xi}(z) = 0$, $\pi_{\Xi}(z) = 1$ and $\sigma_{\Xi}(x) = 1$, for all $z \in \pounds$.*

An svn-set *Ξ on £ is named as an absolute* svn-set *(for short, $\overline{1}$), if $\tau_{\Xi}(z) = 1$, $\pi_{\Xi}(z) = 0$ and $\sigma_{\Xi}(z) = 0$, for all $z \in \pounds$.*

Example 1. *Suppose that $\pounds = \{l_1, l_2, l_3\}$, l_1 is capability, l_2 is trustworthiness and l_3 is price. The values of l_1, l_2 and l_3 are in $\xi = [0,1]$. They are obtained from the questionnaire of some domain experts, their option could be a degree of "good service", a degree of indeterminacy and a degree of "poor service". Ξ is an svn-set of £ defined by*

$$\Xi = \langle 0.2, 0.3, 0.8\rangle / l_1 + \langle 0.8, 0.2, 0.3\rangle / l_2 + \langle 0.7, 0.1, 0.2\rangle / l_3,$$

Θ is an svn-set of £ defined by

$$\Theta = \langle 0.6, 0.1, 0.2\rangle / l_1 + \langle 0.3, 0.2, 0.6\rangle / l_2 + \langle 0.4, 0.1, 0.5\rangle / l_3.$$

To better understand the properties of *svn-sets*, we will now discuss the complement of an *svn-set*.

Definition 3 ([20]). *Let* $\Xi = \{\langle x, \tau_\Xi(z), \pi_\Xi(z), \sigma_\Xi(z)\rangle\}e : x \in \pounds\}$ *be an svn-set on* £. *The complement of the set* Ξ (Ξ^c) *is defined as follows:*

$$\tau_{\Xi^c}(z) = \sigma_\Xi(z),\ \pi_{\Xi^c}(z) = [\pi_\Xi]^c(z),\ \sigma_{\Xi^c}(z) = \tau_\Xi(z).$$

The following definition provides more insight into the relationships between *svn-sets*, introducing the notions of subsets, equality and special sets.

Definition 4 ([34]). *Let* $\Xi, \Theta \in \xi^{\pounds}$, *then,*

(1) Ξ *is said to be contained in* Θ, *denoted by* $\Xi \subseteq \Theta$, *if, for each* $z \in \pounds$,

$$\tau_\Xi(z) \le \tau_\Theta(z),\ \pi_\Xi(z) \ge \pi_\Theta(z),\ \sigma_\Xi(z) \ge \sigma_\Theta(z).$$

(2) Ξ *is said to be equal to* Θ, *denoted by* $\Xi = \Theta$, *iff* $\Xi \subseteq \Theta$ *and* $\Theta \subseteq \Xi$.

In the context of *svn-sets*, we introduce definitions related to the intersection and union of *svn-sets*. Further, we discuss the concept of a single-valued neutrosophic topological space (*svnts*) and the properties it entails.

Definition 5 ([33]). *Let* $\Xi, \Theta \in \xi^{\pounds}$. *Then,*

(a) $\Xi \wedge \Theta$ *is an (svn-set), if* $\forall\ z \in \pounds$,

$$\Xi \wedge \Theta = \langle (\tau_\Xi \wedge \tau_\Theta)(z),\ (\pi_\Xi \vee \pi_\Theta)(z),\ (\sigma_\Xi \vee \sigma_\Theta)(z)\rangle$$

where $(\tau_\Xi \wedge \tau_\Theta)(z) = \tau_\Xi(z) \wedge \tau_\Theta(z)$, $(\pi_\Xi \vee \pi_\Theta)(z) = \pi_\Xi(z) \vee \pi_\Theta(z)$ *and* $(\sigma_\Xi \vee \sigma_\Theta)(z) = \sigma_\Xi(z) \vee \sigma_\Theta(z)$, $\forall\ z \in \pounds$,

(b) $\Xi \vee \Theta$ *is an (svn-set), if* $\forall\ z \in \pounds$,

$$\Xi \vee \Theta = \langle (\tau_\Xi \vee \tau_\Theta)(z),\ (\pi_\Xi \wedge \pi_\Theta)(z),\ (\sigma_\Xi \wedge \sigma_\Theta)(z)\rangle.$$

Now, we discuss the concept of svnts, which consists of a set £ and three mappings $\mathcal{T}^\tau, \mathcal{T}^\pi, \mathcal{T}^\sigma : \zeta^{\pounds} \to \zeta$ that satisfy specific axioms.

Definition 6 ([27]). *An svnts is an ordered* $(\pounds, \mathcal{T}^\tau, \mathcal{T}^\pi, \mathcal{T}^\sigma)$ *where* $\mathcal{T}^\tau, \mathcal{T}^\pi, \mathcal{T}^\sigma : \zeta^{\pounds} \to \zeta$ *is a mapping satisfying the following axioms:*

(SVNT1) $\mathcal{T}^\tau(\bar{0}) = \mathcal{T}^\tau(\bar{1}) = 1$ *and* $\mathcal{T}^\pi(\bar{0}) = \mathcal{T}^\pi(\bar{1}) = \mathcal{T}^\sigma(\bar{0}) = \mathcal{T}^\sigma(\bar{1}) = 0$

(SVNT2) $\mathcal{T}^\tau(\Xi \wedge \Theta) \ge \mathcal{T}^\tau(\Xi) \wedge \mathcal{T}^\tau(\Theta)$, $\quad \mathcal{T}^\pi(\Xi \wedge \Theta) \le \mathcal{T}^\pi(\xi) \vee \mathcal{T}^\pi(\Theta)$,
$\mathcal{T}^\sigma(\Xi \wedge \Theta) \le \mathcal{T}^\sigma(\Xi) \vee \mathcal{T}^\sigma(\Theta)$, *for every* $\Xi, \Theta \in \xi^{\pounds}$,

(SVNT3) $\mathcal{T}^\tau(\bigvee_{j\in J}(\Xi_j) \ge \bigwedge_{j\in J} \mathcal{T}^\tau(\Xi_j)$, $\quad \mathcal{T}^\pi(\bigvee_{j\in J}(\Xi_j) \le \bigvee_{j\in J} \mathcal{T}^\pi(\Xi_j)$,
$\mathcal{T}^\sigma(\bigvee_{j\in J}(\Xi_j) \le \bigvee_{j\in J} \mathcal{T}^\sigma(\Xi_j)$, *for every* $\Xi_j \in \xi^{\pounds}$.

For the sake of brevity and clarity, we sometimes denote $(\mathcal{T}^\tau, \mathcal{T}^\pi, \mathcal{T}^\sigma)$ as $\mathcal{T}^{\tau\pi\sigma}$ without causing any ambiguity.

The following theorem establishes an operator that satisfies specific conditions, which further clarifies the properties of *svnts*.

Theorem 1 ([27]). *Let* $(\pounds, \mathcal{T}^{\tau\pi\sigma})$ *be an svnts. Then, for all* $r \in \zeta_0$ *and* $\Xi \in \xi^{\pounds}$, *we define the operator* $C_{\mathcal{T}^{\tau\pi\sigma}} : \xi^{\pounds} \times \zeta_0 \to \xi^{\pounds}$ *as follows:*

$$C_{\mathcal{T}^{\tau\pi\sigma}}(\Xi, r) = \bigwedge\{\Theta \in \xi^{\pounds} | \Xi \le \Theta,\ \ \mathcal{T}^\tau(\Theta^c)) \ge r,\ \ \mathcal{T}^\pi(\Theta^c)) \le 1 - r,\ \ \mathcal{T}^\sigma(\Theta^c)) \le 1 - r\}.$$

For any $\Xi, \Theta \in \zeta^{\pounds}$ *and* $r, s \in \zeta_0$, *the operator* $\mathcal{C}_{\mathcal{T}\tau\pi\sigma}$ *satisfies the following conditions:*

(C1) $\mathcal{C}_{\mathcal{T}\tau\pi\sigma}(\overline{0}, r) = \overline{0}$.
(C2) $\Xi \leq \mathcal{C}_{\mathcal{T}\tau\pi\sigma}(\Xi, r)$.
(C3) $\mathcal{C}_{\mathcal{T}\tau\pi\sigma}(\Xi, r) \vee \mathcal{C}_{\mathcal{T}\tau\pi\sigma}(\Theta, r) = \mathcal{C}_{\mathcal{T}\tau\pi\sigma}(\Xi \vee \Theta, r)$.
(C4) $\mathcal{C}_{\mathcal{T}\tau\pi\sigma}(\Xi, r) \leq \mathcal{C}_{\mathcal{T}\tau\pi\sigma}(\Theta, s)$ *if* $r \leq s$.
(C5) $\mathcal{C}_{\mathcal{T}\tau\pi\sigma}(\mathcal{C}_{\mathcal{T}\tau\pi\sigma}(\xi, r), r) = \mathcal{C}_{\mathcal{T}\tau\pi\sigma}(\xi, r)$.

3. Stratified Single-Valued Neutrosophic Grill with Single-Valued Neutrosophic Primal

In this section, we explores the interconnections between single-valued neutrosophic grills (*svn-grills*) and single-valued neutrosophic primals (*svn-primals*), along with their stratification. We also present a new structure within the context of single-valued neutrosophic topology, referred to as an svn-primal. This novel structure is the dual counterpart to the *svn-grill*.

We start with the following definition:

Definition 7. *A map* $\mathcal{G}^{\tau}, \mathcal{G}^{\pi}, \mathcal{G}^{\sigma} : \zeta^{\pounds} \to \zeta$ *is called an svn-grill on £, if it meets the following criteria:*

(G_1) $\mathcal{G}^{\tau}(\overline{0}) = 0, \mathcal{G}^{\pi}(\overline{0}) = 1, \mathcal{G}^{\sigma}(\overline{0}) = 1$ *and* $\mathcal{G}^{\tau}(\overline{1}) = 1, \mathcal{G}^{\pi}(\overline{1}) = 0, \mathcal{G}^{\sigma}(\overline{1}) = 0$.
(G_2) *If* $\Xi \leq \Theta$, *then* $\mathcal{G}^{\tau}(\Xi) \leq \mathcal{G}^{\tau}(\Theta)$, $\mathcal{G}^{\pi}(\Xi) \geq \mathcal{G}^{\pi}(\Theta)$, $\mathcal{G}^{\sigma}(\Xi) \geq \mathcal{G}^{\sigma}(\Theta)$, $\forall\, \Xi, \Theta \in \zeta^{\pounds}$.
(G_3) $\mathcal{G}^{\tau}(\Xi \vee \Theta) \leq \mathcal{G}^{\tau}(\Xi) \vee \mathcal{G}^{\tau}(\Theta)$, $\mathcal{G}^{\pi}(\Xi \vee \Theta) \geq \mathcal{G}^{\pi}(\Xi) \wedge \mathcal{G}^{\pi}(\Theta)$, $\mathcal{G}^{\sigma}(\Xi \vee \Theta) \geq \mathcal{G}^{\sigma}(\Xi) \wedge \mathcal{G}^{\sigma}(\Theta)$, $\forall\, \Xi, \Theta \in \zeta^{\pounds}$.

An svn-grill *is called stratified iff* $(\mathcal{G}^{\tau}, \mathcal{G}^{\pi}, \mathcal{G}^{\sigma})$ *satisfies the following condition:*
(G_{st}) $\mathcal{G}^{\tau}(\Xi \vee \overline{\alpha}) \leq \mathcal{G}^{\tau}(\Xi) \vee \alpha$, $\mathcal{G}^{\pi}(\Xi \vee \overline{\alpha}) \geq \mathcal{G}^{\pi}(\Xi) \wedge \alpha$, $\mathcal{G}^{\sigma}(\Xi \vee \overline{\alpha}) \geq \mathcal{G}^{\sigma}(\Xi) \wedge \alpha, \forall\, \Xi \in \zeta^{\pounds}$ *and* $\alpha \in \zeta$.

For the sake of brevity and clarity, we will occasionally denote $(\mathcal{G}^{\tau}, \mathcal{G}^{\pi}, \mathcal{G}^{\sigma})$ *as* $\mathcal{G}^{\tau\pi\sigma}$.

A single-valued neutrosophic grill topological space (svngts) is defined as the triple (£, $\mathcal{T}^{\tau\pi\sigma}$, $\mathcal{G}^{\tau\pi\sigma}$*).*

Theorem 2. *Let* $(\mathcal{G}^{\tau\pi\sigma})$ *be an svn-grill on £. Define* $\mathcal{G}^{\tau}_{st}, \mathcal{G}^{\pi}_{st}, \mathcal{G}^{\sigma}_{st} : \zeta^{\pounds} \to \zeta$

$$\mathcal{G}^{\tau}_{st}(\Xi) = \bigwedge_{\{(\Xi_i,\overline{\alpha_i})|i\in J\}\in\mathcal{K}(\Xi)} \left\{ \bigvee_{(\Xi_l,\overline{\alpha_l})\in\{(\Xi_i,\overline{\alpha_i})|i\in J\}} \mathcal{G}^{\tau}(\Xi_l) \vee \alpha_l \right\},$$

$$\mathcal{G}^{\pi}_{st}(\Xi) = \bigvee_{\{(\Xi_i,\overline{\alpha_i})|i\in J\}\in\mathcal{K}(\Xi)} \left\{ \bigwedge_{(\Xi_l,\overline{\alpha_l})\in\{(\Xi_i,\overline{\alpha_i})|i\in J\}} \mathcal{G}^{\pi}(\Xi_l) \vee \alpha_l \right\},$$

$$\mathcal{G}^{\sigma}_{st}(\Xi) = \bigvee_{\{(\Xi_i,\overline{\alpha_i})|i\in J\}\in\mathcal{K}(\Xi)} \left\{ \bigwedge_{(\Xi_l,\overline{\alpha_l})\in\{(\Xi_i,\overline{\alpha_i})|i\in J\}} \mathcal{G}^{\sigma}(\Xi_l) \vee \alpha_l \right\},$$

where $\mathcal{K}(\xi) = \{\{(\Xi_i, \overline{\alpha_i}) \mid i \in J, J \text{ is finite index set}\} \text{ and } \Xi \leq \bigwedge_{i\in J}(\Xi_i \vee \overline{\alpha_i})\}$. *Then,* $(\mathcal{G}^{\tau}_{st}, \mathcal{G}^{\pi}_{st}, \mathcal{G}^{\sigma}_{st})$ *is the coarsest stratified svn-grill on £ which is finer than* $(\mathcal{G}^{\tau}, \mathcal{G}^{\pi}, \mathcal{G}^{\sigma})$.

Proof. First, we will prove that $(\mathcal{G}^{\tau}_{st}, \mathcal{G}^{\pi}_{st}, \mathcal{G}^{\sigma}_{st})$ is a stratified *svn-grill* on £.

(G_1) and (G_2) are straightforward.

(G_3) Assume that there exist $\Xi, \Theta \in \zeta^{\pounds}$ such that

$$\mathcal{G}^{\tau}(\Xi \vee \Theta) \not\leq \mathcal{G}^{\tau}(\Xi) \vee \mathcal{G}^{\tau}(\Theta), \qquad \mathcal{G}^{\pi}(\Xi \vee \Theta) \not\geq \mathcal{G}^{\pi}(\Xi) \wedge \mathcal{G}^{\pi}(\Theta)$$

$$\mathcal{G}^{\sigma}(\Xi \vee \Theta) \not\geq \mathcal{G}^{\sigma}(\Xi) \wedge \mathcal{G}^{\sigma}(\Theta).$$

By the definition of $(\mathcal{G}^{\tau}_{st}, \mathcal{G}^{\pi}_{st}, \mathcal{G}^{\sigma}_{st})$, there exist $\{(\Xi_t, \overline{\alpha_t}) \mid t \in J\} \in \mathcal{K}(\Xi)$ and $\{(\Theta_\iota, \overline{\omega_\iota}) \mid \iota \in \Gamma\} \in \mathcal{K}(\Theta)$ such that

$$\mathcal{G}^{\tau}(\Xi \vee \Theta) \not\geq \left(\bigvee_{(\Xi_i, \overline{\alpha_i}) \in \{(\Xi_t, \overline{\alpha_t}) | t \in J\}} \mathcal{G}^{\tau}(\Xi_t) \vee \alpha_t \right) \vee \left(\bigvee_{(\Theta_j, \overline{\omega_j}) \in \{(\Theta_\iota, \overline{\omega_\iota}) | \iota \in \Gamma\}} \mathcal{G}^{\tau}(\Theta_j) \vee \omega_j \right).$$

$$\mathcal{G}^{\pi}(\Xi \vee \Theta) \not\leq \left(\bigwedge_{(\Xi_i, \overline{\alpha_i}) \in \{(\Xi_t, \overline{\alpha_t}) | t \in J\}} \mathcal{G}^{\pi}(\Xi_t) \vee \alpha_t \right) \wedge \left(\bigwedge_{(\Theta_j, \overline{\omega_j}) \in \{(\Theta_\iota, \overline{\omega_\iota}) | \iota \in \Gamma\}} \mathcal{G}^{\pi}(\Theta_j) \vee \omega_j \right).$$

$$\mathcal{G}^{\sigma}(\Xi \vee \Theta) \not\leq \left(\bigwedge_{(\Xi_i, \overline{\alpha_i}) \in \{(\Xi_t, \overline{\alpha_t}) | t \in J\}} \mathcal{G}^{\sigma}(\Xi_t) \vee \alpha_t \right) \wedge \left(\bigwedge_{(\Theta_j, \overline{\omega_j}) \in \{(\Theta_\iota, \overline{\omega_\iota}) | \iota \in \Gamma\}} \mathcal{G}^{\sigma}(\Theta_j) \vee \omega_j \right).$$

Set $k \in J \cup \Gamma$ such that

$$\Pi_k \vee \overline{\varrho_k} = \begin{cases} \Xi_k \vee \alpha_k, & \text{if } k \in J - (J \cap \Gamma), \\ \Theta_k \vee \omega_k, & \text{if } k \in \Gamma - (J \cap \Gamma), \\ (\Xi_k \vee \alpha_k) \vee (\Theta_k \vee \omega_k), & \text{if } k \in (J \cap \Gamma). \end{cases}$$

On the other hand,

$$\Xi \vee \Theta \leq \left(\bigwedge_{t \in J} (\Xi_t \vee \alpha_t) \right) \vee \left(\bigwedge_{\iota \in \Gamma} (\Theta_\iota \vee \omega_\iota) \right) = \bigwedge_{k \in (J \cap \Gamma)} (\Pi_k \vee \overline{\varrho_k}) \textit{ and } \{(\Pi_k, \overline{\varrho_k}) \mid k \in (J \cup \Gamma)\} \in \mathcal{K}(\Xi \vee \Theta).$$

Then, we have

$$\begin{aligned} \mathcal{G}^{\tau}_{st}(\Xi \vee \Theta) &\leq \bigvee_{(\Pi_v, \overline{\varrho_v}) \in \{(\Pi_k, \overline{\varrho_k}) | k \in (J \cup \Gamma)\}} \mathcal{G}^{\tau}(\Pi_v) \vee \varrho_v \\ &= \left(\bigvee_{(\Xi_i, \overline{\alpha_i}) \in \{(\Xi_t, \overline{\alpha_t}) | t \in J\}} \mathcal{G}^{\tau}(\Xi_i) \vee \alpha_i \right) \vee \left(\bigvee_{(\Theta_j, \overline{\omega_j}) \in \{(\Theta_\iota, \overline{\omega_\iota}) | \iota \in \Gamma\}} \mathcal{G}^{\tau}(\Theta_j) \vee \omega_j \right). \end{aligned}$$

$$\begin{aligned} \mathcal{G}^{\pi}_{st}(\Xi \vee \Theta) &\geq \bigwedge_{(\Pi_v, \overline{\varrho_v}) \in \{(\Pi_k, \overline{\varrho_k}) | k \in (J \cup \Gamma)\}} \mathcal{G}^{\tau}(\Pi_v) \vee \varrho_v \\ &= \left(\bigwedge_{(\Xi_i, \overline{\alpha_i}) \in \{(\Xi_t, \overline{\alpha_t}) | t \in J\}} \mathcal{G}^{\pi}(\Xi_i) \vee \alpha_i \right) \wedge \left(\bigwedge_{(\Theta_j, \overline{\omega_j}) \in \{(\Theta_\iota, \overline{\omega_\iota}) | \iota \in \Gamma\}} \mathcal{G}^{\pi}(\Theta_j) \vee \omega_j \right). \end{aligned}$$

$$\begin{aligned} \mathcal{G}^{\sigma}_{st}(\Xi \vee \Theta) &\geq \bigwedge_{(\Pi_v, \overline{\varrho_v}) \in \{(\Pi_k, \overline{\varrho_k}) | k \in (J \cup \Gamma)\}} \mathcal{G}^{\tau}(\Pi_v) \vee \varrho_v \\ &= \left(\bigwedge_{(\Xi_i, \overline{\alpha_i}) \in \{(\Xi_t, \overline{\alpha_t}) | t \in J\}} \mathcal{G}^{\sigma}(\Xi_i) \vee \alpha_i \right) \wedge \left(\bigwedge_{(\Theta_j, \overline{\omega_j}) \in \{(\Theta_\iota, \overline{\omega_\iota}) | \iota \in \Gamma\}} \mathcal{G}^{\sigma}(\Theta_j) \vee \omega_j \right). \end{aligned}$$

This is a contradiction. Thus, (G_3) holds.

(G_{st}) Assume that there exist $\Xi \in \xi^{\pounds}$ and $\alpha \in \xi$ such that

$$\mathcal{G}^{\tau}_{st}(\Xi \vee \overline{\alpha}) \not\leq \mathcal{G}^{\tau}_{st}(\Xi) \vee \alpha, \qquad \mathcal{G}^{\pi}_{st}(\Xi \vee \overline{\alpha}) \not\geq \mathcal{G}^{\pi}_{st}(\Xi) \wedge \alpha,$$

$$\mathcal{G}^{\sigma}_{st}(\Xi \vee \overline{\alpha}) \ngeq \mathcal{G}^{\sigma}_{st}(\Xi) \wedge \alpha.$$

By the definition of $(\mathcal{G}^{\tau}_{st}, \mathcal{G}^{\pi}_{st}, \mathcal{G}^{\sigma}_{st})$, there exist $\{(\Xi_t, \overline{\alpha_t}) \mid t \in J\} \in \mathcal{K}(\Xi)$ such that

$$\mathcal{G}^{\tau}_{st}(\Xi \vee \overline{\alpha}) \nleq \left(\bigvee_{(\Xi_i, \overline{\alpha_i}) \in \{(\Xi_t, \overline{\alpha_t}) | t \in J\}} \mathcal{G}^{\tau}(\Xi_i) \vee \alpha_i \right) \vee \alpha$$

$$\mathcal{G}^{\pi}_{st}(\Xi \vee \overline{\alpha}) \ngeq \left(\bigwedge_{(\Xi_i, \overline{\alpha_i}) \in \{(\Xi_t, \overline{\alpha_t}) | t \in J\}} \mathcal{G}^{\pi}(\Xi_i) \vee \alpha_i \right) \wedge \alpha$$

$$\mathcal{G}^{\sigma}_{st}(\Xi \vee \overline{\alpha}) \ngeq \left(\bigwedge_{(\Xi_i, \overline{\alpha_i}) \in \{(\Xi_t, \overline{\alpha_t}) | t \in J\}} \mathcal{G}^{\sigma}(\Xi_i) \vee \alpha_i \right) \wedge \alpha$$

On the other hand, $\Xi \vee \overline{\alpha} \leq \bigwedge_{t \in (J \cap \Gamma)} (\Xi_t \vee \overline{\varrho_t})$ where $\varrho_t = \alpha_i \vee \alpha$; then, $\{(\Xi_t, \overline{\varrho_t}) \mid t \in J\} \in \mathcal{K}(\Xi \vee \overline{\alpha})$. Then, we have

$$\mathcal{G}^{\tau}_{st}(\Xi \vee \overline{\alpha}) \leq \left(\bigvee_{(\Xi_i, \overline{\varrho_i}) \in \{(\Xi_t, \overline{\varrho_t}) | t \in J\}} \mathcal{G}^{\tau}(\Xi_i) \vee \alpha_i \right) = \left(\bigvee_{(\Xi_i, \overline{\alpha_i}) \in \{(\Xi_t, \overline{\alpha_t}) | t \in J\}} \mathcal{G}^{\tau}(\Xi_i) \vee \alpha_i \right) \vee \alpha,$$

$$\mathcal{G}^{\pi}_{st}(\Xi \vee \overline{\alpha}) \geq \left(\bigwedge_{(\Xi_i, \overline{\varrho_i}) \in \{(\Xi_t, \overline{\varrho_t}) | t \in J\}} \mathcal{G}^{\pi}(\Xi_i) \vee \alpha_i \right) = \left(\bigwedge_{(\Xi_i, \overline{\alpha_i}) \in \{(\Xi_t, \overline{\alpha_t}) | t \in J\}} \mathcal{G}^{\pi}(\Xi_i) \vee \alpha_i \right) \wedge \alpha,$$

$$\mathcal{G}^{\sigma}_{st}(\Xi \vee \overline{\alpha}) \geq \left(\bigwedge_{(\Xi_i, \overline{\varrho_i}) \in \{(\Xi_t, \overline{\varrho_t}) | t \in J\}} \mathcal{G}^{\sigma}(\Xi_i) \vee \alpha_i \right) = \left(\bigwedge_{(\Xi_i, \overline{\alpha_i}) \in \{(\Xi_t, \overline{\alpha_t}) | t \in J\}} \mathcal{G}^{\sigma}(\Xi_i) \vee \alpha_i \right) \wedge \alpha.$$

This is a contradiction. Thus, $\mathcal{G}_{st}$ holds. Hence, $(\mathcal{G}^{\tau}_{st}, \mathcal{G}^{\pi}_{st}, \mathcal{G}^{\sigma}_{st})$ is stratified.

Second, for any $\Xi \in \xi^{\pounds}$, there exists a collection $\{\overline{\alpha}\}$ with $\Xi \leq \Xi \vee \overline{\alpha}$ such that $\mathcal{G}^{\tau}_{st}(\Xi) \leq \mathcal{G}^{\tau}(\Xi)$, $\mathcal{G}^{\pi}_{st}(\Xi) \geq \mathcal{G}^{\pi}(\Xi)$ and $\mathcal{G}^{\sigma}_{st}(\Xi) \geq \mathcal{G}^{\sigma}(\Xi)$. Thus, $(\mathcal{G}^{\tau}_{st}, \mathcal{G}^{\pi}_{st}, \mathcal{G}^{\sigma}_{st})$ is finer than $(\mathcal{G}^{\tau}, \mathcal{G}^{\pi}, \mathcal{G}^{\sigma})$.

Finally, consider $(\mathcal{G}^{\star\tau}, \mathcal{G}^{\star\pi}, \mathcal{G}^{\star\sigma})$, a stratified *svn-grill* on £ which is finer than $(\mathcal{G}^{\tau}, \mathcal{G}^{\pi}, \mathcal{G}^{\sigma})$. And we will show that $\mathcal{G}^{\tau}_{st}(\Xi) \geq \mathcal{G}^{\star\tau}(\Xi)$, $\mathcal{G}^{\pi}_{st}(\Xi) \leq \mathcal{G}^{\star\pi}(\Xi)$ and $\mathcal{G}^{\sigma}_{st}(\Xi) \leq \mathcal{G}^{\star\sigma}(\Xi)$. Assume that $\Xi \in \xi^{\pounds}$ such that $\mathcal{G}^{\tau}_{st}(\Xi) \ngeq \mathcal{G}^{\star\tau}(\Xi)$, $\mathcal{G}^{\pi}_{st}(\Xi) \nleq \mathcal{G}^{\star\pi}(\Xi)$ and $\mathcal{G}^{\sigma}_{st}(\Xi) \nleq \mathcal{G}^{\star\sigma}(\Xi)$. By the definition of $(\mathcal{G}^{\tau}_{st}, \mathcal{G}^{\pi}_{st}, \mathcal{G}^{\sigma}_{st})$, there exist $\{(\Xi_t, \overline{\alpha_t}) \mid t \in J\} \in \mathcal{K}(\Xi)$ such that

$$\mathcal{G}^{\star\tau}(\Xi) \nleq \left(\bigvee_{(\Xi_i, \overline{\alpha_i}) \in \{(\Xi_t, \overline{\alpha_t}) | t \in J\}} \mathcal{G}^{\tau}(\Xi_i) \vee \alpha_i \right),$$

$$\mathcal{G}^{\star\pi}(\Xi) \ngeq \left(\bigwedge_{(\Xi_i, \overline{\alpha_i}) \in \{(\Xi_t, \overline{\alpha_t}) | t \in J\}} \mathcal{G}^{\pi}(\Xi_i) \vee \alpha_i \right),$$

$$\mathcal{G}^{\star\sigma}(\Xi) \ngeq \left(\bigwedge_{(\Xi_i, \overline{\alpha_i}) \in \{(\Xi_t, \overline{\alpha_t}) | t \in J\}} \mathcal{G}^{\sigma}(\Xi_i) \vee \alpha_i \right).$$

On the other hand, $(\mathcal{G}^{\star\tau}, \mathcal{G}^{\star\pi}, \mathcal{G}^{\star\sigma})$ is stratified; then, we have

$$\begin{aligned}\mathcal{G}^{\star\tau}(\Xi) &\leq \mathcal{G}^{\star\tau}\left(\bigwedge_{t\in J}(\Xi_t \vee \overline{\alpha_t})\right)\\ &\leq \bigvee_{t\in J}\mathcal{G}^{\star\tau}(\Xi_t \vee \overline{\alpha_t})\\ &\leq \bigvee_{t\in J}(\mathcal{G}^{\star\tau}(\Xi_t) \vee \overline{\alpha_t})\\ &\leq \bigvee_{(\Xi_i,\overline{\alpha_i})\in\{(\Xi_t,\overline{\alpha_t})|t\in J\}} \mathcal{G}^{\tau}(\Xi_i) \vee \alpha_i\end{aligned}$$

Likewise, we can establish through a similar line of reasoning that

$$\mathcal{G}^{\star\pi}(\Xi) \geq \bigwedge_{(\Xi_i,\overline{\alpha_i})\in\{(\Xi_t,\overline{\alpha_t})|t\in J\}} \mathcal{G}^{\pi}(\Xi_i) \vee \alpha_i \quad \mathcal{G}^{\star\sigma}(\Xi) \geq \bigwedge_{(\Xi_i,\overline{\alpha_i})\in\{(\Xi_t,\overline{\alpha_t})|t\in J\}} \mathcal{G}^{\sigma}(\Xi_i) \vee \alpha_i.$$

This is a contradiction. Hence, $(\mathcal{G}^{\tau}_{st}, \mathcal{G}^{\pi}_{st}, \mathcal{G}^{\sigma}_{st})$ is the coarsest stratified *svn-grill* on £ which is finer than $(\mathcal{G}^{\tau}, \mathcal{G}^{\pi}, \mathcal{G}^{\sigma})$. □

In order to better understand the notion of *svn-primal* mappings, let us provide some context for the following definition. Consider a non-empty set £ and a mapping $\mathcal{P}^{\tau}, \mathcal{P}^{\pi}, \mathcal{P}^{\sigma} : \zeta^{£} \to \zeta$. We will now introduce certain conditions that, when satisfied, characterize the mapping as an *svn-primal* on £.

Definition 8. *Let £ be a non-empty set. A mapping $\mathcal{P}^{\tau}, \mathcal{P}^{\pi}, \mathcal{P}^{\sigma} : \zeta^{£} \to \zeta$ is said to be svn-primal on £, if it meets the following conditions:*
(P1) $\mathcal{P}^{\tau}(\overline{1}) = 0, \mathcal{P}^{\pi}(\overline{1}) = 1, \mathcal{P}^{\sigma}(\overline{1}) = 1$ and $\mathcal{P}^{\tau}(\overline{0}) = 1, \mathcal{P}^{\pi}(\overline{0}) = 0, \mathcal{P}^{\sigma}(\overline{0}) = 0$.
(P2) If $\Xi \leq \Theta$, then $\mathcal{P}^{\tau}(\Theta) \leq \mathcal{P}^{\tau}(\Xi)$, $\mathcal{P}^{\pi}(\Theta) \geq \mathcal{P}^{\pi}(\Xi)$, $\mathcal{P}^{\sigma}(\Theta) \geq \mathcal{P}^{\sigma}(\Xi)$, $\forall\, \Xi, \Theta \in \zeta^{£}$.
(P3) $\mathcal{P}^{\tau}(\Xi \wedge \Theta) \leq \mathcal{P}^{\tau}(\Xi) \vee \mathcal{P}^{\tau}(\Theta)$, $\mathcal{P}^{\pi}(\Xi \wedge \Theta) \geq \mathcal{P}^{\pi}(\Xi) \wedge \mathcal{P}^{\pi}(\Theta)$, $\mathcal{P}^{\sigma}(\Xi \wedge \Theta) \geq \mathcal{P}^{\sigma}(\Xi) \wedge \mathcal{P}^{\sigma}(\Theta)$, $\forall\, \Xi, \Theta \in \zeta^{£}$. Sometimes, we will write $\mathcal{P}^{\tau\pi\sigma}$ for $(\mathcal{P}^{\tau}, \mathcal{P}^{\pi}, \mathcal{P}^{\sigma})$.

If $\mathcal{P}^{\tau\pi\sigma}$ and $\mathcal{P}^{\star\tau\pi\sigma}$ are svn-primals on £, then "$\mathcal{P}^{\tau\pi\sigma}$ is finer than $\mathcal{P}^{\star\tau\pi\sigma}$ or ($\mathcal{P}^{\star\tau\pi\sigma}$ is coarser than $\mathcal{P}^{\tau\pi\sigma}$)" denoted by $\mathcal{P}^{\tau\pi\sigma} \leq \mathcal{P}^{\star\tau\pi\sigma}$ if and only if

$$\mathcal{P}^{\tau}(\Xi) \leq \mathcal{P}^{\star\tau}(\Theta), \quad \mathcal{P}^{\pi}(\Xi) \geq \mathcal{P}^{\star\pi}(\Theta), \quad \mathcal{P}^{\sigma}(\Xi) \geq \mathcal{P}^{\star\sigma}(\Theta), \forall, \Xi, \Theta \in \zeta^{£}.$$

The triable $(£, \mathcal{T}^{\tau\pi\sigma}, \mathcal{P}^{\tau\pi\sigma})$ is called a single-valued neutrosophic primal topological space (svnpts). For $\alpha \in \zeta_0$, $(£, \mathcal{T}^{\tau\pi\sigma}_{\alpha}, \mathcal{P}^{\tau\pi\sigma}_{\alpha})$ is primal topological space (pts) in [35].

Remark 1. *The terms (P_2) and (P_3), in Definition 10, correspond to the next condition*

$$\mathcal{P}^{\tau}(\Xi \wedge \Theta) = \mathcal{P}^{\tau}(\Xi) \vee \mathcal{P}^{\tau}(\Theta), \quad \mathcal{P}^{\pi}(\Xi \wedge \Theta) \neq \mathcal{P}^{\pi}(\Xi) \wedge \mathcal{P}^{\pi}(\Theta), \quad \mathcal{P}^{\sigma}(\Xi \wedge \Theta) \neq \mathcal{P}^{\sigma}(\Xi) \wedge \mathcal{P}^{\sigma}(\Theta)$$

Example 2. *Suppose that $£ = \{l_1, l_2, l_3\}$; define the svn-set $\Theta \in \xi^{£}$ as follows*

$$\Theta = \langle (0.4, 0.4, 0.4), (0,0,0), (0,0,0) \rangle$$

Define the mappings $\mathcal{P}^{\tau}, \mathcal{P}^{\pi}, \mathcal{P}^{\sigma} : \xi^{£} \to \xi$ as follows:

$$\mathcal{P}^{\tau}(\Xi) = \begin{cases} 1, & \text{if } \Xi = \overline{0}, \\ \frac{1}{4}, & \text{if } \Xi = \Theta, \\ \frac{1}{2}, & \text{if } \overline{0} < \Xi < \Theta, \\ 0, & \text{otherwise}, \end{cases}$$

$$\mathcal{P}^{\pi}(\Xi) = \begin{cases} 0, & \text{if } \Xi = \overline{0}, \\ \frac{3}{4}, & \text{if } \Xi = \Theta, \\ \frac{1}{2}, & \text{if } \overline{0} < \Xi < \Theta, \\ 1, & \text{otherwise}, \end{cases}$$

$$\mathcal{P}^{\sigma}(\Xi) = \begin{cases} 0, & \text{if } \Xi = \overline{0}, \\ \frac{1}{2}, & \text{if } \Xi = \Theta, \\ \frac{1}{4}, & \text{if } \overline{0} < \Xi < \Theta, \\ 1, & \text{otherwise}, \end{cases}$$

Then, $\mathcal{P}^{\tau\pi\sigma}$ is svn-primal on £.

Theorem 3. *Let $(\mathcal{G}^{\tau}, \mathcal{G}^{\pi}, \mathcal{G}^{\sigma})$ be an svng on £. Then, the collection $\{\Theta \in \xi^{£} : \mathcal{G}^{\tau}(\Theta^c) \geq r,$ $\mathcal{G}^{\pi}(\Theta^c) \leq 1-r, \mathcal{G}^{\sigma}(\Theta^c) \leq 1-r, r \in \xi_0\}$ is an svn-primal on £.*

Proof. (P_1) Since $\mathcal{G}^{\tau}(\overline{0}) = 0, \mathcal{G}^{\pi}(\overline{0}) = 1, \mathcal{G}^{\sigma}(\overline{0}) = 1$ and $\mathcal{G}^{\tau}(\overline{1}) = 1, \mathcal{G}^{\pi}(\overline{1}) = 0, \mathcal{G}^{\sigma}(\overline{1}) = 0$ implies that $\mathcal{P}^{\tau}(\overline{1}) = 0, \mathcal{P}^{\pi}(\overline{1}) = 1, \mathcal{P}^{\sigma}(\overline{1}) = 1$ and $\mathcal{P}^{\tau}(\overline{0}) = 1, \mathcal{G}^{\pi}(\overline{0}) = 0, \mathcal{G}^{\sigma}(\overline{0}) = 0$.

(P_2) Let $\Xi \leq \Theta$; then, $\Theta^c \leq \Xi^c$ and, thus,

$$r \leq \mathcal{G}^{\tau}(\Theta^c) \leq \mathcal{G}^{\tau}(\Xi^c), \;\; 1-r \geq \mathcal{G}^{\pi}(\Theta^c) \geq \mathcal{G}^{\pi}(\Xi^c), \;\; 1-r \geq \mathcal{G}^{\sigma}(\Theta^c) \geq \mathcal{G}^{\sigma}(\Xi^c).$$

Hence, $\mathcal{P}^{\tau}(\Theta) \leq \mathcal{P}^{\tau}(\Xi), \mathcal{P}^{\pi}(\Theta) \geq \mathcal{P}^{\pi}(\Xi), \; \mathcal{P}^{\sigma}(\Theta) \geq \mathcal{P}^{\sigma}(\Xi)$.

(P_3) Suppose

$$\mathcal{P}^{\tau}(\Xi \wedge \Theta) \nleq \mathcal{P}^{\tau}(\Xi) \vee \mathcal{P}^{\tau}(\Theta), \qquad \mathcal{P}^{\pi}(\Xi \wedge \Theta) \ngeq \mathcal{P}^{\pi}(\Xi) \wedge \mathcal{P}^{\pi}(\Theta),$$

$$\mathcal{P}^{\sigma}(\Xi \wedge \Theta) \ngeq \mathcal{P}^{\sigma}(\Xi) \wedge \mathcal{P}^{\sigma}(\Theta).$$

Then, there exists $r \in \xi_0$ such that

$$\mathcal{P}^{\tau}(\Xi \wedge \Theta) \geq r \geq \mathcal{P}^{\tau}(\Xi) \vee \mathcal{P}^{\tau}(\Theta), \qquad \mathcal{P}^{\pi}(\Xi \wedge \Theta) \leq 1-r \leq \mathcal{P}^{\pi}(\Xi) \wedge \mathcal{P}^{\pi}(\Theta),$$

$$\mathcal{P}^{\sigma}(\Xi \wedge \Theta) \leq 1-r \leq \mathcal{P}^{\sigma}(\Xi) \wedge \mathcal{P}^{\sigma}(\Theta).$$

Since $\mathcal{P}^{\tau}(\Xi \wedge \Theta) \geq r, \mathcal{P}^{\pi}(\Xi \wedge \Theta) \leq 1-r$ and $\mathcal{P}^{\sigma}(\Xi \wedge \Theta) \leq 1-r$, we have $\mathcal{G}^{\tau}([\Xi \wedge \Theta]^c) \geq r$, $\mathcal{P}^{\pi}([\Xi \wedge \Theta]^c) \leq 1-r$ and $\mathcal{G}^{\sigma}([\Xi \wedge \Theta]^c) \leq 1-r$ implies that

$$\mathcal{G}^{\tau}(\Xi^c \vee \Theta^c) \geq r, \;\; \mathcal{G}^{\pi}(\Xi^c \vee \Theta^c) \leq 1-r, \;\; \mathcal{G}^{\sigma}(\Xi^c \vee \Theta^c) \leq 1-r.$$

From the definition of $\mathcal{G}^{\tau\pi\sigma}$, we have

$$\mathcal{G}^{\tau}(\Xi^c) \vee \mathcal{G}^{\tau}(\Theta^c) \geq \mathcal{G}^{\tau}(\Xi^c \vee \Theta^c) \geq r, \qquad \mathcal{G}^{\pi}(\Xi^c) \wedge \mathcal{G}^{\pi}(\Theta^c) \leq \mathcal{G}^{\pi}(\Xi^c \vee \Theta^c) \leq 1-r,$$

$$\mathcal{G}^{\sigma}(\Xi^c) \wedge \mathcal{G}^{\sigma}(\Theta^c) \leq \mathcal{G}^{\sigma}(\Xi^c \vee \Theta^c) \leq 1-r.$$

Since $\mathcal{G}^{\tau}(\Xi^c) \vee \mathcal{G}^{\tau}(\Theta^c) \geq r$, $\mathcal{G}^{\pi}(\Xi^c) \wedge \mathcal{G}^{\pi}(\Theta^c) \leq 1-r$ and $\mathcal{G}^{\sigma}(\Xi^c \vee \Theta^c) \leq 1-r$, we obtain $\mathcal{G}^{\tau}(\Theta^c) \geq r$, $\mathcal{G}^{\pi}(\Theta^c) \leq 1-r$, $\mathcal{G}^{\sigma}(\Theta^c) \leq 1-r$ and $\mathcal{G}^{\tau}(\Xi^c) \geq r$, $\mathcal{G}^{\pi}(\Xi^c) \leq 1-r$, $\mathcal{G}^{\sigma}(\Xi^c) \leq 1-r$ implies that $\mathcal{P}^{\tau}(\Theta) \geq r$, $\mathcal{P}^{\pi}(\Theta) \leq 1-r$, $\mathcal{P}^{\sigma}(\Theta) \leq 1-r$ and $\mathcal{P}^{\tau}(\Xi) \geq r$, $\mathcal{P}^{\pi}(\Xi) \leq 1-r$, $\mathcal{P}^{\sigma}(\Xi) \leq 1-r$. Hence,

$$\mathcal{P}^{\tau}(\Xi) \vee \mathcal{P}^{\tau}(\Theta) \geq r, \qquad \mathcal{P}^{\pi}(\Xi) \wedge \mathcal{P}^{\pi}(\Theta) \leq 1-r,$$

$$\mathcal{P}^{\sigma}(\Xi) \wedge \mathcal{P}^{\sigma}(\Theta) \leq 1-r.$$

This is a contradiction. Consequently, (P_3) holds. □

Proposition 1. *Let $\{\mathcal{P}_j^{\tau\pi\sigma}\}_{j\in J}$ be a collection of svn-primals on £. Then, their union $\bigvee_{i\in J} \mathcal{P}_j^{\tau\pi\sigma}$ is also an* svn-primal *on £.*

Proof. Directly from Definition 7. □

4. Single-Valued Neutrosophic Primal Open Local Function in Šostak Sense

In this section, we investigate the concept of svn-primal open local functions within the context of Šostak's sense. Our primary focus is to explore the properties of these functions and their relationship with svnts and neutrosophic primals. Through a series of definitions, theorems and discussions, we aim to provide a comprehensive understanding of this unique concept and its implications in the domain of neutrosophic topology. The introductory results presented here lay the foundation for further exploration of this fascinating topic, shedding light on the details of svn structures in the sense of Šostak.

Definition 9. *Let $n, m, v \in \zeta_0$ and $n + m + v \leq 3$. A single-valued neutrosophic point (svn-point) $y_{n,m,v}$ is an svn-set in $\zeta^{\pounds}$ for each $z \in \Theta$, defined by*

$$y_{n,m,v}(z) = \begin{cases} (n, m, v), & \text{if } y = z, \\ (0, 1, 1), & \text{if } y \neq z, \end{cases}$$

An svn-point $y_{n,m,v}$ *is said to belong to an* svn-set $\Xi = \langle z, \tau_{\Xi}(z), \pi_{\Xi}(z), \sigma_{\Xi}(z) \rangle \in \zeta^{\pounds}$, *denoted by* $y_{n,m,v} \in \Xi$ *iff* $n \leq \tau_{\Xi}(z)$, $m \geq \pi_{\Xi}(z)$ *and* $v \geq \sigma_{\Xi}(z)$. *We indicate the set of all* svn-points *in £ as (svn-point (£)).*

For each $y_{n,m,v} \in$ svn-point(£) *and* $\Theta \in \zeta^{\omega}$ *we shall write* $y_{n,m,v}$ *quasi-coincident with* Ξ, *denoted by* $y_{n,m,v} q \Xi$, *if*

$$n + \tau_{\Xi}(z) > 1, \quad n + \pi_{\Xi}(z) \leq 1, \quad v + \sigma_{\Xi}(z) \leq 1.$$

For all $\Theta, \Xi \in \zeta^{\pounds}$ *we shall write* $\Xi \; q \; \theta$ *to mean that* Ξ *is quasi-coincident with* Θ *if there exists* $z \in \pounds$ *such that*

$$\tau_{\Xi}(z) + \tau_{\Theta}(z) > 1, \quad \pi_{\Xi}(z) + \pi_{\Theta}(z) \leq 1, \quad \sigma_{\Xi}(z) + \sigma_{\Theta}(z) \leq 1.$$

Definition 10. *Let* $(\pounds, \mathcal{T}^{\tau\pi\sigma})$ *be an svnts, for all* $\Xi \in \zeta^{\pounds}$, $y_{n,m,v}$ *∈svn-point (£) and* $r \in \zeta_0$. *Then,* Ξ *is said to be an r-open* $\mathcal{Q}_{\mathcal{T}\tau\pi\sigma}$*-neighborhood (r-OQN) of* $y_{n,m,v}$, *defined as follows*

$$\mathcal{Q}_{\mathcal{T}\tau\pi\sigma}(y_{n,m,v}, r) = \{\Xi \in \zeta^{\pounds} | y_{n,m,v} q \Xi, \;\; \mathcal{T}^{\tau}(\Xi)) \geq r, \;\; \mathcal{T}^{\pi}(\Xi)) \leq 1 - r, \;\; \mathcal{T}^{\sigma}(\Xi)) \leq 1 - r\}.$$

Lemma 1. *An* svn-point $y_{n.m.v} \in \mathcal{C}_{\mathcal{T}\tau\pi\sigma}(\Theta, r)$ *iff every* r-OQN *of* $y_{n,n,v}$ *is quasi-coincident with* Ξ.

Definition 11. *Let* $(\pounds, \mathcal{T}^{\tau\pi\sigma}, \mathcal{P}^{\tau\pi\sigma})$ *be an svnpts, for each* $r \in \zeta_0$ *and* $\Xi \in \zeta^{\pounds}$. *Then, the single-valued neutrosophic primal open local function* $\Xi^{\star}_r(\mathcal{T}^{\tau\pi\sigma}, \mathcal{P}^{\tau\pi\sigma})$ *of* Ξ *is the union of all svn-points* $y_{n,m,v}$ *such that if* $\Theta \in \mathcal{Q}_{\mathcal{T}\tau\pi\sigma}(y_{n,m,v}, r)$ *and* $\mathcal{P}^{\tau}(\Pi) \geq r$, $\mathcal{P}^{\pi}(\Pi) \leq 1 - r$, $\mathcal{P}^{\sigma}(\Pi) \leq 1 - r$, *then there is at least one* $z \in \pounds$, *for which* $\tau_{\Xi}(z) + \tau_{\Theta}(z) - 1 > \tau_{\Pi}(z)$, $\pi_{\Xi}(z) + \pi_{\Theta}(z) - 1 \leq \pi_{\Pi}(z)$, $\sigma_{\Xi}(z) + \sigma_{\Theta}(z) - 1 \leq \sigma_{\Pi}(z)$.

In this article, we will write $\Xi^{\star}_r$ for $\Xi^{\star}_r(\mathcal{T}^{\tau\pi\sigma}, \mathcal{P}^{\tau\pi\sigma})$ without any ambiguity.

Example 3. *Let* $(\pounds, \mathcal{T}^{\tau\pi\sigma}, \mathcal{P}^{\tau\pi\sigma})$ *be an svnpts. The simplest svn-primal on £ is* $\mathcal{P}^{\tau}_{0}, \mathcal{P}^{\pi}_{0}, \mathcal{P}^{\sigma}_{0} : \zeta^{\pounds} \to \zeta$ *where*

$$\mathcal{P}^{\tau}_{0}(\Xi) = \begin{cases} 1, & \text{if } \Xi = \overline{0}, \\ 0, & \text{otherwise}, \end{cases}$$

$$\mathcal{P}^{\pi}_{0}(\Xi) = \begin{cases} 0, & \text{if } \Xi = \overline{0}, \\ 1, & \text{otherwise}, \end{cases}$$

$$\mathcal{P}^{\sigma}_{0}(\Xi) = \begin{cases} 0, & \textit{if } \Xi = \overline{0}, \\ 1, & \textit{otherwise}, \end{cases}$$

If $\mathcal{P}^{\tau\pi\sigma} = \mathcal{P}^{\tau\pi\sigma}_{0}$, *then, for each* $\Xi \in \zeta^{\pounds}$, $r \in \zeta_0$, *we have* $\Xi^{\star}_r = C_{\mathcal{T}^{\tau\pi\sigma}}(\Xi, r)$.

Theorem 4. *Let* $(\pounds, \mathcal{T}^{\tau\pi\sigma})$ *be an svnts and* $\mathcal{P}^{\tau\pi\sigma}_1$, $\mathcal{P}^{\tau\pi\sigma}_2$ *be two svn-primals on* £. *Then,* $\forall$ $\Xi, \Theta \in \zeta^{\pounds}$ *and* $r \in \zeta_0$, *we have*

(1) *If* $\Xi \le \Theta$, *then* $\Xi^{\star}_r \le \Theta^{\star}_r$.
(2) *If* $\mathcal{P}^{\tau}_1 \le \mathcal{P}^{\tau}_2$, $\mathcal{P}^{\pi}_1 \ge \mathcal{P}^{\pi}_2$ *and* $\mathcal{P}^{\sigma}_1 \ge \mathcal{P}^{\sigma}_2$, *then* $\Xi^{\star}_r(\mathcal{P}^{\tau\pi\sigma}_1, \mathcal{T}^{\tau\pi\sigma}) \ge \Xi^{\star}_r(\mathcal{P}^{\tau\pi\sigma}_2, \mathcal{T}^{\tau\pi\sigma})$.
(3) $\Xi^{\star}_r = C_{\mathcal{T}^{\tau\pi\sigma}}(\Xi^{\star}_r, r) \le C_{\mathcal{T}^{\tau\pi\sigma}}(\Xi, r)$.
(4) *If* $(\Xi^{\star}_r)^{\star}_r \le \Xi^{\star}_r$.
(5) *If* $\mathcal{P}^{\tau}(\Theta) \ge r$, $\mathcal{P}^{\pi}(\Theta) \le 1 - r$ *and* $\mathcal{P}^{\sigma}(\Theta) \le 1 - r$, *then* $(\Xi \vee \Theta)^{\star}_r = \Xi^{\star}_r \vee \Theta^{\star}_r = \Xi^{\star}_r$.
(6) $(\Xi^{\star}_r \vee \Theta^{\star}_r) = (\Xi \vee \Theta)^{\star}_r$.
(7) $\mathcal{T}^{\tau}(\Theta) \ge r$, $\mathcal{T}^{\pi}(\Theta) \le 1 - r$ *and* $\mathcal{T}^{\sigma}(\Theta) \le 1 - r$, *then ,* $(\Theta \wedge \Xi^{\star}_r) \le (\Theta \wedge \Xi)^{\star}_r$.
(8) $(\Xi^{\star}_r \wedge \Theta^{\star}_r) \ge (\Xi \wedge \Theta)^{\star}_r$.

Proof. (1) Let $\Xi \in \zeta^{\pounds}$ and $r \in \zeta_0$ such that $\Xi^{\star}_r \not\le \Theta^{\star}_r$. Then, there exists $z \in \pounds$ and $n, m, v \in \zeta_0$ such that

$$\tau_{\Xi^{\star}_r}(z) \ge n > \tau_{\Theta^{\star}_r}(z), \qquad \pi_{\Xi^{\star}_r}(z) < m \le \pi_{\Theta^{\star}_r}(z), \qquad \sigma_{\Xi^{\star}_r}(z) < v \le \sigma_{\Theta^{\star}_r}(z). \tag{1}$$

Since $\tau_{\Theta^{\star}_r}(z) < n$, $\pi_{\Theta^{\star}_r}(z) \ge m$ and $\sigma_{\Theta^{\star}_r}(z) \ge v$, there exists $\mathcal{A} \in \mathcal{Q}_{\mathcal{T}^{\tau\pi\sigma}}(y_{n,m,v}, r)$ with $\mathcal{P}^{\tau}(\Pi) \ge r$, $\mathcal{P}^{\pi}(\Pi) \le 1 - r$, $\mathcal{P}^{\sigma}(\Pi) \le 1 - r$, such that for every $x \in \pounds$, we have,

$$\tau_{\mathcal{A}}(x) + \tau_{\Theta}(z) - 1 \le \tau_{\Pi}(x), \quad \pi_{\mathcal{A}}(x) + \pi_{\Theta}(x) - 1 > \pi_{\Pi}(x), \quad \sigma_{\mathcal{A}}(x) + \sigma_{\Theta}(x) - 1 > \sigma_{\Pi}(x).$$

Since $\Xi \le \Theta$, we have

$$\tau_{\mathcal{A}}(x) + \tau_{\Xi}(z) - 1 \le \tau_{\Pi}(x), \quad \pi_{\mathcal{A}}(x) + \pi_{\Xi}(x) - 1 > \pi_{\Pi}(x), \quad \sigma_{\mathcal{A}}(x) + \sigma_{\Xi}(x) - 1 > \sigma_{\Pi}(x).$$

So, $\tau_{\Xi^{\star}_r}(z) < n$, $\pi_{\Xi^{\star}_r}(z) \ge m$ and $\sigma_{\Xi^{\star}_r}(z) \ge v$, and this is a contradiction for Equation (1). Hence, $\Xi^{\star}_r \le \Theta^{\star}_r$.

(2) Suppose that $\Xi^{\star}_r(\mathcal{P}^{\tau\pi\sigma}_1, \mathcal{T}^{\tau\pi\sigma}) \not\ge \Xi^{\star}_r(\mathcal{P}^{\tau\pi\sigma}_2, \mathcal{T}^{\tau\pi\sigma})$. Then, there exist $z \in \pounds$ and $n, m, v \in \zeta_0$ such that

$$\begin{gathered} \tau_{\Xi^{\star}_r(\mathcal{P}^{\tau\pi\sigma}_1, \mathcal{T}^{\tau\pi\sigma})}(z) < n \le \tau_{\Xi^{\star}_r(\mathcal{P}^{\tau\pi\sigma}_2, \mathcal{T}^{\tau\pi\sigma})}(z), \\ \pi_{\Xi^{\star}_r(\mathcal{P}^{\tau\pi\sigma}_1, \mathcal{T}^{\tau\pi\sigma})}(z) \ge m > \pi_{\Xi^{\star}_r(\mathcal{P}^{\tau\pi\sigma}_2, \mathcal{T}^{\tau\pi\sigma})}(z), \\ \sigma_{\Xi^{\star}_r(\mathcal{P}^{\tau\pi\sigma}_1, \mathcal{T}^{\tau\pi\sigma})}(z) \ge v > \sigma_{\Xi^{\star}_r(\mathcal{P}^{\tau\pi\sigma}_2, \mathcal{T}^{\tau\pi\sigma})}(z). \end{gathered} \tag{2}$$

Since $\tau_{\Xi^{\star}_r(\mathcal{P}^{\tau\pi\sigma}_1, \mathcal{T}^{\tau\pi\sigma})}(z) < n$, $\pi_{\Xi^{\star}_r(\mathcal{P}^{\tau\pi\sigma}_1, \mathcal{T}^{\tau\pi\sigma})}(z) \ge m$ and $\sigma_{\Xi^{\star}_r(\mathcal{P}^{\tau\pi\sigma}_1, \mathcal{T}^{\tau\pi\sigma})}(z) \ge v$, there exists $\mathcal{A} \in \mathcal{Q}_{\mathcal{T}^{\tau\pi\sigma}}(y_{n,m,v}, r)$ with $\mathcal{P}^{\tau}_1(\Pi) \ge r$, $\mathcal{P}^{\pi}_1(\Pi) \le 1 - r$, $\mathcal{P}^{\sigma}_1(\Pi) \le 1 - r$, such that for every $x \in \pounds$, we have

$$\tau_{\mathcal{A}}(x) + \tau_{\Xi}(z) - 1 \le \tau_{\Pi}(x), \quad \pi_{\mathcal{A}}(x) + \pi_{\Xi}(x) - 1 > \pi_{\Pi}(x), \quad \sigma_{\mathcal{A}}(x) + \sigma_{\Xi}(x) - 1 > \sigma_{\Pi}(x).$$

Since, $\mathcal{P}^{\tau}_2(\Pi) \ge \mathcal{P}^{\tau}_1(\Pi) \ge r$, $\mathcal{P}^{\pi}_2(\Pi) \le \mathcal{P}^{\pi}_1(\Pi) \le 1 - r$, $\mathcal{P}^{\sigma}_2(\Pi) \le \mathcal{P}^{\sigma}_1(\Pi) \le 1 - r$, we have

$$\tau_{\mathcal{A}}(x) + \tau_{\Xi}(z) - 1 \le \tau_{\Pi}(x), \quad \pi_{\mathcal{A}}(x) + \pi_{\Xi}(x) - 1 > \pi_{\Pi}(x), \quad \sigma_{\mathcal{A}}(x) + \sigma_{\Xi}(x) - 1 > \sigma_{\Pi}(x).$$

Hence, $\tau_{\Xi^{\star}_r(\mathcal{P}^{\tau\pi\sigma}_2, \mathcal{T}^{\tau\pi\sigma})}(z) < s$, $\pi_{\Xi^{\star}_r(\mathcal{P}^{\tau\pi\sigma}_2, \mathcal{T}^{\tau\pi\sigma})}(z) \ge m$ and $\sigma_{\Xi^{\star}_r(\mathcal{P}^{\tau\pi\sigma}_2, \mathcal{T}^{\tau\pi\sigma})}(z) \ge v$, and this is a contradiction for Equation (2). Thus, $\Xi^{\star}_r(\mathcal{P}^{\tau\pi\sigma}_1, \mathcal{T}^{\tau\pi\sigma}) \ge \Xi^{\star}_r(\mathcal{P}^{\tau\pi\sigma}_2, \mathcal{T}^{\tau\pi\sigma})$.

(3) Assume that $\Xi^{\star}_r \not\leq \mathcal{C}_{\mathcal{T}\tau\pi\sigma}(\Xi, r)$; then, there exist $z \in \pounds$ and $n, m, v \in \zeta_0$ such that

$$\tau_{\Xi^{\star}_r}(z) \geq n > \tau_{\mathcal{C}_{\mathcal{T}\tau\pi\sigma}(\Xi,r)}(z), \quad \pi_{\Xi^{\star}_r}(z) < m \leq \pi_{\mathcal{C}_{\mathcal{T}\tau\pi\sigma}(\Xi,r)}, \quad \sigma_{\Xi^{\star}_r}(z) < v \leq \sigma_{\mathcal{C}_{\mathcal{T}\tau\pi\sigma}(\Xi,r)}(z). \tag{3}$$

Since $\tau_{\Xi^{\star}_r}(z) \geq n$, $\pi_{\Xi^{\star}_r}(z) < m$ and $\pi_{\Xi^{\star}_r}(z) < v$, we have $y_{n,m,v} \in \Xi^{\star}_r$. So, there is at least one $x \in \pounds$, for each $\mathcal{A} \in \mathcal{Q}_{\mathcal{T}\tau\pi\sigma}(y_{n,m,v}, r)$ with $\mathcal{P}^{\tau}(\Pi) \geq r$, $\mathcal{P}^{\pi}(\Pi) \leq 1-r$, $\mathcal{P}^{\sigma}(\Pi) \leq 1-r$ such that

$$\tau_{\mathcal{A}}(x) + \tau_{\Xi}(x) > \tau_{\Pi}(z) + 1, \quad \pi_{\mathcal{A}}(x) + \pi_{\Xi}(x) \leq \pi_{\Pi}(z) + 1, \sigma_{\mathcal{A}}(x) + \sigma_{\Xi}(x) \leq \sigma_{\Pi}(x) + 1.$$

From Lemma 1, we have $y_{n,m,v} \in \mathcal{C}_{\mathcal{T}\tau\pi\sigma}(\Xi, r)$. This is a contradiction for Equation (3). Thus, $\Xi^{\star}_r \leq \mathcal{C}_{\mathcal{T}\tau\pi\sigma}(\Xi, r)$.

We will now prove this relationship $\Xi^{\star}_r \geq \mathcal{C}_{\mathcal{T}\tau\pi\sigma}(\Xi^{\star}_r, r)$. Assume that $\Xi^{\star}_r \not\geq \mathcal{C}_{\mathcal{T}\tau\pi\sigma}(\Xi^{\star}_r, r)$; then, there exist $z \in \pounds$ and $n, m, v \in \zeta_0$ such that

$$\tau_{\Xi^{\star}_r}(z) < n \leq \tau_{\mathcal{C}_{\mathcal{T}\tau\pi\sigma}(\Xi^{\star}_r,r)}(z), \quad \pi_{\Xi^{\star}_r}(z) \geq m > \pi_{\mathcal{C}_{\mathcal{T}\tau\pi\sigma}(\Xi^{\star}_r,r)}(z), \quad \sigma_{\Xi^{\star}_r}(z) \geq v > \sigma_{\mathcal{C}_{\mathcal{T}\tau\pi\sigma}(\Xi^{\star}_r,r)}(z). \tag{4}$$

Since $\tau_{\mathcal{C}_{\mathcal{T}\tau\pi\sigma}(\Xi^{\star}_r,r)}(z) \geq n$, $\pi_{\mathcal{C}_{\mathcal{T}\tau\pi\sigma}(\Xi^{\star}_r,r)}(z) < m$ and $\sigma_{\mathcal{C}_{\mathcal{T}\tau\pi\sigma}(\Xi^{\star}_r,r)}(z) < v$, we have $y_{n,m,v} \in \mathcal{C}_{\mathcal{T}\tau\pi\sigma}(\Xi^{\star}_r, r)$. So, there exists at least one $x \in \pounds$ with $\mathcal{A} \in \mathcal{Q}_{\mathcal{T}\tau\pi\sigma}(y_{n,m,v}, r)$ such that

$$\tau_{\mathcal{A}}(x) + \tau_{\Xi^{\star}_r}(x) > 1, \quad \pi_{\mathcal{A}}(x) + \pi_{\Xi^{\star}_r}(x) \leq 1, \quad \sigma_{\mathcal{A}}(x) + \sigma_{\Xi^{\star}_r}(x) \leq 1.$$

Thus, $\Xi^{\star}_r(x) \neq 0$. Suppose that $n_1 = \tau_{\Xi^{\star}_r}(x)$, $m_1 = \pi_{\Xi^{\star}}(x)$ and $v_1 = \sigma_{\Xi^{\star}_r}(x)$. Then, $x_{n_1,m_1,v_1} \in \Xi^{\star}_r$ and $n_1 + \tau_{\mathcal{A}}(x) > 1$, $m_1 + \pi_{\mathcal{A}} \leq 1$, $v_1 + \sigma_{\mathcal{A}}(x) \leq 1$, so that $\mathcal{A} \in \mathcal{Q}_{\mathcal{T}\tau\pi\sigma}(x_{n_1,m_1,v_1}, r)$. Now, $x_{n_1,m_1,v_1} \in \Xi^{\star}_r$ implies there is at least one $z' \in \pounds$ such that $\tau_{\mathcal{B}}(z') + \tau_{\Xi}(z') - 1 > \tau_{\Pi}(z')$, $\pi_{\mathcal{B}}(z') + \pi_{\Xi}(z') - 1 \leq \pi_{\Pi}(z')$, $\sigma_{\mathcal{B}}(z') + \sigma_{\Xi}(z') - 1 \leq \sigma_{\Pi}(z')$ $\forall$, $\mathcal{P}^{\tau}(\Pi) \geq r$, $\mathcal{P}^{\pi}(\Pi) \leq 1-r$, $\mathcal{P}^{\sigma}(\Pi) \leq 1-r$ and $\mathcal{B} \in \mathcal{Q}_{\mathcal{T}\tau\pi\sigma}(x_{n_1,m_2,v_1}, r)$. This is also true for $\mathcal{A}$. So, there is at least one $z'' \in \pounds$ such that $\tau_{\mathcal{A}}(z'') + \tau_{\Xi}(z'') - 1 > \tau_{\Pi}(z')$, $\pi_{\mathcal{A}}(z'') + \pi_{\Xi}(z') - 1 \leq \pi_{\Pi}(z'')$, $\sigma_{\mathcal{A}}(z'') + \sigma_{\Xi}(z'') - 1 \leq \sigma_{\Pi}(z^{';})$. Since $\mathcal{A}$ is an arbitrary and $\mathcal{A} \in \mathcal{Q}_{\mathcal{T}\tau\pi\sigma}(y_{n,m,v}, r)$, then $\tau_{\Xi^{\star}_r}(z) > n$, $\pi_{\Xi^{\star}_r}(z) \leq m$, $\sigma_{\Xi^{\star}_r}(z) \leq v$. This contradicts Equation (4). Thus, $\Xi^{\star}_r \geq \mathcal{C}_{\mathcal{T}\tau\pi\sigma}(\Xi^{\star}_r, r)$.

(4) Using (3) we obtain that $(\Xi^{\star}_r)^{\star}_r = \mathcal{C}_{\mathcal{T}\tau\pi\sigma}((\Xi^{\star}_r)^{\star}_r, r) \leq \mathcal{C}_{\mathcal{T}\tau\pi\sigma}(\Xi^{\star}_r, r) \leq \Xi^{\star}_r$.

(5) Straightforward.

(6) ($\Rightarrow$) Since $\Xi, \Theta \leq \Xi \vee \Theta$. By (1), we have $\Xi^{\star}_r \leq (\Xi \vee \Theta)^{\star}_r$ and $\Theta^{\star}_r \leq (\Xi \vee \Theta)^{\star}_r$. Thus, $\Xi^{\star}_r \vee \Theta^{\star}_r \leq (\Xi \vee \Theta)^{\star}_r$.

($\Leftarrow$) Let $\Xi^{\star}_r \vee \Theta^{\star}_r \not\geq (\Xi \vee \Theta)^{\star}_r$; then, there exist $z \in \pounds$ and $n.m.v \in \zeta_0$ such that

$$\begin{aligned} &\tau_{(\Xi^{\star}_r \vee \Theta^{\star}_r)}(z) < n \leq \tau_{(\Xi \cup \Theta)^{\star}_r}(z), \\ &\pi_{(\Xi^{\star}_r \vee \Theta^{\star}_r)}(z) \geq m > \pi_{(\Xi \cup \Theta)^{\star}_r}(z), \\ &\sigma_{(\Xi^{\star}_r \vee \Theta^{\star}_r)}(z) \geq v > \sigma_{(\Xi \cup \Theta)^{\star}_r}(z). \end{aligned} \tag{5}$$

Since $\tau_{(\Xi^{\star}_r \vee \Theta^{\star}_r)}(z) < n$, $\pi_{(\Xi^{\star}_r \vee \Theta^{\star}_r)}(z) \geq m$, $\sigma_{(\Xi^{\star}_r \vee \Theta^{\star}_r)}(z) \geq v$, we obtain $\tau_{\Xi^{\star}_r}(z) < n$, $\pi_{\Xi^{\star}_r}(z) \geq m$, $\sigma_{\Xi^{\star}_r}(z) \geq v$ or $\tau_{\Theta^{\star}_r}(z) < n$, $\pi_{\Theta^{\star}_r}(z) \geq m$, $\sigma_{\Theta^{\star}_r}(z) \geq v$. So, there exists $\mathcal{A}_1 \in \mathcal{Q}_{\mathcal{T}\tau\pi\sigma}(y_{n,m,v}, r)$ such that for each $x \in \pounds$ and for some $\mathcal{P}^{\tau}(\Pi_1) \geq r$, $\mathcal{P}^{\pi}(\Pi_1) \leq 1-r$, $\mathcal{P}^{\sigma}(\Pi_1) \leq 1-r$ we have,

$$\begin{aligned} &\tau_{\mathcal{A}_1}(x) + \tau_{\Xi}(x) - 1 \leq \tau_{\Pi_1}(x), \\ &\pi_{\mathcal{A}_1}(x) + \pi_{\Xi}(x) - 1 > \pi_{\Pi_1}(x), \\ &\sigma_{\mathcal{A}_1}(x) + \sigma_{\Xi}(x) - 1 > \sigma_{\Pi_1}(x). \end{aligned}$$

Similarly, there exists $\mathcal{A}_2 \in \mathcal{Q}_{\mathcal{T}^{\tau\pi\sigma}}(y_{n,m,v}, r)$ such that for each $x \in \pounds$ and for some $\mathcal{P}^{\tau}(\Pi_2) \geq r$, $\mathcal{P}^{\pi}(\Pi_2) \leq 1-r$, $\mathcal{P}^{\sigma}(\Pi_2) \leq 1-r$ we have,

$$\tau_{\mathcal{A}_2}(x) + \tau_{\Xi}(x) - 1 \leq \tau_{\Pi_2}(x),$$

$$\pi_{\mathcal{A}_2}(x) + \pi_{\Xi}(x) - 1 > \pi_{\Pi_2}(x),$$

$$\sigma_{\mathcal{A}_2}(x) + \sigma_{\Xi}(x) - 1 > \sigma_{\Pi_2}(x).$$

Since $\mathcal{A} = \mathcal{A}_1 \wedge \mathcal{A}_2 \in \mathcal{Q}_{\mathcal{T}^{\tau\pi\sigma}}(y_{n,m,v}, r)$ and by (P_3), we obtain $\mathcal{P}^{\tau}(\Pi_1 \wedge \Pi_2) \geq r$, $\mathcal{P}^{\pi}(\Pi_1 \wedge \Pi_2) \leq 1-r$, $\mathcal{P}^{\sigma}(\Pi_1 \wedge \Pi_2) \leq 1-r$. Thus, for each $x \in \xi$,

$$\tau_{\mathcal{A}}(x) + \tau_{\Xi\vee\Theta}(x) - 1 \leq \tau_{\Pi_1\wedge\Pi_2}(x),$$

$$\pi_{\mathcal{A}}(x) + \pi_{\Xi\vee\Theta}(x) - 1 > \pi_{\Pi_1\wedge\Pi_2}(x),$$

$$\sigma_{\mathcal{A}}(x) + \sigma_{\Xi\vee\Theta}(x) - 1 > \sigma_{\Pi_1\wedge\Pi_2}(x).$$

Hence, $\tau_{(\Xi\cup\Theta)^{\star}_r}(z) < n$, $\pi_{(\Xi\cup\Theta)^{\star}_r}(z) \geq m$, $\sigma_{(\Xi\cup\Theta)^{\star}_r}(z) \geq v$. This is a conflict with Equation (5). Thus, $\Xi^{\star}_r \vee \Theta^{\star}_r \geq (\Xi \vee \Theta)^{\star}_r$.

(7) and (8) are obvious. □

Example 4. *Suppose that* $\pounds = \{l_1, l_2, l_3\}$*; define the* svns $\mathcal{A}_1, \mathcal{A}_2, \mathcal{A}_3, \Theta \in \xi^{\pounds}$ *as follows*

$$\mathcal{A}_1 = \langle (0.8, 0.8, 0.8), (0.8, 0.8, 0.8), (0.8, 0.8, 0.8) \rangle,$$

$$\mathcal{A}_2 = \langle (0.6, 0.6, 0.6), (0.6, 0.6, 0.6), (0.6, 0.6, 0.6) \rangle,$$

$$\mathcal{A}_3 = \langle (0.5, 0.5, 0.5), (0.5, 0.5, 0.5), (0.5, 0.5, 0.5) \rangle,$$

$$\Theta = \langle (0.2, 0.2, 0.2), (0, 0, 0), (0, 0, 0) \rangle.$$

Define the mappings $\mathcal{T}^{\tau}, \mathcal{T}^{\pi}, \mathcal{T}^{\sigma} : \xi^{\pounds} \to \xi$ *and* $\mathcal{P}^{\tau}, \mathcal{P}^{\pi}, \mathcal{P}^{\sigma} : \xi^{\pounds} \to \xi$ *as follows:*

$$\mathcal{T}^{\tau}(\Xi) = \begin{cases} 1, & \text{if } \Xi = \overline{0}, \\ 1, & \text{if } \Xi = \overline{1}, \\ \frac{1}{2}, & \text{if } \Xi = \mathcal{A}_1, \\ 0, & \text{otherwise}, \end{cases} \qquad \mathcal{P}^{\tau}(\Xi) = \begin{cases} 1, & \text{if } \Xi = \overline{0}, \\ \frac{1}{4}, & \text{if } \Xi = \Theta, \\ \frac{1}{2}, & \text{if } \overline{0} < \Xi < \Theta, \\ 0, & \text{otherwise}, \end{cases}$$

$$\mathcal{T}^{\pi}(\Xi) = \begin{cases} 0, & \text{if } \Xi = \overline{0}, \\ 0, & \text{if } \Xi = \overline{1}, \\ \frac{1}{2}, & \text{if } \Xi = \mathcal{A}_2, \\ 1, & \text{otherwise}, \end{cases} \qquad \mathcal{P}^{\pi}(\Xi) = \begin{cases} 0, & \text{if } \Xi = \overline{0}, \\ \frac{3}{4}, & \text{if } \Xi = \Theta, \\ \frac{1}{2}, & \text{if } \overline{0} < \Xi < \Theta, \\ 1, & \text{otherwise}, \end{cases}$$

$$\mathcal{T}^{\sigma}(\Xi) = \begin{cases} 0, & \text{if } \Xi = \overline{0}, \\ 0, & \text{if } \Xi = \overline{1}, \\ \frac{1}{2}, & \text{if } \Xi = \mathcal{A}_3, \\ 1, & \text{otherwise}, \end{cases} \qquad \mathcal{P}^{\sigma}(\Xi) = \begin{cases} 0, & \text{if } \Xi = \overline{0}, \\ \frac{2}{3}, & \text{if } \Xi = \Theta, \\ \frac{1}{2}, & \text{if } \overline{0} < \Xi < \Theta, \\ 1, & \text{otherwise}, \end{cases}$$

Let $\mathcal{B} = \langle (0.4, 0.4, 0.4), (0.4, 0.4, 0.4), (0.4, 0.4, 0.4) \rangle$*. Then,* $\overline{0} = (\mathcal{B}^{\star}_{\frac{1}{2}})^{\star}_{\frac{1}{2}} \neq \mathcal{B}^{\star}_{\frac{1}{2}} = \overline{0.2}$.

Theorem 5. *Let* $(\pounds, \mathcal{T}^{\tau\pi\sigma}, \mathcal{P}^{\tau\pi\sigma})$ *be an svnpts and* $\{\Xi_i : i \in J\} \subset \xi^{\pounds}$*. Then:*

(1) $(\bigvee (\Xi_i)^{\star}_r : i \in J) \leq (\bigvee \Xi_i : i \in J)^{\star}_r$.
(2) $(\bigwedge \Xi_i : i \in J)^{\star}_r \leq (\bigwedge (\Xi_i)^{\star}_r : i \in J)$.

Proof. (1) Since $\Xi_i \leq \bigvee \Xi_i$, for all $i \in J$, by Theorem 4(1), we obtain $(\Xi_i)^\star_r \leq (\bigvee \Xi_i)^\star_r$, for every $i \in J$. Thus,

$$(\bigvee (\Xi_i)^\star_r : i \in J) \leq (\bigvee \Xi_i : i \in J)^\star_r.$$

(2) Since $\bigwedge \Xi_i \leq \mathcal{A}_i$, and by (1) in Theorem 4, we have $(\bigwedge \Xi_i)^\star_r \leq (\Xi_i)^\star_r, \forall i \in J$. Hence,

$$(\bigwedge (\Xi_i)^\star_r : i \in J) \geq (\bigwedge \Xi_i : i \in J)^\star_r.$$

□

Remark 2. *Let $(\pounds, \mathcal{T}^{\tau\pi\sigma}, \mathcal{P}^{\tau\pi\sigma})$ be an svnpts and $\Xi \in \xi^\pounds$; we can define*

$$\mathcal{C}^\star_{\mathcal{T}^{\tau\pi\sigma}}(\Xi, r) = \Xi \cup \Xi^\star_r, \quad \mathcal{I}^\star_{\mathcal{T}^{\tau\pi\sigma}}(\Xi, r) = \Xi \wedge ((\Xi^c)^\star_r)^c.$$

Clearly, $\mathcal{C}^\star_{\mathcal{T}^{\tau\pi\sigma}}$ is an svn-closure operator and $(\mathcal{T}^\tau(\mathcal{P}^\tau), \mathcal{T}^\pi(\mathcal{P}^\pi), \mathcal{T}^\sigma(\mathcal{P}^\sigma))$ is the svnt generated by $\mathcal{C}^\star_{\mathcal{T}^{\tau\pi\sigma}}$, i.e.,

$$\mathcal{T}^\star(\mathcal{I})(\Xi) = \bigvee \{r \mid \mathcal{C}^\star_{\mathcal{T}^{\tau\pi\sigma}}(\Xi^c, r) = \Xi^c\}.$$

Now, if $\mathcal{P}^{\tau\pi\sigma} = \mathcal{P}^{\tau\pi\sigma}_0, \forall \Xi \in \xi^\pounds$, then $\mathcal{C}^\star_{\mathcal{T}^{\tau\pi\sigma}}(\Xi, r) = \Xi \cup \Xi^\star_r = \Xi \vee \mathcal{C}_{\mathcal{T}^{\tau\pi\sigma}}(\Xi, r) = \mathcal{C}_{\mathcal{T}^{\tau\pi\sigma}}(\Xi, r)$. So, $\mathcal{T}^{\tau\star}(\mathcal{P}^\tau_0) = \mathcal{T}^\tau$, $\mathcal{T}^{\pi\star}(\mathcal{P}^\pi_0) = \mathcal{T}^\pi$ and $\mathcal{T}^{\sigma\star}(\mathcal{P}^\sigma_0) = \mathcal{T}^\sigma$.

Theorem 6. *Let $(\pounds, \mathcal{T}^{\tau\pi\sigma}, \mathcal{P}^{\tau\pi\sigma})$ be an svnpts and $\Xi \in \xi^\pounds$ and $r \in \zeta_0$ and $\Xi \in \xi^\pounds$. Then*

(1) $\mathcal{I}^\star_{\mathcal{T}^{\tau\pi\sigma}}(\Xi \vee \Theta, r) \leq \mathcal{I}^\star_{\mathcal{T}^{\tau\pi\sigma}}(\Xi, r) \vee \mathcal{I}^\star_{\mathcal{T}^{\tau\pi\sigma}}(\Theta, r)$.
(2) $\mathcal{I}_{\mathcal{T}^{\tau\pi\sigma}}(\Xi, r) \leq \mathcal{I}^\star_{\mathcal{T}^{\tau\pi\sigma}}(\Xi, r) \leq \Xi \leq \mathcal{C}^\star_{\mathcal{T}^{\tau\pi\sigma}}(\Xi, r) \leq \mathcal{C}_{\mathcal{T}^{\tau\pi\sigma}}(\Xi, r)$.
(3) $\mathcal{I}^\star_{\mathcal{T}^{\tau\pi\sigma}}(\Xi \wedge \Theta, r) = \mathcal{I}^\star_{\mathcal{T}^{\tau\pi\sigma}}(\Xi, r) \wedge \mathcal{I}^\star_{\mathcal{T}^{\tau\pi\sigma}}(\Theta, r)$.
(4) $\mathcal{C}^\star_{\mathcal{T}^{\tau\pi\sigma}}(\Xi^c, r) = [\mathcal{I}^\star_{\mathcal{T}^{\tau\pi\sigma}}(\Xi, r)]^c$ *and* $[\mathcal{C}^\star_{\mathcal{T}^{\tau\pi\sigma}}(\Xi, r)]^c = \mathcal{I}^\star_{\mathcal{T}^{\tau\pi\sigma}}(\Xi^c, r)$.

Proof. Straightforward from $\mathcal{C}^\star_{\mathcal{T}^{\tau\pi\sigma}}, \mathcal{I}^\star_{\mathcal{T}^{\tau\pi\sigma}}$ and $\mathcal{C}_{\mathcal{T}^{\tau\pi\sigma}}$. □

Theorem 7. *Let $(\pounds, \mathcal{T}_1^{\tau\pi\sigma}, \mathcal{P}^{\tau\pi\sigma})$ and $(\pounds, \mathcal{T}_2^{\tau\pi\sigma}, \mathcal{P}^{\tau\pi\sigma})$ be svnptss and $\mathcal{T}_1^\tau \leq \mathcal{T}_2^\tau$, $\mathcal{T}_1^\pi \geq \mathcal{T}_2^\pi$, $\mathcal{T}_1^\sigma \geq \mathcal{T}_2^\sigma$. Then,*

(1) $\Xi^\star_r(\mathcal{T}_2^\tau, \mathcal{P}^\tau) \leq \Xi^\star_r(\mathcal{T}_1^\tau, \mathcal{P}^\tau)$, $\Xi^\star_r(\mathcal{T}_2^\pi, \mathcal{P}^\pi) \geq \Xi^\star_r(\mathcal{T}_1^\pi, \mathcal{P}^\pi)$ *and* $\Xi^\star_r(\mathcal{T}_2^\sigma, \mathcal{P}^\sigma) \geq \Xi^\star_r(\mathcal{T}_1^\sigma, \mathcal{P}^\sigma)$.
(2) $\mathcal{T}_1^{\star\tau}(\mathcal{P}^\tau) \leq \mathcal{T}_2^{\star\tau}(\mathcal{P}^\tau)$, $\mathcal{T}_1^{\star\pi}(\mathcal{P}^\pi) \geq \mathcal{T}_2^{\star\pi}(\mathcal{P}^\pi)$, $\mathcal{T}_1^{\star\sigma}(\mathcal{P}^\sigma) \geq \mathcal{T}_2^{\star\sigma}(\mathcal{P}^\sigma)$.

Proof. (1) Let

$$\Xi^\star_r(\mathcal{T}_2^\tau, \mathcal{P}^\tau) \not\leq \Xi^\star_r(\mathcal{T}_1^\tau, \mathcal{P}^\tau), \quad \Xi^\star_r(\mathcal{T}_2^\pi, \mathcal{P}^\pi) \not\geq \Xi^\star_r(\mathcal{T}_1^\pi, \mathcal{P}^\pi),$$
$$\Xi^\star_r(\mathcal{T}_2^\sigma, \mathcal{P}^\sigma) \not\geq \Xi^\star_r(\mathcal{T}_1^\sigma, \mathcal{P}^\sigma),$$

then, there exist $z \in \pounds$ and $n, m, v \in \zeta_0$ such that

$$\begin{aligned} &\tau_{\Xi^\star_r(\mathcal{T}_2^\tau, \mathcal{P}^\tau)}(z) \geq n > \tau_{\Xi^\star_r(\mathcal{T}_1^\tau, \mathcal{P}^\tau)}(z), \\ &\pi_{\Xi^\star_r(\mathcal{T}_2^\pi, \mathcal{P}^\pi)}(z) < m \leq \pi_{\Xi^\star_r(\mathcal{T}_1^\pi, \mathcal{P}^\pi)}(z), \\ &\sigma_{\Xi^\star_r(\mathcal{T}_2^\sigma, \mathcal{P}^\sigma)}(z) < v \leq \sigma_{\Xi^\star_r(\mathcal{T}_1^\sigma, \mathcal{P}^\sigma)}(z). \end{aligned} \tag{6}$$

Since $\tau_{\Xi^\star_r(\mathcal{T}_1^\tau, \mathcal{P}^\tau)}(z) < n$, $\pi_{\Xi^\star_r(\mathcal{T}_1^\pi, \mathcal{P}^\pi)}(z) \geq m$, $\sigma_{\Xi^\star_r(\mathcal{T}_1^\sigma, \mathcal{P}^\sigma)}(z) \geq v$, there exists $\mathcal{A} \in \mathcal{Q}_{\mathcal{T}_1^{\tau\pi\sigma}}(y_{n,m,v}, r)$ with $\mathcal{P}^\tau(\Pi) \geq r$, $\mathcal{P}^\pi(\Pi) \leq 1 - r$, $\mathcal{P}^\sigma(\Pi) \leq 1 - r$, such that for each $x \in \pounds$,

$$\tau_{\mathcal{A}}(x) + \tau_\Xi(z) - 1 \leq \tau_\Pi(x), \quad \pi_{\mathcal{A}}(x) + \pi_\Xi(x) - 1 > \pi_\Pi(x), \quad \sigma_{\mathcal{A}}(x) + \sigma_\Xi(x) - 1 > \sigma_\Pi(x).$$

Since $\mathcal{T}_1^\tau \le \mathcal{T}_2^\tau, \mathcal{T}_1^\pi \ge \mathcal{T}_2^\pi, \mathcal{T}_1^\sigma \ge \mathcal{T}_2^\sigma$, we have $\mathcal{A} \in \mathcal{Q}_{\mathcal{T}_2^{\tau\pi\sigma}}(y_{n,m,v}, r)$. Hence, $\tau_{\Xi_r^\star(\mathcal{T}_2^\tau,\mathcal{P}^\tau)}(z) < n, \pi_{\Xi_r^\star(\mathcal{T}_2^\pi,\mathcal{P}^\pi)}(z) \ge m, \sigma_{\Xi_r^\star(\mathcal{T}_2^\sigma,\mathcal{P}^\sigma)}(z) \ge v$. This is a contradiction of Equation (6).

(2) Similar to part (1). □

Theorem 8. *Let* $(\pounds, \mathcal{T}^{\tau\pi\sigma}, \mathcal{P}_1^{\tau\pi\sigma})$ *and* $(\pounds, \mathcal{T}^{\tau\pi\sigma}, \mathcal{P}_2^{\tau\pi\sigma})$ *be svnptss and* $\mathcal{P}_1^\tau \le \mathcal{P}_2^\tau$, $\mathcal{P}_1^\pi \ge \mathcal{P}_2^\pi$, $\mathcal{P}_1^\sigma \ge \mathcal{P}_2^\sigma$. *Then,*

(1) $\Xi_r^\star(\mathcal{P}_1^\tau, \mathcal{T}^\tau) \ge \Xi_r^\star(\mathcal{P}_2^\tau, \mathcal{T}^\pi), \Xi_r^\star(\mathcal{P}_1^\pi, \mathcal{T}^\pi) \le \Xi_r^\star(\mathcal{P}_2^\pi, \mathcal{T}^\pi)$ *and* $\Xi_r^\star(\mathcal{P}_1^\tau, \mathcal{T}^\tau) \le \Xi_r^\star(\mathcal{P}_2^\tau, \mathcal{T}^\tau)$.

(2) $\mathcal{T}^{\star\tau}(\mathcal{P}_1^\tau) \le \mathcal{T}^{\star\tau}(\mathcal{P}_2^\tau), \mathcal{T}^{\star\pi}(\mathcal{P}_1^\pi) \ge \mathcal{T}^{\star\pi}(\mathcal{P}_2^\pi), \mathcal{T}^{\star\sigma}(\mathcal{P}_1^\sigma) \ge \mathcal{T}^{\star\sigma}(\mathcal{P}_2^\sigma)$.

Proof. The same method as the proof of Theorem 7. □

Theorem 9. *Let* $(\pounds, \mathcal{T}^{\tau\pi\sigma})$ *be an svnts and* $\mathcal{P}_1^{\tau\pi\sigma}, \mathcal{P}_2^{\tau\pi\sigma}$ *be two svn-primals on* £. *Then,* $\forall\, \Xi \in \xi^\pounds$ *and* $r \in \xi_0$,

(1)
$$\Xi_r^\star(\mathcal{P}_1^\tau \wedge \mathcal{P}_2^\tau, \mathcal{T}^\tau) = \Xi_r^\star(\mathcal{P}_1^\tau, \mathcal{T}^\tau) \vee \Xi_r^\star(\mathcal{P}_2^\tau, \mathcal{T}^\tau),$$
$$\Xi_r^\star(\mathcal{P}_1^\pi \wedge \mathcal{P}_2^\pi, \mathcal{T}^\pi) = \Xi_r^\star(\mathcal{P}_1^\pi, \mathcal{T}^\pi) \wedge \Xi_r^\star(\mathcal{P}_2^\pi, \mathcal{T}^\pi),$$
$$\Xi_r^\star(\mathcal{P}_1^\sigma \wedge \mathcal{P}_2^\sigma, \mathcal{T}^\sigma) = \Xi_r^\star(\mathcal{P}_1^\sigma, \mathcal{T}^\sigma) \wedge \Xi_r^\star(\mathcal{P}_2^\sigma, \mathcal{T}^\sigma).$$

(2)
$$\Xi_r^\star(\mathcal{P}_1^\tau \vee \mathcal{P}_2^\tau, \mathcal{T}^\tau) = \Xi_r^\star(\mathcal{P}_1^\tau, \mathcal{T}^{\star\tau}(\mathcal{P}_2^\tau)) \wedge \Xi_r^\star(\mathcal{P}_2^\tau, \mathcal{T}^{\star\tau}(\mathcal{P}_1^\tau))),$$
$$\Xi_r^\star(\mathcal{P}_1^\pi \vee \mathcal{P}_2^\pi, \mathcal{T}^\pi) = \Xi_r^\star(\mathcal{P}_1^\pi, \mathcal{T}^{\star\pi}(\mathcal{P}_2^\pi)) \vee \Xi_r^\star(\mathcal{P}_2^\pi, \mathcal{T}^{\star\pi}(\mathcal{P}_1^\pi)),$$
$$\Xi_r^\star(\mathcal{P}_1^\sigma \vee \mathcal{P}_2^\sigma, \mathcal{T}^\sigma) = \Xi_r^\star(\mathcal{P}_1^\sigma, \mathcal{T}^{\star\sigma}(\mathcal{P}_2^\sigma)) \vee \Xi_r^\star(\mathcal{P}_2^\sigma, \mathcal{T}^{\star\sigma}(\mathcal{P}_1^\sigma)).$$

Proof. (1) Let

$$\Xi_r^\star(\mathcal{P}_1^\tau \wedge \mathcal{P}_2^\tau, \mathcal{T}^\tau)) \not\le \Xi_r^\star(\mathcal{P}_1^\tau, \mathcal{T}^\tau) \vee \Xi_r^\star(\mathcal{P}_2^\tau, \mathcal{T}^\tau),$$

$$\Xi_r^\star(\mathcal{P}_1^\pi \wedge \mathcal{P}_2^\pi, \mathcal{T}^\pi) \not\ge \Xi_r^\star(\mathcal{P}_1^\pi, \mathcal{T}^\pi) \wedge \Xi_r^\star(\mathcal{P}_2^\pi, \mathcal{T}^\pi),$$

$$\Xi_r^\star(\mathcal{P}_1^\sigma \wedge \mathcal{P}_2^\sigma, \mathcal{T}^\sigma) \not\ge \Xi_r^\star(\mathcal{P}_1^\sigma, \mathcal{T}^\sigma) \wedge \Xi_r^\star(\mathcal{P}_2^\sigma, \mathcal{T}^\sigma).$$

Then there exist $z \in \pounds$ and $n, m, v \in \xi_0$ s.t.

$$\tau_{\Xi_r^\star(\mathcal{P}_1^\tau \wedge \mathcal{P}_2^\tau, \mathcal{T}^\tau))}(z) \ge n > \tau_{\Xi_r^\star(\mathcal{P}_1^\tau, \mathcal{T}^\tau)}(z) \vee \tau_{\Xi_r^\star(\mathcal{P}_2^\tau, \mathcal{T}^\tau)}(z),$$

$$\pi_{\Xi_r^\star(\mathcal{P}_1^\pi \wedge \mathcal{P}_2^\pi, \mathcal{T}^\pi)}(z) < m \le \pi_{\Xi_r^\star(\mathcal{P}_1^\pi, \mathcal{T}^\pi)}(z) \wedge \pi_{\Xi_r^\star(\mathcal{P}_2^\pi, \mathcal{T}^\pi)}(z), \tag{7}$$

$$\sigma_{\Xi_r^\star(\mathcal{P}_1^\sigma \wedge \mathcal{P}_2^\sigma, \mathcal{T}^\sigma)}(z) < v \le \sigma_{\Xi_r^\star(\mathcal{P}_1^\sigma, \mathcal{T}^\sigma)}(z) \wedge \sigma_{\Xi_r^\star(\mathcal{P}_2^\sigma, \mathcal{T}^\sigma)}(z).$$

Since $[\tau_{\Xi_r^\star(\mathcal{P}_1^\tau,\mathcal{T}^\tau)}(z) \vee \tau_{\Xi_r^\star(\mathcal{P}_2^\tau,\mathcal{T}^\tau)}(z)] < n$, $[\pi_{\Xi_r^\star(\mathcal{P}_1^\pi,\mathcal{T}^\pi)}(z) \wedge \pi_{\Xi_r^\star(\mathcal{P}_2^\pi,\mathcal{T}^\pi)}(z)] \ge m$, $[\sigma_{\Xi_r^\star(\mathcal{P}_1^\sigma,\mathcal{T}^\sigma)}(z) \wedge \sigma_{\Xi_r^\star(\mathcal{P}_2^\sigma,\mathcal{T}^\sigma)}(z)] \ge v$, we obtain $\tau_{\Xi_r^\star(\mathcal{P}_1^\tau,\mathcal{T}^\tau)}(z) < n$, $\pi_{\Xi_r^\star(\mathcal{P}_1^\pi,\mathcal{T}^\pi)}(z) \ge m$, $\sigma_{\Xi_r^\star(\mathcal{P}_1^\sigma,\mathcal{T}^\sigma)}(z) \ge v$ and $\tau_{\Xi_r^\star(\mathcal{P}_2^\tau,\mathcal{T}^\tau)}(z) < n$, $\pi_{\Xi_r^\star(\mathcal{P}_2^\pi,\mathcal{T}^\pi)}(z) \ge m$, $\sigma_{\Xi_r^\star(\mathcal{P}_2^\sigma,\mathcal{T}^\sigma)}(z) \ge v$.

First, by taking the first part, $\tau_{\Xi_r^\star(\mathcal{P}_1^\tau,\mathcal{T}^\tau)}(z) < n$, $\pi_{\Xi_r^\star(\mathcal{P}_1^\pi,\mathcal{T}^\pi)}(z) \ge m$, $\sigma_{\Xi_r^\star(\mathcal{P}_1^\sigma,\mathcal{T}^\sigma)}(z) \ge v$, there will be $\mathcal{A}_1 \in \mathcal{Q}_{\mathcal{T}^{\tau\pi\sigma}}(y_{n,m,v}, r)$ with $\mathcal{P}_1^\tau(\Pi_1) \ge r$, $\mathcal{P}_1^\pi(\Pi_1) \le 1 - r$, $\mathcal{P}_1^\sigma(\Pi_1) \le 1 - r$, such that $\forall$, $x \in \pounds$,

$$\tau_{\mathcal{A}_1}(x) + \tau_\Xi(x) - 1 \le \tau_{\Pi_1}(x),$$

$$\pi_{\mathcal{A}_1}(x) + \pi_\Xi(x) - 1 > \pi_{\Pi_1}(x),$$

$$\sigma_{\mathcal{A}_1}(x) + \sigma_{\Xi}(x) - 1 > \sigma_{\Pi_1}(x).$$

Secondly, by taking the second part, $\tau_{\Xi^{\star}_r(\mathcal{P}^{\tau}_2, \mathcal{T}^{\tau})}(z) < n,\ \pi_{\Xi^{\star}_r(\mathcal{P}^{\pi}_2, \mathcal{T}^{\pi})}(z) \geq m,\ \sigma_{\Xi^{\star}_r(\mathcal{P}^{\sigma}_2, \mathcal{T}^{\sigma})}(z) \geq v$, there will be $\mathcal{A}_2 \in \mathcal{Q}_{\mathcal{T}\tau\pi\sigma}(y_{n,m,v}, r)$ with $\mathcal{P}^{\tau}_2(\Pi_2) \geq r$, $\mathcal{P}^{\pi}_2(\Pi_2) \leq 1 - r$, $\mathcal{P}^{\sigma}_2(\Pi_2) \leq 1 - r$, such that $\forall$, $x \in £$,

$$\tau_{\mathcal{A}_2}(x) + \tau_{\Xi}(x) - 1 \leq \tau_{\Pi_2}(x),$$

$$\pi_{\mathcal{A}_2}(x) + \pi_{\Xi}(x) - 1 > \pi_{\Pi_2}(x),$$

$$\sigma_{\mathcal{A}_2}(x) + \sigma_{\Xi}(x) - 1 > \sigma_{\Pi_2}(x).$$

Thus, $\forall\, y \in £$, we obtain

$$\tau_{(\mathcal{A}_1 \wedge \mathcal{A}_2)}(x) + \tau_{\Xi}(x) - 1 > \tau_{(\Pi_1 \wedge \Pi_2)}(x),$$

$$\pi_{(\mathcal{A}_1 \vee \mathcal{A}_2)}(x) + \pi_{\Xi}(x) - 1 \leq \pi_{(\Pi_1 \vee \Pi_2)}(x),$$

$$\sigma_{(\mathcal{A}_1 \vee \mathcal{A}_2)}(x) + \sigma_{\Xi}(x) - 1 \leq \sigma_{(\Pi_1 \vee \Pi_2)}(x).$$

Since $(\mathcal{A}_1 \wedge \mathcal{A}_2) \in \mathcal{Q}_{\mathcal{T}\tau\pi\sigma}(y_{n,m,v}, r)$ and

$$(\mathcal{P}^{\tau}_1 \wedge \mathcal{P}^{\tau}_2)(\Pi_1 \wedge \Pi_2) \geq r, \quad (\mathcal{P}^{\pi}_1 \wedge \mathcal{P}^{\pi}_2)(\Pi_1 \vee \Pi_2) \leq 1 - r,$$
$$(\mathcal{P}^{\pi}_1 \wedge \mathcal{P}^{\pi}_2)(\Pi_1 \vee \Pi_2) \leq 1 - r,$$

we obtain that $\tau_{\Xi^{\star}_r(\mathcal{P}^{\tau}_1 \wedge \mathcal{P}^{\tau}_2, \mathcal{T}^{\tau}))}(z) \leq n,\ \pi_{\Xi^{\star}_r(\mathcal{P}^{\pi}_1 \wedge \mathcal{P}^{\pi}_2, \mathcal{T}^{\pi})}(z) > m,\ \sigma_{\Xi^{\star}_r(\mathcal{P}^{\sigma}_1 \wedge \mathcal{P}^{\sigma}_2, \mathcal{T}^{\sigma})}(z) > v$ and this is a contradiction of Equation (7). So,

$$\Xi^{\star}_r(\mathcal{P}^{\tau}_1 \wedge \mathcal{P}^{\tau}_2, \mathcal{T}^{\tau})) \leq \Xi^{\star}_r(\mathcal{P}^{\tau}_1, \mathcal{T}^{\tau}) \vee \Xi^{\star}_r(\mathcal{P}^{\tau}_2, \mathcal{T}^{\tau}),$$

$$\Xi^{\star}_r(\mathcal{P}^{\pi}_1 \wedge \mathcal{P}^{\pi}_2, \mathcal{T}^{\pi}) \geq \Xi^{\star}_r(\mathcal{P}^{\pi}_1, \mathcal{T}^{\pi}) \wedge \Xi^{\star}_r(\mathcal{P}^{\pi}_2, \mathcal{T}^{\pi}),$$

$$\Xi^{\star}_r(\mathcal{P}^{\sigma}_1 \wedge \mathcal{P}^{\sigma}_2, \mathcal{T}^{\sigma}) \geq \Xi^{\star}_r(\mathcal{P}^{\sigma}_1, \mathcal{T}^{\sigma}) \wedge \Xi^{\star}_r(\mathcal{P}^{\sigma}_2, \mathcal{T}^{\sigma}).$$

On the other side $\mathcal{P}^{\tau}_1 \wedge \mathcal{P}^{\tau}_2 \leq \mathcal{P}^{\tau}_1$, $\mathcal{P}^{\pi}_1 \vee \mathcal{P}^{\pi}_2 \geq \mathcal{P}^{\pi}_1$, $\mathcal{P}^{\sigma}_1 \vee \mathcal{P}^{\sigma}_2 \geq \mathcal{P}^{\sigma}_1$ and $\mathcal{P}^{\tau}_1 \wedge \mathcal{P}^{\tau}_2 \leq \mathcal{P}^{\tau}_2$, $\mathcal{P}^{\pi}_1 \vee \mathcal{P}^{\pi}_2 \geq \mathcal{P}^{\pi}_2$, $\mathcal{P}^{\sigma}_1 \vee \mathcal{P}^{\sigma}_2 \geq \mathcal{P}^{\sigma}_2$, so by Theorem 4(2),

$$\Xi^{\star}_r(\mathcal{P}^{\tau}_1 \wedge \mathcal{P}^{\tau}_2) \geq \Xi^{\star}_r(\mathcal{P}^{\tau}_1) \vee \Xi^{\star}_r(\mathcal{P}^{\tau}_2), \quad \Xi^{\star}_r(\mathcal{P}^{\pi}_1 \wedge \mathcal{P}^{\pi}_2) \leq \Xi^{\star}_r(\mathcal{P}^{\tau}_1) \wedge \Xi^{\star}_r(\mathcal{P}^{\pi}_2),$$

$$\Xi^{\star}_r(\mathcal{P}^{\sigma}_1 \wedge \mathcal{P}^{\sigma}_2) \leq \Xi^{\star}_r(\mathcal{P}^{\sigma}_1) \wedge \Xi^{\star}_r(\mathcal{P}^{\sigma}_2).$$

Hence, $\Xi^{\star}_r(\mathcal{P}^{\tau}_1 \wedge \mathcal{P}^{\tau}_2, \mathcal{T}^{\tau}) = \Xi^{\star}_r(\mathcal{P}^{\tau}_1, \mathcal{T}^{\tau}) \vee \Xi^{\star}_r(\mathcal{P}^{\tau}_2, \mathcal{T}^{\tau})$, $\Xi^{\star}_r(\mathcal{P}^{\pi}_1 \wedge \mathcal{P}^{\pi}_2, \mathcal{T}^{\pi}) = \Xi^{\star}_r(\mathcal{P}^{\pi}_1, \mathcal{T}^{\pi}) \wedge \Xi^{\star}_r(\mathcal{P}^{\pi}_2, \mathcal{T}^{\pi})$ and $\Xi^{\star}_r(\mathcal{P}^{\sigma}_1 \wedge \mathcal{P}^{\sigma}_2, \mathcal{T}^{\sigma}) = \Xi^{\star}_r(\mathcal{P}^{\sigma}_1, \mathcal{T}^{\sigma}) \wedge \Xi^{\star}_r(\mathcal{P}^{\sigma}_2, \mathcal{T}^{\sigma})$.

(2) Similar to part (1). □

From the previous theory, we can see the important result that $(\mathcal{T}^{\star\tau}(\mathcal{P}^{\tau}), \mathcal{T}^{\star\pi}(\mathcal{P}^{\pi}), \mathcal{T}^{\star\sigma}(\mathcal{P}^{\star}))$ (for short $\mathcal{T}^{\star}(\mathcal{P})$) and $([\mathcal{T}^{\star\tau}(\mathcal{P}^{\tau})]^{\star}(\mathcal{P}^{\tau}), [\mathcal{T}^{\star\pi}(\mathcal{P}^{\pi})]^{\star}((\mathcal{P}^{\pi})),$ $[\mathcal{T}^{\star\sigma}(\mathcal{P}^{\star})]^{\star}(\mathcal{P}^{\sigma}))$ (for short $\mathcal{T}^{\star\star}$) are equal for any *svn-primals* on £.

Theorem 10. *Let $(£, \mathcal{T}^{\tau\pi\sigma}, \mathcal{P}^{\tau\pi\sigma})$ be an svnpts. Then, for each $\Xi \in \zeta^{£}$ and $r \in \zeta_0$,*

(1) $\Xi^{\star}_r(\mathcal{P}^{\tau}) = \Xi^{\star}_r(\mathcal{P}^{\tau}, \mathcal{T}^{\star\tau})$, $\Xi^{\star}_r(\mathcal{P}^{\pi}) = \Xi^{\star}_r(\mathcal{P}^{\pi}, \mathcal{T}^{\star\pi})$ *and* $\Xi^{\star}_r(\mathcal{P}^{\sigma}) = \Xi^{\star}_r(\mathcal{P}^{\sigma}, \mathcal{T}^{\star\sigma}))$.

(2) $(\mathcal{T}^{\star\tau}(\mathcal{P}^{\tau}) = \mathcal{T}^{\star\star\tau}, \mathcal{T}^{\star\pi}(\mathcal{P}^{\pi}) = \mathcal{T}^{\star\star\pi}, \mathcal{T}^{\star\sigma}(\mathcal{P}^{\pi})) = \mathcal{T}^{\star\star\sigma}$.

Proof. By putting $\mathcal{P}_1^{\tau} = \mathcal{P}_2^{\tau}$, $\mathcal{P}_1^{\pi} = \mathcal{P}_2^{\pi}$ and $\mathcal{P}_1^{\sigma} = \mathcal{P}_2^{\sigma}$ in the second part of the above theorem, we obtain the required proof. □

Theorem 11. *Let* $(\pounds, \mathcal{T}^{\tau\pi\sigma})$ *be an svnts and* $\mathcal{P}_1^{\tau\pi\sigma}$, $\mathcal{P}_2^{\tau\pi\sigma}$ *be two svn-primals on* £. *Then,* $\forall$ $r \in \zeta_0$ *and* $\Xi \in \xi^{\pounds}$, $\mathcal{T}^{\star\tau}(\mathcal{P}_1^{\tau} \wedge \mathcal{P}_2^{\tau}) = \mathcal{T}^{\star\tau}(\mathcal{P}_1^{\tau}) \wedge \mathcal{T}^{\star\tau}(\mathcal{P}_2^{\tau})$, $\mathcal{T}^{\star\pi}(\mathcal{P}_1^{\pi} \wedge \mathcal{P}_2^{\pi}) = \mathcal{T}^{\star\pi}(\mathcal{P}_1^{\pi}) \vee \mathcal{T}^{\star\pi}(\mathcal{P}_2^{\pi})$ *and* $\mathcal{T}^{\star\sigma}(\mathcal{P}_1^{\sigma} \wedge \mathcal{P}_2^{\sigma}) = \mathcal{T}^{\star\sigma}(\mathcal{P}_1^{\sigma}) \vee \mathcal{T}^{\star\sigma}(\mathcal{P}_2^{\sigma})$.

Proof. (⇒): Since $\mathcal{P}_1^{\tau} \geq \mathcal{P}_1^{\tau} \wedge \mathcal{P}_2^{\tau}$, $\mathcal{P}_1^{\pi} \leq \mathcal{P}_1^{\pi} \vee \mathcal{P}_2^{\pi}$, $\mathcal{P}_1^{\sigma} \leq \mathcal{P}_1^{\sigma} \vee \mathcal{P}_2^{\sigma}$ and $\mathcal{P}_2^{\tau} \geq \mathcal{P}_1^{\tau} \wedge \mathcal{P}_2^{\tau}$, $\mathcal{P}_2^{\pi} \leq \mathcal{P}_1^{\pi} \vee \mathcal{P}_2^{\pi}$, $\mathcal{P}_2^{\sigma} \leq \mathcal{P}_1^{\sigma} \vee \mathcal{P}_2^{\sigma}$, by Theorem 8(2) we obtain $\mathcal{T}^{\star\tau}(\mathcal{P}_1^{\tau}) \geq \mathcal{T}^{\star\tau}(\mathcal{P}_1^{\tau} \wedge \mathcal{P}_2^{\tau})$, $\mathcal{T}^{\star\pi}(\mathcal{P}_1^{\pi}) \leq \mathcal{T}^{\star\pi}(\mathcal{P}_1^{\pi} \vee \mathcal{P}_2^{\pi})$, $\mathcal{T}^{\star\sigma}(\mathcal{P}_1^{\sigma}) \leq \mathcal{T}^{\star\sigma}(\mathcal{P}_1^{\sigma} \vee \mathcal{P}_2^{\sigma})$ and $\mathcal{T}^{\star\tau}(\mathcal{P}_2^{\tau}) \geq \mathcal{T}^{\star\tau}(\mathcal{P}_1^{\tau} \wedge \mathcal{P}_2^{\tau})$, $\mathcal{T}^{\star\pi}(\mathcal{P}_2^{\pi}) \leq \mathcal{T}^{\star\pi}(\mathcal{P}_1^{\pi} \vee \mathcal{P}_2^{\pi})$, $\mathcal{T}^{\star\sigma}(\mathcal{P}_2^{\sigma}) \leq \mathcal{T}^{\star\sigma}(\mathcal{P}_1^{\sigma} \vee \mathcal{P}_2^{\sigma})$. Hence,

$$\mathcal{T}^{\star\tau}(\mathcal{P}_1^{\tau} \wedge \mathcal{P}_2^{\tau}) \leq \mathcal{T}^{\star\tau}(\mathcal{P}_1^{\tau}) \wedge \mathcal{T}^{\star\tau}(\mathcal{P}_2^{\tau}),$$

$$\mathcal{T}^{\star\pi}(\mathcal{P}_1^{\pi} \wedge \mathcal{P}_2^{\pi}) \geq \mathcal{T}^{\star\pi}(\mathcal{P}_1^{\pi}) \vee \mathcal{T}^{\star\pi}(\mathcal{P}_2^{\pi}),$$

$$\mathcal{T}^{\star\sigma}(\mathcal{P}_1^{\sigma} \wedge \mathcal{P}_2^{\sigma}) \geq \mathcal{T}^{\star\sigma}(\mathcal{P}_1^{\sigma}) \vee \mathcal{T}^{\star\sigma}(\mathcal{P}_2^{\sigma}).$$

(⇐): Suppose that $(\mathcal{T}^{\star\tau}(\mathcal{P}_1^{\tau}) \wedge \mathcal{T}^{\star\tau}(\mathcal{P}_2^{\tau}))(\Xi) \geq r$, $(\mathcal{T}^{\star\pi}(\mathcal{P}_1^{\pi}) \vee \mathcal{T}^{\star\pi}(\mathcal{P}_2^{\pi}))(\Xi) \leq 1 - r$, $(\mathcal{T}^{\star\sigma}(\mathcal{P}_1^{\sigma}) \vee \mathcal{T}^{\star\sigma}(\mathcal{P}_2^{\sigma})(\Xi) \leq 1 - r$. Then, $\mathcal{T}^{\star\tau}(\mathcal{P}_1^{\tau})(\Xi) \geq r$, $\mathcal{T}^{\star\pi}(\mathcal{P}_1^{\pi})(\Xi) \leq 1 - r$, $\mathcal{T}^{\star\sigma}(\mathcal{P}_1^{\sigma})(\Xi) \leq 1 - r$ and $\mathcal{T}^{\star\tau}(\mathcal{P}_2^{\tau})(\Xi) \geq r$, $\mathcal{T}^{\star\pi}(\mathcal{P}_2^{\pi})(\Xi) \leq 1 - r$, $\mathcal{T}^{\star\sigma}(\mathcal{P}_2^{\sigma})(\Xi) \leq 1 - r$; that means $\mathcal{C}_{\mathcal{T}^{\tau\pi\sigma}}(\Xi^c, r) = \Xi^c \vee [\Xi^c]_r^{\star}(\mathcal{P}_1^{\tau\pi\sigma}) = \Xi^c$ and $\mathcal{C}_{\mathcal{T}^{\tau\pi\sigma}}(\Xi^c, r) = \Xi^c \vee [\Xi^c]_r^{\star}(\mathcal{P}_2^{\tau\pi\sigma}) = \Xi^c$. Thus, $[\Xi^c]_r^{\star}(\mathcal{P}_1^{\tau\pi\sigma}) \leq \Xi^c$ and $[\Xi^c]_r^{\star}(\mathcal{P}_2^{\tau\pi\sigma}) \leq \Xi^c$. So, $[\Xi^c]_r^{\star}(\mathcal{P}_1^{\tau\pi\sigma}) \vee [\Xi^c]_r^{\star}(\mathcal{P}_2^{\tau\pi\sigma}) \leq \Xi^c$. From Theorem 9(1), we have $[\Xi^c]_r^{\star}(\mathcal{P}_1^{\tau\pi\sigma} \wedge \mathcal{P}_2^{\tau\pi\sigma}) \leq \Xi^c$. Therefore, $\mathcal{T}^{\star\tau}(\mathcal{P}_1^{\tau} \wedge \mathcal{P}_2^{\tau})(\Xi) \geq r$, $\mathcal{T}^{\star\pi}(\mathcal{P}_1^{\pi} \vee \mathcal{P}_2^{\pi})(\Xi) \leq 1 - r$, $\mathcal{T}^{\star\sigma}(\mathcal{P}_1^{\sigma} \vee \mathcal{P}_2^{\sigma})(\Xi) \leq 1 - r$. This completes the proof. □

Definition 12. *Let* $(\pounds, \mathcal{T}^{\tau\pi\sigma})$ *be an svnts with* $\mathcal{P}^{\tau\pi\sigma}$ *an svn-primal on* £. *Then,* $\mathcal{T}^{\tau\pi\sigma}$ *is called single-valued neutrosophic primal open compatible with* $\mathcal{P}^{\tau\pi\sigma}$*, indicated by* $\mathcal{T}^{\tau\pi\sigma} \models \mathcal{P}^{\tau\pi\sigma}$*, if* $\forall$ $\Xi \in \xi^{\pounds}$, $y_{n,m,v} \in \Xi$ *and* $\Pi \in \xi^{\pounds}$ *with* $\mathcal{P}^{\tau}(\Pi) \geq r$, $\mathcal{P}^{\pi}(\Pi) \leq 1 - r$, $\mathcal{P}^{\sigma}(\Pi) \leq 1 - r$*, there exists* $\mathcal{A} \in \mathcal{Q}_{\mathcal{T}^{\tau\pi\sigma}}(y_{n,m,v}, r)$ *such that*

$$\tau_{\mathcal{A}}(z) + \tau_{\Xi}(z) - 1 \leq \tau_{\Pi}(z), \quad \pi_{\mathcal{A}}(z) + \pi_{\Xi}(z) - 1 > \pi_{\Pi}(z), \quad \sigma_{\mathcal{A}}(z) + \sigma_{\xi}(z) - 1 > \sigma_{\Pi}(z),$$

holds for every $z \in \pounds$*, then* $\mathcal{P}^{\tau}(\Xi) \geq r$, $\mathcal{P}^{\pi}(\Xi) \leq 1 - r$, $\mathcal{P}^{\sigma}(\Xi) \leq 1 - r$.

Definition 13. *Let* $\{\Theta_i : i \in \Gamma\} \sqsubseteq \xi^{\pounds}$ *such that* $\Theta_i q \Xi$, $\forall\, i \in \Gamma$ *and* $\Xi \in \xi^{\pounds}$. *Then,* $\{\Theta_i : i \in \Gamma\}$ *is called an r-single-valued neutrosophic quasi-cover (for short, r-svnq-cover) of* Ξ *iff,* $\forall\, z \in \pounds$,

$$\tau_{\Xi}(z) + \tau_{\bigvee_{i\in\Gamma}(\Theta_i)}(z) \geq 1, \quad \pi_{\Xi}(z) + \pi_{\bigvee_{i\in\Gamma}(\Theta_i)}(z) < 1, \quad \sigma_{\Xi}(z) + \sigma_{\bigvee_{i\in\Gamma}(\Theta_i)}(z) < 1.$$

Further, let $(\pounds, \mathcal{T}^{\tau\pi\sigma})$ be an *svnts*, for any $\mathcal{T}^{\tau}(\Theta_i) \geq r$, $\mathcal{T}^{\pi}(\Theta_i) \leq 1 - r$, $\mathcal{T}^{\sigma}(\Theta_i) \leq 1 - r$. Then, this *r-svnq-cover* will be called a single-valued neutrosophic quasi open-cover (for short, *svnqo-cover*) of Ξ.

Theorem 12. *Let* $(\pounds, \mathcal{T}^{\tau\pi\sigma})$ *be an* svnts *with* svn-primal $\mathcal{P}^{\tau\pi\sigma}$ *on* £. *Then, the following conditions are equivalent*

(1) $\mathcal{T}^{\tau\pi\sigma} \models \mathcal{P}^{\tau\pi\sigma}$.
(2) *If for each* $\Xi \in \xi^{\pounds}$ *has a svnqo-cover of* $\{\Theta_i : i \in \Gamma\}$ *such that* $\tau_{\mathcal{A}}(z) + \tau_{\Theta_i}(z) - 1 \leq \tau_{\Pi}(z)$ $\pi_{\mathcal{A}}(z) + \pi_{\Theta_i}(z) - 1 > \pi_{\Pi}(z)$, $\sigma_{\mathcal{A}}(z) + \sigma_{\Theta_i}(z) - 1 > \sigma_{\Pi}(z)$*, for every* $z \in \pounds$ *and for some* $\mathcal{T}^{\tau}(\Pi) \geq r$, $\mathcal{T}^{\pi}(\Pi) \leq 1 - r$, $\mathcal{T}^{\sigma}(\Pi) \leq 1 - r$*, then* $\mathcal{P}^{\tau}(\Xi) \geq r$, $\mathcal{P}^{\pi}(\Xi) \leq 1 - r$, $\mathcal{P}^{\sigma}(\Xi) \leq 1 - r$.
(3) *For any* $\Xi \in \xi^{\pounds}$, $\Xi \wedge \Xi_r^{\star} = \overline{0}$ *implies* $\mathcal{P}^{\tau}(\Xi) \geq r$, $\mathcal{P}^{\pi}(\Xi) \leq 1 - r$, $\mathcal{P}^{\sigma}(\Xi) \leq 1 - r$.

(4) *For any* $\Xi \in \xi^{\pounds}$, $\mathcal{P}^{\tau}(\widehat{\Xi}) \geq r$, $\mathcal{P}^{\pi}(\widehat{\Xi}) \leq 1-r$, $\mathcal{P}^{\sigma}(\widehat{\Xi}) \leq 1-r$, *where* $\widehat{\Xi} = \bigvee y_{n,m,v}$ *such that* $y_{n,m,v} \in \Xi$ *but* $y_{n,m,v} \notin \Xi^{\star}_r$.

(5) *For all* $\mathcal{T}^{\star\tau}(\Xi^c) \geq r$, $\mathcal{T}^{\star\pi}(\Xi^c) \leq 1-r$, $\mathcal{T}^{\star\sigma}(\Xi^c) \leq 1-r$, *we have* $\mathcal{P}^{\tau}(\widehat{\Xi}) \geq r$, $\mathcal{P}^{\pi}(\widehat{\Xi}) \leq 1-r$, $\mathcal{P}^{\sigma}(\widehat{\Xi}) \leq 1-r$.

(6) *For each* $\Xi \in \xi^{\pounds}$, *if* Ξ *contains no* $\Theta \neq \overline{0}$ *with* $\Theta \leq \Theta^{\star}_r$, *then* $\mathcal{P}^{\tau}(\Xi) \geq r$, $\mathcal{P}^{\pi}(\Xi) \leq 1-r$, $\mathcal{P}^{\sigma}(\Xi) \leq 1-r$.

Proof. $1 \Rightarrow 2$: Let $\{\Theta_i : i \in \Gamma\}$ be an *svnqo-cover* of $\Xi \in \xi^{\pounds}$ such that, $\forall\, i \in \Gamma$, $\tau_{\mathcal{A}}(z) + \tau_{\Theta_i}(z) - 1 \leq \tau_{\Pi}(z)$, $\pi_{\mathcal{A}}(z) + \pi_{\Theta_i}(z) - 1 > \pi_{\Pi}(z)$, $\sigma_{\mathcal{A}}(z) + \sigma_{\Theta_i}(z) - 1 > \sigma_{\Pi}(z)$, for any $z \in \pounds$ and for some $\mathcal{P}^{\tau}(\Xi) \geq r$, $\mathcal{P}^{\pi}(\Xi) \leq 1-r$, $\mathcal{P}^{\sigma}(\Xi) \leq 1-r$. Thus, as $\{\Theta_i : i \in \Gamma\}$ is an *svnqo-cover* of Ξ, for each $y_{n,m,v} \in \Xi$, there exists at least one $\Theta_{i\circ}$ such that $y_{n,m,v} q \Theta_{i\circ}$ and for each $z \in \pounds$, $\tau_{\mathcal{A}}(z) + \tau_{\Theta_{i\circ}}(z) - 1 \leq \tau_{\Pi}(z)$, $\pi_{\mathcal{A}}(z) + \pi_{\Theta_{i\circ}}(z) - 1 > \pi_{\Pi}(z)$, $\sigma_{\mathcal{A}}(z) + \sigma_{\Theta_{i\circ}}(z) - 1 > \sigma_{\Pi}(z)$ for some $\mathcal{P}^{\sigma}(\Xi) \leq 1-r$, $\mathcal{T}^{\tau}(\Pi) \geq r$, $\mathcal{T}^{\pi}(\Pi) \leq 1-r$, $\mathcal{T}^{\sigma}(\Pi) \leq 1-r$. Significantly, $\Theta_{i\circ} \in \mathcal{Q}_{\mathcal{T}\tau\pi\sigma}(y_{n,m,v}, r)$. From (1), we obtain $\mathcal{P}^{\tau}(\Xi) \geq r$, $\mathcal{P}^{\pi}(\Xi) \leq 1-r$, $\mathcal{P}^{\sigma}(\Xi) \leq 1-r$.

$2 \Rightarrow 1$: It is clear from this that the family of $\{\Theta_i : i \in \Gamma\}$ contains at least one $\Theta_{i\circ} \in \mathcal{Q}_{\mathcal{T}\tau\pi\sigma}(y_{n,m,v}, r)$, such that every *svn-point* of Ξ constitutes a *svnqo-cover* of Ξ.

$1 \Rightarrow 3$: Let $\Xi \wedge \Xi^{\star}_r = \overline{0}$, for each $z \in \xi$, $y_{n,m,v} \in \Xi$ implies $y_{n,m,v} \notin \Xi^{\star}_r$. Then, there exists $\mathcal{A} \in \mathcal{Q}_{\mathcal{T}\tau\pi\sigma}(y_{n,m,v}, r)$ and $\mathcal{P}^{\tau}(\Pi) \geq r$, $\mathcal{P}^{\pi}(\Pi) \leq 1-r$, $\mathcal{P}^{\sigma}(\Pi) \leq 1-r$, such that for all $z \in \pounds$

$$\tau_{\mathcal{A}}(z) + \tau_{\Xi}(z) - 1 \leq \tau_{\Pi}(z), \quad \pi_{\mathcal{A}}(z) + \pi_{\Xi}(x) - 1 > \pi_{\Pi}(z), \quad \sigma_{\mathcal{A}}(x) + \sigma_{\Xi}(z) - 1 > \sigma_{\Pi}(x).$$

Since $\mathcal{A} \in \mathcal{Q}_{\mathcal{T}\tau\pi\sigma}(y_{n,m,v}, r)$, from (1), we have $\mathcal{P}^{\tau}(\Xi) \geq r$, $\mathcal{P}^{\pi}(\Xi) \leq 1-r$, $\mathcal{P}^{\sigma}(\Xi) \leq 1-r$.

$3 \Rightarrow 1$: For each $y_{n,m,v} \in \Xi$, there exists an $\mathcal{A} \in \mathcal{Q}_{\mathcal{T}\tau\pi\sigma}(y_{n,m,v}, r)$ such that, for any $z \in \pounds$,

$$\tau_{\mathcal{A}}(z) + \tau_{\Xi}(z) - 1 \leq \tau_{\Pi}(z), \quad \pi_{\mathcal{A}}(z) + \pi_{\Xi}(z) - 1 > \pi_{\Pi}(z), \quad \sigma_{\mathcal{A}}(z) + \sigma_{\Xi}(z) - 1 > \sigma_{\Pi}(z),$$

for some $\mathcal{P}^{\tau}(\Pi) \geq r$, $\mathcal{P}^{\pi}(\Pi) \leq 1-r$, $\mathcal{P}^{\sigma}(\Pi) \leq 1-r$, implies $y_{n,m,v} \notin \Xi^{\star}_r$. Firstly, there are two cases: either $\Xi^{\star}_r = \overline{0}$ or $\Xi^{\star}_r \neq \overline{0}$ but $n > \tau_{\Xi^{\star}_r}(z) \neq \overline{0}$, $m \leq \pi_{\Xi^{\star}_r}(z) \neq \overline{0}$, $v \leq \sigma_{\Xi^{\star}_r}(z) \neq \overline{0}$. Assume, if possible, $y_{n.m.v} \in \Xi$ such that $n > \tau_{\Xi^{\star}_r}(z) \neq \overline{0}$, $m \leq \pi_{\Xi^{\star}_r}(z) \neq \overline{0}$, $v \leq \sigma_{\Xi^{\star}_r}(z) \neq \overline{0}$. Let $n_1 = \tau_{\Xi^{\star}_r}(z)$, $m_1 = \pi_{\Xi^{\star}_r}(z)$, $v_1 = \sigma_{\Xi^{\star}_r}(z)$. Then, $y_{n_1,m_1,v_1} \in \Xi^{\star}_r(z)$. Secondly, $y_{n_1,m_1,v_1} \in \Xi$. Thus, for all $\mathcal{B} \in \mathcal{Q}_{\mathcal{T}\tau\pi\sigma}(y_{n,m,v}, r)$, $\mathcal{P}^{\tau}(\Pi) \geq r$, $\mathcal{P}^{\pi}(\Pi) \leq 1-r$, $\mathcal{P}^{\sigma}(\Pi) \leq 1-r$, there is at least one $z \in \pounds$ such that

$$\tau_{\mathcal{B}}(z) + \tau_{\Xi}(z) - 1 > \tau_{\Pi}(z), \quad \pi_{\mathcal{B}}(z) + \pi_{\Xi}(z) - 1 \leq \pi_{\Pi}(z), \quad \sigma_{\mathcal{B}}(z) + \sigma_{\Xi}(z) - 1 \leq \sigma_{\Pi}(z).$$

Since $y_{n_1,m_1,v_1} \in \Xi$, this contradicts the assumption for each *svn-point* of Ξ. So, $\Xi^{\star}_r = \overline{0}$. That means $y_{n,m,v} \in \Xi$ implies $y_{n,m,v} \notin \Xi^{\star}_r$. Now, this is true for each $\Xi \in \xi^{\pounds}$. So, $\Xi \vee \Xi^{\star}_r = \overline{0}$. Thus, by (3), we obtain $\mathcal{P}^{\tau}(\Xi) \geq r$, $\mathcal{P}^{\pi}(\Xi) \leq 1-r$, $\mathcal{P}^{\sigma}(\Xi) \leq 1-r$ implies $\mathcal{T}^{\tau\pi\sigma} \models \mathcal{P}^{\tau\pi\sigma}$.

$3 \Rightarrow 4$: Let $y_{n,m,v} \in \widehat{\Xi}$. Then, $y_{n,m,v} \in \Xi$ but $y_{n,m,v} \notin \Xi^{\star}_r$. So, there exists an $\mathcal{A} \in \mathcal{Q}_{\mathcal{T}\tau\pi\sigma}(y_{n,m,v}, r)$ such that $\forall\, z \in \pounds$,

$$\tau_{\mathcal{A}}(z) + \tau_{\Xi}(z) - 1 \leq \tau_{\Pi}(z), \quad \pi_{\mathcal{A}}(z) + \pi_{\Xi}(z) - 1 > \pi_{\Pi}(z), \quad \sigma_{\mathcal{A}}(z) + \sigma_{\Xi}(z) - 1 > \sigma_{\Pi}(z),$$

for some $\mathcal{P}^{\tau}(\Pi) \geq r$, $\mathcal{P}^{\pi}(\Pi) \leq 1-r$, $\mathcal{P}^{\sigma}(\Pi) \leq 1-r$. Since $\widehat{\Xi} \leq \Xi$,

$$\tau_{\mathcal{A}}(z) + \tau_{\widehat{\Xi}}(z) - 1 \leq \tau_{\Pi}(z), \quad \pi_{\mathcal{A}}(z) + \pi_{\widehat{\Xi}}(z) - 1 > \pi_{\Pi}(z), \quad \sigma_{\mathcal{A}}(z) + \sigma_{\widehat{\Xi}}(z) - 1 > \sigma_{\Pi}(z),$$

for some $\mathcal{P}^{\tau}(\Pi) \geq r$, $\mathcal{P}^{\pi}(\Pi) \leq 1-r$, $\mathcal{P}^{\sigma}(\Pi) \leq 1-r$. Thus, $y_{n,m,v} \notin \widehat{\Xi^{\star}_r}$ implies that $\widehat{\Xi^{\star}_r} = \overline{0}$ or $\widehat{\Xi^{\star}_r} \neq \overline{0}$ but $n > \tau_{\widehat{\Xi^{\star}_r}}(z)$, $m \leq \pi_{\widehat{\Xi^{\star}_r}}(z)$, $v \leq \sigma_{\widehat{\Xi^{\star}_r}}(z)$. Let $y_{s_1,m_1,v_1} \in$

svn-point($\pounds$) such that $n_1 \leq \tau_{\widehat{\Xi^\star_r}}(z) < n$, $m_1 > \pi_{\widehat{\Xi^\star_r}}(z) \geq m$, $v_1 > \sigma_{\widehat{\Xi^\star_r}}(z) \geq v$; this means $y_{n_1,m_1,v_1} \in \widehat{\Xi^\star_r}$. Then, $\forall\, \mathcal{B} \in \mathcal{Q}_{\mathcal{T}\tau\pi\sigma}(y_{n_1,m_1,v_1}, r)$ and for every $\mathcal{P}^\tau(\Pi) \geq r$, $\mathcal{P}^\pi(\Pi) \leq 1-r$, $\mathcal{P}^\sigma(\Pi) \leq 1-r$, there is at least one $z \in \pounds$ such that

$$\tau_{\mathcal{B}}(z) + \tau_{\widehat{\Xi}}(z) - 1 > \tau_{\Pi}(z), \quad \pi_{\mathcal{B}}(z) + \pi_{\widehat{\Xi}}(z) - 1 \leq \pi_{\Pi}(z), \quad \sigma_{\mathcal{B}}(z) + \sigma_{\widehat{\Xi}}(z) - 1 \leq \sigma_{\Pi}(z).$$

Since $\widehat{\Xi} \leq \Xi$, then for any $\mathcal{B} \in \mathcal{Q}_{\mathcal{T}\tau\pi\sigma}(y_{n_1,m_1,v_1}, r)$ and $\mathcal{P}^\tau(\Pi) \geq r$, $\mathcal{P}^\pi(\Pi) \leq 1-r$, $\mathcal{P}^\sigma(\Pi) \leq 1-r$, there is at least one $z \in \pounds$ such that

$$\tau_{\mathcal{B}}(z) + \tau_{\Xi}(z) - 1 > \tau_{\Pi}(z), \quad \pi_{\mathcal{B}}(z) + \pi_{\Xi}(z) - 1 \leq \pi_{\Pi}(z), \quad \sigma_{\mathcal{B}}(z) + \sigma_{\Xi}(z) - 1 \leq \sigma_{\Pi}(z).$$

This implies $y_{n_1,m_1,v_1} \in \Xi^\star_r$. But $n_1 < n$, $m_1 \geq m$, $v_1 \geq v$ and $y_{n,m,v} \in \widehat{\Xi}$ implies $y_{n_1,m_1,v_1} \in \widehat{\Xi}$ and hence $y_{n_1,m_1,v_1} \notin \widehat{\Xi^\star_r}$. This is a contradiction. Thus, $\widehat{\Xi^\star_r} = \overline{0}$, so that $y_{n,m,v} \in \widehat{\Xi}$ implies $y_{n,m,v} \notin \widehat{\Xi^\star_r}$ with $\widehat{\Xi^\star_r} = \overline{0}$. Thus, $\widehat{\Xi} \wedge \widehat{\Xi^\star_r} = \overline{0}$ for every $\Xi \in \zeta^{\pounds}$. Hence, by (3), $\mathcal{P}^\tau(\widehat{\Xi}) \geq r$, $\mathcal{P}^\pi(\widehat{\Xi}) \leq 1-r$, $\mathcal{P}^\sigma(\widehat{\Xi}) \leq 1-r$.

4 $\Rightarrow$ 5: The same method as the proof of 3 $\Rightarrow$ 4.

4 $\Rightarrow$ 6: Let $\Xi \in \zeta^{\pounds}$, Ξ contains no $\Theta \neq \overline{0}$ with $\Theta \leq \Theta^\star_r$. Then, $\forall\, \Xi \in \zeta^{\pounds}$, $\Xi = \widehat{\Xi} \vee (\Xi \wedge \Xi^\star_r)$. By Theorem 4(5), we have $\Xi^\star_r = [\widehat{\Xi} \vee (\Xi \wedge \Xi^\star_r)]^\star_r = \widehat{\Xi^\star_r} \vee [\Xi \wedge \Xi^\star_r]^\star_r$. Now, by (4), we obtain $\mathcal{P}^\tau(\widehat{\Xi}) \geq r$, $\mathcal{P}^\pi(\widehat{\Xi}) \leq 1-r$, $\mathcal{P}^\sigma(\widehat{\Xi}) \leq 1-r$; then, $\widehat{\Xi^\star_r} = \overline{0}$. Thus, $[\Xi \wedge \Xi^\star_r]^\star_r = \Xi^\star_r$ but $\Xi \wedge \Xi^\star_r \leq \Xi^\star_r$, then $\Xi \wedge \Xi^\star_r \leq (\Xi \wedge \Xi^\star_r)^\star_r$. This contradicts the hypothesis if $\overline{0} \neq \Theta \leq \Xi$ with $\Theta \leq \Theta^\star_r$. Hence, $\Xi \wedge \Xi^\star_r = \overline{0}$, so, $\Xi = \widehat{\Xi}$ by (4), we obtain that $\mathcal{P}^\tau(\Xi) \geq r$, $\mathcal{P}^\pi(\Xi) \leq 1-r$, $\mathcal{P}^\sigma(\Xi) \leq 1-r$.

6 $\Rightarrow$ 4: Since $\forall\, \Xi \in \zeta^{\pounds}$, $\Xi \wedge \Xi^\star_r = \overline{0}$. Hence, by (6), as Ξ contains no non-empty single-valued neutrosophic subset Θ with $\Theta \leq \Theta^\star_r$, $\mathcal{P}^\tau(\Xi) \geq r$, $\mathcal{P}^\pi(\Xi) \leq 1-r$, $\mathcal{P}^\sigma(\Xi) \leq 1-r$.

5 $\Rightarrow$ 1: For every $\Xi \in \zeta^{\pounds}$, $y_{n,m,v} \in \Xi$, there exists $\mathcal{A} \in \mathcal{Q}_{\mathcal{T}\tau\pi\sigma}(y_{n,m,v}, r)$ such that

$$\tau_{\mathcal{A}}(z) + \tau_{\Xi}(z) - 1 \leq \tau_{\Pi}(z), \quad \pi_{\mathcal{A}}(z) + \pi_{\Xi}(z) - 1 > \pi_{\Pi}(z), \quad \sigma_{\mathcal{A}}(z) + \sigma_{\xi}(z) - 1 > \sigma_{\Pi}(z),$$

holds for every $z \in \pounds$ and for some $\mathcal{P}^\tau(\Xi) \geq r$, $\mathcal{P}^\pi(\Xi) \leq 1-r$, $\mathcal{P}^\sigma(\Xi) \leq 1-r$. This implies $y_{n,m,v} \notin \Xi^\star_r$. Let $\Theta = \Xi \vee \Xi^\star_r$. Then, $\Theta^\star_r = (\Xi \vee \Xi^\star_r)^\star_r = \Xi^\star_r \vee (\Xi^\star_r)^\star_r = \Xi^\star_r$ by Theorem 4(4). So, $C^\star_{\mathcal{T}\tau\pi\sigma}(\Theta, r) = \Theta \vee \Theta^\star_r = \Theta$. That means $\mathcal{T}^{\star\tau}(\Theta^c) \geq r$, $\mathcal{T}^{\star\pi}(\Theta^c) \leq 1-r$, $\mathcal{T}^{\star\sigma}(\Theta^c) \leq 1-r$. Thus, by (5), we obtain that $\mathcal{P}^\tau(\Theta) \geq r$, $\mathcal{P}^\pi(\Theta) \leq 1-r$, $\mathcal{P}^\sigma(\Theta) \leq 1-r$.

Again, For any $y_{s,m,v} \in$ *svn-point*($\pounds$), $y_{s,m,v} \notin \widehat{\Theta^\star_r}$ implies $y_{s,m,v} \in \Theta$ but $y_{s,m,v} \notin \Theta^\star_r = \Xi^\star_r$. So, $\Theta = \Xi \vee \Xi^\star_r$, $y_{s,m,v} \in \Xi$. Now, by the hypothesis about Ξ, we have for every $y_{s,m,v} \in \Xi^\star_r$. So, $\widehat{\Theta} = \Xi$. Hence, $\mathcal{P}^\tau(\Theta) \geq r$, $\mathcal{P}^\pi(\Theta) \leq 1-r$, $\mathcal{P}^\sigma(\Theta) \leq 1-r$. Thus, $\mathcal{T}^{\tau\pi\sigma} \models \mathcal{P}^{\tau\pi\sigma}$. □

Theorem 13. *Let $(\pounds, \mathcal{T}^{\tau\pi\sigma})$ be an* svnts *with* svn-primal *$\mathcal{P}^{\tau\pi\sigma}$ on $\pounds$. Then, the following cases are equivalent and implied $\mathcal{T}^{\tau\pi\sigma} \models \mathcal{P}^{\tau\pi\sigma}$.*

(1) *For each $\Xi \in \zeta^{\pounds}$, $\Xi \wedge \Xi^\star_r = \overline{0}$ implies $\Xi^\star_r = \overline{0}$.*

(2) *For each $\Xi \in \zeta^{\pounds}$, $\widehat{\zeta^\star_r} = \overline{0}$.*

(3) *For each $\Xi \in \zeta^{\pounds}$, $\Xi \wedge \Xi^\star_r = \Xi^\star_r$.*

Proof. The proof follows a similar line of reasoning to that of Theorem 12. □

5. Conclusions

In this paper, first, we investigated the complex area of stratification of svn grills and determined some of their fundamental features. The links between svn grills and svn-primals were investigated. We also introduced and explored the concept of svn-primal open local functions in the context of Šostak's sense. By extending the notions of svn sets and related topological structures, we have presented a novel approach to understanding the properties and relationships within this unique framework.

Our investigation began by defining svn-sets and their corresponding notions. Building upon these fundamental definitions, we introduced svnts and explored various operations and properties within these spaces, such as the neutrosophic closure and interior. A central contribution of this work has been the introduction and exploration of svn-primals and their associated operators. We have provided several equivalent conditions characterizing the compatibility of svnts with neutrosophic primals. Additionally, we discussed the properties of primal open local functions, their relationship with svnts, and the induced operators.

In conclusion, the results presented in this paper contribute to the growing field of neutrosophic topology by offering a deeper understanding of svn structures in Šostak's sense. The properties and correlations investigated here establish the framework for further studies in this field, opening options for future investigations and applications of these innovative notions in various fields.

In terms of related and future research directions, it is of great interest to investigate the connections between our findings and the advancements in the field of neural networks (Gu and Sheng [36]; Gu et al. [37]; Deng et al. [38]; Gu et al. [39]). Furthermore, the possible connections to multidimensional systems and signal processing need further investigation, as illustrated by Wang et al. [40] and Xiong et al. [41].

By bridging the gap between svn structures and related domains, we might promote collaboration across disciplines and discover new applications for our findings. This not only enriches the discipline of neutrosophic topology, but also benefits the larger scientific community by providing new insights and fresh approaches to difficult problems.

For forthcoming papers

The theory can be extended in the following normal methods.

1—Basic concepts of neutrosophic metric topological spaces can be studied using the notion of svn-primal present in this article;

2—Examine the connected, separation axioms and soft closure spaces in the context of svn-primals.

Author Contributions: F.A., Writing—review & editing, Writing—original draft; H.A., Writing—review & editing, Writing—original draft, Funding acquisition; Y.S., Writing—review & editing, Writing—original draft; F.S., Writing—review & editing. All authors have read and agreed to the published version of the manuscript.

Funding: The work is supported by King Saud University (Supporting Project number RSPD2024R860), Riyadh, Saudi Arabia).

Data Availability Statement: Data are contained within the article.

Acknowledgments: The authors would like to extend their sincere appreciation to Supporting Project number (RSPD2024R860) King Saud University, Riyadh, Saudi Arabia.

Conflicts of Interest: The authors declare no conflicts of interest.

Abbreviations

The following abbreviations are used in this manuscript:

n-set	neutrosophic set
svn-set	single-valued neutrosophic set
svnits	single-valued neutrosophic ideals
svnts	single-valued neutrosophic topological spaces
svngts	single-valued neutrosophic grill topological spaces
svnpts	single-valued neutrosophic primal topological spaces
svnqo-cover	single-valued neutrosophic quasi open-cover
svns-primal	single-valued neutrosophic primal
$\mathcal{T}^{\tau\pi\sigma} \models \mathcal{P}^{\tau\pi\sigma}$	single-valued neutrosophic primal open compatible
svn-point	single-valued neutrosophic point

References

1. Willard, S. *General Topology*; Courier Corporation: North Chelmsford, MA, USA, 2012.
2. Kuratowski, K. *Topology: Volume I*; Elsevier: Amsterdam, The Netherlands, 2014.
3. Abbas, S.E.; Hebeshi, M.A. Construction of stratified L-fuzzy topological structures. *Appl. Math. Lett.* **2011**, *24*, 1063–1066. [CrossRef]
4. Chattopadhyay, K.C.; Thron, W.J. Extensions of closure spaces. *Can. J. Math.* **1977**, *29*, 1277–1286. [CrossRef]
5. Thron, W.J. Proximity structures and grills. *Math. Ann.* **1973**, *206*, 35–62. [CrossRef]
6. Roy, B.; Mukherjee M.N.; Ghosh, S.K. On a new operator based on a grill and its associated topology. *Arab. J. Math.* **2008**, *14*, 21–32.
7. Roy, B.; Mukherjee, M.N. On a typical topology induced by a grill. *Soochow J. Math.* **2007**, *33*, 771–786.
8. Roy, B.; Mukherjee, M.N. Concerning topologies induced by principal grills. *Analele Stiint. Ale Univ. Mat.* **2009**, *55*, 285–294.
9. Roy, B.; Mukherjee, M.N. On a type of compactness via grills. *Mat. Vesn.* **2007**, *59*, 113–120.
10. Thangamariappan, R.; Renukadevi, V. Topology generated by cluster systems. *Math. Vesn.* **2015**, *67*, 174–184.
11. Azzam, A.A.; Hussein, S.S.; Osman, H.S. Compactness of topological spaces with grills. *Ital. J. Pure Appl. Math.* **2020**, *44*, 198–207.
12. Talabeigi, A. On the Tychonoff's type theorem via grills. *Bull. Iran. Math. Soc.* **2016**, *42*, 37–41.
13. Boroojerdian, N.; Talabeigi, A. One-point λ-compactification via grills. *Iran. J. Sci. Technol. Trans. Sci.* **2017**, *41*, 909–912. [CrossRef]
14. Sulimana, S.S.; Esmaeela, R.B. On some topological concepts via grill. *Int. J. Nonlinear Anal. Appl.* **2022**, *13*, 3765–3772. [CrossRef]
15. Azzam, A.A. Grill Nano topological spaces with grill Nano generalized closed sets. *J. Egypt. Math. Soc.* **2017**, *25*, 164–166. [CrossRef]
16. Hosny, R.A. δ-sets with grill. *Int. Math. Forum* **2012**, *7*, 2107–2113.
17. Janković, D.; Hamlett, T.R. New topologies from old via ideals. *Am. Math. Mon.* **1990**, *97*, 295–310. [CrossRef]
18. Smarandache, F. *A Unifying Field in Logics: Neutrosophic Logic. Neutrosophy, Neutrosophic Set, Neutrosophic Probability and Statistics*, 6th ed.; InfoLearnQuest: Ann Arbor, MI, USA, 2007. Available online: https://philarchive.org/rec/SMAAUF-2 (accessed on 10 February 2019).
19. Salama, A.A.; Alblowi, S.A. Neutrosophic set and neutrosophic topological spaces. *IOSR J. Math.* **2012**, *3*, 31–35. [CrossRef]
20. Wang, H.; Smarandache, F.; Zhang, Y.Q.; Sunderraman, R. Single valued neutrosophic sets. *Multispace Multistruct.* **2010**, *4*, 410–413.
21. Rodrigo, P.A.; Maheswari, S. Neutrosophic gsα*-Open and Closed Maps in Neutrosophic Topological Spaces. *Neutrosophic Syst. Appl.* **2023**, *8*, 42–49. [CrossRef]
22. Ye, J. Single valued neutrosophic cross-entropy for multicriteria decision making problems. *Appl. Math. Modell.* **2014**, *38*, 1–3. [CrossRef]
23. Dhar, R. Compactness and Neutrosophic Topological Space via Grills. *Neutrosophic Syst. Appl.* **2023**, *2*, 1–7. [CrossRef]
24. Dey, S.; Ray, G.C. Separation Axioms in Neutrosophic Topological Spaces. *Neutrosophic Syst. Appl.* **2023**,*2*, 38–54. [CrossRef]
25. Alsharari, F.; Saber, Y.M.; Alohali, H.; Alqahtani, M.H.; Ebodey, M.; Elmasry, T.; Alsharif, J.; Soliman, A.F.; Smarandache, F.; Sikander, F. On stratified single-valued soft topogenous structures. *Heliyon* **2024**, *10*, e27926. [CrossRef]
26. Saber, Y.M.; Alohali, H.; Elmasry, T.; Smarandache, F. On single-valued neutrosophic soft uniform spaces. *AIMS Math.* **2024**, *9*, 412–439. [CrossRef]
27. Saber, Y.M.; Alsharari, F.; Smarandache, F. On Single-valued neutrosophic ideals in Šostak sense. *Symmetry* **2020**, *12*, 193. [CrossRef]
28. Saber, Y.M.; Alsharari, F.; Smarandache, F.; Abdel-Sattar, A. Connectedness and stratification of single-valued neutrosophic topological spaces. *Symmetry* **2020**, *12*, 1464. [CrossRef]
29. Ye, J.; Cui, W. Neutrosophic Compound Orthogonal Neural Network and Its Applications in Neutrosophic Function Approximation. *Symmetry* **2019**, *11*, 147. [CrossRef]
30. Shao, S.; Zhang, X.; Li, Y.; Bo, C. Probabilistic Single-Valued (Interval) Neutrosophic Hesitant Fuzzy Set and Its Application in Multi-Attribute Decision Making. *Symmetry* **2018**, *10*, 419. [CrossRef]

31. Rıdvan, S.; Ahmet, K. Subsethood measure for single valued neutrosophic sets. *J. Intell. Fuzzy Syst.* **2015**, *29*, 525–530.
32. Das, S.; Roy, B.K.; Kar, M.B.; Kar, S.; Pamučar, D. Neutrosophic fuzzy set and its application in decision making. *J. Ambient. Intell. Humaniz. Comput.* **2020**, *11*, 5017–5029. [CrossRef]
33. Yang, H.L.; Guo, Z.L.; Liao, X. On single valued neutrosophic relations. *J. Intell. Fuzzy Syst.* **2016**, *30*, 1045–1056. [CrossRef]
34. Ye, J.A. multicriteria decision-making method using aggregation operators for simplified neutrosophic sets. *J. Intell. Fuzzy Syst.* **2014**, *26*, 2450–2466. [CrossRef]
35. Acharjee, S.; Özkoç, M.; Issaka, F.Y. Primal topological spaces. *arXiv* **2022**, arXiv:2209.12676.
36. Gu, B.; Sheng, V.S. A robust regularization path algorithm for v support vector classification. *IEEE. Trans. Neural. Netw. Learn. Syst.* **2017**, *28*, 1241–1248. [CrossRef] [PubMed]
37. Gu, B.; Sun, X.; Sheng, V.S. Structural minimax probability machine. *IEEE. Trans. Neural. Netw. Learn. Syst.* **2017**, *28*, 1646–1656. [CrossRef] [PubMed]
38. Deng, W.; Zhao, H.M.; Yang, X.H.; Xiong, J.X.; Sun, M.; Li, B. Study on an improved adaptive PSO algorithm for solving multi-objective gate assignment. *Appl. Soft. Comput.* **2017**, *59*, 288–302. [CrossRef]
39. Gu, B.; Sheng, V.S.; Tay, K.Y.; Romano, W.; Li, S. Incremental support vector learning for ordinal regression. *IEEE. Trans. Neural. Netw. Learn. Syst.* **2015**, *26*, 1403–1416. [CrossRef] [PubMed]
40. Wang, B.; Gu, X.; Ma, L.; Yan, S. Temperature error correction based on BP neural network in meteorological WSN. *Int. J. Sens. Netw.* **2017**, *23*, 265–278. [CrossRef]
41. Xiong, L.; Xu, Z.; Shi, Y.Q. An integer wavelet transform-based scheme for reversible data hiding in encrypted images. *Multidim. Syst. Sign. Process.* **2018**, *29*, 1191–1202. [CrossRef]

symmetry

MDPI

Article

Bipolar Fuzzy Supra Topology via (Q-) Neighborhood and Its Application in Data Mining Process

Banu Pazar Varol * and Hami Malkoç

Department of Mathematics, Kocaeli University, Umuttepe Campus, 41001 Kocaeli, Turkey; hami.malkoc.4161@gmail.com
* Correspondence: banupazar@kocaeli.edu.tr

Abstract: The aim of this study is to provide neighborhood structures in bipolar fuzzy supra topological space and to show the applicability of bipolar fuzzy supra topology to the medical diagnosis problem. Firstly, we give some properties related to bipolar fuzzy points and their neighborhood structure in bipolar fuzzy supra topological spaces. Then, we consider another important structure, "quasi-coincident", in the case of bipolar fuzzy points and bipolar fuzzy sets. Then, we introduce the corresponding neighborhood structure called "Q-neighborhood system" by using the quasi-coincident relations. Furthermore, we also investigate the characterization of bipolar fuzzy supra topological space in terms of quasi-neighborhoods. Finally, we present a new method to solve medical diagnosis problems by using the bipolar fuzzy score function.

Keywords: bipolar fuzzy set; bipolar fuzzy point; bipolar fuzzy supra topology; bipolar fuzzy supra neighborhood; bipolar fuzzy supra Q-neighborhood

1. Introduction

Throughout the history of humanity, mankind has put forward various disciplines to produce solutions to problems. Over time, these disciplines have been divided into sub-disciplines by being handled through different aspects. Mathematics is one of the oldest disciplines that has shared this fate. Mathematics is separated into many sub-disciplines and has been used effectively to find solutions in different disciplines such as engineering, medicine, and the humanities, especially through the classical set theory approach. However, classical set theory is insufficient to produce an effective solution to all problems encountered.

The notion of fuzzy sets was given by Zadeh [1] in 1965. The theory of fuzzy sets is a generalization of classical set theory; fuzzy sets grade elements as belonging to a set. A fuzzy set A defined on the universal set U can be denoted as $A = \{< u, \mu_A(u) > | u \in U\}$. Here μ_A is a function of the form $\mu_A : U \to [0,1]$ and $\mu_A(u)$ is called the membership degree of an arbitrary element $u \in U$.

Intuitionistic fuzzy sets [2] were defined by adding the degree of non-membership to fuzzy sets. Thus, this concept helps solve broader, real-life problems. The intuitionistic fuzzy set considers membership and non-membership degrees during analysis. For instance, in the fuzzy set, the degree of sweetness is given in the interval [0, 1], while in an intuitionistic fuzzy set, the degree of sweetness ($\mu_A : U \to [0,1]$) and the degree of non-sweetness ($\nu_A : U \to [0,1]$) are added to handle more general problems. In intuitionistic fuzzy sets, we have $\mu_A(u) + \nu_A(u) \leq 1$. Suppose that $\mu_A(u) = 0.6$ and $\nu_A(u) = 0.5$, we obtain $0.6 + 0.5 \nleq 1$, but $(0.6)^2 + (0.5)^2 \leq 1$. We could not solve this kind of problem in an intuitionistic fuzzy set. Therefore, Pythagorean fuzzy sets [3] were defined, which are more general than intuitionistic fuzzy sets because of their ability to model using incoherent data. These sets are characterized by the condition that the sum of the squares of membership and non-membership grades is less than or equal to 1. Thus, the sum of membership and non-membership grades can exceed 1. Table 1 summarizes the advantages of these structures. By continuing the generalizations of fuzzy sets (neutrosophic fuzzy sets [4], picture fuzzy sets [5], spherical fuzzy sets [6], Pythagorean fuzzy sets [3]), the definition of bipolar fuzzy set was given by Zhang [7]. Bipolar-valued fuzzy sets are an extension of fuzzy sets with bipolarity.

Table 1. Some fuzzy models.

Fuzzy Models	Advantages
Fuzzy set [1]	It can study with imprecise data. $\mu_A(u)$
Intuitionistic fuzzy set [2]	It includes membership and nonmembership values. $\mu_A(u) + \nu_A(u) \leq 1$
Pythagorean fuzzy set [3]	It is suitable when the sum of membership and the nonmembership grade is more than one. $(\mu_A(u))^2 + (\nu_A(u))^2 \leq 1$
Bipolar fuzzy set [8]	It is appropriate the positive and negative aspects of a problem. $\mu_A^+ : U \to [0,1]$ and $\mu_A^- : U \to [-1,0]$

W.R. Zhang [7,9,10] extended the idea of a fuzzy set by introducing the concept of a bipolar fuzzy set. Bipolarity refers to the positive and negative facets of a problem. It is suitable for information containing a feature as well as its opposite, such as sourness and sweetness, competition and cooperation, happiness and grief. Although intuitionistic fuzzy sets and bipolar fuzzy sets appear parallel to each other, they are distinct sets. In comparison, we obtain $\mu_A^+(u) = \mu_A(u)$ and $\mu_A^-(u) = -\nu_A(u)$, which look like similar to each other. However, in bipolar fuzzy sets, the positive membership degree ($\mu_A^+(u)$) of a section shows that the section fairly fulfills the subject and the negative membership degree ($\mu_A^-(u)$) of a section represents that the section fairly fulfills the implicit counter property. In intuitionistic fuzzy sets, the membership degree $\mu_A(u)$ represents the extent to which the element u satisfies property A, while the membership degree $\nu_A(u)$ signifies the degree to which u satisfies the not-property of A. Given that a counter property is distinct from a not-property, bipolar-valued fuzzy sets and intuitionistic fuzzy sets serve as distinct extensions of traditional fuzzy sets. Figure 1 summarizes the relation of them.

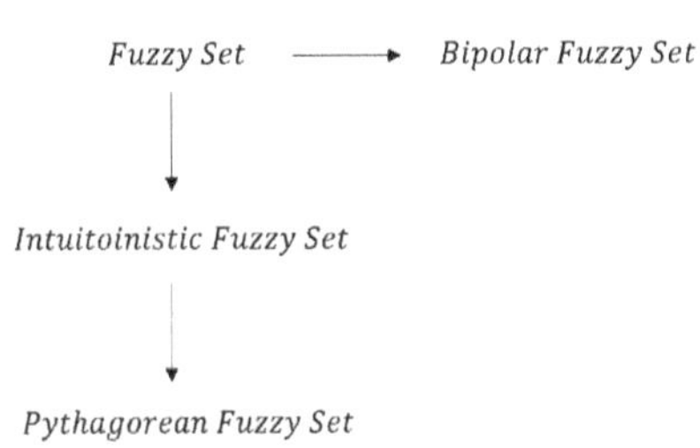

Figure 1. Relation between fuzzy sets, intuitionistic fuzzy sets, and bipolar fuzzy sets.

Recently, bipolar fuzzy sets have been utilized in various fields of research. Lee [8,11], defined bipolar fuzzy set operations and obtained their basic algebraic properties. Abdullah et al. [12] combined the bipolarity, fuzziness, and parameterization and gave the definition of bipolar fuzzy soft sets in 2014. They also gave an application of bipolar fuzzy soft set in decision-making problems. In 2019, Kim et al. [13] defined bipolar fuzzy points and studied the topological structures of bipolar fuzzy sets, such as neighborhood, base, continuity, product, and quotient spaces. In recent years, researchers have also studied the algebraic structures of bipolar fuzzy sets [14–17].

Chang [18] (1968) defined topological spaces on fuzzy sets and examined basic properties such as open-closed sets, continuity, and compactness. In 1976, Lowen [19] gave a new definition of fuzzy topology and guaranteed that the constant functions are continuous in fuzzy topological spaces in this sense. In Chang's fuzzy topology, open sets are fuzzy, but the topology comprising those open sets is a subset of the family of fuzzy sets. Fuzzification of openness was first defined by Hohle [20] and later extended to L-subsets by Shostak [21]. Pao-Ming and Ying-Ming [22,23] defined the concept of a neighborhood of fuzzy points. They also brought out the structures of fuzzy quasi-coincident and Q-neighborhood. The fuzzy topology theory, which has been handled in many ways until today, has now reached a certain maturity. Topological structures of some extensions of fuzzy sets also have been studied. For example intuitonistic fuzzy topology [24], neutrosophic fuzzy topology [25,26], picture fuzzy topology [27], bipolar fuzzy topology [28], etc.

Supra topology [29] was defined by dropping a finite intersection condition of topological spaces. It is fundamental with respect to the investigation of classical topological spaces. Since then, many authors have studied supra topology and its extensions such as (intuitionistic) fuzzy supra topology [30–32]. In 2022, Hami et al. [33] discussed bipolar fuzzy supra topological spaces as a generalization of supra topologies to bipolar fuzzy topologies.

Neighborhood structures play important roles in (supra) topological spaces. As such, we aim to study neighborhood structures and related properties in bipolar fuzzy supra topological spaces. For this, this paper includes the following sections: In Section 2, we list basic definitions and results that are needed in the subsequent sections. In Section 3, we define the concept of neighborhood structure for a bipolar fuzzy point and generate a bipolar fuzzy supra-topology using the system of neighborhoods (see Theorem 11). The characterization of continuous mappings is also provided in this section. In Section 4, we introduce the concept of quasi-coincidence in bipolar fuzzy sets and obtain some of its properties. Subsequently, we study the Q-neighborhood structure of bipolar fuzzy supra-topological space. In the last section, we propose a method for data analysis within a bipolar fuzzy supra-topological environment as a real-life application, and we present numerical examples of the proposed method.

2. Preliminaries

In this section, we give some definitions and several results related to bipolar fuzzy sets.

Definition 1 ([8]). *Let U be a non-empty set. A bipolar fuzzy set A on U is an object having the form $A = \{< u, \mu_A^+(x), \mu_A^-(u) >: u \in U\}$ where $\mu_A^+ : U \to [0,1]$ and $\mu_A^- : U \to [-1,0]$ are mappings. The positive membership degree $\mu_A^+(u)$ represents the satisfaction degree of an element u with respect to the property associated with a bipolar-valued fuzzy set A, while the negative membership degree $\mu_A^-(u)$ indicates the satisfaction degree of u with an implicit counter property of bipolar-valued fuzzy set A.*

If $\mu_A^+(u) = 0$ and $\mu_A^-(u) \neq 0$, it is the situation that u does not satisfy property of A but somewhat satisfies the counter property of A.

If $\mu_A^+(u) \neq 0$ and $\mu_A^-(u) = 0$, it is the situation that u is regarded as having only positive satisfaction of A.

There are cases where the positive membership degree $\mu_A^+(u)$ and the negative membership degree $\mu_A^-(u)$ are both non-zero when the membership function of the property overlaps that of its counter property over certain elements in U.

The set of all bipolar fuzzy sets in U will be denoted as $BPF(U)$.

In the following, we give an example for bipolar fuzzy set.

Example 1. *Let $U = \{u, v, z\}$. $A = \{< u, 0.6, -0.1 >, < v, 0.3, -0.3 >, < z, 0.4, -0.2 >\}$ is a bipolar fuzzy set on U.*

Definition 2 ([28]). *The empty bipolar fuzzy set is defined as $0^+(u) = 0 = 0^-(u)$, for each $u \in U$ and denoted by $\overline{0} = (0^+, 0^-)$.*

The whole bipolar fuzzy set is defined as $1^+(u) = 1$ *and* $1^-(u) = -1$*, for each* $u \in U$ *and denoted by* $\overline{1} = (1^+, 1^-)$.

With the following definition, we give the definitions of some set operations.

Definition 3 ([34])**.** *Let* $A,\ B \in BPF(U)$*. Then;*

(1) $A \subseteq B :\Leftrightarrow \mu_A^+(u) \leq \mu_B^+(u)$ *and* $\mu_A^-(u) \geq \mu_B^-(u)$*, for all* $u \in U$.

(2) $A = B :\Leftrightarrow \mu_A^+(u) = \mu_B^+(u)$ *and* $\mu_A^-(u) = \mu_B^-(u)$*, for all* $u \in U$.

(3) $A \cup B = \{< u, \mu_{A\cup B}^+(u), \mu_{A\cup B}^-(u) >: u \in U\}$*, where* $\mu_{A\cup B}^+(u) = max\{\mu_A^+(u), \mu_B^+(u)\}$ *and* $\mu_{A\cup B}^-(u) = min\{\mu_A^-(u), \mu_B^-(u)\}$

(4) $A \cap B = \{< u, \mu_{A\cap B}^+(u), \mu_{A\cap B}^-(u) >: u \in U\}$*, where* $\mu_{A\cap B}^+(u) = min\{\mu_A^+(u), \mu_B^+(u)\}$ *and* $\mu_{A\cap B}^-(u) = max\{\mu_A^-(u), \mu_B^-(u)\}$

(5) $A^c = \{< u, 1 - \mu_A^+(u), -1 - \mu_A^-(u) >: u \in U\}$.

Proposition 1 ([13])**.** *Let* $A,\ B$ *and* $C \in BPF(U)$*. Then we have the following:*

(1) $A \cup B = B \cup A,\ A \cap B = B \cap A$.

(2) $A \cup (B \cap C) = (A \cup B) \cap (A \cup C),\ A \cap (B \cup C) = (A \cap B) \cup (A \cap C)$.

(3) $A \cup (B \cup C) = (A \cup B) \cup C,\ A \cap (B \cap C) = (A \cap B) \cap C$.

(4) $A \subset A \cup B$ *and* $B \subset A \cup B$.

(5) $A \cap B \subset A$ *and* $A \cap B \subset B$.

(6) $(A \cup B)^c = A^c \cap B^c, (A \cap B)^c = A^c \cup B^c$.

Definition 4 ([13])**.** *Let* $g : U \to V$ *be a function and* $A \in BPF(U)$*,* $B \in BPF(V)$*. The image of a bipolar fuzzy set* A *is a bipolar fuzzy set on* V*, and it is defined by*

$$g(A)(v) = (\mu_{g(A)}^+(v), \mu_{g(A)}^-(v)) = (g(\mu_A^+)(v), g(\mu_A^-)(v)), \forall v \in V$$

where

$$g(\mu_A^+)(v) = \begin{cases} \bigvee \mu_A^+(u), & \text{if } x \in g^{-1}(v); \\ 0, & \text{otherwise} \end{cases},$$

$$g(\mu_A^-)(v) = \begin{cases} \bigwedge \mu_A^-(u), & \text{if } x \in g^{-1}(v); \\ 0, & \text{otherwise.} \end{cases}$$

The preimage of a bipolar fuzzy set B *is a bipolar fuzzy set on* U *and it is defined by*

$$g^{-1}(B)(u) = (\mu_{g^{-1}(B)}^+(u), \mu_{g^{-1}(B)}^-(u)) = (\mu_B^+(g(u)), \mu_B^-(g(u))), \forall u \in U.$$

Theorem 1 ([13])**.** *Let* $g : U \to V$ *be a function and* $A, A_1, A_2, \in BPF(U)$*,* $(A_i)_{i\in J} \subset BPF(U)$ *and* $B, B_1, B_2 \in BPF(V)$*,*$(B_i)_{i\in J} \subset BPF(V)$*. Then we have the following:*

(1) *If* $A_1 \subseteq A_2$*, then* $g(A_1) \subseteq g(A_2)$.

(2) *If* $B_1 \subseteq B_2$*, then* $g^{-1}(B_1) \subseteq g^{-1}(B_2)$.

(3) $A \subseteq g^{-1}(g(A))$*. If* g *is injective, then the equality holds.*

(4) $g(g^{-1}(B)) \subseteq B$*. If* g *is surjective, then the equality holds.*

(5) $g(\bigcup_{i\in J} A_i) = \bigcup_{i\in J} g(A_i)$*,* $g(\bigcap_{i\in J} A_i) \subseteq \bigcap_{i\in J} g(A_i)$.

(6) $g^{-1}(\bigcup_{i\in J} B_i) = \bigcup_{i\in J} g^{-1}(B_i)$*,* $g^{-1}(\bigcap_{i\in J} B_i) = \bigcap_{i\in J} g^{-1}(B_i)$.

Definition 5 ([13])**.** *Let* $u \in U$*,* $(\alpha, \beta) \in (0,1]x[-1,0)$ *and* $A \in BPF(U)$.

(1) $u_{(\alpha,\beta)}$ *is called bipolar fuzzy point in* U*, if for every* $v \in U$

$$(u_{(\alpha,\beta)})(v) = \begin{cases} (\alpha, \beta), & \text{if } v = u; \\ (0,0), & \text{otherwise.} \end{cases}$$

(α, β) *is called the value of this point and* u *is called the support of the bipolar fuzzy point* $u_{(\alpha,\beta)}$.

For simplicity, we will denote bipolar fuzzy point by $\overline{u}$ *instead of* $u_{(\alpha,\beta)}$.

(2) *If* $\mu_A^+(u) \geq \alpha$ *and* $\mu_A^-(u) \leq \beta$*, then* $\overline{u}$ *is called belong to* A *and denoted by* $\overline{u} \in A$.

The set of all bipolar fuzzy points in U will be denoted by $BPF_P(U)$.
$A = \bigcup\{\overline{u} \in BPF_P(U) : \overline{u} \in A\}$, for each $A \in BPF(U)$.

Theorem 2 ([13]). *Let $A, B \in BPF(U)$ and $\overline{u} \in BPF_P(U)$. If $A \subset B$, then $\overline{u} \in B, \forall\, \overline{u} \in A$.*

Proof. Let $A \subset B$ and $\overline{u} \in A$. Then $\mu_A^+(u) \geq \alpha$ and $\mu_A^-(u) \leq \beta$. We have $\mu_A^+(u) \leq \mu_B^+(u)$ and $\mu_A^-(u) \geq \mu_B^-(u)$. Hence $\mu_B^+(u) \geq \alpha$ and $\mu_B^-(u) \leq \beta$. Therefore, $\overline{u} \in B$. □

Theorem 3 ([13]). *Let $A, B \in BPF(U)$ and $\overline{u} \in BPF_P(U)$. Then*
(i) $\overline{u} \in A \cap B \Leftrightarrow \overline{u} \in A$ and $\overline{u} \in B$,
(ii) If $\overline{u} \in A$ or $\overline{u} \in B$, then $\overline{u} \in A \cup B$

Proof. (ii) Let $\overline{u} \in A$ or $\overline{u} \in B$. Then $(\mu_A^+(u) \geq \alpha, \mu_A^-(u) \leq \beta)$ or $(\mu_B^+(u) \geq \alpha, \mu_B^-(u) \leq \beta)$. Thus, $(\mu_A^+(u) \geq \alpha$ or $\mu_B^+(u) \geq \alpha)$ and $(\mu_A^-(u) \leq \beta$ or $\mu_B^-(u) \leq \beta)$. Hence $max\{\mu_A^+(u), \mu_B^+(u)\} \geq \alpha$ and $min\{\mu_A^-(u), \mu_B^-(u)\} \leq \beta$ and so $\overline{u} \in A \cup B$. □

Theorem 4 ([13]). *Let $(A_j)_{j\in J} \subset BPF(U)$ and $\overline{u} \in BPF_P(U)$. Then,*
(i) $\overline{u} \in \bigcap_{j\in J} A_j \Leftrightarrow \overline{u} \in A_j, \forall j \in J$.
(ii) If there exists a $j \in J$ such that $\overline{u} \in A_j$, then $\overline{u} \in \bigcup_{j\in J} A_j$

Proof. (ii) It is easy to see from $A_j \subset \bigcup_{j\in J} A_j$ and Theorem 2. □

Definition 6 ([13]). *Let U be a nonempty set and $\tau \subset BPF(U)$. Then τ is called a bipolar fuzzy topology on U if it satisfies the following conditions;*
(1) $\overline{0}, \overline{1} \in \tau$,
(2) $A \cap B \in \tau$, for any $A, B \in \tau$,
(3) $\bigcup_{j\in J} A_j \in \tau$, for $(A_j)_{j\in J} \in \tau$.
The pair (U, τ) is said to be bipolar fuzzy topological space. Members of τ are called bipolar fuzzy open sets, and members whose complements belong to τ are called bipolar fuzzy closed sets.

Definition 7 ([33]). *Let $\tau \subset BPF(U)$. Then τ is called a bipolar fuzzy supra topology on U if it satisfies the following conditions;*
(1) $\overline{0}, \overline{1} \in \tau$,
(2) $\bigcup_{j\in J} A_j \in \tau$, for $(A_j)_{j\in J} \in \tau$.
The pair (U, τ) is said to be bipolar fuzzy supra topological space. Members of τ are called bipolar fuzzy supra open sets, and members whose complements belong to τ are called bipolar fuzzy supra closed sets.

The family of all bipolar fuzzy supra topologies on U will be denoted by $BPFST(U)$.

Example 2 ([33]).

- *Let U be a nonempty set and $\tau^1 = BPF(U)$. In this case, τ^1 is a bipolar fuzzy supra topology on U. τ^1 is called discrete bipolar fuzzy supra topology and (U, τ^1) is called discrete bipolar fuzzy supra topological space.*
- *Let U be a nonempty set and $\tau^0 = \{\overline{0}, \overline{1}\}$. In this case, τ^0 is a bipolar fuzzy supra topology on U. τ^0 is called indiscrete bipolar fuzzy supra topology and (U, τ^0) is called indiscrete bipolar fuzzy supra topological space.*
- *Let (U, τ) be a bipolar fuzzy supra topological space. The families $\tau^+ = \{\mu_A^+ \in I^U : A \in \tau\}$ and $\tau^- = \{-\mu_A^- \in I^U : A \in \tau\}$ are two fuzzy supra topologies in the sense of Abd-El Monsef and Ramadan [30].*

Theorem 5 ([33]). *Let $A \in BPF(U)$. Then the family of η_τ defined as $\eta_\tau = \{A \in BPF(U) : A \cap B \in \tau, for\ each\ B \in \tau\}$ is a bipolar fuzzy topology on X and $\eta_\tau \subset \tau$.*

Theorem 6 ([33]). *Let κ be the family of all bipolar fuzzy supra closed sets in the bipolar fuzzy supra topological space (U, τ). Then we have following:*

(1) $\overline{0}, \overline{1} \in \kappa$,
(2) $\bigcap_{j \in J} A_j \in \kappa$, *for* $(A_j)_{j \in J} \in \kappa$.

Theorem 7 ([33])**.** *Let* (U, τ^*) *be a bipolar fuzzy topological space and* τ *be a bipolar fuzzy supra topology on* U*. We call* τ *a bipolar fuzzy supra topology associated with* τ^* *if* $\tau^* \subseteq \tau$.

Theorem 8 ([33])**.** *Let* (U, τ) *and* (V, σ) *be two bipolar fuzzy supra topological spaces and* $f : (X, \tau) \rightarrow (Y, \sigma)$ *be a mapping.* f *is called bipolar fuzzy supra continuous, if* $f^{-1}(B) \in \tau$, *for each* $B \in \sigma$.

3. Neighborhood Structure of Bipolar Fuzzy Supra Topological Spaces

In this section, we introduce the concept of neighborhood structure of a bipolar fuzzy point and generate a bipolar fuzzy supra topology by using the system of neighborhood.

Definition 8. *Let* (U, τ) *be a bipolar fuzzy supra topological space,* $\overline{u} \in BPF_P(U)$ *and* $A \in BPF(U)$*.* A *is called a bipolar fuzzy supra neighborhood of* $\overline{u}$ *if there exists a bipolar fuzzy supra open set* B *in* U *such that* $\overline{u} \in B \subseteq A$.

The family of all bipolar fuzzy supra neighborhoods of $\overline{u}$ *is called the bipolar fuzzy supra neighborhood system of* $\overline{u}$ *and denoted by* $N_\tau(\overline{u})$.

Example 3. *Let* $U = \{u, v\}$ *and* $\tau = \{\overline{0}, \overline{1}, A, B, C\}$ *where*
$A = \{< u, 0.5, -0.5 >, < v, 0.7, -0.3 >\}$, $B = \{< u, 0.6, -0.8 >, < v, 0.9, -0.7 >\}$,
$C = \{< u, 0.3, -0.4 >, < v, 0.4, -0.1 >\}$.
Let take two bipolar fuzzy points on U *such that* $\overline{u} = \{< u, 0.8, -0.6 >\}$ *and*
$\overline{v} = \{< v, 0.4, -0.45 >\}$*. Hence, we have the inclusions such that* $\overline{u} \in B \subseteq \overline{1}$ *and*
$\overline{v} \in A \subseteq B$*, so* $\overline{1} \in N_\tau(\overline{u})$ *and* $B \in N_\tau(\overline{v})$.

Example 4. *Let* $U = [0, \pi]$ *and* $\tau = \{\overline{0}, \overline{1}, A, B\}$*. For each* $u \in U$, $A = \{< u, \mu_A^+(u), \mu_A^-(u) >: u \in U\}$ *and* $B = \{< u, \mu_B^+(u), \mu_B^-(u) >: u \in U\}$ *and membership functions given by*

$$\mu_A^+(u) = \frac{sinu}{2},\ \mu_A^-(u) = \frac{-sinu}{2} \text{ and } \mu_B^+(u) = cos(u - \tfrac{\pi}{2}),\ \mu_B^-(u) = \tfrac{1}{3}(u - \tfrac{\pi}{2})^2 - 0.9$$

One can easily see that $A \subseteq B$ with the help of the graphs of membership functions given in Figures 2 and 3.

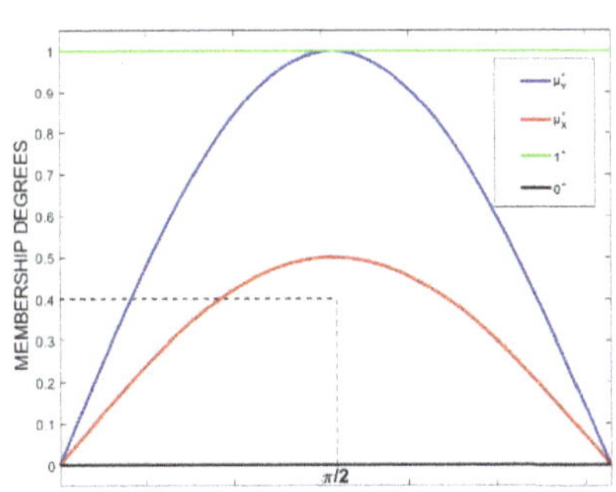

Figure 2. Positive membership degrees of open sets.

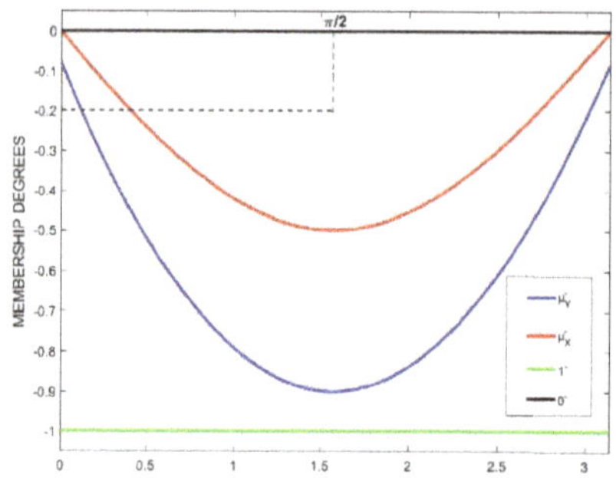

Figure 3. Negative membership degrees of open sets.

It is clear that τ is a bipolar fuzzy supra topology on U. Therefore, for $u = \frac{\pi}{2}$, $\alpha = 0.4, \beta = -0.2$, we have
$\mu_A^+(\frac{\pi}{2}) = 0.5 \geq 0.4\,, \mu_A^-(\frac{\pi}{2}) = -0.5 \leq -0.2$ and $\mu_B^+(\frac{\pi}{2}) = 1 \geq 0.4\,, \mu_B^-(\frac{\pi}{2}) = -0.9 \leq -0.2$ and $\overline{u} \in A \subseteq B$. So, we obtain $B \in N_\tau(\overline{u})$.

With the following theorem, we characterize open sets by using neighborhoods.

Theorem 9. *Let (U, τ) be a bipolar fuzzy supra topological space and $A \in BPF(U)$. Then A is a bipolar fuzzy supra open set if and only if A is a bipolar fuzzy supra neighborhood of each of its bipolar fuzzy points.*

Proof. Let A be a bipolar fuzzy supra open set and $\overline{u} \in A$, then by taking $B = A$, we obtain A is a bipolar fuzzy supra neighborhood of $\overline{u}$.

Conversely, suppose that A is a bipolar fuzzy supra neighborhood of each of its bipolar fuzzy points. Then, for every $\overline{u} \in A$, there exists a bipolar fuzzy supra open set B_j such that $\overline{u} \in B_j \subseteq A$. Let $C = \bigcup_{j \in J} B_j$. From the definition of bipolar fuzzy supra topology, C is a bipolar fuzzy supra open set. $C \subseteq A$ holds because $B_j \subseteq A$ for every $\overline{u} \in A$. Otherwise, every bipolar fuzzy point of A belongs to B_j, and therefore, they belong to C. Finally, we conclude that $A \subseteq C$ and $A = C$. This means that A is bipolar fuzzy supra open set. □

Now, we give the basic properties of the bipolar fuzzy supra neighborhood.

Theorem 10. *Let (U, τ) be a bipolar fuzzy supra topological space and $N_\tau(\overline{u})$ be the neighborhood system of bipolar fuzzy point $\overline{u}$. Then we have the following:*

N1. $N_\tau(\overline{u}) \neq \overline{0}$ for every $\overline{u}$.

N2. If $A \in N_\tau(\overline{u})$, then $\overline{u} \in A$.

N3. If $A \subset B$ and $A \in N_\tau(\overline{u})$, then $B \in N_\tau(\overline{u})$.

N4. Let $A \in N_\tau(\overline{u})$. Then there exists $B \in N_\tau(\overline{u})$ such that $B \subset A$ and $B \in N_\tau(\overline{v})$, $\forall \overline{v} \in B$.

Proof. N1. Let $\overline{u} \in \overline{1}$. Since $\overline{1}$ is a bipolar fuzzy supra open set, then $\overline{1}$ is a neighborhood of each of its bipolar fuzzy points. Therefore $N_\tau(\overline{u}) \neq \overline{0}$.

N2. Let $A \in N_\tau(\overline{u})$, then there exists bipolar fuzzy supra open set C such that $\overline{u} \in C \subseteq A$, so $\overline{u} \in A$.

N3. Let $A \subset B$ and $A \in N_\tau(\overline{u})$. Then there exists a bipolar fuzzy supra open set C such that $\overline{u} \in C \subseteq A$. Since $A \subset B$, then $\overline{u} \in C \subseteq B$ and $B \in N_\tau(\overline{u})$.

N4. Let $A \in N_\tau(\overline{u})$. Then there exists $C \in \tau$ such that $\overline{u} \in C \subseteq A$. Let $C := B$ put a period. Thus we have $B \in N_\tau(\overline{u})$. Now, let take $\overline{v} \in B$, then $B \in N_\tau(\overline{v})$. Since $B \subseteq A$, it follows that $A \in N_\tau(\overline{v})$. □

After proving the last two theorems, we should have a bipolar fuzzy supra topology determined by the neighborhood systems of a bipolar fuzzy point in a bipolar fuzzy supra topological space.

Theorem 11. *Let $N(\overline{u})$ be a nonempty collection of bipolar fuzzy sets on U satisfying (N1)–(N4), for each bipolar fuzzy point $\overline{u}$. Then the family $\tau = \{A \in BPF(U) : A \in N(\overline{v}), \forall \overline{v} \in A\}$ is a bipolar fuzzy supra topology on U such that $N(\overline{u})$ is the family of all neighborhoods of $\overline{u}$ in (U, τ).*

Proof. Let the subfamily $N(\overline{u}) \subset BPF(U)$ satisfy (N1)–(N4) for each $\overline{u}$ and let $\tau = \{A \in BPF(U) : A \in N(\overline{v}), \forall \overline{v} \in A\}$. First, we need to see that τ is a bipolar fuzzy supra topology on U.

Since $\overline{0}$ contains no bipolar fuzzy points then $\overline{0} \in \tau$. We have $N(\overline{u}) \neq \overline{0}$. There must be a bipolar fuzzy supra neighborhood of each bipolar fuzzy points in U, which is $\overline{1}$, so $\overline{1} \in \tau$.

Let $\{A_j : j \in J\} \subseteq \tau$ and $A = \bigcup_{j \in J} A_j$. If $\overline{u} \in A_j$ for any $j \in J$, then $\overline{u} \in \bigcup_{j \in J} A_j$. Since $A_j \in N(\overline{u})$ and $A_j \subseteq A$, we have $A = \bigcup_{j \in J} A_j \in N(\overline{u})$. Therefore, τ is bipolar fuzzy supra topology on U.

For the remaining part of the proof, we need to show that τ is determined by a unique bipolar fuzzy supra neighborhood system, that is $N(\overline{u}) = N_\tau(\overline{u})$. For each $A \in N_\tau(\overline{u})$ there exists a $B \in \tau$ such that $\overline{u} \in B \subset A$. Since $\overline{u} \in B$ and $B \in \tau$, we have $B \in N(\overline{u})$ and $A \in N(\overline{u})$. Hence, $N_\tau(\overline{u}) \subset N(\overline{u})$.

Conversely, let $A \in N(\overline{u})$. Then, there exists a $B \in N(\overline{u})$ such that $B \subseteq A$ and $B \in N(\overline{v})$ for every $\overline{v} \in B$. It yields that $B \in \tau$. This implies that the bipolar fuzzy supra open set B is a bipolar fuzzy supra neighborhood of $\overline{u}$ so $B \in N_\tau(\overline{u})$. Since $B \subseteq A$ we have $A \in N_\tau(\overline{u})$. Then we conclude that $N(\overline{u}) \subset N_\tau(\overline{u})$. Hence we obtain $N(\overline{u}) = N_\tau(\overline{u})$. This completes the proof. □

Here, we present the characterization of continuous mapping by using bipolar fuzzy supra neighborhood.

Theorem 12. *Let (U, τ) and (V, σ) be two bipolar fuzzy supra topological space, $\overline{u} \in BPF_P(U)$ and $f : (U, \tau) \to (V, \sigma)$ be a mapping. Then the following are equivalent:*
1. *f is a bipolar fuzzy supra continuous mapping.*
2. *$f^{-1}(B) \in N_\tau(\overline{u})$ for each $B \in N_\sigma(f(\overline{u}))$.*
3. *For each $\overline{u} \in BPF_P(U)$ and $B \in N_\sigma(f(\overline{u}))$ there exists $A \in N_\tau(\overline{u})$ such that $f(A) \subseteq B$.*

Proof. ($1 \Rightarrow 2$) Suppose that $f : (U, \tau) \to (V, \sigma)$ is a bipolar fuzzy supra continuous mapping. If we take $B \in N_\sigma(f(\overline{u}))$ then it is obvious that there exists a $C \in \sigma$ such that $f(\overline{u}) \in C \subset B$. Since f is bipolar fuzzy supra continuous we have $f^{-1}(C) \in \tau$ and therefore $\overline{u} \in f^{-1}(C)$ and $f^{-1}(C) \subset f^{-1}(B)$ is valid. Hence this implies that $f^{-1}(B) \in N_\tau(\overline{u})$.

($2 \Rightarrow 3$) Let $B \in N_\sigma(f(\overline{u}))$. By hypothesis we obtain $f^{-1}(B) \in N_\tau(\overline{u})$. Let choose $A = f^{-1}(B)$ one can easily see that $f(A) = f(f^{-1}(B)) \subseteq B$.

($3 \Rightarrow 1$) To prove this statement we will show that $f^{-1}(B) \in \tau$ for each $B \in \sigma$. By taking $\overline{u} \in f^{-1}(B)$, we obtain $f(\overline{u}) \in B$ and thus $B \in N_\sigma(f(\overline{u}))$ for each $B \in \sigma$. From the hypothesis there exists $A \in N_\tau(\overline{u})$ such that $f(A) \subseteq B$. Then, by the properties of image and preimage, we have $A \subset f^{-1}(f(A)) \subset f^{-1}(B)$. Finally $A \subset f^{-1}(B)$ for each $A \in N_\tau(\overline{u})$. Hence $f^{-1}(B) \in \tau$. □

4. Q-Neighborhood Structure of Bipolar Fuzzy Supra Topological Spaces

In 1980, Ming et al. [23] defined the concepts of quasi-coincident and Q-neighborhood. In this section, these two concepts are going to extend to bipolar fuzzy sets, and this allows us to study the Q-neighborhood structure of bipolar fuzzy supra topological spaces.

Definition 9. *1. Let $A, B \in BPF(U)$. Then we say that A is called quasi-coincident with B iff $\mu_A^+(u) + \mu_B^+(u) > 1$ and $\mu_A^-(u) + \mu_B^-(u) < -1$ for $u \in U$. It is denoted by AqB.*

2. Bipolar fuzzy point $\overline{u} \in BPF_P(U)$ is called quasi-coincident with A iff $\alpha + \mu_A^+(u) > 1$ and $\beta + \mu_A^-(u) < -1$. It is denoted by $\overline{u}qA$ and opposite situation is denoted as $\overline{u}q^cA$.

In the following, we give an example of a quasi-coincident structure:

Example 5. *Let* $U = \{u,v\}$ $A = \{< u, 0.9, -0.8 >, < v, 0.8, -0.7 >\}$ *and* $B = \{< u, 0.2, -0.3 >, < v, 0.3, -0.4 >\}$. *We obtain* $\mu_A^+(z) + \mu_B^+(z) > 1$ *and* $\mu_A^-(z) + \mu_B^-(z) < -1$ *for each* $z \in U$ *and thus* AqB.

Now, we offer some fundamental properties related to the concept of quasi-coincident.

Theorem 13. *Let* $A, B \in BPF(U)$ *and* $\overline{u} \in BPF_P(U)$. *Then, we have the statements below:*
1. $\overline{u}q^c\overline{0}$.
2. $\overline{u}q\overline{1}$.
3. $AqB = BqA$.
4. $\overline{u} \in A \Leftrightarrow \overline{u}q^cA^c$.
5. $\overline{u}qA \Leftrightarrow \overline{u} \notin A^c$.
6. $A \subseteq B \Leftrightarrow Aq^cB^c$.
7. $AqB \Rightarrow A \cap B \neq \overline{0}$.
8. Aq^cA^c.
9. $AqB \Leftrightarrow$ *There exists* $\overline{u} \in A$ *such that* $\overline{u}qB$.
10. $\overline{u} \in A^c \Leftrightarrow \overline{u}q^cA$.
11. *Let* $A \subseteq B$. *If* $\overline{u}qA$, *then* $\overline{u}qB$.

Proof. 1, 2, and 3 are clear from the definition.

4.
$$\begin{aligned} \overline{u} \in A &\Leftrightarrow \mu_A^+(u) \geq \alpha \text{ and } \mu_A^-(u) \leq \beta \\ &\Leftrightarrow \mu_{(A^c)^c}^+(u) \nless \alpha \text{ and } \mu_{(A^c)^c}^-(u) \ngtr \beta \\ &\Leftrightarrow \overline{u}q^cA^c. \end{aligned}$$

5.
$$\begin{aligned} \overline{u}qA &\Leftrightarrow \alpha + \mu_A^+(u) > 1 \text{ and } \beta + \mu_A^-(u) < -1 \\ &\Leftrightarrow \alpha > 1 - \mu_A^+(u) \text{ and } \beta < -1 - \mu_A^-(u) \\ &\Leftrightarrow \overline{u} \notin A^c. \end{aligned}$$

6. Suppose that $A \subseteq B$. Then $\mu_A^+(u) \leq \mu_B^+(u)$ and $\mu_A^-(u) \geq \mu_B^-(u)$ for each $u \in U$. We can write the following inequality
$$\begin{aligned} \mu_A^+(u) + \mu_{B^c}^+(u) &= \mu_A^+(u) + 1 - \mu_B^+(u) \\ &\leq \mu_B^+(u) + 1 - \mu_B^+(u) \\ &= 1 \end{aligned}$$
and therefore $\mu_A^+(u) + \mu_{B^c}^+(u) \leq 1$.
For the negative part, we have
$$\begin{aligned} \mu_A^-(u) + \mu_{B^c}^-(u) &= \mu_A^-(u) - 1 - \mu_B^-(u) \\ &\geq \mu_B^-(u) - 1 - \mu_B^-(u) \\ &= -1 \end{aligned}$$
By combining the two inequalities, we obtain Aq^cB^c. Converse of the theorem can be shown by the same token.

7.
$$\begin{aligned} AqB &\Rightarrow \mu_A^+(u) + \mu_B^+(u) > 1 \text{ and } \mu_A^-(u) + \mu_B^-(u) < -1 \\ &\Rightarrow \mu_A^+(u), \mu_B^+(u) \neq 0 \text{ and } \mu_A^-(u), \mu_B^-(u) \neq 0 \\ &\Rightarrow \mu_A^+(u) \wedge \mu_B^+(u) \neq 0 \text{ and } \mu_A^-(u) \vee \mu_B^-(u) \neq 0 \\ &\Rightarrow A \cap B \neq \overline{0}. \end{aligned}$$

8. $\mu_A^+(u) + \mu_{A^c}^+(u) = \mu_A^+(u) + 1 - \mu_A^+(u) = 1$ and $\mu_A^-(u) + \mu_{A^c}^-(u) = \mu_A^+(u) - 1 - \mu_A^-(u) = -1$. Thus, we obtain Aq^cA^c.

9. Let AqB and $\overline{u} \in A$. Hence, we obtain $\mu_A^+(u) + \mu_B^+(u) > 1$ and $\mu_A^-(u) + \mu_B^-(u) < -1$. By taking $\alpha = \mu_A^+(u)$ and $\beta = \mu_A^-(u)$ we have what we desired. Thus, $\overline{u}qB$.

Conversely, suppose that $\overline{u} \in A$ and $\overline{u}qB$. Then, $\alpha \leq \mu_A^+(u)$ and $\beta \geq \mu_A^-(u)$. From here, $\mu_A^+(u) + \mu_B^+(u) \geq \alpha + \mu_B^+(u) > 1$ and $\mu_A^-(u) + \mu_B^-(u) \leq \beta + \mu_B^-(u) < -1$ and these inequalities give the result which is AqB.

10.

$$\begin{aligned} \overline{u} \in A^c &\Leftrightarrow \alpha \leq \mu^+_{A^c}(u) \text{ and } \beta \geq +\mu^-_{A^c}(u) \\ &\Leftrightarrow \alpha \leq 1 - \mu^+_A(u) \text{ and } \beta \geq -1 - \mu^-_A(u) \\ &\Leftrightarrow \alpha + \mu^+_A(u) \leq 1 \text{ and } \beta + \mu^-_A(u) \geq -1 \\ &\Leftrightarrow \overline{u} q^c A. \end{aligned}$$

11. Let $A \subseteq B$ and $\overline{u}qA$ be given. Then it follows that $\alpha + \mu^+_A(u) > 1$ and $\beta + \mu^-_A(u) < -1$. Since $A \subseteq B$, we write $\alpha + \mu^+_B(u) \geq \alpha + \mu^+_A(u) > 1$ and $\beta + \mu^-_B(u) \leq \beta + \mu^-_A(u) < -1$. Finally, we conclude that $\overline{u}qB$. □

Proposition 2. *Let $(A_j) \subset BPF(U)$ and $\overline{u} \in BPF_P(U)$. Then the following are hold:*
1. $\overline{u}q(\bigcap_{j\in J} A_j) \Leftrightarrow \overline{u}q(A_j), \forall j \in J$.
2. $\overline{u}q(\bigcup_{j\in J} A_j) \Leftrightarrow \overline{u}q(A_j), \exists j \in J$.

Proof. 1. Let $\overline{u}q(\bigcap_{j\in J} A_j)$. Then we have $\alpha + \wedge_{j\in J}\mu^+_{A_j}(u) > 1$ and $\beta + \vee_{j\in J}\mu^-_{A_j}(u) < -1$. Since $\mu^+_{A_j}(u) \geq \wedge_{j\in J}\mu^+_{A_j}(u)$ and $\mu^-_{A_j}(u) \leq \vee_{j\in J}\mu^-_{A_j}(u), j \in J$, we obtain $\alpha + \mu^+_{A_j}(u) \geq \alpha + \wedge_{j\in J}\mu^+_{A_j}(u) > 1$ and $\beta + \mu^-_{A_j}(u) \leq \beta + \vee_{j\in J}\mu^-_{A_j}(u) < -1$. Hence, $\overline{u}q(A_j), \forall j \in J$.

Conversely, let $\overline{u}q(A_j), \forall j \in J$. Then, $\alpha + \mu^+_{A_j}(u) > 1$ and $\beta + \mu^-_{A_j}(u) < -1$.
$\Rightarrow \alpha + \bigwedge_{j\in J} \mu^+_{A_j}(u) > 1$ and $\beta + \bigvee_{j\in J} \mu^-_{A_j}(u) < -1$.
$\Rightarrow \overline{u}q(\bigcap_{j\in J} A_j)$

2.

$$\begin{aligned} \overline{u}q(\textstyle\bigcup_{j\in J} A_j) &\Leftrightarrow \overline{u} \notin (\textstyle\bigcup_{j\in J} A_j)^c \\ &\Leftrightarrow \overline{u} \notin \textstyle\bigcap_{j\in J}(A_j)^c \\ &\Leftrightarrow \overline{u} \notin (A_j)^c,\ \exists j \in J \\ &\Leftrightarrow \overline{u}qA_j, \exists j \in J. \end{aligned}$$

□

Definition 10. *Let τ be a bipolar fuzzy supra topology on $U, \overline{u} \in BPF_P(U)$ and $A \in BPF(U)$. A is called Q-neighborhood of $\overline{u}$ if there exists $B \in \tau$ such that $\overline{u}qB$ and $B \subseteq A$. The family of all Q-neighborhood of the $\overline{u}$ is denoted by $Q_\tau(\overline{u})$.*

Example 6. *Let $U = \{u,v\}$ and $\tau = \{\overline{0}, \overline{1}, A\}$, where $A = \{< u, 1, -0.6 >, < v, 0.7, -1 >\}$. Take $\overline{u} = \{< x, 0.4, -0.5 >\}$. Since $\overline{u}qA$ and $A \subseteq \overline{1}$ it follows that $\overline{1} \in Q_\tau(\overline{u})$.*

In the next example, we see that a Q-neighborhood of bipolar fuzzy point generally may not contain the point itself.

Example 7. *Let take a bipolar fuzzy supra topology as $\tau = \{\overline{0}, \overline{1}, A, B\}$, where $A = \{< u, 0.7, -0.3 >, < v, 0.5, -0.4 >\}$, $B = \{< u, 0.6, -0.1 >, < v, 0.4, -0.1 >\}$. Now if we take $\overline{u} = \{< u, 0.5, -0.95 >\}$, we thus have $\overline{u}qB$ and $B \subseteq A$, therefore $A \in Q_\tau(\overline{u})$. Considering the given data we obtain $\alpha = 0.5 < 0.7 = \mu^+_A(u)$ and $\beta = -0.95 \not> -0.3 = \mu^-_A(u)$, so $\overline{u} \notin A$.*

In the following theorem, we study the basic properties of the bipolar fuzzy supra Q-neighborhood.

Theorem 14. *Let (U, τ) be a bipolar fuzzy supra topological space and $Q_\tau(\overline{u})$ be the family of all Q neighborhoods of $\overline{u}$. Then we have the following:*
Q1. $\overline{1} \in Q_\tau(\overline{u})$ and if $A \in Q_\tau(\overline{u})$, then $\overline{u}qA$.
Q2. If $B \subseteq A$ and $B \in Q_\tau(\overline{u})$, then $A \in Q_\tau(\overline{u})$.
Q3. Let $A \in Q_\tau(\overline{u})$. Then there exists $B \in Q_\tau(\overline{u})$ such that $B \subseteq A$ and $B \in Q_\tau(\overline{v})$, $\forall \overline{v}qB$.

Proof. Q1. To see $\overline{1} \in Q_\tau(\overline{u})$ we need to show that there exists $B \in \tau$ satisfying $\overline{u}qB$ and $B \subseteq \overline{1}$ for any $\overline{u} \in BPF_P(U)$. If we choose $B := \overline{1}$, then we are done. Now, let $A \in Q_\tau(\overline{u})$.

Then there exists $B \in \tau$ such that $\overline{u}qB$ and $B \subseteq A$ holds. From here, $\alpha + \mu_A^+(u) \geq \alpha + \mu_B^+(u) > 1$ and $\beta + \mu_A^-(u) \leq \beta + \mu_B^-(u) < -1$, consequently $\overline{u}qA$.

Q2. Let $B \subseteq A$ and $B \in Q_\tau(\overline{u})$. Then there exists $C \in \tau$ such that $\overline{u}qC$ and $C \subseteq B$. Since $B \subseteq A$, $\overline{u}qC \subseteq A$ and $A \in Q_\tau(\overline{u})$.

Q3. Let $A \in Q_\tau(\overline{u})$. Then there exists $B \in \tau$ such that $\overline{u}qB$ and $B \subseteq A$. By choosing $B := A$ we obtain $B \in Q_\tau(\overline{u})$. Moreover, since $B \in \tau$, then B is a Q neighborhood of any bipolar fuzzy points that are contained in it. So $\overline{v}qB$ and $B \in Q_\tau(\overline{v})$. □

Theorem 15. *Let $Q(\overline{u})$ be nonempty collection of bipolar fuzzy sets on U satisfying (Q1)–(Q3) for each bipolar fuzzy point $\overline{u}$. Then the family $\tau = \{A \in BPF(U) : A \in Q(\overline{v}), \forall \overline{v}qA\} \cup \{\overline{0}\}$ is a bipolar fuzzy supra topology on U such that $Q(\overline{u})$ is the family of all Q-neighborhoods of $\overline{u}$ in (U, τ).*

Proof. Let the subfamily $Q(\overline{u}) \subset BPF(U)$ satisfies the conditions (Q1)–(Q3) for each $\overline{u}$ and let $\tau = \{A \in BPF(U) : A \in Q(\overline{v}), \forall \overline{v}qA\} \cup \{\overline{0}\}$. Firstly, we need to show that τ is a bipolar fuzzy supra topology. From the definition of τ, we have $\overline{0} \in \tau$ and $\overline{1} \in \tau$ by Theorem 14. Now let $\{A_j : j \in J\} \subseteq \tau$, then $A_j \in \tau, \forall j \in J$, we have $A_j \in Q(\overline{u})$ and $\overline{x}qA_j$. Hence, $\bigcup_{j \in J} A_j \in Q(\overline{u})$. Furthermore, for every $j \in J$ and $u \in U$, we have $1 < \alpha + \mu_{A_j}^+(u) \leq \alpha + \vee_{j \in J} \mu_{A_j}^+(u)$ and $-1 > \beta + \mu_{A_j}^-(u) \geq \beta + \wedge_{j \in J} \mu_{A_j}^-(u)$, then it follows that $\overline{u}q(\bigcup_{j \in J} A_j)$. Finally we conclude that $\bigcup_{j \in J} A_j \in \tau$.

Now we show that $Q(\overline{u}) = Q_\tau(\overline{u})$. Suppose that $A \in Q_\tau(\overline{u})$. Then we have $B \in \tau$ such that $\overline{u}qB$ and $B \subseteq A$. Then $B \in Q(\overline{u})$ and thus $A \in Q(\overline{u})$. So, we obtain $Q_\tau(\overline{u}) \subseteq Q(\overline{u})$. For the converse , take $A \in Q(\overline{u})$. By the Theorem 14 there exists $B \in Q(\overline{u})$ such that for every $\overline{v}qB$ we have $B \subseteq A$ and $B \in Q(\overline{v})$. Moreover, $B \in Q(\overline{u})$, then $\overline{u}qB$ and $B \in \tau$. Since $B \subseteq A$, $A \in Q_\tau(\overline{u})$. Hence, we have $Q(\overline{u}) \subseteq Q_\tau(\overline{u})$. □

5. Bipolar Fuzzy Supra Topology in Data Mining

In the last section, we give an application of bipolar fuzzy set in methodical approach for medical diagnosis problems. The methodical technique to select the appropriate qualities and alternatives in the decision-making problem is given in the following stages. Here, we employ the method in [35].

Step 1: Problem Area Selection:

Examine multi-criteria decision-making problems involving m attributes $A_1, A_2, ..., A_m$ and n alternatives $C_1, C_2, ..., C_n$ and p attributes $D_1, D_2, ..., D_p$, $(n \leq p)$.

	C_1	C_2	·	·	·	C_n
A_1	(a_{11})	(a_{12})	·	·	·	(a_{1n})
A_2	(a_{21})	(a_{22})	·	·	·	(a_{2n})
·	·	·	·	·	·	·
·	·	·	·	·	·	·
·	·	·	·	·	·	·
A_m	(a_{m1})	(a_{m2})	·	·	·	(a_{mn})

	A_1	A_2	·	·	·	A_m
D_1	(d_{11})	(d_{12})	·	·	·	(d_{1m})
D_2	(d_{21})	(d_{22})	·	·	·	(d_{2m})
·	·	·	·	·	·	·
·	·	·	·	·	·	·
·	·	·	·	·	·	·
D_p	(d_{p1})	(d_{p2})	·	·	·	(d_{pm})

All attributes a_{ij} and d_{ki} are bipolar fuzzy numbers for $i = \overline{1,m}, j = \overline{1,n}, k = \overline{1,p}$.

Step 2: Form bipolar fuzzy supra topologies for (C_j) and (D_k):

(i) $\tau_j = E \cup F$, where $E = \{\overline{0}, \overline{1}, a_{1j}, a_{2j}, ..., a_{mj}\}$ and $F = \{a_{1j} \cup a_{2j}, a_{1j} \cup a_{3j}, ..., a_{m-1j} \cup a_{mj}\}$.

(ii) $\sigma_k = G \cup H$, where $G = \{\overline{0}, \overline{1}, d_{k1}, d_{k2}, ..., d_{km}\}$ and $H = \{d_{k1} \cup d_{k2}, d_{k1} \cup d_{k3}, ..., d_{km-1} \cup d_{km}\}$.

Step 3: Find Bipolar fuzzy score functions:

Bipolar fuzzy score functions (BFSF) of E, F, G, H, C_j and D_k are defined as follows:

(i) $BFSF(E) = \frac{1}{2(m+2)}(\sum_{i=1}^{m+2} \frac{1+\mu_i^+ + \mu_i^-}{2})$ and $BFSF(F) = \frac{1}{2t}(\sum_{i=1}^{t} \frac{1+\mu_i^+ + \mu_i^-}{2})$, where t is the number of elements of F.

$$BFSF(C_j) = \begin{cases} BFSF(E), & \text{if } BFSF(F) = 0; \\ \frac{BFSF(E)+BFSF(F)}{2}, & \text{otherwise} \end{cases}, \text{ for } j = \overline{1,n}.$$

(ii) $BFSF(G) = \frac{1}{2(m+2)}(\sum_{i=1}^{m+2} \frac{1+\mu_i^+ + \mu_i^-}{2})$ and $BFSF(H) = \frac{1}{2s}(\sum_{i=1}^{s} \frac{1+\mu_i^+ + \mu_i^-}{2})$, where s is the number of elements of H.

$$BFSF(D_k) = \begin{cases} BFSF(G), & \text{if } BFSF(H) = 0; \\ \frac{BFSF(G)+BFSF(H)}{2}, & \text{otherwise} \end{cases}, \text{ for } k = \overline{1,p}.$$

Step 4: Final Decision:

Determine bipolar fuzzy score values for the alternatives $C_1 \leq C_2 \leq C_3 \leq ... \leq C_n$ and the attributes $D_1 \leq D_2 \leq ... \leq D_p$. Select the attribute D_p for the alternative C_1, D_{p-1} for alternative C_2 and D_{p-2} for alternative C_3, etc. If $n < p$, then ignore D_k, where $k = \overline{1, n-p}$.

Case Study

Dealing with uncertainty is inherent in medical diagnosis problems, and the introduction of bipolar fuzzy sets offers a valuable perspective. In this section, we present an illustrative medical diagnosis problem to demonstrate the applicability of the mentioned approach.

Step 1: Problem Area Selection:

Suppose that $P = \{P_1, P_2, P_3, P_4\}$ be the set of patients,

$S = \{Temperature, Cough, BloodPlates, JointPain, Insulin\}$ be the set symptoms and

$R = \{Tuberculosis, Diabetes, Chikungunya, SwineFlu, Dengue\}$ be the set of diseases corresponding to the symptoms S.

We need to find the patient and to find the disease of the patient.

Patient−Symptom Relation

Symptoms	Patients			
	P1	P2	P3	P4
Temperature	(0.8, −0.1)	(0.4, −0.5)	(0.5, −0.6)	(0.9, −0.4)
Cough	(0.3, −0.5)	(0.4, −0.8)	(0.6, −0.4)	(0.9, −0.2)
Blood Plates	(0.1, −0.3)	(0.7, −0.2)	(0.3, −0.9)	(0.4, −0.7)
Joint pain	(0.4, −0.5)	(0.6, −0.5)	(0.6, −0.3)	(0.5, −0.7)
Insulin	(0.8, −0.2)	(0.7, −0.3)	(0.3, −0.6)	(0.2, −0.5)

Symptom-Disease Relation

Diagnosis	Symptoms				
	Temperature	Cough	Blood Plates	Joint pain	Insulin
Tuberculosis	(0.6, −0.1)	(0.9, −0.1)	(0, −0.8)	(0, −0.8)	(0, −0.9)
Diabetes	(0.1, −0.8)	(0.1, −0.8)	(0.2, −0.1)	(0.2, −0.5)	(0.9, −0.1)
Chikungunya	(0.9, −0.1)	(0, −0.8)	(0.7, −0.1)	(0.9, −0.1)	(0.2, −0.8)
Swine Flue	(0.2, −0.3)	(0.1, −0.3)	(0.2, −0.1)	(0.1, −0.5)	(0.2, −0.1)
Dengeu	(0.9, −0.1)	(0.2, −0.4)	(0.2, −0.4)	(0.3, −0.7)	(0.2, −0.7)

Step 2: Form bipolar fuzzy supra topologies for (C_j) and (D_k):

For (C_j);

(i) $\tau_1 = E \cup F$, where

$E = \{\overline{0}, \overline{1}, a_{11}, a_{21}, a_{31}, a_{41}, a_{51}\} = \{\overline{0}, \overline{1}, (0.8, -0.1), (0.3, -0.5), (0.8, -0.2), (0.4, -0.5), (0.1, -0.3)\}$ and $F = \{a_{11} \cup a_{21}, a_{11} \cup a_{31}, a_{11} \cup a_{41}, a_{11} \cup a_{51}, a_{21} \cup a_{31}, a_{21} \cup a_{41}, a_{21} \cup a_{51}, a_{31} \cup a_{41}, a_{31} \cup a_{51}, a_{41} \cup a_{51}\}$.

We omit some bipolar fuzzy sets of F which are in E and we obtain $F = \{(0.8, -0.3), (0.3, -0.5)\}$.

(ii) $\tau_2 = E \cup F$, where

$E = \{\overline{0}, \overline{1}, a_{12}, a_{22}, a_{32}, a_{42}, a_{52}\} = \{\overline{0}, \overline{1}, (0.4, -0.5), (0.4, -0.8), (0.7, -0.2), (0.6, -0.5), (0.7, -0.3)\}$ and $F = \{a_{12} \cup a_{22}, a_{12} \cup a_{32}, a_{12} \cup a_{42}, a_{12} \cup a_{52}, a_{22} \cup a_{32}, a_{22} \cup a_{42}, a_{22} \cup a_{52}, a_{32} \cup a_{42}, a_{32} \cup a_{52}, a_{42} \cup a_{52}\} = \{(0.7, -0.8), (0.7, -0.5), (0.6, -0.8)\}$.

(iii) $\tau_3 = E \cup F$, where
$E = \{\bar{0}, \bar{1}, a_{13}, a_{23}, a_{33}, a_{43}, a_{53}\} = \{\bar{0}, \bar{1}, (0.5, -0.6), (0.6, -0.4), (0.3, -0.9), (0.6, -0.3), (0.3, -0.6)\}$ and $F = \{a_{13} \cup a_{23}, a_{13} \cup a_{33}, a_{13} \cup a_{43}, a_{13} \cup a_{53}, a_{23} \cup a_{33}, a_{23} \cup a_{43}, a_{23} \cup a_{53}, a_{33} \cup a_{43}, a_{33} \cup a_{53}, a_{43} \cup a_{53}\} = \{(0.6, -0.9), (0.6, -0.6), (0.5, -0.9)\}$.
(iv) $\tau_4 = E \cup F$, where
$E = \{\bar{0}, \bar{1}, a_{14}, a_{24}, a_{34}, a_{44}, a_{54}\} = \{\bar{0}, \bar{1}, (0.9, -0.4), (0.9, -0.2), (0.4, -0.7), (0.5, -0.7), (0.2, -0.5)\}$ and $F = \{a_{14} \cup a_{24}, a_{14} \cup a_{34}, a_{14} \cup a_{44}, a_{14} \cup a_{54}, a_{24} \cup a_{34}, a_{24} \cup a_{44}, a_{24} \cup a_{54}, a_{34} \cup a_{44}, a_{34} \cup a_{54}, a_{44} \cup a_{54}\} = \{(0.9, -0.5), (0.9, -0.7)\}$.
For (D_k);
(i) $\sigma_1 = G \cup H$, where
$G = \{\bar{0}, \bar{1}, d_{11}, d_{12}, d_{13}, d_{14}, d_{15}\} = \{\bar{0}, \bar{1}, (0.6, -0.1), (0.9, -0.1), (0, -0.8), (0, -0.8), (0, -0.9)\}$ and $H = \{d_{11} \cup d_{12}, d_{11} \cup d_{13}, d_{11} \cup d_{14}, d_{11} \cup d_{15}, d_{12} \cup d_{13}, d_{12} \cup d_{14}, d_{12} \cup d_{15}, d_{13} \cup d_{14}, d_{13} \cup d_{15}, d_{14} \cup d_{15}\}$.
We omit some bipolar fuzzy sets of H which are in G and we obtain
$H = \{(0.6, -0.8), (0.6, -0.9), (0.9, -0.8), (0.9, -0.9)\}$.
(ii) $\sigma_2 = G \cup H$, where
$G = \{\bar{0}, \bar{1}, d_{21}, d_{22}, d_{23}, d_{24}, d_{25}\} = \{\bar{0}, \bar{1}, (0.1, -0.8), (0.1, -0.8), (0.2, -0.1), (0.2, -0.5), (0.9, -0.1)\}$ and $H = \{d_{21} \cup d_{22}, d_{21} \cup d_{23}, d_{21} \cup d_{24}, d_{21} \cup d_{25}, d_{22} \cup d_{23}, d_{22} \cup d_{24}, d_{22} \cup d_{25}, d_{23} \cup d_{24}, d_{23} \cup d_{25}, d_{24} \cup d_{25}\} = \{(0.2, -0.8), (0.9, -0.8), (0.9, -0.5)\}$.
(iii) $\sigma_3 = G \cup H$, where
$G = \{\bar{0}, \bar{1}, d_{31}, d_{32}, d_{33}, d_{34}, d_{35}\} = \{\bar{0}, \bar{1}, (0.9, -0.1), (0, -0.8), (0.7, -0.1), (0.9, -0.1), (0.2, -0.8)\}$ and $H = \{d_{31} \cup d_{32}, d_{31} \cup d_{33}, d_{31} \cup d_{34}, d_{31} \cup d_{35}, d_{32} \cup d_{33}, d_{32} \cup d_{34}, d_{32} \cup d_{35}, d_{33} \cup d_{34}, d_{33} \cup d_{35}, d_{34} \cup d_{35}\} = \{(0.9, -0.8), (0.7, -0.8)\}$.
(iv) $\sigma_4 = G \cup H$, where
$G = \{\bar{0}, \bar{1}, d_{41}, d_{42}, d_{43}, d_{44}, d_{45}\} = \{\bar{0}, \bar{1}, (0.2, -0.3), (0.1, -0.3), (0.2, -0.1), (0.1, -0.5), (0.2, -0.1)\}$ and $H = \{d_{41} \cup d_{42}, d_{41} \cup d_{43}, d_{41} \cup d_{44}, d_{41} \cup d_{45}, d_{42} \cup d_{43}, d_{42} \cup d_{44}, d_{42} \cup d_{45}, d_{43} \cup d_{44}, d_{43} \cup d_{45}, d_{44} \cup d_{45}\} = \{(0.2, -0.5)\}$.
(v) $\sigma_5 = G \cup H$, where
$G = \{\bar{0}, \bar{1}, d_{51}, d_{52}, d_{53}, d_{54}, d_{55}\} = \{\bar{0}, \bar{1}, (0.9, -0.1), (0.2, -0.4), (0.2, -0.4), (0.3, -0.7), (0.2, -0.7)\}$ and $H = \{d_{51} \cup d_{52}, d_{51} \cup d_{53}, d_{51} \cup d_{54}, d_{51} \cup d_{55}, d_{52} \cup d_{53}, d_{52} \cup d_{54}, d_{52} \cup d_{55}, d_{53} \cup d_{54}, d_{53} \cup d_{55}, d_{54} \cup d_{55}\} = \{(0.9, -0.4), (0.9, -0.7)\}$.

Step 3: Find Bipolar fuzzy score functions:
For (C_j),
(i) $BFSF(E) = 0.2786$ and $BFSF(F) = 0.2875$, where $t = 2$. $BFSF(C_1) = 0.2831$.
(ii) $BFSF(E) = 0.2679$ and $BFSF(F) = 0.2417$, where $t = 3$. $BFSF(C_2) = 0.2548$.
(iii) $BFSF(E) = 0.2321$ and $BFSF(F) = 0.1917$, where $t = 3$. $BFSF(C_3) = 0.2119$.
(iv) $BFSF(E) = 0.2643$ and $BFSF(F) = 0.3250$, where $t = 2$. $BFSF(C_4) = 0.2947$.
For (D_k),
(i) $BFSF(G) = 0.22071$ and $BFSF(H) = 0.2250$, where $s = 4$. $BFSF(D_1) = 0.2161$.
(ii) $BFSF(G) = 0.2857$ and $BFSF(F) = 0.2417$, where $s = 3$. $BFSF(D_2) = 0.2637$.
(iii) $BFSF(G) = 0.2786$ and $BFSF(H) = 0.2500$, where $s = 2$. $BFSF(D_3) = 0.2643$.
(iv) $BFSF(G) = 0.2321$ and $BFSF(H) = 0.175$, where $s = 1$. $BFSF(D_4) = 0.2036$.
(v) $BFSF(G) = 0.2321$ and $BFSF(H) = 0.3375$, where $s = 2$. $BFSF(D_6) = 0.2848$.

Step 4: Final Decision:
By organizing bipolar fuzzy score values for the alternatives C_1, C_2, C_3, C_4 and the attributes D_1, D_2, D_3, D_4, D_5 in ascending order, we obtain the following order $C_3 \leq C_2 \leq C_1 \leq C_4$ and $D_4 \leq D_1 \leq D_2 \leq D_3 \leq D_5$. Thus the patient P_3 suffers from dengue, the patient P_2 suffers from chikungunya, the patient P_1 suffers from diabetes, the patient P_4 suffers form tuberculosis.

6. Conclusions

With this study, we focus on the notions of bipolar fuzzy neighborhoods and the Q-neighborhood of a bipolar fuzzy point in bipolar fuzzy supra topological spaces and also investigate the necessary conditions for a family of bipolar fuzzy sets to generate a bipolar fuzzy supra topology. Finally, we present a method for data analysis under a bipolar fuzzy supra topological environment as a real-life application. These concepts play useful roles in further research. Generalizations of fuzzy sets have been successfully used in various fields such as economics, environmental science, engineering, and especially in decision-making problems. A bipolar fuzzy set is a new kind of fuzzy set dealing with positive and negative aspects. In recent years, some of the other fuzzy set generalizations have been combined with a bipolar fuzzy set; for instance, bipolar intuitionistic fuzzy sets [36], bipolar picture fuzzy set [37]. With the help of these novel fuzzy sets, similar applications may be studied by defining the supra topology, and also this theory can be developed in other research areas of general topology.

Author Contributions: Conceptualization, B.P.V.; Software, B.P.V.; Formal analysis, H.M.; Investigation, H.M.; Resources, B.P.V.; Data curation, ¸H.M.; Writing—original draft, B.P.V.; Supervision, B.P.V.; Project administration, B.P.V. All authors contributed equally in writing this article. All authors have read and agreed to the published version of the manuscript.

Funding: This research received no external funding.

Data Availability Statement: Data are contained within the article.

Conflicts of Interest: The authors declare no conflict of interest.

References

1. Zadeh, L.A. Fuzzy sets. *Inf. Control* **1965**, *8*, 338–353. [CrossRef]
2. Atanassov, K.T. Intuitionistic fuzzy sets. *Fuzzy Sets Syst.* **1986**, *20*, 87–96. [CrossRef]
3. Yager, R.R. Pythagorean fuzzy subsets. In Proceedings of the IFSA World Congress and NAFIPS Annual Meeting (IFSA/NAFIPS), Edmonton, AL, Canada, 24–28 June 2013; pp. 57–61.
4. Smarandache, F. *A Unifying Field in Logics. Neutrosophy/Neutrosophic Probability, Set and Logic*; American Research Press: Rehoboth, DE, USA, 1998.
5. Cuong, B.C.; Kreinovich, V. Picture fuzzy sets-a new concept for computational intelligence problems. In Proceedings of the 2013 World Congress on Information and Communication Technologies (WICT 2013), Hanoi, Vietnam, 15–18 December 2013; pp. 1–6.
6. Gündogdu, F.K.; Kahraman, C. Spherical fuzzy sets and spherical fuzzy TOPSIS method. *J. Intell. Fuzzy Syst.* **2019**, *36*, 337–352. [CrossRef]
7. Zhang, W.-R. Bipolar fuzzy sets and relations: A computational framework for cognitive modeling and multiagent decision analysis. In Proceedings of the NAFIPS/IFIS/NASA'94, Proceedings of the First International Joint Conference of The North American Fuzzy Information Processing Society Biannual Conference, San Antonio, TX, USA, 18–21 December 1994; pp. 305–309.
8. Lee, K.M. Bipolar-valued fuzzy sets and their operaitons. In Proceedings of the International Conference on Intelligent Technologies, Bangkok, Thailand, 13–15 December 2000; pp. 307–312.
9. Zhang, W.-R. The road from fuzzy sets to definable causality and bipolar quantum intelligence—To the memory of Lotfi A. Zadeh. *J. Intell. Fuzzy Syst.* **2019**, *36*, 3019–3032. [CrossRef]
10. Zhang, W.-R. Science vs. Sophistry—A historical debate on bipolar fuzzy sets and equilibrium-based mathematics for AI and QI. *J. Intell. Fuzzy Syst.* **2021**, *41*, 6781–6799. [CrossRef]
11. Lee, K.M. Bipolar fuzzy subalgebras and bipolar fuzzy ideals of BCK/BCI-algebras. *Bull. Malays. Math. Sci. Soc.* **2009**, *32*, 361–373.
12. Abdullah, S.; Aslam, M.; Ullah, K. Bipolar fuzzy soft sets and its applications in decision making problem. *J. Intell. Fuzzy Syst.* **2014**, *27*, 729–742. [CrossRef]
13. Kim, J.H.; Samanta, S.K.; Lim, P.K.; Lee, j.G.; Hur, K. Bipolar fuzzy topological spaces. *Ann. Fuzzy Math. Inform.* **2019**, *17*, 205–229. [CrossRef]
14. Anitha, M.S.; Muruganantha, K.L.; Arjunan, K. Notes on bipolar valued fuzzy subgroups of a group. *Bull. Soc. Math. Serv. Stand.* **2013**, *7*, 40–45. [CrossRef]
15. Mahmood, T.; Munir, M. On bipolar fuzzy subgroups. *World Appl. Sci. J.* **2013**, *27*, 1806–1811.
16. Pazar Varol, B. An approach to bipolar fuzzy submodules. *Twms J. Appl. Eng. Math.* **2021**, *11*, 168–175.
17. Subbian, S.P.; Kamaraj, M. Bipolar-valued fuzzy ideals of ring and bipolar-valued fuzzy ideal extensions in subrings. *Int. J. Math. Trends Technol.* **2018**, *61*, 155–163. [CrossRef]
18. Chang, C.L. Fuzzy topological spaces. *J. Math. Anal. Appl.* **1968**, *24*, 182–190. [CrossRef]
19. Lowen, R. Fuzzy topological spaces and fuzzy compactness. *J. Math. Anal. Appl.* **1976**, *56*, 621–633. [CrossRef]
20. Höhle, U. Upper semicontinuous fuzzy sets and applications. *J. Math. Anal. Appl.* **1980**, *78*, 659–673. [CrossRef]
21. Shostak, A. On a fuzzy topological structure. *Suppl. Rend. Circ. Matem. Palermo (Ser. II)* **1985**, *11*, 89–103.
22. Pu, P.-M.; Liu, Y.M. Fuzzy topology. II. product and quotient spaces. *J. Math. Anal. Appl.* **1980**, *77*, 20–37.

23. Pu, P.-M.; Liu, Y.M. Fuzzy topology. I. Neighborhood structure of a fuzzy point and Moore-Smith convergence. *J. Math. Anal. Appl.* **1980**, *76*, 571–599.
24. Coker, D. An introduction to intuitionistic fuzzy topological spaces. *Fuzzy Sets Syst.* **1997**, *88*, 81–89. [CrossRef]
25. El-Gayyar, M. Smooth neutrosophic topological spaces. *Neutrosophic Sets Syst.* **2016**, *65*, 65–72.
26. Salama, A.A.; Alblowi, S.A. Neutrosophic set and neutrosophic topological spaces. *Iosr J. Math.* **2012**, *3*, 31–35. [CrossRef]
27. Razaq, A.; Masmali, I.; Garg, H.; Shuaib, U. Picture fuzzy topological spaces and associated continuous functions. *Aims Math.* **2022**, *7*, 14840–14861. [CrossRef]
28. Azhagappan, M.; Kamaraj, M. Notes on bipolar valued fuzzy RW-closaed and bipolar valued fuzzy RW-open sets in bipolar valued fuzzy topological spaces. *Int. J. Math. Arch.* **2016**, *7*, 30–36.
29. Mashhour, A.S.; Allam, A.A.; Mahmoud, F.S.; Khedr, F.H. On supra topological spaces. *Indian J. Pure Appl. Math.* **1983**, *14*, 502–510.
30. Abd El-Monsef, M.E.; Ramadan, A.E. On fuzzy supra topological spaces, Indian. *J. Pure Appl. Math.* **1987**, *18*, 322–329.
31. Al-Shami, T.M. Paracompactness on supra topological spaces. *J. Linear Topol. Algebra* **2020**, *9*, 121–127.
32. Turanlı, N. An overview of intuitionistic fuzzy supratopological spaces. *Hacet. J. Math. Stat.* **2003**, *32*, 17–26.
33. Malkoç, H.; Varol, B.P. Bipolar fuzzy supra topological spaces. *Sak. Univ. J. Sci.* **2022**, *26*, 156–168. [CrossRef]
34. Lee, K.M. Comparison of interval-valued fuzzy sets, intuitionistic fuzzy sets, and bipolar-valued fuzzy sets. *J. Korean Inst. Intell. Syst.* **2004**, *14*, 125–129.
35. Jayaparthasarathy, G.; Little Flower, V.F.; Arockia Dasan, M. Neutrosophic Supra Topological Applications in Data Mining Process. *Neutrosophic Sets Syst.* **2019**, *27*, 80–97.
36. Ezhilmaran, D.; Sankar, K. Morphism of bipolar intuitionistic fuzzy graphs. *J. Discret. Math. Sci. Cryptogr.* **2015**, *18*, 605–621. [CrossRef]
37. Riaz, M.; Garg, H.; Farid, H.M.A.; Chinram, R. Multi-Criteria decision making based on bipolar picture fuzzy operators and new distance measures. *Comput. Model. Eng. Sci.* **2020**, *127*, 771–800. . [CrossRef]

symmetry

MDPI

Article

A Novel Concept of Level Graph in Interval-Valued Fuzzy Graphs with Application

Yongsheng Rao [1], Siran Lei [1], Ali Asghar Talebi [2,3] and Masomeh Mojahedfar [2,3,*]

1 Institute of Computing Science and Technology, Guangzhou University, Guangzhou 510006, China; rysheng@gzhu.edu.cn (Y.R); siranl@e.gzhu.edu.cn (S.L.)
2 Department of Mathematics, University of Mazandaran, Babolsar 4741613534, Iran; a.talebi@umz.ac.ir
3 School of Physics, Damghan University, Damghan 3671641167, Iran
* Correspondence: m.mojahedfar02@umail.umz.ac.ir

Abstract: Many problems of practical interest can be modeled and solved by using interval-valued fuzzy graph (IVFG) algorithms. An IVFG is a very useful and effective tool for studying various calculations, fields of intelligence, and computer science, such as networking, imaging, and other fields, such as biological sciences. In different applications, they present an appropriate construction means. There were limitations in the definition of fuzzy graphs (FGs), which prompted us to propose a new definition for IVFGs. Some interesting properties related to the new IVFGs are investigated, and enough conditions under which the level graph on IVFGs is equivalent are obtained. Therefore, in this study, we present the properties of a level graph (LG) of an IVFG, and four operations, the Cartesian product (CP), composition (CO), union, and join, are investigated on it. Today, in a treatment system, one of the issues that can be very valuable and important to the quality of service to patients is finding qualified and efficient people in each department, which is not an easy task. But the interval-valued fuzzy graph, as an important fuzzy graph, can help us by considering the ability of each person in the form of intervals of numbers and the effectiveness of each one on the other (according to the relationships between them) in order to find the most worthy people. So, an application of IVFG to find the most effective person in a hospital information system has been introduced.

Keywords: fuzzy set; interval-valued fuzzy graph; level graph; Cartesian product; composition; join

1. Introduction

Graph theory started its journey with the famous Konigsberg bridge problem. This problem was the birth of graph theory. Euler finally solved this problem with the help of graphs. Though graph theory is a relatively old subject, its growing applications are shown in research. After the presentation of fuzzy sets by Zadeh [1], fuzzy set (FS) theory has become a massive and strong study area in different fields, including life sciences, management science, statistics, graph theory, and decision making. Zadeh [2] presented the notion of an interval-valued fuzzy set (IVFS) as a continuation of FSs. Since the concept of IVFSs is a very useful issue, some researchers have conducted studies in this regard. Roy and Biswas [3] defined IVF relations. Rosenfeld [4] introduced the concept of fuzzy graphs (FGs). FG theory has various applications in medicine, engineering, psychology, and urban planning. Many researchers are trying to use it to optimize and save time. FG theory is finding an increasing number of applications in modeling real-time systems where the level of information in the system is different with various levels of precision. Some remarks on FGs were expressed by Bhattacharya [5]. Mordeson and Peng [6] described several notations on FGs. Akram et al. [7–10] introduced the definition of an IVFG and examined several of its properties. Hongmei and Lianhua [11] explained the new concept of IVFGs. Turksen [12] defined IVFSs based on normal forms. Some root-level modifications in IVFGs were presented by Jan et al. [13]. Nagoorgani and Radha [14] studied isomorphism on FGs. Rashmanlou and Pal [15] defined antipodal IVFGs. Certain types of m-polar IVFGs were proposed by [16]. Zihni et al. [17] introduced IVF soft graphs. IVFGs are of the FG family and have many abilities when involved with issues that FGs and VGs cannot explain. Since the membership value is not known, impartiality is a good advantage that can be well protected with an IVFG. Therefore, in this study, we extend the FG notion to the IVFG and discuss the well-known problems of level graphs, CP, CO, union, and join, on IVFGs. The level graph has a variety of applications in other sciences. They are used to identify the most effective person in an organization. Krishna et al. [18] explained new information in cubic graphs. Dey et al. [19–21] introduced the fuzzy minimum spanning tree with an interval type 2 fuzzy arc length and an interval type 2 FS in a fuzzy shortest path problem. Qiang et al. [22] expressed a novel description of VG structure and also investigated the new results of it. Some types of FGs were studied in [23,24].

The following points influenced us to write this article:

- Due to the enormous applications of LGs in fuzzy graphs, including level graphs for FGs in distinct decision-making problems, it also seems advantageous to expand the notion of LGs in IVFGs.
- There are numerous applications for the operation of LGs in chemistry, computer science, psychology, and other disciplines.
- Moreover, the LG of an IVFG has not yet been discussed and studied in the literature; therefore, we expanded the notion of a LG of an FG to a LG of an IVFG, and four operations, the Cartesian product, composition, union, and join, are investigated.

The intention of our proposed research work is given as follows:

- The aim of this research study is to investigate the notion of the Cartesian product and the composition of interval-valued fuzzy graphs.
- We introduce the concept of union and join of LGs on IVFGs and study their properties with some examples.
- The properties of LGs in IVFGs under important operations, the Cartesian product, composition, union, and join, are clearly shown.
- Finally, we present an application of an IVFG to find the most effective person in a hospital information system.

This paper is organized as follows.

In the first part, we study some theoretical background. In the second part, we explain some essential definitions of IVFGs and give details of new operations of them, such as the CP, CO, union, and join. In the third part, we introduce some operations of level graphs of IVFGs. In the last part, an application of IVFG is given.

2. Preliminaries

In this part, we present some definition which will be used throughout the paper.

A graph $\mathcal{G}^*$ is a ordered pair (X, E), where X is a nonempty set called the vertex set and $E \subseteq X \times X$ is called the edge set.

Definition 1 ([5])**.** *An FG of a graph $G^* = (X, E)$ is a pair $G = (\delta, \rho)$, where δ is an FS on X and ρ is an FS on E, so that*

$$\rho(ef) \leq \min\{\delta(e), \delta(f)\},$$

for all $ef \in E$.

The set of all closed interval on $[0,1]$ is denoted by $I[0,1]$.

Definition 2. *Let X be a nonempty set. A mapping $R = [\rho^l_R, \rho^u_R] : X \to I[0,1]$, ($x \to [\rho^l_R(x), \rho^u_R(x)] \in I[0,1]$) is called an IVFS on X. The lower and upper values of the vertex interval in IVFS are defined by ρ^l_R and ρ^u_R, respectively.*

Definition 3 ([7]). *A pair $G' = (R,S)$ of a graph $G^* = (X,E)$ is named an IVFG so that $R = [\rho^l_R, \rho^u_R]$ is an IVFS on X and $S = [\rho^l_S, \rho^u_S]$ is an IVFS on E that satisfies the following conditions:*

$$\rho^l_S(ef) \leq \min\{\rho^l_R(e), \rho^l_R(f)\},$$
$$\rho^u_S(ef) \leq \min\{\rho^u_R(e), \rho^u_R(f)\},$$

for all $ef \in E$.

Definition 4. *Assume that $G'_1 = (R_1, S_1)$ and $G'_2 = (R_2, S_2)$ are two IVFGs of $G^*_1 = (X_1, E_1)$ and $G^*_2 = (X_2, E_2)$, respectively.*

(i) The union $G'_1 \cup G'_2$ is defined as the pair (R,S) of IVFSs on the union of graphs G^*_1 and G^*_2, so that

$$(a)\begin{cases}(\rho^l_{R_1} \cup \rho^l_{R_2})(e) = \rho^l_{R_1}(e) & if\ e \in X_1, e \notin X_2\\ (\rho^l_{R_1} \cup \rho^l_{R_2})(e) = \rho^l_{R_2}(e) & if\ e \in X_2, e \notin X_1\\ (\rho^l_{R_1} \cup \rho^l_{R_2})(e) = \max\{\rho^l_{R_1}(e), \rho^l_{R_2}(e)\} & if\ e \in X_1 \cap X_2\end{cases}$$

$$(b)\begin{cases}(\rho^u_{R_1} \cup \rho^u_{R_2})(e) = \rho^u_{R_1}(e) & if\ e \in X_1, e \notin X_2\\ (\rho^u_{R_1} \cup \rho^u_{R_2})(e) = \rho^u_{R_2}(e) & if\ e \in X_2, e \notin X_1\\ (\rho^u_{R_1} \cup \rho^u_{R_2})(e) = \max\{\rho^u_{R_1}(e), \rho^u_{R_2}(e)\} & if\ e \in X_1 \cap X_2\end{cases}$$

$$(c)\begin{cases}(\rho^l_{S_1} \cup \rho^l_{S_2})(ef) = \rho^l_{S_1}(ef) & if\ ef \in E_1, ef \notin E_2\\ \rho^l_{S_1} \cup \rho^l_{S_2})(ef) = \rho^l_{S_2}(ef) & if\ ef \in E_2, ef \notin E_1\\ (\rho^l_{S_1} \cup \rho^l_{S_2})(ef) = \max\{\rho^l_{S_1}(ef), \rho^l_{S_2}(ef)\} & if\ ef \in E_1 \cap E_2\end{cases}$$

$$(d)\begin{cases}(\rho^u_{S_1} \cup \rho^u_{S_2})(ef) = \rho^u_{S_1}(ef) & if\ ef \in E_1, ef \notin E_2\\ (\rho^u_{S_1} \cup \rho^u_{S_2})(ef) = \rho^u_{S_2}(ef) & if\ ef \in E_2, ef \notin E_1\\ (\rho^u_{S_1} \cup \rho^u_{S_2})(ef) = \max\{\rho^u_{S_1}(ef), \rho^u_{S_2}(ef)\} & if\ ef \in E_1 \cap E_2.\end{cases}$$

(ii) The CP of IVFGs G'_1 and G'_2, denoted by $G'_1 \times G'_2$, is the pair (R,S) of IVFSs defined on the CP of graphs G^*_1 and G^*_2, so that

$$(a)\begin{cases}(\rho^l_{R_1} \times \rho^l_{R_2})(e_1, e_2) = \min\{\rho^l_{R_1}(e_1), \rho^l_{R_2}(e_2)\}\\ (\rho^u_{R_1} \times \rho^u_{R_2})(e_1, e_2) = \min\{\rho^u_{R_1}(e_1), \rho^u_{R_2}(e_2)\}\end{cases} \text{for all } (e_1, e_2) \in X_1 \times X_2$$

$$(b)\begin{cases}(\rho^l_{S_1} \times \rho^l_{S_2})((e, e_2)(e, f_2)) = \min\{\rho^l_{R_1}(e), \rho^l_{S_2}(e_2 f_2)\}\\ (\rho^u_{S_1} \times \rho^u_{S_2})((e, e_2)(e, f_2)) = \min\{\rho^u_{R_1}(e), \rho^u_{S_2}(e_2 f_2)\}\end{cases} \text{for all } e \in X_1, e_2 f_2 \in E_2$$

$$(c)\begin{cases}(\rho^l_{S_1} \times \rho^l_{S_2})((e_1, k)(f_1, k)) = \min\{\rho^l_{S_1}(e_1 f_1), \rho^l_{R_2}(k)\}\\ (\rho^u_{S_1} \times \rho^u_{S_2})((e_1, k)(f_1, k)) = \min\{\rho^u_{S_1}(e_1 f_1), \rho^u_{R_2}(k)\}\end{cases} \text{for all } k \in X_2, e_1 f_1 \in E_1.$$

(iii) The CO of two IVFGs G'_1 and G'_2, shown by $G'_1[G'_2]$, is the pair (R,S) of IVFSs defined on the CO $G'^*_1[G'^*_2]$, so that

$$(a)\begin{cases}(\rho^l_{R_1} \circ \rho^l_{R_2})(e_1, e_2) = \min\{\rho^l_{R_1}(e_1), \rho^l_{R_2}(e_2)\}\\ (\rho^u_{R_1} \circ \rho^u_{R_2})(e_1, e_2) = \min\{\rho^u_{R_1}(e_1), \rho^u_{R_2}(e_2)\}\end{cases} \text{for all } (e_1, e_2) \in X_1 \times X_2$$

$$(b)\begin{cases}(\rho^l_{S_1} \circ \rho^l_{S_2})((e, e_2)(e, f_2)) = \min\{\rho^l_{R_1}(e), \rho^l_{S_2}(e_2 f_2)\}\\ (\rho^u_{S_1} \circ \rho^u_{S_2})((e, e_2)(e, f_2)) = \min\{\rho^u_{R_1}(e), \rho^u_{S_2}(e_2 f_2)\}\end{cases} \text{for all } e \in X_1, e_2 f_2 \in E_2$$

$$(c)\begin{cases}(\rho^l_{S_1} \circ \rho^l_{S_2})((e_1, k)(f_1, k)) = \min\{\rho^l_{S_1}(e_1 f_1), \rho^l_{R_2}(k)\}\\ (\rho^u_{S_1} \circ \rho^u_{S_2})((e_1, k)(f_1, k)) = \min\{\rho^u_{S_1}(e_1 f_1), \rho^u_{R_2}(k)\}\end{cases} \text{for all } k \in X_2, e_1 f_1 \in E_1.$$

$$(d)\begin{cases}(\rho^l_{S_1} \circ \rho^l_{S_2})((e_1, e_2)(f_1, f_2)) = \min\{\rho^l_{S_1}(e_1 f_1), \rho^l_{R_2}(e_2), \rho^l_{R_2}(f_2)\}\\ (\rho^u_{S_1} \circ \rho^u_{S_2})((e_1, e_2)(f_1, f_2)) = \min\{\rho^u_{S_1}(e_1 f_1), \rho^u_{R_2}(e_2), \rho^u_{R_2}(f_2)\}\end{cases} \text{for all } e_2, f_2 \in$$
$X_2, e_1 f_1 \in E_1, e_2 \neq f_2$.

3. Level Graphs of the Interval-Valued Fuzzy Graphs

In this section, we introduce a new concept of $[\psi, \theta]-$ level graph on IVFGs.

Definition 5. *For all $[\psi,\theta] \in I[0,1]$, $[\psi,\theta]$-level set of an IVFS R on X is defined to be* $R_{[\psi,\theta]} = \{e \in X : \rho^l_R(e) \geq \psi, \rho^u_R(e) \geq \theta\}$.

Theorem 1. *Suppose that X is a nonempty set, and $R = [\rho^l_R, \rho^u_R]$ and $S = [\rho^l_S, \rho^u_S]$ are IVFGs on X and E, respectively. Then, $G' = (R,S)$ is an IVFG if and only if $(R_{[\psi,\theta]}, S_{[\psi,\theta]})$, named the $[\psi,\theta]$-level graph of G', is a graph for every $[\psi,\theta] \in I[0,1]$.*

Proof. Let $G' = (R,S)$ be an IVFG. For each $[\psi,\theta] \in I[0,1]$, if $ef \in S_{[\psi,\theta]}$, then, $\rho^l_S(ef) \geq \psi, \rho^u_S(ef) \geq \theta$. Since G' is an IVFG,

$$\psi \leq \rho^l_S(ef) \leq \min\{\rho^l_R(e), \rho^l_R(f)\},$$

$$\theta \leq \rho^u_S(ef) \leq \min\{\rho^u_R(e), \rho^u_R(f)\},$$

and so

$\psi \leq \rho^l_R(e), \psi \leq \rho^l_R(f), \theta \leq \rho^u_R(e), \theta \leq \rho^u_R(f)$, that is, $e, f \in R_{[\psi,\theta]}$.

Therefore, $(R_{[\psi,\theta]}, S_{[\psi,\theta]})$ is a graph for every $[\psi,\theta] \in I[0,1]$.

Conversely, suppose $(R_{[\psi,\theta]}, S_{[\psi,\theta]})$ is a graph for all $[\psi,\theta] \in I[0,1]$. For each $ef \in E$, we consider $\rho^l_S(ef) = \psi$ and $\rho^u_S(ef) = \theta$. Then, $ef \in S_{[\psi,\theta]}$. Since $(R_{[\psi,\theta]}, S_{[\psi,\theta]})$ is a graph; thus, we have $e, f \in R_{[\psi,\theta]}$. Hence, $\psi \leq \rho^l_R(e), \psi \leq \rho^l_R(f), \theta \leq \rho^u_R(e)$, and $\theta \leq \rho^u_R(f)$. Therefore,

$$\rho^l_S(ef) = \psi \leq \min\{\rho^l_R(e), \rho^l_R(f)\},$$

$$\rho^u_S(ef) = \theta \leq \min\{\rho^u_R(e), \rho^u_R(f)\},$$

that is, $G' = (R,S)$ is an IVFG. □

Theorem 2. *Suppose $G'_1 = (R_1, S_1)$ and $G'_2 = (R_2, S_2)$ are the IVFGs of $G^*_1 = (X_1, E_1)$ and $G^*_2 = (X_2, E_2)$, respectively. Then, the pair $G' = (R,S)$ of an IVFG on G^*_1 and G^*_2 is the CP of G'_1 and G'_2 if and only if for every $[\psi,\theta] \in I[0,1]$ the $[\psi,\theta]$-level graph $(R_{[\psi,\theta]}, S_{[\psi,\theta]})$ is the CP of $((R_1)_{[\psi,\theta]}, (S_1)_{[\psi,\theta]})$ and $((R_2)_{[\psi,\theta]}, (S_2)_{[\psi,\theta]})$.*

Proof. Suppose that $G' = (R,S)$ is the CP of the IVFGs G'_1 and G'_2. For each $[\psi,\theta] \in I[0,1]$, if $(e,f) \in R_{[\psi,\theta]}$, then

$$\psi \leq \rho^l_R(e,f) = \min\{\rho^l_{R_1}(e), \rho^l_{R_2}(f)\},$$
$$\theta \leq \rho^u_R(e,f) = \min\{\rho^u_{R_1}(e), \rho^u_{R_2}(f)\}.$$

Therefore, $e \in (R_1)_{[\psi,\theta]}$ and $f \in (R_2)_{[\psi,\theta]}$; that is, $(e,f) \in (R_1)_{[\psi,\theta]} \times (R_2)_{[\psi,\theta]}$.

Therefore, $R_{[\psi,\theta]} \subseteq (R_1)_{[\psi,\theta]} \times (R_2)_{[\psi,\theta]}$. If $(e,f) \in (R_1)_{[\psi,\theta]} \times (R_2)_{[\psi,\theta]}$, then $e \in (R_1)_{[\psi,\theta]}$ and $f \in (R_2)_{[\psi,\theta]}$. Here, we have

$$\psi \leq \min\{\rho^l_{R_1}(e), \rho^l_{R_2}(f)\},$$

$$\theta \leq \min\{\rho^u_{R_1}(e), \rho^u_{R_2}(f)\}.$$

Because (R,S) is the CP of G'_1 and G'_2, $\psi \leq \rho^l_R(e,f)$ and $\theta \leq \rho^u_R(e,f)$, so we have $(e,f) \in R_{[\psi,\theta]}$. Thus,

$$(R_1)_{[\psi,\theta]} \times (R_2)_{[\psi,\theta]} \subseteq R_{[\psi,\theta]}$$

and so

$$(R_1)_{[\psi,\theta]} \times (R_2)_{[\psi,\theta]} = R_{[\psi,\theta]}.$$

Now, we prove $S_{[\psi,\theta]} = E$, such that E is the edge set of the CP $(G'_1)_{[\psi,\theta]} \times (G'_2)_{[\psi,\theta]}$ for every $[\psi,\theta] \in I[0,1]$.

Suppose $((e_1, e_2)(f_1, f_2)) \in S_{[\psi,\theta]}$. Therefore,

$$\rho_S^l(e_1, e_2)(f_1, f_2) \geq \psi, \quad \rho_S^u(e_1, e_2)(f_1, f_2) \geq \theta.$$

Since (R, S) is the CP of $G_1^{'}$ and $G_2^{'}$, it satisfies one of the below conditions:

(i) $e_1 = f_1$ and $e_2f_2 \in E_2$,
(ii) $e_2 = f_2$ and $e_1f_1 \in E_1$.

In the first condition (i), we have:

$$\rho_S^l((e_1, e_2)(f_1, f_2)) = \min\{\rho_{R_1}^l(e_1), \rho_{S_2}^l(e_2f_2)\} \geq \psi,$$

$$\rho_S^u((e_1, e_2)(f_1, f_2)) = \min\{\rho_{R_1}^u(e_1), \rho_{S_2}^u(e_2f_2)\} \geq \theta,$$

and so $\rho_{R_1}^l(e_1) \geq \psi, \rho_{R_1}^u(e_1) \geq \theta, \rho_{S_2}^l(e_2f_2) \geq \psi, \rho_{S_2}^u(e_2f_2) \geq \theta$.

It follows that $e_1 = f_1 \in (R_1)_{[\psi,\theta]}$ and $e_2f_2 \in (S_2)_{[\psi,\theta]}$; that is, $((e_1, e_2)(f_1, f_2)) \in E$.

Similarly, for condition (ii), we conclude $((e_1, e_2)(f_1, f_2)) \in E$. Thus, $S_{[\psi,\theta]} \subseteq E$. For each $((e, e_2)(e, f_2)) \in E$, $\rho_{R_1}^l(e) \geq \psi, \rho_{R_1}^u(e) \geq \theta, \rho_{S_2}^l(e_2f_2) \geq \psi, \rho_{S_2}^u(e_2f_2) \geq \theta$.

Because (R, S) is the CP of $G_1^{'}$ and $G_2^{'}$, we have:

$$\rho_S^l((e, e_2)(e, f_2)) = \min\{\rho_{R_1}^l(e), \rho_{S_2}^l(e_2f_2)\} \geq \psi,$$

$$\rho_S^u((e, e_2)(e, f_2)) = \min\{\rho_{R_1}^u(e), \rho_{S_2}^u(e_2f_2)\} \geq \psi.$$

Therefore, $((e, e_2)(e, f_2)) \in S_{[\psi,\theta]}$. Similarly, for each $(e_1, k)(f_1, k) \in E$, we have $((e_1, k)(f_1, k)) \in S_{[\psi,\theta]}$. Thus, $E \subseteq S_{[\psi,\theta]}$, and so $E = S_{[\psi,\theta]}$.

Conversely, suppose the $[\psi, \theta]$-level graph $(R_{[\psi,\theta]}, S_{[\psi,\theta]})$ is the CP of $((R_1)_{[\psi,\theta]}, (S_1)_{[\psi,\theta]})$ and $((R_2)_{[\psi,\theta]}, (S_2)_{[\psi,\theta]})$, for all $[\psi, \theta] \in I[0, 1]$.

Suppose $\min\{\rho_{R_1}^l(e_1), \rho_{R_2}^l(e_2)\} = \psi$ and $\min\{\rho_{R_1}^u(e_1), \rho_{R_2}^u(e_2)\} = \theta$, for $(e_1, e_2) \in X_1 \times X_2$. Then, $e_1 \in R_{1[\psi,\theta]}$ and $e_2 \in R_{2[\psi,\theta]}$. By the hypothesis, $(e_1, e_2) \in R_{[\psi,\theta]}$. Hence,

$$\rho_R^l(e_1, e_2) \geq \psi = \min\{\rho_{R_1}^l(e_1), \rho_{R_2}^l(e_2)\},$$

$$\rho_R^u(e_1, e_2) \geq \theta = \min\{\rho_{R_1}^u(e_1), \rho_{R_2}^u(e_2)\}.$$

Consider $\rho_R^l(e_1, e_2) = \psi^{'}$ and $\rho_R^u(e_1, e_2) = \theta^{'}$. Then, we have $(e_1, e_2) \in R_{[\psi',\theta']}$. Since $(R_{[\psi',\theta']}, S_{[\psi',\theta']})$ is the CP of $(R_{1[\psi',\theta']}, S_{1[\psi',\theta']})$ and $(R_{2[\psi',\theta']}, S_{2[\psi',\theta']})$, then $e_1 \in R_{1[\psi',\theta']}$ and $e_2 \in R_{2[\psi',\theta']}$. Hence,

$$\rho_{R_1}^l(e_1) \geq \psi^{'} = \rho_R^l(e_1, e_2), \quad \rho_{R_1}^u(e_1) \geq \theta^{'} = \rho_R^u(e_1, e_2),$$

$$\rho_{R_2}^l(e_2) \geq \psi^{'} = \rho_R^l(e_1, e_2), \quad \rho_{R_2}^u(e_2) \geq \theta^{'} = \rho_R^u(e_1, e_2).$$

It follows that

$$\rho_R^l(e_1, e_2) \leq \min\{\rho_{R_1}^l(e_1), \rho_{R_2}^l(e_2)\},$$
$$\rho_R^u(e_1, e_2) \leq \min\{\rho_{R_1}^u(e_1), \rho_{R_2}^u(e_2)\}.$$

Therefore,

$$\rho_R^l(e_1, e_2) = \min\{\rho_{R_1}^l(e_1), \rho_{R_2}^l(e_2)\},$$
$$\rho_R^u(e_1, e_2) = \min\{\rho_{R_1}^u(e_1), \rho_{R_2}^u(e_2)\},$$

for all $(e_1, e_2) \in X_1 \times X_2$. That is, $\rho_R^l = \rho_{R_1}^l \times \rho_{R_2}^l, \rho_R^u = \rho_{R_1}^u \times \rho_{R_2}^u$.

For each $e \in X_1$ and $e_2f_2 \in E_2$, suppose

$$\min\{\rho_{R_1}^l(e), \rho_{S_2}^l(e_2f_2)\} = \psi, \quad \min\{\rho_{R_1}^u(e), \rho_{S_2}^u(e_2f_2)\} = \theta,$$

$$\rho^l_S((e,e_2)(e,f_2)) = \psi', \quad \rho^u_S((e,e_2)(e,f_2)) = \theta'.$$

Then, $\rho^l_{R_1}(e) \geq \psi$, $\rho^u_{R_1}(e) \geq \theta$, $\rho^l_{S_2}(e_2f_2) \geq \psi$, $\rho^u_{S_2}(e_2f_2) \geq \theta$ and $((e,e_2)(e,f_2)) \in S_{[\psi',\theta']}$, i.e., $e \in R_1[\psi,\theta]$, $e_2f_2 \in S_2[\psi,\theta]$, and $(e,e_2)(e,f_2) \in S_{[\psi',\theta']}$.

Since $(R_{[\psi,\theta]}, S_{[\psi,\theta]})$ is the CP of $((R_1)_{[\psi,\theta]}, (S_1)_{[\psi,\theta]})$ and $((R_2)_{[\psi,\theta]}, (S_2)_{[\psi,\theta]})$, and also $(R_{[\psi',\theta']}, S_{[\psi',\theta']})$ is the CP of $((R_1)_{[\psi',\theta']}, (S_1)_{[\psi',\theta']})$ and $((R_2)_{[\psi',\theta']}, (S_2)_{[\psi',\theta']})$, we have $(e,e_2)(e,f_2) \in S_{[\psi,\theta]}$, $e \in R_{1[\psi',\theta']}$, and $e_2f_2 \in S_{2[\psi',\theta']}$, which implies $((e,e_2)(e,f_2)) \in S_{[\psi,\theta]}$, $\rho^l_{R1}(e) \geq \psi', \rho^u_{R1}(e) \geq \theta', \rho^l_{S2}(e_2f_2) \geq \psi', \rho^u_{S2}(e_2f_2) \geq \theta'$.

Therefore,

$$\rho^l_S((e,e_2)(e,f_2)) \geq \psi = \min\{\rho^l_{R_1}(e), \rho^l_{S_2}(e_2f_2)\},$$
$$\rho^u_S((e,e_2)(e,f_2)) \geq \theta = \min\{\rho^u_{R_1}(e), \rho^u_{S_2}(e_2f_2)\},$$

and also

$$\min\{\rho^l_{R_1}(e), \rho^l_{S_2}(e_2f_2)\} \geq \psi' = \rho^l_S((e,e_2)(e,f_2)),$$
$$\min\{\rho^u_{R_1}(e), \rho^u_{S_2}(e_2f_2)\} \geq \theta' = \rho^u_S((e,e_2)(e,f_2)).$$

Thus,

$$\min\{\rho^l_{R_1}(e), \rho^l_{S_2}(e_2f_2)\} = \rho^l_S((e,e_2)(e,f_2)),$$
$$\min\{\rho^u_{R_1}(e), \rho^u_{S_2}(e_2f_2)\} = \rho^u_S((e,e_2)(e,f_2)),$$

for all $e \in X_1$ and $e_2f_2 \in E_2$. Also, similarly, we obtain

$$\min\{\rho^l_{S_1}(e_1f_1), \rho^l_{R_2}(k)\} = \rho^l_S((e_1,k)(f_1,k)),$$

$$\min\{\rho^u_{S_1}(e_1f_1), \rho^u_{R_2}(k)\} = \rho^l_S((e_1,k)(f_1,k)),$$

for all $k \in X_2$ and $e_1f_1 \in E_1$. □

Example 1. *Suppose $G_1' = (R_1, S_1)$ and $G_2' = (R_2, S_2)$ are two IVFGs of the graphs $G_1^* = (X_1, E_1)$ and $G_2^* = (X_2, E_2)$, respectively, so that $X_1 = \{a,b,c,d\}$, $X_2 = \{g,h\}$, $E_1 = \{ab, bd, , cd, ac, bc\}$, and $E_2 = \{gh\}$, as is shown in Figure 1.*

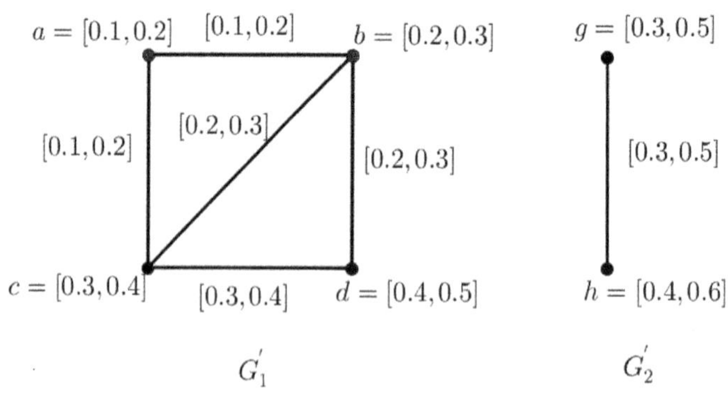

Figure 1. IVFGs G_1' and G_2'.

$$(\rho^l_{S_1} \times \rho^l_{S_2})((a,g)(b,g)) = 0.1, \quad (\rho^u_{S_1} \times \rho^u_{S_2})((a,g)(b,g)) = 0.2$$
$$(\rho^l_{S_1} \times \rho^l_{S_2})((a,g)(a,h)) = 0.1, \quad (\rho^u_{S_1} \times \rho^u_{S_2})((a,g)(a,h)) = 0.2$$
$$(\rho^l_{S_1} \times \rho^l_{S_2})((a,g)(c,g)) = 0.1, \quad (\rho^u_{S_1} \times \rho^u_{S_2})((a,g)(c,g)) = 0.2$$
$$(\rho^l_{S_1} \times \rho^l_{S_2})((b,g)(b,h)) = 0.2, \quad (\rho^u_{S_1} \times \rho^u_{S_2})((b,g)(b,h)) = 0.3$$

$$(\rho^l_{S_1} \times \rho^l_{S_2})((b,g)(d,g)) = 0.2, \quad (\rho^u_{S_1} \times \rho^u_{S_2})((b,g)(d,g)) = 0.3$$
$$(\rho^l_{S_1} \times \rho^l_{S_2})((b,g)(c,g)) = 0.2, \quad (\rho^u_{S_1} \times \rho^u_{S_2})((b,g)(c,g)) = 0.3$$
$$(\rho^l_{S_1} \times \rho^l_{S_2})((b,h)(d,h)) = 0.2, \quad (\rho^u_{S_1} \times \rho^u_{S_2})((b,h)(d,h)) = 0.3$$
$$(\rho^l_{S_1} \times \rho^l_{S_2})((b,h)(a,h)) = 0.1, \quad (\rho^u_{S_1} \times \rho^u_{S_2})((b,h)(a,h)) = 0.2$$
$$(\rho^l_{S_1} \times \rho^l_{S_2})((b,h)(c,h)) = 0.2, \quad (\rho^u_{S_1} \times \rho^u_{S_2})((b,h)(c,h)) = 0.3$$
$$(\rho^l_{S_1} \times \rho^l_{S_2})((d,h)(d,g)) = 0.3, \quad (\rho^u_{S_1} \times \rho^u_{S_2})((d,h)(d,g)) = 0.5$$
$$(\rho^l_{S_1} \times \rho^l_{S_2})((d,h)(c,h)) = 0.3, \quad (\rho^u_{S_1} \times \rho^u_{S_2})((d,h)(c,h)) = 0.4$$
$$(\rho^l_{S_1} \times \rho^l_{S_2})((c,h)(c,g)) = 0.3, \quad (\rho^u_{S_1} \times \rho^u_{S_2})((c,h)(c,g)) = 0.4$$
$$(\rho^l_{S_1} \times \rho^l_{S_2})((c,h)(a,h)) = 0.1, \quad (\rho^u_{S_1} \times \rho^u_{S_2})((c,h)(a,h)) = 0.2$$
$$(\rho^l_{S_1} \times \rho^l_{S_2})((c,g)(d,g)) = 0.3, \quad (\rho^u_{S_1} \times \rho^u_{S_2})((c,g)(d,g)) = 0.4$$

We obtained the CP of the IVFGs G_1' and G_2', which are shown in Figure 2.

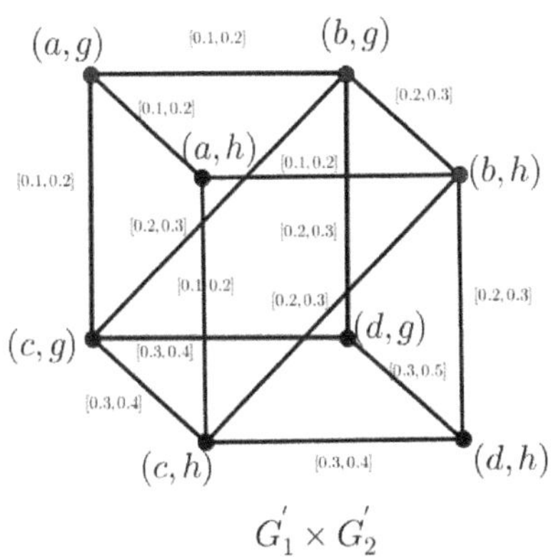

Figure 2. The CP of the IVFGs G_1' and G_2'.

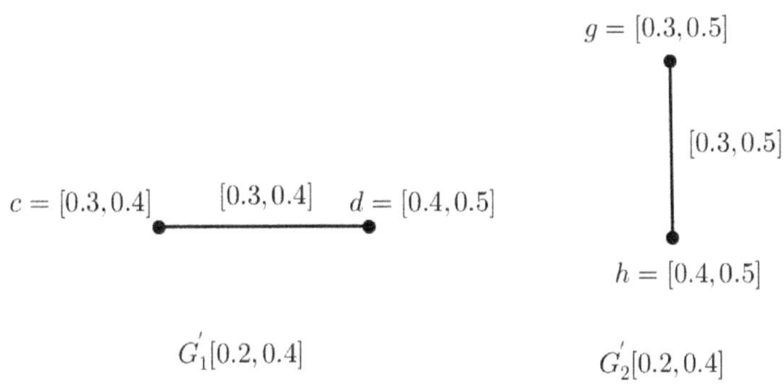

Figure 3. The $[0.2, 0.4]$-level graphs of the IVFGs G_1' and G_2'.

Assume $[\psi, \theta] = [0.2, 0.4]$. *Then,* $R_{1[0.2,0.4]} = \{c, d\}$, $R_{2[0.2,0.4]} = \{g, h\}$, $E_{1[0.2,0.4]} = \{cd\}$, *and* $E_{2[0.2,0.4]} = \{gh\}$, *as is shown in Figure 3.*

We obtain the CP of the IVFGs $G'_{1[0.2,0.4]}$ and $G'_{2[0.2,0.4]}$. The CP of the IVFGs $G'_{1[0.2,0.4]}$ and $G'_{2[0.2,0.4]}$ is shown in Figure 4.

$$(\rho^l_{S_1} \times \rho^l_{S_2})((c,g)(c,h)) = 0.3, \quad (\rho^u_{S_1} \times \rho^u_{S_2})((c,g)(c,h)) = 0.4$$

$$(\rho^l_{S_1} \times \rho^l_{S_2})((d,g)(d,h)) = 0.3, \quad (\rho^u_{S_1} \times \rho^u_{S_2})((d,g)(d,h)) = 0.5$$

$$(\rho^l_{S_1} \times \rho^l_{S_2})((c,h)(d,h)) = 0.3, \quad (\rho^u_{S_1} \times \rho^u_{S_2})((c,h)(d,h)) = 0.4$$

$$(\rho^l_{S_1} \times \rho^l_{S_2})((c,g)(d,g)) = 0.3, \quad (\rho^u_{S_1} \times \rho^u_{S_2})((c,g)(d,g)) = 0.4$$

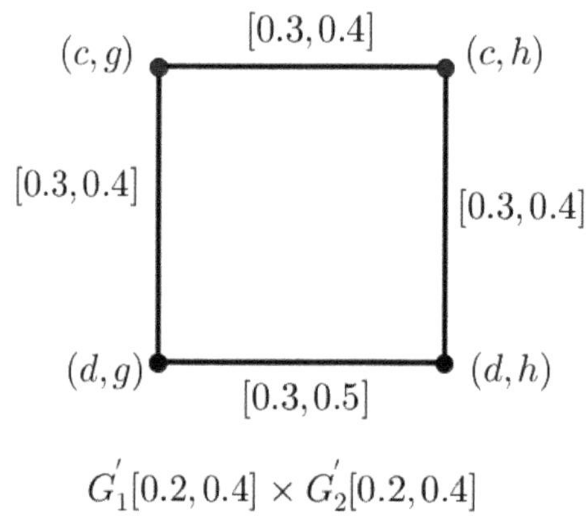

Figure 4. The CP of graphs $G'_{1[0.2,0.4]}$ and $G'_{2[0.2,0.4]}$.

Here, we investigated the properties of the CP IVFGs G'_1 and G'_2 from their $[0.2, 0.4]$-level graphs of G'_1 and G'_2.

We concluded that the pair $G' = (R, S)$ is the CP of G'_1 and G'_2 if and only if the $[0.2, 0.4]$-level graph $(R_{[0.2,0.4]}, S_{[0.2,0.4]})$ is the CP of the two graphs $G'_{1[0.2,0.4]}$ and $G'_{2[0.2,0.4]}$.

Also, we consider $[\psi, \theta] = [0.2, 0.3]$. Then, $R_{1[0.2,0.3]} = \{c, d\}$, $R_{2[0.2,0.3]} = \{g, h\}$, $E_{1[0.2,0.3]} = \{bc, bd, cd\}$, and $E_{2[0.2,0.3]} = \{gh\}$, is shown in Figure 5.

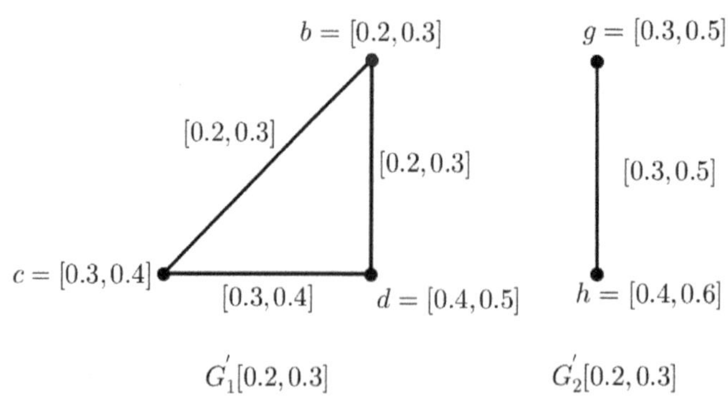

Figure 5. The $[0.2, 0.3]$-level graphs of the IVFGs G'_1 and G'_2.

We obtain the CP of the IVFGs $G'_{1[0.2,0.3]}$ and $G'_{2[0.2,0.3]}$. The CP of the IVFGs $G'_{1[0.2,0.3]}$ and $G'_{2[0.2,0.3]}$ is shown in Figure 6.

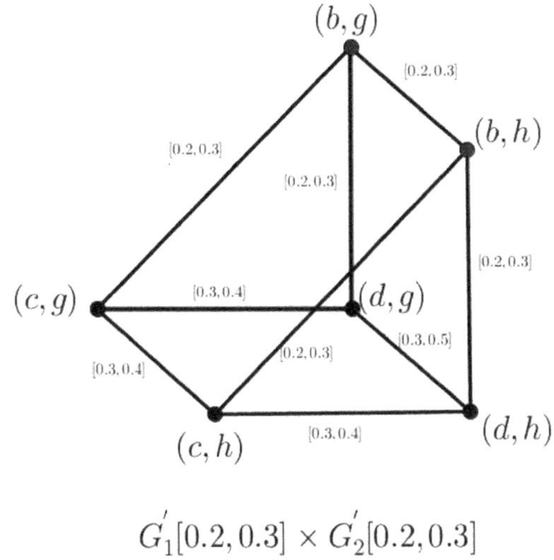

Figure 6. The CP of graphs $G'_{1[0.2,0.3]}$ and $G'_{2[0.2,0.3]}$

$$(\rho^l_{S_1} \times \rho^l_{S_2})((b,g)(b,h)) = 0.2 \quad ,(\rho^u_{S_1} \times \rho^u_{S_2})((b,g)(b,h)) = 0.3$$
$$(\rho^l_{S_1} \times \rho^l_{S_2})((d,g)(d,h)) = 0.3 \quad ,(\rho^u_{S_1} \times \rho^u_{S_2})((d,g)(d,h)) = 0.5$$
$$(\rho^l_{S_1} \times \rho^l_{S_2})((c,g)(c,h)) = 0.3 \quad ,(\rho^u_{S_1} \times \rho^u_{S_2})((c,g)(c,h)) = 0.4$$
$$(\rho^l_{S_1} \times \rho^l_{S_2})((b,g)(d,g)) = 0.2 \quad ,(\rho^u_{S_1} \times \rho^u_{S_2})((b,g)(d,g)) = 0.3$$
$$(\rho^l_{S_1} \times \rho^l_{S_2})((b,g)(c,g)) = 0.2 \quad ,(\rho^u_{S_1} \times \rho^u_{S_2})((b,g)(c,g)) = 0.3$$
$$(\rho^l_{S_1} \times \rho^l_{S_2})((c,g)(d,g)) = 0.3 \quad ,(\rho^u_{S_1} \times \rho^u_{S_2})((c,g)(d,g)) = 0.4$$
$$(\rho^l_{S_1} \times \rho^l_{S_2})((b,h)(d,h)) = 0.2 \quad ,(\rho^u_{S_1} \times \rho^u_{S_2})((b,h)(d,h)) = 0.3$$
$$(\rho^l_{S_1} \times \rho^l_{S_2})((b,h)(c,h)) = 0.2 \quad ,(\rho^u_{S_1} \times \rho^u_{S_2})((b,h)(c,h)) = 0.3$$
$$(\rho^l_{S_1} \times \rho^l_{S_2})((d,h)(c,h)) = 0.3 \quad ,(\rho^u_{S_1} \times \rho^u_{S_2})((d,h)(c,h)) = 0.4$$

In this example, we investigated the properties of the CP IVFGs G'_1 and G'_2 from their $[0.2, 0.3]$-level graphs of G'_1 and G'_2.

We concluded that the pair $G' = (R, S)$ is the CP of G'_1 and G'_2 if and only if the $[0.2, 0.4]$-level graph $(R_{[0.2,0.3]}, S_{[0.2,0.3]})$ is the CP of two graphs $G'_{1[0.2,0.3]}$ and $G'_{2[0.2,0.3]}$.

Corollary 1. *Let $G'_1 = (R_1, S_1)$ and $G'_2 = (R_2, S_2)$ be IVFGs. Then, the CP $G'_1 \times G'_2$ is an IVFG.*

Theorem 3. *Suppose $G'_1 = (R_1, S_1)$ and $G'_2 = (R_2, S_2)$ are two IVFGs of G^*_1 and G^*_2, respectively. Then, the pair $G' = (R, S)$ of the IVFGs on $G^*_1[G^*_2]$ is the CO of G'_1 and G'_2 if and only if for every $[\psi, \theta] \in I[0, 1]$, the $[\psi, \theta]$-level graph $(R_{[\psi,\theta]}, S_{[\psi,\theta]})$ is the CO of $((R_1)_{[\psi,\theta]}, (S_1)_{[\psi,\theta]})$ and $((R_2)_{[\psi,\theta]}, (S_2)_{[\psi,\theta]})$.*

Proof. Suppose that $G' = (R, S)$ is the CO of the IVFGs G'_1 and G'_2. By Theorem 2, we have $R_{[\psi,\theta]} = (R_1)_{[\psi,\theta]} \times (R_2)_{[\psi,\theta]}$. We prove $S_{[\psi,\theta]} = E$, where E is the edge set of the CO $(G'_1)_{[\psi,\theta]}[(G'_2)_{[\psi,\theta]}]$, for all $[\psi, \theta] \in I[0,1]$.

Suppose $(e_1, e_2)(f_1, f_2) \in S_{[\psi,\theta]}$. Then, $\rho^l_S((e_1, e_2)(f_1, f_2)) \geq \psi$ and $\rho^u_S((e_1, e_2)(f_1, f_2)) \geq \theta$.

Since $G' = (R, S)$ is the CO $G'_1[G'_2]$, one of the below conditions holds:

(i) $e_1 = f_1$ and $e_2 f_2 \in E_2$,
(ii) $e_2 = f_2$ and $e_1 f_1 \in E_1$,
(iii) $e_2 \neq f_2$ and $e_1 f_1 \in E_1$.

For conditions (i) and (ii) in the proof of Theorem 2, we obtain $((e_1, e_2)(f_1, f_2)) \in E$. For case (iii), we have

$$\rho^l_S((e_1, e_2)(f_1, f_2)) = \min\{\rho^l_{R_2}(e_2), \rho^l_{R_2}(f_2), \rho^l_{S_1}(e_1 f_1)\} \geq \psi,$$

$$\rho^u_S((e_1, e_2)(f_1, f_2)) = \min\{\rho^u_{R_2}(e_2), \rho^u_{R_2}(f_2), \rho^u_{S_1}(e_1 f_1)\} \geq \theta.$$

Therefore,

$$\rho^l_{R_2}(e_2) \geq \psi, \quad \rho^l_{R_2}(f_2) \geq \psi, \quad \rho^l_{S_1}(e_1 f_1) \geq \psi,$$

$$\rho^u_{R_2}(e_2) \geq \theta, \quad \rho^u_{R_2}(f_2) \geq \theta, \quad \rho^u_{S_1}(e_1 f_1) \geq \theta.$$

It follows that $e_2, f_2 \in (R_2)_{[\psi,\theta]}$ and $e_1 f_1 \in (S_1)_{[\psi,\theta]}$; that is, $((e_1, e_2)(f_1, f_2)) \in E$. Thus, $S_{[\psi,\theta]} \subseteq E$. For each $((e, e_2)(e, f_2)) \in E$,

$$\rho^l_{R_1}(e) \geq \psi, \quad \rho^u_{R_1}(e) \geq \theta, \quad \rho^l_{S_2}(e_2 f_2) \geq \psi, \quad \rho^u_{S_2}(e_2 f_2) \geq \theta.$$

Since $G' = (R, S)$ is the CO $G'_1[G'_2]$, we have

$$\rho^l_S((e, e_2)(e, f_2)) = \min\{\rho^l_{R_1}(e), \rho^l_{S_2}(e_2 f_2)\} \geq \psi$$

$$\rho^u_S((e, e_2)(e, f_2)) = \min\{\rho^u_{R_1}(e), \rho^u_{S_2}(e_2 f_2)\} \geq \theta.$$

Thus, $(e, e_1)(e, f_2) \in S_{[\psi,\theta]}$. Similarly, for each $((e_1, k)(f_1, k)) \in E$, we have $(e, e_2)(e, f_2) \in S_{[\psi,\theta]}$. For each $((e_1, e_2)(f_1, f_2)) \in E$, $e_2 \neq f_2$.

$$\rho^l_{S_1}(e_1 f_1) \geq \psi, \quad \rho^u_{S_1}(e_1 f_1) \geq \theta,$$

$$\rho^l_{R_2}(f_2) \geq \psi, \quad \rho^u_{R_2}(f_2) \geq \theta,$$

$$\rho^l_{R_2}(e_2) \geq \psi, \quad \rho^u_{R_2}(e_2) \geq \theta.$$

Since $G' = (R, S)$ is the CO $G'_1[G'_2]$, we have:

$$\rho^l_S((e_1, e_2)(f_1, f_2)) = \min\{\rho^l_{R_2}(e_2), \rho^l_{R_2}(f_2), \rho^l_{S_1}(e_1 f_1)\} \geq \psi,$$

$$\rho^u_S((e_1, e_2)(f_1, f_2)) = \min\{\rho^u_{R_2}(e_2), \rho^u_{R_2}(f_2), \rho^u_{S_1}(e_1 f_1)\} \geq \theta.$$

Hence, $(e_1, e_2)(f_1, f_2) \in S_{[\psi,\theta]}$. Therefore, $E \in S_{[\psi,\theta]}$ and so $E = S_{[\psi,\theta]}$.

Conversely, let $(R_{[\psi,\theta]}, S_{[\psi,\theta]})$, $[\psi, \theta] \in I[0,1]$ be the CO of $((R_1)_{[\psi,\theta]}, (S_1)_{[\psi,\theta]})$, and $((R_2)_{[\psi,\theta]}, (S_2)_{[\psi,\theta]})$. By Theorem 2, we have

(i) $\begin{cases} \rho^l_R(e_1, e_2) = \min\{\rho^l_{R_1}(e_1), \rho^l_{R_2}(e_2)\} \\ \rho^u_R(e_1, e_2) = \min\{\rho^u_{R_1}(e_1), \rho^u_{R_2}(e_2)\} \end{cases}$ for all $(e_1, e_2) \in X_1 \times X_2$.

(ii) $\begin{cases} \rho^l_S((e, e_2)(e, f_2)) = \min\{\rho^l_{R_1}(e), \rho^l_{S_2}(e_2 f_2)\} \\ \rho^u_S((e, e_2)(e, f_2)) = \min\{\rho^u_{R_1}(e), \rho^u_{S_2}(e_2 f_2)\} \end{cases}$ for all $e \in X_1$ and $e_2 f_2 \in E_2$.

(iii) $\begin{cases} \rho^l_S((e_1, k)(f_1, k)) = \min\{\rho^l_{S_1}(e_1 f_1), \rho^l_{R_2}(k)\} \\ \rho^u_S((e_1, k)(f_1, k)) = \min\{\rho^u_{S_1}(e_1 f_1), \rho^u_{R_2}(k)\} \end{cases}$ for all $k \in X_2$ and $e_1 f_1 \in E_1$.

Also, we obtain:

$$\rho^l_S((e_1,e_2)(f_1,f_2)) = \min\{\rho^l_{R_2}(e_2), \rho^l_{R_2}(f_2), \rho^l_{S_1}(e_1f_1)\},$$

$$\rho^u_S((e_1,e_2)(f_1,f_2)) = \min\{\rho^u_{R_2}(e_2), \rho^u_{R_2}(f_2), \rho^u_{S_1}(e_1f_1)\},$$

for all $e_2, f_2 \in X_2, e_2 \neq f_2$ and $e_1f_1 \in E_1$. □

Corollary 2. *Let $G_1^{'} = (R_1, S_1)$ and $G_2^{'} = (R_2, S_2)$ be IVFGs. Then, the CO $G_1^{'}[G_2^{'}]$ is an IVFG.*

Theorem 4. *Assume $G_1^{'} = (R_1, S_1)$ and $G_2^{'} = (R_2, S_2)$ are IVFGs of $G_1^* = (X_1, E_1)$ and $G_2^* = (X_2, E_2)$, respectively, so that $X_1 \cap X_2 = \emptyset$. Then, $G^{'} = (R, S)$ is the union of $G_1^{'}$ and $G_2^{'}$ if and only if for every $[\psi, \theta] \in I[0,1]$, the level graph $(R_{[\psi,\theta]}, S_{[\psi,\theta]})$ is the union of $((R_1)_{[\psi,\theta]}, (S_1)_{[\psi,\theta]})$ and $((R_2)_{[\psi,\theta]}, (S_2)_{[\psi,\theta]})$.*

Proof. Suppose that $G^{'} = (R, S)$ is the union of the IVFGs $G_1^{'}$ and $G_2^{'}$. We show that $R_{[\psi,\theta]} = (R_1)_{[\psi,\theta]} \cup (R_2)_{[\psi,\theta]}$ for every $[\psi, \theta] \in I[0,1]$.

Assume that $e \in R_{[\psi,\theta]}$, then $e \in X_1 \backslash X_2$ or $e \in X_2 \backslash X_1$. If $e \in X_1 \backslash X_2$, then $\rho^l_{R_1}(e) = \rho^l_R(e) \geq \psi$ and $\rho^u_{R_1}(e) = \rho^u_R(e) \geq \theta$, which implies $e \in (R_1)_{[\psi,\theta]}$. If $e \in X_2 \backslash X_1$, we have $e \in (R_2)_{[\psi,\theta]}$. Therefore, $e \in (R_1)_{[\psi,\theta]} \cup (R_2)_{[\psi,\theta]}$, and so $R_{[\psi,\theta]} \subseteq (R_1)_{[\psi,\theta]} \cup (R_2)_{[\psi,\theta]}$.

Let $e \in (R_1)_{[\psi,\theta]} \cup (R_2)_{[\psi,\theta]}$, then $e \in (R_1)_{[\psi,\theta]}$, $e \notin (R_2)_{[\psi,\theta]}$ or $e \in (R_2)_{[\psi,\theta]}$ and $e \notin (R_1)_{[\psi,\theta]}$. In the first situation, $\rho^l_R(e) = \rho^l_{R1}(e) \geq \psi$ and $\rho^u_R(e) = \rho^u_{R1}(e) \geq \theta$, which implies $e \in R_{[\psi,\theta]}$. In the second condition, $\rho^l_R(e) = \rho^l_{R2}(e) \geq \psi$ and $\rho^u_R(e) = \rho^u_{R2}(e) \geq \theta$, hence $e \in R_{[\psi,\theta]}$.

Consequently, $(R_1)_{[\psi,\theta]} \cup (R_2)_{[\psi,\theta]} \subseteq R_{[\psi,\theta]}$. We prove that $(S_1)_{[\psi,\theta]} \cup (S_2)_{[\psi,\theta]} = S_{[\psi,\theta]}$ for all $[\psi, \theta] \in I[0,1]$. Assume that $ef \in S_{[\psi,\theta]}$, then $ef \in E_1 \backslash E_2$ or $ef \in E_2 \backslash E_1$.

For $ef \in E_1 \backslash E_2$, we have $\rho^l_{S_1}(ef) = \rho^l_S(ef) \geq \psi$ and $\rho^u_{S_1}(ef) = \rho^u_S(ef) \geq \theta$. Therefore, $ef \in S_{1[\psi,\theta]}$. Also, if $ef \in E_2 \backslash E_1$, then $ef \in S_{2[\psi,\theta]}$. Thus, $S_{[\psi,\theta]} \subseteq (S_1)_{[\psi,\theta]} \cup (S_2)_{[\psi,\theta]}$.

If $ef \in (S_1)_{[\psi,\theta]} \cup (S_2)_{[\psi,\theta]}$, then $ef \in (S_1)_{[\psi,\theta]} \backslash (S_2)_{[\psi,\theta]}$ or $ef \in (S_2)_{[\psi,\theta]} \backslash (S_1)_{[\psi,\theta]}$.

In the first situation, $\rho^l_S(ef) = \rho^l_{S1}(ef) \geq \psi$ and $\rho^u_S(ef) = \rho^u_{S1}(ef) \geq \theta$, which implies $e \in S_{[\psi,\theta]}$.

In the second condition, there is also $ef \in S_{[\psi,\theta]}$. Thus, $(S_1)_{[\psi,\theta]} \cup (S_2)_{[\psi,\theta]} \subseteq S_{[\psi,\theta]}$.

Conversely, suppose for all $[\psi, \theta] \in I[0,1]$, $(R_{[\psi,\theta]}, S_{[\psi,\theta]})$ is the union of $((R_{1[\psi,\theta]}), (S_{1[\psi,\theta]}))$ and $((R_{2[\psi,\theta]}), (S_{2[\psi,\theta]}))$. Let $e \in X_1$ and $\rho^l_{R_1}(e) = \psi, \quad \rho^u_{R_1}(e) = \theta, \quad \rho^l_R(e) = \psi^{'}, \quad \rho^u_R(e) = \theta^{'}$, for $\psi, \theta, \psi^{'}, \theta^{'} \in [0,1]$.

Then, $e \in (R_1)_{[\psi,\theta]}$ and $e \in R_{[\psi^{'},\theta^{'}]}$. By the hypothesis, $e \in R_{[\psi,\theta]}$ and $e \in (R_1)_{[\psi^{'},\theta^{'}]}$.

Therefore,

$$\rho^l_R(e) \geq \psi, \quad \rho^u_R(e) \geq \theta, \quad \rho^l_{R_1}(e) \geq \psi^{'}, \quad \rho^u_{R_1}(e) \geq \theta^{'}.$$

It follows, $\rho^l_{R_1}(e) \leq \rho^l_R(e), \quad \rho^u_{R_1}(e) \leq \rho^u_R(e), \quad \rho^l_{R_1}(e) \geq \rho^l_R(e) \; \rho^u_{R_1}(e) \geq \rho^u_R(e)$. Hence, $\rho^l_{R_1}(e) = \rho^l_R(e), \quad \rho^u_{R_1}(e) = \rho^u_R(e)$.

Similarly, for every $e \in X_2$, we obtain $\rho^l_{R_2}(e) = \rho^l_R(e), \quad \rho^u_{R_2}(e) = \rho^u_R(e)$.

Also, we obtain:

(i) $\begin{cases} \rho^l_S(ef) = \rho^l_{S_1}(ef) & if\ ef \in E_1 \\ \rho^l_S(ef) = \rho^l_{S_2}(ef) & if\ ef \in E_2. \end{cases}$

(ii) $\begin{cases} \rho^u_S(ef) = \rho^u_{S_1}(ef) & if\ ef \in E_1 \\ \rho^u_S(ef) = \rho^u_{S_2}(ef) & if\ ef \in E_2 \end{cases}$ □

Corollary 3. *Let $G_1^{'} = (R_1, S_1)$ and $G_2^{'} = (R_2, S_2)$ be IVFGs of $G_1^* = (X_1, E_1)$ and $G_2^* = (X_2, E_2)$, respectively, and $X_1 \cap X_2 = \emptyset$, then $G_1^{'} \cup G_2^{'}$ is an IVFG.*

Theorem 5. *Suppose $G_1^{'} = (R_1, S_1)$ and $G_2^{'} = (R_2, S_2)$ are IVFGs of $G_1^* = (X_1, E_1)$ and $G_2^* = (X_2, E_2)$, respectively, and $X_1 \cap X_2 = \emptyset$. Then, the pair $G^{'} = (R, S)$ of the IVFGd on $G_1^* + G_2^*$ is the join of $G_1^{'}$ and $G_2^{'}$ if and only if for every $[\psi, \theta] \in I[0,1]$, $(R_{[\psi,\theta]}, S_{[\psi,\theta]})$ is the join of $((R_1)_{[\psi,\theta]}, (S_1)_{[\psi,\theta]})$ and $((R_2)_{[\psi,\theta]}, (S_2)_{[\psi,\theta]})$.*

Proof. Suppose that $G^{'} = (R, S)$ is the join of the IVFGs $G_1^{'}$ and $G_2^{'}$. We show that $R_{[\psi,\theta]} = (R_1)_{[\psi,\theta]} \cup (R_2)_{[\psi,\theta]}$ and $S_{[\psi,\theta]} = (S_1)_{[\psi,\theta]} \cup (S_2)_{[\psi,\theta]} \cup E^*_{[\psi,\theta]}$ for all $[\psi, \theta] \in I[0,1]$, where $E^*_{[\psi,\theta]}$ is the set of all edges joining the nodes $(R_1)_{[\psi,\theta]}$ and $(R_2)_{[\psi,\theta]}$.

According to the proof of Theorem 4, $(S_1)_{[\psi,\theta]} \cup (S_2)_{[\psi,\theta]} \subseteq S_{[\psi,\theta]}$. If $ef \in E^*_{[\psi,\theta]}$, then $\rho^l_{R1}(e) \geq \psi, \quad \rho^u_{R1}(e) \geq \theta, \quad \rho^l_{R2}(f) \geq \psi, \quad \rho^u_{R2}(f) \geq \theta$. Hence,

$$\rho^l_S(ef) = \min\{\rho^l_{R_1}(e), \rho^l_{R_2}(f)\} \geq \psi,$$

and

$$\rho^u_S(ef) = \min\{\rho^u_{R_1}(e), \rho^u_{R_2}(f)\} \geq \theta.$$

Therefore, $ef \in S_{[\psi,\theta]}$. It follows, $(S_1)_{[\psi,\theta]} \cup (S_2)_{[\psi,\theta]} \cup E^*_{[\psi,\theta]} \subseteq S_{[\psi,\theta]}$.

For each $ef \in S_{[\psi,\theta]}$, if $ef \in E_1 \cup E_2$, then $ef \in (S_1)_{[\psi,\theta]} \cup (S_2)_{[\psi,\theta]}$. If $e \in X_1$ and $f \in X_2$, then

$$\min\{\rho^l_{R_1}(e), \rho^l_{R_2}(f)\} = \rho^l_S(ef) \geq \psi,$$

and

$$\min\{\rho^u_{R_1}(e), \rho^u_{R_2}(f)\} = \rho^u_S(ef) \geq \theta.$$

Therefore, $e \in (R_1)_{[\psi,\theta]}$, $f \in (R_2)_{[\psi,\theta]}$, and $ef \in E^*_{[\psi,\theta]}$.

Thus, $S_{[\psi,\theta]} \subseteq (S_1)_{[\psi,\theta]} \cup (S_2)_{[\psi,\theta]} \cup E^*_{[\psi,\theta]}$.

Conversely, suppose $(R_{[\psi,\theta]}, S_{[\psi,\theta]})$ is the join of $((R_1)_{[\psi,\theta]}, (S_1)_{[\psi,\theta]})$ and $((R_2)_{[\psi,\theta]}, (S_2)_{[\psi,\theta]})$ for $[\psi, \theta] \in I[0,1]$.

We have

(i) $\begin{cases} \rho^l_R(e) = \rho^l_{R_1}(e) & if\ e \in X_1 \\ \rho^l_R(e) = \rho^l_{R_2}(e) & if\ e \in X_2 \end{cases}$

(ii) $\begin{cases} \rho^u_R(e) = \rho^u_{R_1}(e) & if\ e \in X_1 \\ \rho^u_R(e) = \rho^u_{R_2}(e) & if\ e \in X_2. \end{cases}$

Also, we obtain

(iii) $\begin{cases} \rho^l_S(ef) = \rho^l_{S_1}(ef) & if\ ef \in E_1 \\ \rho^l_S(ef) = \rho^l_{S_2}(ef) & if\ ef \in E_2 \end{cases}$

(iv) $\begin{cases} \rho^u_S(ef) = \rho^u_{S_1}(ef) & if\ ef \in E_1 \\ \rho^u_S(ef) = \rho^u_{S_2}(ef) & if\ ef \in E_2. \end{cases}$

Suppose $e \in X_1$, $f \in X_2$ and consider $min\{\rho^l_{R_1}(e), \rho^l_{R_2}(f)\} = \psi^{'}$, $min\{\rho^u_{R_1}(e), \rho^u_{R_2}(f)\} = \tau^{'}$, $\rho^l_S(ef) = \psi^{'}$, $\rho^u_S(ef) = \theta^{'}$.

Then, $e \in (R_1)_{[\psi,\theta]}$, $f \in (R_2)_{[\psi,\theta]}$ and $ef \in S_{[\psi',\theta']}$.

It follows that $ef \in S_{[\psi,\theta]}$, $e \in (R_1)_{[\psi',\theta']}$ and $f \in (R_2)_{[\psi',\theta']}$. So, $\rho^l_S(ef) \geq \psi, \quad \rho^u_S(ef) \geq \theta, \quad \rho^l_{R_1}(e) \geq \psi^{'}, \quad \rho^u_{R_1}(e) \geq \theta^{'}, \rho^l_{R_2}(f) \geq \psi^{'}, \quad \rho^u_{R_2}(f) \geq \theta^{'}$. Therefore,

$$\rho^l_S(ef) \geq \psi = \min\{\rho^l_{R_1}(e), \rho^l_{R_2}(f)\} \geq \psi^{'} = \rho^l_S(ef),$$

$$\rho^u_S(ef) \geq \theta = \min\{\rho^u_{R_1}(e), \rho^u_{R_2}(f)\} \geq \theta^{'} = \rho^u_S(ef),$$

and then we have

$$\rho^l_S(ef) = \min\{\rho^l_{R_1}(e), \rho^l_{R_2}(f)\}, \quad \rho^u_S(ef) = \min\{\rho^u_{R_1}(e), \rho^u_{R_2}(f)\}.$$

□

4. Application of Interval-Valued Fuzzy Graph to Find the Most Effective Person in a Hospital Information System

The growth of the communication, telecommunication, and informatics industries is facing a new revolution every day. The information and communication technology revolution has had a profound effect on all economic, social, political, and security sectors of the country. One of the most important areas of information technology applications is in the field of health and treatment. A hospital information system is the first and most basic system for providing health care. Hospital information systems are computer systems designed to easily manage medical and hospital information and to improve the quality of health care. Research has shown that the use of hospital information systems has improved the quality of health services and increased customer satisfaction. Some of the problems of health care systems are as follows: the dispersion of patients' information and lack of access to their records, poor cooperation between physicians and health care workers, and poor access to required medical information. These problems can be solved through the development of information technology, especially hospital (health) information systems. Hospital information systems are designed to automate the affairs of hospitals, such as reporting test results, entering doctor's instructions, prescribing medication, controlling pharmacy inventory, central warehouses, feeding units, etc. In the hospital information system, an electronic file is created for each patient that covers all hospital activities (including treatment, diagnosis, finance, etc.) from admission to discharge. In this system, all medical procedures, medication orders, and diagnostic services are sent through the system to clinics and paraclinics and even administrative centers, such as accounting, pharmacies, warehouses, and other units, and their answers are received. Therefore, the start and end times of all actions in the system are clear and traceable. Hence, a hospital information system is an information system in which information is stored in a comprehensive database and is available to consumers in special forms at the time and place of need. Therefore, considering the importance of the hospital information system and its role in improving medical and health services, we intend to specify the most effective employee in the field of technology and information of a hospital in terms of registering information about patients, medicines, finances, laboratories, etc. Suppose the vertices of the IVFG are an information register building and the edges of this graph are the degree of interaction in between. The set of staff is

A = {Moradi, Kamali, Ahmadi, Yegane, Bahmani, Nazari}

(a) Moradi and Bahmani have been co-workers for 16 years.
(b) Yegane is very accurate in calculating and recording information about the hospital's finances, and all employees are satisfied with him.
(c) In recording information about nurses, it is very important to record their expertise, work experience, and the duration of each activity during a day with great care to have the most active nurses serve patients. Kamali is the best choice to undertake this accountability process.
(d) Nazari and Ahmadi have a long history of conflict.
(e) According to Ahmadi's experiences recognizing drugs and their effectiveness, he is the best option for recording information about drugs.

According to the above values, we consider an IVFG. The vertices show each of the department staff members. The edges indicate the level of friendship and fondness between staff. For the weight of the vertices, the lower bound and the upper bound mean the level of staff capability. The lower bound and the upper bound for the weight of the edges mean the amount of friendship and conflict, respectively. The name of the staff and level of staff capability are indicated in Tables 1 and 2. The adjacency matrix corresponding to Figure 7 is indicated in Table 3.

Table 1. The name of employees in hospital and their services.

Name	Services
Moradi	Responsible for recording laboratory information
Kamali	Responsible for registering nurses' information
Ahmadi	Responsible for registering drug information
Yegane	Responsible for registering financial information
Bahmani	Responsible for registering radiological information
Nazari	Responsible for registering clinical information

Table 2. The level of staff capability.

Name	$[\rho_S^l, \rho_S^u]$
Moradi	[0.3, 0.4]
Kamali	[0.4, 0.5]
Ahmadi	[0.2, 0.3]
Yegane	[0.3, 0.4]
Bahmani	[0.2, 0.4]
Nazari	[0.1, 0.2]

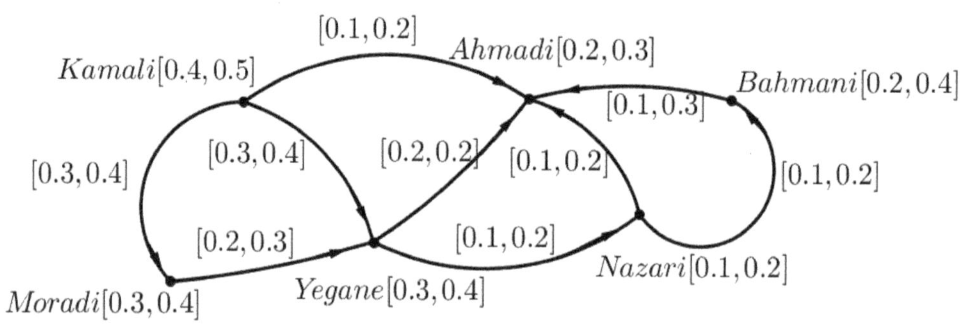

Figure 7. Interval-valued fuzzy digraph.

Table 3. Adjacency matrix corresponding to Figure 7.

Name	Moradi	Kamali	Ahmadi	Yegane	Bahmani	Nazari
Moradi	[0, 0]	[0, 0]	[0, 0]	[0, 0]	[0, 0]	[0, 0]
Kamali	[0.3, 0.4]	[0, 0]	[0.1, 0.2]	[0.3, 0.4]	[0, 0]	[0, 0]
Ahmadi	[0, 0]	[0, 0]	[0, 0]	[0, 0]	[0, 0]	[0, 0]
Yegane	[0, 0]	[0, 0]	[0.2, 0.2]	[0, 0]	[0, 0]	[0.1, 0.2]
Bahmani	[0, 0]	[0, 0]	[0.1, 0.3]	[0, 0]	[0, 0]	[0, 0]
Nazari	[0, 0]	[0, 0]	[0.1, 0.2]	[0, 0]	[0.1, 0.2]	[0, 0]

Figure 7 shows that Ahmadi has 20% of the necessary ability to register drug information in the system, but unfortunately, he does not have the necessary 30% authority to do so. The directional edge Yegane–Nazari indicates that there is only 10% comradeship among these two staff members, and unfortunately they have 20% conflict. Clearly, Kamali has dominion over both Moradi and Yegane, with his dominance over both at 30%. It is clear that Kamali is the most influential staff member of the hospital information system because he inspects both the laboratory information officer and the pecuniary information officer and has 30% of the authority in the hospital.

As we saw in the above example, fuzzy influence graphs play a significant role in determining worthy and effective people in an organization and social institutions, and they are used in the fields of medical and psychological sciences to diagnose diseases. Interval-valued fuzzy influence graphs are useful tools for chemical engineers to model various relationships in a process. These graphs are used to systematically map an entire chain of processes and controllers to describe the effect. The interval-valued fuzzy influence graph theory is growing as a dominant field of research in mathematics because of its application to a variety of problems, including clustering, data mining, decision-making, communication, etc. It has major contribution potential in modeling, preserving, and performing different types of physical problems in networking and trafficking. Several interval-valued fuzzy influence graph parameters are real indicators of network performance and efficiency. They are very useful to handle networks with extraneous support and flows. Especially, the modeling of the ramping system of highways can be performed using interval-valued fuzzy influence graphs in order to control the unpredicted flow between cities and highways.

5. Conclusions

IVFGs are very useful tools for studying different computational intelligence and computer science domains. They have many applications in different sciences, such as optimization, topology, neural networks, and operations research. In graph theory, operations are easily used in many hybrid applications. In different situations, they present appropriate construction means. Hence, in this paper, we introduced four important operations on an IVFG level graph: the Cartesian product, composition, union, and join. Some properties of level graphs of IVFGs were discussed. Finally, an application of IVFG was presented. Our upcoming investigation involves an in-depth exploration of diverse forms of domination on interval-valued fuzzy influence graphs, covering global domination, restrained domination, semi-global domination, and K-domination. We aim to provide a clear understanding of the properties and characteristics of each of these domination types and their practical implications for real-world applications.

Author Contributions: Y.R., S.L. and A.A.T.; methodology, S.L., M.M. and Y.R.; validation, S.L. and A.A.T.; formal analysis, Y.R. and M.M.; investigation, M.M., A.A.T. and S.L.; data curation, A.A.T., S.L. and Y.R.; writing—original draft preparation, Y.R. and A.A.T.; writing—review and editing, S.L., A.A.T. and M.M.; visualization, M.M., Y.R. and S.L.; supervision, S.L.; project administration, Y.R. and A.A.T.; funding acquisition, Y.R. All authors have read and agreed to the published version of the manuscript.

Funding: This work was supported by the National Natural Science Foundation of China (No. 62172116).

Data Availability Statement: Data are contained within the article.

Conflicts of Interest: The authors declare no conflict of interest.

References

1. Zadeh, L.A. Fuzzy sets. *Inf. Control.* **1965**, *8*, 338–353. [CrossRef]
2. Zadeh, L.A. The Concept of a Linguistic Variable and Its Application to Approximate Reasoning-1. *Inf. Sci.* **1975**, *8*, 199–249. [CrossRef]
3. Roy, M.K.; Biswas, R. I-V fuzzy relations and Sanchez's approach for medical diagnosis. *Fuzzy Sets Syst.* **1992**, *47*, 35–38. [CrossRef]
4. Rosenfeld, A. Fuzzy graphs. In *Fuzzy Sets and Their Applications*; Zadeh, L.A., Fu, K.S., Shimura, M., Eds.; Academic Press: New York, NY, USA, 1975; pp. 77–95.
5. Bhattacharya, P. Some remarks on fuzzy graphs. *Pattern Recognit. Lett.* **1987**, *6*, 297–302. [CrossRef]
6. Mordeson, J.N.; Peng, C.S. Operations on fuzzy graphs. *Inf. Sci.* **1994**, *79*, 159–170. [CrossRef]
7. Akram, M.; Dudek, W.A. Interval-valued fuzzy graphs. *Comput. Math. Appl.* **2011**, *61*, 289–299. [CrossRef]
8. Akram, M. Interval-valued fuzzy line graphs. *Neural Comput. Appl.* **2012**, *21*, 145–150. [CrossRef]

9. Akram, M.; Alshehri, N.O.; Dudek, W.A. Certain types of interval-valued fuzzy graphs. *J. Appl. Math.* **2013**, *2013*, 857070. [CrossRef]
10. Akram, M.; Yousaf, M.M.; Dudek, W.A. Self Centered Interval-Valued Fuzzy Graphs. In *African Mathematical Union*; Springer: Berlin/Heidelberg, Germany, 2014.
11. Hongmei, J.; Lianhua, W. Interval-valued fuzzy subsemigroups and subgroups sssociated by intervalvalued suzzy graphs. In Proceedings of the 2009 WRI Global Congress on Intelligent Systems, Xiamen, China, 19–21 May 2009; pp. 484–487.
12. Turksen, I.B. Interval valued fuzzy sets based on normal forms. *Fuzzy Sets Syst.* **1986**, *20*, 191–210. [CrossRef]
13. Jan, N.; Ullah, K.; Mahmood, T.; Garg, H.; Davvaz, B.; Borumand, S.A.; Broumi, S. Some Root Level Modifications in Interval Valued Fuzzy Graphs and Their Generalizations Including Neutrosophic Graphs. *Mathematics* **2019**, *7*, 72. [CrossRef]
14. Nagoorgani, A.; Radha, K. Isomorphism on fuzzy graphs. *Int. J. Comput. Math. Sci.* **2008**, *2*, 190–196.
15. Rashmanlou, H.; Pal, M. Antipodal interval-valued fuzzy graphs. *Int. J. Appl. Fuzzy Sets Artif. Intell.* **2013**, *3*, 107–130.
16. Pal, M. Certain types of m-polar interval-valued fuzzy graph. *J. Intell. Fuzzy Syst.* **2020**, *39*, 3137–3150.
17. Zihni, O.; Kara, G. Interval-valued fuzzy soft graphs. *Topol. Algebra Appl.* **2017**, *5*, 19–27.
18. Krishna, K.K.; Talebi, Y.; Rashmanlou, H.; Talebi, A.A.; Mofidnakhaei, F. New Concept of Cubic Graph with Application. *J. Mult. Valued Log. Soft Comput.* **2019**, *33*, 135–154.
19. Dey, A.; Pal, A.; Pal, T. Interval Type 2 Fuzzy Set in Fuzzy Shortest Path Problem. *Mathematics* **2016**, *4*, 62. [CrossRef]
20. Dey, A.; Pradhan, R.; Pal, A.; Pal, T. A Genetic Algorithm for Solving Fuzzy Shortest Path Problems with Interval Type-2 Fuzzy Arc Lengths. *Malays. J. Comput. Sci.* **2018**, *31*, 255–270. [CrossRef]
21. Dey, A.; Son, L.H.; Pal, A.; Long, H.V. Fuzzy minimum spanning tree with interval type 2 fuzzy arc length: Formulation and a new genetic algorithm. *Soft Comput.* **2020**, *24*, 3963–3974. [CrossRef]
22. Qiang, X.; Akhoundi, M.; Kou, Z.; Liu, X.; Kosari, S. Novel Concepts of Domination in Vague Graphs with Application in Medicine. *Math. Probl. Eng.* **2021**, *2021*, 6121454. [CrossRef]
23. Shao, Z.; Kosari, S.; Rashmanlou, H.; Shoaib, M. New concepts in intuitionistic fuzzy graph with application in water supplier systems. *Mathematics* **2020**, *8*, 1241. [CrossRef]
24. Shi, X.; Kosari, S.; Talebi, A.A.; Sadati, S.H.; Rashmanlou, H. Investigation of the main energies of picture fuzzy graph and its applications. *Int. J. Comput. Intell. Syst.* **2022**, *15*, 31. [CrossRef]

symmetry MDPI

Article

Fuzzy Logic and Its Application in the Assessment of Information Security Risk of Industrial Internet of Things

Seyit Kerimkhulle [1,*], Zhulduz Dildebayeva [2], Akylbek Tokhmetov [1,*], Akzhibek Amirova [1], Jamalbek Tussupov [1], Ulzhan Makhazhanova [1], Alibek Adalbek [1], Roman Taberkhan [1], Alma Zakirova [1] and Alua Salykbayeva [3]

1 Department of Information Systems, L.N. Gumilyov Eurasian National University, 2, Satpayev Street, Astana 010008, Kazakhstan
2 Department of Economics and Business, International Engineering Technological University, 89/21, Al-Farabi Avenue, Almaty 050060, Kazakhstan
3 Department of Supply Chain Management, Tengizchevroil LLP, 3, Satpayev Street, Atyrau 060001, Kazakhstan
* Correspondence: kerimkul_sye@enu.kz (S.K.); tokhmetov_at_2@enu.kz (A.T.); Tel.: +7-701-391-7252 (S.K.); +7-705-651-7480 (A.T.)

Abstract: This article addresses the issue of information security in the Industrial Internet of Things (IIoT) environment. Information security risk assessment in the IIoT is complicated by several factors: the complexity and heterogeneity of the system, the dynamic nature of the system, the distributed network infrastructure, the lack of standards and guidelines, and the increased consequences of security breaches. Given these factors, information security risk assessment in the IIoT requires a comprehensive approach adapted to the peculiarities and requirements of a particular system and industry. It is necessary to use specialized risk assessment methods and to take into account the context and peculiarities of the system. The method of information security risk assessment in the IIoT, based on the mathematical apparatus of fuzzy set theory, is proposed. This paper analyzes information security threats for IIoT systems, from which the most significant criteria are selected. The rules, based on which decisions are made, are formulated in the form of logical formulas containing input parameters. Three fuzzy inference systems are used: one to estimate the probability of threat realization, another to estimate the probable damage, and a final one to estimate the information security risk for the IIoT system. Based on the proposed method, examples of calculating the information security risk assessment in the IIoT environment are provided. The proposed scientific approach can serve as a foundation for creating expert decision support systems for designing IIoT systems.

Keywords: IIoT; security; threat; risk; fuzzy logic application; linguistic variables; fuzzy decision making

1. Introduction

With the rapid evolution of the Industrial Internet of Things (IIoT), there is an urgent need to swiftly respond to, detect, and prevent intrusions. IIoT systems possess specialized features and encounter unique challenges when it comes to defending against cyber-attacks. Information security (IS) risk assessment plays a pivotal role in enterprise management practices, aiding in the identification, quantification, and mitigation of risks based on risk tolerance criteria and organizational objectives.

The necessity of a quick response to intrusions and their timely detection and prevention have arisen during the rapid development of the IIoT. IIoT systems have special features and face unique challenges working with cyber-attacks. IS risk assessment is an important part of the enterprise management practice that helps to identify, quantify, and minimize threats according to organizational risk acceptance criteria and goals.

The most extensive IIoT security research has been made in [1–3]. Hofer [1] presented a late 10-year review on cyber-physical systems architecture considering the concept of Industry 4.0. Using an initial automatic search and iterative refinement, 213 papers were found and studied. In result, the vast majority of architectural styles were categorized and schematized. It is concluded that there is a general increase in security-oriented cyber-physical systems architecture proposals, but no discussion on security in detail. In [2], authors focus on the concepts of the IoT, the Industrial IoT, and Industry 4.0, emphasize issues related to their security and privacy, and present a systematic review of current studies and potential directions for addressing the challenges of the Industrial IoT. The same review article [3] provides a systematic literature review on IIoT security from 2011 until 2019, focusing on IIoT security requirements. Special attention is given to options where the relatively new Fog computing paradigm can be used to fulfil these requirements and serve to enhance IIoT security. Furthermore, it should be noted that in the aforementioned studies, the authors argue that the traditional security strategy is insufficient and not ready to protect modern IIoT systems.

In continuation of the topic, authors [4] pay attention to the fact that IT infrastructure threat identification models—such as Microsoft STRIDE (STRIDE is an acronym that describes the six major threats to information security: Spoofing, Tampering, Repudiation, Information Disclosure, Denial of Service и Elevation of Privilege), OWASP (Open Web Application Security Project), and ENISA (European Network and Information Security Agency)—fully describe the threats of the Internet of Things, but cannot fully identify the threats of the Industrial IoT. This raises a concern related to determining the correct classification of threats to industrial systems. The first step towards threat qualification in industrial systems was made by authors [5]. The study analyzed potential security threats for industries adapting to IIoT. A taxonomy of IIoT attacks was proposed, which would aid in risk—, according to the authors. This taxonomy was considered in terms of four dimensions: attack vector, attack target, attack impact, and attack consequence. However, the disadvantage of this taxonomy is the limited number of threats considered, which does not allow one to fully cover the whole picture of the situation. Authors [6] considered the development of this direction, namely, some types of threats such as spoofing, SQL injection, and DOS attacks on the five-level IIoT architecture. The authors stated that further research is required to obtain a more accurate and complete classification of threats in the IIoT. Considering security models, two main groups can be distinguished: preventive models designed for risk assessment and existing models designed to detect attacks. After the research, it can be stated that there are a significant number of qualitative studies with proposed systems for detecting anomalies and attacks. Various tools such as graph-based methods, blockchain technology, and machine learning algorithms have been used for this purpose [7–10].

IIoT systems have their own dynamics and uniqueness correlated to new approaches for adopting risk assessment because they require special attention. At the moment, there are few studies on this topic. Let us consider a few studies, emphasizing the most significant of them. Authors of [11] proposed an Analytic Hierarchy Process (AHP)-based risk assessment model for IIoT cloud technology. IIoT cloud is a combination of machines, robotic arms, controllers, and drivers in a single platform. This IIoT network risk assessment method is particularly valuable for the core hardware on which cloud services are executed. On other hand, the model does not provide a new solution for decision making and does not address IIoT system assets identification and classification issues. According to [12], the IEC 62443 cybersecurity standard was proposed to implement a cyber-defense platform for industrial IoT systems. This standard contains a set of instructions and measures that need to be implemented to ensure not only the industrial system security but also the operational one. The paper proposes a new approach based on IEC 62443-3-2 and IEC 62443-4-2 to verify, through an in-depth risk assessment, the compliance of objects with basic security requirements. However, despite the advantages described in the paper, the assessment model does not consider security requirements such as system integrity and resource availability, and the model does not propose measures to address the effects of threats on the IIoT system. In [13], it is pointed out that the protection of industrial equipment of IIoT systems is an obligation inherently linked to technological developments and IoT usage, which makes it important to identify the main vulnerabilities and associated risks and threats and to propose the most appropriate countermeasures. In this paper, a description of attacks on IIoT systems is presented, as well as a thorough analysis of solutions to these attacks as they have been proposed in the most recent sources. Authors [14] proposed a fuzzy association rule extraction algorithm based on a fuzzy matrix, and this is applied to the correlation of security events in a network environment. In addition, the embedded system is combined to build an IS risk assessment system and the performance of the system is specified according to the real situation.

An interesting approach to cyber risks in the mining industry is presented in [15]. The mentioned article discusses a method of cyber-attack risk analysis for different levels of automation in mining routines based on the use of fuzzy theory. The focus is a method that combines the Kaplan and Garrick approach and fuzzy theory. Fuzzy theory is implemented to estimate the risk parameters for the cyber-attack scenario execution in the mining industry. The proposed method can be used to identify the current state of the cybersecurity of mine shafts. The article [16] focuses on IS risk assessment and its importance to enterprise management. The authors point out that IS risk assessment helps to identify, quantify, and evaluate risks with respect to risk tolerance criteria and in-organizational objectives. The article also discusses various methods and tools for IS risk assessment such as Operationally Critical Threat, Asset, and Vulnerability Evaluation (OCTAVA), the CCTA Risk Analysis and Management Method (CRAMM), and risk surveillance. These are based on risk analysis, cost-benefit analysis, security subsystem selection, construction and testing, and examination of all aspects of security.

The review of articles on cybersecurity risk assessment methods/models confirms the importance and relevance of studying the problem of the IS of the industrial IoT, such as threat classification and security risk analysis of IIoT systems. An analysis of the studies indicates that a significant amount of research is dedicated to identifying the security measures, but the issue of preventive measures, including analysis and taxonomy of IS risks, is poorly studied.

The IIoT emerges as a network encompassing physical devices, machinery, sensors, and other elements of industrial production. These entities exchange data and interact with control systems to optimize and automate production processes. This paper introduces a method for evaluating IS within the IIoT environment, leveraging the principles of fuzzy logic [17].

Various standards and methods are used in assessing IS risks in the IIoT, including:

- ISO 27400:2022 [18]: This standard offers guidance on principles, information risk assessment, and appropriate IS and privacy controls to mitigate risks associated with the Internet of Things.
- ISA/IEC 62443 [19]: A series of international standards established by the IEC (International Electrotechnical Commission) specifying cybersecurity requirements for Automated Industrial Process Control Systems (APCSs) and Building Control and Management Systems (BCMSs).
- NIST SP 800-XX series of standards [20–22]: These standards provide security recommendations tailored to industrial control systems, considering their unique performance, reliability, and security requirements. The series encompasses various risk assessment methods and approaches.

This paper is organized as follows. Section 2 is devoted to the description of the methodology and algorithms used in the development of the proposed fuzzy information security risk assessment model for the IIoT environment. Section 3 presents the key findings and results of the study aimed at addressing information security issues in the IIoT environment. Section 4 discusses and compares different approaches to information security risk assessment. Some limitations of the study, practical implications, and suggestions for future research are given in the last chapter "Conclusions".

2. Proposed Methodology

The purpose of this study is to develop a model for determining the level of risk of information security of the industrial IoT environment using a fuzzy logic system.

According to [20], risk is a measure of the extent to which an entity is threatened by a potential circumstance or event, and typically a function—the adverse impacts that would arise if the circumstance or event occurs and the likelihood of occurrence. In [21], risk is the product of the probability of a security incident occurring and the damage that will be caused to the organization due to the incident. The probability of a security incident occurring depends on the probability that a threat will occur and the probability that the threat will be able to exploit vulnerabilities in the system successfully. We combine the latter two factors into the probability of a threat occurring and obtain the formula:

$$R = Y_1 \cdot Y_2 \quad (1)$$

where R—risk level, Y_1—probability of a threat occurring, Y_2—level of inflicted damage.

Correctly defining risk criteria is an important step in the risk assessment process as it allows a more accurate determination of the likelihood of risks occurring and the level of potential damage. In addition, identifying risk criteria is also an important step for the subsequent planning and implementation of risk management measures.

According to ISO/IEC 27005:2022 information security, cybersecurity, and privacy protection [22], criteria designed to assess the likelihood of threats occurring include:

1. Asset attractiveness;
2. Asset availability;
3. Asset value;
4. Asset confidentiality;
5. Asset integrity;
6. Software and technical controls;
7. Administrative controls;
8. Procedural controls;
9. Compliance of control measures with information security standards;
10. Previous incidents.

Asset attractiveness is a characteristic that indicates how appealing a particular asset is to potential wrongdoers who may attempt unauthorized access to the asset or its information.

Asset availability is a characteristic that describes how easily access to an asset can be obtained. In other words, if an asset is easily accessible, the probability of threat realization will be very high for that asset.

Asset value is a characteristic that shows how important an asset is to the organization. The value of an asset can be determined by its cost or its significance to the organization's business processes. If an asset has high value, it can lead to a higher probability of threat realization.

Asset confidentiality is a characteristic that reflects the degree of importance in maintaining the confidentiality of information related to the asset. Thus, if an asset is a source of confidential information, it can make it more attractive to potential wrongdoers.

Asset integrity is a characteristic that shows that the asset remains in its original state and is not subject to unauthorized changes or damage. If an asset has high integrity, it maintains its properties and functionality for an extended period without alterations.

Additionally, the first five criteria (asset attractiveness, asset availability, asset value, asset confidentiality, asset integrity) have been consolidated into a single criterion—asset significance, which facilitates the analysis and understanding of asset security within the IIoT system. The inclusion of these criteria into one comprehensive asset assessment criterion is due to their interdependence and their consolidated impact on asset assessment in the context of information security.

For the same reason, the four criteria: (1) software and technical control, (2) administrative control, (3) procedural control, and (4) compliance with information security standards have been consolidated into a single criterion—existing control, as these criteria describe the level of control existing within the organization.

As the third criterion, we have chosen previous incidents. This criterion evaluates whether attacks have been previously committed on the specific asset of an industrial IoT system. If they have, the probability of a threat occurrence will be higher because the wrongdoer is already familiar with this asset and may use past attack experience for the next one.

According to the Factor Analysis of Information Risk (FAIR) methodology [23], criteria designed to assess potential damage include:

1. Damage related to equipment replacement costs;
2. Downtime-related damage to the system;
3. Damage associated with response costs;
4. Reputational damage.

The first three criteria collectively impact financial damage; hence, we consolidated them into the "Financial Damage" criterion.

The "Reputational Damage" criterion reflects potential negative consequences for a company's reputation in the event of risky situations. It represents a kind of "non-material" damage, and we have designated it as a separate criterion, "Reputational Damage". Therefore, we have chosen two criteria to assess the level of incurred damage: Financial Damage and Reputational Damage (non-material losses).

Considering the selected criteria, a fuzzy model was developed to assess the level of information risk in industrial IoT systems. This model divides the process of assessing information risk into three sequential stages. In the first stage, the probability of threats occurring, Y_1, is evaluated. In the second stage, the assessment of damage inflicted on the protected assets of IIoT systems, Y_2, is calculated. In the third stage, the information security risk assessment, R, is computed.

In the process of implementing algorithms for assessing the probability of the occurrence of a threat and the level of inflicted damage, according to the standards and recommendations [18–22], it is necessary to compose input and output linguistic variables—membership functions of the corresponding analytical types. Next, it is necessary to create a rule base—a set of logical expressions that define a cause-and-effect relationship between input and output values. In conclusion, we carry out defuzzification—the calculation of a clear output value based on the resulting membership function of the output block. In particular, the following term sets are used here:

- Very Low (VL);
- Low (L);
- Medium (M);
- High (H);
- Very High (VH).

The next step in the research is:

- Determining the weights of input linguistic variables, the essence of which is to determine the weight of each input linguistic variable in the rule base. To calculate the weight of each criterion, the method of paired comparisons is used [24]. After filling in the matrix of paired comparisons, the eigenvector is calculated, and this makes it possible to find the weights of the criteria of linguistic variables. These, in turn, are used to calculate the risks of information security.
- Implementation of the information security risk assessment model based on fuzzy logic. This takes place in two research stages:

- Formation of a base of fuzzy production rules to determine the assessment of the probability of occurrence of a threat and assess the level of inflicted damage caused both in interval values and in describing the nature of the risk in the following categories:
    - Very low risk;
    - Low risk;
    - Medium risk;
    - High risk;
    - Very high risk.
- Evaluation of the correctness of the risk level determination model, which summarizes the studies by obtaining the value:
- The probability of occurrence of threats and the level of possible damage, and
- The risk of information security of the industrial IoT environment.

3. Results

This section presents the key findings and results of the study aimed at solving information security problems in the IIoT environment. There are many factors that complicate the assessment of information security risks in the IIoT, such as system complexity, heterogeneity, agility, distributed infrastructure, a lack of standards and guidelines, and the increasing potential consequences of a security breach. The authors propose a comprehensive method for assessing information security risks based on the application of fuzzy set theory and the method of hierarchy analysis. The work analyzes information threats to IIoT systems and identifies the most significant criteria. A description of two fuzzy inference systems is presented, used to assess the likelihood of a threat occurring and the potential damage, on the basis of which an assessment of information security in the context of the IIoT is made. The authors also provide specific examples illustrating risk assessment calculations for information security in the IIoT environment based on the proposed method.

3.1. Algorithm for Assessing the Probability of Occurrence of a Threat

To assess the probability of occurrence of a threat, it is necessary to select input linguistic variables (LVs). According to standards and recommendations [18–22], the most preferable are the following LVs:

- C_1—asset attractiveness;
- C_2—existing control;
- C_3 —previous incidents.

The output variable is Y_1—*Probability of a threat occurring*. For linguistic evaluation of input and output variables, the following term sets are used: Very Low (VL); Low (L); Medium (M); High (H); Very High (VH). When setting input and output LVs, it is necessary to set membership functions for fuzzy sets that characterize the term sets of LVs.

Criteria 1: C_1—asset attractiveness. To assess attractiveness, a questionnaire was used with answers "Yes" or "No":

$$C_1 = \begin{cases} 1, & \text{if "Yes"}, \\ 0, & \text{if "No"}, \end{cases} \quad (2)$$

Indeed, for each of the following questions, an affirmative answer is 1, and a negative answer is 0:

1. Is the asset significant to the organization's business processes?
2. Is the asset important to the achievement of the organization's objectives?
3. Is the asset unique to the organization?
4. Are there alternatives that can replace the asset?
5. Does the asset contain sensitive data?
6. Are there safeguards that protect the confidentiality of the information asset?
7. Is the asset intact and not subject to change?

8. Are there safeguards that protect the integrity of the asset?
9. Is the asset easily accessible to the right users?
10. Are there safeguards that protect the asset from unauthorized access?

The maximum number of points is 10; the minimum is 0. To determine the values of the set of linguistic variables "Attractiveness of an asset", a survey of 10 experts with experience and knowledge in the field of information security was used. The results of the experiment in the form of an auxiliary matrix are presented in Table 1 (10 experts attributed the number of points equal to 1 to the term "Very low" and the number of points equal to 2 to the term "Very low"; 7 experts and 3 experts to the term "Low ", etc.)

Table 1. Auxiliary matrix.

Values of Base Terms	Number of Score									
	1	2	3	4	5	6	7	8	9	10
Very Low (VL)	10	7	2	0	0	0	0	0	0	0
Low (L)	0	3	7	5	2	0	0	0	0	0
Medium (M)	0	0	1	5	8	6	3	0	0	0
High (H)	0	0	0	0	0	4	5	6	1	0
Very High (VH)	0	0	0	0	0	0	2	4	9	10

To construct membership functions, we identify the maximum elements in the rows of the auxiliary table. The membership function is then calculated using the following formula [17]:

$$\mu(a_{ij}) = \frac{a_{ij}}{a_{imax}}, \quad (3)$$

where a_{ij} is the matrix element and a_{imax} is the maximum element of the row.

From the obtained values of the membership functions of the terms of the linguistic variable C_1 (asset attractiveness), we created Table 2.

Table 2. Resulting matrix.

Values of Base Terms	Number of Score (γ_{ij})									
	1	2	3	4	5	6	7	8	9	10
Very Low (VL)	1	0.7	0.2	0	0	0	0	0	0	0
Low (L)	0	0.43	1	0.71	0.29	0	0	0	0	0
Medium (M)	0	0	0.125	0.625	1	0.75	0.375	0	0	0
High (H)	0	0	0	0	0	0.5	0.8	1	0.17	0
Very High (VH)	0	0	0	0	0	0	0.2	0.4	0.9	1

Using the data from Table 2, we will plot the membership function LV "Asset attractiveness" (Appendix A, Figure A1).

Criteria 2: C_2,—existing control. The values of the input LV C_2—existing control are determined by the number of security measures in industrial systems and the change in the range [0, 8]. These measures include:

- Protection of network nodes;
- Monitoring of network activity;
- Authentication and authorization;
- Protection from physical attacks;
- Protection against malicious programs;
- Data security;
- Data backup;
- Training.

Hence, the normalized values of the LV C_2 can be determined using Formula (4):

$$C_2 = \frac{N_m}{8}, \quad (4)$$

where N_m—the number of Information Security methods used at an industrial facility—are found in Table 3.

Table 3. Normalized values of C_2.

N_m	1	2	3	4	5	6	7	8
C_2	0.125	0.250	0.375	0.500	0.625	0.750	0.875	1.000

Using the data from Table 3, we will plot the membership function LV "Existing control" (Appendix A, Figure A2).

Criteria 3: C_3—previous incidents. The numeric values of variables C_3—previous incidents—vary in the range [0, 100] and are determined by the percentage of computers attacked in IIoT systems per year and can be expressed by the formula [25]:

$$C_3 = \frac{N_p}{40\%}, \quad (5)$$

where N_p is the percentage of computers attacked in an IIoT system per year, and 40% is the maximum permissible value.

According to the data in Table 4, let us plot the membership functions of the LV "Previous incidents" (Appendix A, Figure A3).

Table 4. Normalized values of C_3.

N_p	5%	10%	15%	20%	25%	30%	35%	40% and Higher
C_3	0.125	0.250	0.375	0.500	0.625	0.750	0.875	1.000

Output variable Y_1—Probability of threat occurrence–is the process of determining the likelihood that a threat will occur in the future. The likelihood of threats being implemented may depend on various factors, such as the importance of information assets, the availability of appropriate security controls at the software, technical, administrative, and procedural control levels, as well as previous cases of security breaches.

Let us define terms for the output LV "Probability of threat occurrence": 'Very Low', 'Low', 'Moderate', 'High', 'Very High'. The descriptions of the terms are provided in Table 5.

Table 5. Description of the terms for the LV "Probability of threat occurrence".

Term	Meaning	Description
Very low	0–0.3	There are no objective prerequisites for the emergence of a threat
Low	0.2–0.5	Some prerequisites for the emergence of a threat exist, but the security measures taken significantly complicate its implementation
Average	0.4–0.7	Objective prerequisites for the emergence of a threat exist, and the number of security measures is sufficient to neutralize it
High	0.6–0.9	Objective prerequisites for the emergence of a threat exist, and the number of security measures is insufficient
Very high	0.8–1	Objective prerequisites for a threat exist, and security measures have not been taken

Using the data from Table 5, we will plot the membership function LV "Probability of threat occurrence" (Appendix A, Figure A4).

As a result, the input linguistic variables for the first stage were set, and the sets of terms and their membership functions were determined. These variables are used to determine the probability of a threat occurrence.

3.2. Algorithm for Assessing the Level of Inflicted Damage

In this section, the following criteria were used to assess the level of inflicted damage caused (input variables):

- C_4—Financial damage;
- C_5—Reputational damage.

The output variable Y_2 reflects the level of inflicted damage.

Criteria 4: C_4,—financial damage. The numerical value of the variable is [0, 100] and it is determined as a percentage of the costs of responding to an attack and restoring systems, fines, the cost of monitoring services, and damage from downtime and disruption of operations. To calculate it, we use the Return on Investment (ROI) method [26]:

$$C_4 = \frac{ALE}{D} \cdot 100\% \tag{6}$$

where ALE is the expected annual losses; D is the annual income. This allows us to obtain normalized values for the fourth criterion of financial damage (see Table 6).

Table 6. Normalized values of C_4.

	1%	2%	3%	4%	5%	6%	7%	8%	9%	10%
C_4	0.1	0.2	0.3	0.4	0.5	0.6	0.7	0.8	0.9	1.0

Let us define terms for the output LV "Financial damage": 'Very Low', 'Low', 'Moderate', 'High', 'Very High'. The descriptions of the terms are provided in Table 7.

Table 7. Description of the terms for the LV "Financial damage".

Term	Description
Very low	Minor damage, less than 1% of annual income
Low	Low damage, 2–4% of annual income
Average	Noticeable damage, 4–7% of annual income
High	Large damage, 7–10% of annual income
Very high	Very large damage, more than 10% of annual income

Using the data from Table 7, we will plot the membership function LV "Financial damage" (Appendix A, Figure A5).

Criteria 4: C_5—Reputational damage. The numerical value of the variable [0, 100] is determined as a percentage of losses due to the negative attitude of customers, partners, and investors towards the company. Let us try to estimate reputational damage as expected losses due to the negative attitude of clients, partners, and investors, divided by annual income [27]:

$$C_5 = \frac{P}{D} \cdot 100\%, \tag{7}$$

where P reflects losses due to the negative attitude of customers, partners, and investors towards the company over the past year; D reflects annual income. This allows us to obtain normalized values for the fifth criterion of reputational damage (see Table 8).

Table 8. Normalized values of C_5.

	1%	2%	3%	4%	5%	6%	7%	8%	9%	10%
C_5	0.1	0.2	0.3	0.4	0.5	0.6	0.7	0.8	0.9	1.0

We understand that reputational damage is difficult to quantify and such an estimate will be approximate. However, this approach can help estimate how much of an organization's annual revenue could be lost due to reputational damage following a cyberattack.

Let us define terms for the output LV "Reputational damage": 'Very Low', 'Low', 'Moderate', 'High', 'Very High'. The descriptions of the terms are provided in Table 9.

Table 9. Description of the terms for the LV "Reputational damage".

Term	Description
Very low	Minor damage, less than 1% of annual income
Low	Low damage, 2–4% of annual income
Average	Noticeable damage, 4–7% of annual income
High	Large damage, 7–10% of annual income
Very high	Very large damage, more than 10% of annual income

Using the data from Table 9, we will plot the membership function LV "Reputational damage" (Appendix A, Figure A6).

The output variable Y_2—the level of inflicted damage is the process of determining the financial, operational, reputational, and other losses that may arise as a result of an information security breach. Potential damage is the sum of all the costs that an organization will incur in the implementation of threats to the assets of an industrial IoT system.

Let us define terms for the output LV "Level of inflicted damage": 'Very Low', 'Low', 'Moderate', 'High', 'Very High'. The descriptions of the terms are provided in Table 10.

Table 10. Description of the terms for the LV "Level of inflicted damage".

Term	Meaning	Description
Very low	0–0.3	The level of damage caused has virtually no effect on the operation of the facility
Low	0.2–0.5	The level of damage caused slightly affects the operation of the facility
Average	0.4–0.7	The level of damage caused makes it difficult for the facility to operate
High	0.6–0.9	The level of damage caused has a significant impact on the operation of the facility
Very high	0.8–1	The level of damage caused greatly affects the operation of the facility

Using the data from Table 10, we will plot the membership function LV "Level of inflicted damage" (Appendix A, Figure A7).

As a result, the input linguistic variables for the second stage were set, and the sets of terms and their membership functions were determined. With the help of these variables, the level of inflicted damage is determined. The output LV "Level of inflicted damage" was also set, and term-sets were defined and described.

3.3. Determining the Weights of Input Linguistic Variables

To assess the risk of information security, it is necessary to determine the weight for each input linguistic variable in the rule base. Let n elements or n objects be given. Then the calculation of the weight of each criterion is made using the method of paired comparisons—a statistical tool that is used to assess the relative preferences between different options or alternatives [17]. Based on the results of the expert's survey, a matrix of paired comparisons is built $= (a_{ij}), i,\ j = 1,\ 2,\ \ldots,\ n$:

$$A = (a_{ij})_{i,\ j=1,\ 2,\ \ldots,\ n} = \begin{bmatrix} a_{11} & a_{12} & \ldots & a_{1n} \\ a_{21} & a_{22} & \ldots & a_{2n} \\ \vdots & \vdots & \vdots & \vdots \\ a_{n1} & a_{n2} & \ldots & a_{nn} \end{bmatrix}, \quad (8)$$

where the number a_{ij} shows how many times, according to the expert, the degree of importance of one element x_i is greater than the degree of importance of element x_j in the set S, or in terms of the membership function, the value $\mu_s(x_i)$ is greater than $\mu_s(x_j)$. At the same time, the expert operates with these concepts guided by the comparison scale according to the Saaty method [24] (see Table 11).

Table 11. Scales for comparing two elements according to the Saaty method.

Comparing Two Elements	Value
Both elements are equally important : $\mu_S(x_i)$ equals $\mu_S(x_j)$	1
One element is slightly more important than another element : $\mu_S(x_i)$ is slightly larger than $\mu_S(x_j)$	3
One element is clearly more important than the other : $\mu_S(x_i)$ is greater than $\mu_S(x_j)$	5
One element is significantly more important than another element : $\mu_S(x_i)$ is noticeably larger than $\mu_S(x_j)$	7
One element is absolutely more important than another element : $\mu_S(x_i)$ is much larger than $\mu_S(x_j)$	9
Values intermediate in degree between those listed	2, 4, 6, 8

The elements of the matrix of paired comparisons, symmetrical with respect to the diagonal of the matrix, must satisfy the requirement:

$$a_{ij} = \frac{1}{a_{ij}}. \quad (9)$$

This condition (8) means that if the membership degree of element x_i is a_{ij} times stronger than the membership degree of element x_j, then the membership degree of element x_j must be $1/a_{ij}$ times stronger than the membership degree of element x_i. Then the problem of constructing the membership function is reduced to finding the eigenvector E of the matrix A corresponding to the largest eigenvalue of the matrix, that is, the vector that is the solution to the equation

$$A{\cdot}E = E{\cdot}e_{max} \quad (10)$$

where e_{max} is the largest eigenvalue of a matrix A.

Further, for each element of the matrix of pairwise comparisons, a certain weight ω_i, $i = 1,\ldots,n$, is determined, and the condition $\omega_1 + \ldots + \omega_n = 1$ is satisfied. Then we can construct a matrix V of relative weights:

$$V = (v_{ij})_{i,\ j=1,\ 2,\ \ldots,\ n} = \begin{bmatrix} \omega_1/\omega_1 & \omega_1/\omega_2 & \ldots & \omega_1/\omega_n \\ \omega_2/\omega_1 & \omega_2/\omega_2 & \ldots & \omega_2/\omega_n \\ \vdots & \vdots & \vdots & \vdots \\ \omega_n/\omega_1 & \omega_n/\omega_2 & \ldots & \omega_n/\omega_n \end{bmatrix} \quad (11)$$

where each element $v_{ij} > 0$ of the matrix of relative weights (38) is the ratio of the weight of the i-th object a_i to the weight of the j-th object a_j, i.e., $v_{ij} = \omega_i/\omega_j$ for any $i,\ j = 1,\ 2,\ \ldots,\ n$. Matrix elements located symmetrically with respect to the main diagonal are inverse to each other, i.e., $v_{ij} = 1/v_{ji}$ for any $i,\ j = 1,\ 2,\ \ldots,\ n$.

After filling in the matrix of paired comparisons (38), the eigenvector is calculated, and for this the sum and product method and the square root method are used ([24,25]):

$$e_i = \sqrt[n]{\prod_{j=1}^{n} a_{ij}},\ i = 1,\ 2,\ \ldots, n. \quad (12)$$

Next, to find the weights of the criteria, we use

$$\omega_i = \frac{e_i}{\sum_{j=1}^{n} e_j},\ i = 1,\ 2,\ \ldots, n. \quad (13)$$

In conclusion, we note that on the basis of the implementation of algorithms (8)–(13), we obtained expert and calculated results of the study:

- Expert estimates of respondents (i)–(v) on the values of pairwise comparison coefficients, $e_i^{(i)}, e_i^{(ii)}, \ldots, e_i^{(v)}$, $i = \overline{1,3}$—eigenvector and $\omega_i^{(i)}, \omega_i^{(ii)}, \ldots, \omega_i^{(v)}$, $i = \overline{1,3}$—values of weights according to criteria C_1, C_2 и C_3 (see Tables A1–A3, Appendix A);
- Calculated ω_i, $i = \overline{1,3}$ values of weights estimating the level Y_1—threat occurrence probability (see Table A3, Appendix A);
- Calculated $\omega_i^{(i)}, \omega_i^{(ii)}, \ldots, \omega_i^{(v)}$, and $\omega{\cdot}i = \overline{4,5}$ values $e_i^{(v)}$ according to criteria C_4 and C_5 assessing the level of Y_2—the damage caused (see Table A4, Appendix A).

3.4. *Implementation of the Information Security Risk Assessment Model Based on Fuzzy Logic*

3.4.1. Formation of a Base of Fuzzy Production Rules

The rule base of fuzzy inference systems is formed on the basis of predefined input and output linguistic variables. After fuzzy input and output variables, membership functions, as well as weight coefficients of criteria $C_1 - C_5$ were defined, the following were created:

- Information base of fuzzy production rules for evaluating Y_1—probability of occurrence of threats (total 125 rules)—with the values of the terms of the input linguistic variable C_1—attractiveness of assets—with a weight coefficient ω_1 = 0.4126; C_2—existing control—with a weight coefficient ω_2 = 0.3952; C_3—previous incidents—with weight coefficient ω_3 = 0.1929; Very low—0.2, Low—0.4, Medium—0.6, High—0.8; Very high—1.0 and the calculated values of the term boundaries of the output linguistic variable Y_1—probability of occurrence of a threat: Very low—[0.0; 0.3], Low—(0.3; 0.5], Medium—(0.5; 0.7], High—(0.7; 0.9], Very High—(0.9; 1.0]) (see Table A5, Appendix A).
- Aggregate fuzzy rules for assessing the probability of occurrence of a threat. Note that aggregation is the process of combining the output parameters of each rule into one fuzzy set. The rules for aggregating fuzzy products are carried out using the classical fuzzy logical operation "AND" of two elementary statements [24,28]. For example, the output variable Y_1 - the probability of occurrence of a threat occurring–takes on the value "Very Low" in rules No. 1, 2, 3, 6, and 26, which can be combined using a conjunction. As a result of the aggregation of the resulting rules, fuzzy causal relationships between antecedents and consequents were obtained (see Table A6, Appendix A).
- Information base of fuzzy production rules for evaluation Y_2—the level of inflicted damage caused by threats to the protected assets of IIoT systems (total 25 rules)–with the values of the terms of the input linguistic variable C_4—financial costs with a weight coefficient ω_4 = 0.5833 and C_5—damage to reputation with a weight coefficient ω_5 = 0.4167: Very low—0.2, Low—0.4, Medium—0.6, High—0.8; Very high—1.0, and the calculated value of the term boundaries of the output linguistic variable Y_2—manifestation of the damage: Very Low—[0.0; 0.3], Low—(0.3; 0.5), Medium—(0.5; 0.7), High—(0.7; 0.9), Very High—(0.9; 1.0] (see Table A7, Appendix A).
- Aggregated fuzzy rules for assessing the level of inflicted damage caused. As a result of the aggregation of the resulting rules, fuzzy causal relationships between antecedents and consequents were obtained (see Table A8, Appendix A).

As a result, we have obtained bases of fuzzy rules for determining the probability of occurrence of a threat and assessing the level of inflicted damage. These two parameters are used to calculate a clear output value of the risk level R, which has the following gradations:

- Very low risk: [0.0000; 0.0625), meaning a slight adverse impact on the activities of the organization and the assets of the organization;
- Low risk: [0.0625; 0.2025), meaning a limited adverse impact on the activities of the organization and the assets of the organization;
- Medium risk: [0.2025; 0.5625), meaning that threats can have a serious adverse effect on the activities of the organization, the assets of the organization, individuals, and other organizations;
- High risk: [0.5625; 0.7225), meaning that threats can have a serious or catastrophic adverse effect on the activities of the organization and the assets of the organization;
- Very high risk: [0.7225; 1.0000], meaning that threats can lead to multiple serious or catastrophic consequences for the organization's activities and the organization's assets.

3.4.2. Evaluation of the Correctness of the Model for Determining the Level of Risk

We will evaluate the correctness of the proposed information security risk model based on fuzzy logic in three scenarios.

Scenario 1: Average Risk. Let the values of the following linguistic variables arrive at the input of the model system to determine the level Y_1—the probability of occurrence of a threat:

- Attractiveness of assets, $C_1 = 0.25$;
- Existing control, $C_2 = 0.20$;
- Previous incidents, $C_3 = 0.55$.

Then, the fuzzification of five fuzzy statements—"Asset assessment is Very Low", "Asset assessment is Low", "Asset assessment is Medium", "Asset assessment is High" and "Asset assessment is Very High" for the input linguistic variable $C_1 - C_3$ asset assessment—gives the following values of the degree of truth of fuzzy statements:

- Attractiveness of assets, C_1: $\mu_1^{VL}(R) = 0.4$, $\mu_1^{L}(R) = 0.6$, $\mu_1^{M}(R) = 0.0$, $\mu_1^{H}(R) = 0.0$, $\mu_1^{VH}(R) = 0.0$;
- Existing control, C_2: $\mu_2^{VL}(R) = 0.3$, $\mu_2^{L}(R) = 0.7$, $\mu_2^{M}(R) = 0.0$, $\mu_2^{H}(R) = 0.0$, $\mu_2^{VH}(R) = 0.0$;
- Previous incidents, C_3: $\mu_3^{VL}(R) = 0.0$, $\mu_3^{L}(R) = 0.8$, $\mu_3^{M}(R) = 0.2$, $\mu_3^{H}(R) = 0.0$, $\mu_3^{VH}(R) = 0.0$.

Next, we determine the degree of truth of the conditions for each of the rules of the fuzzy inference system:

- If the condition of a fuzzy production rule is a simple fuzzy statement, then the degree of its truth corresponds to the value of the membership function of the corresponding term of the linguistic variable.
- If the condition represents a compound statement, then the degree of truth of the compound statement is determined using the logical operation of conjunction.

Therefore, according to the base of production rules (see Table A5, Appendix A) and the fuzzy inference system based on the conjunction operation (see Table A6, Appendix A), for level Y_1 the probability of occurrence of a threat occurring has a non-zero value for rules 3, 8, 28, and 33:

- Rule 3. Y_1 = M: $\mu(R_3) = \min(0.4; 0.3; 1.0) = 0.3$;
- Rule 8. Y_1 = M: $\mu(R_8) = \min(0.4; 0.7; 1.0) = 0.4$;
- Rule 28. Y_1 = M: $\mu(R_{28}) = \min(0.6; 0.3; 1.0) = 0.3$;
- Rule 33. Y_1 = M: $\mu(R_{33}) = \min(0.6; 0.7; 1.0) = 0.6$.

The truth values of all other rules are zero, so there is no need to take them into account. Indeed, the combination of the membership functions of all subsets is usually carried out classically, that is, by taking the maximum from the values of the membership functions of each subset:

$$\mu(R_{Y_1=M}) = \max(\mu(R_3); \mu(R_8); \mu(R_{28}); \mu(R_{33})) = 0.6 \quad (14)$$

Then, as a result of defuzzification, we obtain the value of the level of the output linguistic variable Y_1, the probability of occurrence of a threat occurring in the form of a weighted average value by the degree of membership of values at which all applicable membership functions reach their maximum value (15):

$$Y_1 = \frac{\overline{R}_{Y_1=M} \cdot \mu(R_{Y_1=M})}{\mu(R_{Y_1=M})} = \frac{0.55 \cdot 0.6}{0.6} = 0.55, \quad (15)$$

where (see Figure A1, the histogram of dotted line with dot):

$$\overline{R}_{Y_1=M} = \frac{\min\limits_{Y_1=M} R + \max\limits_{Y_1=M} R}{2} = \frac{0.4 + 0.7}{2} = 0.55$$

Now, let the input of the system of information security risk assessment models based on fuzzy logic determine the level Y_2 (caused damage) and receive the values of the input parameters:

- Financial costs, $C_4 = 0.67$;
- Damage to reputation, $C_5 = 0.33$.

Then, the fuzzification of fuzzy statements by terms for the input linguistic variables $C_4 - C_5$ of the system of risk assessment models of the output linguistic variable Y_2, level of inflicted damage, gives the following values of the degree of truth of the fuzzy inference system:

- Financial costs, C_4: $\mu_4^{VL}(R) = 0.0$, $\mu_4^{L}(R) = 0.0$, $\mu_4^{M}(R) = 0.3$, $\mu_4^{H}(R) = 0.7$, $\mu_4^{VH}(R) = 0.0$;
- Damage to reputation, C_5: $\mu_5^{VL}(R) = 0.0$, $\mu_5^{L}(R) = 0.2$, $\mu_5^{M}(R) = 0.8$, $\mu_5^{H}(R) = 0.0$, $\mu_5^{VH}(R) = 0.0$.

According to the base of production rules (see Table A7, Appendix A) and the fuzzy inference system based on the conjunction operation (see Table A8, Appendix A), the level Y_2, the level of inflicted damage, has a non-zero value for rules 12, 13, 17, and 18:

- Rule 12. Y_2 = M: $\mu(R_{12}) = \min(0.3; 0.2) = 0.2$;
- Rule 13. Y_2 = M: $\mu(R_{13}) = \min(0.3; 0.8) = 0.3$;
- Rule 17. Y_2 = M: $\mu(R_{17}) = \min(0.7; 0.2) = 0.2$;
- Rule 18. Y_2 = H: $\mu(R_{18}) = \min(0.7; 0.8) = 0.7$.

The truth values of all other rules are zero, so there is no need to take them into account. Indeed, the maximum value of the input linguistic variables and the combined value of the membership functions of all subsets, respectively, gives:

$$\begin{gathered} \mu(R_{Y_2=M}) = \max(\mu(R_{12}); \mu(R_{13}); \mu(R_{17})) = 0.3, \\ \mu(R_{Y_2=H}) = \max(\mu(R_{18})) = 0.7 \end{gathered} \quad (16)$$

Then, as a result of defuzzification, we will obtain the value of the level of the output linguistic variable Y_2—level of inflicted damage—in the form of a weighted average value by the degree of membership of the values at which all applicable membership functions reach their maximum value (16):

$$\begin{aligned} Y_2 &= \frac{\overline{R}_{Y_2=M} \cdot \mu(R_{Y_2=M}) + \overline{R}_{Y_2=H} \cdot \mu(R_{Y_2=H})}{\mu(R_{Y_2=M}) + \mu(R_{Y_2=H})} \\ &= \frac{0.55 \cdot 0.3 + 0.75 \cdot 0.7}{0.3 + 0.7} = 0.69 \end{aligned} \quad (17)$$

where (see Figure A1, the histogram of dotted line with dot and the histogram of long dotted line):

$$\overline{R}_{Y_2=M} = \frac{\min\limits_{Y_2=M} R + \max\limits_{Y_2=M} R}{2} = \frac{0.4+0.7}{2} = 0.55,$$

$$\overline{R}_{Y_2=H} = \frac{\min\limits_{Y_2=H} R + \max\limits_{Y_2=H} R}{2} = \frac{0.6+0.9}{2} = 0.75$$

Having determined the values of the probability of the appearance of threats and the level of possible damage by using Formulas (1), (16) and (17), we will find the value of the information security risk:

$$R = Y_1 \cdot Y_2 = 0.55 \cdot 0.69 = 0.38 \quad (18)$$

Thus, we obtained the value which corresponds to the average of the information security risk.

Scenario 2: High Risk. Let the values of the following linguistic variables arrive at the input of the model system:

- Attractiveness of assets, C_1 = 0.85;
- Existing control, C_2 = 0.70;
- Previous incidents, C_3 = 0.90.

Then, fuzzification gives the following values of the degree of truth of fuzzy statements:

- Attractiveness of assets, C_1: $\mu_1^{VL}(R)$ = 0.0, $\mu_1^{L}(R)$ = 0.0, $\mu_1^{M}(R)$ = 0.0, $\mu_1^{H}(R)$ = 0.5, $\mu_1^{VH}(R)$ = 0.5;
- Existing control, C_2:$\mu_2^{VL}(R)$ = 0.0, $\mu_2^{L}(R)$ = 0.0, $\mu_2^{M}(R)$ = 0.08, $\mu_2^{H}(R)$ = 0.12, $\mu_2^{VH}(R)$ = 0.0;
- Previous incidents, C_3: $\mu_3^{VL}(R)$ = 0.0, $\mu_3^{L}(R)$ = 0.0, $\mu_3^{M}(R)$ = 0.0, $\mu_3^{H}(R)$ = 0.2, $\mu_3^{VH}(R)$ = 0.6.

Therefore, according to the base of production rules (see Table A5, Appendix A) and the fuzzy inference system based on the conjunction operation (see Table A6, Appendix A), the level Y_1—the probability of occurrence of a threat occurring—has a non-zero value for rules 89, 90, 94, 95, 114, 115, 119, and 120:

- Rule 89. Y_1 = H: $\mu(R_{89})$ = min(0.5; 0.08; 0.2) = 0.08;
- Rule 90. Y_1 = H: $\mu(R_{90})$ = min(0.5; 0.08; 0.6) = 0.08;
- Rule 94. Y_1 = H: $\mu(R_{94})$ = min(0.5; 0.12; 0.2) = 0.12;
- Rule 95. Y_1 = H: $\mu(R_{95})$ = min(0.5; 0.12; 0.6) = 0.12;
- Rule 114. Y_1 = H: $\mu(R_{114})$ = min(0.5; 0.08; 0.2) = 0.08;
- Rule 115. Y_1 = H: $\mu(R_{115})$ = min(0.5; 0.08; 0.6) = 0.08;
- Rule 119. Y_1 = H: $\mu(R_{119})$ = min(0.5; 0.12; 0.2) = 0.12;
- Rule 120. Y_1 = VH: $\mu(R_{120})$ = min(0.5; 0.12; 0.6) = 0.12.

The value of membership functions for all subsets are:

$$\begin{gathered}\mu(R_{Y_1=H}) = \max(\mu(R_{89}); \mu(R_{90}); \mu(R_{94}); \mu(R_{95}); \mu(R_{114}); \\ \mu(R_{115}); \mu(R_{119})) = 0.12;\ \mu(R_{Y_1=VH}) = \mu(R_{120}) = 0.12\end{gathered} \quad (19)$$

Then, as a result of defuzzification, we obtain the value of the level of the output linguistic variable Y_1—the probability of occurrence of a threat:

$$\begin{aligned} Y_1 &= \frac{\overline{R}_{Y_1=H} \cdot \mu(R_{Y_1=H}) + \overline{R}_{Y_1=VH} \cdot \mu(R_{Y_1=VH})}{\mu(R_{Y_1=H}) + \mu(R_{Y_1=VH})} \\ &= \frac{0.75 \cdot 0.12 + 0.9 \cdot 0.12}{0.12 + 0.12} = 0.82 \end{aligned} \quad (20)$$

where (see Figure A1, the histogram of long dotted line and the histogram of solid line):

$$\overline{R}_{Y_1=H} = \frac{\min\limits_{Y_1=H} R + \max\limits_{Y_1=H} R}{2} = \frac{0.6+0.9}{2} = 0.75,$$

$$\overline{R}_{Y_1=VH} = \frac{\min\limits_{Y_1=VH} R + \max\limits_{Y_1=VH} R}{2} = \frac{0.8+1.0}{2} = 0.90$$

Now, let the input of the system of information security risk assessment models based on fuzzy logic determine the level Y_2—caused damage—and receive the values of the input parameters:

- Financial costs, $C_4 = 0.50$;
- Damage to reputation, $C_5 = 0.75$.

Then, the fuzzification of fuzzy statements by terms for the input linguistic variables $C_4 - C_5$ of the system of risk assessment models of the output linguistic variable Y_2—level of inflicted damage—gives the following values of the degree of truth of the fuzzy inference system:

- Financial costs, C_4: $\mu_4^{VL}(R) = 0.0$, $\mu_4^{L}(R) = 0.0$, $\mu_4^{M}(R) = 0.0$, $\mu_4^{H}(R) = 0.14$, $\mu_4^{VH}(R) = 0.0$;
- Damage to reputation, C_5: $\mu_5^{VL}(R) = 0.0$, $\mu_5^{L}(R) = 0.0$, $\mu_5^{M}(R) = 1.0$, $\mu_5^{H}(R) = 0.0$, $\mu_5^{VH}(R) = 0.0$.

According to the information base of the production rules (see Table A7, Appendix A) of the fuzzy inference system based on the conjunction operation (see Table A8, Appendix A), the level Y_2—level of inflicted damage—has a non-zero value for Rule 18:

- Rule 18. Y_2 = H: $\mu(R_{18}) = \min(0.14; 1.0) = 0.14$.

The value of membership functions for all subsets are:

$$\mu(R_{Y_2=H}) = \max(\mu(R_{18})) = 0.14 \tag{21}$$

Then, as a result of defuzzification, we obtain the value of the level of the output linguistic variable Y_2—level of inflicted damage:

$$Y_2 = \frac{\overline{R}_{Y_2=H} \cdot \mu(R_{Y_2=H})}{\mu(R_{Y_2=H})} = \frac{0.75 \cdot 0.14}{0.14} = 0.75 \tag{22}$$

where (see Figure A1, the histogram of long dotted line):

$$\overline{R}_{Y_2=H} = \frac{\min\limits_{Y_2=H} R + \max\limits_{Y_2=H} R}{2} = \frac{0.6 + 0.9}{2} = 0.75$$

Now determine the values of the probability of the appearance of threats and the level of possible damage by using Formulas (1), (20) and (22), and we will find the value of the information security risk:

$$R = Y_1 \cdot Y_2 = 0.82 \cdot 0.75 = 0.62 \tag{23}$$

Thus, we obtained the value which corresponds to the high information security risk.

Scenario 3: Low Risk. Let the values of the following linguistic variables arrive at the input of the model system:

- Attractiveness of assets, $C_1 = 0.40$;
- Existing control, $C_2 = 0.28$;
- Previous incidents, $C_3 = 0.32$.

Then, fuzzification gives the following values of the degree of truth of fuzzy statements:

- Attractiveness of assets, C_1: $\mu_1^{VL}(R) = 0.0$, $\mu_1^{L}(R) = 0.5$, $\mu_1^{M}(R) = 0.5$, $\mu_1^{H}(R) = 0.0$, $\mu_1^{VH}(R) = 0.0$;
- Existing control, C_2: $\mu_2^{VL}(R) = 0.19$, $\mu_2^{L}(R) = 1.0$, $\mu_2^{M}(R) = 0.0$, $\mu_2^{H}(R) = 0.0$, $\mu_2^{VH}(R) = 0.0$;
- Previous incidents, C_3: $\mu_3^{VL}(R) = 0.21$, $\mu_3^{L}(R) = 1.0$, $\mu_3^{M}(R) = 0.0$, $\mu_3^{H}(R) = 0.0$, $\mu_3^{VH}(R) = 0.0$.

Therefore, according to the base of production rules (see Table A5, Appendix A) and the fuzzy inference system based on the conjunction operation (see Table A6, Appendix A), the level Y_1—the probability of occurrence of a threat occurring—has a non-zero value for rules 89, 90, 94, 95, 114, 115, 119, and 120:

- Rule 26. Y_1 = VL: $\mu(R_{26}) = \min(0.5; 0.19; 0.21) = 0.19$;

- Rule 27. Y_1 = L: $\mu(R_{27})$ = min(0.5; 0.19; 1.0) = 0.19;
- Rule 31. Y_1 = L: $\mu(R_{31})$ = min(0.5; 1.0; 0.21) = 0.21;
- Rule 32. Y_1 = L: $\mu(R_{32})$ = min(0.5; 1.0; 1.0) = 0.5;
- Rule 51. Y_1 = L: $\mu(R_{51})$ = min(0.5; 0.19; 0.21) = 0.19;
- Rule 52. Y_1 = L: $\mu(R_{52})$ = min(0.5; 0.19; 1.0) = 0.19;
- Rule 56. Y_1 = L: $\mu(R_{56})$ = min(0.5; 1.0; 0.21) = 0.21;
- Rule 57. Y_1 = L: $\mu(R_{57})$ = min(0.5; 1.0; 1.0) = 0.5.

The value of membership functions for all subsets are:

$$\begin{gathered}\mu(R_{Y_1=VL}) = \mu(R_{26}) = 0.19; \mu(R_{Y_1=L}) = \max(\mu(R_{27}); \\ \mu(R_{31}); \mu(R_{32}); \mu(R_{51}); \mu(R_{52}); \mu(R_{56}); \mu(R_{57})) = 0.5\end{gathered} \tag{24}$$

Then, as a result of defuzzification, we obtain the value of the level of the output linguistic variable Y_1—the probability of occurrence of a threat:

$$\begin{aligned} Y_1 &= \frac{\overline{R}_{Y_1=VL}\cdot\mu(R_{Y_1=VL})+\overline{R}_{Y_1=L}\cdot\mu(R_{Y_1=L})}{\mu(R_{Y_1=VL})+\mu(R_{Y_1=L})} \\ &= \frac{0.2\cdot 0.19+0.35\cdot 0.5}{0.19+0.5} = 0.31\end{aligned} \tag{25}$$

where (see Figure A1, the histogram dot line (VL) and the histogram dotted line (L)):

$$\overline{R}_{Y_1=VL} = \frac{\min\limits_{Y_1=VL} R + \max\limits_{Y_1=VL} R}{2} = \frac{0.1+0.3}{2} = 0.2,$$

$$\overline{R}_{Y_1=L} = \frac{\min\limits_{Y_1=L} R + \max\limits_{Y_1=L} R}{2} = \frac{0.2+0.5}{2} = 0.35$$

Now, let the input of the system of information security risk assessment models based on fuzzy logic determine the level Y_2—caused damage— and receive the values of the input parameters:

- Financial costs, C_4 = 0.16;
- Damage to reputation, C_5 = 0.84.

Then, the fuzzification of fuzzy statements by terms for the input linguistic variables $C_4 - C_5$ of the system of risk assessment models of the output linguistic variable Y_2—level of inflicted damage—gives the following values of the degree of truth of the fuzzy inference system:

- Financial costs, C_4: $\mu_4^{VL}(R)$ = 0.4, $\mu_4^{L}(R)$ = 0.6, $\mu_4^{M}(R)$ = 0.0, $\mu_4^{H}(R)$ = 0.0, $\mu_4^{VH}(R)$ = 0.0;
- Damage to reputation, C_5: $\mu_5^{VL}(R)$ = 0.0, $\mu_5^{L}(R)$ = 0.0, $\mu_5^{M}(R)$ = 0.0, $\mu_5^{H}(R)$ = 0.6, $\mu_5^{VH}(R)$ = 0.0.

According to the base of production rules (see Table A7, Appendix A) and the fuzzy inference system based on the conjunction operation (see Table A8, Appendix A), the level Y_2—level of inflicted damage—has a non-zero value for Rules 4 and 9:

- Rule 4. Y_2 = L: $\mu(R_4)$ = min(0.4; 0.6) = 0.4;
- Rule 9. Y_2 = M: $\mu(R_9)$ = min(0.6; 0.6) = 0.6.

The value of membership functions for all subsets are:

$$\mu(R_{Y_2=L}) = \mu(R_4) = 0.4,\ \mu(R_{Y_2=M}) = \mu(R_9) = 0.6 \tag{26}$$

Then, as a result of defuzzification, we obtain the value of the level of the output linguistic variable Y_2—level of inflicted damage:

$$\begin{aligned} Y_2 &= \frac{\overline{R}_{Y_2=L}\cdot\mu(R_{Y_2=L})+\overline{R}_{Y_2=M}\cdot\mu(R_{Y_2=M})}{\mu(R_{Y_2=L})+\mu(R_{Y_2=M})} \\ &= \frac{0.35\cdot 0.4+0.55\cdot 0.6}{0.4+0.6} = 0.47\end{aligned} \tag{27}$$

where (see Figure A1, the histogram of dotted line and the histogram of dotted line with dot):

$$\overline{R}_{Y_2=L} = \frac{\min\limits_{Y_2=L} R + \max\limits_{Y_2=L} R}{2} = \frac{0.2+0.5}{2} = 0.35,$$

$$\overline{R}_{Y_2=M} = \frac{\min\limits_{Y_2=M} R + \max\limits_{Y_2=M} R}{2} = \frac{0.4+0.7}{2} = 0.55$$

Now determine the values of the probability of the appearance of threats and the level of possible damage by using Formulas (1), (25) and (27), and we will find the value of the information security risk:

$$R = Y_1 \cdot Y_2 = 0.31 \cdot 0.47 = 0.15 \tag{28}$$

We obtained the value which corresponds to the low level of information security risk in IIoT systems.

Thus, using test sets of fuzzy input variables, we obtained clear values of information security risk level. Using fuzzy input information, it is possible to predict the deterioration of the system's safety level and make timely decisions to prevent possible dangerous situations.

4. Discussion

Fuzzy logic methods have gained traction in recent research for assessing information risks. For instance, [29] introduces a risk assessment approach grounded in an attack tree model, utilizing both fuzzy set theory and probabilistic risk assessment technology. This innovative method is applied to the context of a ship control system risk scenario within industrial control systems. The analysis commences by identifying potential risks, constructing a tree-like attack model, and subsequently employing triangular fuzzy numbers and expert knowledge to gauge factors influencing end-node probabilities. Through fuzzy arithmetic, interval probabilities for both the root node and attack paths are determined, yielding the overall potential risks and probabilities of occurrence for each attack path.

Intriguingly, [30] explores cybersecurity risk assessment of industrial control systems through a unique lens. The paper proposes a methodology reliant on order divergence which measures α within an intuitionistic fuzzy framework characterized by interval values. Departing from conventional methods, where the weights of risk indices remain constant, this approach adapts a novel order α divergence measure to IVIFNs (Interval Intuitionistic Fuzzy Numbers). The integration of IVIFNs facilitates the description of estimated risk indices, while variable weight vectors derived from divergence closeness determine the weights of risk indices. The study presents strategies for node and attack path integration within attack defense trees, leading to risk scores calculation using a designated score function.

Addressing the significance of cybersecurity risk assessment within IIoT systems, [31] proposes a comprehensive model for dynamic IIoT risk assessment. This model, initiated by defining the IIoT context, encompasses diverse risk calculation algorithms, prominently highlighting approaches grounded in artificial intelligence and machine learning. The methodology's application is demonstrated through a case study involving an IIoT-based supervisory control and data acquisition system in a hydroelectric power plant.

In [32], the focus centers on the development of an access control model that dynamically analyzes the security risk of access requests through contextual IoT information. This model employs real-time contextual data associated with the requesting user to compute security risks for each access request. Attributes of the user, action severity, resource sensitivity, and user risk history are considered as inputs to assess and calculate the risk value, ultimately informing access decisions.

In [33], the authors introduce the IORs (Risk Indicator Objects), a notable contribution that leverages the MITRE ATT&CK knowledge base for ICS (Industrial Control Systems) to facilitate ongoing risk monitoring. This approach enables the utilization of existing variables for continuous risk analysis. IORs extend compromise indicators by integrating detection strategies with probabilistic inference, serving as a powerful tool for quantifying cybersecurity risks. The library, endorsed by professionals from major companies, now encompasses 95 IORs.

A compelling study, [34], proposes a model for vulnerability risk analysis based on the widely accepted CVSS (Common Vulnerability Scoring System). This innovative model addresses two key limitations of CVSS: (1) the need for additional indicators beyond those stipulated by CVSS, and (2) CVSS's primary usage within IT environments, rendering it less suitable for industrial settings. To overcome these issues, the study's first part offers an overview of the key protocols, standards, and buses within the IIoT landscape. The second part establishes a comprehensive framework for risk characterization in industrial environments, effectively addressing the limitations of the CVSS index.

A noteworthy contribution comes from the study outlined in [35], proposing a hierarchical structured model for information security risk assessment utilizing fuzzy logic. This new approach extends to the assessment of software risks in learning management systems. The novel risk assessment model is implemented on the MATLAB platform using fuzzy logic through a set of 15 fuzzy machines.

Similarly, [36] delves into the application of a fuzzy expert system for assessing the security of a University Information System (UIS). The authors employed the Visual Basic language and the MATLAB Fuzzy Logic toolkit to tackle the challenge of assessing compliance with the ISO/IEC 27,001 standard—a key foundation for modeling information system security.

In [37], the authors introduce a robust fuzzy model tailored to conducting information security risk assessment within IIoT systems. This model relies on the additive weighting method to establish weighting coefficients for each criterion and leverages fuzzy logic for its implementation. The authors showcase the practical execution of this model using the MATLAB system. Notably, the authors assert that fuzzy logic offers a suitable technological foundation for discerning information security risks and generating dependable practical outcomes.

In [38], the authors embark on an exploration of the cybersecurity landscape in ICS (Industrial Control Systems). The study encompasses several key aspects: (1) elucidating the fundamental principles and unique attributes underlying ICS functionality; (2) presenting a concise history of cyber-attacks targeting ICSs; (3) providing an overview of ICS security-less assessment; (4) conducting a review of "unique ICS" testbeds designed to capture interactions across different levels of ICSs; and (5) outlining current trends in ICS attack and defense strategies.

Turning attention to [39], the article delves into a critical challenge—assessing the creditworthiness of enterprises operating within the trade and services sector. Notably, this assessment poses particular intricacies for borrowers, especially small businesses. Such evaluation necessitates careful consideration of factors such as the developmental stage of small enterprises, their specific activities, and the inherent uncertainty tied to financial outcomes. The study analyzes an array of indicators, including industry and regional specifics, small enterprise activity measures, and financial and economic metrics pertinent to the service and trade domain. Decision-making rules are meticulously formulated in the shape of logical formulas embedded with crucial parameters.

5. Conclusions

This research is devoted to solving the problem of determining the level of IS risks in industrial IoT systems using fuzzy logic. Risk assessment as part of information security (risk management) is an essential tool in building defenses. The risk assessment process is designed to identify the risk to the system and determine the security measures taken to mitigate the risk. The proposed method is based on a new risk analysis model that takes into account multiple risk criteria, such as the attractiveness of the asset, the level of existing controls, the presence of previous threats, and financial and reputational losses as a result of the realization of threats. The main advantage of this method is that it realistically models the system environment, unlike the conventional risk model, which only considers the probability of an event and its impact.

Our method is based on multiple fuzzy inference system MFIS. The first fuzzy inference system FIS1 calculates the overall probability of the realization of threats on the system. The second fuzzy inference system FIS2 calculates the overall probability of damage to the system based on risk factors. The third step of the fuzzy inference system is to calculate the IS risk level based on the output data FIS1, FIS2. The proposed method can be used as a tool for assessing information security and risk analysis in any system.

In information security and risk analysis, the concept of symmetry plays an important role, which can be considered from the point of view of balance and harmony in information security management. Symmetry in this context can be associated with the balance between security and availability of data and resources. Just as symmetry in nature creates harmony and balance, in information security there is a need to find a balance between security measures that may be too strict and restrictive for users and the availability of data and resources that ensures the effective operation of the system.

Symmetry can also be associated with understanding symmetrical threats that can impact information security. Risk analysis involves identifying such threats and developing symmetrical countermeasures that can ensure balance and harmony in security. When information security incidents occur, symmetry can also be important in the context of the response. A symmetric response to incidents may include similar recovery measures to restore balance and functionality to the system.

Thus, there is a clear connection between the concept of symmetry and information security risk analysis, which manifests itself as the desire for balance and harmony in approaches to security and risk management.

In this paper, we have paid little attention to risk management planning, resolution, and control. More research should be conducted on risk management planning. In addition, risk needs to be re-monitored regularly to track the status of identified risks.

Author Contributions: Conceptualization, S.K. and A.T.; methodology, S.K. and A.T.; software, A.A. (Akzhibek Amirova), R.T. and U.M.; validation, S.K., A.T. and U.M.; formal analysis, Z.D., A.A. (Akzhibek Amirova), J.T., U.M., A.A. (Alibek Adalbek), R.T., A.Z. and A.S.; investigation, Z.D., J.T., A.Z., A.A. (Alibek Adalbek), R.T. and A.S.; resources, Z.D., J.T., A.Z., A.A. (Akzhibek Amirova), R.T. and A.S.; data curation, Z.D., J.T., A.Z. and A.S.; writing—original draft preparation, S.K. and A.T.; writing—review and editing, S.K. and A.T.; visualization, S.K., A.T. and U.M.; supervision, S.K. and A.T.; project administration, U.M.; funding acquisition, S.K. All authors have read and agreed to the published version of the manuscript.

Funding: This research was funded by the Committee of Science of the Ministry of Science and Higher Education of the Republic of Kazakhstan (Grant No. AP09259435).

Institutional Review Board Statement: Not applicable.

Informed Consent Statement: Not applicable.

Data Availability Statement: Not applicable.

Acknowledgments: We express gratitude to the Science Committee of the Committee of Science of the Ministry of Science and Higher Education of the Republic of Kazakhstan for its support of the realization this research (Grant No. AP09259435).

Conflicts of Interest: The authors declare no conflict of interest.

Appendix A

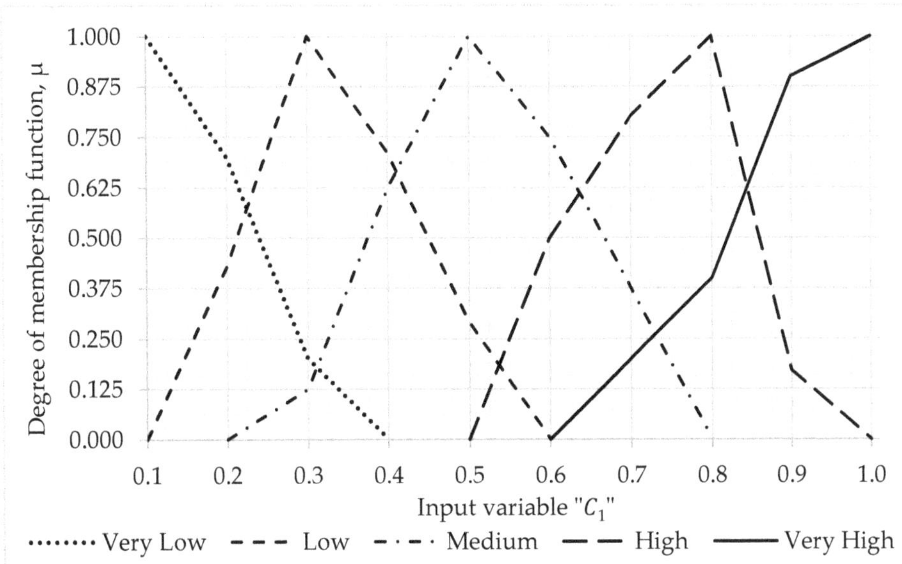

Figure A1. The plot of membership function LV "Asset attractiveness".

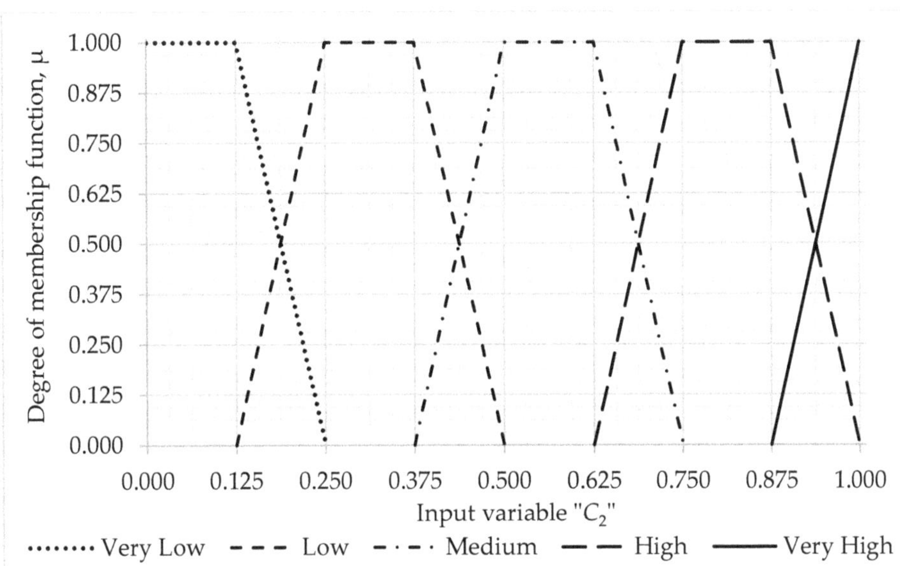

Figure A2. The plot of membership function LV "Existing control".

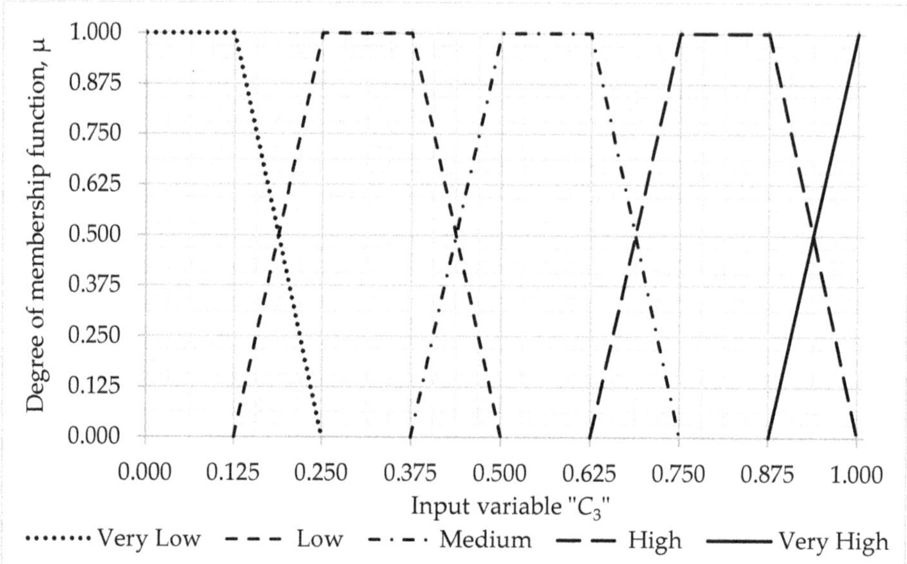

Figure A3. The plot of membership function LV "Previous incidents".

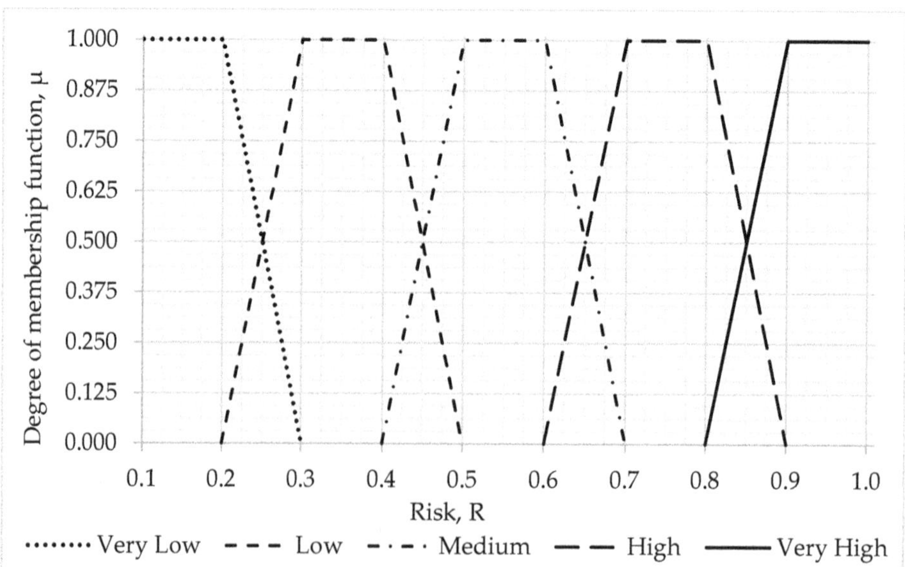

Figure A4. The plot of membership function LV "Probability of threat occurrence".

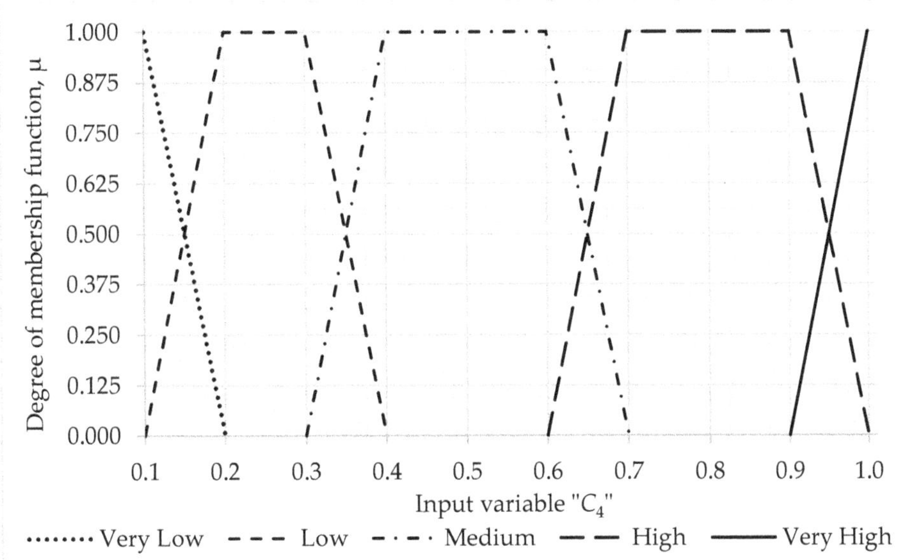

Figure A5. The plot of membership function LV "Financial damage".

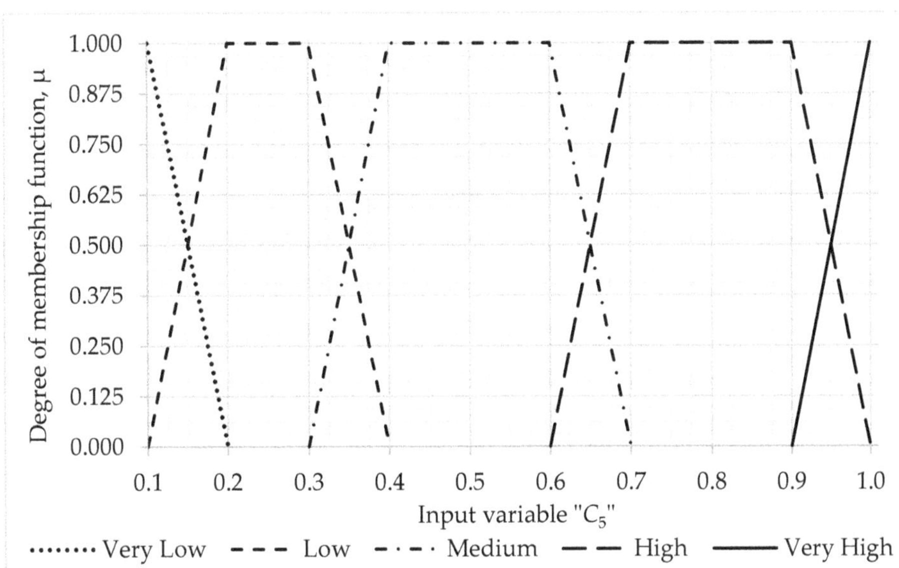

Figure A6. The plot of membership function LV "Reputational damage".

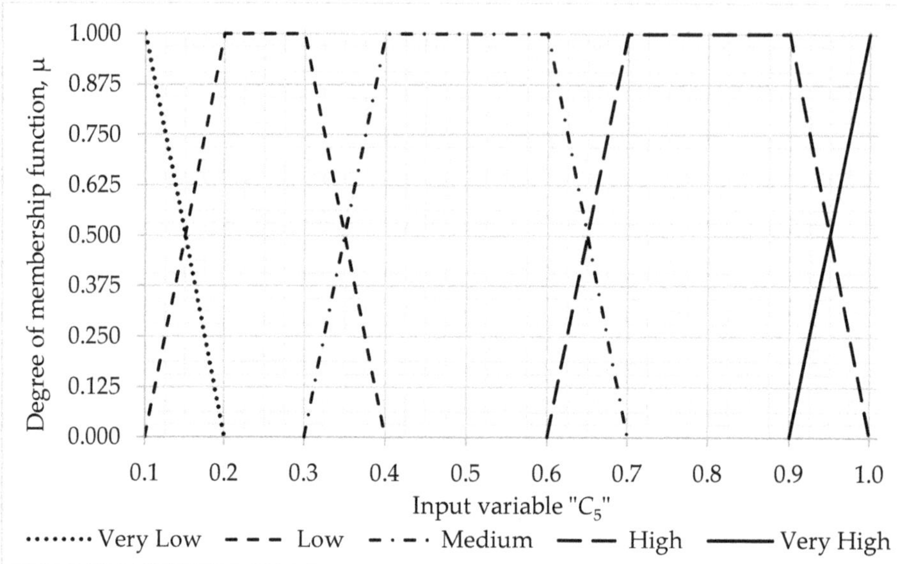

Figure A7. The plot of membership function LV "Level of inflicted damage".

Table A1. The results of assessments by experts (i) and (ii) by pairwise comparison coefficients, eigenvector, and weight values by criteria C_1, C_2, and C_3.

Input Variables			**Expert (i)**					**Expert (ii)**		
	C_1	C_2	C_3	$e_i^{(i)}$	$\omega_i^{(i)}$	C_1	C_2	V_3	$e_i^{(ii)}$	$\omega_i^{(ii)}$
Asset attractiveness (C_1)	1.0	0.5	3.0	1.14	0.3487	1.0	1.0	2.0	1.26	0.3474
Existing control (C_2)	2.0	1.0	2.0	1.59	0.4836	1.0	1.0	3.0	1.44	0.4434
Previous incidents (C_3)	0.3	0.5	1.0	0.55	0.1677	0.3	0.5	1.0	0.55	0.1692

Table A2. Results of evaluations by experts (iii) and (iv) by pairwise comparison coefficients, eigenvector, and weight values by criteria C_1, C_2, and C_3.

Input Variables			**Expert (iii)**					**Expert (iv)**		
	C_1	C_2	C_3	$e_i^{(iii)}$	$\omega_i^{(iii)}$	C_1	C_2	C_3	$e_i^{(iv)}$	$\omega_i^{(iv)}$
Asset attractiveness (C_1)	1.0	2.0	1.0	1.26	0.4126	1.0	0.5	2.0	1.00	0.3711
Existing control (C_2)	0.5	1.0	2.0	1.00	0.3275	0.5	1.0	3.0	1.14	0.4247
Previous incidents (C_3)	1.0	0.5	1.0	0.79	0.2599	0.5	0.3	1.0	0.55	0.2042

Table A3. The results of assessments by experts (v) by the coefficients of pairwise comparison, eigenvector, and weight values according to criteria C_1, C_2, and C_3 and the weight value of those assessing the probability of threats.

Input Variables			**Expert (v)**					**Criteria Weights**		
	C_1	C_2	C_3	$e_i^{(v)}$	$\omega_i^{(v)}$	$\omega_i^{(i)}$	$\omega_i^{(ii)}$	$\omega_i^{(iii)}$	$\omega_i^{(iv)}$	ω_i
Asset attractiveness (C_1)	1.0	2.0	1.0	1.26	0.5396	0.3487	0.3474	0.4126	0.3711	0.4119
Existing control (C_2)	0.5	1.0	2.0	1.00	0.2970	0.4836	0.4434	0.3275	0.4247	0.3952
Previous incidents (C_3)	1.0	0.5	1.0	0.79	0.1634	0.1677	0.1692	0.2599	0.2042	0.1929

Table A4. The results of assessments by experts (i)–(v) by the coefficients of pairwise comparison, eigenvector, and weight values according to criteria C_4, C_5, and the weight value estimating the level of inflicted damage.

Input Variables	Criteria Weights					
	$\omega_i^{(i)}$	$\omega_i^{(ii)}$	$\omega_i^{(iii)}$	$\omega_i^{(iv)}$	$\omega_i^{(v)}$	ω_i
Financial cos ts (C_4)	0.6667	0.3333	0.6667	0.7500	0.5000	0.5833
Reputation damage (C_5)	0.3333	0.6667	0.3333	0.2500	0.5000	0.4167

Table A5. The base of production rules for assessing Y_1—the probability of occurrence of threats.

(i)	(ii)	(iii)	(iv)	(v)	(vi)	(vii)	(viii)	(ix)	(i)	(ii)	(iii)	(iv)	(v)	(vi)	(vii)	(viii)	(ix)
1	VL	0.2	VL	1.0	VL	0.2	0.52	VL	64	M	0.6	M	0.6	H	0.8	0.64	M
2	VL	0.2	VL	1.0	L	0.4	0.55	VL	65	M	0.6	M	0.6	VH	1.0	0.68	M
3	VL	0.2	VL	1.0	M	0.6	0.59	VL	66	M	0.6	H	0.4	VL	0.2	0.44	M
4	VL	0.2	VL	1.0	H	0.8	0.63	L	67	M	0.6	H	0.4	L	0.4	0.48	M
5	VL	0.2	VL	1.0	VH	1.0	0.67	L	68	M	0.6	H	0.4	M	0.6	0.52	M
6	VL	0.2	L	0.8	VL	0.2	0.44	VL	69	M	0.6	H	0.4	H	0.8	0.56	H
7	VL	0.2	L	0.8	L	0.4	0.48	L	70	M	0.6	H	0.4	VH	1.0	0.60	H
8	VL	0.2	L	0.8	M	0.6	0.51	L	71	M	0.6	VH	0.2	VL	0.2	0.36	M
9	VL	0.2	L	0.8	H	0.8	0.55	L	72	M	0.6	VH	0.2	L	0.4	0.40	H
10	VL	0.2	L	0.8	VH	1.0	0.59	L	73	M	0.6	VH	0.2	M	0.6	0.44	H
11	VL	0.2	M	0.6	VL	0.2	0.36	L	74	M	0.6	VH	0.2	H	0.8	0.48	H
12	VL	0.2	M	0.6	L	0.4	0.40	L	75	M	0.6	VH	0.2	VH	1.0	0.52	H
13	VL	0.2	M	0.6	M	0.6	0.44	L	76	H	0.8	VL	1.0	VL	0.2	0.76	L
14	VL	0.2	M	0.6	H	0.8	0.47	L	77	H	0.8	VL	1.0	L	0.4	0.80	L
15	VL	0.2	M	0.6	VH	1.0	0.51	M	78	H	0.8	VL	1.0	M	0.6	0.84	M
16	VL	0.2	H	0.4	VL	0.2	0.28	L	79	H	0.8	VL	1.0	H	0.8	0.88	M
17	VL	0.2	H	0.4	L	0.4	0.32	L	80	H	0.8	VL	1.0	VH	1.0	0.92	M
18	VL	0.2	H	0.4	M	0.6	0.36	M	81	H	0.8	L	0.8	VL	0.2	0.68	M
19	VL	0.2	H	0.4	H	0.8	0.39	M	82	H	0.8	L	0.8	L	0.4	0.72	M
20	VL	0.2	H	0.4	VH	1.0	0.43	M	83	H	0.8	L	0.8	M	0.6	0.76	M
21	VL	0.2	VH	0.2	VL	0.2	0.20	M	84	H	0.8	L	0.8	H	0.8	0.80	M
22	VL	0.2	VH	0.2	L	0.4	0.24	M	85	H	0.8	L	0.8	VH	1.0	0.84	M
23	VL	0.2	VH	0.2	M	0.6	0.28	M	86	H	0.8	M	0.6	VL	0.2	0.61	M
24	VL	0.2	VH	0.2	H	0.8	0.32	M	87	H	0.8	M	0.6	L	0.4	0.64	M
25	VL	0.2	VH	0.2	VH	1.0	0.35	M	88	H	0.8	M	0.6	M	0.6	0.68	M
26	L	0.4	VL	1.0	VL	0.2	0.60	VL	89	H	0.8	M	0.6	H	0.8	0.72	H
27	L	0.4	VL	1.0	L	0.4	0.64	L	90	H	0.8	M	0.6	VH	1.0	0.76	H
28	L	0.4	VL	1.0	M	0.6	0.68	L	91	H	0.8	H	0.4	VL	0.2	0.53	M
29	L	0.4	VL	1.0	H	0.8	0.71	L	92	H	0.8	H	0.4	L	0.4	0.56	H
30	L	0.4	VL	1.0	VH	1.0	0.75	L	93	H	0.8	H	0.4	M	0.6	0.60	H
31	L	0.4	L	0.8	VL	0.2	0.52	L	94	H	0.8	H	0.4	H	0.8	0.64	H
32	L	0.4	L	0.8	L	0.4	0.56	L	95	H	0.8	H	0.4	VH	1.0	0.68	H
33	L	0.4	L	0.8	M	0.6	0.60	L	96	H	0.8	VH	0.2	VL	0.2	0.45	H
34	L	0.4	L	0.8	H	0.8	0.64	L	97	H	0.8	VH	0.2	L	0.4	0.49	H
35	L	0.4	L	0.8	VH	1.0	0.67	M	98	H	0.8	VH	0.2	M	0.6	0.52	H
36	L	0.4	M	0.6	VL	0.2	0.44	L	99	H	0.8	VH	0.2	H	0.8	0.56	H
37	L	0.4	M	0.6	L	0.4	0.48	L	100	H	0.8	VH	0.2	VH	1.0	0.60	VH
38	L	0.4	M	0.6	M	0.6	0.52	M	101	VH	1.0	VL	1.0	VL	0.2	0.85	M
39	L	0.4	M	0.6	H	0.8	0.56	M	102	VH	1.0	VL	1.0	L	0.4	0.88	M
40	L	0.4	M	0.6	VH	1.0	0.59	M	103	VH	1.0	VL	1.0	M	0.6	0.92	M
41	L	0.4	H	0.4	VL	0.2	0.36	M	104	VH	1.0	VL	1.0	H	0.8	0.96	M
42	L	0.4	H	0.4	L	0.4	0.40	M	105	VH	1.0	VL	1.0	VH	1.0	1.00	M
43	L	0.4	H	0.4	M	0.6	0.44	M	106	VH	1.0	L	0.8	VL	0.2	0.77	M
44	L	0.4	H	0.4	H	0.8	0.48	M	107	VH	1.0	L	0.8	L	0.4	0.81	M
45	L	0.4	H	0.4	VH	1.0	0.52	M	108	VH	1.0	L	0.8	M	0.6	0.84	M

Table A5. *Cont.*

(i)	(ii)	(iii)	(iv)	(v)	(vi)	(vii)	(viii)	(ix)	(i)	(ii)	(iii)	(iv)	(v)	(vi)	(vii)	(viii)	(ix)
46	L	0.4	VH	0.2	VL	0.2	0.28	M	109	VH	1.0	L	0.8	H	0.8	0.88	H
47	L	0.4	VH	0.2	L	0.4	0.32	M	110	VH	1.0	L	0.8	VH	1.0	0.92	H
48	L	0.4	VH	0.2	M	0.6	0.36	M	111	VH	1.0	M	0.6	VL	0.2	0.69	M
49	L	0.4	VH	0.2	H	0.8	0.40	H	112	VH	1.0	M	0.6	L	0.4	0.73	H
50	L	0.4	VH	0.2	VH	1.0	0.44	H	113	VH	1.0	M	0.6	M	0.6	0.76	H
51	M	0.6	VL	1.0	VL	0.2	0.68	L	114	VH	1.0	M	0.6	H	0.8	0.80	H
52	M	0.6	VL	1.0	L	0.4	0.72	L	115	VH	1.0	M	0.6	VH	1.0	0.84	H
53	M	0.6	VL	1.0	M	0.6	0.76	L	116	VH	1.0	H	0.4	VL	0.2	0.61	H
54	M	0.6	VL	1.0	H	0.8	0.80	L	117	VH	1.0	H	0.4	L	0.4	0.65	H
55	M	0.6	VL	1.0	VH	1.0	0.84	M	118	VH	1.0	H	0.4	M	0.6	0.69	H
56	M	0.6	L	0.8	VL	0.2	0.60	L	119	VH	1.0	H	0.4	H	0.8	0.72	H
57	M	0.6	L	0.8	L	0.4	0.64	L	120	VH	1.0	H	0.4	VH	1.0	0.76	VH
58	M	0.6	L	0.8	M	0.6	0.68	M	121	VH	1.0	VH	0.2	VL	0.2	0.53	H
59	M	0.6	L	0.8	H	0.8	0.72	M	122	VH	1.0	VH	0.2	L	0.4	0.57	H
60	M	0.6	L	0.8	VH	1.0	0.76	M	123	VH	1.0	VH	0.2	M	0.6	0.61	VH
61	M	0.6	M	0.6	VL	0.2	0.52	M	124	VH	1.0	VH	0.2	H	0.8	0.65	VH
62	M	0.6	M	0.6	L	0.4	0.56	M	125	VH	1.0	VH	0.2	VH	1.0	0.68	VH
63	M	0.6	M	0.6	M	0.6	0.60	M									

where (i)—is a serial number; (ii)–(iii)—the value of the term of the input linguistic variable C_1—Attractiveness of assets with a weighting coefficient $\omega_1 = 0.4126$; (iv)–(v)—value of the term of the input linguistic variable C_2—Existing control with a weight coefficient $\omega_2 = 0.3952$; (vi)–(vii)—value of the term of the input linguistic variable C_3—Previous incidents with a weight coefficient $\omega_3 = 0.1929$; (viii)–(ix)—calculated value of the term of the output linguistic variable Y_1—Probability of occurrence of a threat.

Table A6. Aggregated fuzzy rules for assessing Y_1—the probability of occurrence of a threat.

(i)	(ii)			(iii)
R_1	$(C_1 = VL) \wedge (C_2 = VL) \wedge (C_3 = VL) \vee$	$(C_1 = VL) \wedge (C_2 = VL) \wedge (C_3 = M) \vee$	$(C_1 = L) \wedge (C_2 = VL) \wedge (C_3 = VL)$	$Y_1 = VL$
	$(C_1 = VL) \wedge (C_2 = VL) \wedge (C_3 = L) \vee$	$(C_1 = VL) \wedge (C_2 = L) \wedge (C_3 = VL) \vee$		
	$(C_1 = VL) \wedge (C_2 = VL) \wedge (C_3 = H) \vee$	$(C_1 = VL) \wedge (C_2 = H) \wedge (C_3 = VL) \vee$	$(C_1 = L) \wedge (C_2 = M) \wedge (C_3 = VL) \vee$	
	$(C_1 = VL) \wedge (C_2 = VL) \wedge (C_3 = VH) \vee$	$(C_1 = VL) \wedge (C_2 = H) \wedge (C_3 = L) \vee$	$(C_1 = L) \wedge (C_2 = M) \wedge (C_3 = L) \vee$	
	$(C_1 = VL) \wedge (C_2 = L) \wedge (C_3 = L) \vee$	$(C_1 = L) \wedge (C_2 = VL) \wedge (C_3 = L) \vee$	$(C_1 = M) \wedge (C_2 = VL) \wedge (C_3 = VL) \vee$	
	$(C_1 = VL) \wedge (C_2 = L) \wedge (C_3 = M) \vee$	$(C_1 = L) \wedge (C_2 = VL) \wedge (C_3 = M) \vee$	$(C_1 = M) \wedge (C_2 = VL) \wedge (C_3 = L) \vee$	
	$(C_1 = VL) \wedge (C_2 = L) \wedge (C_3 = H) \vee$	$(C_1 = L) \wedge (C_2 = VL) \wedge (C_3 = H) \vee$	$(C_1 = M) \wedge (C_2 = VL) \wedge (C_3 = M) \vee$	
R_2	$(C_1 = VL) \wedge (C_2 = L) \wedge (C_3 = VH) \vee$	$(C_1 = L) \wedge (C_2 = VL) \wedge (C_3 = VH) \vee$	$(C_1 = M) \wedge (C_2 = VL) \wedge (C_3 = H) \vee$	$Y_1 = L$
	$(C_1 = VL) \wedge (C_2 = M) \wedge (C_3 = VL) \vee$	$(C_1 = L) \wedge (C_2 = L) \wedge (C_3 = VL) \vee$	$(C_1 = M) \wedge (C_2 = L) \wedge (C_3 = VL) \vee$	
	$(C_1 = VL) \wedge (C_2 = M) \wedge (C_3 = L) \vee$	$(C_1 = L) \wedge (C_2 = L) \wedge (C_3 = L) \vee$	$(C_1 = M) \wedge (C_2 = L) \wedge (C_3 = L) \vee$	
	$(C_1 = VL) \wedge (C_2 = M) \wedge (C_3 = M) \vee$	$(C_1 = L) \wedge (C_2 = L) \wedge (C_3 = M) \vee$	$(C_1 = H) \wedge (C_2 = VL) \wedge (C_3 = VL) \vee$	
	$(C_1 = VL) \wedge (C_2 = M) \wedge (C_3 = H) \vee$	$(C_1 = L) \wedge (C_2 = L) \wedge (C_3 = H) \vee$	$(C_1 = H) \wedge (C_2 = VL) \wedge (C_3 = L)$	
	$(C_1 = VL) \wedge (C_2 = M) \wedge (C_3 = VH) \vee$	$(C_1 = L) \wedge (C_2 = VH) \wedge (C_3 = L) \vee$		
	$(C_1 = VL) \wedge (C_2 = H) \wedge (C_3 = M) \vee$	$(C_1 = L) \wedge (C_2 = VH) \wedge (C_3 = M) \vee$	$(C_1 = H) \wedge (C_2 = L) \wedge (C_3 = L) \vee$	
	$(C_1 = VL) \wedge (C_2 = H) \wedge (C_3 = H) \vee$	$(C_1 = M) \wedge (C_2 = VL) \wedge (C_3 = VH) \vee$	$(C_1 = H) \wedge (C_2 = L) \wedge (C_3 = M) \vee$	
	$(C_1 = VL) \wedge (C_2 = H) \wedge (C_3 = VH) \vee$	$(C_1 = M) \wedge (C_2 = L) \wedge (C_3 = M) \vee$	$(C_1 = H) \wedge (C_2 = L) \wedge (C_3 = H) \vee$	
	$(C_1 = VL) \wedge (C_2 = VH) \wedge (C_3 = VL) \vee$	$(C_1 = M) \wedge (C_2 = L) \wedge (C_3 = H) \vee$	$(C_1 = H) \wedge (C_2 = L) \wedge (C_3 = VH) \vee$	
	$(C_1 = VL) \wedge (C_2 = VH) \wedge (C_3 = L) \vee$	$(C_1 = M) \wedge (C_2 = L) \wedge (C_3 = VH) \vee$	$(C_1 = H) \wedge (C_2 = M) \wedge (C_3 = VL) \vee$	
	$(C_1 = VL) \wedge (C_2 = VH) \wedge (C_3 = M) \vee$	$(C_1 = M) \wedge (C_2 = M) \wedge (C_3 = VL) \vee$	$(C_1 = H) \wedge (C_2 = M) \wedge (C_3 = L) \vee$	
	$(C_1 = VL) \wedge (C_2 = VH) \wedge (C_3 = H) \vee$	$(C_1 = M) \wedge (C_2 = M) \wedge (C_3 = L) \vee$	$(C_1 = H) \wedge (C_2 = M) \wedge (C_3 = M) \vee$	
	$(C_1 = VL) \wedge (C_2 = VH) \wedge (C_3 = VH) \vee$	$(C_1 = M) \wedge (C_2 = M) \wedge (C_3 = M) \vee$	$(C_1 = H) \wedge (C_2 = H) \wedge (C_3 = VL) \vee$	
R_3	$(C_1 = L) \wedge (C_2 = L) \wedge (C_3 = VH) \vee$	$(C_1 = M) \wedge (C_2 = M) \wedge (C_3 = H) \vee$	$(C_1 = VH) \wedge (C_2 = VL) \wedge (C_3 = VL) \vee$	$Y_1 = M$
	$(C_1 = L) \wedge (C_2 = M) \wedge (C_3 = M) \vee$	$(C_1 = M) \wedge (C_2 = M) \wedge (C_3 = VH) \vee$	$(C_1 = VH) \wedge (C_2 = VL) \wedge (C_3 = L) \vee$	
	$(C_1 = L) \wedge (C_2 = M) \wedge (C_3 = H) \vee$	$(C_1 = M) \wedge (C_2 = H) \wedge (C_3 = VL) \vee$	$(C_1 = VH) \wedge (C_2 = VL) \wedge (C_3 = M) \vee$	
	$(C_1 = L) \wedge (C_2 = M) \wedge (C_3 = VH) \vee$	$(C_1 = M) \wedge (C_2 = H) \wedge (C_3 = L) \vee$	$(C_1 = VH) \wedge (C_2 = VL) \wedge (C_3 = H) \vee$	
	$(C_1 = L) \wedge (C_2 = H) \wedge (C_3 = VL) \vee$	$(C_1 = M) \wedge (C_2 = H) \wedge (C_3 = M) \vee$	$(C_1 = VH) \wedge (C_2 = VL) \wedge (C_3 = VH) \vee$	
	$(C_1 = L) \wedge (C_2 = H) \wedge (C_3 = L) \vee$	$(C_1 = M) \wedge (C_2 = VH) \wedge (C_3 = VL) \vee$	$(C_1 = VH) \wedge (C_2 = L) \wedge (C_3 = VL) \vee$	
	$(C_1 = L) \wedge (C_2 = H) \wedge (C_3 = M) \vee$	$(C_1 = H) \wedge (C_2 = VL) \wedge (C_3 = M) \vee$	$(C_1 = VH) \wedge (C_2 = L) \wedge (C_3 = L) \vee$	
	$(C_1 = L) \wedge (C_2 = H) \wedge (C_3 = H) \vee$	$(C_1 = H) \wedge (C_2 = VL) \wedge (C_3 = H) \vee$	$(C_1 = VH) \wedge (C_2 = L) \wedge (C_3 = M) \vee$	
	$(C_1 = L) \wedge (C_2 = H) \wedge (C_3 = VH) \vee$	$(C_1 = H) \wedge (C_2 = VL) \wedge (C_3 = VH) \vee$	$(C_1 = VH) \wedge (C_2 = M) \wedge (C_3 = VL)$	
	$(C_1 = L) \wedge (C_2 = VH) \wedge (C_3 = VL) \vee$	$(C_1 = H) \wedge (C_2 = L) \wedge (C_3 = VL) \vee$		

Table A6. *Cont.*

(i)	(ii)			(iii)
R_4	$(C_1 = L) \wedge (C_2 = VH) \wedge (C_3 = H) \vee$ $(C_1 = L) \wedge (C_2 = VH) \wedge (C_3 = VH) \vee$ $(C_1 = M) \wedge (C_2 = H) \wedge (C_3 = H) \vee$ $(C_1 = M) \wedge (C_2 = H) \wedge (C_3 = VH) \vee$ $(C_1 = M) \wedge (C_2 = VH) \wedge (C_3 = L) \vee$ $(C_1 = M) \wedge (C_2 = VH) \wedge (C_3 = M) \vee$ $(C_1 = M) \wedge (C_2 = VH) \wedge (C_3 = H) \vee$ $(C_1 = M) \wedge (C_2 = VH) \wedge (C_3 = VH) \vee$ $(C_1 = H) \wedge (C_2 = M) \wedge (C_3 = H) \vee$ $(C_1 = H) \wedge (C_2 = M) \wedge (C_3 = VH) \vee$	$(C_1 = H) \wedge (C_2 = H) \wedge (C_3 = L) \vee$ $(C_1 = H) \wedge (C_2 = H) \wedge (C_3 = M) \vee$ $(C_1 = H) \wedge (C_2 = H) \wedge (C_3 = H) \vee$ $(C_1 = H) \wedge (C_2 = H) \wedge (C_3 = VH) \vee$ $(C_1 = H) \wedge (C_2 = VH) \wedge (C_3 = VL) \vee$ $(C_1 = H) \wedge (C_2 = VH) \wedge (C_3 = L) \vee$ $(C_1 = H) \wedge (C_2 = VH) \wedge (C_3 = M) \vee$ $(C_1 = H) \wedge (C_2 = VH) \wedge (C_3 = H) \vee$ $(C_1 = VH) \wedge (C_2 = L) \wedge (C_3 = H) \vee$ $(C_1 = VH) \wedge (C_2 = L) \wedge (C_3 = VH) \vee$	$(C_1 = VH) \wedge (C_2 = M) \wedge (C_3 = L) \vee$ $(C_1 = VH) \wedge (C_2 = M) \wedge (C_3 = M) \vee$ $(C_1 = VH) \wedge (C_2 = M) \wedge (C_3 = H) \vee$ $(C_1 = VH) \wedge (C_2 = M) \wedge (C_3 = VH) \vee$ $(C_1 = VH) \wedge (C_2 = H) \wedge (C_3 = VL) \vee$ $(C_1 = VH) \wedge (C_2 = H) \wedge (C_3 = L) \vee$ $(C_1 = VH) \wedge (C_2 = H) \wedge (C_3 = M) \vee$ $(C_1 = VH) \wedge (C_2 = H) \wedge (C_3 = H) \vee$ $(C_1 = VH) \wedge (C_2 = VH) \wedge (C_3 = VL) \vee$ $(C_1 = VH) \wedge (C_2 = VH) \wedge (C_3 = L)$	$Y_1 = H$
R_5	$(C_1 = H) \wedge (C_2 = VH) \wedge (C_3 = VH) \vee$ $(C_1 = VH) \wedge (C_2 = H) \wedge (C_3 = VH) \vee$	$(C_1 = VH) \wedge (C_2 = VH) \wedge (C_3 = M) \vee$ $(C_1 = VH) \wedge (C_2 = VH) \wedge (C_3 = H) \vee$	$(C_1 = VH) \wedge (C_2 = VH) \wedge (C_3 = VH) \vee$	$Y_1 = VH$

where (i)—is the ordinal number of the rules R_j, $j = \overline{1,5}$; (ii)—Rule; (iii)—Consequent.

Table A7. Information base of fuzzy production rules for assessing the level of inflicted damage.

(i)	(ii)	(iii)	(iv)	(v)	(vi)	(vii)	(i)	(ii)	(iii)	(iv)	(v)	(vi)	(vii)	(i)	(ii)	(iii)	(iv)	(v)	(vi)	(vii)
1	VL	1	VL	1	1.000	VL	10	L	2	VH	5	3.251	M	19	H	4	H	4	4.000	H
2	VL	1	L	2	1.417	VL	11	M	3	VL	1	2.166	L	20	H	4	VH	5	4.417	H
3	VL	1	M	3	1.834	L	12	M	3	L	2	2.583	M	21	VH	5	VL	1	3.332	M
4	VL	1	H	4	2.251	L	13	M	3	M	3	3.000	M	22	VH	5	L	2	3.749	H
5	VL	1	VH	5	2.668	M	14	M	3	H	4	3.417	M	23	VH	5	M	3	4.166	H
6	L	2	VL	1	1.583	L	15	M	3	VH	5	3.834	H	24	VH	5	H	4	4.583	VH
7	L	2	L	2	2.000	L	16	H	4	VL	1	2.749	M	25	VH	5	VH	5	5	VH
8	L	2	M	3	2.417	L	17	H	4	L	2	3.166	M							
9	L	2	H	4	2.834	M	18	H	4	M	3	3.583	H							

where (i)—is a serial number; (ii)–(iii)—the value of the term of the input linguistic variable C_4—Financial costs with a weighting coefficient $\omega_4 = 0.5833$; (iv)–(v)—the value of the term of the input linguistic variable C_5—Damage to reputation with a weight coefficient $\omega_5 = 0.4167$; (vi)–(vii)—calculated value of the term of the output linguistic variable Y_2—Manifestation of the damage caused.

Table A8. Aggregated fuzzy rules for assessing the level of inflicted damage.

(i)	(ii)			(iii)
R6	(C4 = VL) ∧ (C5 = VL) ∨	(C4 = VL) ∧ (C5 = L)		Y2 = VL
R7	(C4 = VL) ∧ (C5 = M) ∨ (C4 = VL) ∧ (C5 = H) ∨	(C4 = L) ∧ (C5 = VL) ∨ (C4 = L) ∧ (C5 = L) ∨	(C4 = L) ∧ (C5 = M) ∨ (C4 = M) ∧ (C5 = VL)	Y2 = L
R8	(C4 = VL) ∧ (C5 = VH) ∨ (C4 = L) ∧ (C5 = H) ∨ (C4 = L) ∧ (C5 = VH) ∨	(C4 = M) ∧ (C5 = L) ∨ (C4 = M) ∧ (C5 = M) ∨ (C4 = M) ∧ (C5 = H) ∨	(C4 = H) ∧ (C5 = VL) ∨ (C4 = H) ∧ (C5 = L) ∨ (C4 = VH) ∧ (C5 = VL)	Y2 = M
R9	(C4 = M) ∧ (C5 = VH) ∨ (C4 = H) ∧ (C5 = M) ∨	(C4 = H) ∧ (C5 = H) ∨ (C4 = H) ∧ (C5 = VH) ∨	(C4 = VH) ∧ (C5 = L) ∨ (C4 = VH) ∧ (C5 = M)	Y2 = H
R10	(C4 = VH) ∧ (C5 = H) ∨	(C4 = VH) ∧ (C5 = VH)		Y2 = VH

where (i)—is the ordinal number of rules R_j, $j = \overline{6,10}$; (ii)—Rule; (iii)—Consequent.

References

1. Hofer, F. Architecture, technologies and challenges for cyber-physical systems in industry 4.0: A systematic mapping study. In Proceedings of the 12th ACM/IEEE International Symposium on Empirical Software Engineering and Measurement (ESEM), Oulu, Finland, 11–12 October 2018; pp. 1–10. [CrossRef]
2. Sisinni, E.; Saifullah, A.; Han, S.; Jennehag, U.; Gidlund, M. Industrial Internet of Things: Challenges, opportunities, and directions. *IEEE Trans. Ind. Inform.* **2018**, *14*, 4724–4734. [CrossRef]
3. Tange, K.; De Donno, M.; Fafoutis, X.; Dragoni, N. A Systematic Survey of Industrial Internet of Things Security: Requirements and Fog Computing Opportunities. *IEEE Commun. Surv. Tutor.* **2020**, *22*, 2489–2520. [CrossRef]
4. Yu, X.; Guo, H. A Survey on IIoT Security. In Proceedings of the Conference: IEEE VTS Asia Pacific Wireless Communications Symposium (APWCS), Singapore, 28–30 August 2019; pp. 1–5. [CrossRef]
5. Panchal, A.; Khadse, V.; Mahalle, P. Security Issues in IIoT: A Comprehensive Survey of Attacks on IIoT and Its Countermeasures. In Proceedings of the Conference: 2018 IEEE Global Conference on Wireless Computing and Networking (GCWCN), Lonavala, India, 23–24 November 2018; pp. 124–130. [CrossRef]
6. Shah, Y.; Sengupta, S. A survey on Classification of Cyber-attacks on IoT and IIoT devices. In Proceedings of the Conference: 2020 11th IEEE Annual Ubiquitous Computing, Electronics & Mobile Communication Conference (UEMCON), New York, NY, USA, 28–31 October 2020; pp. 0406–0413. [CrossRef]

7. Tamy, S.; Belhadaoui, H.; Rabbah, M.; Rabbah, N.; Rifi, M. An evaluation of machine learning algorithms to detect attacks in SCADA network. In Proceedings of the Conference: 2019 7th Mediterranean Congress of Telecommunications (CMT), Fez, Morocco, 24–25 October 2019; pp. 1–5. [CrossRef]
8. Al-Hawawreh, M.; Sitnikova, E. Industrial Internet of Things based ransomware detection using stacked variational neural network. In Proceedings of the 2019 Conference on Big Data and Internet of Things (BDIOT), Melbourn, VIC, Australia, 22–24 August 2019; pp. 126–130. [CrossRef]
9. Wang, H.; Chen, Z.; Zhao, J.; Di, X.; Liu, D. A Vulnerability Assessment Method in Industrial Internet of Things Based on Attack Graph and Maximum Flow. *IEEE Access* **2018**, *6*, 8599–8609. [CrossRef]
10. Li, Z.; Kang, J.; Yu, R.; Ye, D.; Deng, Q.; Zhang, Y. Consortium Blockchain for Secure Energy Trading in Industrial Internet of Things. *IEEE Trans. Ind. Inform.* **2017**, *14*, 3690–3700. [CrossRef]
11. Huang, Y.-L.; Sun, W.-L. An AHP-Based Risk Assessment for an Industrial IoT Cloud. In Proceedings of the IEEE International Conference on Software Quality, Reliability and Security Companion (QRS-C), Lisbon, Portugal, 16–20 July 2018; pp. 637–638. [CrossRef]
12. Hassani, H.L.; Bahnasse, A.; Martin, E.; Roland, C.; Bouattane, O.; Diouri, M.E. Vulnerability and security risk assessment in a IIoT environment in compliance with standard IEC 62443. *Procedia Comput. Sci.* **2021**, *191*, 33–40. [CrossRef]
13. Tsiknas, K.; Taketzis, D.; Demertzis, K.; Skianis, C. Cyber Threats to Industrial IoT: A Survey on Attacks and Countermeasures. *IoT* **2021**, *2*, 163–186. [CrossRef]
14. Wentian, C.; Huijun, Y. Research on Information Security Risk Assessment Method Based on Fuzzy Rule Set. *Wirel. Commun. Mob. Comput.* **2021**, 9663520. [CrossRef]
15. Tubis, A.; Werbińska-Wojciechowska, S.; Góralczyk, M.; Wróblewski, A.; Ziętek, B. Cyber-Attacks Risk Analysis Method for Different Levels of Automation of Mining Processes in Mines Based on Fuzzy Theory Use. *Sensors* **2020**, *20*, 7210. [CrossRef]
16. Kuzminykh, I.; Ghita, B.; Sokolov, V.; Bakhshi, T. Information Security Risk Assessment. *Encyclopedia* **2021**, *1*, 602–617. [CrossRef]
17. Zadeh, L.A. Is there a need for fuzzy logic? *Inf. Sci.* **2008**, *178*, 2751–2779. [CrossRef]
18. *ISO/IEC 27400:2022*; Cybersecurity–IoT Security and Privacy. ISO: Geneva, Switzerland, 2023. Available online: www.iso27001security.com (accessed on 21 July 2023).
19. *ISA/IEC 62443*; Series of Standards—Security for Industrial Automation and Control Systems. ISA: Eindhoven, The Netherlands, 2023. Available online: https://www.isa.org/standards-and-publications/isa-standards/isa-iec-62443-series-of-standards (accessed on 21 July 2023).
20. Force, J.T. *Guide for Conducting Risk Assessments*; NIST SP 800-30 Rev. 1; National Institute of Standards and Technology: Gaithersburg, MD, USA, 2012. [CrossRef]
21. Force, J.T. *Risk Management Framework for Information Systems and Organizations: A System Life Cycle Approach for Security and Privacy*; NIST SP 800-37 Rev. 2; National Institute of Standards and Technology: Gaithersburg, MD, USA, 2018. [CrossRef]
22. *ISO/IEC 27005:2022*; Information Security, Cybersecurity and Privacy Protection—Guidance on Managing Information Security Risks. ISO: Geneva, Switzerland, 2022. Available online: https://www.iso.org/standard/80585.html (accessed on 21 July 2023).
23. Freund, J.; Jones, J. *Measuring and Managing Information Risk: A FAIR Approach*; Butterworth-Heinemann: Oxford, UK, 2014; p. 408.
24. Saaty, T.L. There is no mathematical validity for using fuzzy number crunching in the analytic hierarchy process. *J. Syst. Sci. Syst. Eng.* **2006**, *15*, 457–464. [CrossRef]
25. Reports of the Kaspersky Lab Industrial Infrastructure Information Security Incident Response Center (Kaspersky ICS CERT). Available online: https://ics-cert.kaspersky.ru/publications/reports/2023/09/13/threat-landscape-for-industrial-automation-systems-statistics-for-h1-2023/ (accessed on 21 July 2023).
26. Arrow, K.J.; Kruz, M. *Public Investment, the Rate of Return, and Optimal Fiscal Policy*; RFF Press: New York, NY, USA, 2013; p. 218. [CrossRef]
27. Gaultier-Gaillard, S.; Louisot, J.P.; Rayner, J. Managing reputational risk—From theory to practice. In *Reputation Capital: Building and Maintaining Trust in the 21st Century*; Springer: Berlin/Heidelberg, Germany, 2009. [CrossRef]
28. Kureichik, V.M.; Kazharov, A. Using fuzzy logic controller in ant colony optimization. *Adv. Intell. Syst. Comput.* **2015**, *347*, 151–158. [CrossRef]
29. Shang, W.; Gong, T.; Chen, C.; Hou, J.; Zeng, P. Information Security Risk Assessment Method for Ship Control System Based on Fuzzy Sets and Attack Trees. *Secur. Commun. Netw.* **2019**, 3574675. [CrossRef]
30. Huijuan, G.; Lei, D.; Wenchao, X. Cybersecurity Risk Assessment of Industrial Control Systems Based on Order-α Divergence Measures Under an Interval-Valued Intuitionistic Fuzzy Environment. *IEEE Access* **2022**, *10*, 43751–43765. [CrossRef]
31. Stojanović, M.; Markovic-Petrovic, J. A Model for Dynamic Cyber Security Risk Assessment in the Industrial IoT Environment. In Proceedings of the Sinteza 2022—International Scientific Conference on Information Technology and Data Related Research, Online, 16 April 2022; pp. 230–237. [CrossRef]
32. Atlam, H.; Walters, R.; Wills, G.; Daniel, J. Fuzzy Logic with Expert Judgment to Implement an Adaptive Risk-Based Access Control Model for IoT. *Mob. Netw. Appl.* **2021**, *26*, 2545–2557. [CrossRef]
33. Adaros-Boye, C.; Kearney, P.; Josephs, M.; Ulmer, H. An Indicators-of-Risk Library for Industrial Network Security. In Proceedings of the Conference: ARES 2021: The 16th International Conference on Availability, Reliability and Security, Vienna, Austria, 17–20 August 2021. [CrossRef]

34. Figueroa-Lorenzo, S.; Añorga, J.; Arrizabalaga, S. A Survey of IIoT Protocols: A Measure of Vulnerability Risk Analysis Based on CVSS. *ACM Comput. Surv.* **2020**, *53*, 1–53. [CrossRef]
35. Abdymanapov, S.; Muratbekov, M.; Sharipbay, A.; Barlybayev, A. Fuzzy Expert System of Information Security Risk Assessment on the Example of Analysis Learning Management Systems. *IEEE Access* **2021**, *9*, 156556–156565. [CrossRef]
36. Sikman, L.; Latinovic, T.; Sarajlic, N. Modelling of Fuzzy Expert System for an Assessment of Security Information Management System UIS. *Tech. Gaz.* **2022**, *29*, 60–65. [CrossRef]
37. Amirova, A.; Tokhmetov, A. A model for risk analysis in the Industrial Internet of Things. *J. Theor. Appl. Inf. Technol.* **2021**, *99*, 3449–3459.
38. McLaughlin, S.; Konstantinou, C.; Wang, X.; Davi, L.; Sadeghi, A.; Maniatakos, M.; Karri, R. The Cybersecurity Landscape in Industrial Control Systems. *Proc. IEEE* **2016**, *104*, 1039–1057. [CrossRef]
39. Makhazhanova, U.; Kerimkhulle, S.; Mukhanova, A.; Bayegizova, A.; Aitkozha, Z.; Mukhiyadin, A.; Tassuov, B.; Saliyeva, A.; Taberkhan, R.; Azieva, G. The Evaluation of Creditworthiness of Trade and Enterprises of Service Using the Method Based on Fuzzy Logic. *Appl. Sci.* **2022**, *12*, 11515. [CrossRef]

symmetry

MDPI

Article

Baire Category Soft Sets and Their Symmetric Local Properties

Zanyar A. Ameen [1,*] and Mesfer H. Alqahtani [2]

1 Department of Mathematics, College of Science, University of Duhok, Duhok 42001, Iraq
2 Department of Mathematics, University College of Umluj, University of Tabuk, Tabuk 48322, Saudi Arabia; m_halqahtani@ut.edu.sa
* Correspondence: zanyar@uod.ac

Abstract: In this paper, we study soft sets of the first and second Baire categories. The soft sets of the first Baire category are examined to be small soft sets from the point of view of soft topology, while the soft sets of the second Baire category are examined to be large. The family of soft sets of the first Baire category in a soft topological space forms a soft σ-ideal. This contributes to the development of the theory of soft ideal topology. The main properties of these classes of soft sets are discussed. The concepts of soft points where soft sets are of the first or second Baire category are introduced. These types of soft points are subclasses of non-cluster and cluster soft sets. Then, various results on the first and second Baire category soft points are obtained. Among others, the set of all soft points at which a soft set is of the second Baire category is soft regular closed. Moreover, we show that there is symmetry between a soft set that is of the first Baire category and a soft set in which each of its soft points is of the first Baire category. This is equivalent to saying that the union of any collection of soft open sets of the first Baire category is again a soft set of the first Baire category. The last assertion can be regarded as a generalized version of one of the fundamental theorems in topology known as the Banach Category Theorem. Furthermore, it is shown that any soft set can be represented as a disjoint soft union of two soft sets, one of the first Baire category and the other not of the first Baire category at each of its soft points.

Keywords: soft nowhere dense set; soft set of the first category; soft set of the second category; soft codense; Banach Category Theorem; ideal soft topology

MSC: 54A99; 54F65; 03E99

1. Introduction

In the modern world, it is becoming more and more crucial to mathematically describe and manipulate different types of uncertainty in order to solve complicated problems in a variety of disciplines, including economics, environmental science, engineering, medical, and social sciences. Although other theories like theory of the fuzzy set [1], theory of the rough set [2], and the probability theory are well-known and useful methods for treating uncertainty and ambiguity, each has its own set of restrictions. One major weakness shared by these mathematical techniques is the lack of parametrization equipment.

The soft set theory was developed in 1999 by Molodtsov [3] as a solution to the problems associated with the aforementioned theories for managing uncertainty. A collection of parameterized universe possibilities known as soft sets was proposed. The interpretation of sets for modeling uncertainty has been discussed in [4] and then developed in [5]. A standardized framework for modeling uncertain data is provided by the nature of parameter sets linked to soft sets. This results in the quick development of soft set theory and related fields in a short period of time and offers several applications of soft sets in practical settings (see [6–15]).

Several scholars have used soft set theory to study mathematical structures such as soft group theory [16], soft ring theory [17], soft convex structures [18], soft ideals [19], etc.

Khameneh and Kilicman [20] introduced the idea of σ-algebras in soft set configurations. They explored some fundamental characteristics of soft σ-algebras. This concept's other basic features were covered in [21].

Soft topology is one of the structures introduced by Shabir and Naz [22] and Çağman et al. [23] as a novel generalization of the classical topology. The work in [22,23] was crucial to the development of the field of soft topology. Then, many classical concepts in topology have been generalized and extended in soft set settings, including soft separation axioms [24,25], soft connected spaces [26], soft compact spaces [27], soft separable spaces [25], soft paracompact spaces [26], and soft extremally disconnected spaces [28]

It is known that soft open sets are the building blocks of soft topology, but other classes of soft sets can contribute to the growth of soft topology, namely soft dense [29], soft codense [30], soft somewhat open [31], soft nowhere dense [29], soft meager (first-category soft set) [29], and soft somewhere dense open [32].

Another fruitful area of study is determining ways to produce soft topologies over a common universal set. Terepeta provided two exceptional methods for constructing soft topologies from crisp topologies in her paper [33]. The soft topology produced by one of the formulas was then demonstrated by Al-shami [34] to be identical to the enriched soft topology. Alcantud [35] enhanced Terepeta's formulas such that they could be used to create a soft topology from a system of crisp topologies. Jafari et al. proposed a method of inducing soft topologies by soft relations [36]. Al-shami et al. [37] proposed a method of generating a new soft topology, named a primal soft topology, via a mathematical structure called soft primal. Primal soft topologies can be regarded as a generalization of the soft ideal topology studied in [19] under the name of $*$-soft topology. In [38], the authors introduced methods of generating soft topologies by various soft set operators, soft closure and soft derived set operators among them. The cluster soft set [39] can be seen as a generalized version of the latter soft set operators. The set of soft points at which a soft set is of the second Baire category is a special case of a cluster soft set.

The motivations for writing the present work are:

- To study several classes of generalized soft open sets in soft topological spaces, which is an active path of research;
- To introduce the so-called soft points of the first or second category. The latter concept is a verbal generalization of soft limit points and soft closure points. Also, a soft point where a soft set is of the second category is a special case of the cluster soft point. The set of soft points at which a soft set is of the second category plays a crucial role in developing soft ideal topological spaces, which is another method of generating soft topologies.

The following is how the paper's material is organized: Section 2 provides a review of some definitions, properties, and operation of soft set and soft topology. Section 3 investigates some of the features of specific soft sets in soft topological spaces. Section 4 discusses the soft sets of first and second categories along with some operations. It also defines the concepts of soft points at which soft sets are of the first or second Baire category. Then, several properties of these classes of soft points are obtained. Section 5 ends the work with a brief conclusion.

2. Preliminaries

We let 2^X be the family of all subsets of an initial universe X, $\mathcal{T}$ be the associated set of parameters, and I be any index set.

Definition 1 ([3]). *Given a set-valued mapping $A : T \to 2^X$ and $T \subseteq \mathcal{T}$, an ordered pair $(A, T) = \{(t, A(t)) : t \in T\}$ is stated to be the soft set over X. That is, a soft set (A, T) over X is expressed by*

$$(A, T) = \{(t, A(t)) : t \in T, A(t) \in 2^X\}.$$

The collection of all soft subsets of X associated with T (resp. $\mathcal{T}$) is meant by $SS(X_T)$ (resp. $SS(X_{\mathcal{T}})$).

Remark 1. *We can easily extend a soft set (A,T) to the soft set $(A,\mathcal{T})$ by assuming $A(t)=\emptyset$ for any $t\in\mathcal{T}-T$.*

Definition 2 ([40])**.** *A soft set (A,T) is said to be null along with T, Φ_T, if $A(t)=\emptyset$ for each $t\in T$ and is called absolute along with T, X_T, if $A(t)=X$ for each $t\in T$. The absolute and null soft sets are denoted by $\Phi_{\mathcal{T}}$ and $X_{\mathcal{T}}$, respectively.*

Definition 3 ([8])**.** *A soft set $(A,T)^c=(A^c,T)$ is called the soft complement of a soft set (A,T), where $A^c:T\to 2^X$ is a set-valued mapping such that $A^c(t)=X-A(t)$ for all $t\in T$.*

Evidently, $((A,T)^c)^c=(A,T)$, $(\Phi_{\mathcal{T}})^c=X_{\mathcal{T}}$, and $(X_{\mathcal{T}})^c=\Phi_{\mathcal{T}}$.

Definition 4 ([41])**.** *A soft element denoted by x_t is a soft set (A,T) over X whenever $A(t)=\{x\}$ and $F(t')=\emptyset$ for all $t'\in T$ with $t\neq t'$, where $t\in T$ and $x\in X$. The soft element is called a soft point in [42]. We prefer to use the concept of soft point in the sequel. By statement $x_t\in(A,T)$, we mean $x\in A(t)$. By $SP(X_T)$ we denote the set of all soft points over X along with T.*

Definition 5 ([8,43])**.** *Let $T_1,T_2\subseteq\mathcal{T}$. It is said that (A_1,T_1) is a soft subset of (A_2,T_2), written by $(A_1,T_1)\widetilde{\subseteq}(A_2,T_2)$, if $T_1\subseteq T_2$ and $A_1(t)\subseteq A_2(t)$ for all $t\in T_1$. And (A_1,T_1) is soft equal to (A_2,T_1), written by $(A_1,T_1)=(A_2,T_2)$, if $(A_1,T_1)\widetilde{\subseteq}(A_2,T_2)$ and $(A_2,T_2)\widetilde{\subseteq}(A_1,T_1)$.*

Definition 6 ([33,40])**.** *Let $\{(A_i,T):i\in I\}$ be a family of soft sets over X.*
1. *The soft intersection of (A_i,T), for $i\in I$, is a soft set (A,T) such that $A(t)=\bigcap_{i\in I}A_i(t)$ for all $t\in T$ and is denoted by $(A,T)=\widetilde{\bigcap}_{i\in I}(A_i,T)$.*
2. *The soft union of (A_i,T), for $i\in I$, is a soft set (A,T) such that $A(t)=\bigcup_{i\in I}A_i(t)$ for all $t\in T$ and is denoted by $(A,T)=\widetilde{\bigcup}_{i\in I}(A_i,T)$.*

Definition 7 ([39,40])**.** *Let $(A,T),(B,T)\in SS(X_T)$. The soft set difference (A,T) and (B,T) is defined to be the soft set $(C,T)=(A,T)-(B,T)$, where $C(t)=A(t)-B(t)$ for all $t\in T$.*

Definition 8 ([44])**.** *A soft set (A,T) is countable (resp. finite) if $A(t)$ is countable (resp. finite) for each $t\in T$. Otherwise, it is uncountable (resp. infinite).*

In what follows, by two different soft points $x_t,y_{t'}$, we intend either $x\neq y$ or $t\neq t'$, and by two disjoint soft sets $(A,T),(B,T)$ over X we mean $(A,T)\widetilde{\cap}(B,T)=\Phi_T$.

Definition 9 ([22])**.** *Family $\Theta\widetilde{\subseteq}SS(X_T)$ is said to be a soft topology over X if*
1. *$\Phi_T,X_T\in\Theta$,*
2. *$(A_1,T),(A_2,T)\in\Theta$ implies $(A_1,T)\widetilde{\cap}(A_2,T)\in\Theta$, and*
3. *$\{(A_i,T):i\in I\}\widetilde{\subseteq}\Theta$ implies $\widetilde{\bigcup}_{i\in I}(A_i,T)\in\Theta$.*

(X,Θ,T) means a soft topological space. Soft open sets are the elements of Θ, and their complements are soft closed sets. The family of all soft closed sets is meant to be Θ^c. The set of soft topologies over X forms a lattice and it is denoted by $\Theta(X_T)$ (see [45,46]).

Definition 10 ([22])**.** *Let $(Y,T)\neq\Phi_T$ be a soft subset of (X,Θ,T). Then, $\Theta_{(Y,T)}=\{(B,T)\widetilde{\cap}(Y,T):(B,T)\in\Theta\}$ is called a relative soft topology over Y, and $(Y,\Theta_{(Y,T)},T)$ is a soft subspace of (Y,Θ,T).*

Lemma 1 ([22])**.** *Let $(Y,\Theta_{(Y,T)},T)$ be a soft subspace of (Y,Θ,T) and let $(A,T)\widetilde{\subseteq}(Y,T)\in\Theta$. Then, $(A,T)\in\Theta_{(Y,T)}$ if and only if $(A,T)\in\Theta$.*

Definition 11 ([41]). *Let $(B,T) \in SS(X_T)$ and $\Theta \in \Theta(X_T)$. Then, (B,T) is called a soft neighborhood of $x_t \in SP(X_T)$ if there exists $(W,T) \in \Theta(x_t)$ such that $x_t \in (W,T)\widetilde{\subseteq}(B,T)$, where $\Theta(x_t)$ is the family of all elements of Θ that contain x_t.*

Definition 12 ([46]). *A soft topology generated by family $\mathcal{F}\widetilde{\subseteq}SS(X_T)$ is the intersection of all soft topologies over X including $\mathcal{F}$.*

Definition 13 ([23]). *A (countable) soft base for soft topology Θ is a (countable) subfamily $\mathcal{B} \subseteq \Theta$ such that members of Θ are unions of members of $\mathcal{B}$.*

Lemma 2 ([22]). *For soft topological space (X,Θ,T), collection $\Theta(t) = \{A(t) : (A,T) \in \Theta\}$ forms a (crisp) topology on X for each $t \in T$.*

Definition 14 ([22]). *Let $(B,T) \in SS(X_T)$ and $\Theta \in \Theta(X_T)$.*

1. *The soft closure of (B,T) is $cl(B,T) := \widetilde{\cap}\{(A,T) : (B,T)\widetilde{\subseteq}(A,T), (A,T) \in \Theta^c\}$.*
2. *The soft interior of (B,T) is $int(B,T) := \widetilde{\cup}\{(A,T) : (A,T)\widetilde{\subseteq}(B,T), (A,T) \in \Theta\}$.*

Lemma 3 ([47]). *Let $(A,T) \in SS(X_T)$ and $\Theta \in \Theta(X_T)$. Then,*

$$int((A,T)^c) = (cl((A,T)))^c \text{ and } cl((A,T)^c) = (int((A,T)))^c.$$

Definition 15 ([38,47]). *Let $(A,T) \in SS(X_T)$ and $\Theta \in \Theta(X_T)$. The soft boundary of (A,T) is given by $b(A,T) = cl(A,T) - int(A,T)$.*

Definition 16 ([23]). *Let $(B,T) \in SS(X_T)$ and $\Theta \in \Theta(X_T)$. A soft point $x_t \in SP(X_T)$ is called a soft limit point of (B,T) if $(B,T)\widetilde{\cap}(B,T) - \{x_t\} \neq \Phi_T$ for all $(B,T) \in \Theta(x_t)$. The family of all soft limit points is denoted by $\mathcal{D}(B,T)$.*

Then, $cl(A,T) = (A,T)\widetilde{\cup}\mathcal{D}(A,T)$ (see Theorem 5 in [23]).

Definition 17 ([19]). *A non-null class $\tilde{I}\widetilde{\subseteq}SS(X_T)$ is termed a soft ideal over X if $\tilde{I}$ satisfies the following conditions:*

1. *If $(A,T),(B,T) \in \tilde{I}$, then $(A,T)\widetilde{\cup}(B,T) \in \tilde{I}$, and*
2. *If $(B,T) \in \tilde{I}$ and $(A,T)\widetilde{\subseteq}(B,T)$, then $(A,T) \in \tilde{I}$.*

$\tilde{I}$ is called a soft σ-ideal if (1) holds for countably many soft sets. We denote the family of soft ideals over X by $\mathcal{I}(X_T)$.

Definition 18 ([39]). *Let $(A,T) \in SS(X_T)$, $\Theta \in \Theta(X_T)$, and $\tilde{I} \in \mathcal{I}(X_T)$. A soft point $x_t \in SP(X_T)$ is a cluster soft point of (A,T) if $(A,T)\widetilde{\cap}(W,T) \notin \tilde{I}$ for each $(W,T) \in \Theta(x_t)$. The set of all the cluster soft points of (A,T) is called the cluster soft set of (A,T) and is denoted by $\mathfrak{c}_{(\Theta,\tilde{I})}(A,T)$ or shortly $\mathfrak{c}(A,T)$.*

Family $\Theta_{\mathfrak{c}}(\tilde{I}) = \{(A,T) \in SS(X_T) : \mathfrak{c}((A,T)^c)\widetilde{\subseteq}(A,T)^c\}$ is a soft topology over X and is called the cluster soft topology (or soft ideal topology). Lemma 11 and Theorem 6 in [38] guarantee that the cluster soft topology is equivalent to soft Θ^*-topology constructed differently in [19].

Remark 2 ([39]). *Given $(A,T) \in SS(X_T)$, $\Theta \in \Theta(X_T)$, and $\tilde{I} \in \mathcal{I}(X_T)$. We remark that*

1. *If $\tilde{I} = \{\Phi_T\}$, then $\mathfrak{c}(A,T) = cl(A,T)$. That is, the soft cluster points are identical to the soft closure points of (A,T).*
2. *If $\tilde{I} = \{(J,T) : (J,T) \in SS(X_T), (J,T) \text{ is finite}\}$, then $\mathfrak{c}(A,T) = \mathcal{D}(A,T)$. That is, the soft cluster points are identical to the soft limit points of (A,T).*

Now, we present some properties of soft cluster sets.

Proposition 1 ([39]). *Let $(A,T),(B,T) \in SS(X_T)$, $\Theta \in \Theta(X_T)$, and $\tilde{I} \in \mathcal{I}(X_T)$. The properties listed below are true:*

1. *If $(A,T) \in \tilde{I}$, then $\mathfrak{c}(A,T) = \tilde{\Phi}$.*
2. *If $(A,T)\tilde{\subseteq}(B,T)$, then $\mathfrak{c}(A,T)\tilde{\subseteq}\mathfrak{c}(B,T)$.*
3. *$\mathfrak{c}((A,T)\tilde{\cap}(B,T))\tilde{\subseteq}\mathfrak{c}(A,T)\tilde{\cap}\mathfrak{c}(B,T)$.*
4. *$\mathfrak{c}((A,T)\tilde{\cup}(B,T)) = \mathfrak{c}(A,T)\tilde{\cup}\mathfrak{c}(B,T)$.*
5. *$\mathfrak{c}(A,T) - \mathfrak{c}(B,T)\tilde{\subseteq}\mathfrak{c}((A,T) - (B,T))$.*

For any family $\mathfrak{F}$ of finite subsets of I, we have the following statements:

Proposition 2 ([39]). *Let $(A_i,T) \in SS(X_T)$ for $i \in I$, $\Theta \in \Theta(X_T)$, and $\tilde{I} \in \mathcal{I}(X_T)$. The properties listed below are true:*

1. *$\mathfrak{c}\left(\tilde{\bigcup}_{i\in N}(A_i,T)\right) = \tilde{\bigcup}_{i\in N}\mathfrak{c}(A_i,T)$, where $N \in \mathfrak{F}$.*
2. *$\tilde{\bigcup}_{i\in I}\mathfrak{c}(A_i,T)\tilde{\subseteq}\mathfrak{c}\left(\tilde{\bigcup}_{i\in I}(A_i,T)\right)$.*
3. *$\mathfrak{c}\left(\tilde{\bigcap}_{i\in I}(A_i,T)\right)\tilde{\subseteq}\tilde{\bigcap}_{i\in I}\mathfrak{c}(A_i,T)$.*
4. *$\mathfrak{c}\left(\tilde{\bigcup}_{i\in I}(A_i,T)\right) = \tilde{\bigcup}_{i\in I}\mathfrak{c}(A_i,T)\tilde{\cup}\left[\tilde{\bigcap}_{N\in\mathfrak{F}}\mathfrak{c}\left(\tilde{\bigcup}_{i\in I-N}(A_i,T)\right)\right]$.*

Lemma 4 ([39]). *Let $(A,T) \in SS(X_T)$, $\Theta \in \Theta(X_T)$, and $\tilde{I} \in \mathcal{I}(X_T)$. Then,*

1. *$\mathfrak{c}(A,T)\tilde{\subseteq}cl(A,T)$.*
2. *$\mathfrak{c}(A,T) \in \Theta^c$.*
3. *$\mathfrak{c}[\mathfrak{c}(A,T)]\tilde{\subseteq}\mathfrak{c}(A,T)$.*

Definition 19. *Let $(A,T),(B,T) \in SS(X_T)$ and let $\Theta \in \Theta(X_T)$. Then, (A,T) is called*

1. *soft regular closed [48] if $cl(int(A,T)) = (A,T)$.*
2. *soft dense in (B,T) [29,30] if $(B,T)\tilde{\subseteq}cl(A,T)$.*
3. *soft codense [30] if $int(A,T) = \Phi_T$.*
4. *soft somewhat open [31] if $int(A,T) \neq \Phi_T$.*
5. *soft G_δ [49] if $(A,T) = \tilde{\bigcap}_{n=1}^{\infty}(W_n,T)$, where $(W_n,T) \in \Theta$.*
6. *soft F_σ [30] if $(A,T) = \tilde{\bigcup}_{n=1}^{\infty}(A_n,T)$, where $(A_n,T) \in \Theta^c$.*
7. *soft nowhere dense [29] if $int(cl(A,T)) = \Phi_T$.*
8. *soft somewhere dense open [32] if $int(cl(A,T)) \neq \Phi_T$.*

3. Some Properties of Soft Nowhere Dense and Soft Codense Sets

In this section, we start by showing several properties of soft codense and soft nowhere dense sets that are applied in the remainder of the paper. The family of all soft nowhere dense subsets of X_T is denoted by $\mathcal{N}(X_T)$. If we consider the family of all soft nowhere dense subsets of a soft set (A,T), say, the notion is changed to $\mathcal{N}(A,T)$, and this is seen for all other types of families of soft sets. The set of all soft codense subsets of X_T is denoted by $C(X_T)$.

Lemma 5. *Let $(N,T) \in SS(X_T)$ and let $\Theta \in \Theta(X_T)$. The next arguments are equivalent:*

1. *$(N,T) \in \mathcal{N}(X_T)$.*
2. *$X_T - cl(N,T)$ is soft dense in X_T.*
3. *For each $\Phi_T \neq (B,T) \in \Theta$, there exists $(C,T) \in \Theta$ such that $\Phi_T \neq (C,T)\tilde{\subseteq}(B,T)$ and $(C,T)\tilde{\cap}(N,T) = \Phi_T$.*

Proof. (1) $\Longrightarrow$ (2) Let $\Phi_T \neq (D,T) \in \Theta$. Since $int(cl(N,T)) = \Phi_T$, then $X_T - cl(N,T)\tilde{\cap}(D,T) \neq \Phi_T$. Hence, $X_T - cl(N,T)$ is soft dense in X_T.

(2) $\Longrightarrow$ (3) Let $\Phi_T \neq (B,T) \in \Theta$. Set $(C,T) = X_T - cl(N,T)\tilde{\cap}(B,T)$. Then, $\Phi_T \neq (C,T) \in \Theta$ such that $(C,T)\tilde{\subseteq}(B,T)$ and $(C,T)\tilde{\cap}(N,T) = \Phi_T$.

(3) $\Longrightarrow$ (1) If $(N,T) \notin \mathcal{N}(X_T)$, then there exists $(B,T) \in \Theta$ such that $\Phi_T \neq (B,T) \tilde{\subseteq} cl(N,T)$. Therefore, $(B,T)\tilde{\cap} cl(N,T) \neq \Phi_T$ and so $(B,T)\tilde{\cap}(N,T) \neq \Phi_T$. Thus, there exists no $(C,T) \in \Theta$ with $\Phi_T \neq (C,T)\tilde{\subseteq}(B,T)$ such that $(C,T)\tilde{\cap}(N,T) = \Phi_T$. □

Lemma 6. *Let $(A,T) \in SS(X_T)$ and let $\Theta \in \Theta(X_T)$. The next arguments are equivalent:*

1. $(A,T) \in \mathcal{C}(X_T)$.
2. $(A,T)^c$ *is soft dense in* X_T.
3. $(A,T)\tilde{\subseteq} b(A,T)$.

Proof. (1) $\Longrightarrow$ (2) If $(A,T) \in \mathcal{C}(X_T)$, then $int(A,T) = \Phi_T$. By Lemma 3, $cl((A,T)^c) = X_T$ and thus $(A,T)^c$ is soft dense in X_T.

(2) $\Longrightarrow$ (3) Suppose $(A,T)^c$ is soft dense in X_T. Then, $cl((A,T)^c) = X_T$. Therefore, $(A,T)\tilde{\subseteq} cl(A,T)\tilde{\cap} X_T = cl(A,T)\tilde{\cap} cl((A,T)^c) = b(A,T)$.

(3) $\Longrightarrow$ (1) If $(A,T)\tilde{\subseteq} b(A,T)$, then $(A,T)\tilde{\subseteq} = cl(A,T) - int(A,T)$. Since $A \subseteq int(A)$, we must have $int(A,T) = \Phi_T$. Hence, $(A,T) \in \mathcal{C}(X_T)$. □

Lemma 7. *Let $(N,T) \in SS(X_T)$ and let $\Theta \in \Theta(X_T)$. If $(N,T) \in \mathcal{N}(X_T)$, then $cl(N,T) \in \mathcal{N}(X_T)$.*

Proof. Suppose $(N,T) \in \mathcal{N}(X_T)$. Then, $cl(X_T - cl(N,T)) = X_T$. Since $cl(cl(N,T)) = cl(N,T)$, $cl(X_T - cl(cl(N,T))) = cl(X_T - cl(N,T)) = X_T$. Thus, $cl(N,T) \in \mathcal{N}(X_T)$. □

Proposition 3. *Let $(M,T), (Y,T) \in SS(X_T)$ such that $(M,T)\tilde{\subseteq}(Y,T)$ and let $\Theta \in \Theta(X_T)$. If $(Y,T) \in \Theta$, then $(N,T) \in \mathcal{N}(Y,T)$ if and only if $(N,T) \in \mathcal{N}(X_T)$.*

Proof. Let $(N,T) \in \mathcal{N}(Y,T)$ and let $\Phi_T \neq (B,T) \in \Theta$ such that $(B,T)\tilde{\cap}(Y,T) \neq \Phi_T$. Then there exists $\Phi_T \neq (C,T) \in \Theta_{(Y,T)}$ such that $(C,T)\tilde{\subseteq}(B,T)\tilde{\cap}(Y,T)$ and $(C,T)\tilde{\cap}(N,T) = \Phi_T$. Now, we have $(D,T) \in \Theta$ such that $(C,T) = (D,T)\tilde{\cap}(Y,T)$. Therefore, $(D,T)\tilde{\subseteq}(B,T)$ and $(D,T)\tilde{\cap}(N,T) = \Phi_T$. Hence, $(N,T) \in \mathcal{N}(X_T)$.

Conversely, let $(Y,T) \in \Theta$ and $(N,T) \in \mathcal{N}(X_T)$. Let $\Phi_T \neq (C,T) \in \Theta_{(Y,T)}$. Then, $(C,T) \in \Theta$. By assumption, there exists $(B,T) \in \Theta$ such that $\Phi_T \neq (B,T)\tilde{\subseteq}(C,T)$ and $(B,T)\tilde{\cap}(N,T) = \Phi_T$. Since, also, $(B,T) \in \Theta_{(Y,T)}$; hence, $(N,T) \in \mathcal{N}(Y,T)$. □

Remark 3. *In the above proposition, condition $(Y,T) \in \Theta$ can be replaced by (Y,T), which is soft dense in X_T, and the proof remains the same.*

Proposition 4. *Let $\Theta \in \Theta(X_T)$ and let $(M,T), (N,T), (Y,T), (Z,T) \in SS(X_T)$ such that $(M,T)\tilde{\subseteq}(N,T)\tilde{\subseteq}(Y,T)\tilde{\subseteq}(Z,T)$. If $(N,T) \in \mathcal{N}(Y,T)$, then $(M,T) \in \mathcal{N}(Z,T)$.*

Proof. Suppose $(N,T) \in \mathcal{N}(Y,T)$. By the first part of the proof of Proposition 3, $(N,T) \in \mathcal{N}(Z,T)$. Since $(M,T)\tilde{\subseteq}(N,T)$, $(M,T) \in \mathcal{N}(Z,T)$. □

Proposition 5. *Let $\Theta \in \Theta(X_T)$ and let $(M,T), (N,T), (Y,T), (Z,T) \in SS(X_T)$ such that $(M,T)\tilde{\subseteq}(N,T)\tilde{\subseteq}(Y,T)\tilde{\subseteq}(Z,T)$. If $(M,T) \in \mathcal{N}(Z,T)$, (N,T) is soft dense in (Y,T), and (Y,T) is soft open in (Z,T), then $(M,T) \in \mathcal{N}(N,T)$.*

Proof. Suppose $(M,T) \in \mathcal{N}(Z,T)$, (N,T) is soft dense in (Y,T), and (Y,T) is soft open in (Z,T). Let $\Phi_T \neq (B,T) \in \Theta_{(N,T)}$. Then there exists $(C,T) \in \Theta_{(Z,T)}$ such that $(B,T) = (C,T)\tilde{\cap}(N,T)$. Evidently, the soft set $(D,T) = (C,T)\tilde{\cap}(Y,T) \neq \Phi_T$. Since $(M,T) \in \mathcal{N}(Z,T)$, there exists $(W,T) \in \Theta_{(Z,T)}$ such that $\Phi_T \neq (W,T)\tilde{\subseteq}(D,T)$ and $(W,T)\tilde{\cap}(M,T) = \Phi_T$. Set $(V,T) = (W,T)\tilde{\cap}(N,T) \in \Theta_{(N,T)}$ such that $(V,T)\tilde{\subseteq}(B,T)$ and $(V,T)\tilde{\cap}(M,T) = \Phi_T$. Since $\Phi_T \neq (W,T) \in \Theta_{(Z,T)}$ and (N,T) is soft dense in (Y,T), $(V,T) \neq \Phi_T$. Thus, $(M,T) \in \mathcal{N}(N,T)$. □

Definition 20. *Let $\Theta \in \Theta(X_T)$ and let $(A,T) \in SS(X_T)$. Then, (A,T) is called soft nowhere dense (resp. soft codense) at a soft point $x_t \in SP(X_T)$ if there exists $(B,T) \in \Theta(x_t)$ such that $(B,T)\tilde{\sqcap}(A,T) \in \mathcal{N}(X_T)$ (resp. $(B,T)\tilde{\sqcap}(A,T) \in \mathcal{C}(X_T)$).*

The set of soft points at which (A,T) is soft nowhere dense (resp. soft codense) is denoted by $C_N(A,T)$ (resp. $C_0(A,T)$).

Definition 21. *We say (A,T) is not soft nowhere dense (or soft somewhere dense) at a soft point $x_t \in SP(X_T)$ if for each $(B,T) \in \Theta(x_t)$ such that $(B,T)\tilde{\sqcap}(A,T) \notin \mathcal{N}(X_T)$. And it is not soft codense (or soft somewhat open) at a soft point $x_t \in SP(X_T)$ if for each $(B,T) \in \Theta(x_t)$ such that $(B,T)\tilde{\sqcap}(A,T) \notin \mathcal{C}(X_T)$.*

The set of soft points at which (A,T) is soft somewhere dense (resp. soft somewhat open) is denoted by $C_{sd}(A,T)$ (resp. $C_{sw}(A,T)$).

Lemma 8. *Let $\Theta \in \Theta(X_T)$, $(A,T) \in SS(X_T)$, and $x_t \in SP(X_T)$. Then, (A,T) is soft nowhere dense at x_t if and only if $cl(A,T)$ is soft codense at x_t.*

Proof. Suppose (A,T) is not soft nowhere dense at x_t. Then, for each $(C,T) \in \Theta(x_t)$, we have $(C,T)\tilde{\sqcap}(A,T) \notin \mathcal{N}(X_T)$. Therefore, there exists $(B,T) \in \Theta$ such that $\Phi_T \neq (B,T)\tilde{\sqsubseteq}cl[(C,T)\tilde{\sqcap}(A,T)]$. This implies that $(B,T) = (B,T)\tilde{\sqcap}cl[(C,T)\tilde{\sqcap}(A,T)] = cl[(B,T)\tilde{\sqcap}(C,T)\tilde{\sqcap}(A,T)]$, and hence $(C,T)\tilde{\sqcap}(B,T) \neq \Phi_T$. Since $(B,T)\tilde{\sqcap}(C,T)\tilde{\sqsubseteq}(C,T)\tilde{\sqcap}cl[(C,T)\tilde{\sqcap}(A,T)] = (C,T)\tilde{\sqcap}cl(A,T)$. This proves that $(C,T)\tilde{\sqcap}cl(A,T)$ is not soft codense and thus $cl(A,T)$ is not soft codense at x_t.

Conversely, if $cl(A,T)$ is not soft codense at x_t, then for each $(B,T) \in \Theta(x_t)$, we have $(B,T)\tilde{\sqcap}cl(A,T)$ is not soft codense. It follows that there exists $(C,T) \in \Theta$ such that $\Phi_T \neq (C,T)\tilde{\sqsubseteq}(B,T)\tilde{\sqcap}cl(A,T)$. Therefore, $(C,T)\tilde{\sqsubseteq}(B,T)\tilde{\sqcap}cl(A,T)\tilde{\sqsubseteq}cl[(B,T)\tilde{\sqcap}(A,T)]$. This means that $(B,T)\tilde{\sqcap}(A,T)$ is not soft nowhere dense, and hence, (A,T) is not soft nowhere dense at x_t. □

Proposition 6. *Let $\Theta \in \Theta(X_T)$ and $(A,T) \in SS(X_T)$. Then,*

1. $C_{sw}(A,T) = cl(int(A,T))$.
2. $C_{sd}(A,T) = cl(int(cl(A,T)))$.

Proof. (1) Let $x_t \in SP(X_T)$. Suppose that $x_t \in cl(int(A,T))$ and $(C,T) \in \Theta(x_t)$, then $(C,T)\tilde{\sqcap}cl(int(A,T)) \neq \Phi_T$. This means $\Phi_T \neq (C,T)\tilde{\sqcap}int(A,T)\tilde{\sqsubseteq}(C,T)\tilde{\sqcap}(A,T)$. Thus, $x_t \in C_{sw}(A,T)$.

Conversely, suppose $x_t \notin cl(int(A,T))$. Then $x_t \in [cl(int(A,T))]^c$. Set $(C,T) = [cl(int(A,T))]^c$, then $(C,T) \in \Theta(x_t)$ such that $(C,T)\tilde{\sqcap}(A,T) \in \mathcal{C}(X_T)$ because $int((C,T)\tilde{\sqcap}(A,T)) = int(C,T)\tilde{\sqcap}int(A,T) = [cl(int(A,T))]^c\tilde{\sqcap}int(A,T) = \Phi_T$. This implies that $x_t \notin C_{sw}(A,T)$. Consequently, $C_{sw}(A,T) = cl(int(A,T))$.

(2) It follows from (1) and Lemma 8. □

Proposition 7. *Let $\Theta \in \Theta(X_T)$ and $(A,T) \in SS(X_T)$. Then,*

1. $C_0(A,T) \in \mathcal{C}(X_T)$.
2. $C_N(A,T) \in \mathcal{N}(X_T)$.

Proof. (1) Obviously, $C_0(A,T) = (A,T) - C_{sw}(A,T) = (A,T) - cl(int(A,T))\tilde{\sqsubseteq}(A,T) - int(A,T)$. Since $(A,T) - int(A,T) \in \mathcal{C}(X_T)$ and $C_0(A,T)\tilde{\sqsubseteq}(A,T) - int(A,T)$, $C_0(A,T) \in \mathcal{C}(X_T)$.

(2) Similar to (1). □

4. First- and Second-Category Soft Sets

Definition 22. *Let $\Theta \in \Theta(X_T)$. Soft set (M,T) over X is called of the first Baire category or simply first category if*

$$(M,T) = \widetilde{\bigcup}_{n=1}^{\infty}(N_n,T), \tag{1}$$

where $(N_n,T) \in \mathcal{N}(X_T)$ for each n. The set of all soft sets of the first category over X is denoted by $\mathcal{M}(X_T)$.

If (M,T) does not possess the representation in equation (1), it said to be of the second Baire category or simply second category. The set of all soft sets of the second category over X is denoted by $\mathcal{S}(X_T)$.

The definition of soft sets of the first category appeared in the literature under the name of soft meager sets (see [29,50]).

We now have possible connections between the soft sets defined earlier.

first-category soft set $\Longleftarrow$ soft nowhere dense $\Longrightarrow$ soft condense

The reverse of the above arrows is not generally possible.

Example 1. *Let Θ be the soft topology on the set of real number $\mathbb{R}$ generated by $\{\{(t_1,F(t_1)),(t_2,F(t_2))\} : F(t_1) = (r_1,s_1); F(t_1) = (r_1,s_1); F(t_2) = [r_2,s_2); r_1,r_2,s_1,s_2 \in \mathbb{R}; r_i < s_i\}$, where $T = \{t_1,t_2\}$ is a set of parameters and $i = 1,2$. Soft set $(A,T) = \{(t_1,C),(t_2,\{0\})\}$ is soft nowhere dense, which is consequently soft codense and a soft set of the first category, where C is the ternary Cantor set. Soft set $(B,T) = \{(t_1,\mathbb{Q}),(t_2,\mathbb{Z})\}$ is of the first category and soft codense but not soft nowhere dense, where $\mathbb{Z},\mathbb{Q}$ are sets of integers and rationals, respectively. Soft set $(C,T) = \{(t_1,\mathbb{Q}^c),(t_2,\varnothing)\}$ is soft condense but not of the first category.*

We let $(Y,T) = \{(t_1,\mathbb{Q}),(t_2,\varnothing)\}$ and $\Theta_{(Y,T)}$ be the relative soft topology on (Y,T). Given any soft subset (R,T) of (Y,T). Then, we have $(R,T) = \widetilde{\bigcup}_{y_t \in (R,T)}\{(t_1,\{y\}),(t_2,\varnothing)\}$. Evidently, each soft set $\{(t_1,\{y\}),(t_2,\varnothing)\}$ is soft nowhere dense in $\Theta_{(Y,T)}$ implies (R,T) is of the first category. Thus, we show that any soft set of (Y,T) is of the first category. Hence, if $(U,T) \in \Theta_{(Y,T)}$, then (U,T) is of the first category but not soft codense.

Remark 4. *We can apparently conclude that $\mathcal{M}(X_T)$ is closed under soft subsets and countable soft unions. This means that $\mathcal{M}(X_T)$ forms a soft σ-ideal over X.*

Proposition 8. *Let $(M,T) \in SS(X_T)$ and let $\Theta \in \Theta(X_T)$. If $(M,T) \in \mathcal{M}(X_T)$, then $(M,T)\widetilde{\subseteq}(A,T)$, where (A,T) is a soft F_σ set in $\mathcal{M}(X_T)$.*

Proof. Directly follows from Lemma 7. □

Proposition 9. *Let $(M,T) \in SS(X_T)$ and let $\Theta \in \Theta(X_T)$. If $X_T \in \mathcal{S}(X_T)$, then every soft dense G_δ subset of X_T belongs to $\mathcal{S}(X_T)$.*

Proof. $X_T \in \mathcal{S}(X_T)$ and let (B,T) be soft dense G_δ set in $\mathcal{S}(X_T)$. Then $(B,T) = \widetilde{\bigcap}_{n=1}^{\infty}(W_n,T)$, where $(W_n,T) \in \Theta$. Therefore, $X_T - (B,T) = X_T - (\widetilde{\bigcap}_{n=1}^{\infty}(W_n,T)) = \widetilde{\bigcup}_{n=1}^{\infty}(X_T - (W_n,T)) \in \mathcal{M}(X_T)$. Thus, (B,T) must be in $\mathcal{S}(X_T)$, otherwise X_T would be in $\mathcal{M}(X_T)$, a contradiction. □

Proposition 10. *Let $\Theta \in \Theta(X_T)$ and let $(M,T),(Y,T) \in SS(X_T)$ such that $(M,T)\widetilde{\subseteq}(Y,T)$. If $(Y,T) \in \Theta$ or soft dense, then $(M,T) \in \mathcal{M}(Y,T)$ if and only if $(M,T) \in \mathcal{M}(X_T)$.*

Proof. Apply Proposition 3, Remark 3, and Equation (1). □

Proposition 11. *Let* $\Theta \in \Theta(X_T)$ *and let* $(M,T), (N,T), (Y,T), (Z,T) \in SS(X_T)$ *such that* $(M,T)\widetilde{\subseteq}(N,T)\widetilde{\subseteq}(Y,T)\widetilde{\subseteq}(Z,T)$. *If* (N,T) *is soft dense in* (Y,T) *and* (Y,T) *is soft open in* (Z,T), *then* $(M,T) \in \mathcal{M}(Z,T)$ *if and only if* $(M,T) \in \mathcal{M}(N,T)$.

Proof. Apply Propositions 4 and 5, and Equation (1). □

Theorem 1. *Let* $\Theta \in \Theta(X_T)$ *and let* $(M,T) \in SS(X_T)$. *If* $(M,T) \in \mathcal{M}(X_T)$, *then* (M,T) *can be written as the disjoint soft union of a soft nowhere dense set and a soft set of the first category in itself.*

Proof. Let $(M,T) \in \mathcal{M}(X_T)$. Consider the following decomposition:

$$(M,T) = \big[(M,T) - int(cl(M,T)]\widetilde{\bigcup}\big[(M,T)\widetilde{\cap} int(cl(M,T))\big]. \tag{2}$$

We first show that $(M,T) - int(cl(M,T) \in \mathcal{N}(X_T)$. We let $\Phi_T \neq (C,T) \in \Theta$. We suppose for each $(B,T) \in \Theta$ such that $\Phi_T \neq (B,T)\widetilde{\subseteq}(C,T)$; we have $(B,T)\widetilde{\cap}(M,T) \neq \Phi_T$. This means that each soft point in (C,T) is a soft limit point of (M,T) and so is a soft point in $cl(M,T)$. Therefore, $(C,T)\widetilde{\subseteq} int(cl(M,T))$, and hence $(C,T)\widetilde{\cap}[(M,T) - int(cl(M,T))] = \Phi_T$. Thus, for that $\Phi_T \neq (C,T) \in \Theta$, either $(C,T)\widetilde{\cap}[(M,T) - int(cl(M,T))] = \Phi_T$ or there exists $(B,T) \in \Theta$ such that $\Phi_T \neq (B,T)\widetilde{\subseteq}(C,T)$ and $(B,T)\widetilde{\cap}(M,T) = \Phi_T$. The latter case is impossible, so $(C,T)\widetilde{\cap}[(M,T) - int(cl(M,T))] = \Phi_T$. This proves that $(M,T) - int(cl(M,T)) \in \mathcal{N}(X_T)$.

We now prove that $(M',T) = (M,T)\widetilde{\cap} int(cl(M,T))$ is of the first category in itself. Since (M,T) is soft dense in $int(cl(M,T))$, we can easily check that (M',T) is also soft dense in $int(cl(M,T))$. Now, we apply Proposition 11 to $(M,T) = (M',T)$, $(N,T) = (M',T)$, $(Y,T) = int(cl(M,T))$, and $(Z,T) = X_T$; we obtain that $(M',T) \in \mathcal{M}(M',T)$. □

Definition 23. *Let* $(A,T) \in SS(X_T)$ *and* $\Theta \in \Theta(X_T)$. *We say* (A,T) *is of the second category at a soft point* $x_t \in SP(X_T)$ *if* $(A,T)\widetilde{\cap}(W,T) \notin \mathcal{M}(X_T)$ *for each* $(W,T) \in \Theta(x_t)$. *Otherwise, we say* (A,T) *is of the first category at* X_T. *The set of all soft points at which* (A,T) *is of the first (resp. second) category is denoted by* $C_1(A,T)$ *(resp.* $C_2(A,T)$*).*

Remark 5. *Given* $\Theta \in \Theta(X_T)$, *evidently,* $(A,T) \in SS(X_T)$ *is of the first category at a soft point* $x_t \in SP(X_T)$ *if and only if there exists* $(W,T) \in \Theta(x_t)$ *such that* $(A,T)\widetilde{\cap}(W,T) \in \mathcal{M}(X_T)$.

Theorem 2 (Generalized Banach Category Theorem). *Let* $\Theta \in \Theta(X_T)$ *and* $(A,T) \in SS(X_T)$. *The next arguments are equivalent:*

1. *If* $(A,T) \in \mathcal{S}(X_T)$, *then* (A,T) *is of the second category at each soft point in some* $\Phi_T \neq (B,T) \in \Theta$.
2. *If* (A,T) *is of the first category at each of its soft points, then* $(A,T) \in \mathcal{M}(X_T)$.
3. *If* $\{(A_i,T) : i \in I\}\widetilde{\subseteq} SS(X_T)$ *in which* $(A_i,T) \in \mathcal{M}(X_T)$ *and* $(A_i,T) \in \Theta_{(A,T)}$, *where* $(A,T) = \widetilde{\cup}_{i\in I}(A_i,T)$, *then* $(A,T) \in \mathcal{M}(X_T)$.
4. *If* $\{(A_i,T) : i \in I\}\widetilde{\subseteq} SS(X_T)$ *in which* $(A_i,T) \in \mathcal{M}(X_T)$ *and* $(A_i,T) \in \Theta$, *then* $\widetilde{\cup}_{i\in I}(A_i,T) \in \mathcal{M}(X_T)$.

Proof. (1) $\Longrightarrow$ (2) Suppose (1) holds. If $(A,T) \in \mathcal{S}(X_T)$, then, by (1), (A,T) is of the second category at each soft point in some $\Phi_T \neq (B,T) \in \Theta$. Pick any soft point x_t in (B,T), then $(A,T)\widetilde{\cap}(B,T) \in \mathcal{S}(X_T)$ and so $(A,T)\widetilde{\cap}(B,T) \neq \Phi_T$. This means that x_t is a soft point in (A,T) at which (A,T) is not of the first category, a contradiction.

(2) $\Longrightarrow$ (3) Let $x_t \in (A,T)$. Then x_t is in some $(A_{i0},T)\widetilde{\subseteq}(A,T)$. Since (A_{i0},T) is soft open in (A,T), then there exists a soft open (B,T) in X_T containing x_t such that $(A_{i0},T) = (B,T)\widetilde{\cap}(A,T)$. Since $(A_{i0},T) \in \mathcal{M}(X_T)$, so (A,T) is of the first category at each of its soft points. By (2), (A,T) is of the first category.

(3) $\Longrightarrow$ (4) Directly follows from (3).

(4) $\Longrightarrow$ (1) Assume (A,T) is not of the second category at a soft point of any non-null soft open. Therefore, each $\Phi_T \neq (B,T) \in \Theta$ includes $\Phi_T \neq (C,T) \in \Theta$ for which $(A,T)\tilde{\sqcap}(C,T) \in \mathcal{M}(X_T)$. We prove that $(A,T) \in \mathcal{M}(X_T)$. Let $\mathcal{H} = \{(C,T) : \Phi_T \neq (C,T) \in \Theta, (A,T)\tilde{\sqcap}(C,T) \in \mathcal{M}(X_T)\}$. Clearly, $(D,T)\tilde{\sqcap}(A,T) \neq \Phi_T$ for each $\Phi_T \neq (D,T) \in \Theta$, where $(D,T)\tilde{\sqsubseteq}(C,T)$ and $(C,T) \in \mathcal{H}$. Set $(V,T) = \tilde{\sqcup}(\mathcal{H}\tilde{\sqcap}(A,T))$. Then, for each $(C,T) \in \mathcal{H}$, $(C,T)\tilde{\sqcap}(A,T) = (C,T)\tilde{\sqcap}(V,T)$. This implies that $(C,T)\tilde{\sqcap}(A,T)$ is soft open in (V,T). Applying Proposition 11 to $(M,T) = (C,T)$, $(N,T) = (V,T)$, $(Y,T) = \tilde{\sqcup}\mathcal{H}$, and $(Z,T) = X_T$, we see that $(C,T)\tilde{\sqcap}(A,T) \in \mathcal{M}(V,T)$ for each $(C,T) \in \mathcal{H}$. By (4), $(V,T) \in \mathcal{M}(X_T)$.

Let $(B,T) \in \Theta$. Suppose $(C,T) \in \Theta$ such that $\Phi_T \neq (C,T)\tilde{\sqsubseteq}(B,T)$ and $(A,T)\tilde{\sqcap}(C,T) \in \mathcal{M}(X_T)$. If $(C,T) \notin \mathcal{H}$, there exists $(D,T) \in \Theta$ such that $\Phi_T \neq (D,T)\tilde{\sqsubseteq}(C,T)$ and $(D,T)\tilde{\sqcap}(A,T) = \Phi_T$ and so $(D,T)\tilde{\sqcap}[(A,T) - (V,T)] = \Phi_T$. If $(C,T) \in \mathcal{H}$, then $(C,T)\tilde{\sqcap}[X_T - \tilde{\sqcup}\mathcal{H}] = \Phi_T$. Therefore, $(C,T)\tilde{\sqcap}[(A,T) - (V,T)] = \Phi_T$. This proves that $(A,T) - (V,T) \in \mathcal{N}(X_T)$. Consequently, $(A,T) = [(A,T) - (V,T)]\tilde{\sqcup}(V,T) \in \mathcal{M}(X_T)$. □

Proposition 12. *Let $(A,T),(B,T) \in SS(X_T)$ and $\Theta \in \Theta(X_T)$. The properties listed below are true:*

1. *If $(A,T)\tilde{\sqsubseteq}(B,T)$, then $C_2(A,T)\tilde{\sqsubseteq}C_2(B,T)$.*
2. $C_2((A,T)\tilde{\sqcap}(B,T))\tilde{\sqsubseteq}C_2(A,T)\tilde{\sqcap}C_2(B,T)$.
3. $C_2((A,T)\tilde{\sqcup}(B,T)) = C_2(A,T)\tilde{\sqcup}C_2(B,T)$.
4. $C_2(A,T) - C_2(B,T)\tilde{\sqsubseteq}C_2((A,T) - (B,T))$.
5. $C_2(A,T)\tilde{\sqsubseteq}cl(A,T)$.
6. $C_2(A,T) \in \Theta^c$.
7. $C_2[C_2(A,T)]\tilde{\sqsubseteq}C_2(A,T)$.

Proof. It follows from Proposition 1 and Lemma 4. □

Proposition 13. *Let $(A_i,T) \in SS(X_T)$, for $i \in I$, and $\Theta \in \Theta(X_T)$. The properties listed below are true:*

1. $C_2\left(\tilde{\bigsqcup}_{i\in N}(A_i,T)\right) = \tilde{\bigsqcup}_{i\in N}C_2(A_i,T)$, *where $N \in \mathfrak{F}$ and $\mathfrak{F}$ is a collection of finite subsets of I.*
2. $\tilde{\bigsqcup}_{i\in I}C_2(A_i,T)\tilde{\sqsubseteq}C_2\left(\tilde{\bigsqcup}_{i\in I}(A_i,T)\right)$.
3. $C_2\left(\tilde{\bigsqcap}_{i\in I}(A_i,T)\right)\tilde{\sqsubseteq}\tilde{\bigsqcap}_{i\in I}C_2(A_i,T)$.
4. $C_2\left(\tilde{\bigsqcup}_{i\in I}(A_i,T)\right) = \tilde{\bigsqcup}_{i\in I}C_2(A_i,T)\tilde{\sqcup}\left[\tilde{\bigsqcap}_{N\in\mathfrak{F}}C_2\left(\tilde{\bigsqcup}_{i\in I-N}(A_i,T)\right)\right]$.

Proof. It follows from Proposition 2. □

Proposition 14. *Let $\Theta \in \Theta(X_T)$ and $(A,T),(B,T) \in SS(X_T)$. If $(B,T) \in \Theta$, then $(B,T)\tilde{\sqcap}C_2(A,T) = (B,T)\tilde{\sqcap}C_2[(B,T)\tilde{\sqcap}(A,T)]$.*

Proof. Let $x_t \in SP(X_T)$. If $x_t \in (B,T)\tilde{\sqcap}C_2(A,T)$, for each $(C,T) \in \Theta(x_t)$, we have $(C,T)\tilde{\sqcap}(B,T)\tilde{\sqcap}(A,T) \notin \mathcal{M}(X_T)$. Since $(C,T)\tilde{\sqcap}(B,T) \in \Theta(x_t)$, $x_t \in C_2[(B,T)\tilde{\sqcap}(A,T)]$. Therefore, $(B,T)\tilde{\sqcap}C_2(A,T)\tilde{\sqsubseteq}C_2[(B,T)\tilde{\sqcap}(A,T)]$. For the reverse, since $(B,T)\tilde{\sqcap}(A,T)\tilde{\sqsubseteq}(A,T)$, by Proposition 12 (1), $C_2[(B,T)\tilde{\sqcap}(A,T)]\tilde{\sqsubseteq}C_2(A,T)$ and therefore, $(B,T)\tilde{\sqcap}C_2[(B,T)\tilde{\sqcap}(A,T)]\tilde{\sqsubseteq}(B,T)\tilde{\sqcap}C_2(A,T)$. Consequently, $(B,T)\tilde{\sqcap}C_2(A,T) = (B,T)\tilde{\sqcap}C_2[(B,T)\tilde{\sqcap}(A,T)]$. □

Lemma 9. *Let $\Theta \in \Theta(X_T)$ and $(A,T) \in SS(X_T)$. Then $(A,T) \in \mathcal{M}(X_T)$ if and only if $C_2(A,T)\tilde{\sqcap}(A,T) = \Phi_T$ if and only if $C_2(A,T) = \Phi_T$.*

Proof. If $(A,T) \in \mathcal{M}(X_T)$ implies $C_2(A,T) = \Phi_T$ and so $C_2(A,T)\tilde{\sqcap}(A,T) = \Phi_T$.

Conversely, if $C_2(A,T) = \Phi_T$, then $C_2(A,T)\tilde{\sqcap}(A,T) = \Phi_T$ and thus $(A,T) \in \mathcal{M}(X_T)$ from Theorem 2. □

Lemma 10. *Let* $\Theta \in \Theta(X_T)$ *and* $(A,T),(B,T) \in SS(X_T)$. *If* $(B,T) \in \mathcal{M}(X_T)$, *then* $C_2[(A,T)\widetilde{\cup}(B,T)] = C_2(A,T) = C_2[(A,T) - (B,T)]$.

Proof. Applying Proposition 12 (3), we have $C_2[(A,T)\widetilde{\cup}(B,T)] = C_2(A,T)\widetilde{\cup}C_2(B,T)$. Since $(B,T) \in \mathcal{M}(X_T)$, so $C_2(B,T) = \Phi_T$. Therefore, $C_2[(A,T)\widetilde{\cup}(B,T)] = C_2(A,T)$.

On the other hand, by Proposition 12 (4), we have $C_2(A,T) - C_2(B,T)\widetilde{\subseteq}C_2[(A,T) - (B,T)]$. Since $C_2(B,T) = \Phi_T$, then $C_2(A,T)\widetilde{\subseteq}C_2[(A,T) - (B,T)]$. Since $(A,T) - (B,T)\widetilde{\subseteq}(A,T)$, by Proposition 12 (1), $C_2[(A,T) - (B,T)]\widetilde{\subseteq}C_2(A,T)$. Consequently, $C_2[(A,T) - (B,T)] = C_2(A,T)$. Hence, $C_2[(A,T)\widetilde{\cup}(B,T)] = C_2(A,T) = C_2[(A,T) - (B,T)]$. □

Theorem 3. *Let* $\Theta \in \Theta(X_T)$ *and* $(A,T) \in SS(X_T)$. *Then*

1. $C_2(C_1(A,T)) = \Phi_T$, *i.e.*, $C_2((A,T) - C_2(A,T)) = \Phi_T$
2. $C_2(C_2(A,T)) = C_2(A,T)$.
3. $C_2(A,T) = cl(int(C_2(A,T)))$.

Proof. (1) Since $(A,T) - C_2(A,T)\widetilde{\subseteq}(A,T)$, by Proposition 12 (1), $C_2(C_1(A,T)) = C_2((A,T) - C_2(A,T))\widetilde{\subseteq}C_2(A,T)$. Therefore, $(A,T) - C_2(A,T)\widetilde{\cap}C_2(C_1(A,T)) = (A,T) - C_2(A,T)\widetilde{\cap} C_2((A,T) - C_2(A,T))\widetilde{\subseteq}(A,T) - C_2(A,T)\widetilde{\cap}C_2(A,T) = \Phi_T$. Thus, we have $C_2(C_1(A,T)) = \Phi_T$.

(2) Since, from (1), $C_2((A,T) - C_2(A,T)) = \Phi_T$, and by Proposition 12 (4), $C_2(A,T) - C_2(C_2(A,T))\widetilde{\subseteq}C_2((A,T) - C_2(A,T)) = \Phi_T$, therefore, $C_2(A,T) - C_2(C_2(A,T))\widetilde{\subseteq}\Phi_T$ implies $C_2(A,T)\widetilde{\subseteq}C_2(C_2(A,T))$. The converse of the inclusion holds true by Proposition 12 (7). Hence, $C_2(C_2(A,T)) = C_2(A,T)$.

(3) Since $\{\Phi_T\}\widetilde{\subseteq}\mathcal{N}(X_T)\widetilde{\subseteq}\mathcal{M}(X_T)$, by Definition 18 and Proposition 6 (2), it follows that

$$C_2(A,T)\widetilde{\subseteq}cl(int(cl(A,T)))\widetilde{\subseteq}cl(A,T). \tag{3}$$

Substitute $C_2(A,T)$ in expression (3) and since $C_2(A,T)$ is soft closed, by Proposition 12 (6), we obtain that

$$C_2(C_2(A,T))\widetilde{\subseteq}cl(int(C_2(A,T)))\widetilde{\subseteq}C_2(A,T).$$

Since, by (2), $C_2(A,T) = C_2(C_2(A,T))$, hence $C_2(A,T) = cl(int(C_2(A,T)))$. □

Theorem 4. *Let* $\Theta \in \Theta(X_T)$ *and* $(A_n,T) \in SS(X_T)$ *for* $n = 1,2,\ldots$. *Then*

$$C_2(\widetilde{\bigcup}_{n=1}^{\infty}(A_n,T)) - \widetilde{\bigcup}_{n=1}^{\infty}C_2(A_n,T) \in \mathcal{N}(X_T).$$

Proof. Let $\Phi_T \neq (W,T) \in \Theta$. We find $(V,T) \in \Theta$ such that

$$\Phi_T \neq (W,T)\widetilde{\subseteq}(W,T) \text{ and } \left[C_2(\widetilde{\bigcup}_{n=1}^{\infty}(A_n,T)) - \widetilde{\bigcup}_{n=1}^{\infty}C_2(A_n,T)\right]\widetilde{\bigcap}(V,T) = \Phi_T.$$

For each n, if $(W,T)\widetilde{\cap}C_2(A_n,T) = \Phi_T$, then $(W,T)\widetilde{\cap}(A_n,T)\widetilde{\subseteq}(A_n,T) - C_2(A_n,T)$ and hence $(W,T)\widetilde{\cap}(\widetilde{\cup}_{n=1}^{\infty}(A_n,T))\widetilde{\subseteq}\widetilde{\cup}_{n=1}^{\infty}\left[(A_n,T) - C_2(A_n,T)\right]$. It follows from Theorem 3 (1) that $(W,T)\widetilde{\cap}(\widetilde{\cup}_{n=1}^{\infty}(A_n,T)) \in \mathcal{M}(X_T)$. By Lemma 9, $C_2\left[(W,T)\widetilde{\cap}(\widetilde{\cup}_{n=1}^{\infty}(A_n,T))\right] = \Phi_T$ and by Proposition 14, $(W,T)\widetilde{\cap}C_2\left[\widetilde{\cup}_{n=1}^{\infty}(A_n,T)\right] = \Phi_T$. By equaling (V,T) with (W,T) we have $(V,T)\widetilde{\cap}C_2\left[\widetilde{\cup}_{n=1}^{\infty}(A_n,T)\right] - \widetilde{\cup}_{n=1}^{\infty}C_2(A_n,T) = \Phi_T$.

On the other hand, if for some n, $(W,T)\widetilde{\cap}C_2(A_n,T) \neq \Phi_T$. Set $(V,T) = (W,T)\widetilde{\cap} int(C_2(A_n,T))$. By Theorem 3 (3), $(V,T) \neq \Phi_T$. Since $(V,T)\widetilde{\subseteq}C_2(A_n,T)$, we must obtain that $(V,T)\widetilde{\cap} C_2\left[\widetilde{\cup}_{n=1}^{\infty}(A_n,T)\right] - \widetilde{\cup}_{n=1}^{\infty}C_2(A_n,T) = \Phi_T$. This finishes the proof. □

Theorem 5. *Let* $\Theta \in \Theta(X_T)$ *and* $(A,T) \in SS(X_T)$. *Then* (A,T) *can be written as a soft union of two soft sets, one of the first category and the other not of the first category at any of its soft points.*

Proof. Consider the following decomposition

$$(A,T) = ((A,T)\tilde{\cap}C_2(A,T))\tilde{\bigcup}((A,T) - C_2(A,T)).$$

Evidently, $(A,T)\tilde{\cap}C_2(A,T)$ and $(A,T) - C_2(A,T)$ are disjoint. By Theorem 3 (1), $(A,T) - C_2(A,T) \in \mathcal{M}(X_T)$. On the other hand, since, by Lemma 10, $C_2\big((A,T)\tilde{\cap}C_2(A,T)\big) = C_2(A,T)$, so $(A,T)\tilde{\cap}C_2(A,T)\tilde{\subseteq}C_2(A,T) = C_2\big((A,T)\tilde{\cap}C_2(A,T)\big)$. This means that $(A,T)\tilde{\cap} C_2(A,T)$ is not of the first category at any soft point x_t in itself. □

5. Conclusions and Future Work

The ongoing introduction of new classes of topological spaces, examples, and their properties and relations has contributed to the development of topology. As a result, it is critical to expand the area of soft topological spaces in the same manner. We made a new contribution to the field of soft topology by studying certain classes of soft sets in soft topological spaces. The study starts with investigating some important results and operations on soft nowhere dense and soft codense sets. We introduced the concepts of soft points at which a soft set is soft nowhere dense or soft codense followed by their relationships. Correspondingly, we introduced the conceptions and studied soft points at which a soft set is soft somewhere dense or soft somewhat open. We showed that the set of soft points at which a soft set is soft somewhere open is soft regular closed. Then, we recalled the definitions of soft sets of the first and second categories. The main properties of these classes of soft sets were obtained with some operations. In addition, we defined a soft point where a soft set is of the first or second category. The latter type of soft points is a special case of cluster soft points of a soft set. Then, various properties and characterizations of the family of all soft points at which a soft set is of the second category were found. In particular, we proved that the set of soft points at which a soft set is of the second category is soft regular closed, and no soft point in a soft set of the first category can be of the second category. We generalized the so-called "Banach Category Theorem" on soft topologies that states that any soft union of soft open sets of the first category is of the first category. We end this work with a representation that states a soft set can be written as a disjoint soft union of two soft sets, one of the first category and the other not of the first category at any of its soft points.

From a categorical point of view, this study might be seen as a valuable source for advancing the field of soft topology. The results produced in this research can be used to study soft sets and soft functions of the Baire property, and many advanced topics in soft topology.

Author Contributions: Conceptualization, Z.A.A. and M.H.A.; Methodology, Z.A.A.; Formal Analysis, Z.A.A. and M.H.A.; Investigation, Z.A.A. and M.H.A.; Writing Original Draft Preparation, Z.A.A.; Writing Review and Editing, Z.A.A. and M.H.A.; Funding Acquisition, M.H.A. All authors have read and agreed to the published version of the manuscript.

Funding: This research received no external funding.

Data Availability Statement: Not applicable.

Conflicts of Interest: The authors declare no conflict of interest.

References

1. Zadeh, L. Fuzzy sets. *Inf. Control.* **1965**, *8*, 338–353. [CrossRef]
2. Pawlak, Z. Rough sets. *Int. J. Comput. Inf. Sci.* **1982**, *11*, 341–356. [CrossRef]
3. Molodtsov, D. Soft set theory—First results. *Comput. Math. Appl.* **1999**, *37*, 19–31. [CrossRef]
4. Yang, J.; Yao, Y. Semantics of soft sets and three-way decision with soft sets. *Knowl.-Based Syst.* **2020**, *194*, 105538. [CrossRef]
5. Alcantud, J.C.R. The semantics of N-soft sets, their applications, and a coda about three-way decision. *Inf. Sci.* **2022**, *606*, 837–852. [CrossRef]
6. Dalkılıç, O.; Demirtaş, N. Algorithms for covid-19 outbreak using soft set theory: Estimation and application. *Soft Comput.* **2022**, *27*, 3203–3211. [CrossRef]

7. Maji, P.; Roy, A.R.; Biswas, R. An application of soft sets in a decision making problem. *Comput. Math. Appl.* **2002**, *44*, 1077–1083. [CrossRef]
8. Pei, D.; Miao, D. From soft sets to information systems. In Proceedings of the 2005 IEEE International Conference on Granular Computing, Beijing, China, 25–27 July 2005; Volume 2, pp. 617–621.
9. Yuksel, S.; Dizman, T.; Yildizdan, G.; Sert, U. Application of soft sets to diagnose the prostate cancer risk. *J. Inequal. Appl.* **2013**, *2013*, 229. [CrossRef]
10. El-Atik, A.A.; Abu-Gdairi, R.; Nasef, A.A.; Jafari, S.; Badr, M. Fuzzy Soft Sets and Decision Making in Ideal Nutrition. *Symmetry* **2023**, *15*, 1523. [CrossRef]
11. Balcı, M.A.; Batrancea, L.M.; Akgüller, Ö. Network-Induced Soft Sets and Stock Market Applications. *Mathematics* **2022**, *10*, 3964. [CrossRef]
12. Akgüller, Ö. A soft set theoretic approach to network complexity and a case study for Turkish Twitter users. *Appl. Soft Comput.* **2023**, *143*, 110344. [CrossRef]
13. Gwak, J.; Garg, H.; Jan, N. Hybrid integrated decision-making algorithm for clustering analysis based on a bipolar complex fuzzy and soft sets. *Alex. Eng. J.* **2023**, *67*, 473–487. [CrossRef]
14. Qin, H.; Fei, Q.; Ma, X.; Chen, W. A new parameter reduction algorithm for soft sets based on chi-square test. *Appl. Intell.* **2021**, *51*, 7960–7972. [CrossRef]
15. Ma, X.; Qin, H. Soft set based parameter value reduction for decision making application. *IEEE Access* **2019**, *7*, 35499–35511. [CrossRef]
16. Aktaş, H.; Çağman, N. Soft sets and soft groups. *Inf. Sci.* **2007**, *177*, 2726–2735. [CrossRef]
17. Acar, U.; Koyuncu, F.; Tanay, B. Soft sets and soft rings. *Comput. Math. Appl.* **2010**, *59*, 3458–3463. [CrossRef]
18. Alcantud, J.C.R. Convex soft geometries. *J. Comput. Cogn. Eng.* **2022**, *1*, 2–12. [CrossRef]
19. Kandil, A.; Tantawy, O.A.E.; El-Sheikh, S.A.; M Abd El-latif, A. Soft ideal theory soft local function and generated soft topological spaces. *Appl. Math. Inf. Sci.* **2014**, *8*, 1595–1603. [CrossRef]
20. Khameneh, A.Z.; Kilicman, A. On soft σ-algebras. *Malays. J. Math. Sci.* **2013**, *7*, 17–29.
21. Riaz, M.; Naeem, K.; Ahmad, M.O. Novel concepts of soft sets with applications. *Ann. Fuzzy Math. Inf.* **2017**, *13*, 239–251. [CrossRef]
22. Shabir, M.; Naz, M. On soft topological spaces. *Comput. Math. Appl.* **2011**, *61*, 1786–1799. [CrossRef]
23. Çağman, N.; Karataş, S.; Enginoglu, S. Soft topology. *Comput. Math. Appl.* **2011**, *62*, 351–358. [CrossRef]
24. Al-shami, T.M.; El-Shafei, M.E. Partial belong relation on soft separation axioms and decision-making problem, two birds with one stone. *Soft Comput.* **2020**, *24*, 5377–5387. [CrossRef]
25. Bayramov, A.; Gunduz, C. A new approach to separability and compactness in soft topological spaces. *TWMS J. Pure Appl. Math.* **2018**, *9*, 82–93.
26. Lin, F. Soft connected spaces and soft paracompact spaces. *Int. J. Math. Comput. Sci.* **2013**, *7*, 277–283.
27. Aygünoğlu, A.; Aygün, H. Some notes on soft topological spaces. *Neural Comput. Appl.* **2012**, *21*, 113–119. [CrossRef]
28. Asaad, B.A. Results on soft extremally disconnectedness of soft topological spaces. *J. Math. Comput. Sci.* **2017**, *17*, 448–464. [CrossRef]
29. Riaz, M.; Fatima, Z. Certain properties of soft metric spaces. *J. Fuzzy Math.* **2017**, *25*, 543–560.
30. Ameen, Z.A.; Khalaf, A.B. The invariance of soft Baire spaces under soft weak functions. *J. Interdiscip. Math.* **2022**, *25*, 1295–1306. [CrossRef]
31. Ameen, Z.A.; Asaad, B.A.; Al-shami, T.M. Soft somewhat continuous and soft somewhat open functions. *TWMS J. Pure Appl. Math.* **2023**, *13*, 792–806.
32. Al-shami, T.M. Soft somewhere dense sets on soft topological spaces. *Commun. Korean Math. Soc.* **2018**, *33*, 1341–1356.
33. Terepeta, M. On separating axioms and similarity of soft topological spaces. *Soft Comput.* **2019**, *23*, 1049–1057. [CrossRef]
34. Al-shami, T.M.; Kocinac, L.D. The equivalence between the enriched and extended soft topologies. *Appl. Comput. Math.* **2019**, *18*, 149–162.
35. Alcantud, J.C.R. Soft open bases and a novel construction of soft topologies from bases for topologies. *Mathematics* **2020**, *8*, 672. [CrossRef]
36. Jafari, S.; El-Atik, A.A.; Latif, R.M.; El-Bably, M.K. Soft topological spaces induced via soft relations. *WSEAS Trans. Math.* **2021**, *20*, 1–8. [CrossRef]
37. Al-shami, T.M.; Ameen, Z.A.; Abu-Gdairi, R.; Mhemdi, A. On primal soft topology. *Mathematics* **2023**, *11*, 2329. [CrossRef]
38. Azzam, A.; Ameen, Z.A.; Al-shami, T.M.; El-Shafei, M.E. Generating soft topologies via soft set operators. *Symmetry* **2022**, *14*, 914. [CrossRef]
39. Ameen, Z.A.; Al Ghour, S. Cluster soft sets and cluster soft topologies. In *Computational and Applied Mathematics*; Springer: Berlin/Heidelberg, Germany, 2023.
40. Ali, M.I.; Feng, F.; Liu, X.; Min, W.K.; Shabir, M. On some new operations in soft set theory. *Comput. Math. Appl.* **2009**, *57*, 1547–1553. [CrossRef]
41. Nazmul, S.; Samanta, S. Neighbourhood properties of soft topological spaces. *Ann. Fuzzy Math. Inf.* **2013**, *6*, 1–15.
42. Xie, N. Soft points and the structure of soft topological spaces. *Ann. Fuzzy Math. Inf.* **2015**, *10*, 309–322.
43. Maji, P.K.; Biswas, R.R.; Roy, A.R. Soft set theory. *Comput. Math. Appl.* **2003**, *45*, 555–562. [CrossRef]

44. Das, S.; Samanta, S. Soft metric. *Ann. Fuzzy Math. Inf.* **2013**, *6*, 77–94.
45. Al Ghour, S.; Ameen, Z.A. Maximal soft compact and maximal soft connected topologies. *Appl. Comput. Intell. Soft Comput.* **2022**, *2022*, 9860015. [CrossRef]
46. Ameen, Z.A.; Al Ghour, S. Minimal soft topologies. *New Math. Nat. Comput.* **2023**, *19*, 19–31. [CrossRef]
47. Hussain, S.; Ahmad, B. Some properties of soft topological spaces. *Comput. Math. Appl.* **2011**, *62*, 4058–4067. [CrossRef]
48. Yüksel, S.; Tozlu, N.; Ergül, Z.G. Soft regular generalized closed sets in soft topological spaces. *Int. J. Math. Anal.* **2014**, *8*, 355–367. [CrossRef]
49. Asaad, B.A.; Al-shami, T.M.; Ameen, Z.A. On soft somewhere dense open functions and soft Baire spaces. *Iraqi J. Sci.* **2023**, *64*, 373–384. [CrossRef]
50. Ameen, Z.A.; Al-shami, T.M.; Asaad, B.A. Further properties of soft somewhere dense continuous functions and soft Baire spaces. *J. Math. Comput. Sci.* **2024**, *32*, 54–63. [CrossRef]

symmetry

MDPI

Article

Multi-Attribute Group Decision Making Based on Spherical Fuzzy Zagreb Energy

Gang Fang [1], Uzma Ahmad [2,*], Sobia Ikhlaq [2] and Leila Asgharsharghi [3]

1 Institute of Computing Science and Technology, Guangzhou University, Guangzhou 510006, China; gangf@gzhu.edu.cn
2 Department of Mathematics, University of the Punjab, New Campus, Lahore 54590, Pakistan; sobiaikhlaq19@gmail.com
3 Department of Mathematics, Azarbaijan Shahid Madani University, Tabriz P.O. Box 53714-161, Iran; l.sharghi@azaruniv.ac.ir
* Correspondence: uzma.math@pu.edu.pk

Abstract: Based on picture fuzzy sets (PFSs), we use a mathematical model to tackle such types of problems when a person has opinions like yes, no, abstain, and refusal. The spherical fuzzy model is more flexible and practical than the picture fuzzy model, as it enhances the space of uncertainty. It broadens the space of vague information evaluated by decision makers since graphs are the pictorial representation of information. Graphs are a tool to represent a network. To handle some real-world problems, spherical fuzzy graphs can be used more effectively as compared to picture fuzzy graphs (PFGs). In this article, we expand the notion of fuzzy Zagreb indices of the fuzzy graph to the spherical fuzzy Zagreb indices of the spherical fuzzy graph (SFG). The spherical fuzzy Zagreb matrix of SFG and Zagreb energy of SFG are defined with examples. Additionally, we develop several lower and upper bounds of the spherical Zagreb energy of SFG. In addition, we present an application of SFG by computing its Zagreb energy in the decision-making problem of choosing the best location for business purposes.

Keywords: spherical fuzzy graph; spherical fuzzy Zagreb indices; matrix; graph energy; decision making

1. Introduction

In 1965, the notion of fuzzy set theory, which is the generalization of classical set theory, was established by Zadeh [1]. Enormous applications of fuzzy sets are found in telecommunication, control engineering, decision theory, expert systems, logic, management science, operation research, and others, which are all based on Zadeh's exceptional idea. One of the limitations of fuzzy set (FS) is that it deals only with the membership degree ($\breve{\alpha}$). To overcome this deficiency, Atanassov [2] in 1983 initiated the concept of the intuitionistic fuzzy set (IFS), which is the generalization of the fuzzy set (FS) theory. He expanded the notion of FSs by declaring the degree of truthiness ($\breve{\alpha}$) besides the degree of falseness ($\breve{\gamma}$) with the constraint $0 \leq \breve{\alpha} + \breve{\gamma} \leq 1$. On emphasizing the notion of IFS, Yager presented the Pythagorean fuzzy set (PyFS), which enlarged the space with the new constraint, $0 \leq \breve{\alpha}^2 + \breve{\beta}^2 \leq 1$. The situation when a person has an opinion like yes, abstain, no, and refusal can be handled with the picture fuzzy set (PFS) that was initiated by Cuong [3,4] which is an abstraction of IFS. It gives grades to the three parameters, named the degree of truthiness $\breve{\alpha} : R \longrightarrow [0,1]$, degree of abstinence$\breve{\beta} : R \longrightarrow [0,1]$, and the degree of falseness $\breve{\gamma} : R \longrightarrow [0,1]$ with the constraint $0 \leq \breve{\alpha} + \breve{\beta} + \breve{\gamma} \leq 1$, where $\breve{\nabla} = 1 - (\breve{\alpha} + \breve{\beta} + \breve{\gamma})$ is the degree of refusal. Garg [5] proposed some picture fuzzy aggregation operators. The notion of PFS was extended by Gundogdu and Kahraman [6] namely as the spherical fuzzy set (SFS). It gives more space to the degree of truthiness $\breve{\alpha} : R \longrightarrow [0,1]$, degree of abstinence $\breve{\beta} : R \longrightarrow [0,1]$, and degree of falseness $\breve{\gamma} : R \longrightarrow [0,1]$ with the constraint $0 \leq \breve{\alpha}^2 + \breve{\beta}^2 + \breve{\gamma}^2 \leq 1$, where

$\check{\nabla} = \sqrt{1 - (\check{\alpha}^2 + \check{\beta}^2 + \check{\gamma}^2)}$ is the degree of refusal. Ashraf et al. [7] explored the idea of SFSs with an application in multi-criteria decision-making (MCDM) problems using weighted averaging and weighted geometric aggregation operators. Further, Ashraf et al. [8] presented some spherical fuzzy Dombi aggregation operators and their applications in the MCDM problem. Mahmood et al. [9] presented the concept of the spherical fuzzy set and T-spherical fuzzy set as the generalization of the fuzzy set, intuitionistic fuzzy set, and Pythagorean fuzzy set. Some operations of SFSs and T-SFSs were introduced. They utilized these in MCDM of medical diagnostics problems. The q-rung orthopair fuzzy sets (q-ROFs) are the generalized form of IFS and PyFS and provide a more flexible way to handle uncertain information [10,11]. Then, Li et al. [12] introduced the idea of the q-Rung picture fuzzy set (q-RPFS), which is the generalization of SFSs. It provides huge space to the conditions of PFS as well as SFS with $0 \leq \check{\alpha}^q + \check{\beta}^q + \check{\gamma}^q \leq 1, \; q \geq 1$. By this, we can obtain more accurate outcomes as we increase the q-rungs.

In mathematics, graphs are a way to formally represent a network, which is basically just a collection of objects that are all interconnected. The notion of fuzzy graphs (FGs) based on fuzzy relation is presented by Kaufmann [13] and by some other experts who contributed to fuzzy graphs [14–25]. In [26], a MCDM problem is tackled with the help of a certain form of Pythagorean fuzzy graphs. Akram et al. [27] presented an idea of spherical fuzzy graph (SFG) as well as defining some operations on SFGs, namely symmetric difference and rejection. Akram [28] also presented MCDM models involving SFG. Then, Guleria and Bajaj [29] introduced a generalized version of SFGs using T-spherical fuzzy sets.

Topological indices are arithmetical quantities for structural molecular graphs. In 1972, Gutman [30] introduced the first Zagreb index. In 1978, Gutman [31] introduced the idea of the energy of a graph as the sum of the absolute values of the eigenvalues of the adjacency matrix of the graph. Gutman and Zhou [32] presented the term Laplacian energy of a graph as the sum of the absolute values of the differences of the average vertex degree of graph and the Laplacian eigenvalues of the graph.

The research study of topological fuzzy indices (TFIs) seems to be advantageous for multi-criteria decision-making (MCDM) problems and many connected fuzzy networks. Kalathian et al. [33] defined many TFIs for FGs, including the Gutman index, hyper Wiener index, Schultz index, Zagreb indices, Randic index, modified Wiener index, and harmonic index, and they established bounds for few of the indices as well. Islam and Pal [34] investigated the first Zagreb index for various FGs, like path, star, cycle, and fuzzy subgraphs, as well as proving several results. Moreover, a MCDM technique was elaborated that uses the first Zegrab index of a FG for evaluating the best employee in a company. The fuzzy Zagreb index is a degree-based index. Ahmad and Nasir [35] presented Randic and harmonic indices for FGs and derived some upper and lower bounds for different types of products, such as the cross product, Cartesian product and lexicographic product. These fuzzy indices were then utilized to handle a cybercrime problem as well. The Wiener index (based on geodesic distances between the vertices) for directed rough fuzzy graph was defined by Ahmad and Iqra [36], with its application to human trafficking. Some TIs in FGs, which are based on the degree and distance between the vertices, were explored in [37] and used in a multi-criteria decision-making problem.

Anjali and Mathew [38] elaborated the energy for a FG as the sum of the modulus values of the eigenvalues corresponding to the adjacency matrix of FG. The Laplacian energy of FG has defined in [39]. Kale and Minirani [40] presented the fuzzy Zagreb matrix and derived some bounds for fuzzy Zagreb energy. Praba et al.[41] extended the idea of energy of FG to the energy of an IFG and derived several lower and upper bounds. Akram and Naz [42] presented the energy of an IFG to Pythagorean fuzzy graphs (PyFGs) and explored the concepts of energy and Laplacian energy of PyFGs, as well as the energy and Laplacian energy of Pythagorean fuzzy digraphs. Akram et al. [43] introduced the notion of energy of double dominating bipolar fuzzy graphs. Shi et al. [44] extended the notion of the energy of the Pythagorean fuzzy graph to the energy of picture fuzzy graphs (PFGs) and presented the types of energy, including Laplacian energy as well as skew-Laplacian energy in both PFGs and picture fuzzy digraphs. They ranked the suitable locations for business purposes by making use of the picture fuzzy graph and its related energies. Yahya and Mohamed [45] explored the energy of SFG and extracted some bounds of the energy of SFG.

The following points influenced us to write this article:

- Due to the enormous applications of TIs, including Zagreb indices for FGs in distinct decision-making problems, it also seems advantageous to expand the notion of Zagreb indices in SFG.
- There are numerous applications of the spectrum of fuzzy graph theory in solving linear systems, computer science, chemistry, and others.
- The spectrum of the graph plays a crucial role in combinatorial optimization problems in mathematics.
- Moreover, the Zagreb energy of SFG has not yet been discussed and studied in the literature; therefore, we expanded the notion of the energy of SFG to the Zagreb energy of SFG.

The subscription of our proposed research work is given as follows:

- The aim of this research study is to establish the notion of the first and second Zagreb indices of spherical fuzzy graphs.
- We introduce the concept of spherical fuzzy Zagreb matrices of SFGs and corresponding spectra.
- We define the Zagreb energy of SFG and establish the lower and upper bounds for the Zagreb energy of SFGs and some of their results.
- Finally, we utilize the idea of Zagreb energy of SFG in a MCDM problem. In particular, we determine the best place to start a certain business.

This paper is organized as follows.

In Section 2, some definitions are recalled for better understanding. In Section 3, we define fuzzy Zagreb indices of SFG. In Section 4, we discuss the lower and upper bounds of Zagreb energy and some of the main results as well. In addition, in Section 5, we present an application of SFG by computing Zagreb energy in a multi-attribute decision-making problem. Finally, we conclude our proposed work.

Some of the symbols used in this article are mentioned in Table 1.

Table 1. List of symbols.

Symbols	Description	Symbols	Description
$\breve{\alpha}_R(v)$	truthiness membership of v_i	s_t	$\max\{\breve{\alpha}_\mathcal{Y}(v_i)\}$
$\breve{\beta}_R(v)$	abstinence membership of v_i	s_a	$\max\{\breve{\beta}_\mathcal{Y}(v_i)\}$
$\breve{\gamma}_R(v)$	falseness membership of v_i	s_f	$\max\{\breve{\gamma}_\mathcal{Y}(v_i)\}$
g_t	$\min\{\breve{\alpha}_\mathcal{Y}(v_i)\}$	g_a	$\min\{\breve{\beta}_\mathcal{Y}(v_i)\}$
g_f	$\max\{\breve{\gamma}_\mathcal{Y}(v_i)\}$	Δ_t	$\max\{d_t(v_i)\}$
Δ_a	$\max\{d_a(v_i)\}$	Δ_f	$\max\{d_f(v_i)\}$
δ_t	$\min\{d_t(v_i)\}$	δ_a	$\min\{d_a(v_i)\}$
δ_f	$\min\{d_f(v_i)\}$	ZE	Zagreb energy of matrix
SZM	spherical fuzzy Zagreb matrix	$SFM_1(G)$	Zagreb first index of SFG
$SFM_2(G)$	Zagreb second index of SFG	SZE	spherical fuzzy Zagreb energy
e	fuzzy size	e^*	crisp size

2. Preliminaries

Definition 1 ([27]). *Let $\check{V}$ be a nonempty underlying set of vertices. A spherical fuzzy set R over $\check{V}$ is defined as*

$$R = \{(v,\ \check{\alpha}_R(v),\ \check{\beta}_R(v),\ \check{\gamma}_R(v))\ |v \in \check{V}\},$$

where $\check{\alpha}_R(v)$, $\check{\beta}_R(v)$, and $\check{\gamma}_R(v)$ denote the degree of truthiness of v in R, degree of abstinence of v in R, and degree of falseness of v in R, respectively. Moreover, $\check{\alpha}(v)$, $\check{\beta}(v)$, $\check{\gamma}(v) \in [0,1]$, such that $0\leq \check{\alpha}_R^2(v) + \check{\beta}_R^2(v) + \check{\gamma}_R^2(v) \leq 1$. Further, $\check{\nabla}_R(v) = \sqrt{1-(\check{\alpha}_R^2(v) + \check{\beta}_R^2(v) + \check{\gamma}_R^2(v))}$ for all $v \in \check{V}$ is called the degree of refusal of membership of v in R.

Definition 2 ([45]). *Let V be an underlying set of vertices. A spherical fuzzy graph $G = (R,S)$ is a pair of mappings such that $R : V \longrightarrow [0,1]$ and $S : V \times V \longrightarrow [0,1]$, where R is a spherical fuzzy set with constraint $0 \leq \check{\alpha}^2 + \check{\beta}^2 + \check{\gamma}^2 \leq 1$ for all $v \in V$ and S is spherical fuzzy relation on $V \times V$, such that $\check{\alpha}_S(v_1,v_2) \leq min\{\check{\alpha}_R(v_1),\check{\alpha}_R(v_2)\}$, $\check{\beta}_S(v_1,v_2) \leq min\{\check{\beta}_R(v_1),\check{\beta}_R(v_2)\}$, and $\check{\gamma}_S(v_1,v_2) \leq max\{\check{\gamma}_R(v_1),\check{\gamma}_R(v_2)\}$, where $\check{\alpha}$, $\check{\beta}$, and $\check{\gamma}$ denote the degree of truthiness, degree of abstinence, and degree of falseness, respectively, satisfying the following condition:*

$$0 \leq \check{\alpha}_S^2(v_1,v_2) + \check{\beta}_S^2(v_1,v_2) + \check{\gamma}_S^2(v_1,v_2) \leq 1$$

for all $(v_1,v_2) \in \check{V} \times \check{V}$.

Example 1. *The graph $L^* = (V,E)$ is defined on an underlying set of vertices $V = \{\check{v}_1,\check{v}_2,\check{v}_3,\check{v}_4\}$ and $E = \{\check{v}_1\check{v}_2,\check{v}_1\check{v}_3,\check{v}_3\check{v}_4\} \subseteq V \times V$. Consider the graph $\mathcal{C} = (\mathcal{Y},\mathcal{Z})$, where $\mathcal{Y}$ is a spherical fuzzy subset of V and $\mathcal{Z}$ is a spherical fuzzy subset of E defined as in Tables 2 and 3, respectively. The graph $\mathcal{C} = (\mathcal{Y},\mathcal{Z})$ is shown in Figure 1.*

Table 2. Table for $\mathcal{Y}$.

$\mathcal{Y}$	$\check{v}_1$	$\check{v}_2$	$\check{v}_3$	$\check{v}_4$
$\check{\alpha}_{\mathcal{Y}}$	0.2	0.3	0.4	0.4
$\check{\beta}_{\mathcal{Y}}$	0.3	0.5	0.8	0.2
$\check{\gamma}_{\mathcal{Y}}$	0.4	0.7	0.3	0.6

Table 3. Table for $\mathcal{Z}$.

$\mathcal{Z}$	$\check{v}_1\check{v}_2$	$\check{v}_1\check{v}_3$	$\check{v}_3\check{v}_4$
$\check{\alpha}_{\mathcal{Z}}$	0.1	0.2	0.2
$\check{\beta}_{\mathcal{Z}}$	0.2	0.3	0.1
$\check{\gamma}_{\mathcal{Z}}$	0.6	0.4	0.5

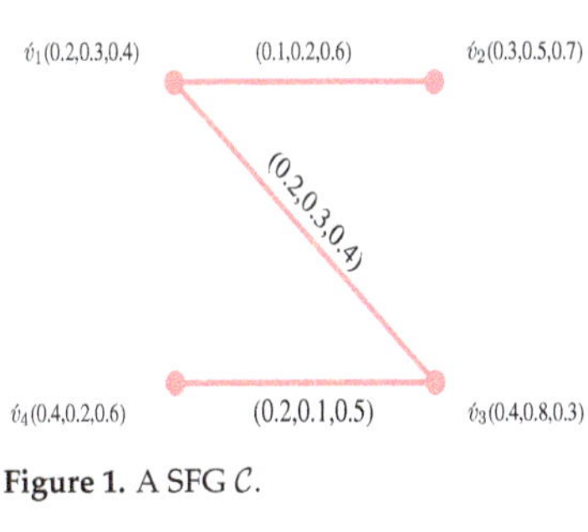

Figure 1. A SFG $\mathcal{C}$.

Definition 3 ([27]). *Consider a SFG $G = (R, S)$ defined on $G^* = (\check{V}, E)$. The degree of a vertex v of G ($d_G(v) = (d_{\check{\alpha}}(v), d_{\check{\beta}}(v), d_{\check{\gamma}}(v))$) is expressed as*

$$d_G(v) = \left(\sum_{v_1 \neq v_2} \check{\alpha}_S(v_1, v_2), \sum_{v_1 \neq v_2} \check{\beta}_S(v_1, v_2), \sum_{v_1 \neq v_2} \check{\gamma}_S(v_1, v_2) \right)$$

for all $(v_1, v_2) \in \check{V} \times \check{V}$.

Definition 4. *Using OWA operator weights for preference aggregation, let wj be the relative importance weight attached to the jth ranking place and vij be the vote candidate i receives in the j-th ranking place. The total score of each candidate is defined as [36], which is a linear function of the relative importance weights. Although the weights are not required to be summed to one, we assume them to be normalized in this paper. That is, once the weights are determined, candidates can be ranked in terms of their total.*

3. Spherical Fuzzy Zagreb Indices

Several topological indices are defined in a crisp graph, but in real life, many issues cannot be tackled by these indices. So, there is a need to define these indices for the fuzzy graph. One of the most famous and useful indices is the Zagreb index, which can be used in several fields of mathematics and chemistry. It is a degree-based topological index. The strength of vertices plays a vital role in fuzzy graph theory. Fuzzy Zagreb indices can be used to measure the connectivity of edges. These can be used to evaluate how much the fuzzy graph is strengthened. In spherical fuzzy Zagreb indices, we involve the membership values of vertices as well as the degree of vertices in terms of truthiness, abstinence, and falseness, which help to encounter the connectivity of neighborhoods of the vertices.

Definition 5. *Let $G = (R, S)$ be a spherical fuzzy graph. Then, the first Zagreb index denoted as $(SFM_1(G) = (SFM_1(G))_t, (SFM_1(G))_a, (SFM_1(G))_f)$ of SFG is defined by*

$$\begin{aligned} SFM_1(G) = \sum_{v_i v_j \in E(G)\ i \neq j} & [\check{\alpha}(v_i) d_{\check{\alpha}}(v_i) + \check{\alpha}(v_j) d_{\check{\alpha}}(v_j),\ \check{\beta}(v_i) d_{\check{\beta}}(v_i) + \check{\beta}(v_j) d_{\check{\beta}}(v_j), \\ & \check{\gamma}(v_i) d_{\check{\gamma}}(v_i) + \check{\gamma}(v_j) d_{\check{\gamma}}(v_j)], \end{aligned} \quad (1)$$

Here , $\check{\alpha}(v_i)$, $\check{\beta}(v_i)$, $\check{\gamma}(v_i)$, $d_{\check{\alpha}}(v_i)$, $d_{\check{\beta}}(v_i)$, and $d_{\check{\gamma}}(v_i)$ are defined in Table 1.

Definition 6. *Let $G = (R, S)$ be a spherical fuzzy graph. Then the second Zagreb index denoted as $(SFM_2(G) = (SFM_2(G))_t, (SFM_2(G))_a, (SFM_2(G))_f)$ of the spherical fuzzy graph is defined as*

$$\begin{aligned} SFM_2(G) = \sum_{v_i v_j \in E(G) i \neq j} & [\check{\alpha}(v_i) d_{\check{\alpha}}(v_i) \check{\alpha}(v_j) d_{\check{\alpha}}(v_j),\ \check{\beta}(v_i) d_{\check{\beta}}(v_i) \\ & \check{\beta}(v_j) d_{\check{\beta}}(v_j),\ \check{\gamma}(v_i) d_{\check{\gamma}}(v_i) \check{\gamma}(v_j) d_{\check{\gamma}}(v_j)], \end{aligned} \quad (2)$$

Here, $\check{\alpha}(v_i)$, $\check{\beta}(v_i)$, $\check{\gamma}(v_i)$, $d_{\check{\alpha}}(v_i)$, $d_{\check{\beta}}(v_i)$, and $d_{\check{\gamma}}(v_i)$ are defined in Table 1.

Remark 1. *From Definitions 5 and 6, it is noted that $(SFM_1(G))_t \leq (SFM_2(G))_t$, $SFM_1(G))_a \leq (SFM_2(G))_a$ and $SFM_1(G))_f \leq (SFM_2(G))_f$.*

Example 2. *Consider the spherical fuzzy graph $J = (D, F)$ as shown in Figure 2.*

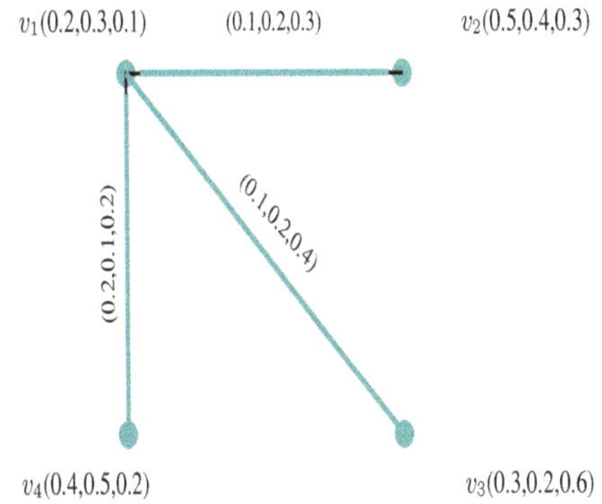

Figure 2. A SFG J.

By using (1), the first Zagreb index of SFG J is calculated as

$$SFM_1(G) = \sum_{v_iv_j \in E(G)\ i \neq j} [\breve{\alpha}(v_i)d_{\breve{\alpha}}(v_i) + \breve{\alpha}(v_j)d_{\breve{\alpha}}(v_j), \breve{\beta}(v_i)d_{\breve{\beta}}(v_i) + \breve{\beta}(v_j) d_{\breve{\beta}}(v_j), \breve{\gamma}(v_i)d_{\breve{\gamma}}(v_i) + \breve{\gamma}(v_j)d_{\breve{\gamma}}(v_j)].$$

$$\begin{aligned} SFM_1(G) =& [\breve{\alpha}(v_1)d_{\breve{\alpha}}(v_1) + \breve{\alpha}(v_2)d_{\breve{\alpha}}(v_2), \breve{\beta}(v_1)d_{\breve{\beta}}(v_1) + \breve{\beta}(v_2)d_{\breve{\beta}}(v_2), \breve{\gamma}(v_1) \\ & d_{\breve{\gamma}}(v_1) + \breve{\gamma}(v_2)d_{\breve{\gamma}}(v_2)] + [\breve{\alpha}(v_1)d_{\breve{\alpha}}(v_1) + \breve{\alpha}(v_3)d_{\breve{\alpha}}(v_3), \breve{\beta}(v_1) \\ & d_{\breve{\beta}}(v_1) + \breve{\beta}(v_3)d_{\breve{\beta}}(v_3), \breve{\gamma}(v_1)d_{\breve{\gamma}}(v_1) + \breve{\gamma}(v_3)d_{\breve{\gamma}}(v_3)] + [\breve{\alpha}(v_1) \\ & d_{\breve{\alpha}}(v_1) + \breve{\alpha}(v_4)d_{\breve{\alpha}}(v_4), \breve{\beta}(v_1)d_{\breve{\beta}}(v_1) + \breve{\beta}(v_4)d_{\breve{\beta}}(v_4), \breve{\gamma}(v_1)d_{\breve{\gamma}}(v_1) \\ & + \breve{\gamma}(v_4)d_{\breve{\gamma}}(v_4)]. \\ =& [(0.2)(0.4) + (0.5)(0.1), (0.3)(0.5) + (0.4)(0.2), (0.1)(0.9) + \\ & (0.3)(0.3)] + [(0.2)(0.4) + (0.3)(0.1), (0.3)(0.5) + (0.2)(0.2), \\ & (0.1)(0.9) + (0.6)(0.4)] + [(0.2)(0.4) + (0.4)(0.2), (0.3)(0.5) + \\ & (0.5)(0.1), (0.1)(0.9) + (0.2)(0.2)]. \\ =& (0.4, 0.62, 0.64). \end{aligned}$$

Now, by using (2), the second Zagreb index of SFG J is computed as

$$SFM_2(G) = \sum_{v_iv_j \in E(G)\ i \neq j} [\breve{\alpha}(v_i)d_{\breve{\alpha}}(v_i) \cdot \breve{\alpha}(v_j)d_{\breve{\alpha}}(v_j), \breve{\beta}(v_i)d_{\breve{\beta}}(v_i) \cdot \breve{\beta}(v_j)d_{\breve{\beta}}(v_j), \breve{\gamma}(v_i)d_{\breve{\gamma}}(v_i) \cdot \breve{\gamma}(v_j)d_{\breve{\gamma}}(v_j)].$$

to remove numbering (before each equation)

$$\begin{aligned} SFM_2(G) =& [\breve{\alpha}(v_1)d_{\breve{\alpha}}(v_1) \cdot \breve{\alpha}(v_2)d_{\breve{\alpha}}(v_2), \breve{\beta}(v_1)d_{\breve{\beta}}(v_1) \cdot \breve{\beta}(v_2)d_{\breve{\beta}}(v_2), \breve{\gamma}(v_1)d_{\breve{\gamma}}(v_1) \\ & \cdot \breve{\gamma}(v_2)d_{\breve{\gamma}}(v_2)] \cdot [\breve{\alpha}(v_1)d_{\breve{\alpha}}(v_1) \cdot \breve{\alpha}(v_3)d_{\breve{\alpha}}(v_3), \beta(v_1)d_{\beta}(v_1) \cdot \beta(v_3)d_{\beta}(v_3), \\ & \breve{\gamma}(v_1)d_{\breve{\gamma}}(v_1) \cdot \breve{\gamma}(v_3)d_{\breve{\gamma}}(v_3)] \cdot [\breve{\alpha}(v_1)d_{\breve{\alpha}}(v_1) \cdot \breve{\alpha}(v_4)d_{\breve{\alpha}}(v_4), \breve{\beta}(v_1) \\ & d_{\breve{\beta}}(v_1) \cdot \breve{\beta}(v_4)d_{\breve{\beta}}(v_4), \breve{\gamma}(v_1)d_{\breve{\gamma}}(v_1) \cdot \breve{\gamma}(v_4)d_{\breve{\gamma}}(v_4)]. \\ =& [(0.2)(0.4) \cdot (0.5)(0.1), (0.3)(0.5) \cdot (0.4)(0.2), (0.1)(0.9) \cdot (0.3)(0.3)] + \\ & [(0.2)(0.4) \cdot (0.3)(0.1), (0.3)(0.5) \cdot (0.2)(0.2), (0.1)(0.9) \cdot (0.6)(0.4)] + \\ & [(0.2)(0.4) \cdot (0.4)(0.2), (0.3)(0.5) \cdot (0.5)(0.1), (0.1)(0.9) \cdot (0.2)(0.2)]. \\ =& (0.0128, 0.0255, 0.0333). \end{aligned}$$

Definition 7. *Consider a SFG $G = (R, S)$ and $\check{V} = \{v_1, v_2, v_3, \ldots, v_n\}$. Then the spherical fuzzy Zagreb matrix (`SZM`) is defined as*

$$[SZM]_{ij} = ([ZM\theta_1]_{ij}, [ZM\theta_2]_{ij}, [ZM\theta_3]_{ij}),$$

where

$$[ZM\theta_1]_{ij} = \begin{cases} \check{\alpha}(v_i)d_{\check{\alpha}}(v_i) + \check{\alpha}(v_j)d_{\check{\alpha}}(v_j), & v_iv_j \in \check{V}; \\ 0, & v_iv_j \notin \check{V}; \\ 0, & v_i = v_j. \end{cases}$$

$$[ZM\theta_2]_{ij} = \begin{cases} \check{\beta}(v_i)d_{\check{\beta}}(v_i) + \check{\beta}(v_j)d_{\check{\beta}}(v_j), & v_iv_j \in \check{V}; \\ 0, & v_iv_j \notin \check{V}; \\ 0, & v_i = v_j. \end{cases}$$

and,

$$[ZM\theta_3]_{ij} = \begin{cases} \check{\gamma}(v_i)d_{\check{\gamma}}(v_i) + \check{\gamma}(v_j)d_{\check{\gamma}}(v_j), & v_iv_j \in \check{V}; \\ 0, & v_iv_j \notin \check{V}; \\ 0, & v_i = v_j. \end{cases}$$

Definition 8. *The spectrum of `SZM` of SFG is expressed as $(\omega^{(1)}, \omega^{(2)}, \omega^{(3)})$, where $\omega^{(1)}$, $\omega^{(2)}$, and $\omega^{(3)}$ are the sets of eigenvalues of $ZM\theta_1$, $ZM\theta_2$, and $ZM\theta_3$, respectively.*

Definition 9. *The spherical fuzzy Zagreb energy (`SZE`) of SFG is defined as*

$$SZE(G) = \Big(ZE(ZM\theta_1),\ ZE(ZM\theta_2),\ ZE(ZM\theta_3)\Big).$$

$$= \left(\sum_{i=1}^{n} |\varsigma_i|, \sum_{i=1}^{n} |\eta_i|, \sum_{i=1}^{n} |\zeta_i|\right), \tag{3}$$

where ς_i, η_i, and ζ_i are the eigenvalues of $ZM\theta_1$, $ZM\theta_2$, and $ZM\theta_3$, respectively. Further, ZE denotes the fuzzy Zagreb energy.

Example 3. *Consider the SFG `W=(P, Q)` as shown in Figure 3.*

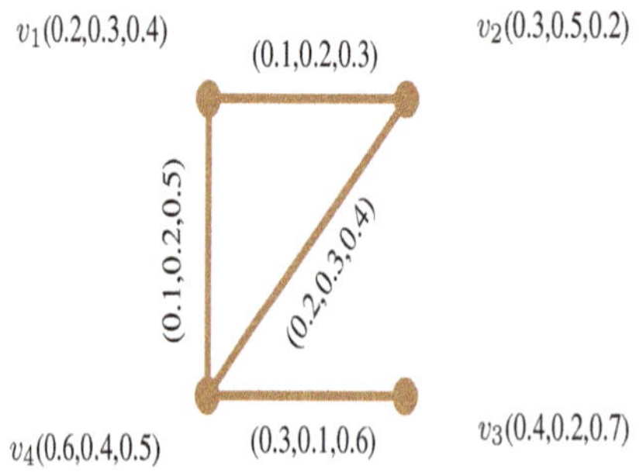

Figure 3. Spherical fuzzy graph `W=(P, Q)`.

The spherical fuzzy Zagreb matrix is obtained according to the definition mentioned as above:

$$SZM = \begin{bmatrix} (0,0,0) & (0.13,0.37,0.46) & (0,0,0) & (0.4,0.36,1.07) \\ (0.13,0.37,0.46) & (0,0,0) & (0,0,0) & (0.45,0.49,0.89) \\ (0,0,0) & (0,0,0) & (0,0,0) & (0.48,0.26,1.17) \\ (0.4,0.36,1.07) & (0.45,0.49,0.89) & (0.48,0.26,1.17) & (0,0,0) \end{bmatrix}.$$

The set of eigenvalues of $ZM\theta_1$, $ZM\theta_2$, and $ZM\theta_3$ is given as

$$\begin{aligned}\omega^{(1)} &= (-0.7340, -0.1296, 0.0503, 0.8133),\\ \omega^{(2)} &= (-0.5566, -0.3461, 0.0568, 0.8459),\end{aligned}$$

and,

$$\omega^{(3)} = (-1.7040, -0.4565, 0.1889, 1.9716),$$

respectively. Also, by using Definition 8, we compute that

$$\begin{aligned} Spectrum \ \ of\, ZM\theta_1 &= \{-0.7340, -0.1296, 0.0503, 0.8133\},\\ Spectrum \ \ of\, ZM\theta_2 &= \{-0.5566, -0.3461, 0.0568, 0.8459\},\\ and, \ \ Spectrum \ \ of\, ZM\theta_3 &= \{-1.7040, -0.4565, 0.1889, 1.9716\}.\end{aligned}$$

Now, by using (3), the spherical fuzzy Zagreb energy of SFG is calculated as

$$SZE(G) = \left(\sum_{i=1}^{n} |\xi_i|, \sum_{i=1}^{n} |\eta_i|, \sum_{i=1}^{n} |\zeta_i|\right).$$

By putting the values, we obtain

$$SZE(G) = (1.7272, 1.8054, 4.321).$$

4. Main Results

In this section, we present some upper and lower bounds related to the maximum eigenvalue and spherical fuzzy energy of SFG. The obtained bounds are then illustrated with the help of examples to show the validity of the results.

Theorem 1. *Let $G = (R, S)$ with order n and size m be a spherical fuzzy undirected and connected graph defined on $G^* = (\check{V}, \check{E})$. Then,*

$$2g_t\delta_t e^* \leq SFM_1(G) \leq 2s_t\Delta_t e^*,$$

$$\begin{aligned} 2g_a\delta_a e^* &\leq SFM_1(G) \leq 2s_a\Delta_a e^*,\\ 2g_f\delta_f e^* &\leq SFM_1(G) \leq 2s_f\Delta_f e^*,\end{aligned}$$

where these symbols s_t, s_a, s_f, g_t, g_a, g_f, Δ_t, Δ_a Δ_f, δ_a, δ_f and e^* are described in Table 1. In particular, the equalities in (5) hold for SFG such that $\breve{\alpha}_{\mathcal{Y}}$, $\check{\beta}_{\mathcal{Y}}$ and $\check{\gamma}_{\mathcal{Y}}$ are constant functions, and each vertex has the same spherical fuzzy degree.

Proof.

$$\begin{aligned}\sum_{v_iv_j\in\check{E}(G)} (\breve{\alpha}_{\mathcal{Y}}(v_i)d_t(v_i) + \breve{\alpha}_{\mathcal{Y}}(v_j)d_t(v_j) &\leq \sum_{v_iv_j\in\check{E}(G)} [s_t d_t(v_i) + s_t d_t(v_j)]\\ &\leq s_t \sum_{v_iv_j\in\check{E}(G)} [d_t(v_i) + d_t(v_j)]\\ &\leq s_t \sum_{v_iv_j\in\check{E}(G)} 2\Delta_t\\ &\leq 2s_t\Delta_t \sum_{v_iv_j\in\check{E}(G)} 1\\ &\leq 2s_t\Delta_t e^*.\end{aligned}$$

It implies that

$$(SFM_1(G))_t \leq 2s_t\Delta_t e^*.$$

Similarly, we can prove other bounds. □

Theorem 2. *Let $G = (R, S)$ with order n and size m be a spherical fuzzy undirected, and connected graph defined on $G^* = (\check{V}, \check{E})$, and let $\mathtt{SZM} = (ZM\theta_1, ZM\theta_2, ZM\theta_3)$ be its spherical fuzzy Zagreb matrix. If $\xi_1 \geq \xi_2 \geq \cdots \geq \xi_n$, $\eta_1 \geq \eta_2 \geq \cdots \geq \eta_n$, and $\zeta_1 \geq \zeta_2 \geq \cdots \geq \zeta_n$ are the eigenvalues of $ZM\theta_1$, $ZM\theta_2$, and $ZM\theta_3$, respectively. Then*

$$8e^*(\delta_t g_t)^2 \leq \sum_{i=1}^{n} \xi_i^2 \leq 8e^*(\Delta_t s_t)^2,$$

$$8e^*(\delta_a g_a)^2 \leq \sum_{i=1}^{n} \eta_i^2 \leq 8e^*(\Delta_a s_a)^2,$$

and

$$8e^*(\delta_f g_f)^2 \leq \sum_{i=1}^{n} \zeta_i^2 \leq 8e^*(\Delta_f s_f)^2.$$

where $s_t = \max\{\breve{\alpha}_{\mathcal{Y}}(v_i)\}$, $s_a = \max\{\breve{\beta}_{\mathcal{Y}}(v_i)\}$, and $s_f = \max\{\breve{\gamma}_{\mathcal{Y}}(v_i)\}$. $g_t = \min\{\breve{\alpha}_{\mathcal{Y}}(v_i)\}$, $g_a = \min\{\breve{\beta}_{\mathcal{Y}}(v_i)\}$, $g_f = \min\{\breve{\gamma}_{\mathcal{Y}}(v_i)\}$. Further, $\Delta_t = \max\{d_t(v_i)\}$, $\Delta_a = \max\{d_a(v_i)\}$ $\Delta_f = \max\{d_f(v_i)\}$, $\delta_t = \min\{d_t(v_i)\}$, $\delta_a = \min\{d_a(v_i)\}$, $\delta_f = \min\{d_f(v_i)\}$ and e^* denotes the number of edges in SFG. In particular, the equalities in (5) hold for SFG such that $\breve{\alpha}_{\mathcal{Y}}$, $\breve{\beta}_{\mathcal{Y}}$ and $\breve{\gamma}_{\mathcal{Y}}$ are constant functions, and each vertex has the same spherical fuzzy degree.

Proof. By the trace properties of a matrix, we have

$$tr(ZM\theta_1)^2 = \sum_{i=1}^{n} \xi_i^2,$$

$$\begin{aligned}
\text{where } tr(ZM\theta_1)^2 =& (0 + (\breve{\alpha}_{\mathcal{Y}}(v_1)d_t(v_1) + \breve{\alpha}_{\mathcal{Y}}(v_2)d_t(v_2))^2 + \cdots + (\breve{\alpha}_{\mathcal{Y}}(v_1) \\
& d_t(v_1) + \breve{\alpha}_{\mathcal{Y}}(v_n)d_t(v_n))^2) + ((\breve{\alpha}_{\mathcal{Y}}(v_2)d_t(v_2) + \breve{\alpha}_{\mathcal{Y}}(v_1) \\
& d_t(v_1))^2 + \cdots + (\breve{\alpha}_{\mathcal{Y}}(v_2)d_t(v_2) + \breve{\alpha}_{\mathcal{Y}}(v_n)d_t(v_n))^2) \\
& + \cdots + (0 + (\breve{\alpha}_{\mathcal{Y}}(v_n)d_t(v_n) + \breve{\alpha}_{\mathcal{Y}}(v_1)d_t(v_1))^2 \\
& + (\breve{\alpha}_{\mathcal{Y}}(v_n)d_t(v_n) + \breve{\alpha}_{\mathcal{Y}}(v_2)d_t(v_2))^2 + \cdots + 0). \\
=& 2 \sum_{v_iv_j \in \check{E}(G)} (\breve{\alpha}_{\mathcal{Y}}(v_i)d_t(v_i) + \breve{\alpha}_{\mathcal{Y}}(v_j)d_t(v_j))^2.
\end{aligned}$$

Hence, we have

$$\sum_{i=1}^{n} \xi_i^2 = 2 \sum_{v_iv_j \in \check{E}(G)} (\breve{\alpha}_{\mathcal{Y}}(v_i)d_t(v_i) + \breve{\alpha}_{\mathcal{Y}}(v_j)d_t(v_j))^2. \tag{4}$$

Let $s_t = \max\{\breve{\alpha}_{\mathcal{Y}}(v_i)\}$ and $\Delta_t = \max\{d_t(v_i)\}$. Now consider,

$$\begin{aligned}\sum_{v_iv_j\in\check{E}(G)}(\check{\alpha}y(v_i)d_t(v_i)+\check{\alpha}y(v_j)d_t(v_j))^2 &\leq \sum_{v_iv_j\in\check{E}(G)}[s_td_t(v_i)+s_td_t(v_j)]^2\\ &\leq s_t^2\sum_{v_iv_j\in\check{E}(G)}[d_t(v_i)+d_t(v_j)]^2\\ &\leq s_t^2\sum_{v_iv_j\in\check{E}(G)}(2\Delta_t)^2\\ &\leq 4s_t^2\Delta_t^2\sum_{v_iv_j\in\check{E}(G)}1\\ &\leq 4s_t^2\Delta_t^2e^*\\ &\leq (2\Delta s_t)^2e^*. \qquad (5)\end{aligned}$$

From (4) and (5), we have

$$\sum_{i=1}^{n}\xi_i^2=2\sum_{v_iv_j\in\check{E}(G)}(\check{\alpha}y(v_i)d_t(v_i)+\check{\alpha}y(v_j)d_t(v_j))^2\leq 8(\Delta_ts_t)^2e^*.$$

Hence,

$$\sum_{i=1}^{n}\xi_i^2\leq 8e^*(\Delta_ts_t)^2. \qquad (6)$$

Similarly, we have

$$\sum_{i=1}^{n}\eta_i^2\leq 8e^*(\Delta_as_a)^2,$$

and

$$\sum_{i=1}^{n}\zeta_i^2\leq 8e^*(\Delta_fs_f)^2.$$

For the lower bound, let $\delta_t=\min\{d_t(v_i)\}$, $g_t=\min\{\check{\alpha}y(v_i)\}$. Now using the same arguments as those used to prove (5), we have

$$\begin{aligned}\sum_{v_iv_j\in\check{E}(G)}(\check{\alpha}y(v_i)d_t(v_i)+\check{\alpha}y(v_j)d_t(v_j))^2 &\geq \sum_{v_iv_j\in\check{E}(G)}[g_td_t(v_i)+g_td_t(v_j)]^2.\\ &\geq 4(\delta_tg_t)^2e^*.\end{aligned}$$

Hence,

$$\sum_{i=1}^{n}|\xi_i|^2\geq 8e^*(\delta_tg_t)^2. \qquad (7)$$

Similarly,

$$\sum_{i=1}^{n}|\eta_i|^2\geq 8e^*(\delta_ag_a)^2.$$

$$\sum_{i=1}^{n}|\zeta_i|^2\geq 8e^*(\delta_fg_f)^2.$$

□

Theorem 3. *Consider a SFG G=(R,S) having n number of vertices and*

$$\mathtt{SZM}(G)=\Big(ZM\theta_1,\ ZM\theta_2,\ ZM\theta_3\Big)$$

as the corresponding SZM *of* G. *Then,*

$$\sqrt{8e^*(\delta_t g_t)^2+n(n-1)|det(ZM\theta_1)|^{\frac{2}{n}}} \leq ZE(ZM\theta_1) \leq 2\sqrt{2ne^*}(s_t\Delta_t).$$

$$\sqrt{8e^*(\delta_a g_a)^2+n(n-1)|det(ZM\theta_2)|^{\frac{2}{n}}} \leq ZE(ZM\theta_2) \leq 2\sqrt{2ne^*}(s_a\Delta_a).$$

and

$$\sqrt{8e^*(\delta_f g_f)^2+n(n-1)|det(ZM\theta_3)|^{\frac{2}{n}}} \leq ZE(ZM\theta_3) \leq 2\sqrt{2ne^*}(s_f\Delta_f).$$

Proof. By considering two sequences (1, 1, 1, ..., 1) and $(|\xi_1|, |\xi_2|, |\xi_3|, ..., |\xi_n|)$ and applying the Cauchy–Schwarz inequality, we have

$$\sum_{i=1}^{n}|\xi_i| \leq \sqrt{n}\sqrt{\sum_{i=1}^{n}|\xi_i|^2} \tag{8}$$

By using (6) from Theorem 2,

$$\sum_{i=1}^{n}|\xi_i|^2 \leq 8e^*(\Delta_t s_t)^2$$

Equation (8) implies

$$\begin{aligned}\sum_{i=1}^{n}|\xi_i| &\leq \sqrt{n}\sqrt{8e^*(\Delta_t s_t)^2}\\ \sum_{i=1}^{n}|\xi_i| &\leq 2\sqrt{2ne^*}(s_t\Delta_t)\end{aligned}$$

Now, by using (3), it follows that

$$\mathrm{ZE}(ZM\theta_1) \leq 2\sqrt{2ne^*}(s_t\Delta_t).$$

Similarly, we have

$$\begin{aligned}\mathrm{ZE}(ZM\theta_2) &\leq 2\sqrt{2ne^*}(s_a\Delta_a),\\ \mathrm{ZE}(ZM\theta_3) &\leq 2\sqrt{2ne^*}(s_f\Delta_f).\end{aligned}$$

Now, for the lower bound, consider

$$\begin{aligned}(\mathrm{ZE}(ZM\theta_1))^2 &= (\sum_{i=1}^{n}|\xi_i|)^2.\\ &= \sum_{i=1}^{n}|\xi_i|^2+2\sum_{1\leq i<j\leq n}|\xi_i\xi_j|.\\ &= \sum_{i=1}^{n}|\xi_i|^2+\frac{2n(n-1)}{2}AM\{|\xi_i\xi_j|\},\end{aligned}$$

where AM represents the arithmetic mean of the terms $\{|\xi_i\xi_j|\}$. As we know that the arithmetic mean (AM) of the terms is always greater than the geometric mean (GM) of these terms $\{|\xi_i\xi_j|\}$ i.e., AM $\{|\xi_i\xi_j|\} \geq GM\{|\xi_i\xi_j|\}, 1 \leq i < j \leq n$; therefore, it follows that

$$\mathrm{ZE}(ZM\theta_1) \geq \sqrt{\sum_{i=1}^{n}|\xi_i|^2+n(n-1)GM\{|\xi_i\xi_j|\}}.$$

Now from Theorem 2, we have

$$\text{ZE}(ZM\theta_1) \geq \sqrt{8e^*(\delta_t g_t)^2 + n(n-1)GM\{|\xi_i\xi_j|\}}. \tag{9}$$

Also,

$$\begin{aligned} GM\{|\xi_i\xi_j|\} &= \left(\prod_{1\leq i<j\leq n} |\xi_i\xi_j|\right)^{\frac{2}{n(n-1)}}. \\ &= \left(\prod_{i=1}^{n} |\xi_i|^{n-1}\right)^{\frac{2}{n(n-1)}}. \\ &= \left(\prod_{i=1}^{n} |\xi_i|\right)^{\frac{2}{n}}. \\ &= \left|det(ZM\theta_1)\right|^{\frac{2}{n}}. \end{aligned} \tag{10}$$

Therefore, by substituting (10) in (9), we obtain

$$\text{ZE}(ZM\theta_1) \geq \sqrt{8e^*(\delta_t g_t)^2 + n(n-1)|det(ZM\theta_1)|^{\frac{2}{n}}}.$$

Thus,

$$\begin{aligned} &\sqrt{8e^*(\delta_t g_t)^2 + n(n-1)|det(ZM\theta_1)|^{\frac{2}{n}}} \\ &\leq \text{ZE}(ZM\theta_1) \leq 2\sqrt{2ne^*}(s_t\Delta_t). \end{aligned}$$

Similarly, we have

$$\begin{aligned} &\sqrt{8e^*(\delta_a g_a)^2 + n(n-1)|det(ZM\theta_2)|^{\frac{2}{n}}} \\ &\leq \text{ZE}(ZM\theta_2) \leq 2\sqrt{2ne^*}(s_a\Delta_a). \end{aligned}$$

and

$$\begin{aligned} &\sqrt{8e^*(\delta_f g_f)^2 + n(n-1)|det(ZM\theta_3)|^{\frac{2}{n}}} \\ &\leq \text{ZE}(ZM\theta_3) \leq 2\sqrt{2ne^*}(s_f\Delta_f). \end{aligned}$$

□

Example 4. *Consider the SFG* `W=(P, Q)` *as shown in Figure 3. The value of* `ZE` *from Example 3 is given as* $ZE(ZM\theta_1) = \sum_{i=1}^{n} |\xi_i| = 1.7272$, $ZE(ZM\theta_2) = \sum_{i=1}^{n} |\eta_i| = 1.8054$, *and* $ZE(ZM\theta_3) = \sum_{i=1}^{n} |\zeta_i| = 4.321$. *Now from Theorem 3, the lower bound for* $ZE(ZM\theta_1) = \sqrt{8e^*(\delta_t g_t)^2 + n(n-1)|det(ZM\theta_1)|^{\frac{2}{n}}}$, *and the upper bound for* $ZE(ZM\theta_1) = 2\sqrt{2ne^*}(\Delta_t s_t)$. *Here,* $n = 4$, $e^* = 4$, $\delta_t = 0.2$, $g_t = 0.2$, $det(ZM\theta_1) = 0.0039$, $\Delta_t = 0.6$, *and* $s_t = 0.6$. *Thus, we obtain*

$$\begin{aligned} \textit{Lower bound for } ZE(ZM\theta_1) &= \sqrt{8e^*(\delta_t g_t)^2 + n(n-1)|det(ZM\theta_1)|^{\frac{2}{n}}} \\ &= \sqrt{8*4(0.2*0.2)^2 + 4(3)(0.0039)^{\frac{2}{4}}} = 0.8947624. \\ \textit{Upper bound for } ZE(ZM\theta_1) &= 2\sqrt{2ne^*}(\Delta_t s_t) \\ &= 2\sqrt{2*4*4}(0.6*0.6) = 4.07293506. \end{aligned}$$

Thus,

$$0.8947624 < ZE(ZM\theta_1) = 1.7272 < 4.07293506.$$

Similarly, we compute that

$$1.08168299 < ZE(ZM\theta_2) = 1.8054 < 3.3941125,$$

and

$$2.6305235 < ZE(ZM\theta_3) = 4.321 < 11.87939392.$$

This shows that the values of spherical Zagreb fuzzy energies lie within the bounds given in Theorem 3.

Remark 2. *In particular, if we take a SFG such that the membership values of the vertices are constant, the spherical fuzzy degree of each vertex is also the same. Then, the bounds given in Theorem 3 seem to be sharp.*

Remark 2 can be explained with the following example:

Example 5. *Let D be a SFG as depicted in Figure 4. Since,* $ZE(ZM\theta_1) = \sum_{i=1}^{n} |\xi_i| = 0.3200$, $ZE(ZM\theta_2) = \sum_{i=1}^{n} |\eta_i| = 0.9600$, *and* $ZE(ZM\theta_3) = \sum_{i=1}^{n} |\zeta_i| = 3.200$. *Now from Theorem 3, Lower bound for* $ZE(ZM\theta_1) = \sqrt{8e^*(\delta_t g_t)^2 + n(n-1)|det(ZM\theta_1)|^{\frac{2}{n}}}$, *Upper bound for* $ZE(ZM\theta_1)$ $= 2\sqrt{2ne^*}(\Delta_t s_t)$. *Here,* $n = 4$, $e^* = 3$, $\delta_t = 0.2$, $g_t = 0.2$, $det(ZM\theta_1) = 0.0010$, $\Delta_t = 0.2$, *and* $s_t = 0.2$. *Thus, we obtain*

$$\begin{aligned} \textit{Lower bound for } ZE(ZM\theta_1) &= \sqrt{8e^*(\delta_t g_t)^2 + n(n-1)|det(ZM\theta_1)|^{\frac{2}{n}}} \\ \sqrt{8 * 3(0.2 * 0.2)^2 + 3(2)(0.0010)^{\frac{2}{3}}} &= 0.3181. \\ \textit{Upper bound for } ZE(ZM\theta_1) &= 2\sqrt{2ne^*}(\Delta_t s_t) \\ 2\sqrt{2 * 3 * 3}(0.2 * 0.2) &= 0.33941. \end{aligned}$$

Thus,

$$0.3181 < ZE(ZM\theta_1) = 0.3200 < 0.33941.$$

Similarly, we compute that

$$0.9459 < ZE(ZM\theta_2) = 0.9600 < 1.0182,$$

and

$$3.1519 < ZE(ZM\theta_3) = 3.200 < 3.3941.$$

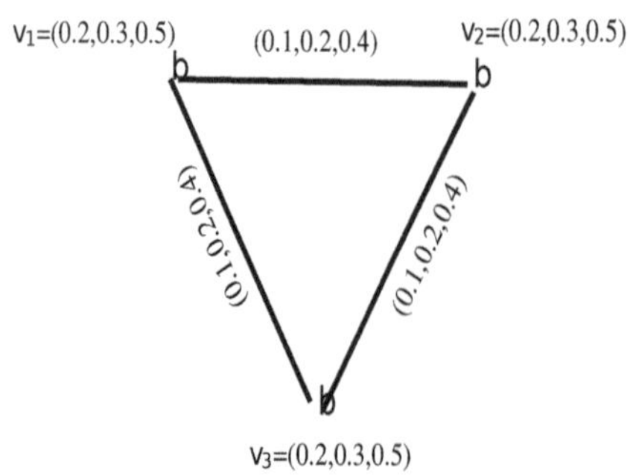

Figure 4. The SFG *D*.

Lemma 1. *If $G = (R, S)$ is a SFG with $\mathtt{SZM}(G) = (ZM\theta_1, ZM\theta_2, ZM\theta_3)$ is its corresponding $\mathtt{SZM}$ such that ξ_1 is the maximum eigenvalue of $ZM\theta_1$, η_1 is the maximum eigenvalue of $ZM\theta_2$, and ζ_1 is the maximum eigenvalue of $ZM\theta_3$, then*

$$\xi_1 \leq 2s_t\Delta_t\Delta^*, \eta_1 \leq 2s_a\Delta_a\Delta^*, \zeta_1 \leq 2s_f\Delta_f\Delta^*,$$

where Δ^* is a maximum crisp degree.

Proof. Given that ξ_1 is the maximum eigenvalue, let T be the eigenvector that corresponds to ξ_1. Then, vividly,

$$\xi_1 T = ZM\theta_1 T.$$

If the vector T has maximum entry $t_0 \geq 0$ corresponding to the vertex v_0 and $[ZM\theta_1]$ has corresponding row $[ZM\theta_1]_{v_0}$, then we obtain

$$\xi_1 t_0 = [ZM\theta_1]_{v_0} v_0 \leq \left(\sum_{v_0 v_j \in \check{E}(G)} \check{\alpha}y(v_0)d_t(v_0) + \check{\alpha}y(v_0)d_t(v_j) \right) t_0$$

By using the same arguments, as we prove (2) in Theorem 2, we have

$$\xi_1 t_0 \leq 2s_t\Delta_t\Delta^* t_0.$$

Hence,

$$\xi_1 \leq 2s_t\Delta_t\Delta^*. \tag{11}$$

Similarly, for $ZM\theta_2$ and $ZM\theta_3$, we have

$$\begin{aligned} \eta_1 &\leq 2s_a\Delta_a\Delta^*, \\ \zeta_1 &\leq 2s_f\Delta_f\Delta^*. \end{aligned}$$

□

Theorem 4. *For a SFG $G = (R, S)$ with n vertices and*

$$\mathtt{SZM}(G) = (ZM\theta_1, ZM\theta_2, ZM\theta_3),$$

$$ZE(ZM\theta_1) \leq 2s_t\Delta_t\Delta^* + \sqrt{(n-1)\{8e^*(\Delta_t s_t)^2 - \left(\frac{2g_t\delta_t e^*}{n}\right)^2\}}.$$

Similarly,

$$ZE(ZM\theta_2) \leq 2s_a\Delta_a\Delta^* + \sqrt{(n-1)\{8e^*(\Delta_a s_a)^2 - \left(\frac{2g_a\delta_a e^*}{n}\right)^2\}},$$

$$ZE(ZM\theta_3) \leq 2s_f\Delta_f\Delta^* + \sqrt{(n-1)\{8e^*(\Delta_f s_f)^2 - \left(\frac{2g_f\delta_f e^*}{n}\right)^2\}}.$$

Proof. Since $ZM\theta_1$, $ZM\theta_2$ and $ZM\theta_3$ are symmetric matrices with zero trace, so we have

$$\xi_{max} \geq \frac{2\sum_{1\leq i\leq j\leq n}[ZM\theta_1]_{ij}}{n}, \eta_{max} \geq \frac{2\sum_{1\leq i\leq j\leq n}[ZM\theta_2]_{ij}}{n}, \zeta_{max} \geq \frac{2\sum_{1\leq i\leq j\leq n}[ZM\theta_3]_{ij}}{n}$$

where ξ_{max}, η_{max} and ζ_{max} are the greatest eigenvalues of $ZM\theta_1$, $ZM\theta_2$, and $ZM\theta_3$, respectively. Let ξ_{max} be the maximum eigenvalue of the matrix $ZM\theta_1$ and by using Definition 7, we can write

$$\xi_{max} \geq \frac{2\sum_{v_i v_j \in E(G)}[\check{\alpha}y(v_i)d_t(v_i) + \check{\alpha}y(v_j)d_t(v_j)]}{n}$$

By using Definition 5 , we can write

$$\geq \frac{2(SFM_1(G))_t}{n}$$

Using Theorem 1,

$$\begin{aligned} \xi_{max} &\geq \frac{2(2g_t\delta_t e_t^*)}{n}. \\ \xi_{max} &\geq \frac{4g_t\delta_t e_t^*}{n}. \end{aligned} \tag{12}$$

Moreover, from Theorem 2, we have $\xi_1 = \xi_{max}$ such that

$$\sum_{i=1}^{n} \xi_i^2 \leq 8e^*(\Delta_t s_t)^2.$$

$$\sum_{i=2}^{n} \xi_i^2 \leq 8e^*(\Delta_t s_t)^2 - \xi_{max}^2. \tag{13}$$

By using (3), we can write

$$\begin{aligned} \mathrm{ZE}(ZM\theta_1) &= \sum_{i=1}^{n} |\xi_i|. \\ &= \sum_{i=2}^{n} |\xi_i| - \xi_{max}. \end{aligned}$$

It implies that

$$\mathrm{ZE}(ZM\theta_1) - \xi_{max} = \sum_{i=2}^{n} |\xi_i|. \tag{14}$$

By considering two sequences $(1, 1, 1, \cdots, 1)$ and $(|\xi_1|, |\xi_2|, \cdots, |\xi_n|)$ and then applying the Cauchy–Schwarz inequality with $n-1$ entries, we have

$$\sum_{i=2}^{n} |\xi_i| \leq \sqrt{(n-1)\sum_{i=2}^{n} |\xi_i|^2}. \tag{15}$$

From (14) and (15), we have

$$\mathrm{ZE}(ZM\theta_1) - \xi_{max} \leq \sqrt{(n-1)\sum_{i=2}^{n} |\xi_i|^2}. \tag{16}$$

By substituting (13) in (16), we attain

$$\mathrm{ZE}(ZM\theta_1) - \xi_{max} \leq \sqrt{(n-1)(8e^*(\Delta_t s_t)^2 - \xi_{max}^2)}.$$

$$\mathrm{ZE}(ZM\theta_1) \leq \xi_{max} + \sqrt{(n-1)(8e^*(\Delta_t s_t)^2 - \xi_{max}^2)}. \tag{17}$$

Using Lemma 1, $\xi_1 = \xi_{max} \leq 2s_t\Delta_t\Delta^*$ and from (12), $-\xi_{max} \leq -\frac{4g_t\delta_t e_t^*}{n}$. Hence,

$$\mathrm{ZE}(ZM\theta_1) \leq 2s_t\Delta_t\Delta^* + \sqrt{(n-1)\{8e^*(\Delta_t s_t)^2 - \left(\frac{2g_t\delta_t e^*}{n}\right)^2\}}.$$

Similarly,

$$\text{ZE}(ZM\theta_2) \leq 2s_a\Delta_a\Delta^* + \sqrt{(n-1)\{8e^*(\Delta_a s_a)^2 - \left(\frac{2g_a\delta_a e^*}{n}\right)^2\}}.$$

$$\text{ZE}(ZM\theta_3) \leq 2s_f\Delta_f\Delta^* + \sqrt{(n-1)\{8e^*(\Delta_f s_f)^2 - \left(\frac{2g_f\delta_f e^*}{n}\right)^2\}}.$$

□

The above Theorem 4 can be explained by the following example:

Example 6. *Consider the SFG* W=(P, Q) *as shown in Figure 3. The value of* ZE *from Example 3 is given as* $ZE(ZM\theta_1) = \sum_{i=1}^{n}|\xi_i| = 1.7272$, $ZE(ZM\theta_2) = \sum_{i=1}^{n}|\eta_i| = 1.8054$, *and* $ZE(ZM\theta_3) = \sum_{i=1}^{n}|\zeta_i| = 4.321$. *Now from Theorem 4, the upper bound for* $ZE(ZM\theta_1)$ $2s_t\Delta_t\Delta^* + \sqrt{(n-1)\{8e^*(\Delta_t s_t)^2 - \left(\frac{2g_t\delta_t e^*}{n}\right)^2\}}$. *Here,* $n = 4$, $e^* = 4$, $\delta_t = 0.2$, $g_t = 0.2$, $\Delta_t = 0.6$, $\Delta^* = 3$ *and* $s_t = 0.6$. *Thus upper bound for* $texttt ZE(ZM\theta_1)$ *is 2.97. Similarly, we compute the upper bounds for* $ZE(ZM\theta_2)$ *as 5.53 and for* $ZE(ZM\theta_3)$ *as 14.37. Thus,*

$$ZE(ZM\theta_1) = 1.7272 < 2.97,$$

$$1.08168299 < ZE(ZM\theta_2) = 1.8054 < 5.53,$$

and

$$2.6305235 < ZE(ZM\theta_3) = 4.321 < 14.37.$$

This shows that the values of the spherical Zagreb fuzzy energies lie within the bounds given in Theorem 4.

Remark 3. *It is observed from Examples 4 and 6 that the upper bound of* $ZE(ZM\theta_1)$ *obtained from Theorem 4 is closer to the exact value than the upper bound obtained from Theorem 1, whereas the upper bounds of* $ZE(ZM\theta_2)$ *and* $ZE(ZM\theta_3)$ *given in Theorem 1 are closer to the exact value as compared to the upper bounds obtained in Theorem 4. This indicates that together with both bounds obtained from Theorems 1 and 4, we can better estimate the exact value of the spherical Zagreb fuzzy energies of SFG.*

5. Application

In this section, we present an application related to the selection of the best location to start a new business to describe the suitability of $SFGs$. Further, we illustrate a comparative analysis with the existing technique.

5.1. Selection of Best Location for Business Purpose

Business depends on profitability and loss; thus, it has a ratio of success or failure with the wide range of variations. Usually, the term business is figured out as a 'company', but it has broad meanings. Business is not just the ownership of a multinational company; the work of a street peddler is a business too. Some of the factors which enhance the profitability of business include high skills of management, mental peace, a broad mental vision , teamwork, patience, and good work performance. But one of the most important factors is location to upgrade the level of business. Since the growth of a business is not certain, a businessman should be mentally ready to accept the decline of a business at any stage of its life. But, if proper consultation is given by an expert, then a business can achieve success at a large scale.

Therefore, we consider five different locations L_i, $(i = 1,2,3,4,5)$ for a new business and taking a panel of four experts U_j, $(j = 1,2,3,4)$ from real estate, finance, law and business communities to decide the most preferable location for the required purpose. The following are the some factors that affect the location.

1. Proximity to target customers.
2. Competitors' locations.
3. Taxes (utilities and other costs).
4. Government laws and policies.
5. Infrastructure and accessibility.
6. Safety.
7. Parking facility.

Each consultant makes distinct judgments based on their experiences between the two different locations. Their opinions depend on three factors, including neutral, appropriate and inappropriate.

An Algorithm 1 to describe our proposed technique is given below:

Algorithm 1: Algorithm to find the best place for business purpose.

INPUT: A discrete set of locations $L = \{\check{l}_1, \check{l}_2, \check{l}_3, \check{l}_4, \check{l}_5\}$, a set of decision-makers $U = \{u_1, u_2, u_3, u_4\}$ in order to attain the goal and fashioning of spherical fuzzy preference relations (SFPRs) $\mathtt{M}_{\check{a}}$, $\check{a} = (1, 2, 3, 4)$ for each consultant.

OUTPUT: The nomination of best location for business.

1. Consider four SFGs corresponding to four spherical fuzzy preference relations. Make spherical fuzzy Zagreb matrices $(\mathtt{SZM})_i$ $(i = 1, 2, 3, 4)$ as defined in Definition 7 corresponding to the given SFGs.
2. Calculate the SZE of all $(\mathtt{SZM})_i$, (i=1, 2, 3, 4) denoted as

$$\mathtt{SZE}(G) = \Big(ZE(ZM\theta_1),\ ZE(ZM\theta_2),\ ZE(ZM\theta_3)\Big).$$

which can be calculated by adding the absolute values of eigenvalues of matrices, i.e.,

$$= \Big(\sum_{i=1}^{n} |\xi_i|, \sum_{i=1}^{n} |\eta_i|, \sum_{i=1}^{n} |\zeta_i|\Big),$$

where $\xi_1 \geq \xi_2 \geq \cdots \geq \xi_n$, $\eta_1 \geq \eta_2 \geq \cdots \geq \eta_n$, and $\zeta_1 \geq \zeta_2 \geq \cdots \geq \zeta_n$ are the eigenvalues of $ZM\theta_1$, $ZM\theta_2$, and $ZM\theta_3$, respectively.
3. Determine the weight vector by using:

$$w_i = ((w_\alpha)_i, (w_\beta)_i, (w_\gamma)_i).$$

$$= \left(\frac{\mathtt{ZE}((\mathtt{SZM})_{\check{\alpha}})_i}{\sum_{j=1}^{4} \mathtt{ZE}((\mathtt{SZM})_{\check{\alpha}})_j}, \frac{\mathtt{ZE}((\mathtt{SZM})_{\check{\beta}})_i}{\sum_{j=1}^{4} \mathtt{ZE}((\mathtt{SZM})_{\check{\beta}})_j}, \frac{\mathtt{ZE}((\mathtt{SZM})_{\check{\gamma}})_i}{\sum_{j=1}^{4} \mathtt{ZE}((\mathtt{SZM})_{\check{\gamma}})_j}\right). \quad (18)$$

4. Now to aggregate the spherical Zagreb preference matrices obtained in step 2, we have to apply one of the suitable aggregation operators to merge the multi-agent information. For this purpose, we apply a well- known simple ordered averaging operator (OWA) [46] given as $\mathtt{SZM} = \sum_{i=1}^{4}(w_i)((\mathtt{SZM})_i)$, where w_i are given from (18) obtained in step 4 to form the combined spherical fuzzy Zagreb preference relation $(SFZPR)$ by aggregating the matrices $(SFZPRs)$ obtained in step 2.
5. Plot an impact model related to collective SFZPR.
6. Plot the partial impact model associated with collective SFZPR using constraint $\alpha_{ij} \geq 0.5$. Determine the degrees of all vertices (alternatives) that appear in the model of SFZPR.
7. All the alternatives are ranked according to the truthiness degree of vertices.
8. *Output*: The best alternative is nominated based on the largest truthiness degree of the vertex.

The flowchart corresponding to the proposed technique is exhibited in Figure 5:

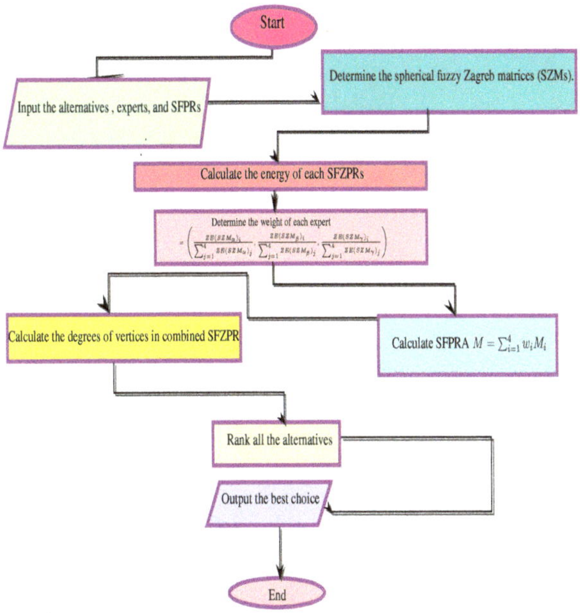

Figure 5. Flowchart for algorithm.

The spherical fuzzy preference relations ($SFPRs$) $M_{\breve{a}}$, $\breve{a} = (1,2,3,4)$ are given in Tables 4–7:

Table 4. SFPRs of the first decision-making expert.

M_1	$\breve{l}_1$	$\breve{l}_2$	$\breve{l}_3$	$\breve{l}_4$	$\breve{l}_5$
$\breve{l}_1$	(0.3, 0.6, 0.5)	(0.1, 0.3, 0.6)	(0.3, 0.1, 0.5)	(0.3, 0.1, 0.3)	(0.3, 0.2, 0.4)
$\breve{l}_2$	(0.1, 0.3, 0.6)	(0.2, 0.4, 0.7)	(0.1, 0.1, 0.5)	(0.2, 0.1, 0.6)	(0.1, 0.2, 0.5)
$\breve{l}_3$	(0.3, 0.1, 0.5)	(0.1, 0.1, 0.5)	(0.3, 0.1, 0.6)	(0.2, 0.1, 0.5)	(0.3, 0.1, 0.5)
$\breve{l}_4$	(0.3, 0.1, 0.3)	(0.2, 0.1, 0.6)	(0.2, 0.1, 0.5)	(0.4, 0.2, 0.4)	(0.3, 0.1, 0.4)
$\breve{l}_5$	(0.3, 0.2, 0.4)	(0.1, 0.2, 0.5)	(0.3, 0.1, 0.5)	(0.3, 0.1, 0.4)	(0.5, 0.2, 0.3)

Table 5. SFPRs of the second decision-making expert.

M_2	$\breve{l}_1$	$\breve{l}_2$	$\breve{l}_3$	$\breve{l}_4$	$\breve{l}_5$
$\breve{l}_1$	(0.3, 0.2, 0.5)	(0.2, 0.1, 0.6)	(0.2, 0.1, 0.4)	(0.2, 0.1, 0.4)	(0.1, 0.1, 0.4)
$\breve{l}_2$	(0.2, 0.1, 0.6)	(0.4, 0.3, 0.7)	(0.4, 0.2, 0.6)	(0.3, 0.2, 0.6)	(0.1, 0.2, 0.5)
$\breve{l}_3$	(0.2, 0.1, 0.4)	(0.4, 0.2, 0.6)	(0.5, 0.6, 0.2)	(0.3, 0.4, 0.3)	(0.1, 0.3, 0.5)
$\breve{l}_4$	(0.2, 0.1, 0.4)	(0.3, 0.2, 0.6)	(0.3, 0.4, 0.3)	(0.4, 0.5, 0.3)	(0.1, 0.3, 0.4)
$\breve{l}_5$	(0.1, 0.1, 0.4)	(0.1, 0.2, 0.5)	(0.1, 0.3, 0.5)	(0.1, 0.3, 0.4)	(0.1, 0.4, 0.6)

Table 6. SFPRs of the third decision-making expert.

M_3	$\breve{l}_1$	$\breve{l}_2$	$\breve{l}_3$	$\breve{l}_4$	$\breve{l}_5$
$\breve{l}_1$	(0.8, 0.4, 0.3)	(0.3, 0.3, 0.4)	(0.1, 0.2, 0.3)	(0.3, 0.2, 0.3)	(0.2, 0.3, 0.4)
$\breve{l}_2$	(0.3, 0.3, 0.4)	(0.4, 0.3, 0.5)	(0.1, 0.2, 0.4)	(0.2, 0.1, 0.4)	(0.1, 0.2, 0.4)
$\breve{l}_3$	(0.1, 0.2, 0.3)	(0.1, 0.2, 0.4)	(0.2, 0.5, 0.6)	(0.2, 0.2, 0.5)	(0.1, 0.2, 0.5)
$\breve{l}_4$	(0.3, 0.2, 0.3)	(0.2, 0.1, 0.4)	(0.2, 0.2, 0.5)	(0.7, 0.3, 0.1)	(0.1, 0.2, 0.3)
$\breve{l}_5$	(0.2, 0.3, 0.4)	(0.1, 0.2, 0.4)	(0.1, 0.2, 0.5)	(0.1, 0.2, 0.3)	(0.2, 0.3, 0.4)

Table 7. SFPRs of the fourth decision-making expert.

$\mathtt{M}_4$	$\check{l}_1$	$\check{l}_2$	$\check{l}_3$	$\check{l}_4$	$\check{l}_5$
$\check{l}_1$	(0.2, 0.7, 0.5)	(0.3, 0.2, 0.4)	(0.1, 0.2, 0.4)	(0.1, 0.3, 0.4)	(0.1, 0.4, 0.6)
$\check{l}_2$	(0.3, 0.2, 0.4)	(0.4, 0.3, 0.1)	(0.2, 0.1, 0.2)	(0.2, 0.3, 0.5)	(0.1, 0.2, 0.6)
$\check{l}_3$	(0.1, 0.2, 0.4)	(0.2, 0.1, 0.2)	(0.5, 0.3, 0.2)	(0.2, 0.3, 0.4)	(0.1, 0.2, 0.6)
$\check{l}_4$	(0.1, 0.3, 0.4)	(0.2, 0.3, 0.5)	(0.2, 0.3, 0.4)	(0.3, 0.4, 0.6)	(0.2, 0.3, 0.5)
$\check{l}_5$	(0.1, 0.4, 0.6)	(0.1, 0.2, 0.6)	(0.1, 0.2, 0.6)	(0.2, 0.3, 0.5)	(0.2, 0.5, 0.7)

The spherical fuzzy graphs $(SFG)_j, j = (1,2,3,4)$ based on spherical fuzzy preference relations $(SFPRs)$ $\mathtt{M}_{\check{a}}$, $\check{a} = (1,2,3,4)$ are constructed by taking each expert's preference between two distinct alternatives as the membership values of the edges, including degree of truthiness, degree of abstinence, and degree of falseness. These spherical fuzzy graphs $(SFG)_j, j = (1,2,3,4)$ are depicted in Figures 6 and 7.

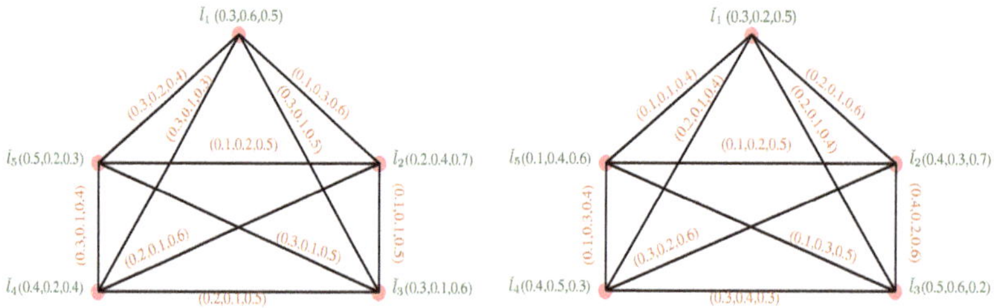

Figure 6. The graphical representations of $\mathtt{M}_{\check{1}}$ and $\mathtt{M}_{\check{2}}$.

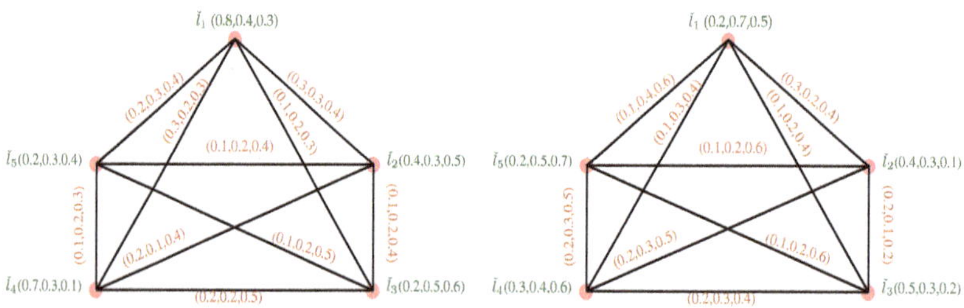

Figure 7. The graphical representations of $\mathtt{M}_{\check{3}}$ and $\mathtt{M}_{\check{4}}$.

Now, we form the spherical fuzzy Zagreb matrices $(\mathtt{SZM})_i$, $i = (1,2,3,4)$ of each $SFGs$. These matrices are based on the degree to which the vertices will give the effect of connectivity in the neighborhood. The $(\mathtt{SZM})_i, i = (1,2,3,4)$ of each $SFGs$ is given below:

$$(\mathtt{SZM})_1 = \begin{bmatrix} (0,0,0) & (0.4,0.7,2.44) & (0.57,0.46,2.1) & (0.7,0.5,1.62) & (0.8,0.54,1.44) \\ (0.4,0.7,2.44) & (0,0,0) & (0.37,0.32,2.74) & (0.5,0.36,2.26) & (0.6,0.4,2.08) \\ (0.57,0.46,2.1) & (0.37,0.32,2.74) & (0,0,0) & (0.67,0.12,1.92) & (0.77,0.16,1.74) \\ (0.7,0.5,1.62) & (0.5,0.36,2.26) & (0.67,0.12,1.92) & (0,0,0) & (0.9,0.2,1.26) \\ (0.8,0.54,1.44) & (0.6,0.4,2.08) & (0.77,0.16,1.74) & (0.9,0.2,1.26) & (0,0,0) \end{bmatrix}.$$

$$(\mathtt{SZM})_2 = \begin{bmatrix} (0,0,0) & (0.61,0.29,2.51) & (0.71,0.68,1.26) & (0.57,0.58,1.41) & (0.25,0.44,1.98) \\ (0.61,0.29,2.51) & (0,0,0) & (0.9,0.81,1.97) & (0.76,0.71,2.12) & (0.44,0.57,2.69) \\ (0.71,0.68,1.26) & (0.9,0.81,1.97) & (0,0,0) & (0.86,1.1,0.87) & (0.54,0.96,1.44) \\ (0.57,0.58,1.41) & (0.76,0.71,2.12) & (0.86,1.1,0.87) & (0,0,0) & (0.4,0.86,1.59) \\ (0.25,0.44,1.98) & (0.44,0.57,2.69) & (0.54,0.96,1.44) & (0.4,0.86,1.59) & (0,0,0) \end{bmatrix}.$$

$$(\mathtt{SZM})_3 = \begin{bmatrix} (0,0,0) & (1,0.64,1.22) & (0.82,0.8,1.44) & (1.28,0.61,0.57) & (0.82,0.67,1.06) \\ (1,0.64,1.22) & (0,0,0) & (0.38,0.64,1.82) & (0.84,0.45,0.95) & (0.38,0.51,1.44) \\ (0.82,0.8,1.44) & (0.38,0.64,1.82) & (0,0,0) & (0.66,0.61,1.17) & (0.2,0.67,1.66) \\ (1.28,0.61,0.57) & (0.84,0.45,0.95) & (0.66,0.61,1.17) & (0,0,0) & (0.66,0.48,0.79) \\ (0.82,0.67,1.06) & (0.38,0.51,1.44) & (0.2,0.67,1.66) & (0.66,0.48,0.79) & (0,0,0) \end{bmatrix}.$$

$$(\mathtt{SZM})_4 = \begin{bmatrix} (0,0,0) & (0.44,1.01,1.07) & (0.42,1.01,1.22) & (0.33,1.25,1.98) & (0.22,1.32,2.51) \\ (0.44,1.01,1.07) & (0,0,0) & (0.62,0.48,0.49) & (0.53,0.72,1.25) & (0.42,0.79,1.78) \\ (0.42,1.01,1.22) & (0.62,0.48,0.49) & (0,0,0) & (0.51,0.72,1.4) & (0.4,0.79,1.93) \\ (0.33,1.25,1.98) & (0.53,0.72,1.25) & (0.51,0.72,1.4) & (0,0,0) & (0.31,1.03,2.69) \\ (0.22,1.32,2.51) & (0.42,0.79,1.78) & (0.4,0.79,1.93) & (0.31,1.03,2.69) & (0,0,0) \end{bmatrix}.$$

The spherical fuzzy Zagreb relations related to $(\mathtt{SZM})_i^{\prime}s$, where i=(1, 2, 3, 4) are shown graphically in Figures 8 and 9. These figures elaborate on the concept of the connectedness of the edges. These graphs corresponding to spherical fuzzy Zagreb relations are more strengthened than the SFGs represented in Figures 6 and 7.

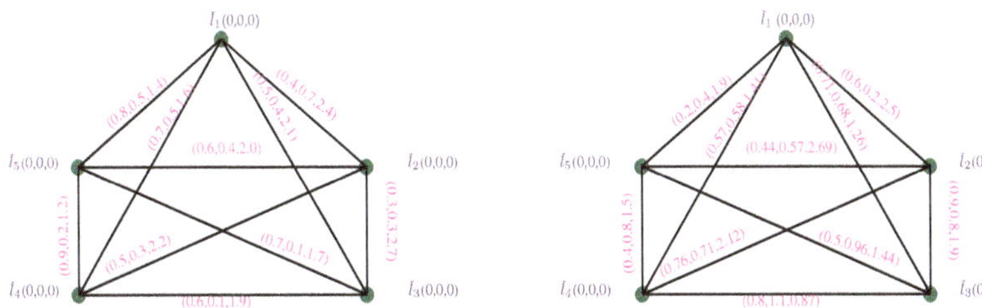

Figure 8. The graphical representation of spherical fuzzy Zagreb relations to $(\mathtt{SZM})_1$, $(\mathtt{SZM})_2$.

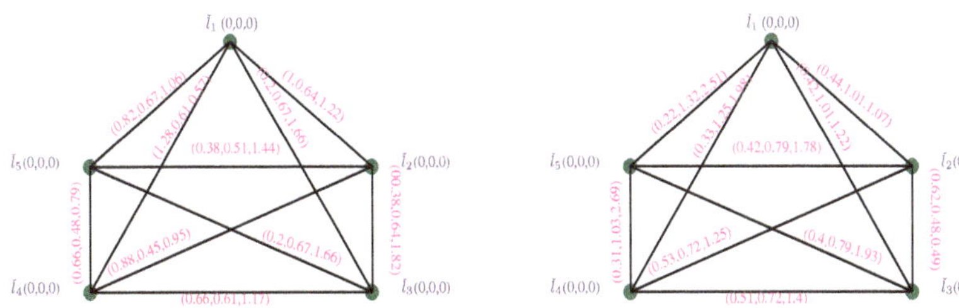

Figure 9. The graphical representation of spherical fuzzy Zagreb relations to $(\mathtt{SZM})_3$ and $(\mathtt{SZM})_4$.

The spherical fuzzy Zagreb energy of each SZMs is calculated as

$$\mathtt{ZE}((\mathtt{SZM})_1) = (5.1283, 3.179, 15.9035).$$

$$\mathtt{ZE}((\mathtt{SZM})_2) = (4.9912, 5.7813, 14.6477).$$

$$\mathtt{ZE}((\mathtt{SZM})_3) = (5.9254, 4.9018, 9.9656).$$

$$\mathtt{ZE}((\mathtt{SZM})_4) = (3.4282, 7.4492, 13.6328).$$

The weight of each expert is computed as

$$w_i = ((w_{\breve{\alpha}})_i, (w_{\breve{\beta}})_i, (w_{\breve{\gamma}})_i).$$

$$w_j = \left(\frac{\mathtt{ZE}((\mathtt{SZM})_{\breve{\alpha}})_j}{\sum_{s=1}^{4} \mathtt{ZE}((\mathtt{SZM})_{\breve{\alpha}})_s}, \frac{\mathtt{ZE}((\mathtt{SZM})_{\breve{\beta}})_j}{\sum_{s=1}^{4} \mathtt{ZE}((\mathtt{SZM})_{\breve{\beta}})_s}, \frac{\mathtt{ZE}((\mathtt{SZM})_{\breve{\gamma}})_j}{\sum_{s=1}^{4} \mathtt{ZE}((\mathtt{SZM})_{\breve{\gamma}})_s} \right).$$

$$w_1 = (0.2633530357, 0.1491696896, 0.2936956434).$$

$$w_2 = (0.2563125542, 0.2712786174, 0.2705043066).$$

$$w_3 = (0.3042864259, 0.2300094316, 0.1840382939).$$

$$w_4 = (0.1760479841, 0.3495422616, 0.2517617859).$$

From the aggregation of four SFZPRs, the collective spherical fuzzy Zagreb preference relation (SFZPR) is calculated as

$$\mathtt{SZM} = \sum_{i=1}^{4} w_i(\mathtt{SZM})_i.$$

$$\mathtt{SZM} = \begin{bmatrix} (0,0,0) & (0.643,0.683,1.88) & (0.655,0.790,1.52) & (0.777,0.808,1.460) & (0.562,0.815,1.192) \\ (0.643,0.683,1.889) & (0,0,0) & (0.55,0.582,1.795) & (0.675,0.601,1.726) & (0.460,0.607,2.051) \\ (0.655,0.790,1.529) & (0.552,0.582,1.795) & (0,0,0) & (0.687,0.708,1.366) & (0.472,0.714,1.691) \\ (0.778,0.809,1.460) & (0.675,0.601,1.72) & (0.687,0.708,1.367) & (0,0,0) & (0.594,0.733,1.622) \\ (0.562,0.815,1.785) & (0.460,0.607,2.051) & (0.472,0.714,1.691) & (0.594,0.733,1.622) & (0,0,0) \end{bmatrix}.$$

The collective SFZPR is shown in Figure 10. In the representation of this collective SFZPR, as exhibited in Figure 10, we choose spherical fuzzy membership, whose truthiness degrees are $\breve{\alpha}_{ij} \geq 0.5$ $(i, j = 1, 2, 3, 4)$. The obtained partial model is depicted in Figure 11.

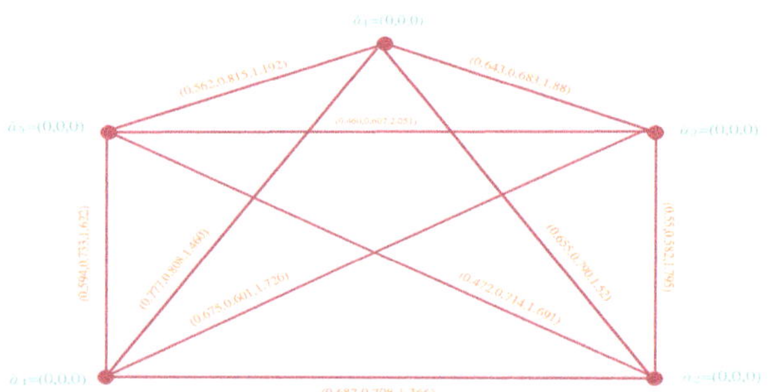

Figure 10. Model of the combined SFZPR.

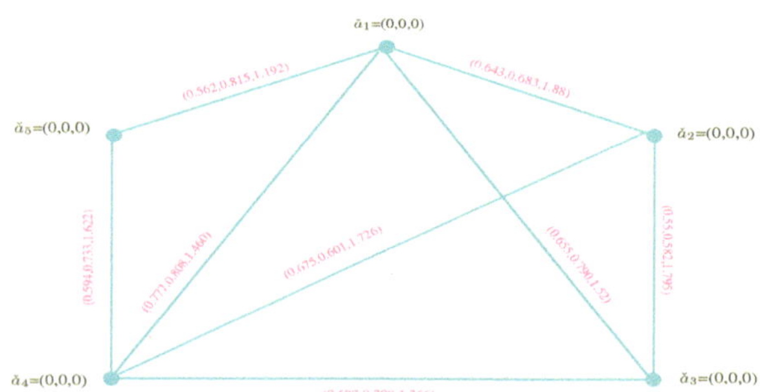

Figure 11. Partial model of the combined SFZPR.

We calculate the degrees $deg(\check{l}_i)$ $(i = 1, 2, 3, 4, 5)$ in a partial directed model as follows: $deg(\check{l}_1) = (2.637, 3.096, 6.052)$, $deg(\check{l}_2) = (2.328, 2.473, 7.452)$, $deg(\check{l}_3) = (2.364, 2.794, 6.372)$, $deg(\check{l}_4) = (2.733, 2.85, 6.174)$, and $deg(\check{l}_5) = (2.088, 2.869, 6.556)$.

Since $\breve{\alpha}_4$ has the largest degree, we have the positioning of the alternatives $\check{l}_i$ $(i = 1, 2, 3, 4, 5)$ as

$$\check{l}_4 \succ \check{l}_1 \succ \check{l}_3 \succ \check{l}_2 \succ \check{l}_5.$$

Thus, the best choice for selecting location is $\breve{\alpha}_4$.

5.2. Comparative Analysis

The comparative inspection with previously existing procedures is needed to examine the feasibility and validity of the proposed technique. By comparative analysis, it can be seen that one adopts whatever techniques and methods are either more accurate to one another or whose results should be the same.Here, we compare our proposed model to the already existing one. In the existing technique, which was proposed in [44], the directed spherical fuzzy graphs with their corresponding adjacency matrices are considered. The spherical fuzzy energy of all adjacency matrices is calculated by adding the absolute value of their eigenvalues. The average operator is applied to aggregate the obtained results. In that technique, the ranking of alternatives is based on the out-degree, which is greater than 0.5 in the partial model of SFGs. In our proposed model, we consider Zagreb spherical fuzzy matrices as compared to the adjacency matrices of SFGs, which give us a more reliable and feasible solution since, in our proposed technique, the concept of the degree of vertices is involved, which encounters the connectivity of the neighborhoods of the vertices. The consequences related to the methodologies are summarized in Tables 8 and 9.

Table 8. Comparison of degrees of the alternatives with existing techniques.

Techniques	Degrees of the Alternatives
Existing technique with adjacency matrices [44]	(0.78, 0.82, 1.69), (0.79, 0.85, 1.85), (0.76, 0.76, 1.7), (0.84, 0.85, 1.70), (0.58, 0.89, 1.88).
Our offered technique with SZMs	(2.63, 3.09, 6.05), (2.32, 2.47, 7.45), (2.36, 2.79, 6.37), (2.73, 2.85, 6.17), (2.08, 2.86, 6.55)

Table 9. Comparison of ranking.

Techniques	Ranking of the Alternatives
Existing technique with adjacency matrices [44]	$\check{\alpha}_4 \succ \check{\alpha}_2 \succ \check{\alpha}_1 \succ \check{\alpha}_3 \succ \check{\alpha}_5$.
Our offered technique with SZMs	$\check{\alpha}_4 \succ \check{\alpha}_1 \succ \check{\alpha}_3 \succ \check{\alpha}_2 \succ \check{\alpha}_5$.

Eventually, the result for the positioning of the options of the existing strategy is similar to the presented technique, which shows the accuracy and viability of the proposed procedure. Clearly, the technique introduced in this paper is more exact, adaptable, and generalized.

The comparison between the proposed and existing techniques, via finding the energy and Zagreb energy of adjacency matrices and SFGs, respectively, is graphically displayed in Figure 12 .

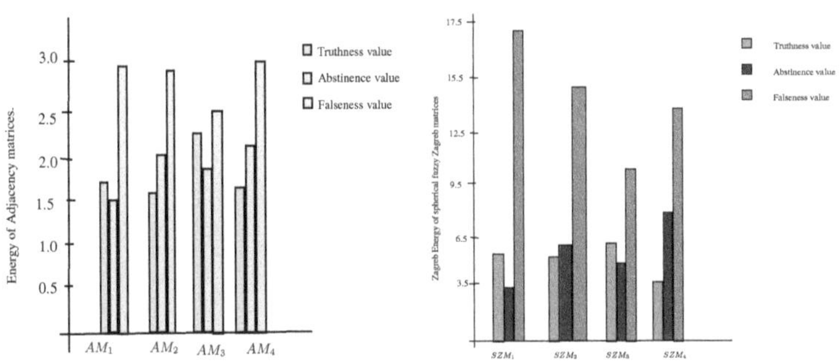

Figure 12. Comparison between energy of AMs and Zagreb energy of SZMs.

6. Conclusions

Spherical fuzzy sets are the generalization of picture fuzzy sets, as they enlarge the space of membership degrees of truthiness, abstinence, and falseness in the unit interval satisfying the condition $0 \leq \check{\alpha}^2 + \check{\beta}^2 + \check{\gamma}^2 \leq 1$. Spherical fuzzy models can handle uncertainty problems more efficiently when a person has different viewpoints like yes, abstain, no, and refusal as compared to the fuzzy set, intuitionistic fuzzy set, Pythagorean fuzzy set, and picture fuzzy set. Topological indices play a crucial role in fuzzy graph theory. One of the important indices are the fuzzy Zagreb index, which includes the fuzzy first, second, and hyper Zagreb index. The Zagreb index is the degree-based index, which encounters the strength of vertices as well as the strength of the fuzzy graph too.

In this research article, we discussed spherical fuzzy Zagreb indices and determined some bounds. Further, we studied how the spherical fuzzy Zagreb matrix of SFG is defined. The concept of the spectrum of SFG was introduced. In addition, we computed the spherical fuzzy Zagreb energy of the spherical fuzzy graph. Further, we extracted some bounds of spherical fuzzy Zagreb energy. Finally, we presented an application to ensure the applicability of our proposed model. In future, our goal is to extend the notion of this work to the following:

1. Hesitant SFGs.
2. SF hypergraphs.
3. Interval-valued SFGs.
4. Single-valued SFGs.
5. Complex spherical fuzzy Hamacher aggregation operators.

Author Contributions: Conceptualization, G.F.; methodology, G.F., L.A. and S.I.; formal analysis, G.F., U.A., L.A. and S.I.; investigation, U.A. and S.I.; writing—review and editing, U.A. and S.I. All authors have read and agreed to the published version of the manuscript.

Funding: This work was supported by the National Natural Science Foundation of China under Grant 61972107.

Data Availability Statement: No data were used to support this study.

Conflicts of Interest: The authors declare no conflict of interest.

References

1. Zadeh, L.A. Fuzzy sets. *Inf. Control* **1965**, *3*, 338–353. [CrossRef]
2. Atanassov, K.T. Intuitionistic fuzzy sets. *Fuzzy Sets Syst.* **1986**, *20*, 87–96. [CrossRef]
3. Cuong, B.C. Picture fuzzy sets-First results, Part 1. In *Seminar Neuro-Fuzzy Systems with Applications*; Institute of Mathematics, Vietnam Academy of Science and Technology: Hanoi, Vietnam, 2013.
4. Cuong, B.C. Picture fuzzy sets-First results, Part 2. In *Seminar Neuro-Fuzzy Systems with Applications*; Institute of Mathematics, Vietnam Academy of Science and Technology: Hanoi, Vietnam, 2013.
5. Garg, H. Some picture fuzzy aggregation operators and their applications to multicriteria decision-making. *Arab. J. Sci. Eng.* **2017**, *42*, 5275–5290. [CrossRef]
6. Gundogdu, F. K.; Kahraman, C. Spherical fuzzy sets and spherical fuzzy TOPSIS method. *J. Intell. Fuzzy Syst.* **2018**, *36*, 1–16.
7. Ashraf, S.; Abdulla, S.; Mahmood, T.; Mahmood, F. T-Spherical fuzzy sets and their applications in multi-attribute decision making problems. *J. Intell. Fuzzy Syst.* **2018**, *36*, 2829–2844. [CrossRef]
8. Ashraf, S.; Abdullah, S.; Mahmood, T. Spherical fuzzy Dombi aggregation operators and their application in group decision making problem. *J. Ambient Intell. Humaniz. Comput.* **2019**, *11*, 2731–2749. [CrossRef]
9. Mahmood, T.; Kifayat, U.; Khan, Q.; Jan, N. An approach toward decision-making and medical diagnosis problems using the concept of spherical fuzzy sets. *Neural Comput. Appl.* **2018**, *31*, 7041–7053. [CrossRef]
10. Alcantud, J.C.R. Complemental Fuzzy Sets: A semantic justification of q-rung orthopair fuzzy sets. *IEEE Trans. Fuzzy Syst.* **2023**, 1–9. [CrossRef]
11. Yager, R.R. Generalized orthopair fuzzy sets. *IEEE Trans. Fuzzy Syst.* **2017**, *25*, 1222–1230. [CrossRef]
12. Li, L.; Zhang, R.; Wang, J.; Shang, X.; Bai, K. A novel approach to multi-attribute group decision-making with q-rung picture linguistic information. *Symmetry* **2018**, *10*, 172. [CrossRef]
13. Kaufmann, A. *Introduction to the Theory of Fuzzy Sets, Fundamental Theoretical Elements*, Academic Press: New York, NY, USA , 1980; Volume 1.
14. Kosari, S.; Shao, Z.; Rao, Y.; Liu, X.; Cai, R.; Rashmanlou, H. Some Types of Domination in Vague Graphs with Application in Medicine. *J. Mult.-Valued Logic Soft Comput.* **2023**, *40*, 203–219.
15. Kou, Z.; Kosari, S.; Akhoundi, M. A Novel Description on Vague Graph with Application in Transportation Systems. *J. Math.* **2021**, *2021*, 4800499. [CrossRef]
16. Qiang, X.; Akhoundi, M.; Kou, Z.; Liu, X.; Kosari, S. Novel Concepts of Domination in Vague Graphs with Application in Medicine. *Math. Probl. Eng.* **2021**, *10*, 6121454. [CrossRef]
17. Kosari, S.; Shao, Z.; Shi, X.; Sheikholeslami, S.M.; Chellali, M.; Khoeilar, R.; Karamib, H. Cubic graphs have paired-domination number at most four-seventh of their orders. *Discret. Math.* **2022**, *345*, 113086. [CrossRef]

18. Rosenfeld, A. *Fuzzy Sets and Their Applications to Cognitive and Decision Processes*; Elsevier: Amsterdam, The Netherlands , 1975; pp. 77–95.
19. Rao, Y.; Kosari, S.; Shao, Z.; Qiang, X.; Akhoundi, M.; Zhang, X. Equitable domination in vague graphs with application in medical sciences. *Front. Phys.* **2021**, *9*, 635–642. [CrossRef]
20. Rao, Y.; Kosari, S.; Shao, Z.; Cai , R.; Xin, L. A Study on Domination in vague incidence graph and its application in medical sciences. *Symmetry* **2020**, *12*, 1885. [CrossRef]
21. Shi, X.; Kosari, S. Certain Properties of Domination in Product VagueGraphs With an Application in Medicine. *Front. Phys.* **2021**, *9*, 680634. [CrossRef]
22. Thomson, M.G. Convergence of powers of a fuzzy matrix. *J. Math. Anal. Appl.* **1977**, *57*, 476–480. [CrossRef]
23. Zimmermann, H.-J. Fuzzy set theory and mathematical programming. In *Fuzzy Sets Theory and Applications*; Springer: Berlin/Heidelberg, Germany, 1986; pp. 99–114.
24. Rashmanlou, H.; Jun, Y.B.; Borzooei, R.A. More results on highly irregular bipolar fuzzy graphs. *Ann. Fuzzy Math. Inform.* **2014**, *8*, 149–168.
25. Zeng, S.S.; Shoaib, M.; Ali, S.; Smarandache, F.; Rashmanlou, H.; Mofidnakhae, F. Certain Properties of Single-Valued Neutrosophic Graph With Application in Food and Agriculture Organization. *Int. J. Comput. Intell. Syst.* **2021**, *14*, 1516–1540. [CrossRef]
26. Akram, M.; Habib, A.; Ilyas, F.; Dar, J. M. Specific types of Pythagorean fuzzy graphs and application to decision-making. *Math. Comput. Appl.* **2018** *23*, 42. [CrossRef]
27. Akram, M.; Saleem, D.; Al-Hawary, T. Spherical Fuzzy Graphs with Application to Decision-Making. *Math. Comput. Appl.* **2020**, *25*, 8. [CrossRef]
28. Akram, M. Decision Making Method Based on Spherical Fuzzy Graphs. In *Studies in Fuzziness and Soft Computing*; Kahraman, C., Otay, L., Eds.; Springer: Berlin, Germany, 2020.
29. Guleria, A.; Bajaj, R.K. T-Spherical Fuzzy Graphs: Operations and Applications in various Selection Processes. *Arab. J. Sci. Eng.* **2019**, *45*, 2177–2193. [CrossRef]
30. Gutman, I.; Trinajstic, N. Graph theory and molecular orbitals, total ϕ-electron energy of alternant hydrocarbons. *Chem. Phys. Lett.* **1972**, *17*, 535–538. [CrossRef]
31. Gutman, I. The energy of a graph. *Ber. Math. Statist. Sekt. Forsch-Ungszentram Graz.* **1978**, *103*, 122.
32. Gutman, I.; Zhou, B. Laplacian energy of a graph, Linear Agebra and its Application. *J. Linear Algebra Appl.* **2006**, *414*, 29–37. [CrossRef]
33. Kalathian, S.; Ramalingam, S.; Sundareswaran, R.; Srinivasan, N. Some topological indices in fuzzy graphs. *J. Intell. Fuzzy Syst.* **2020**, *39*, 6033–6046. [CrossRef]
34. Islam, S.R.; Pal, M. First Zagreb index on a fuzzy graph and its application, Computer science. *J. Intell. Fuzzy Syst.* **2021**, *40*, 10575–10587. [CrossRef]
35. Ahmad, U.; khan, N.K.; Saeid, A.B.; Fuzzy topological indices with application to cybercrime problem. *Granul. Comput.* **2023**, *8*, 967–980. [CrossRef]
36. Ahmad, M.; Nawaz, I. Wiener Index of a Directed Rough Fuzzy Graph and Application to Human Trafficking. *J. Intell. Fuzzy Syst.* **2023**, *44*, 1479–1495 [CrossRef]
37. Ahmad, U.; Sabir, M. Multicriteria Decision Making based on the Degree and Distance Based Indices of Fuzzy Graphs. *Granul. Comput.* **2022**, *8*, 793–807. [CrossRef]
38. Anjali, N.; Mathew, S. Energy of a fuzzy graph. *Ann. Fuzzy Math. Inf.* **2013**, *6*, 455–465.
39. Sharbaf, S.R.; Fayazi, F. Laplacian energy of a fuzzy graph, Iran. *J. Math. Chem.* **2014**, *5*, 1–10.
40. Kale, M.; Minirani, S. Fuzzy Zagreb indices and some bounds for fuzzy Zagreb energy. *Int. J. Anal. Appl.* **2021**, *19*, 252–263.
41. Praba, B.; Chandrasekaran, V.M.; Deepa, G. Energy of an intuitionistic fuzzy graph. *Ital. J. Pure Appl.-Math.-N.* **2014**, *32* 431–444.
42. Akram, M.; Naz, S. Energy of Pythagorean Fuzzy Graphs with Applications. *Mathematics* **2018**, *6*, 136. [CrossRef]
43. Akram, M.; Saleem, D.; Davvaz, B. Energy of double dominating bipolar fuzzy graphs. *J. Appl. Math. Comput.* **2019**, *61*, 219–234. [CrossRef]
44. Shi, X.; Kosari, S.; Asghar Talebi, A.; Hossein Sadati, S.; Rashmanlou, H. Investigation of the main energies of picture fuzzy graph and its applications. *Int. J. Comput. Intell. Syst.* **2022**, *15*, 31. [CrossRef]
45. Yahya, M.S.; Mohamed, A.A. Energy of spherical fuzzy graphs. *Adv. Math. Sci. J.* **2020**, *9*, 321–332.
46. Yager, R.R. Generalized OWA aggregation operators. *Fuzzy Optim Decis Mak.* **2004**, *3*, 93–107. [CrossRef]

symmetry

MDPI

Article

Fuzzy Soft Sets and Decision Making in Ideal Nutrition

Abdelfattah A. El-Atik [1], Radwan Abu-Gdairi [2], Arafa A. Nasef [3], Saeid Jafari [4] and Mohammed Badr [5,*]

[1] Department of Mathematics, Faculty of Science, Tanta University, Tanta 31511, Egypt; aelatik@science.tanta.edu.eg
[2] Department of Mathematics, Faculty of Science, Zarqa University, Zarqa 13133, Jordan; rgdairi@zu.edu.jo
[3] Department of Physics and Engineering Mathematics, Faculty of Engineering, Kafrelsheikh University, Kafrelsheikh 33516, Egypt
[4] Mathematical and Physical Science Foundation, 4200 Slagelse, Denmark; jafaripersia@gmail.com
[5] Department of Mathematics, Faculty of Science, New Valley University, New Valley 72713, Egypt
* Correspondence: m.shaban@sci.nvu.edu.eg

Abstract: Issues in daily life, where making the best decisions is crucial, are frequently encountered. But, in the majority of these situations, the best course of action is uncertain. We must take into account a number of parameters in order to find the best possible solution to these difficulties. The best mathematical instrument for this is fuzzy soft set *FSS* theory in decision making. Nutrition is the process of supplying cells and organisms with the nutrients they need to grow and thrive and to sustain life. A healthy diet has the potential to prevent or mitigate numerous prevalent health issues. The purpose of this paper is to select a burning problem for the nutrition of students and successfully apply the *FSS* theory in decision making. We aim to prove that the approach to decision-making problems with imprecise data via *FSS*s is more accurate than other types of approaches, and we present a new approach to the *FSS* model and its applications in decision-making problems.

Keywords: soft set; fuzzy soft set; information system; rough set; decision making

MSC: 03E72; 54A10; 54B05

1. Introduction and Preliminaries

The attainment of a healthy body and maintenance of a sound physique are contingent upon the presence of a healthy nutrition and diet. People in good physical and mental health are physically and mentally active, including their stamina, body, and mental and physical activity levels. They are resilient, full of vim and vitality, and have a pleasant disposition to boot. They are strong, vivacious, and endowed with an excellent nature. There are six primary categories of nutrients, which include carbs (Cs), fats, minerals (Ms), proteins (Ps), and vitamins (Vs), with water being one of the most important of these. Each nutrient is responsible for one or more of the general functions that are listed below. Vitamin C and lipids are sources of heat, energy, and power. P, M, and V are responsible for the construction and promotion of growth, the renewal of body tissues, and the regulation of body processes. The recommended dietary allowances for each day are broken down into the following fundamental food groups, which are reflected in Table 1 and the food pyramid, which both contain representations of the basic food groups that are used to categorize the recommended daily dietary allowances [1]. These classifications are made for the purpose of making the recommended daily dietary allowances more easily applicable.

Several contemporary theories have been proposed to address the challenges associated with imprecise data, including probability theory, fuzzy sets, intuitionistic fuzzy sets, and rough sets, among others.

Table 1. Basic food groups.

Group	Food Stuff	Main Nutrient Constitution
1	Vegetables and fruits	V, C and M
2	Milk and milk products	C, P and fats
3	Meat, poultry and fish	P and fats
4	Pulses and cereals	C, P and M
5	Oil, ghee and butter	P and fats

Molodtsov [2] showed that each of the above topics has some built-in limitations, for which they do not have a parametrization tool. He also presented a soft set theory with parametrization tools that can be used to deal with a wide range of uncertainties. This fuzzification of soft set theory has seen significant contributions from researchers in the last few years. After that, Maji et al. [3] extended the soft set theory of Molodtsov and introduced FSSs in decision-making problems. The first real-world use of soft sets in problem solving came from Maji et al. [4,5]. They presented and developed the FSS, a notion that combines fuzzy and soft sets and is more widely applicable. Furthermore, Chaudhuriet et al. [6] deployed a few applications of FSSs with the help of the method in [4,5] and compared them with the probability distribution. Also, Çağman et al. [7] developed the case study of the decision-making approach using the fuzzy parametrized FSSs aggregation operator. In 2011, Neog et al. [8] used fuzzy soft matrices, a fuzzy soft complement and a fuzzy matrix operation to solve a decision-making problem.

The objective of this study is to utilize FSSs in a multi-observer multi-criteria decision-making problem as a means of enhancing the approach proposed in [1,9,10]. This paper presents an overview of the fundamental findings regarding soft sets and FSSs stated in [11–14]. In recent years, there have been many applications for soft sets, general topology, and their related topics with applications [15–17]. Moreover, Nasef et al. [18,19] presented some applications of soft sets in decision-making problems.

To solve the reduction issue, Kong et al. [20] defined and developed the heuristic technique for normal parameter reductions (NPRs) in FSS. The NPR soft set algorithm, as proposed in [20], was complex to grasp, required numerous computations, and depended on the dispensability. To lessen its computational complexity, this approach was further investigated by several authors; see [21–24]. A proximity normal parameter reduction (PNPR) of the FSS was proposed by Kong et al. in [25]. Using three-way decision criteria, Khameneh and Kilicman [26] presented an adaptable method for parameterizing FSS. In order to address the issue of FSS parameter reduction based on the score criteria, Kong et al. [27] developed a brand-new NPR method. A distance-based parameter reduction (DBPR) approach for FSS was introduced by Ma and Qin [28]. Its use in decision-making issues was covered, and a problem arose with it because similarity and reduction are different and cannot depend on each other. For more information about the prarametrization reduction in FSS, see [29–34]. Most reduction methods depend on one function.

Throughout this paper, the issue of decision making in the presence of imprecise data holds particular importance when addressing real-life problems. In this example, a multi-observer, multi-criteria decision-making issue is addressed by employing the notion of FSS, which always come equipped with parametrization tools. Also, we give some applications using soft sets and FSSs. By the given results, we prove that the approach to decision-making problems with imprecise data via FSSs is more accurate than other approaches.

Let U_1 be a initial universe set, S be a set of parameters of attributes with respect to U_1, and $P(U_1)$ denote the power set of U_1.

Definition 1 ([2]). *A pair $(\mathfrak{F}, S)$ is called a soft set over U if and only if $\mathfrak{F}$ is a mapping of S into the set of all subsets of U. In other words, a soft set over U is a function from a set of parameters to $P(U)$. We can notice that a soft set is not a set in the usual sense but a parameterized family of subsets of U.*

Definition 2 ([35]). *For a set $A_1 \subseteq X_1$, its indicator function μ_{A_1} is defined as*

$$\mu_{A_1}(x_1) = \begin{cases} 1, & \text{if} \quad x_1 \in A_1; \\ 0, & \text{if} \quad x_1 \notin A_1. \end{cases}$$

A fuzzy set $\mathfrak{F}$ is described by its membership function μ_A. For every $x_1 \in X_1$, this function associates a real number $\mu_F(x_1)$ interpreted for the point as a degree of belonging of x_1 to the fuzzy set $\mathfrak{F}$, written as $\mathfrak{F} = \{(x_1, \mu_{A_1}) : x_1 \in X_1\}$.

Definition 3 ([3]). *Let $\widetilde{P}(U_1)$ be all fuzzy subsets of U_1. A pair $(\widetilde{F}, S)$ is called FSS over U_1 such that $\widetilde{F}$ is a function given by $\widetilde{F} : S \to \widetilde{P}(U_1)$, where S is a set of parameters.*

Similarly, definitions of FSS, null FSS, intersection and union operations [3] are similar to those defined for crisp soft sets (soft sets) [2].

2. Soft Sets through Pawlak Rough Sets

Molodtsov [2] explored various applications of the soft set theory across multiple domains, including the examination of function smoothness, game theory, operations research, probability, etc. In this part, we demonstrate how the rough technique can be utilized to apply soft set theory to a decision-making problem [36,37]. What we will look at is outlined in the following. The information system with set values is outlined in the table that may be found above, where $U = \{\mathfrak{z}_1, \mathfrak{z}_2, \mathfrak{z}_3, \mathfrak{z}_4, \mathfrak{z}_5, \mathfrak{z}_6\}$ are a set of six students. $\mathfrak{V} = \{\mathfrak{v}_1 =$ Food containing preservatives, $\mathfrak{v}_2 =$ C, $\mathfrak{v}_3 =$ P, $\mathfrak{v}_4 =$ V, $\mathfrak{v}_5 =$ Fat, $\mathfrak{v}_6 =$ M, $\mathfrak{v}_7 =$ Junk food, $\mathfrak{v}_8 =$ Icecream $\}$ is a group of parameters that students can use to visualize the nutrients found in food.

Consider the soft set $(\mathfrak{F}, \mathfrak{V})$, which describes the attractiveness of the students given by $(\mathfrak{F}, \mathfrak{V}) =$ Students consume foods with Foods with added preservatives $= \phi$; Students eat food containing C $= \{\mathfrak{z}_1, \mathfrak{z}_2, \mathfrak{z}_3, \mathfrak{z}_4, \mathfrak{z}_5, \mathfrak{z}_6\}$; Students eat food containing P $= \{\mathfrak{z}_1, \mathfrak{z}_2, \mathfrak{z}_3, \mathfrak{z}_4, \mathfrak{z}_6\}$; Students eat food containing V $= \{\mathfrak{z}_1, \mathfrak{z}_2, \mathfrak{z}_3, \mathfrak{z}_4, \mathfrak{z}_5, \mathfrak{z}_6\}$; Students eat food containing Fat $= \{\mathfrak{z}_1, \mathfrak{z}_3, \mathfrak{z}_6\}$; Students eat food containing M $= \{\mathfrak{z}_1, \mathfrak{z}_2, \mathfrak{z}_6\}$; Students eat Junk food $= \{\mathfrak{z}_2, \mathfrak{z}_4, \mathfrak{z}_5\}$; and Students eat Icecream $= \{\mathfrak{z}_1, \mathfrak{z}_3, \mathfrak{z}_6\}$.

Assume that Mr. X possesses an inclination to procure food items based on spečific parameters aligned with his personal preferences $\{\mathfrak{v}_1, \mathfrak{v}_2, \mathfrak{v}_3, \mathfrak{v}_4, \mathfrak{v}_5, \mathfrak{v}_6, \mathfrak{v}_7, \mathfrak{v}_8\}$, which constitute the subset $P = \{\mathfrak{v}_2 =$ C, $\mathfrak{v}_3 =$ P, $\mathfrak{v}_4 =$ V, $\mathfrak{v}_5 =$ Fat, $\mathfrak{v}_6 =$ M$\}$ of the set $\mathfrak{V}$. This implies that the individual must choose from the set of available food items, denoted as U, the food item(s) that satisfy all or the highest number of parameters specified by the soft set. The objective is to identify the food item that aligns with the predetermined selection criteria established by Mr. X.

First, let us build a tabular representation of the problem so we can better understand it. Take into consideration the soft set $(\mathfrak{F}, \mathfrak{P})$, where P is the decision parameter of Mr. X (see Table 2 for further information). In this case, $(\mathfrak{F}, \mathfrak{P})$ can be considered a soft subset of $(\mathfrak{F}, \mathfrak{V})$.

Table 2. Food information system.

Students	$\mathfrak{v}_2$	$\mathfrak{v}_3$	$\mathfrak{v}_4$	$\mathfrak{v}_5$	$\mathfrak{v}_6$
$\mathfrak{z}_1$	1	1	1	1	1
$\mathfrak{z}_2$	1	1	1	0	1
$\mathfrak{z}_3$	1	1	1	1	0
$\mathfrak{z}_4$	1	1	1	0	0
$\mathfrak{z}_5$	1	0	1	0	0
$\mathfrak{z}_6$	1	1	1	1	1

Assume that a hypothetical customer, Mr. Y, intends to make a food purchase based on a predefined set of choice parameters $Q \subset \mathfrak{P}$. So $(\mathfrak{F}, Q)$ is a soft subset of $(\mathfrak{F}, \mathfrak{P})$ and called the reduct soft set of the soft set $(\mathfrak{F}, \mathfrak{P})$. The choice value of an object $\mathfrak{z}_i \in U$ is $\mathfrak{p}_i$, where $\mathfrak{p}_i = \Sigma \mathfrak{z}_{ij}$ such that $\mathfrak{z}_{ij}$ is the entries in the table for reducing the soft set as shown in Table 3.

Table 3. Reduct soft set.

Students	$\mathfrak{v}_2$	$\mathfrak{v}_3$	$\mathfrak{v}_5$	$\mathfrak{v}_6$	Choice Value
$\mathfrak{z}_1$	1	1	1	1	$\mathfrak{p}_1 = 4$
$\mathfrak{z}_2$	1	1	0	1	$\mathfrak{p}_2 = 3$
$\mathfrak{z}_3$	1	1	1	0	$\mathfrak{p}_3 = 3$
$\mathfrak{z}_4$	1	1	0	0	$\mathfrak{p}_4 = 2$
$\mathfrak{z}_5$	1	0	0	0	$\mathfrak{p}_5 = 1$
$\mathfrak{z}_6$	1	1	1	1	$\mathfrak{p}_6 = 4$

So, Mr. Y can choose the food of students $\{\mathfrak{z}_1, \mathfrak{z}_6\}$. The theory of a weighted soft set, or W-soft set, was first presented by Lin [36]. The weighted choice value of an object $\mathfrak{z}_i \in U$ is $W_{\mathfrak{p}_i}$ since $W_{\mathfrak{p}_i} = \Sigma d_{ij}$ such that $d_{ij} = w_j \times c_{ij}$. The following Algorithm 1 is for the selection of students.

Algorithm 1 Decision making for food system.

Step 1: Input the soft set $(\mathfrak{F}, \mathfrak{V})$.
Step 2: Enter the set $\mathfrak{P}$ of choice parameter for Mr. X and $\mathfrak{P} \subseteq \mathfrak{V}$.
Step 3: Reduct soft set of $(\mathfrak{F}, \mathfrak{P})$.
Step 4: Choose one reduct soft set $(\mathfrak{F}, Q)$.
Step 5: Get weighted table of the soft set $(\mathfrak{F}, Q)$ according to the weights decided by Mr. Y.
Step 6: Compute k for which $W_{\mathfrak{p}_i} = max\ w_{\mathfrak{p}_i}$.

The optional choice object is denoted as "c_k". If there are multiple values for k, Mr. Y has the option to choose any one of them. We attempt to resolve the initial problem by employing a modified algorithm. Assume that the weights for the parameter are determined by Mr. Y as presented in Table 4.

Table 4. Weightage for parameters.

w_2	w_3	w_4	w_5	w_6
0.9	0.8	0.7	0.6	0.5

Using these weights, the reduct soft set can be tabulated as in Table 5.

Table 5. Reduct using weightage.

Students	$w_2 \times \mathfrak{v}_2$	$w_3 \times \mathfrak{v}_3$	$w_5 \times \mathfrak{v}_5$	$w_6 \times \mathfrak{v}_6$	Choice Value ($w_{\mathfrak{p}_i}$)
$\mathfrak{z}_1$	0.9	0.8	0.6	0.5	$\mathfrak{p}_1 = 2.8$
$\mathfrak{z}_2$	0.9	0.8	0	0.5	$\mathfrak{p}_2 = 2.2$
$\mathfrak{z}_3$	0.9	0.8	0.6	0	$\mathfrak{p}_3 = 2.3$
$\mathfrak{z}_4$	0.9	0.8	0	0	$\mathfrak{p}_4 = 1.7$
$\mathfrak{z}_5$	0.9	0	0	0	$\mathfrak{p}_5 = 0.9$
$\mathfrak{z}_6$	0.9	0.8	0.6	0.5	$\mathfrak{p}_6 = 2.8$

Therefore, $max \;\; w_{\mathfrak{p}_i} = \{w_{\mathfrak{p}_1}, w_{\mathfrak{p}_6}\}$. The reduct is that Mr. Y chooses the food of students $\mathfrak{z}_1$ and $\mathfrak{z}_6$ among the available food. He seeks counsel from five different counseling agencies $\mathfrak{v}_2, \mathfrak{v}_3, \mathfrak{v}_4, \mathfrak{v}_5, \mathfrak{v}_6$. The five agencies provide the information about food considering parameters C, P, V, Fat and M of the students $\mathfrak{z}_1, \mathfrak{z}_2, \mathfrak{z}_3, \mathfrak{z}_4$, $\mathfrak{z}_5$ and $\mathfrak{z}_6$, respectively.

3. Best Nutrition in Terms of Soft Sets

To address the issues raised above, the following Algorithm 2 is proposed:

Algorithm 2 Decision making for proposed problem.

Step 1: Input the performance evaluation of the similar food for different students as tables.
Step 2: Determine the average value of each relevant entry in each table, and then calculate that average.
Step 3: To obtain the comprehensive decision table, we multiply the weightage of the selection criteria of director (or Mr. Y) to the corresponding entries of each column.
Step 4: Calculate the comparison table.
Step 5: Calculate the column sums and row sums of the comparison table.
Step 6: Obtain the score for every student. The student with maximum score is recommended as the best choice with the best food. So, he has good nutrition.

Suppose Mr. Y is interested in choosing food for students from among the set of students $U = \{\mathfrak{z}_1, \mathfrak{z}_2, \mathfrak{z}_3, \mathfrak{z}_4$, and $\mathfrak{z}_5\}$ on the basis of the set $\mathfrak{P} = \{\mathfrak{p}_1$ (C), $\mathfrak{p}_2$ (M), $\mathfrak{p}_3$ (P), $\mathfrak{p}_4$ (fat), $\mathfrak{p}_5$ (Junk food), $\mathfrak{p}_6(V)\}$ of the selection criteria called the parameters, and assume that Mr. Y wants to choose food for pupils based on his personal preference weightage of the selection criterion. Now to obtain the recent the performance evaluation data, we construct the *FSSs* $(\mathfrak{F}_1, \mathfrak{P})$, $(\mathfrak{F}_2, \mathfrak{P})$, $(\mathfrak{F}_3, \mathfrak{P})$, ($\mathfrak{F}_4$, and $\mathfrak{P}$) over U, where $\mathfrak{F}_1$, $\mathfrak{F}_2$, $\mathfrak{F}_3$, and $\mathfrak{F}_4$ are mappings from $\mathfrak{P}$ into I^U given by four performance evaluation data.
Suppose $\mathfrak{F}_1(\mathfrak{p}_1) = \{(\mathfrak{z}_1, 0.50), (\mathfrak{z}_2, 0.60), (\mathfrak{z}_3, 0.50), (\mathfrak{z}_4, 0.80), (\mathfrak{z}_5, 0.90)\}$,
$\mathfrak{F}_1(\mathfrak{p}_2) = \{(\mathfrak{z}_1, 0.80), (\mathfrak{z}_2, 0.70), (\mathfrak{z}_3, 0.60), (\mathfrak{z}_4, 0.40), (\mathfrak{z}_5, 0.30)\}$,
$\mathfrak{F}_1(\mathfrak{p}_3) = \{(\mathfrak{z}_1, 0.10), (\mathfrak{z}_2, 0.20), (\mathfrak{z}_3, 0.30), (\mathfrak{z}_4, 0.60), (\mathfrak{z}_5, 0.80)\}$,
$\mathfrak{F}_1(\mathfrak{p}_4) = \{(\mathfrak{z}_1, 0.30), (\mathfrak{z}_2, 0.40), (\mathfrak{z}_3, 0.50), (\mathfrak{z}_4, 0.40), (\mathfrak{z}_5, 0.80)\}$,
$\mathfrak{F}_1(\mathfrak{p}_5) = \{(\mathfrak{z}_1, 0.90), (\mathfrak{z}_2, 0.80), (\mathfrak{z}_3, 0.70), (\mathfrak{z}_4, 0.60), (\mathfrak{z}_5, 0.20)\}$,
$\mathfrak{F}_1(\mathfrak{p}_6) = \{(\mathfrak{z}_1, 0.10), (\mathfrak{z}_2, 0.20), (\mathfrak{z}_3, 0.30), (\mathfrak{z}_4, 0.50), (\mathfrak{z}_5, 0.80)\}$,
$\mathfrak{F}_2(\mathfrak{p}_1) = \{(\mathfrak{z}_1, 0.52), (\mathfrak{z}_2, 0.59), (\mathfrak{z}_3, 0.60), (\mathfrak{z}_4, 0.85), (\mathfrak{z}_5, 0.91)\}$,
$\mathfrak{F}_2(\mathfrak{p}_2) = \{(\mathfrak{z}_1, 0.79), (\mathfrak{z}_2, 0.75), (\mathfrak{z}_3, 0.65), (\mathfrak{z}_4, 0.43), (\mathfrak{z}_5, 0.25)\}$,
$\mathfrak{F}_2(\mathfrak{p}_3) = \{(\mathfrak{z}_1, 0.15), (\mathfrak{z}_2, 0.22), (\mathfrak{z}_3, 0.40), (\mathfrak{z}_4, 0.70), (\mathfrak{z}_5, 0.90)\}$,
$\mathfrak{F}_2(\mathfrak{p}_4) = \{(\mathfrak{z}_1, 0.25), (\mathfrak{z}_2, 0.35), (\mathfrak{z}_3, 0.45), (\mathfrak{z}_4, 0.50), (\mathfrak{z}_5, 0.75)\}$,
$\mathfrak{F}_2(\mathfrak{p}_5) = \{(\mathfrak{z}_1, 0.87), (\mathfrak{z}_2, 0.88), (\mathfrak{z}_3, 0.75), (\mathfrak{z}_4, 0.65), (\mathfrak{z}_5, 0.30)\}$,
$\mathfrak{F}_2(\mathfrak{p}_6) = \{(\mathfrak{z}_1, 0.13), (\mathfrak{z}_2, 0.22), (\mathfrak{z}_3, 0.35), (\mathfrak{z}_4, 0.49), (\mathfrak{z}_5, 0.85)\}$,
$\mathfrak{F}_3(\mathfrak{p}_1) = \{(\mathfrak{z}_1, 0.55), (\mathfrak{z}_2, 0.63), (\mathfrak{z}_3, 0.54), (\mathfrak{z}_4, 0.75), (\mathfrak{z}_5, 0.91)\}$,
$\mathfrak{F}_3(\mathfrak{p}_2) = \{(\mathfrak{z}_1, 0.88), (\mathfrak{z}_2, 0.86), (\mathfrak{z}_3, 0.70), (\mathfrak{z}_4, 0.50), (\mathfrak{z}_5, 0.40)\}$,
$\mathfrak{F}_3(\mathfrak{p}_3) = \{(\mathfrak{z}_1, 0.20), (\mathfrak{z}_2, 0.30), (\mathfrak{z}_3, 0.50), (\mathfrak{z}_4, 0.70), (\mathfrak{z}_5, 0.90)\}$,
$\mathfrak{F}_3(\mathfrak{p}_4) = \{(\mathfrak{z}_1, 0.29), (\mathfrak{z}_2, 0.33), (\mathfrak{z}_3, 0.48), (\mathfrak{z}_4, 0.52), (\mathfrak{z}_5, 0.85)\}$,

$\mathfrak{F}_3(\mathfrak{p}_5) = \{(\mathfrak{z}_1, 0.85), (\mathfrak{z}_2, 0.84), (\mathfrak{z}_3, 0.78), (\mathfrak{z}_4, 0.65), (\mathfrak{z}_5, 0.23)\}$,
$\mathfrak{F}_3(\mathfrak{p}_6) = \{(\mathfrak{z}_1, 0.12), (\mathfrak{z}_2, 0.25), (\mathfrak{z}_3, 0.30), (\mathfrak{z}_4, 0.57), (\mathfrak{z}_5, 0.85)\}$,
$\mathfrak{F}_4(\mathfrak{p}_1) = \{(\mathfrak{z}_1, 0.58), (\mathfrak{z}_2, 0.67), (\mathfrak{z}_3, 0.56), (\mathfrak{z}_4, 0.86), (\mathfrak{z}_5, 0.95)\}$,
$\mathfrak{F}_4(\mathfrak{p}_2) = \{(\mathfrak{z}_1, 0.89), (\mathfrak{z}_2, 0.87), (\mathfrak{z}_3, 0.69), (\mathfrak{z}_4, 0.45), (\mathfrak{z}_5, 0.36)\}$,
$\mathfrak{F}_4(\mathfrak{p}_3) = \{(\mathfrak{z}_1, 0.19), (\mathfrak{z}_2, 0.27), (\mathfrak{z}_3, 0.34), (\mathfrak{z}_4, 0.57), (\mathfrak{z}_5, 0.89)\}$,
$\mathfrak{F}_4(\mathfrak{p}_4) = \{(\mathfrak{z}_1, 0.32), (\mathfrak{z}_2, 0.35), (\mathfrak{z}_3, 0.40), (\mathfrak{z}_4, 0.45), (\mathfrak{z}_5, 0.70)\}$,
$\mathfrak{F}_4(\mathfrak{p}_5) = \{(\mathfrak{z}_1, 0.85), (\mathfrak{z}_2, 0.87), (\mathfrak{z}_3, 0.73), (\mathfrak{z}_4, 0.61), (\mathfrak{z}_5, 0.23)\}$,
$\mathfrak{F}_4(\mathfrak{p}_6) = \{(\mathfrak{z}_1, 0.18), (\mathfrak{z}_2, 0.24), (\mathfrak{z}_3, 0.37), (\mathfrak{z}_4, 0.56), (\mathfrak{z}_5, 0.78)\}$.
The following is a table that represents the aforementioned *FSSs* $(\mathfrak{F}_1, \mathfrak{P})$, $(\mathfrak{F}_2, \mathfrak{P})$, $(\mathfrak{F}_3, \mathfrak{P})$, $(\mathfrak{F}_4, \mathfrak{P})$ organized into Tables 6–9.

Table 6. *FSS* for $(\mathfrak{F}_1, \mathfrak{P})$.

$\mathfrak{P} \setminus U$	$\mathfrak{z}_1$	$\mathfrak{z}_2$	$\mathfrak{z}_3$	$\mathfrak{z}_4$	$\mathfrak{z}_5$
$\mathfrak{p}_1$	0.50	0.60	0.50	0.80	0.90
$\mathfrak{p}_2$	0.80	0.70	0.60	0.40	0.30
$\mathfrak{p}_3$	0.10	0.20	0.30	0.60	0.80
$\mathfrak{p}_4$	0.30	0.40	0.50	0.40	0.80
$\mathfrak{p}_5$	0.90	0.80	0.70	0.60	0.20
$\mathfrak{p}_6$	0.10	0.20	0.30	0.50	0.80

Table 7. *FSS* for $(\mathfrak{F}_2, P)$.

$\mathfrak{P} \setminus U$	$\mathfrak{z}_1$	$\mathfrak{z}_2$	$\mathfrak{z}_3$	$\mathfrak{z}_4$	$\mathfrak{z}_5$
$\mathfrak{p}_1$	0.52	0.59	0.60	0.85	0.91
$\mathfrak{p}_2$	0.79	0.75	0.65	0.43	0.25
$\mathfrak{p}_3$	0.15	0.22	0.40	0.70	0.90
$\mathfrak{p}_4$	0.25	0.35	0.45	0.50	0.75
$\mathfrak{p}_5$	0.87	0.88	0.75	0.65	0.30
$\mathfrak{p}_6$	0.13	0.22	0.35	0.49	0.85

Table 8. *FSS* for $(\mathfrak{F}_3, P)$.

$\mathfrak{P} \setminus U$	$\mathfrak{z}_1$	$\mathfrak{z}_2$	$\mathfrak{z}_3$	$\mathfrak{z}_4$	$\mathfrak{z}_5$
$\mathfrak{p}_1$	0.55	0.63	0.54	0.75	0.91
$\mathfrak{p}_2$	0.88	0.86	0.70	0.50	0.40
$\mathfrak{p}_3$	0.20	0.30	0.50	0.70	0.90
$\mathfrak{p}_4$	0.29	0.33	0.48	0.52	0.85
$\mathfrak{p}_5$	0.85	0.84	0.78	0.65	0.23
$\mathfrak{p}_6$	0.12	0.25	0.30	0.57	0.85

Table 9. FSS for $(\mathfrak{F}_4, P)$.

$\mathfrak{P} \setminus U$	$\mathfrak{z}_1$	$\mathfrak{z}_2$	$\mathfrak{z}_3$	$\mathfrak{z}_4$	$\mathfrak{z}_5$
$\mathfrak{p}_1$	0.58	0.67	0.56	0.86	0.95
$\mathfrak{p}_2$	0.89	0.87	0.69	0.45	0.36
$\mathfrak{p}_3$	0.19	0.27	0.34	0.57	0.89
$\mathfrak{p}_4$	0.32	0.35	0.40	0.45	0.70
$\mathfrak{p}_5$	0.85	0.87	0.73	0.61	0.23
$\mathfrak{p}_6$	0.18	0.24	0.37	0.56	0.78

We obtain the performance evaluation shown in Table 10 by averaging the aforementioned four FSSs.

Table 10. Average of FSSs.

$\mathfrak{P} \setminus U$	$\mathfrak{z}_1$	$\mathfrak{z}_2$	$\mathfrak{z}_3$	$\mathfrak{z}_4$	$\mathfrak{z}_5$
$\mathfrak{p}_1$	0.54	0.62	0.55	0.82	0.92
$\mathfrak{p}_2$	0.84	0.80	0.66	0.45	0.33
$\mathfrak{p}_3$	0.16	0.25	0.39	0.64	0.87
$\mathfrak{p}_4$	0.29	0.36	0.46	0.47	0.78
$\mathfrak{p}_5$	0.87	0.85	0.74	0.63	0.24
$\mathfrak{p}_6$	0.13	0.23	0.33	0.53	0.82

Assume that Mr. Y determines the preference weights for the various pupils as shown in Table 11 such that $\sum_{i=1}^{5} w_i = 1$.

Table 11. Weightage for students.

w_1	w_2	w_3	w_4	w_5
0.3	0.3	0.275	0.1	0.025

The comprehensive decision table can be derived by performing a row-wise multiplication of Table 10 with the weightage Table 11, followed by transposing the resulting matrix as depicted in Table 12.

Table 12. Comprehensive decision.

$\mathfrak{P} \setminus (U \times w_i)$	$\mathfrak{z}_1 \times w_1$	$\mathfrak{z}_2 \times w_2$	$\mathfrak{z}_3 \times w_3$	$\mathfrak{z}_4 \times w_4$	$\mathfrak{z}_5 \times w_5$
$\mathfrak{p}_1$	0.162	0.186	0.151	0.082	0.023
$\mathfrak{p}_2$	0.252	0.240	0.182	0.045	0.008
$\mathfrak{p}_3$	0.048	0.075	0.107	0.064	0.022
$\mathfrak{p}_4$	0.087	0.108	0.124	0.047	0.020
$\mathfrak{p}_5$	0.261	0.255	0.204	0.063	0.006
$\mathfrak{p}_6$	0.036	0.069	0.091	0.053	0.006

Now that the comparison table is constructed for the students, we use it to help Mr. Y select the most qualified students possible. The comparison table is in the form of a square and has an equal number of rows and columns. The rows and columns are both labeled with the names of the students as $\mathfrak{z}_1, \mathfrak{z}_2, \mathfrak{z}_3, \mathfrak{z}_4$ and $\mathfrak{z}_5$, and the entries are $\mathfrak{z}_{ij}$ with

$i, j = 1, 2, 3, 4, 5$ given by $\mathfrak{z}_{ij} =$, the number of selection criteria, for which the membership value of $\mathfrak{z}_j$ is greater than or equal to the membership value of $\mathfrak{z}_i$. The comparison table is in Table 13.

Table 13. Comparison table.

$U \setminus U$	$\mathfrak{z}_1$	$\mathfrak{z}_2$	$\mathfrak{z}_3$	$\mathfrak{z}_4$	$\mathfrak{z}_5$
$\mathfrak{z}_1$	6	2	3	4	6
$\mathfrak{z}_2$	4	6	3	5	6
$\mathfrak{z}_3$	3	3	6	6	6
$\mathfrak{z}_4$	1	0	0	6	6
$\mathfrak{z}_5$	0	0	0	0	6

The column sum and the row sum from the comprehensive decision table and the scores for each student are presented in the following Table 14.

Table 14. Score table.

	Column-Sum	Row-Sum	Score Value
$\mathfrak{z}_1$	14	21	−7
$\mathfrak{z}_2$	11	24	−13
$\mathfrak{z}_3$	12	24	−12
$\mathfrak{z}_4$	21	12	9
$\mathfrak{z}_5$	30	6	24

It is concluded that for Table 14 with the score table, the following ordering is suggested: $\mathfrak{z}_5 > \mathfrak{z}_4 > \mathfrak{z}_1 > \mathfrak{z}_3 > \mathfrak{z}_2$.

In this case, we discover that the highest possible score can be achieved by $\mathfrak{z}_5$, the student with the best parameters $\mathfrak{p}_1$, $\mathfrak{p}_2$, $\mathfrak{p}_3$, $\mathfrak{p}_4$, $\mathfrak{p}_5$ and $\mathfrak{p}_6$. Hence, Mr. Y can choose the student with the best ratios of food with parameters $\mathfrak{p}_1$(C), $\mathfrak{p}_2$ (M), $\mathfrak{p}_3$ (P), $\mathfrak{p}_4(fat)$, $\mathfrak{p}_5$ (Junk food), and $\mathfrak{p}_6$ (V) of the selection criteria of FSSs $(\mathfrak{F}_1, \mathfrak{P})$, $(\mathfrak{F}_2, \mathfrak{P})$, $(\mathfrak{F}_3, \mathfrak{P})$, and $(\mathfrak{F}_4, \mathfrak{P})$ over U.

4. Conclusions and Future Work

The application of fuzzy soft sets in decision making for ideal nutrition has proven to be a promising approach. By considering the uncertainty and imprecision associated with dietary recommendations and individual preferences, fuzzy soft sets provide a flexible and adaptive framework for making informed choices. Through the integration of diverse sources of information and the consideration of multiple criteria, this approach can help individuals and health professionals to navigate the complex landscape of nutrition and make decisions that are tailored to their specific needs and goals. Overall, fuzzy soft sets represent a valuable tool for promoting healthy and balanced diets, and further research in this area is likely to yield important insights and practical applications. From the given results, it is clear that the approach to decision-making problems [38–42] with imprecise data via FSSs is more accurate than the other approaches. We are currently working on a new method of reducing FSS to solve the problems that appear in the methods of NPR, $PNPR$ and $DBPR$. The development of homelands begins with building a person, and building a person depends on proper nutrition. Egypt has made many initiatives to build the human being, including 100 million health and a decent life, and the detection of malnutrition diseases. Therefore, in the year 2022, an initiative was launched to detect malnutrition at the beginning of the study, with the follow-up of the Ministry of Health and the Ministry of Education. It examines children in schools (weight, height, and the percentage of hemoglobin in the blood). When a child presents with a positive case of anemia, stunting or obesity, a card is created. It contains the complete data of the child. Upon follow-up, it is re-examined, and a complete treatment plan suitable for the child is drawn up.The examination was carried out for 11 million students. Therefore, attention to nutrition is a very important factor in choosing the appropriate nutrition. In the future, we will work to help identify the best nutrition factors and the best methods of diagnosing malnutrition, help decision makers, and link big data to FSS.

Author Contributions: Conceptualization, A.A.E.-A.; methodology, A.A.N.; validation, S.J. and M.B.; formal analysis, S.J. and R.A.-G.; investigation, A.A.E.-A., S.J., A.A.N. and M.B.; resources, A.A.E.-A., R.A.-G. and M.B.; data curation, R.A.-G. and S.J.; writing—original draft preparation, A.A.E.-A. and M.B.; writing—review and editing, R.A.-G., A.A.N., S.J. and M.B.; visualization, A.A.E.-A.; supervision, A.A.E.-A. and M.B.; project administration, A.A.E.-A., A.A.N. and S.J. All authors have read and agreed to the published version of the manuscript.

Funding: This research received no external funding.

Data Availability Statement: The data are available from the authors on request.

Conflicts of Interest: The authors declare no conflict of interest.

References

1. Thivagar, M.L.; Richard, C. Nutrition Modeling Through Nano Topology. *Int. J. Eng. Res. Appl.* **2014**, *4*, 327–334.
2. Molodtsov, D.A. Soft set theory-first results. *Comput. Math. Appl.* **1999**, *37*, 19–31. [CrossRef]
3. Maji, P.K.; Biswas, R.; Roy, A.R. Fuzzy soft sets. *J. Fuzzy Maths.* **2001**, *9*, 589–602.
4. Maji, P.K.; Roy, A.R.; Biswas, R. An application of soft sets in a decision making problem. *Comput. Math. Appl.* **2002**, *44*, 1077–1083. [CrossRef]
5. Maji, P.K.; Biswas, R.; Roy, A.R. Soft set theory. *Comput. Math. Appl.* **2003**, *45*, 555–562. [CrossRef]
6. Chaudhuri, A.; De, K.; Chatterjee, D. Solution of the decision-making problems using fuzzy soft relations. *Int. J. Inf. Technol.* **2009**, *15*, 78–107.
7. Çağman, N.; Çitak, F.; Enginoğlu, S. Fuzzy parameterized fuzzy soft sets theory and its application. *Turk. J. Fuzzy Syst.* **2010**, *1*, 21–35.
8. Neog, T.J.; Sut, D.K. Application of fuzzy soft sets in decision-making problem using fuzzy soft matrices. *Int. J. Math. Arch.* **2011**, *2*, 2258–2263.
9. Abu-Gdairi, R.; El-Gayar, M.A.; Al-shami, T.M.; Nawar, A.S.; El-Bably, M.K. Some Topological Approaches for Generalized Rough Sets and Their Decision-Making Applications. *Symmetry* **2022**, *14*, 95. [CrossRef]
10. Qin, H.; Wang, Y.; Ma, X.; Wang, G. A Novel Approach to Decision Making Based on Interval-Valued Fuzzy Soft Set. *Symmetry* **2021**, *13*, 2274. [CrossRef]
11. Das, P.K.; Borgohain, R. An Application of Fuzzy Soft Set in Multicriteria decision-making Problem. *Int. J. Comput. Appl.* **2012**, *38*, 33–37.
12. Gogoi, K.; Dutta, A.K.; Chutia, C. Application of Fuzzy Soft Set Theory in Day to Day Problems. *Int. J. Comput. Appl.* **2014**, *85*, 27–31. [CrossRef]
13. Wang, L.; Qin, K. Incomplete Fuzzy Soft Sets and Their Application to Decision-Making. *Symmetry* **2019**, *11*, 535. [CrossRef]
14. Mareay, R.; Noaman, I.; Abu-Gdairi, R.; Badr, M. On Covering-Based Rough Intuitionistic Fuzzy Sets. *Mathematics* **2022**, *10*, 4079. [CrossRef]
15. El-Atik, A.A.; Nasef, A.A. Some topological structures of fractals and their related graphs. *Filomat* **2020**, *34*, 153–165.
16. Mareay, R.; Abu-Gdairi, R.; Badr, M. Modeling of COVID-19 in View of Rough Topology. *Axioms* **2023**, *12*, 663. [CrossRef]
17. Joshi, B.P.; Kumar, A.; Singh, A.; Bhatt, P.K.; Bharti, B.K. Intuitionistic fuzzy parameterized fuzzy soft set theory and its application. *J. Intell. Fuzzy Syst.* **2018**, *35*, 5217–5223. [CrossRef]
18. Nasef, A.A.; ElNashar, E.A. Soft set theory and its application in decision making for textiles and apparel marketing. *Appl. Res. Tech. Technol. Educ.* **2015**, *3*, 32–39.
19. Alzahran, S.; L-Maghrabi, A.I.E.; L-Juhani, M.A.A.; Badr, M.S. New approach of soft M-open sets in soft topological spaces. *J. King Saud-Univ.-Sci.* **2023**, *35*, 12144–12153. [CrossRef]
20. Kong, Z.; Gao, L.; Wang, L.; Li, S. The normal parameter reduction of soft sets and its algorithm. *Comput. Math. Appl.* **2008**, *56*, 3029–3037. [CrossRef]
21. Kong, Z.; Cao, L.; Wang, L. A fuzzy soft set theoretic approach to decision making problems. *J. Cmoput. Appl. Math.* **2009**, *223*, 540–542. [CrossRef]
22. Sani, D.; Maizatul, A.L.; Tutut, H. An alternative approach to normal parameter reduction algorithm for soft set theory. *IEEE Access* **2017**, *5*, 4732–4746.

23. Ma, X.; Sulaiman, N.; Qin, H.; Herawan, T.; Zain, J.M. A new efficient normal parameter reduction algorithm of soft sets. *Comput. Math. Appl.* **2011**, *62*, 588–598. [CrossRef]
24. Khan, A.; Zhu, Y. An improved algorithm for normal parameter reduction of soft set. *J. Intell. Fuzzy Syst.* **2019**, *37*, 2953–2968. [CrossRef]
25. Kong, Z.; Wang, L.; Wu, Z.; Zou, D. A new parameter reduction in fuzzy soft sets. In Proceedings of the 2012 IEEE International Conference on Granular Computing, Hangzhou, China, 11–13 August 2012.
26. Khameneh, A.Z.; Kilicman, A. Parameter reduction of fuzzy soft sets: An adjustable approach based on the three-way decision. *Int. J. Fuzzy Syst.* **2018**, *20*, 928–942. [CrossRef]
27. Kong, Z.; Ai, J.; Wang, L.; Li, P.; Ma, L.; Lu, F. New normal parameter reduction method in fuzzy soft set theory. *IEEE Access* **2018**, *7*, 2986–2998. [CrossRef]
28. Ma, X.; Qin, H. A distance-based parameter reduction algorithm of fuzzy soft sets. *IEEE Access* **2018**, *6*, 10530–10539. [CrossRef]
29. Kong, Z.; Jia, W.; Zhang, G.; Wang, L. Normal parameter reduction in soft set based on particle swarm optimization algorithm. *Appl. Math. Model.* **2015**, *39*, 4808–4820. [CrossRef]
30. Kong, Z.; Wang, L.; Jia, W. Approximate normal parameter reduction of fuzzy soft set based on harmony search algorithm. In Proceedings of the 2015 IEEE Fifth International Conference on Big Data and Cloud Computing, Dalian, China, 26–28 August 2015.
31. Han, B. Comments on 'Normal parameter reduction in soft set based on particle swarm optimization algorithm'. *Appl. Math. Model.* **2016**, *40*, 10828–10834. [CrossRef]
32. Sani, D.; Tutut, H.A.L.; Haruna, C.; Adamu, I.A.; Akram, M.Z. A review on soft set-based parameter reduction and decision making. *IEEE Access* **2017**, *5*, 4671–4689.
33. Zhan, J.; Alcantud, J.C.R. A survey of parameter reduction of soft sets and corresponding algorithms. *Artif. Intell. Rev.* **2018**, *52*, 1839–1872. [CrossRef]
34. Khan, J.A.; Zhu, Y. A Novel Approach to Parameter Reduction of Fuzzy Soft Set. *IEEE Access* **2019**, *7*, 128956–128967. [CrossRef]
35. Zadeh, L.A. Fuzzy set. *Inf. Control.* **1965**, *8*, 338–353. [CrossRef]
36. Lin, T.Y. A set theory for soft computing-a unified view of fuzzy sets via neighborhood. In Proceedings of the IEEE 5th International Fuzzy Systems, New Orleans, LA, USA, 11 September 1996; Volume 2.
37. Pawlak, Z. *Rough Sets: Theoretical Aspects of Reasoning about Data*; Springer Science & Business Media: Berlin, Germany, 1991; Volume 9.
38. Akram, M. *m-Polar Fuzzy Graphs, Studies in Fuzziness and Soft Computing*; Studies in Fuzziness and Soft Computing; Springer: Berlin, Germany, 2019; p. 371.
39. Jiang, H.; Zhan, J.; Chen, D. Covering based variable precision $(\mathcal{I},\mathcal{T})$-fuzzy rough sets with applications to multi-attribute decision-making. *IEEE Trans. Fuzzy Syst.* **2018**, *27*, 1558–1572. [CrossRef]
40. Zhan, J.; Sun, B.; Alcantud, J.C.R. Covering based multigranulation $(\mathcal{I},\mathcal{T})$ -fuzzy rough set models and applications in multi-attribute group decision-making. *Inf. Sci.* **2019**, *476*, 290–318. [CrossRef]
41. Zhang, K.; Zhan, J.; Wu, W.; Alcantud, J.C.R. Fuzzy β-covering based $(\mathcal{I},\mathcal{T})$-fuzzy rough set models and applications to multi-attribute decision-making. *Comput. Ind. Eng.* **2019**, *128*, 605–621. [CrossRef]
42. Zhang, L.; Zhan, J.; Xu, Z. Covering-based generalized IF rough sets with applications to multi-attribute decision-making. *Inf. Sci.* **2019**, *478*, 275–302. [CrossRef]

symmetry

MDPI

Article

Choquet Integral-Based Aczel–Alsina Aggregation Operators for Interval-Valued Intuitionistic Fuzzy Information and Their Application to Human Activity Recognition

Harish Garg [1,2,*], Tehreem [3], Gia Nhu Nguyen [2,4], Tmader Alballa [5,*] and Hamiden Abd El-Wahed Khalifa [6,7]

1 School of Mathematics, Thapar Institute of Engineering & Technology (Deemed University), Patiala 147004, Punjab, India
2 Institute of Research and Development, Duy Tan University, Da Nang 550000, Vietnam
3 Department of Mathematics, Faculty of Basic and Applied Sciences, Air University, PAF Complex E-9, Islamabad 44000, Pakistan
4 School of Computer Science, Duy Tan University, Da Nang 550000, Vietnam
5 Department of Mathematics, College of Sciences, Princess Nourah bint Abdulrahman University, P.O. Box 84428, Riyadh 11671, Saudi Arabia
6 Department of Mathematics, College of Science and Arts, Qassim University, Al-Badaya 51951, Saudi Arabia
7 Department of Operations and Management Research, Faculty of Graduate Studies for Statistical Research, Cairo University, Giza 12613, Egypt
* Correspondence: harishg58iitr@gmail.com (H.G.); tsalballa@pnu.edu.sa (T.A.)

Abstract: Human activity recognition (HAR) is the process of interpreting human activities with the help of electronic devices such as computer and machine version technology. Humans can be explained or clarified as gestures, behavior, and activities that are recorded by sensors. In this manuscript, we concentrate on studying the problem of HAR; for this, we use the proposed theory of Aczel and Alsina, such as Aczel–Alsina (AA) norms, and the derived theory of Choquet, such as the Choquet integral in the presence of Atanassov interval-valued intuitionistic fuzzy (AIVIF) set theory for evaluating the novel concept of AIVIF Choquet integral AA averaging (AIVIFC-IAAA), AIVIF Choquet integral AA ordered averaging (AIVIFC-IAAOA), AIVIF Choquet integral AA hybrid averaging (AIVIFC-IAAHA), AIVIF Choquet integral AA geometric (AIVIFC-IAAG), AIVIF Choquet integral AA ordered geometric (AIVIFC-IAAOG), and AIVIF Choquet integral AA hybrid geometric (AIVIFC-IAAHG) operators. Many essential characteristics of the presented techniques are shown, and we also identify their properties with some results. Additionally, we take advantage of the above techniques to produce a technique to evaluate the HAR multiattribute decision-making complications. We derive a functional model for HAR problems to justify the evaluated approaches and to demonstrate their supremacy and practicality. Finally, we conduct a comparison between the proposed and prevailing techniques for the legitimacy of the invented methodologies.

Keywords: interval-valued intuitionistic fuzzy sets; Choquet integral; Aczel–Alsina; human activity recognition; decision making; fuzzy logic

1. Introduction

Human activity recognition (HAR) [1] is a diverse and universal field of investigation and attention that engages the classification and identification of human activities in the presence of information arranged from different sources, such as computers, the Internet, cameras, sensors, and wearable devices [2,3]. The main theme of HAR is to detect and find human actions, activities, or behaviors in order to know and employ human actions in various contexts directly or automatically. Mostly, it involves working in pattern recognition procedures and machine learning to evaluate and explore the information arranged from sensors or other sources. The arranged information will be given in the shape of motion, orientation, acceleration, audio, video, or physiological signals [4,5]. The practical applications of HAR are diverse and many and can be discovered in various fields, for instance, healthcare, sports and fitness, human–computer interactions, surveillance and security, and ambient-assisted living. Overall, HAR plays a valuable and essential role in considering human performance, qualifying context-conscious systems, and smoothing relevance that needs automated interpretation and reaction to social activities [6,7].

A decision-making technique [8] or procedure signifies a logical approach or technique used to find data, address decisions, and talk about decisions in many complicated situations. In practical applications, managing the symmetry or asymmetry that exists among several sources of information is the main objective of decision-making procedures. There are various decision-making procedures, each with its benefits and advantages, for instance, rational decision making; strength, weakness, opportunities, and threats (SWOT) analysis; cost-benefit analysis; the decision matrix; Pareto analysis; and the Delphi technique [9,10]. These techniques have been utilized by different scholars in various fields in the presence of classical information. But, during the decision-making procedure, we lose a lot of information because of classical information due to limited opinions, such as zero or one. To improve the range of classical set theory, the major concept of fuzzy set (FS) was addressed by Zadeh [11]. The numerical form of the truth grade in FS is given by $\Gamma^{\mathcal{I}} : \mathcal{X} \to [0,1]$, where $\Gamma^{\mathcal{I}}(\nu) \in [0,1], \nu \in \mathcal{X}$. FS theory and classical set theory have the same structure but different features because the range of FS theory is wider compared to crisp set theory. FS theory also has many limitations and restrictions because, in some cases, the experts are faced with two types of information, such as truth and falsity, supporting and opposing, and membership and non-membership. For FS theory, it is not possible to evaluate such a kind of problem; therefore, Atanassov [12] explained the novel concept of intuitionistic FS (IFS) that allows for the show of uncertainty and hesitation in various decision-making techniques. Derived by Atanassov in 1983, IFS aims to depict not only the truth grade but also the falsity of information and neutrality or hesitation between these two data types. In traditional FS, an element can represent the grade of truth between unit intervals. In IFS, however, an element is explained by two types of data called the truth grade "$\Gamma^{\mathcal{I}}(\nu)$" and the falsity grade "$\Lambda^{\mathcal{I}}(\nu)$", with $0 \leq \Gamma^{\mathcal{I}}(\nu) + \Lambda^{\mathcal{I}}(\nu) \leq 1$. In many research articles, FS theory has been employed in the form of combination, modification, and utilization, such as a tribute to Zadeh's extension principle [13], an extension principle of Zadeh's and fuzzy numbers [14], fuzzy superior Mandelbrot sets [15], continuous fuzzy differential equations [16], Cauchy fuzzy differential equations [17], numerical solutions of fuzzy differential and integral equations [18,19], the analysis of the stability of fuzzy differential equations [20], and the analysis and classification of the rise and fall of fuzzy fidelity in Europe [21].

IFS has a lot of applications in the shape of modification, utilization, and combination with other information; for instance, Atanassov [22] invented the interval-valued IFS (IVIFS), Ejegwa and Agbetayo [23] exposed the similarity and distance measures, Tripathi et al. [24] evaluated the divergence measures, Sharma et al. [25] presented the analytical hierarchical process, Rani and Garg [26] derived the trigonometric operators, Hezam et al. [27] examined the MAIRCA techniques, Gong and Wang [28] evaluated different types of inequalities, Jana and Pal [29] presented the decision-making problems, Garg et al. [30] derived the Schweizer–Sklar prioritized operators, Mahmood et al. [31] exposed the power aggregation operators, and finally, Shi et al. [32] examined the Aczel–Alsina power operators.

A lot of scholars have been working on fuzzy set theory, and many of them have utilized different types of operators, techniques, and measures based on fuzzy set theory and its extensions. Additionally, the Choquet integral (CI) operator is one of them, and it was invented by Choquet [33] in 1954. Choquet integral operators have been utilized in fuzzy set theory; for instance, Meyer and Roubens [34] derived Choquet operators based on fuzzy numbers. Moreover, Tan and Chen [35] evaluated CI operators for IFS theory, where the weighted CI operators for IFS theory were exposed by Xu [36]. All these techniques were derived based on algebraic norms. Here, we also talk about the modified version of algebraic norms, such as the Aczel–Alsina norms, which were derived by Aczel and Alsina [37] in 1982. Further, the Aczel–Alsina norms have received a lot of attention from different scholars; for example, Senapati et al. [38] evaluated the Aczel–Alsina averaging operators for IFS theory. Senapati et al. [39] also examined the Aczel–Alsina geometric operators for IFS theory. Ahmad et al. [40] derived the Aczel–Alsina operators for intuitionistic fuzzy rough set theory. Furthermore, Xu [41] exposed the averaging operators for AIFSs, Xu and Yager [42] derived the geometric operators for AIFSs, and Wang et al. [43] presented the aggregation operators for AIVIFSs. Wang and Liu [44] exposed the geometric operators for AIVIFSs. Garg et al. [45] derived the CI operators for AIVIFSs, Meng et al. [46] proposed the geometric CI operators for AIVIFSs, Senapati et al. [47] evaluated the Aczel–Alsina operators for AIVIFSs, and Senapati et al. [48] exposed the Aczel–Alsina geometric operators for AIVIFSs. From the brief analysis above, we noticed that every operator has its own merits, but they have some limitations as well. For instance, the existing operational laws are restricted in nature, and also consider the feature that all the interacting features are independent of each other.

In this paper, we utilize the concept of AIVIFS to model the uncertainties of information and the generalized operational laws based on Aczel–Alsina to determine the membership and nonmembership degrees of AIVIFNs. Also, we state the generalized aggregation operators based on these laws and hence state an MADM algorithm to solve the decision-making problems. The applicability of the proposed algorithm is demonstrated through a numerical example.

The proposed operational laws based on Aczel–Alsina norms are considered as the generalization of several existing laws. In the current study, we considered the AIVIFNs to represent the uncertainties in the data, while the Choquet integral-based Aczel–Alsina norms were used to define their basic operational laws. The Aczel–Alsina explored the theory of triangular norms in the form of Aczel–Alsina triangular norms. Aczel–Alsina triangular norms are robust tools utilized to overcome the loss of information during the aggregation of information. The major advantage of defining these operational laws is that it generalizes the algebraic and Einstein t-norm operations. Another advantage of the proposed method is the utilization of the Choquet integral (CI) to consider an interrelationship between the attribute information. This CI considers the fuzzy measures during the measurement using ordered position. Finally, based on these proposed laws, we summarized the various generalized aggregation operators, namely, weighted averaging or geometric. The theory of Aczel–Alsina Choquet integral operators has many benefits compared to existing operators because the averaging operators, geometric operators, Choquet integral operators, averaging Aczel–Alsina operators, and geometric Aczel–Alsina operators are the special cases of the proposed theory. Also, the proposed Aczel–Alsina averaging and geometric aggregation operators based on FSs, IFSs, interval-valued FSs, and interval-valued IFSs are the special cases of the derived theory. In addition to this, the derived Aczel–Alsina Choquet integral-based aggregation operators under the existing theories are also considered as a special case.

In a nutshell, the main objectives of this work are listed below:

(1) To define some weighted operators using Choquet integral Aczel–Alsina norm operations;
(2) To investigate the basic fundamental features of the proposed operators;
(3) To develop an MADM algorithm based on the stated operators to address the decision-making problems;
(4) To illustrate the stated algorithm, using a numerical example related to HAR problems to demonstrate its supremacy and practicality;
(5) To conduct a comparison between the proposed and prevailing techniques for the legitimacy of the invented methodologies.

The rest of the manuscript is summarized as follows: In Section 2, we recall the idea of fuzzy measure (FM), the Choquet integral (CI), Aczel–Alsina norms and their special cases, AIVIFS, and their operational laws. In Section 3, we derive the AIVIFC-IAAA, AIVIFC-IAAOA, AIVIFC-IAAHA, AIVIFC-IAAG, AIVIFC-IAAOG, and AIVIFC-IAAHG operators. Many essential characteristics of the presented techniques are shown, and we also identify their properties with some results. In Section 4, we take advantage of the above techniques to produce a technique to evaluate the HAR-MADM complications. In Section 5, we derive a functional model for HAR problems to justify the evaluated approaches and to demonstrate their supremacy and practicality. In Section 6, we conduct a comparison between the proposed and prevailing techniques for the legitimacy of the invented methodologies. Some final and concluding remarks are stated in Section 7.

2. Preliminaries

In this section, we revise the FM, CI, Aczel–Alsina norms, AIVIFS, and their operational laws, as this information is very valuable and beneficial for us to evaluate the proposed techniques. Furthermore, all the symbols and their meanings that are used in this manuscript are stated in Table 1.

Table 1. Meaning of different symbols used in this manuscript.

Symbol	Meanings	Symbol	Meanings
$\blacksquare$	Function	z	Ordered of $\boldsymbol{\phi}$, where $\boldsymbol{\phi} = \mathbf{1}, \mathbf{2}, \ldots z$
$\boldsymbol{\mathcal{X}}$	Universal sets	$\varpi \geq \mathbf{1}$	Scaler
$\boldsymbol{\mathcal{P}}(\boldsymbol{\mathcal{X}})$	Power sets	$\zeta \geq \mathbf{1}$	Scaler
$\mathcal{C}_{\blacksquare}(\mathfrak{R})$	Choquet integral		

Definition 1. [33] *A function* $\blacksquare : \boldsymbol{\mathcal{P}}(\boldsymbol{\mathcal{X}}) \rightarrow [\mathbf{0}, \mathbf{1}]$ *is called a fuzzy measure if* $\blacksquare$ *is justified by the following conditions:*

$$\blacksquare(\boldsymbol{\phi}) = \mathbf{0}, \blacksquare(\boldsymbol{\mathcal{X}}) = \mathbf{1}, (\textit{\textbf{Boundary Condition}}) \tag{1}$$

$$\textbf{If } \Xi\rho, \boldsymbol{\mathcal{B}} \in \boldsymbol{\mathcal{P}}(\boldsymbol{\mathcal{X}}) \textbf{ and } \Xi\rho \subseteq \boldsymbol{\mathcal{B}}, \textbf{then } \blacksquare(\Xi\rho) \leq \blacksquare(\boldsymbol{\mathcal{B}}), (\textit{\textbf{Monotonicity}}) \tag{2}$$

where $\blacksquare$ *is a universal set,* $\mathcal{P}(\mathcal{X})$ *is a power set, and* ϕ *represents an empty set.*

Definition 2. [33] *Let* $\blacksquare$ *be a fuzzy measure, and for any* $H, J \in \mathcal{P}(\mathcal{X})$*, we can define*

$$\blacksquare(H \cup J) = \blacksquare(H) + \blacksquare(J) + \lambda\blacksquare(H \cap J)$$

where λ *represents the interaction between the parameters. The basis features of* $\blacksquare$ *are additive, subadditive, supermodular, and submodular.*

Definition 3. [33] *A positive real-valued function* $\mathfrak{R}$ *on fixed set* $\mathcal{X}$ *with a fuzzy measure* $\blacksquare$*. The discrete CI of* $\mathfrak{R}$ *based on* $\blacksquare$ *is demonstrated by:*

$$\mathcal{C}_{\blacksquare}(\mathfrak{R}) = \sum_{\varphi=1}^{z} \mathfrak{R}_{(\varphi)}\left(\blacksquare\left(\Xi\rho_{(\varphi)}\right) - \blacksquare\left(\Xi\rho_{(\varphi+1)}\right)\right) \tag{3}$$

Notice that the (.)*is stated the permutation on* $\mathcal{X}$*, such as* $\mathfrak{R}_{(1)} \leq \mathfrak{R}_{(2)} \leq \cdots \leq \mathfrak{R}_{(z)}$*, where* $\Xi\varrho_{(\varphi)} = \{\varphi = 1, 2, \ldots, z\}, \Xi\varrho_{(z+1)} = \phi$.

Definition 4. [31] *A mapping* $\mathcal{T}_{TN} : [0,1] \times [0,1] \rightarrow [0,1]$ *is called a t-norm if:*

1. $\mathcal{T}_{TN}(\Xi, \Theta) = \mathcal{T}_{TN}(\Theta, \Xi)$;
2. $\mathcal{T}_{TN}(\Xi, \mathcal{T}_{TN}(\Xi', \Theta)) = \mathcal{T}_{TN}(\mathcal{T}_{TN}(\Xi, \Xi'), \Theta)$;
3. *If* $\Xi \leq \Xi'$*and* $\Theta \leq \Theta'$*, then* $\mathcal{T}_{TN}(\Xi, \Theta) \leq \mathcal{T}_{TN}(\Xi', \Theta')$;
4. $\mathcal{T}_{TN}(\Theta.1) = \Theta$.

Definition 5. [31] *A mapping* $\mathcal{S}_{TCN} : [0,1] \times [0,1] \rightarrow [0,1]$ *is called a t-conorm if:*

1. $\mathcal{S}_{TCN}(\Xi, \Theta) = \mathcal{S}_{TCN}(\Theta, \Xi)$;
2. $\mathcal{S}_{TCN}(\Xi, \mathcal{S}_{TCN}(\Xi', \Theta)) = \mathcal{S}_{TCN}(\mathcal{S}_{TCN}(\Xi, \Xi'), \Theta)$;
3. *If* $\Xi \leq \Xi'$ *and* $\Theta \leq \Theta'$, *then* $\mathcal{S}_{TCN}(\Xi, \Theta) \leq \mathcal{S}_{TCN}(\Xi', \Theta')$;
4. $\mathcal{S}_{TCN}(\Theta.1) = \Theta$.

Definition 6. [37] *The mathematical and theoretical shape of an Aczel–Alsina t-norm and t-conorm is stated by:*

$$\mathcal{T}_{TN}^{\varpi}(\Xi, \Theta) = \begin{cases} \mathcal{T}_{TN}^{D}(\Xi, \Theta) & \varpi = 0 \\ min(\Xi, \Theta) & \varpi = \infty \\ e^{-((-\log\Xi)^{\varpi} + (-\log\Theta)^{\varpi})^{\frac{1}{\varpi}}} & otherwise \end{cases} \tag{4}$$

$$\mathcal{S}_{TCN}^{\varpi}(\Xi, \Theta) = \begin{cases} \mathcal{S}_{TCN}^{D}(\Xi, \Theta) & \varpi = 0 \\ max(\Xi, \Theta) & \varpi = \infty \\ 1 - e^{-((-\log(1-\Xi))^{\varpi} + (-\log(1-\Theta))^{\varpi})^{\frac{1}{\varpi}}} & otherwise \end{cases} \tag{5}$$

where $\varpi > 1$, $\mathcal{T}_{TN}^{D}$ *and* $\mathcal{S}_{TCN}^{D}$ *are represented by the discrete t-norm and t-conorm, such as*

$$\mathcal{T}_{TN}^{D}(\Xi, \Theta) = \begin{cases} \Xi & \Theta = 1 \\ \Theta & \Xi = 1 \\ 0 & otherwise \end{cases} \tag{6}$$

$$\mathcal{S}_{TCN}^{D}(\Xi, \Theta) = \begin{cases} \Xi & \Theta = 0 \\ \Theta & \Xi = 0 \\ 1 & otherwise \end{cases} \tag{7}$$

Notice that $\Xi, \Theta \in [0, 1]$.

Definition 7. [22] *The expression of the AIVIFS* $\mathcal{I}^{if}$ *is constructed by:*

$$\mathcal{I}^{if} = \left\{\left(\left[\Gamma^{\mathcal{I}^-}(v), \Gamma^{\mathcal{I}^+}(v)\right], \left[\Lambda^{\mathcal{I}^-}(v), \Lambda^{\mathcal{I}^+}(v)\right]\right) : v \in \mathcal{X}\right\} \tag{8}$$

The information in the pair $\left(\left[\Gamma^{\mathcal{I}^-}(v), \Gamma^{\mathcal{I}^+}(v)\right], \left[\Lambda^{\mathcal{I}^-}(v), \Lambda^{\mathcal{I}^+}(v)\right]\right)$ *represents the membership and nonmembership degrees with a suitable condition:* $0 \leq \Gamma^{\mathcal{I}^+}(v) + \Lambda^{\mathcal{I}^+}(v) \leq 1$. *Moreover, we construct the neutral/refusal information, such as* $\eta^{\mathcal{I}}(v) = \left[\eta^{\mathcal{I}^-}(v), \eta^{\mathcal{I}^+}(v)\right] = \left[1 - \left(\Gamma^{\mathcal{I}^+}(v) + \Lambda^{\mathcal{I}^+}(v)\right), 1 - \left(\Gamma^{\mathcal{I}^-}(v) + \Lambda^{\mathcal{I}^-}(v)\right)\right]$.

Finally, the AIVIFV is constructed in the form of

$$\mathcal{I}_{\varphi}^{if} = \left(\left[\Gamma_{\varphi}^{\mathcal{I}^-}, \Gamma_{\varphi}^{\mathcal{I}^+}\right], \left[\Lambda_{\varphi}^{\mathcal{I}^-}, \Lambda_{\varphi}^{\mathcal{I}^+}\right]\right), \varphi = 1, 2, \ldots, z$$

Definition 8. [22] *For any two AIVIFVs, the basic operational laws are stated as*

$$\mathcal{I}_1^{if} \oplus \mathcal{I}_2^{if} = \left(\left[\Gamma_1^{\mathcal{I}^-} + \Gamma_2^{\mathcal{I}^-} - \Gamma_1^{\mathcal{I}^-}\Gamma_2^{\mathcal{I}^-}, \Gamma_1^{\mathcal{I}^+} + \Gamma_2^{\mathcal{I}^+} - \Gamma_1^{\mathcal{I}^+}\Gamma_2^{\mathcal{I}^+}\right], \left[\Lambda_1^{\mathcal{I}^-}\Lambda_2^{\mathcal{I}^-}, \Lambda_1^{\mathcal{I}^+}\Lambda_2^{\mathcal{I}^+}\right]\right) \tag{9}$$

$$\mathcal{I}_1^{if} \otimes \mathcal{I}_2^{if} = \left(\left[\Gamma_1^{\mathcal{I}^-}\Gamma_2^{\mathcal{I}^-}, \Gamma_1^{\mathcal{I}^+}\Gamma_2^{\mathcal{I}^+}\right], \left[\Lambda_1^{\mathcal{I}^-} + \Lambda_2^{\mathcal{I}^-} - \Lambda_1^{\mathcal{I}^-}\Lambda_2^{\mathcal{I}^-}, \Lambda_1^{\mathcal{I}^+} + \Lambda_2^{\mathcal{I}^+} - \Lambda_1^{\mathcal{I}^+}\Lambda_2^{\mathcal{I}^+}\right]\right) \tag{10}$$

$$\zeta\mathcal{I}_{\varphi}^{if} = \left(\left[1 - \left(1 - \Gamma_{\varphi}^{\mathcal{I}^-}\right)^{\zeta}, 1 - \left(1 - \Gamma_{\varphi}^{\mathcal{I}^+}\right)^{\zeta}\right], \left[\left(\Lambda_{\varphi}^{\mathcal{I}^-}\right)^{\zeta}, \left(\Lambda_{\varphi}^{\mathcal{I}^+}\right)^{\zeta}\right]\right) \tag{11}$$

$$\left(\mathcal{I}_{\varphi}^{if}\right)^{\zeta} = \left(\left[\left(\Gamma_{\varphi}^{\mathcal{I}^-}\right)^{\zeta}, \left(\Gamma_{\varphi}^{\mathcal{I}^+}\right)^{\zeta}\right], \left[1 - \left(1 - \Lambda_{\varphi}^{\mathcal{I}^-}\right)^{\zeta}, 1 - \left(1 - \Lambda_{\varphi}^{\mathcal{I}^+}\right)^{\zeta}\right]\right) \tag{12}$$

Using Equations (9)–(12) and using the idea in Equation (3), Garg et al. *[45] exposed the following theory:*

$$\begin{aligned}&AIVIFCI\left(\mathcal{I}_1^{if},\mathcal{I}_2^{if},\ldots,\mathcal{I}_z^{if}\right)\\&=\mathcal{I}_1^{if}\left(\blacksquare\left(\Xi\rho_{(1)}\right)-\blacksquare\left(\Xi\rho_{(2)}\right)\right)\oplus\mathcal{I}_2^{if}\left(\blacksquare\left(\Xi\rho_{(2)}\right)-\blacksquare\left(\Xi\rho_{(3)}\right)\right)\oplus\ldots\\&\oplus\mathcal{I}_z^{if}\left(\blacksquare\left(\Xi\rho_{(z)}\right)-\blacksquare\left(\Xi\rho_{(z+1)}\right)\right)=\sum_{\varphi=1}^{z}\mathcal{I}_\varphi^{if}\left(\blacksquare\left(\Xi\rho_{(\varphi)}\right)-\blacksquare\left(\Xi\rho_{(\varphi+1)}\right)\right)\\&=\left(\begin{array}{c}\left[\begin{array}{c}1-\prod_{\varphi=1}^{z}\left(1-\Gamma_\varphi^{\mathcal{I}^-}\right)^{\left(\blacksquare\left(\Xi\rho_{(\varphi)}\right)-\blacksquare\left(\Xi\rho_{(\varphi+1)}\right)\right)},\\1-\prod_{\varphi=1}^{z}\left(1-\Gamma_\varphi^{\mathcal{I}^+}\right)^{\left(\blacksquare\left(\Xi\rho_{(\varphi)}\right)-\blacksquare\left(\Xi\rho_{(\varphi+1)}\right)\right)}\end{array}\right],\\\left[\prod_{\varphi=1}^{z}\left(\Lambda_\varphi^{\mathcal{I}^-}\right)^{\left(\blacksquare\left(\Xi\rho_{(\varphi)}\right)-\blacksquare\left(\Xi\rho_{(\varphi+1)}\right)\right)},\prod_{\varphi=1}^{z}\left(\Lambda_\varphi^{\mathcal{I}^+}\right)^{\left(\blacksquare\left(\Xi\rho_{(\varphi)}\right)-\blacksquare\left(\Xi\rho_{(\varphi+1)}\right)\right)}\right]\end{array}\right)\end{aligned}\tag{13}$$

Our aim is to construct the CI in consideration of the Aczel–Alsina t-norm and t-conorm instead of the algebraic norms; therefore, for this, we used the proposed work of Senapati et al. *[47] for the AIVIFVs. The operational laws are defined as the following:*

Definition 9. *For AIVIFVs* $\mathcal{I}_1^{if}=\left(\left[\Gamma_1^{\mathcal{I}^-},\Gamma_1^{\mathcal{I}^+}\right],\left[\Lambda_1^{\mathcal{I}^-},\Lambda_1^{\mathcal{I}^+}\right]\right)$ *and* $\mathcal{I}_2^{if}=\left(\left[\Gamma_2^{\mathcal{I}^-},\Gamma_2^{\mathcal{I}^+}\right],\left[\Lambda_2^{\mathcal{I}^-},\Lambda_2^{\mathcal{I}^+}\right]\right)$ *and* $\zeta>0$ *be a real number, then*

$$\mathcal{I}_1^{if}\oplus\mathcal{I}_2^{if}=\left(\begin{array}{c}\left[\begin{array}{c}1-e^{-\left(\left(-\log\left(1-\Gamma_1^{\mathcal{I}^-}\right)\right)^{\varpi}+\left(-\log\left(1-\Gamma_2^{\mathcal{I}^-}\right)\right)^{\varpi}\right)^{\frac{1}{\varpi}}},\\1-e^{-\left(\left(-\log\left(1-\Gamma_1^{\mathcal{I}^+}\right)\right)^{\varpi}+\left(-\log\left(1-\Gamma_2^{\mathcal{I}^+}\right)\right)^{\varpi}\right)^{\frac{1}{\varpi}}}\end{array}\right],\\\left[e^{-\left(\left(-\log\Lambda_1^{\mathcal{I}^-}\right)^{\varpi}+\left(-\log\Lambda_2^{\mathcal{I}^-}\right)^{\varpi}\right)^{\frac{1}{\varpi}}},e^{-\left(\left(-\log\Lambda_1^{\mathcal{I}^+}\right)^{\varpi}+\left(-\log\Lambda_2^{\mathcal{I}^+}\right)^{\varpi}\right)^{\frac{1}{\varpi}}}\right]\end{array}\right)\tag{14}$$

$$\mathcal{I}_1^{if}\otimes\mathcal{I}_2^{if}=\left(\begin{array}{c}\left[\begin{array}{c}e^{-\left(\left(-\log\left(\Gamma_1^{\mathcal{I}^-}\right)\right)^{\varpi}+\left(-\log\left(\Gamma_2^{\mathcal{I}^-}\right)\right)^{\varpi}\right)^{\frac{1}{\varpi}}},\\e^{-\left(\left(-\log\left(\Gamma_1^{\mathcal{I}^+}\right)\right)^{\varpi}+\left(-\log\left(\Gamma_2^{\mathcal{I}^+}\right)\right)^{\varpi}\right)^{\frac{1}{\varpi}}}\end{array}\right],\\\left[\begin{array}{c}e^{-\left(\left(-\log\left(1-\Lambda_1^{\mathcal{I}^-}\right)\right)^{\varpi}+\left(-\log\left(1-\Lambda_2^{\mathcal{I}^-}\right)\right)^{\varpi}\right)^{\frac{1}{\varpi}}},\\e^{-\left(\left(-\log\left(1-\Lambda_1^{\mathcal{I}^+}\right)\right)^{\varpi}+\left(-\log\left(1-\Lambda_2^{\mathcal{I}^+}\right)\right)^{\varpi}\right)^{\frac{1}{\varpi}}}\end{array}\right]\end{array}\right)\tag{15}$$

$$\zeta\mathcal{I}_1^{if}=\left(\begin{array}{c}\left[1-e^{-\left(\zeta\left(-\log\left(1-\Gamma_1^{\mathcal{I}^-}\right)\right)^{\varpi}\right)^{\frac{1}{\varpi}}},1-e^{-\left(\zeta\left(-\log\left(1-\Gamma_1^{\mathcal{I}^+}\right)\right)^{\varpi}\right)^{\frac{1}{\varpi}}}\right],\\\left[e^{-\left(\zeta\left(-\log\Lambda_1^{\mathcal{I}^-}\right)^{\varpi}\right)^{\frac{1}{\varpi}}},e^{-\left(\zeta\left(-\log\Lambda_1^{\mathcal{I}^+}\right)^{\varpi}\right)^{\frac{1}{\varpi}}}\right]\end{array}\right)\tag{16}$$

$$\left(\mathcal{I}_\varphi^{if}\right)^{\zeta}=\left(\begin{array}{c}\left[e^{-\left(\zeta\left(-\log\left(\Gamma_1^{\mathcal{I}^-}\right)\right)^{\varpi}\right)^{\frac{1}{\varpi}}},e^{-\left(\zeta\left(-\log\left(\Gamma_1^{\mathcal{I}^+}\right)\right)^{\varpi}\right)^{\frac{1}{\varpi}}}\right],\\\left[1-e^{-\left(\zeta\left(-\log\left(1-\Lambda_1^{\mathcal{I}^-}\right)\right)^{\varpi}\right)^{\frac{1}{\varpi}}},1-e^{-\left(\zeta\left(-\log\left(1-\Lambda_1^{\mathcal{I}^+}\right)\right)^{\varpi}\right)^{\frac{1}{\varpi}}}\right]\end{array}\right)\tag{17}$$

Definition 10. *For any AIVIFV* $\mathcal{I}_\varphi^{if}=\left(\left[\Gamma_\varphi^{\mathcal{I}^-},\Gamma_\varphi^{\mathcal{I}^+}\right],\left[\Lambda_\varphi^{\mathcal{I}^-},\Lambda_\varphi^{\mathcal{I}^+}\right]\right)$*, the score and accuracy functions are stated as:*

$$\beth^{SV}\left(\mathcal{I}_{\varphi}^{if}\right) = \frac{1}{2}\left(\Gamma_{\varphi}^{\mathcal{I}^-} + \Gamma_{\varphi}^{\mathcal{I}^+} - \Lambda_{\varphi}^{\mathcal{I}^-} - \Lambda_{\varphi}^{\mathcal{I}^+}\right) \in [-1,1] \tag{18}$$

$$\beth^{AV}\left(\mathcal{I}_{\varphi}^{if}\right) = \frac{1}{2}\left(\Gamma_{\varphi}^{\mathcal{I}^-} + \Gamma_{\varphi}^{\mathcal{I}^+} + \Lambda_{\varphi}^{\mathcal{I}^-} + \Lambda_{\varphi}^{\mathcal{I}^+}\right) \in [0,1] \tag{19}$$

Definition 11. *To compare the two different AIVIFNs $\mathcal{I}_1^{if}$ and $\mathcal{I}_2^{if}$, an order comparison between them is stated below:*

(a) *If $\beth^{SV}\left(\mathcal{I}_1^{if}\right) > \beth^{SV}\left(\mathcal{I}_2^{if}\right)$, then $\mathcal{I}_1^{if} > \mathcal{I}_2^{if}$,*

(b) *If $\beth^{SV}\left(\mathcal{I}_1^{if}\right) = \beth^{SV}\left(\mathcal{I}_2^{if}\right)$, and $\beth^{AV}\left(\mathcal{I}_1^{if}\right) > \beth^{AV}\left(\mathcal{I}_2^{if}\right)$, then $\mathcal{I}_1^{if} > \mathcal{I}_2^{if}$.*

3. Proposed C-IAA Aggregation Operators for AIVIFSs

In this section, we aim to evaluate the theory of AIVIFC-IAAA, AIVIFC-IAAOA, AIVIFC-IAAHA, AIVIFC-IAAG, AIVIFC-IAAOG, and AIVIFC-IAAHG operators. Many essential characteristics of the presented techniques are shown, and we also identify their properties with some results. Throughout this paper, we used the family of AIVIFSs $\mathcal{I}_{\varphi}^{if} = \left(\left[\Gamma_{\varphi}^{\mathcal{I}^-}, \Gamma_{\varphi}^{\mathcal{I}^+}\right], \left[\Lambda_{\varphi}^{\mathcal{I}^-}, \Lambda_{\varphi}^{\mathcal{I}^+}\right]\right), \varphi = 1,2,\ldots,z$.

Definition 12. *For the family of AIVIFSs $\mathcal{I}_{\varphi}^{if}$, an AIVIFC-IAAA operator is demonstrated by:*

$$\begin{aligned}
&AIVIFC - IAAA\left(\mathcal{I}_1^{if}, \mathcal{I}_2^{if}, \ldots, \mathcal{I}_z^{if}\right) \\
&= \mathcal{I}_1^{if}\left(\blacksquare\left(\Xi\rho_{(1)}\right) - \blacksquare\left(\Xi\rho_{(2)}\right)\right) \oplus \mathcal{I}_2^{if}\left(\blacksquare\left(\Xi\rho_{(2)}\right) - \blacksquare\left(\Xi\rho_{(3)}\right)\right) \\
&\oplus \ldots \oplus \mathcal{I}_z^{if}\left(\blacksquare\left(\Xi\rho_{(z)}\right) - \blacksquare\left(\Xi\rho_{(z+1)}\right)\right) \\
&= \sum_{\varphi=1}^{z} \mathcal{I}_{\varphi}^{if}\left(\blacksquare\left(\Xi\rho_{(\varphi)}\right) - \blacksquare\left(\Xi\rho_{(\varphi+1)}\right)\right) \\
&= \oplus_{\varphi=1}^{z} \mathcal{I}_{\varphi}^{if}\left(\blacksquare\left(\Xi\rho_{(\varphi)}\right) - \blacksquare\left(\Xi\rho_{(\varphi+1)}\right)\right)
\end{aligned} \tag{20}$$

Theorem 1. *For the family of AIVIFSs, the aggregated value by the $AIVIFC - IAAA$ operator is also AIVIFV and given as*

$$\begin{aligned}
&AIVIFC - IAAA\left(\mathcal{I}_1^{if}, \mathcal{I}_2^{if}, \ldots, \mathcal{I}_z^{if}\right) \\
&= \left(\begin{array}{c}
\left[\begin{array}{l}
1 - e^{-\left(\sum_{\varphi=1}^{z}\left(\blacksquare\left(\Xi\rho_{(\varphi)}\right) - \blacksquare\left(\Xi\rho_{(\varphi+1)}\right)\right)\left(-\log\left(1-\Gamma_{\varphi}^{\mathcal{I}^-}\right)\right)^{\varpi}\right)^{\frac{1}{\varpi}}}, \\
1 - e^{-\left(\sum_{\varphi=1}^{z}\left(\blacksquare\left(\Xi\rho_{(\varphi)}\right) - \blacksquare\left(\Xi\rho_{(\varphi+1)}\right)\right)\left(-\log\left(1-\Gamma_{\varphi}^{\mathcal{I}^+}\right)\right)^{\varpi}\right)^{\frac{1}{\varpi}}}
\end{array}\right], \\
\left[\begin{array}{l}
e^{-\left(\sum_{\varphi=1}^{z}\left(\blacksquare\left(\Xi\rho_{(\varphi)}\right) - \blacksquare\left(\Xi\rho_{(\varphi+1)}\right)\right)\left(-\log\left(\Lambda_{\varphi}^{\mathcal{I}^-}\right)\right)^{\varpi}\right)^{\frac{1}{\varpi}}}, \\
e^{-\left(\sum_{\varphi=1}^{z}\left(\blacksquare\left(\Xi\rho_{(\varphi)}\right) - \blacksquare\left(\Xi\rho_{(\varphi+1)}\right)\right)\left(-\log\left(\Lambda_{\varphi}^{\mathcal{I}^+}\right)\right)^{\varpi}\right)^{\frac{1}{\varpi}}}
\end{array}\right]
\end{array}\right)
\end{aligned} \tag{21}$$

The proof of Theorem 1 is given in Appendix A.

To demonstrate the functioning of the proposed AIVIFC-IAAA operator, we consider four AIVIFNs as

$$\mathcal{I}_1^{if} = ([0.40,\ 0.41], [0.30,\ 0.31]); \quad \mathcal{I}_2^{if} = ([0.50,\ 0.51], [0.10,\ 0.11])$$

$$\mathcal{I}_3^{if} = ([0.59,\ 0.60], [0.39,\ 0.40]); \quad \mathcal{I}_4^{if} = ([0.70,\ 0.71], [0.20,\ 0.21])$$

To aggregate these numbers, we utilize Equation (21) and obtain the aggregated number as

$$AIVIFC - IAAA\left(\mathcal{I}_1^{if}, \mathcal{I}_2^{if}, \mathcal{I}_3^{if}, \mathcal{I}_4^{if}\right) = ([0.3386, 0.3463], [0.5035, 0.5156]).$$

Further, the proposed operator $AIVIFC - IAAA$ satisfies certain properties, which are listed below.

Property 1. *When $\mathcal{I}_\varphi^{if} = \mathcal{I}^{if} = \left(\left[\Gamma^{\mathcal{I}^-}, \Gamma^{\mathcal{I}^+}\right], \left[\Lambda^{\mathcal{I}^-}, \Lambda^{\mathcal{I}^+}\right]\right), \varphi = 1, 2, \ldots, z$, thus*

$$AIVIFC - IAAA\left(\mathcal{I}_1^{if}, \mathcal{I}_2^{if}, \ldots, \mathcal{I}_z^{if}\right) = \mathcal{I}^{if} \tag{22}$$

The proof of Property 1 is given in Appendix B.

Property 2. *When $\mathcal{I}_\varphi^{if} \le \mathcal{I}^{*if}_\varphi, \varphi = 1, 2, \ldots, z$, then*

$$AIVIFC - IAAA\left(\mathcal{I}_1^{if}, \mathcal{I}_2^{if}, \ldots, \mathcal{I}_z^{if}\right) \le AIVIFC - IAAA\left(\mathcal{I}^{*if}_1, \mathcal{I}^{*if}_2, \ldots, \mathcal{I}^{*if}_z\right) \tag{23}$$

The proof of Property 2 is given in Appendix C.

Property 3. *When $\mathcal{I}_\varphi^- = \left(\left[\min_\varphi \Gamma_\varphi^{\mathcal{I}^-}, \min_\varphi \Gamma_\varphi^{\mathcal{I}^+}\right], \left[\max_\varphi \Lambda_\varphi^{\mathcal{I}^-}, \max_\varphi \Lambda_\varphi^{\mathcal{I}^+}\right]\right)$ and $\mathcal{I}_\varphi^+ = \left(\left[\max_\varphi \Gamma_\varphi^{\mathcal{I}^-}, \max_\varphi \Gamma_\varphi^{\mathcal{I}^+}\right], \left[\min_\varphi \Lambda_\varphi^{\mathcal{I}^-}, \min_\varphi \Lambda_\varphi^{\mathcal{I}^+}\right]\right), \varphi = 1, 2, \ldots, z$, thus*

$$\mathcal{I}_\varphi^- \le AIVIFC - IAAA\left(\mathcal{I}_1^{if}, \mathcal{I}_2^{if}, \ldots, \mathcal{I}_z^{if}\right) \le \mathcal{I}_\varphi^+ \tag{24}$$

The proof of Property 3 is given in Appendix D.

Definition 13. *An AIVIFC-IAAOA operator is demonstrated by:*

$$\begin{aligned} IVIFC - IAAOA \quad & \left(\mathcal{I}_1^{if}, \mathcal{I}_2^{if}, \ldots, \mathcal{I}_z^{if}\right) \\ & = \mathcal{I}_{o(1)}^{if}\left(\blacksquare\left(\Xi\rho_{(1)}\right) - \blacksquare\left(\Xi\rho_{(2)}\right)\right) \oplus \mathcal{I}_{o(2)}^{if}\left(\blacksquare\left(\Xi\rho_{(2)}\right) - \blacksquare\left(\Xi\rho_{(3)}\right)\right) \oplus \ldots \\ & \oplus \mathcal{I}_{o(z)}^{if}\left(\blacksquare\left(\Xi\rho_{(z)}\right) - \blacksquare\left(\Xi\rho_{(z+1)}\right)\right) \\ & = \sum_{\varphi=1}^{z} \mathcal{I}_{o(\varphi)}^{if}\left(\blacksquare\left(\Xi\rho_{(\varphi)}\right) - \blacksquare\left(\Xi\rho_{(\varphi+1)}\right)\right) \\ & = \oplus_{\varphi=1}^{z} \mathcal{I}_{o(\varphi)}^{if}\left(\blacksquare\left(\Xi\rho_{(\varphi)}\right) - \blacksquare\left(\Xi\rho_{(\varphi+1)}\right)\right) \end{aligned} \tag{25}$$

With a dominant condition$o(\varphi) \le o(\varphi - 1)$ and with the data in Equation (18), we find their orders.

Theorem 2. *For the family of AIVIFSs, the aggregated value by the $AIVIFC - IAAOA$ operator is also AIVIFV and given as*

$$AIVIFC - IAAOA\left(\mathcal{I}_1^{if}, \mathcal{I}_2^{if}, \ldots, \mathcal{I}_z^{if}\right) = \left(\begin{array}{c} \left[\begin{array}{c} 1 - e^{-\left(\sum_{\varphi=1}^{z}\left(\blacksquare(\Xi\rho_{(\varphi)}) - \blacksquare(\Xi\rho_{(\varphi+1)})\right)\left(-\log\left(1 - \Gamma_{o(\varphi)}^{\mathcal{I}^-}\right)\right)^{\varpi}\right)^{\frac{1}{\varpi}}}, \\ 1 - e^{-\left(\sum_{\varphi=1}^{z}\left(\blacksquare(\Xi\rho_{(\varphi)}) - \blacksquare(\Xi\rho_{(\varphi+1)})\right)\left(-\log\left(1 - \Gamma_{o(\varphi)}^{\mathcal{I}^+}\right)\right)^{\varpi}\right)^{\frac{1}{\varpi}}} \end{array}\right], \\ \left[\begin{array}{c} e^{-\left(\sum_{\varphi=1}^{z}\left(\blacksquare(\Xi\rho_{(\varphi)}) - \blacksquare(\Xi\rho_{(\varphi+1)})\right)\left(-\log\left(\Lambda_{o(\varphi)}^{\mathcal{I}^-}\right)\right)^{\varpi}\right)^{\frac{1}{\varpi}}}, \\ e^{-\left(\sum_{\varphi=1}^{z}\left(\blacksquare(\Xi\rho_{(\varphi)}) - \blacksquare(\Xi\rho_{(\varphi+1)})\right)\left(-\log\left(\Lambda_{o(\varphi)}^{\mathcal{I}^+}\right)\right)^{\varpi}\right)^{\frac{1}{\varpi}}} \end{array}\right] \end{array}\right) \tag{26}$$

Proof. Similar to the proof of Theorem 1. □

Property 4. *When* $\mathcal{I}_{\varphi}^{if} = \mathcal{I}^{if} = \left(\left[\Gamma^{\mathcal{I}^-}, \Gamma^{\mathcal{I}^+}\right], \left[\Lambda^{\mathcal{I}^-}, \Lambda^{\mathcal{I}^+}\right]\right), \varphi = 1, 2, \ldots, z$, *thus*

$$AIVIFC - IAAOA\left(\mathcal{I}_1^{if}, \mathcal{I}_2^{if}, \ldots, \mathcal{I}_z^{if}\right) = \mathcal{I}^{if} \quad (27)$$

Proof. Similar to the proof of Property 1.□

Property 5. *When* $\mathcal{I}_{\varphi}^{if} \leq \mathcal{I}^{*}{}_{\varphi}^{if}, \varphi = 1, 2, \ldots, z$, *then*

$$AIVIFC - IAAOA\left(\mathcal{I}_1^{if}, \mathcal{I}_2^{if}, \ldots, \mathcal{I}_z^{if}\right) \leq AIVIFC - IAAOA\left(\mathcal{I}^{*}{}_1^{if}, \mathcal{I}^{*}{}_2^{if}, \ldots, \mathcal{I}^{*}{}_z^{if}\right) \quad (28)$$

Proof. Similar to the proof of Property 2.□

Property 6. *When* $\mathcal{I}_{\varphi}^{-} = \left(\left[\min_{\varphi}\Gamma_{\varphi}^{\mathcal{I}^-}, \min_{\varphi}\Gamma_{\varphi}^{\mathcal{I}^+}\right], \left[\max_{\varphi}\Lambda_{\varphi}^{\mathcal{I}^-}, \max_{\varphi}\Lambda_{\varphi}^{\mathcal{I}^+}\right]\right)$ *and* $\mathcal{I}_{\varphi}^{+} = \left(\left[\max_{\varphi}\Gamma_{\varphi}^{\mathcal{I}^-}, \max_{\varphi}\Gamma_{\varphi}^{\mathcal{I}^+}\right], \left[\min_{\varphi}\Lambda_{\varphi}^{\mathcal{I}^-}, \min_{\varphi}\Lambda_{\varphi}^{\mathcal{I}^+}\right]\right), \varphi = 1, 2, \ldots, z$, *thus*

$$\mathcal{I}_{\varphi}^{-} \leq AIVIFC - IAAOA\left(\mathcal{I}_1^{if}, \mathcal{I}_2^{if}, \ldots, \mathcal{I}_z^{if}\right) \leq \mathcal{I}_{\varphi}^{+} \quad (29)$$

Proof. Similar to the proof of Property 3. □

Definition 14. *An AIVIFC-IAAHA operator is demonstrated by:*

$$\begin{aligned} AIVIFC - IAAHA \; &\left(\mathcal{I}_1^{if}, \mathcal{I}_2^{if}, \ldots, \mathcal{I}_z^{if}\right) \\ &= \mathcal{I}_{o(1)}^{*}\left(\blacksquare\left(\Xi\rho_{(1)}\right) - \blacksquare\left(\Xi\rho_{(2)}\right)\right) \oplus \mathcal{I}_{o(2)}^{*}\left(\blacksquare\left(\Xi\rho_{(2)}\right) - \blacksquare\left(\Xi\rho_{(3)}\right)\right) \oplus \ldots \\ &\oplus \mathcal{I}_{o(z)}^{*}\left(\blacksquare\left(\Xi\rho_{(z)}\right) - \blacksquare\left(\Xi\rho_{(z+1)}\right)\right) = \sum_{\varphi=1}^{z} \mathcal{I}_{o(\varphi)}^{*}\left(\blacksquare\left(\Xi\rho_{(\varphi)}\right) - \blacksquare\left(\Xi\rho_{(\varphi+1)}\right)\right) \\ &= \oplus_{\varphi=1}^{z}\mathcal{I}_{o(\varphi)}^{*}\left(\blacksquare\left(\Xi\rho_{(\varphi)}\right) - \blacksquare\left(\Xi\rho_{(\varphi+1)}\right)\right) \end{aligned} \quad (30)$$

With a dominant condition $o(\varphi) \leq o(\varphi - 1)$ *and with the data in Equation (18), we find their order with* $\mathcal{I}_{o(\varphi)}^{*} = z w_{\varphi} \mathcal{I}_{(\varphi)}^{if}, \varphi = 1, 2, \ldots, z$, *where* w_{φ} *represents the weight vector with the rule* $\sum_{\varphi=1}^{z} w_{\varphi} = 1$.

Theorem 3. *For the family of AIVIFSs, the aggregated value by the* $AIVIFC - IAAHA$*operator is also AIVIFV and given as*

$$AIVIFC - IAAHA\left(\mathcal{I}_1^{if}, \mathcal{I}_2^{if}, \ldots, \mathcal{I}_z^{if}\right) = \left(\begin{array}{c} \left[\begin{array}{c} 1 - e^{-\left(\sum_{\varphi=1}^{z}\left(\blacksquare\left(\Xi\rho_{(\varphi)}\right) - \blacksquare\left(\Xi\rho_{(\varphi+1)}\right)\right)\left(-\log\left(1 - \Gamma_{o(\varphi)}^{\mathcal{I}^{-*}}\right)\right)^{\varpi}\right)^{\frac{1}{\varpi}}}, \\ 1 - e^{-\left(\sum_{\varphi=1}^{z}\left(\blacksquare\left(\Xi\rho_{(\varphi)}\right) - \blacksquare\left(\Xi\rho_{(\varphi+1)}\right)\right)\left(-\log\left(1 - \Gamma_{o(\varphi)}^{\mathcal{I}^{+*}}\right)\right)^{\varpi}\right)^{\frac{1}{\varpi}}} \end{array}\right], \\ \left[\begin{array}{c} e^{-\left(\sum_{\varphi=1}^{z}\left(\blacksquare\left(\Xi\rho_{(\varphi)}\right) - \blacksquare\left(\Xi\rho_{(\varphi+1)}\right)\right)\left(-\log\left(\Lambda_{o(\varphi)}^{\mathcal{I}^{-*}}\right)\right)^{\varpi}\right)^{\frac{1}{\varpi}}}, \\ e^{-\left(\sum_{\varphi=1}^{z}\left(\blacksquare\left(\Xi\rho_{(\varphi)}\right) - \blacksquare\left(\Xi\rho_{(\varphi+1)}\right)\right)\left(-\log\left(\Lambda_{o(\varphi)}^{\mathcal{I}^{+*}}\right)\right)^{\varpi}\right)^{\frac{1}{\varpi}}} \end{array}\right] \end{array}\right) \quad (31)$$

Property 7. *When* $\mathcal{I}_{\varphi}^{if} = \mathcal{I}^{if} = \left(\left[\Gamma^{\mathcal{I}^-}, \Gamma^{\mathcal{I}^+}\right], \left[\Lambda^{\mathcal{I}^-}, \Lambda^{\mathcal{I}^+}\right]\right), \varphi = 1, 2, \ldots, z$, *thus*

$$AIVIFC - IAAHA\left(\mathcal{I}_1^{if}, \mathcal{I}_2^{if}, \ldots, \mathcal{I}_z^{if}\right) = \mathcal{I}^{if} \quad (32)$$

Property 8. *When* $\mathcal{I}_\varphi^{if} \leq \mathcal{I}^{*if}_\varphi, \varphi = 1, 2, \ldots, z$, *then*

$$AIVIFC - IAAHA\left(\mathcal{I}_1^{if}, \mathcal{I}_2^{if}, \ldots, \mathcal{I}_z^{if}\right) \leq AIVIFC - IAAHA\left(\mathcal{I}^{*if}_1, \mathcal{I}^{*if}_2, \ldots, \mathcal{I}^{*if}_z\right) \quad (33)$$

Property 9. *When* $\mathcal{I}_\varphi^- = \left(\left[\min_\varphi \Gamma_\varphi^{\mathcal{I}^-}, \min_\varphi \Gamma_\varphi^{\mathcal{I}^+}\right], \left[\max_\varphi \Lambda_\varphi^{\mathcal{I}^-}, \max_\varphi \Lambda_\varphi^{\mathcal{I}^+}\right]\right)$ *and* $\mathcal{I}_\varphi^+ = \left(\left[\max_\varphi \Gamma_\varphi^{\mathcal{I}^-}, \max_\varphi \Gamma_\varphi^{\mathcal{I}^+}\right], \left[\max_\varphi \Gamma_\varphi^{\mathcal{I}^-}, \max_\varphi \Gamma_\varphi^{\mathcal{I}^+}\right]\right), \varphi = 1, 2, \ldots, z$, *thus*

$$\mathcal{I}_\varphi^- \leq AIVIFC - IAAHA\left(\mathcal{I}_1^{if}, \mathcal{I}_2^{if}, \ldots, \mathcal{I}_z^{if}\right) \leq \mathcal{I}_\varphi^+ \quad (34)$$

Definition 15. *An AIVIFC-IAAG operator is demonstrated by:*

$$\begin{aligned} AIVIFC - IAAG&\left(\mathcal{I}_1^{if}, \mathcal{I}_2^{if}, \ldots, \mathcal{I}_z^{if}\right) \\ &= \left(\mathcal{I}_1^{if}\right)^{(\blacksquare(\Xi\rho_{(1)}) - \blacksquare(\Xi\rho_{(2)}))} \otimes \left(\mathcal{I}_2^{if}\right)^{(\blacksquare(\Xi\rho_{(2)}) - \blacksquare(\Xi\rho_{(3)}))} \otimes \ldots \otimes \left(\mathcal{I}_z^{if}\right)^{(\blacksquare(\Xi\rho_{(z)}) - \blacksquare(\Xi\rho_{(z+1)}))} \\ &= \prod_{\varphi=1}^{z} \left(\mathcal{I}_\varphi^{if}\right)^{(\blacksquare(\Xi\rho_{(\varphi)}) - \blacksquare(\Xi\rho_{(\varphi+1)}))} \\ &= \otimes_{\varphi=1}^{z} \left(\mathcal{I}_\varphi^{if}\right)^{(\blacksquare(\Xi\rho_{(\varphi)}) - \blacksquare(\Xi\rho_{(\varphi+1)}))} \end{aligned} \quad (35)$$

Theorem 4. *For the family of AIVIFSs, the aggregated value by the* $AIVIFC - IAAG$ *operator is also AIVIFV and given as*

$$AIVIFC - IAAG\left(\mathcal{I}_1^{if}, \mathcal{I}_2^{if}, \ldots, \mathcal{I}_z^{if}\right) = \left(\begin{array}{c} \left[\begin{array}{c} e^{-\left(\sum_{\varphi=1}^{z}(\blacksquare(\Xi\rho_{(\varphi)}) - \blacksquare(\Xi\rho_{(\varphi+1)}))(-\log(\Gamma_\varphi^{\mathcal{I}^-}))^{\varpi}\right)^{\frac{1}{\varpi}}}, \\ e^{-\left(\sum_{\varphi=1}^{z}(\blacksquare(\Xi\rho_{(\varphi)}) - \blacksquare(\Xi\rho_{(\varphi+1)}))(-\log(\Gamma_\varphi^{\mathcal{I}^+}))^{\varpi}\right)^{\frac{1}{\varpi}}} \end{array}\right], \\ \left[\begin{array}{c} 1 - e^{-\left(\sum_{\varphi=1}^{z}(\blacksquare(\Xi\rho_{(\varphi)}) - \blacksquare(\Xi\rho_{(\varphi+1)}))(-\log(1-\Lambda_\varphi^{\mathcal{I}^-}))^{\varpi}\right)^{\frac{1}{\varpi}}}, \\ 1 - e^{-\left(\sum_{\varphi=1}^{z}(\blacksquare(\Xi\rho_{(\varphi)}) - \blacksquare(\Xi\rho_{(\varphi+1)}))(-\log(1-\Lambda_\varphi^{\mathcal{I}^+}))^{\varpi}\right)^{\frac{1}{\varpi}}} \end{array}\right] \end{array}\right) \quad (36)$$

The proof of Theorem 4 is given in Appendix E.

To demonstrate the functioning of the proposed AIVIFC-IAAG operator, we consider four AIVIFNs:

$$\mathcal{I}_1^{if} = ([0.40, 0.41], [0.30, 0.31]); \quad \mathcal{I}_2^{if} = ([0.50, 0.51], [0.10, 0.11])$$

$$\mathcal{I}_3^{if} = ([0.59, 0.60], [0.39, 0.40]); \; \mathcal{I}_4^{if} = ([0.70, 0.71], [0.20, 0.21])$$

To aggregate these numbers, we utilize Equation (36) and obtain the aggregated number

$$AIVIFC - IAAG\left(\mathcal{I}_1^{if}, \mathcal{I}_2^{if}, \mathcal{I}_3^{if}, \mathcal{I}_4^{if}\right) = ([0.7763, 0.7823], \; [0.1326, 0.1326]).$$

Further, the proposed operator $AIVIFC - IAAG$ *satisfies certain properties, which are listed below.*

Property 10. *When* $\mathcal{I}_\varphi^{if} = \mathcal{I}^{if} = \left(\left[\Gamma^{\mathcal{I}^-}, \Gamma^{\mathcal{I}^+}\right], \left[\Lambda^{\mathcal{I}^-}, \Lambda^{\mathcal{I}^+}\right]\right), \varphi = 1, 2, \ldots, z$, *thus*

$$AIVIFC - IAAG\left(\mathcal{I}_1^{if}, \mathcal{I}_2^{if}, \ldots, \mathcal{I}_z^{if}\right) = \mathcal{I}^{if} \tag{37}$$

Property 11. *When* $\mathcal{I}_\varphi^{if} \leq \mathcal{I}^{*if}_\varphi, \varphi = 1, 2, \ldots, z$, *then*

$$AIVIFC - IAAG\left(\mathcal{I}_1^{if}, \mathcal{I}_2^{if}, \ldots, \mathcal{I}_z^{if}\right) \leq AIVIFC - IAAG\left(\mathcal{I}^{*if}_1, \mathcal{I}^{*if}_2, \ldots, \mathcal{I}^{*if}_z\right) \tag{38}$$

Property 12. *When* $\mathcal{I}_\varphi^- = \left(\left[\min_\varphi \Gamma_\varphi^{\mathcal{I}^-}, \min_\varphi \Gamma_\varphi^{\mathcal{I}^+}\right], \left[\max_\varphi \Lambda_\varphi^{\mathcal{I}^-}, \max_\varphi \Lambda_\varphi^{\mathcal{I}^+}\right]\right)$ *and* $\mathcal{I}_\varphi^+ = \left(\left[\max_\varphi \Gamma_\varphi^{\mathcal{I}^-}, \max_\varphi \Gamma_\varphi^{\mathcal{I}^+}\right], \left[\min_\varphi \Lambda_\varphi^{\mathcal{I}^-}, \min_\varphi \Lambda_\varphi^{\mathcal{I}^+}\right]\right), \varphi = 1, 2, \ldots, z$, *thus*

$$\mathcal{I}_\varphi^- \leq AIVIFC - IAAG\left(\mathcal{I}_1^{if}, \mathcal{I}_2^{if}, \ldots, \mathcal{I}_z^{if}\right) \leq \mathcal{I}_\varphi^+ \tag{39}$$

Definition 16. *An AIVIFC-IAAOA operator is demonstrated by:*

$$\begin{aligned} AIVIFC - IAAOG & \left(\mathcal{I}_1^{if}, \mathcal{I}_2^{if}, \ldots, \mathcal{I}_z^{if}\right) \\ &= \left(\mathcal{I}_{o(1)}^{if}\right)^{(\blacksquare(\Xi\rho_{(1)}) - \blacksquare(\Xi\rho_{(2)}))} \otimes \left(\mathcal{I}_{o(2)}^{if}\right)^{(\blacksquare(\Xi\rho_{(2)}) - \blacksquare(\Xi\rho_{(3)}))} \otimes \ldots \otimes \left(\mathcal{I}_{o(z)}^{if}\right)^{(\blacksquare(\Xi\rho_{(z)}) - \blacksquare(\Xi\rho_{(z+1)}))} \\ &= \prod_{\varphi=1}^{z} \left(\mathcal{I}_{o(\varphi)}^{if}\right)^{(\blacksquare(\Xi\rho_{(\varphi)}) - \blacksquare(\Xi\rho_{(\varphi+1)}))} = \otimes_{\varphi=1}^{z} \left(\mathcal{I}_{o(\varphi)}^{if}\right)^{(\blacksquare(\Xi\rho_{(\varphi)}) - \blacksquare(\Xi\rho_{(\varphi+1)}))} \end{aligned} \tag{40}$$

With a dominant condition $o(\varphi) \leq o(\varphi - 1)$ *and with the data in Equation (18), we find their orders.*

Theorem 5. *For the family of AIVIFSs, the aggregated value by the* $AIVIFC - IAAOG$ *operator is also AIVIFV and given as*

$$AIVIFC - IAAOG\left(\mathcal{I}_1^{if}, \mathcal{I}_2^{if}, \ldots, \mathcal{I}_z^{if}\right) = \left(\begin{array}{c} \left[\begin{array}{c} e^{-\left(\sum_{\varphi=1}^{z} (\blacksquare(\Xi\rho_{(\varphi)}) - \blacksquare(\Xi\rho_{(\varphi+1)}))(-\log(\Gamma_{o(\varphi)}^{\mathcal{I}^-}))^{\varpi}\right)^{\frac{1}{\varpi}}}, \\ e^{-\left(\sum_{\varphi=1}^{z} (\blacksquare(\Xi\rho_{(\varphi)}) - \blacksquare(\Xi\rho_{(\varphi+1)}))(-\log(\Gamma_{o(\varphi)}^{\mathcal{I}^+}))^{\varpi}\right)^{\frac{1}{\varpi}}} \end{array}\right], \\ \left[\begin{array}{c} 1 - e^{-\left(\sum_{\varphi=1}^{z} (\blacksquare(\Xi\rho_{(\varphi)}) - \blacksquare(\Xi\rho_{(\varphi+1)}))(-\log(1 - \Lambda_{o(\varphi)}^{\mathcal{I}^-}))^{\varpi}\right)^{\frac{1}{\varpi}}}, \\ 1 - e^{-\left(\sum_{\varphi=1}^{z} (\blacksquare(\Xi\rho_{(\varphi)}) - \blacksquare(\Xi\rho_{(\varphi+1)}))(-\log(1 - \Lambda_{o(\varphi)}^{\mathcal{I}^+}))^{\varpi}\right)^{\frac{1}{\varpi}}} \end{array}\right] \end{array}\right) \tag{41}$$

Property 13. *When* $\mathcal{I}_\varphi^{if} = \mathcal{I}^{if} = \left(\left[\Gamma^{\mathcal{I}^-}, \Gamma^{\mathcal{I}^+}\right], \left[\Lambda^{\mathcal{I}^-}, \Lambda^{\mathcal{I}^+}\right]\right), \varphi = 1, 2, \ldots, z$, *thus*

$$AIVIFC - IAAOG\left(\mathcal{I}_1^{if}, \mathcal{I}_2^{if}, \ldots, \mathcal{I}_z^{if}\right) = \mathcal{I}^{if} \tag{42}$$

Property 14. *When* $\mathcal{I}_\varphi^{if} \leq \mathcal{I}^{*if}_\varphi, \varphi = 1, 2, \ldots, z$, *then*

$$AIVIFC - IAAOG\left(\mathcal{I}_1^{if}, \mathcal{I}_2^{if}, \ldots, \mathcal{I}_z^{if}\right) \leq AIVIFC - IAAOG\left(\mathcal{I}^{*if}_1, \mathcal{I}^{*if}_2, \ldots, \mathcal{I}^{*if}_z\right) \tag{43}$$

Property 15. *When* $\mathcal{I}_{\varphi}^{-} = \left(\left[\min\limits_{\varphi}\Gamma_{\varphi}^{\mathcal{I}^{-}}, \min\limits_{\varphi}\Gamma_{\varphi}^{\mathcal{I}^{+}}\right], \left[\max\limits_{\varphi}\Lambda_{\varphi}^{\mathcal{I}^{-}}, \max\limits_{\varphi}\Lambda_{\varphi}^{\mathcal{I}^{+}}\right]\right)$ *and* $\mathcal{I}_{\varphi}^{+} = \left(\left[\max\limits_{\varphi}\Gamma_{\varphi}^{\mathcal{I}^{-}}, \max\limits_{\varphi}\Gamma_{\varphi}^{\mathcal{I}^{+}}\right], \left[\min\limits_{\varphi}\Lambda_{\varphi}^{\mathcal{I}^{-}}, \min\limits_{\varphi}\Lambda_{\varphi}^{\mathcal{I}^{+}}\right]\right), \varphi = 1, 2, \ldots, z$, *thus*

$$\mathcal{I}_{\varphi}^{-} \leq AIVIFC - IAAOG\left(\mathcal{I}_1^{if}, \mathcal{I}_2^{if}, \ldots, \mathcal{I}_z^{if}\right) \leq \mathcal{I}_{\varphi}^{+} \tag{44}$$

Definition 17. *An AIVIFC-IAAHG operator is demonstrated by:*

$$\begin{aligned} AIVIFC - IAAHG & \left(\mathcal{I}_1^{if}, \mathcal{I}_2^{if}, \ldots, \mathcal{I}_z^{if}\right) \\ &= \left(\mathcal{I}_{o(1)}^{*}\right)^{(\blacksquare(\Xi\rho_{(1)}) - \blacksquare(\Xi\rho_{(2)}))} \otimes \left(\mathcal{I}_{o(2)}^{*}\right)^{(\blacksquare(\Xi\rho_{(2)}) - \blacksquare(\Xi\rho_{(3)}))} \otimes \ldots \otimes \left(\mathcal{I}_{o(z)}^{*}\right)^{(\blacksquare(\Xi\rho_{(z)}) - \blacksquare(\Xi\rho_{(z+1)}))} \\ &= \prod_{\varphi=1}^{z} \left(\mathcal{I}_{o(\varphi)}^{*}\right)^{(\blacksquare(\Xi\rho_{(\varphi)}) - \blacksquare(\Xi\rho_{(\varphi+1)}))} = \otimes_{\varphi=1}^{z} \left(\mathcal{I}_{o(\varphi)}^{*}\right)^{(\blacksquare(\Xi\rho_{(\varphi)}) - \blacksquare(\Xi\rho_{(\varphi+1)}))} \end{aligned} \tag{45}$$

With a dominant condition $o(\varphi) \leq o(\varphi - 1)$ *and with the data in Equation (18), we find their order with* $\mathcal{I}_{o(\varphi)}^{*} = zw_{\varphi}\mathcal{I}_{(\varphi)}^{if}, \varphi = 1, 2, \ldots, z$, *where* w_{φ} *represents the weight vector with the rule* $\sum\limits_{\varphi=1}^{z} w_{\varphi} = 1$.

Theorem 6. *For the family of AIVIFSs, the aggregated value by the* $AIVIFC - IAAHG$ *operator is also AIVIFV and given as*

$$AIVIFC - IAAHG\left(\mathcal{I}_1^{if}, \mathcal{I}_2^{if}, \ldots, \mathcal{I}_z^{if}\right) = \left(\begin{array}{c} \left[\begin{array}{c} e^{-\left(\sum_{\varphi=1}^{z}(\blacksquare(\Xi\rho_{(\varphi)}) - \blacksquare(\Xi\rho_{(\varphi+1)}))(-\log(\Gamma_{o(\varphi)}^{\mathcal{I}^{-*}}))^{\varpi}\right)^{\frac{1}{\varpi}}}, \\ e^{-\left(\sum_{\varphi=1}^{z}(\blacksquare(\Xi\rho_{(\varphi)}) - \blacksquare(\Xi\rho_{(\varphi+1)}))(-\log(\Gamma_{o(\varphi)}^{\mathcal{I}^{+*}}))^{\varpi}\right)^{\frac{1}{\varpi}}} \end{array}\right], \\ \left[\begin{array}{c} 1 - e^{-\left(\sum_{\varphi=1}^{z}(\blacksquare(\Xi\rho_{(\varphi)}) - \blacksquare(\Xi\rho_{(\varphi+1)}))(-\log(1 - \Lambda_{o(\varphi)}^{\mathcal{I}^{-*}}))^{\varpi}\right)^{\frac{1}{\varpi}}}, \\ 1 - e^{-\left(\sum_{\varphi=1}^{z}(\blacksquare(\Xi\rho_{(\varphi)}) - \blacksquare(\Xi\rho_{(\varphi+1)}))(-\log(1 - \Lambda_{o(\varphi)}^{\mathcal{I}^{+*}}))^{\varpi}\right)^{\frac{1}{\varpi}}} \end{array}\right] \end{array}\right) \tag{46}$$

Property 16. *When* $\mathcal{I}_{\varphi}^{if} = \mathcal{I}^{if} = \left(\left[\Gamma^{\mathcal{I}^{-}}, \Gamma^{\mathcal{I}^{+}}\right], \left[\Lambda^{\mathcal{I}^{-}}, \Lambda^{\mathcal{I}^{+}}\right]\right), \varphi = 1, 2, \ldots, z$, *thus*

$$AIVIFC - IAAHG\left(\mathcal{I}_1^{if}, \mathcal{I}_2^{if}, \ldots, \mathcal{I}_z^{if}\right) = \mathcal{I}^{if} \tag{47}$$

Property 17. *When* $\mathcal{I}_{\varphi}^{if} \leq \mathcal{I}^{*}{}_{\varphi}^{if}, \varphi = 1, 2, \ldots, z$, *then*

$$AIVIFC - IAAHG\left(\mathcal{I}_1^{if}, \mathcal{I}_2^{if}, \ldots, \mathcal{I}_z^{if}\right) \leq AIVIFC - IAAHG\left(\mathcal{I}^{*}{}_1^{if}, \mathcal{I}^{*}{}_2^{if}, \ldots, \mathcal{I}^{*}{}_z^{if}\right) \tag{48}$$

Property 18. *When* $\mathcal{I}_{\varphi}^{-} = \left(\left[\min\limits_{\varphi}\Gamma_{\varphi}^{\mathcal{I}^{-}}, \min\limits_{\varphi}\Gamma_{\varphi}^{\mathcal{I}^{+}}\right], \left[\max\limits_{\varphi}\Lambda_{\varphi}^{\mathcal{I}^{-}}, \max\limits_{\varphi}\Lambda_{\varphi}^{\mathcal{I}^{+}}\right]\right)$ *and* $\mathcal{I}_{\varphi}^{+} = \left(\left[\max\limits_{\varphi}\Gamma_{\varphi}^{\mathcal{I}^{-}}, \max\limits_{\varphi}\Gamma_{\varphi}^{\mathcal{I}^{+}}\right], \left[\min\limits_{\varphi}\Lambda_{\varphi}^{\mathcal{I}^{-}}, \min\limits_{\varphi}\Lambda_{\varphi}^{\mathcal{I}^{+}}\right]\right), \varphi = 1, 2, \ldots, z$, *thus*

$$\mathcal{I}_{\varphi}^{-} \leq AIVIFC - IAAHG\left(\mathcal{I}_1^{if}, \mathcal{I}_2^{if}, \ldots, \mathcal{I}_z^{if}\right) \leq \mathcal{I}_{\varphi}^{+} \tag{49}$$

4. Proposed MADM Technique

The multi-attribute decision-making (MADM) technique is a procedure or technique, which is especially used, for evaluating the optimal decision in the presence of multiple criteria or attributes. It is used in situations when an expert or decision-maker needs to find the best one among a finite number of alternatives or possibilities.

In MADM, each alternative contains many criteria or attributes, and these attributes can be qualitative or quantitative, which are very important for the procedure of the decision-making technique. Every example of attributes or criteria could contain cost, quality, time, environmental impact, and many others, whereas every MADM procedure contains the following major themes, such as the identification of criteria, the weighting of criteria, the evaluation of alternatives, the aggregation of sources, and finally, the selection of the best decision. Therefore, to evaluate some real-life problems, first, we need to develop the procedure of the MADM technique. For this, we have a collection of alternatives, such as $\mathcal{I}_1^{if},\mathcal{I}_2^{if},\ldots,\mathcal{I}_z^{if}$, where each alternative covers the finite family of attributes or criteria, such as $\mathcal{I}_1^{cr},\mathcal{I}_2^{cr},\ldots,\mathcal{I}_y^{cr}$ with w_φ, where w_φ represents the weight vector with the rule $\sum_{\varphi=1}^{z} w_\varphi = 1$. Further, we aim to assign AIVIFN to each attribute in every alternative, where the information in the pair $\left(\left[\Gamma^{\mathcal{I}^-}(v),\Gamma^{\mathcal{I}^+}(v)\right],\left[\Lambda^{\mathcal{I}^-}(v),\Lambda^{\mathcal{I}^+}(v)\right]\right)$ represents the membership and non-membership degrees with a suitable condition: $0 \leq \Gamma^{\mathcal{I}^+}(v) + \Lambda^{\mathcal{I}^+}(v) \leq 1$. Moreover, we constructed the neutral/refusal information, such as $\eta^{\mathcal{I}}(v) = \left[\eta^{\mathcal{I}^-}(v),\eta^{\mathcal{I}^+}(v)\right] = \left[1-\left(\Gamma^{\mathcal{I}^-}(v)+\Lambda^{\mathcal{I}^-}(v)\right),1-\left(\Gamma^{\mathcal{I}^+}(v)+\Lambda^{\mathcal{I}^+}(v)\right)\right]$. Finally, the AIVIFV was constructed in the shape $\mathcal{I}_\varphi^{if} = \left(\left[\Gamma_\varphi^{\mathcal{I}^-},\Gamma_\varphi^{\mathcal{I}^+}\right],\left[\Lambda_\varphi^{\mathcal{I}^-},\Lambda_\varphi^{\mathcal{I}^+}\right]\right),\varphi = 1,2,\ldots,z$. All the information was arranged in the shape of a matrix, and then for evaluating the data in the matrix, we aimed to construct the procedure of the MADM technique; therefore, we have the following procedure:

Step 1: First, we arrange the AIVIFSs in the form of the matrix, but during the collection of information, we will face two types of data, such as benefit and cost types of information. These attributes show the positive and negative features of each alternative. For both kinds of data, we have the following rules, for instance:

Rule 1: (Benefit type of data.) We are not required to normalize the arranged data in the matrix;

Rule 2: (Cost type of data.) We are required to normalize the arranged data in a matrix; for instance,

$$N = \begin{cases} \left(\left[\Gamma_\varphi^{\mathcal{I}^-},\Gamma_\varphi^{\mathcal{I}^+}\right],\left[\Lambda_\varphi^{\mathcal{I}^-},\Lambda_\varphi^{\mathcal{I}^+}\right]\right) & for\ B \\ \left(\left[\Lambda_\varphi^{\mathcal{I}^-},\Lambda_\varphi^{\mathcal{I}^+}\right],\left[\Gamma_\varphi^{\mathcal{I}^-},\Gamma_\varphi^{\mathcal{I}^+}\right]\right) & for\ C \end{cases}$$

where B and C represent the benefit and cost types of data.

Step 2: After normalization (if necessary), we aggregate the arranged information based on the proposed AIVIFC-IAAA operator and AIVIFC-IAAG operator, such as

$$AIVIFC-IAAA\left(\mathcal{I}_1^{if},\mathcal{I}_2^{if},\ldots,\mathcal{I}_z^{if}\right) = \left(\begin{array}{c} \left[\begin{array}{l} 1-e^{-\left(\sum_{\varphi=1}^{z}\left(\blacksquare(\Xi\rho_{(\varphi)})-\blacksquare(\Xi\rho_{(\varphi+1)})\right)\left(-\log\left(1-\Gamma_\varphi^{\mathcal{I}^-}\right)\right)^{\varpi}\right)^{\frac{1}{\varpi}}}, \\ 1-e^{-\left(\sum_{\varphi=1}^{z}\left(\blacksquare(\Xi\rho_{(\varphi)})-\blacksquare(\Xi\rho_{(\varphi+1)})\right)\left(-\log\left(1-\Gamma_\varphi^{\mathcal{I}^+}\right)\right)^{\varpi}\right)^{\frac{1}{\varpi}}} \end{array}\right], \\ \left[\begin{array}{l} e^{-\left(\sum_{\varphi=1}^{z}\left(\blacksquare(\Xi\rho_{(\varphi)})-\blacksquare(\Xi\rho_{(\varphi+1)})\right)\left(-\log\left(\Lambda_\varphi^{\mathcal{I}^-}\right)\right)^{\varpi}\right)^{\frac{1}{\varpi}}}, \\ e^{-\left(\sum_{\varphi=1}^{z}\left(\blacksquare(\Xi\rho_{(\varphi)})-\blacksquare(\Xi\rho_{(\varphi+1)})\right)\left(-\log\left(\Lambda_\varphi^{\mathcal{I}^+}\right)\right)^{\varpi}\right)^{\frac{1}{\varpi}}} \end{array}\right] \end{array}\right)$$

$$AIVIFC-IAAG\left(\mathcal{I}_1^{if},\mathcal{I}_2^{if},\ldots,\mathcal{I}_z^{if}\right)=\left(\begin{array}{c}\left[\begin{array}{c}e^{-\left(\sum_{\varphi=1}^{z}\left(\blacksquare(\Xi\rho_{(\varphi)})-\blacksquare(\Xi\rho_{(\varphi+1)})\right)\left(-\log\left(\Gamma_{\varphi}^{\mathcal{I}^-}\right)\right)^{\varpi}\right)^{\frac{1}{\varpi}}},\\ e^{-\left(\sum_{\varphi=1}^{z}\left(\blacksquare(\Xi\rho_{(\varphi)})-\blacksquare(\Xi\rho_{(\varphi+1)})\right)\left(-\log\left(\Gamma_{\varphi}^{\mathcal{I}^+}\right)\right)^{\varpi}\right)^{\frac{1}{\varpi}}}\end{array}\right],\\ \left[\begin{array}{c}1-e^{-\left(\sum_{\varphi=1}^{z}\left(\blacksquare(\Xi\rho_{(\varphi)})-\blacksquare(\Xi\rho_{(\varphi+1)})\right)\left(-\log\left(1-\Lambda_{\varphi}^{\mathcal{I}^-}\right)\right)^{\varpi}\right)^{\frac{1}{\varpi}}},\\ 1-e^{-\left(\sum_{\varphi=1}^{z}\left(\blacksquare(\Xi\rho_{(\varphi)})-\blacksquare(\Xi\rho_{(\varphi+1)})\right)\left(-\log\left(1-\Lambda_{\varphi}^{\mathcal{I}^+}\right)\right)^{\varpi}\right)^{\frac{1}{\varpi}}}\end{array}\right]\end{array}\right)$$

Step 3: After aggregating the normalized data, we evaluate their score values (if the score function has failed, then we will use the accuracy function), which are given in Equations (18) and (19);

Step 4: Finally, we derive the ranking results of each alternative based on their score or accuracy values and try to examine the optimal or best decision.

After the successful implementation of the MADM technique for evaluating the problems, we aimed to choose some real-life applications and tried to resolve them with the help of the proposed four techniques.

5. Numerical Example (Human Activity Recognition)

The HAR technique is used for the identification or classification of human activities based on the analysis of sensor information. There are many kinds of HAR techniques, which are used in the field, varying on the concern, problems, and their requirements. The major theme of this application is to point out the best HAR technique among the five best HAR techniques, which are represented by a family of five alternatives, whose major and brief analyses are stated below:

Rule-based Systems "$\mathcal{I}_1^{if}$": To identify certain actions, rule-based systems employ predetermined rules or heuristics. These regulations are frequently founded on professional expertise or industry-specific standards. A rule-based system, for instance, may employ thresholds on accelerometer measurements to identify movements like walking or running.

Machine Learning-based Approaches "$\mathcal{I}_2^{if}$": The identification of human behavior makes extensive use of machine learning techniques. These methods use labeled datasets for model training to discover patterns and connections between sensor data and actions. Typical machine learning algorithms include the following:

(1) Supervised learning;
(2) Unsupervised learning;
(3) Deep learning.

Sensor Fusions"$\mathcal{I}_3^{if}$": To increase the precision of activity detection, sensor fusion combines data from various sensors. The system may record a more complete description of human actions by combining data from many sensors, including accelerometers, gyroscopes, and magnetometers.

Hidden Markov Models (HMMs) "$\mathcal{I}_4^{if}$": HMMs are popular probabilistic models for recognizing activities. To estimate the most likely sequence of activities given the observed sensor data, they model the temporal relationships of the activities and employ the Viterbi algorithm or forward–backward algorithm.

Dynamic Time Warping (DTW) "$\mathcal{I}_5^{if}$": DTW is a method for aligning two-time series in a nonlinear warping manner and measuring how similar they are. It is ideal for activity detection tasks, as it is frequently utilized for contrasting and identifying temporal patterns in sensor data.

Under the presence of the above five alternatives, we aimed to find the best one based on their features, which were used as attributes or criteria, such as $\mathcal{I}_1^{cr}$: data collection, $\mathcal{I}_2^{cr}$: preprocessing and data extraction, $\mathcal{I}_3^{cr}$: classification and evaluations, and $\mathcal{I}_4^{cr}$: monitoring and facilitating. Then, the steps of the proposed approach, as shown below, were implemented, to find the best alternative(s).

Step 1: First, we arrange the AIVIFSs in the form of the matrix (see Table 2), but during the collection of information, we will face two types of data, such as benefit and cost types information. These attributes show the positive and negative features of each alternative. For both kinds of data, we have the following rules, for instance:

Rule 1: (Benefit type of data.) We are not required to normalize the arranged data in the matrix;

Rule 2: (Cost type of data.) We are required to normalize the arranged data in a matrix; for instance,

$$N = \begin{cases} \left(\left[\Gamma_{\varphi}^{\mathcal{I}^-}, \Gamma_{\varphi}^{\mathcal{I}^+}\right], \left[\Lambda_{\varphi}^{\mathcal{I}^-}, \Lambda_{\varphi}^{\mathcal{I}^+}\right]\right) & for\ B \\ \left(\left[\Lambda_{\varphi}^{\mathcal{I}^-}, \Lambda_{\varphi}^{\mathcal{I}^+}\right], \left[\Gamma_{\varphi}^{\mathcal{I}^-}, \Gamma_{\varphi}^{\mathcal{I}^+}\right]\right) & for\ C \end{cases}$$

where B and C represent the benefit and cost types of data. But we used Rule 1 because we had positive types of criteria.

Table 2. AIVIF decision matrix.

	$\mathcal{I}_1^{cr}$	$\mathcal{I}_2^{cr}$	$\mathcal{I}_3^{cr}$	$\mathcal{I}_4^{cr}$
$\mathcal{I}_1^{if}$	([0.4, 0.41], [0.3, 0.31])	([0.5, 0.51], [0.1, 0.11])	([0.59, 0.6], [0.39, 0.4])	([0.7, 0.71], [0.2, 0.21])
$\mathcal{I}_2^{if}$	([0.4, 0.41], [0.2, 0.21])	([0.3, 0.31], [0.1, 0.11])	([0.5, 0.51], [0.3, 0.31])	([0.1, 0.11], [0.2, 0.21])
$\mathcal{I}_3^{if}$	([0.5, 0.51], [0.3, 0.31])	([0.4, 0.41], [0.3, 0.31])	([0.3, 0.31], [0.2, 0.21])	([0.2, 0.21], [0.1, 0.11])
$\mathcal{I}_4^{if}$	([0.4, 0.41], [0.2, 0.21])	([0.6, 0.61], [0.3, 0.31])	([0.5, 0.51], [0.4, 0.41])	([0.5, 0.51], [0.2, 0.21])
$\mathcal{I}_5^{if}$	([0.1, 0.11], [0.2, 0.21])	([0.2, 0.21], [0.2, 0.21])	([0.3, 0.31], [0.2, 0.21])	([0.6, 0.61], [0.1, 0.11])

Step 2: After normalization (if necessary), we aggregate the arranged information based on the proposed AIVIFC-IAAA operator and AIVIFC-IAAG operator (see Table 3);

Table 3. AIVIF aggregated decision matrix.

	AIVIFC-IAAA	**AIVIFC-IAAG**
$\mathcal{I}_1^{if}$	([0.3386, 0.3463], [0.5035, 0.5156])	([0.7763, 0.7823], [0.1326, 0.1326])
$\mathcal{I}_2^{if}$	([0.1768, 0.1821], [0.4827, 0.4948])	([0.4994, 0.5129], [0.1038, 0.1038])
$\mathcal{I}_3^{if}$	([0.1657, 0.1711], [0.5249, 0.4713])	([0.5748, 0.5842], [0.1129, 0.1129])
$\mathcal{I}_4^{if}$	([0.2692, 0.2758], [0.552, 0.5617])	([0.7386, 0.745], [0.142, 0.142])
$\mathcal{I}_5^{if}$	([0.2311, 0.2371], [0.4376, 0.451])	([0.5616, 0.5728], [0.0781, 0.0781])

Step 3: After aggregating the normalized data, we evaluate their score values (if the score function has failed, then we will use the accuracy function), which are given in Equations (18) and (19) (see Table 4);

Table 4. AIVIF score matrix.

	AIVIFC-IAAA	AIVIFC-IAAG
$\mathcal{I}_1^{if}$	−0.1671	0.6467
$\mathcal{I}_2^{if}$	−0.3093	0.4023
$\mathcal{I}_3^{if}$	−0.3298	0.4666
$\mathcal{I}_4^{if}$	−0.2844	0.5998
$\mathcal{I}_5^{if}$	−0.2102	0.4891

Step 4: Finally, we derive the ranking results of each alternative based on their score or accuracy values and try to examine the optimal or best decision (see Table 5).

Table 5. Ranking matrix.

Methods	Ranking Values	Best One
AIVIFC-IAAA	$\mathcal{I}_1^{if} > \mathcal{I}_5^{if} > \mathcal{I}_4^{if} > \mathcal{I}_2^{if} > \mathcal{I}_4^{if}$	$\mathcal{I}_1^{if}$ (Rule-Based Systems)
AIVIFC-IAAG	$\mathcal{I}_1^{if} > \mathcal{I}_4^{if} > \mathcal{I}_5^{if} > \mathcal{I}_3^{if} > \mathcal{I}_2^{if}$	$\mathcal{I}_1^{if}$ (Rule-Based Systems)

According to the analysis in Table 5, we noticed that all the proposed techniques obtained the same ranking results, where the best decision is $\mathcal{I}_1^{if}$ (a rule-based system). After the successful evaluation of the problem of HAR with the help of the MADM technique, we further aimed to compare the proposed operators with some existing operators to show the supremacy and validity of the proposed approaches.

6. Comparative Analysis

This section shows the supremacy and validity of the proposed techniques by comparing them with some prevailing methods or techniques. Comparative analysis is the best way to prove the advantages and disadvantages between the proposed and prevailing methods. Therefore, in this section, we aim to compare the proposed techniques with some prevailing methods. For this, we have the following ideas: Wang et al. [43] presented the aggregation operators for AIVIFSs, Wang and Liu [44] exposed the geometric operators for AIVIFSs, Garg et al. [45] derived the CI operators for AIVIFSs, Meng et al. [46] proposed the geometric CI operators for AIVIFSs, Senapati et al. [47] evaluated the Aczel–Alsina operators for AIVIFSs, and Senapati et al. [48] exposed the Aczel–Alsina geometric operators for AIVIFSs. Therefore, to consider the data in Table 2, the comparison is listed in Table 6.

Table 6. Comparative analysis of the derived and existing techniques.

Approaches	Score Values					Ranking
	$\mathcal{I}_1^{if}$	$\mathcal{I}_2^{if}$	$\mathcal{I}_3^{if}$	$\mathcal{I}_4^{if}$	$\mathcal{I}_5^{if}$	
Wang et al. [43]	0.3452	0.1713	0.145	0.2499	0.0981	$\mathcal{I}_1^{if} > \mathcal{I}_4^{if} > \mathcal{I}_3^{if} > \mathcal{I}_2^{if} > \mathcal{I}_5^{if}$
Wang and Liu [44]	0.2804	0.0936	0.1002	0.2005	0.0239	$\mathcal{I}_1^{if} > \mathcal{I}_4^{if} > \mathcal{I}_3^{if} > \mathcal{I}_5^{if} > \mathcal{I}_2^{if}$
Garg et al. [45]	0.3794	0.119	0.1424	0.1919	0.1646	$\mathcal{I}_1^{if} > \mathcal{I}_4^{if} > \mathcal{I}_5^{if} > \mathcal{I}_3^{if} > \mathcal{I}_2^{if}$

Table 6. *Cont.*

Approaches	Score Values					Ranking
	$\mathcal{I}_1^{if}$	$\mathcal{I}_2^{if}$	$\mathcal{I}_3^{if}$	$\mathcal{I}_4^{if}$	$\mathcal{I}_5^{if}$	
Meng et al. [46]	0.3212	0.0264	0.0921	0.1466	0.0691	$\mathcal{I}_1^{if} > \mathcal{I}_4^{if} > \mathcal{I}_3^{if} > \mathcal{I}_5^{if} > \mathcal{I}_2^{if}$
Senapati et al. [47]	−0.1817	−0.2772	−0.3138	−0.2818	−0.3275	$\mathcal{I}_1^{if} > \mathcal{I}_2^{if} > \mathcal{I}_4^{if} > \mathcal{I}_3^{if} > \mathcal{I}_5^{if}$
Senapati et al. [48]	0.6177	0.4557	0.4933	0.5798	0.4107	$\mathcal{I}_1^{if} > \mathcal{I}_4^{if} > \mathcal{I}_3^{if} > \mathcal{I}_2^{if} > \mathcal{I}_5^{if}$
Proposed AIFC-IAAA	−0.164	−0.3059	−0.2923	−0.3256	−0.2973	$\mathcal{I}_1^{if} > \mathcal{I}_3^{if} > \mathcal{I}_5^{if} > \mathcal{I}_2^{if} > \mathcal{I}_4^{if}$
Proposed AIFC-IAAG	0.6424	0.3955	0.4728	0.5523	0.4465	$\mathcal{I}_1^{if} > \mathcal{I}_4^{if} > \mathcal{I}_3^{if} > \mathcal{I}_5^{if} > \mathcal{I}_2^{if}$

According to the analysis in Table 6, we noticed that all the proposed techniques and some existing techniques obtained the same ranking results, where the best decision is $\mathcal{I}_1^{if}$ (a rule-based system). From this table, we observe that Wang et al. [43] presented the aggregation operators for AIVIFSs, which can easily evaluate the data in Table 2; the ranking result is stated in the shape $\mathcal{I}_1^{if} > \mathcal{I}_4^{if} > \mathcal{I}_3^{if} > \mathcal{I}_2^{if} > \mathcal{I}_5^{if}$, hence the best decision is $\mathcal{I}_1^{if}$. On the other hand, Wang and Liu [44] exposed the geometric operators for AIVIFSs, which can easily evaluate the data in Table 2; the ranking result is stated in the shape: $\mathcal{I}_1^{if} > \mathcal{I}_4^{if} > \mathcal{I}_3^{if} > \mathcal{I}_2^{if} > \mathcal{I}_5^{if}$, hence the best decision is $\mathcal{I}_1^{if}$. Garg et al. [45] derived the CI operators for AIVIFSs, which can easily evaluate the data in Table 2; the ranking result is stated in the shape $\mathcal{I}_1^{if} > \mathcal{I}_4^{if} > \mathcal{I}_3^{if} > \mathcal{I}_2^{if} > \mathcal{I}_5^{if}$, hence the best decision is $\mathcal{I}_1^{if}$. Meng et al. [46] proposed the geometric CI operators for AIVIFSs, which can easily evaluate the data in Table 2; the ranking result is stated in the shape $\mathcal{I}_1^{if} > \mathcal{I}_4^{if} > \mathcal{I}_3^{if} > \mathcal{I}_2^{if} > \mathcal{I}_5^{if}$, hence the best decision is $\mathcal{I}_1^{if}$. Senapati et al. [47] evaluated the Aczel–Alsina operators for AIVIFSs, which can easily evaluate the data in Table 2; the ranking result is stated in the shape $\mathcal{I}_1^{if} > \mathcal{I}_4^{if} > \mathcal{I}_3^{if} > \mathcal{I}_2^{if} > \mathcal{I}_5^{if}$, hence the best decision is $\mathcal{I}_1^{if}$. Senapati et al. [48] exposed the Aczel–Alsina geometric operators for AIVIFSs, which can easily evaluate the data in Table 2; the ranking result is stated in the shape $\mathcal{I}_1^{if} > \mathcal{I}_4^{if} > \mathcal{I}_3^{if} > \mathcal{I}_2^{if} > \mathcal{I}_5^{if}$, hence the best decision is $\mathcal{I}_1^{if}$. All these existing approaches are based on algebraic norm operations; however, the proposed operators are based on the Choquet integral-based Aczel–Alsina (AA) norms. The Aczel–Alsina explored the theory of triangular norms in the form of Aczel–Alsina triangular norms. Aczel–Alsina triangular norms are robust tools utilized to overcome the loss of information during the aggregation of information. The major advantage of defining these operational laws is that it generalizes the algebraic and Einstein t-norm operations. Another advantage of the proposed method is the utilization of the Choquet integral (CI) to consider an inter-relationship between the attribute information. This CI considers the fuzzy measures during the measurement using ordered position. Therefore, the proposed techniques are more reliable and more general than existing techniques, such as the theory of Wang et al. [43], Wang and Liu [44], Garg et al. [45], Meng et al. [46], Senapati et al. [47], and Senapati et al. [48]. Hence, the proposed technique is superior to existing methodologies.

7. Conclusions

In this paper, we addressed the algorithm related to the decision-making problem using the concept of the aggregation operators under an AIVIFS environment. In this work, the uncertainties present in the information were handled with the help of AIVIFNs, and the Choquet integral-based operators were defined by incorporating the Aczel–Alsina norm operations. The defined operational laws based on Aczel–Alsina norms are considered as the generalization of several existing laws. The key merit of such operational laws is that they generalize the algebraic and Einstein t-norm operations. Also, the Choquet integral was utilized in the study to consider an inter-relationship between the attribute information. This CI considers the fuzzy measures during the measurement using ordered position. Based on these CI and operational laws, we stated some weighted averaging and geometric operators, namely, AIVIFC-IAAA, AIVIFC-IAAG, AIVIFC-IAAOA, AIVIFC-IAAOG, AIVIF AIFC-IAAHA, and AIVIFC-IAAHG operators to aggregate the information of the AIVIFNs. Finally, we addressed the MADM algorithm, and the applicability of the proposed algorithm was demonstrated through a numerical example. A comparative analysis with some of the existing studies shows the feasibility of the proposed algorithm.

In the future, on the one hand, the proposed method has the potential to be extended to several areas, such as classification-based strategy [49], heterogeneous preference information [50], consensus [51], and addressing multicriteria problems in large-scale group decision making [52]. Further, the presented idea has been extended to different extensions of the fuzzy sets, such as the T-spherical fuzzy set, the multiplicative set, the neutrosophic set, etc. On the other hand, we shall extend our approach to analyze different applications related to evidence theory [53,54], support vector machines [55], supply chains [56], and different tools of artificial intelligence, such as optimization or neural networks, etc. [57].

Author Contributions: Conceptualization, T. and H.G.; methodology, T., H.G. and G.N.N.: investigation, T. and H.G.; writing—original draft preparation, T. and H.G.; writing—review and editing, T. and H.G.; supervision, T. and H.G.; project administration, T.A. and H.A.E.-W.K.; funding acquisition, T.A. All authors have read and agreed to the published version of the manuscript.

Funding: Princess Nourah bint Abdulrahman University Researchers Supporting project number (PNURSP2023R404), Princess Nourah bint Abdulrahman University, Riyadh, Saudi Arabia.

Data Availability Statement: No data were used to support this study.

Acknowledgments: Princess Nourah bint Abdulrahman University Researchers Supporting Project number (PNURSP2023R404), Princess Nourah bint Abdulrahman University, Riyadh, Saudi Arabia.

Conflicts of Interest: The authors declare no conflict of interest.

Appendix A

Proof. Considering the procedure of mathematical induction, we proved that the data in Equation (21) also hold for all positive integers. For this, we have the following procedure: Step 1: Let $z = 2$, and we have

$$\mathcal{I}_1^{if}\left(\blacksquare\left(\Xi\rho_{(1)}\right) - \blacksquare\left(\Xi\rho_{(1+1)}\right)\right) = \mathcal{I}_1^{if}\left(\blacksquare\left(\Xi\rho_{(1)}\right) - \blacksquare\left(\Xi\rho_{(2)}\right)\right)$$
$$= \left(\begin{array}{c}\left[\begin{array}{c}1 - e^{-\left(\left(\blacksquare(\Xi\rho_{(1)}) - \blacksquare(\Xi\rho_{(2)})\right)\left(-\log\left(1-\Gamma_1^{\mathcal{I}^-}\right)\right)^{\varpi}\right)^{\frac{1}{\varpi}}}, \\ 1 - e^{-\left(\left(\blacksquare(\Xi\rho_{(1)}) - \blacksquare(\Xi\rho_{(2)})\right)\left(-\log\left(1-\Gamma_1^{\mathcal{I}^+}\right)\right)^{\varpi}\right)^{\frac{1}{\varpi}}}\end{array}\right], \\ \left[\begin{array}{c}e^{-\left(\left(\blacksquare(\Xi\rho_{(1)}) - \blacksquare(\Xi\rho_{(2)})\right)\left(-\log\Lambda_1^{\mathcal{I}^-}\right)^{\varpi}\right)^{\frac{1}{\varpi}}}, \\ e^{-\left(\left(\blacksquare(\Xi\rho_{(1)}) - \blacksquare(\Xi\rho_{(2)})\right)\left(-\log\Lambda_1^{\mathcal{I}^+}\right)^{\varpi}\right)^{\frac{1}{\varpi}}}\end{array}\right]\end{array}\right)$$

$$\mathcal{I}_2^{if}\left(\blacksquare\left(\Xi\rho_{(2)}\right)-\blacksquare\left(\Xi\rho_{(2+1)}\right)\right)=\mathcal{I}_2^{if}\left(\blacksquare\left(\Xi\rho_{(2)}\right)-\blacksquare\left(\Xi\rho_{(3)}\right)\right)$$

$$=\left(\begin{array}{c}\left[\begin{array}{c}1-e^{-\left(\left(\blacksquare(\Xi\rho_{(2)})-\blacksquare(\Xi\rho_{(3)})\right)\left(-\log\left(1-\Gamma_2^{\mathcal{I}-}\right)\right)^{\varpi}\right)^{\frac{1}{\varpi}}},\\ 1-e^{-\left(\left(\blacksquare(\Xi\rho_{(2)})-\blacksquare(\Xi\rho_{(3)})\right)\left(-\log\left(1-\Gamma_2^{\mathcal{I}+}\right)\right)^{\varpi}\right)^{\frac{1}{\varpi}}}\end{array}\right],\\ \left[\begin{array}{c}e^{-\left(\left(\blacksquare(\Xi\rho_{(2)})-\blacksquare(\Xi\rho_{(3)})\right)\left(-\log\Lambda_2^{\mathcal{I}-}\right)^{\varpi}\right)^{\frac{1}{\varpi}}},\\ e^{-\left(\left(\blacksquare(\Xi\rho_{(2)})-\blacksquare(\Xi\rho_{(3)})\right)\left(-\log\Lambda_2^{\mathcal{I}+}\right)^{\varpi}\right)^{\frac{1}{\varpi}}}\end{array}\right]\end{array}\right)$$

Then, we have

$$AIVIFC-IAAA\left(\mathcal{I}_1^{if},\mathcal{I}_2^{if}\right)=\mathcal{I}_1^{if}\left(\blacksquare\left(\Xi\rho_{(1)}\right)-\blacksquare\left(\Xi\rho_{(2)}\right)\right)\oplus\mathcal{I}_2^{if}\left(\blacksquare\left(\Xi\rho_{(2)}\right)-\blacksquare\left(\Xi\rho_{(3)}\right)\right)$$

$$=\left(\begin{array}{c}\left[\begin{array}{c}1-e^{-\left(\left(\blacksquare(\Xi\rho_{(1)})-\blacksquare(\Xi\rho_{(2)})\right)\left(-\log\left(1-\Gamma_1^{\mathcal{I}-}\right)\right)^{\varpi}\right)^{\frac{1}{\varpi}}},\\ 1-e^{-\left(\left(\blacksquare(\Xi\rho_{(1)})-\blacksquare(\Xi\rho_{(2)})\right)\left(-\log\left(1-\Gamma_1^{\mathcal{I}+}\right)\right)^{\varpi}\right)^{\frac{1}{\varpi}}}\end{array}\right],\\ \left[\begin{array}{c}e^{-\left(\left(\blacksquare(\Xi\rho_{(1)})-\blacksquare(\Xi\rho_{(2)})\right)\left(-\log\Lambda_1^{\mathcal{I}-}\right)^{\varpi}\right)^{\frac{1}{\varpi}}},\\ e^{-\left(\left(\blacksquare(\Xi\rho_{(1)})-\blacksquare(\Xi\rho_{(2)})\right)\left(-\log\Lambda_1^{\mathcal{I}+}\right)^{\varpi}\right)^{\frac{1}{\varpi}}}\end{array}\right]\end{array}\right)$$

$$\oplus\left(\begin{array}{c}\left[\begin{array}{c}1-e^{-\left(\left(\blacksquare(\Xi\rho_{(2)})-\blacksquare(\Xi\rho_{(3)})\right)\left(-\log\left(1-\Gamma_2^{\mathcal{I}-}\right)\right)^{\varpi}\right)^{\frac{1}{\varpi}}},\\ 1-e^{-\left(\left(\blacksquare(\Xi\rho_{(2)})-\blacksquare(\Xi\rho_{(3)})\right)\left(-\log\left(1-\Gamma_2^{\mathcal{I}+}\right)\right)^{\varpi}\right)^{\frac{1}{\varpi}}}\end{array}\right],\\ \left[\begin{array}{c}e^{-\left(\left(\blacksquare(\Xi\rho_{(2)})-\blacksquare(\Xi\rho_{(3)})\right)\left(-\log\Lambda_2^{\mathcal{I}-}\right)^{\varpi}\right)^{\frac{1}{\varpi}}},\\ e^{-\left(\left(\blacksquare(\Xi\rho_{(2)})-\blacksquare(\Xi\rho_{(3)})\right)\left(-\log\Lambda_2^{\mathcal{I}+}\right)^{\varpi}\right)^{\frac{1}{\varpi}}}\end{array}\right]\end{array}\right)$$

$$=\left(\begin{array}{c}\left[\begin{array}{c}1-e^{-\left(\sum_{\varphi=1}^{2}\left(\blacksquare(\Xi\rho_{(\varphi)})-\blacksquare(\Xi\rho_{(\varphi+1)})\right)\left(-\log\left(1-\Gamma_\varphi^{\mathcal{I}-}\right)\right)^{\varpi}\right)^{\frac{1}{\varpi}}},\\ 1-e^{-\left(\sum_{\varphi=1}^{2}\left(\blacksquare(\Xi\rho_{(\varphi)})-\blacksquare(\Xi\rho_{(\varphi+1)})\right)\left(-\log\left(1-\Gamma_\varphi^{\mathcal{I}+}\right)\right)^{\varpi}\right)^{\frac{1}{\varpi}}}\end{array}\right],\\ \left[\begin{array}{c}e^{-\left(\sum_{\varphi=1}^{2}\left(\blacksquare(\Xi\rho_{(\varphi)})-\blacksquare(\Xi\rho_{(\varphi+1)})\right)\left(-\log\left(\Lambda_\varphi^{\mathcal{I}-}\right)\right)^{\varpi}\right)^{\frac{1}{\varpi}}},\\ e^{-\left(\sum_{\varphi=1}^{2}\left(\blacksquare(\Xi\rho_{(\varphi)})-\blacksquare(\Xi\rho_{(\varphi+1)})\right)\left(-\log\left(\Lambda_\varphi^{\mathcal{I}-}\right)\right)^{\varpi}\right)^{\frac{1}{\varpi}}}\end{array}\right]\end{array}\right)$$

Information in Equation (21) is fully suitable for $z=2$. Additionally, we are letting the data in Equation (21) also be suitable for $z=q$, and then we have

$$AIVIFC-IAAA\left(\mathcal{I}_1^{if},\mathcal{I}_2^{if},\ldots,\mathcal{I}_q^{if}\right)=\oplus_{\varphi=1}^{q}\mathcal{I}_\varphi^{if}\left(\blacksquare\left(\Xi\rho_{(\varphi)}\right)-\blacksquare\left(\Xi\rho_{(\varphi+1)}\right)\right)$$

$$=\left(\begin{array}{c}\left[\begin{array}{c}1-e^{-\left(\sum_{\varphi=1}^{q}\left(\blacksquare(\Xi\rho_{(\varphi)})-\blacksquare(\Xi\rho_{(\varphi+1)})\right)\left(-\log\left(1-\Gamma_\varphi^{\mathcal{I}-}\right)\right)^{\varpi}\right)^{\frac{1}{\varpi}}},\\ 1-e^{-\left(\sum_{\varphi=1}^{q}\left(\blacksquare(\Xi\rho_{(\varphi)})-\blacksquare(\Xi\rho_{(\varphi+1)})\right)\left(-\log\left(1-\Gamma_\varphi^{\mathcal{I}+}\right)\right)^{\varpi}\right)^{\frac{1}{\varpi}}}\end{array}\right],\\ \left[\begin{array}{c}e^{-\left(\sum_{\varphi=1}^{q}\left(\blacksquare(\Xi\rho_{(\varphi)})-\blacksquare(\Xi\rho_{(\varphi+1)})\right)\left(-\log\left(\Lambda_\varphi^{\mathcal{I}-}\right)\right)^{\varpi}\right)^{\frac{1}{\varpi}}},\\ e^{-\left(\sum_{\varphi=1}^{q}\left(\blacksquare(\Xi\rho_{(\varphi)})-\blacksquare(\Xi\rho_{(\varphi+1)})\right)\left(-\log\left(\Lambda_\varphi^{\mathcal{I}+}\right)\right)^{\varpi}\right)^{\frac{1}{\varpi}}}\end{array}\right]\end{array}\right)$$

Thus, we prove that the data in Equation (21) are also suitable for $z = q + 1$, and we have

$$IVIFC - IAAA\left(\mathcal{I}_1^{if}, \mathcal{I}_2^{if}, \ldots, \mathcal{I}_q^{if}, \mathcal{I}_{q+1}^{if}\right)$$

$$= \oplus_{\varphi=1}^{q} \mathcal{I}_\varphi^{if}\left(\blacksquare\left(\Xi\rho_{(\varphi)}\right) - \blacksquare\left(\Xi\rho_{(\varphi+1)}\right)\right) \oplus \mathcal{I}_{q+1}^{if}\left(\blacksquare\left(\Xi\rho_{(q+1)}\right) - \blacksquare\left(\Xi\rho_{(q+2)}\right)\right)$$

$$= \left(\begin{array}{c} \left[\begin{array}{c} 1 - e^{-\left(\sum_{\varphi=1}^{q}\left(\blacksquare(\Xi\rho_{(\varphi)}) - \blacksquare(\Xi\rho_{(\varphi+1)})\right)\left(-\log\left(1-\Gamma_\varphi^{\mathcal{I}^-}\right)\right)^{\varpi}\right)^{\frac{1}{\varpi}}}, \\ 1 - e^{-\left(\sum_{\varphi=1}^{q}\left(\blacksquare(\Xi\rho_{(\varphi)}) - \blacksquare(\Xi\rho_{(\varphi+1)})\right)\left(-\log\left(1-\Gamma_\varphi^{\mathcal{I}^+}\right)\right)^{\varpi}\right)^{\frac{1}{\varpi}}} \end{array}\right], \\ \left[\begin{array}{c} e^{-\left(\sum_{\varphi=1}^{q}\left(\blacksquare(\Xi\rho_{(\varphi)}) - \blacksquare(\Xi\rho_{(\varphi+1)})\right)\left(-\log\left(\Lambda_\varphi^{\mathcal{I}^-}\right)\right)^{\varpi}\right)^{\frac{1}{\varpi}}}, \\ e^{-\left(\sum_{\varphi=1}^{q}\left(\blacksquare(\Xi\rho_{(\varphi)}) - \blacksquare(\Xi\rho_{(\varphi+1)})\right)\left(-\log\left(\Lambda_\varphi^{\mathcal{I}^+}\right)\right)^{\varpi}\right)^{\frac{1}{\varpi}}} \end{array}\right] \end{array}\right)$$

$$\oplus \left(\begin{array}{c} \left[\begin{array}{c} 1 - e^{-\left(\left(\blacksquare(\Xi\rho_{(q+1)}) - \blacksquare(\Xi\rho_{(q+2)})\right)\left(-\log\left(1-\Gamma_{q+1}^{\mathcal{I}^-}\right)\right)^{\varpi}\right)^{\frac{1}{\varpi}}}, \\ 1 - e^{-\left(\left(\blacksquare(\Xi\rho_{(q+1)}) - \blacksquare(\Xi\rho_{(q+2)})\right)\left(-\log\left(1-\Gamma_{q+1}^{\mathcal{I}^+}\right)\right)^{\varpi}\right)^{\frac{1}{\varpi}}} \end{array}\right], \\ \left[\begin{array}{c} e^{-\left(\left(\blacksquare(\Xi\rho_{(q+1)}) - \blacksquare(\Xi\rho_{(q+2)})\right)\left(-\log\Lambda_{q+1}^{\mathcal{I}^-}\right)^{\varpi}\right)^{\frac{1}{\varpi}}}, \\ e^{-\left(\left(\blacksquare(\Xi\rho_{(q+1)}) - \blacksquare(\Xi\rho_{(q+2)})\right)\left(-\log\Lambda_{q+1}^{\mathcal{I}^+}\right)^{\varpi}\right)^{\frac{1}{\varpi}}} \end{array}\right] \end{array}\right)$$

$$= \left(\begin{array}{c} \left[\begin{array}{c} 1 - e^{-\left(\sum_{\varphi=1}^{q+1}\left(\blacksquare(\Xi\rho_{(\varphi)}) - \blacksquare(\Xi\rho_{(\varphi+1)})\right)\left(-\log\left(1-\Gamma_\varphi^{\mathcal{I}^-}\right)\right)^{\varpi}\right)^{\frac{1}{\varpi}}}, \\ 1 - e^{-\left(\sum_{\varphi=1}^{q+1}\left(\blacksquare(\Xi\rho_{(\varphi)}) - \blacksquare(\Xi\rho_{(\varphi+1)})\right)\left(-\log\left(1-\Gamma_\varphi^{\mathcal{I}^+}\right)\right)^{\varpi}\right)^{\frac{1}{\varpi}}} \end{array}\right], \\ \left[\begin{array}{c} e^{-\left(\sum_{\varphi=1}^{q+1}\left(\blacksquare(\Xi\rho_{(\varphi)}) - \blacksquare(\Xi\rho_{(\varphi+1)})\right)\left(-\log\left(\Lambda_\varphi^{\mathcal{I}^-}\right)\right)^{\varpi}\right)^{\frac{1}{\varpi}}}, \\ e^{-\left(\sum_{\varphi=1}^{q+1}\left(\blacksquare(\Xi\rho_{(\varphi)}) - \blacksquare(\Xi\rho_{(\varphi+1)})\right)\left(-\log\left(\Lambda_\varphi^{\mathcal{I}^+}\right)\right)^{\varpi}\right)^{\frac{1}{\varpi}}} \end{array}\right] \end{array}\right)$$

Hence, we evaluated that the data in Equation (21) are suitable for all positive values of z. □

Appendix B

Proof. Consider $\mathcal{I}_\varphi^{if} = \mathcal{I}^{if} = \left(\left[\Gamma^{\mathcal{I}^-}, \Gamma^{\mathcal{I}^+}\right], \left[\Lambda^{\mathcal{I}^-}, \Lambda^{\mathcal{I}^+}\right]\right), \varphi = 1, 2, \ldots, z$, and then using the data in Equation (21), we have

$$AIVIFC-IAAA\left(\mathcal{I}_1^{if},\mathcal{I}_2^{if},\ldots,\mathcal{I}_z^{if}\right)=\left(\begin{array}{c}\left[\begin{array}{l}1-e^{-\left(\sum_{\varphi=1}^{z}\left(\blacksquare(\Xi\rho_{(\varphi)})-\blacksquare(\Xi\rho_{(\varphi+1)})\right)\left(-\log\left(1-\Gamma_{\varphi}^{\mathcal{I}^-}\right)\right)^{\varpi}\right)^{\frac{1}{\varpi}}},\\1-e^{-\left(\sum_{\varphi=1}^{z}\left(\blacksquare(\Xi\rho_{(\varphi)})-\blacksquare(\Xi\rho_{(\varphi+1)})\right)\left(-\log\left(1-\Gamma_{\varphi}^{\mathcal{I}^+}\right)\right)^{\varpi}\right)^{\frac{1}{\varpi}}}\end{array}\right],\\\left[\begin{array}{l}e^{-\left(\sum_{\varphi=1}^{z}\left(\blacksquare(\Xi\rho_{(\varphi)})-\blacksquare(\Xi\rho_{(\varphi+1)})\right)\left(-\log\left(\Lambda_{\varphi}^{\mathcal{I}^-}\right)\right)^{\varpi}\right)^{\frac{1}{\varpi}}},\\e^{-\left(\sum_{\varphi=1}^{z}\left(\blacksquare(\Xi\rho_{(\varphi)})-\blacksquare(\Xi\rho_{(\varphi+1)})\right)\left(-\log\left(\Lambda_{\varphi}^{\mathcal{I}^+}\right)\right)^{\varpi}\right)^{\frac{1}{\varpi}}}\end{array}\right]\end{array}\right)$$

$$=\left(\begin{array}{c}\left[\begin{array}{l}1-e^{-\left(\sum_{\varphi=1}^{z}\left(\blacksquare(\Xi\rho)-\blacksquare(\Xi\rho_{(1)})\right)\left(-\log\left(1-\Gamma^{\mathcal{I}^-}\right)\right)^{\varpi}\right)^{\frac{1}{\varpi}}},\\1-e^{-\left(\sum_{\varphi=1}^{z}\left(\blacksquare(\Xi\rho)-\blacksquare(\Xi\rho_{(1)})\right)\left(-\log\left(1-\Gamma^{\mathcal{I}^+}\right)\right)^{\varpi}\right)^{\frac{1}{\varpi}}}\end{array}\right],\\\left[\begin{array}{l}e^{-\left(\sum_{\varphi=1}^{z}\left(\blacksquare(\Xi\rho)-\blacksquare(\Xi\rho_{(1)})\right)\left(-\log\left(\Lambda^{\mathcal{I}^-}\right)\right)^{\varpi}\right)^{\frac{1}{\varpi}}},\\e^{-\left(\sum_{\varphi=1}^{z}\left(\blacksquare(\Xi\rho)-\blacksquare(\Xi\rho_{(1)})\right)\left(-\log\left(\Lambda^{\mathcal{I}^+}\right)\right)^{\varpi}\right)^{\frac{1}{\varpi}}}\end{array}\right]\end{array}\right)$$

$$=\left(\begin{array}{c}\left[1-e^{-\left(\left(-\log\left(1-\Gamma^{\mathcal{I}^-}\right)\right)^{\varpi}\right)^{\frac{1}{\varpi}}},1-e^{-\left(\left(-\log\left(1-\Gamma^{\mathcal{I}^+}\right)\right)^{\varpi}\right)^{\frac{1}{\varpi}}}\right],\\\left[e^{-\left(\left(-\log\left(\Lambda^{\mathcal{I}^-}\right)\right)^{\varpi}\right)^{\frac{1}{\varpi}}},e^{-\left(\left(-\log\left(\Lambda^{\mathcal{I}^+}\right)\right)^{\varpi}\right)^{\frac{1}{\varpi}}}\right]\end{array}\right)$$

$$=\left(\left[1-e^{-\left(-\log\left(1-\Gamma^{\mathcal{I}^-}\right)\right)},1-e^{-\left(-\log\left(1-\Gamma^{\mathcal{I}^+}\right)\right)}\right],\left[e^{-\left(-\log\left(\Lambda^{\mathcal{I}^-}\right)\right)},e^{-\left(-\log\left(\Lambda^{\mathcal{I}^+}\right)\right)}\right]\right)$$

$$=\left(\left[1-e^{\log\left(1-\Gamma^{\mathcal{I}^-}\right)},1-e^{\log\left(1-\Gamma^{\mathcal{I}^+}\right)}\right],\left[e^{\log\left(\Lambda^{\mathcal{I}^-}\right)},e^{\log\left(\Lambda^{\mathcal{I}^+}\right)}\right]\right)$$

$$=\left(\left[1-\left(1-\Gamma^{\mathcal{I}^-}\right),1-\left(1-\Gamma^{\mathcal{I}^+}\right)\right],\left[\Lambda^{\mathcal{I}^-},\Lambda^{\mathcal{I}^+}\right]\right)$$

$$=\left(\left[\Gamma^{\mathcal{I}^-},\Gamma^{\mathcal{I}^+}\right],\left[\Lambda^{\mathcal{I}^-},\Lambda^{\mathcal{I}^+}\right]\right)=\mathcal{I}^{if}.$$

Hence, we successfully proved our required results

$$AIVIFC-IAAA\left(\mathcal{I}_1^{if},\mathcal{I}_2^{if},\ldots,\mathcal{I}_z^{if}\right)=\mathcal{I}^{if}.$$

□

Appendix C

Proof. Suppose $\mathcal{I}_{\varphi}^{if}\leq\mathcal{I}^{*if}_{\varphi}$, then we have $\Gamma_{\varphi}^{\mathcal{I}^-}\leq\Gamma_{\varphi}^{\mathcal{I}^{-*}},\Gamma_{\varphi}^{\mathcal{I}^+}\leq\Gamma_{\varphi}^{\mathcal{I}^{+*}}$ and $\Lambda_{\varphi}^{\mathcal{I}^-}\geq\Lambda_{\varphi}^{\mathcal{I}^{-*}}$, $\Lambda_{\varphi}^{\mathcal{I}^+}\geq\Lambda_{\varphi}^{\mathcal{I}^{+*}}$; thus,

$$\Gamma_{\varphi}^{\mathcal{I}^-} \leq \Gamma_{\varphi}^{\mathcal{I}^{-*}} \Rightarrow 1-\Gamma_{\varphi}^{\mathcal{I}^-} \geq 1-\Gamma_{\varphi}^{\mathcal{I}^{-*}} \Rightarrow \log\left(1-\Gamma_{\varphi}^{\mathcal{I}^-}\right) \geq \log\left(1-\Gamma_{\varphi}^{\mathcal{I}^{-*}}\right)$$
$$\Rightarrow \left(-\log\left(1-\Gamma_{\varphi}^{\mathcal{I}^-}\right)\right)^{\varpi} \leq \left(-\log\left(1-\Gamma_{\varphi}^{\mathcal{I}^{-*}}\right)\right)^{\varpi}$$
$$\Rightarrow \sum_{\varphi=1}^{z}\left(■\left(\Xi\rho_{(\varphi)}\right)-■\left(\Xi\rho_{(\varphi+1)}\right)\right)\left(-\log\left(1-\Gamma_{\varphi}^{\mathcal{I}^-}\right)\right)^{\varpi}$$
$$\leq \sum_{\varphi=1}^{z}\left(■\left(\Xi\rho_{(\varphi)}\right)-■\left(\Xi\rho_{(\varphi+1)}\right)\right)\left(-\log\left(1-\Gamma_{\varphi}^{\mathcal{I}^{-*}}\right)\right)^{\varpi}$$
$$\Rightarrow -\left(\sum_{\varphi=1}^{z}\left(■\left(\Xi\rho_{(\varphi)}\right)-■\left(\Xi\rho_{(\varphi+1)}\right)\right)\left(-\log\left(1-\Gamma_{\varphi}^{\mathcal{I}^-}\right)\right)^{\varpi}\right)^{\frac{1}{\varpi}}$$
$$\geq -\left(\sum_{\varphi=1}^{z}\left(■\left(\Xi\rho_{(\varphi)}\right)-■\left(\Xi\rho_{(\varphi+1)}\right)\right)\left(-\log\left(1-\Gamma_{\varphi}^{\mathcal{I}^{-*}}\right)\right)^{\varpi}\right)^{\frac{1}{\varpi}}$$
$$\Rightarrow e^{-(\sum_{\varphi=1}^{z}(■(\Xi\rho_{(\varphi)})-■(\Xi\rho_{(\varphi+1)}))(-\log(1-\Gamma_{\varphi}^{\mathcal{I}^-}))^{\varpi})^{\frac{1}{\varpi}}} \geq e^{-(\sum_{\varphi=1}^{z}(■(\Xi\rho_{(\varphi)})-■(\Xi\rho_{(\varphi+1)}))(-\log(1-\Gamma_{\varphi}^{\mathcal{I}^{-*}}))^{\varpi})^{\frac{1}{\varpi}}}$$
$$\Rightarrow -e^{-(\sum_{\varphi=1}^{z}(■(\Xi\rho_{(\varphi)})-■(\Xi\rho_{(\varphi+1)}))(-\log(1-\Gamma_{\varphi}^{\mathcal{I}^-}))^{\varpi})^{\frac{1}{\varpi}}} \geq -e^{-(\sum_{\varphi=1}^{z}(■(\Xi\rho_{(\varphi)})-■(\Xi\rho_{(\varphi+1)}))(-\log(1-\Gamma_{\varphi}^{\mathcal{I}^{-*}}))^{\varpi})^{\frac{1}{\varpi}}}$$
$$\Rightarrow 1-e^{-(\sum_{\varphi=1}^{z}(■(\Xi\rho_{(\varphi)})-■(\Xi\rho_{(\varphi+1)}))(-\log(1-\Gamma_{\varphi}^{\mathcal{I}^-}))^{\varpi})^{\frac{1}{\varpi}}}$$
$$\leq 1-e^{-(\sum_{\varphi=1}^{z}(■(\Xi\rho_{(\varphi)})-■(\Xi\rho_{(\varphi+1)}))(-\log(1-\Gamma_{\varphi}^{\mathcal{I}^{-*}}))^{\varpi})^{\frac{1}{\varpi}}}$$
$$\Rightarrow 1-e^{-(\sum_{\varphi=1}^{z}(■(\Xi\rho_{(\varphi)})-■(\Xi\rho_{(\varphi+1)}))(-\log(1-\Gamma_{\varphi}^{\mathcal{I}^+}))^{\varpi})^{\frac{1}{\varpi}}}$$
$$\leq 1-e^{-(\sum_{\varphi=1}^{z}(■(\Xi\rho_{(\varphi)})-■(\Xi\rho_{(\varphi+1)}))(-\log(1-\Gamma_{\varphi}^{\mathcal{I}^{+*}}))^{\varpi})^{\frac{1}{\varpi}}}$$

Furthermore, we evaluated the nonmembership grade, such as

$$\Lambda_{\varphi}^{\mathcal{I}^-} \geq \Lambda_{\varphi}^{\mathcal{I}^{-*}} \Rightarrow -\log\left(\Lambda_{\varphi}^{\mathcal{I}^-}\right) \leq -\log\left(\Lambda_{\varphi}^{\mathcal{I}^{-*}}\right)$$
$$\Rightarrow \left(■\left(\Xi\rho_{(\varphi)}\right)-■\left(\Xi\rho_{(\varphi+1)}\right)\right)\left(-\log\left(\Lambda_{\varphi}^{\mathcal{I}^-}\right)\right)^{\varpi} \leq \left(■\left(\Xi\rho_{(\varphi)}\right)-■\left(\Xi\rho_{(\varphi+1)}\right)\right)\left(-\log\left(\Lambda_{\varphi}^{\mathcal{I}^{-*}}\right)\right)^{\varpi}$$
$$\Rightarrow \left(\sum_{\varphi=1}^{z}\left(■\left(\Xi\rho_{(\varphi)}\right)-■\left(\Xi\rho_{(\varphi+1)}\right)\right)\left(-\log\left(\Lambda_{\varphi}^{\mathcal{I}^-}\right)\right)^{\varpi}\right)^{\frac{1}{\varpi}}$$
$$\leq \left(\sum_{\varphi=1}^{z}\left(■\left(\Xi\rho_{(\varphi)}\right)-■\left(\Xi\rho_{(\varphi+1)}\right)\right)\left(-\log\left(\Lambda_{\varphi}^{\mathcal{I}^{-*}}\right)\right)^{\varpi}\right)^{\frac{1}{\varpi}}$$
$$\Rightarrow -\left(\sum_{\varphi=1}^{z}\left(■\left(\Xi\rho_{(\varphi)}\right)-■\left(\Xi\rho_{(\varphi+1)}\right)\right)\left(-\log\left(\Lambda_{\varphi}^{\mathcal{I}^-}\right)\right)^{\varpi}\right)^{\frac{1}{\varpi}}$$
$$\geq -\left(\sum_{\varphi=1}^{z}\left(■\left(\Xi\rho_{(\varphi)}\right)-■\left(\Xi\rho_{(\varphi+1)}\right)\right)\left(-\log\left(\Lambda_{\varphi}^{\mathcal{I}^{-*}}\right)\right)^{\varpi}\right)^{\frac{1}{\varpi}}$$
$$\Rightarrow e^{-(\sum_{\varphi=1}^{z}(■(\Xi\rho_{(\varphi)})-■(\Xi\rho_{(\varphi+1)}))(-\log(\Lambda_{\varphi}^{\mathcal{I}^-}))^{\varpi})^{\frac{1}{\varpi}}} \geq e^{-(\sum_{\varphi=1}^{z}(■(\Xi\rho_{(\varphi)})-■(\Xi\rho_{(\varphi+1)}))(-\log(\Lambda_{\varphi}^{\mathcal{I}^{-*}}))^{\varpi})^{\frac{1}{\varpi}}}$$

Finally, we used the theory in Equations (18) and (19), and we have

$$AIVIFC-IAAA\left(\mathcal{I}_1^{if},\mathcal{I}_2^{if},\ldots,\mathcal{I}_z^{if}\right) \leq AIVIFC-IAAA\left(\mathcal{I}^{*if}_1,\mathcal{I}^{*if}_2,\ldots,\mathcal{I}^{*if}_z\right).$$

□

Appendix D

Proof. We combined the statement of Property 1 and Property 2, such as

$$AIVIFC-IAAA\left(\mathcal{I}_1^{if},\mathcal{I}_2^{if},\ldots,\mathcal{I}_z^{if}\right)\leq AIVIFC-IAAA\left(\mathcal{I}_1^{+},\mathcal{I}_2^{+},\ldots,\mathcal{I}_z^{+}\right)=\mathcal{I}_\varphi^{+}$$

$$AIVIFC-IAAA\left(\mathcal{I}_1^{if},\mathcal{I}_2^{if},\ldots,\mathcal{I}_z^{if}\right)\geq AIVIFC-IAAA\left(\mathcal{I}_1^{-},\mathcal{I}_2^{-},\ldots,\mathcal{I}_z^{-}\right)=\mathcal{I}_\varphi^{-}$$

Thus,

$$\mathcal{I}_\varphi^{-}\leq AIVIFC-IAAA\left(\mathcal{I}_1^{if},\mathcal{I}_2^{if},\ldots,\mathcal{I}_z^{if}\right)\leq\mathcal{I}_\varphi^{+}.$$

□

Appendix E

Proof. Considering the procedure of mathematical induction, we proved that the data in Equation (36) also hold for all positive integers. For this, we have the following procedure: Step 1: Let $z=2$, and we have

$$\left(\mathcal{I}_1^{if}\right)^{(\blacksquare(\Xi\rho_{(1)})-\blacksquare(\Xi\rho_{(1+1)}))}=\left(\mathcal{I}_1^{if}\right)^{(\blacksquare(\Xi\rho_{(1)})-\blacksquare(\Xi\rho_{(2)}))}$$

$$=\left(\begin{array}{c}\left[\begin{array}{c}e^{-((\blacksquare(\Xi\rho_{(1)})-\blacksquare(\Xi\rho_{(2)}))(-\log(\Gamma_1^{\mathcal{I}-}))^{\varpi})^{\frac{1}{\varpi}}},\\ e^{-((\blacksquare(\Xi\rho_{(1)})-\blacksquare(\Xi\rho_{(2)}))(-\log(\Gamma_1^{\mathcal{I}+}))^{\varpi})^{\frac{1}{\varpi}}}\end{array}\right],\\ \left[\begin{array}{c}1-e^{-((\blacksquare(\Xi\rho_{(1)})-\blacksquare(\Xi\rho_{(2)}))(-\log(1-\Lambda_1^{\mathcal{I}-}))^{\varpi})^{\frac{1}{\varpi}}},\\ 1-e^{-((\blacksquare(\Xi\rho_{(1)})-\blacksquare(\Xi\rho_{(2)}))(-\log(1-\Lambda_1^{\mathcal{I}+}))^{\varpi})^{\frac{1}{\varpi}}}\end{array}\right]\end{array}\right)$$

$$\left(\mathcal{I}_2^{if}\right)^{(\blacksquare(\Xi\rho_{(2)})-\blacksquare(\Xi\rho_{(2+1)}))}=\left(\mathcal{I}_2^{if}\right)^{(\blacksquare(\Xi\rho_{(2)})-\blacksquare(\Xi\rho_{(3)}))}$$

$$=\left(\begin{array}{c}\left[\begin{array}{c}e^{-((\blacksquare(\Xi\rho_{(2)})-\blacksquare(\Xi\rho_{(3)}))(-\log(\Gamma_2^{\mathcal{I}-}))^{\varpi})^{\frac{1}{\varpi}}},\\ e^{-((\blacksquare(\Xi\rho_{(2)})-\blacksquare(\Xi\rho_{(3)}))(-\log(\Gamma_2^{\mathcal{I}+}))^{\varpi})^{\frac{1}{\varpi}}}\end{array}\right],\\ \left[\begin{array}{c}1-e^{-((\blacksquare(\Xi\rho_{(2)})-\blacksquare(\Xi\rho_{(3)}))(-\log(1-\Lambda_2^{\mathcal{I}-}))^{\varpi})^{\frac{1}{\varpi}}},\\ 1-e^{-((\blacksquare(\Xi\rho_{(2)})-\blacksquare(\Xi\rho_{(3)}))(-\log(1-\Lambda_2^{\mathcal{I}+}))^{\varpi})^{\frac{1}{\varpi}}}\end{array}\right]\end{array}\right)$$

Then, we have

$$AIVIFC-IAAG\left(\mathcal{I}_1^{if},\mathcal{I}_2^{if}\right)=\left(\mathcal{I}_1^{if}\right)^{(\blacksquare(\Xi\rho_{(1)})-\blacksquare(\Xi\rho_{(2)}))}\otimes\left(\mathcal{I}_2^{if}\right)^{(\blacksquare(\Xi\rho_{(2)})-\blacksquare(\Xi\rho_{(3)}))}$$

$$=\left(\begin{array}{c}\left[\begin{array}{c}e^{-((\blacksquare(\Xi\rho_{(1)})-\blacksquare(\Xi\rho_{(2)}))(-\log(\Gamma_1^{\mathcal{I}-}))^{\varpi})^{\frac{1}{\varpi}}},\\ e^{-((\blacksquare(\Xi\rho_{(1)})-\blacksquare(\Xi\rho_{(2)}))(-\log(\Gamma_1^{\mathcal{I}+}))^{\varpi})^{\frac{1}{\varpi}}}\end{array}\right],\\ \left[\begin{array}{c}1-e^{-((\blacksquare(\Xi\rho_{(1)})-\blacksquare(\Xi\rho_{(2)}))(-\log(1-\Lambda_1^{\mathcal{I}-}))^{\varpi})^{\frac{1}{\varpi}}},\\ 1-e^{-((\blacksquare(\Xi\rho_{(1)})-\blacksquare(\Xi\rho_{(2)}))(-\log(1-\Lambda_1^{\mathcal{I}+}))^{\varpi})^{\frac{1}{\varpi}}}\end{array}\right]\end{array}\right)$$

$$\oplus\left(\begin{array}{c}\left[\begin{array}{c}e^{-((\blacksquare(\Xi\rho_{(2)})-\blacksquare(\Xi\rho_{(3)}))(-\log(\Gamma_2^{\mathcal{I}-}))^{\varpi})^{\frac{1}{\varpi}}},\\ e^{-((\blacksquare(\Xi\rho_{(2)})-\blacksquare(\Xi\rho_{(3)}))(-\log(\Gamma_2^{\mathcal{I}+}))^{\varpi})^{\frac{1}{\varpi}}}\end{array}\right],\\ \left[\begin{array}{c}1-e^{-((\blacksquare(\Xi\rho_{(2)})-\blacksquare(\Xi\rho_{(3)}))(-\log(1-\Lambda_2^{\mathcal{I}-}))^{\varpi})^{\frac{1}{\varpi}}},\\ 1-e^{-((\blacksquare(\Xi\rho_{(2)})-\blacksquare(\Xi\rho_{(3)}))(-\log(1-\Lambda_2^{\mathcal{I}+}))^{\varpi})^{\frac{1}{\varpi}}}\end{array}\right]\end{array}\right)$$

$$=\left(\begin{array}{c}\left[\begin{array}{c}e^{-(\sum_{\varphi=1}^{2}(\blacksquare(\Xi\rho_{(\varphi)})-\blacksquare(\Xi\rho_{(\varphi+1)}))(-\log(\Gamma_\varphi^{\mathcal{I}-}))^{\varpi})^{\frac{1}{\varpi}}},\\ e^{-(\sum_{\varphi=1}^{2}(\blacksquare(\Xi\rho_{(\varphi)})-\blacksquare(\Xi\rho_{(\varphi+1)}))(-\log(\Gamma_\varphi^{\mathcal{I}+}))^{\varpi})^{\frac{1}{\varpi}}}\end{array}\right],\\ \left[\begin{array}{c}1-e^{-(\sum_{\varphi=1}^{2}(\blacksquare(\Xi\rho_{(\varphi)})-\blacksquare(\Xi\rho_{(\varphi+1)}))(-\log(1-\Lambda_\varphi^{\mathcal{I}-}))^{\varpi})^{\frac{1}{\varpi}}},\\ 1-e^{-(\sum_{\varphi=1}^{2}(\blacksquare(\Xi\rho_{(\varphi)})-\blacksquare(\Xi\rho_{(\varphi+1)}))(-\log(1-\Lambda_\varphi^{\mathcal{I}+}))^{\varpi})^{\frac{1}{\varpi}}}\end{array}\right]\end{array}\right)$$

Information in Equation (36) is fully suitable for $z=2$. Additionally, we are letting the data in Equation (36) also be suitable for $z=q$, and then we have

$$AIVIFC-IAAG\left(\mathcal{I}_1^{if},\mathcal{I}_2^{if},\ldots,\mathcal{I}_q^{if}\right)=\otimes_{\varphi=1}^{q}\left(\mathcal{I}_\varphi^{if}\right)^{(\blacksquare(\Xi\rho_{(\varphi)})-\blacksquare(\Xi\rho_{(\varphi+1)}))}$$

$$=\left(\begin{array}{c}\left[\begin{array}{c}e^{-(\sum_{\varphi=1}^{q}(\blacksquare(\Xi\rho_{(\varphi)})-\blacksquare(\Xi\rho_{(\varphi+1)}))(-\log(\Gamma_\varphi^{\mathcal{I}-}))^{\varpi})^{\frac{1}{\varpi}}},\\ e^{-(\sum_{\varphi=1}^{q}(\blacksquare(\Xi\rho_{(\varphi)})-\blacksquare(\Xi\rho_{(\varphi+1)}))(-\log(\Gamma_\varphi^{\mathcal{I}+}))^{\varpi})^{\frac{1}{\varpi}}}\end{array}\right],\\ \left[\begin{array}{c}1-e^{-(\sum_{\varphi=1}^{q}(\blacksquare(\Xi\rho_{(\varphi)})-\blacksquare(\Xi\rho_{(\varphi+1)}))(-\log(1-\Lambda_\varphi^{\mathcal{I}-}))^{\varpi})^{\frac{1}{\varpi}}},\\ 1-e^{-(\sum_{\varphi=1}^{q}(\blacksquare(\Xi\rho_{(\varphi)})-\blacksquare(\Xi\rho_{(\varphi+1)}))(-\log(1-\Lambda_\varphi^{\mathcal{I}+}))^{\varpi})^{\frac{1}{\varpi}}}\end{array}\right]\end{array}\right)$$

Thus, we prove that the data in Equation (36) are also suitable for $z = q + 1$, and we have

$$AIVIFC - IAAG\left(\mathcal{I}_1^{if}, \mathcal{I}_2^{if}, \ldots, \mathcal{I}_q^{if}, \mathcal{I}_{q+1}^{if}\right)$$

$$= \otimes_{\varphi=1}^{q}\left(\mathcal{I}_\varphi^{if}\right)^{(\blacksquare(\Xi\rho_{(\varphi)})-\blacksquare(\Xi\rho_{(\varphi+1)}))} \otimes \left(\mathcal{I}_{q+1}^{if}\right)^{(\blacksquare(\Xi\rho_{(q+1)})-\blacksquare(\Xi\rho_{(q+2)}))}$$

$$= \left(\begin{array}{c} \left[\begin{array}{c} e^{-(\sum_{\varphi=1}^{q}(\blacksquare(\Xi\rho_{(\varphi)})-\blacksquare(\Xi\rho_{(\varphi+1)}))(-\log(\Gamma_\varphi^{\mathcal{I}-}))^{\varpi})^{\frac{1}{\varpi}}}, \\ e^{-(\sum_{\varphi=1}^{q}(\blacksquare(\Xi\rho_{(\varphi)})-\blacksquare(\Xi\rho_{(\varphi+1)}))(-\log(\Gamma_\varphi^{\mathcal{I}+}))^{\varpi})^{\frac{1}{\varpi}}} \end{array}\right], \\ \left[\begin{array}{c} 1-e^{-(\sum_{\varphi=1}^{q}(\blacksquare(\Xi\rho_{(\varphi)})-\blacksquare(\Xi\rho_{(\varphi+1)}))(-\log(1-\Lambda_\varphi^{\mathcal{I}-}))^{\varpi})^{\frac{1}{\varpi}}}, \\ 1-e^{-(\sum_{\varphi=1}^{q}(\blacksquare(\Xi\rho_{(\varphi)})-\blacksquare(\Xi\rho_{(\varphi+1)}))(-\log(1-\Lambda_\varphi^{\mathcal{I}+}))^{\varpi})^{\frac{1}{\varpi}}} \end{array}\right] \end{array}\right)$$

$$\oplus \left(\begin{array}{c} \left[\begin{array}{c} e^{-((\blacksquare(\Xi\rho_{(q+1)})-\blacksquare(\Xi\rho_{(q+2)}))(-\log(\Gamma_{q+1}^{\mathcal{I}-}))^{\varpi})^{\frac{1}{\varpi}}}, \\ e^{-((\blacksquare(\Xi\rho_{(q+1)})-\blacksquare(\Xi\rho_{(q+2)}))(-\log(\Gamma_{q+1}^{\mathcal{I}+}))^{\varpi})^{\frac{1}{\varpi}}} \end{array}\right], \\ \left[\begin{array}{c} 1-e^{-((\blacksquare(\Xi\rho_{(q+1)})-\blacksquare(\Xi\rho_{(q+2)}))(-\log(1-\Lambda_{q+1}^{\mathcal{I}-}))^{\varpi})^{\frac{1}{\varpi}}}, \\ 1-e^{-((\blacksquare(\Xi\rho_{(q+1)})-\blacksquare(\Xi\rho_{(q+2)}))(-\log(1-\Lambda_{q+1}^{\mathcal{I}+}))^{\varpi})^{\frac{1}{\varpi}}} \end{array}\right] \end{array}\right)$$

$$= \left(\begin{array}{c} \left[\begin{array}{c} e^{-(\sum_{\varphi=1}^{q+1}(\blacksquare(\Xi\rho_{(\varphi)})-\blacksquare(\Xi\rho_{(\varphi+1)}))(-\log(\Gamma_\varphi^{\mathcal{I}-}))^{\varpi})^{\frac{1}{\varpi}}}, \\ e^{-(\sum_{\varphi=1}^{q+1}(\blacksquare(\Xi\rho_{(\varphi)})-\blacksquare(\Xi\rho_{(\varphi+1)}))(-\log(\Gamma_\varphi^{\mathcal{I}+}))^{\varpi})^{\frac{1}{\varpi}}} \end{array}\right], \\ \left[\begin{array}{c} 1-e^{-(\sum_{\varphi=1}^{q+1}(\blacksquare(\Xi\rho_{(\varphi)})-\blacksquare(\Xi\rho_{(\varphi+1)}))(-\log(1-\Lambda_\varphi^{\mathcal{I}-}))^{\varpi})^{\frac{1}{\varpi}}}, \\ 1-e^{-(\sum_{\varphi=1}^{q+1}(\blacksquare(\Xi\rho_{(\varphi)})-\blacksquare(\Xi\rho_{(\varphi+1)}))(-\log(1-\Lambda_\varphi^{\mathcal{I}+}))^{\varpi})^{\frac{1}{\varpi}}} \end{array}\right] \end{array}\right)$$

Hence, we evaluated that the data in Equation (36) are suitable for all positive values of z.□

References

1. Kim, E.; Helal, S.; Cook, D. Human activity recognition and pattern discovery. *IEEE Pervasive Comput.* **2009**, *9*, 48–53. [CrossRef] [PubMed]
2. Chen, B.; Meng, F.; Tang, H.; Tong, G. Two-level attention module based on spurious-3d residual networks for human action recognition. *Sensors* **2023**, *23*, 1707. [CrossRef] [PubMed]
3. Suh, S.; Rey, V.F.; Lukowicz, P. TASKED: Transformer-based Adversarial learning for human activity recognition using wearable sensors via Self-KnowledgE Distillation. *Knowl. Based Syst.* **2023**, *260*, 110143. [CrossRef]
4. Morshed, M.G.; Sultana, T.; Alam, A.; Lee, Y.K. Human Action Recognition: A Taxonomy-Based Survey, Updates, and Opportunities. *Sensors* **2023**, *23*, 2182. [CrossRef] [PubMed]
5. Kumar Jain, D.; Liu, X.; Neelakandan, S.; Prakash, M. Modeling of human action recognition using hyperparameter tuned deep learning model. *J. Electron. Imaging* **2023**, *32*, 011211. [CrossRef]
6. Chen, Z.; Cai, C.; Zheng, T.; Luo, J.; Xiong, J.; Wang, X. Rf-based human activity recognition using signal adapted convolutional neural network. *IEEE Trans. Mob. Comput.* **2021**, *22*, 487–499. [CrossRef]
7. Saleem, G.; Bajwa, U.I.; Raza, R.H. Toward human activity recognition: A survey. *Neural Comput. Appl.* **2023**, *35*, 4145–4182. [CrossRef]
8. Merigó, J.M.; Gil-Lafuente, A.M. New decision-making techniques and their application in the selection of financial products. *Inf. Sci.* **2010**, *180*, 2085–2094. [CrossRef]
9. Høybye-Mortensen, M. Decision-making tools and their influence on caseworkers' room for discretion. *Br. J. Soc. Work* **2015**, *45*, 600–615. [CrossRef]

10. Maniya, K.; Bhatt, M.G. A selection of material using a novel type decision-making method: Preference selection index method. *Mater. Des.* **2010**, *31*, 1785–1789. [CrossRef]
11. Zadeh, L.A. Fuzzy sets. *Inf. Control* **1965**, *8*, 338–353. [CrossRef]
12. Atanassov, K. Intuitionistic fuzzy sets. *Fuzzy Sets Syst.* **1986**, *20*, 87–96. [CrossRef]
13. Kerre, E.E. A tribute to Zadeh's extension principle. *Sci. Iran.* **2011**, *18*, 593–595. [CrossRef]
14. de Barros, L.C.; Bassanezi, R.C.; Lodwick, W.A.; de Barros, L.C.; Bassanezi, R.C.; Lodwick, W.A. The extension principle of Zadeh and fuzzy numbers. In *A First Course in Fuzzy Logic, Fuzzy Dynamical Systems, and Biomathematics: Theory and Applications*; Springer: Berlin/Heidelberg, Germany, 2017; pp. 23–41.
15. Mahmood, T.; Ali, Z. Fuzzy superior mandelbrot sets. *Soft Comput.* **2022**, *26*, 9011–9020. [CrossRef]
16. Nieto, J.J. The Cauchy problem for continuous fuzzy differential equations. *Fuzzy Sets Syst.* **1999**, *102*, 259–262. [CrossRef]
17. Congxin, W.; Shiji, S. Existence theorem to the Cauchy problem of fuzzy differential equations under compactness-type conditions. *Inf. Sci.* **1998**, *108*, 123–134. [CrossRef]
18. Ma, M.; Friedman, M.; Kandel, A. Numerical solutions of fuzzy differential equations. *Fuzzy Sets Syst.* **1999**, *105*, 133–138. [CrossRef]
19. Friedman, M.; Ma, M.; Kandel, A. Numerical solutions of fuzzy differential and integral equations. *Fuzzy Sets Syst.* **1999**, *106*, 35–48. [CrossRef]
20. Song, S.; Wu, C.; Lee, E.S. Asymptotic equilibrium and stability of fuzzy differential equations. *Comput. Math. Appl.* **2005**, *49*, 1267–1277. [CrossRef]
21. Voas, D. The rise and fall of fuzzy fidelity in Europe. *Eur. Sociol. Rev.* **2009**, *25*, 155–168. [CrossRef]
22. Atanassov, K.T.; Gargov, G. Interval valued intuitionistic fuzzy sets. *Fuzzy Sets Syst.* **1999**, *31*, 139–177.
23. Ejegwa, P.A.; Agbetayo, J.M. Similarity-distance decision-making technique and its applications via intuitionistic fuzzy pairs. *J. Comput. Cogn. Eng.* **2023**, *2*, 68–74. [CrossRef]
24. Tripathi, D.K.; Nigam, S.K.; Rani, P.; Shah, A.R. New intuitionistic fuzzy parametric divergence measures and score function-based CoCoSo method for decision-making problems. *Decis. Mak. Appl. Manag. Eng.* **2023**, *6*, 535–563. [CrossRef]
25. Sharma, K.; Singh, V.P.; Ebrahimnejad, A.; Chakraborty, D. Solving a multi-objective chance constrained hierarchical optimization problem under intuitionistic fuzzy environment with its application. *Expert Syst. Appl.* **2023**, *217*, 119595. [CrossRef]
26. Rani, D.; Garg, H. Multiple attributes group decision-making based on trigonometric operators, particle swarm optimization and complex intuitionistic fuzzy values. *Artif. Intell. Rev.* **2023**, *56*, 1787–1831. [CrossRef]
27. Hezam, I.M.; Vedala NR, D.; Kumar, B.R.; Mishra, A.R.; Cavallaro, F. Assessment of Biofuel Industry Sustainability Factors Based on the Intuitionistic Fuzzy Symmetry Point of Criterion and Rank-Sum-Based MAIRCA Method. *Sustainability* **2023**, *15*, 6749. [CrossRef]
28. Gong, Z.; Wang, F. Operation properties and (α,β)-equalities of complex intuitionistic fuzzy sets. *Soft Comput.* **2023**, *27*, 4369–4391. [CrossRef]
29. Jana, C.; Pal, M. Application of bipolar intuitionistic fuzzy soft sets in decision making problem. *Int. J. Fuzzy Syst. Appl.* **2018**, *7*, 32–55. [CrossRef]
30. Garg, H.; Ali, Z.; Mahmood, T.; Ali, M.R.; Alburaikan, A. Schweizer-Sklar prioritized aggregation operators for intuitionistic fuzzy information and their application in multi-attribute decision-making. *Alex. Eng. J.* **2023**, *67*, 229–240. [CrossRef]
31. Mahmood, T.; Ali, W.; Ali, Z.; Chinram, R. Power aggregation operators and similarity measures based on improved intuitionistic hesitant fuzzy sets and their applications to multiple attribute decision making. *Comput. Model. Eng. Sci.* **2021**, *126*, 1165–1187. [CrossRef]
32. Shi, X.; Ali, Z.; Mahmood, T.; Liu, P. Power Aggregation Operators of Interval-Valued Atanassov-Intuitionistic Fuzzy Sets Based on Aczel–Alsina t-Norm and t-Conorm and Their Applications in Decision Making. *Int. J. Comput. Intell. Syst.* **2023**, *16*, 43. [CrossRef]
33. Choquet, G. Theory of capacities. *Ann. De L'institut Fourier* **1954**, *5*, 131–295. [CrossRef]
34. Meyer, P.; Roubens, M. On the use of the Choquet integral with fuzzy numbers in multiple criteria decision support. *Fuzzy Sets Syst.* **2006**, *157*, 927–938. [CrossRef]
35. Tan, C.; Chen, X. Intuitionistic fuzzy Choquet integral operator for multi-criteria decision making. *Expert Syst. Appl.* **2010**, *37*, 149–157. [CrossRef]
36. Xu, Z. Choquet integrals of weighted intuitionistic fuzzy information. *Inf. Sci.* **2010**, *180*, 726–736. [CrossRef]
37. Aczél, J.; Alsina, C. Characterizations of some classes of quasilinear functions with applications to triangular norms and to synthesizing judgements. *Aequationes Math.* **1982**, *25*, 313–315. [CrossRef]
38. Senapati, T.; Chen, G.; Yager, R.R. Aczel–Alsina aggregation operators and their application to intuitionistic fuzzy multiple attribute decision making. *Int. J. Intell. Syst.* **2022**, *37*, 1529–1551. [CrossRef]
39. Senapati, T.; Chen, G.; Mesiar, R.; Yager, R.R. Intuitionistic fuzzy geometric aggregation operators in the framework of Aczel-Alsina triangular norms and their application to multiple attribute decision making. *Expert Syst. Appl.* **2023**, *212*, 118832. [CrossRef]
40. Ahmmad, J.; Mahmood, T.; Mehmood, N.; Urawong, K.; Chinram, R. Intuitionistic Fuzzy Rough Aczel-Alsina Average Aggregation Operators and Their Applications in Medical Diagnoses. *Symmetry* **2022**, *14*, 2537. [CrossRef]
41. Xu, Z. Intuitionistic fuzzy aggregation operators. *IEEE Trans. Fuzzy Syst.* **2007**, *15*, 1179–1187.

42. Xu, Z.; Yager, R.R. Some geometric aggregation operators based on intuitionistic fuzzy sets. *Int. J. Gen. Syst.* **2006**, *35*, 417–433. [CrossRef]
43. Wang, W.; Liu, X.; Qin, Y. Interval-valued intuitionistic fuzzy aggregation operators. *J. Syst. Eng. Electron.* **2012**, *23*, 574–580. [CrossRef]
44. Wang, W.; Liu, X. Some interval-valued intuitionistic fuzzy geometric aggregation operators based on einstein operations. In Proceedings of the 2012 9th International Conference on Fuzzy Systems and Knowledge Discovery, Chongqing, China, 29–31 May 2012; pp. 604–608.
45. Garg, H.; Agarwal, N.; Tripathi, A. Choquet integral-based information aggregation operators under the interval-valued intuitionistic fuzzy set and its applications to decision-making process. *Int. J. Uncertain. Quantif.* **2017**, *7*, 249–269. [CrossRef]
46. Meng, F.; Zhang, Q.; Zhan, J. The interval-valued intuitionistic fuzzy geometric choquet aggregation operator based on the generalized banzhaf index and 2-additive measure. *Technol. Econ. Dev. Econ.* **2015**, *21*, 186–215. [CrossRef]
47. Senapati, T.; Chen, G.; Mesiar, R.; Yager, R.R. Novel Aczel–Alsina operations-based interval-valued intuitionistic fuzzy aggregation operators and their applications in multiple attribute decision-making process. *Int. J. Intell. Syst.* **2022**, *37*, 5059–5081. [CrossRef]
48. Senapati, T.; Mesiar, R.; Simic, V.; Iampan, A.; Chinram, R.; Ali, R. Analysis of interval-valued intuitionistic fuzzy Aczel–Alsina geometric aggregation operators and their application to multiple attribute decision-making. *Axioms* **2022**, *11*, 258. [CrossRef]
49. Liu, Y.; Li, Y.; Zhang, Z.; Xu, Y.; Dong, Y. Classification-based strategic weight manipulation in multiple attribute decision making. *Expert Syst. Appl.* **2022**, *197*, 116781. [CrossRef]
50. Li, Z.; Zhang, Z.; Yu, W. Consensus reaching for ordinal classification-based group decision making with heterogeneous preference information. *J. Oper. Res. Soc.* **2023**, 1–22. [CrossRef]
51. Li, Z.; Zhang, Z. Threshold-Based Value-Driven Method to Support Consensus Reaching in Multicriteria Group Sorting Problems: A Minimum Adjustment Perspective. *IEEE Trans. Comput. Soc. Syst.* **2023**, 1–14. [CrossRef]
52. Yang, Y.; Gai, T.; Cao, M.; Zhang, Z.; Zhang, H.; Wu, J. Application of group decision making in shipping industry 4.0: Bibliometric Analysis, Trends, and Future Directions. *Systems* **2023**, *11*, 69. [CrossRef]
53. Cheng, L.; Yin, F.; Theodoridis, S.; Chatzis, S.; Chang, T. Rethinking Bayesian Learning for Data Analysis: The art of prior and inference in sparsity-aware modeling. *IEEE Signal Process. Mag.* **2022**, *39*, 18–52. [CrossRef]
54. Xie, X.; Huang, L.; Marson, S.M.; Wei, G. Emergency response process for sudden rainstorm and flooding: Scenario deduction and Bayesian network analysis using evidence theory and knowledge meta-theory. *Nat. Hazards* **2023**, *117*, 3307–3329. [CrossRef]
55. Li, X.; Sun, Y. Stock intelligent investment strategy based on support vector machine parameter optimization algorithm. *Neural Comput. Appl.* **2020**, *32*, 1765–1775. [CrossRef]
56. Li, Q.; Lin, H.; Tan, X.; Du, S. H_∞ Consensus for Multiagent-Based Supply Chain Systems under Switching Topology and Uncertain Demands. *IEEE Trans. Syst. Man Cybern. Syst.* **2020**, *50*, 4905–4918. [CrossRef]
57. Li, X.; Sun, Y. Application of RBF neural network optimal segmentation algorithm in credit rating. *Neural Comput. Appl.* **2021**, *33*, 8227–8235. [CrossRef]

symmetry

MDPI

Article

Cosine Similarity Measures of (m, n)-Rung Orthopair Fuzzy Sets and Their Applications in Plant Leaf Disease Classification

Arpan Singh Rajput [1], Shailja Shukla [2] and Samajh Singh Thakur [3,*]

1 Department of Electronics and Communication, Jabalpur Engineering College, Jabalpur 482011, India; arpansinghrajput@gmail.com
2 Department of Electrical Engineering, Jabalpur Engineering College, Jabalpur 482011, India; shailja270@gmail.com
3 Department of Applied Mathematics, Jabalpur Engineering College, Jabalpur 482011, India
* Correspondence: ssthakur@jecjabalpur.ac.in

Abstract: A fuzzy set is a powerful tool to handle uncertainty and ambiguity, and generally, the notions of symmetry and similarity are also exhibited in the fuzzy set theory. The class of (m, n)-rung orthopair fuzzy sets through two universes are more flexible and efficient than the q-rung orthopair fuzzy sets when discussing the symmetry and similarity between multiple objects. This research article comprehensively investigates ten similarity measures that employ cosine and cotangent functions for comparing (m, n)-rung orthopair fuzzy sets, which are a superclass of q-rung orthopair fuzzy sets. Moreover, the proposed weighted similarity measures are applied to real-world problems in building material analysis. A comparative analysis is conducted between the proposed measures and the existing cosine and cotangent measures of q-rung orthopair fuzzy sets, showing that the proposed measures are more efficient than existing ones. Additionally, a numerical example demonstrates the practical and scientific applications of these similarity measures in classifying plant leaf diseases. The sensitivity analysis shows that the existing measures cannot be applied to (m, n)-fuzzy data for distinct values of m and n. The results are supported by graphical interpretations, further illustrating the efficacy of the proposed measures.

Keywords: (m, n)-rung orthopair fuzzy sets; cosine similarity measure; pattern recognition; plant leaf disease

1. Introduction

The concept of symmetry holds tremendous significance in science and engineering and is widely observed in nature, fine arts, and various human creative pursuits. Its foundations are rooted in mathematics, while its artistic expression and communication medium can be traced back to early human endeavors. Symmetry can be defined as an object's property that identifies two or more parts as identical concerning a point, line, or plane. In geometry, symmetry is formally defined as the invariance of a configuration of elements under a group of automorphic transformations [1–3]. Recent research has emphasized the versatility of symmetry as a tool for establishing connections across a wide range of disciplines, encompassing mathematics, physics, chemistry, biology, archaeology, geology, and pattern recognition. By integrating the deep theoretical foundations of symmetry and similarity with its practical applications in various domains, this research aims to advance our understanding and utilization of this fundamental concept. This interdisciplinary exploration will contribute to the comprehension of symmetry and its implications for diverse fields, opening the path to novel discoveries and practical advancements.

The fusion of technology and generalized forms of classical sets is instrumental in solving many real-world complex problems, which involve incomplete and uncertain information. A classical set is defined by its characteristic function from a universe of discourse to two point sets {0, 1}. The classical set theory falls short when dealing with intricate issues that encompass vague and uncertain information. To handle the vagueness and impreciseness in complex problems, fuzzy sets (FSs) were created by Zadeh [4] as a generalization of classical sets. The application of the Fuzzy set theory extends to multiple fields, including control theory, artificial intelligence, pattern recognition, database system, and medical diagnosis. In 1986, Atanassov [5] created intuitionistic fuzzy sets (IFSs), a superclass of FSs. After the occurrence of the Atanassov [5] paper, several generalizations of IFSs have appeared in the literature. In 2013, Yager [6] presented a superclass of IFSs called Pythagorean fuzzy sets (PFSs). PFSs are more extensive than the IFSs and can describe more imprecise and vague information in the decision-making process. In 2017, Yager introduced the q-rung ortho-pair fuzzy sets (q-ROFSs) [7]. This innovative approach offers a highly effective and powerful tool to manage imprecise and uncertain information across various real-world applications and problems. In 2019, Senapati and Yager [8] developed and introduced the concept of Fermatean fuzzy sets (FFSs), a specific instance of q-ROFSs when q = 3. Recently, Ibrahim and Alshamari [9] initiated the study of (m, n)-rung orthopair fuzzy sets ((m, n)-ROFSs) as a superclass of q-ROFSs. They discuss the applications of these fuzzy sets in the context of multi-criteria decision-making methods. This concept is also independently investigated by Jun and hur [10] and AI-Shami [11] with the name of (m, n)-fuzzy sets. The (m, n)-ROFSs are more flexible and effective as compared to q-ROFSs in handling the uncertainty and vagueness in MADM and MCDM.

Symmetry plays a fundamental role in shape analysis and object recognition, as it is considered a pre-attentive feature that enhances object recognition and reconstruction. After the invention of fuzzy sets, several authors have proposed methods and algorithms based on fuzzy measures of symmetry and similarity for pattern recognition and classification of fuzzy objects. Helgason and Jobe [12] investigated fuzzy measures of symmetry breaking, similarity, and comparison within the context of non-statistical information pertaining to a single patient. This research may be relevant to healthcare and medical decision-making. Zainuddin and Pauline [13] presented an effective fuzzy C-means algorithm based on a symmetry–similarity approach. The algorithm aims to improve the performance of fuzzy C-means clustering in handling symmetric patterns in data. Miranda and Grabisch [14] created p-symmetric fuzzy measures and explored the properties and applications of these measures in uncertainty, fuzziness, and knowledge-based systems. Saha and Bandyopadhyay [15] presented a new point symmetry-based fuzzy genetic clustering technique for automatically evolving clusters. This technique combines symmetry principles and genetic algorithms to improve the clustering process. Colliota and Tuzikovb [16] studied approximate reflectional symmetries of fuzzy objects and their application in model-based object recognition. This research focused on developing fuzzy models to recognize and analyze objects based on their approximate reflectional symmetries and similarities.

The similarity measure is a crucial metric that can evaluate the degree of similarity between two objects, making it an essential tool for distinguishing diverse patterns in practical applications. Adlassnig [17], Zwick et al. [18], Pappis and Karacapilidis [19], Chen et al. [20], Zeng and Li [21], Mitchel [22], and others, have extensively studied the similarity measures between fuzzy sets. Their research explored the potential of fuzzy sets to facilitate the development of corresponding applications in areas such as image processing, medical diagnosis, pattern recognition, and decision-making. Since the emergence of interval type-2 fuzzy sets (IFSs), several similarity measures between IFSs have appeared in this literature [23–36]. Some researchers have investigated and studied these similarity measures between IFSs based on cosine functions, including Ye [37–39], Shi and Ye [40], Zhau et al. [41], and Liu et al. [42,43]. Tian [44] and Rajarajeswari and Uma [45] proposed similarity measures between IFSs based on cotangent functions and demonstrated their applications in medical diagnoses. Recently, Garg et al. [46] proposed Choquet integral-based cosine similarity measures for interval-valued IFSs and presented their applications in pattern recognition.

PFS is a powerful tool for depicting vagueness and impreciseness in MADM and MCDM. Recently, many researchers, such as Garg [47], Zeng, Li, and Yin [48], Peng, Yuan, and Yang [49], Husain, and Yang [50], Wei and Wei [51], Ejeiwa et al. [52–54], and others, presented different similarity measures between PFSs for solving MADM problems. Recently, different similarity measures between FFSs and their applications in MADM and MCDM have appeared in the literature [55–60]. q-ROFSs are powerful mathematical tools for handling uncertain, imprecise, and vague information in real-world problems, surpassing PFS and FFS regarding capability. In 2019, Peng and Dai [61] introduced a similarity measure between q-ROFSs that assessed the quality of classroom teaching. Jan et al. [62] considered the generalized dice similarity between ROFSs. Farhadinia et al. explored a range of similarity measures for q-ROFSs. Peng and Liu [63] investigated information measures for q-ROFSs. Liu, Chen, and Peng [64], as well as Wang et al. [65], introduced several similarity measures between q-ROFSs based on cosine and cotangent functions and explored their properties and applications.

The existing generalizations of PFSs, FSSs, and q-ROFSs of IFSs exhibit symmetry between the powers of MD and NMD of an attribute within the universe of discourse. In decision-making, it is not flexible in prioritizing different powers of the MD or NMD of an attribute in these extensions of IFSs. The motivations for writing this research are to consider a new class of IFSs, called (m, n)-round orthopair fuzzy sets((m, n)-ROFSs) for creating cosine and cotangent similarity measures, which helps to expand the MD and NMD more than all types of q-ROFSs. Classes with distinct powers enable us to evaluate the input data with different levels of significance for MD and NMD, which is appropriate in MADM problems. This matter does not apply to the other generalizations of IFSs because they give equal significance to MD and NMD viz 1 in IFSs, 2 in PFSs, 3 in FFSs, and q in q-ROFSs. In (m, n)-orthopair fuzzy sets, different power function scales are utilized to widen the scope of the decision-making problems.(m, n)-rung orthopair fuzzy sets can be applied to more diverse scenarios than FFSs, PFSs, and IFSs sets, due to their wider range in depicting membership grades. The main advantage of(m, n)-rung orthopair fuzzy sets is that they can describe more uncertainties than q-ROFSs, which can be applied to many decision-making problems. The (m, n)-ROFSs through double universes are more flexible and efficient than m-ROFS and n-ROFS when discussing the similarity between multiple objects. In other words, (m, n)-ROFSs can more effectively address MADM problems, including all q-ROFS decision-making problems as a special case.

The structure of this article is as follows. Section two presents a review of generalized fuzzy structures along with their cosine and cotangent similarity measures. Section three establishes similarity and weighted similarity measures between (m, n)-ROFSs based on cosine and cotangent functions. Section four compares the newly established similarity measures for (m, n)-ROFSs with existing q-ROFSs, PFSs, and IFSs based on cosine and cotangent functions. The comparison is made by considering pattern recognition, medical diagnosis, and building material problems discussed in the literature. In section five, the established similarity measures are utilized to classify plant leaf disease, and the effectiveness and reasonableness of the proposed measures are demonstrated. Finally, section six concludes the article with some closing remarks.

All the abbreviations and their description used in the paper are presented in Table 1.

Table 1. Abbreviations and their description.

Abbreviation	Description
FS	Fuzzy set
IFS	Intuitionistic fuzzy set
PFS	Pythagorean fuzzy set
FFS	Fermatean fuzzy set
q-ROFS	q-rung orthopair fuzzy set
(m, n)-ROFS	(m, n)-rung orthopair fuzzy set
$(m,n)-ROFS(\mathbb{P})$	The family of all (m, n)-ROFSs defined over $\mathbb{P}$
MD	Membership degree
NMD	Non-membership degree
IMD	Indeterminacy membership degree
$\vartheta_{\mathbb{E}}(p)$	MD of p to $\mathbb{E}$
$\varsigma_{\mathbb{E}}(p)$	NMD of p to $\mathbb{E}$
$\pi_{\mathbb{E}}(p)$	IMD of p to $\mathbb{E}$

2. Preliminaries

In this section, we will examine different types of generalized fuzzy structures and the cosine and cotangent similarity measures currently used for these structures. In the remainder of the paper, we will assume that $\mathbb{P}$ is a finite, discrete, and non-empty discourse set consisting of r elements, denoted as $p_1, p_2, \ldots, p_r$.

2.1. Generalized Fuzzy Structures

Definition 1. *Let us consider that $\mathbb{P}$ is a fixed set. A structure $\mathbb{E} = \{\langle p, \vartheta_{\mathbb{E}}(p), \varsigma_{\mathbb{E}}(p)\rangle : p \in \mathbb{P}\}$, where $\vartheta_{\mathbb{E}} : \mathbb{P} \to [0,1]$ and $\varsigma_{\mathbb{E}} : \mathbb{P} \to [0,1]$ denotes the membership and non-membership functions of $\mathbb{E}$, called:*

(a) Intuitionistic fuzzy set [5] in $\mathbb{P}$ if $0 \le \vartheta_{\mathbb{E}}(p) + \varsigma_{\mathbb{E}}(p) \le 1,\ \forall\ p \in \mathbb{P}$.
(b) Pythagorean fuzzy set [6] in $\mathbb{P}$ if $0 \le (\vartheta_{\mathbb{E}}(p))^2 + (\varsigma_{\mathbb{E}}(p))^2 \le 1,\ \forall\ p \in \mathbb{P}$.
(c) Fermatean fuzzy set [8] in $\mathbb{P}$ if $0 \le (\vartheta_{\mathbb{E}}(p))^3 + (\varsigma_{\mathbb{E}}(p))^3 \le 1,\ \forall\ p \in \mathbb{P}$.
(d) q-rung orthopair fuzzy set [7] in $\mathbb{P}$ if $0 \le (\vartheta_{\mathbb{E}}(p))^q + (\varsigma_{\mathbb{E}}(p))^q \le 1,\ \forall\ p \in \mathbb{P}$ and $q \in$ N.

Definition 2 ([9–11])**.** *A(m, n)-rung orthopair fuzzy set $\mathbb{E}$ in a universe of discourse $\mathbb{P}$ is a structure defined as follows:*

$$\mathbb{E} = \{\langle p, (\vartheta_{\mathbb{E}}(p), \varsigma_{\mathbb{E}}(p))\rangle : p \in \mathbb{P}\}$$

where $\vartheta_{\mathbb{E}} : \mathbb{P} \to [0,1]$ and $\varsigma_{\mathbb{E}} : \mathbb{P} \to [0,1]$ denote the membership and non-membership functions of $\mathbb{E}$, which satisfies the following condition:

$$0 \le (\vartheta_{\mathbb{E}}(p))^m + (\varsigma_{\mathbb{E}}(p))^n \le 1$$

$\forall$ p$\in \mathbb{P}$ and m, n $\in$ N.

Remark 1 ([9–11])**.** *A (m, n)-ROFS $\mathbb{E}$ in $\mathbb{P}$ coincides with IFS (resp., PFS, FFS, q-ROFS) if m = n = 1 (resp., m = n = 2, m = n = 3, m = n = q).*

Proposition 1 ([11])**.** *For any universe of discourse $\mathbb{P}$:*

(a) Every IFS is an (m, n)-ROFS.
(b) If $m \ge 2$ and $n \ge 2$ then a PFS is an (m, n)-ROFS.
(c) If $m \ge 3$ and $n \ge 3$ then a FFS is an (m, n)-ROFS.
(d) If $m \ge q$ and $n \ge q$ then a q-ROFS is an (m, n)-ROFS.

Remark 2. *The converse of the relationships presented in Proposition 1 is false.*

Definition 3 ([9–11]). *For any (m, n)-ROFSs* $\mathbb{E} = \{\langle p, \vartheta_{\mathbb{E}}(p), \varsigma_{\mathbb{E}}(p)\rangle : p \in \mathbb{P}\}$, $\mathbb{E}_1 = \{\langle p, \vartheta_{\mathbb{E}_1}(p), \varsigma_{\mathbb{E}_1}(p)\rangle : p \in \mathbb{P}\}$, *and* $\mathbb{E}_2 = \{\langle p, \vartheta_{\mathbb{E}_2}(p), \varsigma_{\mathbb{E}_2}(p)\rangle : p \in \mathbb{P}\}$ *in* $\mathbb{P}$.

The subset, equality, union, intersection, and complement operations over $(m,n) - ROFS(\mathbb{P})$ *are defined as follows:*

(a) $\mathbb{E}_1 \Subset \mathbb{E}_2 \Leftrightarrow \vartheta_{\mathbb{E}_1}(p) \leq \vartheta_{\mathbb{E}_2}(p)$ *and* $\varsigma_{\mathbb{E}_1}(p) \geq \varsigma_{\mathbb{E}_2}(p)\ \forall\ p \in \mathbb{P}$.

(b) $\mathbb{E}_1 = \mathbb{E}_2 \Leftrightarrow \vartheta_{\mathbb{E}_1} = \vartheta_{\mathbb{E}_2}$ *and* $\varsigma_{\mathbb{E}_1} = \varsigma_{\mathbb{E}_2}$.

(c) $\mathbb{E}_1 \Cup \mathbb{E}_2 = \left\{ \begin{array}{c} \langle p, \vartheta_{E_1}(p) \bigvee \vartheta_{\mathbb{E}_2}(p), \\ \varsigma_{\mathbb{E}_1}(p) \bigwedge \varsigma_{\mathbb{E}_2}(p)\rangle : p \in \mathbb{P} \end{array} \right\}$.

(d) $\mathbb{E}_1 \Cap \mathbb{E}_2 = \left\{ \begin{array}{c} \langle p, \vartheta_{\mathbb{E}_1}(p) \bigwedge \vartheta_{\mathbb{E}_2}(p), \\ \varsigma_{\mathbb{E}_1}(p) \bigvee \varsigma_{\mathbb{E}_2}(p)\rangle : p \in \mathbb{P} \end{array} \right\}$.

(e) $\mathbb{E}^c = \{\langle p, (\varsigma_{\mathbb{E}}(p))^{\frac{n}{m}}, (\vartheta_{\mathbb{E}}(p))^{\frac{m}{n}} : p \in \mathbb{P}\}$.

Proposition 2 ([9–11]). *Let* $\mathbb{E}_1 = \{\langle p, \vartheta_{\mathbb{E}_1}(p), \varsigma_{\mathbb{E}_1}(p)\rangle : p \in \mathbb{P}\}$ *and* $\mathbb{E}_2 = \{\langle p, \vartheta_{\mathbb{E}_2}(p), \varsigma_{\mathbb{E}_2}(p)\rangle : p \in \mathbb{P}\}$ *be two (m, n)-ROFS on* $\mathbb{P}$. *Then,*

(a) $\mathbb{E}_1 \Cup \mathbb{E}_2 = \mathbb{E}_2 \Cup \mathbb{E}_1$.
(b) $\mathbb{E}_1 \Cap \mathbb{E}_2 = \mathbb{E}_2 \Cap \mathbb{E}_1$.
(c) $(\mathbb{E}_1^c)^c = \mathbb{E}_1$.
(d) $(\mathbb{E}_1 \Cup \mathbb{E}_2)^c = \mathbb{E}_1^c \Cap \mathbb{E}_2^c$.
(e) $(P_1 \Cap \mathbb{E}_2)^c = \mathbb{E}_1^c \Cup \mathbb{E}_2^c$.

Definition 4 ([5–8]). *Let* $\mathbb{P}$ *be a universe of discourse. Then, for any*

(a) *IFS* $\mathbb{E} = \{\langle p, \vartheta_{\mathbb{E}}(p), \varsigma_{\mathbb{E}}(p)\rangle : p \in \mathbb{P}\}$ *in* $\mathbb{P}$, *the expression*

$$\pi_{\mathbb{E}}(p) = (1 - \vartheta_{\mathbb{E}}(p) + \varsigma_{\mathbb{E}}(p))$$

is called the IMD of $p \in \mathbb{P}$.

(b) *PFS* $\mathbb{E} = \{\langle p, \vartheta_{\mathbb{E}}(p), \varsigma_{\mathbb{E}}(p)\rangle : p \in \mathbb{P}\}$, *in* $\mathbb{P}$, *the expression*

$$\pi_{\mathbb{E}}(p) = \sqrt{(1 - \vartheta_{\mathbb{E}}(p))^2 + (\varsigma_{\mathbb{E}}(p))^2}$$

is called the IMD of $p \in \mathbb{P}$.

(c) *FFS* $\mathbb{E} = \{\langle p, \vartheta_{\mathbb{E}}(p), \varsigma_{\mathbb{E}}(p)\rangle : p \in \mathbb{P}\}$, *in* $\mathbb{P}$, *the expression*

$$\pi_{\mathbb{E}}(p) = \sqrt[3]{(1 - \vartheta_{\mathbb{E}}(p))^3 + (\varsigma_{\mathbb{E}}(p))^3}$$

is called the IMD of $p \in \mathbb{P}$.

(d) *q-ROFS* $\mathbb{E} = \{\langle p, \vartheta_{\mathbb{E}}(p), \varsigma_{\mathbb{E}}(p)\rangle : p \in \mathbb{P}\}$ *in* $\mathbb{P}$, *the expression*

$$\pi_{\mathbb{E}}(p) = \sqrt[q]{(1 - \vartheta_{\mathbb{E}}(p))^q + (\varsigma_{\mathbb{E}}(p))^q}$$

is called the IMD of $p \in \mathbb{P}$.

Definition 5. *For any (m, n)-ROFS* $\mathbb{E} = \{\langle p, \vartheta_{\mathbb{E}}(p), \varsigma_{\mathbb{E}}(p)\rangle : p \in \mathbb{P}\}$ *over* $\mathbb{P}$, *the expression*

$$\pi_{\mathbb{E}}(p) = \sqrt[\frac{m+n}{2}]{(1 - \vartheta_{\mathbb{E}}(p))^m + (\varsigma_{\mathbb{E}}(p))^n}$$

is called the IMD of $p \in \mathbb{P}$.

Remark 3. *The IMD* $\pi_{\mathbb{E}}(p)$ *of* $p \in \mathbb{P}$ *to IFS (resp., PFS, FFS, q-ROFS)* $\mathbb{E}$ *is a special case of IMD* $\pi_{\mathbb{E}}(p)$ *of p to (m, n)-ROFS* $\mathbb{E}$ *for m = n = 1 (resp., m = n = 2 m = n = 3, m = n = q).*

Remark 4. *Clearly, for each (m, n)-ROFS $\mathbb{E}$ in $\mathbb{P}$,*

$$\pi_{\mathbb{E}}^{\frac{m+n}{2}}(p) + (\vartheta_{\mathbb{E}}(p))^m + (\varsigma_{\mathbb{E}}(p))^n = 1,$$

$\forall\, p \in \mathbb{P}$.

2.2. *Cosine and Cotangent Similarity Measures for Generalized Fuzzy Structures*

The cosine and cotangent similarity measures have been applied in numerous MADM and MCDM methods to calculate the degree of proximity between any two objects. The study of the cosine measure between two IFSs $\mathbb{E}$ and $\mathbb{F}$ was initiated by Ye [37] in 2011. In 2013, Shi and Ye [40] created new cosine similarity measures for IFSs, which extend the measures proposed by Ye [37] and are applied to the fault diagnosis of turbines. In 2016, Ye [38] created two cosine similarity measures for IFSs based on cosine functions and applied them to MADM. The cotangent function-based similarity measures for IFSs were created by Tian [44] and Rajeshwari and Uma [45] in 2013. The weighted cosine and cotangent similarity measures between IFSs were defined by Ye [37], Shi and Ye [40], Tian [44], and Rajarajeshwari and Uma [45]. In 2018, Wei and Wei [51] proposed cosine and cotangent measures and weighted cosine and cotangent measures between PFSs. In 2019, Wang et al. [65] extended cosine and cotangent measures of similarity for q-ROFSs, which are shown in Tables 2 and 3. The cosine and cotangent similarity and weighted similarity measures for IFSs and PFSs are exceptional cases of corresponding similarity measures defined by Wang et al. [65]. Recently, Kirisci [58] created some cosine similarity measures for Fermatean fuzzy sets, which is a particular case of q-ROFS for q = 3.

Table 2. Cosine and cotangent-based measures of similarity between q-ROFSs [51].

S. N.	Similarity Measure
1	$q-ROFC^1(\mathbb{E},\mathbb{F}) = \frac{1}{r}\sum_{j=1}^{r}\frac{\vartheta_{\mathbb{E}}^q(p_j)\vartheta_{\mathbb{F}}^q(p_j)+\varsigma_{\mathbb{E}}^q(p_j)\varsigma_{\mathbb{F}}^q(p_j)}{\sqrt{(\vartheta_{\mathbb{E}}^q(p_j))^2+(\varsigma_{\mathbb{E}}^q(p_j))^2}\sqrt{(\vartheta_{\mathbb{F}}^q(p_j))^2+(\varsigma_{\mathbb{F}}^q(p_j))^2}}$
2	$q-ROFC^2(\mathbb{E},\mathbb{F}) = \frac{1}{r}\sum_{j=1}^{r}[\frac{(\vartheta_{\mathbb{E}}^q(p_j)\vartheta_{\mathbb{F}}^q(p_j)+\varsigma_{\mathbb{E}}^q(p_j)\varsigma_{\mathbb{F}}^q(p_j)+\pi_{\mathbb{E}}^q(p_j)\pi_{\mathbb{F}}^q(p_j))}{\sqrt{(\vartheta_{\mathbb{E}}^q(p_j))^2+(\varsigma_{\mathbb{E}}^q(p_j))^2+(\pi_{\mathbb{E}}^q(p_j))^2}\sqrt{(\vartheta_{\mathbb{F}}^q(p_j))^2+(\varsigma_{\mathbb{F}}^q(p_j))^2+(\pi_{\mathbb{F}}^q(p_j))^2}}]$
3	$q-ROFCS^1(\mathbb{E},\mathbb{F}) = \frac{1}{r}\sum_{j=1}^{r}cos[\frac{\pi}{2}(max(\lvert\vartheta_{\mathbb{E}}^q(p_j)-\vartheta_{\mathbb{F}}^q(p_j)\rvert,\lvert\varsigma_{\mathbb{E}}^q(p_j)-\varsigma_{\mathbb{F}}^q(p_j)\rvert))]$
4	$q-ROFCS^2(\mathbb{E},\mathbb{F}) = \frac{1}{r}\sum_{j=1}^{r}cos[\frac{\pi}{4}(\lvert\vartheta_{\mathbb{E}}^q(p_j)-\vartheta_{\mathbb{F}}^q(p_j)\rvert+\lvert\varsigma_{\mathbb{E}}^q(p_j)-\varsigma_{\mathbb{F}}^q(p_j)\rvert)]$
5	$q-ROFCS^3(\mathbb{E},\mathbb{F}) = \frac{1}{r}\sum_{j=1}^{r}cos[\frac{\pi}{2}(max(\lvert\vartheta_{\mathbb{E}}^q(p_j)-\vartheta_{\mathbb{F}}^q(p_j)\rvert,\lvert\varsigma_{\mathbb{E}}^q(p_j)-\varsigma_{\mathbb{F}}^q(p_j)\rvert,\lvert\pi_{\mathbb{E}}^q(p_j)-\pi_{\mathbb{F}}^q(p_j)\rvert))]$
6	$q-ROFCS^4(\mathbb{E},\mathbb{F}) = \frac{1}{r}\sum_{j=1}^{r}cos[\frac{\pi}{4}(\lvert\vartheta_{\mathbb{E}}^q(p_j)-\vartheta_{\mathbb{F}}^q(p_j)\rvert+\lvert\varsigma_{\mathbb{E}}^q(p_j)-\varsigma_{\mathbb{F}}^q(p_j)\rvert+\lvert\pi_{\mathbb{E}}^q(p_j)-\pi_{\mathbb{F}}^q(p_j)\rvert)]$
7	$q-ROFCot^1(\mathbb{E},\mathbb{F}) = \frac{1}{r}\sum_{j=1}^{r}cot[\frac{\pi}{4}+\frac{\pi}{4}(max(\lvert\vartheta_{\mathbb{E}}^q(p_j)-\vartheta_{\mathbb{F}}^q(p_j)\rvert,\lvert\varsigma_{\mathbb{E}}^q(p_j)-\varsigma_{\mathbb{F}}^q(p_j)\rvert))]$
8	$q-ROFCot^2(\mathbb{E},\mathbb{F}) = \frac{1}{r}\sum_{j=1}^{r}cot[\frac{\pi}{4}+\frac{\pi}{8}(\lvert\vartheta_{\mathbb{E}}^q(p_j)-\vartheta_{\mathbb{F}}^q(p_j)\rvert+\lvert\varsigma_{\mathbb{E}}^q(p_j)-\varsigma_{\mathbb{F}}^q(p_j)\rvert)]$
9	$q-ROFCot^3(\mathbb{E},\mathbb{F})=\frac{1}{r}\sum_{j=1}^{r}cot[\frac{\pi}{4}+\frac{\pi}{4}(max(\lvert\vartheta_{\mathbb{E}}^q(p_j)-\vartheta_{\mathbb{F}}^q(p_j)\rvert,\lvert\varsigma_{\mathbb{E}}^q(p_j)-\varsigma_{\mathbb{F}}^q(p_j)\rvert,\lvert\pi_{\mathbb{E}}^q(p_j)-\pi_{\mathbb{F}}^q(p_j)\rvert))]$
10	$q-ROFCot^4(\mathbb{E},\mathbb{F}) = \frac{1}{r}\sum_{j=1}^{r}cot[\frac{\pi}{4}+\frac{\pi}{8}(\lvert\vartheta_{\mathbb{E}}^q(p_j)-\vartheta_{\mathbb{F}}^q(p_j)\rvert+\lvert\varsigma_{\mathbb{E}}^q(p_j)-\varsigma_{\mathbb{F}}^q(p_j)\rvert+\lvert\pi_{\mathbb{E}}^q(p_j)-\pi_{\mathbb{F}}^q(p_j)\rvert))]$

Table 3. Cosine and cotangent-based weighted similarity measures between q-ROFSs [65].

S. N.	Similarity Measure
1	$q-ROFWC^1(\mathbb{E},\mathbb{F}) = \sum_{j=1}^{r}\omega_j[\frac{(\vartheta^q_{\mathbb{E}}(p_j)\vartheta^q_{\mathbb{F}}(p_j)+\varsigma^q_{\mathbb{E}}(p_j)\varsigma^q_{\mathbb{F}}(p_j))}{\sqrt{(\vartheta^q_{\mathbb{E}}(p_j))^2+(\varsigma^q_{\mathbb{E}}(p_j))^2}\sqrt{(\vartheta^q_{\mathbb{F}}(p_j))^2+(\varsigma^q_{\mathbb{F}}(p_j))^2}}]$
2	$q-ROFWC^2(\mathbb{E},\mathbb{F}) = \sum_{j=1}^{r}\omega_j[\frac{(\vartheta^q_{\mathbb{E}}(p_j)\vartheta^q_{\mathbb{F}}(p_j)+\varsigma^q_{\mathbb{E}}(p_j)\varsigma^q_{\mathbb{F}}(p_j)+\pi^q_{\mathbb{E}}(p_j)\pi^q_{\mathbb{F}}(p_j))}{\sqrt{(\vartheta^q_{\mathbb{E}}(p_j))^2+(\varsigma^q_{\mathbb{E}}(p_j))^2+(\pi^q_{\mathbb{E}}(p_j))^2}\sqrt{(\vartheta^q_{\mathbb{F}}(p_j))^2+(\varsigma^q_{\mathbb{F}}(p_j))^2+(\pi^q_{\mathbb{F}}(p_j))^2}}]$
3	$q-ROFWCS^1(\mathbb{E},\mathbb{F}) = \sum_{j=1}^{r}\omega_j cos[\frac{\pi}{2}(max(\lvert\vartheta^q_{\mathbb{E}}(p_j)-\vartheta^q_{\mathbb{F}}(p_j)\rvert,\lvert\varsigma^q_{\mathbb{E}}(p_j)-\varsigma^q_{\mathbb{F}}(p_j)\rvert))]$
4	$q-ROFWCS^2(\mathbb{E},\mathbb{F}) = \sum_{j=1}^{r}\omega_j cos[\frac{\pi}{4}(\lvert\vartheta^q_{\mathbb{E}}(p_j)-\vartheta^q_{\mathbb{F}}(p_j)\rvert+\lvert\varsigma^q_{\mathbb{E}}(p_j)-\varsigma^q_{\mathbb{F}}(p_j)\rvert)]$
5	$q-ROFWCS^3(\mathbb{E},\mathbb{F}) = \sum_{j=1}^{r}\omega_j cos[\frac{\pi}{2}(max(\lvert\vartheta^q_{\mathbb{E}}(p_j)-\vartheta^q_{\mathbb{F}}(p_j)\rvert,\lvert\varsigma^q_{\mathbb{E}}(p_j)-\varsigma^q_{\mathbb{F}}(p_j)\rvert,\lvert\pi^q_{\mathbb{E}}(p_j)-\pi^q_{\mathbb{F}}(p_j)\rvert))]$
6	$q-ROFWCS^4(\mathbb{E},\mathbb{F}) = \sum_{j=1}^{r}\omega_j cos[\frac{\pi}{4}(\lvert\vartheta^q_{\mathbb{E}}(p_j)-\vartheta^q_{\mathbb{F}}(p_j)\rvert+\lvert\varsigma^q_{\mathbb{E}}(p_j)-\varsigma^q_{\mathbb{F}}(p_j)\rvert+\lvert\pi^q_{\mathbb{E}}(p_j)-\pi^q_{\mathbb{F}}(p_j)\rvert)]$
7	$q-ROFWCot^1(\mathbb{E},\mathbb{F}) = \sum_{j=1}^{r}\omega_j cot[\frac{\pi}{4}+\frac{\pi}{4}(max(\lvert\vartheta^q_{\mathbb{E}}(p_j)-\vartheta^q_{\mathbb{F}}(p_j)\rvert,\lvert\varsigma^q_{\mathbb{E}}(p_j)-\varsigma^q_{\mathbb{F}}(p_j)\rvert))]$
8	$q-ROFWCot^2(\mathbb{E},\mathbb{F}) = \sum_{j=1}^{r}\omega_j cot[\frac{\pi}{4}+\frac{\pi}{8}(\lvert\vartheta^q_{\mathbb{E}}(p_j)-\vartheta^q_{\mathbb{F}}(p_j)\rvert+\lvert\varsigma^q_{\mathbb{E}}(p_j)-\varsigma^q_{\mathbb{F}}(p_j)\rvert)]$
9	$q-ROFWCot^3(\mathbb{E},\mathbb{F}) = \sum_{j=1}^{r}\omega_j cot[\frac{\pi}{4}+\frac{\pi}{4}(max(\lvert\vartheta^q_{\mathbb{E}}(p_j)-\vartheta^q_{\mathbb{F}}(p_j)\rvert,\lvert\varsigma^q_{\mathbb{E}}(p_j)-\varsigma^q_{\mathbb{F}}(p_j)\rvert,\lvert\pi^q_{\mathbb{E}}(p_j)-\pi^q_{\mathbb{F}}(p_j)\rvert))]$
10	$q-ROFWCot^4(\mathbb{E},\mathbb{F}) = \sum_{j=1}^{r}\omega_j cot[\frac{\pi}{4}+\frac{\pi}{8}(\lvert\vartheta^q_{\mathbb{E}}(p_j)-\vartheta^q_{\mathbb{F}}(p_j)\rvert+\lvert\varsigma^q_{\mathbb{E}}(p_j)-\varsigma^q_{\mathbb{F}}(p_j)\rvert+\lvert\pi^q_{\mathbb{E}}(p_j)-\pi^q_{\mathbb{F}}(p_j)\rvert)]$

3. Cosine and Cotangent Similarity Measures for (m, n)-ROFSs

The (m, n)-ROFSs described by the degrees of membership and non-membership, for which the sum of the n-th power of the membership degree and the n-th power of the non-membership degree lies between 0 and 1, are more general than the IFSs, PFSs, and q-ROFSs, and can describe more vague and imprecise information. In other words, the (m, n)-ROFSs can deal with the MADM and MCDM problems, which IFSs, PFSs, and q-ROFSs cannot, and it is clear that IFSs, PFSs, and q-ROFSs are the special (m, n)-ROFSs, which indicates that (m, n)-ROFSs can be a more effective and powerful tool to deal with the vagueness and impreciseness involved in MADM and MCDM problems. In this section, we shall propose the(m, n)-rung ortho-pair fuzzy cosine similarity measures and (m, n)-rung orthopair fuzzy cotangent similarity measures under the (m, n)-ROFSs environment, which are new extensions of the similarity measures of IFSs, PFSs, and q-ROFSs.

3.1. Cosine Similarity Measures for (m, n)-ROFSs

This section introduces a cosine similarity measure and a weighted cosine similarity measure using (m, n)-ROFSs information in a manner analogous to the cosine similarity measure and weighted cosine similarity measure for IFSs, PFSs, and q-ROFSs.

Definition 6. *Let $\mathbb{P}=\{p_1,p_2,\ldots,p_r\}$ be a fixed set. Assume that $\mathbb{E}=\{\langle p_j,\vartheta_{\mathbb{E}}(p_j),\varsigma_{\mathbb{E}}(p_j)\rangle \mid p_j\in\mathbb{P}\}$ and $\mathbb{F}=\{\langle p_j,\vartheta_{\mathbb{F}}(p_j),\varsigma_{\mathbb{F}}(p_j)\rangle \mid p_j\in\mathbb{P}\}$ are two (m, n)-ROFSs of $\mathbb{P}$, then the (m, n)-ROFSs cosine measure $(m,n)-ROFC^1$ between $\mathbb{E}$ and $\mathbb{F}$ is defined as follows:*

$$(m,n)-ROFC^1(\mathbb{E},\mathbb{F})=\frac{1}{r}\sum_{j=1}^{r}\frac{\vartheta^m_{\mathbb{E}}(p_j)\vartheta^m_{\mathbb{F}}(p_j)+\varsigma^n_{\mathbb{E}}(p_j)\varsigma^n_{\mathbb{F}}(p_j)}{\sqrt{(\vartheta^m_{\mathbb{E}}(p_j))^2+(\varsigma^n_{\mathbb{E}}(p_j))^2}\sqrt{(\vartheta^m_{\mathbb{F}}(p_j))^2+(\varsigma^n_{\mathbb{F}}(p_j))^2}} \tag{1}$$

Remark 5. *The cosine measures $IFC^1(\mathbb{E},\mathbb{F})$ (resp., $PFC^1(\mathbb{E},\mathbb{F})$, $q-ROFC^1(\mathbb{E},\mathbb{F})$) for IFSs (resp., PFSs, q-ROFSs) are special cases of cosine similarity measures of $(m,n)-ROFC^1(\mathbb{E},\mathbb{F})$ of (m, n)-ROFSs for m = n = 1 (resp., m = n = 2, m = n = q).*

Proposition 3. *Let $\mathbb{P} = \{p_1, p_2, \ldots, p_r\}$ and $\mathbb{E}, \mathbb{F} \in (m,n) - ROFS(\mathbb{P})$, then the cosine similarity measure of $(m,n) - ROFC^1(\mathbb{E},\mathbb{F})$ satisfies the following conditions:*

(i) $0 \leq (m,n) - ROFC^1(\mathbb{E},\mathbb{F}) \leq 1$.
(ii) $(m,n) - ROFC^1(\mathbb{E},\mathbb{F}) = (m,n) - ROFC^1(\mathbb{F},\mathbb{E})$.
(iii) $\mathbb{E} = \mathbb{F} \Rightarrow (m,n) - ROFC^1(\mathbb{E},\mathbb{F}) = 1$.

Proof.

(i) It is true because of the cosine values within the closed interval [0,1].
(ii) It follows, noting that:

$$\begin{aligned}(m,n) - ROFC^1(\mathbb{E},\mathbb{F}) &= \frac{1}{r}\sum_{j=1}^{r} \frac{\vartheta_{\mathbb{E}}^m(p_j)\vartheta_{\mathbb{F}}^m(p_j) + \varsigma_{\mathbb{E}}^n(p_j)\varsigma_{\mathbb{F}}^n(p_j)}{\sqrt{(\vartheta_{\mathbb{E}}^m(p_j))^2 + (\varsigma_{\mathbb{E}}^n(p_j))^2}\sqrt{(\vartheta_{\mathbb{F}}^m(p_j))^2 + (\varsigma_{\mathbb{F}}^n(p_j))^2}} \\ &= \frac{1}{r}\sum_{j=1}^{r} \frac{\vartheta_{\mathbb{F}}^m(p_j)\vartheta_{\mathbb{E}}^m(p_j) + \varsigma_{\mathbb{F}}^n(p_j)\varsigma_{\mathbb{E}}^n(p_j)}{\sqrt{(\vartheta_{\mathbb{F}}^m(p_j))^2 + (\varsigma_{\mathbb{F}}^n(p_j))^2}\sqrt{(\vartheta_{\mathbb{E}}^m(p_j))^2 + (\varsigma_{\mathbb{E}}^n(p_j))^2}} \\ &= (m,n) - ROFC^1(\mathbb{F},\mathbb{E}).\end{aligned}$$

(iii) If $\mathbb{E} = \mathbb{F}$, then $\vartheta_{\mathbb{E}}(p_j) = \vartheta_{\mathbb{F}}(p_j)$ and $\varsigma_{\mathbb{E}}(p_j) = \varsigma_{\mathbb{F}}(p_j)$ for j = 1, 2, ..., n. Thus, from Equation (1), we have the following: $(m,n) - ROFC^1(\mathbb{E},\mathbb{F})$ = 1

□

Proposition 4. *Let $\mathbb{P} = \{p_1, p_2, \ldots, p_r\}$ and $\mathbb{E}, \mathbb{F} \in (m,n) - ROFS(\mathbb{P})$. The distance measure of angle is defined as follows:*

$$d(\mathbb{E},\mathbb{F}) = arccos((m,n) - ROFC^1(\mathbb{E},\mathbb{F}))$$

meeting the specified conditions:

(i) $0 \leq d(\mathbb{E},\mathbb{F}) \leq 1$.
(ii) $\mathbb{E} = \mathbb{F} \Rightarrow d(\mathbb{E},\mathbb{F})$=0.
(iii) $d(\mathbb{E},\mathbb{F}) = d(\mathbb{F},\mathbb{E})$.
(iv) $d(\mathbb{E},\mathbb{G}) \leq d(\mathbb{E},\mathbb{F}) + d(\mathbb{F},\mathbb{G})$ *if* $\mathbb{E} \Subset \mathbb{F} \Subset \mathbb{G}$ *for any* $\mathbb{G} \in (m,n) - ROFS(\mathbb{P})$.

Proof. Proof of conditions (i), (ii), and (iii) follows from Proposition 3.

(iv) Suppose that $\mathbb{E} \subseteq \mathbb{F} \subseteq \mathbb{G}$ for any (m, n)-ROFS $\mathbb{G} = \{\langle p_j, \vartheta_T(p_j), \varsigma_T(p_j)\rangle | p_j \in \mathbb{P}\}$ over $\mathbb{P}$. Since Equation (1) is a sum of terms, it is appropriate to examine the distance measures based on the angle between the vectors:
$d_j(\mathbb{E}(p_j),\mathbb{F}(p_j)) = arccos((m,n) - ROFC_j^1(\mathbb{E}(p_j),\mathbb{F}(p_j)))$,
$d_j(\mathbb{E}(p_j),\mathbb{G}(p_j)) = arccos((m,n) - ROFC_j^1(\mathbb{E}(p_j),\mathbb{G}(p_j)))$,
$d_j(\mathbb{F}(p_j),\mathbb{G}(p_j)) = arccos((m,n) - ROFC_j^1(\mathbb{F}(p_j),\mathbb{G}(p_j)))$,
$(j = 1,2,\ldots r)$, where,

$$(m,n) - ROFC_j^1(\mathbb{E}(p_j),\mathbb{F}(p_j)) = \frac{\vartheta_{\mathbb{E}}^m(p_j)\vartheta_{\mathbb{F}}^m(p_j) + \varsigma_{\mathbb{E}}^n(p_j)\varsigma_{\mathbb{F}}^n(p_j)}{\sqrt{(\vartheta_{\mathbb{E}}^m(p_j))^2 + (\varsigma_{\mathbb{E}}^n(p_j))^2}\sqrt{(\vartheta_{\mathbb{F}}^m(p_j))^2 + (\varsigma_{\mathbb{F}}^n(p_j))^2}}$$

$$(m,n) - ROFC_j^1(\mathbb{E}(p_j),\mathbb{G}(p_j)) = \frac{\vartheta_{\mathbb{E}}^m(p_j)\vartheta_{\mathbb{G}}^m(p_j) + \varsigma_{\mathbb{E}}^n(p_j)\varsigma_{\mathbb{G}}^n(p_j)}{\sqrt{(\vartheta_{\mathbb{E}}^m(p_j))^2 + (\varsigma_{\mathbb{E}}^n(p_j))^2}\sqrt{(\vartheta_{\mathbb{G}}^m(p_j))^2 + (\varsigma_{\mathbb{G}}^n(p_j))^2}}$$

$$(m,n) - ROFC_j^1(\mathbb{F}(p_j),\mathbb{G}(p_j)) = \frac{\vartheta_{\mathbb{F}}^m(p_j)\vartheta_{\mathbb{G}}^m(p_j) + \varsigma_{\mathbb{F}}^n(p_j)\varsigma_{\mathbb{G}}^n(p_j)}{\sqrt{(\vartheta_{\mathbb{F}}^m(p_j))^2 + (\varsigma_{\mathbb{F}}^n(p_j))^2}\sqrt{(\vartheta_{\mathbb{G}}^m(p_j))^2 + (\varsigma_{\mathbb{G}}^n(p_j))^2}}$$

For three vectors, $\mathbb{E}(p_j) = \langle \vartheta_{\mathbb{E}}(p_j), \varsigma_{\mathbb{E}}(p_j) \rangle$, $\mathbb{F}(p_j) = \langle \vartheta_{\mathbb{F}}(p_j), \varsigma_{\mathbb{F}}(p_j) \rangle$, $\mathbb{G}(p_j) = \langle \vartheta_{\mathbb{G}}(p_j), \varsigma_{\mathbb{G}}(p_j) \rangle$ in one plane, if the $\mathbb{E}(p_j) \subseteq \mathbb{F}(p_j) \subseteq \mathbb{G}(p_j)$, $j = 1, 2, \ldots,$ r, then by the triangle inequality, we have the following: $d_j(\mathbb{E}(p_j), \mathbb{G}(p_j)) \leq d_j(\mathbb{E}(p_j), \mathbb{F}(p_j)) + d_j(\mathbb{F}(p_j), \mathbb{G}(p_j))$. Combining the inequality with Equation (1), we can obtain $d(\mathbb{E}, \mathbb{G}) \leq d(\mathbb{E}, \mathbb{F}) + d(\mathbb{F}, \mathbb{G})$. Hence, the distance measure of angle $\mathrm{d}(\mathbb{E}, \mathbb{F})$ satisfies the property (iv). □

Now, we define the (m, n)-ROFS cosine measure by considering three terms, i.e.; MD, NMD, and IMD of (m, n)-ROFSs.

Definition 7. *Let* $\mathbb{E} = \{\langle p_j, \vartheta_{\mathbb{E}}(p_j), \varsigma_{\mathbb{E}}(p_j) \rangle | p_j \in \mathbb{P}\}$, *and* $\mathbb{F} = \{\langle p_j, \vartheta_{\mathbb{F}}(p_j), \varsigma_{\mathbb{F}}(p_j) \rangle | p_j \in \mathbb{P}\}$ *be two (m, n)-ROFSs in* $\mathbb{P}$, *then the (m, n)-rung orthopair fuzzy cosine measure* ($(m,n) - ROFC^2$) *between* $\mathbb{E}$ *and* $\mathbb{F}$ *can be expressed as follows:*

$(m,n) - ROFC^2(\mathbb{E}, \mathbb{F})=$

$$\frac{1}{r}\sum_{j=1}^{r} \frac{\left(\vartheta_{\mathbb{E}}^{m}(p_j)\vartheta_{\mathbb{F}}^{m}(p_j) + \varsigma_{\mathbb{E}}^{n}(p_j)\varsigma_{\mathbb{F}}^{n}(p_j) + \pi_{\mathbb{E}}^{\frac{m+n}{2}}(p_j)\pi_{\mathbb{F}}^{\frac{m+n}{2}}(p_j)\right)}{\left((\sqrt{(\vartheta_{\mathbb{E}}^{m}(p_j))^2 + (\varsigma_{\mathbb{E}}^{n}(p_j))^2 + (\pi_{\mathbb{E}}^{\frac{m+n}{2}}(p_j))^2})(\sqrt{(\vartheta_{\mathbb{F}}^{m}(p_j))^2 + (\varsigma_{\mathbb{F}}^{n}(p_j))^2 + (\pi_{\mathbb{F}}^{\frac{m+n}{2}}(p_j))^2})\right)} \tag{2}$$

Proposition 5. *Consider two (m, n)-ROFSs, denoted by* $\mathbb{E}$ *and* $\mathbb{F}$, *defined over* $\mathbb{P}$, *the cosine similarity measure* $(m,n) - ROFC^2(\mathbb{E}, \mathbb{F})$ *satisfies the following conditions:*

(i) $0 \leq (m,n) - ROFC^2(\mathbb{E}, \mathbb{F}) \leq 1$.
(ii) $(m,n) - ROFC^2(\mathbb{E}, \mathbb{F}) = (m,n) - ROFC^2(\mathbb{F}, \mathbb{E})$.
(iii) $\mathbb{E} = \mathbb{F} \Rightarrow (m,n) - ROFC^2(\mathbb{E}, \mathbb{F}) = 1$.

Remark 6. *The cosine measures* $IFC^2(\mathbb{E}, \mathbb{F})$ *(resp.,* $PFC^2(\mathbb{E}, \mathbb{F})$, $q - ROFC^2(\mathbb{E}, \mathbb{F})$*) for IFSs (resp., PFSs, q-ROFSs) are special cases of cosine similarity measures* $(m,n) - ROFC^2(\mathbb{E}, \mathbb{F})$ *of (m, n)-ROFSs for m = n = 1 (resp., m = n = 2, m = n = q).*

Now, we define the (m, n)-ROFS-weighted cosine measures between two (m, n)-ROFSs, $\mathbb{E}$ and $\mathbb{F}$, by considering the weighting vector of the elements in (m, n)-ROFSs.

Definition 8. *Let* $\mathbb{P} = \{p_1, p_2, \ldots, p_r\}$ *be a fixed set and* $\mathbb{E}, \mathbb{F} \in (m,n) - ROFS(\mathbb{P})$. *Assume* $\omega = (\omega_1, \omega_2, \ldots, \omega_n)^T$ *is the weighting vector of the elements* p_j *(j = 1, 2, …, r), satisfying the condition* $\sum_{j=1}^{r} \omega_j = 1$, $\forall\ \omega_j \in [0, 1]$ *and j = 1, 2, …, r. Then, the (m, n)-rung orthopair fuzzy-weighted cosine measures, i.e.,* $(m,n) - ROFWC^1$ *and* $(m,n) - ROFWC^2$, *between* $\mathbb{E}$ *and* $\mathbb{F}$, *can be expressed as follows:*

$(m,n) - ROFWC^1(\mathbb{E}, \mathbb{F})=$

$$\sum_{j=1}^{r} \omega_j \frac{(\vartheta_{\mathbb{E}}^{m}(p_j)\vartheta_{\mathbb{F}}^{m}(p_j) + \varsigma_{\mathbb{E}}^{n}(p_j)\varsigma_{\mathbb{F}}^{n}(p_j))}{\left((\sqrt{(\vartheta_{\mathbb{E}}^{m}(p_j))^2 + (\varsigma_{\mathbb{E}}^{n}(p_j))^2})(\sqrt{(\vartheta_{\mathbb{F}}^{m}(p_j))^2 + (\varsigma_{\mathbb{F}}^{n}(p_j))^2})\right)} \tag{3}$$

$(m,n) - ROFWC^2(\mathbb{E}, \mathbb{F}) =$

$$\sum_{j=1}^{r} \omega_j \frac{\left(\vartheta_{\mathbb{E}}^{m}(p_j)\vartheta_{\mathbb{F}}^{m}(p_j) + \varsigma_{\mathbb{E}}^{n}(p_j)\varsigma_{\mathbb{F}}^{n}(p_j) + \pi_{\mathbb{E}}^{\frac{m+n}{2}}(p_j)\pi_{\mathbb{F}}^{\frac{m+n}{2}}(p_j)\right)}{\left((\sqrt{(\vartheta_{\mathbb{E}}^{m}(p_j))^2 + (\varsigma_{\mathbb{E}}^{n}(p_j))^2 + (\pi_{\mathbb{E}}^{\frac{m+n}{2}}(p_j))^2})(\sqrt{(\vartheta_{\mathbb{F}}^{m}(p_j))^2 + (\varsigma_{\mathbb{F}}^{n}(p_j))^2 + (\pi_{\mathbb{F}}^{\frac{m+n}{2}}(p_j))^2})\right)} \tag{4}$$

When we take the weighting vector $\omega = (\frac{1}{r}, \frac{1}{r}, \ldots, \frac{1}{r})^T$, then the weighted cosine similarity measures $(m,n) - ROFWC^1(\mathbb{E}, \mathbb{F})$, and $(m,n) - ROFWC^2(\mathbb{E}, \mathbb{F})$ will reduce to cosine similarity measures $(m,n) - ROFC^1(\mathbb{E}, \mathbb{F})$ and $(m,n) - ROFC^2(\mathbb{E}, \mathbb{F})$, respectively.

Remark 7. *The weighted cosine similarity measures* $WIFC^k(\mathbb{E}, \mathbb{F})$ *(resp.,* $WPFC^k(\mathbb{E}, \mathbb{F})$, $q - ROFWC^k(\mathbb{E}, \mathbb{F})$*) for IFSs (resp., PFSs, q-ROFSs) are special cases of the weighted cosine similarity measures* $(m,n) - ROFWC^k(\mathbb{E}, \mathbb{F})$ *(k = 1, 2) of (m, n)-ROFSs for m = n = 1 (resp., m = n = 2, m = n = q).*

Example 1. *Let* $\mathbb{P} = \{p_1, p_2, p_3\}$ *and*

$$\mathbb{E} = \{(p_1, 0.5, 0.8), (p_2, 0.6, 0.4), (p_3, 0.8, 0.3)\}$$
$$\mathbb{F} = \{(p_1, 0.7, 0.6), (p_2, 0.8, 0.2), (p_3, 0.4, 0.3)\}$$

be two (m, n)-ROFSs over $\mathbb{P}$. *Assuming* $m = 4$, $n = 3$, *and* $\omega = (0.20, 0.45, 0.35)^T$ *is a weighting vector of the elements* p_1, p_2, p_3, *then,* $(m,n) - ROFWC^1(\mathbb{E}, \mathbb{F}) = 0.8150$ *and* $(m,n) - ROFWC^2(\mathbb{E}, \mathbb{F}) = 0.8610$.

Proposition 6. *Let* $\mathbb{E}$ *and* $\mathbb{F}$ *be two (m, n)-ROFSs over a fixed set* $\mathbb{P} = \{p_1, p_2, \ldots, p_r\}$. *Assuming* $\omega = (\omega_1, \omega_2, \ldots, \omega_n)^T$ *is the weighting vector of the elements* p_j $(j = 1, 2, \ldots, r)$, *satisfying the conditions* $\sum_{j=1}^{r} \omega_j = 1$, $\forall\ \omega_j \in [0, 1]$ *and* $j = 1, 2, \ldots, r$, *then the weighted cosine similarity measures* $(m,n) - ROFWC^k(\mathbb{E}, \mathbb{F})$ $(k = 1, 2)$ *meet the following conditions:*

(a) $0 \leq (m,n) - ROFWC^k(\mathbb{E}, \mathbb{F}) \leq 1$.
(b) $(m,n) - ROFWC^k(\mathbb{E}, \mathbb{F}) = (m,n) - ROFWC^k(\mathbb{F}, \mathbb{E})$.
(c) $\mathbb{E} = \mathbb{F} \Rightarrow (m,n) - ROFWC^k(\mathbb{E}, \mathbb{F}) = 1$.

3.2. Similarity Measures of (m, n)-ROFSs Based on the Cosine Function

This section introduces several (m, n)-ROFS cosine similarity measures between (m, n)-ROFSs, which are based on the cosine function, and examines their properties.

Definition 9. *Let* $\mathbb{P} = \{p_j : j = 1, 2, \ldots, r\}$ *and*

$$\mathbb{E} = \{\langle p_j, (\vartheta_{\mathbb{E}}(p_j), \varsigma_{\mathbb{E}}(p_j))\rangle | p_j \in \mathbb{P}\}$$
$$\mathbb{F} = \{\langle p_j, (\vartheta_{\mathbb{F}}(p_j), \varsigma_{\mathbb{F}}(p_j))\rangle | p_j \in \mathbb{P}\}$$

be two (m, n)-ROFSs over $\mathbb{P}$, *then two (m, n)-ROFS cosine similarity measures* $(m,n) - ROFCS^k$ $(k = 1, 2)$ *between* $\mathbb{E}$ *and* $\mathbb{F}$ *can be expressed as follows:*

$(m,n) - ROFCS^1(\mathbb{E}, \mathbb{F})=$

$$\frac{1}{r}\sum_{j=1}^{r} \cos\left[\frac{\pi}{2}\left(|\vartheta^m_{\mathbb{E}}(p_j) - \vartheta^m_{\mathbb{F}}(p_j)| \vee |\varsigma^n_{\mathbb{E}}(p_j) - \varsigma^n_{\mathbb{F}}(p_j)|\right)\right] \tag{5}$$

$(m,n) - ROFCS^2(\mathbb{E}, \mathbb{F})=$

$$\frac{1}{r}\sum_{j=1}^{r} \cos\left[\frac{\pi}{4}\left(|\vartheta^m_{\mathbb{E}}(p_j) - \vartheta^m_{\mathbb{F}}(p_j)| + |\varsigma^n_{\mathbb{E}}(p_j) - \varsigma^n_{\mathbb{F}}(p_j)|\right)\right] \tag{6}$$

Proposition 7. *Let* $\mathbb{P} = \{p_1, p_2, \ldots, p_r\}$ *and* $\mathbb{E}, \mathbb{F} \in (m,n) - ROFS(\mathbb{P})$, *then the (m, n)-rung orthopair fuzzy cosine similarity measures* $(m,n) - ROFCS^k(\mathbb{E}, \mathbb{F})$ $(k = 1, 2)$ *meet the following properties:*

(a) $0 \leq (m,n) - ROFCS^k(\mathbb{E}, \mathbb{F}) \leq 1$.
(b) $(m,n) - ROFCS^k(\mathbb{E}, \mathbb{F}) = 1 \Leftrightarrow \mathbb{E} = \mathbb{F}$.
(c) $(m,n) - ROFCS^k(\mathbb{E}, \mathbb{F}) = (m,n) - ROFCS^k(\mathbb{F}, \mathbb{E})$.
(d) *If* $\mathbb{E} \subseteq \mathbb{F} \subseteq \mathbb{G}$, $\forall\ \mathbb{G} \in (m,n) - ROFS(\mathbb{P})$. *Then,* $(m,n) - ROFCS^k(\mathbb{E}, \mathbb{G}) \leq (m,n) - ROFCS^k(\mathbb{E}, \mathbb{F})$ *and* $(m,n) - ROFCS^k(\mathbb{E}, \mathbb{G}) \leq (m,n) - ROFCS^k(\mathbb{F}, \mathbb{G})$.

Proof.

(a) The values of cosine functions lie between 0 and 1, which makes it evident.
(b) If $\mathbb{E} = \mathbb{F}$ for any two (m, n)-ROFSs $\mathbb{E}$ and $\mathbb{F}$ in $\mathbb{P} = \{p_1, p_2, \ldots, p_r\}$, then for each j = 1, 2, …, r, $\vartheta^m_{\mathbb{E}}(p_j) = \vartheta^m_{\mathbb{F}}(p_j)$ and $\varsigma^n_{\mathbb{E}}(p_j) = \varsigma^n_{\mathbb{F}}(p_j)$. It implies that $|\ \vartheta^m_{\mathbb{E}}(p_j) - \vartheta^m_{\mathbb{F}}(p_j)\ | = 0$ and $|\ \varsigma^n_{\mathbb{E}}(p_j) - \varsigma^n_{\mathbb{F}}(p_j)\ | = 0$. Hence, $(m,n) - ROFCS^k(\mathbb{E}, \mathbb{F}) = 1$ for $k = 1, 2$. Suppose that

$(m,n) - ROFCS^k(\mathbb{E},\mathbb{F}) = 1, k = 1, 2$, then $|\ \vartheta^m_{\mathbb{E}}(p_j) - \vartheta^m_{\mathbb{F}}(p_j)\ | = 0$ and $|\ \varsigma^n_{\mathbb{E}}(p_j) - \varsigma^n_{\mathbb{F}}(p_j)\ | = 0$, for all $j= 1, 2, \ldots, r$. Since $\cos(0) = 1$, there are $\vartheta^m_{\mathbb{E}}(p_j) = \vartheta^m_{\mathbb{F}}(p_j), \varsigma^n_{\mathbb{E}}(p_j) = \varsigma^n_{\mathbb{F}}(p_j)$ ($j = 1, 2, \ldots, r$). Hence, $\mathbb{E} = \mathbb{F}$.

(c) Obvious.

(d) If $\mathbb{E}(p_j) \subseteq \mathbb{F}(p_j) \subseteq \mathbb{G}(p_j)$, $\forall\ j = 1, 2, \ldots, r$, then $\vartheta_{\mathbb{E}}(p_j) \leq \vartheta_{\mathbb{F}}(p_j) \leq \vartheta_{\mathbb{G}}(p_j)$ and $\varsigma_{\mathbb{E}}(p_j) \geq \varsigma_{\mathbb{F}}(p_j) \geq \varsigma_{\mathbb{G}}(p_j)$, $j = 1, 2, \ldots, r$. It follows that $\vartheta^m_{\mathbb{E}}(p_j) \leq \vartheta^m_{\mathbb{F}}(p_j) \leq \vartheta^m_{\mathbb{G}}(p_j)$ and $\varsigma^n_{\mathbb{E}}(p_j) \geq \varsigma^n_{\mathbb{F}}(p_j) \geq \varsigma^n_{\mathbb{G}}(p_j)$. Thus, we obtain the following:
$|\ \vartheta^m_{\mathbb{E}}(p_j) - \vartheta^m_{\mathbb{F}}(p_j)\ | \leq |\ \vartheta^m_{\mathbb{E}}(p_j) - \vartheta^m_{\mathbb{G}}(p_j)\ |$,
$|\ \vartheta^m_{\mathbb{F}}(p_j) - \vartheta^m_{\mathbb{G}}(p_j)\ | \leq |\ \vartheta^m_{\mathbb{E}}(p_j) - \vartheta^m_{\mathbb{G}}(p_j)\ |$,
$|\ \varsigma^n_{\mathbb{E}}(p_j) - \varsigma^n_{\mathbb{F}}(p_j)\ | \leq |\ \varsigma^n_{\mathbb{E}}(p_j) - \varsigma^n_{\mathbb{G}}(p_j)\ |$,
$|\ \varsigma^n_{\mathbb{F}}(p_j) - \varsigma^n_{\mathbb{G}}(p_j)\ | \leq |\ \varsigma^n_{\mathbb{E}}(p_j) - \varsigma^n_{\mathbb{G}}(p_j)\ |$.
□

The cosine function is a decreasing function with the interval $[0, \frac{\pi}{2}]$; therefore, we obtain that $(m,n) - ROFCS^k(\mathbb{E},\mathbb{G}) \leq (m,n) - ROFCS^k(\mathbb{E},\mathbb{F})$, $(m,n) - ROFCS^k(\mathbb{E},\mathbb{G}) \leq (m,n) - ROFCS^k(\mathbb{F},\mathbb{G})$ for $k = 1, 2$.

Next, we introduce (m, n)-rung orthopair fuzzy cosine measures based on the cosine function. These measures are obtained by considering MD, NMD, and IMD for two (m, n)-ROFSs, i.e., $\mathbb{E}$ and $\mathbb{F}$ of $\mathbb{P}$.

Definition 10. *Let* $\mathbb{P} = \{p_j : j = 1, 2, \ldots, r\}$ *and*

$$\mathbb{E} = \{\langle p_j, (\vartheta_{\mathbb{E}}(p_j), \varsigma_{\mathbb{E}}(p_j))\rangle | p_j \in \mathbb{P}\}$$
$$\mathbb{F} = \{\langle p_j, (\vartheta_{\mathbb{F}}(p_j), \varsigma_{\mathbb{F}}(p_j))\rangle | p_j \in \mathbb{P}\}$$

be the two (m, n)-ROFSs over $\mathbb{P}$, *then two (m, n)-ROFS cosine similarity measures, i.e.,* $(m,n) - ROFCS^k)$ *(k = 3, 4) between* $\mathbb{E}$ *and* $\mathbb{F}$, *by considering MD, NMD, and IMD, can be expressed as follows:*

$(m,n) - ROFCS^3(\mathbb{E},\mathbb{F})=$

$$\frac{1}{r}\sum_{j=1}^{r} cos\left[\frac{\pi}{2}\left(|\vartheta^m_{\mathbb{E}}(p_j) - \vartheta^m_{\mathbb{F}}(p_j)|, \vee|\varsigma^n_{\mathbb{E}}(p_j) - \varsigma^n_{\mathbb{F}}(p_j)|, \vee|\pi_{\mathbb{E}}^{\frac{m+n}{2}}(p_j) - |\pi_{\mathbb{F}}^{\frac{m+n}{2}}(p_j)|\right)\right] \tag{7}$$

$(m,n) - ROFCS^4(\mathbb{E},\mathbb{F})=$

$$\frac{1}{r}\sum_{j=1}^{r} cos\left[\frac{\pi}{4}\left(|\vartheta^m_{\mathbb{E}}(p_j) - \vartheta^m_{\mathbb{F}}(p_j)| + |\varsigma^n_{\mathbb{E}}(p_j) - \varsigma^n_{\mathbb{F}}(p_j)| + |\pi_{\mathbb{E}}^{\frac{m+n}{2}}(p_j) - |\pi_{\mathbb{F}}^{\frac{m+n}{2}}(p_j)|\right)\right] \tag{8}$$

Remark 8. *The cosine measures* $IFCS^k(\mathbb{E},\mathbb{F})$ *(resp.,* $PFCS^k(\mathbb{E},\mathbb{F})$, $q - ROFWCS^k(\mathbb{E},\mathbb{F})$*) for IFSs (resp., PFSs, q-ROFSs) are special cases of cosine measures* $(m,n) - ROFCS^k(\mathbb{E},\mathbb{F})$ *(k = 1, 2, 3, 4) of (m, n)-ROFSs for m = n = 1 (resp., m = n = 2, m = n = q).*

We will now introduce the (m, n)-ROFS weighted cosine measures between two (m, n)-ROFSs, which are based on cosine functions $\mathbb{E}$ and $\mathbb{F}$, by taking into account the weighting vector associated with the elements in (m, n)-ROFSs.

Definition 11. *Let* $\mathbb{E} = \{\langle p_j, \vartheta_{\mathbb{E}}(p_j), \varsigma_{\mathbb{E}}(p_j)\rangle | p_j \in \mathbb{P}\}$ *and* $\mathbb{F} = \{\langle p_j, \vartheta_{\mathbb{F}}(p_j), \varsigma_{\mathbb{F}}(p_j)\rangle | p_j \in \mathbb{P}\}$ *be two (m, n)-ROFSs in* $\mathbb{P}$ *and let* $\omega = (\omega_1, \omega_2, \ldots, \omega_r)^T$ *be the weighting vector of the elements* p_j *(j = 1, 2, ..., r) that satisfies the condition* $\sum_{j=1}^{r} \omega = 1$, $\forall\ \omega_j \in [0, 1]$ *and j = 1, 2, ..., r. The (m, n)-ROFS weighted cosine measures* $(m,n) - ROFWCS^k$, *(k = 1, 2, 3, 4) between* $\mathbb{E}$ *and* $\mathbb{F}$ *on the bases of cosine functions can be presented as follows:*

$(m,n) - ROFWCS^1(\mathbb{E},\mathbb{F})=$

$$\frac{1}{r}\sum_{j=1}^{r}\omega_j cos\left[\frac{\pi}{2}(|\vartheta^m_{\mathbb{E}}(p_j) - \vartheta^m_{\mathbb{F}}(p_j)| \vee |\varsigma^n_{\mathbb{E}}(p_j) - \varsigma^n_{\mathbb{F}}(p_j)|)\right] \quad (9)$$

$(m,n) - ROFWCS^2(\mathbb{E},\mathbb{F})=$

$$\frac{1}{r}\sum_{j=1}^{r}\omega_j cos\left[\frac{\pi}{4}(|\vartheta^m_{\mathbb{E}}(p_j) - \vartheta^m_{\mathbb{F}}(p_j)| + |\varsigma^n_{\mathbb{E}}(p_j) - \varsigma^n_{\mathbb{F}}(p_j)|)\right] \quad (10)$$

$(m,n) - -ROFWCS^3\,(\mathbb{E},\mathbb{F}) =$

$$\frac{1}{r}\sum_{j=1}^{r}\omega_j cos\left[\frac{\pi}{2}\left(|\vartheta^m_{\mathbb{E}}(p_j) - \vartheta^m_{\mathbb{F}}(p_j)| \vee |\varsigma^n_{\mathbb{E}}(p_j) - \varsigma^n_{\mathbb{F}}(p_j)| \vee |\pi_{\mathbb{E}}^{\frac{m+n}{2}}(p_j) - \pi_{\mathbb{F}}^{\frac{m+n}{2}}(p_j)|\right)\right] \quad (11)$$

$(m,n) - ROFWCS^4(\mathbb{E},\mathbb{F})=$

$$\frac{1}{r}\sum_{j=1}^{r}\omega_j cos\left[\frac{\pi}{4}\left(|\vartheta^m_{\mathbb{E}}(p_j) - \vartheta^m_{\mathbb{F}}(p_j)| + |\varsigma^n_{\mathbb{E}}(p_j) - \varsigma^n_{\mathbb{F}}(p_j)| + |\pi_{\mathbb{E}}^{\frac{m+n}{2}}(p_j) - \pi_{\mathbb{F}}^{\frac{m+n}{2}}(p_j)|\right)\right] \quad (12)$$

When the weighting vector $\omega_j = \frac{1}{r}$, $j = 1, 2, \ldots r$, then for k = 1, 2, 3, 4, we have (m, n)-ROFWCS $^k(\mathbb{E},\mathbb{F})$ = (m, n)-ROFCS$^k(\mathbb{E},\mathbb{F})$.

Remark 9. *The weighted cosine similarity measures $WIFCS^k(\mathbb{E},\mathbb{F})$ (resp., $WPFCS^k(\mathbb{E},\mathbb{F})$, $q-ROFWCS^k(\mathbb{E},\mathbb{F})$) for IFSs (resp., PFSs, q-ROFSs) are special cases of weighted cosine measures $(m,n) - ROFWCS^k(\mathbb{E},\mathbb{F})$($k$ = 1, 2, 3, 4) of (m, n)-ROFSs for $m = n = 1$ (resp., $m = n = 2$, $m = n = q$).*

Example 2. *Let $\mathbb{P} = \{p_1, p_2, p_3\}$ and*

$$\mathbb{E} = \{(p_1, 0.8, 0.5), (p_2, 0.4, 0.6), (p_3, 0.3, 0.8)\}$$
$$\mathbb{F} = \{(p_1, 0.6, 0.7), (p_2, 0.2, 0.8), (p_3, 0.4, 0.3)\}$$

be two (m, n)-ROFSs over $\mathbb{P}$. Assuming $m = 4$, $n = 6$ and $\omega = (0.25, 0.55, 0.20)^T$ are the weights for the elements p_1, p_2, p_3, then:

$$(m,n) - ROFWCS^1(\mathbb{E},\mathbb{F}) = 0.9283.$$
$$(m,n) - ROFWCS^2(\mathbb{E},\mathbb{F}) = 0.9743.$$
$$(m,n) - ROFWCS^3(\mathbb{E},\mathbb{F}) = 0.9283.$$
$$(m,n) - ROFWCS^4(\mathbb{E},\mathbb{F}) = 0.9283.$$

Proposition 8. *Assuming that there are any two (m, n)-ROFSs, $\mathbb{E}$ and $\mathbb{F}$ in $\mathbb{P} = \{p_1, p_2, \ldots, p_r\}$, the (m, n)-ROFS weighted cosine similarity measures (m, n)-ROFWCS^k $(\mathbb{E},\mathbb{F})$(k = 1, 2, 3, 4) should satisfy properties (a)–(b):*

(a) $0 \le (m,n) - ROFWCS^k(\mathbb{E},\mathbb{F}) \le 1.$

(b) $(m,n) - ROFWCS^k(\mathbb{E},\mathbb{F}) = 1 \Leftrightarrow \mathbb{E} = \mathbb{F}.$

(c) $(m,n) - ROFWCS^k(\mathbb{E},\mathbb{F})$
$= (m,n) - ROFWCS^k(\mathbb{F},\mathbb{E}).$

(d) *If $\mathbb{E} \subseteq \mathbb{F} \subseteq \mathbb{G}$, $\forall\, \mathbb{G} \in (m,n) - ROFS(\mathbb{P})$. Then (m, n)-ROFWCS^k $(\mathbb{E},\mathbb{G})$ $\le$(m, n)-ROFWCS^k $(\mathbb{E},\mathbb{F})$, (m, n)-ROFWCS^k $(\mathbb{E},\mathbb{G})$ $\le$ (m, n)-ROFWCS^k $(\mathbb{F},\mathbb{G})$.*

3.3. Cotangent-Based Similarity Measures for (m, n)-ROFSs

Definition 12. *Let* $\mathbb{P} = \{p_1, p_2, \ldots, p_r\}$ *and*
$\mathbb{E}= \{\langle p_j, (\vartheta_{\mathbb{E}}(p_j), \varsigma_{\mathbb{E}}(p_j))\rangle | p_j \in \mathbb{P}\}$,
Let $\mathbb{F}= \{\langle p_j, (\vartheta_{\mathbb{F}}(p_j), \varsigma_{\mathbb{F}}(p_j))\rangle | p_j \in \mathbb{P}\}$ *be two (m, n)-ROFSs; the (m, n)-ROFS cotangent measures* $(m,n)-ROFCot^1$ *and* $(m,n)-ROFCot^2$ *between* $\mathbb{E}$ *and* $\mathbb{F}$ *are defined as follows:*
$(m,n)-ROFCot^1(\mathbb{E},\mathbb{F})=$

$$\frac{1}{r}\sum_{j=1}^{r} cot\left[\frac{\pi}{4}+\frac{\pi}{4}(|\vartheta_{\mathbb{E}}^{m}(p_j)-\vartheta_{\mathbb{F}}^{m}(p_j)| \vee |\varsigma_{\mathbb{E}}^{n}(p_j)-\varsigma_{\mathbb{F}}^{n}(p_j)|)\right] \tag{13}$$

$(m,n)-ROFCot^2(\mathbb{E},\mathbb{F})=$

$$\frac{1}{r}\sum_{j=1}^{r} cot\left[\frac{\pi}{4}+\frac{\pi}{8}(|\vartheta_{\mathbb{E}}^{m}(p_j)-\vartheta_{\mathbb{F}}^{m}(p_j)| + |\varsigma_{\mathbb{E}}^{n}(p_j)-\varsigma_{\mathbb{F}}^{n}(p_j)|)\right] \tag{14}$$

We will now incorporate MD, NMD, and IMD, all of which are components of (m, n)-ROFSs, to define two additional cotangent similarity measures between two (m, n)-ROFSs.

Definition 13. *Let* $\mathbb{P} = \{p_j : j = 1, 2, \ldots, r\}$ *and*

$$\mathbb{E} = \{\langle p_j, (\vartheta_{\mathbb{E}}(p_j), \varsigma_{\mathbb{E}}(p_j)\rangle : p_j \in \mathbb{P}\}$$
$$\mathbb{F} = \{\langle p_j, (\vartheta_{\mathbb{F}}(p_j), \varsigma_{\mathbb{F}}(p_j))\rangle : p_j \in \mathbb{P}\}.$$

be two (m, n)-ROFSs in $\mathbb{P}$, *then the (m, n)-ROFSs cotangent similarity measures* $(m,n)-ROFCot^3$ *and* $(m,n)-ROFCot^4$ *between* $\mathbb{E}$ *and* $\mathbb{F}$ *can be expressed as follows:*
$(m,n)-ROFCot^3(\mathbb{E},\mathbb{F})=$

$$\frac{1}{r}\sum_{j=1}^{r} cot\left[\frac{\pi}{4}+\frac{\pi}{4}\left(|\vartheta_{\mathbb{E}}^{m}(p_j)-\vartheta_{\mathbb{F}}^{m}(p_j)| \vee |\varsigma_{\mathbb{E}}^{n}(p_j)-\varsigma_{\mathbb{F}}^{n}(p_j)| \vee |\pi_{\mathbb{E}}^{\frac{m+n}{2}}(p_j)-\pi_{\mathbb{F}}^{\frac{m+n}{2}}(p_j)|\right)\right] \tag{15}$$

$(m,n)-ROFCot^4(\mathbb{E},\mathbb{F})=$

$$\frac{1}{r}\sum_{j=1}^{r} cot\left[\frac{\pi}{4}+\frac{\pi}{8}\left(|\vartheta_{\mathbb{E}}^{m}(p_j)-\vartheta_{\mathbb{F}}^{m}(p_j)| + |\varsigma_{\mathbb{E}}^{n}(p_j)-\varsigma_{\mathbb{F}}^{n}(p_j)| + |\pi_{\mathbb{E}}^{\frac{m+n}{2}}(p_j)-\pi_{\mathbb{F}}^{\frac{m+n}{2}}(p_j)|\right)\right] \tag{16}$$

Remark 10. *The cotangent measures* $IFCT^k(\mathbb{E},\mathbb{F})$ *(resp.,* $PFCT^k(\mathbb{E},\mathbb{F})$, $q-ROFCot^k(\mathbb{E},\mathbb{F})$*) for IFSs (resp., PFSs, q-ROFSs) are special cases of cotangent measures* $(m,n)-ROFCot^k(\mathbb{E},\mathbb{F})$ *(k = 1, 2, 3, 4) of (m, n)-ROFSs for m = n = 1 (resp., m = n = 2, m = n = q).*

We will now introduce the (m, n)-ROFS weighted cotangent measures between two (m, n)-ROFSs, $\mathbb{E}$ and $\mathbb{F}$, by taking into account the weighting vector associated with the elements in (m, n)-ROFSs.

Definition 14. *Let* $\mathbb{P} = \{p_1, p_2, \ldots, p_r\}$ *be a fixed set and* $\mathbb{E} = \{\langle p_j, \vartheta_{\mathbb{E}}(p_j), \varsigma_{\mathbb{E}}(p_j)\rangle | p_j \in \mathbb{P}\}$, $\mathbb{F} = \{\langle p_j, \vartheta_{\mathbb{F}}(p_j), \varsigma_{\mathbb{F}}(p_j)\rangle | p_j \in \mathbb{P}\}$ *be two (m, n)-ROFSs in* $\mathbb{P}$. *Assume that* $\omega = (\omega_1, \omega_2, \ldots, \omega_r)^T$ *is the weighting vector of the elements* p_j *(j = 1, 2, ..., r) that satisfies the condition* $\sum_{j=1}^{r} \omega_j = 1$, $\forall\, \omega_j \in [0,1]$ *and j = 1, 2, ..., r.*

The (m, n)-ROFS weighted cotangent measures $(m,n)-ROFWCot^k$ *(k = 1, 2, 3, 4) between* $\mathbb{E}$ *and* $\mathbb{F}$ *are expressed as follows:*
$(m,n)-ROFWCot^1(\mathbb{E},\mathbb{F})=$

$$\sum_{j=1}^{r} \omega_j cot\left[\frac{\pi}{4}+\frac{\pi}{4}(|\vartheta_{\mathbb{E}}^{m}(p_j)-\vartheta_{\mathbb{F}}^{m}(p_j)| \vee |\varsigma_{\mathbb{E}}^{n}(p_j)-\varsigma_{\mathbb{F}}^{n}(p_j)|)\right] \tag{17}$$

$(m,n) - ROFWCot^2(\mathbb{E},\mathbb{F}) =$

$$\sum_{j=1}^{r} \omega_j cot\left[\frac{\pi}{4} + \frac{\pi}{8}(|\vartheta_{\mathbb{E}}^{m}(p_j) - \vartheta_{\mathbb{F}}^{m}(p_j)| + |\varsigma_{\mathbb{E}}^{n}(p_j) - \varsigma_{\mathbb{F}}^{n}(p_j)|)\right] \quad (18)$$

$(m,n) - ROFWCot^3(\mathbb{E},\mathbb{F}) =$

$$\sum_{j=1}^{r} \omega_j cot\left[\frac{\pi}{4} + \frac{\pi}{4}\left(|\vartheta_{\mathbb{E}}^{m}(p_j) - \vartheta_{\mathbb{F}}^{m}(p_j)| \vee |\varsigma_{\mathbb{E}}^{n}(p_j) - \varsigma_{\mathbb{F}}^{n}(p_j)| \vee |\pi_{\mathbb{E}}^{\frac{m+n}{2}}(p_j) - \pi_{\mathbb{F}}^{\frac{m+n}{2}}(p_j)|\right)\right] \quad (19)$$

$(m,n) - ROFWCot^4(\mathbb{E},\mathbb{F}) =$

$$\sum_{j=1}^{r} \omega_j cot\left[\frac{\pi}{4} + \frac{\pi}{8}\left(|\vartheta_{\mathbb{E}}^{m}(p_j) - \vartheta_{\mathbb{F}}^{m}(p_j)| + |\varsigma_{\mathbb{E}}^{n}(p_j) - \varsigma_{\mathbb{F}}^{n}(p_j)| + |\pi_{\mathbb{E}}^{\frac{m+n}{2}}(p_j) - \pi_{\mathbb{F}}^{\frac{m+n}{2}}(p_j)|\right)\right] \quad (20)$$

When we let the weighting vector $\omega = (\frac{1}{r}, \frac{1}{r}, \dots \frac{1}{r})^T$, then $(m,n) - ROFWCot^k(\mathbb{E},\mathbb{F})$ coincides with $(m,n) - ROFCot^k(\mathbb{E},\mathbb{F})$, for $k = 1, 2, 3, 4$.

Example 3. *Let* $X = \{p_1, p_2, p_3\}$ *and*

$$\mathbb{E} = \{(p_1, 0.4, 0.9), (p_2, 0.9, 0.3), (p_3, 0.9, 0.6)\}$$
$$\mathbb{F} = \{(p_1, 0.3, 0.7), (p_2, 0.8, 0.3), (p_3, 0.7, 0.4)\}$$

be two (m, n)-ROFSs over $\mathbb{P}$*. Assuming that* $m = 5$, $n = 7$ *and* $\omega_1 = 0.25$, $\omega_2 = 0.35$ *and* $\omega_1 = 0.40$ *are the weights for the elements* p_1, p_2, p_3*, then*

$$(m,n) - ROFWCot^1(\mathbb{E},\mathbb{F}) = 0.5290.$$
$$(m,n) - ROFWCot^2(\mathbb{E},\mathbb{F}) = 0.7206.$$
$$(m,n) - ROFWCot^3(\mathbb{E},\mathbb{F}) = 0.5253.$$
$$(m,n) - ROFWCot^4(\mathbb{E},\mathbb{F}) = 0.5253.$$

Remark 11. *The weighted cotangent similarity measures* $WIFCT^k(\mathbb{E},\mathbb{F})$ *(resp.,* $WPFCT^k(\mathbb{E},\mathbb{F})$, $q - ROFWCot^k(\mathbb{E},\mathbb{F})$ *for IFSs (resp., PFSs, q-ROFSs) are special cases of weighted cotangent measures* $(m,n) - ROFWCot^k(\mathbb{E},\mathbb{F})$ *(k = 1, 2, 3, 4) of (m, n)-ROFSs for* $m = n = 1$ *(resp.,* $m = n = 2$, $m = n = q$*).*

4. Comparisons of Existing Similarity Measures and Proposed Similarity Measures

The following section presents a comparison between the cosine and cotangent similarity measures for q-ROFSs and the newly introduced cosine and cotangent similarity measures for (m, n)-ROFSs. The evaluation is based on the example of the building material classification by Wang et al. [65].

Example 4 ([65]). *Let us consider a scenario where there are five known building construction materials, represented by q-ROFSs* $\mathbb{Z}_i$ *(i = 1, 2, 3, 4, 5), in the feature space* $\mathbb{P} = \{p_1, p_2, p_3, p_4, p_5\}$*, as shown in Table 4. We also have an unknown building material* $\mathbb{Z}$ *that needs to be classified into one of the following classes:* $\mathbb{Z}_1, \mathbb{Z}_2, \mathbb{Z}_3, \mathbb{Z}_4, \mathbb{Z}_5$*. Assuming that the weights* $w = (0.15, 0.20, 0.25, 0.10, 0.30)^T$*, we aim to determine the degree of similarity between* $\mathbb{Z}_3$ *and* $\mathbb{Z}$*.*

According to the findings presented in Table 5, the degree of weighted similarity between $\mathbb{Z}_3$ and $\mathbb{Z}$ is the highest among all ten weighted similarity measures from Table 3 for most building materials, except for $q - ROFWC^1$ and $q - ROFWC^2$. As a result, based on the principle of maximum weighted q-ROFWS similarity, the unknown building material

$\mathbb{Z}$ can be classified as similar to the known building material $\mathbb{Z}_2$ using these ten similarity measures.

Table 4. q-Orthopair fuzzy data for the material pattern (for q = 3) [65].

Feature	$\mathbb{Z}_1$	$\mathbb{Z}_2$	$\mathbb{Z}_3$	$\mathbb{Z}_4$	$\mathbb{Z}_5$	$\mathbb{Z}$
p_1	(0.5, 0.8)	(0.6, 0.7)	(0.3, 0.4)	(0.5, 0.3)	(0.4, 0.7)	(0.7, 0.6)
p_2	(0.6, 0.4)	(0.7, 0.3)	(0.7, 0.5)	(0.4, 0.4)	(0.2, 0.6)	(0.8, 0.2)
p_3	(0.8, 0.3)	(0.6, 0.2)	(0.9, 0.3)	(0.6, 0.2)	(0.5, 0.4)	(0.4, 0.3)
p_4	(0.6, 0.9)	(0.8, 0.6)	(0.4, 0.8)	(0.4, 0.7)	(0.5, 0.3)	(0.7, 0.8)
p_5	(0.1, 0.4)	(0.3, 0.5)	(0.2, 0.3)	(0.2, 0.6)	(0.4, 0.2)	(0.4, 0.2)

Table 5. q-ROF weighted similarity measures for the data presented in Table 4 for q = 3.

Weighted Similarity Measures	$(\mathbb{Z}_1, \mathbb{Z})$	$(\mathbb{Z}_2, \mathbb{Z})$	$(\mathbb{Z}_3, \mathbb{Z})$	$(\mathbb{Z}_4, \mathbb{Z})$	$(\mathbb{Z}_5, \mathbb{Z})$	Ranking
$q - ROFWC^1$	0.6728	0.7515	**0.7553**	0.6584	0.7336	$\mathbb{Z}_3 > \mathbb{Z}_2 > \mathbb{Z}_5 > \mathbb{Z}_1 > \mathbb{Z}_4$
$q - ROFWC^2$	0.8457	0.8901	**0.8937**	0.8406	0.8735	$\mathbb{Z}_3 > \mathbb{Z}_2 > \mathbb{Z}_5 > \mathbb{Z}_1 > \mathbb{Z}_4$
$q - ROFWCS^1$	0.8962	**0.9673**	0.8398	0.9114	0.8976	$\mathbb{Z}_2 > \mathbb{Z}_4 > \mathbb{Z}_5 > \mathbb{Z}_1 > \mathbb{Z}_3$
$q - ROFWCS^2$	0.9601	**0.9838**	0.9487	0.9621	0.9464	$\mathbb{Z}_2 > \mathbb{Z}_4 > \mathbb{Z}_1 > \mathbb{Z}_3 > \mathbb{Z}_5$
$q - ROFWCS^3$	0.8962	**0.9673**	0.8299	0.8986	0.8910	$\mathbb{Z}_2 > \mathbb{Z}_4 > \mathbb{Z}_1 > \mathbb{Z}_5 > \mathbb{Z}_3$
$q - ROFWCS^4$	0.8961	**0.9693**	0.8830	0.8883	0.8830	$\mathbb{Z}_2 > \mathbb{Z}_1 > \mathbb{Z}_4 > \mathbb{Z}_3 = \mathbb{Z}_3$
$q - ROFWCot^1$	0.6740	**0.7831**	0.6478	0.6735	0.7474	$\mathbb{Z}_2 > \mathbb{Z}_5 > \mathbb{Z}_1 > \mathbb{Z}_4 > \mathbb{Z}_3$
$q - ROFWCot^2$	0.7740	**0.8482**	0.7700	0.7733	0.8065	$\mathbb{Z}_2 > \mathbb{Z}_5 > \mathbb{Z}_1 > \mathbb{Z}_4 > \mathbb{Z}_3$
$q - ROFWCot^3$	0.6740	**0.7831**	0.6356	0.6522	0.7324	$\mathbb{Z}_2 > \mathbb{Z}_5 > \mathbb{Z}_1 > \mathbb{Z}_4 > \mathbb{Z}_3$
$q - ROFWCot^4$	0.6727	**0.7866**	0.6356	0.6389	0.7284	$\mathbb{Z}_2 > \mathbb{Z}_5 > \mathbb{Z}_1 > \mathbb{Z}_4 > \mathbb{Z}_3$

Table 6 shows the results obtained by the proposed weighted similarity measures $(m,n) - ROFWSs$ for $m = 4$ and $n = 3$. Based on these results, it is evident in Table 6 that all ten similarity measures allocate unknown building material $\mathbb{Z}$ to building material $\mathbb{Z}_2$, with the degree of weighted similarity between $\mathbb{Z}$ and $\mathbb{E}_2$ being the largest. This result suggests that the proposed weighted $(m,n) - ROFWSs$ method accurately allocates unknown building materials to known building materials.

Table 6. Weighted (m, n)-ROFSs for the data presented in Table 4 for m = 4, n = 3.

Weighted Similarity Measures	$(\mathbb{Z}_1, \mathbb{Z})$	$(\mathbb{Z}_2, \mathbb{Z})$	$(\mathbb{Z}_3, \mathbb{Z})$	$(\mathbb{Z}_4, \mathbb{Z})$	$(\mathbb{Z}_5, \mathbb{Z})$	Ranking
$(m,n) - ROFWC^1$	0.7353	**0.7620**	0.7334	0.5957	0.6426	$\mathbb{Z}_2 > \mathbb{Z}_1 > \mathbb{Z}_3 > \mathbb{Z}_5 > \mathbb{Z}_4$
$(m,n) - ROFWC^2$	0.9008	**0.9527**	0.8244	0.8947	0.8481	$\mathbb{Z}_2 > \mathbb{Z}_1 > \mathbb{Z}_4 > \mathbb{Z}_5 > \mathbb{Z}_3$
$(m,n) - ROFWCS^1$	0.9073	**0.9648**	0.8614	0.9203	0.8930	$\mathbb{Z}_2 > \mathbb{Z}_4 > \mathbb{Z}_1 > \mathbb{Z}_5 > \mathbb{Z}_3$
$(m,n) - ROFWCS^2$	0.9661	**0.9828**	0.9557	0.9669	0.9417	$\mathbb{Z}_2 > \mathbb{Z}_4 > \mathbb{Z}_1 > \mathbb{Z}_3 > \mathbb{Z}_5$
$(m,n) - ROFWCS^3$	0.9073	**0.9648**	0.8503	0.8906	0.8590	$\mathbb{Z}_2 > \mathbb{Z}_1 > \mathbb{Z}_4 > \mathbb{Z}_5 > \mathbb{Z}_3$
$(m,n) - ROFWCS^4$	0.9073	**0.9648**	0.8503	0.8906	0.8590	$\mathbb{Z}_2 > \mathbb{Z}_1 > \mathbb{Z}_4 > \mathbb{Z}_5 > \mathbb{Z}_3$
$(m,n) - ROFWCot^1$	0.6726	**0.7819**	0.6717	0.6936	0.7215	$\mathbb{Z}_2 > \mathbb{Z}_5 > \mathbb{Z}_4 > \mathbb{Z}_1 > \mathbb{Z}_3$
$(m,n) - ROFWCot^2$	0.7853	**0.8515**	0.7818	0.7895	0.7803	$\mathbb{Z}_2 > \mathbb{Z}_4 > \mathbb{Z}_1 > \mathbb{Z}_3 > \mathbb{Z}_5$
$(m,n) - ROFWCot^3$	0.6497	**0.7664**	0.6277	0.6119	0.6500	$\mathbb{Z}_2 > \mathbb{Z}_5 > \mathbb{Z}_1 > \mathbb{Z}_3 > \mathbb{Z}_4$
$(m,n) - ROFWCot^4$	0.6530	**0.7704**	0.6372	0.6183	0.6603	$\mathbb{Z}_2 > \mathbb{Z}_5 > \mathbb{Z}_1 > \mathbb{Z}_3 > \mathbb{Z}_4$

By comparing the results presented in Tables 5 and 6, it is clear that the proposed weighted $(m,n) - ROFWSs$ method is more accurate than the method proposed by Wang et al. [65] for assigning unknown building materials to the consistent class ($\mathbb{Z}_2$, $\mathbb{Z}$). Therefore, our results are more reliable and accurate.

Figure 1 shows that for the weighted q-ROFWS values of all building materials, except for $q - ROFWC^1$ and $q - ROFWC^2$, the degree of weighted similarity between ($\mathbb{Z}_3$, $\mathbb{Z}$) is the largest among the ten weighted similarity measures, and the proposed weighted (m, n)-ROFWSs for $m = 4, n = 3$ show that $\mathbb{Z}_3$ has the most significant and consistent value. This result indicates that the unknown pattern $\mathbb{Z}$ is the most similar to $\mathbb{Z}_3$.

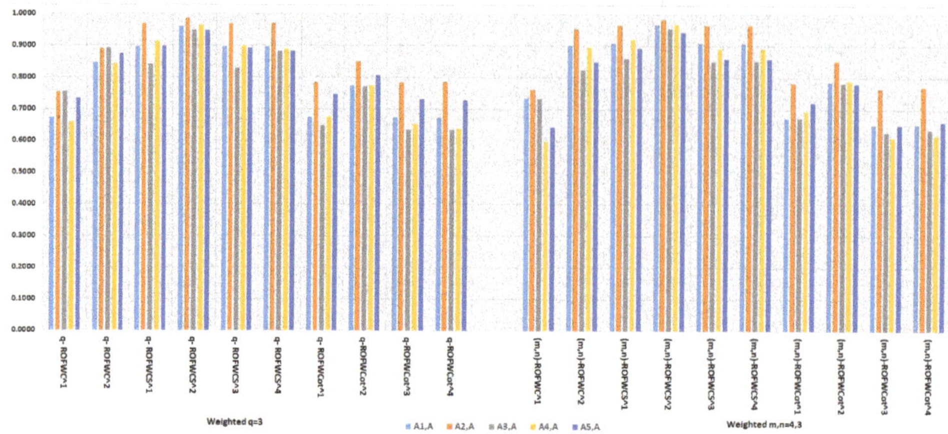

Figure 1. Comparison graph between weighted q-ROFWSs and the proposed weighted (m, n)-ROFWSs.

5. Applications of Proposed Similarity Measures in the Classification of Plant Leaf Disease

Plants are integral components of our ecosystem that provide us with vital resources such as oxygen and food. However, these crucial organisms are vulnerable to diseases that can significantly impact their growth and survival. One of the most prevalent problems plants face is leaf disease, which can considerably reduce crop yield and quality, significantly affecting farmers' livelihoods and the economy. This section aims to explore the issue of plant leaf disease and the measures that can be taken to prevent and manage it.

Several factors, such as bacteria, fungi, viruses, and other pathogens, can cause plant leaf diseases. Common types of leaf diseases include powdery mildew, downy mildew, leaf spot, and rust. These diseases can affect various parts of plants, including leaves, stems, and fruits, leading to discoloration, distortion, and wilting. The leaves may fall off in severe cases, leading to stunted growth and reduced yield. Several factors can facilitate the spread of plant leaf diseases, such as high humidity, poor air circulation, and contaminated soil or water. Additionally, using infected planting materials and inadequate crop management practices can contribute to the spreading of these diseases.

Plant leaf diseases pose significant problems that can adversely affect crop yield and quality, ultimately impacting farmers' livelihoods and the economy. Preventing and managing these diseases require a combination of preventive and curative measures, including disease-resistant plant varieties, good agricultural practices, and judicious chemical treatments. By taking these measures, we can ensure that our plants remain healthy and continue to provide us with the essential resources that we need for our survival.

Tomato plants are susceptible to various leaf diseases that can negatively impact their growth and yield. These diseases can be prevented by planting disease-resistant tomato varieties, keeping the soil well-drained, and avoiding overhead watering. Additionally, it is essential to remove any infected plant parts and keep the garden clean to prevent the spread of disease.

In the following illustrative example, we proposed a method to classify the plant leaf disease using the proposed cosine and cotangent similarity and weighted similarity measures for the study of the leaf disease classification that we generated Table 7 after carefully studying the dataset (the plant village dataset) [66] containing the different diseases and their symptoms.

Example 5. *Let us consider a set of five symptoms $q = \{q_1, q_2, q_3, q_4, q_5\}$, where q_1 = dark brown leaf, q_2 = brown leaf, q_3 = yellow leaf, q_4 = patches, q_5 = spots and five diagnoses $\mathbb{Z}_i(i = 1,2,3,4,5)$, which are presented by (m, n)-ROFSs, $\mathbb{Z}_1$(Gray leaf spot), $\mathbb{Z}_2$ (Bacterial Canker), $\mathbb{Z}_3$ (Bacterial Speck), $\mathbb{Z}_4$ (Bacterial Spot), and $\mathbb{Z}_5$ (Early Blight), defined in Table 7; let us also consider a sample pattern $\mathbb{Z}$ that will be recognized.*

Table 7. (m, n)-orthopair fuzzy data for the pattern of plant leaf diseases.

Symptom	$\mathbb{Z}_1$	$\mathbb{Z}_2$	$\mathbb{Z}_3$	$\mathbb{Z}_4$	$\mathbb{Z}_5$	$\mathbb{Z}$
q_1	(0.45, 0.95)	(0.25, 0.75)	(0.95, 0.55)	(0.85, 0.45)	(0.15, 0.95)	(0.35, 0.70)
q_2	(0.95, 0.35)	(0.85, 0.25)	(0.35, 0.85)	(0.65, 0.45)	(0.25, 0.65)	(0.80, 0.30)
q_3	(0.95, 0.65)	(0.75, 0.35)	(0.95, 0.45)	(0.15, 0.95)	(0.95, 0.15)	(0.70, 0.40)
q_4	(0.45, 0.65)	(0.15, 0.95)	(0.85, 0.15)	(0.45, 0.75)	(0.95, 0.55)	(0.20, 0.90)
q_5	(0.55, 0.95)	(0.15, 0.85)	(0.55, 0.35)	(0.95, 0.15)	(0.55, 0.95)	(0.25, 0.80)

For the given plant leaf disease example, the proposed cosine and cotangent similarity measures for $(m, n) - ROFSs$ for the values m = 5, n = 7, and m = 6, n = 10, and m = 10, n = 100, and m = 100, n = 10 are shown in Tables 8–11. The results show consistent and accurate results, indicating that all ten proposed similarity measures show $\mathbb{Z}_2$ as having the largest value, suggesting that sample $\mathbb{Z}$ is the most similar to $\mathbb{Z}_2$.

For the given plant leaf disease example, the cosine and cotangent similarity measures $q - ROFSs$ for the values $q = 100$ and $q = 50$ are shown in Tables 12 and 13. The similarity measures for $q = 100$ and $q = 50$, respectively, show inconsistent results, indicating that the six $q - ROFSs$ similarity measures of Table 2, given by Wang et al [65], failed to classify.

Table 8. (m, n)-ROF similarity measures for the data presented in Table 7 for m = 7, n = 5.

Similarity Measure	$(\mathbb{Z}_1, \mathbb{Z})$	$(\mathbb{Z}_2, \mathbb{Z})$	$(\mathbb{Z}_3, \mathbb{Z})$	$(\mathbb{Z}_4, \mathbb{Z})$	$(\mathbb{Z}_5, \mathbb{Z})$	Ranking
(m, n)-$ROFC^1$	0.9897	**0.9993**	0.2821	0.4250	0.6132	$\mathbb{Z}_2 > \mathbb{Z}_1 > \mathbb{Z}_5 > \mathbb{Z}_4 > \mathbb{Z}_3$
(m, n)-$ROFC^2$	0.5495	**0.9802**	0.5954	0.6602	0.5617	$\mathbb{Z}_2 > \mathbb{Z}_4 > \mathbb{Z}_3 > \mathbb{Z}_5 > \mathbb{Z}_1$
(m, n)-$ROFCS^1$	0.6733	**0.9836**	0.6536	0.7028	0.6630	$\mathbb{Z}_2 > \mathbb{Z}_4 > \mathbb{Z}_1 > \mathbb{Z}_5 > \mathbb{Z}_3$
(m, n)-$ROFCS^2$	0.9047	**0.9958**	0.8552	0.8728	0.8472	$\mathbb{Z}_2 > \mathbb{Z}_1 > \mathbb{Z}_4 > \mathbb{Z}_3 > \mathbb{Z}_5$
(m, n)-$ROFCS^3$	0.6400	**0.9836**	0.6515	0.7028	0.6598	$\mathbb{Z}_2 > \mathbb{Z}_4 > \mathbb{Z}_5 > \mathbb{Z}_3 > \mathbb{Z}_1$
(m, n)-$ROFCS^4$	0.6400	**0.9836**	0.6515	0.7028	0.6598	$\mathbb{Z}_2 > \mathbb{Z}_4 > \mathbb{Z}_5 > \mathbb{Z}_3 > \mathbb{Z}_1$
(m, n)-$ROFCot^1$	0.3917	**0.8477**	0.3889	0.4705	0.4105	$\mathbb{Z}_2 > \mathbb{Z}_4 > \mathbb{Z}_5 > \mathbb{Z}_1 > \mathbb{Z}_3$
(m, n)-$ROFCot^2$	0.6402	**0.9194**	0.5816	0.6395	0.5958	$\mathbb{Z}_2 > \mathbb{Z}_1 > \mathbb{Z}_4 > \mathbb{Z}_5 > \mathbb{Z}_3$
(m, n)-$ROFCot^3$	0.3699	**0.8477**	0.3875	0.4705	0.4076	$\mathbb{Z}_2 > \mathbb{Z}_4 > \mathbb{Z}_5 > \mathbb{Z}_3 > \mathbb{Z}_1$
(m, n)-$ROFCot^4$	0.3699	**0.8477**	0.3875	0.4705	0.4076	$\mathbb{Z}_2 > \mathbb{Z}_4 > \mathbb{Z}_5 > \mathbb{Z}_3 > \mathbb{Z}_1$

Table 9. (m, n)-ROF similarity measures for the data presented in Table 7 for m = 6, n = 10.

Similarity Measure	$(\mathbb{Z}_1, \mathbb{Z})$	$(\mathbb{Z}_2, \mathbb{Z})$	$(\mathbb{Z}_3, \mathbb{Z})$	$(\mathbb{Z}_4, \mathbb{Z})$	$(\mathbb{Z}_5, \mathbb{Z})$	Ranking
(m, n)-$ROFC^1$	0.9698	**0.9996**	0.2162	0.4117	0.6037	$\mathbb{Z}_2 > \mathbb{Z}_1 > \mathbb{Z}_5 > \mathbb{Z}_4 > \mathbb{Z}_3$
(m, n)-$ROFC^2$	0.6335	**0.9703**	0.6921	0.7239	0.5816	$\mathbb{Z}_2 > \mathbb{Z}_4 > \mathbb{Z}_3 > \mathbb{Z}_1 > \mathbb{Z}_5$
(m, n)-$ROFCS^1$	0.7015	**0.9784**	0.7411	0.7358	0.6455	$\mathbb{Z}_2 > \mathbb{Z}_3 > \mathbb{Z}_4 > \mathbb{Z}_1 > \mathbb{Z}_5$
(m, n)-$ROFCS^2$	0.9185	**0.9946**	0.8969	0.9093	0.8682	$\mathbb{Z}_2 > \mathbb{Z}_1 > \mathbb{Z}_4 > \mathbb{Z}_3 > \mathbb{Z}_5$
(m, n)-$ROFCS^3$	0.6903	**0.9784**	0.7410	0.7358	0.6394	$\mathbb{Z}_2 > \mathbb{Z}_3 > \mathbb{Z}_4 > \mathbb{Z}_1 > \mathbb{Z}_5$
(m, n)-$ROFCS^4$	0.6903	**0.9784**	0.7410	0.7358	0.6394	$\mathbb{Z}_2 > \mathbb{Z}_3 > \mathbb{Z}_4 > \mathbb{Z}_1 > \mathbb{Z}_5$
(m, n)-$ROFCot^1$	0.4195	**0.8474**	0.5111	0.4871	0.3897	$\mathbb{Z}_2 > \mathbb{Z}_3 > \mathbb{Z}_4 > \mathbb{Z}_1 > \mathbb{Z}_5$
(m, n)-$ROFCot^2$	0.6648	**0.9193**	0.6545	0.6832	0.6141	$\mathbb{Z}_2 > \mathbb{Z}_4 > \mathbb{Z}_1 > \mathbb{Z}_3 > \mathbb{Z}_5$
(m, n)-$ROFCot^3$	0.4110	**0.8474**	0.5111	0.4871	0.3847	$\mathbb{Z}_2 > \mathbb{Z}_3 > \mathbb{Z}_4 > \mathbb{Z}_1 > \mathbb{Z}_5$
(m, n)-$ROFCot^4$	0.4110	**0.8474**	0.5111	0.4871	0.3847	$\mathbb{Z}_2 > \mathbb{Z}_3 > \mathbb{Z}_4 > \mathbb{Z}_1 > \mathbb{Z}_5$

Table 10. (m, n)-ROF similarity measures for the data presented in Table 7 for m = 10, n = 100.

Similarity Measure	$(\mathbb{Z}_1, \mathbb{Z})$	$(\mathbb{Z}_2, \mathbb{Z})$	$(\mathbb{Z}_3, \mathbb{Z})$	$(\mathbb{Z}_4, \mathbb{Z})$	$(\mathbb{Z}_5, \mathbb{Z})$	Ranking
(m, n)-ROFC^1	0.4910	**0.8132**	0.8008	0.6008	0.4795	$\mathbb{Z}_2 > \mathbb{Z}_3 > \mathbb{Z}_4 > \mathbb{Z}_1 > \mathbb{Z}_5$
(m, n)-ROFC^2	0.8465	**0.9984**	0.8203	0.9044	0.8260	$\mathbb{Z}_2 > \mathbb{Z}_4 > \mathbb{Z}_1 > \mathbb{Z}_5 > \mathbb{Z}_3$
(m, n)-ROFCS^1	0.8682	**0.9978**	0.8305	0.9060	0.8400	$\mathbb{Z}_2 > \mathbb{Z}_4 > \mathbb{Z}_1 > \mathbb{Z}_5 > \mathbb{Z}_3$
(m, n)-ROFCS^2	0.9655	**0.9995**	0.9555	0.9753	0.9578	$\mathbb{Z}_2 > \mathbb{Z}_4 > \mathbb{Z}_1 > \mathbb{Z}_5 > \mathbb{Z}_3$
(m, n)-ROFCS^3	0.8682	**0.9978**	0.8305	0.9060	0.8399	$\mathbb{Z}_2 > \mathbb{Z}_4 > \mathbb{Z}_1 > \mathbb{Z}_5 > \mathbb{Z}_3$
(m, n)-ROFCS^4	0.8682	**0.9978**	0.8305	0.9060	0.8399	$\mathbb{Z}_2 > \mathbb{Z}_4 > \mathbb{Z}_1 > \mathbb{Z}_5 > \mathbb{Z}_3$
(m, n)-ROFCot^1	0.7508	**0.9632**	0.6495	0.7750	0.7005	$\mathbb{Z}_2 > \mathbb{Z}_5 > \mathbb{Z}_1 > \mathbb{Z}_5 > \mathbb{Z}_3$
(m, n)-ROFCot^2	0.8580	**0.9811**	0.8031	0.8744	0.8300	$\mathbb{Z}_2 > \mathbb{Z}_4 > \mathbb{Z}_1 > \mathbb{Z}_5 > \mathbb{Z}_3$
(m, n)-ROFCot^3	0.7499	**0.9632**	0.6495	0.7750	0.6997	$\mathbb{Z}_2 > \mathbb{Z}_4 > \mathbb{Z}_1 > \mathbb{Z}_5 > \mathbb{Z}_3$
(m, n)-ROFCot^4	0.7499	**0.9632**	0.6495	0.7750	0.6997	$\mathbb{Z}_2 > \mathbb{Z}_4 > \mathbb{Z}_1 > \mathbb{Z}_5 > \mathbb{Z}_3$

Table 11. (m, n)-ROF similarity measures for the data presented in Table 7 for m = 100, n = 10.

Similarity Measure	$(\mathbb{Z}_1, \mathbb{Z})$	$(\mathbb{Z}_2, \mathbb{Z})$	$(\mathbb{Z}_3, \mathbb{Z})$	$(\mathbb{Z}_4, \mathbb{Z})$	$(\mathbb{Z}_5, \mathbb{Z})$	Ranking
(m, n)-ROFC^1	0.7840	**0.9992**	0.5033	0.8000	0.6787	$\mathbb{Z}_2 > \mathbb{Z}_4 > \mathbb{Z}_1 > \mathbb{Z}_5 > \mathbb{Z}_3$
(m, n)-ROFC^2	0.8241	**0.9750**	0.9691	0.8915	0.8231	$\mathbb{Z}_2 > \mathbb{Z}_3 > \mathbb{Z}_4 > \mathbb{Z}_1 > \mathbb{Z}_5$
(m, n)-ROFCS^1	0.8411	**0.9826**	0.9582	0.8942	0.8394	$\mathbb{Z}_2 > \mathbb{Z}_3 > \mathbb{Z}_4 > \mathbb{Z}_1 > \mathbb{Z}_5$
(m, n)-ROFCS^2	0.9586	**0.9956**	0.9894	0.9722	0.9579	$\mathbb{Z}_2 > \mathbb{Z}_3 > \mathbb{Z}_4 > \mathbb{Z}_1 > \mathbb{Z}_5$
(m, n)-ROFCS^3	0.8411	**0.9826**	0.9582	0.8942	0.8394	$\mathbb{Z}_2 > \mathbb{Z}_3 > \mathbb{Z}_4 > \mathbb{Z}_1 > \mathbb{Z}_5$
(m, n)-ROFCS^4	0.8411	**0.9826**	0.9582	0.8942	0.8394	$\mathbb{Z}_2 > \mathbb{Z}_3 > \mathbb{Z}_4 > \mathbb{Z}_1 > \mathbb{Z}_5$
(m, n)-ROFCot^1	0.6637	**0.8987**	0.8174	0.7496	0.6614	$\mathbb{Z}_2 > \mathbb{Z}_3 > \mathbb{Z}_4 > \mathbb{Z}_1 > \mathbb{Z}_5$
(m, n)-ROFCot^2	0.8097	**0.9462**	0.9007	0.8599	0.8085	$\mathbb{Z}_2 > \mathbb{Z}_3 > \mathbb{Z}_4 > \mathbb{Z}_1 > \mathbb{Z}_5$
(m, n)-ROFCot^3	0.6618	**0.8987**	0.8173	0.7496	0.6614	$\mathbb{Z}_2 > \mathbb{Z}_3 > \mathbb{Z}_4 > \mathbb{Z}_1 > \mathbb{Z}_5$
(m, n)-ROFCot^4	0.6618	**0.8987**	0.8173	0.7496	0.6614	$\mathbb{Z}_2 > \mathbb{Z}_3 > \mathbb{Z}_4 > \mathbb{Z}_1 > \mathbb{Z}_5$

Table 12. q-ROF similarity measures for the data presented in Table 7 for q = 100.

Similarity Measure	$(\mathbb{Z}_1, \mathbb{Z})$	$(\mathbb{Z}_2, \mathbb{Z})$	$(\mathbb{Z}_3, \mathbb{Z})$	$(\mathbb{Z}_4, \mathbb{Z})$	$(\mathbb{Z}_5, \mathbb{Z})$	Ranking
q-ROFC^1	**1.0000**	**1.0000**	0.2000	0.4000	0.6000	cannot be classified
q-ROFC^2	**1.0000**	**1.0000**	**1.0000**	**1.0000**	**1.0000**	cannot be classified
q-ROFCS^1	**1.0000**	**1.0000**	**1.0000**	**1.0000**	**1.0000**	cannot be classified
q-ROFCS^2	**1.0000**	**1.0000**	**1.0000**	**1.0000**	**1.0000**	cannot be classified
q-ROFCS^3	**1.0000**	**1.0000**	**1.0000**	**1.0000**	**1.0000**	cannot be classified
q-ROFCS^4	**1.0000**	**1.0000**	**1.0000**	**1.0000**	**1.0000**	cannot be classified
q-ROFCot^1	0.9926	**0.9982**	0.9963	0.9963	0.9926	$\mathbb{Z}_2 > \mathbb{Z}_3 = \mathbb{Z}_4 > \mathbb{Z}_5 = \mathbb{Z}_1$
q-ROFCot^2	0.9963	**0.9991**	0.9981	0.9981	0.9963	$\mathbb{Z}_2 > \mathbb{Z}_3 = \mathbb{Z}_4 > \mathbb{Z}_5 = \mathbb{Z}_1$
q-ROFCot^3	0.9926	**0.9982**	0.9963	0.9963	0.9926	$\mathbb{Z}_2 > \mathbb{Z}_3 = \mathbb{Z}_4 > \mathbb{Z}_5 = \mathbb{Z}_1$
q-ROFCot^4	0.9926	**0.9982**	0.9963	0.9963	0.9926	$\mathbb{Z}_2 > \mathbb{Z}_3 = \mathbb{Z}_4 > \mathbb{Z}_5 = \mathbb{Z}_1$

If we consider the weights of $w = (0.10, 0.30, 0.25, 0.15, 0.20)^T$, the proposed weighted cosine and cotangent similarity measures for (m, n)-ROFWSs with values of m = 5, n = 7, m = 6, n = 10, m = 10, n = 100, and m = 100, n = 10 are presented in Tables 14–17, respectively. The accurate and consistent results indicate that all ten proposed weighted similarity measures show $\mathbb{Z}_2$ as having the largest value, suggesting that the sample $\mathbb{Z}$ is the most similar to $\mathbb{Z}_2$.

Table 13. q-ROF similarity measures for the data presented in Table 7 for q = 50.

Similarity Measure	$(\mathbb{Z}_1, \mathbb{Z})$	$(\mathbb{Z}_2, \mathbb{Z})$	$(\mathbb{Z}_3, \mathbb{Z})$	$(\mathbb{Z}_4, \mathbb{Z})$	$(\mathbb{Z}_5, \mathbb{Z})$	Ranking
q-ROFC^1	**1.0000**	**1.0000**	0.2000	0.4000	0.6000	cannot be classified
q-ROFC^2	**1.0000**	**1.0000**	**1.0000**	**1.0000**	**1.0000**	cannot be classified
q-ROFCS^1	0.9900	**1.0000**	**1.0000**	**1.0000**	0.9900	cannot be classified
q-ROFCS^2	**1.0000**	**1.0000**	**1.0000**	**1.0000**	**1.0000**	cannot be classified
q-ROFCS^3	0.9900	**1.0000**	**1.0000**	**1.0000**	0.9900	cannot be classified
q-ROFCS^4	0.9900	**1.0000**	**1.0000**	**1.0000**	0.9900	cannot be classified
q-ROFCot^1	0.9100	**0.9800**	0.9500	0.9500	0.9100	$\mathbb{Z}_2 > \mathbb{Z}_3 = \mathbb{Z}_4 > \mathbb{Z}_5 = \mathbb{Z}_1$
q-ROFCot^2	0.9500	**0.9900**	0.9800	0.9800	0.9500	$\mathbb{Z}_2 > \mathbb{Z}_3 = \mathbb{Z}_4 > \mathbb{Z}_5 = \mathbb{Z}_1$
q-ROFCot^3	0.9100	**0.9800**	0.9500	0.9500	0.9100	$\mathbb{Z}_2 > \mathbb{Z}_3 = \mathbb{Z}_4 > \mathbb{Z}_5 = \mathbb{Z}_1$
q-ROFCot^4	0.9100	**0.9800**	0.9500	0.9500	0.9100	$\mathbb{Z}_2 > \mathbb{Z}_3 = \mathbb{Z}_4 > \mathbb{Z}_5 = \mathbb{Z}_1$

Table 14. Weighted (m, n)-ROFSs for the data presented in Table 7 for m = 7, n = 5.

Weighted Similarity Measures	$(\mathbb{Z}_1, \mathbb{Z})$	$(\mathbb{Z}_2, \mathbb{Z})$	$(\mathbb{Z}_3, \mathbb{Z})$	$(\mathbb{Z}_4, \mathbb{Z})$	$(\mathbb{Z}_5, \mathbb{Z})$	Ranking
(m, n)-$ROFWC^1$	0.9897	**0.9991**	0.3256	0.4690	0.5595	$\mathbb{Z}_2 > \mathbb{Z}_1 > \mathbb{Z}_5 > \mathbb{Z}_4 > \mathbb{Z}_3$
(m, n)-$ROFWC^2$	0.5483	**0.9815**	0.6338	0.6444	0.6225	$\mathbb{Z}_2 > \mathbb{Z}_4 > \mathbb{Z}_3 > \mathbb{Z}_5 > \mathbb{Z}_1$
(m, n)-$ROFWCS^1$	0.6789	**0.9846**	0.6832	0.6876	0.7051	$\mathbb{Z}_2 > \mathbb{Z}_5 > \mathbb{Z}_4 > \mathbb{Z}_3 > \mathbb{Z}_1$
(m, n)-$ROFWCS^2$	0.9042	**0.9961**	0.8687	0.8699	0.8710	$\mathbb{Z}_2 > \mathbb{Z}_1 > \mathbb{Z}_5 > \mathbb{Z}_4 > \mathbb{Z}_3$
(m, n)-$ROFWCS^3$	0.6384	**0.9846**	0.6805	0.6876	0.7020	$\mathbb{Z}_2 > \mathbb{Z}_5 > \mathbb{Z}_4 > \mathbb{Z}_3 > \mathbb{Z}_1$
(m, n)-$ROFWCS^4$	0.6384	**0.9846**	0.6805	0.6876	0.7020	$\mathbb{Z}_2 > \mathbb{Z}_5 > \mathbb{Z}_4 > \mathbb{Z}_3 > \mathbb{Z}_1$
(m, n)-$ROFWCot^1$	0.3958	**0.8507**	0.4105	0.4704	0.4534	$\mathbb{Z}_2 > \mathbb{Z}_4 > \mathbb{Z}_5 > \mathbb{Z}_3 > \mathbb{Z}_1$
(m, n)-$ROFWCot^2$	0.6401	**0.9209**	0.5972	0.6447	0.6266	$\mathbb{Z}_2 > \mathbb{Z}_4 > \mathbb{Z}_1 > \mathbb{Z}_5 > \mathbb{Z}_3$
(m, n)-$ROFWCot^3$	0.3696	**0.8507**	0.4088	0.4704	0.4506	$\mathbb{Z}_2 > \mathbb{Z}_4 > \mathbb{Z}_5 > \mathbb{Z}_3 > \mathbb{Z}_1$
(m, n)-$ROFWCot^4$	0.3696	**0.8507**	0.4088	0.4704	0.4506	$\mathbb{Z}_2 > \mathbb{Z}_4 > \mathbb{Z}_5 > \mathbb{Z}_3 > \mathbb{Z}_1$

Table 15. Weighted (m, n)-ROF similarity measures for the data presented in Table 7 for m = 6, n = 10.

Weighted Similarity Measures	$(\mathbb{Z}_1, \mathbb{Z})$	$(\mathbb{Z}_2, \mathbb{Z})$	$(\mathbb{Z}_3, \mathbb{Z})$	$(\mathbb{Z}_4, \mathbb{Z})$	$(\mathbb{Z}_5, \mathbb{Z})$	Ranking
(m, n)-$ROFWC^1$	0.9773	**0.9998**	0.2603	0.4557	0.5556	$\mathbb{Z}_2 > \mathbb{Z}_1 > \mathbb{Z}_5 > \mathbb{Z}_4 > \mathbb{Z}_3$
(m, n)-$ROFWC^2$	0.6175	**0.9740**	0.7352	0.7171	0.6258	$\mathbb{Z}_2 > \mathbb{Z}_3 > \mathbb{Z}_4 > \mathbb{Z}_5 > \mathbb{Z}_1$
(m, n)-$ROFWCS^1$	0.6978	**0.9805**	0.7789	0.7331	0.6828	$\mathbb{Z}_2 > \mathbb{Z}_3 > \mathbb{Z}_4 > \mathbb{Z}_1 > \mathbb{Z}_5$
(m, n)-$ROFWCS^2$	0.9176	**0.9951**	0.9099	0.9069	0.8870	$\mathbb{Z}_2 > \mathbb{Z}_1 > \mathbb{Z}_3 > \mathbb{Z}_4 > \mathbb{Z}_5$
(m, n)-$ROFWCS^3$	0.6865	**0.9805**	0.7788	0.7331	0.6766	$\mathbb{Z}_2 > \mathbb{Z}_3 > \mathbb{Z}_4 > \mathbb{Z}_1 > \mathbb{Z}_5$
(m, n)-$ROFWCS^4$	0.6865	**0.9805**	0.7788	0.7331	0.6766	$\mathbb{Z}_2 > \mathbb{Z}_3 > \mathbb{Z}_4 > \mathbb{Z}_1 > \mathbb{Z}_5$
(m, n)-$ROFWCot^1$	0.4151	**0.8471**	0.5444	0.4931	0.4251	$\mathbb{Z}_2 > \mathbb{Z}_3 > \mathbb{Z}_4 > \mathbb{Z}_5 > \mathbb{Z}_1$
(m, n)-$ROFWCot^2$	0.6624	**0.9196**	0.6736	0.6852	0.6430	$\mathbb{Z}_2 > \mathbb{Z}_4 > \mathbb{Z}_3 > \mathbb{Z}_1 > \mathbb{Z}_5$
(m, n)-$ROFWCot^3$	0.4066	**0.8471**	0.5443	0.4931	0.4200	$\mathbb{Z}_2 > \mathbb{Z}_3 > \mathbb{Z}_4 > \mathbb{Z}_5 > \mathbb{Z}_1$
(m, n)-$ROFWCot^4$	0.4066	**0.8471**	0.5443	0.4931	0.4200	$\mathbb{Z}_2 > \mathbb{Z}_3 > \mathbb{Z}_4 > \mathbb{Z}_5 > \mathbb{Z}_1$

Table 16. Weighted (m, n)-ROF similarity measures for the data presented in Table 7 for m = 10, n = 100.

Weighted Similarity Measures	$(\mathbb{Z}_1, \mathbb{Z})$	$(\mathbb{Z}_2, \mathbb{Z})$	$(\mathbb{Z}_3, \mathbb{Z})$	$(\mathbb{Z}_4, \mathbb{Z})$	$(\mathbb{Z}_5, \mathbb{Z})$	Ranking
(m, n)-$ROFWC^1$	0.6350	**0.8506**	0.8132	0.6006	0.6293	$\mathbb{Z}_2 > \mathbb{Z}_3 > \mathbb{Z}_1 > \mathbb{Z}_5 > \mathbb{Z}_4$
(m, n)-$ROFWC^2$	0.7907	**0.9977**	0.8444	0.9067	0.8265	$\mathbb{Z}_2 > \mathbb{Z}_4 > \mathbb{Z}_3 > \mathbb{Z}_5 > \mathbb{Z}_1$
(m, n)-$ROFWCS^1$	0.8211	**0.9968**	0.8537	0.9096	0.8403	$\mathbb{Z}_2 > \mathbb{Z}_4 > \mathbb{Z}_3 > \mathbb{Z}_5 > \mathbb{Z}_1$
(m, n)-$ROFWCS^2$	0.9533	**0.9992**	0.9616	0.9762	0.9580	$\mathbb{Z}_2 > \mathbb{Z}_4 > \mathbb{Z}_3 > \mathbb{Z}_5 > \mathbb{Z}_1$
(m, n)-$ROFWCS^3$	0.8211	**0.9968**	0.8537	0.9096	0.8403	$\mathbb{Z}_2 > \mathbb{Z}_4 > \mathbb{Z}_3 > \mathbb{Z}_5 > \mathbb{Z}_1$
(m, n)-$ROFWCS^4$	0.8211	**0.9968**	0.8537	0.9096	0.8403	$\mathbb{Z}_2 > \mathbb{Z}_4 > \mathbb{Z}_3 > \mathbb{Z}_5 > \mathbb{Z}_1$
(m, n)-$ROFWCot^1$	0.6615	**0.9484**	0.6823	0.7860	0.6870	$\mathbb{Z}_2 > \mathbb{Z}_4 > \mathbb{Z}_5 > \mathbb{Z}_3 > \mathbb{Z}_1$
(m, n)-$ROFWCot^2$	0.8073	**0.9735**	0.8223	0.8803	0.8232	$\mathbb{Z}_2 > \mathbb{Z}_4 > \mathbb{Z}_5 > \mathbb{Z}_3 > \mathbb{Z}_1$
(m, n)-$ROFWCot^3$	0.6606	**0.9484**	0.6823	0.7860	0.6863	$\mathbb{Z}_2 > \mathbb{Z}_4 > \mathbb{Z}_5 > \mathbb{Z}_3 > \mathbb{Z}_1$
(m, n)-$ROFWCot^4$	0.6606	**0.9484**	0.6823	0.7860	0.6863	$\mathbb{Z}_2 > \mathbb{Z}_4 > \mathbb{Z}_5 > \mathbb{Z}_3 > \mathbb{Z}_1$

Table 17. Weighted (m, n)-ROF similarity measures for the data presented in Table 7 for m = 100, n = 10.

Weighted Similarity Measures	$(\mathbb{Z}_1, \mathbb{Z})$	$(\mathbb{Z}_2, \mathbb{Z})$	$(\mathbb{Z}_3, \mathbb{Z})$	$(\mathbb{Z}_4, \mathbb{Z})$	$(\mathbb{Z}_5, \mathbb{Z})$	Ranking
(m, n)-ROFWC^1	0.6803	**0.9987**	0.5636	0.8000	0.6590	$\mathbb{Z}_2 > \mathbb{Z}_4 > \mathbb{Z}_1 > \mathbb{Z}_5 > \mathbb{Z}_3$
(m, n)-ROFWC^2	0.8716	**0.9809**	0.9721	0.8739	0.8708	$\mathbb{Z}_2 > \mathbb{Z}_3 > \mathbb{Z}_4 > \mathbb{Z}_1 > \mathbb{Z}_5$
(m, n)-ROFWCS^1	0.8854	**0.9865**	0.9609	0.8789	0.8841	$\mathbb{Z}_2 > \mathbb{Z}_3 > \mathbb{Z}_1 > \mathbb{Z}_5 > \mathbb{Z}_4$
(m, n)-ROFWCS^2	0.9702	**0.9966**	0.9901	0.9681	0.9697	$\mathbb{Z}_2 > \mathbb{Z}_3 > \mathbb{Z}_1 > \mathbb{Z}_5 > \mathbb{Z}_4$
(m, n)-ROFWCS^3	0.8853	**0.9865**	0.9609	0.8789	0.8841	$\mathbb{Z}_2 > \mathbb{Z}_3 > \mathbb{Z}_1 > \mathbb{Z}_5 > \mathbb{Z}_4$
(m, n)-ROFWCS^4	0.8853	**0.9865**	0.9609	0.8789	0.8841	$\mathbb{Z}_2 > \mathbb{Z}_3 > \mathbb{Z}_1 > \mathbb{Z}_5 > \mathbb{Z}_4$
(m, n)-ROFWCot^1	0.7478	**0.9196**	0.8159	0.7391	0.7455	$\mathbb{Z}_2 > \mathbb{Z}_3 > \mathbb{Z}_1 > \mathbb{Z}_5 > \mathbb{Z}_4$
(m, n)-ROFWCot^2	0.8573	**0.9573**	0.9007	0.8531	0.8565	$\mathbb{Z}_2 > \mathbb{Z}_3 > \mathbb{Z}_1 > \mathbb{Z}_5 > \mathbb{Z}_4$
(m, n)-ROFWCot^3	0.7456	**0.9196**	0.8158	0.7391	0.7455	$\mathbb{Z}_2 > \mathbb{Z}_3 > \mathbb{Z}_1 > \mathbb{Z}_5 > \mathbb{Z}_4$
(m, n)-ROFWCot^4	0.7456	**0.9196**	0.8158	0.7391	0.7455	$\mathbb{Z}_2 > \mathbb{Z}_3 > \mathbb{Z}_1 > \mathbb{Z}_5 > \mathbb{Z}_4$

The $q - ROFWs$ weighted similarity measures in Table 3, given by Wang et al. [65], for the values q = 100 and q = 50 with same weighted values, and the results presented in Tables 18 and 19, shows that six weighted similarity measures failed to classify.

Table 18. Weighted (m, n)-ROF similarity measures for the data presented in Table 7 for q = 100.

Weighted Similarity Measures	$(\mathbb{Z}_1, \mathbb{Z})$	$(\mathbb{Z}_2, \mathbb{Z})$	$(\mathbb{Z}_3, \mathbb{Z})$	$(\mathbb{Z}_4, \mathbb{Z})$	$(\mathbb{Z}_5, \mathbb{Z})$	Ranking
q-ROFWC^1	**1.0000**	**1.0000**	0.2500	0.4500	0.5500	cannot be classified
q-ROFWC^2	**1.0000**	**1.0000**	**1.0000**	**1.0000**	**1.0000**	cannot be classified
q-ROFWCS^1	**1.0000**	**1.0000**	**1.0000**	**1.0000**	**1.0000**	cannot be classified
q-ROFWCS^2	**1.0000**	**1.0000**	**1.0000**	**1.0000**	**1.0000**	cannot be classified
q-ROFWCS^3	**1.0000**	**1.0000**	**1.0000**	**1.0000**	**1.0000**	cannot be classified
q-ROFWCS^4	**1.0000**	**1.0000**	**1.0000**	**1.0000**	**1.0000**	cannot be classified
q-ROFWCot^1	0.9921	**0.9986**	0.9968	0.9958	0.9935	$\mathbb{Z}_2 > \mathbb{Z}_3 > \mathbb{Z}_4 > \mathbb{Z}_5 > \mathbb{Z}_1$
q-ROFWCot^2	0.9961	**0.9993**	0.9984	0.9979	0.9967	$\mathbb{Z}_2 > \mathbb{Z}_3 > \mathbb{Z}_4 > \mathbb{Z}_5 > \mathbb{Z}_1$
q-ROFWCot^3	0.9921	**0.9986**	0.9968	0.9958	0.9935	$\mathbb{Z}_2 > \mathbb{Z}_3 > \mathbb{Z}_4 > \mathbb{Z}_5 > \mathbb{Z}_1$
q-ROFWCot^4	0.9921	**0.9986**	0.9968	0.9958	0.9935	$\mathbb{Z}_2 > \mathbb{Z}_3 > \mathbb{Z}_4 > \mathbb{Z}_5 > \mathbb{Z}_1$

Table 19. Weighted (m, n)-ROF similarity measures for the data presented in Table 7 for q = 50.

Weighted Similarity Measure	$(\mathbb{Z}_1, \mathbb{Z})$	$(\mathbb{Z}_2, \mathbb{Z})$	$(\mathbb{Z}_3, \mathbb{Z})$	$(\mathbb{Z}_4, \mathbb{Z})$	$(\mathbb{Z}_5, \mathbb{Z})$	Ranking
q-ROFWC^1	**1.0000**	**1.0000**	0.2500	0.4500	0.5500	cannot be classified
q-ROFWC^2	**1.0000**	**1.0000**	**1.0000**	**1.0000**	**1.0000**	cannot be classified
q-ROFWCS^1	0.9900	**1.0000**	**1.0000**	**1.0000**	0.9900	cannot be classified
q-ROFWCS^2	**1.0000**	**1.0000**	**1.0000**	**1.0000**	**1.0000**	cannot be classified
q-ROFWCS^3	0.9900	**1.0000**	**1.0000**	**1.0000**	0.9900	cannot be classified
q-ROFWCS^4	0.9900	**1.0000**	**1.0000**	**1.0000**	0.9900	cannot be classified
q-ROFWCot^1	0.9000	**0.9800**	0.9600	0.9500	0.9200	$\mathbb{Z}_2 > \mathbb{Z}_3 > \mathbb{Z}_4 > \mathbb{Z}_5 > \mathbb{Z}_1$
q-ROFWCot^2	0.9500	**0.9900**	0.9800	0.9700	0.9600	$\mathbb{Z}_2 > \mathbb{Z}_3 > \mathbb{Z}_4 > \mathbb{Z}_5 > \mathbb{Z}_1$
q-ROFWCot^3	0.9000	**0.9800**	0.9600	0.9500	0.9200	$\mathbb{Z}_2 > \mathbb{Z}_3 > \mathbb{Z}_4 > \mathbb{Z}_5 > \mathbb{Z}_1$
q-ROFWCot^4	0.9000	**0.9800**	0.9600	0.9500	0.9200	$\mathbb{Z}_2 > \mathbb{Z}_3 > \mathbb{Z}_4 > \mathbb{Z}_5 > \mathbb{Z}_1$

6. Discussion

The existing cosine and cotangent similarity measures for IFS, PFS, and q-ROFs are special cases of the proposed (m, n)-ROFS similarity measure in the paper. The flexibility of the power of the MD and NMD attributes represents the uncertainty of attributes reflecting better performances for different values of m and n, compared to the other cases where the powers of the MD and NMD attributes are the same. The results of different values of m and n show consistent and accurate results for higher values of m and n in this paper. In q-ROFS, the similarity measure failed to classify the sets for the higher values of q, as shown in the paper.

After analyzing the data presented in several tables, it is clear that the most reliable classification of the plant leaf sample disease $\mathbb{Z}$ can be achieved using (m, n)-ROFSs and (m, n)-ROFWs. As a result, the plant leaf can be identified as disease $\mathbb{Z}_2$, a bacterial canker. However, other tables show that q-ROFSs and q-ROFWs are ineffective at classifying plant leaf diseases. These findings highlight the significance of the (m, n) condition for precise results and accurate disease classification. Overall, this analysis emphasizes the importance of selecting appropriate similarity measures for the specific type of fuzzy information to achieve accurate disease classification.

7. Conclusions

This research article demonstrates the effectiveness of (m, n)-ROFS, a generalized fuzzy structure, in addressing uncertainty and imprecision in decision-making problems. The (m, n)-ROFS framework surpasses other fuzzy structures, such as IFS, PFS, FFS, and q-ROFS (for $q > 3$), by accommodating a wider range of information. Our study introduces cosine, cotangent, and weighted similarity measures specifically designed for (m, n)-ROFSs, including measures for q-ROFSs information in special cases. We applied these similarity measures to evaluate their performances in building material problems. We compared the q-ROFSs cosine and cotangent measures with the existing ones. We also presented a numerical example to demonstrate the practical applications of these similarity measures in plant leaf disease classification.

The findings of our study indicate that the defined similarity measures are more suitable and applicable to real-world problems than existing measures. This research significantly contributes to decision-making under uncertainty and imprecision, providing improved tools for measuring similarity within the (m, n)-ROFSs framework. These findings have broad implications in domains such as medicine, pattern recognition, and material engineering, where robust decision-making techniques are essential. Future research can build upon this work by further exploring and expanding the (m, n)-ROFS framework and its similarity measures to address complex decision-making problems in diverse applications, by continually advancing the (m, n)-ROFS methodology, we can foster the innovation and improve the decision-making processes in various domains.

Author Contributions: All authors (A.S.R., S.S. and S.S.T.) contributed equally to the design, implementation of the research, analysis of the results, and writing of the manuscript. All authors have read and approved the final version of the manuscript for publication.

Funding: This research did not receive any specific grant from funding agencies in the public, commercial, or non-profit sectors.

Acknowledgments: We would like to thank the anonymous reviewers for their comments, which helped us improve this manuscript.

Conflicts of Interest: The authors declare that they have no known competing financial interests or personal relationships that could have appeared to influence the work reported in this paper.

References

1. Weyl, H. *Symmetry*; University Press: Princeton, NJ, USA, 1952.
2. Bernal, I.; Hamilton, W.C.; Ricci, J.S. *Symmetry*; Freeman: San Francisco, CA, USA, 1972.
3. Shubnikov, A.V.; Koptsik, V.A. *Symmetry in Science and Art*; Plenum: New York, NY, USA, 1974; p. 308.
4. Zadeh, L.A. Fuzzy sets. *Inf. Control* **1965**, *8*, 338–356. [CrossRef]
5. Atanassov, K. Intuitionistic fuzzy sets. *Fuzzy Sets Syst.* **1986**, *20*, 87–96. [CrossRef]
6. Yager, R.R. Pythagorean fuzzy subsets. In Proceedings of the Joint IFSA World Congress, and NAFIPS Annual Meeting (IFSA/-NAFIPS), Edmonton, AB, Canada, 24–28 June 2013; pp. 57–61.
7. Yager, R.R. Generalized orthopair fuzzy sets. *IEEE Trans. Fuzzy Syst.* **2017**, *25*, 1222–1230. [CrossRef]
8. Senapati, T.; Yager, R.R. Fermatean fuzzy sets. *J. Ambient. Intell. Humaniz. Comput.* **2020**, *11*, 663–674. [CrossRef]
9. Ibrahim, H.Z.; Alshammari, I. n, m-Rung Orthopair Fuzzy Sets with applications to multicriteria decision making. *IEEE Access* **2022**, *10*, 99562–99572. [CrossRef]
10. Jun, Y.B.; Hur, H. The (m, n)-fuzzy set, and its application in BCK-algebras. *Ann. Fuzzy Math. Inform.* **2022**, *24*, 17–29.

11. Al-shami, T.; Mhemdi, A. Generalized Frame for Orthopair Fuzzy Sets: (m, n)-fuzzy sets, and their Applications to Multicriteria Decision Making Methods. *Information* **2023**, *14*, 56. [CrossRef]
12. Helgason, C.M.; Jobe, T.H. Fuzzy Measures of Symmetry Breaking of Conditions, Similarity and Comparison: Non-Statistical Information for the Single Patient. *Open Cybern. Syst. J.* **2008**, 2, 11–19. [CrossRef]
13. Zainuddin, Q.Z.; Paulinea, O. An Effective Fuzzy C-means Algorithm Based on Symmetry Similarity Approach. *Appl. Soft Comput.* **2015**, 35, 433–448. [CrossRef]
14. Miranda, P.; Grabisch, M.; Gil, P. p-symmetric fuzzy measures. *Int. J. Uncertain. Fuzziness Knowl.-Based Syst.* **2002**, *10*, 105–123. [CrossRef]
15. Saha, S.; Bandyopadhyay, S. A new point symmetry-based fuzzy genetic clustering technique for automatic evolution of clusters. *Inf. Sci.* **2009**, 179, 3230–3246. [CrossRef]
16. Colliota, O.; Tuzikovb, A.V.; Cesarc, R.M.; Blocha, I. Approximate reflectional symmetries of fuzzy objects with an application in model-based object recognition. *Fuzzy Sets Syst.* **2004**, 147, 141–163. [CrossRef]
17. Adlassnig, K.P. Fuzzy set theory in medical diagnosis. *IEEE Trans. Syst. Man Cybern. Syst.* **1986**, *16*, 260–265. [CrossRef]
18. Zwick, R.; Carlstein, E.; Budescu, D.V. Measures of similarity among fuzzy concepts: A comparative analysis. *Int. J. Approx. Reason.* **1987**, *1*, 221–242. [CrossRef]
19. Pappis, C.P.; Karacapilidis, N.I. A comparative assessment of measures of similarity of fuzzy values. *Fuzzy Sets Syst.* **1993**, *56*, 171–174. [CrossRef]
20. Chen, S.M. A comparison of measures of similarity of fuzzy values. *Fuzzy Sets Syst.* **1994**, *56*, 152–159.
21. Zeng, W.; Li, H. Relationship between similarity measure, and entropy of interval valued fuzzy sets. *Fuzzy Sets Syst.* **2006** *157* 1477–1484. [CrossRef]
22. Mitchell, H.B. On the Dengfeng-Chuntian similarity measure, and its application to pattern recognition. *Pattern Recognit. Lett.* **2003**, *24*, 3101–3104. [CrossRef]
23. Li, D.F.; Cheng, C.T. New similarity measures of intuitionistic fuzzy sets, and application to pattern recognition. *Pattern Recognit. Lett.* **2002**, *23*, 221–225.
24. Liang, Z.; Shi, P. Similarity Measures on intuitionistic fuzzy sets. *Pattern Recognit. Lett.* **2003**, *24*, 2687–2693. [CrossRef]
25. Szmidt, E.; Kacprzyk, J. Distances between intuitionistic fuzzy sets. *Fuzzy Sets Syst.* **2000**, *114*, 505–518. [CrossRef]
26. Lee, S.H.; Pedrycz, W.; Sohn, G. Design of similarity, and dissimilarity measures for fuzzy sets on the basis of distance measures. *Int. J. Fuzzy Syst.* **2009**, *11*, 67–72.
27. De, S.K.; Biswas, R.; Roy, A.R. An application of intuitionistic fuzzy sets in medical diagnosis. *Fuzzy Sets Syst.* **2001**, *117*, 209–213. [CrossRef]
28. Khatibi, V.; Montazer, G.A. Intuitionistic fuzzy set vs. fuzzy set application in medical pattern recognition. *Artif. Intell. Med.* **2009**, *47*, 43–52. [CrossRef]
29. Xia, M.; Xu, Z. Some new similarity measures for intuitionistic fuzzy values, and their application in group decision making. *J. Syst. Sci. Syst. Eng.* **2010**, *19*, 430–452. [CrossRef]
30. Szmidt, E.; Kacprzyk, J. A new concept of similarity measure for intuitionistic fuzzy sets, and its use in group decision making. *Lect. Notes Comput. Sci. (Subseries LNAI)* **2005**, *3558*, 272–282.
31. Szmidt, E. *Distances, and Similarities in Intuitionistic Fuzzy Sets*; Springer: Berlin/Heidelberg, Germany, 2014.
32. Chen, S.M.; Chang, C.H. A new similarity measure between intuitionistic fuzzy sets based on transformation techniques. In Proceedings of the International Conference on Machine Learning, and Cybernetics, Lanzhou, China, 13–16 July 2014; pp. 396–402.
33. Hoang, L.; Pham, H.S.P. On the performance evaluation of intuitionistic vector similarity measures for medical diagnosis. *J. Intell. Fuzzy Syst.* **2016**, *31*, 1597–1608.
34. Nguyen, H. A novel similarity dissimilarity measure for intuitionistic fuzzy sets, and its application in pattern recognition. *Expert Syst. Appl.* **2016**, *45*, 97–107. [CrossRef]
35. Laijun, L.; Haiping, R. A new similarity measure of intuitionistic fuzzy set, and application in MADM problem. *AMSE J.* **2016**, *53*, 204–223.
36. Zhou, Y.; Ejegwa, P.A.; Johnny, S.E. Generalized Similarity Operator for Intuitionistic Fuzzy Sets and its Applications Based on Recognition Principle and Multiple Criteria Decision Making Technique. *Int. J. Comput. Intell. Syst.* **2023**, *16*, 85. [CrossRef]
37. Ye, J. Cosine similarity measures for intuitionistic fuzzy sets, and their applications. *Math. Comput. Model.* **2011**, *53*, 91–97. [CrossRef]
38. Ye, J. Similarity measures of intuitionistic fuzzy sets based on cosine function for the decision making of mechanical design schemes. *J. Intell. Fuzzy Syst* **2016**, *30*, 151–158. [CrossRef]
39. Ye, J. Interval-valued intuitionistic fuzzy similarity measures for multiple attribute decision-making. *Int. J. Gen. Syst.* **2013**, *42*, 883–891. [CrossRef]
40. Shi, L.L.; Ye, J. Study on fault diagnosis of turbine using an improved cosine similarity measure for vague sets. *J. Appl. Sci.* **2013**, *13*, 1781–1786. [CrossRef]
41. Zhou, L.; Tao, Z.; Chen, H. Intuitionistic fuzzy ordered weighted cosine similarity measure. *Group Decis. Negot.* **2014**, *23*, 879–900. [CrossRef]
42. Liu, D.; Chen, X.; Peng, D. Interval-valued intuitionistic fuzzy ordered weighted cosine similarity measure, and its application in investment decision-making. *Complexity* **2017**, *2017*, 1891923. [CrossRef]

43. Liu, D.; Chen, X.; Peng, D. The intuitionistic fuzzy linguistic cosine similarity measure, and its application in pattern recognition. *Complexity* **2018**, *1*, 9073597. [CrossRef]
44. Tian, M.Y. A new fuzzy similarity based on cotangent function for medical diagnosis. *Adv. Model. Optim.* **2013**, *15*, 151–156.
45. Rajarajeswari, P.; Uma, N. Intuitionistic fuzzy multi similarity measure based on cotangent function. *Int. J. Eng. Res. Technol.* **2013**, *2*, 1323–1329.
46. Garg, H.; Olgun, M.; Türkarslan, E.; Ünver, M. A Choquet Integral Based Cosine Similarity Measure for Interval-Valued Intuitionistic Fuzzy Sets and an Application to Pattern Recognition. *Lobachevskii J. Math.* **2022**, *43*, 2444–2452. [CrossRef]
47. Garg, H. A novel correlation coefficient between Pythagorean fuzzy sets, and its applications to decision-making processes. *Int. J. Intell. Syst.* **2016**, *31*, 1234–1252. [CrossRef]
48. Zeng, W.; Li, D.; Yin, Q. Distance, and similarity measures of Pythagorean fuzzy sets, and their applications to multiple criteria group decision making. *Int. J. Intell. Syst.* **2018**, *33*, 2236–2254. [CrossRef]
49. Peng, X.D.; Yuan, H.Y.; Yang, Y. Pythagorean Fuzzy Information Measures, and Their Applications. *Int. J. Intell. Syst.* **2017**, *32*, 991–1029. [CrossRef]
50. Hussian, Z.; Yang, M.S. Distance, and similarity measures of Pythagorean fuzzy sets based on Hausdorff metric with application to fuzzy TOPSIS. *J. Intell. Syst.* **2019**, *34*, 2633–2654. [CrossRef]
51. Wei, G.W.; Wei, Y. Similarity measures of Pythagorean fuzzy sets based on the cosine function, and their applications. *Int. J. Intell. Syst.* **2018**, *33*, 634–652. [CrossRef]
52. Ejegwa P. A.; Jana C.; Pal, M. Medical diagnostic process based on modified composite relation on Pythagorean fuzzy multisets. *Granul. Comput.* **2022**, *7*, 15–23. [CrossRef]
53. Ejegwa P.A.; Onyeke I.C. Some new distance and similarity algorithms for Pythagorean fuzzy sets with application in decision-making problems. In *Handbook of Research on Advances and Applications of Fuzzy Sets and Logic*; Broumi, S., Ed.; Hershey: Pennsylvania, PA, USA, 2022; pp. 192–211.
54. Ejegwa, P.A.; Feng, Y.; Tang, S.; Agbetayo, J.M.; Dai X. New Pythagorean fuzzy-based distance operators and their applications in pattern classification and disease diagnostic analysis. *Neural Comput. Appl.* **2023**, *35*, 10083–10095. [CrossRef]
55. Aydın, S. A fuzzy MCDM method based on new Fermatean fuzzy theories. *Int. J. Inf. Technol. Decis. Mak. (IJITDM)* **2021**, *20*, 881–902. [CrossRef]
56. Ejegwa, P.A.; Onyeke, I.C. Fermatean fuzzy similarity measure algorithm, and its application in students admission process. *Int. J. Fuzzy Comput. Model.* **2022**, *4*, 34–50. [CrossRef]
57. Sahoo, L. Similarity measures for Fermatean fuzzy sets, and applications in group decision making. *Decis. Sci. Lett.* **2022**, *11*, 167–180. [CrossRef]
58. Khan, F.M.; Khan, I.; Ahmed, W. A benchmark similarity measure for Fermatean fuzzy sets. *Bull. Sect. Logic* **2022**, *51*, 207–226. [CrossRef]
59. Kirişci, M. New cosine similarity, and distance measures for Fermatean fuzzy sets, and TOPSIS approach. *Knowledge, Inf. Syst.* **2023**, *65*, 855–868. [CrossRef]
60. Rahim, M.; Garg, H.; Amin, F.; Perez-Dominguez, L.; Alkhayyat, A. Improved cosine similarity and distance measures-based TOPSIS method for cubic Fermatean fuzzy sets. *Alex. Eng. J.* **2023**, *73*, 309–319. [CrossRef]
61. Peng, X.; Dai, J. Research on the assessment of classroom teaching quality with q-rung orthopair fuzzy information based on multiparametric similarity measure, and combinative distance-based assessment. *Int. J. Intell. Syst.* **2019**, *34*, 1543–1555. [CrossRef]
62. Zedam, N.J.L.; Mahmood, T.; Rak, E.; Ali, Z. Generalized dice similarity measures for q-rung orthopair fuzzy sets with applications. *Complex, Intell. Syst.* **2020**, *6*, 545–558. [CrossRef]
63. Peng, X.; Liu, L. Information measures for q-rung orthopair fuzzy sets. *Int. J. Intell. Syst.* **2019**, *34*, 1795–1834. [CrossRef]
64. Liu, D.; Chen, X.; Peng, D. Some cosine similarity measures, and distance measures between q-rung orthopair fuzzy sets. *Int. J. Intell. Syst.* **2019**, *34*, 2454–2469. [CrossRef]
65. Wang, P.; Wang, J.; Wei, G.; Wei, C. Similarity measures of q-Rung orthopair fuzzy sets based on cosine function, and their applications. *Mathematics* **2019**, *7*, 1037. [CrossRef]
66. Plant Village Dataset. Available online: https://www.kaggle.com/datasets/abdallahalidev/plantvillage-dataset (accessed on 25 June 2023).

symmetry

MDPI

Article

Application of the Double Fuzzy Sawi Transform for Solving a Telegraph Equation

Atanaska Tencheva Georgieva [1,*] and Albena Pavlova [2]

[1] Department of Mathematical Analysis, University of Plovdiv Paisii Hilendarski, 24 Tzar Asen, 4003 Plovdiv, Bulgaria

[2] Department of MPC, Technical University-Sofia, Plovdiv Branch, 25 Tzanko Djustabanov Str., 4000 Plovdiv, Bulgaria

* Correspondence: atanaska@uni-plovdiv.bg

Abstract: The main purpose of this study is to introduce a new double fuzzy transform called the double fuzzy Sawi transform. A proof of some basic properties of the single fuzzy Sawi transform and the double fuzzy Sawi transform are provided. These new results are implemented to obtain the exact solution of a non-homogeneous linear fuzzy telegraph equation under a generalized Hukuhara partial differentiability. In addition, by using the symmetric triangular fuzzy numbers, numerical examples are given to demonstrate the validity and superiority of the double fuzzy Sawi transform in solving the fuzzy linear telegraph equation.

Keywords: double fuzzy Sawi transform; linear fuzzy telegraph equation; generalized Hukuhara partial differentiability

MSC: 44A30; 35A22; 35N05

1. Introduction

A lot of scientific fields, such as engineering, biology, and physics, use fuzzy differential equations for modeling uncertainty in various mathematical models [1–4]. Furthermore, fuzzy derivative definitions and concepts provide additional support in methods for solving these equations. In [5], Feuring and Buckley introduce fuzzy partial differential equations. Allahviranloo [6], who found solution for these equations based on a difference method via Taylor series, continues this work to a greater extent. Subsequently, Pownuk [7] uses algorithm-based sensitivity analysis applied to a finite element method model to obtain a solution of fuzzy partial differential equations. Another technique that was of high consideration in finding an approximate solution of the fuzzy heat equation in [8] pertains to the Adomian decomposition method. That method, along with the fuzzy variational iteration method, was applied by Osman, Gong, and Mustafa [9] to solve fuzzy heat-like and wave-like equations with variable coefficients in the sense of gH-differentiability. In later work [10], Gouyandeh and others introduced a fuzzy Fourier transformation. Based on this transformation, they examined analytical solutions of a fuzzy heat equation under a generalized Hukuhara partial differentiability. Many authors have presented various analytical and computational methods that led to solving these equations [11–15].

The Sawi transform was proposed by Mahgub [16] and is applied to ordinary linear differential equations with constant coefficients. Aggarwal and Gupta [17] provided supportive evidence for the relationship between the Sawi transformation and other fundamental transformations. Aggarwal discussed the application of the Sawi transform in finding solutions to biological problems such as growth and decay in [18]. Higary et al. demonstrated another example of how the Sawi transform can be used in finding a solution to a system of ordinary differential equations by its application in determining the concentration of chemical reactants of a chemical reaction in a series [19]. In [20], one-dimensional shallow water wave equations are solved using a new hybrid technique that involves homotopy perturbation based on the Sawi transformation.

In recent years, some scholars [21–25] applied different double fuzzy integral transforms (Laplace; Natural; Elzaki) to find the solution of a fuzzy partial differential equation. These transforms are very useful in solving linear fuzzy partial differential equations. They convert the fuzzy partial equations to algebraic equations about the unknown function.

The objective of the present paper is to obtain the solution of the linear fuzzy telegraph equation under generalized Hukuhara partial derivatives using a double fuzzy Sawi transform. To begin with, we define a single fuzzy Sawi transform. Then, we provide sufficient conditions for its existence and prove some key properties of this transformation. The fuzzy Sawi transform for a one-variable fuzzy function is used to define a new double fuzzy integral transformation for multivariate fuzzy functions, known as the double fuzzy Sawi transform (DFST). We introduce basic theorems and properties of the DFST and present some results related to the generalized Hukuhara partial derivatives. Based on the full DFST, we obtain a simple formula for the solution of the non-homogeneous linear fuzzy telegraph equation without converting it to two crisp equations. Finally, by using the symmetric triangular fuzzy numbers, we give numerical examples of homogeneous and non-homogeneous linear fuzzy telegraph equations with symmetric characteristics to demonstrate the usefulness of the provided double fuzzy integral transform in solving fuzzy partial differential equations.

The rest of this paper can be summarized as follows: in Section 2, we introduce theorems and some of the principal definitions that will be used. In Section 3, we illustrate fundamental facts and properties of the single fuzzy Sawi transformation. Section 4 presents the new double fuzzy Sawi transform: its basic properties; theorems; and several relationships related to its existence and gH-partial derivatives. In Section 5, we apply a double fuzzy Sawi transform to the linear fuzzy telegraph equation under partial gH-differentiability and obtain a formula for its solution. In Section 6, we provide numerical examples to be solved with this new double fuzzy transform. Finally, in Section 7, we summarize our results.

2. Basic Preliminaries

This section consists of some definitions and notations, which will be used in the paper. Let $\mathbb{R}$ be the set of all real numbers.

Definition 1 ([26]). *A fuzzy number is a mapping $u : \mathbb{R} \to [0,1]$ that possesses the following properties:*

(i) *u is normal, i.e., there exists $x \in \mathbb{R}$ with $u(x) = 1$;*
(ii) *u is upper semi-continuous on $\mathbb{R}$;*
(iii) *u is a convex fuzzy set, i.e., $u(rx + (1-r)y) \geq \min\{u(x), u(y)\}$ for any $x, y \in \mathbb{R}$, $r \in [0,1]$;*
(iv) *$supp\ u = \{x \in \mathbb{R} :\ u(x) > 0\}$ is the support of u, and its closure $cl(suppu)$ is compact.*

Denote E^1 as the set of all fuzzy numbers. Any real number $a \in \mathbb{R}$ can be interpreted as a fuzzy number $\tilde{a} = \chi(a)$, and therefore, $\mathbb{R} \subset E^1$.

Definition 2 ([27]). *Let $u \in E^1$. The r-level set of u is denoted by*

$$[u]^r = \begin{cases} \{x \in \mathbb{R} : u(x) \geq r\}, & 0 < r \leq 1, \\ cl(supp\ u), & r = 0. \end{cases}$$

Denote $[u]^r = [\underline{u}(r), \overline{u}(r)]$, so the r-level set $[u]^r$ is a bounded and closed interval for all $r \in [0,1]$.

Definition 3 ([27]). *A parametric form of the fuzzy number u is an ordered pair* $u(r) = (\underline{u}(r), \overline{u}(r))$ *of functions* $\underline{u}(r)$ *and* $\overline{u}(r)$ *for any* $r \in [0,1]$, *which satisfies the following conditions:*

(i) *the function* $\underline{u}(r)$ *is a bounded left continuous monotonic increasing in* $[0,1]$;
(ii) *the function* $\overline{u}(r)$ *is a bounded left continuous monotonic decreasing in* $[0,1]$;
(iii) $\underline{u}(r) \leq \overline{u}(r)$.

Definition 4 ([27]). *A triangular fuzzy number u is said to be an ordered triple* $u = (a,b,c)$ *with the conditions* $a \leq b \leq c$ *and* $a,\ b,\ c \in \mathbb{R}$. *The r-cuts associated with triangular fuzzy number u are* $[a + (b-a)r, c - (c-b)r]$.

Definition 5 ([28]). *A trapezoidal fuzzy number u is said to be an ordered four* $u = (a,b,c,d)$ *with the conditions* $a \leq b \leq c \leq d$ *and* $a,\ b,\ c\ d \in \mathbb{R}$. *The r-cuts associated with trapezoidal fuzzy number u are* $[a + (b-a)r, d - (d-c)r]$.

For fuzzy numbers $[u]^r = [\underline{u}(r), \overline{u}(r)]$, $[v]^r = [\underline{v}(r), \overline{v}(r)]$, and $\lambda \in \mathbb{R}$, the addition and scalar multiplication are defined by

$$[u \oplus v]^r = [u]^r + [v]^r = [\underline{u}(r) + \underline{v}(r), \overline{u}(r) + \overline{v}(r)]$$

and

$$[\lambda \odot u]^r = k.[u]^r = \begin{cases} [\lambda \underline{u}(r), \lambda \overline{u}(r)], & \lambda \geq 0 \\ [\lambda \overline{u}(r), \lambda \underline{u}(r)], & \lambda < 0. \end{cases}$$

Denote $\tilde{0} = \chi_{\{0\}}$ as the neutral element with respect to $\oplus$ in E^1. In [26], the basic algebraic properties of fuzzy numbers are given.

In this study, we suppose $\mathbb{R}_+ = [0, +\infty)$.

Definition 6 ([26]). *The Hausdorff distance between fuzzy numbers is given by* $D : E^1 \times E^1 \to \mathbb{R}_+$ *as*

$$D(u,v) = \sup_{r \in [0,1]} d([u]^r, [v]^r) = \sup_{r \in [0,1]} \max\{|\underline{u}(r) - \underline{v}(r)|, |\overline{u}(r) - \overline{v}(r)|\},$$

where d is the Hausdorff metric.

Some basic properties of the metric D are given in [26].

(i) (E^1, D) is a complete metric space;
(ii) $D(u \oplus w, v \oplus w) = D(u,v)$ for all $u,\ v,\ w \in E^1$;
(ii) $D(\lambda u, \lambda v) = |\lambda| D(u,v)$ for all $u,\ v \in E^1$ and $\lambda \in \mathbb{R}$;
(iii) $D(u \oplus v, w \oplus z) \leq D(u,w) + D(v,z)$ for all $u,\ v,\ w,\ z \in E^1$;
(iv) $D(u \ominus v, w \ominus z) \leq D(u,w) + D(v,z)$ for all $u,\ v,\ w,\ z \in E^1$, assuming that $u \ominus v$ and $w \ominus z$ exist.

The Hukuhara difference (H-difference) $\ominus$ between fuzzy numbers u and v is defined by $u \ominus v = w$ if and only if $v \oplus w = u$. For the r-level, we have

$$[u \ominus v]^r = [\underline{u}(r) - \underline{v}(r), \overline{u}(r) - \overline{v}(r)].$$

The H-difference does not always exist, but it is unique. A necessary condition is that u contains a translate $\{c\} \oplus v$ of v.

Definition 7 ([28]). *The generalized Hukuhara difference (gH-difference)* $\ominus_{gH}$ *between two fuzzy numbers* $u, v \in E^1$ *is defined by:*

$$u \ominus_{gH} v = w \Leftrightarrow \begin{cases} (i) & u = v \oplus w, \\ or\ (ii) & v = u \oplus (-1) \odot w. \end{cases}$$

For the r-level, we obtain

$$[u \ominus_{gH} v]^r = [\min\{\underline{u}(r) - \underline{v}(r), \overline{u}(r) - \overline{v}(r)\}, \max\{\underline{u}(r) - \underline{v}(r), \overline{u}(r) - \overline{v}(r)\}].$$

If the H-difference exists, then $u \ominus v = u \ominus_{gH} v$. The sufficient conditions for the existence of $u \ominus_{gH} v$ are

$$\text{(i)} \quad \begin{cases} \underline{u}(r) - \underline{v}(r) = \underline{w}(r) \text{ and } \overline{u}(r) - \overline{v}(r) = \overline{w}(r), \text{ for all } 0 \le r \le 1, \\ \text{with } \underline{w}(r) \text{ increasing, } \overline{w}(r) \text{ decreasing, } \underline{w}(r) \le \overline{w}(r). \end{cases}$$

$$\text{(ii)} \quad \begin{cases} \overline{u}(r) - \overline{v}(r) = \underline{w}(r) \text{ and } \underline{u}(r) - \underline{v}(r) = \overline{w}(r), \text{ for all } 0 \le r \le 1, \\ \text{with } \underline{w}(r) \text{ increasing, } \overline{w}(r) \text{ decreasing, } \underline{w}(r) \le \overline{w}(r). \end{cases}$$

It is easy to show that both (i) and (ii) are true if and only if w is a crisp number.

In the fuzzy case, it is possible that the gH-difference of two fuzzy numbers does not exist.

Example 1. *Let $u = (0,2,2,4)$ and $v = (0,1,2,3)$ be a triangular and trapezoidal fuzzy number. In this case, $u(r) = (2r, 4-2r)$ and $v(r) = (r, 3-r)$. For the level-wise, the gH-differences exist, but the gH-difference $u \ominus_{gH} v$ does not exist. If we suppose that it exists, then either case (i) or (ii) of Definition 2.7 should hold for any $r \in [0,1]$. However,*

$$\underline{w}(0) = \underline{u}(0) - \underline{v}(0) = 0 < \overline{w}(0) = \overline{u}(0) - \overline{v}(0),$$

while

$$\underline{w}(1) = \underline{u}(1) - \underline{v}(1) = 1 > \overline{w}(1) = \overline{u}(1) - \overline{v}(1) = 0,$$

so neither case (i) or (ii) is true from Definition 2.7.

Proposition 1 ([28]). *Let $u, v \in E^1$ be two fuzzy numbers. Then*

(i) $(-1)[u]^r = [-\overline{u}(r), -\underline{u}(r)]$;

(ii) $\ominus[u]^r = [-\underline{u}(r), -\overline{u}(r)]$ *if a Hukuhara difference exists;*

(iii) $\tilde{0} \ominus_{gH} [u]^r = [-\overline{u}(r), -\underline{u}(r)] = (-1)[u]^r$;

(iv) $\tilde{0} \ominus_{gH} (-1)[u]^r = [\underline{u}(r), \overline{u}(r)] = [u]^r$;

(v) $[u]^r \ominus_{gH} [v]^r = [u]^r \ominus [v]^r$ *or* $[u]^r \ominus_{gH} [v]^r = -([v]^r \ominus [u]^r)$ *whenever the expressions on the right exist;*

(vi) $[v]^r \ominus_{gH} (-1)[u]^r \neq [v]^r + [u]^r$.

2.1. Fuzzy Function of One-Variable

Now, we present some definitions, theorems, and notations for a fuzzy-valued function of one-variable.

Consider the fuzzy-valued function $f : D \to E^1$. The parametric representation of this function is the ordered pair

$$f(x,r) = \left(\underline{f}(x,r), \overline{f}(x,r)\right) \text{ for any } 0 \le r \le 1.$$

Definition 8 ([29]). *A fuzzy-valued function $f : (a,b) \to E^1$ is said to be continuous at $x_0 \in (a,b)$ if for each $\varepsilon > 0$, there is $\delta > 0$ such that $D(f(x), f(x_0)) < \varepsilon$ whenever $|x - x_0| < \delta$.*

If the function f is continuous for each $x \in (a,b)$, then we say that f is continuous on $[a,b]$.

Definition 9 ([28]). *The generalized Hukuhara derivative (gH-derivative) of a fuzzy-valued function $f : (a,b) \to E^1$ at $x_0 \in (a,b)$ is defined as*

$$f'(x_0) = \lim_{h \to 0} \frac{1}{h}\left[f(x_0 + h) \ominus_{gH} f(x_0)\right]. \tag{1}$$

If $f'(x_0) \in E^1$ satisfying (1) exists, we say that f is a generalized Hukuhara differentiable at x_0.

Example 2. *Let $f(x) = g(x) \odot u$, where $a(x)$ is a crips differentiable function and $u \in E^1$. Then, it follows that the gH-derivative exists, and it is $f'(x) = g'(x) \odot u$.*

Definition 10 ([28]). *Let $f : (a,b) \to E^1$ and $x_0 \in (a,b)$, with $\underline{f}(.,r)$ and $\overline{f}(.,r)$ both differentiable at x_0. We say that*

(i) *the function f is (i)-gH-differentiable at x_0 if*

$$f'_{(i)}(x_0,r) = \left(\underline{f}'(x_0,r), \overline{f}'(x_0,r)\right) \text{ for each } r \in [0,1], \tag{2}$$

(ii) *the function f is (ii)-gH-differentiable at x_0 if*

$$f'_{(ii)}(x_0,r) = \left(\overline{f}'(x_0,r), \underline{f}'(x_0,r)\right) \text{ for each } r \in [0,1]. \tag{3}$$

We will use the following theorem and the formula for integration by parts to obtain the formulas of the fuzzy Sawi transform from derivatives of the function $f : (a,b) \to E'$.

Theorem 1 ([28]). *Let $f : [a,b] \to E^1$ be gH-differentiable with no switching point in the interval $[a,b]$. Then,*

$$(FR)\int_a^b f'(x)dx = f(b) \ominus_{gH} f(a).$$

Lemma 1 ([25]). *Let $f,\ g : \mathbb{R}_+ \to E^1$ be fuzzy-valued functions, which are improper fuzzy Riemann-integrable on $\mathbb{R}_+$. Then,*

(i) $(FR)\int_0^\infty [a \odot f(x) \ominus_{gH} b \odot g(x)]dx = a \odot (FR)\int_0^\infty f(x)dx \ominus_{gH} b \odot (FR)\int_0^\infty g(x)dx;$

(ii) $(FR)\int_0^\infty [a \odot f(x) \oplus b \odot g(x)]dx = a \odot (FR)\int_0^\infty f(x)dx \oplus b \odot (FR)\int_0^\infty g(x)dx,$

where a and b are nonzero constants.

Theorem 2 ([10], Integration by part). *Let $f : [a,b] \to E^1$ be gH-differentiable with no switching point in the interval $[a,b]$ and $g : [a,b] \to \mathbb{R}$ be differentiable functions. Then,*

$$(FR)\int_a^b f'(x) \odot g(x)dx = (f(b) \odot g(b)) \ominus_{gH} (f(a) \odot g(a)) \ominus_{gH} (FR)\int_a^b f(x) \odot g'(x)dx.$$

2.2. Fuzzy Function of a Two-Variable

In this section, we present some definitions and theorems for the fuzzy-valued function of a two-variable. Furthermore, we introduce the generalized Hukuhara partial derivative.

Consider $f : D \subset \mathbb{R} \times \mathbb{R} \to E^1$ as a fuzzy-valued function of a two-variable. The parametric representation of this function is the ordered pair

$$f(x,y,r) = \left(\underline{f}(x,y,r), \overline{f}(x,y,r)\right) \text{ for any } 0 \le r \le 1.$$

Definition 11 ([22]). *A fuzzy-valued function $f : D \to E^1$ is said to be continuous at $(x_0, y_0) \in D$ if for each $\varepsilon > 0$, there is $\delta > 0$ such that $D(f(x,y), f(x_0,y_0)) < \varepsilon$ whenever $|x - x_0| + |y - y_0| < \delta$. If f is continuous for each $(x,y) \in D$, then we say that f is continuous on D.*

Definition 12 ([12]). *The first generalized Hukuhara partial derivative (gH-p-derivative) of a fuzzy-valued function* $f : D \to E^1$ *at* $(x_0, y_0) \in D$ *with respect to variables x and y are the functions* $f'_x(x_0, y_0)$ *and* $f'_y(x_0, y_0)$*, defined by*

$$f'_x(x_0, y_0) = \lim_{h \to 0} \frac{1}{h}[f(x_0 + h, y_0) \ominus_{gH} f(x_0, y_0)],$$

$$f'_y(x_0, y_0) = \lim_{k \to 0} \frac{1}{k}[f(x_0, y_0 + k) \ominus_{gH} f(x_0, y_0)]$$

provided that $f'_x(x_0, y_0),\ f'_y(x_0, y_0) \in E^1$.

Definition 13 ([12]). *Let* $f : D \to E^1$*, and* $\underline{f}(x, y, r)$ *and* $\overline{f}(x, y, r)$ *are partial differentiable at* $(x_0, y_0) \in D$ *with respect to variable x. We say that*

(i) *the function* $f(x, y)$ *is* (i)*-gH-p-differentiable at* (x_0, y_0) *with respect to variable x if*

$$f'_{x_{(i)}}(x_0, y_0, r) = \left(\underline{f}'_x(x_0, y_0, r), \overline{f}'_x(x_0, y_0, r)\right) \ \textit{for each } r \in [0, 1], \tag{4}$$

(ii) *the function* $f(x, y)$ *is* (ii)*-gH-p -differentiable at* (x_0, y_0) *with respect to variable x if*

$$f'_{x_{(ii)}}(x_0, y_0, r) = \left(\overline{f}'_x(x_0, y_0, r), \underline{f}'_x(x_0, y_0, r)\right) \ \textit{for each } r \in [0, 1]. \tag{5}$$

Theorem 3 ([10]). *Let* $f : [a, \infty) \times [c, \infty) \to E^1$ *be a fuzzy-valued function. Suppose that* $(FR) \int_c^\infty f(x, y)dy$ *is convergent for each* $[a, \infty)$*, and* $(FR) \int_a^\infty f(x, y)dx$ *as a function y is convergent on* $[c, \infty)$*. Then,*

$$(FR) \int_a^\infty (FR) \int_c^\infty f(x, y)dydx = (FR) \int_c^\infty (FR) \int_a^\infty f(x, y)dxdy,$$

for all $a,\ c \in \mathbb{R}$.

3. Fuzzy Sawi Transform

In this section, we introduce the fuzzy Sawi transform (FST) [30] and prove some basic properties for it.

Definition 14. *Let* $f : \mathbb{R}_+ \to E^1$ *be a fuzzy-valued function, and for* $\sigma > 0$*, the function* $e^{-\frac{x}{\sigma}} \odot f(x)$ *is an improper fuzzy Riemann-integrable on* $\mathbb{R}_+$*. Then, the FST of a function* $f(x)$ *is defined as*

$$F(\sigma) = S_x[f(x)] = (FR) \int_0^\infty \frac{1}{\sigma^2} e^{-\frac{x}{\sigma}} \odot f(x)dx, \tag{6}$$

where the variables σ *are used to factor the variable x in the argument of the fuzzy-valued function.*

Definition 15. *Let* $f : \mathbb{R}_+ \to E^1$ *and* $F(\sigma) = S_2[f(x)]$*. The fuzzy inverse Sawi transform of the function* $F(\sigma)$ *is defined as*

$$S_\sigma^{-1}[F(\sigma)] = f(x). \tag{7}$$

Definition 16. *A fuzzy-number-valued function* $f : \mathbb{R}_+ \to E^1$ *is said to be of exponential order* $\alpha > 0$ *if there exists a positive constant M such that for all* $x > X$

$$D(f(x), \tilde{0}) \le Me^{\alpha x}.$$

The below theorem shows the sufficient existence condition for a fuzzy Sawi transform.

Theorem 4. *Let $f : \mathbb{R}_+ \to E^1$ be a continuous or piece-wise continuous fuzzy-valued function in every finite interval $(0, X)$ and of exponential order $\alpha > 0$. Then, the FST of $f(x)$ exists for all σ, provided $Re(\frac{1}{\sigma}) > \alpha$.*

Proof. Let $S_x[f(x)] = F(\sigma)$. From the definition of FST, we have

$$\begin{aligned} D(F(\sigma), \tilde{0}) &= D\left((FR)\int_0^\infty \frac{1}{\sigma^2}e^{-\frac{x}{\sigma}} \odot f(x)dx, \tilde{0}\right) \le \int_0^\infty \frac{1}{\sigma^2}e^{-\frac{x}{\sigma}} D(f(x), \tilde{0})dx \\ &\le \frac{M}{\sigma^2}\int_0^\infty e^{-(\frac{1}{\sigma}-\alpha)x}dx = \frac{M}{\sigma^2(\frac{1}{\sigma}-\alpha)} = \frac{M}{\sigma(1-\sigma\alpha)}, \end{aligned}$$

for $Re(\frac{1}{\sigma}) > \alpha$. □

In [19], a classical Sawi transform is applied on some special functions.

Let $F(\sigma) = S_x[f(x)]$. Then,

(i) if $f(x) = 1$ for $x > 0$, then $F(\sigma) = \frac{1}{\sigma}$;
(ii) if $f(x) = x^n$, where n are positive integers, then $F(\sigma) = (n!)\sigma^{n-1}$;
(iii) if $f(x) = e^{ax}$, then $F(\sigma) = \frac{1}{\sigma(1-a\sigma)}$;
(iv) if $f(x) = \sin ax$, then $F(\sigma) = \frac{a}{1+a^2\sigma^2}$;
(v) if $f(x) = \cos ax$, then $F(\sigma) = \frac{1}{\sigma(1+a^2\sigma^2)}$.

Now, we present some basic properties of FST. To start with, we will prove the linearity property of the fuzzy Sawi transform.

Theorem 5. *Let $f,\ g : \mathbb{R}_+ \to E^1$ be fuzzy-valued functions for which the FST exists. Then, the FST of a $a \odot f(x) \oplus b \odot g(x)$ and $a \odot f(x) \ominus_{gH} b \odot g(x)$ exists, and*

(i) $a \odot S_x[f(x)] \ominus_{gH} b \odot S_x[g(x)] = S_x[a \odot f(x) \ominus_{gH} b \odot g(x)]$;
(ii) $a \odot S_x[f(x)] \oplus b \odot S_x[g(x)] = S_x[a \odot f(x) \oplus b \odot g(x)]$,

where a and b are nonzero constants.

Proof. Using Definition 15 and Lemma 1, we obtain

$$\begin{aligned} a \odot S_x[f(x)] \ominus_{gH} b \odot S_x[g(x)] &= (FR)\int_0^\infty \frac{a}{\sigma^2}e^{-\frac{x}{\sigma}} \odot f(x)dx \ominus_{gH} (FR)\int_0^\infty \frac{b}{\sigma^2}e^{-\frac{x}{\sigma}} \odot g(x)dx \\ &= (FR)\int_0^\infty \left(\frac{a}{\sigma^2}e^{-\frac{x}{\sigma}} \odot f(x) \ominus_{gH} \frac{b}{\sigma^2}e^{-\frac{x}{\sigma}} \odot g(x)\right)dx \\ &= (FR)\int_0^\infty \frac{1}{\sigma^2}e^{-\frac{x}{\sigma}}(a \odot f(x) \ominus_{gH} b \odot g(x))dx \\ &= S_x[a \odot f(x) \ominus_{gH} b \odot g(x)]. \end{aligned}$$

In a similar manner, we obtain the proof for part (ii). □

The fuzzy Sawi transform for a derivative of a continuous fuzzy-valued function is given in the following theorem.

Theorem 6. *Let $f : \mathbb{R}_+ \to E^1$ be a continuous fuzzy-valued function of exponential order $\alpha > 0$. Moreover, let $f'(x)$ be piece-wise continuous in every finite closed interval $0 \le x \le b$. Then, for $Re(\frac{1}{\sigma}) > \alpha$, we have*

(i) $S_x[f'(x)] = (-1)\frac{1}{\sigma^2} \odot f(0) \ominus_{gH} (-1)\frac{1}{\sigma} \odot F(\sigma)$;
(ii) $S_x[f''(x)] = (-1)\frac{1}{\sigma^2} \odot f'(0) \ominus_{gH} \left(\frac{1}{\sigma^3} \odot f(0) \ominus_{gH} \frac{1}{\sigma^2} \odot F(\sigma)\right)$,

where $S_x[f(x)] = F(\sigma)$.

Proof. From the definition of the improper fuzzy Riemann-integral, we have

$$S_x[f'(x)] = (FR)\int_0^\infty \frac{1}{\sigma^2}e^{-\frac{x}{\sigma}} \odot f'(x)dx = \lim_{R\to\infty}(FR)\int_0^R \frac{1}{\sigma^2}e^{-\frac{x}{\sigma}} \odot f'(x)dx$$

provided this limit exist, which is, Theorem 2

$$(FR)\int_0^R \tfrac{1}{\sigma^2}e^{-\frac{x}{\sigma}} \odot f'(x)dx = \tfrac{1}{\sigma^2}e^{-\frac{x}{\sigma}} \odot f(x)|_0^R \ominus_{gH} (-1)(FR)\int_0^R \tfrac{1}{\sigma^3}e^{-\frac{x}{\sigma}} \odot f(x)dx$$
$$= \tfrac{1}{\sigma^2}e^{-\frac{R}{\sigma}} \odot f(R) \ominus_{gH} \tfrac{1}{\sigma^2} \odot f(0) \ominus_{gH} (-1)(FR)\int_0^R \tfrac{1}{\sigma^3}e^{-\frac{x}{\sigma}} \odot f(x)dx.$$

The fuzzy-valued function f is of exponential order $\alpha > 0$. Thus, there exists $M > 0$ and $x_0 > 0$ such that $D(f(x),\tilde{0}) \leq Me^{\alpha x}$ for $x > x_0$. Thus, if $Re(\frac{1}{\sigma}) > \alpha$, we have

$$\lim_{R\to\infty} D(e^{-\frac{R}{\sigma}} \odot f(R),\tilde{0}) \leq \lim_{R\to\infty} Me^{-(\frac{1}{\sigma}-\alpha)x} = 0$$

and

$$\lim_{R\to\infty}(FR)\int_0^R \frac{1}{\sigma^3}e^{-\frac{x}{\sigma}} \odot f(x)dx = \frac{1}{\sigma} \odot S_x[f(x)].$$

Hence, by the above equations and Proposition 1, we obtain

$$S_x[f'(x)] = (-1)\frac{1}{\sigma^2} \odot f(0) \ominus_{gH} (-1)\frac{1}{\sigma} \odot S_x[f(x)].$$

Using Definition 14, Proposition 1, and equation (i) of this theorem, we obtain

$$\begin{aligned} S_x[f''(x)] &= (-1)\tfrac{1}{\sigma^2} \odot f'(0) \ominus_{gH} (-1)\tfrac{1}{\sigma} \odot S_x[f'(x)] \\ &= (-1)\tfrac{1}{\sigma^2} \odot f'(0) \ominus_{gH} (-1)\tfrac{1}{\sigma}\Big((-1)\tfrac{1}{\sigma^2} \odot f(0) \ominus_{gH} (-1)\tfrac{1}{\sigma} \odot S_x[f(x)]\Big) \\ &= (-1)\tfrac{1}{\sigma^2} \odot f'(0) \ominus_{gH} \Big(\tfrac{1}{\sigma^3} \odot f(0) \ominus_{gH} \tfrac{1}{\sigma^2} \odot S_x[f(x)]\Big). \end{aligned}$$

Hence, the proof of (ii) is established. □

Corollary 1. *Let $f : \mathbb{R}_+ \times \mathbb{R}_+ \to E^1$ be continuous fuzzy-valued functions and of exponential order $\alpha > 0$. Moreover, let $f'_x(x,y)$ be piece-wise continuous in every finite closed interval $0 \leq x \leq b$. Then, for $Re(\frac{1}{\sigma}) > \alpha$, we have*

(i) $S_x[f'_x(x,y)] = (-1)\frac{1}{\sigma^2} \odot f(0,y) \ominus_{gH} (-1)\frac{1}{\sigma} \odot F(\sigma,y)$;

(ii) $S_x[f''_{xx}(x,y)] = (-1)\frac{1}{\sigma^2} \odot f'_x(0,y) \ominus_{gH} \Big(\frac{1}{\sigma^3} \odot f(0,y) \ominus_{gH} \frac{1}{\sigma^2} \odot F(\sigma,y)\Big)$,

where $S_x[f(x,y)] = F(\sigma,y)$.

4. Double Fuzzy Sawi Transform

In this section, we introduce a new double fuzzy integral transform that combines two fuzzy Sawi transforms of order one. We prove basic properties concerning the existence, linearity, and the double fuzzy inverse Sawi transform. Moreover, we provide the double fuzzy Sawi transform of some basic functions. We establish new results relative to gH-partial derivatives of the new transform.

Definition 17. *Let $f : \mathbb{R}_+ \times \mathbb{R}_+ \to E^1$ be a fuzzy-valued function, and for $\sigma > 0$, $\delta > 0$, the function $e^{-\frac{x}{\sigma}-\frac{y}{\delta}} \odot f(x,y)$ is improper fuzzy Riemann-integrable on $\mathbb{R}_+ \times \mathbb{R}_+$. Then, the double fuzzy Sawi transform of a function $f(x,y)$ is defined as*

$$\begin{aligned} F(\sigma,\delta) &= S_2[f(x,y)] = S_x[S_y[f(x,y)]] \\ &= (FR)\int_0^\infty (FR)\int_0^\infty \frac{1}{\sigma^2\delta^2} e^{-\frac{x}{\sigma}-\frac{y}{\delta}} \odot f(x,y)dxdy, \end{aligned} \tag{8}$$

where the variables σ and δ are used to factor the variable x and y in the arguments of the fuzzy-valued function.

Definition 18. *Let $f : \mathbb{R}_+ \times \mathbb{R}_+ \to E^1$ and $F(\sigma,\delta) = S_2[f(x,y)]$. The double fuzzy inverse Sawi transform of the function $F(\sigma,\delta)$ is defined as*

$$S_\sigma^{-1}[S_\delta^{-1}[F(\sigma,\delta)]] = S_\sigma^{-1}[F(\sigma,y)] = f(x,y). \tag{9}$$

Definition 19. *A fuzzy-number-valued function $f : \mathbb{R}_+ \times \mathbb{R}_+ \to E^1$ is said to be of exponential order $\alpha > 0$ and $\beta > 0$ if there exists a positive constant M such that for all $x > X$ and $y > Y$*

$$D(f(x,y),\tilde{0}) \leq Me^{\alpha x+\beta x}.$$

The following theorem gives the existence conditions for a double fuzzy Sawi transform.

Theorem 7. *Let $f : \mathbb{R}_+ \times \mathbb{R}_+ \to E^1$ be a continuous or piece-wise continuous fuzzy-valued function in every finite interval $(0,X)$ and $(0,Y)$ and of exponential order $\alpha > 0$ and $\beta > 0$. Then, the DFST of $f(x,y)$ exists for all σ an δ provided $Re(\frac{1}{\sigma}) > \alpha$ and $Re(\frac{1}{\delta}) > \beta$.*

Proof. Let $S_2[f(x,y)] = F(\sigma,\delta)$. From the definition of DFST, we have

$$\begin{aligned} D(F(\sigma,\delta),\tilde{0}) &= D\left((FR)\int_0^\infty (FR)\int_0^\infty \frac{1}{\sigma^2\delta^2} e^{-\frac{x}{\sigma}-\frac{y}{\delta}} \odot f(x,y)dxdy, \tilde{0}\right) \\ &\leq \int_0^\infty \frac{1}{\sigma^2\delta^2} e^{-\frac{x}{\sigma}-\frac{y}{\delta}} D(f(x,y),\tilde{0})dxdy \\ &\leq \frac{M}{\sigma^2}\int_0^\infty e^{-(\frac{1}{\sigma}-\alpha)x}\left(\frac{1}{\delta^2}\int_0^\infty e^{-(\frac{1}{\delta}-\beta)y}dy\right)dx \\ &= \frac{M}{\sigma^2\delta^2(\frac{1}{\sigma}-\alpha)(\frac{1}{\delta}-\beta)} = \frac{M}{\sigma\delta(1-\sigma\alpha)(1-\delta\beta)}, \end{aligned}$$

for $Re(\frac{1}{\sigma}) > \alpha$, $Re(\frac{1}{\delta}) > \beta$. □

Lemma 2. *Let $f(x,y) = a \in E^1$. Then, for $x > 0$ and $y > 0$, we have*

$$S_2[f(x,y)] = \frac{1}{\sigma\delta} \odot a.$$

Proof. By Definition 17, we can write

$$\begin{aligned} S_2[f(x,y)] &= (FR)\int_0^\infty (FR)\int_0^\infty \frac{1}{\sigma^2\delta^2} e^{-\frac{x}{\sigma}-\frac{y}{\delta}} \odot adxdy \\ &= a \odot \lim_{\tau\to\infty}\int_0^\tau \frac{1}{\sigma^2} e^{-\frac{x}{\sigma}}dx \lim_{\xi\to\infty}\int_0^\xi \frac{1}{\delta^2} e^{-\frac{y}{\delta}}dy \\ &= a \odot \lim_{\tau\to\infty}\left(-\frac{1}{\tau}e^{-\frac{\tau}{\sigma}}+\frac{1}{\sigma}\right) \lim_{\xi\to\infty}\left(-\frac{1}{\xi}e^{-\frac{\xi}{\delta}}+\frac{1}{\delta}\right) = \frac{1}{\sigma\delta} \odot a. \end{aligned}$$

Hence, the proof is obtained. □

A classical double Sawi transform is performed on some special functions.

Let $F(\sigma,\delta) = S_2[f(x,y)]$. Then,

(i) if $f(x,y) = 1$ for $x > 0,\ y > 0$, then $F(\sigma,\delta) = \frac{1}{\sigma\delta}$;

(ii) if $g(x,y) = x^m y^n$, where $m,\ n$ are positive integers, then $F(\sigma,\delta) = (m!)(n!)\sigma^{m-1}\delta^{n-1}$;

(iii) if $f(x,y) = e^{ax+by}$, where $a,\ b$ are any constants, then $F(\sigma,\delta) = \frac{1}{\sigma\delta(1-a\sigma)(1-b\delta)}$;

(iv) if $f(x,y) = e^{i(ax+by)}$, where $a,\ b \in \mathbb{R}$, then

$F(\sigma,\delta) = \frac{1}{\sigma\delta(1-ia\sigma)(1-ib\delta)} = \frac{(1-ia\sigma)(1-ib\delta)}{\sigma\delta(1+a^2\sigma^2)(1+b^2\delta^2)} = \frac{1-ab\sigma\delta+i(a\sigma+b\delta)}{\sigma\delta(1+a^2\sigma^2)(1+b^2\delta^2)}$.

Consequently,

$$S_2[\cos(ax+by)] = \frac{1-ab\sigma\delta}{\sigma\delta(1+a^2\sigma^2)(1+b^2\delta^2)},\quad S_2[\sin(ax+by)] = \frac{a\sigma+b\delta}{\sigma\delta(1+a^2\sigma^2)(1+b^2\delta^2)}.$$

Clearly, the double fuzzy Sawi transform is a linear transformation as shown below.

Theorem 8. *Let $f,\ g : \mathbb{R}_+ \times \mathbb{R}_+ \to E^1$ be fuzzy-valued functions for which the DFST exists. Then, the DFST of a $a \odot f(x,y) \oplus b \odot g(x,y)$ and $a \odot f(x,y) \ominus_{gH} b \odot g(x,y)$ exists, and*

(i) $a \odot S_2[f(x,y)] \ominus_{gH} b \odot S_2[g(x,y)] = S_2[a \odot f(x,y) \ominus_{gH} b \odot g(x,y)]$;

(ii) $a \odot S_2[f(x,y)] \oplus b \odot S_2[g(x,y)] = S_2[a \odot f(x,y) \oplus b \odot g(x,y)]$,

where a and b are nonzero constants.

Proof. The proof follows from Definition 17 and Theorem 5. □

Now, we present some fundamental properties of DFST.

Theorem 9. *(Shifting property) Let $f(x,y)$ be a continuous fuzzy-valued function. If $F(\sigma,\delta)$ is the double fuzzy Sawi transform of $f(x,y)$ and $a,\ b$ are arbitrary constants, then*

$$S_2[e^{ax+by} \odot f(x,y)] = \frac{1}{(1-a\sigma)^2(1-b\delta)^2} \odot F\left(\frac{\sigma}{1-a\sigma}, \frac{\delta}{1-b\delta}\right). \tag{10}$$

Proof. From Definition 17, we have

$$\begin{aligned} S_2[e^{ax+by} \odot f(x,y)] &= (FR)\int_0^\infty (FR)\int_0^\infty \tfrac{1}{\sigma^2\delta^2} e^{-x(\frac{1}{\sigma}-a)-y(\frac{1}{\delta}-b)} \odot f(x,y)dxdy \\ &= (FR)\int_0^\infty (FR)\int_0^\infty \tfrac{1}{\sigma^2\delta^2} e^{-x(\frac{1-a\sigma}{\sigma})-y(\frac{1-b\delta}{\delta})} \odot f(x,y)dxdy \\ &= (FR)\int_0^\infty (FR)\int_0^\infty \tfrac{1}{(1-a\sigma)^2(1-b\delta)^2} e^{-x(\frac{1-a\sigma}{\sigma})-y(\frac{1-b\delta}{\delta})} \odot f(x,y)dxdy \\ &= \tfrac{1}{(1-a\sigma)^2(1-b\delta)^2} \odot F\left(\tfrac{\sigma}{1-a\sigma}, \tfrac{\delta}{1-b\delta}\right). \end{aligned}$$

Hence, the proof is obtained. □

Theorem 10. *(Change of scale property) Let $f(x,y)$ be a continuous fuzzy-valued function. If $F(\sigma,\delta)$ is the double fuzzy Sawi transform of $f(x,y)$ and $a,\ b$ are arbitrary constants, then*

$$S_2[f(ax,by)] = ab \odot F(\sigma,\delta). \tag{11}$$

Proof. From Definition 17, we have

$$S_2[f(ax,by)] = (FR)\int_0^\infty (FR)\int_0^\infty \frac{1}{\sigma^2\delta^2} e^{-\frac{x}{\sigma}-\frac{y}{\delta}} \odot f(ax,by)dxdy.$$

Put $ax = x_1, adx = dx_1, by = y_1, bdy = dy_1$ in the above equation, and we have

$$S_2[f(ax,by)] = (FR)\int_0^\infty (FR)\int_0^\infty \frac{ab}{a^2\sigma^2 b^2\delta^2} e^{-\frac{x_1}{a\sigma}-\frac{y_1}{b\delta}} \odot f(x_1,y_1)dx_1dy_1 = ab \odot F(\sigma,\delta). \quad \square$$

Theorem 11. *(Derivatives' properties)*
If $S_2[f(x,y)] = F(\sigma,\delta)$, *then*

(i) $S_2[f'_x(x,y)] = (-1)\frac{1}{\sigma^2} \odot S_y[f(0,y)] \ominus_{gH} (-1)\frac{1}{\sigma} \odot F(\sigma,\delta)$;
(ii) $S_2[f'_y(x,y)] = (-1)\frac{1}{\delta^2} \odot S_x[f(x,0)] \ominus_{gH} (-1)\frac{1}{\delta} \odot F(\sigma,\delta)$;
(iii) $S[f''_{xx}(x,y)] = (-1)\frac{1}{\sigma^2} \odot S_y[f'_x(0,y)] \ominus_{gH} \left(\frac{1}{\sigma^3} S_y[f(0,y)] \ominus_{gH} \frac{1}{\sigma^2} \odot F(\sigma,\delta)\right)$;
(iv) $S_2[f''_{yy}(x,y)] = (-1)\frac{1}{\delta^2} \odot S_x[f'_y(x,0)] \ominus_{gH} \left(\frac{1}{\delta^3} \odot S_x[f(x,0)] \ominus \frac{1}{\delta^2} \odot F(\sigma,\delta)\right)$;
(v) $S_2[f''_{xy}(x,y)] = (-1)\frac{1}{\delta^2} \odot S_x[f'_x(x,0)] \ominus_{gH} \left(\frac{1}{\sigma^2\delta} \odot S_y[f(0,y)] \ominus \frac{1}{\sigma\delta} \odot F(\sigma,\delta)\right)$;
(vi) $S_2[f''_{yx}(x,y)] = (-1)\frac{1}{\sigma^2} \odot S_y[f'_y(0,y)] \ominus_{gH} \left(\frac{1}{\sigma\delta^2} \odot S_x[f(x,0)] \ominus_{gH} \frac{1}{\sigma\delta} \odot F(\sigma,\delta)\right)$.

Proof. From Definition 17, Theorem 5, and Corollary 1, we obtain

$$\begin{aligned} S_2[f'_x(x,y)] &= S_y[S_x[f'_x(x,y)]] \\ &= S_y\left[(-1)\frac{1}{\sigma^2} \odot f(0,y) \ominus_{gH} (-1)\frac{1}{\sigma} \odot S_x[f(x,y)]\right] \\ &= (-1)\frac{1}{\sigma^2} \odot S_y[f(0,y)] \ominus_{gH} (-1)\frac{1}{\sigma} \odot S_y[S_x[f(x,y)]] \\ &= (-1)\frac{1}{\sigma^2} \odot S_y[f(0,y)] \ominus_{gH} (-1)\frac{1}{\sigma} \odot F(\sigma,\delta). \end{aligned}$$

A similar procedure can be used to prove the case (ii).

$$\begin{aligned} &S_2[f''_{xx}(x,y)] = S_y[S_x[f''_{xx}(x,y)]] \\ &= S_y\left[(-1)\frac{1}{\sigma^2} \odot f'_x(0,y) \ominus_{gH} \left(\frac{1}{\sigma^3} \odot f(0,y) \ominus_{gH} \frac{1}{\sigma^2} \odot S_x[f(x,y)]\right)\right] \\ &= (-1)\frac{1}{\sigma^2} \odot S_y[f'_x(0,y)] \ominus_{gH} \left(\frac{1}{\sigma^3} \odot S_y[f(0,y)] \ominus_{gH} \frac{1}{\sigma^2} \odot S_y[S_x[f(x,y)]]\right) \\ &= (-1)\frac{1}{\sigma^2} \odot S_y[f'_x(0,y)] \ominus_{gH} \left(\frac{1}{\sigma^3} \odot S_y[f(0,y)] \ominus_{gH} \frac{1}{\sigma^2} \odot F(\sigma,\delta)\right). \end{aligned}$$

The proof of case (iv) is analogous to the proof of case (iii).

$$\begin{aligned} &S_2[f''_{xy}(x,y)] = S_x[S_y[f''_{xy}(x,y)]] \\ &= S_x\left[(-1)\frac{1}{\delta^2} \odot f'_x(x,0) \ominus_{gH} \frac{1}{\delta} \odot S_y[f'_x(x,y)]\right] \\ &= (-1)\frac{1}{\delta^2} \odot S_x[f'_x(x,0)] \ominus_{gH} \frac{1}{\delta} \odot S_y[S_x[f'_x(x,y)]] \\ &= (-1)\frac{1}{\delta^2} \odot S_x[f'_x(x,0)] \ominus_{gH} \frac{1}{\delta} \odot S_y\left[(-1)\frac{1}{\sigma^2} \odot f(0,y) \ominus_{gH} (-1)\frac{1}{\sigma} \odot S_x[f(x,y)]\right] \\ &= (-1)\frac{1}{\delta^2} \odot S_x[f'_x(x,0)] \ominus_{gH} \left(\frac{1}{\delta\sigma^2} \odot S_y[f(0,y)] \ominus_{gH} \frac{1}{\delta\sigma} \odot S_y[S_x[f(x,y)]]\right) \\ &= (-1)\frac{1}{\delta^2} \odot S_x[f'_x(x,0)] \ominus_{gH} \left(\frac{1}{\delta\sigma^2} \odot S_y[f(0,y)] \ominus_{gH} \frac{1}{\delta\sigma} \odot F(\sigma,\delta)\right). \end{aligned}$$

The proof of case (vi) is analogous to the proof of case (v). $\square$

5. Double Fuzzy Sawi Transform to Solve Fuzzy Telegraph Equation

In this section, we demonstrate the application of the DFST method for solving of the linear fuzzy telegraph equation. This equation is defined as

$$w''_{xx}(x,t) = a \odot w''_{tt}(x,t) \oplus b \odot w'_t(x,t) \oplus c \odot w(x,t) \oplus g(x,t), \tag{12}$$

where $a,\ b,\ c \in \mathbb{R}_+$, with initial conditions

$$w(x,0) = \psi_0(x),\ \ w'_t(x,0) = \psi_1(x) \tag{13}$$

and boundary conditions

$$w(0,t) = \varphi_0(t),\ \ w'_x(0,t) = \varphi_1(t). \tag{14}$$

We apply DFST for Definition 17 on both side of the Equation (12). By using Theorem 8, we obtain the following

$$S_2[w''_{xx}(x,t)] = a \odot S_2[w''_{tt}(x,t)] \oplus b \odot S_2[w'_t(x,t)] \oplus c \odot S_2[w(x,t)] \oplus S_2[g(x,t)].$$

Applying Theorem 11, we have

$$\begin{aligned}
&(-1)\tfrac{1}{\sigma^2} \odot S_t[w'_x(0,t)] \ominus_{gH} \left(\tfrac{1}{\sigma^3} S_t[w(0,t)] \ominus_{gH} \tfrac{1}{\sigma^2} \odot W(\sigma,\delta)\right) \\
&= a \odot \left[(-1)\tfrac{1}{\delta^2} \odot S_x[w'_t(x,0)] \ominus_{gH} \left(\tfrac{1}{\delta^3} \odot S_x[w(x,0)] \ominus_{gH} \tfrac{1}{\delta^2} \odot W(\sigma,\delta)\right)\right] \\
&\oplus b \odot \left[(-1)\tfrac{1}{\delta^2} \odot S_x[w(x,0)] \ominus_{gH} (-1)\tfrac{1}{\delta} \odot W(\sigma,\delta)\right] \oplus c \odot W(\sigma,\delta) \oplus G(\sigma,\delta),
\end{aligned}$$

where $W(\sigma,\delta) = S_2[w(x,t)]$ and $G(\sigma,\delta) = S_2[g(x,t)]$. Then, from initial conditions (13) and boundary conditions (14), we have

$$\begin{aligned}
&(-1)\tfrac{1}{\sigma^2} \odot S_t[\varphi_1(t)] \ominus_{gH} \left(\tfrac{1}{\sigma^3} S_t[\varphi_0(t)] \ominus_{gH} \tfrac{1}{\sigma^2} \odot W(\sigma,\delta)\right) \\
&= a \odot \left[(-1)\tfrac{1}{\delta^2} \odot S_x[\psi_1(x)] \ominus_{gH} \left(\tfrac{1}{\delta^3} \odot S_x[\psi_0(x)] \ominus_{gH} \tfrac{1}{\delta^2} \odot W(\sigma,\delta)\right)\right] \\
&\oplus b \odot \left[(-1)\tfrac{1}{\delta^2} \odot S_x[\psi_0(x)] \ominus_{gH} (-1)\tfrac{1}{\delta} \odot W(\sigma,\delta)\right] \oplus c \odot W(\sigma,\delta) \oplus G(\sigma,\delta).
\end{aligned}$$

Denote $\Psi_0(\sigma) = S_x[\psi_0(x)]$, $\Psi_1(\sigma) = S_x[\psi_1(x)]$, $\Phi_0(\delta) = S_t[\varphi_0(t)]$ and $\Phi_1(\delta) = S_t[\varphi_1(t)]$. Then, we obtain

$$\begin{aligned}
&(-1)\tfrac{1}{\sigma^2} \odot \Phi_1(\delta) \ominus_{gH} \left(\tfrac{1}{\sigma^3} \Phi_0(\delta) \ominus_{gH} \tfrac{1}{\sigma^2} \odot W(\sigma,\delta)\right) \\
&= a \odot \left[(-1)\tfrac{1}{\delta^2} \odot \Psi_1(\sigma) \ominus_{gH} \left(\tfrac{1}{\delta^3} \odot \Psi_0(\sigma) \ominus_{gH} \tfrac{1}{\delta^2} \odot W(\sigma,\delta)\right)\right] \\
&\oplus b \odot \left[(-1)\tfrac{1}{\delta^2} \odot \Psi_0(\sigma) \ominus_{gH} (-1)\tfrac{1}{\delta} \odot W(\sigma,\delta)\right] \oplus c \odot W(\sigma,\delta) \oplus G(\sigma,\delta).
\end{aligned}$$

Using Proposition 1, we have

$$\begin{aligned}
&\left(\tfrac{1}{\sigma^2} - \tfrac{a}{\delta^2} - \tfrac{b}{\delta} - c\right) \odot W(\sigma,\delta) \\
&= \tfrac{1}{\sigma^2} \odot \Phi_1(\delta) \oplus \tfrac{1}{\sigma^3} \odot \Phi_0(\delta) \oplus \tfrac{-a}{\delta^2} \odot \Psi_1(\sigma) \oplus \left(\tfrac{-a}{\delta^3} - \tfrac{b}{\delta^2}\right) \odot \Psi_0(\sigma) \oplus G(\sigma,\delta).
\end{aligned}$$

Hence,

$$\begin{aligned}
W(\sigma,\delta) &= \tfrac{A}{\sigma^2} \odot \Phi_1(\delta) \oplus \tfrac{A}{\sigma^3} \odot \Phi_0(\delta) \\
&\oplus \tfrac{-a}{\delta^2} A \odot \Psi_1(\sigma) \oplus A\left(\tfrac{-a}{\delta^3} - \tfrac{b}{\delta^2}\right) \odot \Psi_0(\sigma) \oplus A \odot G(\sigma,\delta),
\end{aligned} \tag{15}$$

where

$$A = \frac{\sigma^2\delta^2}{\delta^2 - a\sigma^2 - b\sigma^2\delta - c\sigma^2\delta^2}. \tag{16}$$

Finally, by using the inverse of DFST, we obtain $w(x,t)$.

6. Examples

Example 3. *Consider the homogeneous linear fuzzy telegraphic equation given by*

$$w''_{xx}(x,t) = w''_{tt}(x,t) \oplus w'_t(x,t) \oplus w(x,t), \;\; x \geq 0, \; t \geq 0 \tag{17}$$

with initial conditions

$$w(x,0,r) = e^x \odot (1,2,3), \;\; w'_t(x,0,r) = -e^x \odot (1,2,3) \tag{18}$$

and boundary conditions

$$w(0,t,r) = e^{-t} \odot (1,2,3), \;\; w'_x(0,t,r) = e^{-t} \odot (1,2,3). \tag{19}$$

In this case, $a = b = c = 1$, the functions

$$\psi_0(x) = e^x \odot (1,2,3), \;\; \psi_1(x) = -e^x \odot (1,2,3),$$

$$\varphi_0(t) = e^{-t} \odot (1,2,3), \;\; \varphi_1(t) = e^{-t} \odot (1,2,3).$$

From Definition 14, we have

$$S_x[\psi_0(x)] = \Psi_0(\sigma) = \frac{1}{\sigma(1-\sigma)} \odot (1,2,3), \;\; S_x[\psi_1(x)] = \Psi_1(\sigma) = -\frac{1}{\sigma(1-\sigma)} \odot (1,2,3),$$

$$S_t[\varphi_0(t)] = \Phi_0(\delta) = \frac{1}{\delta(1+\delta)} \odot (1,2,3), \;\; S_t[\varphi_1(t)] = \Phi_1(\delta) = \frac{1}{\delta(1+\delta)} \odot (1,2,3).$$

By using the Equations (15) and (16), we obtain

$$\begin{aligned} W(\sigma,\delta) &= \tfrac{A}{\sigma^2}\tfrac{1}{\delta(1+\delta)} \odot (1,2,3) \oplus \tfrac{A}{\sigma^3}\tfrac{1}{\delta(1+\delta)} \odot (1,2,3) \\ &\oplus \tfrac{A}{\delta^2\sigma(1-\sigma)} \odot (1,2,3) \oplus A\left(\tfrac{-1}{\delta^3} - \tfrac{1}{\delta^2}\right)\tfrac{1}{\sigma(1-\sigma)} \odot (1,2,3), \end{aligned}$$

where

$$A = \frac{\sigma^2\delta^2}{\delta^2 - \sigma^2 - \sigma^2\delta - \sigma^2\delta^2}.$$

Hence,

$$\begin{aligned} W(\sigma,\delta) &= A\left(\tfrac{1}{\sigma^2\delta(1+\delta)} + \tfrac{1}{\sigma^3\delta(1+\delta)} - \tfrac{1}{\sigma\delta^3(1-\sigma)}\right) \odot (1,2,3) \\ &= \tfrac{1}{\sigma(1-\sigma)\delta(1+\delta)} \odot (1,2,3). \end{aligned}$$

Applying the inverse double fuzzy Sawi transform, we find the solution of the Equations (17)–(19) is

$$w(x,t) = e^{x-t} \odot (1,2,3).$$

Example 4. *Suppose the non-homogeneous linear fuzzy telegraph equation that is given as*

$$w''_{xx}(x,t) = w''_{tt}(x,t) \oplus w'_t(x,t) \oplus w(x,t) \oplus g(x,t) \tag{20}$$

with initial conditions

$$w(x,0,r) = e^x \odot (1,2,3), \;\; w'_t(x,0,r) = e^x \odot (1,2,3) \tag{21}$$

and boundary conditions

$$w(0,t,r) = e^t \odot (1,2,3), \;\; w'_x(0,t,r) = e^t \odot (1,2,3), \tag{22}$$

where the function $g(x,t) = -2e^{x+t} \odot (1,2,3)$.

In this case, $a = b = c = 1$, *the functions*

$$\psi_0(x) = e^x \odot (1,2,3), \ \ \psi_1(x) = e^x \odot (1,2,3),$$

$$\varphi_0(t) = e^t \odot (1,2,3), \ \ \varphi_1(t) = e^t \odot (1,2,3).$$

From Definition 14, we have

$$S_x[\psi_0(x)] = \Psi_0(\sigma) = \frac{1}{\sigma(1-\sigma)} \odot (1,2,3), \ \ S_x[\psi_1(x)] = \Psi_1(\sigma) = \frac{1}{\sigma(1-\sigma)} \odot (1,2,3),$$

$$S_t[\varphi_0(t)] = \Phi_0(\delta) = \frac{1}{\delta(1-\delta)} \odot (1,2,3), \ \ S_t[\varphi_1(t)] = \Phi_1(\delta) = \frac{1}{\delta(1-\delta)} \odot (1,2,3),$$

$$G(\sigma,\delta) = \frac{-2}{\sigma\delta(1-\sigma)(1-\delta)} \odot (1,2,3).$$

By using the Equations (15) and (16), we obtain

$$\begin{aligned} W(\sigma,\delta) &= \tfrac{A}{\sigma^2}\tfrac{1}{\delta(1-\delta)} \odot (1,2,3) \oplus \tfrac{A}{\sigma^3}\tfrac{1}{\delta(1-\delta)} \odot (1,2,3) \\ &\oplus \tfrac{-A}{\delta^2}\tfrac{1}{\sigma(1-\sigma)} \odot (1,2,3) \oplus A\left(\tfrac{-1}{\delta^3} - \tfrac{1}{\delta^2}\right)\tfrac{1}{\sigma(1-\sigma)} \odot (1,2,3) \oplus \tfrac{-2A}{\sigma\delta(1-\sigma)(1-\delta)} \odot (1,2,3), \end{aligned}$$

where

$$A = \frac{\sigma^2\delta^2}{\delta^2 - \sigma^2 - \sigma^2\delta - \sigma^2\delta^2}.$$

Hence,

$$\begin{aligned} W(\sigma,\delta) &= A\left(\tfrac{1}{\sigma^2\delta(1-\delta)} + \tfrac{1}{\sigma^3\delta(1-\delta)} - \tfrac{2}{\sigma\delta^2(1-\sigma)} - \tfrac{1-\delta+2\delta^2}{\sigma\delta^3(1-\sigma)(1-\delta)}\right) \odot (1,2,3) \\ &= \tfrac{1}{\sigma(1-\sigma)\delta(1-\delta)} \odot (1,2,3). \end{aligned}$$

Applying the inverse double fuzzy Sawi transform, we find the solution of the Equations (20)–(22) is

$$w(x,t) = e^{x+t} \odot (1,2,3).$$

7. Conclusions

The main idea of this paper is to develop the double fuzzy Sawi transform to solve a fuzzy telegraph equation under gH-differentiability. Fundamental properties of the new double fuzzy transformation are introduced and proven. New results on DFST for fuzzy partial gH-derivatives are obtained. Finally, we apply DFST to solve the linear non-homogeneous fuzzy telegraph equation. A simple formula for its solution is obtained. Some illustrative examples are given to show the validity and efficiency of DFST in solving the linear fuzzy telegraph equations with symmetric characteristics. The results obtained of this study show the strength and simplicity of DFST in solving linear fuzzy partial differential equations.

For future research, we intend to use DFST in solving some fuzzy integro-differential equations, as well as fuzzy partial differential equations from mathematical physics [31,32] due to the advantage of this transform in preserving the constants' values, which reduces the calculations in comparison to other double fuzzy integral transforms.

Author Contributions: Conceptualization, A.T.G., A.P.; methodology, A.T.G., A.P.; validation, A.T.G., A.P.; formal analysis, A.T.G., A.P.; writing—original draft preparation, A.T.G., A.P.; writing—review and editing A.T.G., A.P. All authors have read and agreed to the published version of the manuscript.

Funding: This research received no external funding.

Institutional Review Board Statement: Not applicable.

Informed Consent Statement: Not applicable.

Data Availability Statement: Not applicable.

Conflicts of Interest: The authors declare no conflict of interest.

References

1. Araour, M.; Mennouni, A. A New Procedures for Solving Two Classes of Fuzzy Singular Integro-Differential Equations: Airfoil Collocation Methods. *Int. J. Appl. Comput. Math.* **2022**, *8*, 35. [CrossRef]
2. Kadham, S.; Alkiffai, A. Model Tumor Response to Cancer Treatment Using Fuzzy Partial SH-Transform: An Analytic Study. *Int. J. Math. Comput. Sci.* **2022**, *18*, 23–28.
3. Di Martino, F.; Perfilieva, I.; Sessa, S. A Summary of F-Transform Techniques in Data Analysis. *Electronics* **2021**, *10*, 1771. [CrossRef]
4. Napole, C.; Derbeli, M.; Barambones, O. Experimental Analysis of a Fuzzy Scheme against a Robust Controller for a Proton Exchange Membrane Fuel Cell System. *Symmetry* **2022**, *14*, 139. [CrossRef]
5. Buckley, J.; Feuring, T. Introduction to fuzzy partial differential equations. *Fuzzy Sets Syst.* **1999**, *105*, 241–248. [CrossRef]
6. Allahveranloo, T. Difference methods for fuzzy partial differential equations. *Comput. Methods Appl. Math.* **2002**, *2*, 233–242. [CrossRef]
7. Pownuk, A. Numerical solutions of fuzzy partial differential equations and its applications in computational mechanics. *Stud. Fuzziness Soft Comput.* **2004**, *142*, 308–347.
8. Allahviranloo, T.; Taheri, N. An analytic approximation to the solution of fuzzy heat equation by adomian decomposition method. *Int. J. Contemp. Math. Sci.* **2009**, *4*, 105–114.
9. Osman, M.; Gong, Z.; Mustafa, A. Comparison of fuzzy Adomian decomposition method with fuzzy VIM for solving fuzzy heat-like and wave-like equations with variable coefficients. *Adv. Differ. Equ.* **2020**, 327.. [CrossRef]
10. Gouyandeh, Z.; Allahviranloo, T.; Abbasbandy, S.; Armand, A. A fuzzy solution of heat equation under generalized Hukuhara differentiability by fuzzy Fourier transform. *Fuzzy Sets Syst.* **2017**, *309*, 81–97. [CrossRef]
11. Allahviranloo, T.; Kermani, M.A. Numerical methods for fuzzy linear partial differential equations under new definition for derivative. *Iran. J. Fuzzy Syst.* **2010**, *7*, 33–50.
12. Allahviranloo, T.; Gouyndeh, Z.; Ahmand, A. and Hasanoglu, A. On fuzzy solutions of heat equation based on generalized Hukuhara differentiability. *Fuzzy Sets Syst.* **2015**, *265*, 1–23. [CrossRef]
13. Osman, M.; Xia, Y.; Omer, O.A.; Hamoud, A. On the Fuzzy Solution of Linear-Nonlinear Partial Differential Equations. *Mathematics* **2022**, *10*, 2295. [CrossRef]
14. Rahman, N.A.; Ahmad, M.Z. Fuzzy Sumudu transform for solving fuzzy partial differential equations. *J. Nonlinear Sci. Appl.* **2016**, *9*, 3226–3239. [CrossRef]
15. Rashid, S.; Ashraf, R.; El-Deeb, A.A.; García Guirao, J.L.; Althobaiti, A. A Novel Configuration of the Fuzzy Elzaki Transform for Solving Nonlinear Partial Differential Equations via Fuzzy Fractional Derivative with General Order. *Fractal Fract.* 2021, *in preparation*.
16. Mahgoub, M.M.A.; Mohand, M. The new integral transform "Sawi Transform". *Adv. Theor. Appl. Math.* **2019**, *14*, 81–87.
17. Aggarwal, S.; Gupta, A.R. Dualities between some useful integral transforms and Sawi transform. *Int. J. Recent Technol. Eng.* **2019**, *8*, 5978–5982. [CrossRef]
18. Singh, G.P.; Aggarwal, S. Sawi transform for population growth and decay problems. *Int. J. Latest Technol. Eng.* **2019**, *8*, 157–162.
19. Higazy, M.; Aggarwal, S. Sawi transformation for system of ordinary differential equations with application. *Ain Shams Eng. J.* **2021**, *12*, 3173–3182. [CrossRef]
20. Sahoo, M.; Chakraverty, S. Sawi Transform Based Homotopy Perturbation Method for Solving Shallow Water Wave Equations in Fuzzy Environment. *Mathematics* **2022**, *10*, 2900. [CrossRef]
21. Abdeljawad,T.; Younus, A.; Alqudah, M.A.; Atta, U. On Fuzzy Conformable Double Laplace Transform with Applications to Partial Differential Equations. *Comput. Model. Eng. Sci.* **2023**, *134*, 2163–2191.
22. Georgieva, A. Double Fuzzy Sumudu transform to solve partial Volterra fuzzy integro-differential equations. *Mathematics* **2020**, *8*, 692. [CrossRef]
23. Georgieva, A. Application of double fuzzy Natural transform for solving fuzzy partial equations. *AIP Conf. Proc.* **2021**, *2333*, 080006-1–080006-8.
24. Kshirsagar, K.A.; Nikam, V.R.; Gaikwad, S.B.; Tarate, S.A. The double fuzzy Elzaki transform for solving fuzzy partial differential equations. *J. Chungcheong Math. Soc.* **2022**, *35*, 2.
25. Stabestari, R.M.; Ezzati, R. The Fuzzy Double Laplace Transforms and their Properties with Applications to Fuzzy Wave Equation. *New Math. Nat. Comp.* **2021**, *17*, 319–338. [CrossRef]
26. Goetschel, R.; Voxman, W. Elementary fuzzy calculus. *Fuzzy Sets Syst.* **1986**, *18*, 31–43. [CrossRef]
27. Kaufmann, A.; Gupta, M.M. *Introduction to Fuzzy Arithmetic: Theory and Applications;* Van Nostrand Reinhold Co.: New York, NY, USA, 1991.
28. Bede, B.; Stefanini, L. Generalized differentiability of fuzzy-valued functions. *Fuzzy Sets Syst.* **2013**, *230*, 119–141. [CrossRef]

29. Wu, C.; Wu, C. The supremum and infimum of these to fuzzy-numbers and its applications. *J. Math. Anal. Appl.* **1997**, *210*, 499–511.
30. Georgieva, A.; Pavlova, A. Fuzzy Sawi Decomposition Method for Solving Nonlinear Partial Fuzzy Differential Equations. *Symmetry* **2021**, *13*, 1580. [CrossRef]
31. Issa, M.S.; Hamoud, A.A; Ghadle, K.P. Numerical solutions of fuzzy integro-differential equations of the second kind. *J. Math. Comput. Sci.* **2021**, *23*, 67–74. [CrossRef]
32. Harir, A.; Melliani, S.; Chadli, L.S. Solving fuzzy Burgers equation by variational iteration method. *J. Math. Comput. Sci.* **2020**, *21*, 136–149. [CrossRef]

symmetry

MDPI

Article

Multiple-Attribute Decision Making Based on Intuitionistic Hesitant Fuzzy Connection Set Environment

Wajid Ali [1,*], Tanzeela Shaheen [1], Iftikhar Ul Haq [1], Hamza Ghazanfar Toor [2], Faraz Akram [2], Saeid Jafari [3], Md. Zia Uddin [4] and Mohammad Mehedi Hassan [5]

1 Department of Mathematics, Air University, E-9, Islamabad 44000, Pakistan
2 Biomedical Engineering Department, Riphah International University, Islamabad 46000, Pakistan
3 Mathematical and Physical Science Foundation, 4200 Slagelse, Denmark
4 Software and Service Innovation, SINTEF Digital, 0373 Oslo, Norway
5 Information Systems Department, College of Computer and Information Sciences, King Saud University, Riyadh 11543, Saudi Arabia
* Correspondence: wajidali00258@gmail.com

Abstract: The intuitionistic hesitant fuzzy set (IHFS) is an enriched version of hesitant fuzzy sets (HFSs) that can cover both fuzzy sets (FSs) and intuitionistic fuzzy sets (IFSs). By assigning membership and non-membership grades as subsets of [0, 1], the IHFS can model and handle situations more proficiently. Another related theory is the theory of set pair analysis (SPA), which considers both certainties and uncertainties as a cohesive system and represents them from three aspects: identity, discrepancy, and contrary. In this article, we explore the suitability of combining the IHFS and SPA theories in multi-attribute decision making (MADM) and present the hybrid model named intuitionistic hesitant fuzzy connection number set (IHCS). To facilitate the design of a novel MADM algorithm, we first develop several averaging and geometric aggregation operators on IHCS. Finally, we highlight the benefits of our proposed work, including a comparative examination of the recommended models with a few current models to demonstrate the practicality of an ideal decision in practice. Additionally, we provide a graphical interpretation of the devised attempt to exhibit the consistency and efficiency of our approach.

Keywords: intuitionistic fuzzy set; hesitant fuzzy set; power aggregation operators; connection number; set pair analysis theory

1. Introduction

The technique for picking the most acceptable alternative based on the provided criteria is known as decision making (DM). Various DM procedures are originated via one feature only, but most often, these are dependent upon multiple attributes. The area of DM is then called multiple-attribute DM (MADM). MADM is a highly crucial testing domain, which helps choose the correct option associated with several leading features [1–3]. Mainly, the DM uses crisp figures to describe the preferences concerning the choices in usual MADM problems. Nevertheless, due to the inadequacy of statistics, shortage of time, and lack of data and quality values, fuzzy values may be used to specify the preferences exclusively for the attribute values.

The idea of fuzzy sets (FSs) was introduced by Zadeh [4] in 1965 and, after they have come into existence, several researchers have applied them to solve various problems and developed symmetrical decision models [5–7]. Every fuzzy set has a pair of each component with a function of membership, where this function provides a membership grade in $[0,1]$. Later, several extensions of this fuzzy set have been proposed by the researchers. Atanassov [8,9] proposed an intuitionistic fuzzy set (IFS) in 1986. The IFS expresses ambiguous and complex information with the aid of the membership as well as non-membership grades, where the sum of both grades cannot exceed 1. The IFS has been getting a lot of attention since its initiation. For instance, Garg and Arora [10] stated a decision-making algorithm for the DMPs ("decision-making problems") with "interval-valued intuitionistic fuzzy soft set" features. Zeng et al. [11] defined the generalized probabilistic ordered operators for DMPs. Eom and Lee [12] elaborated the intuitionistic fuzzy theta-compact space. In Refs. [13,14], the authors have defined an application of the intuitionistic fuzzy pairs to solve the different DMPs. Bustince and Burillo [15] and Park et al. [16] defined the correlation coefficients for an interval-valued IFS. Atanassov [17] stated some novel topological operators over the IFS. In terms of ranking the different pairs of IFSs, several researchers have defined various measures such as the accuracy function [18], similarity measures [19], and grey relational analysis [20]-based algorithms for DMPs. Jiang et al. [21] defined the distance measures based on the transformation techniques of IFSs and their application to the "pattern recognition" problems. In [22,23], the authors have defined some generalized aggregation operators to aggregate the different pairs of IFSs and their applications to the DMPs.

In the above-mentioned literature, all the studies considered the input as a real number. However, to address the uncertainties in a more generalized manner, Torra [24,25] presented the concept of the hesitant fuzzy set (HFS). An HFS agrees to the membership grade holding a set of possible values of the interval from 0 to 1. An HFS is also an expanded form of the FS. The idea of the HFS is broadly applied in several complications. Most scholars performed a critical investigation on HF data accumulation procedures and their effects in DMPs. For instance, Mahmood et al. [26] defined the aggregation operators of the pairs of the bipolar-valued hesitant fuzzy set to solve the DMPs. Mockor et al. [27] explored the relationship of HFSs with some generalized form of fuzzy sets. Alcantud [28] ranked the different pairs of HFSs for multi-agent decisions. Zhang et al. [29] presented an extended LINMAP method with HFS information for green-supplier selection problems. Xia et al. [30] stated some operators for HFSs. Shaheen et al. [31] defined the concept of hesitant fuzzy rough sets. Sun and Ouyang [32] stated a TOPSIS-based decision-making algorithm for the DMPs. Ni et al. [33] stated a projection method for DMPs using the dual HFS. Liu and Sun [34] proposed generalized power operators for DMPs using the pairs of HFSs. Tahir et al. [35] described the concept of an IHFS ("intuitionistic hesitant fuzzy set") which is a fusion of the IFS and the HFS. In the IHFS, the grades reflect in the form of a set of possible values from $[0,1]$. Admittedly, the IHFS has developed as a potent tool for explaining the fuzziness of the DM complexities.

Aside from the aforementioned ideas, Zhao [36] suggested another approach, recognized as set pair analysis (SPA), to cope with uncertainty. This concept harmonizes the system of assurance and apprehension in a specific evaluation. The most important part of this concept is the CN ("connection number"); it is split into three kinds of senses: identity, inconsistency, and opposition. The fundamental properties of the CNs are defined by Jiang et al. [37]. Later, several researchers showed interest in explaining DM difficulties using set pair analysis (SPA) [38–40]. However, Kumar and Garg [41,42] outlined the different formulae of connection numbers to resolve the DM problems applying the TOPSIS method. Zhang [43] developed the relationship between fuzzy sets and the theory of SPA. After considering the relationship between both theories, Hu et al. [44] defined a dynamic stochastic multiple-attribute DM course. Jia et al. [45] determined the distance measures for MADM based on CNs.

The two foremost steps involved in MADM are, firstly, the aggregation phase to determine the total value of the selected option by combining the given performance values of all the attributes through the suitable integration process; and, secondly, the manipulation phase for choosing the best option. In this paper [46], the authors employ many approaches to support the MD process, such as a combination of the DEA window analysis with the Malmquist index approach to assess the efficiency of the cybersecurity industry, and a framework based on multicriteria decision making (MCDM) is provided that integrates the spherical fuzzy analytical hierarchical process (SF-AHP) and the grey complex proportional assessment (G-COPRAS), in which spherical fuzzy sets and grey numbers are used to express the ambiguous linguistic evaluation statements of experts [47]. For the aggregation phase, during the last twenty years, experts have worked hard to develop aggregation operators, used to tackle DM difficulties. For example, Xu and Yager [48] established a few fundamental geometric aggregation (GA) operators named the IF-WGA operator and IF-OWG operator, which are applied for DM based upon the intuitionistic fuzzy set. Zhang [49] established some aggregation operators and aggregated the hesitant fuzzy environment. Yager [50] demonstrated a power aggregation operator and confirmed its role in MADM. Ahmmad et al. [51] used the Aczel–Alsina Average aggregation operator for medical diagnosis. Mehmood et al. [52] produced the Hamacher Choquet-integral aggregation operators for ranking. Moreover, Tahir et al. [35] established some AOs for IHFSs and PHFSs for decision making.

The above-described aggregation operators are extensively applied to aggregate the preference values for getting the best results. However, during the research, these operators exceeded the association between the data provided. Through research, we have explored the idea that the CN of the theory of SPA can be applied extensively for MADM. Considering this aspect, we define the intuitionistic hesitant fuzzy connection number set (IHCS) by merging the prominent features of the IHFS and the SPA, and the applications of fuzzy logic in different fields should also be mentioned in the literature review. The related works were suggested as follows [53–56]. In addition, this article establishes a sequence of aggregation operators. The inspiration and attainments of this paper are presented below:

1. The origination of some PA operators, such as the IHCPA, IHCPWA, IHCPOWA, IHCPHA, IHCPG, IHCPWG, IHCPOWG, and IHCPHG operators, and verifying their properties;
2. Proposing a novel MADM technique that involves the developed operations;
3. Furnishing specific mathematical examples to validate the consistency and supremacy of the presented approach.

The rest of the article is organized as follows: In Section 2, we briefly overview the concept of the HFS and SPA theory. In Section 3, we defined the concept of IHFCNS ("intuitionistic hesitant fuzzy connection number set") and stated its properties. In Section 4, we proposed an MADM algorithm with the stated operators to address the DMPs. To validate the performance of the proposed algorithm, a numerical example is given in Section 5. Finally, a conclusion is drawn in Section 6. The detailed flow chart of the proposed study is shown in Figure 1.

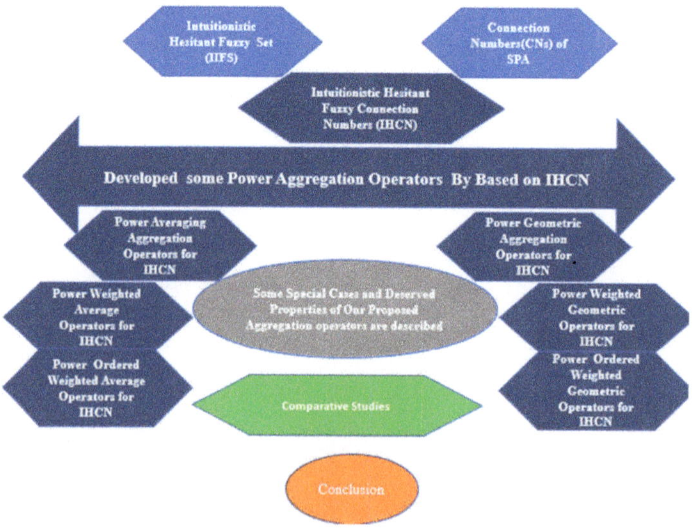

Figure 1. Flow chart of the manuscript.

2. Preliminaries

This section includes a few fundamental concepts related to the present studies on the intuitionistic hesitant fuzzy set and the theory of SPA.

Definition 1 ([35]). *The supporting mappings for an IHFS are ϕ, ψ: $\mathcal{F} \rightarrow [0,1]$. With the aid of these mappings, IHFS $\mathcal{Z}_i$ over $\mathcal{F}$ is described as below:*

$$\mathcal{Z}_i = \{(\varsigma_i, \phi_{\mathcal{Z}}(\varsigma_i), \psi_{\mathcal{Z}}(\varsigma_i)) | \varsigma_i \in \mathcal{F}\} \tag{1}$$

where $0 \leq max(\phi_{\mathcal{Z}}(\varsigma_i)) + max(\psi_{\mathcal{Z}}(\varsigma_i)) \leq 1$. $\phi_{\mathcal{Z}}(\varsigma_i)$ and $\psi_{\mathcal{Z}}(\varsigma_i)$ are collections of certain amounts in [0, 1], representing the membership grades and non-membership grades of the component $\varsigma_i \in \mathcal{F}$.

Remark 1.

1. *For each $\varsigma_i \in \mathcal{F}$, $\mathcal{Z}_i = (\phi_{\mathcal{Z}}(\varsigma_i), \psi_{\mathcal{Z}}(\varsigma_i))$ is the IHFE.*
2. *It is assumed that the largest element will be repeated to make the lengths of the two IHFEs the same in the IHFSs.*
3. *The elements in the IHFSs will be arranged in ascending order for comparison purposes.*

Definition 2 ([35]). *For IHFS $\mathcal{Z} = (\phi_{\mathcal{Z}}, \psi_{\mathcal{Z}})$, the score function ($\mathcal{S}c(\mathcal{Z})$) as well as accuracy function ($\mathcal{T}(\mathcal{Z})$) are expressed as:*

$$\mathcal{S}c(\mathcal{Z}) = \frac{\mathcal{S}c(\phi_{\mathcal{Z}}) - \mathcal{S}c(\psi_{\mathcal{Z}})}{2}, \mathcal{S}c(\mathcal{Z}) \in [-1,\ 1]$$

$$\mathcal{T}(\mathcal{Z}) = \frac{\mathcal{S}c(\phi_{\mathcal{Z}}) + \mathcal{S}c(\psi_{\mathcal{Z}})}{2}, \mathcal{T}(\mathcal{Z}) \in [0,\ 1]$$

where $\mathcal{S}c(\phi_{\mathcal{Z}}) = \frac{sum\ of\ all\ elements\ in\ (\phi_{\mathcal{Z}})}{order\ of\ (\phi_{\mathcal{Z}})}$ and $\mathcal{S}c(\psi_{\mathcal{Z}}) = \frac{sum\ of\ all\ elements\ in\ (\psi_{\mathcal{Z}})}{order\ of\ (\psi_{\mathcal{Z}})}$.

Definition 3 ([35]). *An IHFS $\mathcal{Z}_1$ will be preferred over $\mathcal{Z}_2$, denoted by $\mathcal{Z}_1 > \mathcal{Z}_2$, based upon the following criteria:*

(i) $\mathcal{S}c(\mathcal{Z}_1) > \mathcal{S}c(\mathcal{Z}_2)$;
(ii) $\mathcal{S}c(\mathcal{Z}_1) = \mathcal{S}c(\mathcal{Z}_2)$ and $\mathcal{T}(\mathcal{Z}_1) > \mathcal{T}(\mathcal{Z}_2)$

Definition 4 ([35]). *The intuitionistic hesitant fuzzy power average and geometric operators are denoted and defined, respectively, as follows:*

$$IHFPA(\mathcal{Z}_1\mathcal{Z}_2 \ldots, \mathcal{Z}_n)$$

$$= \bigcup_{\substack{h_i \varepsilon \phi_i \\ f_i \varepsilon \psi_i}} \left(1 - \prod_{i=1}^{n}\left(1 - (h_i)^{\frac{(1+T(\mathcal{Z}_i))}{\sum_{i=1}^{n}(1+T(\mathcal{Z}_i))}}\right), \prod_{i=1}^{n}(f_i)^{\frac{(1+T(\mathcal{Z}_i))}{\sum_{i=1}^{n}(1+T(\mathcal{Z}_i))}}\right)$$

and

$$IHFPG\ (\mathcal{Z}_1\mathcal{Z}_2 \ldots, \mathcal{Z}_n)$$

$$= \bigcup_{\substack{h_i \varepsilon \phi_i \\ f_i \varepsilon \psi_i}} \left(\prod_{i=1}^{n}(h_i)^{\frac{(1+T(\mathcal{Z}_i))}{\sum_{i=1}^{n}(1+T(\mathcal{Z}_i))}}, 1 - \prod_{i=1}^{n}(1 - (f_i)^{\frac{(1+T(\mathcal{Z}_i))}{\sum_{i=1}^{n}(1+T(\mathcal{Z}_i))}})\right)$$

where

$$T(\mathcal{Z}_i) = \bigcup_{\substack{\phi_i \varepsilon \mathcal{Z}_i \\ \psi_i \varepsilon \mathcal{Z}_i}} \left(\sum_{\substack{i=1 \\ i \neq j}}^{n} Sup(\mathcal{Z}_i, \mathcal{Z}_j)\right)$$

The theory of SPA is based on a pair of sets that are interrelated and unified under a certain construction. The examples may include the system and surroundings, the system and engineering, military problems, state security, etc. SPA analyzes the common attributes and establishes a connection degree ($\mathcal{J} = \alpha + \beta i + \gamma j$) of two such sets according to the given settings. The theory is further extended for more than two sets.

Definition 5 ([36]). *The connection degree is defined as*

$$\mathcal{J} = \frac{S}{N} + \frac{F}{N}i + \frac{P}{N}j$$

$$\mathcal{J} = \alpha + \beta i + \gamma \quad (2)$$

where N represents "all attributes", S represents "identity attributes", P represents "contrary attributes", and $F = N - S - P$ represents the amount of "mutual attributes" of the two sets that are neither identity nor contrary. $\alpha = \frac{S}{N}, \beta = \frac{F}{N}, \gamma = \frac{P}{N}$ are, respectively, called the identity degree, discrepancy degree, and contrary degree of the two sets. According to the given circumstances, i (contrary degree) and j (discrepancy degree) can be specified from $[-1,\ 1]$. Clearly, $\alpha + \beta + \gamma = 1$.

3. Proposed IHCS and Aggregation Operators

This portion includes the establishment of a new concept by combining the IHFS and CN of the theory of SPA, called the intuitionistic hesitant fuzzy connection number set (IHCS). Based on this definition, a sequence of new aggregation operators is developed. These proposed operators and their properties have been analyzed and their suitability is portrayed in some newly developed algorithm.

Definition 6. *An intuitionistic hesitant fuzzy CN set (IHCS) corresponding to IHFS $\mathcal{Z} = \{(\varsigma_i, \phi(\varsigma_i), \psi(\varsigma_i)) | \varsigma_i \in \mathcal{F}\}$ is denoted and defined as*

$$\mathcal{J}_{\mathcal{Z}} = \{(\varsigma_i, \alpha_{\mathcal{Z}}(\varsigma_i) + \beta_{\mathcal{Z}}(\varsigma_i)i + \gamma_{\mathcal{Z}}(\varsigma_i)j | \varsigma_i \in \mathcal{F}\} \quad (3)$$

where $\alpha_{\mathcal{Z}}(\varsigma_i) = \frac{1}{m}\sum_{l=1}^{m}(\{h_l(1-f_l)\}), \beta_{\mathcal{Z}}(\varsigma_i) = \frac{1}{m}\sum_{l=1}^{m}(\{1 - h_l(1-f_l) - f_l(1-h_l)\})$, and $\gamma_{\mathcal{Z}}(\varsigma_i) = \frac{1}{m}\sum_{l=1}^{m}(\{f_l(1-h_l)\})$, and $h_l \in \phi_{\mathcal{Z}}(\varsigma_i)$ and $f_l \in \psi_{\mathcal{Z}}(\varsigma_i)$ are arbitrary elements of the membership and non-membership sets. Here, $\alpha_{\mathcal{Z}}(\varsigma_i), \beta_{\mathcal{Z}}(\varsigma_i)$, and $\gamma_{\mathcal{Z}}(\varsigma_i)$ signify the "identity," "discrepancy", and "contrary" degrees.

For a particular $k, \alpha_{\mathcal{Z}}(\varsigma_k) + \beta_{\mathcal{Z}}(\varsigma_k)i + \gamma_{\mathcal{Z}}(\varsigma_k)j$, this represents the intuitionistic hesitant fuzzy connection number IHCN. Without loss of generality, it will be written as $\alpha_k + \beta_k i + \gamma_k j$.

Remark 2.

1. *For each $\varsigma_i \in \mathcal{F}, \mathcal{J}_{\mathcal{Z}} = \alpha_{\mathcal{Z}}(\varsigma_i) + \beta_{\mathcal{Z}}(\varsigma_i)i + \gamma_{\mathcal{Z}}(\varsigma_i)j$ will be considered as an intuitionistic hesitant fuzzy connection number element.*
2. *Throughout the article, the lengths of the IHFEs will be kept similar by repeating the maximum value in the smaller one.*
3. *h_l, f_l $(l = 1, 2, \ldots, m)$ represents the IHFEs in ascending order.*
4. *The components of the IHCS are considered as IHCEs.*

Definition 7. *For two IHCEs $\mathcal{J}_1 = \alpha_1 + \beta_1 i + \gamma_1 j$ and $\mathcal{J}_2 = \alpha_2 + \beta_2 i + \gamma_2(\varsigma_i)j$, we have*

i. $\mathcal{J}_1(\varsigma_i) = \mathcal{J}_2(.\varsigma_i) \Leftrightarrow \alpha_1(\varsigma_i) = \alpha_2(\varsigma_i), \beta_1(\varsigma_i) = \beta_1(\varsigma_i), \gamma_1(\varsigma_i) = \gamma_2(\varsigma_i)$;
ii. $\mathcal{J}_1(\varsigma_i) \leq \mathcal{J}_2(\varsigma_i)\ if\ \alpha_1(\varsigma_i) \leq \alpha_2(\varsigma_i), \gamma_1(\varsigma_i) \geq \gamma_2(\varsigma_i)$;
iii. $\mathcal{J}_1(\varsigma_i)^c = \gamma_1(\varsigma_i) + \beta_1(\varsigma_i)i + \alpha_1(\varsigma_i)j$ represents the complement of the IHCE $\mathcal{J}_1(\varsigma_i)$.

Definition 8. *Let $\mathcal{J}_1 = \alpha_1 + \beta_1 i + \gamma_1 j$ and $\mathcal{J}_2 = \alpha_2 + \beta_2 i + \gamma_2 j$ be two IHCEs; then,*

i. $\mathcal{J}_1 \oplus \mathcal{J}_2 = (1 - (1-\alpha_1)(1-\alpha_2)) + ((\beta_1 + \gamma_1)(\beta_2 + \gamma_2) - \beta_1\beta_2)i + (\beta_1\beta_2)j$;

ii. $\mathcal{J}_1 \otimes \mathcal{J}_2 = \alpha_1\alpha_2 + (1-(1-\beta_1)(1-\beta_2))i + ((\alpha_1+\gamma_1)(\alpha_2+\gamma_2) - \alpha_1\alpha_2)j$;
iii. $\mathcal{J}_1{}^{\lambda} = a_1{}^{\lambda} + \left(1-(1-b_1)^{\lambda}\right)i + \left((a_1+c_1)^{\lambda} - a_1^{\lambda}\right)j, \lambda > 0$.

It is straightforward to prove that these operators generate IHCEs.

Definition 9. *For a group of IHCEs $\mathcal{J}_i (i = 1, 2, \ldots, n)$, the power averaging operator IHCPA: $\mathcal{J}^n \to \mathcal{J}$ is defined as*

$$IHCPA(\mathcal{J}_1, \mathcal{J}_2, \ldots \mathcal{J}_n) = \frac{\bigoplus_{i=1}^{n} (1+T(\mathcal{J}_i))\mathcal{J}_i}{\sum_{i=1}^{n}(1+T(\mathcal{J}_i))} \tag{4}$$

$$= \left(1 - \prod_{i=1}^{n}\left(1-(\alpha_i)^{\frac{(1+T(\mathcal{J}_i)))}{\sum_{i=1}^{n}(1+T(\mathcal{J}_i))}}\right)\right) + \left(\prod_{i=1}^{n}(\beta_i+\gamma_i)^{\frac{(1+T(\mathcal{J}_i))}{\sum_{i=1}^{n}(1+T(\mathcal{J}_i))}} - \prod_{i=1}^{n}(\beta_i)^{\frac{(1+T(\mathcal{J}_i))}{\sum_{i=1}^{n}(1+T(\mathcal{J}_i))}}\right)i + \left(\prod_{i=1}^{n}(\beta_i)^{\frac{(1+T(\mathcal{J}_i))}{\sum_{i=1}^{n}(1+T(\mathcal{J}_i))}}\right) \tag{5}$$

wherever $T(\mathcal{J}_i)$ is the Sup of the ith biggest IHCE ($\mathcal{J}_i$) by all the other IHCEs, that is,

$$T(\mathcal{J}_i) = \sum_{\substack{j=1 \\ j \neq i}}^{n} Sup(\mathcal{J}_i, \mathcal{J}_j)$$

Here, $Sup(\mathcal{J}_i, \mathcal{J}_j)$ is the Sup for $\mathcal{J}_i$ from $\mathcal{J}_j$, and it is calculated by:

$$Sup(\mathcal{J}_i, \mathcal{J}_j) = 1 - d(\mathcal{J}_i, \mathcal{J}_j)$$

Sup satisfies the given properties:

i. $Sup\ (\mathcal{J}_i, \mathcal{J}_j) \in [0, 1]$;
ii. $Sup\ (\mathcal{J}_i, \mathcal{J}_j) = Sup\ (\mathcal{J}_j, \mathcal{J}_i)$;
iii. $Sup\ (\mathcal{J}_i, \mathcal{J}_j) \geq Sup\ (\mathcal{J}_s, \mathcal{J}_t), if\ d(\mathcal{J}_i - \mathcal{J}_j) < d(\mathcal{J}_s - \mathcal{J}_t)$ where d is distance.

The support (Sup) amount is a similarity indicator.

Definition 10. *Let $\mathcal{J}_i$ be a group of IHCEs and $\omega = (\omega_1, \omega_2, \ldots, \omega_n)^T$ by the weight vector of $\mathcal{J}_i$, $\omega_i > 0$, and $\sum_{i=1}^{n} \omega_i = 1$. The power weight averaging operator IHCPWA: $\mathcal{J}^n \to \mathcal{J}$ is defined as*

$$IHCPWA(\mathcal{J}_1, \mathcal{J}_2, \ldots, \mathcal{J}_n) = \frac{\bigoplus_{i=1}^{n} (\omega_i(1+T(\mathcal{J}_i)\mathcal{J}_i)}{\sum_{i=1}^{n}\omega_i(1+T(\mathcal{J}_i))}$$

$$= 1 - \prod_{i=1}^{n}\left(1-(\alpha_i)^{\frac{\omega_i(1+T(\mathcal{J}_i))}{\sum_{i=1}^{n}\omega_i(1+T(\mathcal{J}_i))}}\right) + \left(\prod_{i=1}^{n}(\beta_i+\gamma_i)^{\frac{\omega_i(1+T(\mathcal{J}_i))}{\sum_{i=1}^{n}\omega_i(1+T(\mathcal{J}_i))}} - \prod_{i=1}^{n}(\beta_i)^{\frac{\omega_i(1+T(\mathcal{J}_i))}{\sum_{i=1}^{n}\omega_i(1+T(\mathcal{J}_i))}}\right)i + \left(\prod_{i=1}^{n}(\beta_i)^{\frac{\omega_i(1+T(\mathcal{J}_i))}{\sum_{i=1}^{n}\omega_i(1+T(\mathcal{J}_i))}}\right)j \tag{6}$$

The following properties can be easily justified for the IHCPWA operators.

Property 1: (Idempotency) *Suppose* $\mathcal{J}_i$ $(i = 1, 2, 3 \cdots, n)$ *are* $\mathcal{J}_i = \mathcal{J}$ *for each i ; then,*

$$IHCPWA(\mathcal{J}_1, \mathcal{J}_2, \ldots, \mathcal{J}_n) = \mathcal{J}$$

Property 2: (Boundedness) *Suppose* $\mathcal{J}_i$ *is a collection of IHCEs, and permits*

$$\mathcal{J}^- = \min_i \mathcal{J}_i, \mathcal{J}^+ = \max_i \mathcal{J}_i (i = 1, 2, \ldots, n)$$

then

$$\mathcal{J}^- \leq IHCPWA(\mathcal{J}_1, \mathcal{J}_2, \ldots, \mathcal{J}_n) \leq \mathcal{J}^+$$

Property 3: (Monotonicity) *Suppose* $\mathcal{J}_i$ *and* $\mathcal{J}'_i$ *are collections of IHCEs; if* $\mathcal{J}_i \leq \mathcal{J}'_i$ *for all i , then*

$$IHCPWA(\mathcal{J}_1, \mathcal{J}_2, \ldots, \mathcal{J}_n) \leq IHCPWA(\mathcal{J}'_1, \mathcal{J}'_2, \ldots, \mathcal{J}'_n)$$

Definition 11. *Let* $\mathcal{J}_i$ *be a group of IHCEs; the power order weight averaging operator of dimension "n", related with the weight vector* $\omega = (\omega_1, \omega_2, \ldots, \omega_i)^T$ *such that* $\omega_i > 0$ *and* $\sum_{i=1}^n \omega_i = 1$ *, IHCPOWA:* $\mathcal{J}^n \to \mathcal{J}$ *, is defined as*

$$IHCPOWA(\mathcal{J}_1, \mathcal{J}_2, \ldots, \mathcal{J}_n) = \frac{\bigoplus_{i=1}^{n} (\omega_i(1 + T(\mathcal{J}_{\sigma(i)})\mathcal{J}_{\sigma(i)}))}{\sum_{i=1}^n \omega_i(1 + T(\mathcal{J}_{\sigma(i)}))}$$
$$= 1 - \prod_{i=1}^{n}\left(1 - \left(\alpha_{\sigma(i)}\right)^{\frac{\omega_i(1+T(\mathcal{J}_{\sigma(i)}))}{\sum_{i=1}^n \omega_i(1+T(\mathcal{J}_{\sigma(i)}))}} + \left(\prod_{i=1}^{n}\left(\beta_{\sigma(i)} + \gamma_{\sigma(i)}\right)^{\frac{\omega_i(1+T(\mathcal{J}_{\sigma(i)}))}{\sum_{i=1}^n \omega_i(1+T(\mathcal{J}_{\sigma(i)}))}} - \prod_{i=1}^{n}\left(\beta_{\sigma(i)}\right)^{\frac{\omega_i(1+T(\mathcal{J}_{\sigma(i)}))}{\sum_{i=1}^n \omega_i(1+T(\mathcal{J}_{\sigma(i)}))}}\right) i + \left(\prod_{i=1}^{n}\left(\beta_{\sigma(i)}\right)^{\frac{\omega_i(1+T(\mathcal{J}_{\sigma(i)}))}{\sum_{i=1}^n \omega_i(1+T(\mathcal{J}_{\sigma(i)}))}}\right) j\right) \quad (7)$$

where $\sigma(1), \sigma(2), \ldots, \sigma(n)$ indicates a permutation of $(1, 2, \ldots, n)$, in which $\mathcal{J}_{\sigma(i-1)} \geq \mathcal{J}_{\sigma(i)}$, $\omega_i(i = 1, 2, \ldots, n)$ is a group of weights so that

$$\omega_i = g\left(\frac{R_i}{TV}\right) - g\left(\frac{R_{i-1}}{TV}\right), R_i = \sum_{i=1}^n V_{\sigma(i)}, TV = \sum_{i=1}^n V_{\sigma(i)}, V_{\sigma(i.)} = 1. + T\left(\mathcal{J}_{\sigma(i)}\right)$$

and $T\left(\mathcal{J}_{\sigma(j)}\right)$ implies the Sup of the jth largest IHCE $T\left(\mathcal{J}_{\sigma(j)}\right)$ by all the other (IHCEs), that is,

$$T\left(\mathcal{J}_{\sigma(j)}\right) = \sum_{\substack{i=1 \\ i \neq j}}^{n} Sup\left(\mathcal{J}_{\sigma(j)}, \mathcal{J}_{\sigma(i)}\right)$$

where $\sum_{\substack{i=1 \\ i \neq j}}^{n} Sup\left(\mathcal{J}_{\sigma(j)}, \mathcal{J}_{\sigma(i)}\right)$ shows the Sup of the jth is the biggest IHCE $\mathcal{J}_{\sigma(j)}$, for the ith largest IHCE $\mathcal{J}_{\sigma(i)}$.

Some properties of the IHCPOWA operator are as follows:

Property 4: (Idempotency) *Suppose* $\mathcal{J}_i(i = 1, 2, 3 \cdots, n)$ *are* $\mathcal{J}_i = \mathcal{J}$ *for every i; then,*

$$\text{IHCPOWA}(\mathcal{J}_1, \mathcal{J}_2, \ldots, \mathcal{J}_n) = \mathcal{J}$$

Property 5: (Boundedness) *Let $\mathcal{J}_i$ be a group of IHCEs and allow*

$$\mathcal{J}^- = \min_i \mathcal{J}_i, \quad \mathcal{J}^+ = \max_i \mathcal{J}_i \; (i = 1, 2, \ldots, n)$$

then

$$\mathcal{J}^- \leq IHCPOWA((\mathcal{J}_1, \mathcal{J}_2, \ldots, \mathcal{J}_n) \leq \mathcal{J}^+$$

Property 6: (Monotonicity) *Let $\mathcal{J}_i$ and $\mathcal{J}'_i$ be two set of IHCEs; if $\mathcal{J}_i \leq \mathcal{J}'_i$ for all i , then*

$$IHCPOWA(\mathcal{J}_1, \mathcal{J}_2, \ldots, \mathcal{J}_n) \leq IHCPOWA(\mathcal{J}'_1, \mathcal{J}'_2, \ldots, \mathcal{J}'_n)$$

Property 7: (Commutativity) *Let $\mathcal{J}_i$ and $\mathcal{J}'_i$ be two set of IHCEs; if $\mathcal{J}_i \leq \mathcal{J}'_i$ for all i, then*

$$IHCPOWA(\mathcal{J}_1, \mathcal{J}_2, \ldots, \mathcal{J}_n) = IHCPOWA(\mathcal{J}'_1, \mathcal{J}'_2, \ldots, \mathcal{J}'_n)$$

where $\mathcal{J}'_j$ is a permutation of $\mathcal{J}_j$.

Definition 12. *Suppose $\mathcal{J}_i$ is group of IHCEs; the power hybrid averaging operator IHCPHA: $\mathcal{J}^n \to \mathcal{J}$ is defined as*

$$IHCNPHA(\mathcal{J}_1, \mathcal{J}_2, \ldots, \mathcal{J}_n) = \frac{\overset{n}{\underset{i=1}{\oplus}} (\omega_i(1 + T(\dot{\mathcal{J}}_{\sigma(i)})\dot{\mathcal{J}}_{\sigma(i)}))}{\sum_{i=1}^n \omega_i \left(1 + T\left(\dot{\mathcal{J}}_{\sigma(i)}\right)\right)}$$

$$= 1 - \prod_{i=1}^n \left(1 - \left(\dot{\alpha}_{\sigma(i)}\right)^{\frac{\omega_i(1+T(\dot{\mathcal{J}}_{\sigma(i)}))}{\sum_{i=1}^n \omega_i(1+T(\dot{\mathcal{J}}_{\sigma(i)}))}}\right) + \left(\begin{array}{l} \prod_{i=1}^n \left(\dot{\beta}_{\sigma(i)} + \dot{\gamma}_{\sigma(i)}\right)^{\frac{\omega_i(1+T(\dot{\mathcal{J}}_{\sigma(i)}))}{\sum_{i=1}^n \omega_i(1+T(\dot{\mathcal{J}}_{\sigma(i)}))}} \\ -\prod_{i=1}^n \left(\dot{\beta}_{\sigma(i)}\right)^{\frac{\omega_i(1+T(\dot{\mathcal{J}}_{\sigma(i)}))}{\sum_{i=1}^n \omega_i(1+T(\dot{\mathcal{J}}_{\sigma(i)}))}} \end{array}\right) i + \left(\prod_{i=1}^n \left(\dot{\beta}_{\sigma(i)}\right)^{\frac{\omega_i(1+T(\dot{\mathcal{J}}_{\sigma(i)}))}{\sum_{i=1}^n \omega_i(1+T(\dot{\mathcal{J}}_{\sigma(i)}))}}\right) j \quad (8)$$

where $\omega = (\omega_1, \omega_2, \ldots, \omega_i)^T$ is a represented weight vector, where $\omega_i \in [0, 1]$ and $\sum_{i=1}^n \omega_i = 1$ and $\mathcal{J}_{\sigma(i)}$ is the ith largest objects in the IHCE arguments $\dot{\mathcal{J}}_i$ ($\dot{\mathcal{J}} = (n\omega_i)$ $\mathcal{J}_i$, $i = 1, 2, \ldots, n$), $\omega = (\omega_1, \omega_2, \ldots, \omega_n)$ is the weighting vector of the IHCE arguments $\mathcal{J}_i (i = 1, 2, \ldots, n)$, $\omega_i \in [0, 1]$, and $\sum_{i=1}^n \omega_i = 1$ with ω_i being a group such that

$$\omega_i = g\left(\frac{R_i}{TV}\right) - g\left(\frac{R_{i-1}}{TV}\right), R_i = \sum_{i=1}^j V_{\sigma(i)}, TV = \sum_{i=1}^n V_{\sigma(i)}, V_{\sigma(i)} = 1 + T\left(\dot{\mathcal{J}}_{\sigma(i)}\right)$$

and $T\left(\dot{\mathcal{J}}_{\sigma(i)}\right)$ is the Sup of the jth biggest IHCEs $\dot{\mathcal{J}}_{\sigma(i)}$ by all the other (IHCEs), that is,

$$T\left(\dot{\mathcal{J}}_{\sigma(i)}\right) = \sum_{\substack{i=1 \\ i \neq j}}^n Sup\left(\dot{\mathcal{J}}_{\sigma(j)}, \mathcal{J}_{\sigma(i)}\right)$$

where $\sum_{\substack{i=1 \\ i \neq j}}^{n} Sup\left(\dot{\mathcal{J}}_{\sigma(j)}, \mathcal{J}_{\sigma(i)}\right)$ shows the Sup of the jth biggest IHCE $\dot{\mathcal{J}}_{\sigma(j)}$, for the ith biggest IHCE $\dot{\mathcal{J}}_{\sigma(i)}$. Specifically, the IHCPHA is reduced to the IHCPWA operator if $\omega = \left(\frac{1}{n}, \frac{1}{n}, \ldots, \frac{1}{n}\right)^T$ and the IHCPHA is reduced to the IHCPOWA operator if $\omega = \left(\frac{1}{n}, \frac{1}{n}, \ldots, \frac{1}{n}\right)$.

Definition 13. *Suppose $\mathcal{J}_i$ is family of IHCEs; the power geometric operator IHCPG: $\mathcal{J}^n \rightarrow \mathcal{J}$ is defined as*

$$IHCPG(\mathcal{J}_1, \mathcal{J}_2, \ldots, \mathcal{J}_n) = \underset{i=1}{\overset{n}{\otimes}} (\mathcal{J})^{\frac{1+T(\mathcal{J}_i)}{\sum_{i=1}^{n}(1+T(\mathcal{J}_i))}} \tag{9}$$

$$= \prod_{i=1}^{n}(\alpha_i)^{\frac{(1+T(\mathcal{J}_i))}{\sum_{i=1}^{n}(1+T(\mathcal{J}_i))}} + \left(1 - \prod_{i=1}^{n}(1-\beta_i)^{\frac{(1+T(\mathcal{J}_i))}{\sum_{i=1}^{n}(1+T(\mathcal{J}_i))}}\right)i + \left(\prod_{i=1}^{n}(\alpha_i+\gamma_i)^{\frac{(1+T(\mathcal{J}_i))}{\sum_{i=1}^{n}(1+T(\mathcal{J}_i))}} - \prod_{i=1}^{n}(\alpha_i)^{\frac{(1+T(\mathcal{J}_i))}{\sum_{i=1}^{n}(1+T(\mathcal{J}_i))}}\right)j \tag{10}$$

where

$$T(\mathcal{J}_i) = \sum_{\substack{j=1 \\ i \neq j}}^{n} Sup\,(\mathcal{J}_i, \mathcal{J}_j)$$

Definition 14. *Let $\mathcal{J}_i$ be a group of IHCEs and $\omega = (\omega_1, \omega_2, \ldots, \omega_n)^T$ be the weight vector of $\mathcal{J}_i$, $\omega_i > 0$ and $\sum_{i=1}^{n}\omega_i = 1$. The power weight geometric operator IHCPWG: $\mathcal{J}^n \rightarrow \mathcal{J}$ is defined as*

$$IHCPWG(\mathcal{J}_1, \mathcal{J}_2, \ldots, \mathcal{J}_n) = \underset{i=1}{\overset{n}{\otimes}} (\mathcal{J})^{\frac{\omega_i(1+T(\mathcal{J}_i))}{\sum_{i=1}^{n}\omega_i(1+T(\mathcal{J}_i))}}$$

$$= \prod_{i=1}^{n}(\alpha_i)^{\frac{\omega_i(1+T(\mathcal{J}_i))}{\sum_{i=1}^{n}\omega_i(1+T(\mathcal{J}_i))}} + \left(1 - \prod_{i=1}^{n}(1-\beta_i)^{\frac{\omega_i(1+T(\mathcal{J}_i))}{\sum_{i=1}^{n}\omega_i(1+T(\mathcal{J}_i))}}\right)i + \left(\prod_{i=1}^{n}(\alpha_i+\gamma_i)^{\frac{\omega_i(1+T(\mathcal{J}_i))}{\sum_{i=1}^{n}\omega_i(1+T(\mathcal{J}_i))}} - \prod_{i=1}^{n}(\alpha_i)^{\frac{\omega_i(1+T(\mathcal{J}_i))}{\sum_{i=1}^{n}\omega_i(1+T(\mathcal{J}_i))}}\right)j \tag{11}$$

The following characteristics can be easily proven for the IHCPWG operator.

Property 8: (Idempotency) *When $\mathcal{J}_i(i = 1, 2, 3 \cdots, n)$ are $\mathcal{J}_i = \mathcal{J}$ for each i, then*

$$IHCPWG(\mathcal{J}_1, \mathcal{J}_2, \ldots, \mathcal{J}_n) = \mathcal{J}$$

Property 9: (Boundedness) *Suppose $\mathcal{J}_i$ is a group of IHCEs, and permits*

$$\mathcal{J}^- = \min_i \mathcal{J}_i, \mathcal{J}^+ = \max_i \mathcal{J}_i \ (i = 1, 2, \ldots, n)$$

then

$$\mathcal{J}^- \leq IHCPWG(\mathcal{J}_1, \mathcal{J}_2, \ldots, \mathcal{J}_n) \leq \mathcal{J}^+$$

Property 10: (Monotonicity) *Let $\mathcal{J}_i$ and $\mathcal{J}'_i$ be two sets of IHCEs; if $\mathcal{J}_i \leq \mathcal{J}'_i$ for all i, then*

$$IHCPWG(\mathcal{J}_1, \mathcal{J}_2, \ldots, \mathcal{J}_n) \leq IHCPWG(\mathcal{J}'_1, \mathcal{J}'_2, \ldots, \mathcal{J}'_n)$$

Definition 15. *Let $\mathcal{J}_i$ be group of IHCEs; the power order weight geometric operator of dimension 'n', related with the weight vector $\omega = (\omega_1, \omega_2, \ldots, \omega_i)^T$ such that $\omega_i > 0$ and $\sum_{i=1}^n \omega_i = 1$, IHCPOWG: $\mathcal{J}^n \to \mathcal{J}$, is defined as*

$$IHCPOWG(\mathcal{J}_1, \mathcal{J}_2, \ldots, \mathcal{J}_n) = \underset{i=1}{\overset{n}{\otimes}} \left(\mathcal{J}_{\sigma(i)}\right)^{\frac{\omega_i(1+T(\mathcal{J}_{\sigma(i)}))}{\sum_{i=1}^n \omega_i(1+T(\mathcal{J}_{\sigma(i)}))}}$$

$$= \prod_{i=1}^n \left(\left(\alpha_{\sigma(i)}\right)^{\frac{\omega_i(1+T(\mathcal{J}_{\sigma(i)}))}{\sum_{i=1}^n \omega_i(1+T(\mathcal{J}_{\sigma(i)}))}} \right) + \left(1 - \prod_{i=1}^n \left(1-\beta_{\sigma(i)}\right)^{\frac{\omega_i(1+T(\mathcal{J}_{\sigma(i)}))}{\sum_{i=1}^n \omega_i(1+T(\mathcal{J}_{\sigma(i)}))}}\right) i + \left(\prod_{i=1}^n \left(\alpha_{\sigma(i)} + \gamma_{\sigma(i)}\right)^{\frac{\omega_i(1+T(\mathcal{J}_{\sigma(i)}))}{\sum_{i=1}^n \omega_i(1+T(\mathcal{J}_{\sigma(i)}))}} - \prod_{i=1}^n \left(\alpha_{\sigma(i)}\right)^{\frac{\omega_i(1+T(\mathcal{J}_{\sigma(i)}))}{\sum_{i=1}^n \omega_i(1+T(\mathcal{J}_{\sigma(i)}))}} \right) j \tag{12}$$

where $\sigma(1), \sigma(2), \ldots, \sigma(n)$ indicates a permutation of $(1, 2, \ldots, n)$, where $\mathcal{J}_{\sigma(i-1)} \geq \mathcal{J}_{\sigma(i)}$, and $\omega_i (i = 1, 2, \ldots, n)$ is group of weights so that

$$\omega_i = g\left(\frac{R_i}{TV}\right) - g\left(\frac{R_{i-1}}{TV}\right), R_j = \sum_{i=1}^{j} V_{\sigma(i)}, TV = \sum_{i=1}^{n} V_{\sigma(i)}, V_{\sigma(i.)} = 1. + T\left(\mathcal{J}_{\sigma(i)}\right)$$

and $T\left(\mathcal{J}_{\sigma(i)}\right)$ implies the Sup of the ith biggest IHCE $\mathcal{J}_{\sigma(i)}$ by all the other (IHCEs), that is,

$$T\left(\mathcal{J}_{\sigma(i)}\right) = \sum_{\substack{j=1 \\ i \neq j}}^{n} Sup\left(\mathcal{J}_{\sigma(i)}, \mathcal{J}_{\sigma(j)}\right)$$

where $\sum_{\substack{j=1 \\ i \neq j}}^{n} Sup\left(\mathcal{J}_{\sigma(i)}, \mathcal{J}_{\sigma(j)}\right)$ shows the Sup of the ith is the biggest IHCE $\mathcal{J}_{\sigma(i)}$, for the jth largest IHCE $\mathcal{J}_{\sigma(j)}$.

Some properties of the IHCPOWG operator are as follows:

Property 11: (Idempotency) *Let $\mathcal{J}_i$ $(i = 1, 2, 3 \cdots, n)$ be $\mathcal{J}_i = \mathcal{J}$ for every i; then,*

$$IHCPOWG(\mathcal{J}_1, \mathcal{J}_2, \ldots, \mathcal{J}_n) = \mathcal{J}$$

Property 12: (Boundedness) *Suppose $\mathcal{J}_i$ is a group of IHCEs, and permits*

$$\mathcal{J}^- = \min_i \mathcal{J}_i, \quad \mathcal{J}^+ = \max_i \mathcal{J}_i (i = 1, 2, \ldots, n)$$

then

$$\mathcal{J}^- \leq IHCPOWG(\mathcal{J}_1, \mathcal{J}_2, \ldots, \mathcal{J}_n) \leq \mathcal{J}^+$$

Property 13: (Monotonicity) *Let $\mathcal{J}_i$ and $\mathcal{J}'_i$ be two sets of IHCEs; if $\mathcal{J}_i \leq \mathcal{J}'_i$ for all i, then*

$$IHCPOWG(\mathcal{J}_1, \mathcal{J}_2, \ldots, \mathcal{J}_n) \leq IHCPOWG(\mathcal{J}'_1, \mathcal{J}'_2, \ldots, \mathcal{J}'_n)$$

Property 14: (Commutativity) *Let $\mathcal{J}_i$ and $\mathcal{J}'_i$ be two sets of IHCEs; if $\mathcal{J}_i \leq \mathcal{J}'_i$ for all i, then*

$$IHCPOWG(\mathcal{J}_1, \mathcal{J}_2, \ldots, \mathcal{J}_n) = IHCPOWG(\mathcal{J}'_1, \mathcal{J}'_2, \ldots, \mathcal{J}'_n)$$

where $\mathcal{J}'_j$ is a permutation of $\mathcal{J}_j$.

Definition 16. *Suppose $\mathcal{J}_i$ is group of IHCEs; the power hybrid geometric operator of objects 'n' IHCPHG: $\mathcal{J}^n \to \mathcal{J}$ is defined as*

$$IHCPHG(\mathcal{J}_1, \mathcal{J}_2, \ldots, \mathcal{J}_n) = \underset{i=1}{\overset{n}{\otimes}} \left(\dot{\mathcal{J}}_{\sigma(i)}\right)^{\frac{\omega_i(1+T(\dot{\mathcal{J}}_{\sigma(i)}))}{\sum_{i=1}^{n}\omega_i(1+T(\dot{\mathcal{J}}_{\sigma(i)}))}}$$

$$= \prod_{i=1}^{n}\left(\dot{\alpha}_{\sigma(i)}\right)^{\frac{\omega_i(1+T(\dot{\mathcal{J}}_{\sigma(i)}))}{\sum_{i=1}^{n}\omega_i(1+T(\dot{\mathcal{J}}_{\sigma(i)}))}} + \left(1-\prod_{i=1}^{n}\left(1-\dot{\beta}_{\sigma(i)}\right)^{\frac{\omega_i(1+T(\dot{\mathcal{J}}_{\sigma(i)}))}{\sum_{i=1}^{n}\omega_i(1+T(\dot{\mathcal{J}}_{\sigma(i)}))}}\right)i + \left(\prod_{i=1}^{n}\left(\dot{\alpha}_{\sigma(i)}+\dot{\gamma}_{\sigma(i)}\right)^{\frac{\omega_i(1+T(\dot{\mathcal{J}}_{\sigma(i)}))}{\sum_{i=1}^{n}\omega_i(1+T(\dot{\mathcal{J}}_{\sigma(i)}))}} - \prod_{i=1}^{n}\left(\dot{\alpha}_{\sigma(i)}\right)^{\frac{\omega_i(1+T(\dot{\mathcal{J}}_{\sigma(i)}))}{\sum_{i=1}^{n}\omega_i(1+T(\dot{\mathcal{J}}_{\sigma(i)}))}}\right)j \quad (13)$$

where $\omega = (\omega_1, \omega_2, \ldots, \omega_i)^T$ is a represented weight vector, where $\omega_i \in [0,1]$ and $\sum_{i=1}^{n}\omega_i = 1$, and $\mathcal{J}_{\sigma(i)}$ is the ith largest object in the IHCEs arguments $\dot{\mathcal{J}}_i$ ($\dot{\mathcal{J}} = (n\omega_i)\,\mathcal{J}_i$, $i = 1, 2, \ldots, n$), $\omega = (\omega_1, \omega_2, \ldots, \omega_n)$ is the weighting vector of the IHCE influences $\mathcal{J}_i (i = 1, 2, \ldots, n)$, $\omega_i \in [0,1]$. $\sum_{i=1}^{n}\omega_i = 1$, as well as ω_i, is a group where

$$\omega_i = g\left(\frac{R_i}{TV}\right) - g\left(\frac{R_{i-1}}{TV}\right), R_i = \sum_{i=1}^{j} V_{\sigma(i)}, TV = \sum_{i=1}^{n} V_{\sigma(i)}, V_{\sigma(i)} = 1 + T\left(\dot{\mathcal{J}}_{\sigma(i)}\right)$$

and $T\left(\dot{\mathcal{J}}_{\sigma(i)}\right)$ is the Sup of the jth biggest IHCEs $\dot{\mathcal{J}}_{\sigma(i)}$ by all the other IHCEs, that is,

$$T\left(\dot{\mathcal{J}}_{\sigma(i)}\right) = \sum_{\substack{j=1 \\ i \neq j}}^{n} Sup\left(\dot{\mathcal{J}}_{\sigma(i)}, \mathcal{J}_{\sigma(j)}\right)$$

where $\sum_{\substack{j=1 \\ i \neq j}}^{n} Sup\left(\dot{\mathcal{J}}_{\sigma(i)}, \mathcal{J}_{\sigma(j)}\right)$ shows the Sup of the jth largest IHCE $\dot{\mathcal{J}}_{\sigma(j)}$, for the ith biggest IHCE $\dot{\mathcal{J}}_{\sigma(i)}$. Specifically, the IHCPHG is reduced to the IHCPWG operator if $\omega = \left(\frac{1}{n}, \frac{1}{n}, \ldots, \frac{1}{n}\right)^T$ and the IHCPHG is reduced to the IHCNPOWG operator if $\omega = \left(\frac{1}{n}, \frac{1}{n}, \ldots, \frac{1}{n}\right)$.

Theorem 1. *The IHCPA operator aggregates the "n" IHCEs and again generates IHCE.*

Proof 1. *The proof is straightforward.* □

Remark 3. *Similarly, the IHCPWA, IHCPOWA, IHCPHA, IHCPG IHCPWG, IHCPOWG, and IHCPHG also generate the IHCE.*

4. Proposed MADM Algorithm Based on IHCS

This section includes the execution of the proposed operators to DMPs through IHF data. The proposed concepts are applied to denote the MADM challenges for the promising computation of developing technology companies with IHF data. Suppose $\mathfrak{H} = \{\mathfrak{H}_1, \mathfrak{H}_2, \ldots, \mathfrak{H}_m\}$ is the distinctive collection of alternatives, and $\mathfrak{G} = \{\mathfrak{G}_1, \mathfrak{G}_2, \ldots, \mathfrak{G}_n\}$ is the collection of attributes. Suppose $\omega = (\omega_t)(t = 1, 2, \ldots n)$ is the weight vector of the attributes, such that $\omega_t \geq 0$, $\sum_{t=1}^{n} \omega_t = 1$. Therefore, both the IHCPWA and IHCWG operators are applied to the MADM problems for the possible calculation of emerging technology commercialization by the IHF environment.

Step 1. Arrange all data about the alternative in matrix $\mathcal{M} = \left(\check{Y}_{it}\right)_{m \times n}$ in such a way:

$$\mathcal{M} = \begin{matrix} & \mathfrak{G}_1 & \mathfrak{G}_2 & \cdots & \mathfrak{G}_n \\ \mathfrak{H}_1 \\ \mathfrak{H}_2 \\ \vdots \\ \mathfrak{H}_m \end{matrix} \begin{pmatrix} \check{Y}_{11} & \check{Y}_{12} & \cdots & \check{Y}_{1n} \\ \check{Y}_{21} & \check{Y}_{22} & & \check{Y}_{2n} \\ \vdots & \ddots & \ddots & \vdots \\ \check{Y}_{m1} & \check{Y}_{m2} & \cdots & \check{Y}_{mn} \end{pmatrix}$$

Step 2. Formulate the IHCEs $\mathcal{J}_{it} = \alpha_{it} + \beta_{it} i + \gamma_{it} j$ from the IHFEs given in $\check{Y}_{it}$, by using Definition 6.

Step 3. Compute the supports:

$$Sup(\mathcal{J}_{it}, \mathcal{J}_{ik}) = 1 - d(\mathcal{J}_{it}, \mathcal{J}_{ik}), (t, k = 1, 2, \ldots, n) \tag{14}$$

where

$$d(\mathcal{J}_{it}, \mathcal{J}_{ik}) = \frac{1}{3}(|\alpha_{it} - \alpha_{ik}| + |\beta_{it} - \beta_{ik}| + |\gamma_{it} - \gamma_{ik}|) \tag{15}$$

Step 4. Utilize the weights ω_j of attribute $\mathfrak{G}_j$ to calculate the weighted Sup T ($\mathcal{J}_{it}$) of the IHCEs $\mathcal{J}_{it}$ by other IHCEs $\mathcal{J}_{ik}$ $(t, k = 1, 2, \ldots, n, t \neq k)$

$$T(\mathcal{J}_{it}) = \sum_{\substack{k=1 \\ k \neq j}}^{n} \omega_j Sup(\mathcal{J}_{it}, \mathcal{J}_{ik}) \tag{16}$$

and calculate the weight ξ_{it} connected with the IHCEs $\mathcal{J}_{it}$, $(i = 1, 2, \ldots, n, t = 1, 2, \ldots, m)$

$$\xi_{it} = \frac{\omega_t((1 + T(\mathcal{J}_{it}))}{\sum_{i=1}^{n} \omega_t(1 + T(\mathcal{J}_{it}))} \tag{17}$$

where $\xi_{it} \geq 0$ and $\sum_{i=1}^{n} \xi_{it} = 1$.

Step 5. Use the decision data, the IHCPWA operator, and IHCPWG operators

$$\mathcal{J}_t = IHCPWA(\mathcal{J}_{i1}, \mathcal{J}_{i2}, \ldots, \mathcal{J}_{in}) = \frac{\overset{n}{\underset{i=1}{\oplus}} (\omega_i(1 + T(\mathcal{J}_i)\mathcal{J}_i)}{\sum_{i=1}^{n} \omega_i(1 + T(\mathcal{J}_i))}$$

$$= 1 - \prod_{i=1}^{n}\left(1 - (\alpha_{it})^{\xi_{it}}\right) + \left(\prod_{i=1}^{n}(\beta_{it} + \gamma_{it})^{\xi_{it}} - \prod_{i=1}^{n}(\beta_{it})^{\xi_{it}}\right) i + \left(\prod_{i=1}^{n}(\beta_{it})^{\xi_{it}}\right) j \tag{18}$$

and

$$IHCPWG_{\omega}(\mathcal{J}_{t1}, \mathcal{J}_{t2}, \ldots, \mathcal{J}_{tn}) = \underset{i=1}{\overset{n}{\otimes}} (\mathcal{J})^{\xi_{it}}$$

$$= \prod_{i=1}^{n} (\alpha_{it})^{\xi_{it}} + \left(1 - \prod_{i=1}^{n} (1-\beta_{it})^{\xi_{it}}\right) i + \left(\prod_{i=1}^{n} (\alpha_{it} + \gamma_{it})^{\xi_{it}} - \prod_{i=1}^{n} (\alpha_{it})^{\xi_{it}}\right) j \quad (19)$$

to obtain the complete preference elements $\mathcal{J}_i$ of $\mathfrak{H}_t (t = 1, 2, \ldots, m)$.

Step 6. Calculate the scores $Sc(\mathcal{J}_i)$ for the total IHCEs $\mathcal{J}_i$ to rank the $\mathfrak{H}_i$ each, then choose the best one(s).

$$Sc(\mathcal{J}_i) = \frac{1 + (\alpha_i - \gamma_i)(1 + \beta_i)}{2} \quad (20)$$

Step 7. Rank the alternative $\mathfrak{H}_i$ values and select the biggest, considering $(\mathcal{J}_i)$ $(i = 1, 2, \ldots, n)$.

5. Illustrative Example

In this section, we illustrate a mathematical problem to express the potential evaluation of companies of emerging technology by IHF information, demonstrating the method suggested in this paper. In a state of Pakistan, the government wants to contest an election and to overcome fraud and make it fair. The government decided to use technology for this election, so the government decided to develop an electronic voting machine (EVM). To complete this task, the government invites some electronics companies and configures five attributes for selecting the best company for the effort—"project cost" ($\mathfrak{G}_1$),"completion time" ($\mathfrak{G}_2$), "technical capability" ($\mathfrak{G}_3$), "business status" ($\mathfrak{G}_4$), and "company background" ($\mathfrak{G}_5$)—and allocate the weights of the relative importance of every attribute. The weight vector relating to it has been given as $\omega = (0.25, 0.3, 0.1, 0.2, 0.15)^T$ based on the decision maker's preferences. The four electronics companies have taken in this structure of the alternatives, namely, "Noor Manufacturers Ltd." ($\mathfrak{H}_1$), "F&I Electronics Ltd." ($\mathfrak{H}_2$), "Pakistan Software Company" ($\mathfrak{H}_3$), and "Sial Group of Technological Companies" ($\mathfrak{H}_4$), who are interested in these tasks. The major purpose of the task is to select the best company for the project. The steps for the suggested technique are executed as follows:

Step 1: The specialist has calculated all alternatives for the distinct attributes based on the IHFSs as given in Table 1.

Table 1. IHF information corresponding to attributes.

$\mathfrak{G}_1$	$\mathfrak{G}_2$	$\mathfrak{G}_3$	$\mathfrak{G}_4$	$\mathfrak{G}_5$
$(\{0.2, 0.1\}, \{0.1, 0.4\})$	$(\{0.1, 0.2\}, \{0.6, 0.3\})$	$(\{0.1, 0.3\}, \{0.5, 0.1\})$	$(\{0.2, 0.4\}, \{0.1, 0.2\})$	$(\{0.2, 0.1\}, \{0.5, 0.1\})$
$(\{0.1, 0.0\}, \{0.2, 0.2\})$	$(\{0.0, 0.1\}, \{0.1, 0.2\})$	$(\{0.1, 0.1\}, \{0.1, 0.3\})$	$(\{0.1, 0.2\}, \{0.1, 0.3\})$	$(\{0.1, 0.4\}, \{0.1, 0.2\})$
$(\{0.3, 0.2\}, \{0.2, 0.1\})$	$(\{0.1, 0.2\}, \{0.0, 0.1\})$	$(\{0.2, 0.5\}, \{0.2, 0.1\})$	$(\{0.0, 0.6\}, \{0.2, 0.1\})$	$(\{0.2, 0.2\}, \{0.5, 0.2\})$
$(\{0.3, 0.1\}, \{0.2, 0.5\})$	$(\{0.3, 0.5\}, \{0.1, 0.1\})$	$(\{0.1, 0.0\}, \{0.1, 0.2\})$	$(\{0.3, 0.2\}, \{0.2, 0.2\})$	$(\{0.3, 0.5\}, \{0.2, 0.2\})$

Step 2: The IHCE for every IHFS is calculated by using Definition 6, and thus, the calculated results are summarized in Table 2.

Table 2. Developed IHCEs.

$\mathfrak{G}_1$	$\mathfrak{G}_2$	$\mathfrak{G}_3$	$\mathfrak{G}_4$	$\mathfrak{G}_5$
$0.12 + 0.66i + 0.22j$	$0.09 + 0.52i + 0.39j$	$0.16 + 0.58i + 0.26j$	$0.25 + 0.65i + 0.1j$	$0.095 + 0.66i + 0.245j$
$0.04 + 0.77i + 0.19j$	$0.04 + 0.82i + 0.14j$	$0.08 + 0.74i + 0.18j$	$0.115 + 0.72i + 0.165j$	$0.205 + 0.69i + 0.105j$
$0.21 + 0.68i + 0.11j$	$0.14 + 0.82i + 0.04j$	$0.305 + 0.59i + 0.105j$	$0.27 + 0.61i + 0.12j$	$0.13 + 0.59i + 0.28j$
$0.145 + 0.56i + 0.295j$	$0.36 + 0.58i + 0.06j$	$0.045 + 0.81i + 0.145j$	$0.2 + 0.65i + 0.15j$	$0.32 + 0.56i + 0.12j$

Now, we apply the proposed operators to show the possible assessment of the emerging technology companies of the participants developing technology enterprises.
Step 3: Using Equation (14), we calculate the supports $Sup\ (\mathcal{J}_{kt}, \mathcal{J}_{kl})$ among the IHCEs. $(k = 1,2,3,4; t,l = 1,2,3,4,5)$
Step 4: Evaluate the weights $\xi_{it}(i = 1,2,3,4, t = 1,2,3,4,5)$ by applying Equation (17) that are associated with the IHCEs, that include $R = \gamma_{4\times 5}$

$$\xi = \begin{bmatrix} 0.266868\ 0.34021\ 0.075676\ 0.18803\ 0.129215 \\ 0.2630690.3455470.0748770.1910870.125421 \\ 0.2662250.338625\ 0.07573\ \ 0.19356\ \ 0.12686 \\ 0.2608040.3431850.0745490.1925590.128904 \end{bmatrix}$$

Step 5: Utilize the IHCPWA operators and IHCPWG operators given in Equations (18) and (19), respectively, to obtain all IHCEs $\mathcal{J}_{it}(i = 1,2,3,4, t = 1,2,3,4,5)$ of the emerging enterprises $\mathfrak{H}_i$. The aggregating values are reflected in Table 3.

Table 3. Aggregate the finding of the developing enterprises by IHCPWA and IHCPWG operators.

	IHFCNPWA	IHFCNPWG
$\mathfrak{H}_1$	$0.136176 + 0.262893i + 0.600931j$	$0.123867 + 0.609392i + 0.266741$
$\mathfrak{H}_2$	$0.079838 + 0.156161i + 0.76399j$	$0.063278 + 0.770114i + 0.166608j$
$\mathfrak{H}_3$	$0.1972 + 0.113411i + 0.68939j$	$0.185977 + 0.712337i + 0.101686j$
$\mathfrak{H}_4$	$0.251833 + 0.148609i + 0.599558j$	$0.213909 + 0.610781i + 0.17531j$

Step 6: By Equation (20), the values obtained by applying the score function are produced in Table 4.

Table 4. Results after applying score function.

	IHCPWA	IHCPWG
$\mathfrak{H}_1$	0.206531	0.38503
$\mathfrak{H}_2$	0.1045	0.408546
$\mathfrak{H}_3$	0.225995	0.572167
$\mathfrak{H}_4$	0.3003	0.531087

Step 7: Agreeing to the score values given in Table 4 and evaluating the formula of score functions, the rank of the emerging technology companies is stated in Table 5. Recall that this idea " > " indicates "preference."

Table 5. Ranking of the best attributes.

	Ranking
IHCPWA	$\mathfrak{H}_4 > \mathfrak{H}_3 > \mathfrak{H}_1 > \mathfrak{H}_2$
IHCPWG	$\mathfrak{H}_3 > \mathfrak{H}_4 > \mathfrak{H}_2 > \mathfrak{H}_1$

Comparative Study

Now, we will evaluate the execution of the suggested method with the current operators, power averaging aggregation, and power geometric aggregation based on intuitionistic hesitant fuzzy data as proposed by Tahir et al. [35]. We will consider the data of Example 1 for this comparative study, and the outcomes are presented in Table 6.

Table 6. Comparative study with some existing approach discussed.

Methods		Ranking
Tahir et al. [35]	IHFPWA	$\mathfrak{H}_3 > \mathfrak{H}_4 > \mathfrak{H}_2 > \mathfrak{H}_1$
	IHFPWG	$\mathfrak{H}_3 > \mathfrak{H}_4 > \mathfrak{H}_1 > \mathfrak{H}_2$
Proposed method	IHCPWA	$\mathfrak{H}_4 > \mathfrak{H}_3 > \mathfrak{H}_1 > \mathfrak{H}_2$
	IHCPWG	$\mathfrak{H}_3 > \mathfrak{H}_4 > \mathfrak{H}_2 > \mathfrak{H}_1$

By comparison, we obtain the existing approach and the proposed method and their ranking results in Table 6 and Figure 2, which show the geometrical representation that will be helpful for understanding this comparative analysis.

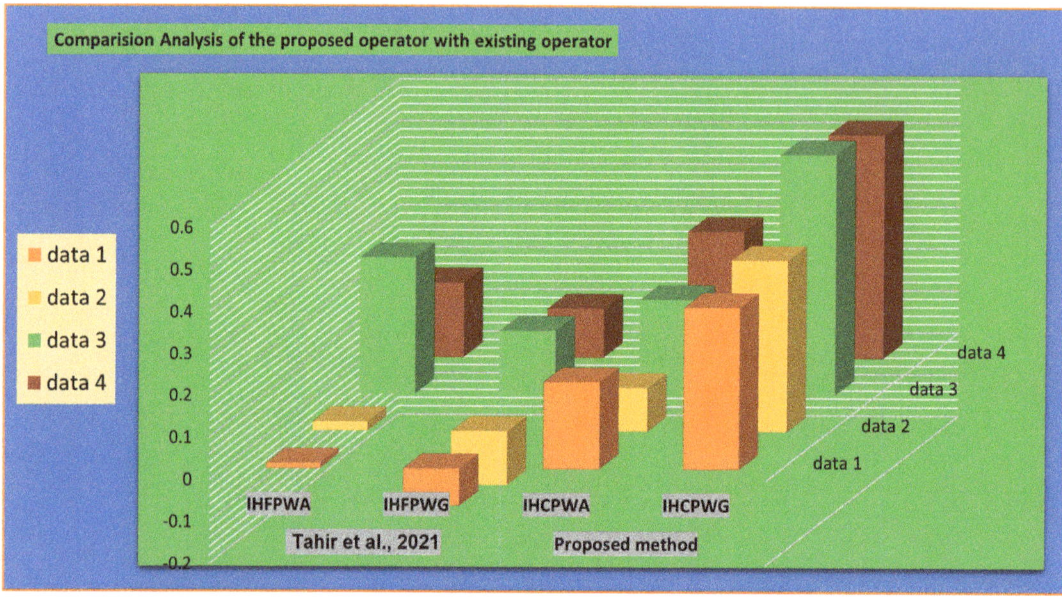

Figure 2. Graphical illustration of the developed and existing operator. Tahir et al. [35].

The advantages and benefits of the proposed notion defined in this paper is a generalized form of the CN defined for the IFS. If we have a singleton set, then the IHFS reduces to the IFS and Definition 6 for the IHFCS reduces to the IFCNS. Therefore, the IHCS is capable of coping with the ambiguity and vagueness of the environment.

6. Conclusions

We have proposed an extension of the intuitionistic hesitant fuzzy set IHFS by integrating it with the CN of SPA, resulting in the intuitionistic hesitant fuzzy connection number set (IHCS). This development has filled certain existing gaps in MADM by facilitating the design of a novel MADM algorithm. The primary contribution of this manuscript is the presentation of novel aggregation operators and basic operational laws of the IHCNs. We explored the concept of power aggregation operators and developed a series of novel operators, including the IHCPA, IHCPG, IHCPWA, IHCPWG, IHCPOWA, IHCPOWG, IHCPHA, and IHCPHG, and verified their novelty with the deserved properties. We validated the proposed methodology by applying it to a real-life problem and demonstrating its feasibility and competency. Additionally, we conducted a comparison analysis of our approach with some existing AO models to establish its validity, authenticity, and effectiveness, and presented a graphical interpretation of the proposed approach. These operators and techniques have numerous applications, including networking analysis, risk assessment, cognitive science, and other areas in uncertain situations. We plan to construct more broadly applicable information metrics to comprehend the information that affects our daily life and investigate our novel techniques in the context of multi-criteria development in the fuzzy environment. We also intend to examine the idea behind our suggested methods within the perspective of square root fuzzy information [57] and ongoing research using a Pythagorean fuzzy system [58].

Author Contributions: Conceptualization, W.A., T.S., I.U.H., H.G.T., F.A., S.J., M.Z.U. and M.M.H.; methodology, W.A. and T.S.; software, W.A.; validation, W.A., T.S., I.U.H., H.G.T., F.A., S.J., M.Z.U. and M.M.H.; formal analysis, W.A. and T.S.; investigation, W.A., T.S., I.U.H., H.G.T., F.A. and S.J.; resources, M.Z.U. and M.M.H.; data curation, W.A., T.S. and I.U.H.; writing—original draft preparation, W.A., T.S., I.U.H., H.G.T., F.A. and S.J.; writing—review and editing, M.Z.U. and M.M.H.; visualization, W.A.; supervision, W.A., T.S. and I.U.H.; funding acquisition, M.M.H. All authors have read and agreed to the published version of the manuscript.

Funding: The authors are grateful to King Saud University, Riyadh, Saudi Arabia for funding this work through Researchers Supporting Project Number (RSP2023R18).

Institutional Review Board Statement: Not applicable.

Informed Consent Statement: Not applicable.

Data Availability Statement: Not applicable.

Conflicts of Interest: The authors declare no conflict of interest.

References

1. Zhang, F.; Ma, W.; Ma, H. Dynamic Chaotic Multi-Attribute Group Decision Making under Weighted T-Spherical Fuzzy Soft Rough Sets. *Symmetry* **2023**, *15*, 307. [CrossRef]
2. Senapati, T. Approaches to multi-attribute decision-making based on picture fuzzy Aczel–Alsina average aggregation operators. *Comput. Appl. Math.* **2022**, *41*, 1–19. [CrossRef]
3. Ullah, K.; Ali, Z.; Jan, N.; Mahmood, T.; Maqsood, S. Multi-Attribute Decision Making Based on Averaging Aggregation Operators for Picture Hesitant Fuzzy Sets. *Tech. J.* **2018**, *23*, 84–95.
4. Zadeh, L.A. Fuzzy sets. *Inf. Control.* **2018**, *8*, 338–353. [CrossRef]
5. Sarfraz, M.; Ullah, K.; Akram, M.; Pamucar, D.; Božanić, D. Prioritized Aggregation Operators for Intuitionistic Fuzzy Information Based on Aczel–Alsina T-Norm and T-Conorm and Their Applications in Group Decision-Making. *Symmetry* **2022**, *14*, 2655. [CrossRef]
6. Jin, H.; Hussain, A.; Ullah, K.; Javed, A. Novel Complex Pythagorean Fuzzy Sets under Aczel–Alsina Operators and Their Application in Multi-Attribute Decision Making. *Symmetry* **2022**, *15*, 68. [CrossRef]
7. Shaheen, T.; Ali, M.I.; Toor, H. Why do we need q-rung orthopair fuzzy sets? Some evidence established via mass assignment. *Int. J. Intell. Syst.* **2021**, *36*, 5493–5505. [CrossRef]
8. Atanassov, K.T. New operations defined over the intuitionistic fuzzy sets. *Fuzzy Sets Syst.* **1994**, *61*, 137–142. [CrossRef]
9. Atanassov, K.T. On the concept of intuitionistic fuzzy sets. In *On Intuitionistic Fuzzy Sets Theory*; Springer: Berlin/Heidelberg, Germany, 2012; pp. 1–16.
10. Garg, H.; Arora, R. A nonlinear-programming methodology for multi-attribute decision-making problem with interval-valued intuitionistic fuzzy soft sets information. *Appl. Intell.* **2018**, *48*, 2031–2046. [CrossRef]
11. Zeng, S.; Su, W.; Zhang, C. Intuitionistic fuzzy generalized probabilistic ordered weighted averaging operator and its application to group decision making. *Technol. Econ. Dev. Econ.* **2016**, *22*, 177–193. [CrossRef]
12. Eom, Y.S.; Lee, S.J. Intuitionistic Fuzzy Theta-Compact Spaces. *Int. J. Fuzzy Log. Intell. Syst.* **2013**, *13*, 224–230. [CrossRef]
13. Liu, P.; Mahmood, T.; Khan, Q. Multi-attribute decision-making based on prioritized aggregation operator under hesitant intuitionistic fuzzy linguistic environment. *Symmetry* **2017**, *9*, 270. [CrossRef]
14. Alcantud, J.C.R.; Khameneh, A.Z.; Kilicman, A. Aggregation of infinite chains of intuitionistic fuzzy sets and their application to choices with temporal intuitionistic fuzzy information. *Inf. Sci.* **2020**, *514*, 106–117. [CrossRef]
15. Bustince, H.; Burillo, P. Correlation of interval-valued intuitionistic fuzzy sets. *Fuzzy Sets Syst.* **1995**, *74*, 237–244. [CrossRef]
16. Park, D.G.; Kwun, Y.C.; Park, J.H.; Park, I.Y. Correlation coefficient of interval-valued intuitionistic fuzzy sets and its application to multiple attribute group decision making problems. *Math. Comput. Model.* **2009**, *50*, 1279–1293. [CrossRef]
17. Atanassov, K.T. New Topological Operator Over Intuitionistic Fuzzy Sets. *J. Comput. Cogn. Eng.* **2022**, *1*, 94–102.
18. Ye, J. Multicriteria fuzzy decision-making method based on a novel accuracy function under interval-valued intuitionistic fuzzy environment. *Expert Syst. Appl.* **2009**, *36*, 6899–6902. [CrossRef]

19. Fei, L.; Wang, H.; Chen, L.; Deng, Y. A new vector valued similarity measure for intuitionistic fuzzy sets based on OWA operators. *Iran. J. Fuzzy Syst.* **2019**, *16*, 113–126.
20. Wei, G.W. Gray relational analysis method for intuitionistic fuzzy multiple attribute decision making. *Expert Syst. Appl.* **2011**, *38*, 11671–11677. [CrossRef]
21. Jiang, Q.; Jin, X.; Lee, S.J.; Yao, S. A new similarity/distance measure between intuitionistic fuzzy sets based on the transformed isosceles triangles and its applications to pattern recognition. *Expert Syst. Appl.* **2019**, *116*, 439–453. [CrossRef]
22. Zhao, H.; Xu, Z.; Ni, M.; Liu, S. Generalized aggregation operators for intuitionistic fuzzy sets. *Int. J. Intell. Syst.* **2010**, *25*, 1–30. [CrossRef]
23. Senapati, T.; Chen, G.; Mesiar, R.; Yager, R.R. Intuitionistic fuzzy geometric aggregation operators in the framework of Aczel-Alsina triangular norms and their application to multiple attribute decision making. *Expert Syst. Appl.* **2023**, *212*, 118832. [CrossRef]
24. Torra, V. Hesitant fuzzy sets. *Int. J. Intell. Syst.* **2010**, *25*, 529–539. [CrossRef]
25. Torra, V.; Narukawa, Y. On hesitant fuzzy sets and decision. In Proceedings of the 2009 IEEE International Conference on Fuzzy Systems, Jeju Island, Republic of Korea, 20–24 2009 August; pp. 1378–1382.
26. Mahmood, T.; Ullah, K.; Jan, N.; Deli, I.; Khan, Q. Some aggregation operators for bipolar-valued hesitant fuzzy information based on Einstein operational laws. *J. Eng. Appl. Sci.* **2017**, 36.
27. Močkoř, J.; Hýnar, D. On unification of methods in theories of fuzzy sets, hesitant fuzzy set, fuzzy soft sets and intuitionistic fuzzy sets. *Mathematics* **2021**, *9*, 447. [CrossRef]
28. Alcantud, J.C.R. Ranked hesitant fuzzy sets for multi-criteria multi-agent decisions. *Expert Syst. Appl.* **2022**, *209*, 118276. [CrossRef]
29. Zhang, N.; Zhou, Q.; Wei, G. Research on Green Supplier Selection Based on Hesitant Fuzzy Set and Extended LINMAP Method. *Int. J. Fuzzy Syst.* **2022**, *24*, 3057–3066. [CrossRef]
30. Xia, M.; Xu, Z.; Chen, N. Some hesitant fuzzy aggregation operators with their application in group decision making. *Group Decis. Negot.* **2013**, *22*, 259–279. [CrossRef]
31. Shaheen, T.; Ali, M.I.; Shabir, M. Generalized hesitant fuzzy rough sets (GHFRS) and their application in risk analysis. *Soft Comput.* **2020**, *24*, 14005–14017. [CrossRef]
32. Sun, Q.; Ouyang, J. Hesitant fuzzy multi-attribute decision making based on TOPSIS with entropy-weighted method. *Manag. Sci. Eng.* **2015**, *9*, 1–6.
33. Ni, Y.; Zhao, H.; Xu, Z.; Wang, Z. Multiple attribute decision-making method based on projection model for dual hesitant fuzzy set. *Fuzzy Optim. Decis. Mak.* **2022**, *21*, 263–289. [CrossRef]
34. Liu, J.; Sun, M. Generalized power average operator of hesitant fuzzy numbers and its application in multiple attribute decision making. *J. Comput. Inf. Syst.* **2013**, *9*, 3051–3058.
35. Mahmood, T.; Ali, W.; Ali, Z.; Chinram, R. Power Aggregation Operators and Similarity Measures Based on Improved Intuitionistic Hesitant Fuzzy Sets and their Applications to Multiple Attribute Decision Making. *Comput. Model. Eng. Sci.* **2021**, *126*, 1165–1187. [CrossRef]
36. Zhao, K.Q. *Set pair and set pair analysis-a new concept and systematic analysis method*; National Conference on System Theory and Regional Planning: Baotou, China, 1989; Volume 5.
37. Jiang, Y.L.; Xu, C.F.; Yao, Y.; Zhao, K.Q. Systems information in set pair analysis and its applications. In Proceedings of the 2004 International Conference on Machine Learning and Cybernetics (IEEE Cat. No. 04EX826), Shanghai, China, 26–29 August 2004; Volume 3, p. 171.
38. ChangJian, W. Application of the set pair analysis theory in multiple attribute decision-making. *J. Mech. Strength* **2007**, *6*, 1009–1012.
39. Lü, W.S.; Zhang, B. Set pair analysis method of containing target constraint mixed interval multi-attribute decision-making. In *Applied Mechanics and Materials*; Trans Tech Publications Ltd.: Stafa-Zurich, Switzerland, 2012; Volume 226, pp. 2222–2226.
40. Xie, Z.; Zhang, F.; Cheng, J.; Li, L. Fuzzy multi-attribute decision making methods based on improved set pair analysis. In Proceedings of the 2013 Sixth International Symposium on Computational Intelligence and Design, Hangzhou, China, 28–29 October 2013; Volume 2, pp. 386–389.
41. Kumar, K.; Garg, H. TOPSIS method based on the connection number of set pair analysis under interval-valued intuitionistic fuzzy set environment. *Comput. Appl. Math.* **2018**, *37*, 1319–1329. [CrossRef]
42. Kumar, K.; Garg, H. Connection number of set pair analysis based TOPSIS method on intuitionistic fuzzy sets and their application to decision making. *Appl. Intell.* **2018**, *48*, 2112–2119. [CrossRef]
43. Shen, Q.; Huang, X.; Liu, Y.; Jiang, Y.; Zhao, K. Multiattribute decision making based on the binary connection number in set pair analysis under an interval-valued intuitionistic fuzzy set environment. *Soft Comput.* **2020**, *24*, 7801–7809. [CrossRef]
44. Hu, J.; Yang, L. Dynamic stochastic multi-criteria decision-making method based on cumulative prospect theory and set pair analysis. *Syst. Eng. Procedia* **2011**, *1*, 432–439. [CrossRef]
45. Liu, J.B.; Malik, M.A.; Ayub, N.; Siddiqui, H.M.A. Distance Measures for Multiple-Attributes Decision-Making Based on Connection Numbers of Set Pair Analysis with Dual Hesitant Fuzzy Sets. *IEEE Access* **2020**, *8*, 9172–9184. [CrossRef]
46. Wang, C.-N.; Yang, F.-C.; Vo, N.T.M.; Nguyen, V.T.T. Wireless communications for data security: Efficiency assessment of cybersecurity industry—A promising application for UAVs. *Drones* **2022**, *6*, 363. [CrossRef]
47. Dang, T.-T.; Nguyen, N.-A.; Nguyen, V.-T.; Dang, L.-T. A two-stage multi-criteria supplier selection model for sustainable automotive supply chain under uncertainty. *Axioms* **2022**, *11*, 228. [CrossRef]

48. Xu, Z.; Yager, R.R. Some geometric aggregation operators based on intuitionistic fuzzy sets. *Int. J. Gen. Syst.* **2006**, *35*, 417–433. [CrossRef]
49. Zhang, Z. Hesitant fuzzy power aggregation operators and their application to multiple attribute group decision making. *Inf. Sci.* **2013**, *234*, 150–181. [CrossRef]
50. Yager, R.R. The power average operator. *IEEE Trans. Syst. Man Cybern.-Part A Syst. Hum.* **2001**, *31*, 724–731. [CrossRef]
51. Ahmmad, J.; Mahmood, T.; Mehmood, N.; Urawong, K.; Chinram, R. Intuitionistic Fuzzy Rough Aczel-Alsina Average Aggregation Operators and Their Applications in Medical Diagnoses. *Symmetry* **2022**, *14*, 2537. [CrossRef]
52. Mahmood, T.; Ali, Z.; Baupradist, S.; Chinram, R. TOPSIS Method Based on Hamacher Choquet-Integral Aggregation Operators for Atanassov-Intuitionistic Fuzzy Sets and Their Applications in Decision-Making. *Axioms* **2022**, *11*, 715. [CrossRef]
53. Peng, F.; Wang, Y.; Xuan, H.; Nguyen, T.V.T. Efficient road traffic anti-collision warning system based on fuzzy nonlinear programming. *Int. J. Syst. Assur. Eng. Manag.* **2022**, *13*, 456–461. [CrossRef]
54. Huynh, N.T.; Nguyen, T.V.; Nguyen, Q.M. Optimum Design for the Magnification Mechanisms Employing Fuzzy Logic-ANFIS. *CMC-COMPUTERS MATERIALS CONTINUA* **2022**, *73*, 5961–5983. [CrossRef]
55. Nguyen, T.V.T.; Huynh, N.-T.; Vu, N.-C.; Kieu, V.N.D.; Huang, S.-C. Optimizing compliant gripper mechanism design by employing an effective bi-algorithm: Fuzzy logic and ANFIS. *Microsyst. Technol.* **2021**, *27*, 3389–3412. [CrossRef]
56. Patel, U.D.; Radenović, S. An Application to Nonlinear Fractional Differential Equation via α-Γ F-Fuzzy Contractive Mappings in a Fuzzy Metric Space. *Mathematics* **2022**, *10*, 2831. [CrossRef]
57. Radenovic, S.; Ali, W.; Shaheen, T.; ul Haq, I.; Akram, F.; Toor, H. Multiple Attribute Decision-Making Based on Bonferroni Mean Operators under Square Root Fuzzy Set Environment. *J. Comput. Cogn. Eng.* **2022**. [CrossRef]
58. Ul Haq, I.; Shaheen, T.; Ali, W.; Senapati, T. A Novel SIR Approach to Closeness Coefficient-Based MAGDM Problems Using Pythagorean Fuzzy Aczel–Alsina Aggregation Operators for Investment Policy. *Discret. Dyn. Nat. Soc.* **2022**, *2022*, 5172679. [CrossRef]

symmetry

Article

Fermatean Fuzzy CODAS Approach with Topology and Its Application to Sustainable Supplier Selection

Hafiz Muhammad Athar Farid [1], Mohamed Bouye [2,*], Muhammad Riaz [1] and Nimra Jamil [1]

1 Department of Mathematics, University of the Punjab, Lahore 54590, Pakistan
2 Department of Mathematics, College of Science, King Khalid University, P.O. Box 9004, Abha 61413, Saudi Arabia
* Correspondence: medeni.doc@gmail.com

Abstract: A Fermatean fuzzy set (FFS) is a reliable method for representing uncertainty in "multi-criteria decision-making" (MCDM). This research seeks to examine the topological properties of FFSs and to establish the notion of "Fermatean fuzzy topology" (FFT). An FFT is the generalisation of existing fuzzy topologies. Several aspects of FFT are examined and various novel concepts are proposed, which include Fermatean fuzzy α-continuity between FFTSs and Fermatean fuzzy connectedness. To deal multiple challenges in sustainable supply chain management, a Fermatean fuzzy "combinative distance-based assessment" (CODAS) method was developed. The proposed FF CODAS technique involves various key features for MCDM. Firstly, a known reputation vector or equal expert weights is determined based on the reputation, experience and qualifications of the experts. Secondly, the Fermatean fuzzy direct rating approach is used to establish the relative relevance of criteria based on the expert group's evaluation preferences. Thirdly, the Fermatean fuzzy CODAS approach is used to construct alternative orderings based on their assessment scores. Finally, an application is developed to show the benefit of the suggested supplier selection approach. Additionally, the symmetry of an optimal decision in application is carried out by a comparison analysis of the suggested models with some existing models.

Keywords: Fermatean fuzzy topology; Fermatean fuzzy α-continuity; topological data analysis; CODAS; supplier selection

MSC: 03E72; 94D05; 90B50

1. Introduction

In computational intelligence challenges, inferring topological and geometrical information from data can provide a novel perspective in mathematical modelling. Methods for "topological data analysis" (TDA) are rapidly expanding methodologies for inferring the permanent and essential characteristics for potentially complicated data. TDA can be utilised autonomously or in tandem with other information-processing and analytical instructional methods. In modern data science, topological methods have been utilised to evaluate the structural aspects of big data, leading to additional information analysis. Utilising a variety of mathematical techniques, topology and geometry are natural instruments for evaluating big datasets. Traditional and basic analysis in a range of computer intelligence domains are inspired by topology and big data. In addition, topology is the link between geographical structures and characteristics, and it may be utilised to explain certain spatial functions and create datasets with a greater level of dependability and integrity. Topological notions such as continuity, convergence and homeomorphisms have a solid geometrical interpretation.

Researchers have investigated a lot of key features in classical set theory and classical topology. Nevertheless, traditional approaches cannot handle ambiguous and unclear information. To solve these concerns, Zadeh [1] developed the concept of "fuzzy set" (FS) theory and "membership function" (MSF), Pawlak [2] proposed rough set theory and approximation spaces, and Molodtsov [3] developed soft set theory and parameterisation. Chang [4] expanded the concept of FSs to fuzzy topological space (TS) and studied several essential features, including open set, closed set, compactness, and continuity in terms of FS theory. Lowen presented a different notion of fuzzy TSs [5,6]. Atanassov [7] further revealed the notion of an "intuitionistic fuzzy set" (IFS) using MSF and "non-membership function" (NMSF). Later, Coker established the concept of intuitionistic fuzzy TS and researched the equivalent versions of traditional topology concepts such as continuity and compactness [8,9]. Additional results on intuitionistic fuzzy TSs are defined in [10,11]. Fuzzy metric spaces provided solutions to the topics concerning distance-like functions, etc. [12]. Thus, instead of particular fixed components, the idea of topology incorporates the MSF structure of fuzziness. The concepts of open and alpha open maps in terms of fuzzy and continuous functions were introduced by Singal and Rajvanshi [13]. Ajmal and Kohli [14] developed the idea of "connectedness in fuzzy TSs" and Chaudhuri and Das [15] initiated the notion of "some fuzzy connected sets in fuzzy TSs". Olgun et al. [16] introduced the "Pythagorean fuzzy TSs", Turkarslan et al. [17] proposed some sort of "q-rung orthopair fuzzy TSs", Joseline and Ajay [18] gave the idea of "Pythagorean fuzzy α-continuity". Haydar defined connectedness for the fuzzy Pythagorean TS [19].

In the modern scientific era, modelling uncertainty as part of MCDM approaches is essential for addressing problems that occur in the actual world. In order to determine how reliable human judgments are, many MCDM techniques have been devised. These procedures include comparing a group of potential outcomes to a set of criteria and rating each possibility accordingly. The gathering and synthesis of information is essential to the operation of a wide variety of technological processes, including machine learning, pattern classification, photogrammetry, and selection. In a general sense, the process of aggregation involves the combination of a great deal of data in order to obtain a conclusion. It was also shown that fundamental data processing algorithms that are based on crisp integers cannot be used to accurately reflect the operating circumstances of human cognitive processes. Because of these strategies, "decision makers" (DMs) are left with confusing facts and judgements that are difficult to understand. As a consequence of this, in order to cope with the ambiguous and fuzzy situations that are present in the world, DMs look for new philosophies that will enable them to understand confusing data values and preserve their judgement demands in response to a variety of settings.

Fuzzy logic is a sort of multi-valued logic in which variable values might vary between 0 and 1. The premise of fuzzy logic is that individuals make judgments based on confusing and non-numerical information. Fuzzy sets are mathematical representations of ambiguity and inaccurate information. They are commonly known as fuzzy models. It is a word used to explain the concept of partial truth, according to which the truth value might vary between false and true. Zadeh proposed a formal framework for making decisions based on imprecise data representations. This concept is based on the fuzzy set, which is a set with no obvious bounds and can only contain things to a given degree; in other words, elements can only be members to a certain degree. Researchers have noticed that the structure of the membership grades is a big concern when utilising fuzzy sets as a result of this. The uncertainty associated with giving an exact numerical membership value to each element in the supplied fuzzy collection is the source of the difficulty. Yager introduced the "Pythagorean fuzzy set" (PFS) [20–22] as well as the "q-rung orthopair fuzzy set" [23]. Senapati and Yager [24] developed the concept of FFSs.

Data processing is crucial for decision making in business, government, sociology, science, intellectual, cognitive, and autonomous systems. In general, awareness of the alternatives has been regarded as a numerical or verbal quantity. Unfortunately, the data cannot easily be amalgamated with regard to ambiguity. Xu et al. [25,26] established geometric and averaging AOs for IFS. Akram et al. [27] proposed the idea of complex Fermatean fuzzy N-soft sets as a hybrid model of N-soft set, FFS, and complex FS. They developed a new hybrid method for decision making with regard to the terrific capability problem based on the Fermatean fuzzy TOPSIS technique approach. A robust work related to the proposed work can be seen in [28].

Riaz et al. [29] developed "linear Diophantine fuzzy prioritised AOs" and Iampan et al. [30] proposed Einstein AOs for LDFSs. Ashraf and Abdullah [31] proposed some mathematical modelling for COVID-19 under a spherical fuzzy set. Some extensive work related to AOs can be seen in [32–37]. Peng et al. [38] introduced some AOs for a "single-valued neutrosophic number" (SVNN). Liu et al. [39] developed some AOs for SVNNs based on "Hamacher operations". Farid and Riaz [40] proposed Einstein interactive AOs for SVNNs. Some extensive work related to operational science in a fuzzy framework was given in [41–44]. The main goals of this study are given as follows:

1. To define the topological structure of FSSs and to propose the concept of fuzzy Fermatean topology;
2. To address the characterisation of Fermatean fuzzy TSs, such as interior, closure, and boundary, etc.;
3. Examining noteworthy results regarding images and inverse images of FFSs under Fermatean fuzzy mapping;
4. To define Fermatean fuzzy α-continuity between FFTSs and Fermatean fuzzy connectedness;
5. Modelling uncertain information in MCDM with Fermatean fuzzy CODAS methods.
6. Data analysis with Fermatean fuzzy CODAS approach for supplier selection and supply chain. A numerical example is illustrated to explain FF CODAS for supplier selection.

The remaining sections of the paper are structured as follows. Section 2 covers the fundamental FFS ideas. In Section 3, the concept of FFT is defined and associated findings are examined. In Section 4, the idea of FF α-continuity is introduced. Section 5 provides basic ideas pertaining to FF connectivity, whereas Section 6 suggests a CODAS structure under the FFSs. Section 7 provides an application regarding the selection of suppliers. Section 8 provides a summary of the planned outcomes, techniques, findings, and their benefits. This section also includes future directions.

2. Fundamental Concepts

In this section of the manuscript, we will review some of the fundamental notions.

Definition 1 ([24])**.** *Assume FFS $\hbar$ in $\overline{\Im}$ is defined as*

$$\hbar = \{\langle \rho, \mu^{\eta}{}_{\hbar}(\rho), \nu^{\eta}{}_{\hbar}(\rho) \rangle : \rho \in \overline{\Im}\}$$

where $\mu^{\eta}{}_{\hbar}, \nu^{\eta}{}_{\hbar} : \overline{\Im} \to [0,1]$ denotes the MSF and NMSF of the alternative $\rho \in \overline{\Im}$ and $\forall \rho$, so we have

$$0 \leq \mu^{\eta 3}_{\hbar}(\rho) + \nu^{\eta 3}_{\hbar}(\rho) \leq 1.$$

Furthermore, $\pi_{\hbar}(\rho) = \sqrt[3]{1 - \mu^{\eta 3}_{\hbar}(\rho) - \nu^{\eta 3}_{\hbar}(\rho)}$ is called the "indeterminacy degree" of ρ to $\hbar$.

Definition 2 ([24])**.** *Let $\tilde{\delta}_1^{\curlywedge} = \langle \mu^{\eta}{}_1, \nu^{\eta}{}_1 \rangle$ and $\tilde{\delta}_2^{\curlywedge} = \langle \mu^{\eta}{}_2, \nu^{\eta}{}_2 \rangle$ be FFNs. Since $\sigma > 0$, then*

(1) $(\tilde{\delta}_1^{\curlywedge})^c = \langle \nu^{\eta}{}_1, \mu^{\eta}{}_1 \rangle$

(2) $\tilde{\delta}_1^{\curlywedge} \vee \tilde{\delta}_2^{\curlywedge} = \langle \max\{\mu^{\eta}{}_1, \nu^{\eta}{}_1\}, \min\{\mu^{\eta}{}_2, \nu^{\eta}{}_2\} \rangle$

(3) $\tilde{\delta}_1^{\curlywedge} \wedge \tilde{\delta}_2^{\curlywedge} = \langle \min\{\mu^{\eta}{}_1, \nu^{\eta}{}_1\}, \max\{\mu^{\eta}{}_2, \nu^{\eta}{}_2\} \rangle$

(4) $\tilde{\delta}_1^{\curlywedge} \oplus \tilde{\delta}_2^{\curlywedge} = \langle \sqrt[3]{\mu^{\eta 3}_1 + \mu^{\eta 3}_2 - \mu^{\eta 3}_1 \mu^{\eta 3}_2}, \nu^{\eta}{}_1 \nu^{\eta}{}_2 \rangle$

(5) $\tilde{\delta}_1^{\curlywedge} \otimes \tilde{\delta}_2^{\curlywedge} = \langle \mu^{\eta}{}_1 \mu^{\eta}{}_2, \sqrt[3]{\nu^{\eta 3}_1 + \nu^{\eta 3}_2 - \nu^{\eta 3}_1 \nu^{\eta 3}_2} \rangle$

(6) $\sigma \tilde{\delta}_1^{\curlywedge} = \langle \sqrt[3]{1 - (1 - \mu^{\eta 3}_1)^{\sigma}}, \nu^{\eta \sigma}_1 \rangle$

(7) $(\tilde{\delta}_1^{\curlywedge})^{\sigma} = \langle \mu^{\eta \sigma}_1, \sqrt[3]{1 - (1 - \nu^{\eta 3}_1)^{\sigma}} \rangle$

Definition 3 ([24]). *Let $\tilde{\delta}^{\curlywedge} = \langle \mu^{\eta}, \nu^{\eta} \rangle$ be the FFN, and the "score function" (SF) S of $\tilde{\delta}^{\curlywedge}$ is defined as*

$$S(\tilde{\delta}^{\curlywedge}) = \mu^{\eta 3} - \nu^{\eta 3}$$

$S(\tilde{\delta}^{\curlywedge}) \in [-1, 1]$. The FFN score will determine its ranking, with the greatest score dictating the FFN's top priority. In other instances, however, the SF is not favourable for FFN. Consequently, using the SF to examine FFNs is inadequate. We are introducing a new function, namely the "accuracy function" (AF).

Definition 4 ([24]). *Let $\tilde{\delta}^{\curlywedge} = \langle \mu^{\eta}, \nu^{\eta} \rangle$ be the FFN, then an AF $\check{L}$ of $\tilde{\delta}^{\curlywedge}$ is defined as*

$$\check{L}(\tilde{\delta}^{\curlywedge}) = \mu^{\eta 3} + \nu^{\eta 3}$$

$\check{L}(\tilde{\delta}^{\curlywedge}) \in [0, 1]$.

Definition 5. *Consider $\tilde{\delta}^{\curlywedge} = \langle \mu^{\eta}{}_{\tilde{\delta}^{\curlywedge}}, \nu^{\eta}{}_{\tilde{\delta}^{\curlywedge}} \rangle$ and $\breve{\mho} = \langle \mu^{\eta}{}_{\breve{\mho}}, \nu^{\eta}{}_{\breve{\mho}} \rangle$ as two FFN, and $S(\tilde{\delta}^{\curlywedge}), S(\breve{\mho})$ are the SF of $\tilde{\delta}^{\curlywedge}$ and $\breve{\mho}$, and $\check{L}(\tilde{\delta}^{\curlywedge}), \check{L}(\breve{\mho})$ are the AFs of $\tilde{\delta}^{\curlywedge}$ and $\breve{\mho}$, respectively, then:*
(a) If $S(\tilde{\delta}^{\curlywedge}) > S(\breve{\mho})$, then $\tilde{\delta}^{\curlywedge} > \breve{\mho}$;
(b) If $S(\tilde{\delta}^{\curlywedge}) = S(\breve{\mho})$ then;

If $\check{L}(\tilde{\delta}^{\curlywedge}) > \check{L}(\breve{\mho})$ then $\tilde{\delta}^{\curlywedge} > \breve{\mho}$;
If $\check{L}(\tilde{\delta}^{\curlywedge}) = \check{L}(\breve{\mho})$, then $\tilde{\delta}^{\curlywedge} = \breve{\mho}$.

Definition 6 ([45]). *Considering $\tilde{\delta}_1^{\curlywedge} = \langle \mu^{\eta}{}_1, \nu^{\eta}{}_1 \rangle$ and $\tilde{\delta}_2^{\curlywedge} = \langle \mu^{\eta}{}_2, \nu^{\eta}{}_2 \rangle$ as FFNs, we define the subtraction and division of FFNs as*

- $\tilde{\delta}_1^{\curlywedge} \ominus \tilde{\delta}_2^{\curlywedge} = \left(\sqrt[3]{\frac{\mu^{\eta 3}_1 - \mu^{\eta 3}_2}{1 - \mu^{\eta 3}_2}}, \frac{\nu^{\eta}1}{\nu^{\eta}2} \right)$, *if* $\mu^{\eta}{}_1 \geq \mu^{\eta}{}_2, \nu^{\eta}{}_1 \leq \min\left\{ \nu^{\eta}{}_2, \frac{\nu^{\eta}{}_2 \pi_1}{\pi_2} \right\}$
- $\tilde{\delta}_1^{\curlywedge} \oslash \tilde{\delta}_2^{\curlywedge} = \left(\frac{\mu^{\eta}{}_1}{\mu^{\eta}{}_2}, \sqrt[3]{\frac{\nu^{\eta}1^3 - \nu^{\eta}2^3}{1 - \nu^{\eta}2^3}} \right)$ *if* $\nu^{\eta}{}_1 \geq \nu^{\eta}{}_2, \mu^{\eta}{}_1 \leq \min\left\{ \mu^{\eta}{}_2, \frac{\mu^{\eta}{}_2 \pi_1}{\pi_2} \right\}$

3. Main Results

In this section, the concept of Fermatean fuzzy topology (FFT) and numerous related results are proposed.

Definition 7. *Let $\Im \neq \emptyset$ be the universe and $\hbar^{\daleth}$ be the assemblage of FF subsets of $\Im$. If $\hbar^{\daleth}$ satisfies the axioms:*

T1 $0_{\Im}, 1_{\Im} \in \hbar^{\daleth}$;

T2 *For any $\chi^{\zeta}{}_1, \chi^{\zeta}{}_2 \in \hbar^{\daleth}$, we have $\chi^{\zeta}{}_1 \cap \chi^{\zeta}{}_2 \in \hbar^{\daleth}$;*

T3 *For any $\{\chi^{\zeta}{}_i\}_{i \in I} \subseteq \hbar^{\daleth}$, we have $\cup_{i \in I} \chi^{\zeta}{}_i \in \hbar^{\daleth}$.*

Then, $\hbar^{\daleth}$ is called an FFT on $\Im$ and the pair $(\Im, \hbar^{\daleth})$ is said to be an FFTS. Each member of $\hbar^{\daleth}$ is called an FF open set (FFOS). The complement of an FF open set is called an FF closed set (FFCS).

Remark 1. *Each IFS and PFS may be considered as an FFS, leading to the conclusion that any IFS topology and PFS topology is an FFT. However, the converse fails to hold.*

Example 1. *Let $\Im = \{\breve{\alpha}_1^{\curlyvee}, \breve{\alpha}_2^{\curlyvee}, \breve{\alpha}_3^{\curlyvee}\}$. Consider the following family of FF subsets $\hbar^{\daleth} = \{0_{\Im}, 1_{\Im}, \chi^{\zeta}{}_1, \dots, \chi^{\zeta}{}_4\}$, where*

$$\chi^{\zeta}{}_1 = \{\langle \breve{\alpha}_1^{\curlyvee}, 0.58, 0.78 \rangle, \langle \breve{\alpha}_2^{\curlyvee}, 0.67, 0.58 \rangle, \langle \breve{\alpha}_3^{\curlyvee}, 0.28, 0.18 \rangle\},$$
$$\chi^{\zeta}{}_2 = \{\langle \breve{\alpha}_1^{\curlyvee}, 0.60, 0.76 \rangle, \langle \breve{\alpha}_2^{\curlyvee}, 0.72, 0.53 \rangle, \langle \breve{\alpha}_3^{\curlyvee}, 0.30, 0.16 \rangle\},$$
$$\chi^{\zeta}{}_3 = \{\langle \breve{\alpha}_1^{\curlyvee}, 0.64, 0.72 \rangle, \langle \breve{\alpha}_2^{\curlyvee}, 0.74, 0.48 \rangle, \langle \breve{\alpha}_3^{\curlyvee}, 0.34, 0.14 \rangle\},$$
$$\chi^{\zeta}{}_4 = \{\langle \breve{\alpha}_1^{\curlyvee}, 0.71, 0.67 \rangle, \langle \breve{\alpha}_2^{\curlyvee}, 0.80, 0.43 \rangle, \langle \breve{\alpha}_3^{\curlyvee}, 0.44, 0.10 \rangle\}.$$

One can see that $(\overline{\Im}, \hbar^{\daleth})$ *is an FFTS.*

Moreover, $\hbar^{\daleth}_1 = \{0_{\overline{\Im}}, 1_{\overline{\Im}}, \chi^{\zeta}_1\}$, $\hbar^{\daleth}_2 = \{0_{\overline{\Im}}, 1_{\overline{\Im}}, \chi^{\zeta}_2\}$, $\hbar^{\daleth}_3 = \{0_{\overline{\Im}}, 1_{\overline{\Im}}, \chi^{\zeta}_3\}$, $\hbar^{\daleth}_4 = \{0_{\overline{\Im}}, 1_{\overline{\Im}}, \chi^{\zeta}_4\}$, $\hbar^{\daleth}_5 = \{0_{\overline{\Im}}, 1_{\overline{\Im}}, \chi^{\zeta}_1, \chi^{\zeta}_2\}$, $\hbar^{\daleth}_6 = \{0_{\overline{\Im}}, 1_{\overline{\Im}}, \chi^{\zeta}_1, \chi^{\zeta}_3\}$, $\hbar^{\daleth}_7 = \{0_{\overline{\Im}}, 1_{\overline{\Im}}, \chi^{\zeta}_1, \chi^{\zeta}_4\}$, $\hbar^{\daleth}_8 = \{0_{\overline{\Im}}, 1_{\overline{\Im}}, \chi^{\zeta}_2, \chi^{\zeta}_3\}$, $\hbar^{\daleth}_9 = \{0_{\overline{\Im}}, 1_{\overline{\Im}}, \chi^{\zeta}_2, \chi^{\zeta}_4\}$, $\hbar^{\daleth}_{10} = \{0_{\overline{\Im}}, 1_{\overline{\Im}}, \chi^{\zeta}_3, \chi^{\zeta}_4\}$, $\hbar^{\daleth}_{11} = \{0_{\overline{\Im}}, 1_{\overline{\Im}}, \chi^{\zeta}_1, \chi^{\zeta}_2, \chi^{\zeta}_3\}$ $\hbar^{\daleth}_{12} = \{0_{\overline{\Im}}, 1_{\overline{\Im}}, \chi^{\zeta}_1, \chi^{\zeta}_3, \chi^{\zeta}_4\}$ are also FFTSs.

Definition 8. *Let* $\overline{\Im}$ *and* $\breve{\Pi}$ *be two non-empty sets, let* $\beth : \overline{\Im} \to \breve{\Pi}$ *be a mapping, and let* $\check{D}$ *and* $\tilde{F}$ *be FF subsets of* $\overline{\Im}$ *and* $\breve{\Pi}$*, respectively. The image of* $\check{D}$ *under mapping* $\beth$ *is denoted by* $\beth[\check{D}]$*. Then, the MSF and NMSF of the image set* $\beth[\check{D}]$ *are defined by*

$$\mu^{\eta}{}_{\beth[\check{D}]}(y) = \begin{cases} \sup_{z \in \beth^{-1}(y)} \mu^{\eta}{}_{\check{D}}(z), & \text{if } \beth^{-1}(y) \neq \emptyset \\ 0, & \text{otherwise} \end{cases}$$

and

$$\nu^{\eta}{}_{\beth[\check{D}]}(y) = \begin{cases} \inf_{z \in \beth^{-1}(y)} \nu^{\eta}{}_{\check{D}}(z), & \text{if } \beth^{-1}(y) \neq \emptyset \\ 0, & \text{otherwise} \end{cases}$$

respectively. The MSF and NMSF of the pre-image of $\tilde{F}$ *with respect to* $\beth$ *that is denoted by* $\beth^{-1}[\tilde{F}]$ *are defined by*

$$\mu^{\eta}{}_{\beth^{-1}[\tilde{F}]}(x) = \mu^{\eta}{}_{\tilde{F}}(\beth(x)) \text{ and } \nu^{\eta}{}_{\beth^{-1}[\tilde{F}]}(x) = \nu^{\eta}{}_{\tilde{F}}(\beth(x)) \text{ respectively.}$$

which show that the $\mu^{\eta 3}_{\beth[\check{D}]} + \nu^{\eta 3}_{\beth[\check{D}]} \leq 1$ *FF membership condition is provided for the FF image and pre-image.*

Proposition 1. *Let* $\overline{\Im}$ *and* $\breve{\Pi}$ *be two non-empty sets and* $\beth : \overline{\Im} \to \breve{\Pi}$ *be an FF mapping. Then, we have*

1. $\beth^{-1}[\tilde{F}^c] = (\beth^{-1}[\tilde{F}])^c$ *for any FF subset* $\tilde{F}$ *of* $\breve{\Pi}$;
2. $(\beth[\check{D}])^c \subseteq \beth[\check{D}^c]$ *for any FF subset* $\check{D}$ *of* $\overline{\Im}$;
3. *If* $\tilde{F}_1 \subseteq \tilde{F}_2$*, then* $\beth^{-1}[\tilde{F}_1] \subseteq \beth^{-1}[\tilde{F}_2]$ *where* $\tilde{F}_1$ *and* $\tilde{F}_2$ *are FF subsets of* $\breve{\Pi}$;
4. *If* $\check{D}_1 \subseteq \check{D}_2$ *then* $\beth[\check{D}_1] \subseteq \beth[\check{D}_2]$ *where* $\check{D}_1$ *and* $\check{D}_2$ *are FF subsets of* $\overline{\Im}$;
5. $\beth[\beth^{-1}[\tilde{F}]] \subseteq \tilde{F}$ *for any FF subset* $\tilde{F}$ *of* $\breve{\Pi}$;
6. $\check{D} \subseteq \beth^{-1}[\beth[\check{D}]]$ *for any FF subset* $\check{D}$ *of* $\overline{\Im}$.

Definition 9. *Let* $\left\{\chi^{\zeta}_i = \left\{\left\langle \breve{\aleph}, \mu^{\eta}{}_{\chi^{\zeta}_i}(\breve{\aleph}), \nu^{\eta}{}_{\chi^{\zeta}_i}(\breve{\aleph}) \right\rangle : \breve{\aleph} \in \overline{\Im}\right\}\right\}_{i \in I}$ *be the assemblage of FF sets over* $\overline{\Im}$*. Then,*

$$\bigcap_{i \in I} \chi^{\zeta}_i = \left\{\left\langle \breve{\aleph}, \in \beth\left\{\mu^{\eta}{}_{\chi^{\zeta}_i}(\breve{\aleph})\right\}, \sup\left\{\nu^{\eta}{}_{\chi^{\zeta}_i}(\breve{\aleph})\right\}\right\rangle : \breve{\aleph} \in \overline{\Im}\right\},$$

$$\bigcup_{i \in I} \chi^{\zeta}_i = \left\{\left\langle \breve{\aleph}, \sup\left\{\mu^{\eta}{}_{\chi^{\zeta}_i}(\breve{\aleph})\right\}, \in \beth\left\{\nu^{\eta}{}_{\chi^{\zeta}_i}(\breve{\aleph})\right\}\right\rangle : \breve{\aleph} \in \overline{\Im}\right\}.$$

Note that $\bigcap_{i \in I} \chi^{\zeta}_i$ *and* $\bigcup_{i \in I} \chi^{\zeta}_i$ *are FF sets over* $\overline{\Im}$*. We shall* $\bigcap_{i \in I} \chi^{\zeta}_i$ *define* $\bigcap_{i \in I} \chi^{\zeta}_i = \left\{\left\langle \breve{\aleph}, \alpha_{\cap \cap_i}, \beta_{i \in I} \chi^{\zeta}_i \right\rangle : \breve{\aleph} \in \overline{\Im}\right\}$ *such that* $\alpha_{n \in \chi^{\zeta}_i} = \in \beth\left\{\mu^{\eta}{}_{\chi^{\zeta}_i}(\breve{\aleph})\right\}$ *and* $\beta_{i \in I} \chi^{\zeta}_i = \sup\left\{\nu^{\eta}{}_{\chi^{\zeta}_i}(\breve{\aleph})\right\}$*. In order to for* $\bigcap_{i \in I} \chi^{\zeta}_i$ *to be an FF set, we must have that* $\alpha^3_{i \in I} \chi^{\zeta}_i(\breve{\aleph}) + \beta^3_{i \in I} \chi^{\zeta}_i(\breve{\aleph}) \leq 1$*. We see since* $\beta^3_{i \in I} \chi^{\zeta}_i(\breve{\aleph}) = \sup\left\{\nu^{\eta 3}_{\chi^{\zeta}_i}(\breve{\aleph})\right\}$*, then*

$$\beta^3_{\cap \in I}\chi^\zeta{}_i(\breve{\aleph}) = \sup\left\{\nu^{\eta 3}{}_{\chi^\zeta{}_i}(\breve{\aleph})\right\} = \sup\left\{r_i^3 - \mu^{\eta 3}{}_{\chi^\zeta{}_i}, r_i^3 - \nu^{\eta 3}{}_{\chi^\zeta{}_i}\right\}$$
$$\leq \sup\left\{r_i^3 - \in \beth\left\{\mu^{\eta 3}{}_{\chi^\zeta{}_i}, \nu^{\eta 3}{}_{\chi^\zeta{}_i}\right\}, r_i^3 - \in \beth\left\{\mu^{\eta 3}{}_{\chi^\zeta{}_i}, \nu^{\eta 3}{}_{\chi^\zeta{}_i}\right\}\right\}$$
$$\beta^3_{i\in I}(\breve{\aleph}) \leq \sup\left\{1 - \in \beth\left\{\mu^{\eta 3}{}_{\chi^\zeta{}_i}, \nu^{\eta 3}{}_{\chi^\zeta{}_i}\right\}\right\}, 1 - \in \beth\left\{\mu^{\eta 3}{}_{\chi^\zeta{}_i}, \nu^{\eta 3}{}_{\chi^\zeta{}_i}\right\}$$
$$\leq 1 - \in \beth\left\{\mu^{\eta 3}{}_{\chi^\zeta{}_i}, \nu^{\eta 3}{}_{\chi^\zeta{}_i}\right\}$$

where $\mu^{\eta 3}{}_{\chi^\zeta{}_i} + \nu^{\eta 3}{}_{\chi^\zeta{}_i} = r_i^3$ *for every* $i \in I$. *From this, we see that* $\alpha^3_{\cap \in I}\chi^\zeta{}_i(\breve{\aleph}) + \beta^3_{\cap \in I}\chi^\zeta{}_i(\breve{\aleph}) \leq \in \beth\left\{\mu^{\eta 3}{}_{\chi^\zeta{}_i}, \nu^{\eta 3}{}_{\chi^\zeta{}_i}\right\} + 1 - \in \beth\left\{\mu^{\eta 3}{}_{\chi^\zeta{}_i}, \nu^{\eta 3}{}_{\chi^\zeta{}_i}\right\} \leq 1$. *Thus,* $\bigcap_{i\in I}\chi^\zeta{}_i$ *is an FF set.*
The proof is trivial for $\cup_{i\in I}\chi^\zeta{}_i$.

Theorem 1. *Let* $\left\{\chi^\zeta{}_i = \left\{\left\langle \breve{\aleph}, \mu^\eta{}_{\chi^\zeta{}_i}(\breve{\aleph}), \nu^\eta{}_{\chi^\zeta{}_i}(\breve{\aleph})\right\rangle : \breve{\aleph} \in \overline{\Im}\right\}\right\}_{i\in I}$ *be the assemblage of FF sets over* $\overline{\Im}$. *Then,*
1. $\overline{\bigcap_{i\in I}\chi^\zeta{}_i} = \cup_{i\in I}\overline{\chi^\zeta{}_i}$;
2. $\overline{\bigcup_{i\in I}\chi^\zeta{}_i} = \bigcap_{i\in I}\overline{\chi^\zeta{}_i}$.

Proof. (1) We have $\bigcap_{i\in I}\chi^\zeta{}_i = \left\{\left\langle \breve{\aleph}, \in \beth\left\{\mu^\eta{}_{\chi^\zeta{}_i}(\breve{\aleph})\right\}, \sup\left\{\nu^\eta{}_{\chi^\zeta{}_i}(\breve{\aleph})\right\}\right\rangle : \breve{\aleph} \in \overline{\Im}\right\}$. Then,

$$\overline{\bigcap_{i\in I}\chi^\zeta{}_i} = \left\{\left\langle \breve{\aleph}, \sup\left\{\nu^\eta{}_{\chi^\zeta{}_i}(\breve{\aleph}), \in \beth\left\{\mu^\eta{}_{\chi^\zeta{}_i}(\breve{\aleph})\right\}\right\}\right\rangle : \breve{\aleph} \in \overline{\Im}\right\}$$

and $\overline{\chi^\zeta{}_i} = \left\{\left\langle \breve{\aleph}, \nu^\eta{}_{\chi^\zeta{}_i}(\breve{\aleph}), \mu^\eta{}_{\chi^\zeta{}_i}(\breve{\aleph})\right\rangle : \breve{\aleph} \in \overline{\Im}\right\}$ and so
$\cup \bar{u}_{i\in I}\overline{\chi^\zeta{}_i} = \left\{\left\langle \breve{\aleph}, \sup\left\{\nu^\eta{}_{\chi^\zeta{}_i}(\breve{\aleph}), \in \beth\left\{\mu^\eta{}_{\chi^\zeta{}_i}(\breve{\aleph})\right\}\right\}\right\rangle : \breve{\aleph} \in \overline{\Im}\right\}$. That is, $\overline{\bigcap_{i\in I}\chi^\zeta{}_i} = \cup_{i\in I}\overline{\chi^\zeta{}_i}$.

(2) It is proven similar to (1). □

Definition 10. *Let* $(\overline{\Im}, \hbar^\beth)$ *be an FFTS and* $\chi^\zeta = \left\{\left\langle \breve{\aleph}, \mu^\eta{}_{\chi^\zeta}(\breve{\aleph}), \nu^\eta{}_{\chi^\zeta}(\breve{\aleph})\right\rangle : \breve{\aleph} \in \overline{\Im}\right\}$ *be an FFS over* $\overline{\Im}$. *Then, the FF interior, FF closure, and FF boundary of* χ^ζ *are defined by:*
1. $Int(\chi^\zeta) = \cup\{\mathfrak{G} : \mathfrak{G}$ *is an FFOS in* $\overline{\Im}$ *and* $\mathfrak{G} \subseteq \chi^\zeta\}$;
2. $Cl(\chi^\zeta) = \cap\{\mathfrak{K} : \mathfrak{K}$ *is an FFCS in* $\overline{\Im}$ *and* $\chi^\zeta \subseteq \mathfrak{K}\}$;
3. $Fr(\chi^\zeta) = Cl(\chi^\zeta) \cap Cl\left(\chi^{\zeta^c}\right)$;
4. $Ext(\chi^\zeta) = Int(\chi^{\zeta^c})$.

It is clear that:
(a) Int (χ^ζ) *is the largest FFOS containing* χ^ζ;
(b) $Cl(\chi^\zeta)$ *is the smallest FFCS containing* χ^ζ.

Example 2. *Assume* $\overline{\Im} = \{\breve{\alpha}^\gamma_1, \breve{\alpha}^\gamma_2, \breve{\alpha}^\gamma_3\}$. *Consider the family of FFSs*

$$\hbar^\beth = \left\{1_{\overline{\Im}}, 0_{\overline{\Im}}, \chi^\zeta{}_1, \chi^\zeta{}_2, \chi^\zeta{}_3, \chi^\zeta{}_4, \right\},$$

where

$$\chi^\zeta{}_1 = \{\langle\breve{\alpha}^\gamma_1, 0.58, 0.78\rangle, \langle\breve{\alpha}^\gamma_2, 0.67, 0.58\rangle, \langle\breve{\alpha}^\gamma_3, 0.28, 0.18\rangle\},$$
$$\chi^\zeta{}_2 = \{\langle\breve{\alpha}^\gamma_1, 0.60, 0.76\rangle, \langle\breve{\alpha}^\gamma_2, 0.72, 0.53\rangle, \langle\breve{\alpha}^\gamma_3, 0.30, 0.16\rangle\},$$
$$\chi^\zeta{}_3 = \{\langle\breve{\alpha}^\gamma_1, 0.64, 0.72\rangle, \langle\breve{\alpha}^\gamma_2, 0.74, 0.48\rangle, \langle\breve{\alpha}^\gamma_3, 0.34, 0.14\rangle\},$$
$$\chi^\zeta{}_4 = \{\langle\breve{\alpha}^\gamma_1, 0.71, 0.67\rangle, \langle\breve{\alpha}^\gamma_2, 0.80, 0.43\rangle, \langle\breve{\alpha}^\gamma_3, 0.44, 0.10\rangle\}.$$

It is clear that $(\overline{\Im}, \hbar^{\beth})$ is an FF TS. Now, assume that

$$\daleth = \{\langle \breve{\alpha}_1^{\gamma}, 0.78, 0.48\rangle, \langle \breve{\alpha}_2^{\gamma}, 0.88, 0.28\rangle, \langle \breve{\alpha}_3^{\gamma}, 0.57, 0.08\rangle\}$$

is an FF subset over $\overline{\Im}$. Then,

$$\begin{aligned} Int(\daleth) &= 0_{\overline{\Im}} \cup \chi^{\zeta}{}_1 \cup \chi^{\zeta}{}_2 \cup \chi^{\zeta}{}_3 \cup \chi^{\zeta}{}_4 \\ &= \chi^{\zeta}{}_4 = \{\langle \breve{\alpha}_1^{\gamma}, 0.71, 0.67\rangle, \langle \breve{\alpha}_2^{\gamma}, 0.80, 0.43\rangle, \langle \breve{\alpha}_3^{\gamma}, 0.44, 0.10\rangle\} \end{aligned}$$

In fact, $Int(\daleth)$ is the largest FFOS contained in FFS $\daleth$.
On the other hand, in order to find the FF closure of χ^{ζ}, it necessary to determine the FFCSs over $\overline{\Im}$. Then,

$$\begin{aligned} \chi^{\zeta c}{}_1 &= \{\langle \breve{\alpha}_1^{\gamma}, 0.78, 0.58\rangle, \langle \breve{\alpha}_2^{\gamma}, 0.58, 0.67\rangle, \langle \breve{\alpha}_3^{\gamma}, 0.18, 0.28\rangle\}, \\ \chi^{\zeta c}{}_2 &= \{\langle \breve{\alpha}_1^{\gamma}, 0.76, 0.60\rangle, \langle \breve{\alpha}_2^{\gamma}, 0.53, 0.72\rangle, \langle \breve{\alpha}_3^{\gamma}, 0.16, 0.30\rangle\}, \\ \chi^{\zeta c}{}_3 &= \{\langle \breve{\alpha}_1^{\gamma}, 0.72, 0.64\rangle, \langle \breve{\alpha}_2^{\gamma}, 0.48, 0.74\rangle, \langle \breve{\alpha}_3^{\gamma}, 0.14, 0.34\rangle\}, \\ \chi^{\zeta c}{}_4 &= \{\langle \breve{\alpha}_1^{\gamma}, 0.67, 0.71\rangle, \langle \breve{\alpha}_2^{\gamma}, 0.43, 0.80\rangle, \langle \breve{\alpha}_3^{\gamma}, 0.10, 0.44\rangle\}. \end{aligned}$$

Now, we obtain

$$\daleth^c = \{\langle \breve{\alpha}_1^{\gamma}, 0.48, 0.78\rangle, \langle \breve{\alpha}_2^{\gamma}, 0.28, 0.88\rangle, \langle \breve{\alpha}_3^{\gamma}, 0.08, 0.57\rangle\}$$

The computations for $Cl(\daleth)$, $Fr(\daleth)$, and $Ext(\daleth)$ are as follows,

$$\begin{aligned} Cl(\daleth) &= 1_{\overline{\Im}} \qquad (1_{\overline{\Im}} \text{ is only closed superset of } \daleth) \\ Cl(\daleth^c) &= 1_{\overline{\Im}} \cap \chi^{\zeta c}{}_1 \cap \chi^{\zeta c}{}_2 \cap \chi^{\zeta c}{}_3 \cap \chi^{\zeta c}{}_4 \\ &= \chi^{\zeta c}{}_4 \qquad (\chi^{\zeta c}{}_4 \text{ is the smallest closed superset of } \daleth) \\ Fr(\daleth) &= Cl(\daleth) \cap Cl(\daleth^c) \\ &= 1_{\overline{\Im}} \cap \chi^{\zeta c}{}_4 \\ &= \chi^{\zeta c}{}_4 \qquad (\chi^{\zeta c}{}_4 \subseteq 1_{\overline{\Im}}) \\ Ext(\daleth) &= Int(\daleth^c) \\ &= 0_{\overline{\Im}} \end{aligned}$$

Remark 2. *In addition, we analyse why certain findings that hold in crisp topology fail in FFT. The results of crisp topology and FFT are shown in Table 1.*

Table 1. Comparison of some results of crisp topology and FFT.

Crisp Topology	Fermatean Fuzzy Topology
$Int(\daleth) \bigcup Ext(\daleth) \bigcup Fr(\daleth) = \overline{\Im}$	$Int(\daleth) \bigcup Ext(\daleth) \bigcup Fr(\daleth) \neq 1_{\overline{\Im}}$
$Int(\daleth) \bigcap Ext(\daleth) = \varnothing$	$Int(\daleth) \bigcap Ext(\daleth) \neq 0_{\overline{\Im}}$
$Ext(\daleth) \bigcap Fr(\daleth) = \varnothing$	$Ext(\daleth) \bigcap Fr(\daleth) \neq 0_{\overline{\Im}}$
$Int(\daleth) \bigcap Fr(\daleth) = \varnothing$	$Int(\daleth) \bigcap Fr(\daleth) \neq 0_{\overline{\Im}}$

Proposition 2. *Let $(\overline{\Im}, \hbar^{\beth})$ be an FFTS and $\chi^{\zeta}, \chi^{\zeta}{}_1, \chi^{\zeta}{}_2$ be FFSs over $\overline{\Im}$. Then, the following properties hold.*

1. $Int(\chi^{\zeta}) \subseteq \chi^{\zeta}$;
2. $Int(Int(\chi^{\zeta})) = Int(\chi^{\zeta})$;
3. $\chi^{\zeta}{}_1 \subseteq \chi^{\zeta}{}_2 \Rightarrow Int(\chi^{\zeta}{}_1) \subseteq Int(\chi^{\zeta}{}_2)$;
4. $Int(\chi^{\zeta}{}_1 \cap \chi^{\zeta}{}_2) = Int(\chi^{\zeta}{}_1) \cap Int(\chi^{\zeta}{}_2)$;
5. $Int(1_{\overline{\Im}}) = 1_{\overline{\Im}}, Int(0_{\overline{\Im}}) = 0_{\overline{\Im}}$;
6. $Int(\chi^{\zeta}{}_1 \cup \chi^{\zeta}{}_2) \subseteq Int(\chi^{\zeta}{}_1) \cap Int(\chi^{\zeta}{}_2)$.

Proof. We can see that (1), (2), (3), and (5) are readily available from the FF interior description.
For (4), we obtain
$Int(\chi^{\zeta}{}_1 \cap \chi^{\zeta}{}_2) \subseteq Int(\chi^{\zeta}{}_1) \cap$ Int $(\chi^{\zeta}{}_2)$ from $Int(\chi^{\zeta}{}_1 \cap \chi^{\zeta}{}_2) \subseteq Int(\chi^{\zeta}{}_1)$ and $Int(\chi^{\zeta}{}_1 \cap \chi^{\zeta}{}_2) \subseteq Int(\chi^{\zeta}{}_2)$. On the other hand, from the facts $Int(\chi^{\zeta}{}_1) \subseteq \chi^{\zeta}{}_1$ and $Int(\chi^{\zeta}{}_2) \subseteq \chi^{\zeta}{}_2 \Rightarrow Int(\chi^{\zeta}{}_1) \cap Int(\chi^{\zeta}{}_2) \subseteq \chi^{\zeta}{}_1 \cap \chi^{\zeta}{}_2$ and $Int(\chi^{\zeta}{}_1) \cap Int(\chi^{\zeta}{}_2) \in \hbar^{\daleth}$, we have $Int(\chi^{\zeta}{}_1) \cap Int(\chi^{\zeta}{}_2) \subseteq Int(\chi^{\zeta}{}_1 \cap \chi^{\zeta}{}_2)$. Thus, the proof of the axioms (4) is obtained from these two inequalities. □

Theorem 2. *Let $\mathcal{P}^{\xi} : FFS(\overline{\Im}) \rightarrow FFS(\overline{\Im})$ be a mapping. The family $\hbar^{\daleth} = \{\chi^{\zeta} \in FFS(\overline{\Im}) : \mathcal{P}^{\xi}(\chi^{\zeta}) = \chi^{\zeta}\}$ is an FF topology over $\overline{\Im}$, if the mapping $\mathcal{P}^{\xi}$ satisfies the following conditions:*
(i) $\mathcal{P}^{\xi}(\chi^{\zeta}) \subseteq \chi^{\zeta}$;
(ii) $\mathcal{P}^{\xi}(1_{\overline{\Im}}) = 1_{\overline{\Im}}$;
(iii) $\mathcal{P}^{\xi}(\mathcal{P}^{\xi}(\chi^{\zeta})) = \mathcal{P}^{\xi}(\chi^{\zeta})$;
(iv) $\mathcal{P}^{\xi}(\chi^{\zeta}{}_1 \cap \chi^{\zeta}{}_2) = \mathcal{P}^{\xi}(\chi^{\zeta}{}_1) \cap \mathcal{P}^{\xi}(\chi^{\zeta}{}_2)$. $\mathcal{P}^{\xi}(\chi^{\zeta}) = Int(\chi^{\zeta})$ for each FF set χ^{ζ} in this FF TS.

Proposition 3. *Let $(\overline{\Im}, \hbar^{\daleth})$ be an FFTS and $\chi^{\zeta}, \chi^{\zeta}{}_1, \chi^{\zeta}{}_2$ be FFSs over $\overline{\Im}$. Then, the following properties hold.*

1. $\chi^{\zeta} \subseteq Cl(\chi^{\zeta})$;
2. $Cl(Cl(\chi^{\zeta})) = Cl(\chi^{\zeta})$;
3. $\chi^{\zeta}{}_1 \subseteq \chi^{\zeta}{}_2 \Rightarrow Cl(\chi^{\zeta}{}_1) \subseteq Cl(\chi^{\zeta}{}_2)$;
4. $Cl(\chi^{\zeta}{}_1 \cup \chi^{\zeta}{}_2) = Cl(\chi^{\zeta}{}_1) \cup Cl(\chi^{\zeta}{}_2)$;
5. $Cl(1_{\overline{\Im}}) = 1_{\overline{\Im}}, Cl(0_{\overline{\Im}}) = 0_{\overline{\Im}}$.

Proof. Here, (1), (2), (3) and (5) can be easily obtained from the definition of the FF closure. For (4), we obtain $Cl(\chi^{\zeta}{}_1) \cup Cl(\chi^{\zeta}{}_2) \subseteq Cl(\chi^{\zeta}{}_1 \cup \chi^{\zeta}{}_2)$ from $Cl(\chi^{\zeta}{}_1) \subseteq Cl(\chi^{\zeta}{}_1 \cup \chi^{\zeta}{}_2)$ and $Cl(\chi^{\zeta}{}_2) \subseteq Cl(\chi^{\zeta}{}_1 \cup \chi^{\zeta}{}_2)$. On the other hand, from the facts $\chi^{\zeta}{}_1 \subseteq Cl(\chi^{\zeta}{}_1)$ and $\chi^{\zeta}{}_2 \subseteq Cl(\chi^{\zeta}{}_2) \Rightarrow \chi^{\zeta}{}_1 \cup \chi^{\zeta}{}_2 \subseteq Cl(\chi^{\zeta}{}_1) \cup Cl(\chi^{\zeta}{}_2)$ and $Cl(\chi^{\zeta}{}_1) \cup Cl(\chi^{\zeta}{}_2) \in \chi^{\zeta}$, we have $Cl(\chi^{\zeta}{}_1 \cup \chi^{\zeta}{}_2) \subseteq Cl(\chi^{\zeta}{}_1) \cup Cl(\chi^{\zeta}{}_2)$. Thus, the proof of the axioms (4) is obtained from these two inequalities. □

Theorem 3. *Let $C : FFS(\overline{\Im}) \rightarrow FFS(\overline{\Im})$ be a mapping. The family*
$\hbar^{\daleth} = \left\{\chi^{\zeta} \in FFS(\overline{\Im}) : C\left(\chi^{\zeta^c}\right) = \chi^{\zeta^c}\right\}$ is an FF topology over $\overline{\Im}$ if the mapping C satisfies the following conditions:

1. $\chi^{\zeta} \subseteq C(\chi^{\zeta})$;
2. $C(0_{\overline{\Im}}) = 0_{\overline{\Im}}$;
3. $C(C(\chi^{\zeta})) = C(\chi^{\zeta})$;
4. $C(\chi^{\zeta}{}_1 \cup \chi^{\zeta}{}_2) = C(\chi^{\zeta}{}_1) \cup C(\chi^{\zeta}{}_2)$.

Furthermore, $C(\chi^{\zeta}) = Cl(\chi^{\zeta})$ for each FF set χ^{ζ} in this FF TS.

Theorem 4. *Let $(\overline{\Im}, \hbar^{\daleth})$ be an FFTS and χ^{ζ} be an FFS over $\overline{\Im}$. Then,*

(a) $Cl\left(\chi^{\zeta^c}\right) = (Int(\chi^{\zeta}))^c$;

(b) $Int\left(\chi^{\zeta^c}\right) = (Cl(\chi^{\zeta}))^c$.

Proof. **(a)** Let $\chi^{\zeta} = \left\{\left\langle \breve{\aleph}, \mu^{\eta}{}_{\chi^{\zeta}}(\breve{\aleph}), \nu^{\eta}{}_{\chi^{\zeta}}(\breve{\aleph}) \right\rangle : \breve{\aleph} \in \overline{\Im}\right\}$ and assume that the family of FFSs contained in χ^{ζ} are indexed by the family $\left\{\chi^{\zeta}{}_i = \left\{\left\langle \breve{\aleph}, \mu^{\eta}{}_{\chi^{\zeta}{}_i}(\breve{\aleph}), \nu^{\eta}{}_{\chi^{\zeta}{}_i}(\breve{\aleph}) \right\rangle : \breve{\aleph} \in \overline{\Im}\right\}\right\}_{i \in I}$. Then, we see that $Int(\chi^{\zeta}) = \left\{\left\langle \breve{\aleph}, \sup\left\{\mu^{\eta}{}_{\chi^{\zeta}{}_i}(\breve{\aleph})\right\}, \in \beth\left\{\nu^{\eta}{}_{\chi^{\zeta}{}_i}(\breve{\aleph})\right\} \right\rangle : \breve{\aleph} \in \overline{\Im}\right\}$ and hence $(Int(\chi^{\zeta}))^c = \left\{\left\langle \breve{\aleph}, \in \beth\left\{\nu^{\eta}{}_{\chi^{\zeta}{}_i}(\breve{\aleph})\right\}, \sup\left\{\mu^{\eta}{}_{\chi^{\zeta}{}_i}(\breve{\aleph})\right\} \right\rangle : \breve{\aleph} \in \overline{\Im}\right\}$. Since $\chi^{\zeta^c} = \left\{\left\langle \breve{\aleph}, \nu^{\eta}{}_{\chi^{\zeta}}(\breve{\aleph}), \mu^{\eta}{}_{\chi^{\zeta}}(\breve{\aleph}) \right\rangle : \breve{\aleph} \in \overline{\Im}\right\}$ and $\mu^{\eta}{}_{\chi^{\zeta}{}_i}(\breve{\aleph}) \leq \mu^{\eta}{}_{\chi^{\zeta}}(\breve{\aleph}), \nu^{\eta}{}_{\chi^{\zeta}{}_i}(\breve{\aleph}) \geq \nu^{\eta}{}_{\chi^{\zeta}}(\breve{\aleph})$ for

each $i \in I$, we obtain that
$\left\{\chi^{\zeta}_i = \left\{\left\langle \breve{\aleph}, \mu^{\eta}{}_{\chi^{\zeta}_i}(\breve{\aleph}), \nu^{\eta}{}_{\chi^{\zeta}_i}(\breve{\aleph})\right\rangle : \breve{\aleph} \in \overline{\Im}\right\}\right\}_{i \in I}$ is the family of *FFS*s containing χ^{ζ^c}, i.e.,
$Cl\left(\chi^{\zeta^c}\right) = \left\{\left\langle \breve{\aleph}, \in \beth\left\{\nu^{\eta}{}_{\chi^{\zeta}_i}(\breve{\aleph})\right\}, \sup\left\{\mu^{\eta}{}_{\chi^{\zeta}_i}(\breve{\aleph})\right\}\right\rangle : \breve{\aleph} \in \overline{\Im}\right\}$. Therefore,
$Cl\left(\chi^{\zeta^c}\right) = (Int(\chi^{\zeta}))^c$ immediately.

(b) This is analogous to **(a)**. □

Definition 11. *A Fermatean fuzzy number (FFN) or Fermatean fuzzy point (FF point)* $\aleph = (\mu^{\eta}, \nu^{\eta})$ *is said to be contained in FFS* $\mathcal{K}$

$$\mathcal{K} = \{\langle \rho, \mu^{\eta}{}_{\mathcal{K}}(\rho), \nu^{\eta}{}_{\mathcal{K}}(\rho)\rangle : \rho \in \overline{\Im}\}$$

written as $\aleph \in \mathcal{K}$, *if* $\mu^{\eta} \leq \mu^{\eta}{}_{\mathcal{K}}$ *and if* $\nu^{\eta} \geq \nu^{\eta}{}_{\mathcal{K}}, \forall \rho \in \overline{\Im}$.

Definition 12. *An FFN* $\aleph = (\mu^{\eta}, \nu^{\eta})$ *contained in an FFS* $\mathcal{K}$ *is said to be an FF interior point if there exists FFOS* $\mathcal{U}$ *such that,* $\aleph \in \mathcal{U} \subseteq \mathcal{K}$. *Then,* $\mathcal{K}$ *is called an FF neighbourhood of FFN* $\aleph$. *Note that* $\aleph$ *in the FF interior point of FFS* $\mathcal{K}$ *if and only if* $\mathcal{K}$ *is an FF neighbourhood of FFN* $\aleph$.

Theorem 5. *Let* $(\overline{\Im}, \hbar^{\daleth})$ *be an FFTS.*
(i) If ϕ *and* φ *are the neighbourhoods of FFN* $\aleph$, *then* $\phi \cap \varphi$ *and* $\phi \cup \varphi$ *are also neighbourhoods of* $\aleph$.
(ii) If ψ *is a neighbourhood of FFN* $\aleph$, *then each FF superset* δ *of* ψ *is also a neighbourhood of* $\aleph$.

Proposition 4. *Let* $\left(\overline{\Im}, \hbar^{\daleth}{}_1\right)$ *and* $\left(\overline{\Im}, \hbar^{\daleth}{}_2\right)$ *be two FFTSs and* $\beth : \overline{\Im} \to \breve{\Pi}$ *be an FF mapping. Then, the following are equivalent to each other:*

a $\beth$ *is FF continuous mapping;*
b $\beth[Cl(\chi^{\zeta})] \subseteq Cl(\beth[\chi^{\zeta}])$ *for each FFS* χ^{ζ} *in* $\overline{\Im}$;
c $Cl(\beth^{-1}[K]) \subseteq \beth^{-1}[Cl(K)]$ *for each FFSK in* $\breve{\Pi}$;
d $\beth^{-1}[Int(K)] \subseteq Int(\beth^{-1}[K])$ *for each FFSK in* $\breve{\Pi}$.

Proof. (a) $\Rightarrow$ (b) Let $\beth : \overline{\Im} \to \breve{\Pi}$ be FF continuous mapping and χ^{ζ} be an FFS over $\overline{\Im}$. Then, $\beth[\chi^{\zeta}] \subseteq Cl(\beth[\chi^{\zeta}])$ and $\chi^{\zeta} \subseteq \beth^{-1}[Cl(\beth[\chi^{\zeta}])]$. Since $Cl(\beth[\chi^{\zeta}])$ is an FFCS in $\breve{\Pi}$ and $\beth$ is FF continuous mapping, $\beth^{-1}[Cl(\beth[\chi^{\zeta}])]$ is an FFCS in $\overline{\Im}$. On the other hand, if $Cl(\chi^{\zeta})$ is the smallest FFCS containing χ^{ζ}, then $Cl(\chi^{\zeta}) \subseteq \beth^{-1}[Cl(\beth[\chi^{\zeta}])]$ and so, $\beth[Cl(\chi^{\zeta})] \subseteq Cl(\beth[\chi^{\zeta}])$.

(b) $\Rightarrow$ (c) Suppose that $\chi^{\zeta} = \beth^{-1}[K]$. From (b), $\beth[Cl(\chi^{\zeta})] = \beth[Cl(\beth^{-1}[K])] \subseteq Cl(\beth[\chi^{\zeta}]) = Cl(\beth[\beth^{-1}[K]]) \subseteq Cl(K)$. Then, $Cl(\beth^{-1}[K]) = Cl(\chi^{\zeta}) \subseteq \beth^{-1}[\beth[Cl(\chi^{\zeta})]] \subseteq \beth^{-1}[Cl(K)]$.

(c) $\Rightarrow$ (d) Since Int $(K) = (Cl(K^c))^c$, then $Cl(\beth^{-1}[K]) = Cl(\chi^{\zeta}) \subseteq \beth^{-1}[\beth[Cl(\chi^{\zeta})]] \subseteq \beth^{-1}[Cl(K)]$.

Assume that G is an FFOS in $\breve{\Pi}$. Then, Int $(G) = G$. From (d), $\beth^{-1}[G] = \beth^{-1}[Int(G)] \subseteq Int(\beth^{-1}[G]) \subseteq \beth^{-1}[G]$. Therefore, $\beth$ is an FF continuous mapping. □

Definition 13. *Let* $(\overline{\Im}, \hbar^{\daleth})$ *be an FFTS.*
(i) A subfamily Γ *of* $\hbar^{\daleth}$ *is called an FF basis (FFB) for* $\hbar^{\daleth}$ *if for each* $\chi^{\zeta} \in \hbar^{\daleth}$, *there exists* $\Gamma' \subseteq \Gamma$ *such that* $\chi^{\zeta} = \cup\Gamma'$.
(ii) A collection Φ *of some FFSs on* $\overline{\Im}$ *is called an FF subbase (FFSB) for some FFT* $\hbar^{\daleth}$ *if the finite intersections of members of* Φ *form an FF basis for* $\hbar^{\daleth}$.

Theorem 6. $\left(\overline{\Im}, \hbar^{\daleth}{}_1\right)$ *and* $\left(\overline{\Im}, \hbar^{\daleth}{}_2\right)$ *are two FFTSs and* $\beth : \overline{\Im} \to \breve{\Pi}$ *is an FF mapping. Then,*

1. $\beth$ *is an FF continuous mapping iff for each* $\tilde{F} \in \Gamma$, *we have* $\beth^{-1}[\tilde{F}]$ *as an FF open subset of* $\overline{\Im}$ *such that* Γ *is an FF basis for* $\hbar^{\daleth}{}_2$.

2. $\sqsupset$ *is an FF continuous mapping iff for each* $K \in \chi^{\zeta}$, *we have* $\sqsupset^{-1}[K]$ *as an FF open subset of* $\overline{\Im}$ *such that* Φ *is an FF subbase for* $\hbar^{\daleth}{}_2$.

Proof. (i) Let $\sqsupset$ be an FF continuous mapping. Since each $\tilde{F} \in \Gamma \subseteq \hbar^{\daleth}{}_2$ and $\sqsupset$ is an FF continuous mapping, then $\sqsupset^{-1}[\tilde{F}] \in \hbar^{\daleth}{}_1$.
Conversely, suppose that Γ is an FF basis for $\hbar^{\daleth}{}_2$ and $\sqsupset^{-1}[\tilde{F}] \in \hbar^{\daleth}{}_1$ for each $\tilde{F} \in \Gamma$. Then, for an arbitrary FFOS $\chi^{\zeta} \in \hbar^{\daleth}{}_2$,

$$\sqsupset^{-1}[\chi^{\zeta}] = \sqsupset^{-1}\left[\cup_{\tilde{F}\in\Gamma}\tilde{F}\right] = \underset{\tilde{F}\in\Gamma}{\cup}\sqsupset^{-1}[\tilde{F}] \in \hbar^{\daleth}{}_1.$$

That is, $\sqsupset$ is an FF continuous mapping.
(ii) Let $\sqsupset$ be an FF continuous mapping. Since each $K \in \Phi \subseteq \hbar^{\daleth}{}_2$ and $\sqsupset$ is an FF continuous mapping, then $\sqsupset^{-1}[K] \in \hbar^{\daleth}{}_1$.

Conversely, assume that Φ is an FF subbase for $\hbar^{\daleth}{}_2$ and $\sqsupset^{-1}[K] \in \hbar^{\daleth}{}_1$ for each $K \in \Phi$. Then, for an arbitrary FFOS $\chi^{\zeta} \in \hbar^{\daleth}{}_2$,

$$\begin{aligned}\sqsupset^{-1}[\chi^{\zeta}] &= \sqsupset^{-1}\left[\cup_{i_j\in I}(K_{i_1}\cap K_{i_2}\cap\ldots\cap K_{i_n})\right]\\ &= \bigcup_{i_j\in I}\left(\sqsupset^{-1}[K_{i_1}]\cap\sqsupset^{-1}[K_{i_2}]\cap\ldots\cap\sqsupset^{-1}[K_{i_n}]\right) \in \hbar^{\daleth}{}_1\end{aligned}$$

That is, $\sqsupset$ is an FF continuous mapping. □

Definition 14. *Let* $\left(\overline{\Im}, \hbar^{\daleth}{}_1\right)$ *and* $\left(\overline{\Im}, \hbar^{\daleth}{}_2\right)$ *be two FFTSs and* $\sqsupset : \overline{\Im} \to \breve{\Pi}$ *be an FF mapping. Then:*
(i) $\sqsupset$ *is called an FF open function if* $\sqsupset[\chi^{\zeta}]$ *is an FFOS over* $\breve{\Pi}$ *for every FFOS* χ^{ζ} *over* $\overline{\Im}$. *(ii)* $\sqsupset$ *is called an FF closed function if* $\sqsupset[K]$ *is an FFCS over* $\breve{\Pi}$ *for every FFCS K over* $\overline{\Im}$.

Example 3. *Let* $\overline{\Im} = \{\breve{\alpha}^{\gamma}_1, \breve{\alpha}^{\gamma}_2, \breve{\alpha}^{\gamma}_3\}$ *and* $\breve{\Pi} = \{y_1, y_2, y_3\}$. *Consider the following families of FF sets* $\hbar^{\daleth}{}_1 = \{0_{\overline{\Im}}, 1_{\overline{\Im}}, \chi^{\zeta}{}_1, \chi^{\zeta}{}_2, \chi^{\zeta}{}_3, \chi^{\zeta}{}_4\}$ *and* $\hbar^{\daleth}{}_2 = \{0_{\breve{\Pi}}, 1_{\breve{\Pi}}, S_1, S_2, S_3, S_4\}$ *where*

$$\begin{aligned}\chi^{\zeta}{}_1 &= \{\langle\breve{\alpha}^{\gamma}_1, 0.27, 0.43\rangle, \langle\breve{\alpha}^{\gamma}_2, 0.57, 0.17\rangle, \langle\breve{\alpha}^{\gamma}_3, 0.57, 0.47\rangle\}\\ \chi^{\zeta}{}_2 &= \{\langle\breve{\alpha}^{\gamma}_1, 0.57, 0.47\rangle, \langle\breve{\alpha}^{\gamma}_2, 0.77, 0.27\rangle, \langle\breve{\alpha}^{\gamma}_3, 0.67, 0.57\rangle\}\\ \chi^{\zeta}{}_3 &= \{\langle\breve{\alpha}^{\gamma}_1, 0.57, 0.38\rangle, \langle\breve{\alpha}^{\gamma}_2, 0.77, 0.17\rangle, \langle\breve{\alpha}^{\gamma}_3, 0.67, 0.47\rangle\}\\ \chi^{\zeta}{}_4 &= \{\langle\breve{\alpha}^{\gamma}_1, 0.27, 0.40\rangle, \langle\breve{\alpha}^{\gamma}_2, 0.57, 0.27\rangle, \langle\breve{\alpha}^{\gamma}_3, 0.57, 0.57\rangle\}\end{aligned}$$

$$\begin{aligned}S_1 &= \{\langle y_1, 0.57, 0.17\rangle, \langle y_2, 0.27, 0.43\rangle, \langle y_3, 0.57, 0.47\rangle\},\\ S_2 &= \{\langle y_1, 0.77, 0.27\rangle, \langle y_2, 0.57, 0.47\rangle, \langle y_3, 0.67, 0.57\rangle\},\\ S_3 &= \{\langle y_1, 0.77, 0.17\rangle, \langle y_2, 0.57, 0.38\rangle, \langle y_3, 0.67, 0.47\rangle\},\\ S_4 &= \{\langle y_1, 0.57, 0.27\rangle, \langle y_2, 0.27, 0.40\rangle, \langle y_3, 0.57, 0.57\rangle\},\end{aligned}$$

It is clear that $\left(\overline{\Im}, \hbar^{\daleth}{}_1\right)$ *and* $\left(\overline{\Im}, \hbar^{\daleth}{}_2\right)$ *are FFTSs. If FF mapping* $\sqsupset : \overline{\Im} \to \breve{\Pi}$ *is defined as*

$$\begin{aligned}\sqsupset(\breve{\alpha}^{\gamma}_1) &= y_2\\ \sqsupset(\breve{\alpha}^{\gamma}_2) &= y_1\\ \sqsupset(\breve{\alpha}^{\gamma}_3) &= y_3\end{aligned}$$

Then $\sqsupset$ *is an FF open function. However,* $\sqsupset$ *is not an FF closed function on FFTSs* $\left(\overline{\Im}, \hbar^{\daleth}{}_1\right)$.

Theorem 7. *Let* $\left(\overline{\Im}, \hbar^{\daleth}{}_1\right)$ *and* $\left(\overline{\Im}, \hbar^{\daleth}{}_2\right)$ *be two FFTSs and* $\sqsupset : \overline{\Im} \to \breve{\Pi}$ *be an FF mapping. Then:*

1. $\sqsupset$ *is an FF open function if* $\sqsupset[Int(\chi^{\zeta})] \subseteq Int(\sqsupset[\chi^{\zeta}])$ *for each FF set* χ^{ζ} *over* $\overline{\Im}$.

2. $\beth$ *is an FF closed function if* $Cl(\beth[\chi^{\zeta}]) \subseteq \beth[Cl(\chi^{\zeta})]$ *for each FF set* χ^{ζ} *over* $\overline{\Im}$.

Proof. (1) Let $\beth$ be an FF open function and χ^{ζ} be an FFS over $\overline{\Im}$. Then, $Int(\chi^{\zeta})$ is an FFOS and $Int(\chi^{\zeta}) \subseteq \chi^{\zeta}$. Since $\beth$ is an FF open function, $\beth[Int(\chi^{\zeta})]$ is an FFOS over $\breve{\Pi}$ and $\beth[Int(\chi^{\zeta})] \subseteq \beth[\chi^{\zeta}]$. Thus, $\beth[Int(\chi^{\zeta})] \subseteq Int(\beth[\chi^{\zeta}])$ is obtained.
Conversely, suppose that χ^{ζ} is any FFOS over $\overline{\Im}$. Then, $\chi^{\zeta} = Int(\chi^{\zeta})$. From the condition of theorem, we have $\beth[Int(\chi^{\zeta})] \subseteq Int(\beth[\chi^{\zeta}])$. Then, $\beth[\chi^{\zeta}] = \beth[Int(\chi^{\zeta})] \subseteq Int(\beth[\chi^{\zeta}]) \subseteq \beth[\chi^{\zeta}]$. This implies that $\beth[\chi^{\zeta}] = Int(\beth[\chi^{\zeta}])$. That is, $\beth$ is an FF open function.
(2) Let $\beth$ be an FF closed function and χ^{ζ} be a FFS over $\overline{\Im}$. Since $\beth$ is an FF closed function, then $\beth[Cl(\chi^{\zeta})]$ is an FFCS over $\breve{\Pi}$ and $\beth[\chi^{\zeta}] \subseteq \beth[Cl(\chi^{\zeta})]$. Thus, $Cl(\beth[\chi^{\zeta}]) \subseteq \beth[Cl(\chi^{\zeta})]$ is obtained.

Conversely, assume that χ^{ζ} is any FFCS over $\overline{\Im}$. Then, $\chi^{\zeta} = Cl(\chi^{\zeta})$. From the condition of theorem, we have $Cl(\beth[\chi^{\zeta}]) \subseteq \beth[Cl(\chi^{\zeta})] = \beth[\chi^{\zeta}] \subseteq Cl(\beth[\chi^{\zeta}])$. This means that, $Cl(\beth[\chi^{\zeta}]) = \beth[\chi^{\zeta}]$. That is, $\beth$ is an FF closed function. □

Definition 15. *Let* $\left(\overline{\Im}, \hbar^{\daleth}{}_1\right)$ *and* $\left(\overline{\Im}, \hbar^{\daleth}{}_2\right)$ *be two FFTSs and* $\beth : \overline{\Im} \to \breve{\Pi}$ *be an FF mapping. Then,* $\beth$ *is a called an FF homeomorphism if:*
(i) $\beth$ *is a bijective mapping;*
(ii) $\beth$ *is an FF continuous mapping;*
(iii) $\beth^{-1}$ *is an FF continuous mapping.*

Theorem 8. *Let* $\left(\overline{\Im}, \hbar^{\daleth}{}_1\right)$ *and* $\left(\overline{\Im}, \hbar^{\daleth}{}_2\right)$ *be two FFTSs and* $\beth : \overline{\Im} \to \breve{\Pi}$ *be an FF mapping. Then, the following conditions are equivalent:*
(a) $\beth$ *is an FF homeomorphism;*
(b) $\beth$ *is an FF continuous mapping and FF open function; (c)* $\beth$ *is an FF continuous mapping and FF closed function.*

Proof. The proof can be easily obtained by using the previous theorems on continuity, openness and closedness are omitted. □

4. Ff Connectedness

In this section, we define the generalised concept of IF-connected TS and provide the related results with illustrations.

Definition 16. *Let A be an FF subset in* $(\overline{\Im}, \hbar^{\daleth}{}_{\overline{\Im}})$.
(a) If there exist FFOSs $\mathcal{U}^{\varsigma}$ *and* $\mathcal{V}^{\tau}$ *in* $\overline{\Im}$ *satisfying the following properties, then* A^{ζ} *is called FF* $\mathfrak{C}_i$*-disconnected* $(i = 1,2,3,4)$:

C_1 $A^{\zeta} \subseteq \mathcal{U}^{\varsigma} \cup \mathcal{V}^{\tau}, \mathcal{U}^{\varsigma} \cap \mathcal{V}^{\tau} \subseteq A^{\zeta^c}, A^{\zeta} \cap \mathcal{U}^{\varsigma} \neq 0_x, A^{\zeta} \cap \mathcal{V}^{\tau} \neq 0_x;$

C_2 $A^{\zeta} \subseteq \mathcal{U}^{\varsigma} \cup \mathcal{V}^{\tau}, A^{\zeta} \cap \mathcal{U}^{\varsigma} \cap \mathcal{V}^{\tau} \neq 0_x, A^{\zeta} \cap \mathcal{U}^{\varsigma} \neq 0_x, A^{\zeta} \cap \mathcal{V}^{\tau} \neq 0_x;$

C_3 $A^{\zeta} \subseteq \mathcal{U}^{\varsigma} \cup \mathcal{V}^{\tau}, \mathcal{U}^{\varsigma} \cap \mathcal{V}^{\tau} \subseteq A^{\zeta^c}, \mathcal{U}^{\varsigma} \nsubseteq A^{\zeta^c}, \mathcal{V}^{\tau} \nsubseteq A^{\zeta^c};$

C_4 $A^{\zeta} \subseteq \mathcal{U}^{\varsigma} \cup \mathcal{V}^{\tau}, A^{\zeta} \cap \mathcal{U}^{\varsigma} \cap \mathcal{V}^{\tau} \neq 0_x, \mathcal{U}^{\varsigma} \nsubseteq A^{\zeta^c}, \mathcal{V}^{\tau} \nsubseteq A^{\zeta^c}.$

(b) A^{ζ} *is said to be FF* $\mathfrak{C}_i$*-connected* $(i = 1,2,3,4)$ *if* A^{ζ} *is not FF* $\mathfrak{C}_i$*-disconnected* $(i = 1,2,3,4)$.

It is clear that, in FFTSs, we have the following implications:

$$\begin{array}{ccc} \mathfrak{C}_1\text{-connectedness} & \rightarrow & \mathfrak{C}_2\text{-connectedness} \\ \downarrow & & \downarrow \\ \mathfrak{C}_3\text{-connectedness} & \rightarrow & \mathfrak{C}_4\text{-connectedness.} \end{array}$$

Example 4. *Let* $\overline{\Im} = \{\breve{\alpha}_1^{\gamma}, \breve{\alpha}_2^{\gamma}, \breve{\alpha}_3^{\gamma}\}$. *Consider the following family of FF sets*

$$\begin{aligned}
\chi^{\zeta}{}_1 &= \{\langle \breve{\alpha}_1^{\gamma}, 0.50, 0.20\rangle, \langle \breve{\alpha}_2^{\gamma}, 0.50, 0.40\rangle, \langle \breve{\alpha}_3^{\gamma}, 0.40, 0.40\rangle\},\\
\chi^{\zeta}{}_2 &= \{\langle \breve{\alpha}_1^{\gamma}, 0.40, 0.50\rangle, \langle \breve{\alpha}_2^{\gamma}, 0.60, 0.30\rangle, \langle \breve{\alpha}_3^{\gamma}, 0.20, 0.30\rangle\},\\
\chi^{\zeta}{}_3 &= \{\langle \breve{\alpha}_1^{\gamma}, 0.50, 0.20\rangle, \langle \breve{\alpha}_2^{\gamma}, 0.60, 0.30\rangle, \langle \breve{\alpha}_3^{\gamma}, 0.40, 0.30\rangle\},\\
\chi^{\zeta}{}_4 &= \{\langle \breve{\alpha}_1^{\gamma}, 0.40, 0.50\rangle, \langle \breve{\alpha}_2^{\gamma}, 0.50, 0.40\rangle, \langle \breve{\alpha}_3^{\gamma}, 0.20, 0.40\rangle\}.
\end{aligned}$$

Then, $\hbar^{\daleth} = \{1_{\overline{\Im}}, 0_{\overline{\Im}}, \chi^{\zeta}{}_1, \chi^{\zeta}{}_2, \chi^{\zeta}{}_3, \chi^{\zeta}{}_4\}$ *is an FFTS on* $\overline{\Im}$, *and consider the FFSE given below*

$$E = \{\langle \breve{\alpha}_1^{\gamma}, 0.60, 0.20\rangle, \langle \breve{\alpha}_2^{\gamma}, 0.50, 0.20\rangle, \langle \breve{\alpha}_3^{\gamma}, 0.40, 0.30\rangle\},$$

in $\overline{\Im}$. *Then, E is FF* $\mathfrak{C}_1$*-connected, and E is also FF*$\mathfrak{C}_2$*-connected, FF*$\mathfrak{C}_3$*-connected, and FF*$\mathfrak{C}_4$*-connected.*

Example 5. *Consider the FFTS* $(\overline{\Im}, \hbar^{\daleth}{}_{\overline{\Im}})$ *given in Example 4 and consider the FFS F given below*

$$F = \{\langle \breve{\alpha}_1^{\gamma}, 0.20, 0.40\rangle, \langle \breve{\alpha}_2^{\gamma}, 0.30, 0.60\rangle, \langle \breve{\alpha}_3^{\gamma}, 0.20, 0.40\rangle\},$$

One can verify whether F is FF$\mathfrak{C}_1$*-disconnected and hence not FF*$\mathfrak{C}_1$*-connected.*

Definition 17. *Let* $(\overline{\Im}, \hbar^{\daleth}{}_{\overline{\Im}})$ *be an FFTS:*

(i) $\overline{\Im}$ *is said to be FFC*$_5$*-disconnected if there exists an FFOS and FFCS G such that* $G \neq 1_x$ *and* $G \neq 0_x$.

(ii) $\overline{\Im}$ *is said to be FF*$\mathfrak{C}_5$*-connected if it is not FF*$\mathfrak{C}_5$*-disconnected.*

Example 6. *Let* $\overline{\Im} = \{1, 2\}$ *and define the FF subsets* $A^{\zeta}, S^{\varsigma}, C, andD$ *as follows ;*
Let $\overline{\Im} = \{\breve{\alpha}_1^{\gamma}, \breve{\alpha}_2^{\gamma}, \breve{\alpha}_3^{\gamma}\}$. *Consider the following family of FF sets:*

$$\begin{aligned}
\chi^{\zeta}{}_1 &= \{\langle \breve{\alpha}_1^{\gamma}, 0.40, 0.30\rangle, \langle \breve{\alpha}_2^{\gamma}, 0.20, 0.70\rangle\},\\
\chi^{\zeta}{}_2 &= \{\langle \breve{\alpha}_1^{\gamma}, 0.30, 0.40\rangle, \langle \breve{\alpha}_2^{\gamma}, 0.70, 0.20\rangle\},\\
\chi^{\zeta}{}_3 &= \{\langle \breve{\alpha}_1^{\gamma}, 0.30, 0.40\rangle, \langle \breve{\alpha}_2^{\gamma}, 0.20, 0.70\rangle\},\\
\chi^{\zeta}{}_4 &= \{\langle \breve{\alpha}_1^{\gamma}, 0.40, 0.30\rangle, \langle \breve{\alpha}_2^{\gamma}, 0.70, 0.20\rangle\},
\end{aligned}$$

Then, the family $\hbar^{\daleth} = \{1_{\overline{\Im}}, 0_{\overline{\Im}}, \chi^{\zeta}{}_1, \chi^{\zeta}{}_2, \chi^{\zeta}{}_3, \chi^{\zeta}{}_4\}$ *is an FFTS on* $\overline{\Im}$ *and* $(\overline{\Im}, \hbar^{\daleth})$ *is an FF*$\mathfrak{C}_5$*-disconnected, since* A^{ζ} *is a nonzero FFOS and FFCS in* $\overline{\Im}$.

Definition 18. *Let* $(\overline{\Im}, \hbar^{\daleth}{}_{\overline{\Im}})$ *be an FFTS:*
(i) $\overline{\Im}$ *is called FF disconnected if there exist FFOSs* $A^{\zeta} \neq 0_x$ *and* $S^{\varsigma} \neq 0_x$ *such that* $A^{\zeta}\mathcal{U}^{\varsigma}S^{\varsigma} = 1_x$ *and* $A^{\zeta} \cap S^{\varsigma} = 0_x$.
(ii) $\overline{\Im}$ *is called FF connected if* $\overline{\Im}$ *is not FF disconnected.*

Proposition 5. *FF* $\mathfrak{C}_5$*-connectedness implies FF connectedness.*

Proposition 6. *Let* $\left(\overline{\Im} and \hbar^{\daleth}{}_1\right), (\breve{\Pi}, \hbar^{\daleth}{}_2)$ *be two FFTSs and let* $f : \overline{\Im} \to \breve{\Pi}$ *be an FF continuous surjection. If* $\left(\overline{\Im}, \hbar^{\daleth}{}_1\right)$ *is FF connected, then so is* $(\breve{\Pi}, \hbar^{\daleth}{}_2)$.

Proof. On the contrary, suppose that $(\breve{\Pi}, \hbar^{\daleth}{}_2)$ is FF disconnected. Then, there exist FFOSs $A^{\zeta} \neq 0_{\breve{\Pi}}, S^{\varsigma} \neq 0_{\breve{\Pi}}$ in $\breve{\Pi}$ such that $A^{\zeta}\mathcal{U}^{\varsigma}S^{\varsigma} = 1_y, A^{\zeta} \cap S^{\varsigma} = 0_{\breve{\Pi}}$. Now, we see that $\mathcal{U}^{\varsigma} = f^1(A^{\zeta}), \mathcal{V}^{\tau} = f^1(S^{\varsigma})$ are FFOSs in $\overline{\Im}$ since f is FF continuous. From $A^{\zeta} \neq 0_{\breve{\Pi}}$, we obtain $\mathcal{U}^{\varsigma} = f^1(A^{\zeta}) \neq 0_x$. Similarly, $\mathcal{V}^{\tau} \neq 0_x$. Hence, $A^{\zeta}\mathcal{U}^{\varsigma}S^{\varsigma} = 1_y \Rightarrow f^1(A^{\zeta})f^1(S^{\varsigma}) = f^1(1_y) = 1_x \Rightarrow \mathcal{U}_u^{\varsigma}\mathcal{V}^{\tau} = 1_{\overline{\Im}}; A^{\zeta} \cap S^{\varsigma} = 0_{\breve{\Pi}} \Rightarrow f^1(A^{\zeta}) \cap f^1(S^{\varsigma}) = f^1(0_{\breve{\Pi}}) = 0_{\overline{\Im}} \Rightarrow \mathcal{U}^{\varsigma} \cap \cap S^{\varsigma} = 0_{\breve{\Pi}} \Rightarrow f^1(A^{\zeta}) \cap f^1(S^{\varsigma}) = f^1(0_{\breve{\Pi}}) = 0_{\overline{\Im}} \Rightarrow \mathcal{U}^{\varsigma} \cap$ □

Corollary 1. *Let* $\left(\overline{\Im}, \hbar^{\daleth}{}_1\right), \left(\breve{\Pi}, \hbar^{\daleth}{}_2\right)$ *be two FFTSs and let* $f : \overline{\Im} \rightarrow \breve{\Pi}$ *be an FF continuous surjection. If* $\left(\overline{\Im}, \hbar^{\daleth}{}_1\right)$ *is FF* $\mathfrak{C}_5$*-connected, then so is* $\left(\breve{\Pi}, \hbar^{\daleth}{}_2\right)$.

Definition 19. *An FFTS* $(\overline{\Im}, \hbar^{\daleth})$ *is said to be FF strongly connected, if there exists nonzero FFCSs* A^{ζ} *and* S^{ς} *such that* $\mu^{\eta}{}_{A^{\zeta}} + \mu^{\eta}{}_{S^{\varsigma}} \leq 1$ *and* $\vartheta_{A^{\zeta}} + \vartheta_{S^{\varsigma}} \geq 1$.

Proposition 7. *Let* $\left(\overline{\Im}, \hbar^{\daleth}{}_1\right), \left(\breve{\Pi}, \hbar^{\daleth}{}_2\right)$ *be two FFTSs and let* $f : \overline{\Im} \rightarrow \breve{\Pi}$ *be an FF continuous surjection. If* $\left(\overline{\Im}, \hbar^{\daleth}{}_1\right)$ *is FF strongly connected, then so is* $\left(\breve{\Pi}, \hbar^{\daleth}{}_2\right)$.

Proof. This is analogous to the proof of Proposition 6. It is clear that, in FFTSs, strong FF connectedness does not imply FF $\mathfrak{C}_5$-connectedness, and the same is true for its converse. □

5. Fermatean Fuzzy α-Continuity

Definition 20. *An FFS* $\chi^{\zeta} = < x, \mu^{\eta}{}_{\chi^{\zeta}}, \gamma_{\chi^{\zeta}} >$ *of an FFTS* $(\overline{\Im}, \hbar^{\daleth})$ *is called an FF α open set if* $\chi^{\zeta} \subseteq Int(Cl(Int(\chi^{\zeta})))$. *An FFS whose complement is an FF α open set (FFαOS) is called an FF α closed set (FFαCS).*

Proposition 8. *Let* $(\overline{\Im}, \hbar^{\daleth})$ *be an FFTS. Then, the arbitrary union of FFαOS is an FFαOS and an arbitrary intersection of FFαCSs is FFαCS.*

Proof. Let $\{\chi^{\zeta}{}_i = \langle x, \mu^{\eta}{}_{\chi^{\zeta}}, \gamma_{\chi^{\zeta}} > | i \in I\}$ be a family of FFαOSs. Then, for each $i \in I, \chi^{\zeta}{}_i \subseteq Int(Cl(\text{ Int }(\chi^{\zeta}{}_i)))$. Thus, $\cup\chi^{\zeta}{}_i \subseteq \cup Int((Cl(\text{ Int }(\chi^{\zeta}{}_i))))$ $\subseteq Int(\cup Cl(\text{ Int }(\chi^{\zeta}{}_i)))) \subseteq Int(Cl(\cup Int(\chi^{\zeta}{}_i)))) \subseteq Int(Cl(Int(\cup\chi^{\zeta}{}_i))))$
Hence, $\cup\chi^{\zeta}{}_i$ is an FFαOS set. If we take the complement of this part, the following will be proven (i.e., the arbitrary intersection of FFαOS is also an FFαOS).

Every FFOS is an FFαOS and every FFCS is an FFαCS but the converse is not true. □

Definition 21. *The FF α closure of an FFS* χ^{ζ} *in an FFTS* $(\overline{\Im}; \hbar^{\daleth})$ *represented as* $Cl_{\alpha}(\chi^{\zeta})$ *and defined by* $Cl_{\alpha}(\chi^{\zeta}) = \cap\{C_i | C_i \textit{is an FF}\alpha C \textit{ set and } \chi^{\zeta} \subseteq C_i\}$

Proposition 9. *In an FFTS* $(\overline{\Im}, \hbar^{\daleth})$, *an FFS* χ^{ζ} *is FFαC if and only if* $\chi^{\zeta} = Cl_{\alpha}(\chi^{\zeta})$.

Proof. Assume that χ^{ζ} is an $FF\alpha C$ set. Then,
$\chi^{\zeta} \in \{C_i | C_i$ is a $FF\alpha C$ set and $\chi^{\zeta} \subseteq C_i\}$, so $\chi^{\zeta} = \cap\{C_i | C_i$ is a $FF\alpha C$ and $\chi^{\zeta} \subseteq C_i\}$
$= Cl_{\alpha}(\chi^{\zeta})$.
Conversely, consider $\chi^{\zeta} = Cl_{\alpha}(\chi^{\zeta})$,
$\chi^{\zeta} \in \{C_i | C_i$ is a $FF\alpha C$ set and $\chi^{\zeta} \subseteq C_i\}$
Thus, χ^{ζ} is an FFα-closed set. □

Proposition 10. *In an FFTS* $(\overline{\Im}, \hbar^{\daleth})$, *the following hold for q-ROα-closure:*
(1) $Cl_{\alpha}(\underline{0}) = \underline{0}$;
(2) $Cl_{\alpha}(\chi^{\zeta})$ *is a q-ROαC in* $(\overline{\Im}, \hbar^{\daleth})$ *for every FFS* χ^{ζ} *in* $\overline{\Im}$;
(3) $Cl_{\alpha}(\chi^{\zeta}) \subseteq Cl_{\alpha}(R)$ *whenever* $\chi^{\zeta} \subseteq R$ *for every* χ^{ζ} *and R in* $\overline{\Im}$;
(4) $Cl_{\alpha}(Cl_{\alpha}(\chi^{\zeta})) = Cl_{\alpha}(\chi^{\zeta})$ *for every FFS* χ^{ζ} *in* $\overline{\Im}$.

Proof. (1) The proof is obvious;
(2) By preposition, χ^{ζ} is FFαC iff the $\chi^{\zeta} = Cl_{\alpha}(\chi^{\zeta})$ we obtain $Cl_{\alpha}(\chi^{\zeta})$ is an FFαC for every χ^{ζ} in $\overline{\Im}$.
(3) By the same preposition, we obtain $\chi^{\zeta} = Cl_{\alpha}(\chi^{\zeta})$ and $R = Cl_{\alpha}(R)$. whenever $\chi^{\zeta} \subseteq R$, we have $Cl_{\alpha}(\chi^{\zeta}) \subseteq Cl_{\alpha}(R)$.

(4) Let χ^{ζ} be an FFFS in $\overline{\Im}$. We know that $\chi^{\zeta} = Cl_{\alpha}(\chi^{\zeta})$,
$Cl_{\alpha}(\chi^{\zeta}) = Cl_{\alpha}(Cl_{\alpha}(\chi^{\zeta}))$. Thus, $Cl_{\alpha}(Cl_{\alpha}(\chi^{\zeta})) = Cl_{\alpha}(\chi^{\zeta})$ for every χ^{ζ} in $\overline{\Im}$. □

Definition 22. *Let* $\left(\overline{\Im}, \hbar^{\daleth}_{\overline{\Im}}\right)$ *and* $(\breve{\Pi}, \hbar^{\daleth}_{\breve{\Pi}})$ *be FFTSs. A mapping* $\beth : \overline{\Im} \to \breve{\Pi}$ *is named FF*α*-continuous (FF*α*CN) if the inverse image of each FFOS of* $\breve{\Pi}$ *is an FF*α*O set in* $\overline{\Im}$.

Theorem 9. *Let* $\beth : \left(\overline{\Im}, \hbar^{\daleth}_{\overline{\Im}}\right) \to (\breve{\Pi}, \hbar^{\daleth}_{\breve{\Pi}})$ *be a mapping from a* $FFTS\left(\overline{\Im}, \hbar^{\daleth}_{\overline{\Im}}\right)$ *to an* $FFTS(\breve{\Pi}, \hbar^{\daleth}_{\breve{\Pi}})$. *If* $\beth$ *is FF*α*-continues, then:*
(1) $\beth(Cl(Int(Cl(\chi^{\zeta})))) \subseteq Cl(\beth(\chi^{\zeta}))$ *for all FFS* χ^{ζ} *in* $\overline{\Im}$.
(2) $Cl(Int(\beth^{-1}(\tilde{F}))) \subseteq \beth^{-1}(Cl(\tilde{F}))$ *for all* $\tilde{F}$ *in* $\breve{\Pi}$.

6. Fermatean Fuzzy Codas Approach

Combinative distance-based assessment (CODAS) is a method for evaluating the similarity between two sets of data. This method is particularly useful in applications where the datasets are complex and may not be easily compared using traditional methods such as Euclidean distance. One of the main advantages of CODAS is its ability to handle data with missing or incomplete values. This is important because, in many real-world applications, data are often missing or incomplete due to various reasons such as errors in data collection or missing information. CODAS can handle such data using a combination of different distance measures which can be customised based on the needs of the application. CODAS is also highly flexible and can be applied to a wide range of data types, including numerical, categorical, and ordinal data. This makes it an ideal method for applications where datasets may contain a mix of different data types.

The CODAS method is a useful tool for evaluating the similarity between two sets of data, particularly when the data are complex or contain missing or incomplete values. It is flexible and can be applied to a wide range of data types, making it a valuable tool for many different applications.

The fundamental task in general MCDM problems is that of selecting one or even more options from a set of available alternatives based on numerous criteria. The CODAS method is a comparatively recent MCDM method introduced by Ghorabaee et al. [46] in 2016. Ghorabaee et al. [47] also extended the CODAS approach to the fuzzy set. We extended the CODAS approach to FFSs with an application to supplier selection. To begin, in contrast to the vast majority of existing group decision-making techniques, which assume either a known reputation vector or equal expert weights, the experts' reputation is determined by their qualifications and experience. Second, the Fermatean fuzzy direct rating approach is used to establish the relative relevance of criteria based on the expert group's evaluation preferences. Thirdly, the Fermatean fuzzy CODAS approach is used to construct alternative orderings based on their assessment scores. Assume that there are n alternatives given as $\aleph^{\daleth} = \{\aleph^{\daleth}_1, \ldots, \aleph^{\daleth}_i, \ldots, \aleph^{\daleth}_n\}(n \geq 2)$ and $\aleph^{\urcorner} = \left\{\aleph^{\urcorner}_1, \ldots, \aleph^{\urcorner}_j, \ldots, \aleph^{\urcorner}_m\right\}(m \geq 2)$ is the finite set of m criteria. Suppose that $\wp^{\mho} = \{\wp^{\mho}_1, \ldots, \wp^{\mho}_e, \ldots, \wp^{\mho}_z\}(z \geq 2)$ constitute the assemblage of invited DMs. The FF-CODAS approach consists of the following steps.

Step 1: Determine the reputation of the experts:

$$\widehat{\Delta}_e = \operatorname{avg}\left(\Theta^{(1)}_e, \Theta^{(2)}_e\right) = \left(\frac{\mu^{\eta}{}_{\Theta^{(1)}_e} + \mu^{\eta}{}_{\Theta^{(2)}_e}}{2}, \frac{\nu^{\eta}{}_{\Theta^{(1)}_e} + \nu^{\eta}{}_{\Theta^{(2)}_e}}{2}\right), \quad e = 1, 2, \ldots, z \tag{1}$$

here, $\widehat{\Delta}_e$ indicates the FF average reputation of the invited DM $\wp^{\mho}_e$. $\Theta^{(1)}_e$ and $\Theta^{(2)}_e$ are FFNs that express the education and expertise of the invited DM $\wp^{\mho}_e$, respectively. Table 2 shows an FF linguistic scale that can be used to distinguish specialists based on their credentials and expertise.

Table 2. FF linguistic scale to distinct DMs

Qualifications	Experience (Years)	FFNs
F.Sc. (Higher Secondary)	$[6.5, 10)$	$(0.150, 0.900)$
B.Sc. (Graduate)	$[10, 15.5)$	$(0.250, 0.700)$
M.Sc. (Master's)	$[15.5, 20)$	$(0.500, 0.500)$
M.S./M.Phil. (Postgraduate)	$[20, 35)$	$(0.700, 0.250)$
Ph.D. (Doctorate)	≥ 35	$(0.900, 0.150)$

Step 2: Normalise the importance of the DMs:

$$\daleth_e = \frac{\text{score}^P\left(\widehat{\Delta}_e\right)}{\sum_{t=1}^{z} \text{score}^P\left(\widehat{\Delta}_t\right)} = \frac{1 + \mu\eta^3_{\widehat{\Delta}_e} - \nu\eta^3_{\widehat{\Delta}_e}}{\sum_{t=1}^{z}\left(1 + \mu\eta^3_{\widehat{\Delta}_t} - \nu\eta^3_{\widehat{\Delta}_t}\right)}, \quad e = 1, \ldots, z \tag{2}$$

here, $\daleth = (\daleth_1, \ldots, \daleth_e, \ldots, \daleth_z)^T$ is the importance vector of the DMs, with $\daleth_e \in [0, 1]$ and $\sum_{e=1}^{z} \daleth_e = 1$.

Step 3: Evaluate the criteria importance matrices $V^e = \left[V_j^e\right]_{m \times 1}$:

$$\aleph_1^\daleth(\mu\eta^e_{V_1}, \nu\eta^e_{V_1})[t]\aleph_2^\daleth(\mu\eta^e_{V_2}, \nu\eta^e_{V_2}) \vdots\vdots\vdots \aleph_m^\daleth(\mu\eta^e_{V_m}, \nu\eta^e_{V_m})[b]$$

where $V_j^e = \left(\mu\eta^e_{V_j}, \nu\eta^e_{V_j}\right)(j = 1, \ldots, m; e = 1, \ldots, z)$ is an FFN representing the important assessment of the criterion $\aleph_j^\daleth$ provided by the DM $\wp_e^\mho$. It is defined by utilising an FF linguistic importance scale, which is shown in Table 3 and can be used to offer expert criteria importance preferences.

Table 3. FF linguistic scale to evaluate criteria importance.

Linguistic Term	FFN
Extremely unimportant (EU)	$(0.100, 0.975)$
Not important (NI)	$(0.200, 0.850)$
Slightly important (SI)	$(0.350, 0.700)$
Moderately important (MI)	$(0.550, 0.500)$
Important (I)	$(0.700, 0.350)$
Very important (VI)	$(0.850, 0.200)$
Extremely important (EI)	$(0.975, 0.100)$

Step 4: Compute the consolidated criterion significance matrix:

$$\begin{aligned}
\widehat{W} &= \left[\widehat{W}_j\right]_{m \times 1}: \\
\widehat{W}_j &= \left(\mu\eta_{\widehat{W}_j}, \nu\eta_{\widehat{W}_j}\right) \\
&= FFWG_\daleth\left(V_j^1, \ldots, V_j^e, \ldots, V_j^z\right) = \bigotimes_{e=1}^{z}\left(V_j^e\right)^{\daleth_e}
\end{aligned}$$

$$= \left(\prod_{e=1}^{z} \mu\eta^{\daleth_e}_{V_j^e}, \sqrt[3]{1 - \prod_{e=1}^{z}\left(1 - \nu\eta^3_{V_j^e}\right)^{\daleth_e}}\right), \quad j = 1, \ldots, m \tag{3}$$

where $\widehat{W}_j = \left(\mu\eta_{\widehat{W}_j}, \nu\eta_{\widehat{W}_j}\right)$ is the FF aggregated importance evaluation of the criterion $\aleph_j^\daleth$ given by the DMs.

Step 5: Normalise the aggregated criteria importance:

$$\beth_j = \frac{\text{score}^P\left(\widehat{W}_j\right)}{\sum_{l=1}^m \text{score}^P\left(\widehat{W}_l\right)} = \frac{1 + \mu^{\eta 3}_{\widehat{W}_j} - \nu^{\eta 3}_{\widehat{W}_j}}{\sum_{l=1}^m \left(1 + \mu^{\eta 3}_{\widehat{W}_l} - \nu^{\eta 3}_{\widehat{W}_l}\right)}$$

where $\beth = (\beth_1, \ldots, \beth_j, \ldots, \beth_m)^T$ is the importance vector of the criteria, with $\beth_j \in [0,1](j = 1, \ldots, n)$ and $\sum_{j=1}^n \beth_j = 1$.

Step 6: Obtain the decision matrices $\Gamma^e = \left[\Gamma^e_{ij}\right]_{n\times m}$:

where $\Gamma^e_{ij} = \left(\mu^\eta{}_{\Gamma^e_{ij}}, \nu^\eta{}_{\Gamma^e_{ij}}\right)(i = 1, \ldots, n; j = 1, \ldots, m; e = 1, \ldots, z\ )$ is an FFN that represents the assessment of the alternative $\aleph^\daleth_i$ with respect to the criterion $\aleph^\urcorner_j$ given by the invited expert $\wp^\mho_e$. It is defined using a Fermatean fuzzy linguistic assessment scale. The nine-point Fermatean fuzzy linguistic scale presented in Table 4 can be used to present the alternative assessment preferences of experts.

Table 4. FF linguistic scale to evaluate alternatives.

Linguistic Term	FFNs
Inadequate (I)	(0.100, 0.975)
Very poor (VP)	(0.200, 0.900)
Poor (P)	(0.300, 0.800)
Medium poor (MP)	(0.400, 0.650)
Medium (M)	(0.550, 0.500)
Medium good (MG)	(0.650, 0.400)
Good (G)	(0.800, 0.300)
Very good (VG)	(0.900, 0.200)
Exceptional (E)	(0.975, 0.100)

Step 7: Determine the aggregated decision matrix $G = \left[G_{ij}\right]_{n\times m}$:

$$\begin{aligned} G_{ij} &= \text{FFWG}_\beth\left(\Gamma^1_{ij}, \ldots, \widehat{\Gamma}^e_{ij}, \ldots, \Gamma^k_{ij}\right) \\ &= \left(\prod_{e=1}^z \mu^{\eta\,\beth_e}_{\Gamma^e_{ij}}, \sqrt[3]{1 - \prod_{e=1}^z \left(1 - \nu^\eta{}_{\Gamma^e_{ij}}\right)^{\beth_e}}\right) \end{aligned} \tag{4}$$

where the aggregation is determined by applying the "Fermatean fuzzy weighted geometric (FFWG) operator" [48] and $G_{ij} = \left(\mu^\eta{}_{G_{ij}}, \nu^\eta{}_{G_{ij}}\right)$ is the Fermatean fuzzy aggregated assessment of the alternative $\aleph^\daleth_i$ with respect to the criterion $\aleph^\urcorner_j$ given by the experts.

Step 8: Determine the normalised decision matrix $\widehat{R} = \left[\widehat{R}_{ij}\right]_{n\times m}$:

$$\widehat{R}_{ij} = \begin{cases} (G_{ij})^c; & \mid \aleph^\urcorner_j \in C^- \\ G_{ij}; & \mid \aleph^\urcorner_j \in C^+. \end{cases} \tag{5}$$

where $\widehat{R}_{ij} = \left(\mu^\eta{}_{\widehat{R}_{ij}}, \nu^\eta{}_{\widehat{R}_{ij}}\right)$ denotes the FF normalised assessment of the alternative $\aleph^\daleth_i$ with respect to the criterion $\aleph^\urcorner_j$ given by the experts, $C^+ \subseteq C$ is the set of benefit criteria, $C^- \subseteq C$ is the set of cost criteria, and $C^+ \cup C^- = C$. Only alternative assessments with respect to cost criteria are transformed by utilising the complement operation.

Step 9: Determine the Fermatean fuzzy negative-ideal solution (FFNIS).

$$\widehat{S_j^-} = \left(\mu^{\eta}{}_{\widehat{S_j^-}}, \nu^{\eta}{}_{\widehat{S_j^-}}\right) = \widehat{R_j^-} \mid \text{score}\left(\widehat{R_j^-}\right)$$
$$= \min_{1 \le i \le n}\left[\text{score}(R_{ij})\right], j = 1, \ldots, m$$

$\widehat{S^-} = \left\{\widehat{S_1^-}, \ldots, \widehat{S_j^-}, \ldots, \widehat{S_m^-}\right\}$ is a collection of FFNs that represent the FFNIS and $\widehat{R_j^-}$ is an FFN with the lowest score function value of alternatives with respect to the criterion $\aleph_j^{ℸ}$.

Step 10: Calculate the weighted Euclidean distance (H_i) and weighted Hamming distance (E_i) of the alternatives from the FFNIS given in Equations (6) and (7), respectively.

$$H_i\left(\aleph_i^{ℷ}, \widehat{S^-}\right) = \frac{1}{2}\sum_{j=1}^{n}\omega_j\left(\left|\mu^{\eta 3}_{\widehat{R}_{ij}} - \mu^{\eta 3}_{\widehat{R_j^-}}\right| + \left|\nu^{\eta 3}_{\widehat{R}_{ij}} - \nu^{\eta 3}_{\widehat{S_j^-}}\right| + \left|\pi^{3}_{\widehat{R}_{ij}} - \pi^{3}_{\widehat{S_j^-}}\right|\right) \tag{6}$$

$$E_i\left(\aleph_i^{ℷ}, \widehat{S^-}\right) = \sqrt{\frac{1}{2}\sum_{j=1}^{n}\omega_j\left[\left(\mu^{\eta 3}_{\widehat{R}_{ij}} - \mu^{\eta 3}_{\widehat{R_j^-}}\right)^2 + \left(\nu^{\eta 3}_{\widehat{R}_{ij}} - \nu^{\eta 3}_{\widehat{S_j^-}}\right)^2 + \left(\pi^{3}_{\widehat{R}_{ij}} - \pi^{3}_{\widehat{S_j^-}}\right)^2\right]} \tag{7}$$

Step 11: Construct the relative assessment matrix $\text{P} = [\text{P}_{it}]_{n \times n}$:

$$\text{P}_{it} = E_i\left(\aleph_i^{ℷ}, \widehat{S^-}\right) - E_t\left(\aleph_t^{ℷ}, \widehat{S^-}\right) + \Phi_{it}\left(E_i\left(\aleph_i^{ℷ}, \widehat{S^-}\right) - E_t\left(\aleph_t^{ℷ}, \widehat{S^-}\right)\right) \cdot \left[H_i\left(\aleph_i^{ℷ}, \widehat{S^-}\right) - H_t\left(\aleph_t^{ℷ}, \widehat{S^-}\right)\right]$$

$i, t = 1, \ldots, n$, where Φ is a threshold function to recognise the equality of Euclidean distance measures of two alternatives. It is defined as follows

$$\Phi_{it}\left(E_i\left(\aleph_i^{ℷ}, \widehat{S^-}\right) - E_t\left(\aleph_t^{ℷ}, \widehat{S^-}\right)\right) = \begin{cases} 1 & \phi \le |E_i\left(\aleph_i^{ℷ}, \widehat{S^-}\right) - E_t\left(\aleph_t^{ℷ}, \widehat{S^-}\right)| \\ 0 & \phi > |E_i\left(\aleph_i^{ℷ}, \widehat{S^-}\right) - E_t\left(\aleph_t^{ℷ}, \widehat{S^-}\right)| \end{cases} \tag{8}$$

where ϕ is the threshold parameter.

Step 12: Calculate the assessment scores and rank the alternatives:

$$R_i = \sum_{t=1}^{n} \text{P}_{it}, \quad i = 1, 2, \ldots, n \tag{9}$$

where R_i represents the assessment scores of the alternative $\aleph_i^{ℷ}$. The alternatives are ranked according to the decreasing values of their assessment score. The highest score is the most desirable alternative.

7. Case Study

Sustainable supplier selection (SSS) is the process of evaluating and choosing suppliers based on their ability to meet the needs of an organisation while also considering the environmental and social impact of their practices. This approach to sourcing is becoming increasingly important as organisations recognise the need to minimise their environmental footprint and promote ethical business practices.

There are several reasons for which SSS is important. Firstly, it helps organisations meet their sustainability goals and reduce their environmental impact. By choosing suppliers that are committed to sustainability, organisations can minimise the environmental impact of their supply chain and reduce their greenhouse gas emissions. This can help organisations meet their sustainability targets and reduce their carbon footprint. Secondly,

SSS can help organisations reduce their risk. By choosing suppliers that are committed to sustainability, organisations can reduce the risk of supply chain disruptions caused by environmental disasters or social unrest. This is particularly important for organisations that rely on global supply chains, as these may be vulnerable to risks such as natural disasters or political instability. Thirdly, SSS can help organisations build and maintain a positive reputation. Consumers and other stakeholders are increasingly concerned about the environmental and social impact of the products and services they consume, and are more likely to choose companies that are transparent about their supply chain practices and that have a strong commitment to sustainability. By choosing sustainable suppliers, organisations can demonstrate their commitment to sustainability and build trust among their stakeholders.

There are several approaches that organisations can take to implementing SSS. One approach is to incorporate sustainability criteria into the supplier selection process. This can involve evaluating suppliers based on their environmental performance, labour practices, and social impact. Organisations can use tools such as sustainability assessment frameworks or rating systems to evaluate suppliers based on these criteria.

Another approach is to work with suppliers to improve their sustainability practices. This can involve setting sustainability targets for suppliers and providing them with support to meet these targets. Organisations can also work with suppliers to implement sustainability initiatives, such as reducing waste or increasing the use of renewable energy. SSS is often approached as an MCDM problem, as it involves the evaluation of multiple criteria such as cost, quality, delivery performance, and sustainability. MCDM methods are used to weigh these criteria and determine the most suitable supplier based on the organisation's specific needs and priorities.

SSS is an important aspect of corporate responsibility and can be approached as a MCDM problem. By choosing suppliers that are committed to sustainability and incorporating sustainability criteria into the supplier selection process, organisations can minimise their environmental impact, reduce risk, and build a positive reputation. Using MCDM methods, organisations can evaluate multiple criteria and choose suppliers that best meet their needs while also considering the environmental and social impacts of their practices.

Supplier selection is a critical process for firms to conduct in order to maintain a competitive edge and achieve their supply chain objectives. According to industry statistics, manufacturers spend up to 70% of their total product costs on products and services, while high-technology businesses spend up to 80% of their total product costs on goods and services. To properly manage this strategically critical purchasing function, it is crucial to choose the most appropriate strategy and parameters for the situation. In today's dynamic business environment, all the aspects of delivering goods must be considered, including reliability, versatility, and fast response, through the successful structure and implementation of the distribution chain. Vendor assessment is a critical part of the supply network, as it has an impact on the organisation's long objectives and productivity. Manufacturers have a variety of qualities and shortcomings that must be carefully evaluated by purchasers before they are ranked according to certain criteria. As a result, each choice must be integrated by weighing the performance of various suppliers at each supply chain level.

The problem becomes much more acute in manufacturing plants because considerable amounts of effort and money are spent on acquiring. Reliable vendors assist organisations in achieving the highest levels of their manufacturing strategy while also supplying practitioners with the greatest number of benefits. Supplier selection is regarded as a challenging task due to the high number of variables and the interactions among them. In general, the supply chain supplier selection problem is a group decision-making problem with a large number of criteria that must be met. Because group decision making involves human judgement, precise facts are insufficient to convey these judgments, which are based on human preferences. The more pragmatic approach is to make judgments based on language rather than numerical qualities. As a result, linguistic variables are utilised to assess the grades and weights given to the problem's criteria.

Supplier selection is an MCDM dilemma that is influenced by a number of competing considerations, including cost, reliability, and execution. Dickson conducted a study questionnaire-based distributed to 273 purchasing professionals, which resulted in the identification of 23 different regularly utilised criteria for the supplier selection problem. Dickson came to the conclusion that quality, delivery, and performance history are the most essential criteria out of the 23 elements considered [49]. Numerous strategies have been developed over the years to efficiently handle the challenge. In the literature, methods such as "analytic hierarchy process" (AHP), "analytic network process" (ANP), "linear programming" (LP), "mathematical programming", "multi-objective programming", "data envelopment analysis" (DEA), "neural networks" (NN), "case-based reasoning" (CBR), and "fuzzy set theory" (FST) have been used [50]. Additionally, the integration of many approaches has been developed by academics, and the integration capitalises on the strengths of each method while compensating for its flaws.

7.1. Criterion for SSS

There are several criteria that organisations can use to evaluate the sustainability of their suppliers. These criteria can be grouped into three main categories: environmental, social, and economic.

7.1.1. Environmental Criteria

- Carbon emissions: Organisations can evaluate suppliers based on their carbon emissions and the steps they are taking to reduce them. This can include evaluating the energy efficiency of their facilities, their use of renewable energy sources, and their transportation practices.
- Resource use: Organisations can evaluate suppliers based on their use of natural resources such as water and raw materials and their efforts to conserve these resources.
- Waste reduction: Organisations can evaluate suppliers based on their waste reduction efforts, including the recycling of materials and the implementation of zero waste initiatives.
- Environmental compliance: Organisations can evaluate suppliers based on their compliance with environmental regulations and their efforts to minimise the environmental impact of their operations.

7.1.2. Social Criteria

- Labour practices: Organisations can evaluate suppliers based on their treatment of employees, including their working conditions, wages, and benefits. This can also include evaluating the suppliers' policies on issues such as diversity, equity, and inclusion.
- Community involvement: Organisations can evaluate suppliers based on their involvement in and impact on the local community, including their charitable activities and efforts to address community needs.
- Human rights: Organisations can evaluate suppliers based on their respect for human rights and their efforts to prevent human rights abuses in their operations.

7.1.3. Economic Criteria

- Cost: Organisations can evaluate suppliers based on the cost of their products or services and the value they provide.
- Quality: Organisations can evaluate suppliers based on the quality of their products or services and their ability to meet the needs of the organisation.
- Delivery performance: Organisations can evaluate suppliers based on their ability to deliver products or services on time and in the required quantities.

- Innovation: Organisations can evaluate suppliers based on their ability to bring innovative products or services into the market and their willingness to collaborate on new product development.

There are several criteria that organisations can use to evaluate the sustainability of their suppliers. These criteria can be grouped into environmental, social, and economic categories and can be customised based on the specific needs and priorities of the organisation.

7.2. Decision-Making Application

A high-tech industrial business wishes to find an appropriate material supplier from whom to procure critical components for future products. Following preliminary screening, five candidates ($\aleph_1^{\daleth}, \aleph_2^{\daleth}, \aleph_3^{\daleth}, \aleph_4^{\daleth}$, and $\aleph_5^{\daleth}$) will be evaluated further. To pick the best acceptable supplier, a committee of four DMs, $\wp_1^{\mho}, \wp_2^{\mho}, \wp_3^{\mho}$, and $\wp_4^{\mho}$, has been constituted. Seven criteria are taken into account, as given in Table 5.

Table 5. Criterion for the assessment.

	Criteria
$\aleph_1^{\daleth}$	Quality
$\aleph_2^{\daleth}$	Technical support
$\aleph_3^{\daleth}$	Performance history
$\aleph_4^{\daleth}$	Cost
$\aleph_5^{\daleth}$	Reputation in industry
$\aleph_6^{\daleth}$	Risk factor
$\aleph_7^{\daleth}$	Professionalism

Step 1: Four DMs participated in the provided case study. The five-point FF linguistic scale was applied to various DMs given in Table 6. The table contains FFNs that denote the experts' credentials and expertise. Then, utilising Equation (1) and the related FFNs, a Fermatean fuzzy average distinction of an expert is calculated, as given in Table 7.

Table 6. Information about the DMs.

DMs	Qualifications	Experience (Years)	Gender
$\wp_1^{\mho}$	Ph.D.	15	Male
$\wp_2^{\mho}$	M.S.	19	Female
$\wp_3^{\mho}$	Ph.D.	23	Male
$\wp_4^{\mho}$	Ph.D.	35	Male

Table 7. Information about the DMs in terms of FFNs.

DMs	Qualifications	Experience (Years)	Average	Positive Score
$\wp_1^{\mho}$	$(0.900, 0.150)$	$(0.250, 0.700)$	$(0.575, 0.425)$	1.113
$\wp_2^{\mho}$	$(0.700, 0.250)$	$(0.500, 0.500)$	$(0.600, 0.375)$	1.163
$\wp_3^{\mho}$	$(0.900, 0.150)$	$(0.700, 0.250)$	$(0.800, 0.200)$	1.504
$\wp_4^{\mho}$	$(0.900, 0.150)$	$(0.900, 0.150)$	$(0.900, 0.150)$	1.726

Step 2: The FF average reputations of DMs are normalised using Equation 2. Because a DM cannot have a negative reputation value, the positive score algorithm is employed to obtain a crisp average result. The obtained reputation vector of the DMs is $\beth = (0.2021, 0.2112, 0.2732, 0.3135)$.

Step 3: The seven-point FF linguistic scale shown in Table 3 is used to determine the relative relevance of criteria. DMs examine predefined factors that influence the supplier evaluation process. Table 8 contains the ratings of the criteria's linguistic significance. Table 9 has seven matrices of criterion importance, one for each DM. These are generated using the matching FF linguistic importance scale and linguistic evaluations gathered from the field.

Table 8. DM evaluations of the criteria using linguistic terms.

Criterion	DMs			
	$\wp_1^{\mho}$	$\wp_2^{\mho}$	$\wp_3^{\mho}$	$\wp_4^{\mho}$
$\aleph_1^{\daleth}$	EI	VI	MI	I
$\aleph_2^{\daleth}$	VI	I	VI	MI
$\aleph_3^{\daleth}$	I	MI	VI	I
$\aleph_4^{\daleth}$	VI	VI	MI	VI
$\aleph_5^{\daleth}$	MI	I	VI	MI
$\aleph_6^{\daleth}$	I	MI	EI	VI
$\aleph_7^{\daleth}$	EI	I	VI	MI

Table 9. DM evaluations of the criteria in terms of corresponding FFNs.

Criterion	DMs			
	$\wp_1^{\mho}$	$\wp_2^{\mho}$	$\wp_3^{\mho}$	$\wp_4^{\mho}$
$\aleph_1^{\daleth}$	(0.975, 0.100)	(0.850, 0.200)	(0.550, 0.500)	(0.700, 0.350)
$\aleph_2^{\daleth}$	(0.850, 0.200)	(0.700, 0.350)	(0.850, 0.200)	(0.550, 0.500)
$\aleph_3^{\daleth}$	(0.700, 0.350)	(0.550, 0.500)	(0.850, 0.200)	(0.700, 0.350)
$\aleph_4^{\daleth}$	(0.850, 0.200)	(0.850, 0.200)	(0.550, 0.500)	(0.850, 0.200)
$\aleph_5^{\daleth}$	(0.550, 0.500)	(0.700, 0.350)	(0.850, 0.200)	(0.550, 0.500)
$\aleph_6^{\daleth}$	(0.700, 0.350)	(0.550, 0.500)	(0.975, 0.100)	(0.850, 0.200)
$\aleph_7^{\daleth}$	(0.975, 0.100)	(0.700, 0.350)	(0.850, 0.200)	(0.550, 0.500)

Step 4: Equation (3) aggregates the FF significance ratings of the parameters by taking into account the DMs' repute vector. Table 10 contains the calculated value.

Table 10. Aggregated FFNs for the criteria.

Criterion	Importance		
	Aggregated FFNs	**Positive Score**	**Normalised**
$\aleph_1^{\daleth}$	(0.730090, 0.370315)	1.33838	0.1440
$\aleph_2^{\daleth}$	(0.711773, 0.376696)	1.30715	0.1407
$\aleph_3^{\daleth}$	(0.701479, 0.372318)	1.29357	0.1392
$\aleph_4^{\daleth}$	(0.754690, 0.346039)	1.38840	0.1494
$\aleph_5^{\daleth}$	(0.651828, 0.425725)	1.19979	0.2150
$\aleph_6^{\daleth}$	(0.773977, 0.339312)	1.42458	0.1533
$\aleph_7^{\daleth}$	(0.731785, 0.373507)	1.33977	0.1442

Step 5: In this step, we normalise the FF aggregated importance evaluations of the criteria. Because criteria cannot have a negative significance, the positive score function is used to calculate the crisp aggregated values. Normalised values are given in Table 10.

Step 6: The alternatives are evaluated using the nine-point FF linguistic scale listed in Table 4. Table 11 contains the linguistic assessments of the options in relation to four DMs' decision criteria. Table 12 contains the initial decision matrices. These were designed using the FF linguistic assessment scale as a guide.

Table 11. DM evaluations for the alternatives in linguistic terms.

Experts	Alternatives	Criterion						
		$\aleph_1^{\urcorner}$	$\aleph_2^{\urcorner}$	$\aleph_3^{\urcorner}$	$\aleph_4^{\urcorner}$	$\aleph_5^{\urcorner}$	$\aleph_6^{\urcorner}$	$\aleph_7^{\urcorner}$
$\wp_1^{\mho}$	$\aleph_1^{\daleth}$	VG	G	MG	G	VG	VG	G
	$\aleph_2^{\daleth}$	MP	M	G	MG	VG	P	G
	$\aleph_3^{\daleth}$	MG	I	G	MP	M	VG	P
	$\aleph_4^{\daleth}$	G	I	MP	VG	M	G	MP
	$\aleph_5^{\daleth}$	P	MP	G	VG	M	VG	MP
$\wp_2^{\mho}$	$\aleph_1^{\daleth}$	VG	VG	G	MG	VG	G	MG
	$\aleph_2^{\daleth}$	M	G	MP	VG	M	P	G
	$\aleph_3^{\daleth}$	MP	I	VG	MP	M	P	VG
	$\aleph_4^{\daleth}$	M	MP	VP	G	M	VG	G
	$\aleph_5^{\daleth}$	G	M	MP	P	MP	P	VG
$\wp_3^{\mho}$	$\aleph_1^{\daleth}$	VG	G	VG	G	G	MG	G
	$\aleph_2^{\daleth}$	MP	M	VG	P	MP	MP	MG
	$\aleph_3^{\daleth}$	G	VG	MP	P	VG	VG	MG
	$\aleph_4^{\daleth}$	M	I	G	MP	VP	G	VG
	$\aleph_5^{\daleth}$	M	MP	P	VP	VG	I	G
$\wp_4^{\mho}$	$\aleph_1^{\daleth}$	VG	VG	G	MG	VG	G	MG
	$\aleph_2^{\daleth}$	M	G	MP	VG	M	P	G
	$\aleph_3^{\daleth}$	MP	I	VG	MP	M	P	VG
	$\aleph_4^{\daleth}$	M	MP	VP	G	M	VG	G
	$\aleph_5^{\daleth}$	G	M	MP	P	MP	P	VG

Table 12. DM evaluations for the alternative terms of the corresponding FFNs.

Experts	Alternatives	Criterion						
		$\aleph_1^{\urcorner}$	$\aleph_2^{\urcorner}$	$\aleph_3^{\urcorner}$	$\aleph_4^{\urcorner}$	$\aleph_5^{\urcorner}$	$\aleph_6^{\urcorner}$	$\aleph_7^{\urcorner}$
$\wp_1^{\mho}$	$\aleph_1^{\daleth}$	(0.900, 0.200)	(0.800, 0.300)	(0.650, 0.400)	(0.800, 0.300)	(0.900, 0.200)	(0.900, 0.200)	(0.800, 0.300)
	$\aleph_2^{\daleth}$	(0.400, 0.650)	(0.550, 0.500)	(0.800, 0.300)	(0.650, 0.400)	(0.900, 0.200)	(0.300, 0.800)	(0.800, 0.300)
	$\aleph_3^{\daleth}$	(0.650, 0.400)	(0.100, 0.975)	(0.800, 0.300)	(0.400, 0.650)	(0.550, 0.500)	(0.900, 0.200)	(0.300, 0.800)
	$\aleph_4^{\daleth}$	(0.800, 0.300)	(0.100, 0.975)	(0.400, 0.650)	(0.900, 0.200)	(0.550, 0.500)	(0.800, 0.300)	(0.400, 0.650)
	$\aleph_5^{\daleth}$	(0.300, 0.800)	(0.400, 0.650)	(0.800, 0.300)	(0.900, 0.200)	(0.550, 0.500)	(0.900, 0.200)	(0.400, 0.650)
$\wp_2^{\mho}$	$\aleph_1^{\daleth}$	(0.900, 0.200)	(0.900, 0.200)	(0.800, 0.300)	(0.650, 0.400)	(0.900, 0.200)	(0.800, 0.300)	(0.650, 0.400)
	$\aleph_2^{\daleth}$	(0.550, 0.500)	(0.800, 0.300)	(0.400, 0.650)	(0.900, 0.200)	(0.550, 0.500)	(0.300, 0.800)	(0.800, 0.300)
	$\aleph_3^{\daleth}$	(0.400, 0.650)	(0.100, 0.975)	(0.900, 0.200)	(0.400, 0.650)	(0.550, 0.500)	(0.300, 0.800)	(0.900, 0.200)
	$\aleph_4^{\daleth}$	(0.550, 0.500)	(0.400, 0.650)	(0.200, 0.900)	(0.800, 0.300)	(0.550, 0.500)	(0.900, 0.200)	(0.800, 0.300)
	$\aleph_5^{\daleth}$	(0.800, 0.300)	(0.550, 0.500)	(0.400, 0.650)	(0.300, 0.800)	(0.400, 0.650)	(0.300, 0.800)	(0.900, 0.200)
$\wp_3^{\mho}$	$\aleph_1^{\daleth}$	(0.900, 0.200)	(0.800, 0.300)	(0.900, 0.200)	(0.800, 0.300)	(0.800, 0.300)	(0.650, 0.400)	(0.800, 0.300)
	$\aleph_2^{\daleth}$	(0.400, 0.650)	(0.550, 0.500)	(0.900, 0.200)	(0.300, 0.800)	(0.400, 0.650)	(0.400, 0.650)	(0.650, 0.400)
	$\aleph_3^{\daleth}$	(0.800, 0.300)	(0.900, 0.200)	(0.400, 0.650)	(0.300, 0.800)	(0.900, 0.200)	(0.900, 0.200)	(0.650, 0.400)
	$\aleph_4^{\daleth}$	(0.550, 0.500)	(0.100, 0.975)	(0.800, 0.300)	(0.400, 0.650)	(0.200, 0.900)	(0.800, 0.300)	(0.900, 0.200)
	$\aleph_5^{\daleth}$	(0.550, 0.500)	(0.400, 0.650)	(0.300, 0.800)	(0.200, 0.900)	(0.900, 0.200)	(0.100, 0.975)	(0.800, 0.300)
$\wp_4^{\mho}$	$\aleph_1^{\daleth}$	(0.900, 0.200)	(0.900, 0.200)	(0.800, 0.300)	(0.650, 0.400)	(0.900, 0.200)	(0.800, 0.300)	(0.650, 0.400)
	$\aleph_2^{\daleth}$	(0.550, 0.500)	(0.800, 0.300)	(0.400, 0.650)	(0.900, 0.200)	(0.550, 0.500)	(0.300, 0.800)	(0.800, 0.300)
	$\aleph_3^{\daleth}$	(0.400, 0.650)	(0.100, 0.975)	(0.900, 0.200)	(0.400, 0.650)	(0.550, 0.500)	(0.300, 0.800)	(0.900, 0.200)
	$\aleph_4^{\daleth}$	(0.550, 0.500)	(0.400, 0.650)	(0.200, 0.900)	(0.800, 0.300)	(0.550, 0.500)	(0.900, 0.200)	(0.800, 0.300)
	$\aleph_5^{\daleth}$	(0.800, 0.300)	(0.550, 0.500)	(0.400, 0.650)	(0.300, 0.800)	(0.400, 0.650)	(0.300, 0.800)	(0.900, 0.200)

Step 7: Four decision matrices are aggregated using the FFWG operator specified in Equation (4), which take the DMs' reputational vector into consideration. Table 13 contains the derived FF aggregated assessments of the alternatives in relation to the criteria specified by four DMs.

Table 13. FF aggregated assessments of the alternatives.

Criterion	Alternatives				
	$\aleph_1^{\daleth}$	$\aleph_2^{\daleth}$	$\aleph_3^{\daleth}$	$\aleph_4^{\daleth}$	$\aleph_5^{\daleth}$
$\aleph_1^{\urcorner}$	(0.900, 0.200)	(0.473, 0.584)	(0.533, 0.557)	(0.593, 0.473)	(0.592, 0.562)
$\aleph_2^{\urcorner}$	(0.851, 0.258)	(0.669, 0.421)	(0.182, 0.948)	(0.207, 0.911)	(0.473, 0.584)
$\aleph_3^{\urcorner}$	(0.792, 0.309)	(0.574, 0.545)	(0.704, 0.459)	(0.336, 0.809)	(0.425, 0.676)
$\aleph_4^{\urcorner}$	(0.717, 0.360)	(0.624, 0.577)	(0.369, 0.693)	(0.677, 0.462)	(0.335, 0.804)
$\aleph_5^{\urcorner}$	(0.872, 0.236)	(0.557, 0.528)	(0.629, 0.455)	(0.417, 0.714)	(0.532, 0.563)
$\aleph_6^{\urcorner}$	(0.774, 0.322)	(0.325, 0.769)	(0.506, 0.681)	(0.851, 0.258)	(0.277, 0.872)
$\aleph_7^{\urcorner}$	(0.717, 0.359)	(0.755, 0.333)	(0.659, 0.536)	(0.718, 0.428)	(0.740, 0.419)

Step 8: Table 14 contains the normalised decision matrix. Equation (5) is used to determine it based on the aggregated decision matrix. The complement operation is used solely for the cost type attributes. Here, $\aleph_4^{\urcorner}$ and $\aleph_6^{\urcorner}$ are the cost-type attributes.

Table 14. Normalised assessment matrix.

Criterion	Alternatives				
	$\aleph_1^{\daleth}$	$\aleph_2^{\daleth}$	$\aleph_3^{\daleth}$	$\aleph_4^{\daleth}$	$\aleph_5^{\daleth}$
$\aleph_1^{\urcorner}$	(0.900, 0.200)	(0.473, 0.584)	(0.533, 0.557)	(0.593, 0.473)	(0.592, 0.562)
$\aleph_2^{\urcorner}$	(0.851, 0.258)	(0.669, 0.421)	(0.182, 0.948)	(0.207, 0.911)	(0.473, 0.584)
$\aleph_3^{\urcorner}$	(0.792, 0.309)	(0.574, 0.545)	(0.704, 0.459)	(0.336, 0.809)	(0.425, 0.676)
$\aleph_4^{\urcorner}$	(0.360, 0.717)	(0.577, 0.624)	(0.693, 0.369)	(0.462, 0.677)	(0.804, 0.335)
$\aleph_5^{\urcorner}$	(0.872, 0.236)	(0.557, 0.528)	(0.629, 0.455)	(0.417, 0.714)	(0.532, 0.563)
$\aleph_6^{\urcorner}$	(0.322, 0.774)	(0.769, 0.325)	(0.681, 0.506)	(0.258, 0.851)	(0.872, 0.277)
$\aleph_7^{\urcorner}$	(0.717, 0.359)	(0.755, 0.333)	(0.659, 0.536)	(0.718, 0.428)	(0.740, 0.419)

Step 9: To begin, the values of the FF normalised assessments' score functions are determined using the formulation of the FFNs' score function. Then, the FFNIS is calculated and provided as

$$\Big\{(0.473,0.584),(0.182,0.948),(0.336,0.809),(0.462,0.677),(0.417,0.714),$$
$$(0.258,0.851),(0.659,0.536)\Big\}.$$

Step 10: Evaluate the weighted Euclidean distances and weighted Hamming distances using Equations (6) and (7), given in Table 15.

Table 15. Weighted Euclidean distances and weighted Hamming distances.

Distance Measure	Alternatives				
	$\aleph_1^{\daleth}$	$\aleph_2^{\daleth}$	$\aleph_3^{\daleth}$	$\aleph_4^{\daleth}$	$\aleph_5^{\daleth}$
Weighted Euclidean	0.372646	0.266123	0.211559	0.0420982	0.278918
Weighted Hamming	0.599526	0.478071	0.364525	0.1012120	0.493522

Step 11: Construct the relative assessment matrix, which is given in Table 16. In the base case scenario, the threshold parameter $\phi > 0$ is set to 0.40.

Table 16. Relative assessment matrix.

Alternatives	$\aleph_1^{\daleth}$	$\aleph_2^{\daleth}$	$\aleph_3^{\daleth}$	$\aleph_4^{\daleth}$	$\aleph_5^{\daleth}$
$\aleph_1^{\daleth}$	0	0.106523	0.161087	0.330548	0.093728
$\aleph_2^{\daleth}$	0.106523	0	0.054564	0.224025	−0.012795
$\aleph_3^{\daleth}$	−0.161087	−0.054564	0	0.169461	−0.067359
$\aleph_4^{\daleth}$	−0.330548	−0.224025	−0.169461	0	−0.236820
$\aleph_5^{\daleth}$	−0.093728	0.012795	0.067359	-0.236820	0

Step 12: Calculate assessment scores and rank the alternatives using Equation (9) given in Table 17.

Table 17. Assessment scores and final ranking.

Alternatives	Assessment Score	Rank
$\aleph_1^{\daleth}$	0.691886	1
$\aleph_2^{\daleth}$	0.372317	2
$\aleph_3^{\daleth}$	−0.113549	4
$\aleph_4^{\daleth}$	−0.960854	5
$\aleph_5^{\daleth}$	0.250394	3

7.3. Comparison Analysis

We compare our findings to existing models to confirm their veracity and validity, as shown in Table 18.

Table 18. Comparison analysis.

Methods	Authors	Top Ranking
TOPSIS method	Aydemir and Gunduz [51]	$\aleph_1^{\daleth}$
VIKOR method	Gül [52]	$\aleph_1^{\daleth}$
CODAS method	Simic et. al. [53]	$\aleph_1^{\daleth}$

8. Conclusions

Numerous practitioners and academics have emphasised the benefits of supply chain management. Many organisations have learned that a well-managed supply chain system is a vital instrument for strengthening their competitive edge. Under these circumstances, establishing strong and long-term connections between customers and suppliers is important to the supply chain system's performance. As a result, the issue of supplier selection becomes the key concern when developing an effective supply chain system. We invented the Fermatean fuzzy "Combinative Distance-based Assessment" CODAS approach for the selection of optimum provider. To begin, in contrast to the overwhelming majority of existing group decision-making systems, which assume either a known reputation vector or equal expert weights, experts' reputation is established by their qualifications and experience. Second, the Fermatean fuzzy direct rating approach is utilised to establish the relative significance of criteria based on the expert group's evaluation preferences. Thirdly, the Fermatean fuzzy CODAS technique is utilised to generate alternative orderings based on their assessment scores. Topological data analysis (TDA) techniques are quickly gaining traction as methods for managing massive amounts of data. Moreover, numerous concepts relevant to FFTSs are explored in this paper. Examples are supplied for the FF interior, FF closure, and FF border of any FFS. The notions of FF base, FF subbase, FF continuous mapping, FF homeomorphism, FF open function, and FF closed function are also introduced, along with several crucial proofs. Furthermore, the novel idea of "Fermatean fuzzy α-continuous mapping" between FFTSs and "Fermatean fuzzy connectedness" is introduced and studied.

Author Contributions: M.B.: Methodology, Formal analysis, Writing—review & editing. H.M.A.F.: Methodology, Formal analysis, Writing—review & editing. M.R.: Investigation, Methodology, Supervision. N.J.: Methodology, Investigation. All authors made a significant scientific contribution to the research in the manuscript. All authors have read and agreed to the published version of the manuscript.

Funding: This research received no external funding.

Institutional Review Board Statement: Not applicable.

Informed Consent Statement: Not applicable.

Data Availability Statement: The data used to support the findings of the study are included within the article.

Acknowledgments: The authors extend their appreciation to the Deanship of Scientific Research at King Khalid University, Abha, Saudi Arabia, for funding this work through a research group program under grant number R.G.P. 2/217/43.

Conflicts of Interest: The authors declare that they have no conflict of interest.

References

1. Zadeh, L.A. Fuzzy sets . *Inf. Control* **1965**, *8*, 338–353. [CrossRef]
2. Pawlak, Z. Rough sets. *Int. J. Inf. Comput. Sci.* **1982**, *11*, 341–356. [CrossRef]
3. Molodtsov, D. Soft set theory-first results. *Comput. Math. Appl.* **1999**, *37*, 19–31. [CrossRef]
4. Chang, C.L. Fuzzy topological spaces. *J. Math. Anal. Appl.* **1968**, *24*, 182–190. [CrossRef]
5. Lowen, R. Fuzzy topological spaces and fuzzy compactness. *J. Math. Anal. Appl.* **1976**, *56*, 621–633. [CrossRef]
6. Lowen, R. Initial and final fuzzy topologies and the fuzzy Tychonoff theorem. *J. Math. Anal. Appl.* **1977**, *58*, 11–21. [CrossRef]
7. Atanassov, K.T. Intuitionistic fuzzy sets. *Fuzzy Sets Ans Syst.* **1986**, *20*, 87–96. [CrossRef]
8. Coker, D. An introduction to intuitionistic fuzzy topological spaces. *Fuzzy Sets Syst.* **1997**, *88*, 81–89. [CrossRef]
9. Coker, D.; Haydar, E.A. On fuzzy compactness in intuitionistic fuzzy topological spaces. *J. Fuzzy Math.* **1995**, *3*, 899–910.
10. Turanli, N.; Coker, D. Fuzzy connectedness in intuitionistic fuzzy topological spaces. *Fuzzy Sets Syst.* **2000**, *116*, 369–375. [CrossRef]
11. Ozcag, S.; Coker, D. On connectedness in intuitionistic fuzzy special topological spaces. *Int. J. Math. Math. Sci.* **1998**, *21*, 33–40. [CrossRef]
12. Kramosil, I.; Michalek, J. Fuzzy metrics and statistical metric spaces. *Kybernetika* **1975**, *11*, 336–344.
13. Singal, M.K.; Rajvanshi, N. Fuzzy alpha-sets and alpha-continuous maps. *Fuzzy Sets Syst.* **1992**, *483*, 383–390. [CrossRef]
14. Ajmal, N.; Kohli, J.K. Connectedness in fuzzy topological spaces. *Fuzzy Sets Syst.* **1989**, *31*, 369–388. [CrossRef]
15. Chaudhuri, A.K.; Das, P. Fuzzy connected sets in fuzzy topological spaces. *Fuzzy Sets Syst.* **1992**, *49*, 223–229. [CrossRef]
16. Olgun, M.; Unver, M.; Yardymcy, P. Pythagorean fuzzy topological spaces. *Complex Intell. Syst.* **2019**, *5*, 177–183. [CrossRef]
17. Turkarslan, E.; Unver, M.; Olgun, M. q-Rung orthopair fuzzy topological spaces. *Lobachevskii J. Math.* **2021**, *42*, 470–478. [CrossRef]
18. Charisma, J.; Ajay, D. Pythagorean fuzzy α-continuity. *J. Comput. Math.* **2020**, *4*, 10–15.
19. Haydar, A. Connectedness in Pythagorean fuzzy topological spaces. *Int. J. Math. Trends Technol.* **2019**, *65*, 110–116. [CrossRef]
20. Yager, R.R.; Abbasov, A.M. Pythagorean membership grades, complex numbers, and decision making. *Int. J. Intell. Syst.* **2013**, *28*, 436–452. [CrossRef]
21. Yager, R.R. Pythagorean fuzzy subsets. In Proceedings of the 2013 Joint IFSA World Congress, NAFIPS Annual Meeting (IFSA/NAFIPS), Edmonton, Canada, 24–28 June 2013; pp. 57–61.
22. Yager, R.R. Pythagorean membership grades in multi criteria decision-making. *IEEE Trans. Fuzzy Syst.* **2014**, 22, 958–965. [CrossRef]
23. Yager, R.R. Generalized orthopair fuzzy sets. *IEEE Trans. Fuzzy Syst.* **2017**, *25*, 1222–1230. [CrossRef]
24. Senapati, T.; Yager, R.R. Fermatean fuzzy sets. *J. Ambient. Intell. Humaniz. Comput.* **2020**, *11*, 663–674. [CrossRef]
25. Xu, Z.S. Intuitionistic fuzzy aggregation operators. *IEEE Transections Fuzzy Syst.* **2007**, *15*, 1179–1187.
26. Xu, Z.S.; Yager, R.R. Some geometric aggregation operators based on intuitionistic fuzzy sets. *Int. J. Gen. Syst.* **2006**, *35*, 417–433. [CrossRef]
27. Akram, M.; Amjad, U.; Alcantud, J.C.R.; Garcia, G.S. Complex fermatean fuzzy N-soft sets: a new hybrid model with applications. *J. Ambient. Intell. Humaniz. Comput.* **2022**. [CrossRef]
28. Feng, F.; Zheng, Y.; Sun, B.; Akram, M. Novel score functions of generalized orthopair fuzzy membership grades with application to multiple attribute decision making., *Granul. Comput.* **2022**, *7*, 95–111. [CrossRef]
29. Riaz, M.; Farid, H.M.A.; Aslam, M.; Pamucar, D.; Bozanic, D. Novel approach for third-party reverse logistic provider selection process under linear Diophantine fuzzy prioritized aggregation operators. *Symmetry* **2021**, *13*, 1152. [CrossRef]
30. Iampan, A.; Garcia, G.S.; Riaz, M.; Farid, H.M.A.; Chinram, R. Linear Diophantine fuzzy Einstein aggregation operators for multi-criteria decision-making problems. *J. Math.* **2021**, *2021*, 5548033. [CrossRef]

31. Ashraf, S.; Abdullah, S. Emergency decision support modeling for COVID-19 based on spherical fuzzy information. *Int. J. Intell. Syst.* **2020**, *35*, 1–45. [CrossRef]
32. Saha, A.; Dutta, D.; Kar, S. Some new hybrid hesitant fuzzy weighted aggregation operators based on Archimedean and Dombi operations for multi-attribute decision making. Neural Comput. Appl. **2021**, *33*, 8753–8776. [CrossRef]
33. Saha, A.; Majumder, P.; Dutta, D.; Debnath, B.K. Multi-attribute decision making using q-rung orthopair fuzzy weighted fairly aggregation operators. *J. Ambient. Intell. Humaniz. Comput.* **2021**, *12*, 8149–8171. [CrossRef]
34. Wei, G.; Zhang, Z. Some single-valued neutrosophic bonferroni power aggregation operators in multiple attribute decision making. *J. Ambient. Intell. Humaniz. Comput.* **2019**, *10*, 863–882. [CrossRef]
35. Wei, G.; Wei, Y. Some single-valued neutrosophic dombi prioritized weighted aggregation operators in multiple attribute decision making. *J. Intell. Fuzzy Syst.* **2018**, *35*, 2001–2013. [CrossRef]
36. Garg, H. Multi-attribute group decision-making process based on possibility degree and operators for intuitionistic multiplicative set. *Complex Intell. Syst.* **2021**, *7*, 1099–1121. [CrossRef]
37. Naeem, K.; Riaz, M.; Peng, X.; Afzal, D. Pythagorean m-polar fuzzy topology with TOPSIS approach in exploring most effectual method for curing from COVID-19. *Int. J. Biomath.* **2020**, *13*, 2050075. [CrossRef]
38. Peng, J.J.; Wang, J.Q.; Wang, J.; Zhang, H.Y.; Chen, Z.H. Simplified neutrosophic sets and their applications in multi-criteria group decision-making problems. *Int. J. Syst. Sci.* **2016**, *47*, 2342–2358. [CrossRef]
39. Liu, P.; Chu, Y.; Li, Y.; Chen, Y. Some generalized neutrosophic number Hamacher aggregation operators and their application to group decision making. *Int. J. Fuzzy Syst.* **2014**, *16*, 242–255.
40. Farid, H.M.A.; Riaz, M. Single-valued neutrosophic Einstein interactive aggregation operators with applications for material selection in engineering design: case study of cryogenic storage tank. *Complex Intell. Syst.* **2022**, *8*, 2131–2149. [CrossRef]
41. Lin, M.; Huang, C.; Xu, Z.; Chen, R. Evaluating IoT Platforms Using Integrated Probabilistic Linguistic MCDM Method. *IEEE Internet Things J.* **2020**, *7*, 11195–11208. [CrossRef]
42. Huang, C.; Lin, M.; Xu, Z. Pythagorean fuzzy MULTIMOORA method based on distance measure and score function: its application in multicriteria decision making process. *Knowl. Inf. Syst.* **2020**, *62*, 4373–4406. [CrossRef]
43. Lin, M.; Huang, C.; Xu, Z. TOPSIS Method Based on Correlation Coefficient and Entropy Measure for Linguistic Pythagorean Fuzzy Sets and Its Application to Multiple Attribute Decision Making. *Complexity* **2019**, *2019*, 6967390. [CrossRef]
44. Lin, M.; Li, X.; Chen, R.; Fujita, H.; Lin, J. Picture fuzzy interactional partitioned Heronian mean aggregation operators: an application to MADM process. *Artif. Intell. Rev.* **2022**, *55*, 1171–1208. [CrossRef]
45. Senapati, T.; Yager, R.R. Some new operations over Fermatean fuzzy numbers and application of fermatean fuzzy WPM in multiple criteria decision making. *Informatica* **2019**, *30*, 391–412. [CrossRef]
46. Ghorabaee, M.K.; Zavadskas, E.K.; Turskis, Z.; Antucheviciene, J. A new combinative distance-based assessment (CODAS) method for multi-criteria decision-making. *Econ. Comput. Econ. Cybern. Stud. Res.* **2016**, *50*, 25–44.
47. Ghorabaee, M.K.; Amiri, M.; Zavadskas, E.K.; Hooshmand, R.; Antuchevieiene, J. Fuzzy extension of the CODAS method for multi-criteria market segment evaluation. *Journal Of Bus. Econ. Manag.* **2017**, *18*, 1–19.
48. Ghorabaee, M.K.; Amiri, M.; Tabatabaei, M.H.; Zavadskas, E.K.; Kaklauskas, A. A new decision-making approach based on Fermatean fuzzy sets and WASPAS for green construction supplier evaluation. *Mathematics* **2020**, *8*, 2202. [CrossRef]
49. Dickson, G.W. An analysis of vendor selection systems and decisions. *J. Purch.* **1966**, *2*, 5–17. [CrossRef]
50. Guneri, A.F.; Yucel, A.; Ayyildiz, G. An integrated fuzzy-lp approach for a supplier selection problem in supply chain management. *Expert Syst. Appl.* **2009**, *36*, 9223–9228. [CrossRef]
51. Aydemir, S.B.; Gunduz, S.Y. Fermatean Fuzzy TOPSIS Method with Dombi Aggregation Operators and Its Application in Multi-criteria Decision Making. *J. Intell. Fuzzy Syst.* **2020**, *39*, 851–869. [CrossRef]
52. Gül, S. Fermatean fuzzy set extensions of SAW, ARAS, and VIKOR with applications in COVID-19 testing laboratory selection problem. *Expert Syst.* **2021**, *38*, 12769. [CrossRef] [PubMed]
53. Simic, V.; Gokasar, I.; Deveci, M.; Isik, M. Fermatean Fuzzy Group Decision-Making Based CODAS Approach for Taxation of Public Transit Investments. *IEEE Trans. Eng. Manag.* **2021**. [CrossRef]

symmetry

MDPI

Article

A Novel GDMD-PROMETHEE Algorithm Based on the Maximizing Deviation Method and Social Media Data Mining for Large Group Decision Making

Juxiang Wang [1,2,*], Si Li [1] and Xiangyu Zhou [1]

[1] School of Mathematics and Physics, Anhui Jianzhu University, Hefei 230601, China
[2] School of Management, Hefei University of Technology, Hefei 230009, China
* Correspondence: wjxahjzdx@ahjzu.edu.cn

Abstract: Multi-attribute group decision making is widely used in the real world, and many scholars have done a lot of research on it. The public's focus on emergencies can provide an important reference for emergency handling decision making in the social media big data environment. Due to the complexity of emergency handling decision making, the asymmetry of user evaluation information is easy to cause the loss of important information. It is very important to mine valuable information for decision making through online reviews. Then, a generalized extended hybrid distance measure method between the probabilistic linguistic term sets is proposed. Based on this, an extended GDMD-PROMETHEE large-scale multi-attribute group decision-making method is proposed as well, which can be used to decision making under symmetric information and asymmetric information. Firstly, web crawler technology is used to explore the topics of public concern of emergency handling on social media platforms, and use *k*-means cluster analysis to classify the crawling variables, then the attributes and subjective weights of emergency handling plans are obtained by TF-IDF and Word2vec technology. Secondly, in order to better retain the linguistic evaluation information from decision-makers, a new generalized probabilistic hybrid distance measure method based on Hamming distance is proposed. Considering the difference of decision makers' evaluation, the objective weight of decision makers is calculated by combining the maximum deviation method with the new extended hybrid Euclidean distance. On this basis, the comprehensive weights of the attributes are calculated by combining subjective and objective factors. Meanwhile, this paper realizes the distance measures and information fusion of probabilistic linguistic term sets under cumulative prospect theory, and the ranking results of the emergency handling plans based on the extended GDMD-PROMETHEE algorithm are given. Finally, the feasibility and effectiveness of the extended GDMD-PROMETHEE algorithm are verified by the case study of the explosion accident handling decision making of Shanghai "6.18" Petrochemical, and the comparative analyses between the several traditional algorithms demonstrate the extended GDMD-PROMETHEE algorithm is more scientific and superior in this paper.

Keywords: probabilistic linguistic term set; cumulative prospect theory; maximum deviation method; PROMETHEE

1. Introduction

In recent years, the frequency of unconventional emergencies has been increasing, and such events not only constrain economic and social development, but also pose a serious threat to human livelihood security. Therefore, in the new situation, it is important to focus on improving the emergency management capabilities of emergency management agencies and reducing the adverse effects caused by emergencies. Since emergency decision-making events are uncertain, risky, and variable, different emergency management options need to be developed for different types of events [1–4]. How to decide the best solution among various alternatives is a major problem that needs to be solved urgently and is the research of this paper.

Unlike traditional decision problems, the complexity and asymmetry of large group decision problems and the differences in decision makers' own knowledge level, life experience and research direction lead to the difficulty of decision makers to make accurate judgments on decision options under a short time pressure in the decision process. At this time, they often choose to express their preferences in the form of fuzzy numbers. In the actual multi-attribute decision making (MADM), Herrera et al. [5] extended linguistic forms of decision making to group decision making (GDM), where the use of linguistic terms allows for a convenient and intuitive representation of the evaluator's uncertainty preferences. This allows experts to scientifically weigh the choice of emergency response options for major disaster relief, corporate investment choices and large constructive projects [6].

With the popularity and development of the Internet, more and more social media platforms encourage the public to post their opinions and form text comments on the web, such as Weibo, Douban, AutoZone, and GoWhere. How to help decision makers (DMs) make choices based on text comments after an emergency event is a meaningful study and an essential task of this paper. So far, some scholars have mined and studied the behavior of social media users. Xu et al. [7–9] mined the topics of public concern events through social media platforms, introduced the social relationship network of experts, and built a consensus model to complete the selection of alternatives. The traditional GDM with multi-granularity linguistic details, on the other hand, focuses more on the expert side's opinions and loses the original data's complete information [10]. In this paper, the study of academic, social network user clustering based on user behavior data, mining the degree of utilization and behavior patterns of different user groups, better retains the integrity of the information, solves the problem of completely unknown attribute weights [11] and helps to understand the information behavior patterns of academic and social network users.

For complex large-group decision problems, the representation and fusion of information are crucial. Many aggregation operators have developed in the literature, such as the ordered weighted average operator (OWA), the induced ordered weighted average operator (IOWA) and so on. Many scholars have also applied foreground theory in different linguistic value situations recently. Gao et al. [12] introduced foreground theory into the probabilistic language environment and proposed a foreground decision method based on a probabilistic linguistic term set (PLTS). Yu Zhang et al. [13] proposed an improved probabilistic linguistic multicriteria compromise solution group decision method PL-VIKOR based on cumulative prospect theory (CPT) and learned ratings.

Determining weights is an essential part of decision making. According to the source of the original data for calculating weights, these methods can be divided into three categories: subjective assignment method, objective assignment method, and combined assignment method. The subjective assignment method is an early and mature method, which determines the weight of attributes according to the importance of the DMs subjectively, and the DMs' subjective judgment obtains the original data based on experience. The commonly used subjective assignment methods are the expert's survey method (Delphi method) [14], analytic hierarchy process [15] (AHP), the binomial coefficient method [16], and ring score methods [17]. Furthermore, the original data of the objective assignment method is formed by the actual data of each attribute in the decision scheme. The commonly used objective assignment methods are principal component analysis, entropy value method [18], multi-objective planning method, deviation [19] and mean square difference methods. In order to make the decision results accurate and reliable, scholars propose a third type of assignment method, namely, the subjective–objective integrated assignment method. The subjective–objective assignment method includes the compromise coefficient integrated weighting method, linear-weighted single-objective optimization method, combined assignment method [20], Frank–Wolfe method, etc.

In the past decades, MADM methods have been successfully applied in several fields and disciplines, and different MADM methods yield similarity in the final rankings [21]. These methods include the technique of preference ranking with similarity to the ideal solution (TOPSIS) [22], VIekriterijumsko KOmpromisno Rangiranje (VIKOR) [13], the preference ranking organization method for enrichment of evaluations (PROMETHEE) [23], to better solve the complex problem. However, many problems in real life have vague and uncertain information, thus leading to the language of probability. In 1965, Zadeh [24] introduced the concept of "fuzzy set," then, Pang [11] and others extended the set of hesitant fuzzy linguistic terms by adding probability values and gave the first definition of the probabilistic linguistic term set. Wang [25] proposed the comparative algorithm of the score function, deviation function, and probabilistic hesitant fuzzy set. In this paper, we use the probabilistic language PROMETHEE, which is an outer ranking method proposed by Brans and Vincle [26] in 1985 for obtaining partial (PROMETHEE I) and complete (PROMETHEE II) rankings of alternatives based on multiple attributes or criteria.

Considering the timeliness of emergency decision making, the weight of each decision expert is more quickly obtained by using maximizing deviation method [27–29] in this paper. Gong et al. [30] proposed a method based on cardinal deviations to measure the differences between multiplicative linguistic term sets and combined it with VIKOR. Akram et al. [31] proposed a decision method based on the maximum deviation method by TOPSIS to solve the MADM problem with incomplete attribute weight information. This paper combined the maximum deviation method with PROMETHEE on the basis of mixed distance to solve the multi-attribute group decision-making (MAGDM) problem.

Based on the above discussion, this paper addresses the problem of complex large-group emergency decision making in the social media big data environment. This paper is organized as follows. In Section 2, we define basic concepts of probabilistic languages and a new generalized extended hybrid distance based on PLTS. In Section 3, we collect public opinions on social media platforms, extract keywords, and explore the attributes of emergency decision-making events as an essential basis for expert evaluation of solutions. Then, we use a combination of subjective and objective weighting models to integrate public opinions with expert decision making by CPT. In Section 4, we provide a specific flow on the GDMD-PROMETHEE algorithm. In Section 5, we verify the validity and feasibility of this paper's method through the "6–18" Shanghai Petrochemical explosion and compare it with other methods. Meanwhile, a sensitivity analysis was conducted. In Section 6, we present conclusions.

2. Preliminaries

2.1. Probabilistic Linguistic Term Sets

PLTS is one of the most widely used research tool in MAGDM. In this section, we introduce the basic concepts of linguistic term sets (LTSs) and distance measure between them. On this basis, the basic concepts of PLTSs, as well as distance improvement are given.

Definition 1. [1] *Let $S = \{s_\alpha | \alpha = 0, 1, 2, \cdots, 2g, g \in N^+\}$ be a LTS, then different language terms may be used. For example, let S be the following LTS: $S_9 = \{s_0 = extremely\ low$, $s_1 = very\,low, s_2 = low, s_3 = slightly\,low, s_4 = fair, s_5 = slightly\,high, s_6 = high, s_7 = very$ $high, s_8 = extremely\ high\}$, s_α satisfies the following conditions:*

1. *The set is ordered: $s_{\alpha_1} > s_{\alpha_2}$, if $\alpha_1 > \alpha_2$;*
2. *The negation operator is defined: $neg(s_\alpha) = s_{2g-\alpha}$,*

where s_α can be expressed by the linguistic scale transformation function f as: $f(s_\alpha) = \alpha/2g$, α is the subscript of s_α.

Definition 2. [1] *Let $S = \{s_\alpha | \alpha = 0, 1, 2, \cdots, 2g, g \in N^+\}$ be a LTS, a PLTS can be defined as:*

$$L(p) = \left\{ L^{(k)}(p^{(k)}) \middle| L^{(k)} \in S, p^{(k)} \geq 0, k = 1, 2, \cdots, \#L(p), \sum_{k=1}^{\#L(p)} p^{(k)} \leq 1 \right\} \tag{1}$$

where $L^{(k)}(p^{(k)})$ *denotes the associated probability of the set of linguistic terms* $L^{(k)}$ *with* $p^{(k)}$*;* $\#L(p)$ *denotes the number of linguistic terms in the set of probabilistic linguistic terms.*

Note that if $\sum_{k=1}^{\#L(p)} p^{(k)} = 1$, then we have the complete information of probabilistic distribution of all possible linguistic terms; if $\sum_{k=1}^{\#L(p)} p^{(k)} \leq 1$, then partial ignorance exists because current knowledge is not enough to provide complete assessment information, which is not rare in practical GDM problems. Especially, $\sum_{k=1}^{\#L(p)} p^{(k)} = 0$ means completely ignorance. Obviously, handling the ignorance of $L(p)$ is a crucial work for the use of PLTSs.

Definition 3. [32] *Given a PLTS* $L(p)$ *with* $\sum_{k=1}^{\#L(p)} p^{(k)} \leq 1$*, then the normalized PLTS* $\dot{L}(p)$ *is defined by:*

$$\dot{L}(p) = \{L^{(k)}(\dot{p}^{(k)})|L^{(k)} \in S, p^{(k)} \geq 0, k = 1, 2, \cdots, \#L(p), \dot{p}^{(k)} = p^{(k)}/\sum_{k=1}^{\#L(p)} p^{(k)}\} \quad (2)$$

Definition 4. [11] *Let* $L(p)$ *be a PLTS, the score of* $L(p)$ *is* $E(L(p)) = s_{\overline{\alpha}}$*, where:*

$$\overline{\alpha} = \sum_{k=1}^{\#L(p)} \alpha^{(k)} p^{(k)} / \sum_{k=1}^{\#L(p)} p^{(k)} \quad (3)$$

Definition 5. [11] *The deviation degree of* $L(p)$ *is:*

$$\sigma(L(p)) = \left(\sum_{k=1}^{\#L(p)} (p^{(k)}(\alpha^{(k)} - \overline{\alpha}))^2\right)^{1/2} / \sum_{k=1}^{\#L(p)} p^{(k)} \quad (4)$$

where $\alpha^{(k)}$ *is the subscript of linguistic term* $L^{(k)}$*, given two PLTSs* $L_1(p)$ *and* $L_2(p)$ *then:*

(1) *If* $E(L_1(p)) > E(L_2(p))$*, then* $L_1(p) \succ L_2(p)$*;*
(3) *If* $E(L_1(p)) < E(L_2(p))$*, then* $L_1(p) \prec L_2(p)$*;*
(3) *If* $E(L_1(p)) = E(L_2(p))$*, while* $\sigma(L_1(p)) < \sigma(L_2(p))$*, then* $L_1(p) \succ L_2(p)$*; while* $\sigma(L_1(p)) > \sigma(L_2(p))$*, then* $L_1(p) \prec L_2(p)$*; while* $\sigma(L_1(p)) = \sigma(L_2(p))$*, then* $L_1(p) \approx L_2(p)$*.*

2.2. Distance Measures between PLTSs

PLTSs can more accurately represent qualitative information of DMs in complex linguistic environments. However, existing distance measures may distort the original information and lead to unreasonable results. For this reason, a new generalized hybrid distance based on the classical distance is proposed.

Definition 6. *Let* $L_1(p) = \left\{L_1^{(k)}(p_1^{(k)})\middle|L_1^{(k)} \in S, p_1^{(k)} \geq 0, k = 1, 2, \cdots, \#L_1(p), \sum_{k=1}^{\#L_1(p)} p_1{}^{(k)} = 1\right\}$ *and* $L_2(p) = \left\{L_2^{(k)}(p_2^{(k)})\middle|L_2^{(k)} \in S,\ p_2^{(k)} \geq 0,\ k = 1, 2, \cdots, \#L_2(p), \sum_{k=1}^{\#L_2(p)} p_2{}^{(k)} = 1\right\}$ *be two PLTSs,* $\#L_1(p) = \#L_2(p)$*,* $L_1^{(k)}$ *and* $L_2^{(k)}$ *are the kth linguistic terms of* $L_1(p)$ *and* $L_2(p)$ *respectively,* $p_1^{(k)}$ *and* $p_2^{(k)}$ *are the probabilities of the kth linguistic terms of* $L_1(p)$ *and* $L_2(p)$ *respectively,* $\alpha_1^{(k)}$ *and* $\alpha_2^{(k)}$ *are the subscripts of the linguistic terms corresponding to* $L_1^{(k)}$ *and* $L_2^{(k)}$*, respectively, then a new probabilistic linguistic distance based on Reference* [33] *is defined as:*

$$d(L_1(p), L_2(p)) = \frac{1}{2}\left(\frac{1}{2}\sum_{k=1}^{\#L(p)} \left|p_1^{(k)} - p_2^{(k)}\right| + \left|\sum_{k=1}^{\#L(p)} f(\alpha_1^{(k)})p_1^{(k)} - \sum_{k=1}^{\#L(p)} f(\alpha_2^{(k)})p_2^{(k)}\right|\right) \quad (5)$$

Definition 7. [34] *Let* $L_1(p) = \left\{L_1^{(k)}(p_1^{(k)}) \middle| L_1^{(k)} \in S, p_1^{(k)} \geq 0, k = 1,2,\cdots,\#L_1(p), \sum_{k=1}^{\#L_1(p)} p_1^{(k)} = 1\right\}$ *and* $L_2(p) = \left\{L_2^{(k)}(p_2^{(k)}) \middle| L_2^{(k)} \in S,\ p_2^{(k)} \geq 0,\ k = 1,2,\cdots,\#L_2(p), \sum_{k=1}^{\#L_2(p)} p_2^{(k)} = 1\right\}$ *be two PLTSs,* $\#L_1(p) = \#L_2(p)$, $L_1^{(k)}$ *and* $L_2^{(k)}$ *are the kth linguistic terms of* $L_1(p)$ *and* $L_2(p)$ *respectively,* $p_1^{(k)}$ *and* $p_2^{(k)}$ *are the probabilities of the kth linguistic terms of* $L_1(p)$ *and* $L_2(p)$ *respectively. Then, the extended Hausdorff distance is:*

$$d_h(L_1(p), L_2(p)) = \max_{k=1}^{\#L_1(p)} \left\{ \left\{ \frac{1}{2} \left[\min_{k'=1}^{\#L_2(p)} \left(\left| f(\alpha_1^{(k)}) - f(\alpha_2^{(k')}) \right|^{\lambda} + \left| f(\alpha_1^{(k)}) p_1^{(k)} - f(\alpha_2^{(k')}) p_2^{(k')} \right|^{\lambda} \right) \right] \right\}^{\frac{1}{\lambda}} \right\} \quad (6)$$

where f is the linguistic scale function, $\lambda > 0$, *when* $\lambda = 1$, *the above Equation(6) is Hamming-Hausdorff distance; when* $\lambda = 2$, *the above Equation is Euclidean-Hausdorff distance.*

In MAGDM, when the above distances cannot meet the decision needs, this paper creatively introduces probability-related distances to achieve perfect integration with the probabilistic linguistic, and also fully considers the wishes of each decision maker, the new distance is given as follow.

Definition 8. *Let* $S = \{s_\alpha | \alpha = 0,1,2,\cdots,2g, g \in N^+\}$ *is an LTS. Let* $L_1(p) = \left\{L_1^{(k)}(p_1^{(k)}) \middle| L_1^{(k)} \in S, p_1^{(k)} \geq 0, k = 1,2,\cdots,\#L_1(p), \sum_{k=1}^{\#L_1(p)} p_1^{(k)} = 1\right\}$ *and* $L_2(p) = \left\{L_2^{(k)}(p_2^{(k)}) \middle| L_2^{(k)} \in S, p_2^{(k)} \geq 0, k = 1,2,\cdots, \#L_2(p), \sum_{k=1}^{\#L_2(p)} p_2^{(k)} = 1\right\}$ *be two PLTSs, then the generalized hybrid distance between PLTSs is defined as:*

$$\begin{aligned} D_{gh}(L_1(p), L_2(p)) = \Bigg\{ \eta \Bigg[\frac{1}{2} \Bigg(\frac{1}{2} \sum_{k=1}^{\#L(p)} \left| p_1^{(k)} - p_2^{(k)} \right| + \left| \sum_{k=1}^{\#L(p)} f(\alpha_1^{(k)}) p_1^{(k)} - \sum_{k=1}^{\#L(p)} f(\alpha_2^{(k)}) p_2^{(k)} \right| \Bigg)^{\lambda} \Bigg] + (1-\eta) \\ \max_{k=1}^{\#L(p)} \left\{ \frac{1}{2} \left[\min_{k=1}^{\#L(p)} \left(\left| f(\alpha_1^{(k)}) - f(\alpha_2^{(k)}) \right|^{\lambda} + \left| f(\alpha_1^{(k)}) p_1^{(k)} - f(\alpha_2^{(k)}) p_2^{(k)} \right|^{\lambda} \right) \right] \right\} \Bigg\}^{\frac{1}{\lambda}} \end{aligned} \quad (7)$$

From Equation (7), $\lambda \geq 1$, $\eta \in [0,1]$, the generalized hybrid distance combines the generalized probabilistic linguistic distance and the extended Hausdorff distance through the parameter η. The parameter λ can be considered as the expert's risk attitude, so the proposed distance allows more options for the experts to decide their risk preferences through the parameters.

Theorem 1. *Let* $L_1(p)$, $L_2(p)$ *and* $L_3(p)$ *be three complete probabilistic linguistic term sets, the three PLTSs are* $L_1(p) = \left\{L_1^{(k)}(p_1^{(k)}) \middle| L_1^{(k)} \in S, p_1^{(k)} \geq 0, k = 1,2,\cdots,\#L_1(p), \sum_{k=1}^{\#L_1(p)} p_1^{(k)} = 1\right\}$ $L_2(p) = \left\{L_2^{(k)}(p_2^{(k)}) \middle| L_2^{(k)} \in S, p_2^{(k)} \geq 0, k = 1,2,\cdots,\#L_2(p), \sum_{k=1}^{\#L_2(p)} p_2^{(k)} = 1\right\}$ *and* $L_3(p) = \left\{L_3^{(k)}(p_3^{(k)}) \middle| L_3^{(k)} \in S, p_3^{(k)} \geq 0, k = 1,2,\cdots,\#L_3(p), \sum_{k=1}^{\#L_3(p)} p_3^{(k)} = 1\right\}$, *where* $L_1^{(k)}$, $L_2^{(k)}$ *and* $L_3^{(k)}$ *are the kth linguistic terms in* $L_1(p)$, $L_2(p)$ *and* $L_3(p)$, $\alpha_1^{(k)}$, $\alpha_2^{(k)}$ *and* $\alpha_3^{(k)}$ *are the probabilities of the kth linguistic terms in* $L_1(p)$, $L_2(p)$ *and* $L_3(p)$ *respectively. Then, the generalized hybrid distance has the following properties:*

(1) $D_{gh}(L_1(p), L_2(p)) \geq 0$;
(2) $D_{gh}(L_1(p), L_2(p)) = 0 \Leftrightarrow L_1(p) = L_2(p)$;
(3) *If* $L_1(p) < L_2(p) < L_3(p)$, *then* $D_{gh}(L_1(p), L_2(p)) < D_{gh}(L_1(p), L_3(p))$, $D_{gh}(L_2(p), L_3(p)) < D_{gh}(L_1(p), L_3(p))$.

The proof of Theorem 1 is given in Appendix A.

2.3. *Probabilistic Linguistic CPT*

2.3.1. Classical CPT

To better retain the true evaluation information of DMs, probabilistic fusion is performed using CPT. CPT [35] is an improved version of prospect theory (PT) [36] to address stochastic dominance proposed by Tversky et al. in 1992, which well explains phenomena such as stochastic dominance, and its measure of the total value of a prospect through a value function and probability weights. The forms are shown as follows:

Combined prospect value:

$$V(x) = \sum_{i=0}^{n} v(x_i) w(p_i) \tag{8}$$

CPT asserts that there exist a strictly increasing weighted value function $v(x_i)$. The value function $v(x_i)$ is defined on the deviations from a reference point, which represents the behavior of the DMs and can be expressed as follows.

Value function:

$$v(x_i) = \begin{cases} (x_i - \mathrm{b})^{\xi}, x_i \geq b \\ -\theta(b - x_i)^{\beta}, x_i < b \end{cases} \tag{9}$$

The key difference between CPT and PT is that the weight function used in CPT is no longer a linear function, but an inverse S-shaped curve, indicating that individual decision makers tend to overestimate the possibility of small probability events and underestimate the possibility of medium and high probability events, so the probability weights of gains and losses are formulated as follows.

Weighting function:

$$w(p_i) = \begin{cases} w^{+}(p_i) = \frac{p_i^{\delta}}{[p_i^{\delta} + (1-p_i)^{\delta}]^{1/\delta}}, x_i \geq b \\ w^{-}(p_i) = \frac{p_i^{\varepsilon}}{[p_i^{\varepsilon} + (1-p_i)^{\varepsilon}]^{1/\varepsilon}}, x_i < b \end{cases} \tag{10}$$

where b denotes the reference point; ξ, β are the risk attitude coefficients towards value in the face of gain or loss, $\xi, \beta \in (0,1)$; θ is the loss aversion coefficient, $\theta > 1$; δ, ε are the risk attitude coefficients towards probability weights about gain or loss, $\delta, \varepsilon \in (0,1)$. Combined with Reference [35], it is generally considered to take $\xi = \beta = 0.88$, $\theta = 2.25$, $\delta = 0.61$, $\varepsilon = 0.69$.

Considering the risk preferences of DMs facing gains and losses in real problems, CPT gives a specific form of the value function and a form of decision weights, which let it be combined with probabilistic linguistic as follows. It would be more meaningful to integrate CPT into the practical application of GDM.

2.3.2. The Measures between PLTSs Based on CPT

In order to measure probabilistic linguistic terms more accurately, a new probabilistic linguistic terminology measure is obtained by fusing information based on the value function of the relative reference point variables and the probability weight function.

Definition 9. [13] *The measures between PLTSs based on CPT. The forms are shown as follows: Score value:*

$$V(L(p)) = \sum_{k=1}^{\#L(p)} (v(\alpha_k) w(p_k)) \tag{11}$$

$$v(\alpha_k) = \begin{cases} (\alpha_k)^{\xi}, \alpha_k \geq 2 \\ -\theta(-\alpha_k)^{\beta}, \alpha_k < 2 \end{cases} \tag{12}$$

$$w(p_k) = \begin{cases} \frac{p_k^{\delta}}{[p_k^{\delta} + (1-p_k)^{\delta}]^{1/\delta}}, \alpha_k \geq 2 \\ \frac{p_k^{\varepsilon}}{[p_k^{\varepsilon} + (1-p_k)^{\varepsilon}]^{1/\varepsilon}}, \alpha_k < 2 \end{cases} \tag{13}$$

Variance value:

$$\delta(L(p)) = \left(\sum_{k=1}^{\#L(p)} v(\alpha_k) - E(\alpha_k)^2 \cdot w(p_k)\right)^{1/2} \quad (14)$$

where α_k *is the subscript of* S, $S = \{s_\alpha | \alpha = 0, 1, 2, \cdots, 2g, g \in N^+\}$, *here* $\alpha_k = 0, 1, 2, 3, 4$, ${p_k}^\delta$ *is the probability of* α_k.

CPT not only analyzes the risk psychological factors of human in the decision making process. It also considers the value function and probability weight function of the relative reference point variables, which makes up for the shortcomings of PT.

3. Comprehensive Assignment Method to Determine Attribute Weights

3.1. Obtain Objective Weights Based on Social Media Data Mining

3.1.1. Data Clustering of Large Groups Based on Data Attention

The typical way for the public to express their feelings, views, opinions, etc., is through behavior [7]. Public behavior data are mainly divided into operational (interaction) behavior data and content behavior data. The first refers to published texts, while the second mainly involves data on public commenting, liking, and retweeting behaviors. This study uses a Python-based crawler technique to obtain the raw microblog data, which mainly includes the blogger's ID screen name, blog post text, posting time, number of likes, number of retweets, number of comments, and others. The flow of obtaining event attributes and attribute weights are shown in Figure 1.

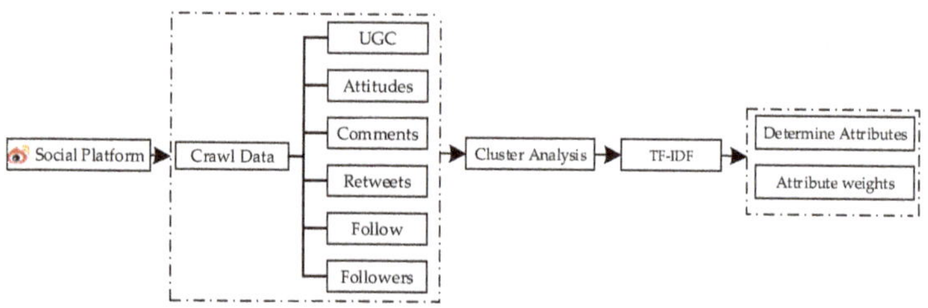

Figure 1. Attribute acquisition framework.

First, use Python-based crawler technique to collect a large amount of information about user behavior on social media networks. Each piece of data can be denoted as $D = (UGC, AN, CN, RN, FN, FSN)$. AN, CN, RN, FN, FSN and UGC represent the number of likes, comments, retweets, followers and tweet texts (user-generated content), respectively. Then, each text data is pre-processed using the Python natural language processing package, including word separation, cleaning, lexical annotation, and entity word recognition. Finally, after the data pre-processing, the k-means clustering algorithm is chosen to classify the data based on the public attention level.

In order to obtain the optimal number of clusters in the process of cluster analysis and ensure more scientific results of data classification, the elbow method and the contour coefficient method are generally adopted to determine the optimal value. In contrast, the optimal k value determined by the contour coefficient method is not necessarily optimal. Sometimes it needs to be obtained with the aid of SSE; therefore, in this paper, we first consider using the elbow method of Equation (13) to determine the optimal number of clusters. The core index of the elbow method is sum of the squared errors SSE:

$$SSE = \sum_{i=1}^{k} \sum_{p \in C_i} |p - m_i|^2 \quad (15)$$

where C_i is the ith cluster, p is the sample points in C_i, m_i is the center of mass of C_i (the mean of all samples in C_i) and SSE is the clustering error of all models, representing the good or lousy clustering effect. The core idea of the elbow method is that as the number of clusters k increases, the sample division will be finer, and the degree of aggregation of each cluster will gradually increase. Then, SSE will naturally become smaller gradually.

Each dataset is obtained after classifying the data containing multiple data objects. Based on the information of each data item in the dataset, the attention coefficient of the dataset is calculated, where $DS_i(AN)$, $DS_i(CN)$, $DS_i(RN)$, $DS_i(FN)$ and $DS_i(FSN)$ denote the average number of likes, average number of comments, the average number of retweets, the average number of followers and average number of fans of the ith dataset, respectively. The denominator n_i denotes the number of data in the dataset, and the attention factor γ_i formula [7] is as follows:

$$\gamma_i = \frac{\partial_a \cdot DS_i(AN) + \partial_c \cdot DS_i(CN) + \partial_r \cdot DS_i(RN) + \partial_f \cdot DS_i(FN) + \partial_s DS_i(FSN)}{\sum_{i=1}^{t} \partial_a \cdot DS_i(AN) + \partial_c \cdot DS_i(CN) + \partial_r \cdot DS_i(RN) + \partial_f \cdot DS_i(FN) + \partial_s DS_i(FSN)} \tag{16}$$

where $DS_i(AN) = \frac{\sum_{D_{ij} \in DS_i} AN_{ij}}{n_i}$, $DS_i(CN) = \frac{\sum_{D_{ij} \in DS_i} CN_{ij}}{n_i}$, $DS_i(RN) = \frac{\sum_{D_{ij} \in DS_i} RN_{ij}}{n_i}$, $DS_i(FN) = \frac{\sum_{D_{ij} \in DS_i} FN_{ij}}{n_i}$,

$$DS_i(FSN) = \frac{\sum_{D_{ij} \in DS_i} FSN_{ij}}{n_i} \tag{17}$$

A linear programming model is developed to maximize the influence of the data, where Z is the influence of the data, A, B, C, D, E determine the number of likes, comments, retweets, followers and followers of the data, respectively, and $\partial_a, \partial_c, \partial_r, \partial_f, \partial_s$ mean the weights of each index, respectively. If the influence of each factor is equal, find the data's maximum influence and the indicator's weight as follows:

$$\begin{aligned} MaxZ = A \cdot \partial_a + B \cdot \partial_c + C \cdot \partial_r + D\partial_f + E\partial_s \\ s.t. \begin{cases} A \cdot \partial_a - B \cdot \partial_c = 0 \\ A \cdot \partial_a - C \cdot \partial_r = 0 \\ A \cdot \partial_a - D \cdot \partial_f = 0 \\ \cdots \\ D \cdot \partial_f - E\partial_s = 0 \\ \partial_a + \partial_c + \partial_r + \partial_f + \partial_s = 1 \\ \partial_a, \partial_c, \partial_r, \partial_f, \partial_s \geq 0 \end{cases} \end{aligned} \tag{18}$$

Obtain the weights of each indicator by solving this linear programming model. The method of using the model to determine the indicator weights is more objective than others. It can effectively avoid the risk of decision making caused by experts' subjective determination of the indicator weights, which makes the method to be more scientific and applicable.

3.1.2. Obtain Attributes and Weights

Once an emergency breaks out, the microblogging platform forms real-time hot topics, and the text of microblogs representing public views proliferates to form a significant data stream. Term frequency–inverse document frequency (TF-IDF) is a widely used keyword extraction technique in the field of data miningand evolved from IDF which is proposed by Sparck Jones [37,38] with heuristic intuition. It is a common weighting technique used in information retrieval and text mining to evaluate the importance of a word in a document collection by considering the word frequency and the inverse document frequency to determine the weight of the keyword.

The specific steps of the algorithm are as follows:

Step1. Calculate the word frequency.

Word frequency is the number of times a word appears in an article. The word frequency is standardized to facilitate the comparison of different articles and explained the difference in length of the articles.

$$\mathrm{tf}_{ij} = \frac{n_{i,j}}{\sum_k n_{k,j}} \tag{19}$$

where $n_{i,j}$ is the number of occurrences of the word in a document d_j, and the denominator is the sum of the occurrences of all words in the document d_j.

Step2. Calculate inverse document frequency as

$$idf_i = \log \frac{|D|}{|\{j : t_i \in d_j\}|} \tag{20}$$

where $|D|$ is the total number of documents in the corpus and $|\{j : t_i \in d_j\}|$ denotes the number of documents containing the word t_i. If the word is not in the corpus, it will result in a denominator of 0. Therefore, in general, $1 + |\{j : t_i \in d_j\}|$ is used, i.e.,

Step3. Calculate TF-IDF as

$$TF - IDF = TF \times IDF \tag{21}$$

Finally, the weights of public attributes are obtained by combining the attention coefficients γ_i of the dataset, and the standard decision attribute weights are obtained after normalization. Combining the attention coefficients obtained by Equation (16), the weights of public attributes are obtained and normalized to get the standard decision attribute weights.

3.2. Determine Expert Subjective Weights Based on Disparity Maximization

In this paper, the idea of disparity maximization is used to determine the weight of each decision. Wang [34] proposed the maximum deviation method to deal with MADM problems with numerical information [39]. For the MAGDM problem, if the variance of a DMs' attribute evaluation value is more minor for all solutions, it means that the DMs' decision plays a smaller role in the ranking of solutions; conversely, if the variance of a DMs' attribute evaluation value is larger for all solutions, it means that the DMs' decision plays a larger role in the ranking of solutions, and the DMs should be given a larger weight at this time. This method can motivate DMs' to make an objective and reasonable evaluation of known solutions.

Suppose all the attribute indicators in this paper are benefit-based indicators, which do not need to be normalized.

The specific steps are as follows:

Step1. Obtain the decision-making matrix $R = (r_{ij})_{n \times m}$ from the expert e_k. The evaluated value of the alternative A_i on C_j can be expressed as v_{ij}^k, which is expressed in PLTS.

Step2. Based on the maximum deviation method, construct the objective function:

$$\begin{gathered} Max \cdot F(w_j) = \textstyle\sum_{j=1}^{m} w_j \sum_{i=1}^{n} \sum_{k=1,k\neq i}^{n} D(r_{ij}, r_{kj}) \\ s.t \begin{cases} \sum_{j=1}^{m} {w_j}^2 = 1 \\ w_j \geq 0, j = 1, 2, \cdots, m \end{cases} \end{gathered} \tag{22}$$

Solve this optimal model as a Lagrange function:

$$F(w_j, \lambda) = \sum_{j=1}^{m} w_j \sum_{i=1}^{n} \sum_{k=1,k\neq i}^{n} D(r_{ij}, r_{kj}) + \frac{\lambda}{2}\left(\sum_{j=1}^{m} {w_j}^2 - 1\right) \tag{23}$$

Derive the partial derivative of Equation (23) and let:

$$\begin{cases} \frac{\partial F(w_j,\lambda)}{\partial w_j} = \sum_{i=1}^{n} \sum_{k=1,k\neq i}^{n} D(r_{ij}, r_{kj}) + \lambda w_j = 0 \\ \frac{\partial F(w_j,\lambda)}{\partial \lambda} = \sum_{j=1}^{m} w_j{}^2 - 1 = 0 \end{cases} \tag{24}$$

Find the optimal solution:

$$w_j^* = \frac{\sum_{i=1}^{n} \sum_{k=1,k\neq i}^{n} D(r_{ij}, r_{kj})}{\sqrt{\sum_{i=1}^{n} \sum_{k=1,k\neq i}^{n} D(r_{ij}, r_{kj})^2}} \tag{25}$$

Step3. Normalize the weights as

$$w_j = \frac{w_j^*}{\sum_{j=1}^{m} w_j^*} = \frac{\sum_{i=1}^{n} \sum_{k=1,k\neq i}^{n} D(r_{ij}, r_{kj})}{\sum_{j=1}^{m} \left(\sum_{i=1}^{n} \sum_{k=1,k\neq i}^{n} D(r_{ij}, r_{kj}) \right)} \tag{26}$$

3.3. *Combined Weights*

Let w_{ij}^k denotes the combined weight of expert e_k for alternative A_i on the attribute C_j, by combining the subjective weight w_j' with the objective weight w_{ij}^k:

$$w_{ij}^k = \alpha W_{ij}^k + \beta w_j' \tag{27}$$

where α, β are the linear expression coefficients of the combined weights and satisfy $0 \leq \alpha, \beta \leq 1, \alpha + \beta = 1$, $i = 1, 2, \cdots, n, j = 1, 2, \cdots, m, k = 1, 2, \cdots, n$. When $\alpha = 0$ and $\beta = 1$ only subjective weights are considered in GDM; when $\alpha = 1$ and $\beta = 0$, only objective weights are considered in GDM.

4. GDMD-PROMETHEE Algorithm Based on CPT

This section provides a new extended PROMETHEE using probabilistic linguistic information, namely the GDMD-PROMETHEE method, to evaluate multi-criterion GDM. Let $A_i (i = 1, 2, \cdots, n)$ be the alternative, $C_j (j = 1, 2, \cdots, m)$ be the criterion mined through social media, and $E_k (k \in N^+, k \geq 20)$ be the decision-making experts from relevant fields. Based on a two-by-two comparison of $A_i (i = 1, 2, \cdots, n)$, $A_i (i = 1, 2, \cdots, n)$ are ranked by GDMD-PROMETHEE. The flow chart of GDMD-PROMETHEE is shown in Figure 2.

Based on the above analysis, the specific steps of GDMD-PROMETHEE are as follows:

Step1. Combine big data network behavior data to mine event keywords, obtain event evaluation criteria, and use TF-IDF technique to find the subjective weights of event attributes.

Step2. Solve the objective weights of experts using Equations (22)–(26) to determine the comprehensive weights w_{ij}^k.

Step3. Combine Equations (12)–(14) to fuse the probabilistic linguistic evaluation information into specific real values to obtain the fused initial evaluation matrix.

Step4. Combine the integrated weights with the initial evaluation matrix to obtain the group evaluation matrix $V = [v_{ij}^l]_{n \times n}$.

Step5. Calculate the priority indices of two solutions under different attributes as

$$r_{jk} = \sum_{l=1}^{t} \sum_{h=1}^{l} v_j^l v_k^h - \frac{1}{2} \sum_{l=1}^{t} v_j^l v_k^l, j, k = 1, 2, \cdots, n \tag{28}$$

$$r_{kj} = \sum_{l=1}^{t} \sum_{h=1}^{l} v_j^l v_k^h - \frac{1}{2} \sum_{l=1}^{t} v_j^l v_k^l, j, k = 1, 2, \cdots, n \tag{29}$$

Step6. Construct the dominance matrix for pairwise comparisons between solutions, when the solution is compared with itself, then the dominance ratio is 0.5, and the rest of the cases satisfy $r_{jk} + r_{kj} = 1$.

$$R = [r_{jk}]_{n\times n} = \begin{matrix} & A_1 & A_2 & \cdots & A_n \\ A_1 & r_{11} & r_{12} & \cdots & r_{1n} \\ A_2 & r_{21} & r_{22} & \cdots & r_{2n} \\ \vdots & \vdots & \vdots & & \vdots \\ A_n & r_{n1} & r_{n2} & \cdots & r_{nn} \end{matrix} \quad (30)$$

Step7. From Equation (33), the net flow value $\phi(i)$ of each solution is obtained, and the larger $\phi(i)$ is, the better the solution is. The outflow $\phi^+(A_j)$ of A_j indicates the extent to which A_j outperforms the other $(n-1)$ scenarios in the set, and the larger the outflow $\phi^+(A_j)$, the better A_j is. The inflow indicates the extent to which the other $(n-1)$ solutions in the solution set out perform A_j. The smaller $\phi^-(A_j)$, the better A_j is. The formulas are as follows:

$$\phi^+(A_j) = \frac{1}{n}\sum\nolimits_{k=1}^{n} r_{jk}, j = 1, 2, \cdots n. \quad (31)$$

$$\phi^-(A_j) = \frac{1}{n}\sum\nolimits_{k=1}^{n} r_{kj}, j = 1, 2, \cdots n. \quad (32)$$

$$\phi(A_j) = \frac{1}{n}\sum\nolimits_{k=1}^{n} r_{jk}, j = 1, 2, \cdots n. \quad (33)$$

As one of the most widely used ranking methods in MAGDM, PROMETHEE is convenient and flexible to use due to its ease of understanding. Based on this paper, we propose the GDMD-PROMETHEE algorithm based on CPT.

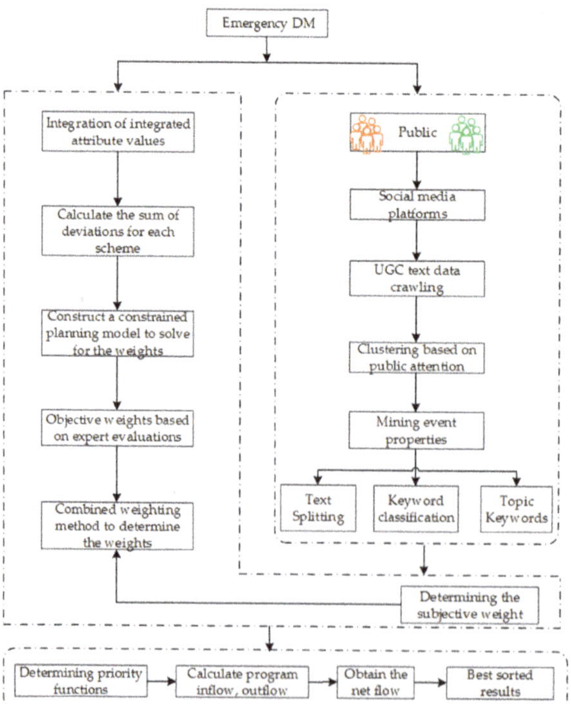

Figure 2. Emergency DM flow chart.

5. Case Study

5.1. Case Background

Take the Shanghai Petrochemical explosion on 18 June 2022 as an example to verify the method's feasibility in this paper. At 4:28 pm on 18 June 2022, the chemical department of Shanghai Petrochemical caught fire, and the fireball shot up to the sky with explosions in many places. In order to protect the basic life safety of the public and ensure the emergency command carries out the coordination work quickly. After consulting professional information, four alternatives were identified, and 20 emergency decision-making experts from firefighting, medical, chemical and other related departments evaluated each option in terms of attributes, and the four options were:

A_1 Timely understanding of the destruction of the surrounding traffic, communications, power supply, water supply and other facilities, the deployment of drones to draw a 360-degree panoramic map of the explosion site, survey the hidden fire point, determine the rescue route, organize a rescue, reasonable arrangement of firefighting and rescue forces, to protect the safety of people and property. After the fire is extinguished, the organization will organize forces to seal the leak point for repair work to ensure the successful completion of the anti-disaster work.

A_2 After the fire, the attacking team was sent to the scene to detect the gas, strengthen the personal protection of rescue personnel and quickly rescue the trapped personnel. Moreover, take the initial battle to control the fire, cooling, and explosion suppression tactical measures, synchronization of multiple fire points and surrounding storage tanks, devices for cooling protection, to prevent heating, pressure and cause secondary fire explosion.

A_3 Immediately after discovering the leaking device, stop transmission, close the cut-off valves on both sides of the pipeline leak point, take necessary protective measures for other pipelines near the leaking pipeline and, at the same time, be alert to electricity leakage, highly toxic and highly corrosive substances. Make every effort to help the injured, and take isolation, caution and evacuation measures to avoid extraneous personnel from entering the danger area. Activate the environmental emergency plan and arrange to test the surrounding air and water quality.

A_4 To avoid the secondary explosion of unknown hazardous materials, suspend large-scale firefighting, dispatch the chemical prevention regiment, nuclear, biological and chemical emergency rescue team to search and rescue the scene in depth, and sample burning materials, according to the composition of burning materials selected to correspond to the firefighting methods. Take anti-leakage and anti-proliferation control measures to prevent the spread of fire. After the fire was controlled, protective burning was implemented.

Using Python to crawl microblog data, keywords such as Shanghai petrochemical fire accident has set up an investigation team, Shanghai petrochemical fire information, aerial photography of Shanghai petrochemical fire scene, Shanghai petrochemical fire latest progress. A total of 1200 pieces of data were extracted; each piece of data consisted of $D = (UGC, AN, CN, RN, FN, FSN)$ pieces of data. Data Availability Statement: The data of this study are available from the authors upon request. Relevant data are available from the "Wei Bo" website (https://weibo.com/ (accessed on 18 June 2022)).

After cleaning and filtering the data, about 400 pieces of valid data were retained and used to generate a word cloud map as Figure 3.

Figure 3. "6·18" Shanghai petrochemical explosion word cloud map.

5.2. Data Analysis

Step1. After data pre-processing, the number of likes, comments and retweets of the data as distance measures, the k-means clustering algorithm is applied to complete the behavioral big data clustering based on public attention, as the number of categories of classification increases, the decline of SSE will plummet and then level off as the k-value continues to increase, the elbow method is to select that the inflection point, so as shown in Figure 4, $k = 3$ should be selected.

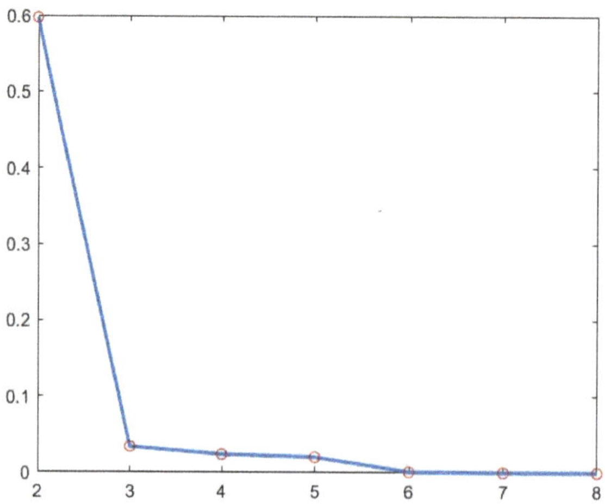

Figure 4. SSE values for clustering.

After converting the distances into probability distributions using Gaussian distributions in high-dimensional space, determining the optimal number of clusters $k = 3$ T-SNE Python by reducing the 3D features of high-dimensional data to 2D visualization. The different colors in the diagram represent a small group, and each small group is a category. Blue, green and red represent DS_1, DS_2 and DS_3 at low dimension, respectively. It makes it possible to maintain the information they carry in high-dimensional, even in low-dimensional space, as shown in Figure 5.

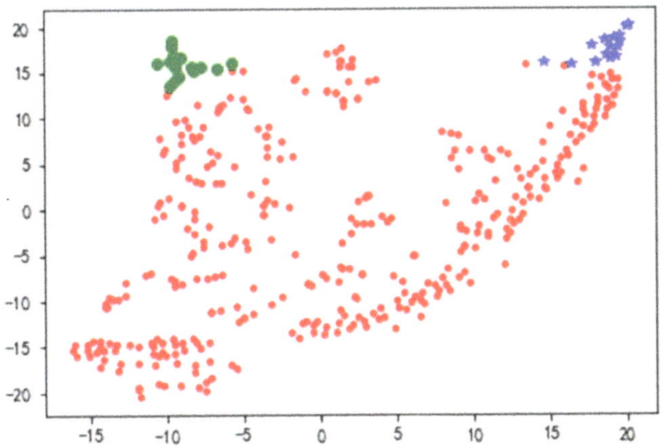

Figure 5. Visualization of data clustering results.

Using the linear programming model established by Equation (18), the weights of the resulting indicators are calculated as shown in Table 1, and the concern coefficients for each data set are obtained according to Equation (16), which is presented in Table 2 as follows:

Table 1. Information on the weight of each index.

Projects	Attitudes	Comments	Retweets	Follow	Followers (Thousand)
Number of indicators	19,806	4073	4417	456,413	170,401.8639
Weights	0.095	0.463	0.427	0.004	0.011

Table 2. Attention factor for each data set.

Dataset	Average Number of Attitudes	Average Number of Comments	Average Number of Retweets	Average Number of Follow	Average Number of Followers	Attention Factor
DS_1	155	11	12	877	151.4908	0.118
DS_2	10	4	2	4306	81.1671	0.085
DS_3	806	93	76	1382	4112.3652	0.797

In this paper, the words with high TF-IDF values are selected as keywords for the subsequent extensive data use Jieba Python. In order to facilitate the subsequent analysis, some words that are not highly related to the emergency event and have dark themes are deleted. For example, the words that are not related to the explosion are "original", "good night", "takeout", etc. Based on the above analysis, the emergency decision guidelines and their corresponding keywords considering the topic of public concern for mega emergencies are shown in Table 3. Determine four attributes $C_j = \{C_1, C_2, C_3, C_4\}$, where C_1 is "emergency response", including emergency response, control, preplanning, etc. C_2 is "fire suppression and derivative disaster control", including fire, burning, etc. C_3 is "site and surrounding environment detection", including photography, smoke, pollution, etc. C_4 is "casualty and rescue", including injury, death, rescue, etc. The corresponding weights of each attribute are $w'_j = \{w'_1, w'_2, w'_3, w'_4\} = \{0.250, 0.204, 0.174, 0.372\}$.

Table 3. Attributes and weights.

Criterion	Weight DS_1	Weight DS_2	Weight DS_3	Weight
C_1	0.230	0.148	0.264	0.250
C_2	0.179	0.340	0.193	0.204
C_3	0.305	0.106	0.162	0.174
C_4	0.286	0.407	0.381	0.372

Step2. The objective weights are obtained using Equations (22)–(26) as in Table 4, and there is no difference in the deviation values of experts e_7, e_9 and e_{15}, so the weights are assigned to 0.

Table 4. The Weights of 20 experts.

Expert	e_1	e_2	e_3	e_4	e_5	e_6	e_7	e_8	e_9	e_{10}
Weight	0.011	0.061	0.032	0.154	0.009	0.014	0.000	0.079	0.000	0.070
Expert	e_{11}	e_{12}	e_{13}	e_{14}	e_{15}	e_{16}	e_{17}	e_{18}	e_{19}	e_{20}
Weight	0.009	0.046	0.044	0.130	0.000	0.029	0.057	0.009	0.167	0.079

Step3. According to Equation (27), the integrated weights are calculated, here let $\alpha = \beta = 0.5$, and Table 5 is obtained.

Table 5. Integrated weights.

Expert \ Attribute	C_1	C_2	C_3	C_4	Expert \ Attribute	C_1	C_2	C_3	C_4
e_1	0.131	0.108	0.093	0.192	e_{11}	0.130	0.107	0.092	0.191
e_2	0.155	0.132	0.117	0.216	e_{12}	0.148	0.125	0.110	0.209
e_3	0.141	0.118	0.103	0.202	e_{13}	0.147	0.124	0.109	0.208
e_4	0.202	0.179	0.164	0.263	e_{14}	0.190	0.167	0.152	0.251
e_5	0.130	0.107	0.092	0.191	e_{15}	0.125	0.102	0.087	0.186
e_6	0.132	0.109	0.094	0.193	e_{16}	0.139	0.116	0.101	0.200
e_7	0.125	0.102	0.087	0.186	e_{17}	0.154	0.131	0.116	0.215
e_8	0.165	0.142	0.127	0.226	e_{18}	0.130	0.107	0.092	0.191
e_9	0.125	0.102	0.087	0.186	e_{19}	0.208	0.185	0.170	0.269
e_{10}	0.160	0.137	0.122	0.221	e_{20}	0.165	0.142	0.127	0.226

Step4. Combined with the four attributes identified in Table 3, the experts gave the ratings in terms of the four attributes under the five-grain language $S = \{s_0, s_1, s_2, s_3, s_4\}$ = {very low, low, fair, high, very high}, due to space issues, the rating matrices of the top two experts are listed, as shown in Tables 6 and 7 below.

Table 6. The decision matrix given by e_1.

Alternative \ Attribute	C_1	C_2	C_3	C_4
A_1	s_4	s_0	s_4	s_1
A_2	s_3	s_2	s_1	s_3
A_3	s_4	s_1	s_3	s_2
A_4	s_0	s_3	s_1	s_4

Table 7. The decision matrix given by e_2.

Alternative \ Attribute	C_1	C_2	C_3	C_4
A_1	s_3	s_3	s_4	s_3
A_2	s_4	s_4	s_4	s_4
A_3	s_4	s_4	s_4	s_4
A_4	s_4	s_4	s_3	s_4

The evaluation information was fused based on the cumulative Equations (11) to (13), then obtain the initial evaluation matrix transformed into real values, and the results are shown in Table 8, additional complementary results are in Appendix B.

Table 8. The initial evaluation matrix.

Expert	Alternative	C_1	C_2	C_3	C_4
e_1	A_1	3.387	0.000	3.387	−2.250
	A_2	2.629	1.840	−2.250	2.629
	A_3	3.387	−2.250	2.629	1.840
	A_4	0.000	2.629	−2.250	3.387
e_2	A_1	2.629	2.629	3.387	2.629
	A_2	3.387	3.387	3.387	3.387
	A_3	3.387	3.387	3.387	3.387
	A_4	3.387	3.387	2.629	3.387
e_3	A_1	−2.250	−2.250	1.840	1.840
	A_2	1.840	1.840	1.840	1.840
	A_3	2.629	2.629	2.629	2.629
	A_4	−2.250	−2.250	1.840	1.840
		……			
e_{20}	A_1	3.387	3.387	3.387	3.387
	A_2	3.387	3.387	3.387	2.629
	A_3	3.387	3.387	3.387	3.387
	A_4	3.387	2.629	2.629	2.629

Step5. The weights were combined with the evaluation information to obtain the normalized group evaluation matrix, as shown in Table 9.

Table 9. The group evaluation matrices.

Alternative \ Attribute	C_1	C_2	C_3	C_4
A_1	0.255	0.118	0.199	0.429
A_2	0.251	0.183	0.084	0.482
A_3	0.292	0.172	0.120	0.416
A_4	0.185	0.369	0.148	0.297

Step6. The advantage ratios between the two solutions are calculated using Equations (29)–(30), as shown in Table 10.

Table 10. Priority index of each program.

Alternative	A_1	A_2	A_3	A_4
A_1	0.500	0.492	0.525	0.557
A_2	0.508	0.500	0.532	0.554
A_3	0.475	0.468	0.500	0.520
A_4	0.443	0.446	0.480	0.500

Step7. By calculating the inflow, outflow and net flow for each scenario, the net flow for each scenario is derived and the results are shown in Table 11.

Table 11. Ranking of alternatives.

Alternative	$\phi^+(i)$	$\phi^-(i)$	$\phi(i)$	Rank
A_1	0.519	0.481	0.037	2
A_2	0.523	0.477	0.046	1
A_3	0.491	0.509	−0.018	3
A_4	0.467	0.533	−0.065	4

By comparing the size of the net flow, the final program ranking: $A_2 \succ A_1 \succ A_3 \succ A_4$, that is, the choice of program A_2: After the fire, the attack team was sent to the scene to detect the gas, strengthen the personal protection of rescue personnel and quickly rescue the trapped personnel. Take the initial battle to control the fire, cooling and explosion suppression tactical measures, simultaneous cooling protection of multiple fire points and surrounding tanks and devices to prevent heating and pressure and cause a fire secondary explosion.

5.3. Sensitivity Analysis

5.3.1. Ranking Results under Different Parameters by the Same Decision Method

For sensitivity analysis, the effect of different sizes of α and β under the combined weights on the ranking results was investigated, where the coefficient α represents the percentage of objective weights and coefficient β represents the percentage of subjective weights. The results are shown in Table 12.

Table 12. Comparison of different parameters.

Parameter	Rank
$\alpha = 0, \beta = 1$	$A_2 \succ A_1 \succ A_3 \succ A_4$
$\alpha = 0.1, \beta = 0.9$	$A_2 \succ A_1 \succ A_3 \succ A_4$
$\alpha = 0.2, \beta = 0.8$	$A_2 \succ A_1 \succ A_3 \succ A_4$
$\alpha = 0.3, \beta = 0.7$	$A_2 \succ A_1 \succ A_3 \succ A_4$
$\alpha = 0.4, \beta = 0.6$	$A_2 \succ A_1 \succ A_3 \succ A_4$
$\alpha = 0.5, \beta = 0.5$	$A_2 \succ A_1 \succ A_3 \succ A_4$
$\alpha = 0.6, \beta = 0.4$	$A_2 \succ A_1 \succ A_3 \succ A_4$
$\alpha = 0.7, \beta = 0.3$	$A_2 \succ A_1 \succ A_3 \succ A_4$
$\alpha = 0.8, \beta = 0.2$	$A_2 \succ A_1 \succ A_3 \succ A_4$
$\alpha = 0.9, \beta = 0.1$	$A_2 \succ A_1 \succ A_3 \succ A_4$
$\alpha = 1, \beta = 0$	$A_1 \succ A_2 \succ A_3 \succ A_4$

As can be seen from Table 12, the optimal solution is A_1 except when $\alpha = 1, \beta = 0$ (i.e., only objective weights are considered); in all other cases, the solution ranking results maintain good consistency, i.e., $A_2 \succ A_1 \succ A_3 \succ A_4$. It shows that the goodness of the schemes is not affected by the large fluctuations of the parameters regardless of the cases, and the comparison with the method in Reference [40] confirms that the GDMD-PROMETHEE method combining generalized probability distance and Hausdorff is more stable. By observing the scores obtained in Figures 6 and 7, it can be seen that the scores of scenarios and schemes are relatively close under each parameter, but A_2 is the best and A_4 is the worst, and it is obviously undesirable to consider only the objective weights.

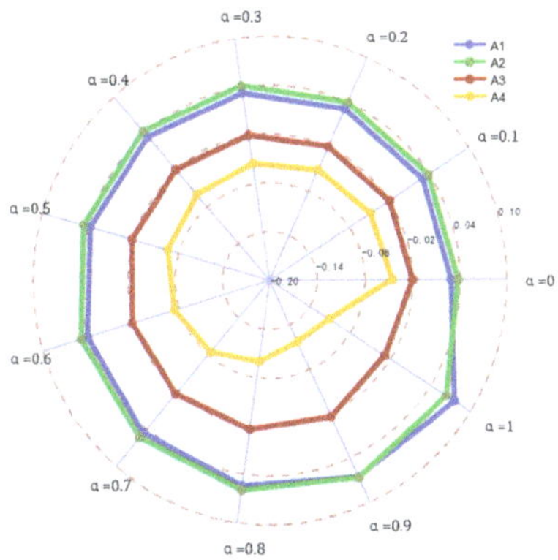

Figure 6. Parameter comparison radar chart.

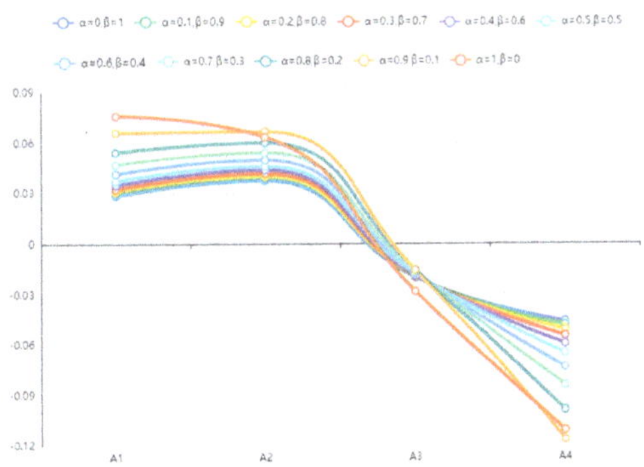

Figure 7. Scheme scores under different parameter fluctuations.

5.3.2. Comparison the Ranking Results of Different Decision Methods

To verify the validity and feasibility of the model in this paper, the methods of literature [40,41] and TOPSIS analysis were selected to make a comparison of the results, as shown in the following table.

(1) By observing Table 13, it can be obtained that the result of PROMETHEE ranking based on the literature [41] is$A_3 \succ A_2 \succ A_1 \succ A_4$, which is different from the result of this paper. The main reason is that this paper considers the weights of individual decision experts. The literature [41] only assigns the same average weight to decision groups. The method of assigning expert weights based on the maximum deviation value extracted from the evaluation of individual decision experts in this paper is more consistent with the individual decision risk levels and attitudes of experts compared to the simple average weight.

Table 13. Comparison results with other literature methods.

Programs	A_1	A_2	A_3	A_4	Rank
GDMD-PROMETHEE method	0.037	0.046	−0.018	−0.065	$A_2 \succ A_1 \succ A_3 \succ A_4$
Traditional TOPSIS method	0.519	0.591	0.529	0.374	$A_2 \succ A_3 \succ A_1 \succ A_4$
GDM-PROMETHEE II method [40]	0.128	0.198	−0.117	−0.209	$A_2 \succ A_1 \succ A_3 \succ A_4$
Probabilistic linguistic PROMETHEE method [41]	−0.142	0.044	0.256	−0.158	$A_3 \succ A_2 \succ A_1 \succ A_4$

(2) As can be seen from Table 13, the PROMETHEE method based on CPT has the same ranking results as the traditional TOPSIS method and the literature [40]. Combined with Figure 8, it can be seen that the comparative analysis results of the first three methods are relatively consistent, i.e., the best solution A_2, the worst solution A_4, which further verifies the validity and reasonableness of the method in this paper.

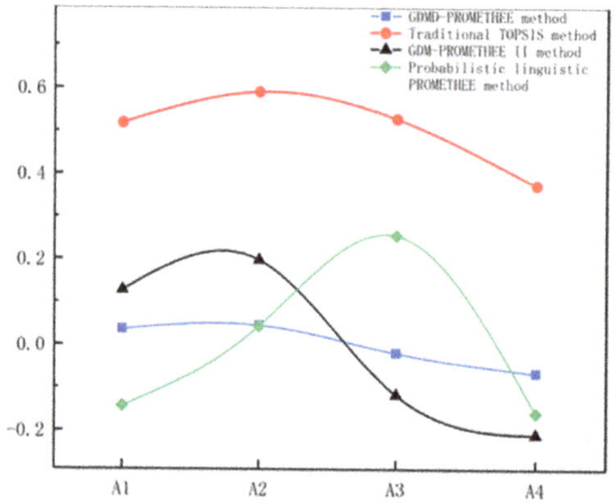

Figure 8. Comparison of the results of the four methods.

6. Conclusions

In this paper, we study emergency decision making in the social media environment in the era of big data and use probabilistic language methods to cluster the decision results. Compared with traditional GDM, this paper not only extracts event attributes from public information but also combines public opinion with weights, which effectively and quickly incorporates public opinion into the final decision information and helps to grasp the actual development of the emergency. A new generalized extended hybrid distance is proposed to determine the objective weights of each decision expert based on the expert decision information using the maximum difference method. The decision weight coefficients are used to adjust the proportion of subject, object, and view weights to obtain the total weights. The influence on the decisions made under the weights of different perspectives is studied. Using the CPT to combine the probabilistic linguistic evaluation information with the total weights and finally taking the Shanghai Petrochemical "6.18" explosion as an example, the rationality and feasibility of GDMD-PROMETHEE method are verified. Combining the external influences of public opinion with the influence of each public member in decision making needs to be studied further in future. In addition, the dynamic change process of experts' opinion can be described so that the decision-making process is closer to the actual situation and the decision results are more scientific.

Author Contributions: Conceptualization, J.W. and S.L.; methodology, J.W.; software, S.L.; validation, S.L. and X.Z.; formal analysis, J.W. and S.L.; investigation, X.Z.; resources, J.W.; data curation, X.Z.; writing—original draft preparation, J.W. and S.L.; writing—review and editing, J.W. and S.L.; visualization, S.L.; supervision, S.L.; project administration, S.L.; funding acquisition, J.W. All authors have read and agreed to the published version of the manuscript.

Funding: This study was funded by the Projects of Natural Science Research in Anhui Colleges and Universities (2020jyxm0335, KJ2021JD20), the Projects of College Mathematics Teaching Research and Development Center (CMC20210414), the Projects of Natural Science Research in Anhui Jianzhu University (2021xskc01) (2020jy62) (2020szkc01) (HYB20220179).

Institutional Review Board Statement: Not applicable.

Informed Consent Statement: Not applicable.

Data Availability Statement: The data used to support the findings of this study can be used by anyone without prior permission of the authors by just citing this article.

Conflicts of Interest: The authors declare no conflict of interests regarding the publication for the paper.

Appendix A

Proof must be formatted as follows: it is easy to verify properties 1 and 2 in Theorem 1. Proof of property 3 is shown in the following formula:

$$D_{gh}(L_1(p), L_2(p)) = \left\{\eta\left[\frac{1}{2}\left(\left|\frac{1}{2}\sum_{k=1}^{\#L(p)}\left|p_1^{(k)} - p_2^{(k)}\right| + \left|\sum_{k=1}^{\#L(p)} f(\alpha_1^{(k)})p_1^{(k)} - \sum_{k=1}^{\#L(p)} f(\alpha_2^{(k)})p_2^{(k)}\right|\right|\right)^{\lambda}\right] + \right.$$
$$\left.(1-\eta)\max_{k=1}^{\#L(p)}\left\{\frac{1}{2}\left[\min_{k=1}^{\#L(p)}\left(\left|f(\alpha_1^{(k)}) - f(\alpha_2^{(k)})\right|^{\lambda} + \left|f(\alpha_1^{(k)})p_1^{(k)} - f(\alpha_2^{(k)})p_2^{(k)}\right|^{\lambda}\right)\right]\right\}\right\}^{\frac{1}{\lambda}}$$
$$D_{gh}(L_1(p), L_3(p)) = \left\{\eta\left[\frac{1}{2}\left(\left|\frac{1}{2}\sum_{k=1}^{\#L(p)}\left|p_1^{(k)} - p_3^{(k)}\right| + \left|\sum_{k=1}^{\#L(p)} f(\alpha_1^{(k)})p_1^{(k)} - \sum_{k=1}^{\#L(p)} f(\alpha_3^{(k)})p_3^{(k)}\right|\right|\right)^{\lambda}\right] + \right.$$
$$\left.(1-\eta)\max_{k=1}^{\#L(p)}\left\{\frac{1}{2}\left[\min_{k=1}^{\#L(p)}\left(\left|f(\alpha_1^{(k)}) - f(\alpha_3^{(k)})\right|^{\lambda} + \left|f(\alpha_1^{(k)})p_1^{(k)} - f(\alpha_3^{(k)})p_3^{(k)}\right|^{\lambda}\right)\right]\right\}\right\}^{\frac{1}{\lambda}}$$

As $L_1(p) < L_2(p) < L_3(p)$ and Definition 2, $\max f(\alpha_1^{(k)}) < \min f(\alpha_2^{(k)})$, $\max f(\alpha_2^{(k)}) < \min f(\alpha_3^{(k)})$, Given that all three are complete sets of probabilistic linguistic terms, it follows that:

$$\sum_{k=1}^{\#L(p)} f(\alpha_1^{(k)})p_1^{(k)} \le (\max f(\alpha_1^{(k)})) \times \sum_{k=1}^{\#L(p)} p_1^{(k)} \Leftrightarrow \sum_{k=1}^{\#L(p)} f(\alpha_1^{(k)})p_1^{(k)} \le \max f(\alpha_1^{(k)})$$
$$(\min f(\alpha_2^{(k)})) \times \sum_{k=1}^{\#L(p)} p_2^{(k)} \le \sum_{k=1}^{\#L(p)} f(\alpha_2^{(k)})p_2^{(k)} \le (\max f(\alpha_2^{(k)})) \times \sum_{k=1}^{\#L(p)} p_2^{(k)} \Leftrightarrow \min f(\alpha_2^{(k)}) \le \sum_{k=1}^{\#L(p)} f(\alpha_2^{(k)})p_2^{(k)} \le \max f(\alpha_2^{(k)})$$
$$\sum_{k=1}^{\#L(p)} f(\alpha_3^{(k)})p_3^{(k)} \ge (\min f(\alpha_3^{(k)})) \times \sum_{k=1}^{\#L(p)} p_3^{(k)} \Leftrightarrow \sum_{k=1}^{\#L(p)} f(\alpha_3^{(k)})p_3^{(k)} \ge \min f(\alpha_3^{(k)})$$

Combining the above Equation gives:

$$\sum_{k=1}^{\#L(p)} f(\alpha_1^{(k)})p_1^{(k)} \le \max f(\alpha_1^{(k)}) < \min f(\alpha_2^{(k)}) \le \sum_{k=1}^{\#L(p)} f(\alpha_2^{(k)})p_2^{(k)} \le \max f(\alpha_2^{(k)}) < \min f(\alpha_3^{(k)}) \le \sum_{k=1}^{\#L(p)} f(\alpha_3^{(k)})p_3^{(k)}$$
$$\Leftrightarrow \sum_{k=1}^{\#L(p)} f(\alpha_1^{(k)})p_1^{(k)} < \sum_{k=1}^{\#L(p)} f(\alpha_2^{(k)})p_2^{(k)} < \sum_{k=1}^{\#L(p)} f(\alpha_3^{(k)})p_3^{(k)}$$
$$0 < \sum_{k=1}^{\#L(p)} f(\alpha_2^{(k)})p_2^{(k)} - \sum_{k=1}^{\#L(p)} f(\alpha_1^{(k)})p_1^{(k)} < \sum_{k=1}^{\#L(p)} f(\alpha_3^{(k)})p_3^{(k)} - \sum_{k=1}^{\#L(p)} f(\alpha_1^{(k)})p_1^{(k)}$$
$$\left|\sum_{k=1}^{\#L(p)} f(\alpha_1^{(k)})p_1^{(k)} - \sum_{k=1}^{\#L(p)} f(\alpha_2^{(k)})p_2^{(k)}\right| = \sum_{k=1}^{\#L(p)} f(\alpha_2^{(k)})p_2^{(k)} - \sum_{k=1}^{\#L(p)} f(\alpha_1^{(k)})p_1^{(k)} < \sum_{k=1}^{\#L(p)} f(\alpha_3^{(k)})p_3^{(k)} - \sum_{k=1}^{\#L(p)} f(\alpha_1^{(k)})p_1^{(k)}$$
$$= \left|\sum_{k=1}^{\#L(p)} f(\alpha_1^{(k)})p_1^{(k)} - \sum_{k=1}^{\#L(p)} f(\alpha_3^{(k)})p_3^{(k)}\right|$$
$$\frac{1}{2}\sum_{k=1}^{\#L(p)}\left|p_1^{(k)} - p_2^{(k)}\right| = \frac{1}{2}\sum_{k=1}^{\#L_1(p)}\left|p_1^{(k)} - p_2^{(k)}\right| + \frac{1}{2}\sum_{k=1}^{\#L_2(p)}\left|p_1^{(k)} - p_2^{(k)}\right| + \frac{1}{2}\sum_{k=1}^{\#L_3(p)}\left|p_1^{(k)} - p_2^{(k)}\right| = \frac{1}{2}\sum_{k=1}^{\#L_1(p)} p_1^{(k)} + \frac{1}{2}\sum_{k=1}^{\#L_2(p)} p_2^{(k)} + 0 = 1$$
$$\Leftrightarrow \frac{1}{2}\sum_{k=1}^{\#L(p)}\left|p_1^{(k)} - p_2^{(k)}\right| = \frac{1}{2}\sum_{k=1}^{\#L(p)}\left|p_1^{(k)} - p_3^{(k)}\right| = 1$$

Thus:

$$\frac{1}{2}\left(\frac{1}{2}\sum_{k=1}^{\#L(p)}\left|p_1^{(k)} - p_2^{(k)}\right| + \left|\sum_{k=1}^{\#L(p)} f(\alpha_1^{(k)})p_1^{(k)} - \sum_{k=1}^{\#L(p)} f(\alpha_2^{(k)})p_2^{(k)}\right|\right) = \frac{1}{2}\left(\frac{1}{2}\sum_{k=1}^{\#L(p)}\left|p_1^{(k)} - p_3^{(k)}\right| + \left|\sum_{k=1}^{\#L(p)} f(\alpha_1^{(k)})p_1^{(k)} - \sum_{k=1}^{\#L(p)} f(\alpha_2^{(k)})p_2^{(k)}\right|\right)$$
$$< \frac{1}{2}\left(\frac{1}{2}\sum_{k=1}^{\#L(p)}\left|p_1^{(k)} - p_3^{(k)}\right| + \left|\sum_{k=1}^{\#L(p)} f(\alpha_1^{(k)})p_1^{(k)} - \sum_{k=1}^{\#L(p)} f(\alpha_3^{(k)})p_3^{(k)}\right|\right)$$

The same can be proven:

$$f(\alpha_1^{(k)}) - f(\alpha_2^{(k)}) < f(\alpha_1^{(k)}) - f(\alpha_3^{(k)}), f(\alpha_1^{(k)}) \cdot p_1^{(k)} - f(\alpha_2^{(k)}) \cdot p_2^{(k)} < f(\alpha_1^{(k)}) \cdot p_1^{(k)} - f(\alpha_3^{(k)}) \cdot p_3^{(k)}$$
$$\Rightarrow \left|f(\alpha_1^{(k)}) - f(\alpha_2^{(k)})\right|^{\lambda} < \left|f(\alpha_1^{(k)}) - f(\alpha_3^{(k)})\right|^{\lambda}$$
$$\left|f(\alpha_1^{(k)}) \cdot p_1^{(k)} - f(\alpha_2^{(k)}) \cdot p_2^{(k)}\right|^{\lambda} < \left|f(\alpha_1^{(k)}) \cdot p_1^{(k)} - f(\alpha_3^{(k)}) \cdot p_3^{(k)}\right|^{\lambda} \Rightarrow \min_{k=1}^{\#L(p)}\left\{\left|f(\alpha_1^{(k)}) - f(\alpha_2^{(k)})\right|^{\lambda} + \left|f(\alpha_1^{(k)}) \cdot p_1^{(k)} - f(\alpha_2^{(k)}) \cdot p_2^{(k)}\right|^{\lambda}\right\}$$
$$< \min_{k=1}^{\#L(p)}\left\{\left|f(\alpha_1^{(k)}) - f(\alpha_2^{(k)})\right|^{\lambda} + \left|f(\alpha_1^{(k)}) \cdot p_1^{(k)} - f(\alpha_3^{(k)}) \cdot p_3^{(k)}\right|^{\lambda}\right\}$$
$$\Rightarrow \max_{k=1}^{\#L(p)}\left\{\left(\frac{1}{2}\left(\min_{j=1}^{t}\left\{\left|f(\alpha_1^{(k)}) - f(\alpha_2^{(k)})\right|^{\lambda} + \left|f(\alpha_1^{(k)})p_1^{(k)} - f(\alpha_2^{(k)})p_2^{(k)}\right|^{\lambda}\right\}\right)\right)^{\frac{1}{\lambda}}\right\}$$
$$< \max_{k=1}^{\#L(p)}\left\{\left(\frac{1}{2}\left(\min_{j=1}^{m}\left\{\left|f(\alpha_1^{(k)}) - f(\alpha_3^{(k)})\right|^{\lambda} + \left|f(\alpha_1^{(k)})p_1^{(k)} - f(\alpha_3^{(k)})p_3^{(k)}\right|^{\lambda}\right\}\right)\right)^{\frac{1}{\lambda}}\right\}.$$

Combining the above equations, when $\lambda = 1$ or $\lambda = 2$, yields the following Equation.

$$\left(\frac{1}{2}\left(\left|\frac{1}{2}\sum_{k=1}^{\#L(p)}\left|p_1^{(k)} - p_2^{(k)}\right| + \frac{1}{2g}\left|\sum_{k=1}^{\#L(p)} f(\alpha_1^{(k)})p_1^{(k)} - \sum_{k=1}^{\#L(p)} f(\alpha_2^{(k)})p_2^{(k)}\right|\right|\right)^{\lambda}\right)$$
$$\leq \left(\frac{1}{2}\left(\left|\frac{1}{2}\sum_{k=1}^{\#L(p)}\left|p_1^{(k)} - p_3^{(k)}\right| + \frac{1}{2g}\left|\sum_{k=1}^{\#L(p)} f(\alpha_1^{(k)})p_1^{(k)} - \sum_{k=1}^{\#L(p)} f(\alpha_3^{(k)})p_3^{(k)}\right|\right|\right)^{\lambda}\right),$$
$$\max_{k=1}^{\#L(p)}\left\{\left(\frac{1}{2}\left(\min_{k=1}^{\#L(p)}\left\{\left|f(\alpha_1^{(k)}) - f(\alpha_2^{(k)})\right|^{\lambda} + \left|f(\alpha_1^{(k)})p_1^{(k)} - f(\alpha_2^{(k)})p_2^{(k)}\right|^{\lambda}\right\}\right)\right)\right\}$$
$$\leq \max_{k=1}^{\#L(p)}\left\{\left(\frac{1}{2}\left(\min_{k=1}^{\#L(p)}\left\{\left|f(\alpha_1^{(k)}) - f(\alpha_3^{(k)})\right|^{\lambda} + \left|f(\alpha_1^{(k)})p_1^{(k)} - f(\alpha_3^{(k)})p_3^{(k)}\right|^{\lambda}\right\}\right)\right)\right\},$$
$$\left\{\eta\left[\frac{1}{2}\left(\left|\frac{1}{2}\sum_{k=1}^{\#L(p)}\left|p_1^{(k)} - p_2^{(k)}\right| + \left|\sum_{k=1}^{\#L(p)} f(\alpha_1^{(k)})p_1^{(k)} - \sum_{k=1}^{\#L(p)} f(\alpha_2^{(k)})p_2^{(k)}\right|\right|\right)^{\lambda}\right] + (1-\eta)\right.$$
$$\left.\max_{k=1}^{\#L(p)}\left\{\frac{1}{2}\left[\min_{k=1}^{\#L(p)}\left(\left|f(\alpha_1^{(k)}) - f(\alpha_2^{(k)})\right|^{\lambda} + \left|f(\alpha_1^{(k)})p_1^{(k)} - f(\alpha_2^{(k)})p_2^{(k)}\right|^{\lambda}\right)\right]\right\}\right\}^{\frac{1}{\lambda}}$$
$$\leq \left\{\eta\left[\frac{1}{2}\left(\left|\frac{1}{2}\sum_{k=1}^{\#L(p)}\left|p_1^{(k)} - p_3^{(k)}\right| + \left|\sum_{k=1}^{\#L(p)} f(\alpha_1^{(k)})p_1^{(k)} - \sum_{k=1}^{\#L(p)} f(\alpha_3^{(k)})p_3^{(k)}\right|\right|\right)^{\lambda}\right] +\right.$$
$$\left.(1-\eta)\max_{k=1}^{\#L(p)}\left\{\frac{1}{2}\left[\min_{k=1}^{\#L(p)}\left(\left|f(\alpha_1^{(k)}) - f(\alpha_3^{(k)})\right|^{\lambda} + \left|f(\alpha_1^{(k)})p_1^{(k)} - f(\alpha_3^{(k)})p_3^{(k)}\right|^{\lambda}\right)\right]\right\}\right\}^{\frac{1}{\lambda}}$$
$$\Rightarrow D_{gh}(L_1(p), L_2(p)) \leq D_{gh}(L_1(p), L_3(p))$$

Ditto for easy proof: $D_{gh}(L_2(p), L_3(p)) \leq D_{gh}(L_1(p), L_3(p))$. Thus, Theorem 1 is proved.

Appendix B

All the results of Table 8 are as follows:

Table A1. The complete evaluation matrix.

Expert	Alternative	C_1	C_2	C_3	C_4
e_1	A_1	3.387	0.000	3.387	−2.250
	A_2	2.629	1.840	−2.250	2.629
	A_3	3.387	−2.250	2.629	1.840
	A_4	0.000	2.629	−2.250	3.387
e_2	A_1	2.629	2.629	3.387	2.629
	A_2	3.387	3.387	3.387	3.387
	A_3	3.387	3.387	3.387	3.387
	A_4	3.387	3.387	2.629	3.387

Table A1. *Cont.*

Expert	Alternative	C_1	C_2	C_3	C_4
e_3	A_1	−2.250	−2.250	1.840	1.840
	A_2	1.840	1.840	1.840	1.840
	A_3	2.629	2.629	2.629	2.629
	A_4	−2.250	−2.250	1.840	1.840
e_4	A_1	2.629	2.629	3.387	2.629
	A_2	3.387	3.387	1.840	3.387
	A_3	2.629	2.629	2.629	2.629
	A_4	1.840	3.387	2.629	−2.250
e_5	A_1	2.629	3.387	3.387	3.387
	A_2	3.387	2.629	3.387	2.629
	A_3	3.387	2.629	2.629	3.387
	A_4	3.387	3.387	3.387	2.629
e_6	A_1	2.629	1.840	1.840	2.629
	A_2	2.629	3.387	1.840	3.387
	A_3	2.629	3.387	3.387	1.840
	A_4	1.840	3.387	3.387	−2.250
e_7	A_1	3.387	3.387	3.387	3.387
	A_2	3.387	3.387	3.387	3.387
	A_3	3.387	3.387	3.387	3.387
	A_4	3.387	3.387	3.387	3.387
e_8	A_1	3.387	3.387	3.387	3.387
	A_2	3.387	3.387	3.387	2.629
	A_3	3.387	3.387	3.387	3.387
	A_4	3.387	2.629	2.629	2.629
e_9	A_1	1.840	1.840	1.840	1.840
	A_2	1.840	1.840	1.840	1.840
	A_3	3.387	3.387	3.387	3.387
	A_4	0.000	0.000	0.000	0.000
e_{10}	A_1	2.629	2.629	1.840	1.840
	A_2	3.387	3.387	1.840	2.629
	A_3	3.387	3.387	3.387	3.387
	A_4	2.629	3.387	2.629	3.387
e_{11}	A_1	2.629	2.629	1.840	2.629
	A_2	3.387	2.629	2.629	2.629
	A_3	2.629	2.629	1.840	2.629
	A_4	2.629	2.629	2.629	2.629
e_{12}	A_1	−2.250	−2.250	1.840	0.000
	A_2	2.629	−2.250	1.840	3.387
	A_3	2.629	2.629	2.629	2.629
	A_4	2.629	2.629	1.840	2.629

Table A1. *Cont.*

Expert	Alternative	C_1	C_2	C_3	C_4
e_{13}	A_1	2.629	−2.250	0.000	−2.250
	A_2	2.629	1.840	−2.250	2.629
	A_3	3.387	2.629	2.629	2.629
	A_4	1.840	2.629	0.000	1.840
e_{14}	A_1	2.629	1.840	2.629	1.840
	A_2	1.840	2.629	2.629	1.840
	A_3	2.629	2.629	2.629	2.629
	A_4	−2.250	1.840	−2.250	−2.250
e_{15}	A_1	2.629	2.629	2.629	2.629
	A_2	2.629	2.629	2.629	2.629
	A_3	2.629	2.629	2.629	2.629
	A_4	2.629	2.629	2.629	2.629
e_{16}	A_1	2.629	1.840	3.387	2.629
	A_2	1.840	3.387	3.387	3.387
	A_3	2.629	3.387	2.629	2.629
	A_4	2.629	3.387	2.629	2.629
e_{17}	A_1	1.840	2.629	2.629	2.629
	A_2	2.629	1.840	−2.250	−2.250
	A_3	3.387	2.629	−2.250	−2.250
	A_4	−2.250	−2.250	−2.250	−2.250
e_{18}	A_1	2.629	3.387	3.387	3.387
	A_2	3.387	3.387	2.629	2.629
	A_3	3.387	3.387	2.629	2.629
	A_4	2.629	3.387	3.387	2.629
e_{19}	A_1	0.000	0.000	0.000	0.000
	A_2	−2.250	1.840	2.629	1.840
	A_3	2.629	2.629	2.629	2.629
	A_4	−2.250	1.840	1.840	−2.250
e_{20}	A_1	3.387	3.387	3.387	3.387
	A_2	3.387	3.387	3.387	2.629
	A_3	3.387	3.387	3.387	3.387
	A_4	3.387	2.629	2.629	2.629

References

1. Lv, J.; Mao, Q.; Li, Q.; Yu, R. A group emergency decision-making method for epidemic prevention and control based on probabilistic hesitant fuzzy prospect set considering quality of information. *Int. J. Comput. Intell. Syst.* **2022**, *15*, 33. [CrossRef]
2. Deng, X.; Kong, Z. Humanitarian rescue scheme selection under the COVID-19 crisis in China: Based on group decision-making method. *Symmetry* **2021**, *13*, 668. [CrossRef]
3. Xu, X.H.; Liu, S.L.; Chen, X.H. Dynamic adjustment method of emergency decision scheme for major incidents based on big data analysis of public preference. *Oper. Res. Manag. Sci.* **2020**, *29*, 41–51.
4. Xu, X.H.; Yin, X.P.; Zhong, X.Y.; Wan, Q.F.; Yang, Z. Summary of research on theory and methods in large-group decision-making: Problems and challenges. *Inf. Control* **2021**, *50*, 54–64.
5. Herrera, F.; Herrera-Viedma, E.; Verdegay, J.L. A model of consensus in group decision making under linguistic assessments. *Fuzzy Sets Syst.* **1996**, *78*, 73–87. [CrossRef]

6. Liu, Y.; Li, L.; Tu, Y.; Mei, Y. Fuzzy TOPSIS-EW method with multi-granularity linguistic assessment information for emergency logistics performance evaluation. *Symmetry* **2020**, *12*, 1331. [CrossRef]
7. Xu, X.H.; Xiao, T. Consensus model for large group emergency decision making driven by social network behavior data. *Syst. Eng. Electron.* **2022**, 1–15. Available online: https://kns.cnki.net/kcms/detail/11.2422.tn.20220518.2134.007.html (accessed on 18 June 2022).
8. Xu, X.H.; Wang, L.L.; Chen, X.H. Large group risky emergency decision-making under the public concern themes. *J. Syst. Eng.* **2019**, *34*, 511–525.
9. Xu, X.H.; Yu, Z.X. A large group emergency decision making method and application based on attribute mining of public behavior big data in social network environment. *Control Decis. Mak.* **2022**, *37*, 175–184.
10. Wang, J.X. A MAGDM Algorithm with Multi-Granular Probabilistic Linguistic Information. *Symmetry* **2019**, *11*, 127. [CrossRef]
11. Pang, Q.; Wang, H.; Xu, Z.S. Probabilistic linguistic term sets in multi-attribute group decision making. *Inf. Sci.* **2016**, *369*, 128–143. [CrossRef]
12. Gao, J.; Li, X. Prospective decision-making method based on probabilistic language terminology. *Comput. Appl. Res.* **2021**, *38*, 1973–1978.
13. Zhang, Y.; Wang, L.; Lu, L.; Ye, Y.P.; Wan, L. PL-VIKOR group decision-making based on cumulative prospect theory and knowledge rating. *Syst. Eng. Electron.* **2022**, 1–12. Available online: https://kns.cnki.net/kcms/detail/11.2422.TN.20220615.1203.007.html (accessed on 18 June 2022).
14. Sforzini, L.; Worrell, C.; Kose, M.; Anderson, I.M.; Aouizerate, B.; Arolt, V.; Bauer, M.; Baune, B.T.; Blier, P.; Cleare, A.J.; et al. A Delphi-method-based consensus guideline for definition of treatment-resistant depression for clinical trials. *Mol. Psychiatry* **2022**, *27*, 1286–1299. [CrossRef]
15. Krishankumar, R.; Ravichandran, K.S.; Ahmed, M.I.; Kar, S.; Tyagi, S.K. Probabilistic linguistic preference relation-based decision framework for multi-attribute group decision making. *Symmetry* **2018**, *11*, 2. [CrossRef]
16. Campbell, J.M.; Chen, K.W. Explicit identities for infinite families of series involving squared binomial coefficients. *J. Math. Anal. Appl.* **2022**, *513*, 126219. [CrossRef]
17. Carlson, D.A.; Shehata, C.; Gonsalves, N.; Hirano, I.; Peterson, S.; Prescott, J.; Farina, D.A.; Schauer, J.M.; Kou, W.; Kahrilas, P.J.; et al. Esophageal dysmotility is associated with disease severity in eosinophilic esophagitis. *Clin. Gastroenterol. Hepatol.* **2022**, *20*, 1719–1728. [CrossRef]
18. Zhao, H.; You, J.X.; Liu, H.C. Failure mode and effect analysis using MULTI- MOORA method with continuous weighted entropy under interval-valued intuitionistic fuzzy environment, Soft Comput. 2017, 21, 5355–5367. *Soft Comput.* **2017**, *21*, 5355–5367. [CrossRef]
19. Wang, Y. Using the method of maximizing deviation to make decision for multiindices. *J. Syst. Eng. Electron.* **1997**, *8*, 21–26.
20. Zhang, Z.; Geng, Y.; Wu, X.; Zhou, H.; Lin, B. A method for determining the weight of objective indoor environment and subjective response based on information theory. *Build. Environ.* **2022**, *207*, 108426. [CrossRef]
21. Sałabun, W.; Wątróbski, J.; Shekhovtsov, A. Are mcda methods benchmarkable? a comparative study of topsis, vikor, copras, and promethee ii methods. *Symmetry* **2020**, *12*, 1549. [CrossRef]
22. Farrokhizadeh, E.; Seyfi-Shishavan, S.A.; Gündoğdu, F.K.; Donyatalab, Y.; Kahraman, C.; Seifi, S.H. A spherical fuzzy methodology integrating maximizing deviation and TOPSIS methods. *Eng. Appl. Artif. Intell.* **2021**, *101*, 104212. [CrossRef]
23. Akram, M.; Al-Kenani, A.N. Multi-criteria group decision-making for selection of green suppliers under bipolar fuzzy PROMETHEE process. *Symmetry* **2020**, *12*, 77. [CrossRef]
24. Zadeh, L.A. The concept of a linguistic variable and its application to approximate reasoning-I. *Inf. Sci.* **1975**, *8*, 199–249. [CrossRef]
25. Wang, L.J. Multi-criteria decision-making method based on dominance degree and BWM with probabilistic hesitant fuzzy information. *Int. J. Mach. Learn. Cybern.* **2019**, *10*, 1671–1685.
26. Brans, J.P.; Vincke, P.; Mareschal, B. How to select and how to rank projects: The PROMETHEE method. *Eur. J. Oper. Res.* **1986**, *24*, 228–238. [CrossRef]
27. Rani, P.; Mishra, A.R. Fermatean fuzzy Einstein aggregation operators-based MULTIMOORA method for electric vehicle charging station selection. *Expert Syst. Appl.* **2021**, *182*, 115267. [CrossRef]
28. Narayanamoorthy, S.; Pragathi, S.; Parthasarathy, T.N.; Kalaiselvan, S.; Kureethara, J.V.; Saraswathy, R.; Nithya, P.; Kang, D. The COVID-19 vaccine preference for youngsters using promethee-ii in the ifss environment. *Symmetry* **2021**, *13*, 1030. [CrossRef]
29. Goswami, S.S.; Behera, D.K.; Afzal, A.; Kaladgi, A.R.; Khan, S.A.; Rajendran, P.; Asif, M. Analysis of a robot selection problem using two newly developed hybrid MCDM models of TOPSIS-ARAS and COPRAS-ARAS. *Symmetry* **2021**, *13*, 1331. [CrossRef]
30. Gong, Z.; Lin, J.; Weng, L. A Novel Approach for Multiplicative Linguistic Group Decision Making Based on Symmetrical Linguistic Chi-Square Deviation and VIKOR Method. *Symmetry* **2022**, *14*, 136. [CrossRef]
31. Akram, M.; Naz, S.; Smarandache, F. Generalization of maximizing deviation and TOPSIS method for MADM in simplified neutrosophic hesitant fuzzy environment. *Symmetry* **2019**, *11*, 1058. [CrossRef]
32. Bao, G.Y.; Lian, X.L.; He, M.; Wang, L.L. Improved two-tuple linguistic representation model based on new linguistic evaluation scale. *Control Decis.* **2010**, *25*, 780–784.
33. Zhang, X.; Liao, H.; Xu, B.; Xiong, M. A probabilistic linguistic-based deviation method for multi-expert qualitative decision making with aspirations. *Appl. Soft Comput.* **2020**, *93*, 106362. [CrossRef]

34. Wang, X.; Wang, J.; Zhang, H. Distance-based multicriteria group decision-making approach with probabilistic linguistic term sets. *Expert Syst.* **2019**, *36*, e12352. [CrossRef]
35. Tversky, A.; Kahneman, D. *Advances in Prospect Theory: Cumulative Representation of Uncertainty*; Cambridge University Press: Cambridge, UK, 2000; pp. 44–66.
36. Tversky, K.A. Prospect theory: An analysis of decision under risk. *Econometrica* **1979**, *47*, 263–291.
37. Sparck Jones, K. A statistical interpretation of term specificity and its application in retrieval. *J. Doc.* **1972**, *28*, 11–21. [CrossRef]
38. Sparck Jones, K. IDF term weighting and IR research lessons. *J. Doc.* **2004**, *60*, 521–523. [CrossRef]
39. Yu, L.; Lai, K.K. A distance-based group decision-making methodology for multi-person multicriteria emergency decision support. *Decis. Support Syst.* **2011**, *51*, 307–315. [CrossRef]
40. Liu, Y.; Fan, Z.P.; Zhang, X. A method for large group decision-making based on evaluation information provided by participators from multiple groups. *Inf. Fusion* **2016**, *29*, 132–141. [CrossRef]
41. Xu, Z.S.; Luo, S.Q.; Liao, H.C. Probabilistic linguistic PROMETHEE method and its application in medical service. *J. Syst. Eng.* **2019**, *34*, 760–769.

symmetry

MDPI

Article

Confidence Levels-Based Cubic Fermatean Fuzzy Aggregation Operators and Their Application to MCDM Problems

Harish Garg [1,2,3,*], Muhammad Rahim [4], Fazli Amin [4], Saeid Jafari [5] and Ibrahim M. Hezam [6]

1 School of Mathematics, Thapar Institute of Engineering & Technology, Deemed University, Patiala 147004, Punjab, India
2 Department of Mathematics, Graphic Era Deemed to be University, Dehradun 248002, Uttarakhand, India
3 Applied Science Research Center, Applied Science Private University, Amman 11931, Jordan
4 Department of Mathematics, Hazara University Mansehra, Mansehra 21120, Pakistan
5 College of Vestsjaelland South, Herrestraede 11, 4200 Slagelse, Denmark
6 Department of Statistics & Operations Research, College of Sciences King Saud University, Riyadh 11451, Saudi Arabia
* Correspondence: harishg58iitr@gmail.com; Tel.: +91-86990-31147

Abstract: Assessment specialists (experts) are sometimes expected to provide two types of information: knowledge of rating domains and the performance of rating objects (called confidence levels). Unfortunately, the results of previous information aggregation studies cannot be properly used to combine the two categories of data covered above. Additionally, a significant range of symmetric/asymmetric events and structures are frequently included in the implementation process or practical use of fuzzy systems. The primary goal of the current study was to use cubic Fermatean fuzzy set features to address such situations. To deal with the ambiguous information of the aggregated arguments, we defined information aggregation operators with confidence degrees. Two of the aggregation operators we initially proposed were the confidence cubic Fermatean fuzzy weighted averaging (CCFFWA) operator and the confidence cubic Fermatean fuzzy weighted geometric (CCFFWG) operator. They were used as a framework to create an MCDM process, which was supported by an example to show how effective and applicable it is. The comparison of computed results was carried out with the help of existing approaches.

Keywords: cubic Fermatean fuzzy sets; MCDM; confidence levels; aggregation operators

1. Introduction

Researchers working in the general area of fuzzy decision-making have drawn inspiration from the Bellman–Zadeh conception of a symmetrical decision model in an uncertain environment, with complete symmetry between constraints and decision variables. A significant range of symmetric/asymmetric events and structures is frequently included in the implementation process or practical use of fuzzy systems. Multi-criteria decision-making (MCDM) is one of the fast-developing active research problems for obtaining conclusive results in a reasonable time. However, due to different restrictions, it is not always possible to express the requirements precisely, hence the corresponding solutions are not always optimal. The intuitionistic fuzzy set (IFS) [1] theory is one of the most effective and promising strategies scholars usually apply to manage the ambiguity and imprecision of information. In this context, different scholars focus more on IFSs for integrating the different alternatives using various aggregation algorithms. The performances of the criteria for alternatives are aggregated throughout the data synthesis process using weighted and ordered weighted aggregation operators (AOs) [2,3]. In an IFS environment, Xu and Yager [4] presented a geometric aggregation operator (GAO) while Xu [5] proposed a weighted averaging aggregation operator (AAO). Wang and Liu [6] proposed Einstein aggregation operators by using Einstein norm operations in the IFS context. Lai et al. [7] presented a matching algorithm based on similarity measures and adaptive weights. Ye [8] proposed an accuracy function (ac) for interval-valued IFS to compare them to interval-valued intuitionistic fuzzy numbers. Garg [9] presented a series of communicating AOs for IFSs. Garg [10,11] introduced interacting geometric operators employing Einstein t-norm and Einstein t-conorm operations to aggregate intuitionistic fuzzy data. Xu et al. [12] introduced the intuitionistic fuzzy Einstein–Choquet integral-based operators for decision-making (DM) problems. According to the results of the research mentioned above, they are legitimate as long as the sum of the membership grades does not exceed one. However, in real life, it is not always possible to communicate one's preferences within this restriction. For instance, if someone were to review an option according to their preferences, they would give it a satisfaction rating of 0.7 and an unsatisfaction rating of 0.6. As a result, the review would be unable to meet the IFS condition, as $0.7 + 0.6 > 1$. Because the effectiveness cannot be tested under these circumstances, the IFS theory has some limits and disadvantages. To address these issues, Yager [13,14] introduced Pythagorean fuzzy sets (PFSs) as an extension of the IFS theory. PFSs relax the limitations of IFS. Furthermore, it has been demonstrated that all intuitionistic fuzzy values are part of Pythagorean fuzzy values, which specifies that PFSs have superior ability to manage ambiguous issues (See Figure 1). Following his pioneering work, scholars are continually attempting to improve PFSs. According to Yager and Abbasov [15], Pythagorean fuzzy grades are subclasses of complex numbers. Moreover, Zhang and Xu [16] provided a method for determining the optimal alternative based on an ideal solution in a Pythagorean fuzzy environment. Yager [14] presented a series of aggregation operators in a PFS environment. Peng and Yang [17] defined some basic operational laws and their related properties for Pythagorean fuzzy numbers. Garg presented correlation and correlation coefficients for PFSs. Geo and Deng [18] proposed a Pythagorean fuzzy generation technique based on probability negativity to handle MCDM problems. Zhang [19] presented the notions of interval-valued PFSs (IVPFSs) by extending PFSs. Some important properties of IVPFSs were presented by Peng and Yang [20]. To relax the limitations of PFSs, Senapati and Yager [21] proposed Fermatean fuzzy sets (FFSs) and some operational laws of FFSs. Senapati and Yager [22] proposed weighted averaging and weighted geometric aggregation operators under an FFS environment. Rani and Mishra proposed interval-valued FFSs.

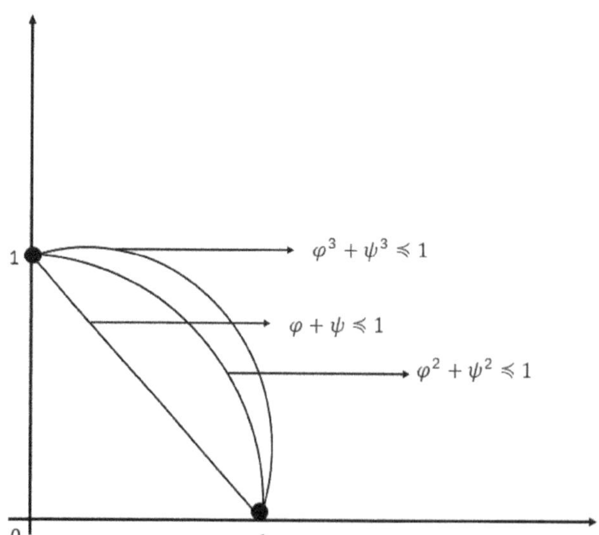

Figure 1. Space analysis between IFS, PFS and FFS.

According to the available research, fuzzy sets, IFS, PFS, and their corresponding implementations are the main topics of all current research. Later on, Jun et al. proposed cubic sets (CSs) by integrating fuzzy sets and interval-valued fuzzy sets. Kaur and Garg [23] presented cubic IFSs and a series of AOs based on t-norm operations. Khan et al. [24,25] suggested CS operations and their characteristics. Abbas et al. [26] proposed cubic PFSs (CPFSs) by combining PFSs and IVPFSs for solving MCDM problems. The flaws and ambiguities of CPFSs were investigated by Amin et al. [27]. Rahim et al. [28] proposed Bonferroni mean aggregation operators under a CPFS environment. Rong and Mishra [29] proposed cubic FFSs and their application in MCDM problems.

Despite the popularity of the aforementioned work, the level of confidence in the criteria was not assessed in any of the studies described above. To put it another way, every researcher has approached the studies with the premise that decision-makers are unquestionably competent in the subjects being investigated. However, these types of prerequisites are only partially accomplished in real-world situations. To compensate for this limitation, decision-makers may examine the alternatives in terms of cubic Fermatean fuzzy numbers (CFFNs) and their associated confidence levels based on their familiarity with the evaluation. As a result, during the evaluation of the alternative in terms of CFFNs, the present study proposes the concept of confidence levels in the optimization processes. First, some basic operations such as P-union (rep. P-intersection), R-union (rep. R-intersection) and so on are defined. Based on these investigations a series of weighted and geometric operators and are proposed in this paper. Additionally, a method to address MCDM issues is suggested. The following is a summary of the study's primary goals:

(1) Define some basic operations of CFFSs and their properties.
(2) Based on these operational laws, propose a series of aggregation operators with confidence levels in a CFFS environment.
(3) Develop a new approach to solve MCDM problems under CFFSs.
(4) Provide an example to evaluate the accuracy and reliability of the proposed approach.
(5) Compare the results of the proposed framework with some existing approaches.

2. Preliminaries

In this section, we briefly present some concepts of PFS, IVPFS, and others to understand the paper.

2.1. PFSs, IVPFSs, and CPFSs

Definition 1 Ref. [13]. *Let F be a non-empty finite set. A PFS over element $t \in F$ is defined as*

$$A = \{\langle t,\ \varphi_A(t),\ \psi_A(t)\rangle | t \in F\}, \tag{1}$$

where $\varphi_A(t) \in [0,\ 1]$ and $\psi_A(t) \in [0,1]$ are the membership and non-membership function of an element $t \in F$ such that $(\varphi_A(t))^2 + (\psi_A(t))^2 \leq 1$.

For convenience, Zhang and Xu [16] called $\langle \varphi_A(t),\ \psi_A(t)\rangle$ a PFN denoted by $\langle \varphi_A, \psi_A\rangle$. The score function of A can be calculated as $sc(A) = \varphi_A^2 - \psi_A^2$.

Definition 2 Ref. [19]. *For a non-empty set F, an IVPFS over an element $t \in F$ is defined as follows:*

$$B = \{\langle t, \widetilde{\varphi}_B(t),\ \widetilde{\psi}_B(t)\rangle | t \in F\}, \tag{2}$$

where $\widetilde{\varphi}_B(t)$ and $\widetilde{\psi}_B(t)$ are interval-valued fuzzy numbers representing the interval membership and non-membership grades of set B, respectively. Let $\widetilde{\varphi}_B(t) = [\widetilde{\varphi}_B^L(t), \widetilde{\varphi}_B^U(t)]$ and $\widetilde{\psi}_B(t) = [\widetilde{\psi}_B^L(t), \widetilde{\psi}_B^U(t)]$ then IVPFS can be written as $B = \{\langle t, [\widetilde{\varphi}_B^L(t), \widetilde{\varphi}_B^U(t)], [\widetilde{\psi}_B^L(t), \widetilde{\psi}_B^U(t)]\rangle | t \in F\}$.

For convenience, we denote these pairs as $\langle [\tilde{\varphi}_B^L, \tilde{\varphi}_B^U], [\tilde{\psi}_B^L, \tilde{\psi}_B^U] \rangle$ and call this an interval-valued PFN (IVPFN). We also set, $0 \le \tilde{\varphi}_B^L, \tilde{\varphi}_B^U, \tilde{\psi}_B^L, \tilde{\psi}_B^U \le 1$ such that $(\tilde{\varphi}_B^U)^2 + (\tilde{\psi}_B^U)^2 \le 1$. The score function of B can be calculated as $sc(B) = \frac{1}{2}\left((\tilde{\varphi}_B^L)^2 + (\tilde{\varphi}_B^U)^2 - (\tilde{\psi}_B^L)^2 - (\tilde{\varphi}_B^U)^2 \right)$.

Definition 3 Refs. [26,27]. *Let F be a non-empty finite set. A CPFS over an element $t \in F$ is defined as*

$$C = \left\{ \langle t, \tilde{\mathcal{B}}_C(t), \mathcal{A}_C(t) \rangle | t \in F \right\}, \tag{3}$$

where $\tilde{\mathcal{B}}_C(t) = \left(\left[\tilde{\varphi}_{\tilde{B}_c}^L(t), \tilde{\varphi}_{\tilde{B}_c}^U(t) \right], \left[\tilde{\psi}_{\tilde{B}_c}^L(t), \tilde{\psi}_{\tilde{B}_c}^U(t) \right] \right)$ *represents an IVPFS while* $\mathcal{A}_C(t) = \left(\varphi_{\tilde{B}_C}(t), \psi_{\tilde{B}_C}(t) \right)$ *represents a PFS. We also set,* $0 \le \tilde{\varphi}_{\tilde{B}_c}^L(t), \tilde{\varphi}_{\tilde{B}_c}^U(t), \tilde{\psi}_{\tilde{B}_c}^L(t), \tilde{\psi}_{\tilde{B}_c}^U(t) \le 1$ *such that* $\left(\tilde{\varphi}_{\tilde{B}_c}^U(t) \right)^2 + \left(\tilde{\psi}_{\tilde{B}_c}^U(t) \right)^2 \le 1$.

For convenience, we denote the pairs as $\langle \left[\tilde{\varphi}_{\tilde{B}_c}^L, \tilde{\varphi}_{\tilde{B}_c}^U \right], \left[\tilde{\psi}_{\tilde{B}_c}^L, \tilde{\psi}_{\tilde{B}_c}^U \right], \varphi_{\tilde{B}_C}, \psi_{\tilde{B}_C} \rangle$ and call this a CPFN.

Definition 4 Ref. [28]. *Let* $C_1 = \left(\langle \left[\varphi_{C_1}^L, \varphi_{C_1}^U \right], \left[\psi_{C_1}^L, \psi_{C_1}^U \right] \rangle, \langle \varphi_{C_1}, \psi_{C_1} \rangle \right)$ *be a CPFN, then the score function is defined under R-order as*

$$sc(C_1) = \frac{\left(\varphi_{C_1}^L \right)^2 + \left(\varphi_{C_1}^L \right)^2 - \left(\psi_{C_1}^L \right)^2 - \left(\psi_{C_1}^L \right)^2}{2} + (\psi_{C_1})^2 - (\varphi_{C_1})^2, \tag{4}$$

and for P-order as

$$sc(C_1) = \frac{\left(\varphi_{C_1}^L \right)^2 + \left(\varphi_{C_1}^L \right)^2 - \left(\psi_{C_1}^L \right)^2 - \left(\psi_{C_1}^L \right)^2}{2} + (\varphi_{C_1})^2 - (\psi_{C_1})^2, \tag{5}$$

where $-2 \le sc(\beta_1) \le 2$.

Definition 5 Ref. [28]. *Let* $C_1 = \left(\langle \left[\varphi_{C_1}^L, \varphi_{C_1}^U \right], \left[\psi_{C_1}^L, \psi_{C_1}^U \right] \rangle, \langle \varphi_{C_1}, \psi_{C_1} \rangle \right)$ *be a CPFN, then the accuracy function is defined as*

$$ac(C_1) = \frac{\left(\varphi_{C_1}^L \right)^2 + \left(\varphi_{C_1}^L \right)^2 + \left(\psi_{C_1}^L \right)^2 + \left(\psi_{C_1}^L \right)^2}{2} + (\varphi_{C_1})^2 + (\psi_{C_1})^2, \tag{6}$$

where $0 \le ac(C_1) \le 2$.

Definition 6 Ref. [28]. *Let* $C_1 = \left(\langle \left[\varphi_{C_1}^L, \varphi_{C_1}^U \right], \left[\psi_{C_1}^L, \psi_{C_1}^U \right] \rangle, \langle \varphi_{C_1}, \psi_{C_1} \rangle \right)$ *and* $C_2 = \left(\langle \left[\varphi_{C_2}^L, \varphi_{C_2}^U \right], \left[\psi_{C_2}^L, \psi_{C_2}^U \right] \rangle, \langle \varphi_{C_2}, \psi_{C_2} \rangle \right)$ *be two CPFSs in F. Then:*

- *(Equality):* $C_1 = C_2$, *if and only if* $\left[\varphi_{C_1}^L, \varphi_{C_1}^U \right] = \left[\varphi_{C_2}^L, \varphi_{C_2}^U \right], \psi_{C_1}^L, \psi_{C_1}^U = \psi_{C_2}^L, \psi_{C_2}^U$, $\varphi_{C_1} = \varphi_{C_2}$ *and* $\psi_{C_1} = \psi_{C_2}$;
- *(P-order):* $C_1 \subseteq_P C_2$ if $\left[\varphi_{C_1}^L, \varphi_{C_1}^U \right] \subseteq \left[\varphi_{C_2}^L, \varphi_{C_2}^U \right], \left[\psi_{C_1}^L, \psi_{C_1}^U \right] \supseteq \left[\psi_{C_2}^L, \psi_{C_2}^U \right], \varphi_{C_1} \le \varphi_{C_2}$ *and* $\psi_{C_1} \ge \psi_{C_2}$;
- *(R-order):* $C_1 \subseteq_R C_2$ if $\left[\varphi_{C_1}^L, \varphi_{C_1}^U \right] \subseteq \left[\varphi_{C_2}^L, \varphi_{C_2}^U \right], \left[\psi_{C_1}^L, \psi_{C_1}^U \right] \supseteq \left[\psi_{C_2}^L, \psi_{C_2}^U \right], \varphi_{C_1} \ge \varphi_{C_2}$ *and* $\psi_{C_1} \le \psi_{C_2}$.

Definition 7 Ref. [27]. *For the CPFNs* $C_i = \left(\langle \left[\varphi_{C_i}^L, \varphi_{C_i}^U \right], \left[\psi_{C_i}^L, \psi_{C_i}^U \right] \rangle, \langle \varphi_{C_i}, \psi_{C_i} \rangle \right)$ (1, 2, 3, 4) *we have:*

(a) *If* $C_1 \subseteq_P C_2$ *and* $C_2 \subseteq_P C_3$ *then* $C_1 \subseteq_P C_3$;

(b) *If* $C_1 \subseteq_P C_2$ *then* $C_2^c \subseteq_P C_1^c$;
(c) *If* $C_1 \subseteq_P C_2$ *and* $C_1 \subseteq_P C_3$ *then* $C_1 \subseteq_P C_2 \cap C_3$;
(d) *If* $C_1 \subseteq_P C_2$ *and* $C_3 \subseteq_P C_4$ *then* $C_1 \cup C_3 \subseteq_P C_2 \cup C_4$ *and* $C_1 \cap C_3 \subseteq_P C_2 \cap C_4$;
(e) *If* $C_1 \subseteq_P C_2$ *and* $C_3 \subseteq_P C_2$ *then* $C_1 \cup C_3 \subseteq_P C_2$;
(f) *If* $C_1 \subseteq_R C_2$ *and* $C_2 \subseteq_R C_3$ *then* $C_1 \subseteq_R C_3$;
(g) *If* $C_1 \subseteq_R C_2$ *then* $C_2^c \subseteq_R C_1^c$;
(h) *If* $C_1 \subseteq_R C_2$ *and* $C_1 \subseteq_R C_3$ *then* $C_1 \subseteq_R C \cap C_3$;
(i) *If* $C_1 \subseteq_R C_2$ *and* $C_3 \subseteq_R C_4$ *then* $C_1 \cup C_3 \subseteq_R C_2 \cup C_4$ *and* $C_1 \cap C_3 \subseteq_R C_2 \cap C_4$;
(j) *If* $C_1 \subseteq_R C_2$ *and* $C_3 \subseteq_R C_2$ *then* $C_1 \cup C_3 \subseteq_R C_2$.

2.2. FFSs, IVFFSs, and CFFSs

Definition 8 Ref. [21]. *Let F be a non-empty set and* $t \in F$. *The FFS over element t is defined as*

$$\mathcal{F} = \{\langle t, \varphi_{\mathcal{F}}(t), \psi_{\mathcal{F}}(t)\rangle | t \in F\}, \tag{7}$$

where $\varphi_{\mathcal{F}}(t) \in [0, 1]$ *and* $\psi_{\mathcal{F}}(t) \in [0, 1]$ *are the membership and non-membership function of an element* $t \in F$ *such that* $(\varphi_{\mathcal{F}}(t))^3 + (\psi_{\mathcal{F}}(t))^3 \in 1$.

For convenience, Senapati and Yager [21] called $\langle \varphi_{\mathcal{F}}(t), \psi_{\mathcal{F}}(t)\rangle$ an FFN denoted by $\langle \varphi_{\mathcal{F}}, \psi_{\mathcal{F}}\rangle$. The score function of A can be calculated as $sc(A) = \varphi_{\mathcal{F}}^3 - \psi_{\mathcal{F}}^3$.

Definition 9 Ref. [30]. *For a non-empty set F, an interval-valued FFS (IVFFS) over an element* $t \in F$ *is defined as follows:*

$$\mathcal{G} = \{\langle t, \widetilde{\varphi}_{\mathcal{G}}(t), \widetilde{\psi}_{\mathcal{G}}(t)\rangle | t \in F\}, \tag{8}$$

where $\widetilde{\varphi}_{\mathcal{G}}(t)$ *and* $\widetilde{\psi}_{\mathcal{G}}(t)$ *are interval-valued fuzzy numbers representing the interval membership and non-membership grades of the set* $\mathcal{G}$ *repectively. Let* $\widetilde{\varphi}_{\mathcal{G}}(t) = \left[\widetilde{\varphi}_{\mathcal{G}}^L(t), \widetilde{\varphi}_{\mathcal{G}}^U(t)\right]$ *and* $\widetilde{\psi}_{\mathcal{G}}(t) = \left[\widetilde{\psi}_{\mathcal{G}}^L(t), \widetilde{\psi}_{\mathcal{G}}^U(t)\right]$ *then IVPFS can be written as* $\mathcal{G} = \left\{\langle t, \left[\widetilde{\varphi}_{\mathcal{G}}^L(t), \widetilde{\varphi}_{\mathcal{G}}^U(t)\right], \left[\widetilde{\psi}_{\mathcal{G}}^L(t), \widetilde{\psi}_{\mathcal{G}}^U(t)\right]\rangle | t \in F\right\}$.

For convenience, we denote these pairs as $\langle \left[\widetilde{\varphi}_{\mathcal{G}}^L, \widetilde{\varphi}_{\mathcal{G}}^U\right], \left[\widetilde{\psi}_{\mathcal{G}}^L, \widetilde{\psi}_{\mathcal{G}}^U\right]\rangle$ and call this an interval-valued FFN (IVFFN). We also set, $0 \leq \widetilde{\varphi}_{\mathcal{G}}^L, \widetilde{\varphi}_{\mathcal{G}}^U, \widetilde{\psi}_{\mathcal{G}}^L, \widetilde{\psi}_{\mathcal{G}}^U \leq 1$ such that $\left(\widetilde{\varphi}_{\mathcal{G}}^U\right)^3 + \left(\widetilde{\psi}_{\mathcal{G}}^U\right)^3 \leq 1$. The score function of $\mathcal{G}$ can be calculated as $sc(B) = \frac{1}{2}\left((\widetilde{\varphi}_B^L)^3 + (\widetilde{\varphi}_B^U)^3 - (\widetilde{\psi}_B^L)^3 - (\widetilde{\varphi}_B^U)^3\right)$.

Definition 10 Ref. [29]. *Let F be a non-empty finite set. A CPFS* $\mathcal{L}$ *over an element* $t \in F$ *is defined as*

$$\mathcal{L} = \{\langle t, \mathcal{G}_{\mathcal{L}}(t), \mathcal{F}_{\mathcal{L}}(t)\rangle | t \in F\}, \tag{9}$$

where $\mathcal{G}_{\mathcal{L}}(t) = ([\widetilde{\varphi}_{\mathcal{L}}^L(t), \widetilde{\varphi}_{\mathcal{L}}^U(t)], [\widetilde{\psi}_{\mathcal{L}}^L(t), \widetilde{\psi}_{\mathcal{L}}^U(t)])$ *represents an IVFFS while* $\mathcal{F}_{\mathcal{L}}(t) = (\varphi_{\mathcal{L}}(t), \psi_{\mathcal{L}}(t))$ *represents PFS. We also set,* $0 \leq \widetilde{\varphi}_{\mathcal{L}}^L(t), \widetilde{\varphi}_{\mathcal{L}}^U(t), \widetilde{\psi}_{\mathcal{L}}^L(t), \widetilde{\psi}_{\mathcal{L}}^U(t) \leq 1$ *such that* $(\widetilde{\varphi}_{\mathcal{L}}^U(t))^2 + (\widetilde{\psi}_{\mathcal{L}}^U(t))^2 \leq 1$.

For convenience, we denote the pairs as $\langle [\widetilde{\varphi}_{\mathcal{L}}^L, \widetilde{\varphi}_{\mathcal{L}}^U], [\widetilde{\psi}_{\mathcal{L}}^L, \widetilde{\psi}_{\mathcal{L}}^U], \varphi_{\mathcal{L}}, \psi_{\mathcal{L}}\rangle$ and call this a CPFN.

3. New Operational Laws and Aggregation Operators under CFFSs with Confidence Levels

In this section, the existing operations defined by Rong et al. [29] are modified. Furthermore, the order relations such as P-order and R-order of CFFNs are presented. Finally, based on these modified operations some series aggregation operators with confidence levels are proposed.

3.1. Modified Operations of CFFSs

Definition 11. *For a family of CFFS* $\{\mathcal{L}_i,\ i \in \Delta\}$, *it follows that*

(a) (*P-union*): $\bigcup_{i\in\Delta}^{P} \mathcal{L}_i = \left(\begin{matrix} \langle \begin{bmatrix} max_{i\in\Delta}\left(\varphi^L_{\mathcal{L}_i}\right), \\ max_{i\in\Delta}\left(\varphi^U_{\mathcal{L}_i}\right) \end{bmatrix}, \begin{bmatrix} min_{i\in\Delta}\left(\psi^L_i\right), \\ min_{i\in\Delta}\left(\psi^U_{\mathcal{L}_i}\right) \end{bmatrix} \rangle, \\ \langle max_{i\in\Delta}\mu_{\mathcal{L}_i}, min_{i\in\Delta}\nu_{\mathcal{L}_i}\rangle \end{matrix} \right)$;

(b) (*P-intersection*): $\bigcap_{i\in\Delta}^{R} \mathcal{L}_i = \left(\begin{matrix} \langle \begin{bmatrix} min_{i\in\Delta}\left(\varphi^L_{\mathcal{L}_i}\right), \\ min_{i\in\Delta}\left(\varphi^U_{\mathcal{L}_i}\right) \end{bmatrix}, \begin{bmatrix} max_{i\in\Delta}\left(\psi^L_{\mathcal{L}_i}\right), \\ max_{i\in\Delta}\left(\psi^U_{\mathcal{L}_i}\right) \end{bmatrix} \rangle, \\ \langle min_{i\in\Delta}\mu_{\mathcal{L}_i}, max_{i\in\Delta}\nu_{\mathcal{L}_i}\rangle \end{matrix} \right)$;

(c) (*R-union*): $\bigcup_{i\in\Delta}^{R} \mathcal{L}_i = \left(\begin{matrix} \langle \begin{bmatrix} max_{i\in\Delta}\left(\varphi^L_{\mathcal{L}_i}\right), \\ max_{i\in\Delta}\left(\varphi^U_{\mathcal{L}_i}\right) \end{bmatrix}, \begin{bmatrix} min_{i\in\Delta}\left(\psi^L_{\mathcal{L}_i}\right), \\ min_{i\in\Delta}\left(\psi^U_{\mathcal{L}_i}\right) \end{bmatrix} \rangle, \\ \langle min_{i\in\Delta}\mu_{\mathcal{L}_i}, max_{i\in\Delta}\nu_{\mathcal{L}_i}\rangle \end{matrix} \right)$;

(d) (*R-intersection*): $\bigcup_{i\in\Delta}^{P} \mathcal{L}_i = \left(\begin{matrix} \langle \begin{bmatrix} max_{\mathcal{L}_i\in\Delta}\left(\varphi^L_{\mathcal{L}_i}\right), \\ max_{i\in\Delta}\left(\varphi^U_{\mathcal{L}_i}\right) \end{bmatrix}, \begin{bmatrix} min_{i\in\Delta}\left(\psi^L_{\mathcal{L}_i}\right), \\ min_{i\in\Delta}\left(\psi^U_{\mathcal{L}_i}\right) \end{bmatrix} \rangle, \\ \langle min_{i\in\Delta}\varphi_{\mathcal{L}_i}, max_{i\in\Delta}\psi_{\mathcal{L}_i}\rangle \end{matrix} \right)$.

Definition 12. *Let* $\mathcal{L}_1 = \left(\langle\left[\varphi^L_{\mathcal{L}_1}, \varphi^U_{\mathcal{L}_1}\right], \left[\psi^L_{\mathcal{L}_1}, \psi^U_{\mathcal{L}_1}\right]\rangle, \langle\varphi_{\mathcal{L}_1}, \psi_{\mathcal{L}_1}\rangle\right)$ *and* $\mathcal{L}_2 = \left(\langle\left[\varphi^L_{\mathcal{L}_2}, \varphi^U_{\mathcal{L}_2}\right], \left[\psi^L_{\mathcal{L}_2}, \psi^U_{\mathcal{L}_2}\right]\rangle, \langle\varphi_{\mathcal{L}_2}, \psi_{\mathcal{L}_2}\rangle\right)$ *be two CFFSs in F. Then*

(a) (*Equality*): $\mathcal{L}_1 = \mathcal{L}_2$, *if and only if* $\left[\varphi^L_{\mathcal{L}_1}, \varphi^U_{\mathcal{L}_1}\right] = \left[\varphi^L_2, \varphi^U_2\right]$, $\left[\psi^L_{\mathcal{L}_1}, \psi^U_{\mathcal{L}_1}\right] = \left[\psi^L_{\mathcal{L}_2}, \psi^U_{\mathcal{L}_2}\right]$, $\varphi_{\mathcal{L}_1} = \varphi_{\mathcal{L}_2}$ *and* $\psi_{\mathcal{L}_1} = \psi_{\mathcal{L}_2}$:

(b) (*P-order*): $\mathcal{L}_1 \subseteq_P \mathcal{L}_2$ *if* $\left[\varphi^L_{\mathcal{L}_1}, \varphi^U_{\mathcal{L}_1}\right] \subseteq \left[\varphi^L_{\mathcal{L}_2}, \varphi^U_{\mathcal{L}_2}\right]$, $\left[\psi^L_{\mathcal{L}_1}, \psi^U_{\mathcal{L}_1}\right] \supseteq \left[\psi^L_{\mathcal{L}_2}, \psi^U_{\mathcal{L}_2}\right]$, $\varphi_{\mathcal{L}_1} \leq \varphi_{\mathcal{L}_2}$ *and* $\psi_{\mathcal{L}_1} \geq \psi_{\mathcal{L}_2}$;

(c) (*R-order*): $\mathcal{L}_1 \subseteq_R \mathcal{L}_2$ *if* $\left[\varphi^L_{\mathcal{L}_1}, \varphi^U_{\mathcal{L}_1}\right] \subseteq \left[\varphi^L_{\mathcal{L}_2}, \varphi^U_{\mathcal{L}_2}\right]$, $\left[\psi^L_{\mathcal{L}_1}, \psi^U_{\mathcal{L}_1}\right] \supseteq \left[\psi^L_{\mathcal{L}_2}, \psi^U_{\mathcal{L}_2}\right]$, $\varphi_{\mathcal{L}_1} \geq \varphi_{\mathcal{L}_2}$ *and* $\psi_{\mathcal{L}_1} \leq \psi_{\mathcal{L}_2}$.

Definition 13. *Let* $\mathcal{L}_1 = \left(\langle\left[\varphi^L_{\mathcal{L}_1}, \varphi^U_{\mathcal{L}_1}\right], \left[\psi^L_{\mathcal{L}_1}, \psi^U_{\mathcal{L}_1}\right]\rangle, \langle\varphi_{\mathcal{L}_1}, \psi_{\mathcal{L}_1}\rangle\right)$ *be a CFFN, then the score function is defined under R-order as*

$$sc(\mathcal{L}_1) = \frac{\left(\varphi^L_{\mathcal{L}_1}\right)^3 + \left(\varphi^U_{\mathcal{L}_1}\right)^3 - \left(\psi^L_{\mathcal{L}_1}\right)^3 - \left(\psi^U_{\mathcal{L}_1}\right)^3}{2} + \left(\psi^3_{\mathcal{L}_1} - \varphi^3_{\mathcal{L}_1}\right), \tag{10}$$

and for P-order as

$$sc(\mathcal{L}_1) = \frac{\left(\varphi^L_{\mathcal{L}_1}\right)^3 + \left(\varphi^U_{\mathcal{L}_1}\right)^3 - \left(\psi^L_{\mathcal{L}_1}\right)^3 - \left(\psi^U_{\mathcal{L}_1}\right)^3}{2} + \left(\varphi^3_{\mathcal{L}_1} - \psi^3_{\mathcal{L}_1}\right), \tag{11}$$

where $-2 \leq sc(\mathcal{L}_1) \leq 2$.

Definition 14. *Let* $\mathcal{L}_1 = \left(\langle\left[\varphi^L_{\mathcal{L}_1}, \varphi^U_{\mathcal{L}_1}\right], \left[\psi^L_{\mathcal{L}_1}, \psi^U_{\mathcal{L}_1}\right]\rangle, \langle\varphi_{\mathcal{L}_1}, \psi_{\mathcal{L}_1}\rangle\right)$ *be a CFFN, then the accuracy function is defined under R-order as*

$$ac(\mathcal{L}_1) = \frac{\left(\varphi^L_{\mathcal{L}_1}\right)^3 + \left(\varphi^U_{\mathcal{L}_1}\right)^3 + \left(\psi^L_{\mathcal{L}_1}\right)^3 + \left(\psi^U_{\mathcal{L}_1}\right)^3}{2} + \left(\varphi^3_{\mathcal{L}_1} + \psi^3_{\mathcal{L}_1}\right), \tag{12}$$

where $0 \leq ac(\mathcal{L}_1) \leq 2$.

Theorem 1. For the CPFNs $\mathcal{L}_i = \left(\langle\left[\varphi^L_{\mathcal{L}_i}, \varphi^U_{\mathcal{L}_i}\right], \left[\psi^L_{\mathcal{L}_i}, \psi^U_{\mathcal{L}_i}\right]\rangle, \langle\varphi_{\mathcal{L}_i}, \psi_{\mathcal{L}_i}\rangle\right)$ (1, 2, 3, 4) we have:

(a) *If* $\mathcal{L}_1 \subseteq_P \mathcal{L}_2$ *and* $\mathcal{L}_2 \subseteq_P \mathcal{L}_3$ *then* $\mathcal{L}_1 \subseteq_P \mathcal{L}_3$;
(b) *If* $\mathcal{L}_1 \subseteq_P \mathcal{L}_2$ *then* $\mathcal{L}_2^c \subseteq_P \mathcal{L}_1^c$;
(c) *If* $\mathcal{L}_1 \subseteq_P \mathcal{L}_2$ *and* $\mathcal{L}_1 \subseteq_P \mathcal{L}_3$ *then* $\mathcal{L}_1 \subseteq_P \mathcal{L}_2 \cap \mathcal{L}_3$;
(d) *If* $\mathcal{L}_1 \subseteq_P \mathcal{L}_2$ *and* $\mathcal{L}_3 \subseteq_P \mathcal{L}_4$ *then* $\mathcal{L}_1 \cup \mathcal{L}_3 \subseteq_P \mathcal{L}_2 \cup \mathcal{L}_4$ *and* $\mathcal{L}_1 \cap \mathcal{L}_3 \subseteq_P \mathcal{L}_2 \cap \mathcal{L}_4$;
(e) *If* $\mathcal{L}_1 \subseteq_P \mathcal{L}_2$ *and* $\mathcal{L}_3 \subseteq_P \mathcal{L}_2$ *then* $\mathcal{L}_1 \cup \mathcal{L}_3 \subseteq_P \mathcal{L}_2$;
(f) *If* $\mathcal{L}_1 \subseteq_R \mathcal{L}_2$ *and* $\mathcal{L}_2 \subseteq_R \mathcal{L}_3$ *then* $\mathcal{L}_1 \subseteq_R \mathcal{L}_3$;
(g) *If* $\mathcal{L}_1 \subseteq_R \mathcal{L}_2$ *then* $\mathcal{L}_2^c \subseteq_R \mathcal{L}_1^c$;
(h) *If* $\mathcal{L}_1 \subseteq_R \mathcal{L}_2$ *and* $\mathcal{L}_1 \subseteq_R \mathcal{L}_3$ *then* $\mathcal{L}_1 \subseteq_R \mathcal{L}_2 \cap \mathcal{L}_3$;
(i) *If* $\mathcal{L}_1 \subseteq_R \mathcal{L}_2$ *and* $\mathcal{L}_3 \subseteq_R \mathcal{L}_4$ *then* $\mathcal{L}_1 \cup \mathcal{L}_3 \subseteq_R \mathcal{L}_2 \cup \mathcal{L}_4$ *and* $\mathcal{L}_1 \cap \mathcal{L}_3 \subseteq_R \mathcal{L}_2 \cap \mathcal{L}_4$;
(j) *If* $\mathcal{L}_1 \subseteq_R \mathcal{L}_2$ *and* $\mathcal{L}_3 \subseteq_R \mathcal{L}_2$ *then* $\mathcal{L}_1 \cup \mathcal{L}_3 \subseteq_R \mathcal{L}_2$.

Proof. (a) Since $\mathcal{L}_1 = \left(\langle\left[\varphi^L_{\mathcal{L}_1}, \varphi^U_{\mathcal{L}_1}\right], \left[\psi^L_{\mathcal{L}_1}, \psi^U_{\mathcal{L}_1}\right]\rangle, \langle\varphi_{\mathcal{L}_1}, \psi_{\mathcal{L}_1}\rangle\right)$, $\mathcal{L}_2 = \left(\langle\left[\varphi^L_{\mathcal{L}_2}, \varphi^U_{\mathcal{L}_2}\right], \left[\psi^L_{\mathcal{L}_2}, \psi^U_{\mathcal{L}_2}\right]\rangle, \langle\varphi_{\mathcal{L}_2}, \psi_{\mathcal{L}_2}\rangle\right)$, and $\mathcal{L}_3 = \left(\langle\left[\varphi^L_{\mathcal{L}_3}, \varphi^U_{\mathcal{L}_3}\right], \left[\psi^L_{\mathcal{L}_3}, \psi^U_{\mathcal{L}_3}\right]\rangle, \langle\varphi_{\mathcal{L}_3}, \psi_{\mathcal{L}_3}\rangle\right)$ be CPFNs. Using Definition 12, if $\mathcal{L}_1 \subseteq_P \mathcal{L}_2$ then $\left[\varphi^L_{\mathcal{L}_1}, \varphi^U_{\mathcal{L}_1}\right] \subseteq \left[\varphi^L_{\mathcal{L}_2}, \varphi^U_{\mathcal{L}_2}\right]$, $\left[\psi^L_{\mathcal{L}_1}, \psi^U_{\mathcal{L}_1}\right] \supseteq \left[\psi^L_{\mathcal{L}_2}, \psi^U_{\mathcal{L}_2}\right]$, $\varphi_{\mathcal{L}_1} \leq \varphi_{\mathcal{L}_2}$, and $\psi_{\mathcal{L}_1} \geq \psi_{\mathcal{L}_2}$. Similarly, if $\mathcal{L}_2 \subseteq_P \mathcal{L}_3$, then $\left[\varphi^L_{\mathcal{L}_2}, \varphi^U_{\mathcal{L}_2}\right] \subseteq \left[\varphi^L_{\mathcal{L}_3}, \varphi^U_{\mathcal{L}_3}\right]$, $\left[\psi^L_{\mathcal{L}_2}, \psi^U_{\mathcal{L}_2}\right] \supseteq \left[\psi^L_{\mathcal{L}_3}, \psi^U_{\mathcal{L}_3}\right]$, $\varphi_{\mathcal{L}_2} \leq \varphi_{\mathcal{L}_3}$, and $\psi_{\mathcal{L}_2} \geq \psi_{\mathcal{L}_3}$ which implies that $\left[\varphi^L_{\mathcal{L}_1}, \varphi^U_{\mathcal{L}_1}\right] \subseteq \left[\varphi^L_{\mathcal{L}_2}, \varphi^U_{\mathcal{L}_2}\right] \subseteq \left[\varphi^L_{\mathcal{L}_3}, \varphi^U_{\mathcal{L}_3}\right]$; $\left[\psi^L_{\mathcal{L}_1}, \psi^U_{\mathcal{L}_1}\right] \supseteq \left[\psi^L_{\mathcal{L}_2}, \psi^U_{\mathcal{L}_2}\right] \supseteq \left[\psi^L_{\mathcal{L}_3}, \psi^U_{\mathcal{L}_3}\right]$; $\varphi_{\mathcal{L}_1} \leq \varphi_{\mathcal{L}_2} \leq \varphi_{\mathcal{L}_3}$; and $\psi_{\mathcal{L}_1} \geq \psi_{\mathcal{L}_2} \geq \psi_{\mathcal{L}_3}$ and hence $\left[\varphi^L_{\mathcal{L}_1}, \varphi^U_{\mathcal{L}_1}\right] \subseteq \left[\varphi^L_{\mathcal{L}_3}, \varphi^U_{\mathcal{L}_3}\right]$; $\left[\psi^L_{\mathcal{L}_1}, \psi^U_{\mathcal{L}_1}\right] \supseteq \left[\psi^L_{\mathcal{L}_3}, \psi^U_{\mathcal{L}_3}\right]$; $\varphi_{\mathcal{L}_1} \leq \varphi_{\mathcal{L}_3}$; and $\psi_{\mathcal{L}_1} \geq \psi_{\mathcal{L}_3}$. Therefore, if $\mathcal{L}_1 \subseteq_P \mathcal{L}_2$ and $\mathcal{L}_2 \subseteq_P \mathcal{L}_3$, then $\mathcal{L}_1 \subseteq_P \mathcal{L}_3$. Similarly, for the others. □

Definition 15. *Let* $\mathcal{L} = (\langle[\varphi^L_{\mathcal{L}}, \varphi^U_{\mathcal{L}}], [\psi^L_{\mathcal{L}}, \psi^U_{\mathcal{L}}]\rangle, \langle\varphi_{\mathcal{L}}, \psi_{\mathcal{L}}\rangle)$*and* $\mathcal{L}_i = \left(\langle\left[\varphi^L_{\mathcal{L}_i}, \varphi^U_{\mathcal{L}_i}\right], \left[\psi^L_{\mathcal{L}_i}, \psi^U_{\mathcal{L}_i}\right]\rangle, \langle\varphi_{\mathcal{L}_i}, \psi_{\mathcal{L}_i}\rangle\right)$ $(i = 1, 2)$ *be the collections of CFFNs, and* $\zeta \succ 0$ *be a real number then*

(a) $$\mathcal{L}_1 \oplus \mathcal{L}_2 = \left(\begin{array}{c} \langle\left[\begin{array}{c} \sqrt[3]{1 - \prod_{i=1}^2\left(1 - \left(\varphi^L_{\mathcal{L}_i}\right)^3\right)}, \\ \sqrt[3]{1 - \prod_{i=1}^2\left(1 - \left(\varphi^U_{\mathcal{L}_i}\right)^3\right)} \end{array}\right], \left[\prod_{i=1}^2 \psi^L_{\mathcal{L}_i}, \prod_i^2 \psi^U_{\mathcal{L}_i}\right]\rangle, \\ \langle\prod_{i=1}^2 \varphi_{\mathcal{L}_i}, \sqrt[3]{1 - \prod_{i=1}^2\left(1 - \left(\psi_{\mathcal{L}_i}\right)^3\right)}\rangle \end{array}\right);$$

(b) $$\mathcal{L}_1 \otimes \mathcal{L}_2 = \left(\begin{array}{c} \langle\left[\prod_{i=1}^2 \varphi^L_{\mathcal{L}_i}, \prod_i^2 \varphi^U_{\mathcal{L}_i}\right], \left[\begin{array}{c} \sqrt[3]{1 - \prod_{i=1}^2\left(1 - \left(\psi^L_{\mathcal{L}_i}\right)^3\right)}, \\ \sqrt[3]{1 - \prod_{i=1}^2\left(1 - \left(\psi^U_{\mathcal{L}_i}\right)^3\right)} \end{array}\right]\rangle, \\ \langle\sqrt[3]{1 - \prod_{i=1}^2\left(1 - \left(\varphi_{\mathcal{L}_i}\right)^3\right)}, \prod_{i=1}^2 \psi_{\mathcal{L}_i}\rangle \end{array}\right);$$

(c) $$\zeta\mathcal{L} = \left(\begin{array}{c} \langle\left[\begin{array}{c} \sqrt[3]{1 - \left(1 - \left(\varphi^L_{\mathcal{L}}\right)^3\right)^\zeta}, \\ \sqrt[3]{1 - \left(1 - \left(\varphi^U_{\mathcal{L}}\right)^3\right)^\zeta} \end{array}\right], \left[\left(\psi^L_{\mathcal{L}}\right)^\zeta, \left(\psi^U_{\mathcal{L}}\right)^\zeta\right]\rangle, \\ \langle\varphi^\zeta_{\mathcal{L}}, \sqrt[3]{1 - \left(1 - \psi^3_{\mathcal{L}}\right)^\zeta}\rangle \end{array}\right);$$

$$\text{(d)} \quad \mathcal{L}^{\zeta} = \begin{pmatrix} \langle \left[(\varphi_{\mathcal{L}}^{L})^{\zeta}, (\varphi_{\mathcal{L}}^{U})^{\zeta} \right], \begin{bmatrix} \sqrt[3]{1-\left(1-(\psi_{\mathcal{L}}^{L})^{3}\right)^{\zeta}}, \\ \sqrt[3]{1-\left(1-(\psi_{\mathcal{L}}^{U})^{3}\right)^{\zeta}} \end{bmatrix} \rangle, \\ \langle \sqrt[3]{1-(1-\varphi_{\mathcal{L}}^{3})^{\zeta}}, \varphi_{\mathcal{L}}^{\zeta} \rangle \end{pmatrix}.$$

Theorem 2. *For two CFFNs* $\mathcal{L}_1 = \left(\langle\left[\varphi_{\mathcal{L}_1}^{L}, \varphi_{\mathcal{L}_1}^{U}\right], \left[\psi_{\mathcal{L}_1}^{L}, \psi_{\mathcal{L}_1}^{U}\right]\rangle, \langle\varphi_{\mathcal{L}_1}, \psi_{\mathcal{L}_1}\rangle\right)$ *and* $\mathcal{L}_2 = \left(\langle\left[\varphi_{\mathcal{L}_2}^{L}, \varphi_{\mathcal{L}_2}^{U}\right], \left[\psi_{\mathcal{L}_2}^{L}, \psi_{\mathcal{L}_2}^{U}\right]\rangle, \langle\varphi_{\mathcal{L}_2}, \psi_{\mathcal{L}_2}\rangle\right)$*, provided* $\zeta \succ 0$ *is a real number, then* $\mathcal{L}_1 \oplus \mathcal{L}_2$*,* $\mathcal{L}_1 \otimes \mathcal{L}_2$*,* $\mathcal{L}^{\zeta}$*, and* $\zeta\mathcal{L}_1$ *are also CFFNs.*

Proof. Since $\mathcal{L}_1 = \left(\langle\left[\varphi_{\mathcal{L}_1}^{L}, \varphi_{\mathcal{L}_1}^{U}\right], \left[\psi_{\mathcal{L}_1}^{L}, \psi_{\mathcal{L}_1}^{U}\right]\rangle, \langle\varphi_{\mathcal{L}_1}, \psi_{\mathcal{L}_1}\rangle\right)$ and $\mathcal{L}_2 = \left(\langle\left[\varphi_{\mathcal{L}_2}^{L}, \varphi_{\mathcal{L}_2}^{U}\right], \left[\psi_{\mathcal{L}_2}^{L}, \psi_{\mathcal{L}_2}^{U}\right]\rangle, \langle\varphi_{\mathcal{L}_2}, \psi_{\mathcal{L}_2}\rangle\right)$ are two CFFNs such that $0 \leq \varphi_{\mathcal{L}_1}^{L}, \varphi_{\mathcal{L}_1}^{U}, \psi_{\mathcal{L}_1}^{L}, \psi_{\mathcal{L}_i}^{U}, \varphi_{\mathcal{L}_2}^{L}, \varphi_{\mathcal{L}_2}^{U}, \psi_{\mathcal{L}_2}^{L}, \psi_{\mathcal{L}_2}^{U} \leq 1$ and $\left(\varphi_{\mathcal{L}_1}^{U}\right)^3 + \left(\psi_{\mathcal{L}_1}^{U}\right)^3 \leq 1$ this implies that $0 \leq \left(1-\left(\varphi_{\mathcal{L}_1}^{L}\right)^3\right)\left(1-\left(\varphi_{\mathcal{L}_1}^{L}\right)^3\right) \leq 1$ and hence $0 \leq \sqrt[3]{\left(\varphi_{\mathcal{L}_1}^{L}\right)^3 + \left(\varphi_{\mathcal{L}_2}^{L}\right)^3 - \left(\varphi_{\mathcal{L}_1}^{L}\right)^3\left(\varphi_{\mathcal{L}_i}^{L}\right)^3} \leq 1$. Similarly, we can prove that $0 \leq \sqrt[3]{\left(\varphi_{\mathcal{L}_2}^{L}\right)^3 + \left(\varphi_{\mathcal{L}_2}^{L}\right)^3 - \left(\varphi_{\mathcal{L}_2}^{L}\right)^3\left(\varphi_{\mathcal{L}_2}^{L}\right)^3} \leq 1$, $0 \leq \psi_{\mathcal{L}_1}^{L}\psi_{\mathcal{L}_2}^{L} \leq 1$ and $0 \leq \psi_{\mathcal{L}_1}^{U}\psi_{\mathcal{L}_2}^{U} \leq 1$. We also set, $0 \leq \varphi_{\mathcal{L}_1}, \psi_{\mathcal{L}_2}, \varphi_{\mathcal{L}_1}, \psi_{\mathcal{L}_2} \leq 1$ and $\varphi_{\mathcal{L}_1}^3 + \psi_{\mathcal{L}_1}^3 \leq 1$, $\varphi_{\mathcal{L}_2}^3 + \psi_{\mathcal{L}_2}^3 \leq 1$, which implies that $\varphi_{\mathcal{L}_1}\varphi_{\mathcal{L}_2} \leq 1$ and $\sqrt[3]{\varphi_{\mathcal{L}_1}^3 + \varphi_{\mathcal{L}_2}^3 - \varphi_{\mathcal{L}_1}^3\mu_{\mathcal{L}_2}^3} \leq 1$.

Finally, we have

$$\begin{gathered} \sqrt[3]{\left(\varphi_{\mathcal{L}_1}^{U}\right)^3 + \left(\varphi_{\mathcal{L}_2}^{U}\right)^3 - \left(\varphi_{\mathcal{L}_1}^{U}\right)^3\left(\varphi_{\mathcal{L}_2}^{U}\right)^3 + \left(\varphi_{\mathcal{L}_1}^{U}\right)^3\left(\varphi_{\mathcal{L}_2}^{U}\right)^3} \\ = \sqrt[3]{1-\left(1-\left(\varphi_{\mathcal{L}_1}^{U}\right)^3\right)\left(1-\left(\varphi_{\mathcal{L}_2}^{U}\right)^3\right) + \left(\varphi_{\mathcal{L}_1}^{U}\right)^3\left(\varphi_{\mathcal{L}_2}^{U}\right)^3} \\ \leq \sqrt[3]{1-\left(\varphi_{\mathcal{L}_1}^{U}\right)^3\left(\varphi_{\mathcal{L}_2}^{U}\right)^3 + \left(\varphi_{\mathcal{L}_1}^{U}\right)^3\left(\varphi_{\mathcal{L}_2}^{U}\right)^3} \\ \leq 1, \end{gathered}$$

and

$$\begin{gathered} \sqrt[3]{\varphi_{\mathcal{L}_1}\varphi_{\mathcal{L}_2} + \psi_{\mathcal{L}_1}^3 + \psi_{\mathcal{L}_2}^3 - \left(\psi_{\mathcal{L}_1}^{U}\right)^3\left(\psi_{\mathcal{L}_1}^{U}\right)^3} \\ = \sqrt[3]{\varphi_{\mathcal{L}_1}\varphi_{\mathcal{L}_2} + 1 - \left(1-\left(\varphi_{\mathcal{L}_1}^{U}\right)^3\right)\left(1-\left(\varphi_{\mathcal{L}_2}^{U}\right)^3\right)} \\ \leq \sqrt[3]{\varphi_{\mathcal{L}_1}\varphi_{\mathcal{L}_2} + 1 - \varphi_{\mathcal{L}_1}\varphi_{\mathcal{L}_2}} \\ \leq 1. \end{gathered}$$

Therefore, $\mathcal{L}_1 \oplus \mathcal{L}_2$ is a CFFN. Furthermore, for any positive real number ψ and CFFN $\beta = (\langle[\varphi_{\mathcal{L}}^{L}, \varphi_{\mathcal{L}}^{U}], [\psi_{\mathcal{L}}^{L}, \psi_{\mathcal{L}}^{U}]\rangle, \langle\varphi_{\mathcal{L}}, \psi_{\mathcal{L}}\rangle)$, we have $0 \leq \varphi^{\zeta} \leq 1$, $0 \leq \sqrt[3]{1-\left(1-(\varphi_{\mathcal{L}})^3\right)^{\zeta}} \leq 1$, $0 \leq (\psi_{\mathcal{L}}^{L})^{\zeta}(\psi_{\mathcal{L}}^{U})^{\zeta} \leq 1$ and $0 \leq \sqrt[3]{1-\left(1-(\varphi_{\mathcal{L}}^{L})^3\right)^{\zeta}\left(1-(\varphi_{\mathcal{L}}^{U})^3\right)^{\zeta}} \leq 1$. Hence $\zeta\mathcal{L}$ is also a CFFN. Similarly, we can prove that $\mathcal{L}_1 \otimes \mathcal{L}_2$ and $\mathcal{L}^{\zeta}$ are also CFFNs. □

3.2. Cubic Fermatean AOs with Confidence Levels

In the available studies, all scholars have approached the studies by taking the postulation that decision-makers are confident in using the estimated objects. However, these kinds of prerequisites are only partially met in real-world situations. To address this problem, in this section we propose a set of averaging and geometric operators with different confidence levels in a cubic Fermatean fuzzy environment. Those are named confidence cubic Fermatean fuzzy weighted averaging (CCFFWA) operator and confidence cubic Fermatean fuzzy weighted geometric (CCFFWG) operator.

3.2.1. Weighted Averaging Operators

Definition 16. *A CCFFWA operator is a mapping* CCFFWA : $\Gamma^p \to \Gamma$ *defined as*

$$\mathrm{CCFFWA}(\mathcal{L}_1, \mathcal{L}_2, \ldots, \mathcal{L}_p) = \sigma_1(\xi_1\mathcal{L}_1) \oplus \sigma_2(\xi_2\mathcal{L}_2) \oplus \ldots \oplus \sigma_p(\xi_p\mathcal{L}_p) \tag{13}$$

where Γ *is the collection of CPFNs with confidence level* $\mathcal{L}_i = \left(\langle \left[\varphi^L_{\mathcal{L}_i}, \varphi^U_{\mathcal{L}_i}\right], \left[\psi^L_{\mathcal{L}_i}, \psi^U_{\mathcal{L}_i}\right]\rangle, \langle \varphi_{\mathcal{L}_i}, \psi_{\mathcal{L}_i}\rangle, \sigma_i\right)$ *for* $i = 1, 2, \ldots, p$; $\xi = (\xi_1, \xi_2, \ldots, \xi_p)^T$ *is the weight vector of* ξ_i *such that* $\xi_i > 0$ *and* $\sum_{i=1}^n \xi_i = 1$; *and* σ_i *are the confidence levels of the CFFNs* $\mathcal{L}_i$.

Theorem 3. *For the group of CCFFNs* $\mathcal{L}_1, \mathcal{L}_2, \ldots, \mathcal{L}_n$, *the value obtained via CCFFWA is a CFFN, which can be calculated as*

$$\mathrm{CCFFWA}(\mathcal{L}_1, \mathcal{L}_2, \ldots, \mathcal{L}_p) = \begin{pmatrix} \langle \begin{bmatrix} \sqrt[3]{1 - \prod_{i=1}^p \left(1 - \left(\varphi^L_{\mathcal{L}_i}\right)^3\right)^{\xi_i\sigma_i}}, \\ \sqrt[3]{1 - \prod_{i=1}^p \left(1 - \left(\varphi^U_{\mathcal{L}_i}\right)^3\right)^{\xi_i\sigma_i}} \end{bmatrix}, \begin{bmatrix} \prod_{i=1}^p \left(\psi^L_{\mathcal{L}_i}\right)^{\xi_i\sigma_i}, \\ \prod_{i=1}^p \left(\psi^U_{\mathcal{L}_i}\right)^{\xi_i\sigma_i} \end{bmatrix} \rangle, \\ \langle \prod_{i=1}^p (\varphi_{\mathcal{L}_i})^{\xi_i\sigma_i}, \sqrt[3]{1 - \prod_{i=1}^p \left(1 - (\psi_{\mathcal{L}_i})^3\right)^{\xi_i\sigma_i}} \rangle \end{pmatrix}. \tag{14}$$

Proof. We apply induction principle on $\mathcal{L}_1, \mathcal{L}_2, \ldots, \mathcal{L}_P$

Step 1 For $p = 2$, using Definition 15, we get

$$\mathrm{CCFFWA}(\mathcal{L}_1, \mathcal{L}_2) = \sigma_1\xi_1\mathcal{L}_1 \oplus \sigma_2\xi_2\mathcal{L}_2$$

$$= \begin{pmatrix} \langle \begin{bmatrix} \sqrt[3]{1 - \left(1 - \left(\varphi^L_{\mathcal{L}_1}\right)^3\right)^{\sigma_1\xi_1} \left(1 - \left(\varphi^L_{\mathcal{L}_2}\right)^3\right)^{\sigma_2\xi_2}}, \\ \sqrt[3]{1 - \left(1 - \left(\varphi^U_{\mathcal{L}_1}\right)^3\right)^{\sigma_1\xi_1} \left(1 - \left(\varphi^L_{\mathcal{L}_2}\right)^3\right)^{\sigma_2\xi_2}} \end{bmatrix}, \begin{bmatrix} \left(\psi^L_{\mathcal{L}_1}\right)^{\sigma_1\xi_1} \left(\psi^L_{\mathcal{L}_2}\right)^{\sigma_2\xi_2}, \\ \left(\psi^U_{\mathcal{L}_1}\right)^{\sigma_1\xi_1} \left(\psi^U_{\mathcal{L}_2}\right)^{\sigma_2\xi_2} \end{bmatrix} \rangle, \\ \langle (\varphi_{\mathcal{L}_1})^{\sigma_1\xi_1} (\varphi_{\mathcal{L}_2})^{\sigma_2\xi_2}, \sqrt[3]{1 - \left(1 - \psi^3_{\mathcal{L}_1}\right)^{\sigma_1\xi_1} \left(1 - \psi^3_{\mathcal{L}_1}\right)^{\sigma_1\xi_1}} \rangle \end{pmatrix}$$

$$= \begin{pmatrix} \langle \begin{bmatrix} \sqrt[3]{1 - \prod_{i=1}^2 \left(1 - \left(\varphi^L_{\mathcal{L}_i}\right)^3\right)^{\xi_i\sigma_i}}, \\ \sqrt[3]{1 - \prod_{i=1}^2 \left(1 - \left(\varphi^U_{\mathcal{L}_i}\right)^3\right)^{\xi_i\sigma_i}} \end{bmatrix}, \begin{bmatrix} \prod_{i=1}^2 \left(\psi^L_{\mathcal{L}_i}\right)^{\xi_i\sigma_i}, \\ \prod_{i=1}^2 \left(\psi^U_{\mathcal{L}_i}\right)^{\xi_i\sigma_i} \end{bmatrix} \rangle, \\ \langle \prod_{i=1}^2 (\varphi_{\mathcal{L}_i})^{\xi_i\sigma_i}, \sqrt[3]{1 - \prod_{i=1}^2 \left(1 - (\psi_{\mathcal{L}_i})^3\right)^{\xi_i\sigma_i}} \rangle \end{pmatrix}.$$

Hence, it holds for $P = 2$.

Step 2 Assume Equation (14) holds for $p = \kappa$, then

$$\mathrm{CCFFWA}(\mathcal{L}_1, \mathcal{L}_2, \ldots, \mathcal{L}_k) = \begin{pmatrix} \langle \begin{bmatrix} \sqrt[3]{1 - \prod_{i=1}^k \left(1 - \left(\varphi^L_{\mathcal{L}_i}\right)^3\right)^{\xi_i\sigma_i}}, \\ \sqrt[3]{1 - \prod_{i=1}^k \left(1 - \left(\varphi^U_{\mathcal{L}_i}\right)^3\right)^{\xi_i\sigma_i}} \end{bmatrix}, \begin{bmatrix} \prod_{i=1}^k \left(\psi^L_{\mathcal{L}_i}\right)^{\xi_i\sigma_i}, \\ \prod_{i=1}^k \left(\psi^U_{\mathcal{L}_i}\right)^{\xi_i\sigma_i} \end{bmatrix} \rangle, \\ \langle \prod_{i=1}^k (\varphi_{\mathcal{L}_i})^{\xi_i\sigma_i}, \sqrt[3]{1 - \prod_{i=1}^k \left(1 - (\psi_{\mathcal{L}_i})^3\right)^{\xi_i\sigma_i}} \rangle \end{pmatrix}. \tag{15}$$

Step 3 For $p = \kappa + 1$, we have

$$\mathrm{CCFFWA}(\mathcal{L}_1, \mathcal{L}_2, \ldots, \mathcal{L}_\kappa, \mathcal{L}_{\kappa+1}) = \mathcal{L}_1 \oplus \mathcal{L}_2 \oplus \ldots. \oplus \mathcal{L}_\kappa \oplus \mathcal{L}_{\kappa+1}$$

$$= \begin{pmatrix} \langle \begin{bmatrix} \sqrt[3]{1 - \prod_{i=1}^{\kappa}\left(1 - \left(\varphi^L_{\mathcal{L}_i}\right)^3\right)^{\xi_i\sigma_i}}, \\ \sqrt[3]{1 - \prod_{i=1}^{\kappa}\left(1 - \left(\varphi^U_{\mathcal{L}_i}\right)^3\right)^{\xi_i\sigma_i}} \end{bmatrix}, \begin{bmatrix} \prod_{i=1}^{\kappa}\left(\psi^L_{\mathcal{L}_i}\right)^{\xi_i\sigma_i}, \\ \prod_{i=1}^{\kappa}\left(\psi^U_{\mathcal{L}_i}\right)^{\xi_i\sigma_i} \end{bmatrix} \rangle, \\ \langle \prod_{i=1}^{\kappa}\left(\varphi_{\mathcal{L}_i}\right)^{\xi_i\sigma_i}, \sqrt[3]{1 - \prod_{i=1}^{\kappa}\left(1 - \left(\psi_{\mathcal{L}_i}\right)^3\right)^{\xi_i\sigma_i}} \rangle \end{pmatrix}$$

$$\oplus \begin{pmatrix} \langle \begin{bmatrix} \sqrt[3]{1 - \left(1 - \left(\varphi^L_{\mathcal{L}_{\kappa+1}}\right)^3\right)^{\sigma_{\kappa+1}\xi_{\kappa+1}}}, \\ \sqrt[3]{1 - \left(1 - \left(\varphi^U_{\mathcal{L}_{\kappa+1}}\right)^3\right)^{\sigma_{\kappa+1}\xi_{\kappa+1}}} \end{bmatrix}, \begin{bmatrix} \left(\psi^L_{\mathcal{L}_{\kappa+1}}\right)^{\sigma_{\kappa+1}\xi_{\kappa+1}}, \\ \left(\psi^U_{\mathcal{L}_{\kappa+1}}\right)^{\sigma_{\kappa+1}\xi_{\kappa+1}} \end{bmatrix} \rangle, \\ \langle \left(\varphi_{\mathcal{L}_{\kappa+1}}\right)^{\sigma_{\kappa+1}\xi_{\kappa+1}}, \sqrt[3]{1 - \left(1 - \left(\psi_{\mathcal{L}_{\kappa+1}}\right)^3\right)^{\sigma_{\kappa+1}\xi_{\kappa+1}}} \rangle \end{pmatrix}$$

$$= \begin{pmatrix} \langle \begin{bmatrix} \sqrt[3]{1 - \prod_{i=1}^{\kappa+1}\left(1 - \left(\varphi^3_{\mathcal{L}_i}\right)^3\right)^{\xi_i\sigma_i}}, \\ \sqrt[3]{1 - \prod_{i=1}^{\kappa+1}\left(1 - \left(\varphi^U_{\mathcal{L}_i}\right)^3\right)^{\xi_i\sigma_i}} \end{bmatrix}, \begin{bmatrix} \prod_{i=1}^{\kappa+1}\left(\psi^U_{\mathcal{L}_i}\right)^{\xi_i\sigma_i}, \\ \prod_{i=1}^{\kappa+1}\left(\psi^U_{\mathcal{L}_i}\right)^{\xi_i\sigma_i} \end{bmatrix} \rangle, \\ \langle \prod_{i=1}^{\kappa+1}\left(\varphi_{\mathcal{L}_i}\right)^{\xi_i\sigma_i}, \sqrt[3]{1 - \prod_{i=1}^{\kappa+1}\left(1 - \left(\psi_{\mathcal{L}_i}\right)^3\right)^{\xi_i\sigma_i}} \rangle \end{pmatrix}.$$

As a result, the result is valid for $p = \kappa + 1$, and hence

$$\mathrm{CCFFWA}(\mathcal{L}_1, \mathcal{L}_2, \ldots, \mathcal{L}_p) = \begin{pmatrix} \langle \begin{bmatrix} \sqrt[3]{1 - \prod_{i=1}^{p}\left(1 - \left(\varphi^L_{\mathcal{L}_i}\right)^3\right)^{\xi_i\sigma_i}}, \\ \sqrt[3]{1 - \prod_{i=1}^{p}\left(1 - \left(\varphi^U_{\mathcal{L}_i}\right)^3\right)^{\xi_i\sigma_i}} \end{bmatrix}, \begin{bmatrix} \prod_{i=1}^{p}\left(\psi^L_{\mathcal{L}_i}\right)^{\xi_i\sigma_i}, \\ \prod_{i=1}^{p}\left(\psi^U_{\mathcal{L}_i}\right)^{\xi_i\sigma_i} \end{bmatrix} \rangle, \\ \langle \prod_{i=1}^{p}\left(\varphi_{\mathcal{L}_i}\right)^{\xi_i\sigma_i}, \sqrt[3]{1 - \prod_{i=1}^{p}\left(1 - \left(\psi_{\mathcal{L}_i}\right)^3\right)^{\xi_i\sigma_i}} \rangle \end{pmatrix}.$$

The proof is completed. □

Example 1. *Let* $\mathcal{L}_1 = (\langle[0.4, 0.6], [0.3.0.7], (0.3, 0.5)\rangle; 0.8)$, $\mathcal{L}_2 = (\langle[0.5, 0.6], [0.4.0.5], (0.2, 0.4)\rangle; 0.7)$, *and* $\mathcal{L}_3 = (\langle[0.2, 0.3], [0.4.0.5], (0.7, 0.2)\rangle; 0.6)$ *be three CFFNs with confidence levels and* $\xi = (0.25, 0.35, 0.4)$ *be their corresponding weight vector then*

$$\sqrt[3]{1 - \prod_{i=1}^{3}\left(1 - \left(\varphi^L_{\mathcal{L}_i}\right)^3\right)^{\xi_i\sigma_i}} = \left(1 - \left(\begin{matrix}\left(1 - (0.4)^3\right)^{(0.25)(0.8)} \times \left(1 - (0.5)^3\right)^{(0.35)(0.7)} \\ \times \left(1 - (0.2)^3\right)^{(0.4)(0.6)}\end{matrix}\right)\right)^{\frac{1}{3}} = 0.3602;$$

$$\sqrt[3]{1 - \prod_{i=1}^{3}\left(1 - \left(\varphi^U_{\mathcal{L}_i}\right)^3\right)^{\xi_i\sigma_i}} = \left(1 - \left(\begin{matrix}\left(1 - (0.6)^3\right)^{(0.25)(0.8)} \times \left(1 - (0.6)^3\right)^{(0.35)(0.7)} \\ \times \left(1 - (0.3)^3\right)^{(0.4)(0.6)}\end{matrix}\right)\right)^{\frac{1}{3}} = 0.477;$$

$$\prod_{i=1}^{3}\left(\psi^L_{\mathcal{L}_i}\right)^{\xi_i\sigma_i} = (0.3)^{(0.25)(0.8)} \times (0.4)^{(0.35)(0.7)} \times (0.4)^{(0.4)(0.6)} = 0.5040;$$

$$\prod_{i=1}^{3}\left(\psi^L_{\mathcal{L}_i}\right)^{\xi_i\sigma_i} = (0.7)^{(0.25)(0.8)} \times (0.5)^{(0.35)(0.7)} \times (0.6)^{(0.4)(0.6)} = 0.6653;$$

$$\prod_{i=1}^{p}(\varphi_{\mathcal{L}_i})^{\xi_i\sigma_i} = (0.3)^{(0.25)(0.8)} \times (0.2)^{(0.35)(0.7)} \times (0.7)^{(0.4)(0.6)} = 0.4864;$$

$$\sqrt[3]{1-\prod_{i=1}^{p}\left(1-(\psi_{\mathcal{L}_i})^3\right)^{\xi_i\sigma_i}} = \left(1-\left(\begin{array}{c}\left(1-(0.5)^3\right)^{(0.25)(0.8)} \times \left(1-(0.4)^3\right)^{(0.35)(0.7)} \\ \times\left(1-(0.2)^3\right)^{(0.4)(0.6)}\end{array}\right)\right)^{1/3} = 0.3526.$$

Thus, using Equation (14) we get

$$\text{CCFFWA}(\mathcal{L}_1,\ \mathcal{L}_2, \mathcal{L}_3) = \left(\begin{array}{c}\langle\left[\begin{array}{c}\sqrt[3]{1-\prod_{i=1}^{3}\left(1-\left(\varphi^L_{\mathcal{L}_i}\right)^3\right)^{\xi_i\sigma_i}}, \\ \sqrt[3]{1-\prod_{i=1}^{3}\left(1-\left(\varphi^U_{\mathcal{L}_i}\right)^3\right)^{\xi_i\sigma_i}}\end{array}\right], \left[\begin{array}{c}\prod_{i=1}^{3}\left(\psi^L_{\mathcal{L}_i}\right)^{\xi_i\sigma_i}, \\ \prod_{i=1}^{3}\left(\psi^U_{\mathcal{L}_i}\right)^{\xi_i\sigma_i}\end{array}\right]\rangle, \\ \langle\prod_{i=1}^{3}(\varphi_{\mathcal{L}_i})^{\xi_i\sigma_i}, \sqrt[3]{1-\prod_{i=1}^{3}\left(1-(\psi_{\mathcal{L}_i})^3\right)^{\xi_i\sigma_i}}\rangle\end{array}\right)$$

$$= \left(\begin{array}{c}\langle[0.3602, 0.4770], [0.5040.0.6653]\rangle, \\ \langle 0.4864,\ 0.3526\rangle\end{array}\right).$$

According to Theorem 3, the CCFFWA operator fulfils the certain properties listed below.

Property 1. *For $\mathcal{L}_i = \mathcal{L}\ i = 1, 2, \ldots, p$, where $\mathcal{L} = (\langle[\varphi^L_{\mathcal{L}}, \varphi^u_{\mathcal{L}}], [\psi^L_{\mathcal{L}}, \psi^U_{\mathcal{L}}]\rangle, \langle\varphi_{\mathcal{L}}, \psi_{\mathcal{L}}\rangle)$, it follows that $\text{CCFFWA}(\mathcal{L}_1,\ \mathcal{L}_2, \ldots, \mathcal{L}_n) = \mathcal{L}$. This property is called idempotency.*

Proof. As $\xi_i \succ 0, \sum_{I=1}^{n}\xi_i = 1$ and $\xi_i = \xi$ for all i, then

$$\text{CCFFWA}(\mathcal{L},\ \mathcal{L}, \ldots, \mathcal{L}) = \left(\begin{array}{c}\langle\left[\begin{array}{c}\sqrt[3]{1-\prod_{i=1}^{p}\left(1-(\varphi^L_{\mathcal{L}})^3\right)^{\xi_i\sigma_i}}, \\ \sqrt[3]{1-\prod_{i=1}^{p}\left(1-(\varphi^U_{\mathcal{L}})^3\right)^{\xi_i\sigma_i}}\end{array}\right], \left[\begin{array}{c}\prod_{i=1}^{p}(\psi^L_{\mathcal{L}})^{\xi_i\sigma_i}, \\ \prod_{i=1}^{p}(\psi^U_{\mathcal{L}})^{\xi_i\sigma_i}\end{array}\right]\rangle, \\ \langle\prod_{i=1}^{p}(\varphi_{\mathcal{L}})^{\xi_i\sigma_i}, \sqrt[3]{1-\prod_{i=1}^{p}\left(1-(\psi_{\mathcal{L}})^3\right)^{\xi_i\sigma_i}}\rangle\end{array}\right)$$

$$= \left(\begin{array}{c}\langle\left[1-\left(1-(\varphi^L_{\mathcal{L}})^3\right)^{\xi_i\sigma_i}, 1-\left(1-(\varphi^U_{\mathcal{L}})^3\right)^{\xi_i\sigma_i}\right], \left[(\psi^L_{\mathcal{L}})^{\xi_i\sigma_i}, (\psi^U_{\mathcal{L}})^{\xi_i\sigma_i}\right]\rangle, \\ \langle(\varphi_{\mathcal{L}})^{\xi_i\sigma_i}, 1-\left(1-(\psi_{\mathcal{L}})^3\right)^{\xi_i\sigma_i}\rangle\end{array}\right)$$

$$= (\langle[\varphi^L_{\mathcal{L}}, \varphi^u_{\mathcal{L}}], [\psi^L_{\mathcal{L}}, \psi^U_{\mathcal{L}}]\rangle, \langle\varphi_{\mathcal{L}}, \psi_{\mathcal{L}}\rangle)$$
$$= \mathcal{L}.$$

□

Property 2. *Let $\mathcal{L}_i = \left(\langle\left[\varphi^L_{\mathcal{L}_i}, \varphi^U_{\mathcal{L}_i}\right], \left[\psi^L_{\mathcal{L}_i}, \psi^U_{\mathcal{L}_i}\right]\rangle, \langle\varphi_{\mathcal{L}_i}, \psi_{\mathcal{L}_i}\rangle\right)$ and $\widetilde{\mathcal{L}}_i = \left(\langle\left[\widetilde{\varphi}^L_{\mathcal{L}_i}, \widetilde{\varphi}^U_{\mathcal{L}_i}\right], \left[\widetilde{\psi}^L_{\mathcal{L}_i}, \widetilde{\psi}^U_{\mathcal{L}_i}\right]\rangle, \langle\widetilde{\varphi}_{\mathcal{L}_i}, \widetilde{\psi}_{\mathcal{L}_i}\rangle\right)$ be CCFFNs where $(i = 1, 2, \ldots, p)$, such that $\mathcal{L}_i \leq \widetilde{\mathcal{L}}_i$, then*

$$\text{CPFWA}(\mathcal{L}_1,\ \mathcal{L}_2, \ldots, \mathcal{L}_n) \leq \text{CCFFWA}\left(\widetilde{\mathcal{L}}_1,\ \widetilde{\mathcal{L}}_2, \ldots, \widetilde{\mathcal{L}}_p\right). \quad (16)$$

This property is called monotonicity.

Proof. First let us express the term of CCFFN as follows:

$$\sqrt[3]{1-\prod_{i=1}^{p}\left(1-\left(\varphi_{\mathcal{L}_i}^{L}\right)^3\right)^{\xi_i\sigma_i}}=\alpha,\ \sqrt[3]{1-\prod_{i=1}^{p}\left(1-\left(\varphi_{\mathcal{L}_i}^{U}\right)^3\right)^{\xi_i\sigma_i}}=\beta,$$
$$\prod_{i=1}^{p}\left(\psi_{\mathcal{L}_i}^{L}\right)^{\xi_i\sigma_i}=\gamma,\ \prod_{i=1}^{p}\left(\psi_{\mathcal{L}_i}^{U}\right)^{\xi_i\sigma_i}=\delta,$$
$$\prod_{i=1}^{p}\left(\varphi_{\mathcal{L}_i}\right)^{\xi_i\sigma_i}=\varepsilon,\ \sqrt[3]{1-\prod_{i=1}^{p}\left(1-\left(\psi_{\mathcal{L}_i}\right)^3\right)^{\xi_i\sigma_i}}=\zeta,$$
$$\sqrt[3]{1-\prod_{i=1}^{p}\left(1-\left(\widetilde{\varphi}_{\mathcal{L}_i}^{L}\right)^3\right)^{\xi_i\sigma_i}}=\widetilde{\alpha},\ \sqrt[3]{1-\prod_{i=1}^{p}\left(1-\left(\widetilde{\varphi}_{\mathcal{L}_i}^{U}\right)^3\right)^{\xi_i\sigma_i}}=\widetilde{\beta},$$
$$\prod_{i=1}^{p}\left(\widetilde{\psi}_{\mathcal{L}_i}^{L}\right)^{\xi_i\sigma_i}=\widetilde{\gamma},\ \prod_{i=1}^{p}\left(\widetilde{\psi}_{\mathcal{L}_i}^{L}\right)^{\xi_i\sigma_i}=\widetilde{\delta},$$
$$\prod_{i=1}^{p}\left(\widetilde{\varphi}_{\mathcal{L}_i}\right)^{\xi_i\sigma_i}=\widetilde{\varepsilon}\text{ and }\sqrt[3]{1-\prod_{i=1}^{p}\left(1-\left(\widetilde{\psi}_{\mathcal{L}_i}\right)^3\right)^{\xi_i\sigma_i}}=\widetilde{\zeta}.$$

Also, $\mathcal{L}_i \le \widetilde{\mathcal{L}}_i$ for all i, then we have $\varphi_{\mathcal{L}_i}^{L} \le \widetilde{\varphi}_{\mathcal{L}_i}^{L}$, $\varphi_{\mathcal{L}_i}^{U} \le \widetilde{\varphi}_{\mathcal{L}_i}^{U}$, $\psi_{\mathcal{L}_i}^{L} \ge \widetilde{\psi}_{\mathcal{L}_i}^{L}$, $\psi_{\mathcal{L}_i}^{U} \ge \widetilde{\psi}_{\mathcal{L}_i}^{U}$; $\varphi_{\mathcal{L}_i} \ge \widetilde{\varphi}_{\mathcal{L}_i}$ and $\psi_{\mathcal{L}_i} \le \widetilde{\psi}_{\mathcal{L}_i}$, then we have $\alpha \le \widetilde{\alpha}$, $\beta \le \widetilde{\beta}$, $\gamma \ge \widetilde{\gamma}$, $\delta \ge \widetilde{\delta}$, $\varepsilon \ge \widetilde{\varepsilon}$, and $\zeta \le \widetilde{\zeta}$. Therefore, using the score function defined in Definition 10 and 11, we have

$$sc(\text{CCFFWA}(\mathcal{L}_1,\ \mathcal{L}_2,\ldots,\mathcal{L}_p))=\frac{\alpha^3+\beta^3-\gamma^3-\delta^3}{2}+\left(\zeta^3-\varepsilon^3\right)$$
$$\le\frac{\widetilde{\alpha}^3+\widetilde{\beta}^3-\widetilde{\gamma}^3-\widetilde{\delta}^3}{2}+\left(\widetilde{\zeta}^3-\widetilde{\varepsilon}^3\right)=sc\left(\text{CCFFWA}\left(\widetilde{\mathcal{L}}_1,\ \widetilde{\mathcal{L}}_2,\ldots,\widetilde{\mathcal{L}}_p\right)\right).$$

Thus, $\text{CCFFWA}(\mathcal{L}_1,\ \mathcal{L}_2,\ldots,\mathcal{L}_p)\le\text{CCFFWA}\left(\widetilde{\mathcal{L}}_1,\ \widetilde{\mathcal{L}}_2,\ldots,\widetilde{\mathcal{L}}_p\right)$. □

Property 3. *For any group of CCFFNs $\mathcal{L}_i$ $(i = 1,\ 2,\ldots,\ p)$. If*

$$\mathcal{L}^-=\left(\left\langle\begin{bmatrix}min_i\left(\varphi_{\mathcal{L}_i}^{L}\right),\\ min_i\left(\varphi_{\mathcal{L}_i}^{U}\right)\end{bmatrix},\begin{bmatrix}max_i\left(\psi_{\mathcal{L}_i}^{L}\right),\\ max_i\left(\psi_{\mathcal{L}_i}^{U}\right)\end{bmatrix}\right\rangle,\left\langle\begin{matrix}max_i\left(\varphi_{\mathcal{L}_i}\right),\\ min_i\left(\psi_{\mathcal{L}_i}\right)\end{matrix}\right\rangle\right)\text{ and}$$
$$\mathcal{L}^+=\left(\left\langle\begin{bmatrix}max_i\left(\varphi_{\mathcal{L}_i}^{L}\right),\\ max_i\left(\varphi_{\mathcal{L}_i}^{U}\right)\end{bmatrix},\begin{bmatrix}min_i\left(\psi_{\mathcal{L}_i}^{L}\right),\\ min_i\left(\psi_{\mathcal{L}_i}^{U}\right)\end{bmatrix}\right\rangle,\left\langle\begin{matrix}min_i\left(\varphi_{\mathcal{L}_i}\right),\\ max_i\left(\psi_{\mathcal{L}_i}\right)\end{matrix}\right\rangle\right)$$

then $\mathcal{L}^- \le \text{CCFFWA}(\mathcal{L}_1,\ \mathcal{L}_2,\ldots,\mathcal{L}_n) \le \mathcal{L}^+$. This property is called Boundedness.

Proof. As $min_i\left(\varphi_{\mathcal{L}_i}^{L}\right) \le \varphi_{\mathcal{L}_i}^{L} \le max_i\left(\varphi_{\mathcal{L}_i}^{L}\right)$, $min_i\left(\varphi_{\mathcal{L}_i}^{U}\right) \le \varphi_{\mathcal{L}_i}^{U} \le max_i\left(\varphi_{\mathcal{L}_i}^{U}\right)$, $min_i\left(\psi_{\mathcal{L}_i}^{L}\right) \le \psi_{\mathcal{L}_i}^{L} \le max_i\left(\psi_{\mathcal{L}_i}^{L}\right)$, $min_i\left(\psi_{\mathcal{L}_i}^{U}\right) \le \psi_{\mathcal{L}_i}^{U} \le max_i\left(\psi_{\mathcal{L}_i}^{U}\right)$, $min_i(\varphi_{\mathcal{L}_i}) \le \varphi_{\mathcal{L}_i} \le max_i(\varphi_{\mathcal{L}_i})$, and $min_i(\psi_{\mathcal{L}_i}) \le \psi_{\mathcal{L}_i} \le max_i(\psi_{\mathcal{L}_i})$ it follows that

$$\sqrt[3]{1-\prod_{i=1}^{n}\left(1-min_i\left(\varphi_{\mathcal{L}_i}^{L}\right)^3\right)^{\xi_i\sigma_i}}\le\sqrt[3]{1-\prod_{i=1}^{n}\left(1-\left(\varphi_{\mathcal{L}_i}^{L}\right)^3\right)^{\xi_i\sigma_i}}\le\sqrt[3]{1-\prod_{i=1}^{n}\left(1-max_i\left(\varphi_{\mathcal{L}_i}^{L}\right)^3\right)^{\xi_i\sigma_i}};$$
$$\sqrt[3]{1-\prod_{i=1}^{n}\left(1-min_i\left(\varphi_{\mathcal{L}_i}^{U}\right)^3\right)^{\xi_i\sigma_i}}\le\sqrt[3]{1-\prod_{i=1}^{n}\left(1-\left(\varphi_{\mathcal{L}_i}^{U}\right)^3\right)^{\xi_i\sigma_i}}\le\sqrt[3]{1-\prod_{i=1}^{n}\left(1-max_i\left(\varphi_{\mathcal{L}_i}^{U}\right)^3\right)^{\xi_i\sigma_i}};$$
$$\prod_{i=1}^{n}max_i\left(\psi_{\mathcal{L}_i}^{L}\right)^{\xi_i\sigma_i}\le\prod_{i=1}^{n}\left(\psi_{\mathcal{L}_i}^{L}\right)^{\xi_i\sigma_i}\le\prod_{i=1}^{n}min_i\left(\psi_{\mathcal{L}_i}^{L}\right)^{\xi_i\sigma_i};$$
$$\prod_{i=1}^{n}max_i\left(\psi_{\mathcal{L}_i}^{U}\right)^{\xi_i\sigma_i}\le\prod_{i=1}^{n}\left(\psi_{\mathcal{L}_i}^{U}\right)^{\xi_i\sigma_i}\le\prod_{i=1}^{n}min_i\left(\psi_{\mathcal{L}_i}^{U}\right)^{\xi_i\sigma_i};$$
$$\prod_{i=1}^{n}max_i\left(\varphi_{\mathcal{L}_i}\right)^{\xi_i\sigma_i}\le\prod_{i=1}^{n}\left(\varphi_{\mathcal{L}_i}\right)^{\xi_i\sigma_i}\le\prod_{i=1}^{n}min_i\left(\varphi_{\mathcal{L}_i}\right)^{\xi_i\sigma_i};$$
$$\sqrt[3]{1-\prod_{i=1}^{n}\left(1-min_i\left(\psi_{\mathcal{L}_i}\right)^3\right)^{\xi_i\sigma_i}}\le\sqrt[3]{1-\prod_{i=1}^{n}\left(1-\left(\psi_{\mathcal{L}_i}\right)^3\right)^{\xi_i\sigma_i}}\le\sqrt[3]{1-\prod_{i=1}^{n}\left(1-max_i\left(\psi_{\mathcal{L}_i}\right)^3\right)^{\xi_i\sigma_i}}$$

which implies that

$$min_i\left(\varphi^L_{\mathcal{L}_i}\right)^3 \leq \sqrt[3]{1-\prod_{i=1}^n\left(1-\left(\varphi^L_{\mathcal{L}_i}\right)^3\right)^{\xi_i\sigma_i}} \leq max_i\left(\varphi^L_{\mathcal{L}_i}\right)^3;$$
$$min_i\left(\varphi^U_{\mathcal{L}_i}\right)^3 \leq \sqrt[3]{1-\prod_{i=1}^n\left(1-\left(\varphi^U_{\mathcal{L}_i}\right)^3\right)^{\xi_i\sigma_i}} \leq max_i\left(\varphi^U_{\mathcal{L}_i}\right)^3;$$
$$max_i\left(\psi^L_{\mathcal{L}_i}\right) \leq \prod_{i=1}^n\left(\psi^L_{\mathcal{L}_i}\right)^{\xi_i\sigma_i} \leq min_i\left(\psi^L_{\mathcal{L}_i}\right);$$
$$max_i\left(\psi^U_{\mathcal{L}_i}\right) \leq \prod_{i=1}^n\left(\psi^U_{\mathcal{L}_i}\right)^{\xi_i\sigma_i} \leq min_i\left(\psi^U_{\mathcal{L}_i}\right);$$
$$max_i(\varphi_{\mathcal{L}_i}) \leq \prod_{i=1}^n(\varphi_{\mathcal{L}_i})^{\xi_i\sigma_i} \leq min_i(\varphi_{\mathcal{L}_i});$$
$$min_i(\psi_{\mathcal{L}_i})^3 \leq \sqrt[3]{1-\prod_{i=1}^n\left(1-(\psi_{\mathcal{L}_i})^3\right)^{\xi_i\sigma_i}} \leq max_i(\psi_{\mathcal{L}_i})^3.$$

Thus, $\mathcal{L}^- \leq \text{CCFFWA}(\mathcal{L}_1,\ \mathcal{L}_2,\ldots,\mathcal{L}_n) \leq \mathcal{L}^+$. □

Property 4. *For the CCFFNs $\mathcal{L}_1,\ \mathcal{L}_2,\ldots,\ \mathcal{L}_p$ and $\widetilde{\mathcal{L}} = \left(\langle\left[\widetilde{\varphi}^L_{\widetilde{\mathcal{L}}},\ \widetilde{\varphi}^U_{\widetilde{\mathcal{L}}}\right],\ \left[\widetilde{\psi}^L_{\widetilde{\mathcal{L}}},\widetilde{\psi}^U_{\widetilde{\mathcal{L}}}\right]\rangle,\ \langle\widetilde{\varphi}_{\widetilde{\mathcal{L}}},\ \widetilde{\psi}_{\widetilde{\mathcal{L}}}\rangle\right)$, we have*

$$\text{CCFFWA}\left(\mathcal{L}_1\widetilde{\mathcal{L}} \oplus \mathcal{L}_2\widetilde{\mathcal{L}} \oplus \ldots \oplus \mathcal{L}_p\widetilde{\mathcal{L}}\right) = \text{CCFFWA}(\mathcal{L}_1,\mathcal{L}_2,\ldots,\mathcal{L}_p) \oplus \widetilde{\mathcal{L}}.$$

Proof. Straightforward. □

Property. 5. *For a positive real number ζ, we have*

$$\text{CCFFWA}(\zeta\mathcal{L}_1,\zeta\ \mathcal{L}_2,\ldots,\zeta\mathcal{L}_p) = \zeta\text{CCFFWA}(\mathcal{L}_1,\ \mathcal{L}_2,\ldots,\mathcal{L}_p).$$

Proof. Straightforward. □

3.2.2. Ordered weighted Averaging Operator

Definition. 17. *A CCFFOWA is a mapping defined as* CCFFOWA : $\Gamma^n \to \Gamma$ *on a collection of CPFNs $\mathcal{L}_i$, $(i = 1,2,\ldots p)$ as follows*

$$\text{CCFFOWA}(\mathcal{L}_1,\ \mathcal{L}_2,\ldots,\ \mathcal{L}_p) = \xi_1\sigma_1\mathcal{L}_{\delta(1)} \oplus \xi_2\sigma_2\beta_{\delta(2)} \oplus \ldots \oplus\ \xi_p\sigma_p\mathcal{L}_{\sigma(p)} \tag{17}$$

where δ is a permutation of $(1,\ 2,\ldots,n)$, such that $\mathcal{L}_{\delta(i-1)} \geq \mathcal{L}_i$ for $i = 1,2,\ldots,p$ and $\xi = (\xi_1,\xi_2\ldots,\xi_n)^T$ is its weight vector, such that $\xi \succ 0$ and $\sum_{i=1}^p \xi_i = 1$ with confidence levels $0 \leq \sigma_i \leq 1$. Furthermore, the ith *largest CFFN among $\mathcal{L}_i'$s is $\mathcal{L}_{\delta(i)}$.*

Theorem. 4. *The value obtained by using the CCFFOWA operator for CFFNs $\mathcal{L}_i$ $(i = 1,2,\ldots,p)$ is again a CFFN and given by*

$$\text{CCFFWA}(\mathcal{L}_1,\ \mathcal{L}_2,\ldots,\mathcal{L}_n) = \left(\begin{array}{c}\langle\left[\begin{array}{c}\sqrt[3]{1-\prod_{i=1}^p\left(1-\left(\varphi^L_{\mathcal{L}_{\delta(i)}}\right)^3\right)^{\xi_i\sigma_i}},\\ \sqrt[3]{1-\prod_{i=1}^p\left(1-\left(\varphi^U_{\mathcal{L}_{\delta(i)}}\right)^3\right)^{\xi_i\sigma_i}}\end{array}\right],\left[\begin{array}{c}\prod_{i=1}^p\left(\psi^L_{\mathcal{L}_{\delta(i)}}\right)^{\xi_i\sigma_i},\\ \prod_{i=1}^p\left(\psi^U_{\mathcal{L}_{\delta(i)}}\right)^{\xi_i\sigma_i}\end{array}\right]\rangle,\\ \langle\prod_{i=1}^p\left(\varphi_{\mathcal{L}_{\delta(i)}}\right)^{\xi_i\sigma_i},\sqrt[3]{1-\prod_{i=1}^p\left(1-\left(\psi_{\mathcal{L}_{\delta(i)}}\right)^3\right)^{\xi_i\sigma_i}}\rangle\end{array}\right). \tag{18}$$

Proof. Similar proof as Theorem 3. □

Example 2. *Let* $\mathcal{L}_1 = (\langle[0.3, 0.4], [0.2.0.3], (0.2, 0.6)\rangle; 0.5)$, $\mathcal{L}_2 = (\langle[0.4, 0.5], [0.3.0.4], (0.6, 0.2)\rangle; 0.4)$, *and* $\mathcal{L}_3 = (\langle[0.6, 0.7], [0.5.0.6], (0.4, 0.3)\rangle; 0.7)$ *be three CFFNs with confidence levels, and* $\xi = (0.5, 0.3, 0.2)$ *be their corresponding weight vector. By using Equations (10) and (11) to calculate the score values of each CFFN it follows that*

$$\begin{aligned} sc(\mathcal{L}_1) &= \tfrac{(0.3)^3+(0.4)^3-(0.2)^3-(0.3)^3}{2} + ((0.6)^3 - (0.2)^3) = 0.2360; \\ sc(\mathcal{L}_2) &= \tfrac{(0.4)^3+(0.5)^3-(0.3)^3-(0.4)^3}{2} + ((0.2)^3 - (0.6)^3) = -0.1590; \\ sc(\mathcal{L}_3) &= \tfrac{(0.6)^3+(0.7)^3-(0.5)^3-(0.6)^3}{2} + ((0.3)^3 - (0.4)^3) = 0.0720. \end{aligned}$$

The order of these CFFNs with respect to score values is $\mathcal{L}_1 \succ \mathcal{L}_3 \succ \mathcal{L}_2$.
Arrange these CFFNs with respect to score values, i.e.,

$$\mathcal{L}_1 = (\langle[0.3, 0.4], [0.2.0.3], (0.2, 0.6)\rangle; 0.5), \mathcal{L}_3 = (\langle[0.6, 0.7], [0.5.0.6], (0.4, 0.3)\rangle; 0.7);$$

and

$$\mathcal{L}_2 = (\langle[0.4, 0.5], [0.3.0.4], (0.6, 0.2)\rangle; 0.4).$$

Therefore, $\mathcal{L}_{\delta(1)} = \mathcal{L}_1$, $\mathcal{L}_{\delta(2)} = \mathcal{L}_3$, and $\mathcal{L}_{\delta(3)} = \mathcal{L}_2$.
Now, we have

$$\begin{aligned} \sqrt[3]{1 - \prod_{i=1}^{3}\left(1 - \left(\varphi^L_{\mathcal{L}_{\delta(i)}}\right)^3\right)^{\xi_i\sigma_i}} &= \left(1 - \left(\begin{array}{c}(1-(0.3)^3)^{(0.5)(0.5)} \times (1-(0.6)^3)^{(0.3)(0.7)} \\ \times (1-(0.4)^3)^{(0.2)(0.4)}\end{array}\right)\right)^{1/3} = 0.3942; \\ \sqrt[3]{1 - \prod_{i=1}^{3}\left(1 - \left(\varphi^U_{\mathcal{L}_{\delta(i)}}\right)^3\right)^{\xi_i\sigma_i}} &= \left(1 - \left(\begin{array}{c}(1-(0.4)^3)^{(0.5)(0.5)} \times (1-(0.7)^3)^{(0.3)(0.7)} \\ \times (1-(0.5)^3)^{(0.2)(0.4)}\end{array}\right)\right)^{1/3} = 0.4777; \\ \prod_{i=1}^{3}\left(\psi^L_{\mathcal{L}_{\delta(i)}}\right)^{\xi_i\sigma_i} &= (0.2)^{(0.5)(0.5)} \times (0.5)^{(0.3)(0.7)} \times (0.3)^{(0.2)(0.4)} = 0.5251; \\ \prod_{i=1}^{3}\left(\psi^L_{\mathcal{L}_{\delta(i)}}\right)^{\xi_i\sigma_i} &= (0.3)^{(0.5)(0.5)} \times (0.6)^{(0.3)(0.7)} \times (0.4)^{(0.2)(0.4)} = 0.6178; \\ \prod_{i=1}^{p}\left(\varphi_{\mathcal{L}_{\delta(i)}}\right)^{\xi_i\sigma_i} &= (0.2)^{(0.5)(0.5)} \times (0.4)^{(0.3)(0.7)} \times (0.6)^{(0.2)(0.4)} = 0.5296; \\ \sqrt[3]{1 - \prod_{i=1}^{p}\left(1 - \left(\psi_{\mathcal{L}_{\delta(i)}}\right)^3\right)^{\xi_i\sigma_i}} &= \left(1 - \left(\begin{array}{c}(1-(0.6)^3)^{(0.5)(0.5)} \times (1-(0.3)^3)^{(0.3)(0.7)} \\ \times (1-(0.2)^3)^{(0.2)(0.4)}\end{array}\right)\right)^{1/3} = 0.4021. \end{aligned}$$

Hence,

$$\text{CCFFOWA}(\mathcal{L}_1, \mathcal{L}_2, \mathcal{L}_3) = \left(\begin{array}{c}\langle[0.3942, 0.4777], [0.5251.0.6178]\rangle, \\ \langle 0.5296,\ 0.4021\rangle\end{array}\right).$$

3.2.3. Geometric Operator

Definition 18. *A CCFFWG operator is a mapping* $\text{CCFFWG} : \Gamma^n \to \Gamma$ *defined as*

$$\text{CCFFWG}(\mathcal{L}_1, \mathcal{L}_2, \ldots, \mathcal{L}_p) = \beth_1\mathcal{L}_1 \otimes \beth_2\mathcal{L}_2 \otimes \ldots \otimes \beth_p\mathcal{L}_p \tag{19}$$

where Ω *is the collection of CPFNs* $\mathcal{L}_i (i = 1, 2, \ldots, p)$, *and* $\xi = (\xi_1, \xi_2, \ldots, \xi_p)^T$ *is the weight vector of* $\mathcal{L}_i$ *such that* $\xi_i \succ 0$ *and* $\sum_{i=1}^{n} \xi_i = 1$. *We also set,* σ_p *be the confidence levels of CFFN* $\mathcal{L}_p$.

Theorem 5. *For* $\mathcal{L}_1, \mathcal{L}_2, \ldots, \mathcal{L}_n$, *the value obtained by CCFFWG is a CFFN, which is determined by*

$$\text{CCFFWG}(\mathcal{L}_1, \mathcal{L}_2, \ldots, \mathcal{L}_n) = \left(\begin{array}{c} \langle \begin{bmatrix} \prod_{i=1}^{p} \left(\varphi_{\mathcal{L}_i}^{L} \right)^{\xi_i \sigma_i}, \\ \prod_{i=1}^{p} \left(\varphi_{\mathcal{L}_i}^{U} \right)^{\xi_i \sigma_i} \end{bmatrix}, \begin{bmatrix} \sqrt[3]{1 - \prod_{i=1}^{p} \left(1 - \left(\psi_{\mathcal{L}_i}^{L} \right)^3 \right)^{\xi_i \sigma_i}}, \\ \sqrt[3]{1 - \prod_{i=1}^{p} \left(1 - \left(\psi_{\mathcal{L}_i}^{U} \right)^3 \right)^{\xi_i \sigma_i}} \end{bmatrix} \rangle, \\ \langle \sqrt[3]{1 - \prod_{i=1}^{p} \left(1 - (\varphi_{\mathcal{L}_i})^3 \right)^{\xi_i \sigma_i}}, \prod_{i=1}^{p} (\psi_{\mathcal{L}_i})^{\xi_i \sigma_i} \rangle \end{array} \right). \tag{20}$$

Proof. Similar to Theorem 3, therefore omitted here. □

Example 3. *Let* $\mathcal{L}_1 = (\langle [0.4, 0.6], [0.3.0.7], (0.3, 0.5) \rangle; 0.8)$, $\mathcal{L}_2 = (\langle [0.5, 0.6], [0.4.0.5], (0.2, 0.4) \rangle; 0.7)$, *and* $\mathcal{L}_3 = (\langle [0.2, 0.3], [0.4.0.5], (0.7, 0.2) \rangle; 0.6)$ *be three CFFNs with confidence levels and* $\xi = (0.25, 0.35, 0.4)$ *be their corresponding weight vector then*

$$\prod_{i=1}^{3} \left(\varphi_{\mathcal{L}_i}^{L} \right)^{\xi_i \sigma_i} = (0.4)^{(0.25)(0.8)} \times (0.5)^{(0.35)(0.7)} \times (0.2)^{(0.4)(0.6)} = 0.4774;$$

$$\prod_{i=1}^{3} \left(\varphi_{\mathcal{L}_i}^{L} \right)^{\xi_i \sigma_i} = (0.6)^{(0.25)(0.8)} \times (0.6)^{(0.35)(0.7)} \times (0.3)^{(0.4)(0.6)} = 0.5967;$$

$$\sqrt[3]{1 - \prod_{i=1}^{3} \left(1 - \left(\psi_{\mathcal{L}_i}^{L} \right)^3 \right)^{\xi_i \sigma_i}} = \left(1 - \left(\begin{array}{c} (1 - (0.3)^3)^{(0.25)(0.8)} \times (1 - (0.4)^3)^{(0.35)(0.7)} \\ \times (1 - (0.4)^3)^{(0.4)(0.6)} \end{array} \right) \right)^{\frac{1}{3}} = 0.3328;$$

$$\sqrt[3]{1 - \prod_{i=1}^{3} \left(1 - \left(\psi_{\mathcal{L}_i}^{U} \right)^3 \right)^{\xi_i \sigma_i}} = \left(1 - \left(\begin{array}{c} (1 - (0.7)^3)^{(0.25)(0.8)} \times (1 - (0.5)^3)^{(0.35)(0.7)} \\ \times (1 - (0.5)^3)^{(0.4)(0.6)} \end{array} \right) \right)^{\frac{1}{3}} = 0.5171;$$

$$\sqrt[3]{1 - \prod_{i=1}^{p} \left(1 - (\varphi_{\mathcal{L}_i})^3 \right)^{\xi_i \sigma_i}} = \left(1 - \left(\begin{array}{c} (1 - (0.3)^3)^{(0.25)(0.8)} \times (1 - (0.2)^3)^{(0.35)(0.7)} \\ \times (1 - (0.7)^3)^{(0.4)(0.6)} \end{array} \right) \right)^{\frac{1}{3}} = 0.4682 :$$

$$\prod_{i=1}^{p} (\psi_{\mathcal{L}_i})^{\xi_i \sigma_i} = (0.5)^{(0.25)(0.8)} \times (0.4)^{(0.35)(0.7)} \times (0.2)^{(0.4)(0.6)} = 0.4727.$$

Hence, we have

$$\text{CCFFWG}(\mathcal{L}_1, \mathcal{L}_2, \mathcal{L}_3) = \left(\begin{array}{c} \langle [0.4774, 0.5967], [0.3328, 0.5171] \rangle, \\ \langle 0.4682, 0.4727 \rangle \end{array} \right).$$

3.2.4. Ordered Weighted Geometric Operator

Definition 19. *A CPFOWG is a mapping* $\text{CPFOWG} : \Gamma^n \to \Gamma$ *defined over a collection of CCFFNs* $\mathcal{L}_i$ *with confidence levels* σ_i $(i = 1, 2, \ldots p)$ *as follows*

$$\text{CCFFOWG}(\mathcal{L}_1, \mathcal{L}_2, \ldots, \mathcal{L}_p) = \sigma_1 \xi_1 \mathcal{L}_{\sigma(1)} \otimes \sigma_2 \xi_2 \mathcal{L}_{\sigma(2)} \otimes \ldots \otimes \sigma_p \xi_p \mathcal{L}_{\delta(p)} \tag{21}$$

where δ *is a permutation of* $(1, 2, \ldots, p)$, *such that* $\mathcal{L}_{\delta(i-1)} \geq \mathcal{L}_i$ *for* $i = 1, 2, \ldots, n$ *and* $\xi = (\xi_1, \xi_2 \ldots, \xi_p)^T$ *is its weight vector, such that* $\xi \succ 0$ *and* $\sum_{i=1}^{n} \xi_i = 1$. *Moreover, the* ith *largest CFFN among* $\mathcal{L}_i$*s is* $\mathcal{L}_{\delta(i)}$.

Theorem 6. *The value obtained by using the CPFOWG operator for CFFNs* $\mathcal{L}_i$ $(i = 1, 2, \ldots, p)$ *is again a CFFN and given by*

$$\text{CCFFWG}(\mathcal{L}_1,\ \mathcal{L}_2,\ldots,\mathcal{L}_n) = \left(\begin{array}{c}\langle\left[\begin{array}{c}\prod_{i=1}^{p}\left(\varphi^L_{\mathcal{L}_{\delta(i)}}\right)^{\xi_i\sigma_i},\\ \prod_{i=1}^{p}\left(\varphi^U_{\mathcal{L}_{\delta(i)}}\right)^{\xi_i\sigma_i}\end{array}\right],\left[\begin{array}{c}\sqrt[3]{1-\prod_{i=1}^{p}\left(1-\left(\varphi^L_{\mathcal{L}_{\delta(i)}}\right)^3\right)^{\xi_i\sigma_i}},\\ \sqrt[3]{1-\prod_{i=1}^{p}\left(1-\left(\varphi^U_{\mathcal{L}_{\delta(i)}}\right)^3\right)^{\xi_i\sigma_i}}\end{array}\right]\rangle,\\ \langle\sqrt[3]{1-\prod_{i=1}^{p}\left(1-\left(\varphi_{\mathcal{L}_{\delta(i)}}\right)^3\right)^{\xi_i\sigma_i}},\prod_{i=1}^{p}\left(\psi_{\mathcal{L}_{\delta(i)}}\right)^{\xi_i\sigma_i}\rangle\end{array}\right). \tag{22}$$

Theorem 7. *Let $\mathcal{L}_i(i = 1,2,\ldots,p)$, and $\xi = (\xi_1,\ \xi_2,\ldots,\xi_p)^T$ be the weight vector of $\mathcal{L}_i$ such that $\xi_i \succ 0$ and $\sum_{i=1}^{p}\xi_i = 1$,* then we *have*

1. $\text{CCFFWA}\left(\mathcal{L}_1^c,\ \mathcal{L}_2^c,\ldots,\mathcal{L}_p^c\right) = (\text{CPFWG}(\mathcal{L}_1,\ \mathcal{L}_2,\ldots,\mathcal{L}_p))^c$;
2. $\text{CCFFWG}\left(\mathcal{L}_1^c,\ \mathcal{L}_2^c,\ldots,\mathcal{L}_p^c\right) = (\text{CPFWA}(\mathcal{L}_1,\ \mathcal{L}_2,\ldots,\mathcal{L}_p))^c$.

Proof. Since $\mathcal{L}_i = \left(\langle\left[\varphi^L_{\mathcal{L}_i},\ \varphi^U_{\mathcal{L}_i}\right],\ \left[\psi^L_{\mathcal{L}_i},\psi^U_{\mathcal{L}_i}\right]\rangle,\ \langle\varphi_{\mathcal{L}_i},\ \psi_{\mathcal{L}_i}\rangle\right)$ and $\mathcal{L}_i^c = \left(\langle\left[\psi^L_{\mathcal{L}_i},\psi^U_{\mathcal{L}_i}\right],\ \left[\varphi^L_{\mathcal{L}_i},\ \varphi^U_{\mathcal{L}_i}\right]\rangle,\ \langle\psi_{\mathcal{L}_i},\ \varphi_{\mathcal{L}_i}\rangle\right)$, then using Equation (17), we have

$$\text{CCFFWA}\left(\mathcal{L}_1^c,\ \mathcal{L}_2^c,\ldots,\mathcal{L}_p^c\right) = \left(\begin{array}{c}\langle\left[\begin{array}{c}\prod_{i=1}^{n}\left(\psi^L_{\mathcal{L}_i}\right)^{\xi_i\sigma_i},\\ \prod_{i=1}^{n}\left(\psi^L_{\mathcal{L}_i}\right)^{\xi_i\sigma_i}\end{array}\right],\left[\begin{array}{c}\sqrt[3]{1-\prod_{i=1}^{n}\left(1-\left(\varphi^L_{\mathcal{L}_i}\right)^2\right)^{\xi_i\sigma_i}},\\ \sqrt[3]{1-\prod_{i=1}^{n}\left(1-\left(\varphi^L_{\mathcal{L}_i}\right)^2\right)^{\xi_i\sigma_i}}\end{array}\right]\rangle,\\ \langle\sqrt[3]{1-\prod_{i=1}^{n}\left(1-(\psi_{\mathcal{L}_i})^2\right)^{\xi_i\sigma_i}},\prod_{i=1}^{n}(\varphi_{\mathcal{L}_i})^{\xi_i\sigma_i}\rangle\end{array}\right)$$
$$= (\text{CCFFWG}(\mathcal{L}_1,\ \mathcal{L}_2,\ldots,\mathcal{L}_p))^c.$$

Similarly, we can prove that $\text{CCFFWG}\left(\mathcal{L}_1^c,\ \mathcal{L}_2^c,\ldots,\mathcal{L}_p^c\right) = (\text{CCPFWA}(\mathcal{L}_1,\ \mathcal{L}_2,\ldots,\mathcal{L}_p))^c$. □

Theorem 8. *Let $\mathcal{L}_i(i = 1,2,\ldots,p)$,* and *$\xi = (\xi_1,\ \xi_2,\ldots,\xi_p)^T$ be the weight vector of $\mathcal{L}_i$ such that $\xi_i \succ 0$ and $\sum_{i=1}^{p}\xi_i = 1$, then we have*

$$\text{CCFFWG}(\mathcal{L}_1,\ \mathcal{L}_2,\ldots,\mathcal{L}_p) \le \text{CCFFWA}(\mathcal{L}_1,\ \mathcal{L}_2,\ldots,\mathcal{L}_p) \tag{23}$$

Proof. Easy to prove. □

Definition. 20. *For the CFFNs $\mathcal{L}_i$ $(i = 1,\ 2,\ldots,p)$ the operator* CCFFHA : $\Gamma^n \to \Gamma$ *is given as*

$$\text{CCFFHA}(\mathcal{L}_1,\ \mathcal{L}_2,\ldots,\mathcal{L}_p) = \sigma_1\xi_1\dot{\mathcal{L}}_{\sigma(1)} \oplus \sigma_2\xi_2\dot{\mathcal{L}}_{\sigma(2)} \oplus \ldots \oplus \sigma_p\xi_p\dot{\mathcal{L}}_{\sigma(p)} \tag{24}$$

*where, $\xi = (\xi_1,\ \xi_2,\ldots,\xi_p)^T$ be the weight vector, such that $\xi_i \succ 0$ and $\sum_{i=1}^{n}\xi_i = 1$ and $\dot{\mathcal{L}}_i$'*s $\left(\dot{\mathcal{L}}_i = n\zeta_i\mathcal{L}_i\right)$ is $\dot{\mathcal{L}}_{\sigma(i)}$, *where n is the number of CPFNs and $\eta = (\eta_1,\ \eta_2,\ldots,\eta_p)^T$ is the vector corresponding to $\mathcal{L}_i$ with $\zeta_i \succ 0$ and $\sum_{i=1}^{p}\zeta_i = 1$.*

Theorem. 9. *The value obtained using the CCFFHA operator for the CFFNs $\mathcal{L}_i$ $(i = 1,2,\ldots,p)$ is again a CFFN and given by*

$$\mathrm{CCFFHA}(\mathcal{L}_1, \mathcal{L}_2, \ldots, \mathcal{L}_n) = \left(\begin{array}{c} \langle \begin{bmatrix} \sqrt[3]{1 - \prod_{i=1}^{p}\left(1 - \left(\dot{\varphi}^{L}_{\mathcal{L}_{\delta(i)}}\right)^2\right)^{\xi_i\sigma_i}}, \\ \sqrt[3]{1 - \prod_{i=1}^{p}\left(1 - \left(\dot{\mu}^{U}_{\mathcal{L}_{\delta(i)}}\right)^2\right)^{\xi_i\sigma_i}} \end{bmatrix}, \begin{bmatrix} \prod_{i=1}^{n}\left(\dot{\psi}^{L}_{\mathcal{L}_{\delta(i)}}\right)^{\xi_i\sigma_i}, \\ \prod_{i=1}^{n}\left(\dot{\psi}^{U}_{\mathcal{L}_{\delta(i)}}\right)^{\xi_i\sigma_i} \end{bmatrix} \rangle \\ \langle \prod_{i=1}^{p}\left(\dot{\varphi}_{\mathcal{L}_{\delta(i)}}\right)^{\xi_i\sigma_i}, \sqrt[3]{1 - \prod_{i=1}^{n}\left(1 - \left(\dot{\psi}_{\mathcal{L}_{\delta(i)}}\right)^2\right)^{\xi_i\sigma_i}} \rangle \end{array} \right). \quad (25)$$

Proof. Easy to prove. □

Example 4. *Consider three CPFNs* β_i $(i = 1, 2, 3)$, *such that* $\mathcal{L}_1 = (\langle[0.30, 0.50], [0.60, 0.70]\rangle, \langle 0.50, 0.40\rangle, 0.3)$, $\mathcal{L}_2 = (\langle[0.60, 0.70], [0.40, 0.50]\rangle, \langle 0.50, 0.60\rangle, 0.4)$, *and* $\mathcal{L}_3 = (\langle[0.70, 0.80], [0.20, 0.40]\rangle, \langle 0.50, 0.40\rangle, 0.5)$. *Additionally, if* $\eta = (0.25, 0.35, 0.40)^T$ *is the weight vector of* $\mathcal{L}_i$ *then* $\dot{\mathcal{L}}_i = 3\eta_i\mathcal{L}_i = \left(\langle\left[\dot{\varphi}^{L}_{\mathcal{L}_{\delta(i)}}, \dot{\varphi}^{U}_{\mathcal{L}_{\delta(i)}}\right], \left[\dot{\psi}^{L}_{\mathcal{L}_{\delta(i)}}, \dot{\psi}^{U}_{\mathcal{L}_{\delta(i)}}\right]\rangle, \langle\dot{\varphi}_{\mathcal{L}_{\delta(i)}}, \dot{\psi}_{\mathcal{L}_{\delta(i)}}\rangle\right)$ $(i = 1, 2, 3)$ *is computed for each CFFN as*

$$\begin{aligned} \dot{\mathcal{L}}_1 &= \left(\langle\begin{bmatrix} \sqrt[3]{1 - \left(1 - (0.30)^3\right)^{3\times0.25}}, \\ \sqrt[3]{1 - (1 - (0.50)^3)^{3\times0.25}} \end{bmatrix}, \begin{bmatrix} (0.60)^{3\times0.25}, \\ (0.70)^{3\times0.25} \end{bmatrix}\rangle, \langle \begin{array}{c} (0.50)^{3\times0.25}, \\ \sqrt[3]{1 - (1 - (0.40)^3)^{3\times0.25}} \end{array}\rangle\right) \\ &= \left(\langle\begin{bmatrix} 0.2729, \\ 0.4568 \end{bmatrix}, \begin{bmatrix} 0.6817, \\ 0.7653 \end{bmatrix}\rangle, \langle \begin{array}{c} 0.5946, \\ 0.3644 \end{array}\rangle\right); \\ \dot{\mathcal{L}}_2 &= \left(\langle\begin{bmatrix} \sqrt[3]{1 - \left(1 - (0.60)^3\right)^{3\times0.35}}, \\ \sqrt[3]{1 - (1 - (0.70)^3)^{3\times0.35}} \end{bmatrix}, \begin{bmatrix} (0.40)^{3\times0.35}, \\ (0.50)^{3\times0.35} \end{bmatrix}\rangle, \langle \begin{array}{c} (0.50)^{3\times0.35}, \\ \sqrt[3]{1 - (1 - (0.60)^3)^{3\times0.35}} \end{array}\rangle\right) \\ &= \left(\langle\begin{bmatrix} 0.6087, \\ 0.7092 \end{bmatrix}, \begin{bmatrix} 0.3821, \\ 0.4830 \end{bmatrix}\rangle, \langle \begin{array}{c} 0.4830, \\ 0.6087 \end{array}\rangle\right); \\ \dot{\mathcal{L}}_3 &= \left(\langle\begin{bmatrix} \sqrt[3]{1 - \left(1 - (0.70)^3\right)^{3\times0.4}}, \\ \sqrt[3]{1 - (1 - (0.80)^3)^{3\times0.4}} \end{bmatrix}, \begin{bmatrix} (0.20)^{3\times0.4}, \\ (0.40)^{3\times0.4} \end{bmatrix}\rangle, \langle \begin{array}{c} (0.50)^{3\times0.4}, \\ \sqrt[3]{1 - (1 - (0.40)^3)^{3\times0.4}} \end{array}\rangle\right) \\ &= \left(\langle\begin{bmatrix} 0.7343, \\ 0.8326 \end{bmatrix}, \begin{bmatrix} 0.1450, \\ 0.3330 \end{bmatrix}\rangle, \langle \begin{array}{c} 0.4353, \\ 0.4241 \end{array}\rangle\right). \end{aligned}$$

The score values of these numbers are calculated as

$$\begin{aligned} sc\left(\dot{\mathcal{L}}_1\right) &= \tfrac{(0.2729)^3 + (0.4568)^3 - (0.6817)^3 - (0.7653)^3}{2} - \left((0.5946)^3 - (0.3644)^3\right) = -0.4865; \\ sc\left(\dot{\mathcal{L}}_2\right) &= \tfrac{(0.6087)^3 + (0.7092)^3 - (0.3821)^3 - (0.4830)^3}{2} - \left((0.4830)^3 - (0.6087)^3\right) = 0.0948; \\ sc\left(\dot{\mathcal{L}}_3\right) &= \tfrac{(0.7343)^3 + (0.8326)^3 - (0.1450)^3 - (0.3330)^3}{2} - \left((0.4353)^3 - (0.4241)^3\right) = 0.3841. \end{aligned}$$

Thus, $sc\left(\dot{\mathcal{L}}_3\right) \succcurlyeq sc\left(\dot{\mathcal{L}}_2\right) \succcurlyeq sc\left(\dot{\mathcal{L}}_1\right)$, *which gives*

$$\begin{aligned} \dot{\beta}_{\sigma(1)} &= \left(\langle\begin{bmatrix} 0.7343, \\ 0.8326 \end{bmatrix}, \begin{bmatrix} 0.1450, \\ 0.3330 \end{bmatrix}\rangle, \langle \begin{array}{c} 0.4353, \\ 0.4241 \end{array}\rangle\right), \\ \dot{\beta}_{\sigma(2)} &= \left(\langle\begin{bmatrix} 0.6087, \\ 0.7092 \end{bmatrix}, \begin{bmatrix} 0.3821, \\ 0.4830 \end{bmatrix}\rangle, \langle \begin{array}{c} 0.4830, \\ 0.6087 \end{array}\rangle\right), \end{aligned}$$

and

$$\dot{\beta}_{\delta(3)} = \left(\langle\begin{bmatrix} 0.2729, \\ 0.4568 \end{bmatrix}, \begin{bmatrix} 0.6817, \\ 0.7653 \end{bmatrix}\rangle, \langle \begin{array}{c} 0.5946, \\ 0.3644 \end{array}\rangle\right)$$

Let $\xi = (0.35, 0.4, 0.25)$ *be the position vector, then by using Equation (25), we have*

$$\sqrt[3]{1-\prod_{i=1}^{p}\left(1-\left(\dot{\varphi}^{L}_{\mathcal{L}_{\delta(i)}}\right)^{3}\right)^{\xi_i\sigma_i}} = \sqrt[3]{1-\left(\begin{array}{c}\left(1-(0.7343)^3\right)^{0.35\times0.5}\times\left(1-(0.6087)^3\right)^{0.4\times0.4}\\ \times\left(1-(0.2729)^3\right)^{0.25\times0.3}\end{array}\right)} = 0.4966;$$

$$\sqrt[3]{1-\prod_{i=1}^{n}\left(1-\left(\dot{\varphi}^{U}_{\sigma(i)}\right)^{3}\right)^{\xi_i\sigma_i}} = \sqrt[3]{1-\left(\begin{array}{c}\left(1-(0.8326)^3\right)^{0.35\times0.5}\times\left(1-(0.7092)^3\right)^{0.4\times0.4}\\ \times\left(1-(0.4568)^3\right)^{0.25\times0.3}\end{array}\right)} = 0.5891;$$

$$\prod_{i=1}^{p}\left(\dot{\psi}^{L}_{\mathcal{L}_{\delta(i)}}\right)^{\xi_i\sigma_i} = (0.1450)^{0.35\times0.5}(0.3821)^{0.4\times0.4}(0.6817)^{0.25\times0.3} = 0.5942;$$

$$\prod_{i=1}^{p}\left(\dot{\psi}^{U}_{\mathcal{L}_{\delta(i)}}\right)^{\xi_i\sigma_i} = (0.3330)^{0.35\times0.5}(0.4830)^{0.4\times0.4}(0.7653)^{0.25\times0.3} = 0.7197;$$

$$\prod_{i=1}^{p}\left(\dot{\psi}_{\mathcal{L}_{\delta(i)}}\right)^{\xi_i\sigma_i} = (0.4353)^{0.35\times0.5}(0.4830)^{0.4\times0.4}(0.5946)^{0.25\times0.3} = 0.7401;$$

$$\sqrt[3]{1-\prod_{i=1}^{p}\left(1-\left(\dot{\psi}_{\mathcal{L}_{\delta(i)}}\right)^{3}\right)^{\xi_i\sigma_i}} = \sqrt[3]{1-\left(\begin{array}{c}\left(1-(0.4241)^3\right)^{0.35\times0.5}\times\left(1-(0.6087)^3\right)^{0.4\times0.4}\\ \times\left(1-(0.3644)^3\right)^{0.25\times0.3}\end{array}\right)} = 0.3844.$$

Therefore,

$$\text{CCFFHA}(\mathcal{L}_1,\mathcal{L}_2,\mathcal{L}_3) = \left(\langle\begin{bmatrix}0.4966,\\0.5891\end{bmatrix},\begin{bmatrix}0.5942,\\0.7197\end{bmatrix}\rangle,\langle\begin{matrix}0.7401,\\0.3844\end{matrix}\rangle\right).$$

4. Decision-Making Approach under Cubic Fermatean Fuzzy Sets with Confidence Levels

This section presents an MCDM approach to deal with MCDM problems by using the proposed aggregation operators under a cubic Fermatean fuzzy environment. The MCDM problem is presented for evaluation with a cubic Fermatean fuzzy environment with the following presumptions and abbreviations. Let $X = \{X_1, X_2, \ldots, X_p\}$ be the set of m different alternatives which have to be analyzed under the set of q different criteria $C = \{C_1, C_2, \ldots, C_q\}$. Suppose that all these possibilities are examined by experts, which provide their choices for each X_i $(i = 1,2,\ldots,p)$, under a cubic Fermatean fuzzy environment, and that these values can be considered as CFFNs $\mathcal{D} = \left[\daleth_{ij}\right]_{p\times q}$ where $\daleth_{ij} = \left(\langle\left[\varphi^L_{\mathcal{L}_{ij}}, \varphi^U_{\mathcal{L}_{ij}}\right], \left[\psi^L_{\mathcal{L}_{ij}}, \psi^U_{\mathcal{L}_{ij}}\right]\rangle, \langle\varphi_{\mathcal{L}_{ij}}, \psi_{\mathcal{L}_{ij}}\rangle\right)$ characterizes the importance values of alternative X_i given by the decision-maker such that $0 \le \varphi^L_{\mathcal{L}_{ij}}, \varphi^U_{\mathcal{L}_{ij}}, \psi^L_{\mathcal{L}_{ij}}, \psi^U_{\mathcal{L}_{ij}}, \varphi_{\mathcal{L}_{ij}}, \psi_{\mathcal{L}_{ij}} \le 1$, $\left[\varphi^L_{\mathcal{L}_{ij}}, \varphi^U_{\mathcal{L}_{ij}}\right], \left[\psi^L_{\mathcal{L}_{ij}}, \psi^U_{\mathcal{L}_{ij}}\right] \subseteq [0,1]$, which satisfy the conditions that $\left(\varphi^U_{ij}\right)^3 + \left(\psi^U_{ij}\right)^3 \le 1$ and $\left(\varphi_{\mathcal{L}_{ij}}\right)^3 + \left(\psi_{\mathcal{L}_{ij}}\right)^3 \le 1$. Let $\xi = (\xi_1, \xi_2, \ldots, \xi_p)$ be the weight vector of the criteria such that $\xi_i \succ 0$ and $\sum_{i=1}^{p}\xi_i = 1$. Additionally, let σ_i be the confidence levels of the CFFNs $\mathcal{L}_i$ such that $0 \le \sigma_i \le 1$. In order to identify the optimal alternative(s), the presented approach is divided into the following steps.

Step 1. Arrange the confidence and capability for each alternative X_i in the form of $\daleth_{ij} = \left(\langle\left[\varphi^L_{\mathcal{L}_{ij}}, \varphi^U_{\mathcal{L}_{ij}}\right], \left[\psi^L_{\mathcal{L}_{ij}}, \psi^U_{\mathcal{L}_{ij}}\right]\rangle, \langle\varphi_{\mathcal{L}_{ij}}, \psi_{\mathcal{L}_{ij}}\rangle\right)$. These rating values are expressed as a decision matrix $\mathcal{D}$ as:

$$\mathcal{D} = \begin{matrix} X_1 \\ X_2 \\ \vdots \\ X_p \end{matrix}\begin{pmatrix} \daleth_{11} & \daleth_{12} & \cdots & \daleth_{1p} \\ \daleth_{21} & \daleth_{22} & \cdots & \daleth_{2p} \\ \vdots & \vdots & \ddots & \vdots \\ \daleth_{q1} & \daleth_{q2} & \cdots & d_{pq} \end{pmatrix}. \tag{26}$$

Step 2. Convert the cost-type criteria into benefit-type criteria by using the normalization formula as given below:

$$r_{ij} = \begin{cases} \left(\langle\left[\varphi^L_{\mathcal{L}_{ij}}, \varphi^U_{\mathcal{L}_{ij}}\right], \left[\psi^L_{\mathcal{L}_{ij}}, \psi^U_{\mathcal{L}_{ij}}\right]\rangle, \langle\varphi_{\mathcal{L}_{ij}}, \psi_{\mathcal{L}_{ij}}\rangle\right); \text{ if the benefit} - \text{type conditions are met} \\ \left(\left[\psi^L_{\mathcal{L}_{ij}}, \psi^U_{\mathcal{L}_{ij}}\right], \left[\varphi^L_{\mathcal{L}_{ij}}, \varphi^U_{\mathcal{L}_{ij}}\right], \langle\nu_{\mathcal{L}_{ij}}, \mu_{ij}\rangle\right); \text{ if the cost} - \text{type conditions are met} \end{cases} \tag{27}$$

Step 3. Calculate the aggregated value $r_i\ (i = 1, 2, \ldots, p)$ of the alternative X_i, using CCFFWA, CCFFOWA, CCFFHA, CCFFWG, or CCFFOWG operators.

(a) Using a CCFFWA operator

$$\begin{aligned} r_i &= \left(\langle\left[\varphi^L_{\mathcal{L}_i}, \varphi^U_{\mathcal{L}_i}\right], \left[\psi^L_{\mathcal{L}_i}, \psi^U_{\mathcal{L}_i}\right]\rangle, \langle\varphi_{\mathcal{L}_i}, \psi_{\mathcal{L}_i}\rangle\right) = \mathrm{CCFFWA}(\mathcal{L}_{i1}, \mathcal{L}_{i2}, \ldots, \mathcal{L}_{ip}) \\ &= \left(\begin{array}{c} \left[\begin{array}{c} \sqrt[3]{1 - \prod_{j=1}^{p}\left(1 - \left(\varphi^L_{\mathcal{L}_{ij}}\right)^3\right)^{\xi_i\sigma_i}}, \\ \sqrt[3]{1 - \prod_{j=1}^{n}\left(1 - \left(\varphi^U_{\mathcal{L}_{ij}}\right)^3\right)^{\xi_i\sigma_i}} \end{array}\right], \left[\begin{array}{c} \prod_{j=1}^{p}\left(\psi^L_{\mathcal{L}_{ij}}\right)^{\xi_i\sigma_i}, \\ \prod_{j=1}^{p}\left(\psi^L_{\mathcal{L}_{ij}}\right)^{\xi_i\sigma_i} \end{array}\right], \\ \prod_{j=1}^{p}\left(\varphi_{\mathcal{L}_{ij}}\right)^{\xi_i\sigma_i}, \sqrt[3]{1 - \prod_{j=1}^{p}\left(1 - \left(\psi_{\mathcal{L}_{ij}}\right)^3\right)^{\xi_i\sigma_i}} \end{array}\right); \end{aligned} \tag{28}$$

(b) using a CCFFOWA operator

$$\begin{aligned} r_i &= \left(\langle\left[\varphi^L_{\mathcal{L}_i}, \varphi^U_{\mathcal{L}_i}\right], \left[\psi^L_{\mathcal{L}_i}, \psi^U_{\mathcal{L}_i}\right]\rangle, \langle\varphi_{\mathcal{L}_i}, \psi_{\mathcal{L}_i}\rangle\right) = \mathrm{CCFFOWA}\left(r_{\delta(i1)}, r_{\delta(i2)}, \ldots, r_{\delta(ip)}\right) \\ &= \left(\begin{array}{c} \langle\left[\begin{array}{c} \sqrt[3]{1 - \prod_{j=1}^{p}\left(1 - \left(\varphi^L_{\mathcal{L}_{\delta(ij)}}\right)^3\right)^{\xi_i\sigma_i}}, \\ \sqrt[3]{1 - \prod_{j=1}^{n}\left(1 - \left(\varphi^U_{\mathcal{L}_{\delta(ij)}}\right)^3\right)^{\xi_i\sigma_i}} \end{array}\right], \left[\begin{array}{c} \prod_{j=1}^{p}\left(\psi^L_{\mathcal{L}_{\delta(ij)}}\right)^{\xi_i\sigma_i}, \\ \prod_{j=1}^{p}\left(\psi^U_{\mathcal{L}_{\delta(i)}}\right)^{\xi_i\sigma_i} \end{array}\right]\rangle, \\ \langle\prod_{j=1}^{p}\left(\varphi_{\mathcal{L}_{\delta(ij)}}\right)^{\xi_i\sigma_i}, \sqrt[3]{1 - \prod_{j=1}^{p}\left(1 - \left(\psi_{\mathcal{L}_{\delta(ij)}}\right)^3\right)^{\xi_i\sigma_i}}\rangle \end{array}\right); \end{aligned} \tag{29}$$

(c) using a CCFFHA operator

$$\begin{aligned} r_i &= \left(\langle\left[\varphi^L_{\mathcal{L}_i}, \varphi^U_{\mathcal{L}_i}\right], \left[\psi^L_{\mathcal{L}_i}, \psi^U_{\mathcal{L}_i}\right]\rangle, \langle\varphi_{\mathcal{L}_i}, \psi_{\mathcal{L}_i}\rangle\right) = \mathrm{CPFFHA}\left(\dot{r}_{\delta(i1)}, \dot{r}_{\delta(i2)}, \ldots, \dot{r}_{\delta(ip)}\right) \\ &= \left(\begin{array}{c} \langle\left[\begin{array}{c} \sqrt[3]{1 - \prod_{j=1}^{p}\left(1 - \left(\dot{\varphi}^L_{\mathcal{L}_{\delta(ij)}}\right)^3\right)^{\xi_i\sigma_i}}, \\ \sqrt[3]{1 - \prod_{j=1}^{n}\left(1 - \left(\dot{\mu}^U_{\mathcal{L}_{\delta(ij)}}\right)^3\right)^{\xi_i\sigma_i}} \end{array}\right], \left[\begin{array}{c} \prod_{j=1}^{p}\left(\dot{\psi}^L_{\mathcal{L}_{\delta(ij)}}\right)^{\xi_i\sigma_i}, \\ \prod_{j=1}^{p}\left(\dot{\psi}^U_{\mathcal{L}_{\delta(iJ)}}\right)^{\xi_i\sigma_i} \end{array}\right]\rangle, \\ \langle\prod_{j=1}^{p}\left(\dot{\varphi}_{\mathcal{L}_{\delta(ij)}}\right)^{\xi_i\sigma_i}, \sqrt[3]{1 - \prod_{j=1}^{p}\left(1 - \left(\dot{\psi}_{\mathcal{L}_{\delta(ij)}}\right)^3\right)^{\xi_i\sigma_i}}\rangle \end{array}\right); \end{aligned} \tag{30}$$

(d) using a CCFFWG operator

$$\begin{aligned} r_i &= \left(\langle\left[\varphi^L_{\mathcal{L}_i}, \varphi^U_{\mathcal{L}_i}\right], \left[\psi^L_{\mathcal{L}_i}, \psi^U_{\mathcal{L}_i}\right]\rangle, \varphi_{\mathcal{L}_i}, \psi_{\mathcal{L}_i}\right) = \mathrm{CCFFWG}(r_{i1}, r_{i2}, \ldots, r_{ip}) \\ &= \left(\begin{array}{c} \langle\left[\begin{array}{c} \prod_{i=1}^{p}\left(\varphi^L_{\mathcal{L}_{ij}}\right)^{\xi_i\sigma_i}, \\ \prod_{i=1}^{p}\left(\varphi^U_{\mathcal{L}_{ij}}\right)^{\xi_i\sigma_i} \end{array}\right], \left[\begin{array}{c} \sqrt[3]{1 - \prod_{i=1}^{p}\left(1 - \left(\psi^L_{\mathcal{L}_{ij}}\right)^3\right)^{\xi_i\sigma_i}}, \\ \sqrt[3]{1 - \prod_{i=1}^{p}\left(1 - \left(\psi^U_{\mathcal{L}_{ij}}\right)^3\right)^{\xi_i\sigma_i}} \end{array}\right]\rangle, \\ \langle\sqrt[3]{1 - \prod_{i=1}^{p}\left(1 - \left(\varphi_{\mathcal{L}_{ij}}\right)^3\right)^{\xi_i\sigma_i}}, \prod_{i=1}^{p}\left(\psi_{\mathcal{L}_{ij}}\right)^{\xi_i\sigma_i}\rangle \end{array}\right); \end{aligned} \tag{31}$$

(e) using a CCFFOWG operator

$$
\begin{aligned}
\mathcal{r}_i &= \left(\langle \left[\varphi^L_{\mathcal{L}_i}, \varphi^U_{\mathcal{L}_i}\right], \left[\psi^L_{\mathcal{L}_i}, \psi^U_{\mathcal{L}_i}\right]\rangle, \langle \varphi_{\mathcal{L}_i}, \psi_{\mathcal{L}_i}\rangle\right) = \mathrm{CCFFOWG}(\mathcal{r}_{i1}, \mathcal{r}_{i2}, \ldots, \mathcal{r}_{ip}) \\
&= \left(\begin{array}{c} \langle \left[\begin{array}{c} \prod_{i=1}^{p}\left(\varphi^L_{\mathcal{L}_{\delta(ij)}}\right)^{\xi_i\sigma_i}, \\ \prod_{i=1}^{p}\left(\varphi^U_{\mathcal{L}_{\delta(ij)}}\right)^{\xi_i\sigma_i} \end{array}\right], \left[\begin{array}{c} \sqrt[3]{1-\prod_{i=1}^{p}\left(1-\left(\psi^L_{\mathcal{L}_{\delta(ij)}}\right)^3\right)^{\xi_i\sigma_i}}, \\ \sqrt[3]{1-\prod_{i=1}^{p}\left(1-\left(\psi^U_{\mathcal{L}_{\delta(ij)}}\right)^3\right)^{\xi_i\sigma_i}} \end{array}\right]\rangle, \\ \langle \sqrt[3]{1-\prod_{i=1}^{p}\left(1-\left(\varphi_{\mathcal{L}_{\delta(ij)}}\right)^3\right)^{\xi_i\sigma_i}}, \prod_{i=1}^{p}\left(\psi_{\mathcal{L}_{\delta(ij)}}\right)^{\xi_i\sigma_i}\rangle \end{array}\right).
\end{aligned}
\tag{32}
$$

Step 4. Compute the collected score values of each alternative as follows:

$$
sc(\mathcal{r}_i) = \frac{\left(\varphi^L_{\mathcal{L}_{ij}}\right)^3 + \left(\varphi^U_{\mathcal{L}_{ij}}\right)^3 - \left(\psi^L_{\mathcal{L}_{ij}}\right)^3 - \left(\psi^U_{\mathcal{L}_{ij}}\right)^3}{2} + \left(\psi^3_{\mathcal{L}_{ij}} - \varphi^3_{\mathcal{L}_{ij}}\right). \tag{33}
$$

If $sc(\mathcal{r}_{i_1}) = sc(\mathcal{r}_{i_2})$ for any two indices i_1 and i_2, then compute accuracy values as

$$
ac(\mathcal{r}_i) = \frac{\left(\varphi^L_{\mathcal{L}_{ij}}\right)^3 + \left(\varphi^U_{\mathcal{L}_{ij}}\right)^3 + \left(\psi^L_{\mathcal{L}_{ij}}\right)^3 + \left(\psi^U_{\mathcal{L}_{ij}}\right)^3}{2} + \left(\varphi^3_{\mathcal{L}_{ij}} + \psi^3_{\mathcal{L}_{ij}}\right). \tag{34}
$$

Step 5. By rating all of the alternatives in order of importance of the score values choose the best alternative.

4.1. Case Study

Inventory management is a major subject these days. From an industrial standpoint, a corporation cannot achieve targeted levels of manufacturing unless its inventory is adequately maintained. Therefore, appropriate inventory management is the first stage of the ladder of suitable levels of production. Any scarcity of raw materials in stock might cause a disruption of the entire manufacturing process, which would result in a significant loss for the industry. Suppose a food corporation wishes to monitor different inventory products. The corporation primarily manufactures four different types of food: drinks (X_1), palm oil (X_2), pickles (X_3), and sweets (X_4). Three factors namely cost price (C_1), storage facilities (C_2), and staleness level (C_3) must be taken into consideration while deciding whether to reorder ingredients for making these food products such that $\xi = (0.25, 0.35, 0.4)$ is the weight vector of these factors. The presented alternatives are examined under these three factors and their values are scored in terms of CFFNs. In each CFFN, the interval-valued FFNs (IVFFNs) indicate the current stock level in the inventory, and the FFNs represent the estimate of agreement and disagreement towards the present stock level for a coming week. Since the corporation does not sacrifice product quality, reducing staleness levels is given top attention. The main objective is then to determine the food products for which the ingredient stock must be reordered frequently. The following steps of the proposed approach were carried out for it.

Step 1. As described in Table 1, the desired data for each alternative is presented in CFFNs, and the collection evaluation is provided in a decision matrix.

Table 1. Assessment values of alternatives in terms of CFFNs with confidence levels.

Alternatives	C_1	C_2	C_3
X_1	$\left(\langle [0.55, 0.65], [0.15, 0.25] \rangle; 0.4 \; (0.45, 0.25)\right)$	$\left(\langle [0.25, 0.35], [0.45, 0.55] \rangle; 0.6 \; (0.35, 0.25)\right)$	$\left(\langle [0.45, 0.65], [0.25, 0.35] \rangle; 0.5 \; (0.25, 0.40)\right)$
X_2	$\left(\langle [0.25, 0.35], [0.45, 0.55] \rangle; 0.5 \; (0.45, 0.65)\right)$	$\left(\langle [0.20, 0.30], [0.35, 0.40] \rangle; 0.4 \; (0.25, 0.35)\right)$	$\left(\langle [0.25, 0.45], [0.15, 0.25] \rangle; 0.6 \; (0.45, 0.55)\right)$
X_3	$\left(\langle [0.55, 0.65], [0.25, 0.35] \rangle; 0.3 \; (0.25, 0.45)\right)$	$\left(\langle [0.45, 0.65], [0.30, 0.40] \rangle; 0.3 \; (0.35, 0.45)\right)$	$\left(\langle [0.55, 0.75], [0.15, 0.20] \rangle; 0.7 \; (0.35, 0.55)\right)$
X_4	$\left(\langle [0.35, 0.55], [0.15, 0.35] \rangle; 0.5 \; (0.15, 0.35)\right)$	$\left(\langle [0.45, 0.60], [0.20, 0.25] \rangle; 0.7 \; (0.35, 0.45)\right)$	$\left(\langle [0.45, 0.55], [0.25, 0.35] \rangle; 0.8 \; (0.50, 0.40)\right)$

Step 2. Using Equation (26), it is possible to derive a normalized decision matrix which is summarized in Table 2.

Table 2. Normalized decision matrix.

Alternatives	C_1	C_2	C_3
X_1	$\left(\langle [0.15, 0.25], [0.55, 0.65] \rangle; 0.4 \; (0.25, 0.45)\right)$	$\left(\langle [0.25, 0.35], [0.45, 0.55] \rangle; 0.6 \; (0.35, 0.25)\right)$	$\left(\langle [0.25, 0.35], [0.45, 0.65] \rangle; 0.5 \; (0.40, 0.25)\right)$
X_2	$\left(\langle [0.45, 0.55], [0.25, 0.35] \rangle; 0.5 \; (0.65, 0.45)\right)$	$\left(\langle [0.20, 0.30], [0.35, 0.40] \rangle; 0.4 \; (0.25, 0.35)\right)$	$\left(\langle [0.15, 0.25], [0.25, 0.45] \rangle; 0.6 \; (0.55, 0.45)\right)$
X_3	$\left(\langle [0.25, 0.35], [0.55, 0.65] \rangle; 0.3 \; (0.45, 0.25)\right)$	$\left(\langle [0.45, 0.65], [0.30, 0.40] \rangle; 0.3 \; (0.35, 0.45)\right)$	$\left(\langle [0.15, 0.20], [0.55, 0.75] \rangle; 0.7 \; (0.55, 0.35)\right)$
X_4	$\left(\langle [0.15, 0.35], [0.35, 0.55] \rangle; 0.5 \; (0.35, 0.15)\right)$	$\left(\langle [0.45, 0.60], [0.20, 0.25] \rangle; 0.7 \; (0.35, 0.45)\right)$	$\left(\langle [0.25, 0.35], [0.45, 0.55] \rangle; 0.8 \; (0.40, 0.50)\right)$

Step 3. Aggregate the values of Table 2 with the proposed operators:

(a) Using Equation (28) we get

$$\begin{aligned}
r_1 &= (\langle [0.1892, 0.2685], [0.6790, 0.7751] \rangle, (0.5814, 0.2514));\\
r_2 &= (\langle [0.2398, 0.3104], [0.5205, 0.6369] \rangle, (0.6761, 0.3425));\\
r_3 &= (\langle [0.2295, 0.3376], [0.5715, 0.7032] \rangle, (0.7135, 0.5335));\\
r_4 &= (\langle [0.3053, 0.4237], [0.4579, 0.5457] \rangle, (0.5058, 0.4008)).
\end{aligned}$$

(b) Using Equation (29) we get

$$\begin{aligned}
r_1 &= (\langle [0.1757, 0.2536], [0.6941, 0.7895] \rangle, (0.5603, 0.2904));\\
r_2 &= (\langle [0.2773, 0.3507], [0.5100, 0.6239] \rangle, (0.7056, 0.3493));\\
r_3 &= (\langle [0.2855, 0.4200], [0.5999, 0.6988] \rangle, (0.6441, 0.4218));\\
r_4 &= (\langle [0.2766, 0.3923], [0.5368, 0.6297] \rangle, (0.5933, 0.3195)).
\end{aligned}$$

(c) Using Equation (30) we get

$$\begin{aligned}
r_1 &= (\langle [0.4724, 0.5803], [0.4016, 0.5234] \rangle, (0.2971, 0.5310));\\
r_2 &= (\langle [0.4612, 0.5723], [0.2154, 0.3146] \rangle, (0.4333, 0.6352));\\
r_3 &= (\langle [0.4321, 0.5276], [0.2311, 0.3214] \rangle, (0.4523, 0.5876));\\
r_4 &= (\langle [0.5889, 0.6794], [0.4023, 0.3367] \rangle, (0.4429, 0.6054)).
\end{aligned}$$

(d) Using Equation (31) we get

$$\begin{aligned} r_1 &= (\langle[0.4686, 0.5661], [0.3820, 0.5012]\rangle, (0.2873, 0.5230)); \\ r_2 &= (\langle[0.4582, 0.5621], [0.2277, 0.3331]\rangle, (0.4352, 0.6450)); \\ r_3 &= (\langle[0.4872, 0.5629], [0.2746, 0.3829]\rangle, (0.3932, 0.7646)); \\ r_4 &= (\langle[0.4163, 0.5530], [0.3341, 0.4333]\rangle, (0.3323, 0.5197)). \end{aligned}$$

(e) Using Equation (32) we get

$$\begin{aligned} r_1 &= (\langle[0.3390, 0.4463], [0.4369, 0.5695]\rangle, (0.3109, 0.4437)); \\ r_2 &= (\langle[0.3665, 0.4768], [0.2426, 0.3644]\rangle, (0.5061, 0.5586)); \\ r_3 &= (\langle[0.3768, 0.4715], [0.3237, 0.4366]\rangle, (0.4268, 0.6303)); \\ r_4 &= (\langle[0.4092, 0.5759], [0.2921, 0.4118]\rangle, (0.3191, 0.4462)). \end{aligned}$$

Step 4. Compute the score values by using Equation (33); the results are listed in Table 3.

Table 3. Score values and ranking order of alternatives with different operators.

Operators	$sc(r_1)$	$sc(r_2)$	$sc(r_3)$	$sc(r_4)$	Ranking
CCFFWA	−0.5569	−0.4467	−0.4533	−0.1420	$X_4 \succ X_2 \succ X_3 \succ X_1$
CCFFOWA	−0.5538	−0.4202	−0.4221	−0.3376	$X_4 \succ X_2 \succ X_3 \succ X_1$
CCFFHA	0.1698	0.1971	0.2014	0.3423	$X_4 \succ X_2 \succ X_3 \succ X_1$
CCFFWG	0.1650	0.2948	0.1707	0.4732	$X_4 \succ X_2 \succ X_3 \succ X_1$
CCFFOWG	−0.0128	0.1932	0.0922	0.2387	$X_4 \succ X_2 \succ X_3 \succ X_1$

Step 5. Rankings of all the alternatives based on the score values and ordering are listed in the last column of Table 3. From this analysis, it is seen that X_4 is the best one among the others.

4.2. Validity Tests

To illustrate the feasibility of the proposed strategy in a multitude of environments, we used testing procedures defined by Wang and Trianaphyllou [31] as follows:

Test 1. If we replace the rating values of the non-optimal alternatives with those of a worse alternative, the best alternative should remain stable as long as the relative weighted criteria remain fixed.

Test 2. The procedure should be transitive.

Test 3. When a specific problem is separated into smaller ones while the same decision-making approach is used, the aggregated ranking of the alternatives should be equivalent to the original ranking.

Validity test using criterion 1

The ranking order of alternatives obtained by the proposed approach is $X_4 \succ X_2 \succ X_3 \succ X_1$. To test the corresponding nature of the proposed approach by test criterion 1, the non-optimal alternative X_1 was replaced with the worst alternative X_1^* where rating values of X_1^* were assumed to be $([\langle 0.1, 0.2], [0.6, 0.7], (0.2, 0.6)\rangle)$, $(\langle[0.2, 0.3], [0.5, 0.6], (0.3, 0.5)\rangle)$, and $(\langle[0.25, 0.35], [0.3, 0.4], (0.1, 0.5)\rangle)$. Following the observations, the presented approach was used, and the aggregated score values of the alternatives were $sc(X_1) = 0.1606$, $sc(X_1^*) = 0.0031$, $sc(X_3) = 0.3676$, and $sc(X_4) = 0.3646$. As a result, the ranking order was $X_4 \succ X_3 \succ X_1 \succ X_1^*$ with the best alternative remaining the same as in the proposed approach. Thus, the presented approach yielded consistent findings in term of test criterion 1.

Validity test using criteria 2 and 3

For testing validity according to criteria 2 and 3, the fragmented decision-making subcases are taking as $\{X_1, X_2, X_4\}$, $\{X_2, X_3, X_4\}$, and $\{X_2, X_3, X_1\}$. Then, using the described process, their rank order is as follows: $X_4 \succ X_2 \succ X_1$, $X_4 \succ X_2 \succ X_3$ and $X_2 \succ X_3 \succ X_1$, for criterion 2 and 3, respectively. When all of the results are combined, the overall ranking is $X_4 \succ X_2 \succ X_3 \succ X_1$ which is the same as the outcomes of the original decision-making approach. Hence, our proposed approach is valid under test criteria 2 and 3.

4.3. Comparative Analysis

In the literature, there are numerous types of fuzzy sets that are used for specific situations based on their properties. The fuzzy sets, intuitionistic fuzzy sets, Pythagorean fuzzy sets, and Fermatean fuzzy sets are some of the most popular sets of fuzzy set theory. Cubic Fermatean fuzzy sets with confidence levels are an innovative variation of the fuzzy set theory that we introduce in this study. Table 4 compares each of these fuzzy sets with respect to a number of attributes. Each of them has a graded membership value and the capacity to describe uncertainty across multiple attributes.

Table 4. Different type of fuzzy sets and their features.

Characteristics	Different Types of Fuzzy Sets					
	Fuzzy Set	IFS	PFS	FFS	CFFS	CFFSCL
Membership value	✓	✓	✓	✓	✓	✓
Describe ambiguity	MG	MG and NMG	MG and NMG	MG and NMG	MG and NMG	MG and NMG with confidence levels
Unknown parameters	×	×	×	×	×	✓
Ability of multi-attribute modeling	✓	✓	✓	✓	✓	✓
Modeling of increasing uncertainty	×	×	×	×	×	✓
Taking reluctance into account while making decisions	×	✓	×	✓	×	✓

Abbreviations: IFS: intuitionistic fuzzy set; PFS: Pythagorean fuzzy set; FFS: Fermatean fuzzy set; CFFS: Cubic Fermatean fuzzy set; CFFSCL: Cubic Fermatean fuzzy set with confidence levels; MG: membership grade; NMG: Non-membership grade.

4.4. Comparison with Some Existing Approaches

An evaluation was conducted to examine the performance of the new method compared to existing approaches [23,27,28,32] in the context of CPFSs and CIFSs. Sacrificing flexibility, we examined the situation by using the weight of decision-makers as $\xi = (0.25, 0.35, 40)$ which allows for the existing approaches to be used with the original dataset. The results obtained with different methods are summarized in Table 5 and we conclude that the ranking order of the given alternatives is $X_4 \succ X_2 \succ X_3 \succ X_1$, hence the best alternative is X_4 which coincides with the proposed approach results given in Table 3, which validates the stability of our approach. Furthermore, the structure of the relative score values follows the same pattern, demonstrating that the presented approach is conservative in nature.

Table 5. Comparison with existing studies.

Existing Approaches	$sc(X_1)$	$sc(X_2)$	$sc(X_3)$	$sc(X_4)$	Ranking Order
Garg and Kaur [32]	−0.6294	−0.4567	−0.5321	−0.2310	$X_4 \succ X_2 \succ X_3 \succ X_1$
Amin et al. [27]	−0.7312	−0.5438	−0.4877	−0.3421	$X_4 \succ X_2 \succ X_3 \succ X_1$
Rahim et al. [28]	−0.3643	−0.3241	−0.3575	−0.2783	$X_4 \succ X_2 \succ X_3 \succ X_1$
Kaur and Garg [23]	−0.5666	−0.4763	−0.5198	−0.3417	$X_4 \succ X_2 \succ X_3 \succ X_1$

According to the comparative study described above, the presented strategy for handling decision-making problems has significant improvements over existing ones.

(1) Cubic Fermatean fuzzy sets are a new development in fuzzy set theory, which can handle the uncertainty more accurately in real situations. Therefore, the proposed approach is more suitable than existing approaches to solve real-life and engineering decision problems.
(2) Furthermore, Table 4 demonstrates that the findings calculated using the different available methods are performed without taking the confidence levels of the attributes into account throughout the analysis. In other words, all of these techniques examined their theories on the premise that decision-makers are completely confident in the analyzed objects. However, in practice these sorts of prerequisites are only partially met.
(3) The existing aggregation operators are a special case of the presented operators. As a result, we conclude that the presented aggregation operators are more general in nature and more appropriate to solve real-world issues than the existing ones.

5. Conclusions

The main purpose of this research was to modify the existing operational laws of cubic Fermatean fuzzy sets, and propose a number of aggregation operators by taking into account the degree of confidence levels of each decision-maker during evaluation. Previously, all decision-makers were considered to express their opinions of numerous alternatives with a same level of certainty. However, this issue has been solved in the current article by factoring in the decision- maker's confidence levels. We introduced a number of aggregating operators under the cubic Fermatean fuzzy framework, including CCFFWA, CCFFOWA, CCFFWG, and CCFFHA, by taking confidence levels into account. A few significant traits of each were also described. Additionally, the standard cubic Fermatean fuzzy weighted averaging and cubic Fermatean fuzzy weighted geometric operators were transformed into the provided aggregation operators when $\sigma = 1$ for all preferences. A comparison with several existing operators was performed to show that the provided operators offer a reducible approach to the MCDM problem.

Future research may further develop the outlined technique to support a wider range of applications and address a variety of uncertain programming difficulties, such as K-mean clustering [33] and fuzzy controllers [34,35]. The application will also be expanded to include neural networks and convolutional networks [36–39].

Author Contributions: Conceptualization, H.G., M.R., F.A. and S.J.; Methodology, H.G., M.R. and F.A.; Software, H.G.; Formal analysis, H.G., M.R., F.A. and I.M.H.; Investigation, S.J.; Writing—original draft, H.G., M.R. and F.A.; Writing—review & editing, H.G.; Visualization, S.J. and I.M.H.; Funding acquisition, H.G. All authors have read and agreed to the published version of the manuscript.

Funding: This paper was supported by the Researchers Supporting Project (project number RSP2023R389), King Saud University, Riyadh, Saudi Arabia.

Institutional Review Board Statement: This article does not contain any studies with human participants or animals performed by any of the authors.

Data Availability Statement: Data sharing is not applicable to this article as no datasets were generated or analyzed during the current study.

Acknowledgments: This paper was supported by the Researchers Supporting Project (project number RSP2023R389), King Saud University, Riyadh, Saudi Arabia.

Conflicts of Interest: The authors declare that they have no conflict of interest.

References

1. Atanassov, K.T. Intuitionistic fuzzy sets. *Fuzzy Sets Syst.* **1986**, *20*, 87–96. [CrossRef]
2. Yager, R.R. Heavy OWA operators. *Fuzzy Optim. Decis. Mak.* **2002**, *1*, 379–397. [CrossRef]
3. Yager, R.R. On ordered weighted averaging aggregation operators in multicriteria decisionmaking. *IEEE Trans. Syst. Man Cybern.* **1988**, *18*, 183–190. [CrossRef]
4. Xu, Z.; Yager, R.R. Some geometric aggregation operators based on intuitionistic fuzzy sets. *Int. J. Gen. Syst.* **2006**, *35*, 417–433. [CrossRef]
5. ZXu, Z. Intuitionistic Fuzzy Aggregation Operators. *IEEE Trans. Fuzzy Syst.* **2007**, *15*, 1179–1187.
6. Wang, W.; Liu, X. Intuitionistic fuzzy geometric aggregation operators based on einstein operations. *Int. J. Intell. Syst.* **2011**, *26*, 1049–1075. [CrossRef]
7. Lai, X.; Yang, B.; Ma, B.; Liu, M.; Yin, Z.; Yin, L.; Zheng, W. An Improved Stereo Matching Algorithm Based on Joint Similarity Measure and Adaptive Weights. *Appl. Sci.* **2022**, *13*, 514. [CrossRef]
8. Ye, J. Multicriteria fuzzy decision-making method based on a novel accuracy function under interval-valued intuitionistic fuzzy environment. *Expert Syst. Appl.* **2009**, *36*, 6899–6902. [CrossRef]
9. Garg, H. Some series of intuitionistic fuzzy interactive averaging aggregation operators. *SpringerPlus* **2016**, *5*, 999. [CrossRef]
10. Garg, H. Generalized intuitionistic fuzzy multiplicative interactive geometric operators and their application to multiple criteria decision making. *Int. J. Mach. Learn. Cybern.* **2015**, *7*, 1075–1092. [CrossRef]
11. Garg, H. Generalized intuitionistic fuzzy interactive geometric interaction operators using Einstein t-norm and t-conorm and their application to decision making. *Comput. Ind. Eng.* **2016**, *101*, 53–69. [CrossRef]
12. Xu, Y.; Wang, H.; Merigó, J.M. Intuitionistic fuzzy einstein choquet integral operators for multiple attribute decision making. *Technol. Econ. Dev. Econ.* **2014**, *20*, 227–253. [CrossRef]
13. Yager, R.R. Pythagorean fuzzy subsets. In Proceedings of the 2013 Joint IFSA World Congress and NAFIPS Annual Meeting (IFSA/NAFIPS), Edmonton, AB, Canada, 24–28 June 2013; pp. 57–61.
14. Yager, R.R. Properties and applications of Pythagorean fuzzy sets. In *Imprecision and Uncertainty in Information Representation and Processing*; Springer: Berlin/Heidelberg, Germany, 2016; pp. 119–136.
15. Yager, R.R.; Abbasov, A.M. Pythagorean membership grades, complex numbers, and decision making. *Int. J. Intell. Syst.* **2013**, *28*, 436–452. [CrossRef]
16. Zhang, X.; Xu, Z. Extension of TOPSIS to Multiple Criteria Decision Making with Pythagorean Fuzzy Sets. *Int. J. Intell. Syst.* **2014**, *29*, 1061–1078. [CrossRef]
17. Peng, X.; Yang, Y. Pythagorean Fuzzy Choquet Integral Based MABAC Method for Multiple Attribute Group Decision Making. *Int. J. Intell. Syst.* **2016**, *31*, 989–1020. [CrossRef]
18. Gao, X.; Deng, Y. Generating method of Pythagorean fuzzy sets from the negation of probability. *Eng. Appl. Artif. Intell.* **2021**, *105*, 104403. [CrossRef]
19. Zhang, X. Multicriteria Pythagorean fuzzy decision analysis: A hierarchical QUALIFLEX approach with the closeness index-based ranking methods. *Inf. Sci.* **2016**, *330*, 104–124. [CrossRef]
20. Peng, X.; Yang, Y. Fundamental Properties of Interval-Valued Pythagorean Fuzzy Aggregation Operators. *Int. J. Intell. Syst.* **2015**, *31*, 444–487. [CrossRef]
21. Senapati, T.; Yager, R.R. Fermatean fuzzy sets. *J. Ambient. Intell. Humaniz. Comput.* **2020**, *11*, 663–674. [CrossRef]
22. Senapati, T.; Yager, R.R. Fermatean fuzzy weighted averaging/geometric operators and its application in multi-criteria decision-making methods. *Eng. Appl. Artif. Intell.* **2019**, *85*, 112–121. [CrossRef]
23. Kaur, G.; Garg, H. Generalized cubic intuitionistic fuzzy aggregation operators using t-norm operations and their applications to group decision-making process. *Arab. J. Sci. Eng.* **2019**, *44*, 2775–2794. [CrossRef]
24. Khan, F.; Khan, M.S.A.; Shahzad, M.; Abdullah, S. Pythagorean cubic fuzzy aggregation operators and their application to multi-criteria decision making problems. *J. Intell. Fuzzy Syst.* **2019**, *36*, 595–607. [CrossRef]
25. Khan, F.; Abdullah, S.; Mahmood, T.; Shakeel, M.; Rahim, M.; Amin, N.U. Pythagorean cubic fuzzy aggregation information based on confidence levels and its application to multi-criteria decision making process. *J. Intell. Fuzzy Syst.* **2019**, *36*, 5669–5683. [CrossRef]
26. Abbas, S.Z.; Khan, M.S.A.; Abdullah, S.; Sun, H.; Hussain, F. Cubic Pythagorean fuzzy sets and their application to multi-attribute decision making with unknown weight information. *J. Intell. Fuzzy Syst.* **2019**, *37*, 1529–1544. [CrossRef]
27. Amin, F.; Rahim, M.; Ali, A.; Ameer, E. Generalized Cubic Pythagorean Fuzzy Aggregation Operators and their Application to Multi-attribute Decision-Making Problems. *Int. J. Comput. Intell. Syst.* **2022**, *15*, 92. [CrossRef]

28. Rahim, M.; Amin, F.; Ali, A.; Shah, K. An Extension of Bonferroni Mean under Cubic Pythagorean Fuzzy Environment and Its Applications in Selection-Based Problems. *Math. Probl. Eng.* **2022**, *2022*, 9735100. [CrossRef]
29. Rong, Y.; Yu, L.; Niu, W.; Liu, Y.; Senapati, T.; Mishra, A.R. MARCOS approach based upon cubic Fermatean fuzzy set and its application in evaluation and selecting cold chain logistics distribution center. *Eng. Appl. Artif. Intell.* **2022**, *116*, 105401. [CrossRef]
30. Jeevaraj, S. Ordering of interval-valued Fermatean fuzzy sets and its applications. *Expert Syst. Appl.* **2021**, *185*, 115613.
31. Wang, X.; Triantaphyllou, E. Ranking irregularities when evaluating alternatives by using some ELECTRE methods. *Omega* **2008**, *36*, 45–63. [CrossRef]
32. Garg, H.; Kaur, G. Cubic Intuitionistic Fuzzy Sets and its Fundamental Properties. *J. Mult.-Valued Log. Soft Comput.* **2019**, *33*, 507–537.
33. Talib, R. How we can use Energy Efficiency built upon the method of K-means clustering to extend the lifetime of WSN. *Al-Salam J. Eng. Technol.* **2022**, *2*, 40–45. [CrossRef]
34. Wang, S.; Sun, Y.; Yang, C.; Yu, Y. Advanced design and tests of a new electrical control seeding system with genetic algorithm fuzzy control strategy. *J. Comput. Methods Sci. Eng.* **2021**, *21*, 703–712. [CrossRef]
35. Mercorelli, P. Using Fuzzy PD Controllers for Soft Motions in a Car-like Robot. *Adv. Sci. Technol. Eng. Syst. J.* **2018**, *3*, 380–390. [CrossRef]
36. Qin, X.; Liu, Z.; Liu, Y.; Liu, S.; Yang, B.; Yin, L.; Liu, M.; Zheng, W. User OCEAN Personality Model Construction Method Using a BP Neural Network. *Electronics* **2022**, *11*, 3022. [CrossRef]
37. Yi, Y.; Wang, J.; Ding, X.; Li, C. A convolutional neural network model of multi-scale feature fusion: MFF-Net. *J. Comput. Methods Sci. Eng.* **2022**, *22*, 2217–2225. [CrossRef]
38. Alajanbi, M.; Malerba, D.; Liu, H. Distributed Reduced Convolution Neural Networks. *Mesop. J. Big Data* **2021**, *2021*, 26–29. [CrossRef]
39. Nentwig, M.; Mercorelli, P. Inversion of Fuzzy Neural Networks for the Reduction of Noise in the Control Loop. *IFAC Proc. Vol.* **2008**, *41*, 157–162. [CrossRef]

symmetry

MDPI

Article

Novel Complex Pythagorean Fuzzy Sets under Aczel–Alsina Operators and Their Application in Multi-Attribute Decision Making

Huanhuan Jin [1,*], Abrar Hussain [2], Kifayat Ullah [2,*] and Aqib Javed [2]

1 Department of Statistics, Zhejiang University City College, Hangzhou 310015, China
2 Department of Mathematics, Riphah International University Lahore, Lahore 5400, Pakistan
* Correspondence: jinhh1988@mail.zjgsu.edu.cn (H.J.); Kifayat.khan.dr@gmail.com (K.U.)

Abstract: Aggregation operators (AOs) are utilized to overcome the influence of uncertain and vague information in different fuzzy environments. A multi-attribute decision-making (MADM) technique plays a vital role in several fields of different environments such as networking analysis, risk assessment, cognitive science, recommender systems, signal processing, and many more domains in ambiguous circumstances. In this article, we elaborated the notion of Aczel–Alsina t-norm (TNM) and t-conorm (TCNM) under the system of complex Pythagorean fuzzy (CPyF) sets (CPyFSs). Some basic operational laws of Aczel–Alsina TNM and TCNM are established including Aczel–Alsina sum, product, scalar multiplication, and power operations based on CPyFSs. We established several AOs of CPyFSs such as CPyF Aczel–Alsina weighted average (CPyFAAWA), and CPyF Aczel–Alsina weighted geometric (CPyFAAWG) operators. The proposed CPyFAAWA and CPyFAAWG operators are symmetric in nature and satisfy the properties of idempotency, monotonicity, boundedness and commutativity. To solve an MADM technique, we established an illustrative example to select a suitable candidate for a vacant post in a multinational company. To see the advantages of our proposed AOs, we compared the results of existing AOs with the results of newly established AOs.

Keywords: complex pythagorean fuzzy values; aggregation operators; Aczel–Alsina t-norm; multi-attribute decision-making method

1. Introduction

The purpose of the MADM technique is to categorize and deal with problems using a variety of different criteria. The MADM methodology has become increasingly popular among decision-makers as a consequence of its numerous applications in a variety of disciplines, including operation research, engineering technology management science, etc., through collecting the information into a single useful form, AOs are essential in helping to address all MADM issues. The decision-makers in real decision making categorize the alternatives using a variety of evaluation techniques, such as interval numbers or crisp numbers. Due to the growing uncertainty involved and the ambiguities of data, it has become more challenging for decision makers to solve decision-making problems using precise numerical values. Zadeh [1] introduced the novel idea of the fuzzy set (FS) in 1965, by launching the membership value (MV), whose range lies between 0 and 1, to address this issue. In order to tackle decision-making problems involving uncertainties and ambiguities in the data more precisely than a crisp set, Zadeh's creation of the FS gives decision making a plate form. To overcome the decision-making difficulties, Atanassov [2] enlarged the concepts of FS in the form of intuitionistic FS (IFS) in which the sum of the MV and the non-membership value (NMV) lies on interval $[0,1]$. i.e., $0 \leq \Pi + \Xi \leq 1$, where $\Pi \in [0,1]$ represents MV and $\Xi \in [0,1]$ represents NMV in an IFSs. In some scenarios, when IFSs failed to deal with uncertain and vague information in fuzzy system, Yager [3] provided an innovative idea of IFS in the form of Pythagorean FS (PyFS) in such a way that the sum of the square of MV and NMV lies on interval $[0,1]$, i.e., $0 \leq \Pi^2 + \Xi^2 \leq 1$. Several researchers have plenty of commentary the above-discussed fuzzy environment. Adlassnig [4] generalized the theory of FSs to formalize the uncertain information under the system of medical diagnosis. Atanassov [5] also explored concepts of IFS in the framework of interval-valued IFS (IVIFS) with upper and lower cases of MV and NMV of an IVIFS. Mohd and Abdullah [6] proposed a study of several similarity measured distances based on PyFSs.

It has been determined that the MCDM concerns were resolved, as the above current research in FS, IFS, and extended sets, such as PyFSs settings, are only capable of handling the vagueness and ambiguity of the data. All of these models are unable to address the lack of historical knowledge and data sensitivity. However, a complex data collection can handle both the periodicity and the uncertainty of the data at the same time. To deal with these circumstances, Ramot et al. [7,8] proposed the idea of a complex fuzzy set (CFS). They suggested that $\Pi e^{i\alpha_\Pi}$, whose range is expanded from unit disc to a complex plane, where $\Pi \in [0,\ 1]$ represents the MV of an amplitude term of a CFS and $\alpha_\Pi \in [0,\ 2\pi]$ represents MV of phase terms of a CFS. Alkouri and Salleh [9] extended the theory of CFSs in the form of complex IFS (CIFS), having two aspects of MV and NMV in such a way that $\left(\Pi e^{i\alpha}, \Xi e^{\pi i\beta}\right)$, $i = \sqrt{-1}$. A CIFS satisfied the conditions $0 \leq \Pi + \Xi \leq 1$ and $0 \leq \alpha + \beta \leq 2\pi$, where $\Pi \in [0,1]$ and $\Xi \in [0,1]$ represent the MV and NMV of amplitude terms, respectively. In the same way, $\alpha \in [0,2\pi]$ and $\beta \in [0,2\pi]$ represents the MV and NMV of phase terms, respectively. Ullah et al. [10] developed an innovative concept of CIFS in the framework of complex PyFS (CPyFSs), and relaxed the condition of CIFS with the square of amplitude and phase terms of MV and NMV, respectively. Riaz and Hashmi [11] provided a new extension of FSs in the form of linear Diophantine FS to handle vagueness and uncertainty in the fuzzy system. Akram and Naz [12] introduced an innovative idea of PyFS in the framework of CPyFS to cope with uncertain information under an MADM approach. Khan et al. [13] utilized the theory of complex T-SFSs to provide some new averaging and geometric operators based on power aggregation tools. Ali et al. [14] explored the idea of complex q-ROFS and developed some new AOs to solve real life problem using an MADM technique. Mahmood [15] worked on a bipolar soft set to cope with uncertain and ambiguous information. We also studied some basic notions of the fuzzy environment related to our research work, which are not discussed in the above paragraphs, seen in [15–18].

AOs are essential tools to cope with uncertain and vague information in different fuzzy environments. Several researchers worked on a distinct model of classical set theory and fuzzy systems. We studied some AOs developed by Xu [19] in the form of weighted averaging operators and some special cases based on IFSs. Wei [20] invented some AOs in the form of induced weighted geometric operators, and ordered weighted geometric operators and hybrid weighted geometric operators. Peng and Yuan [21] explored some inequalities and invented some AOs of PyF value (PyFV) in the form of generalized weighted averaging operators. Akram et al. [22] explored the idea of interval valued T-FSs based on a Bonferroni mean operator, and established an MADM technique under the solar system. Khan et al. [23] extended the concepts of spherical FSs (SFSs) and introduced some new AOs of SFSs based on Dombi aggregation tools. Rahman et al. [24] presented a list of new AOs of PyFSs-like weighted averaging, and weighted geometric operators with some basic deserved characteristics. Mahmood et al. [25] presented some new AOs, an innovative concept of PyFS in the form of complex PyFS (CPyFS), to overcome the influence of vague and ambiguous information under the CPyFS system. Liu et al. [26] explored the concepts of IFS to deal with vague information, and also developed a list of new AOs by utilizing the concepts of Maclaurin symmetric mean operators. Ullah [27] utilized the concepts of Maclaurin symmetric mean operators and developed a list of new AOs based on picture FS (PFS). Akram et al. [28] provided some new AOs of PyFS and also studied an MADM technique to complete a selection process for the textile industry. Chen [29] developed new approaches by utilizing the innovative concept of prioritized AOs based on IVIFS.

Liu and Wang [30] presented a list of new AOs by using the concepts of Archimedean Bonferroni tools under the system of q-rung orthopair FS (q-ROFS) to solve a real-life problems based on MADM techniques. Hussain et al. [31] explored a list of new AOs and gave an illustrative example to solve an MADM problem for the selection of suitable tourism destinations. Garg [32] developed a series of new AOs with entropy weight vectors based on IF information. Akram and Shahzadi [33] worked on a new concept of Yager AOs and gave an MADM technique under the system of q-ROFS. Jan et al. [34] introduced some new AOs under the system of linguistic cubic information to solve an MADM technique. Yang et al. [35] explored an innovative idea of the TOPSIS method and developed some new aggregation tools of Fermatean fuzzy integrated weighted distance to process fuzzy information. Mahmood [18] modified traditional Maclaurin symmetric mean operators and developed a list of new AOs in the environment of a bipolar complex fuzzy system. Ullah et al. [36] utilized the concepts of T-spherical FSs (T-SFSs) and provided some AOs of T-SFSs to solve an MADM problem.

Menger [37] introduced a new concept of triangular norms based on probabilistic metric space in 1942. Klement [38] presented some new aggregated tools by utilizing the theory of t-norm (TNM) and t-conorm (TCNM) in different fuzzy information. To aggregate the information in numerous mathematical structures, a series of triangular norms were constructed. Information aggregation is critical for solving various MADM issues. Many different types of TN and TCN have been applied to the increase in the average and geometric aggregation process. The invented TNMs and TCNMs are the Lukasiewicz TNM and TCNM [39], drastic TNM and TCNM [40], nilpotent TNM and TCNM [41], Frank TNM and TCNM [42], Archimedean TNM and TCNM [43], Einstein TNM and TCNM [44], probabilistic TNM and TCNM [45] and Dombi TNM and TCNM [46]. Recently Mahmood et al. [47] proposed a new idea to cope with unpredictable and vague information by developing a list of AOs based on the Frank TNM and TCNM under a system of interval-valued picture FSs. Liu [48] explored the theory of algebraic and Einstein AOs in the form of Hamacher AOs based on IVIF information. Garg [49] generated the concepts of PyFSs and developed some new approaches to geometric AOs by utilizing the operations of the Einstein TNM and TCNM in the environment of PyFSs. Liu and Wang [30] proposed a list of new AOs by using the fundamental operations of Archimedean Bonferroni operators under the system of q-ROFSs with an MADM technique. We also studied existing research work seen in the references [50,51].

Aczel and Alsina [52] discovered some more reliable and flexible TNMs and TCNMs like the Aczel–Alsina TNM (AA-TNM) and the Aczel–Alsina TCNM (AA-TCNM) in 1982. We can overcome the impact of unreasonable and unpredictable information in different fuzzy environments. Babu and Ahmed [53] worked on several TNMs and TCNMs to classify the best TNM and TCNM from a family of TNMs and TCNMs. After evaluation, they found that AA-TNM and AA-TCNM are more suitable aggregation tools than other ones. To see the advantages and benefits of AA-TNM and AA-TCNM, several researchers utilized these aggregation tools in their research works. Recently, Senapati et al. [54] explored the concepts of AA-TNM and AA-TCNM and established an illustrative example to solve an MAMD technique under the system of IFSs. Senapati et al. [55] also generalized the theory of AA-TNM and AA-TCNM and gave a list of new AOs based on IVIFSs. Naeem et al. [56] enlarged the concepts of AA-TNM and AA-TCNM with more extensive information in the framework of picture FSs (PFSs). Hussain et al. [57] enlarged the concepts of T-SFSs and developed some new AOs using the basic operations of AA-TNM and AA-TCNM. All of the aforementioned invented AOs to handle two tuple information; there is a chance of losing information during the aggregation process, whereby a decision maker cannot obtain original results for the decision's purpose. A CPyFS contains more information than FSs, IFSs and PyFSs. Keeping in mind the significance of CPyFSs, we developed some innovative concepts of AA-TNM and AA-TCNM within the framework of CPyFSs. The main contributions of this article are in the following forms:

(1) We presented some new AOs and fundamental operational laws of CPyFSs. We also generalized the basic idea of Aczel–Alsina TNM and TCNM, with their operational laws and illustrative examples.
(2) By using the operational laws of Aczel–Alsina TNM and TCNM, we developed a list of new AOs like the CPyFAAWA operator and verified invented AOs with some deserved properties.
(3) Furthermore, we also established the CPyFAAWAG operator based on the defined fundamental operational laws of Aczel–Alsina TNM and TCNM.
(4) To find the feasibility and reliability of our invented methodologies, we explored some special cases, like CPyFAA ordered weighted (CPyFAAWAG), average (CPyFAAWAG) and CPyFAAOW geometric (CPyFAAOWG) operators, CPyFAA hybrid weighted (CPyFAAHW), average (CPyFAAHWA) and CPyFAAHW geometric (CPyFAAOWG) operators with some basic properties.
(5) By utilizing our invented approaches, we solved an MADM technique. We established an illustrative example to select a suitable candidate for a vacant post at a multinational company.
(6) To analyse the effectiveness of different parametric values of Υ on the results of our proposed approaches, we discussed an influence study.
(7) We checked the reliability and flexibility of our invented approaches, by comparing the results of existing AOs with the results of our discussed technique.

The structure of this manuscript is presented as follows and also displayed in the Figure 1: in Section 1, we thoroughly overviewed all previous history of our research work; in Section 2, we recall the notions of CFSs, CPyFSs and fundamental operations of CPyFSs. In Section 3, we studied the concepts of some existing AOs under the different environments of fuzzy systems. In Section 4, we introduced innovative concepts of Aczel–Alsina operations under the system of CPyF information. In Section 5, we developed several AOs of CPyFAAWA operators, and some special cases are also present here. In Section 6, we enlarged the idea of CPyFSs and introduced some AOs in the form of CPyFAAWG operators with some deserved characteristics. In Section 7, we solved an MADM technique to find the reliability and flexibility of our invented AOs, and we gave an illustrative example to select a suitable candidate for a multinational company. In Section 8, we studied the advantages and verified our invented AOs by comparing the results of existing AOs with the results of our invented AOs. In Section 9, we summarized the whole article in a single paragraph.

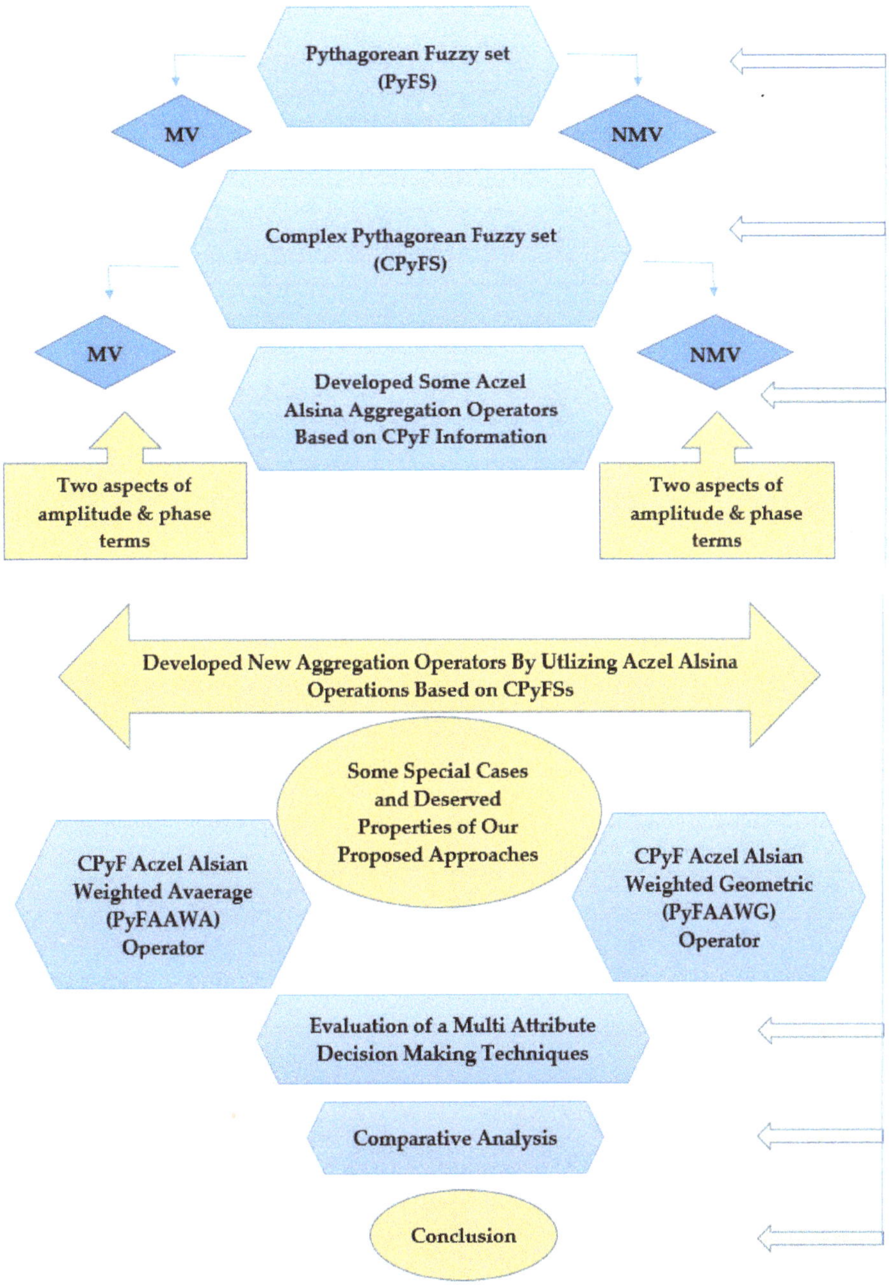

Figure 1. Flow chart of this article.

2. Preliminaries

We recall the notions of CFS and CPyFSs, and also discussed some basic operations of CPyFSs. Further, we studied the notion of score and accuracy function to compare CPyF values (CPyFVs).

Definition 1 ([7]). *Consider* $\grave{\text{W}}$ *to be a non-empty set, and a CFS* Λ *is defined as:*

$$\Lambda = \left\{ \left(x,\ \Pi_\Lambda(\varkappa) e^{2\pi i(\alpha_\Lambda(\varkappa))} \right) : x \in \grave{\text{W}} \right\},\ i = \sqrt{-1}$$

where $\Pi_\Lambda(\varkappa) \in [0,\ 1]$ *and* $\alpha_\Lambda(\varkappa) \in [0,\ 1]$ *represents the membership value (MV) of amplitude terms and phase terms of* Λ*, respectively. A CFS must satisfy the condition:*

$$0 \leq \Pi_\Lambda(\varkappa) \leq 1 \text{ and } 0 \leq \alpha_\Lambda(\varkappa) \leq 1.$$

In the following Table 1, we define the symbols and their meanings.

Table 1. Symbols and their meanings.

Symbol	Meaning	Symbol	Meaning
$\grave{\text{W}}$	Non-empty set	$R^{\breve{}}$	Score function
Π	MV of amplitude term	$A^{\breve{}}$	Accuracy function
α	MV of phase term	Ω	CPyFV
Ξ	NMV of amplitude term	$\mathfrak{D}$	Weight vector
β	NMV of phase term	Ŧ	TNM
ψ	Alternative	Ṩ	TCNM
ʊ	Attribute	$\mathcal{R}$	Decision matrix

Definition 2 ([9]). *A CPyFS* Λ *on a* $\grave{\text{W}}$ *is defined as:*

$$\Lambda = \left\{ \Pi_\Lambda(\varkappa) e^{2\pi i(\alpha_\Lambda(\varkappa))}, \Xi_\Lambda(\varkappa) e^{2\pi i(\beta_\Lambda(\varkappa))} : x\ \grave{\text{W}} \right\},\ i = \sqrt{-1}$$

where $\Pi_\Lambda(\varkappa) \in [0,\ 1]$ *and* $\alpha_\Lambda(\varkappa) \in [0,\ 1]$ *represents amplitude terms and phase terms of MV, respectively. Similarly* $\Xi_\Lambda(\varkappa) \in [0,\ 1]$ *and* $\beta_\Lambda(\varkappa) \in [0,\ 1]$ *represents amplitude and phase terms of NMV, respectively. A CPyFS must satisfy these conditions:*

$$0 \leq \Pi^2_\Lambda(x) + \Xi^2_\Lambda(\varkappa) \leq 1 \text{ and } 0 \leq (\alpha_\Lambda(\varkappa))^2 + (\beta_\Lambda(\varkappa))^2 \leq 1$$

For the sake of convenience, the pair $\Lambda = \left(\Pi(\varkappa) e^{2\pi i(\alpha(\varkappa))}, \Xi(\varkappa) e^{2\pi i(\beta(\varkappa))} \right)$ *is known as CPyFV.*

Definition 3 ([31]). *Let* $\Omega = \left(\Pi(\varkappa) e^{2\pi i(\alpha(\varkappa))}, \Xi(\varkappa) e^{2\pi i(\beta(\varkappa))} \right)$ *be a CPyFV; then, the score function* $R^{\breve{}}(\Omega)$ *of CPyFVs is given as:*

$$R^{\breve{}}(\Omega) = \frac{(\Pi(\varkappa))^2 - (\Xi(\varkappa))^2 + (\alpha(\varkappa))^2 - (\beta(\varkappa))^2}{2} \tag{1}$$

and the accuracy function is given as:

$$A^{\breve{}}(\Omega) = \frac{(\Pi(\varkappa))^2 + (\Xi(\varkappa))^2 + (\alpha(\varkappa))^2 + (\beta(\varkappa))^2}{2} \tag{2}$$

where $R^{\breve{}}\ (\Omega) \in [-1,\ 1]$ *and* $A^{\breve{}}\ (\Omega) \in [0,\ 1]$.

Definition 4 ([33]). *Let* $\Omega_1 = \left(\Pi_1(\varkappa) e^{2\pi i(\alpha_1(\varkappa))}, \Xi_1(\varkappa) e^{2\pi i(\beta_1(\varkappa))} \right)$ *and* $\Omega_2 = \left(\Pi_2(\varkappa) e^{2\pi i(\alpha_2(\varkappa))}, \Xi_2(\varkappa) e^{2\pi i(\beta_2(\varkappa))} \right)$ *be two CPyFVs. Then*

i. *If* $R^{\breve{}}(\Omega_1) < R^{\breve{}}(\Omega_2)$*, then* $\Omega_1 < \Omega_2$*,*
ii. *If* $R^{\breve{}}(\Omega_1) = R^{\breve{}}(\Omega_2)$*, then we need to find out the accuracy function:*

i. *If* $\breve{A}(\Omega_1) < \breve{A}(\Omega_2)$, *then* $\Omega_1 < \Omega_2$,
ii. *If* $\breve{A}(\Omega_1) = \breve{A}(\Omega_2)$, *then* $\Omega_1 = \Omega_2$.

Definition 5 ([32]). *Let* $\Omega_1 = \left(\Pi_1(\varkappa)e^{2\pi i(\alpha_1(\varkappa))}, \Xi_1(\varkappa)e^{2\pi i(\beta_1(\varkappa))}\right)$ *and* $\Omega_2 = \left(\Pi_2(\varkappa)e^{2\pi i(\alpha_2(\varkappa))}, \Xi_2(\varkappa)e^{2\pi i(\beta_2(\varkappa))}\right)$ *be two CPyFVs. Then*

i. $\Omega_1 \subseteq \Omega_2$ *if* $\Pi_1 \leq \Pi_2,\ \alpha_1 \leq \alpha_2,\ \Xi_1 \geq \Xi_2$ *and* $\beta_1 \geq \beta_2$.
ii. $\Omega_1 \subseteq \Omega_2$ *if* $\Pi_1 = \Pi_2,\ \alpha_1 = \alpha_2,\ \Xi_1 = \Xi_2$ *and* $\beta_1 = \beta_2$.
iii. $\Omega_1^c = \left(\Xi_1(\varkappa)e^{2\pi i(\beta_1(\varkappa))}, \Pi_1(\varkappa)e^{2\pi i(\alpha_1(\varkappa))}\right)$.

3. Existing Aggregation Operators

In this part, we recall the existing concepts of Aczel–Alsina AOs under the system of IFS and PyFs.

Definition 6 ([55]). *Let* $\Omega_{\mathfrak{z}} = \left(\Pi_{\Omega_{\mathfrak{z}}}(\varkappa), \Xi_{\Omega_{\mathfrak{z}}}(\varkappa)\right)$, $\mathfrak{z} = 1,2,\ldots,\mathfrak{n}$ *be a collection of IF numbers, with weight vector* $\mathfrak{D}_{\mathfrak{z}} = (\mathfrak{D}_1, \mathfrak{D}_2, \mathfrak{D}_3, \ldots, \mathfrak{D}_n)^T$ *of* $\Omega_{\mathfrak{z}}\left(\mathfrak{z} = 1,2,3,\ldots\mathfrak{n}\right)$, *such that* $\mathfrak{D}_{\mathfrak{z}} \in [0,1]$, $\mathfrak{z} = 1,2,\ldots,\mathfrak{n}$ *and* $\sum_{\mathfrak{z}=1}^{\mathfrak{n}} \mathfrak{D}_{\mathfrak{z}} = 1$. *Then, the IF Aczel–Alsina weighted averaging operator is given as:*

$$IFAAWA\left(\Omega_1, \Omega_2, \ldots, \Omega_{\mathfrak{z}}\right) = \overset{\mathfrak{n}}{\underset{\mathfrak{z}=1}{\oplus}}\left(\mathfrak{D}_{\mathfrak{z}}\Omega\right) = 1 - e^{-\left(\sum_{\mathfrak{z}=1}^{\mathfrak{n}} \mathfrak{D}_{\mathfrak{z}}(-ln(1-\Pi_{\Omega}))^{\Upsilon}\right)^{\frac{1}{\Upsilon}}}, e^{-\left(\sum_{\mathfrak{z}=1}^{\mathfrak{n}} \mathfrak{D}_{\mathfrak{z}}(-ln(\Xi_{\Omega}))^{\Upsilon}\right)^{\frac{1}{\Upsilon}}}$$

Definition 7 ([58]). *Let* $\Omega_{\mathfrak{z}} = \left(\Pi_{\Omega_{\mathfrak{z}}}(\varkappa), \Xi_{\Omega_{\mathfrak{z}}}(\varkappa)\right)$, $\mathfrak{z} = 1,2,\ldots,\mathfrak{n}$ *be the collection of PyF numbers with weight vector* $\mathfrak{D}_{\mathfrak{z}} = (\mathfrak{D}_1, \mathfrak{D}_2, \mathfrak{D}_3, \ldots, \mathfrak{D}_n)^T$ *of* $\Omega_{\mathfrak{z}}\left(\mathfrak{z} = 1,2,3,\ldots\mathfrak{n}\right)$ *such that* $\mathfrak{D}_{\mathfrak{z}} \in [0,1]$, $\mathfrak{z} = 1,2,\ldots,\mathfrak{n}$ *and* $\sum_{\mathfrak{z}=1}^{\mathfrak{n}} \mathfrak{D}_{\mathfrak{z}} = 1$. *Then, the PyF Aczel–Alsina weighted averaging operator is given as:*

$$PyFAAWA\left(\Omega_1, \Omega_2, \ldots, \Omega_{\mathfrak{n}}\right) = \overset{\mathfrak{n}}{\underset{\mathfrak{z}=1}{\oplus}}\left(\mathfrak{D}_{\mathfrak{z}}\Omega\right) = \sqrt{1 - e^{-\left(\sum_{\mathfrak{z}=1}^{\mathfrak{n}} \mathfrak{D}_{\mathfrak{z}}(-ln(1-\Pi_{\Omega}^2))^{\Upsilon}\right)^{\frac{1}{\Upsilon}}}}, e^{-\left(\sum_{\mathfrak{z}=1}^{\mathfrak{n}} \mathfrak{D}_{\mathfrak{z}}(-ln(\Xi_{\Omega}))^{\Upsilon}\right)^{\frac{1}{\Upsilon}}}$$

Definition 8 ([58]). *Let* $\Omega_{\mathfrak{z}} = \left(\Pi_{\Omega_{\mathfrak{z}}}(\varkappa), \Xi_{\Omega_{\mathfrak{z}}}(\varkappa)\right)$, $\mathfrak{z} = 1,2,\ldots,\mathfrak{n}$ *be the collection of PyF numbers with weight vector* $\mathfrak{D}_{\mathfrak{z}} = (\mathfrak{D}_1, \mathfrak{D}_2, \mathfrak{D}_3, \ldots, \mathfrak{D}_n)^T$ *of* $\Omega_{\mathfrak{z}}\left(\mathfrak{z} = 1,2,3,\ldots\mathfrak{n}\right)$ *such that* $\mathfrak{D}_{\mathfrak{z}} \in [0,1]$, $\mathfrak{z} = 1,2,\ldots,\mathfrak{n}$ *and* $\sum_{\mathfrak{z}=1}^{\mathfrak{n}} \mathfrak{D}_{\mathfrak{z}} = 1$. *Then, the PyF Aczel–Alsina weighted geometric operator is given as:*

$$PyFAAWG\left(\Omega_1, \Omega_2, \ldots, \Omega_{\mathfrak{n}}\right) = \overset{\mathfrak{n}}{\underset{\mathfrak{z}=1}{\oplus}}\left(\Omega_{\mathfrak{z}}^{\mathfrak{D}_{\mathfrak{z}}}\right) = e^{-\left(\sum_{\mathfrak{z}=1}^{\mathfrak{n}} \mathfrak{D}_{\mathfrak{z}}(-ln(\Pi_{\Omega}))^{\Upsilon}\right)^{\frac{1}{\Upsilon}}}, \sqrt{1 - e^{-\left(\sum_{\mathfrak{z}=1}^{\mathfrak{n}} \mathfrak{D}_{\mathfrak{z}}(-ln(1-\Xi_{\Omega}^2))^{\Upsilon}\right)^{\frac{1}{\Upsilon}}}}$$

4. Aczel–Alsina Operations Based on CPyFSs

By utilizing the notions of Aczel–Alsina TNM and TCNM, we explored some fundamental operational laws of CPyFSs. We also study the generalization of union and intersection of CPyFSs and established some operations of the Aczel–Alsina-like Aczel–Alsina sum, product, scalar multiplication and power role. Then, we have:

Definition 9. *Let* $\Omega_1 = \left(\Pi_1(\varkappa)e^{2\pi i(\alpha_1(\varkappa))}, \Xi_1(\varkappa)e^{2\pi i(\beta_1(\varkappa))}\right)$ *and* $\Omega_2 = \left(\Pi_2(\varkappa)e^{2\pi i(\alpha_2(\varkappa))}, \Xi_2(\varkappa)e^{2\pi i(\beta_2(\varkappa))}\right)$ *be any two CPyFVs. The extension of intersection and the union of the given CPyFVs are defined as follows:*

i. $$\Omega_1 \cup_{\text{Ŧ},\dot{\text{Ś}}} \Omega_2 = \left\{ \left(\begin{array}{c} \dot{\text{Ś}}\left(\Xi_1(\varkappa)e^{2\pi i(\beta_1(\varkappa))}, \Xi_2(\varkappa)e^{2\pi i(\beta_2(\varkappa))}\right), \\ \text{Ŧ}\left(\Pi_1(\varkappa)e^{2\pi i(\alpha_1(\varkappa))}, \Pi_2(\varkappa)e^{2\pi i(\alpha_2(\varkappa))}\right) \end{array} \right) | \varkappa \in \dot{W} \right\}$$

ii. $$\Omega_1 \cap_{\text{Ŧ},\dot{\text{Ś}}} \Omega_2 = \left\{ \left(\begin{array}{c} \text{Ŧ}\left(\Pi_1(\varkappa)e^{2\pi i(\alpha_1(\varkappa))}, \Pi_2(\varkappa)e^{2\pi i(\alpha_2(\varkappa))}\right), \\ \dot{\text{Ś}}\left(\Xi_1(\varkappa)e^{2\pi i(\beta_1(\varkappa))}, \Xi_2(\varkappa)e^{2\pi i(\beta_2(\varkappa))}\right) \end{array} \right) | \varkappa \in \dot{W} \right\}$$

where TNM and TCNM are denoted by Ŧ *and* $\dot{\text{Ś}}$*, respectively.*

Definition 10. *Consider* $\Omega = \left(\Pi_\Omega(\varkappa)e^{2\pi i(\alpha_\Omega(\varkappa))}, \Xi_\Omega(\varkappa)e^{2\pi i(\beta_\Omega(\varkappa))}\right)$, $\Omega_1 = (\Pi_{\Omega_1}(\varkappa)e^{2\pi i(\alpha_{\Omega_1}(\tau))}, \Xi_{\Omega_1}(\varkappa)e^{2\pi i(\beta_{\Omega_1}(\varkappa))})$ *and* $\Omega_2 = (\Pi_{\Omega_2}(\varkappa)e^{2\pi i(\alpha_{\Omega_2}(\varkappa))}, \Xi_{\Omega_2}(\varkappa)e^{2\pi i(\beta_{\Omega_2}(\varkappa))})$ *as the three CPyFVs,* $\Upsilon \geq 1$ *and* $\Psi > 0$*. Then, we have:*

$$\Omega_1 \oplus \Omega_2 = \left(\begin{array}{c} \sqrt{1 - e^{-((-ln(1-\Pi^2_{\Omega_1}))^{\Upsilon} + (-ln(1-\Pi^2_{\Omega_2}))^{\Upsilon})^{\frac{1}{\Upsilon}}}} \\ e^{2\pi i\left(\sqrt{1-e^{-((-ln(1-\alpha^2_{\Omega_1}))^{\Upsilon} + (-ln(1-\alpha^2_{\Omega_2}))^{\Upsilon})^{\frac{1}{\Upsilon}}}}\right)}, \\ e^{-\left((-ln(\Xi_{\Omega_1}))^{\Upsilon} + (-ln(\Xi_{\Omega_2}))^{\Upsilon}\right)^{\frac{1}{\Upsilon}}} \\ e^{2\pi i\left(-((-ln(\beta_{\Omega_1}))^{\Upsilon} + (-ln(\beta_{\Omega_2}))^{\Upsilon})^{\frac{1}{\Upsilon}}\right)} \end{array} \right)$$

$$\Omega_1 \otimes \Omega_2 = \left(\begin{array}{c} e^{-\left((-ln(\Pi_{\Omega_{\mathfrak{z}}}))^{\Upsilon} + (-ln(\Pi_{\Omega_{\mathfrak{z}}}))^{\Upsilon}\right)^{\frac{1}{\Upsilon}}} \\ e^{2\pi i\left(e^{-((-ln(\alpha_{\Omega_{\mathfrak{z}}}))^{\Upsilon} + (-ln(\alpha_{\Omega_{\mathfrak{z}}}))^{\Upsilon})^{\frac{1}{\Upsilon}}}\right)}, \\ \sqrt{1 - e^{-\left((-ln(1-\Xi^2_{\Omega_1}))^{\Upsilon} + (-ln(1-\Xi^2_{\Omega_2}))^{\Upsilon}\right)^{\frac{1}{\Upsilon}}}} \\ e^{2\pi i\left(\sqrt{1-e^{-\left((-ln(1-\beta^2_{\Omega_1}))^{\Upsilon} + (-ln(1-\beta^2_{\Omega_2}))^{\Upsilon}\right)^{\frac{1}{\Upsilon}}}}\right)} \end{array} \right)$$

$$\Psi\Omega = \begin{pmatrix} \sqrt{1-e^{-\left(\Psi\left(\left(-ln\left(1-\Pi_{\Omega}^{2}\right)\right)^{\Upsilon}\right)\right)^{\frac{1}{\Upsilon}}}} e^{2\pi i\left(\sqrt{1-e^{-\left(\Psi\left(\left(-ln\left(1-\alpha_{\Omega}^{2}\right)\right)^{\Upsilon}\right)\right)^{\frac{1}{\Upsilon}}}}\right)}, \\ e^{-\left(\Psi\left(-ln\left(\Xi_{\Omega_{\mathfrak{Z}}}\right)\right)^{\Upsilon}\right)^{\frac{1}{\Upsilon}}} e^{2\pi i\left(e^{-\left(\Psi\left(-ln\left(\beta_{\Omega_{\mathfrak{Z}}}\right)\right)^{\Upsilon}\right)^{\frac{1}{\Upsilon}}}\right)} \end{pmatrix}$$

$$\Omega^{\Psi} = \begin{pmatrix} e^{-\left(\Psi\left(-ln\left(\Pi_{\Omega_{\mathfrak{Z}}}\right)\right)^{\Upsilon}\right)^{\frac{1}{\Upsilon}}} e^{2\pi i\left(e^{-\left(\Psi\left(-ln\left(\alpha_{\Omega_{\mathfrak{Z}}}\right)\right)^{\Upsilon}\right)^{\frac{1}{\Upsilon}}}\right)}, \\ \sqrt{1-e^{-\left(\Psi\left(\left(-ln\left(1-\Xi_{\Omega}^{2}\right)\right)^{\Upsilon}\right)\right)^{\frac{1}{\Upsilon}}}} e^{2\pi i\left(\sqrt{1-e^{-\left(\Psi\left(\left(-ln\left(1-\beta_{\Omega}^{2}\right)\right)^{\Upsilon}\right)\right)^{\frac{1}{\Upsilon}}}}\right)} \end{pmatrix}$$

Example 1. *Consider* $\Omega = \left(0.56e^{2\pi i(0.35)},\ 0.88e^{2\pi i(0.47)}\right)$, $\Omega_1 = \left(0.66e^{2\pi i(0.05)},\ 0.37e^{2\pi i(0.67)}\right)$ *and* $\Omega_2 = \left(0.43e^{2\pi i(0.08)},\ 0.69e^{2\pi i(0.24)}\right)$ *as the three CPyFVs. Then, we have: For* $\Upsilon = 3$ *and* $\Psi = 4$*:*

$$\begin{aligned} \Omega_1 \oplus \Omega_2 &= \begin{pmatrix} \sqrt{1-e^{-\left(\left(-ln\left(1-(0.66)^2\right)\right)^3+\left(-ln\left(1-(0.43)^2\right)\right)^3\right)^{\frac{1}{3}}}} e^{2\pi i\left(\sqrt{1-e^{-\left(\left(-ln\left(1-(0.05)^2\right)\right)^3+\left(-ln\left(1-(0.08)^2\right)\right)^3\right)^{\frac{1}{3}}}}\right)}, \\ e^{-\left(\left(-ln(0.37)\right)^3+\left(-ln(0.69)\right)^3\right)^{\frac{1}{3}}} e^{2\pi i\left(-\left(\left(-ln(0.67)\right)^3+\left(-ln(0.24)\right)^3\right)^{\frac{1}{3}}\right)} \end{pmatrix} \\ &= \left(0.2513e^{2\pi i(0.0003)}, 0.3638e^{2\pi i(0.2375)}\right) \end{aligned}$$

$$\begin{aligned} \Omega_1 \otimes \Omega_2 &= \begin{pmatrix} e^{-\left(\left(-ln(0.66)\right)^3+\left(-ln(0.43)\right)^3\right)^{\frac{1}{3}}} e^{2\pi i\left(e^{-\left(\left(-ln(0.05)\right)^3+\left(-ln(0.08)\right)^3\right)^{\frac{1}{3}}}\right)}, \\ \sqrt{1-e^{-\left(\left(-ln\left(1-(0.37)^2\right)\right)^3+\left(-ln\left(1-(0.69)^2\right)\right)^3\right)^{\frac{1}{3}}}} e^{2\pi i\left(\sqrt{1-e^{-\left(\left(-ln\left(1-(0.67)^2\right)\right)^3+\left(-ln\left(1-(0.24)^2\right)\right)^3\right)^{\frac{1}{3}}}}\right)} \end{pmatrix} \\ &= \left(0.4163e^{2\pi i(0.0301)}, 0.2951e^{2\pi i(0.2611)}\right) \end{aligned}$$

$$4\Omega = \begin{pmatrix} \sqrt{1-e^{-\left(4\left(\left(-ln\left(1-(0.66)^2\right)\right)^3\right)\right)^{\frac{1}{3}}}} e^{2\pi i\left(\sqrt{1-e^{-\left(4\left(\left(-ln\left(1-(0.05)^2\right)\right)^3\right)\right)^{\frac{1}{3}}}}\right)}, \\ e^{-\left(4(-ln(0.37))^3\right)^{\frac{1}{3}}} e^{2\pi i\left(e^{-\left(4(-ln(0.67))^3\right)^{\frac{1}{3}}}\right)} \end{pmatrix} = \left(0.6706e^{2\pi i(0.4328)}, 0.8316e^{2\pi i(0.3366)}\right)$$

$$\Omega^4 = \begin{pmatrix} e^{-\left(4(-ln(0.66))^3\right)^{\frac{1}{3}}} e^{2\pi i\left(e^{-\left(4(-ln(0.05))^3\right)^{\frac{1}{3}}}\right)}, \\ \sqrt{1-e^{-\left(4\left(\left(-ln\left(1-(0.37)^2\right)\right)^3\right)\right)^{\frac{1}{3}}}} e^{2\pi i\left(\sqrt{1-e^{-\left(4\left(\left(-ln\left(1-(0.67)^2\right)\right)^3\right)\right)^{\frac{1}{3}}}}\right)} \end{pmatrix} = \left(0.4333e^{2\pi i(0.2200)}, 0.9518e^{2\pi i(0.5720)}\right)$$

Theorem 1. *Let* $\Omega = \left(\Pi_\Omega(\varkappa)e^{2\pi i(\alpha_\Omega(\varkappa))}, \Xi_\Omega(\varkappa)e^{2\pi i(\beta_\Omega(\varkappa))}\right)$, $\Omega_1 = \left(\Pi_{\Omega_1}(\varkappa)e^{2\pi i(\alpha_{\Omega_1}(\varkappa))}, \Xi_{\Omega_1}(\varkappa)e^{2\pi i(\beta_{\Omega_1}(\varkappa))}\right)$ *and* $\Omega_2 = \left(\Pi_{\Omega_2}(\varkappa)e^{2\pi i(\alpha_{\Omega_2}(\varkappa))}, \Xi_{\Omega_2}(\varkappa)e^{2\pi i(\beta_{\Omega_2}(\varkappa))}\right)$ *be three CPyFVs. Then we have:*

(1) $\Pi_{\Omega_1} \oplus \Pi_{\Omega_2} = \Pi_{\Omega_2} \oplus \Pi_{\Omega_1}$
(2) $\Pi_{\Omega_1} \otimes \Pi_{\Omega_2} = \Pi_{\Omega_2} \otimes \Pi_{\Omega_1}$
(3) $\Psi(\Pi_{\Omega_1} \oplus \Pi_{\Omega_2}) = \Psi\Pi_{\Omega_1} \oplus \Psi\Pi_{\Omega_2}, \Psi > 0$
(4) $(\Psi_1 + \Psi_2)\Pi_\Omega = \Psi_1\Pi_\Omega \oplus \Psi_2\Pi_\Omega, \Psi_1, \Psi_2 > 0$
(5) $(\Pi_{\Omega_1} \otimes \Pi_{\Omega_2})^\Psi = \Pi_{\Omega_1}^\Psi \otimes \Pi_{\Omega_2}^\Psi, \Psi > 0$
(6) $\Pi_\Omega^{\Psi_1} \otimes \Pi_\Omega^{\Psi_2} = \Pi_\Omega^{(\Psi_1+\Psi_2)}, \Psi_1, \Psi_2 > 0$

Proof. Given that $\Omega = \left(\Pi_\Omega(\varkappa)e^{2\pi i(\alpha_\Omega(\varkappa))}, \Xi_\Omega(\varkappa)e^{2\pi i(\beta_\Omega(\varkappa))}\right)$, $\Omega_1 = \left(\Pi_{\Omega_1}(\varkappa)e^{2\pi i(\alpha_{\Omega_1}(\varkappa))}, \Xi_{\Omega_1}(\varkappa)e^{2\pi i(\beta_{\Omega_1}(\varkappa))}\right)$ and $\Omega_2 = \left(\Pi_{\Omega_2}(\varkappa)e^{2\pi i(\alpha_{\Omega_2}(\varkappa))}, \Xi_{\Omega_2}(\varkappa)e^{2\pi i(\beta_{\Omega_2}(\varkappa))}\right)$ are the three CPyFVs, and $\Psi, \Psi_1, \Psi_2 > 0$, we have:

$$(1)\quad \Pi_{\Omega_1} \oplus \Pi_{\Omega_2} = \begin{pmatrix} \sqrt{1-e^{-\left(\left(-ln\left(1-\Pi_{\Omega_1}^2\right)\right)^{\Upsilon}+\left(-ln\left(1-\Pi_{\Omega_2}^2\right)\right)^{\Upsilon}\right)^{\frac{1}{\Upsilon}}}} e^{2\pi i\left(\sqrt{1-e^{-\left(\left(-ln\left(1-\alpha_{\Omega_1}^2\right)\right)^{\Upsilon}+\left(-ln\left(1-\alpha_{\Omega_2}^2\right)\right)^{\Upsilon}\right)^{\frac{1}{\Upsilon}}}}\right)} \\ , e^{-\left(\left(-ln(\Xi_{\Omega_1})\right)^{\Upsilon}+\left(-ln(\Xi_{\Omega_2})\right)^{\Upsilon}\right)^{\frac{1}{\Upsilon}}} e^{2\pi i\left(e^{-\left(\left(-ln(\beta_{\Omega_1})\right)^{\Upsilon}+\left(-ln(\beta_{\Omega_2})\right)^{\Upsilon}\right)^{\frac{1}{\Upsilon}}}\right)} \end{pmatrix}$$

$$= \left(\begin{array}{c} \sqrt{1-e^{-\left(\left(-ln\left(1-\Pi_{\Omega_2}^2\right)\right)^{\Upsilon}+\left(-ln\left(1-\Pi_{\Omega_1}^2\right)\right)^{\Upsilon}\right)^{\frac{1}{\Upsilon}}}} e^{2\pi i\left(\sqrt{1-e^{-\left(\left(-ln\left(1-\alpha_{\Omega_2}^2\right)\right)^{\Upsilon}+\left(-ln\left(1-\alpha_{\Omega_1}^2\right)\right)^{\Upsilon}\right)^{\frac{1}{\Upsilon}}}}\right)}, \\ e^{-\left(\left(-ln\left(\Xi_{\Omega_2}\right)\right)^{\Upsilon}+\left(-ln\left(\Xi_{\Omega_1}\right)\right)^{\Upsilon}\right)^{\frac{1}{\Upsilon}}} e^{2\pi i\left(e^{-\left(\left(-ln\left(\beta_{\Omega_2}\right)\right)^{\Upsilon}+\left(-ln\left(\beta_{\Omega_1}\right)\right)^{\Upsilon}\right)^{\frac{1}{\Upsilon}}}\right)} \end{array} \right) = \Pi_{\Omega_2} \oplus \Pi_{\Omega_1}.$$

(2) We can prove this easily by following Property 1.
(3) Now, we have to prove this property $\Psi\left(\Pi_{\Omega_1} \oplus \Pi_{\Omega_2}\right) = \Psi\Pi_{\Omega_1} \oplus \Psi\Pi_{\Omega_2}$, $\Psi > 0$. We know that

$$\Psi\left(\Pi_{\Omega_1} \oplus \Pi_{\Omega_2}\right) = \Psi \left(\begin{array}{c} \sqrt{1-e^{-\left(\left(-ln\left(1-\Pi_{\Omega_1}^2\right)\right)^{\Upsilon}+\left(-ln\left(1-\Pi_{\Omega_2}^2\right)\right)^{\Upsilon}\right)^{\frac{1}{\Upsilon}}}} e^{2\pi i\left(\sqrt{1-e^{-\left(\left(-ln\left(1-\alpha_{\Omega_1}^2\right)\right)^{\Upsilon}+\left(-ln\left(1-\alpha_{\Omega_2}^2\right)\right)^{\Upsilon}\right)^{\frac{1}{\Upsilon}}}}\right)}, \\ e^{-\left(\left(-ln\left(\Xi_{\Omega 1}\right)\right)^{\Upsilon}+\left(-ln\left(\Xi_{\Omega 2}\right)\right)^{\Upsilon}\right)^{\frac{1}{\Upsilon}}} e^{2\pi i\left(e^{-\left(\left(-ln\left(\beta_{\Omega 1}\right)\right)^{\Upsilon}+\left(-ln\left(\beta_{\Omega 2}\right)\right)^{\Upsilon}\right)^{\frac{1}{\Upsilon}}}\right)} \end{array} \right)$$

$$= \left(\begin{array}{c} \sqrt{1-e^{-\Psi\left(\left(-ln\left(1-\Pi_{\Omega_1}^2\right)\right)^{\Upsilon}+\left(-ln\left(1-\Pi_{\Omega_2}^2\right)\right)^{\Upsilon}\right)^{\frac{1}{\Upsilon}}}} e^{2\pi i\left(\sqrt{1-e^{-\Psi\left(\left(-ln\left(1-\alpha_{\Omega_1}^2\right)\right)^{\Upsilon}+\left(-ln\left(1-\alpha_{\Omega_2}^2\right)\right)^{\Upsilon}\right)^{\frac{1}{\Upsilon}}}}\right)}, \\ e^{-\Psi\left(\left(-ln\left(\Xi_{\Omega 1}\right)\right)^{\Upsilon}+\left(-ln\left(\Xi_{\Omega 2}\right)\right)^{\Upsilon}\right)^{\frac{1}{\Upsilon}}} e^{2\pi i\left(e^{-\Psi\left(\left(-ln\left(\beta_{\Omega 1}\right)\right)^{\Upsilon}+\left(-ln\left(\beta_{\Omega 2}\right)\right)^{\Upsilon}\right)^{\frac{1}{\Upsilon}}}\right)} \end{array} \right)$$

$$= \left(\begin{array}{c} \sqrt{1 - e^{-\left(\Psi\left(-ln\left(1-\Pi^2_{\Omega_1}\right)\right)^{\Upsilon} + \Psi\left(-ln\left(1-\Pi^2_{\Omega_2}\right)\right)^{\Upsilon}\right)^{\frac{1}{\Upsilon}}}} \\ e^{2\pi i\left(\sqrt{1-e^{-\left(\Psi\left(-ln\left(1-\alpha^2_{\Omega_1}\right)\right)^{\Upsilon} + \Psi\left(-ln\left(1-\alpha^2_{\Omega_2}\right)\right)^{\Upsilon}\right)^{\frac{1}{\Upsilon}}}}\right)}, \\ e^{-\left(\Psi(-ln(\Xi_{\Omega 1}))^{\Upsilon} + \Psi\ (-ln(\Xi_{\Omega 2}))^{\Upsilon}\right)^{\frac{1}{\Upsilon}}} \\ e^{2\pi i\left(e^{-\left(\Psi(-ln(\beta_{\Omega 1}))^{\Upsilon} + \Psi\ (-ln(\beta_{\Omega 2}))^{\Upsilon}\right)^{\frac{1}{\Upsilon}}}\right)} \end{array} \right)$$

$$= \left(\begin{array}{c} \left(\begin{array}{c} \sqrt{1 - e^{-\left(\Psi\left(\left(-ln\left(1-\Pi^2_{\Omega_1}\right)\right)^{\Upsilon}\right)\right)^{\frac{1}{\Upsilon}}}}\, e^{2\pi i\left(\sqrt{1-e^{-\left(\Psi\left(\left(-ln\left(1-\alpha^2_{\Omega_1}\right)\right)^{\Upsilon}\right)\right)^{\frac{1}{\Upsilon}}}}\right)}, \\ e^{-\left(\Psi(-ln(\Xi_{\Omega 1}))^{\Upsilon}\right)^{\frac{1}{\Upsilon}}}\, e^{2\pi i\left(e^{-\left(\Psi(-ln(\beta_{\Omega 1}))^{\Upsilon}\right)^{\frac{1}{\Upsilon}}}\right)} \end{array} \right) \oplus \\ \left(\begin{array}{c} \sqrt{1 - e^{-\left(\Psi\left(\left(-ln\left(1-\Pi^2_{\Omega_2}\right)\right)^{\Upsilon}\right)\right)^{\frac{1}{\Upsilon}}}}\, e^{2\pi i\left(\sqrt{1-e^{-\left(\Psi\left(\left(-ln\left(1-\alpha^2_{\Omega_2}\right)\right)^{\Upsilon}\right)\right)^{\frac{1}{\Upsilon}}}}\right)}, \\ e^{-\left(\Psi(-ln(\Xi_{\Omega 2}))^{\Upsilon}\right)^{\frac{1}{\Upsilon}}}\, e^{2\pi i\left(e^{-\left(\Psi(-ln(\beta_{\Omega 2}))^{\Upsilon}\right)^{\frac{1}{\Upsilon}}}\right)} \end{array} \right) \end{array} \right)$$

$$= \Psi\Pi_{\Omega_1} \oplus \Psi\Pi_{\Omega_2}$$

(4) Now we have to prove $(\Psi_1 + \Psi_2)\Pi_{\Omega} = \Psi_1\Pi_{\Omega} + \Psi_2\Pi_{\Omega}$, $\Psi_1, \Psi_2 > 0$. We have that

$$\Psi_1\Pi_{\Omega} \oplus \Psi_2\Pi_{\Omega} = \left(\begin{array}{c} \left(\begin{array}{c} \sqrt{1 - e^{-\left(\Psi_1\left(\left(-ln\left(1-\Pi^2_{\Omega}\right)\right)^{\Upsilon}\right)\right)^{\frac{1}{\Upsilon}}}}\, e^{2\pi i\left(\sqrt{1-e^{-\left(\Psi_1\left(\left(-ln\left(1-\alpha^2_{\Omega}\right)\right)^{\Upsilon}\right)\right)^{\frac{1}{\Upsilon}}}}\right)}, \\ e^{-\left(\Psi_1(-ln(\Xi_{\Omega}))^{\Upsilon}\right)^{\frac{1}{\Upsilon}}}\, e^{2\pi i\left(e^{-\left(\Psi_1(-ln(\beta_{\Omega}))^{\Upsilon}\right)^{\frac{1}{\Upsilon}}}\right)} \end{array} \right) \\ \left(\begin{array}{c} \sqrt{1 - e^{-\left(\Psi_2\left(\left(-ln\left(1-\Pi^2_{\Omega}\right)\right)^{\Upsilon}\right)\right)^{\frac{1}{\Upsilon}}}}\, e^{2\pi i\left(\sqrt{1-e^{-\left(\Psi_2\left(\left(-ln\left(1-\alpha^2_{\Omega}\right)\right)^{\Upsilon}\right)\right)^{\frac{1}{\Upsilon}}}}\right)}, \\ e^{-\left(\Psi_2(-ln(\Xi_{\Omega}))^{\Upsilon}\right)^{\frac{1}{\Upsilon}}}\, e^{2\pi i\left(e^{-\left(\Psi_2(-ln(\beta_{\Omega}))^{\Upsilon}\right)^{\frac{1}{\Upsilon}}}\right)} \end{array} \right) \end{array} \right)$$

$$= \left(\begin{array}{c} \sqrt{1 - e^{-\left((\Psi_1+\Psi_2)\left(\left(-ln\left(1-\Pi_{\Omega}^2\right)\right)^{'\Upsilon}\right)\right)^{\frac{1}{'\Upsilon}}}} e^{2\pi i \left(\sqrt{1-e^{-\left((\Psi_1+\Psi_2)\left(\left(-ln\left(1-\alpha_{\Omega}^2\right)\right)^{'\Upsilon}\right)\right)^{\frac{1}{'\Upsilon}}}}\right)}, \\ e^{-\left((\Psi_1+\Psi_2)(-ln(\Xi_{\Omega}))^{'\Upsilon}\right)^{\frac{1}{'\Upsilon}}} e^{2\pi i \left(e^{-\left((\Psi_1+\Psi_2)(-ln(\beta_{\Omega}))^{'\Upsilon}\right)^{\frac{1}{'\Upsilon}}}\right)} \end{array} \right)$$

$$= (\Psi_1 + \Psi_2)\Pi_{\Omega}.$$

(5) We must now prove that $\left(\Pi_{\Omega_1} \oplus \Pi_{\Omega_2}\right)^{\Psi} = \Pi_{\Omega_1}^{\Psi} \otimes \Pi_{\Omega_2}^{\Psi}$, $\Psi > 0$. We have that

$$\left(\Pi_{\Omega_1} \otimes \Pi_{\Omega_2}\right)^{\Psi} = \left(\begin{array}{c} e^{-\left((-ln(\Pi_{\Omega}))^{'\Upsilon} + (-ln(\Pi_{\Omega}))^{'\Upsilon}\right)^{\frac{1}{'\Upsilon}}} e^{2\pi i \left(e^{-\left((-ln(\alpha_{\Omega}))^{'\Upsilon} + (-ln(\alpha_{\Omega}))^{'\Upsilon}\right)^{\frac{1}{'\Upsilon}}}\right)}, \\ \sqrt{1 - e^{-\left(\left(-ln\left(1-\Xi_{\Omega_1}^2\right)\right)^{'\Upsilon} + \left(-ln\left(1-\Xi_{\Omega_2}^2\right)\right)^{'\Upsilon}\right)^{\frac{1}{'\Upsilon}}}} \\ e^{2\pi i \left(\sqrt{1-e^{-\left(\left(-ln\left(1-\beta_{\Omega_1}^2\right)\right)^{'\Upsilon} + \left(-ln\left(1-\beta_{\Omega_2}^2\right)\right)^{'\Upsilon}\right)^{\frac{1}{'\Upsilon}}}}\right)} \end{array} \right)^{\Psi}$$

$$= \left(\begin{array}{c} e^{-\left(\Psi\left((-ln(\Pi_{\Omega}))^{'\Upsilon} + (-ln(\Pi_{\Omega}))^{'\Upsilon}\right)\right)^{\frac{1}{'\Upsilon}}} e^{2\pi i \left(e^{-\left(\Psi\left((-ln(\alpha_{\Omega}))^{'\Upsilon} + (-ln(\alpha_{\Omega}))^{'\Upsilon}\right)\right)^{\frac{1}{'\Upsilon}}}\right)}, \\ \sqrt{1 - e^{-\left(\Psi\left(\left(-ln\left(1-\Xi_{\Omega_1}^2\right)\right)^{'\Upsilon} + \left(-ln\left(1-\Xi_{\Omega_2}^2\right)\right)^{'\Upsilon}\right)\right)^{\frac{1}{'\Upsilon}}}} \\ e^{2\pi i \left(\sqrt{1-e^{-\left(\Psi\left(\left(-ln\left(1-\beta_{\Omega_1}^2\right)\right)^{'\Upsilon} + \left(-ln\left(1-\beta_{\Omega_2}^2\right)\right)^{'\Upsilon}\right)\right)^{\frac{1}{'\Upsilon}}}}\right)} \end{array} \right)$$

$$= \left(\begin{array}{c} \left(\begin{array}{c} e^{-\left(\Psi(-ln(\Pi_{\Omega}))^{\Upsilon}\right)^{\frac{1}{\Upsilon}}} e^{2\pi i \left(e^{-\left(\Psi(-ln(\alpha_{\Omega}))^{\Upsilon}\right)^{\frac{1}{\Upsilon}}} \right)}, \\ \sqrt{1-e^{-\left(\Psi\left(\left(-ln\left(1-\Xi^{2}_{\Omega_1}\right)\right)^{\Upsilon}\right)\right)^{\frac{1}{\Upsilon}}}} e^{2\pi i \left(\sqrt{1-e^{-\left(\Psi\left(\left(-ln\left(1-\beta^{2}_{\Omega_1}\right)\right)^{\Upsilon}\right)\right)^{\frac{1}{\Upsilon}}}} \right)} \end{array} \right) \otimes \\ \left(\begin{array}{c} e^{-\left(\Psi(-ln(\Pi_{\Omega}))^{\Upsilon}\right)^{\frac{1}{\Upsilon}}} e^{2\pi i \left(e^{-\left(\Psi(-ln(\alpha_{\Omega}))^{\Upsilon}\right)^{\frac{1}{\Upsilon}}} \right)}, \\ \sqrt{1-e^{-\left(\Psi\left(\left(-ln\left(1-\Xi^{2}_{\Omega_2}\right)\right)^{\Upsilon}\right)\right)^{\frac{1}{\Upsilon}}}} e^{2\pi i \left(\sqrt{1-e^{-\left(\Psi\left(\left(-ln\left(1-\beta^{2}_{\Omega_2}\right)\right)^{\Upsilon}\right)\right)^{\frac{1}{\Upsilon}}}} \right)} \end{array} \right) \end{array} \right)$$

$$= \Pi^{\Psi}_{\Omega_1} \otimes \Pi^{\Psi}_{\Omega_2}.$$

(6) In order to prove that $\Pi^{\Psi_1}_{\Omega} \otimes \Pi^{\Psi_2}_{\Omega} = \Pi^{(\Psi_1+\Psi_2)}_{\Omega}, \Psi_1, \Psi_2 > 0$, we have that

$$\Pi^{\Psi_1}_{\Omega} \otimes \Pi^{\Psi_2}_{\Omega} = \left(\begin{array}{c} \left(\begin{array}{c} e^{-\left(\Psi_1(-ln(\Pi_{\Omega}))^{\Upsilon}\right)^{\frac{1}{\Upsilon}}} e^{2\pi i \left(e^{-\left(\Psi_1(-ln(\alpha_{\Omega}))^{\Upsilon}\right)^{\frac{1}{\Upsilon}}} \right)} \\ , \sqrt{1-e^{-\left(\Psi_1\left(\left(-ln\left(1-\Xi^{2}_{\Omega}\right)\right)^{\Upsilon}\right)\right)^{\frac{1}{\Upsilon}}}} e^{2\pi i \left(\sqrt{1-e^{-\left(\Psi_1\left(\left(-ln\left(1-\beta^{2}_{\Omega}\right)\right)^{\Upsilon}\right)\right)^{\frac{1}{\Upsilon}}}} \right)} \end{array} \right) \otimes \\ \left(\begin{array}{c} e^{-\left(\Psi_2(-ln(\Pi_{\Omega}))^{\Upsilon}\right)^{\frac{1}{\Upsilon}}} e^{2\pi i \left(e^{-\left(\Psi_2(-ln(\alpha_{\Omega}))^{\Upsilon}\right)^{\frac{1}{\Upsilon}}} \right)}, \\ \sqrt{1-e^{-\left(\Psi_2\left(\left(-ln\left(1-\Xi^{2}_{\Omega}\right)\right)^{\Upsilon}\right)\right)^{\frac{1}{\Upsilon}}}} e^{2\pi i \left(\sqrt{1-e^{-\left(\Psi_2\left(\left(-ln\left(1-\beta^{2}_{\Omega}\right)\right)^{\Upsilon}\right)\right)^{\frac{1}{\Upsilon}}}} \right)} \end{array} \right) \end{array} \right)$$

$$= \left(\begin{array}{c} e^{-\left((\Psi_1+\Psi_2)(-ln(\Pi_{\Omega}))^{\Upsilon}\right)^{\frac{1}{\Upsilon}}} e^{2\pi i \left(e^{-\left((\Psi_1+\Psi_2)(-ln(\alpha_{\Omega}))^{\Upsilon}\right)^{\frac{1}{\Upsilon}}} \right)}, \\ \sqrt{1-e^{-\left((\Psi_1+\Psi_2)\left(\left(-ln\left(1-\Xi^{2}_{\Omega}\right)\right)^{\Upsilon}\right)\right)^{\frac{1}{\Upsilon}}}} e^{2\pi i \left(\sqrt{1-e^{-\left((\Psi_1+\Psi_2)\left(\left(-ln\left(1-\beta^{2}_{\Omega}\right)\right)^{\Upsilon}\right)\right)^{\frac{1}{\Upsilon}}}} \right)} \end{array} \right)$$

$$= \Pi^{(\Psi_1+\Psi_2)}_{\Omega}.$$

□

5. Complex Pythagorean Fuzzy Aczel–Alsina Weighted Averaging Operators

A CPyFS contains more extensive information than IFSs and PyFSs because a CPyFS has the two aspects of MV and NMV in terms of amplitude and phase terms. We develop a list of new AOs of CPyFSs by utilizing the basic operational laws of Aczel–Alsina TNM and TCNM.

Definition 11. *Consider* $\Omega_{\mathfrak{z}} = \left(\Pi_{\Omega_{\mathfrak{z}}}(\varkappa)e^{2\pi i(\alpha_{\Omega_{\mathfrak{z}}}(\varkappa))}, \Xi_{\Omega_{\mathfrak{z}}}(\varkappa)e^{2\pi i(\beta_{\Omega_{\mathfrak{z}}}(\varkappa))}\right)$, $\mathfrak{z} = 1,2,\ldots,\mathfrak{n}$ *to be the family of CPyFVs and its corresponding weight vectors* $\mathfrak{D}_{\mathfrak{z}} = (\mathfrak{D}_1, \mathfrak{D}_2, \mathfrak{D}_3, \ldots, \mathfrak{D}_n)^T$ *of* $\Omega_{\mathfrak{z}}\left(\mathfrak{z} = 1,2,3,\ldots\mathfrak{n}\right)$, *such that* $\mathfrak{D}_{\mathfrak{z}} \in [0,1]$, $\mathfrak{z} = 1,2,\ldots,\mathfrak{n}$ *and* $\sum_{\mathfrak{z}=1}^{\mathfrak{n}} \mathfrak{D}_{\mathfrak{z}} = 1$. *Then, the CPyFAAWA operator is defined as:*

$$CPyFAAWA\left(\Omega_1, \Omega_2, \ldots, \Omega_{\mathfrak{n}}\right) = \underset{\mathfrak{z}=1}{\overset{\mathfrak{n}}{\oplus}}\left(\mathfrak{D}_{\mathfrak{z}}\Omega_{\mathfrak{z}}\right) = \mathfrak{D}_1\Omega_1 \oplus \mathfrak{D}_2\Omega_2 \oplus, \ldots, \oplus \mathfrak{D}_{\mathfrak{n}}\Omega_{\mathfrak{n}} \tag{3}$$

Theorem 2. *Consider* $\Omega_{\mathfrak{z}} = \left(\Pi_{\Omega_{\mathfrak{z}}}(\varkappa)e^{2\pi i(\alpha_{\Omega_{\mathfrak{z}}}(\varkappa))}, \Xi_{\Omega_{\mathfrak{z}}}(\varkappa)e^{2\pi i(\beta_{\Omega_{\mathfrak{z}}}(\varkappa))}\right)$, $\mathfrak{z} = 1,2,\ldots,\mathfrak{n}$ *to be the family of CPyFVs and its corresponding weight vectors* $\mathfrak{D}_{\mathfrak{z}} = (\mathfrak{D}_1, \mathfrak{D}_2, \mathfrak{D}_3, \ldots, \mathfrak{D}_n)^T$ *of* $\Omega_{\mathfrak{z}}\left(\mathfrak{z} = 1,2,3,\ldots\mathfrak{n}\right)$, *such that* $\mathfrak{D}_{\mathfrak{z}} \in [0,1]$, $\mathfrak{z} = 1,2,\ldots,\mathfrak{n}$ *and* $\sum_{\mathfrak{z}=1}^{\mathfrak{n}} \mathfrak{D}_{\mathfrak{z}} = 1$. *Then, the CPyFAAWA operator is particularized as:*

$$CPyFAAWA\left(\Omega_1, \Omega_2, \ldots, \Omega_{\mathfrak{n}}\right) = \begin{pmatrix} \sqrt{1 - e^{-(\sum_{\mathfrak{z}=1}^{\mathfrak{n}} \mathfrak{D}_{\mathfrak{z}}(-ln(1-\Pi_{\mathfrak{z}}^2))^{\Upsilon})^{\frac{1}{\Upsilon}}}} e^{2\pi i(\sqrt{1-e^{-(\sum_{\mathfrak{z}=1}^{\mathfrak{n}} \mathfrak{D}_{\mathfrak{z}}(-ln(1-\alpha_{\mathfrak{z}}^2))^{\Upsilon})^{\frac{1}{\Upsilon}}}})}, \\ e^{-(\sum_{\mathfrak{z}=1}^{\mathfrak{n}} \mathfrak{D}_{\mathfrak{z}}(-ln(\Xi_{\mathfrak{z}}))^{\Upsilon})^{\frac{1}{\Upsilon}}} e^{2\pi i(e^{-(\sum_{\mathfrak{z}=1}^{\mathfrak{n}} \mathfrak{D}_{\mathfrak{z}}(-ln(\beta))^{\Upsilon})^{\frac{1}{\Upsilon}}})} \end{pmatrix}, \tag{4}$$

Proof. Consider $\Omega_{\mathfrak{z}} = \left(\Pi_{\Omega_{\mathfrak{z}}}(\varkappa)e^{2\pi i(\alpha_{\Omega_{\mathfrak{z}}}(\varkappa))}, \Xi_{\Omega_{\mathfrak{z}}}(\varkappa)e^{2\pi i(\beta_{\Omega_{\mathfrak{z}}}(\varkappa))}\right)$, $\mathfrak{z} = 1,2,\ldots,\mathfrak{n}$ to be the family of CPyFVs. By using an induction method, we prove Theorem 1 based on Aczel–Alsina operations. For $\mathfrak{n} = 2$, we have:

$$\mathfrak{D}_1\Pi_{\Omega_1} = \begin{pmatrix} \sqrt{1 - e^{-\left(\mathfrak{D}_1\left(-ln\left(1-\Pi_{\Omega_1}^2\right)\right)^{\Upsilon}\right)^{\frac{1}{\Upsilon}}}} e^{2\pi i\left(\sqrt{1-e^{-\left(\mathfrak{D}_1\left(-ln\left(1-\alpha_{\Omega_1}^2\right)\right)^{\Upsilon}\right)^{\frac{1}{\Upsilon}}}}\right)}, \\ e^{-\left(\mathfrak{D}_1\left(-ln\left(\Xi_{\Omega_1}\right)\right)^{\Upsilon}\right)^{\frac{1}{\Upsilon}}} e^{2\pi i\left(e^{-\left(\mathfrak{D}_1\left(-ln\left(\beta_{\Omega_1}\right)\right)^{\Upsilon}\right)^{\frac{1}{\Upsilon}}}\right)} \end{pmatrix}$$

$$\mathfrak{D}_2\Pi_{\Omega_2} = \begin{pmatrix} \sqrt{1 - e^{-\left(\mathfrak{D}_2\left(-ln\left(1-\Pi_{\Omega_2}^2\right)\right)^{\Upsilon}\right)^{\frac{1}{\Upsilon}}}} e^{2\pi i\left(\sqrt{1-e^{-\left(\mathfrak{D}_2\left(-ln\left(1-\alpha_{\Omega_2}^2\right)\right)^{\Upsilon}\right)^{\frac{1}{\Upsilon}}}}\right)}, \\ e^{-\left(\mathfrak{D}_2\left(-ln\left(\Xi_{\Omega_2}\right)\right)^{\Upsilon}\right)^{\frac{1}{\Upsilon}}} e^{2\pi i\left(e^{-\left(\mathfrak{D}_2\left(-ln\left(\beta_{\Omega_2}\right)\right)^{\Upsilon}\right)^{\frac{1}{\Upsilon}}}\right)} \end{pmatrix}$$

By Definition 11, $CPyFAAWA(\Omega_1,\ \Omega_2) = \underset{\mathfrak{z}=1}{\overset{2}{\oplus}}\left(\mathfrak{D}_{\mathfrak{z}}\Omega_{\mathfrak{z}}\right) = \mathfrak{D}_1\Omega_1 \oplus \mathfrak{D}_2\Omega_2$

$$= \left(\begin{array}{c} \sqrt{1-e^{-\left(\mathfrak{D}_1\left(-ln\left(1-\Pi^2_{\Omega_1}\right)\right)^{\Upsilon}\right)^{\frac{1}{\Upsilon}}}}\, e^{2\pi i\left(\sqrt{1-e^{-\left(\mathfrak{D}_1\left(-ln\left(1-\alpha^2_{\Omega_1}\right)\right)^{\Upsilon}\right)^{\frac{1}{\Upsilon}}}}\right)}, \\ e^{-\left(\mathfrak{D}_1\left(-ln\left(\Xi_{\Omega_1}\right)\right)^{\Upsilon}\right)^{\frac{1}{\Upsilon}}}\, e^{2\pi i\left(e^{-\left(\mathfrak{D}_1\left(-ln\left(\beta_{\Omega_1}\right)\right)^{\Upsilon}\right)^{\frac{1}{\Upsilon}}}\right)} \end{array}\right) \oplus \left(\begin{array}{c} \sqrt{1-e^{-\left(\mathfrak{D}_2\left(-ln\left(1-\Pi^2_{\Omega_2}\right)\right)^{\Upsilon}\right)^{\frac{1}{\Upsilon}}}}\, e^{2\pi i\left(\sqrt{1-e^{-\left(\mathfrak{D}_2\left(-ln\left(1-\alpha^2_{\Omega_2}\right)\right)^{\Upsilon}\right)^{\frac{1}{\Upsilon}}}}\right)}, \\ e^{-\left(\mathfrak{D}_2\left(-ln\left(\Xi_{\Omega_2}\right)\right)^{\Upsilon}\right)^{\frac{1}{\Upsilon}}}\, e^{2\pi i\left(e^{-\left(\mathfrak{D}_2\left(-ln\left(\beta_{\Omega_2}\right)\right)^{\Upsilon}\right)^{\frac{1}{\Upsilon}}}\right)} \end{array}\right)$$

$$= \left(\begin{array}{c} \sqrt{1-e^{-\left(\mathfrak{D}_1\left(-ln\left(1-\Pi^2_{\Omega_1}\right)\right)^{\Upsilon}+\mathfrak{D}_2\left(-ln\left(1-\Pi^2_{\Omega_2}\right)\right)^{\Upsilon}\right)^{\frac{1}{\Upsilon}}}}\, e^{2\pi i\left(\sqrt{1-e^{-\left(\mathfrak{D}_1\left(-ln\left(1-\alpha^2_{\Omega_1}\right)\right)^{\Upsilon}+\mathfrak{D}_2\left(-ln\left(1-\alpha^2_{\Omega_2}\right)\right)^{\Upsilon}\right)^{\frac{1}{\Upsilon}}}}\right)}, \\ e^{-\left(\mathfrak{D}_1\left(-ln\left(\Xi_{\Omega_1}\right)\right)^{\Upsilon}+\mathfrak{D}_2\left(-ln\left(\Xi_{\Omega_2}\right)\right)^{\Upsilon}\right)^{\frac{1}{\Upsilon}}}\, e^{2\pi i\left(e^{-\left(\mathfrak{D}_1\left(-ln\left(\beta_{\Omega_1}\right)\right)^{\Upsilon}+\mathfrak{D}_2\left(-ln\left(\beta_{\Omega_2}\right)\right)^{\Upsilon}\right)^{\frac{1}{\Upsilon}}}\right)} \end{array}\right)$$

$$= \left(\begin{array}{c} \sqrt{1-e^{-\left(\sum_{\mathfrak{z}=1}^{2}\mathfrak{D}_{\mathfrak{z}}\left(-ln\left(1-\Pi^2_{\Omega_{\mathfrak{z}}}\right)\right)^{\Upsilon}\right)^{\frac{1}{\Upsilon}}}}\, e^{2\pi i\left(\sqrt{1-e^{-\left(\sum_{\mathfrak{z}=1}^{2}\mathfrak{D}_{\mathfrak{z}}\left(-ln\left(1-\alpha^2_{\Omega_{\mathfrak{z}}}\right)\right)^{\Upsilon}\right)^{\frac{1}{\Upsilon}}}}\right)}, \\ e^{-\left(\sum_{\mathfrak{z}=1}^{2}\mathfrak{D}_{\mathfrak{z}}\left(-ln\left(\Xi_{\Omega_{\mathfrak{z}}}\right)\right)^{\Upsilon}\right)^{\frac{1}{\Upsilon}}}\, e^{2\pi i\left(e^{-\left(\sum_{\mathfrak{z}=1}^{2}\mathfrak{D}_{\mathfrak{z}}\left(-ln\left(\beta_{\Omega_{\mathfrak{z}}}\right)\right)^{\Upsilon}\right)^{\frac{1}{\Upsilon}}}\right)} \end{array}\right).$$

is true for $\mathfrak{n} = 2$.

Consider that $\mathfrak{n} = k$. Then,

$$CPyFAAWA(\Omega_1,\ \Omega_2,\ \ldots,\ \Omega_k) = \underset{\mathfrak{z}=1}{\overset{\mathfrak{n}}{\oplus}}\left(\mathfrak{D}_{\mathfrak{z}}\Omega_{\mathfrak{z}}\right) = \mathfrak{D}_1\Omega_1 \oplus \mathfrak{D}_2\Omega_2 \oplus, \ldots, \oplus \mathfrak{D}_k\Omega_k$$

$$= \left(\sqrt{1 - e^{-\left(\sum_{\mathfrak{z}=1}^{k} \mathfrak{D}_{\mathfrak{z}} \left(-ln\left(1 - \Pi_{\Omega_{\mathfrak{z}}}^{2}\right)\right)^{\Upsilon}\right)^{\frac{1}{\Upsilon}}}} e^{2\pi i \left(\sqrt{1 - e^{-\left(\sum_{\mathfrak{z}=1}^{k} \mathfrak{D}_{\mathfrak{z}} \left(-ln\left(1 - \alpha_{\Omega_{\mathfrak{z}}}^{2}\right)\right)^{\Upsilon}\right)^{\frac{1}{\Upsilon}}}} \right)}, e^{-\left(\sum_{\mathfrak{z}=1}^{k} \mathfrak{D}_{\mathfrak{z}} \left(-ln\left(\Xi_{\Omega_{\mathfrak{z}}}\right)\right)^{\Upsilon}\right)^{\frac{1}{\Upsilon}}} e^{2\pi i \left(e^{-\left(\sum_{\mathfrak{z}=1}^{k} \mathfrak{D}_{\mathfrak{z}} \left(-ln\left(\beta_{\Omega_{\mathfrak{z}}}\right)\right)^{\Upsilon}\right)^{\frac{1}{\Upsilon}}} \right)} \right),$$

For a further process, we have to show that this is true for $\eta = k + 1$ We have that

$$CPyFAAWA(\Omega_1, \Omega_2, \ldots, \Omega_k, \Omega_{k+1}) = \mathfrak{D}_1\Omega_1 \oplus \mathfrak{D}_2\Omega_2 \oplus, \ldots, \oplus \mathfrak{D}_k\Omega_k \oplus \mathfrak{D}_{k+1}\Omega_{k+1} = \overset{\eta}{\underset{\mathfrak{z}=1}{\oplus}} \left(\mathfrak{D}_{\mathfrak{z}}\Omega_{\mathfrak{z}}\right) \oplus \left(\mathfrak{D}_{k+1}\Omega_{k+1}\right)$$

$$= \left(\left(\sqrt{1 - e^{-\left(\sum_{\mathfrak{z}=1}^{k} \mathfrak{D}_{\mathfrak{z}} \left(-ln\left(1 - \Pi_{\Omega_{\mathfrak{z}}}^{2}\right)\right)^{\Upsilon}\right)^{\frac{1}{\Upsilon}}}} e^{2\pi i \left(\sqrt{1 - e^{-\left(\sum_{\mathfrak{z}=1}^{k} \mathfrak{D}_{\mathfrak{z}} \left(-ln\left(1 - \alpha_{\Omega_{\mathfrak{z}}}^{2}\right)\right)^{\Upsilon}\right)^{\frac{1}{\Upsilon}}}} \right)}, e^{e^{-\left(\sum_{\mathfrak{z}=1}^{k} \mathfrak{D}_{\mathfrak{z}} \left(-ln\left(\Xi_{\Omega_{\mathfrak{z}}}\right)\right)^{\Upsilon}\right)^{\frac{1}{\Upsilon}}} } e^{2\pi i \left(e^{-\left(\sum_{\mathfrak{z}=1}^{k} \mathfrak{D}_{\mathfrak{z}} \left(-ln\left(\beta_{\Omega_{\mathfrak{z}}}\right)\right)^{\Upsilon}\right)^{\frac{1}{\Upsilon}}} \right)} \right) \oplus \left(\sqrt{1 - e^{-\left(\mathfrak{D}_{k+1} \left(-ln\left(1 - \Pi_{\Omega_{k+1}}^{2}\right)\right)^{\Upsilon}\right)^{\frac{1}{\Upsilon}}}} e^{2\pi i \left(\sqrt{1 - e^{-\left(\mathfrak{D}_{k+1} \left(-ln\left(1 - \alpha_{\Omega_{k+1}}^{2}\right)\right)^{\Upsilon}\right)^{\frac{1}{\Upsilon}}}} \right)}, e^{-\left(\mathfrak{D}_{k+1} \left(-ln\left(\Xi_{\Omega_{k+1}}\right)\right)^{\Upsilon}\right)^{\frac{1}{\Upsilon}}} e^{2\pi i \left(e^{-\left(\mathfrak{D}_{k+1} \left(-ln\left(\beta_{\Omega_{k+1}}\right)\right)^{\Upsilon}\right)^{\frac{1}{\Upsilon}}} \right)} \right) \right)$$

$$= \left(\sqrt{1 - e^{-\left(\sum_{\mathfrak{z}=1}^{k+1} \mathfrak{D}_{\mathfrak{z}} \left(-ln\left(1 - \Pi_{\Omega_{\mathfrak{z}}}^{2}\right)\right)^{\Upsilon}\right)^{\frac{1}{\Upsilon}}}} e^{2\pi i \left(\sqrt{1 - e^{-\left(\sum_{\mathfrak{z}=1}^{k+1} \mathfrak{D}_{\mathfrak{z}} \left(-ln\left(1 - \alpha_{\Omega_{\mathfrak{z}}}^{2}\right)\right)^{\Upsilon}\right)^{\frac{1}{\Upsilon}}}} \right)}, e^{-\left(\sum_{\mathfrak{z}=1}^{k+1} \mathfrak{D}_{\mathfrak{z}} \left(-ln\left(\Xi_{\Omega_{\mathfrak{z}}}\right)\right)^{\Upsilon}\right)^{\frac{1}{\Upsilon}}} e^{2\pi i \left(e^{-\left(\sum_{\mathfrak{z}=1}^{k+1} \mathfrak{D}_{\mathfrak{z}} \left(-ln\left(\beta_{\Omega_{\mathfrak{z}}}\right)\right)^{\Upsilon}\right)^{\frac{1}{\Upsilon}}} \right)} \right)$$

We observed that $\eta = k + 1$ holds. Therefore, this theorem is proved and completed for $\forall, \eta$. □

Theorem 3. *Consider* $\Omega_{\mathfrak{z}} = \left(\Pi_{\Omega_{\mathfrak{z}}}(\mathfrak{z}) e^{2\pi i(\alpha_{\Omega_{\mathfrak{z}}}(\varkappa))}, \Xi_{\Omega_{\mathfrak{z}}}(\varkappa) e^{2\pi i(\beta_{\Omega_{\mathfrak{z}}}(\varkappa))}\right)$, $\mathfrak{z} = 1,2,\ldots,\mathfrak{n}$ *to be all the same CPyFVs,* $\forall$, $\mathfrak{z} = 1,2,\ldots,\mathfrak{n}$. *Then,* $CPyFAAWA\left(\Omega_1, \Omega_2, \ldots, \Omega_{\mathfrak{n}}\right) = \Omega$.

Proof. Show that $\Omega_{\mathfrak{z}} = \left(\Pi_{\Omega_{\mathfrak{z}}}(\varkappa) e^{2\pi i(\alpha_{\Omega_{\mathfrak{z}}}(\varkappa))}, \Xi_{\Omega_{\mathfrak{z}}}(\varkappa) e^{2\pi i(\beta_{\Omega_{\mathfrak{z}}}(\varkappa))}\right)$, $\mathfrak{z} = 1,2,\ldots,\mathfrak{n}$ are all the same CPyFVs, for $\mathfrak{z} = 1,2,\ldots,\mathfrak{n}$. Then,

$$CPyFAAWA\left(\Omega_1, \Omega_2, \ldots, \Omega_{\mathfrak{n}}\right) = \oplus_{\mathfrak{z}=1}^{\mathfrak{n}}\left(\mathfrak{D}_{\mathfrak{z}}\Omega_{\mathfrak{z}}\right)$$

$$= \left(\begin{array}{c} \sqrt{1-e^{-\left(\Sigma_{\mathfrak{z}=1}^{\mathfrak{n}}\mathfrak{D}_{\mathfrak{z}}\left(-ln\left(1-\Pi_{\Omega_{\mathfrak{z}}}^2\right)\right)^{\Upsilon}\right)^{\frac{1}{\Upsilon}}}}\, e^{2\pi i\left(\sqrt{1-e^{-\left(\Sigma_{\mathfrak{z}=1}^{\mathfrak{n}}\mathfrak{D}_{\mathfrak{z}}\left(-ln\left(1-\alpha_{\Omega_{\mathfrak{z}}}^2\right)\right)^{\Upsilon}\right)^{\frac{1}{\Upsilon}}}}\right)}, \\ e^{-\left(\Sigma_{\mathfrak{z}=1}^{\mathfrak{n}}\mathfrak{D}_{\mathfrak{z}}\left(-ln\left(\Xi_{\Omega_{\mathfrak{z}}}\right)\right)^{\Upsilon}\right)^{\frac{1}{\Upsilon}}}\, e^{2\pi i\left(e^{-\left(\Sigma_{\mathfrak{z}=1}^{\mathfrak{n}}\mathfrak{D}_{\mathfrak{z}}\left(-ln\left(\beta_{\Omega_{\mathfrak{z}}}\right)\right)^{\Upsilon}\right)^{\frac{1}{\Upsilon}}}\right)} \end{array}\right)$$

$$\left(\begin{array}{c} \sqrt{1-e^{-\left(\left(-ln\left(1-\Pi_{\Omega}^2\right)\right)^{\Upsilon}\right)^{\frac{1}{\Upsilon}}}}\, e^{2\pi i\left(\sqrt{1-e^{-\left(\left(-ln\left(1-\alpha_{\Omega}^2\right)\right)^{\Upsilon}\right)^{\frac{1}{\Upsilon}}}}\right)}, \\ e^{-\left(\left(-ln\left(\Xi_{\Omega}\right)\right)^{\Upsilon}\right)^{\frac{1}{\Upsilon}}}\, e^{2\pi i\left(e^{-\left(\left(-ln\left(\beta_{\Omega}\right)\right)^{\Upsilon}\right)^{\frac{1}{\Upsilon}}}\right)} \end{array}\right) = \Omega.$$

Hence,

$$CPyFAAWA\left(\Omega_1, \Omega_2, \ldots, \Omega_{\mathfrak{n}}\right) = \Omega$$

□

Theorem 4. *Consider* $\Omega_{\mathfrak{z}} = \left(\Pi_{\Omega_{\mathfrak{z}}}(\varkappa) e^{2\pi i(\alpha_{\Omega_{\mathfrak{z}}}(\varkappa))}, \Xi_{\Omega_{\mathfrak{z}}}(\varkappa) e^{2\pi i(\beta_{\Omega_{\mathfrak{z}}}(\varkappa))}\right)$, $\mathfrak{z} = 1,2,\ldots,\mathfrak{n}$ *to be the family of CPyFVs, and consider* $\Omega^- = min\left(\Omega_1, \Omega_2, \Omega_3, \ldots, \Omega_{\mathfrak{n}}\right)$ *and* $\Omega^+ = max\left(\Omega_1, \Omega_2, \Omega_3, \ldots, \Omega_{\mathfrak{n}}\right)$. *Then, the associated value* $CPyFAAWA(\Omega_1, \Omega_2, \ldots, \Omega_k)$ *is defined as:*

$$\Omega^- \leq CPyFAAWA\left(\Omega_1, \Omega_2, \ldots, \Omega_{\mathfrak{n}}\right) \leq \Omega^+$$

Proof. Let $\Omega_{\mathfrak{z}} = \left(\Pi_{\Omega_{\mathfrak{z}}}(\varkappa) e^{2\pi i(\alpha_{\Omega_{\mathfrak{z}}}(\varkappa))}, \Xi_{\Omega_{\mathfrak{z}}}(\varkappa) e^{2\pi i(\beta_{\Omega_{\mathfrak{z}}}(\varkappa))}\right)$, $\mathfrak{z} = 1,2,\ldots,\mathfrak{n}$ as a collection of CPyFVs. Let $\Omega^- = min\left(\Omega_1, \Omega_2, \Omega_3, \ldots, \Omega_{\mathfrak{n}}\right) = \left(\Pi_{\Omega}^-(\varkappa), \Xi_{\Omega}^-(\varkappa)\right)$ and $\Omega^+ = max\left(\Omega_1, \Omega_2, \Omega_3, \ldots, \Omega_{\mathfrak{n}}\right) = \left(\Pi_{\Omega}^+(\varkappa), \Xi_{\Omega}^+(\varkappa)\right)$ such that $\Pi_{\Omega}^-(\varkappa) = \min\left\{\Pi_{\Omega_{\mathfrak{z}}}^-(\varkappa)\right\}$,

$\Pi^{+}_{\Omega}(\varkappa) = \max\left\{\Pi^{+}_{\Omega_{\mathfrak{z}}}(\varkappa)\right\}$ and $\Xi^{-}_{\Omega}(\varkappa) = \max\left\{\Xi^{-}_{\Omega_{\mathfrak{z}}}(\varkappa)\right\}$, $\Xi^{+}_{\Omega}(\varkappa) = \min\left\{\Xi^{+}_{\Omega_{\mathfrak{z}}}(\varkappa)\right\}$.

Then, the associated value $CPyFAAWA(\Omega_1, \Omega_2, \ldots, \Omega_{\mathfrak{y}})$ must satisfy the following conditions:

$$\left(\begin{array}{c}\sqrt{1-e^{-\left(\sum_{\mathfrak{z}=1}^{\mathfrak{y}}\mathfrak{D}_{\mathfrak{z}}\left(-ln\left(1-\left(\Pi^{-}_{\Omega_{\mathfrak{z}}}\right)^{2}\right)\right)^{\Upsilon}\right)^{\frac{1}{\Upsilon}}}} \leq \\ \sqrt{1-e^{-\left(\sum_{\mathfrak{z}=1}^{\mathfrak{y}}\mathfrak{D}_{\mathfrak{z}}\left(-ln\left(1-\Pi^{2}_{\Omega_{\mathfrak{z}}}\right)\right)^{\Upsilon}\right)^{\frac{1}{\Upsilon}}}} \leq \\ \sqrt{1-e^{-\left(\sum_{\mathfrak{z}=1}^{\mathfrak{y}}\mathfrak{D}_{\mathfrak{z}}\left(-ln\left(1-\left(\Pi^{+}_{\Omega_{\mathfrak{z}}}\right)^{2}\right)\right)^{\Upsilon}\right)^{\frac{1}{\Upsilon}}}}\end{array}\right)$$

$$\left(\begin{array}{c} e^{2\pi i\left(\sqrt{1-e^{-\left(\sum_{\mathfrak{z}=1}^{\mathfrak{y}}\mathfrak{D}_{\mathfrak{z}}\left(-ln\left(1-\left(\alpha^{-}_{\Omega_{\mathfrak{z}}}\right)^{2}\right)\right)^{\Upsilon}\right)^{\frac{1}{\Upsilon}}}}\right)} \leq \\ e^{2\pi i\left(\sqrt{1-e^{-\left(\sum_{\mathfrak{z}=1}^{\mathfrak{y}}\mathfrak{D}_{\mathfrak{z}}\left(-ln\left(1-\alpha^{2}_{\Omega_{\mathfrak{z}}}\right)\right)^{\Upsilon}\right)^{\frac{1}{\Upsilon}}}}\right)} \leq \\ e^{2\pi i\left(\sqrt{1-e^{-\left(\sum_{\mathfrak{z}=1}^{\mathfrak{y}}\mathfrak{D}_{\mathfrak{z}}\left(-ln\left(1-\left(\alpha^{+}_{\Omega_{\mathfrak{z}}}\right)^{2}\right)\right)^{\Upsilon}\right)^{\frac{1}{\Upsilon}}}}\right)}\end{array}\right)$$

and

$$\left(\begin{array}{c}\left(\begin{array}{c}\sqrt{1-e^{-\left(\Sigma_{\mathfrak{z}=1}^{\mathfrak{y}}\mathfrak{D}_{\mathfrak{z}}=1\left(-ln\left(1-\left(\Pi^{-}_{\Omega_{\mathfrak{z}}}\right)^{2}\right)\right)^{\Upsilon}\right)^{\frac{1}{\Upsilon}}}}\\ e^{2\pi i\left(\sqrt{1-e^{-\left(\Sigma_{\mathfrak{z}=1}^{\mathfrak{y}}\mathfrak{D}_{\mathfrak{z}}=1\left(-ln\left(1-\left(\alpha^{-}_{\Omega_{\mathfrak{z}}}\right)^{2}\right)\right)^{\Upsilon}\right)^{\frac{1}{\Upsilon}}}}\right)}\end{array}\right)\leq\\ \left(\begin{array}{c}\sqrt{1-e^{-\left(\Sigma_{\mathfrak{z}=1}^{\mathfrak{y}}\mathfrak{D}_{\mathfrak{z}}=1\left(-ln\left(1-\Pi^{2}_{\mathfrak{z}}\right)\right)^{\Upsilon}\right)^{\frac{1}{\Upsilon}}}}\\ e^{2\pi i\left(\sqrt{1-e^{-\left(\Sigma_{\mathfrak{z}=1}^{\mathfrak{y}}\mathfrak{D}_{\mathfrak{z}}=1\left(-ln\left(1-\alpha^{2}_{\mathfrak{z}}\right)\right)^{\Upsilon}\right)^{\frac{1}{\Upsilon}}}}\right)}\end{array}\right)\leq\\ \left(\begin{array}{c}\sqrt{1-e^{-\left(\Sigma_{\mathfrak{z}=1}^{\mathfrak{y}}\mathfrak{D}_{\mathfrak{z}}=1\left(-ln\left(1-\left(\Pi^{+}_{\Omega_{\mathfrak{z}}}\right)^{2}\right)\right)^{\Upsilon}\right)^{\frac{1}{\Upsilon}}}}\\ e^{2\pi i\left(\sqrt{1-e^{-\left(\Sigma_{\mathfrak{z}=1}^{\mathfrak{y}}\mathfrak{D}_{\mathfrak{z}}=1\left(-ln\left(1-\left(\alpha^{+}_{\Omega_{\mathfrak{z}}}\right)^{2}\right)\right)^{\Upsilon}\right)^{\frac{1}{\Upsilon}}}}\right)}\end{array}\right)\end{array}\right)$$

$$\left(\left(\begin{array}{c}\left(e^{-(\Sigma_{\mathfrak{z}=1}^{\mathfrak{y}}\mathfrak{D}_{\mathfrak{z}}(-ln(\Xi^{-}_{\Omega_{\mathfrak{z}}}))^{\Upsilon})^{\frac{1}{\Upsilon}}}\; e^{2\pi i((\Sigma_{\mathfrak{z}=1}^{\mathfrak{y}}\mathfrak{D}_{\mathfrak{z}}(-ln(\Xi^{-}_{\Omega_{\mathfrak{z}}}))^{\Upsilon})^{\frac{1}{\Upsilon}})}\right)\leq\\ \left(e^{-(\Sigma_{\mathfrak{z}=1}^{\mathfrak{y}}\mathfrak{D}_{\mathfrak{z}}(-ln(\Xi_{\Omega_{\mathfrak{z}}}))^{\Upsilon})^{\frac{1}{\Upsilon}}}\; e^{2\pi i((\Sigma_{\mathfrak{z}=1}^{\mathfrak{y}}\mathfrak{D}_{\mathfrak{z}}(-ln(\Xi^{-}_{\Omega_{\mathfrak{z}}}))^{\Upsilon})^{\frac{1}{\Upsilon}})}\right)\leq\\ \left(e^{-(\Sigma_{\mathfrak{z}=1}^{\mathfrak{y}}\mathfrak{D}_{\mathfrak{z}}(-ln(\Xi^{+}_{\Omega_{\mathfrak{z}}}))^{\Upsilon})^{\frac{1}{\Upsilon}}}\; e^{2\pi i((\Sigma_{\mathfrak{z}=1}^{\mathfrak{y}}\mathfrak{D}_{\mathfrak{z}}(-ln(\Xi^{-}_{\Omega_{\mathfrak{z}}}))^{\Upsilon})^{\frac{1}{\Upsilon}})}\right)\end{array}\right)\right).$$

This shows that:

$$\Omega^{-}\leq CPyFAAWA\left(\Omega_{1},\,\Omega_{2},\,\ldots,\,\Omega_{\mathfrak{y}}\right)\leq\Omega^{+}$$

□

Theorem 5. *If* $\Omega_{\mathfrak{z}} = \left(\Pi_{\Omega_{\mathfrak{z}}}(\varkappa)e^{2\pi i(\alpha_{\Omega_{\mathfrak{z}}}(\varkappa))}, \Xi_{\Omega_{\mathfrak{z}}}(\varkappa)e^{2\pi i(\beta_{\Omega_{\mathfrak{z}}}(\varkappa))}\right)$, $\mathfrak{z} = 1,2,\ldots,\eta$ *and* $\Omega'_{\mathfrak{z}} = \left(\Pi_{\Omega'_{\mathfrak{z}}}(\varkappa)e^{2\pi i(\alpha_{\Omega'_{\mathfrak{z}}}(\varkappa))}, \Xi_{\Omega'_{\mathfrak{z}}}(\varkappa)e^{2\pi i(\beta_{\Omega'_{\mathfrak{z}}}(\varkappa))}\right)$, $\mathfrak{z} = 1,2,\ldots,\eta$ *are two CPyFSs and if* $\Omega_{\mathfrak{z}} \leq \Omega'_{\mathfrak{z}}$, $\forall$, $(\mathfrak{z} = 1,2,\ldots,\eta)$, *then we have:*

$$CPyFAAWA\left(\Omega_1, \Omega_2, \ldots, \Omega_\eta\right) \leq CPyFAAWA\left(\Omega'_1, \Omega'_2, \ldots, \Omega'_\eta\right)$$

Proof. We can prove this by using the steps of Theorem 2. □

Example 2. *Consider* $\Omega_1 = (0.46e^{2i\pi(0.15)}, 0.61e^{2i\pi(0.22)})$, $\Omega_2 = (0.17e^{2i\pi(0.37)}, 0.27e^{2i\pi(0.54)})$, $\Omega_3 = (0.63e^{2i\pi(0.45)}, 0.16e^{2i\pi(0.67)})$ *and* $\Omega_4 = (0.36e^{2i\pi(0.29)}, 0.49e^{2i\pi(0.24)})$ *are four CpyFVs with corresponding weight vector* $\mathfrak{D} = (0.20, 0.35, 0.30, 0.15)$. *Then, the aggregated values of CPyFAAWA operator are given for* $\Upsilon = 3$.

Solution. *Since we have: for* $\mathfrak{z} = 1, 2, 3, 4$

$$CPyFAAWA(\Omega_1, \Omega_2, \ldots, \Omega_4) = \begin{pmatrix} \sqrt{1-e^{-\left(\sum_{\mathfrak{z}=1}^{4}\mathfrak{D}_{\mathfrak{z}}\left(-ln\left(1-\Pi_{\mathfrak{z}}^2\right)\right)^3\right)^{\frac{1}{3}}}}\, e^{2\pi i\left(\sqrt{1-e^{-\left(\sum_{\mathfrak{z}=1}^{4}\mathfrak{D}_{\mathfrak{z}}\left(-ln\left(1-\alpha_{\mathfrak{z}}^2\right)\right)^3\right)^{\frac{1}{3}}}}\right)}, \\ e^{-\left(\sum_{\mathfrak{z}=1}^{4}\mathfrak{D}_{\mathfrak{z}}\left(-ln\left(\Xi_{\mathfrak{z}}\right)\right)^3\right)^{\frac{1}{3}}}\, e^{2\pi i\left(e^{-\left(\sum_{\mathfrak{z}=1}^{4}\mathfrak{D}_{\mathfrak{z}}(-ln(\beta))^3\right)^{\frac{1}{3}}}\right)} \end{pmatrix}$$

$$= \begin{pmatrix} \sqrt{1-e^{-\left(\left((0.20)\left(-ln\left(1-(0.46)^2\right)\right)^3+(0.35)\left(-ln\left(1-(0.17)^2\right)\right)^3+ (0.30)\left(-ln\left(1-(0.63)^2\right)\right)^3+(0.15)\left(-ln\left(1-(0.36)^2\right)\right)^3\right)\right)^{\frac{1}{3}}}}\, e^{2\pi i\left(\sqrt{1-e^{-\left(\left((0.20)\left(-ln\left(1-(0.15)^2\right)\right)^3+(0.35)\left(-ln\left(1-(0.37)^2\right)\right)^3+ (0.30)\left(-ln\left(1-(0.45)^2\right)\right)^3+(0.15)\left(-ln\left(1-(0.29)^2\right)\right)^3\right)\right)^{\frac{1}{3}}}}\right)}, \\ e^{-\left(\left((0.20)(-ln(0.61))^3+(0.35)(-ln(0.27))^3+ (0.30)(-ln(0.16))^3+(0.15)(-ln(0.49))^3\right)\right)^{\frac{1}{3}}}\, e^{2\pi i\left(e^{-\left(\left((0.20)(-ln(0.22))^3+(0.35)(-ln(0.54))^3+ (0.30)(-ln(0.67))^3+(0.15)(-ln(0.24))^3\right)\right)^{\frac{1}{3}}}\right)} \end{pmatrix}$$

$$= \left(0.5417e^{2i\pi(0.3927)},\ 0.2480e^{2i\pi(0.3424)}\right)$$

We explore our invented AOs and presented new AOs of CPyF using an Aczel–Alsina-order weighted averaging (CPyFAAOWA) operator based on Aczel–Alsina operations.

Definition 12. *Consider* $\Omega_{\mathfrak{z}} = (\Pi_{\Omega_{\mathfrak{z}}}(\varkappa)e^{2\pi i(\alpha_{\Omega_{\mathfrak{z}}}(\varkappa))}, \Xi_{\Omega_{\mathfrak{z}}}(\varkappa)e^{2\pi i(\beta_{\Omega_{\mathfrak{z}}}(\varkappa))})$, $\mathfrak{z} = 1,2,\ldots,\mathfrak{n}$ *to be the family of CPyFVs, and its corresponding weight vectors* $\mathfrak{D}_{\mathfrak{z}} = (\mathfrak{D}_1, \mathfrak{D}_2, \mathfrak{D}_3, \ldots, \mathfrak{D}_n)^T$ *of* $\Omega_{\mathfrak{z}}\left(\mathfrak{z} = 1,2,3,\ldots\mathfrak{n}\right)$*, such that* $\mathfrak{D}_{\mathfrak{z}} \in [0,1]$, $\mathfrak{z} = 1,2,\ldots,\mathfrak{n}$ *and* $\sum_{\mathfrak{z}=1}^{\mathfrak{n}} \mathfrak{D}_{\mathfrak{z}} = 1$. *Then, the CPyFAAOWA operator is particularized as:*

$$CPyFAAOWA\left(\Omega_1,\ \Omega_2,\ \ldots,\ \Omega_{\mathfrak{n}}\right) = \oplus_{\mathfrak{z}=1}^{\mathfrak{n}}\left(\mathfrak{D}_{\mathfrak{z}}\Omega_{\mathfrak{b}(\mathfrak{z})}\right) = \mathfrak{D}_1\Omega_{\mathfrak{b}(1)} \oplus \mathfrak{D}_2\Omega_{\mathfrak{b}(2)} \oplus, \ldots, \oplus \mathfrak{D}_{\mathfrak{n}}\Omega_{\mathfrak{b}(\mathfrak{n})} \tag{5}$$

where $(\mathfrak{b}(1),\ \mathfrak{b}(2),\ \mathfrak{b}(3),\ \ldots,\ \mathfrak{b}(\mathfrak{z}))$ *is a permutation of* $(\mathfrak{z} = 1,\ 2,\ 3, \ldots \mathfrak{n})$ *and* $\Omega_{\mathfrak{b}(\mathfrak{z}-1)} \geq \Omega_{\mathfrak{b}(\mathfrak{z})}$, $\forall,\ \mathfrak{z} = 1,2,3,\ldots\mathfrak{n}$.

Theorem 6. *Let* $\Omega_{\mathfrak{z}} = \left(\Pi_{\Omega_{\mathfrak{z}}}(\varkappa)e^{2\pi i(\alpha_{\Omega_{\mathfrak{z}}}(\varkappa))}, \Xi_{\Omega_{\mathfrak{z}}}(\varkappa)e^{2\pi i(\beta_{\Omega_{\mathfrak{z}}}(\varkappa))}\right)$, $\mathfrak{z} = 1,2,\ldots,\mathfrak{n}$ *be the family of CPyFVs and its corresponding weight vector* $\mathfrak{D}_{\mathfrak{z}} = (\mathfrak{D}_1, \mathfrak{D}_2, \mathfrak{D}_3, \ldots, \mathfrak{D}_n)^T$ *of* $\Omega_{\mathfrak{z}}\left(\mathfrak{z} = 1,2,3,\ldots\mathfrak{n}\right)$*, such that* $\mathfrak{D}_{\mathfrak{z}} \in [0,1]$, $\mathfrak{z} = 1,2,\ldots,\mathfrak{n}$ *and* $\sum_{\mathfrak{z}=1}^{\mathfrak{n}} \mathfrak{D}_{\mathfrak{z}} = 1$. *Then, the associated values of the CPyFAAOWA operator are particularized as:*

$$CPyFAAOWA\left(\Omega_1,\ \Omega_2,\ \ldots,\ \Omega_{\mathfrak{n}}\right) = \left(\begin{array}{c} \sqrt{1 - e^{-\left(\sum_{\mathfrak{z}=1}^{\mathfrak{n}} \mathfrak{D}_{\mathfrak{z}}\left(-ln\left(1-\Pi^2_{\Omega_{\mathfrak{b}(\mathfrak{z})}}\right)\right)^{\Upsilon}\right)^{\frac{1}{\Upsilon}}}}\ e^{2\pi i\left(\sqrt{1-e^{-\left(\sum_{\mathfrak{z}=1}^{\mathfrak{n}} \mathfrak{D}_{\mathfrak{z}}\left(-ln\left(1-\alpha^2_{\Omega_{\mathfrak{b}(\mathfrak{z})}}\right)\right)^{\Upsilon}\right)^{\frac{1}{\Upsilon}}}}\right)}, \\ e^{-\left(\sum_{\mathfrak{z}=1}^{\mathfrak{n}} \mathfrak{D}_{\mathfrak{z}}\left(-ln\left(\Xi_{\Omega_{\mathfrak{b}(\mathfrak{z})}}\right)\right)^{\Upsilon}\right)^{\frac{1}{\Upsilon}}}\ e^{2\pi i\left(e^{-\left(\sum_{\mathfrak{z}=1}^{\mathfrak{n}} \mathfrak{D}_{\mathfrak{z}}\left(-ln\left(\beta_{\Omega_{\mathfrak{b}(\mathfrak{z})}}\right)\right)^{\Upsilon}\right)^{\frac{1}{\Upsilon}}}\right)} \end{array}\right) \tag{6}$$

$(\mathfrak{b}(1),\ \mathfrak{b}(2),\ \mathfrak{b}(3),\ \ldots,\ \mathfrak{b}(\mathfrak{z}))$ *is the set of permutations of* $\left(\mathfrak{z} = 1,\ 2,\ 3, \ldots,\ \mathfrak{n}\right)$ *and* $\Omega_{\mathfrak{b}(\mathfrak{z}-1)} \geq \Omega_{\mathfrak{b}(\mathfrak{z})}$, $\forall,\ \mathfrak{z} = 1,2,3,\ldots\mathfrak{n}$.

Proof. We can prove this by using the steps of Theorem 3. □

Theorem 7. *Consider* $\Omega_{\mathfrak{z}} = \left(\Pi_{\Omega_{\mathfrak{z}}}(\varkappa)e^{2\pi i(\alpha_{\Omega_{\mathfrak{z}}}(\varkappa))}, \Xi_{\Omega_{\mathfrak{z}}}(\varkappa)e^{2\pi i(\beta_{\Omega_{\mathfrak{z}}}(\varkappa))}\right)$*, to be the family of all same CPyFVs,* $\forall$*,* $\mathfrak{z} = 1, 2, \ldots, \mathfrak{n}$*. Then we have:*

$$CPyFAAOWA\left(\Omega_1, \Omega_2, \ldots, \Omega_{\mathfrak{n}}\right) = \Omega$$

Proof. We can prove this theorem easily. □

Theorem 8. *Let* $\Omega_{\mathfrak{z}} = \left(\Pi_{\Omega_{\mathfrak{z}}}(\varkappa)e^{2\pi i(\alpha_{\Omega_{\mathfrak{z}}}(\varkappa))}, \Xi_{\Omega_{\mathfrak{z}}}(\varkappa)e^{2\pi i(\beta_{\Omega_{\mathfrak{z}}}(\varkappa))}\right)$*,* $\mathfrak{z} = 1, 2, \ldots, \mathfrak{n}$ *be the family of CPyFVs, and* $\Omega^- = min(\Omega_1, \Omega_2, \Omega_3, \ldots, \Omega_{\mathfrak{n}})$ *and* $\Omega^+ = max(\Omega_1, \Omega_2, \Omega_3, \ldots, \Omega_{\mathfrak{n}})$*. Then, we have:*

$$\Omega^- \leq CPyFAAOWA\left(\Omega_1, \Omega_2, \ldots, \Omega_{\mathfrak{n}}\right) \leq \Omega^+$$

Proof. We can prove this theorem easily by following the steps of Theorem 4. □

Theorem 9. Consider that $\Omega_{\mathfrak{z}} = \left(\Pi_{\Omega_{\mathfrak{z}}}(\varkappa)e^{2\pi i(\alpha_{\Omega_{\mathfrak{z}}}(\varkappa))}, \Xi_{\Omega_{\mathfrak{z}}}(\varkappa)e^{2\pi i(\beta_{\Omega_{\mathfrak{z}}}(\varkappa))}\right)$, and $\Omega'_{\mathfrak{z}} = \left(\Pi_{\Omega'_{\mathfrak{z}}}(\varkappa)e^{2\pi i(\alpha_{\Omega'_{\mathfrak{z}}}(\varkappa))}, \Xi_{\Omega'_{\mathfrak{z}}}(\varkappa)e^{2\pi i(\beta_{\Omega'_{\mathfrak{z}}}(\varkappa))}\right)$, $\mathfrak{z} = 1, 2, \ldots, \mathfrak{n}$ are two CPyFSs; if $\Omega_{\mathfrak{z}} \leq \Omega'_{\mathfrak{z}}$, $\forall$, $\left(\mathfrak{z} = 1, 2, \ldots, \mathfrak{n}\right)$, then we have:

$$CPyFAAOWA\left(\Omega_1, \Omega_2, \ldots, \Omega_{\mathfrak{n}}\right) \leq CPyFAAOWA\left(\Omega'_1, \Omega'_2, \ldots, \Omega'_{\mathfrak{n}}\right)$$

Proof. We can prove this theorem easily. □

Theorem 10. *If* $\Omega_{\mathfrak{z}} = \left(\Pi_{\Omega_{\mathfrak{z}}}(\varkappa)e^{2\pi i(\alpha_{\Omega_{\mathfrak{z}}}(\varkappa))}, \Xi_{\Omega_{\mathfrak{z}}}(\varkappa)e^{2\pi i(\beta_{\Omega_{\mathfrak{z}}}(\varkappa))}\right)$*, and* $\Omega'_{\mathfrak{z}} = \left(\Pi_{\Omega'_{\mathfrak{z}}}(\varkappa)e^{2\pi i(\alpha_{\Omega'_{\mathfrak{z}}}(\varkappa))}, \Xi_{\Omega'_{\mathfrak{z}}}(\varkappa)e^{2\pi i(\beta_{\Omega'_{\mathfrak{z}}}(\varkappa))}\right)$*,* $\mathfrak{z} = 1, 2, \ldots, \mathfrak{n}$ *are the two CPyFSs, and if* $\Omega_{\mathfrak{z}} \leq \Omega'_{\mathfrak{z}}$*,* $\forall$*,* $\left(\mathfrak{z} = 1, 2, \ldots, \mathfrak{n}\right)$*, then we have:*

$$CPyFAAOWA\left(\Omega_1, \Omega_2, \ldots, \Omega_{\mathfrak{n}}\right) \leq CPyFAAOWA\left(\Omega'_1, \Omega'_2, \ldots, \Omega'_{\mathfrak{n}}\right)$$

where $(\mathfrak{b}(1), \mathfrak{b}(2), \mathfrak{b}(3), \ldots, \mathfrak{b}(\mathfrak{z}))$ is the set of permutations of $\left(\Omega'_{\mathfrak{z}} : \mathfrak{z} = 1, 2, 3, \ldots, \mathfrak{n}\right)$.

Proof. We can prove this theorem easily. □

We also discussed another extension, like the CPyFAA hybrid averaging (CPyFAAHA) operator of the CPyFAAWA and CPyFAAOWA operators, based on Aczel–Alsina operations.

Definition 13. *Consider* $\Omega_{\mathfrak{z}} = \left(\Pi_{\Omega_{\mathfrak{z}}}(\varkappa)e^{2\pi i(\alpha_{\Omega_{\mathfrak{z}}}(\varkappa))}, \Xi_{\Omega_{\mathfrak{z}}}(\varkappa)e^{2\pi i(\beta_{\Omega_{\mathfrak{z}}}(\varkappa))}\right)$*,* $\mathfrak{z} = 1, 2, \ldots, \mathfrak{n}$ *is the family of CPyFVs. Then, a CPyFAAHA operator is particularized as:*

$$CPyFAAHA\left(\Omega_1, \Omega_2, \ldots, \Omega_{\mathfrak{n}}\right) = \overset{\mathfrak{n}}{\underset{\mathfrak{z}=1}{\oplus}}\left(\mathfrak{A}_{\mathfrak{z}}\mathcal{X}_{\mathfrak{b}(\mathfrak{z})}\right) = \mathfrak{A}_1\mathcal{X}_{\mathfrak{b}(1)} \oplus \mathfrak{A}_2\mathcal{X}_{\mathfrak{b}(2)} \oplus, \ldots, \oplus \mathfrak{A}_{\mathfrak{n}}\mathcal{X}_{\mathfrak{b}(\mathfrak{n})} \quad (7)$$

where the corresponding weight vector of CPyFAAHA operator is denoted by $\mathfrak{A} = (\mathfrak{A}_1, \mathfrak{A}_2, \mathfrak{A}_3, \ldots, \mathfrak{A}_{\mathfrak{y}})^T$, *such that* $\mathfrak{A}_{\mathfrak{z}} \in [0,1]$, $\mathfrak{z} = 1,2,\ldots,\mathfrak{y}$ *and* $\sum_{\mathfrak{z}=1}^{\mathfrak{y}} \mathfrak{A}_{\mathfrak{z}} = 1$ *and* $\mathcal{X}_{\mathfrak{z}} = k\mathfrak{D}_{\mathfrak{z}}\Omega_{\mathfrak{z}}$, $\left(\mathfrak{z} = 1,2,3,\ldots\mathfrak{y}\right)$ *is the set of any permutations* $\left(\mathcal{X}_{\mathfrak{b}(1)}, \mathcal{X}_{\mathfrak{b}(2)}, \mathcal{X}_{\mathfrak{b}(3)}, \ldots, \mathcal{X}_{\mathfrak{b}(\mathfrak{z})}\right)$ *of CPyFVs. The associated weight vector of CPyFVs of* $\Omega_{\mathfrak{z}}$ *is represented by* $\mathfrak{D}_{\mathfrak{z}} = (\mathfrak{D}_1, \mathfrak{D}_2, \mathfrak{D}_3, \ldots, \mathfrak{D}_n)^T$, *such that* $\mathfrak{D}_{\mathfrak{z}} \in [0,1]$, $\mathfrak{z} = 1,2,\ldots,\mathfrak{y}$ *and* $\sum_{\mathfrak{z}=1}^{\mathfrak{y}} \mathfrak{D}_{\mathfrak{z}} = 1$; $\mathcal{X}_{\mathfrak{b}(\mathfrak{z}-1)} \geq \mathcal{X}_{\mathfrak{b}(\mathfrak{z})}$, $\forall$, $\mathfrak{z} = 1, 2, 3, \ldots \mathfrak{y}$ *and a balancing coefficient are denoted by* k.

Theorem 11. *Let* $\Omega_{\mathfrak{z}} = \left(\Pi_{\Omega_{\mathfrak{z}}}(\varkappa)e^{2\pi i(\alpha_{\Omega_{\mathfrak{z}}}(\varkappa))}, \Xi_{\Omega_{\mathfrak{z}}}(\varkappa)e^{2\pi i(\beta_{\Omega_{\mathfrak{z}}}(\varkappa))}\right)$, $\mathfrak{z} = 1,2,\ldots,\mathfrak{y}$ *be the family of CPyFVs. Then, the CPyFAAHA operator is particularized as:*

$$CPyFAAHA\left(\Omega_1, \Omega_2, \ldots, \Omega_{\mathfrak{y}}\right) = \begin{pmatrix} \sqrt{1 - e^{-\left(\sum_{\mathfrak{z}=1}^{\mathfrak{y}} \mathfrak{A}_{\mathfrak{z}}\left(-ln\left(1-\Pi^2_{\mathcal{X}_{\mathfrak{b}(\mathfrak{z})}}\right)\right)^{\Upsilon}\right)^{\frac{1}{\Upsilon}}}} \, e^{2\pi i\left(\sqrt{1 - e^{-\left(\sum_{\mathfrak{z}=1}^{\mathfrak{y}} \mathfrak{A}_{\mathfrak{z}}\left(-ln\left(1-\alpha^2_{\mathcal{X}_{\mathfrak{b}(\mathfrak{z})}}\right)\right)^{\Upsilon}\right)^{\frac{1}{\Upsilon}}}}\right)}, \\ e^{-\left(\sum_{\mathfrak{z}=1}^{\mathfrak{y}} \mathfrak{A}_{\mathfrak{z}}\left(-ln\left(\Xi_{\mathcal{X}_{\mathfrak{b}(\mathfrak{z})}}\right)\right)^{\Upsilon}\right)^{\frac{1}{\Upsilon}}} \, e^{2\pi i\left(e^{-\left(\sum_{\mathfrak{z}=1}^{\mathfrak{y}} \mathfrak{A}_{\mathfrak{z}}\left(-ln\left(\beta_{\mathcal{X}_{\mathfrak{b}(\mathfrak{z})}}\right)\right)^{\Upsilon}\right)^{\frac{1}{\Upsilon}}}\right)} \end{pmatrix} \quad (8)$$

Proof. We can prove this theorem analogously. □

6. Complex Pythagorean Fuzzy Aczel–Alsina Weighted Geometric Aggregation Operators

By utilizing the theory of Aczel–Alsina operations, we explored the concept of CPyFSs in the framework of CPyFAAWG operators with some reversed properties. To support our proposed technique, we established a numerical example.

Definition 14. *Consider* $\Omega_{\mathfrak{z}} = (\Pi_{\Omega_{\mathfrak{z}}}(\varkappa)e^{2\pi i(\alpha_{\Omega_{\mathfrak{z}}}(\varkappa))}, \Xi_{\Omega_{\mathfrak{z}}}(\varkappa)e^{2\pi i(\beta_{\Omega_{\mathfrak{z}}}(\varkappa))})$, $\mathfrak{z} = 1,2,\ldots,\mathfrak{y}$ *to be the family of CPyFVs and weight vector* $\mathfrak{D}_{\mathfrak{z}} = (\mathfrak{D}_1, \mathfrak{D}_2, \mathfrak{D}_3, \ldots, \mathfrak{D}_n)^T$ *of* $\Omega_{\mathfrak{z}}(\mathfrak{z} = 1,2,3,\ldots\mathfrak{y})$,.

such that $\mathfrak{D}_{\mathfrak{z}} \in [0,1]$, $\mathfrak{z} = 1,2,\ldots,\mathfrak{n}$ *and* $\sum_{\mathfrak{z}=1}^{\mathfrak{n}} \mathfrak{D}_{\mathfrak{z}} = 1$. *Then, the CPyFAAWG operator is particularized as:*

$$CPyFAAWG\left(\Omega_1,\ \Omega_2,\ \ldots,\ \Omega_{\mathfrak{n}}\right) = \underset{\mathfrak{z}=1}{\overset{\mathfrak{n}}{\otimes}}\left(\Omega_{\mathfrak{z}}^{\mathfrak{D}_{\mathfrak{z}}}\right) = \Omega_1^{\mathfrak{D}_1} \otimes \Omega_2^{\mathfrak{D}_2} \otimes, \ldots, \otimes \Omega_{\mathfrak{n}}^{\mathfrak{D}_{\mathfrak{n}}} \tag{9}$$

Theorem 12. *Consider* $\Omega_{\mathfrak{z}} = \left(\Pi_{\Omega_{\mathfrak{z}}}(\varkappa)e^{2\pi i(\alpha_{\Omega_{\mathfrak{z}}}(\varkappa))}, \Xi_{\Omega_{\mathfrak{z}}}(\varkappa)e^{2\pi i(\beta_{\Omega_{\mathfrak{z}}}(\varkappa))}\right)$, $\mathfrak{z} = 1,2,\ldots,\mathfrak{n}$ *to be the family of CPyFVs and weight vector* $\mathfrak{D}_{\mathfrak{z}} = (\mathfrak{D}_1, \mathfrak{D}_2, \mathfrak{D}_3, \ldots, \mathfrak{D}_n)^T$ *of* $\Omega_{\mathfrak{z}}(\mathfrak{z} = 1,2,3,\ldots\mathfrak{n})$, *such that* $\mathfrak{D}_{\mathfrak{z}} \in [0,1]$, $\mathfrak{z} = 1,2,\ldots,\mathfrak{n}$ *and* $\sum_{\mathfrak{z}=1}^{\mathfrak{n}} \mathfrak{D}_{\mathfrak{z}} = 1$. *Then, the associated value of the CPyFAAWG operator is also a CPyFV, and we have:*

$$CPyFAAWG\left(\Omega_1,\ \Omega_2,\ \ldots,\ \Omega_{\mathfrak{n}}\right) = \left(\begin{array}{c} e^{-\left(\sum_{\mathfrak{z}=1}^{k} \mathfrak{D}_{\mathfrak{z}}\left(-ln\left(\Pi_{\Omega_{\mathfrak{z}}}\right)\right)^{\Upsilon}\right)^{\frac{1}{\Upsilon}}} e^{2\pi i\left(e^{-\left(\sum_{\mathfrak{z}=1}^{k} \mathfrak{D}_{\mathfrak{z}}\left(-ln\left(\alpha_{\Omega_{\mathfrak{z}}}(\varkappa)\right)\right)^{\Upsilon}\right)^{\frac{1}{\Upsilon}}}\right)}, \\ \sqrt{1-e^{-\left(\sum_{\mathfrak{z}=1}^{k} \mathfrak{D}_{\mathfrak{z}}\left(-ln\left(1-\left(\Xi_{\Omega_{\mathfrak{z}}}\right)^2\right)\right)^{\Upsilon}\right)^{\frac{1}{\Upsilon}}}} e^{2\pi i\left(\sqrt{1-e^{-\left(\sum_{\mathfrak{z}=1}^{k} \mathfrak{D}_{\mathfrak{z}}\left(-ln\left(1-\left(\beta_{\Omega_{\mathfrak{z}}}(\varkappa)\right)^2\right)\right)^{\Upsilon}\right)^{\frac{1}{\Upsilon}}}}\right)}, \end{array}\right) \tag{10}$$

Theorem 13. *Consider* $\Omega_{\mathfrak{z}} = \left(\Pi_{\Omega_{\mathfrak{z}}}(\varkappa)e^{2\pi i(\alpha_{\Omega_{\mathfrak{z}}}(\varkappa))}, \Xi_{\Omega_{\mathfrak{z}}}(\varkappa)e^{2\pi i(\beta_{\Omega_{\mathfrak{z}}}(\varkappa))}\right)$, *to be the set of all same CPyFVs,* $\forall$, $\mathfrak{z} = 1,\ 2,\ldots,\mathfrak{n}$. *Then, we have:*

$$CPyFAAWG\left(\Omega_1,\ \Omega_2,\ \ldots,\ \Omega_{\mathfrak{n}}\right) = \Omega$$

Proof. We can prove this theorem by following the steps of Theorem 3. □

Theorem 14. *Let* $\Omega_{\mathfrak{z}} = \left(\Pi_{\Omega_{\mathfrak{z}}}(\varkappa)e^{2\pi i(\alpha_{\Omega_{\mathfrak{z}}}(\varkappa))}, \Xi_{\Omega_{\mathfrak{z}}}(\varkappa)e^{2\pi i(\beta_{\Omega_{\mathfrak{z}}}(\varkappa))}\right)$, $\mathfrak{z} = 1,2,\ldots,\mathfrak{n}$ *be the family of CPyFVs, and* $\Omega^- = min(\Omega_1, \Omega_2,\ \Omega_3, \ldots,\ \Omega_{\mathfrak{n}})$ *and* $\Omega^+ = max(\Omega_1, \Omega_2,\ \Omega_3, \ldots,\ \Omega_{\mathfrak{n}})$. *Then, the associated value* $CPyFAAWG(\Omega_1,\ \Omega_2,\ \ldots,\ \Omega_k)$ *has that*

$$\Omega^- \leq CPyFAAWG\left(\Omega_1,\ \Omega_2,\ \ldots,\ \Omega_{\mathfrak{n}}\right) \leq \Omega^+$$

Proof. The proof of this theorem is similar to that of Theorem 4. □

Theorem 15. *If* $\Omega_\mathfrak{z} = \left(\Pi_{\Omega_\mathfrak{z}}(\varkappa)e^{2\pi i(\alpha_{\Omega_\mathfrak{z}}(\varkappa))}, \Xi_{\Omega_\mathfrak{z}}(\varkappa)e^{2\pi i(\beta_{\Omega_\mathfrak{z}}(\varkappa))}\right)$ *and* $\Omega'_\mathfrak{z} = \left(\Pi_{\Omega'_\mathfrak{z}}(\varkappa)e^{2\pi i(\alpha_{\Omega'_\mathfrak{z}}(\varkappa))}, \Xi_{\Omega'_\mathfrak{z}}(\varkappa)e^{2\pi i(\beta_{\Omega'_\mathfrak{z}}(\varkappa))}\right)$, $\mathfrak{z} = 1, 2, \ldots, \mathfrak{n}$ *are two CPyFSs, and if* $\Omega_\mathfrak{z} \leq \Omega'_\mathfrak{z}, \forall, \left(\mathfrak{z} = 1, 2, \ldots, \mathfrak{n}\right)$*, then, we have:*

$$CPyFAAWG\left(\Omega_1, \Omega_2, \ldots, \Omega_\mathfrak{n}\right) \leq CPyFAAWG\left(\Omega'_1, \Omega'_2, \ldots, \Omega'_\mathfrak{n}\right)$$

Proof. We can prove this theorem easily. □

Example 3. *Consider* $\Omega_1 = (0.46e^{2i\pi(0.67)}, 0.45e^{2i\pi(0.09)}), \Omega_2 = (0.46e^{2i\pi(0.67)}, 0.45e^{2i\pi(0.09)})$, $\Omega_3 = (0.46e^{2i\pi(0.67)}, 0.45e^{2i\pi(0.09)})$ *and* $\Omega_4 = (0.46e^{2i\pi(0.67)}, 0.45e^{2i\pi(0.09)})$ *are four CPyFVs with corresponding weight vector* $\mathfrak{D} = (0.20, 0.35, 0.30, 0.15)$*. Then, the aggregated values of CPyFAAWG operators is given as* $\Upsilon = 3$.

Solution. *Since we have: for* $\mathfrak{z} = 1, 2, 3, 4$

$$CPyFAAWG(\Omega_1, \Omega_2, \ldots, \Omega_4) = \begin{pmatrix} e^{-\left(\Sigma_{\mathfrak{z}=1}^{4}\mathfrak{D}_\mathfrak{z}\left(-ln\left(\Pi_\mathfrak{z}\right)\right)^3\right)^{\frac{1}{3}}} e^{2\pi i\left(e^{-\left(\Sigma_{\mathfrak{z}=1}^{4}\mathfrak{D}_\mathfrak{z}(-ln(\alpha_\mathfrak{z}))^3\right)^{\frac{1}{3}}}\right)}, \\ \sqrt{1-e^{-\left(\Sigma_{\mathfrak{z}=1}^{4}\mathfrak{D}_\mathfrak{z}\left(-ln\left(1-\Xi_\mathfrak{z}^2\right)\right)^3\right)^{\frac{1}{3}}}} e^{2\pi i\left(\sqrt{1-e^{-\left(\Sigma_{\mathfrak{z}=1}^{4}\mathfrak{D}_\mathfrak{z}\left(-ln\left(1-\beta_\mathfrak{z}^2\right)\right)^3\right)^{\frac{1}{3}}}}\right)} \end{pmatrix}$$

$$= \begin{pmatrix} e^{-\left(\begin{pmatrix}(0.20)(-ln(0.55))^3+(0.35)(-ln(0.17))^3+\\(0.30)(-ln(0.55))^3+(0.15)(-ln(0.47))^3\end{pmatrix}\right)^{\frac{1}{3}}} e^{2\pi i\left(e^{-\left(\begin{pmatrix}(0.20)(-ln(0.29))^3+(0.35)(-ln(0.27))^3+\\(0.30)(-ln(0.78))^3+(0.15)(-ln(0.57))^3\end{pmatrix}\right)^{\frac{1}{3}}}\right)}, \\ \sqrt{1-e^{-\left(\begin{pmatrix}(0.20)\left(-ln\left(1-(0.46)^2\right)\right)^3+(0.35)\left(-ln\left(1-(0.45)^2\right)\right)^3+\\(0.30)\left(-ln\left(1-(0.18)^2\right)\right)^3+(0.15)\left(-ln\left(1-(0.47)^2\right)\right)^3\end{pmatrix}\right)^{\frac{1}{3}}}} e^{2\pi i\left(\sqrt{1-e^{-\left(\begin{pmatrix}(0.20)\left(-ln\left(1-(0.71)^2\right)\right)^3+(0.35)\left(-ln\left(1-(0.61)^2\right)\right)^3+\\(0.30)\left(-ln\left(1-(0.28)^2\right)\right)^3+(0.15)\left(-ln\left(1-(0.48)^2\right)\right)^3\end{pmatrix}\right)^{\frac{1}{3}}}}\right)} \end{pmatrix}$$

$$= \left(0.2768e^{2i\pi(0.3459)}, 0.4340e^{2i\pi(0.6149)}\right)$$

Now, we explored the AOs of the CPyFAAWG operator, and also studied some special cases of the CPyFAAWG operator in the framework of a CPyF Aczel–Alsina ordered weighted geometric (CPyFAAOWG) operator, based on Aczel–Alsina operations.

Definition 15. *Let* $\Omega_{\mathfrak{z}} = \left(\Pi_{\Omega_{\mathfrak{z}}}(\varkappa)e^{2\pi i(\alpha_{\Omega_{\mathfrak{z}}}(\varkappa))}, \Xi_{\Omega_{\mathfrak{z}}}(\varkappa)e^{2\pi i(\beta_{\Omega_{\mathfrak{z}}}(\varkappa))}\right)$, $\mathfrak{z} = 1,2,\ldots,\mathfrak{n}$ *be the family of CPyFVs and weight vectors* $\mathfrak{D}_{\mathfrak{z}} = (\mathfrak{D}_1, \mathfrak{D}_2, \mathfrak{D}_3, \ldots, \mathfrak{D}_n)^T$ *of* $\Omega_{\mathfrak{z}}(\mathfrak{z} = 1,2,3,\ldots\mathfrak{n})$, *such that* $\mathfrak{D}_{\mathfrak{z}} \in [0,1]$, $\mathfrak{z} = 1,2,\ldots,\mathfrak{n}$ *and* $\sum_{\mathfrak{z}=1}^{\mathfrak{n}} \mathfrak{D}_{\mathfrak{z}} = 1$. *Then, the associated values of the CPyFAAOWG operator are particularized as:*

$$CPyFAAOWG\left(\Omega_1, \Omega_2, \ldots, \Omega_{\mathfrak{n}}\right) = \underset{\mathfrak{z}=1}{\overset{\mathfrak{n}}{\otimes}} \left(\Omega_{\mathfrak{b}(\mathfrak{z})}^{\mathfrak{D}_{\mathfrak{z}}}\right) = \Omega_{\mathfrak{b}(1)}^{\mathfrak{D}_1} \otimes \Omega_{\mathfrak{b}(2)}^{\mathfrak{D}_2} \otimes, \ldots, \otimes \Omega_{\mathfrak{b}(\mathfrak{n})}^{\mathfrak{D}_{\mathfrak{n}}} \quad (11)$$

where $(\mathfrak{b}(1), \mathfrak{b}(2), \mathfrak{b}(3), \ldots, \mathfrak{b}(\mathfrak{z}))$ *is the set of permutations of* $\left(\mathfrak{z} = 1,2,3,\ldots\mathfrak{n}\right)$ *and* $\Omega_{\mathfrak{b}(\mathfrak{z}-1)} \geq \Omega_{\mathfrak{b}(\mathfrak{z})}, \forall, \mathfrak{z} = 1, 2, 3, \ldots\mathfrak{n}$.

Theorem 16. *Let* $\Omega_{\mathfrak{z}} = \left(\Pi_{\Omega_{\mathfrak{z}}}(\varkappa)e^{2\pi i(\alpha_{\Omega_{\mathfrak{z}}}(\varkappa))}, \Xi_{\Omega_{\mathfrak{z}}}(\varkappa)e^{2\pi i(\beta_{\Omega_{\mathfrak{z}}}(\varkappa))}\right)$, $\mathfrak{z} = 1,2,\ldots,\mathfrak{n}$ *be the family of CPyFVs and weight vectors* $\mathfrak{D}_{\mathfrak{z}} = (\mathfrak{D}_1, \mathfrak{D}_2, \mathfrak{D}_3, \ldots, \mathfrak{D}_n)^T$ *of* $\Omega_{\mathfrak{z}}\left(\mathfrak{z} = 1,2,3,\ldots\mathfrak{n}\right)$, *such that* $\mathfrak{D}_{\mathfrak{z}} \in [0,1]$, $\mathfrak{z} = 1,2,\ldots,\mathfrak{n}$ *and* $\sum_{\mathfrak{z}=1}^{\mathfrak{n}} \mathfrak{D}_{\mathfrak{z}} = 1$. *Then associated values of the CPyFAAOWG operator are also a CPyFV, and we can write them in the following way:*

$$CPyFAAOWG\left(\Omega_1, \Omega_2, \ldots, \Omega_{\mathfrak{n}}\right) = \left(\begin{array}{c} e^{-(\sum_{\mathfrak{z}=1}^{\mathfrak{n}}(-ln(\Pi_{\Omega_{\mathfrak{b}(\mathfrak{z})}}))^{\Upsilon})^{\frac{1}{\Upsilon}}} e^{2\pi i(e^{-(\sum_{\mathfrak{z}=1}^{\mathfrak{n}}(-ln(\alpha_{\Omega_{\mathfrak{b}(\mathfrak{z})}}))^{\Upsilon})^{\frac{1}{\Upsilon}}})}, \\ \sqrt{1-e^{-(\sum_{\mathfrak{z}=1}^{\mathfrak{n}}(-ln(1-\Xi^2_{\Omega_{\mathfrak{b}(\mathfrak{z})}}))^{\Upsilon})^{\frac{1}{\Upsilon}}}} e^{2\pi i(\sqrt{1-e^{-(\sum_{\mathfrak{z}=1}^{\mathfrak{n}}(-ln(1-\beta^2_{\Omega_{\mathfrak{b}(\mathfrak{z})}}))^{\Upsilon})^{\frac{1}{\Upsilon}}}})} \end{array}\right) \quad (12)$$

where $(\mathfrak{b}(1), \mathfrak{b}(2), \mathfrak{b}(3), \ldots, \mathfrak{b}(\mathfrak{z}))$ *is the set of permutations of* $\left(\mathfrak{z} = 1, 2, 3, \ldots, \mathfrak{n}\right)$ *and* $\Omega_{\mathfrak{b}(\mathfrak{z}-1)} \geq \Omega_{\mathfrak{b}(\mathfrak{z})}, \forall, \mathfrak{z} = 1,2,3,\ldots\mathfrak{n}$.

Proof. We can prove this theorem easily. □

Now, we explored the AOs of the CPyFAAWG operator, and also studied some special cases of the CPyFAAWG operator in the framework of CPyF Aczel–Alsina hybrid geometric (CPyFAAHG) operator, based on Aczel–Alsina operations.

Definition 16. *Consider* $\Omega_{\mathfrak{z}} = (\Pi_{\Omega_{\mathfrak{z}}}(\varkappa)e^{2\pi i(\alpha_{\Omega_{\mathfrak{z}}}(\varkappa))}, \Xi_{\Omega_{\mathfrak{z}}}(\varkappa)e^{2\pi i(\beta_{\Omega_{\mathfrak{z}}}(\varkappa))})$, $\mathfrak{z} = 1,2,\ldots,\mathfrak{n}$ *to be the family of CPyFVs. Then, a CPyFAAHG operator is particularized as:*

$$CPyFAAHG\left(\Omega_1, \Omega_2, \ldots, \Omega_{\mathfrak{n}}\right) = \underset{\mathfrak{z}=1}{\overset{\mathfrak{n}}{\otimes}} \left(\mathfrak{R}_{\mathfrak{z}} \mathcal{X}_{\mathfrak{b}(\mathfrak{z})}\right) = \mathfrak{R}_1 \mathcal{X}_{\mathfrak{b}(1)} \otimes \mathfrak{R}_2 \mathcal{X}_{\mathfrak{b}(2)} \otimes, \ldots, \otimes \mathfrak{R}_{\mathfrak{n}} \mathcal{X}_{\mathfrak{b}(\mathfrak{n})} \quad (13)$$

where $(\mathfrak{b}(1), \mathfrak{b}(2), \mathfrak{b}(3), \ldots, \mathfrak{b}(\mathfrak{z}))$ *is the set of permutations of* $\left(\mathfrak{z} = 1,2,3,\ldots\mathfrak{n}\right)$ *with the weight vector* $\mathfrak{R} = (\mathfrak{R}_1, \mathfrak{R}_2, \mathfrak{R}_3, \ldots, \mathfrak{R}_{\mathfrak{n}})^T$, *such that* $\mathfrak{R}_{\mathfrak{z}} \in [0,1]$, $\mathfrak{z} = 1,2,\ldots,\mathfrak{n}$ *and* $\sum_{\mathfrak{z}=1}^{\mathfrak{n}} \mathfrak{R}_{\mathfrak{z}} = 1$. *A balancing coefficient is denoted by k and* $\mathcal{X}_{\mathfrak{z}} = k\mathfrak{R}_{\mathfrak{z}}\Omega_{\mathfrak{z}}$, $\left(\mathfrak{z} = 1,2,3,\ldots\mathfrak{n}\right)$ *with* $\mathcal{X}_{\mathfrak{b}(\mathfrak{z}-1)} \geq \mathcal{X}_{\mathfrak{b}(\mathfrak{z})}, \forall, \mathfrak{z} = 1,2,3,\ldots\mathfrak{n}$.

Theorem 17. *Let* $\Omega_{\mathfrak{z}} = \left(\Pi_{\Omega_{\mathfrak{z}}}(\varkappa)e^{2\pi i(\alpha_{\Omega_{\mathfrak{z}}}(\varkappa))}, \Xi_{\Omega_{\mathfrak{z}}}(\varkappa)e^{2\pi i(\beta_{\Omega_{\mathfrak{z}}}(\varkappa))}\right)$, $\mathfrak{z} = 1,2,\ldots,\mathfrak{n}$ *be the family of CPyFVs. Then, the CPyFAAHG operator is particularized as:*

$$CPyFAAHG\left(\Omega_1, \Omega_2, \ldots, \Omega_{\mathfrak{n}}\right) = \left(\begin{array}{c} \frac{e^{-\left(\sum_{\mathfrak{z}=1}^{\mathfrak{n}}\left(-ln\left(\Pi_{\chi_{\mathfrak{b}(\mathfrak{z})}}\right)\right)^{\Upsilon}\mathfrak{A}_{\mathfrak{z}}\right)^{\frac{1}{\Upsilon}}}}{\sqrt{1-e^{-\left(\sum_{\mathfrak{z}=1}^{\mathfrak{n}}\left(-ln\left(1-\Xi^2_{\chi_{\mathfrak{b}(\mathfrak{z})}}\right)\right)^{\Upsilon}\mathfrak{A}_{\mathfrak{z}}\right)^{\frac{1}{\Upsilon}}}}} \\ e^{2\pi i\left(e^{-\left(\sum_{\mathfrak{z}=1}^{\mathfrak{n}}\left(-ln\left(\alpha_{\chi_{\mathfrak{b}(\mathfrak{z})}}\right)\right)^{\Upsilon}\mathfrak{A}_{\mathfrak{z}}\right)^{\frac{1}{\Upsilon}}}\right)}, e^{2\pi i\left(\sqrt{1-e^{-\left(\sum_{\mathfrak{z}=1}^{\mathfrak{n}}\left(-ln\left(1-\beta^2_{\chi_{\mathfrak{b}(\mathfrak{z})}}\right)\right)^{\Upsilon}\mathfrak{A}_{\mathfrak{z}}\right)^{\frac{1}{\Upsilon}}}}\right)} \end{array}\right) \quad (14)$$

Proof. We can prove this theorem analogously. □

7. Evaluation of an MADM Technique Using Our Proposed Methodologies

An MADM technique may be solved by utilizing our proposed methodologies under the system of CPyF information. Consider $\psi = \{\psi_1, \psi_2, \psi_3, \ldots, \psi_n\}$ is the set of alternative with the associated weight vector of ψ, $\mathfrak{D} = \{\mathfrak{D}_1, \mathfrak{D}_2, \mathfrak{D}_3, \ldots, \mathfrak{D}_n\}$, such that $\mathfrak{D}_{\mathfrak{z}} \in [0,1]$, $\mathfrak{z} = 1, 2, 3, \ldots, n$, and $\sum_{\mathfrak{z}=1}^{n} \mathfrak{D}_{\mathfrak{z}} = 1$. The decision maker assigns some characteristics to select suitable alternatives like $\upsilon = \{\upsilon_1, \upsilon_2, \upsilon_3, \ldots, \upsilon_n\}$. Consider that $\mathcal{R} = \left(\mathcal{Y}_{\backslash\wr}\right)_{\Updownarrow\times\backslash}$ is the decision matrix and $\mathcal{Y}_{\backslash\wr} = \chi_{\backslash\wr} = \left(\Pi_{\chi_{\backslash\wr}}(\varkappa)e^{2\pi i(\alpha_{\chi_{\backslash\wr}}(\varkappa))}, \Xi_{\chi_{\backslash\wr}}(\varkappa)e^{2\pi i(\beta_{\chi_{\backslash\wr}}(\varkappa))}\right)$ denotes the CPyF numbers (CPyFVs), where $\Pi_{\Omega_{\mathfrak{z}}} \in [0,1]$ and $\Xi_{\Omega_{\mathfrak{z}}} \in [0,1]$ represent the MV and NMV of alternatives, sequentially. The following decision matrix is constructed by the decision maker:

$$\mathcal{R} = \left(\mathcal{Y}_{\backslash\wr}\right)_{\Updownarrow\times\backslash} = \begin{bmatrix} \chi_{11} & \chi_{12} & \cdots & \chi_{1n} \\ \chi_{21} & \chi_{22} & \cdots & \chi_{2n} \\ \vdots & \vdots & & \ddots \\ \chi_{m1} & \chi_{m2} & \cdots & \chi_{mn} \end{bmatrix}$$

In the above decision matrix, each 2-tuple $\left(\Pi_{\chi_{\backslash\wr}}(\varkappa)e^{2\pi i(\alpha_{\chi_{\backslash\wr}}(\varkappa))}, \Xi_{\chi_{\backslash\wr}}(\varkappa)e^{2\pi i(\beta_{\chi_{\backslash\wr}}(\varkappa))}\right)$, has two aspects MV and NMV of CPyFVs in the environment of CPyF information. To select a suitable alternative, we utilized our proposed methodologies of CPyFAAWA and CPyFAAWG operators based on Aczel–Alsina operations. We evaluated the given decision matrix by using the following steps of the algorithm.

7.1. Algorithim

Step 1: Collect the information in the form of CPyFVs and display in a decision matrix using the decision maker.
Step 2: The set of attributes is of two types: beneficial factor attributes and cost factor attributes. A normalized matrix of a decision matrix $\mathcal{R} = (\mathcal{Y}_{no})_{m\times n}$ is denoted by the $\mathcal{R}' = (\mathcal{Y}'_{no})_{m\times n}$. We can obtain them in the following way:

$$\mathcal{Y}'_{no} = \begin{vmatrix} \mathcal{Y}_{no} & \text{for benefit attributes} \\ (\mathcal{Y}_{no})' & \text{for cos t attributes} \end{vmatrix}$$

We can obtain a normalized matrix $\mathcal{R}' = (\mathcal{Y}'_{no})_{m\times n} = \left(\Xi_{\chi_{no}}(\varkappa)e^{2\pi i(\beta_{\chi_{no}}(\varkappa))}, \Pi_{\chi_{no}}(\varkappa)e^{2\pi i(\alpha_{\chi_{no}}(\varkappa))}\right)$ of a decision matrix $\mathcal{R} = (\mathcal{Y}_{no})_{m\times n}$ using the complement of the 2-tuple $\left(\Pi_{\chi_{no}}(\varkappa)e^{2\pi i(\alpha_{\chi_{no}}(\varkappa))}, \Xi_{\chi_{no}}(\varkappa)e^{2\pi i(\beta_{\chi_{no}}(\varkappa))}\right)$. There is no need to transform the decision matrix into a normalized matrix if all attributes are of different kinds and there is no involved cost-type attribute.

Step 3: Investigate the given information $\mathcal{R} = (\mathcal{Y}_{no})_{m\times n}$ of the alternatives in the form of a CPyF system, using proposed AOs of CPyFAAWA and CPyFAAWG operators.

$$\text{CPyFAAWA}\left(\mathcal{Y}'_{n1}, \mathcal{Y}'_{n2}, \mathcal{Y}'_{n3}, \ldots, \mathcal{Y}'_{no}\right) = \overset{\eta}{\underset{\mathfrak{z}=1}{\oplus}}\left(\mathfrak{D}_{\mathfrak{z}}, \mathcal{Y}'_{n\mathfrak{z}}\right)$$

$$= \left(\begin{array}{c} \sqrt{1-e^{-\left(\sum_{\mathfrak{z}=1}^{o}\mathfrak{D}_{\mathfrak{z}}\left(-\ln\left(1-\Pi^2_{\Omega_{\mathfrak{z}}}\right)\right)^{\Upsilon}\right)^{\frac{1}{\Upsilon}}}}\; e^{2\pi i\left(\sqrt{1-e^{-\left(\sum_{\mathfrak{z}=1}^{o}\mathfrak{D}_{\mathfrak{z}}\left(-\ln\left(1-\alpha^2_{\Omega_{\mathfrak{z}}}\right)\right)^{\Upsilon}\right)^{\frac{1}{\Upsilon}}}}\right)}, \\ e^{-\left(\sum_{\mathfrak{z}=1}^{o}\mathfrak{D}_{\mathfrak{z}}\left(-\ln\left(\Xi_{\Omega_{\mathfrak{z}}}\right)\right)^{\Upsilon}\right)^{\frac{1}{\Upsilon}}}\; e^{2\pi i\left(e^{-\left(\sum_{\mathfrak{z}=1}^{l}\mathfrak{D}_{\mathfrak{z}}\left(-\ln\left(\beta_{\Omega_{\mathfrak{z}}}\right)\right)^{\Upsilon}\right)^{\frac{1}{\Upsilon}}}\right)} \end{array}\right)$$

$$\text{CPyFAAWG}\left(\Omega_1, \Omega_2, \ldots, \Omega_\eta\right) = \overset{\eta}{\underset{\mathfrak{z}=1}{\otimes}}\left(\Omega_{\mathfrak{z}}^{\mathfrak{D}_{\mathfrak{z}}}\right)$$

$$= \left(\begin{array}{c} e^{-\left(\sum_{\mathfrak{z}=1}^{k}\mathfrak{D}_{\mathfrak{z}}\left(-\ln\left(\Pi_{\Omega_{\mathfrak{z}}}\right)\right)^{\Upsilon}\right)^{\frac{1}{\Upsilon}}}\; e^{2\pi i\left(e^{-\left(\sum_{\mathfrak{z}=1}^{k}\mathfrak{D}_{\mathfrak{z}}\left(-\ln\left(\alpha_{\Omega_{\mathfrak{z}}}(\varkappa)\right)\right)^{\Upsilon}\right)^{\frac{1}{\Upsilon}}}\right)}, \\ \sqrt{1-e^{-\left(\sum_{\mathfrak{z}=1}^{k}\mathfrak{D}_{\mathfrak{z}}\left(-\ln\left(1-\left(\Xi_{\Omega_{\mathfrak{z}}}\right)^2\right)\right)^{\Upsilon}\right)^{\frac{1}{\Upsilon}}}}\; e^{2\pi i\left(\sqrt{1-e^{-\left(\sum_{\mathfrak{z}=1}^{k}\mathfrak{D}_{\mathfrak{z}}\left(-\ln\left(1-\left(\beta_{\Omega_{\mathfrak{z}}}(\varkappa)\right)^2\right)\right)^{\Upsilon}\right)^{\frac{1}{\Upsilon}}}}\right)}, \end{array}\right)$$

Step 4: After evaluation of the given information by the decision maker, we find the score values by using the consequences of CPyFAAWA and CPyFAAWG operators.
Step 5: To find out suitable alternative, we have to perform the task of ordering and ranking the score values obtained by the previous step.

7.2. Exmaple

A multinational company want to fill their vacant post of a general manager. Consider $x_n\,; n(1, 2, 3, 4, 5)$ be the set of five different applicants. The decision maker wants to complete the selection process according to the following attributes. J_1 represents the qualification of the applicants, J_2 represents the experience of the applicants, J_3 represents the behavior and character of the applicants and J_4 represents the personality of the applicants. The decision maker explored the selection process by using the weight vector $\mathfrak{D} = (0.30,\ 0.25,\ 0.35,\ 0.10)$ for the applicants. The decision maker presented information in the form of CPyFVs and depicted in the decision matrix of Table 2.

Table 2. Decision matrix using the information of the CPyFVs.

	J_1	J_2
x_1	$\left(0.55e^{2i\pi(0.29)},\ 0.46e^{2i\pi(0.71)}\right)$	$\left(0.46e^{2i\pi(0.67)},\ 0.45e^{2i\pi(0.09)}\right)$
x_2	$\left(0.46e^{2i\pi(0.33)},\ 0.09e^{2i\pi(0.41)}\right)$	$\left(0.17e^{2i\pi(0.27)},\ 0.45e^{2i\pi(0.61)}\right)$
x_3	$\left(0.45e^{2i\pi(0.61)},\ 0.88e^{2i\pi(0.28)}\right)$	$\left(0.67e^{2i\pi(0.45)},\ 0.62e^{2i\pi(0.45)}\right)$
x_4	$\left(0.36e^{2i\pi(0.71)},\ 0.46e^{2i\pi(0.67)}\right)$	$\left(0.36e^{2i\pi(0.68)},\ 0.36e^{2i\pi(0.56)}\right)$
x_5	$\left(0.48e^{2i\pi(0.67)},\ 0.19e^{2i\pi(0.37)}\right)$	$\left(0.56e^{2i\pi(0.67)},\ 0.19e^{2i\pi(0.37)}\right)$
	J_3	J_4
x_1	$\left(082e^{2i\pi(0.27)},\ 0.43e^{2i\pi(0.61)}\right)$	$\left(0.56e^{2i\pi(0.81)},\ 0.23e^{2i\pi(0.09)}\right)$
x_2	$\left(0.39e^{2i\pi(0.36)},\ 0.35e^{2i\pi(0.55)}\right)$	$\left(0.19e^{2i\pi(0.46)},\ 0.53e^{2i\pi(0.47)}\right)$
x_3	$\left(0.55e^{2i\pi(0.78)},\ 0.18e^{2i\pi(0.28)}\right)$	$\left(0.49e^{2i\pi(0.47)},\ 0.29e^{2i\pi(0.38)}\right)$
x_4	$\left(0.47e^{2i\pi(0.58)},\ 0.42e^{2i\pi(0.38)}\right)$	$\left(0.8e^{2i\pi(0.48)},\ 0.53e^{2i\pi(0.45)}\right)$
x_5	$\left(0.57e^{2i\pi(0.61)},\ 0.38e^{2i\pi(0.63)}\right)$	$\left(0.47e^{2i\pi(0.57)},\ 0.47e^{2i\pi(0.48)}\right)$

7.3. *Method of the Selection Process*

The decision maker evaluates given information by using our proposed methodologies based on the following steps in the algorithm

Step 1: Collection of information in the form of CPyFVs and displayed in Table 2 by the decision maker.

Step 2: In this step, perform the transformation of the decision matrix into the normalizer matrix. There is no need to perform such a task because there is no cost factor involved in the set of attributes/characteristics for the section model.

Step 3: Investigate the given information by using proposed AOs of CPyFAAWA and CPyFAAWG operators. The consequences of such as are displayed in the following Table 3.

Step 4: Evaluate score values by using the consequences of the CPyFAAWA and CPyFAAWG operators, using Definition 11 and the Definition14. The results shown in Table 4.

Step 5: To analyse suitable applicants, we arranged score values and performed ranking and ordering of the score values in Table 4. We can see that x_1 and x_5 are suitable applicants obtained by CPyFAAWA and CPyFAAWG operators. We also explored obtained score values in the following graphical representation of Figure 2.

Table 3. Consequences of CPyFAAWA and CPyFAAWG operators.

CPyFAAWA	CPyFAAWG
$\left(0.7416e^{2i\pi(0.6545)},\ 0.3959e^{2i\pi(0.1821)}\right)$	$\left(0.5554e^{2i\pi(0.3292)},\ 0.4398e^{2i\pi(0.6357)}\right)$
$\left(04035e^{2i\pi(0.3635)},\ 0.1863e^{2i\pi(0.4908)}\right)$	$\left(0.2681e^{2i\pi(0.3276)},\ 0.4196e^{2i\pi(0.5471)}\right)$
$\left(0.5864e^{2i\pi(0.7046)},\ 0.2847e^{2i\pi(0.3137)}\right)$	$\left(0.5199e^{2i\pi(0.5509)},\ 0.7965e^{2i\pi(0.3774)}\right)$
$\left(0.6195e^{2i\pi(0.6609)},\ 0.4185e^{2i\pi(0.4685)}\right)$	$\left(0.4050e^{2i\pi(0.6086)},\ 0.4456e^{2i\pi(0.5909)}\right)$
$\left(0.5409e^{2i\pi(0.6461)},\ 0.2411e^{2i\pi(0.4273)}\right)$	$\left(0.5229e^{2i\pi(0.6333)},\ 0.3648e^{2i\pi(0.5533)}\right)$

Table 4. Ranking and ordering of the score values.

Operators	$S(x_1)$	$S(x_2)$	$S(x_3)$	$S(x_4)$	$S(x_5)$	Ranking and Ordering
CPyFAAWA	0.3942	0.0097	0.3304	0.2130	0.2347	$x_1 \succ x_3 \succ x_5 \succ x_4 \succ x_2$
CPyFAAWG	−0.0904	−0.1481	−0.1015	−0.0067	0.1176	$x_5 \succ x_4 \succ x_1 \succ x_3 \succ x_2$

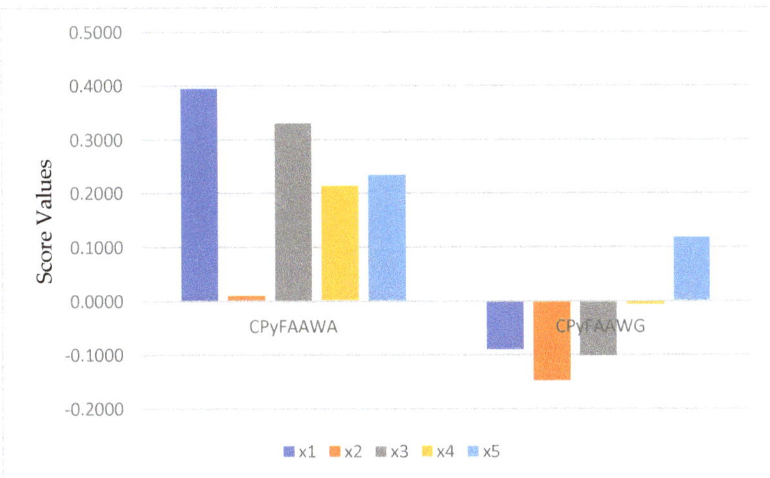

Figure 2. The score values of the CPyFAAWA and CPyFAAWG operators.

7.4. Influence Study

We deploy several parameters Υ inside the approaches we have mentioned to characterize the alternatives and to demonstrate the influence of various parameter Υ magnitudes. Tables 5 and 6 report the ordering consequences of the CPyFAAWA and CPyFAAWG operator-based option selections. It is obvious that as the magnitude Υ for the CPyFAAWA and CPyFAAWG operators increases; the score values of the alternatives continue rising, but the best option stays the same. This suggests that the provided strategies have the property of isotonicity and that the decision makers can choose the most appropriate value based on their preferences. Furthermore, we see that the results generated by the alternatives seem to be consistent, even when the value varies throughout the demonstration, illustrating the stability of the recommended operators.

We also illustrate the consequences of CPyFAAWA and CPyFAAWG operators as the geometrical representation of Figures 3 and 4, respectively.

Table 5. The ordering and ranking of the obtained consequences of CPyFAAWA operators.

	$S(x_1)$	$S(x_2)$	$S(x_3)$	$S(x_4)$	$S(x_5)$	Ordering and Ranking
$\Upsilon = 1$	0.2169	−0.0383	0.2275	0.1062	0.2082	$x_3 \succ x_1 \succ x_5 \succ x_4 \succ x_2$
$\Upsilon = 3$	0.3942	0.0097	0.3304	0.2130	0.2347	$x_1 \succ x_3 \succ x_5 \succ x_4 \succ x_2$
$\Upsilon = 11$	0.5562	0.0771	0.4259	0.3534	0.2733	$x_1 \succ x_3 \succ x_4 \succ x_5 \succ x_2$
$\Upsilon = 25$	0.6004	0.1024	0.4524	0.3967	0.2874	$x_1 \succ x_3 \succ x_4 \succ x_5 \succ x_2$
$\Upsilon = 75$	0.6228	0.1164	0.4663	0.4222	0.2957	$x_1 \succ x_3 \succ x_4 \succ x_5 \succ x_2$
$\Upsilon = 105$	0.6260	0.1184	0.4683	0.4259	0.2970	$x_1 \succ x_3 \succ x_4 \succ x_5 \succ x_2$
$\Upsilon = 155$	0.6285	0.1201	0.4699	0.4288	0.2981	$x_1 \succ x_3 \succ x_4 \succ x_5 \succ x_2$
$\Upsilon = 201$	0.6297	0.1209	0.4707	0.4303	0.2986	$x_1 \succ x_3 \succ x_4 \succ x_5 \succ x_2$
$\Upsilon = 265$	0.6307	0.1215	0.4713	0.4314	0.2991	$x_1 \succ x_3 \succ x_4 \succ x_5 \succ x_2$
$\Upsilon = 313$	0.6311	0.1218	0.4716	0.4320	0.2993	$x_1 \succ x_3 \succ x_4 \succ x_5 \succ x_2$
$\Upsilon = 395$	0.6317	0.1222	0.4719	0.4326	0.2995	$x_1 \succ x_3 \succ x_4 \succ x_5 \succ x_2$
$\Upsilon = 475$	0.6320	0.1224	0.4722	0.4330	0.2997	$x_1 \succ x_3 \succ x_4 \succ x_5 \succ x_2$

Table 6. The ordering and ranking of the obtained consequences of CPyFAAWG operators.

	$S(x_1)$	$S(x_2)$	$S(x_3)$	$S(x_4)$	$S(x_5)$	Ordering and Ranking
$\Upsilon = 1$	0.0089	−0.0982	0.0436	0.0485	0.1721	$x_5 \succ x_4 \succ x_3 \succ x_1 \succ x_2$
$\Upsilon = 3$	−0.0904	−0.1481	−0.1015	−0.0067	0.1176	$x_5 \succ x_4 \succ x_1 \succ x_3 \succ x_2$
$\Upsilon = 11$	−0.1653	−0.2190	−0.2223	−0.1033	0.0403	$x_5 \succ x_4 \succ x_1 \succ x_2 \succ x_2$
$\Upsilon = 25$	−0.1911	−0.2487	−0.2566	−0.1474	0.0043	$x_5 \succ x_4 \succ x_1 \succ x_2 \succ x_3$
$\Upsilon = 75$	−0.2070	−0.2666	−0.2760	−0.1724	−0.0208	$x_5 \succ x_4 \succ x_1 \succ x_2 \succ x_3$
$\Upsilon = 105$	−0.2094	−0.2691	−0.2788	−0.1760	−0.0249	$x_5 \succ x_4 \succ x_1 \succ x_2 \succ x_3$
$\Upsilon = 155$	−0.2114	−0.2712	−0.2811	−0.1788	−0.0284	$x_5 \succ x_4 \succ x_1 \succ x_2 \succ x_3$
$\Upsilon = 201$	−0.2124	−0.2722	−0.2822	−0.1802	−0.0301	$x_5 \succ x_4 \succ x_1 \succ x_2 \succ x_3$
$\Upsilon = 265$	−0.2131	−0.2730	−0.2831	−0.1814	−0.0315	$x_5 \succ x_4 \succ x_1 \succ x_2 \succ x_3$
$\Upsilon = 313$	−0.2135	−0.2734	−0.2836	−0.1819	−0.0322	$x_5 \succ x_4 \succ x_1 \succ x_2 \succ x_3$
$\Upsilon = 395$	−0.2140	−0.2739	−0.2841	−0.1825	−0.0330	$x_5 \succ x_4 \succ x_1 \succ x_2 \succ x_3$
$\Upsilon = 475$	−0.2142	−0.2742	−0.2844	−0.1829	−0.0335	$x_5 \succ x_4 \succ x_1 \succ x_2 \succ x_3$

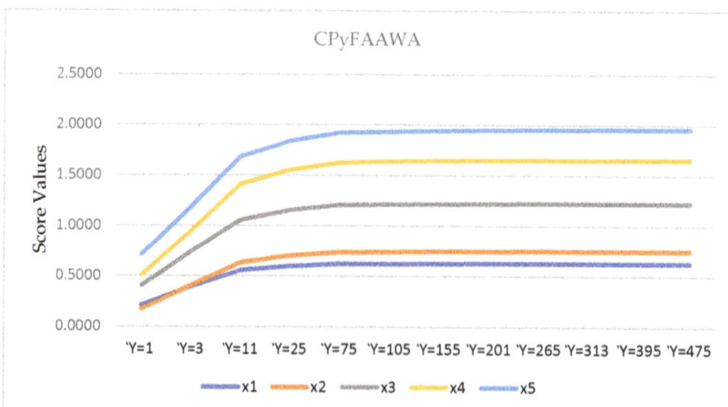

Figure 3. The results of CPyFAAWA operators for Υ.

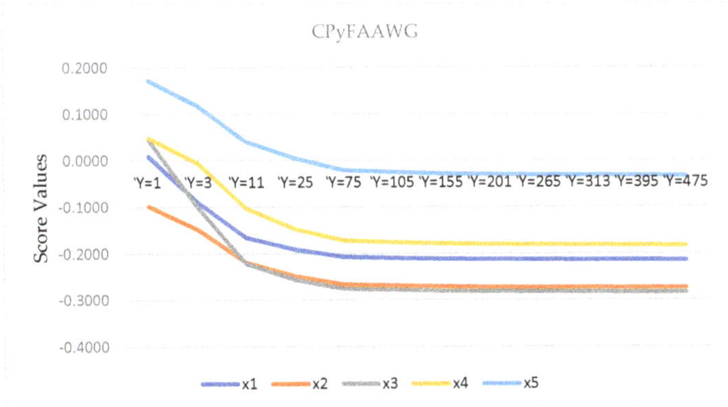

Figure 4. The results of CPyFAAWG operators for 'Υ.

8. Comparative Study

To classify the validity and feasibility of our proposed methodologies, we applied several existing AOs to demonstrate information given by the decision makers and displayed in Table 2: the AOs of CPyF-weighted average, (CPyFWA) and CPyF-weighted geometric (CPyFWG) operators by Mahmood et al. [25], AOs of CPyF Dombi-weighted average and CPyF Dombi-weighted operators by Akram et al. [59], AOs of PyF Aczel–Alsina-weighted average (PyFAAWA) and PyF Aczel–Alsina-weighted geometric (PyFAAWG) given by Hussain et al. [58], AOs of interval-valued CPyFWA (IVCPyFWA) and interval-valued CPyFWG (IVCPyFWG) operators by Ali et al. [60], AOs of PyF-weighted average (PyFWA) and PyF-weighted geometric (PyFWG) operators by Rahman et al. [24], and AOs of PyF Einstein-weighted (PyFEW) average (PyFEW) and geometric (PyFEWG) operators by Garg, 2016 [61]. The results of aforementioned existing AOs operators are shown in the following Table 7.

Table 7. The results of existing AOs and our proposed methodologies.

Aggregation Operators	Environment	Ranking and Ordering
CPyFAAWA	CPyFVs	$x_1 \succ x_3 \succ x_5 \succ x_4 \succ x_2$
CPyFAAWG	CPyFVs	$x_5 \succ x_4 \succ x_1 \succ x_3 \succ x_2$
CPyFWA [25]	CPyFVs	$x_3 \succ x_1 \succ x_5 \succ x_4 \succ x_2$
CPyFWG [25]	CPyFVs	$x_5 \succ x_4 \succ x_3 \succ x_1 \succ x_2$
CPyFDWAA [59]	CPyFVs	$x_1 \succ x_3 \succ x_5 \succ x_4 \succ x_2$
CPyFDWGA [59]	CPyFVs	$x_5 \succ x_4 \succ x_3 \succ x_1 \succ x_2$
PFAAWA/PFAAWG [58]	PyFVs	Failed
IVCPyFWA/IVCPyFWA [60]	IVCPyFVs	Failed
PyFWA/PyFWG [24]	PyFVs	Failed
PyFEWA/PyFEWG [61]	PyFVs	Failed

Furthermore, we also illustrate the results of existing AOs as a graphical representation in Figure 5, which is shown above Table 7.

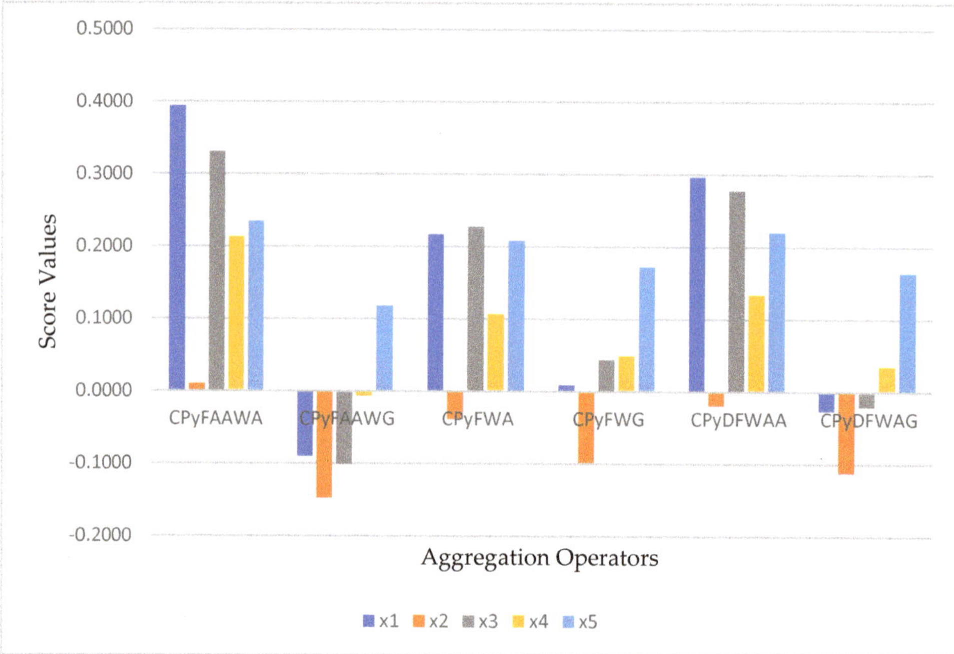

Figure 5. The results of the comparative analysis.

9. Conclusions

Decision-making problems are widespread throughout multiple sectors, including marketing, business and technology. There are a lot of difficulties that decision makers face during the aggregation process due to insufficient information. We used an innovative concept of CPyFSs and developed a list of new AOs based on Aczel–Alsina operations: a CPyFS that has extensive information, including two aspects of MV and NMV in the form of amplitude and phase terms. The main purposes of this article are as follows.

(1) The main contribution of this article is to present some new AOs and fundamental operational laws of CPyFSs. We generalized the basic idea of Aczel–Alsina TNM and TCNM with operational laws and illustrative examples.
(2) By using the operational laws of Aczel–Alsina TNM and TCNM, we developed a list of new AOs, like the CPyFAAWA operator, and verified invented AOs with some deserved properties.
(3) Furthermore, we also established the CPyFAAWAG operator based on the defined fundamental operational laws of Aczel–Alsina TNM and TCNM.
(4) To find the feasibility and reliability of our invented methodologies, we explored some special cases like CPyFAA-ordered weighted (CPyFAAOW), average (CPyFAAOWA) and CPyFAAOW geometric (CPyFAAOWG) operators, and CPyFAA hybrid-weighted (CPyFAAHW), average (CPyFAAHWA) and CPyFAAHW geometric (CPyFAAHWG) operators with some basic properties.
(5) By utilizing our invented approaches, we solved an MADM technique. We established an illustrative example to select a suitable candidate for the vacant post of a multinational company.
(6) To analyze the effectiveness of different parametric values of Υ on the results of our proposed approaches, we discussed an influence study.
(7) We checked the reliability and flexibility of our invented approaches by comparing the results of existing AOs with the results of our discussed technique.

The aforementioned operators and approaches will be gradually applied to a range of applications, such as networking analysis, risk assessment, cognitive science, recommender systems, signal processing and many more domains in ambiguous circumstances. Additionally, the interrelationships between the pairs of attributes throughout the aggregation process are not taken into consideration in the current study, but they will be in future ones. To better understand the information in our daily lives, we will also try to establish some more generalized information measurements. We will explore our invented methodologies within the framework of multi-criteria development in the system of the fuzzy environment [62]. We will also explore the concepts of our proposed approaches within the framework of bipolar-valued hesitant fuzzy information [63]. Moreover, we will also explore our current work within the framework of interval type-2 fuzzy systems with quantized output tools [64].

Author Contributions: Conceptualization, H.J., A.H., K.U. and A.J.; Formal analysis, K.U.; Investigation, H.J., A.H., K.U. and A.J.; Software, A.H. and A.J.; Supervision, H.J. and K.U.; Validation, A.H. and A.J.; Visualization, A.H.; Writing—original draft, H.J., A.H., K.U. and A.J.; Writing—review & editing, H.J., A.H., K.U. and A.J. All authors have read and agreed to the published version of the manuscript.

Funding: This research received no external funding.

Institutional Review Board Statement: Not applicable.

Informed Consent Statement: Not applicable.

Data Availability Statement: Not applicable.

Conflicts of Interest: The authors have no conflict of interest regarding this paper.

References

1. Zadeh, L.A. Fuzzy Sets. *Inf. Control* **1965**, *8*, 338–353. [CrossRef]
2. Atanassov, K.T. Intuitionistic Fuzzy Sets. *Fuzzy Sets Syst.* **1986**, *20*, 87–96. [CrossRef]
3. Yager, R.R. Pythagorean Fuzzy Subsets. In Proceedings of the 2013 Joint IFSA World Congress and NAFIPS Annual Meeting (IFSA/NAFIPS), Edmonton, AB, Canada, 24–28 June 2013; pp. 57–61.
4. Adlassnig, K.-P. Fuzzy Set Theory in Medical Diagnosis. *IEEE Trans. Syst. Man Cybern.* **1986**, *16*, 260–265. [CrossRef]
5. Atanassov, K.T. Interval Valued Intuitionistic Fuzzy Sets. In *Intuitionistic Fuzzy Sets*; Springer: Berlin/Heidelberg, Germany, 1999; pp. 139–177.
6. Mohd, W.R.W.; Abdullah, L. Similarity Measures of Pythagorean Fuzzy Sets Based on Combination of Cosine Similarity Measure and Euclidean Distance Measure. *AIP Conf. Proc.* **2018**, *1974*, 030017.
7. Ramot, D.; Milo, R.; Friedman, M.; Kandel, A. Complex Fuzzy Sets. *IEEE Trans. Fuzzy Syst.* **2002**, *10*, 171–186. [CrossRef]
8. Ramot, D.; Friedman, M.; Langholz, G.; Kandel, A. Complex Fuzzy Logic. *IEEE Trans. Fuzzy Syst.* **2003**, *11*, 450–461. [CrossRef]
9. Alkouri, A.M.J.S.; Salleh, A.R. Complex Intuitionistic Fuzzy Sets. *AIP Conf. Proc.* **2012**, *1482*, 464–470.
10. Ullah, K.; Mahmood, T.; Ali, Z.; Jan, N. On Some Distance Measures of Complex Pythagorean Fuzzy Sets and Their Applications in Pattern Recognition. *Complex Intell. Syst.* **2020**, *6*, 15–27. [CrossRef]
11. Riaz, M.; Hashmi, M.R. Linear Diophantine Fuzzy Set and Its Applications towards Multi-Attribute Decision-Making Problems. *J. Intell. Fuzzy Syst.* **2019**, *37*, 5417–5439. [CrossRef]
12. Akram, M.; Naz, S. A Novel Decision-Making Approach under Complex Pythagorean Fuzzy Environment. *Math. Comput. Appl.* **2019**, *24*, 73. [CrossRef]
13. Khan, R.; Ullah, K.; Pamucar, D.; Bari, M. Performance Measure Using a Multi-Attribute Decision Making Approach Based on Complex T-Spherical Fuzzy Power Aggregation Operators. *J. Comput. Cogn. Eng.* **2022**. [CrossRef]
14. Ali, Z.; Mahmood, T.; Pamucar, D.; Wei, C. Complex Interval-Valued q-Rung Orthopair Fuzzy Hamy Mean Operators and Their Application in Decision-Making Strategy. *Symmetry* **2022**, *14*, 592. [CrossRef]
15. Mahmood, T. A Novel Approach towards Bipolar Soft Sets and Their Applications. *J. Math.* **2020**, *2020*, 4690808. [CrossRef]
16. Zhang, N.; Su, W.; Zhang, C.; Zeng, S. Evaluation and Selection Model of Community Group Purchase Platform Based on WEPLPA-CPT-EDAS Method. *Comput. Ind. Eng.* **2022**, *172*, 108573. [CrossRef]
17. Vojinović, N.; Stević, Ž.; Tanackov, I. A Novel IMF $SWARA - FDWGA - PES^{TEL}$ Analysis for Assessment of Healthcare System. *Oper. Res. Eng. Sci. Theory Appl.* **2022**, *5*, 139–151. [CrossRef]
18. Mahmood, T. Multi-Attribute Decision-Making Method Based on Bipolar Complex Fuzzy Maclaurin Symmetric Mean Operators. *Comput. Appl. Math.* **2022**, *41*, 331. [CrossRef]
19. Xu, Z. Intuitionistic Fuzzy Aggregation Operators. *IEEE Trans. Fuzzy Syst.* **2007**, *15*, 1179–1187.

20. Wei, G. Some Induced Geometric Aggregation Operators with Intuitionistic Fuzzy Information and Their Application to Group Decision Making. *Appl. Soft Comput.* **2010**, *10*, 423–431. [CrossRef]
21. Peng, X.; Yuan, H. Fundamental Properties of Pythagorean Fuzzy Aggregation Operators. *Fundam. Inform.* **2016**, *147*, 415–446. [CrossRef]
22. Akram, M.; Ullah, K.; Pamucar, D. Performance Evaluation of Solar Energy Cells Using the Interval-Valued T-Spherical Fuzzy Bonferroni Mean Operators. *Energies* **2022**, *15*, 292. [CrossRef]
23. Khan, Q.; Mahmood, T.; Ullah, K. Applications of Improved Spherical Fuzzy Dombi Aggregation Operators in Decision Support System. *Soft Comput.* **2021**, *25*, 9097–9119. [CrossRef]
24. Rahman, K.; Ali, A.; Shakeel, M.; Khan, M.A.; Ullah, M. Pythagorean Fuzzy Weighted Averaging Aggregation Operator and Its Application to Decision Making Theory. *Nucleus* **2017**, *54*, 190–196.
25. Mahmood, T.; Ali, Z.; Ullah, K.; Khan, Q.; AlSalman, H.; Gumaei, A.; Rahman, S.M.M. Complex Pythagorean Fuzzy Aggregation Operators Based on Confidence Levels and Their Applications. *Math. Biosci. Eng.* **2022**, *19*, 1078–1107. [CrossRef] [PubMed]
26. Liu, P.; Chen, S.-M.; Wang, Y. Multiattribute Group Decision Making Based on Intuitionistic Fuzzy Partitioned Maclaurin Symmetric Mean Operators. *Inf. Sci.* **2020**, *512*, 830–854. [CrossRef]
27. Ullah, K. Picture Fuzzy Maclaurin Symmetric Mean Operators and Their Applications in Solving Multiattribute Decision-Making Problems. *Math. Probl. Eng.* **2021**, *2021*, 1098631. [CrossRef]
28. Akram, M.; Dudek, W.A.; Dar, J.M. Pythagorean Dombi Fuzzy Aggregation Operators with Application in Multicriteria Decision-Making. *Int. J. Intell. Syst.* **2019**, *34*, 3000–3019. [CrossRef]
29. Chen, T.-Y. A Prioritized Aggregation Operator-Based Approach to Multiple Criteria Decision Making Using Interval-Valued Intuitionistic Fuzzy Sets: A Comparative Perspective. *Inf. Sci.* **2014**, *281*, 97–112. [CrossRef]
30. Liu, P.; Wang, P. Multiple-Attribute Decision-Making Based on Archimedean Bonferroni Operators of q-Rung Orthopair Fuzzy Numbers. *IEEE Trans. Fuzzy Syst.* **2018**, *27*, 834–848. [CrossRef]
31. Hussain, A.; Ullah, K.; Ahmad, J.; Karamti, H.; Pamucar, D.; Wang, H. Applications of the Multiattribute Decision-Making for the Development of the Tourism Industry Using Complex Intuitionistic Fuzzy Hamy Mean Operators. *Comput. Intell. Neurosci.* **2022**, *2022*, 8562390. [CrossRef]
32. Garg, H. Intuitionistic Fuzzy Hamacher Aggregation Operators with Entropy Weight and Their Applications to Multi-Criteria Decision-Making Problems. *Iran. J. Sci. Technol. Trans. Electr. Eng.* **2019**, *43*, 597–613. [CrossRef]
33. Akram, M.; Shahzadi, G. A Hybrid Decision-Making Model under q-Rung Orthopair Fuzzy Yager Aggregation Operators. *Granul. Comput.* **2021**, *6*, 763–777. [CrossRef]
34. Jan, N.; Zedam, L.; Mahmood, T.; Ullah, K.; Ali, Z. Multiple Attribute Decision Making Method under Linguistic Cubic Information. *J. Intell. Fuzzy Syst.* **2019**, *36*, 253–269. [CrossRef]
35. Yang, S.; Pan, Y.; Zeng, S. Decision Making Framework Based Fermatean Fuzzy Integrated Weighted Distance and TOPSIS for Green Low-Carbon Port Evaluation. *Eng. Appl. Artif. Intell.* **2022**, *114*, 105048. [CrossRef]
36. Ullah, K.; Mahmood, T.; Jan, N.; Ahmad, Z. Policy Decision Making Based on Some Averaging Aggregation Operators of T-Spherical Fuzzy Sets; a Multi-Attribute Decision Making Approach. *Ann. Optim. Theory Pract.* **2020**, *3*, 69–92.
37. Menger, K. Statistical Metrics. *Proc. Natl. Acad. Sci. USA* **1942**, *28*, 535. [CrossRef]
38. Klement, E.P. *Triangular Norms*; Springer: Berlin/Heidelberg, Germany, 2000; Volume 8, ISBN 978-90-481-5507-1.
39. Klement, E.P.; Navara, M. A Characterization of Tribes with Respect to the Łukasiewicz T-Norm. *Czechoslov. Math. J.* **1997**, *47*, 689–700. [CrossRef]
40. Wang, S. A Fuzzy Logic for the Revised Drastic Product T-Norm. *Soft Comput.* **2007**, *11*, 585–590. [CrossRef]
41. Fodor, J.C. Nilpotent Minimum and Related Connectives for Fuzzy Logic. In Proceedings of the 1995 IEEE International Conference on Fuzzy Systems, Yokohama, Japan, 20–24 March 1995; Volume 4, pp. 2077–2082.
42. Mesiar, R. Nearly Frank T-Norms. *Tatra Mt. Math. Publ.* **1999**, *16*, 127–134.
43. Nguyen, H.T.; Kreinovich, V.; Wojciechowski, P. Strict Archimedean T-Norms and t-Conorms as Universal Approximators. *Int. J. Approx. Reason.* **1998**, *18*, 239–249. [CrossRef]
44. Wang, W.; Liu, X. Some Operations over Atanassov's Intuitionistic Fuzzy Sets Based on Einstein t-Norm and t-Conorm. *Int. J. Uncertain. Fuzziness Knowl.-Based Syst.* **2013**, *21*, 263–276. [CrossRef]
45. Egbert, R.J. Products and Quotients of Probabilistic Metric Spaces. *Pac. J. Math.* **1968**, *24*, 437–455. [CrossRef]
46. Dombi, J. A General Class of Fuzzy Operators, the DeMorgan Class of Fuzzy Operators and Fuzziness Measures Induced by Fuzzy Operators. *Fuzzy Sets Syst.* **1982**, *8*, 149–163. [CrossRef]
47. Mahmood, T.; Waqas, H.M.; Ali, Z.; Ullah, K.; Pamucar, D. Frank Aggregation Operators and Analytic Hierarchy Process Based on Interval-Valued Picture Fuzzy Sets and Their Applications. *Int. J. Intell. Syst.* **2021**, *36*, 7925–7962. [CrossRef]
48. Liu, P. Some Hamacher Aggregation Operators Based on the Interval-Valued Intuitionistic Fuzzy Numbers and Their Application to Group Decision Making. *IEEE Trans. Fuzzy Syst.* **2013**, *22*, 83–97. [CrossRef]
49. Garg, H. Generalized Pythagorean Fuzzy Geometric Aggregation Operators Using Einstein T-Norm and t-Conorm for Multicriteria Decision-Making Process. *Int. J. Intell. Syst.* **2017**, *32*, 597–630. [CrossRef]
50. Yan, S.-R.; Guo, W.; Mohammadzadeh, A.; Rathinasamy, S. Optimal Deep Learning Control for Modernized Microgrids. *Appl. Intell.* **2022**. [CrossRef]

51. Mousavi, S.M.; Salimain, S.; Antucheviciene, J. Evaluation of Infrastructure Projects by A Decision Model with Interval-Valued Intuitionistic Fuzzy Sets. *Int. J. Strateg. Prop. Manag.* **2022**, *26*, 106–118.
52. Aczél, J.; Alsina, C. Characterizations of Some Classes of Quasilinear Functions with Applications to Triangular Norms and to Synthesizing Judgements. *Aequ. Math.* **1982**, *25*, 313–315. [CrossRef]
53. Babu, M.S.; Ahmed, S. Function as the Generator of Parametric T-Norms. *Am. J. Appl. Math.* **2017**, *5*, 114–118. [CrossRef]
54. Senapati, T.; Chen, G.; Yager, R.R. Aczel–Alsina Aggregation Operators and Their Application to Intuitionistic Fuzzy Multiple Attribute Decision Making. *Int. J. Intell. Syst.* **2022**, *37*, 1529–1551. [CrossRef]
55. Senapati, T.; Chen, G.; Mesiar, R.; Yager, R.R. Novel Aczel–Alsina Operations-Based Interval-Valued Intuitionistic Fuzzy Aggregation Operators and Their Applications in Multiple Attribute Decision-Making Process. *Int. J. Intell. Syst.* **2021**, *38*, 5059–5081. [CrossRef]
56. Naeem, M.; Khan, Y.; Ashraf, S.; Weera, W.; Batool, B. A Novel Picture Fuzzy Aczel-Alsina Geometric Aggregation Information: Application to Determining the Factors Affecting Mango Crops. *AIMS Math.* **2022**, *7*, 12264–12288. [CrossRef]
57. Hussain, A.; Ullah, K.; Yang, M.-S.; Pamucar, D. Aczel-Alsina Aggregation Operators on T-Spherical Fuzzy (TSF) Information with Application to TSF Multi-Attribute Decision Making. *IEEE Access* **2022**, *10*, 26011–26023. [CrossRef]
58. Hussain, A.; Ullah, K.; Alshahrani, M.N.; Yang, M.-S.; Pamucar, D. Novel Aczel–Alsina Operators for Pythagorean Fuzzy Sets with Application in Multi-Attribute Decision Making. *Symmetry* **2022**, *14*, 940. [CrossRef]
59. Akram, M.; Khan, A.; Borumand Saeid, A. Complex Pythagorean Dombi Fuzzy Operators Using Aggregation Operators and Their Decision-Making. *Expert Syst.* **2021**, *38*, e12626. [CrossRef]
60. Ali, Z.; Mahmood, T.; Ullah, K.; Khan, Q. Einstein Geometric Aggregation Operators Using a Novel Complex Interval-Valued Pythagorean Fuzzy Setting with Application in Green Supplier Chain Management. *Rep. Mech. Eng.* **2021**, *2*, 105–134. [CrossRef]
61. Garg, H. A New Generalized Pythagorean Fuzzy Information Aggregation Using Einstein Operations and Its Application to Decision Making. *Int. J. Intell. Syst.* **2016**, *31*, 886–920. [CrossRef]
62. Zeng, S.; Hu, Y.; Llopis-Albert, C. Stakeholder-Inclusive Multi-Criteria Development of Smart Cities. *J. Bus. Res.* **2023**, *154*, 113281. [CrossRef]
63. Khan, M.U.; Mahmood, T.; Ullah, K.; Jan, N.; Deli, I. Some Aggregation Operators for Bipolar-Valued Hesitant Fuzzy Information Based on Einstein Operational Laws. *J. Eng. Appl. Sci. JEAS* **2017**, *36*, 63–72.
64. Sakthivel, R.; Kavikumar, R.; Mohammadzadeh, A.; Kwon, O.-M.; Kaviarasan, B. Fault Estimation for Mode-Dependent IT2 Fuzzy Systems with Quantized Output Signals. *IEEE Trans. Fuzzy Syst.* **2020**, *29*, 298–309. [CrossRef]

symmetry

MDPI

Article

Prioritized Aggregation Operators for Intuitionistic Fuzzy Information Based on Aczel–Alsina T-Norm and T-Conorm and Their Applications in Group Decision-Making

Mehwish Sarfraz [1], Kifayat Ullah [1,*], Maria Akram [1], Dragan Pamucar [2,*] and Darko Božanić [3]

[1] Department of Mathematics, Riphah International University (Lahore Campus), Lahore 54000, Pakistan
[2] Department of Operations Research and Statistics, Faculty of Organizational Sciences, University of Belgrade, 11000 Belgrade, Serbia
[3] Military Academy, University of Defense in Belgrade, 11000 Belgrade, Serbia
* Correspondence: kifayat.khan.dr@gmail.com (K.U.); dragan.pamucar@fon.bg.ac.rs (D.P.)

Abstract: In multi-attribute group decision-making (MAGDM) problems, prioritization is sometimes important. Several techniques and methods have been introduced in fuzzy systems to use prioritization. The main purpose of this paper is to propose prioritized aggregation operators (AOs) for intuitionistic fuzzy (IF) information. These AOs are symmetric in nature and are based on the novel Aczel–Alsina t-norm and t-conorm. Herein, we propose IF-prioritized Aczel–Alsina averaging (IFPAAA) and IF-prioritized Aczel–Alsina geometric (IFPAAG) operators. It is shown that these AOs satisfy the basic features of aggregation. Some additional results for these AOs are also investigated. These proposed operators can capture the prioritization phenomenon among the aggregated arguments, and the weights for prioritization are obtained from expert information. Finally, the proposed AOs are used in an MAGDM problem where a doctor is selected for a hospital. A comparison of the proposed prioritized AOs is also established with other well-known AOs to show the significance of the IFPAAA and IFPAAG operators.

Keywords: intuitionistic fuzzy set; Aczel–Alsina t-norm; decision-making; prioritized aggregation operators

1. Introduction

The classical set is characterized so that the universe of elements is split into two groups, i.e., members and non-members. This kind of system can appoint just two numeric values, for example 0 or 1. There are numerous phenomena that cannot be depicted utilizing the classical theory, for example knowledge, age, beauty, intelligence, etc. Zadeh [1] tried to describe such phenomena by introducing the theory of fuzzy sets (FSs) in 1965. Human assessment of some phenomena is not generally unidirectional, and the framework of FSs depicts only one aspect of a questionable occasion by using a membership grade (MG), thus not giving any information about the second aspect, i.e., the non-membership grade (NMG). Atanassov [2] introduced the notion of intuitionistic FSs (IFSs) that describe the MG and NMG of any unsure phenomena. IFSs have a few certain limits, i.e., the sum of MG and NMG cannot exceed $[0, 1]$. This implies that the duplet $(0.9, 0.7)$ cannot be considered an IF value (IFV). IFSs also describe doubts in human opinion using the hesitancy grade (HG), which is defined as the information left when the sum of the MG and NMG is subtracted from 1. Some further work on the theory and applications of FSs and IFSs can be seen in [3,4].

MAGDM is a hot research area, and the most useful tools that has been extensively used in dealing with MAGDM problems are AOs. Most AOs are based on triangular norms (TNs) and triangular conorms (TCNs). These TNs and TCNs include algebraic [5], Einstein [6], Hamacher [7], Frank [8], Dombi [9], Aczel–Alsina [10], etc. There is a wide range of research that has been conducted on the theory of AOs. Xu [11] and Xu and Yager [12] first investigated the algebraic AOs for IF information. The Einstein AOs of IFVs were investigated for MAGDM problems by Wang and Liu [13,14]. The theory and applications of Hamacher AOs for IFSs was investigated by Huang [15]. Zhang et al. [16] used Frank TN and TCN to introduce IF Frank AOs for decision-making problems. Recently, Senapati et al. [17] used IF information for MAGDM using the Aczel–Alsina TN and TCN. This led researchers to produce some useful results for the Aczel–Alsina TN and TCN. Hussain et al. [18] introduced Aczel–Alsina AOs for Pythagorean fuzzy information for MAGDM problems. Khan et al. [19] studied the construction material selection problem using novel Aczel–Alsina AOs for generalized orthopair fuzzy information. Hussain et al. [20] studied MAGDM problems using T-spherical fuzzy (TSF) Aczel–Alsina AOs. Some further recent work on the theory and application of AOs based on TNs and TCNs can be seen in [21–25].

In MAGDM problems, sometimes one attribute has priority over other attributes, while sometimes experts have prioritizations. To keep in mind the prioritization of attributes and experts, the concept of prioritized AOs was introduced for the first time by Yager [26] in 2008. Yager [27] also investigated prioritized ordered weighted averaging operators. Yan et al. [28] extended the study of prioritization. Yu and Xu [29] introduced prioritized AOs for IF information. Ali et al. [30] studied the significance of prioritization in the frame of complex IF soft sets for MAGDM problems. Arora and Garg [31] introduced prioritization for linguistic IF information aggregation. Arora and Garg [32] also investigated prioritized AOs for IF soft sets. Chen [33] discussed some comparison perspectives of interval-valued prioritized AOs for MAGDM problems. Gao [34] developed some prioritized AOs for Pythagorean fuzzy information based on the Einstein TN and TCN. Jana et al. [35] developed some prioritized AOs for bipolar fuzzy information based on the Dombi TN and TCN. Riaz et al. [36] studied prioritized AOs for generalized orthopair fuzzy sets. More recent work on prioritized AOs can be found in [37–42].

The concept of Aczel–Alsina AOs is a recent contribution to the theory of fuzzy mathematics, where some significant results have already been established in [17,19–22]. Farahbod and Eftekhari [43] utilized some TNs and TCNs in a classification problem and declared the Aczel–Alsina TN as the most efficient. Keeping in mind the significance of the Aczel–Alsina TN- and TCN-based AOs and prioritization in aggregation phenomena, the goal of this paper is to introduce prioritized AOs for IFSs based on the Aczel–Alsina TN and TCN. The proposed results are novel, and the main advantage of such AOs is to aggregate IF information by using the prioritization phenomenon. To show the effectiveness of the proposed AOs, a few comparisons are provided to understand the advantages of the suggested approaches. It emerges that the results proposed by the IFPAAA and IFPAAG operators are reliable. Such AOs will enable us to aggregate information based on IFVs and keep the attributes or experts in a prioritization order. The key features of the manuscript are as follows:

(1) To propose prioritized AOs for IF information based on the Aczel–Alsina TN and TCN, i.e., IFPAAA and IFPAAG operators, to overcome shortcomings.
(2) To study the importance of the proposed IFPAAA and IFPAAG operators.
(3) To study some properties of the proposed prioritized AOs.
(4) To apply the IFPAAA and IFPAAG operators in a MAGDM problem.
(5) To compare the results obtained using the proposed prioritized AOs of IFVs with other existing AOs.

This paper is organized as follows: Section 1 covers the introduction and brief history of previous concepts with relevant literature. In Section 2, we discuss some basic concepts of IFSs, the Aczel–Alsina TN and TCN, and Aczel–Alsina AOs. In Section 3, we propose the IFPAAA and IFPAAG operators and study their relevant properties. In Section 4, we discuss the MAGDM algorithm based on IFPAAA and IFPAAG operators, followed by a comprehensive decision-making example in Section 5. In Section 6, we establish a comparison study of the proposed and existing theories, while in Section 7, we summarize the article with some concluding remarks.

2. Preliminaries

As an extension of an FS, Atanassov [2] proposed IFSs. IFSs deliver both an MD and an NMD simultaneously, whereas fuzzy sets only deliver the MD of an element in a specific set. The MD in the context of fuzzy sets is a real number between 0 and 1. Similar results are obtained for the NMD, and additionally the sum of the two degrees is less than or equal to 1. IFSs are defined by means of the following:

Definition 1 [2]. *Let F be considered a universe of discourse; an IFS in F is an expression ϱ given by*

$$\beta = \{(\xi, \gamma_\beta(\xi), \delta_\beta(\xi) : \xi \in F)\}$$

where $\gamma_\beta : F \to [0,1]$, $\delta_\beta : F \to [0,1]$, *including the condition* $0 \le \gamma_\beta(\xi) + \delta_\beta(\xi) \le 1$, *for each* ξ *in F. The numbers* $\gamma_\beta(\xi)$ *and* $\delta_\beta(\xi)$ *serve as the MD and NMD of the element* ξ *in the set F, respectively. For every IFS* β *in F, we denote* $\pi_\beta(\xi) = 1 - \gamma_\beta(\xi) - \delta_\beta(\xi), \forall \xi \in F$. *Then* $\pi_\beta(\xi)$ *is known as the hesitancy degree (HD) of* ξ *to* β. *Especially, if* $\pi_\beta(\xi) = 1 - \gamma_\beta(\xi) - \delta_\beta(\xi) = 0, \forall \xi \in F$, *then the IFS* β *is diminished to an FS. Furthermore,* $(\gamma_\beta(\xi), \delta_\beta(\xi))$ *is known as the intuitionistic fuzzy value (IFV).*

Definition 2 [12]. *Let* $\beta_1 = (\gamma_{\beta_1}, \delta_{\beta_1})$ *be an IFV. Then*

$$Sco(\beta_1) = \gamma_{\beta_1} - \delta_{\beta_1} \quad (1)$$

is the score value of β_1.

Definition 3 [12]. *Let* $\beta_1 = (\gamma_{\beta_1}, \delta_{\beta_1})$ *be an IFV. Then*

$$Acc\ (\beta_1) = \gamma_{\beta_1} + \delta_{\beta\ 1} \quad (2)$$

is the degree of accuracy of β_1.

(1) *If* $Sco(\beta_1) < Sco(\beta_2)$, *then* β_1 *has less preference than* β_2.
(2) *If* $Sco(\beta_1) = Sco(\beta_2)$, *then* β_1 *and* β_2 *are the same.*
(3) *If* $Acc\ (\beta_1) < Acc\ (\beta_2)$, *then* β_1 *has less preference than* β_2.
(4) *If* $Acc\ (\beta_1) = Acc\ (\beta_2)$, *then* β_1 *and* β_2 *are the same.*

Definition 4. *The Aczel–Alsina t-norm* $(T_A^{\eta})_{\eta\in[0,\infty]}$ *is ascertained by*

$$(T_A^{\eta})_{(\ell,v)} = \begin{cases} T_D(\ell,v) & if\ \eta = 0 \\ min(\ell,v) & if\ \eta = \infty \\ e^{-((-In\ell)^{\eta}+(-Inv)^{\eta})^{\frac{1}{\eta}}} & otherwise \end{cases}$$

The Aczel–Alsina t-conorm $(S_A^{\eta})_{\eta\in[0,\infty]}$ *is ascertained by*

$$(S_A^{\eta})_{(\ell,v)} = \begin{cases} S_D(\ell,v) & if\ \eta = 0 \\ max(\ell,v) & if\ \eta = \infty \\ 1 - e^{-((-In(1-\ell))^{\eta}+(-In(1-v))^{\eta})^{\frac{1}{\eta}}} & otherwise \end{cases}$$

Limiting values: $T_A^{\infty} = min$, $T_A^0 = T_D$, $T_A^1 = T_p$, $S_A^{\infty} = max$, $S_A^0 = S_D$, *and* $S_A^1 = S_p$. *The t-norm* T_A^{η} *and t-conorm* S_A^{η} *are dual with regard to each other for all* $\eta\in[0,\infty]$. *Both the Aczel–Alsina t-norm family and the Aczel–Alsina t-conorm family show strictly expanding and strictly reducing trends, respectively.*

Furthermore, the Aczel–Alsina t-norms are the only ones that truly satisfy the equivalence $T(\ell^{\lambda}, v^{\lambda}) = T(\ell, v)^{\lambda}$ *for any* $\lambda > 0$ *and* $\ell, v \in [0,1]$.

Definition 5 [17]. *Let* $\beta = (\gamma_{\beta}, \delta_{\beta})$, $\beta_1 = (\gamma_{\beta_1}, \delta_{\beta_1})$, *and* $\beta_2 = (\gamma_{\beta_2}, \delta_{\beta_2})$ *be three IFVs,* $\eta \geq 1$ *and* $\Phi \geq 0$. *Then the Aczel–Alsina t-norm and t-conorm operations of IFVs are defined as:*

$$(i)\quad \beta_1 \oplus \beta_2 = \left(1 - e^{-((-ln(1-\gamma_{\beta_1}))^{\eta} + (-ln(1-\gamma_{\beta_2}))^{\eta})^{1/\eta}}, e^{-((-ln(\delta_{\beta_1}))^{\eta} + (-ln(\delta_{\beta_2}))^{\eta})^{1/\eta}}\right),$$

$$(ii)\quad \beta_1 \otimes \beta_2 = \left(e^{-((-ln(\gamma_{\beta_1}))^{\eta} + (-ln(\gamma_{\beta_2}))^{\eta})^{1/\eta}}, 1 - e^{-((-ln(1-\delta_{\beta_1}))^{\eta} + (-ln(1-\delta_{\beta_2}))^{\eta})^{1/\eta}}\right),$$

$$(iii)\quad \Phi\beta = \left(1 - e^{-(\Phi(-ln(1-\gamma_{\beta}))^{\eta})^{1/\eta}}, e^{-(\Phi(-ln(\delta_{\beta}))^{\eta})^{1/\eta}}\right),$$

$$(iv)\quad \beta^{\Phi} = \left(e^{-(\Phi(-ln(\gamma_{\beta}))^{\eta})^{1/\eta}}, 1 - e^{-(\Phi(-ln(1-\delta_{\beta}))^{\eta})^{1/\eta}}\right),$$

Definition 6. *Let* $\beta_j = \left(\gamma_{\beta_j}, \delta_{\beta_j}\right)$ *be a collection of IFVs and* $\frac{T_1}{\sum_{j=1}^{\vartheta} T_j}\beta_j = (\frac{T_1}{\sum_{j=1}^{\vartheta} T_j}\beta_1, \frac{T_1}{\sum_{j=1}^{\vartheta} T_j}\beta_2, \ldots \frac{T_1}{\sum_{j=1}^{\vartheta} T_j}\beta_{\vartheta})^T$ *shows a weight vector of* $\beta_j (j = 1,2,\ldots,\vartheta)$ *in a manner allowing* $\beta_j \in [0,1]$, $j = 1,2,\ldots \vartheta$ *and* $\sum_{j=1}^{\vartheta} \vartheta_j = 1$.
So, the IFPAAA operator of dimension ϑ *is a function IFPAAA:* $L^{*\vartheta} \to L^*$

$$IFPAAA(\beta_1, \beta_2, \ldots, \beta_{\vartheta}) = \left(\left(1 - \prod_{j=1}^{\vartheta}\left(1 - \gamma_{\beta_j}^{L}\right)^{\vartheta_j}, 1 - \prod_{j=1}^{\vartheta}\left(1 - \gamma_{\beta_j}^{U}\right)^{\vartheta_j}\right), \left(\prod_{j=1}^{\vartheta}\left(\delta_{\beta_j}^{L}\right)^{\vartheta_j}, \prod_{j=1}^{\vartheta}\left(\delta_{\beta_j}^{U}\right)^{\vartheta_j}\right)\right)$$

3. Intuitionistic Fuzzy Prioritized Aczel–Alsina Averaging Aggregation Operators

In this section, we present a few IFPAAA operators by means of the Aczel–Alsina operations. Throughout this article, $(j = 1,2\ldots,\vartheta)$ will stand for indexing terms.

Definition 7. *Let* $\beta_j = \left(\gamma_{\beta_j}, \delta_{\beta_j}\right)$ *be an accumulation of IFVs. Then, the (IFPAAA) operator is a function IFPAAA:* $L^{*\vartheta} \to L^*$ *and defined as:*

$$IFPAAA(\beta_1, \beta_2, \ldots \beta_{\vartheta}) = \oplus_{j=1}^{\vartheta} \frac{T_j}{\sum_{j=1}^{\vartheta} T_j}\beta_j$$

Using Aczel–Alsina operations on IFVs, we prove the following theorem.

Theorem 1. *Let* $\beta_j = \left(\gamma_{\beta_j}, \delta_{\beta_j}\right)$ *be a collection of IFVs. Then, the aggregated value of* β_j *utilizing the IFPAAA operator is also an IFV, given by:*

$$IFPAAA(\beta_1, \beta_2, \ldots \beta_{\vartheta}) = \begin{pmatrix} 1 - e^{-(\sum_{j=1}^{\vartheta} \frac{T_j}{\sum_{j=1}^{\vartheta} T_j}(-ln(1-\gamma_{\beta_j}))^{\eta})^{\frac{1}{\eta}}}, \\ e^{-(\sum_{j=1}^{\vartheta} \frac{T_j}{\sum_{j=1}^{\vartheta} T_j}(-ln(\delta_{\beta_j}))^{\eta})^{1/\eta}} \end{pmatrix} \quad (3)$$

Proof. Theorem 1 can be demonstrated in the following way using the mathematical induction approach.

(I) For $\vartheta = 2$, using Aczel–Alsina operations of IFVs, we obtain

$$\frac{T_1}{\sum_{j=1}^{\vartheta} T_j}\beta_1 = \left(1 - e^{-\left(\frac{T_1}{\sum_{j=1}^{\vartheta} T_j}(-ln(1-\gamma_{\beta_1}))^{\eta}\right)^{1/\eta}}, e^{-\left(\frac{T_1}{\sum_{j=1}^{\vartheta} T_j}(-ln(\delta_{\beta_1}))^{\eta}\right)^{1/\eta}}\right)$$

$$\frac{T_2}{\sum_{j=1}^{\vartheta} T_j}\beta_2 = \left(1 - e^{-\left(\frac{T_2}{\sum_{j=1}^{\vartheta} T_j}(-ln(1-\gamma_{\beta_2}))^{\eta}\right)^{\frac{1}{\eta}}}, e^{-\left(\frac{T_2}{\sum_{j=1}^{\vartheta} T_j}(-ln(\delta_{\beta_2}))^{\eta}\right)^{\frac{1}{\eta}}}\right)$$

$$IFPAAA(\beta_1, \beta_2) = \frac{T_1}{\sum_{j=1}^{2} T_j}\beta_1 \oplus \frac{T_2}{\sum_{j=1}^{2} T_j}\beta_2$$

$$= \left(1 - e^{-\left(\frac{T_1}{\sum_{j=1}^{2} T_j}(-ln(1-\gamma_{\beta_1}))^{\eta}\right)^{\frac{1}{\eta}}}, e^{-\left(\frac{T_1}{\sum_{j=1}^{2} T_j}(-ln(\delta_{\beta_1}))^{\eta}\right)^{\frac{1}{\eta}}}\right)$$

$$\oplus \left(1 - e^{-\left(\frac{T_2}{\sum_{j=1}^{2} T_j}(-ln(1-\gamma_{\beta_2}))^{\eta}\right)^{1/\eta}}, e^{-\left(\frac{T_2}{\sum_{j=1}^{2} T_j}(-ln(\delta_{\beta_2}))^{\eta}\right)^{1/\eta}}\right)$$

$$= \left(\begin{array}{c} 1 - e^{-\left(\frac{T_1}{\sum_{j=1}^{2} T_j}(-ln(1-\gamma_{\beta_1}))^{\eta} + \frac{T_2}{\sum_{j=1}^{2} T_j}(-ln(1-\gamma_{\beta_2}))^{\eta}\right)^{\frac{1}{\eta}}}, \\ e^{-\left(\frac{T_1}{\sum_{j=1}^{2} T_j}(-ln(\delta_{\beta_1}))^{\eta} + \frac{T_2}{\sum_{j=1}^{2} T_j}(-ln(\delta_{\beta_2}))^{\eta}\right)^{1/\eta}} \end{array}\right)$$

$$= \left(1 - e^{-\left(\sum_{j=1}^{\vartheta} \frac{T_j}{\sum_{j=1}^{2} T_j}(-ln(1-\gamma_{\beta_j}))^{\eta}\right)^{1/\eta}}, e^{-\left(\sum_{j=1}^{\vartheta} \frac{T_j}{\sum_{j=1}^{2} T_j}(-ln(\delta_{\beta_j}))^{\eta}\right)^{1/\eta}}\right)$$

Hence, Equation (3) is true for $\vartheta = 2$.

(II) Assume that Equation (3) is true for $\vartheta = k$, then we have

$$IFPAAA(\beta_1, \beta_2, \ldots \beta_k) = \oplus_{j=1}^{k} \frac{T_j}{\sum_{j=1}^{k} T_j}(\beta_j) = \left(\begin{array}{c} 1 - e^{-\left(\sum_{j=1}^{k} \frac{T_j}{\sum_{j=1}^{k} T_j}(-ln(1-\gamma_{\beta_j}))^{\eta}\right)^{\frac{1}{\eta}}}, \\ e^{-\left(\sum_{j=1}^{k} \frac{T_j}{\sum_{j=1}^{k} T_j}(-ln(\delta_{\beta_j}))^{\eta}\right)^{1/\eta}} \end{array}\right)$$

Now for $\vartheta = k + 1$, we obtain

$$IFPAAA(\beta_1, \beta_2, \ldots \beta_{k+1}) = \oplus_{j=1}^{k} \frac{T_j}{\sum_{j=1}^{k+1} T_j}(\beta_j) \oplus \frac{T_{k+1}}{\sum_{j=1}^{k+1} T_j}(\beta_{k+1})$$

$$= \left(\left(1 - e^{-\left(\sum_{j=1}^{k} \frac{T_j}{\sum_{j=1}^{k+1} T_j}(-ln(1-\gamma_{\beta_j}))^{\eta}\right)^{\frac{1}{\eta}}}, e^{-\left(\sum_{j=1}^{k} \frac{T_j}{\sum_{j=1}^{k+1} T_j}(-ln(\delta_{\beta_j}))^{\eta}\right)^{\frac{1}{\eta}}}\right) \oplus \left(1 - e^{-\left(\frac{T_{k+1}}{\sum_{j=1}^{k+1} T_j}(-ln(1-\gamma_{\beta_{k+1}}))^{\eta}\right)^{1/\eta}}, e^{-\left(\frac{T_{k+1}}{\sum_{j=1}^{k+1} T_j}(-ln(1-\delta_{\beta_{k+1}}))^{\eta}\right)^{1/\eta}}\right)\right)$$

$$= \left(1 - e^{-\left(\sum_{j=1}^{k+1} \frac{T_j}{\sum_{j=1}^{k+1} T_j}(-ln(1-\gamma_{\beta_j}))^{\eta}\right)^{1/\eta}}, e^{-\left(\sum_{j=1}^{k+1} \frac{T_j}{\sum_{j=1}^{k+1} T_j}(-ln(\delta_{\beta_j}))^{\eta}\right)^{1/\eta}}\right)$$

Equation (3) is therefore valid for $\vartheta = k + 1$.
We conclude that Equation (3) holds for any value of ϑ as a result of forms (I) and (II).
Every aggregation operator must satisfy the boundedness and monotonicity condition; idempotency is also one the famous properties of aggregation. Below, we show that the IFPAAA operator satisfies the condition of boundedness, monotonicity, idempotency.

The following properties, given in Theorems 2, 3, and 4, are likely to satisfy using the IFPAAA operator. □

Theorem 2. *If all $\beta_j = \left(\gamma_{\beta_j}, \delta_{\beta_j}\right) = (\gamma_\beta, \delta_\beta) = \beta$, that is $\beta_j = \beta$ for all j, then $IFPAAA(\beta_1, \beta_2, \ldots, \beta_\vartheta) = \beta$.*

Proof. Since $\beta_j = \left(\gamma_{\beta_j}, \delta_{\beta_j}\right) = \beta = (\gamma_\beta, \delta_\beta)$, then we have by Equation (3)

$$IFPAAA(\beta_1, \beta_2, \ldots \beta_\vartheta) = \left(1 - e^{-\left(\sum_{j=1}^{\vartheta} \frac{T_j}{\sum_{j=1}^{\vartheta} T_j}(-ln(1-\gamma_{\beta_j}))^{\eta}\right)^{1/\eta}}, e^{-\left(\sum_{j=1}^{\vartheta} \frac{T_j}{\sum_{j=1}^{\vartheta} T_j}(-ln(\delta_{\beta_j}))^{\eta}\right)^{1/\eta}}\right)$$
$$= \left(1 - e^{-((-ln(1-\gamma_\beta))^{\eta})^{1/\eta}}, e^{-((-ln(\delta_\beta))^{\eta})^{1/\eta}}\right)$$
$$= \left(1 - e^{-ln(1-\gamma_\beta)}, e^{ln\delta_\beta}\right) = (\gamma_\beta, \delta_\beta) = \beta$$

Thus, $IFPAAA(\beta_1, \beta_2, \ldots, \beta_\varrho) = \beta$ holds. □

Theorem 3. *Let $\beta_j = \left(\gamma_{\beta_j}, \delta_{\beta_j}\right)$ be a collection of IFVs. Let $\beta^- = min(\beta_1, \beta_2, \ldots, \beta_\vartheta)$ and $\beta^+ = max(\beta_1, \beta_2, \ldots, \beta_\vartheta)$. Then $\beta^- \leq IFPAAA(\beta_1, \beta_2, \ldots, \beta_\vartheta) \leq \beta^+$.*

Proof. Let $\beta_j = \left(\gamma_{\beta_j}, \delta_{\beta_j}\right)$ be a collection of IFVs. Let $\beta^- = min(\beta_1, \beta_2, \ldots, \beta_\vartheta) = \left(\gamma_\beta^-, \delta_\beta^-\right)$ and $\beta^+ = max(\beta_1, \beta_2, \ldots, \beta_\vartheta) = \left(\gamma_\beta^+, \delta_\beta^+\right)$. Hence, there are the subsequent inequalities:

$$1 - e^{-\left(\sum_{j=1}^{\vartheta} \frac{T_j}{\sum_{j=1}^{\vartheta} T_j}(-ln(1-\gamma_\beta^-))^{\eta}\right)^{\frac{1}{\eta}}} \leq 1 - e^{-\left(\sum_{j=1}^{\vartheta} \frac{T_j}{\sum_{j=1}^{\vartheta} T_j}(-ln(1-\gamma_{\beta_j}))^{\eta}\right)^{\frac{1}{\eta}}}$$
$$\leq 1 - e^{-\left(\sum_{j=1} \frac{T_j}{\sum_{j=1}^{\vartheta} T_j}(-ln(1-\gamma_{\beta_j}))^{\eta}\right)^{1/\eta}}$$
$$e^{-\left(\sum_{j=1}^{\vartheta} \frac{T_j}{\sum_{j=1}^{\vartheta} T_j}(-ln(\delta_\beta^+))^{\eta}\right)^{1/\eta}} \geq e^{-\left(\sum_{j=1}^{\vartheta} \frac{T_j}{\sum_{j=1}^{\vartheta} T_j}(-ln(\delta_{\beta_j}))^{\eta}\right)^{1/\eta}} \geq e^{-\left(\sum_{j=1}^{\vartheta} \frac{T_j}{\sum_{j=1}^{\vartheta} T_j}(-ln(\delta_\beta^-))^{\eta}\right)^{1/\eta}}$$

Therefore, $\beta^- \leq IFPAAA(\beta_1, \beta_2, \ldots, \beta_\vartheta \leq \beta^+)$. □

Theorem 4. *Let β_j and β_j' be two sets of IFVs. If $\beta_j \leq \beta_j'$ for all j, then*

$$IFPAAA(\beta_1, \beta_2, \ldots, \beta_\vartheta) \leq IFPAAA(\beta_1', \beta_2', \ldots, \beta_\vartheta')$$

Proof. Straightforward. □

Theorem 5. *Let $\beta_j = \left(\gamma_{\beta_j}, \delta_{\beta_j}\right)$ be a collection of IFVs, where $T_j = \prod_{k=1}^{j-1} S(\beta_k)(j = 2, \ldots \vartheta)$, $T_1 = 1$, and $S(\beta_k)$ is the score of IFVs (β_k). If $\alpha = (\gamma_\alpha, \delta_\alpha)$ is IFVs on k, then:*

$$IFPAAA(\beta_1 \oplus \alpha, \beta_2 \oplus \alpha, \ldots, \beta_\vartheta \oplus \alpha) = IFPAAA(\beta_1, \beta_2, \ldots, \beta_\vartheta) \oplus \alpha$$

Proof. First, we compute $IFPAAA(\beta_1 \oplus \alpha, \beta_2 \oplus \alpha, \ldots, \beta_\vartheta \oplus \alpha)$.

$$IFPAAA(\beta_1,\beta_2,\ldots\beta_\vartheta)=\left(1-e^{-\left(\sum_{j=1}^{\vartheta}\frac{T_j}{\sum_{j=1}^{\vartheta}T_j}(-ln(1-\gamma_{\beta_j}))^{ɳ}\right)^{1/ɳ}},e^{-\left(\sum_{j=1}^{\vartheta}\frac{T_j}{\sum_{j=1}^{\vartheta}T_j}(-ln(\delta_{\beta_j}))^{ɳ}\right)^{1/ɳ}}\right)$$

$$\beta_j\oplus\alpha=\left(1-e^{-((-ln(1-\gamma_{\beta_j}))^{ɳ}+(-ln(1-\gamma_\alpha))^{ɳ})^{1/ɳ}},e^{-((-ln(\delta_{\beta_j}))^{ɳ}+(-ln(\delta_\alpha))^{ɳ})^{1/ɳ}}\right)$$

$$IFPAAA(\beta_1\oplus\alpha,\beta_2\oplus\alpha,\ldots,\beta_\vartheta\oplus\alpha)$$

$$=\left(\begin{array}{c}1-e^{-\left(\sum_{j=1}^{\vartheta}\frac{T_j}{\sum_{j=1}^{\vartheta}T_j}\left(-ln\left(1-\left(1-e^{-((-ln(1-\gamma_{\beta_j}))^{ɳ}+(-ln(1-\gamma_\alpha))^{ɳ})^{\frac{1}{ɳ}}}\right)\right)\right)^{ɳ}\right)^{\frac{1}{ɳ}}},\\ e^{-\left(\sum_{j=1}^{\vartheta}\frac{T_j}{\sum_{j=1}^{\vartheta}T_j}\left(-ln\left(e^{-((-ln(\delta_{\beta_j}))^{ɳ}+(-ln(\delta_\alpha))^{ɳ})^{1/ɳ}}\right)\right)^{ɳ}\right)^{1/ɳ}}\end{array}\right)$$

$$IFPAAA(\beta_1\oplus\alpha,\beta_2\oplus\alpha,\ldots,\beta_\vartheta\oplus\alpha)=\left(\begin{array}{c}1-e^{-\left(\left(\sum_{j=1}^{\vartheta}\frac{T_j}{\sum_{j=1}^{\vartheta}T_j}(-ln(1-\gamma_{\beta_j}))^{ɳ}\right)+(-ln(1-(\gamma_\alpha)))^{ɳ}\right)^{\frac{1}{ɳ}}},\\ e^{-\left(\left(\sum_{j=1}^{\vartheta}\frac{T_j}{\sum_{j=1}^{\vartheta}T_j}(-ln(\delta_{\beta_j}))^{ɳ}\right)+(-ln(\delta_\alpha))^{ɳ}\right)^{1/ɳ}}\end{array}\right)$$

$$IFPAAA(\beta_1\oplus\alpha,\beta_2\oplus\alpha,\ldots,\beta_\vartheta\oplus\alpha)$$

$$=\left(1-e^{-\left(\sum_{j=1}^{\vartheta}\frac{T_j}{\sum_{j=1}^{\vartheta}T_j}(-ln(1-\gamma_{\beta_j\oplus\alpha}))^{ɳ}\right)^{1/ɳ}},e^{-\left(\sum_{j=1}^{\vartheta}\frac{T_j}{\sum_{j=1}^{\vartheta}T_j}(-ln(\delta_{\beta_j\oplus\alpha}))^{ɳ}\right)^{1/ɳ}}\right)$$

Then, we make an expression for $IFPAAA(\beta_1,\beta_2,\ldots,\beta_\vartheta)\oplus\alpha$

$$IFPAAA(\beta_1,\beta_2,\ldots\beta_\vartheta)=\left(1-e^{-\left(\sum_{j=1}^{\vartheta}\frac{T_j}{\sum_{j=1}^{\vartheta}T_j}(-ln(1-\gamma_{\beta_j}))^{ɳ}\right)^{1/ɳ}},e^{-\left(\sum_{j=1}^{\vartheta}\frac{T_j}{\sum_{j=1}^{\vartheta}T_j}(-ln(\delta_{\beta_j}))^{ɳ}\right)^{1/ɳ}}\right)$$

$$IFPAAA(\beta_1,\beta_2,\ldots\beta_\vartheta)\oplus\alpha=\left(\begin{array}{c}1-e^{-\left(\sum_{j=1}^{\vartheta}\frac{T_j}{\sum_{j=1}^{\vartheta}T_j}(-ln(1-\gamma_{\beta_j}))^{ɳ}\right)^{\frac{1}{ɳ}}},\\ e^{-\left(\sum_{j=1}^{\vartheta}\frac{T_j}{\sum_{j=1}^{\vartheta}T_j}(-ln(\delta_{\beta_j}))^{ɳ}\right)^{1/ɳ}}\end{array}\right)\oplus\alpha$$

$$IFPAAA(\beta_1,\beta_2,\ldots\beta_\vartheta)\oplus\alpha=\left(\begin{array}{c}1-e^{-\left(\sum_{j=1}^{\vartheta}\frac{T_j}{\sum_{j=1}^{\vartheta}T_j}(-ln(1-\gamma_{\beta_j}))^{ɳ}\right)^{\frac{1}{ɳ}}},\\ e^{-\left(\sum_{j=1}^{\vartheta}\frac{T_j}{\sum_{j=1}^{\vartheta}T_j}(-ln(\delta_{\beta_j}))^{ɳ}\right)^{1/ɳ}}\end{array}\right)\oplus(\gamma_\alpha,\delta_\alpha)$$

$$IFPAAA(\beta_1,\beta_2,\ldots\beta_\vartheta)\oplus\alpha$$

$$=\left(\begin{array}{c}1-e^{-\left(\left(-ln\left(1-\left(1-e^{-\left(\sum_{j=1}^{\vartheta}\frac{T_j}{\sum_{j=1}^{\vartheta}T_j}(-ln(1-\gamma_{\beta_j}))^{ɳ}\right)^{\frac{1}{ɳ}}}\right)\right)\right)^{ɳ}+(-ln(1-(\gamma_\alpha)))^{ɳ}\right)^{\frac{1}{ɳ}}},\\ e^{-\left(\left(-ln\left(e^{-\left(\sum_{j=1}^{\vartheta}\frac{T_j}{\sum_{j=1}^{\vartheta}T_j}(-ln(\delta_{\beta_j}))^{ɳ}\right)^{1/ɳ}}\right)\right)^{ɳ}+(-ln(\delta_\alpha))^{ɳ}\right)^{1/ɳ}}\end{array}\right)$$

$$=\left(\begin{array}{c}1-e^{-\left(\left(\sum_{j=1}^{\vartheta}\frac{T_j}{\sum_{j=1}^{\vartheta}T_j}(-ln(1-\gamma_{\beta_j}))^{ɳ}\right)+(-ln(1-(\gamma_\alpha)))^{ɳ}\right)^{\frac{1}{ɳ}}},\\ e^{-\left(\left(\sum_{j=1}^{\vartheta}\frac{T_j}{\sum_{j=1}^{\vartheta}T_j}(-ln(\delta_{\beta_j}))^{ɳ}\right)+(-ln(\delta_\alpha))^{ɳ}\right)^{1/ɳ}}\end{array}\right)$$

Hence:

$$IFPAAA(\beta_1\oplus\alpha,\beta_2\oplus\alpha,\ldots,\beta_\vartheta\oplus\alpha)=IFPAAA(\beta_1,\beta_2,\ldots,\beta_\vartheta)\oplus\alpha$$

□

Theorem 6. *Let* $\beta_j = \left(\gamma_{\beta_j}, \delta_{\beta_j}\right)$ *be a collection of IFVs, and* $T_j = \prod_{k=1}^{j-1} S\ (\beta_k)(j = 2, \ldots \vartheta)$, $T_1 = 1$ *, and* $S\ (\beta_k)$ *is the score of* β_k*, if* $\Phi > 0$*, then:*

$$IFPAAA(\Phi\beta_1, \Phi\beta_2, \ldots, \Phi\beta_\vartheta) = \Phi IFPAAA(\beta_1, \beta_2, \ldots, \beta_\vartheta)$$

Proof. We have the following based on the operational laws listed in Section 2:

$$\Phi\beta = \left(1 - e^{-\left(\Phi\left(-ln\left(1-\gamma_{\beta_j}\right)\right)^{\eta}\right)^{1/\eta}}, e^{-\left(\Phi\left(-ln\left(\delta_{\beta_j}\right)\right)^{\eta}\right)^{1/\eta}} \right)$$

According to Theorem 1, we have:

$$\text{IFPAAA}(\Phi\beta_1, \Phi\beta_2, \ldots, \Phi\beta_\vartheta)$$

$$= \left(\begin{array}{c} 1 - e^{-\left(\sum_{j=1}^{\vartheta} \frac{T_j}{\sum_{j=1}^{\vartheta} T_j}\left(-\ln\left(1-\left(1-e^{-\left(\Phi\left(-\ln\left(1-\gamma_{\beta_j}\right)\right)^{\eta}\right)^{\frac{1}{\eta}}}\right)\right)\right)^{\eta}\right)^{\frac{1}{\eta}}}, \\ e^{-\left(\sum_{j=1}^{\vartheta} \frac{T_j}{\sum_{j=1}^{\vartheta} T_j}\left(-\ln\left(e^{-\left(\Phi\left(-\ln\left(\delta_{\beta_j}\right)\right)^{\eta}\right)^{1/\eta}}\right)\right)^{\eta}\right)^{1/\eta}} \end{array} \right)$$

$$= \left(1 - e^{-\left(\sum_{j=1}^{\vartheta} \frac{T_j}{\sum_{j=1}^{\vartheta} T_j}\left(\left(\Phi\left(-\ln\left(1-\gamma_{\beta_j}\right)\right)^{\eta}\right)\right)\right)^{\frac{1}{\eta}}}, e^{-\left(\sum_{j=1}^{\vartheta} \frac{T_j}{\sum_{j=1}^{\vartheta} T_j}\left(\left(\Phi\left(-\ln\left(\delta_{\beta_j}\right)\right)^{\eta}\right)\right)\right)^{\frac{1}{\eta}}} \right)$$

$$\Phi IFPAAA(\beta_1, \beta_2, \ldots, \beta_\vartheta) = \Phi \left(1 - e^{-\left(\sum_{j=1}^{\vartheta} \frac{T_j}{\sum_{j=1}^{\vartheta} T_j}\left(-ln\left(1-\gamma_{\beta_j}\right)\right)^{\eta}\right)^{\frac{1}{\eta}}}, e^{-\left(\sum_{j=1}^{\vartheta} \frac{T_j}{\sum_{j=1}^{\vartheta} T_j}\left(-ln\left(\delta_{\beta_j}\right)\right)^{\eta}\right)^{\frac{1}{\eta}}} \right)$$

$$= \left(\begin{array}{c} 1 - e^{-\left(\Phi\left(-ln\left(1-\left(1-e^{-\left(\sum_{j=1}^{\vartheta} \frac{T_j}{\sum_{j=1}^{\vartheta} T_j}\left(-ln\left(1-\gamma_{\beta_j}\right)\right)^{\eta}\right)^{\frac{1}{\eta}}}\right)\right)\right)^{\eta}\right)^{\frac{1}{\eta}}}, \\ e^{-\left(\Phi\left(-ln\left(e^{-\left(\sum_{j=1}^{\vartheta} \frac{T_j}{\sum_{j=1}^{\vartheta} T_j}\left(-ln\left(\delta_{\beta_j}\right)\right)^{\eta}\right)^{1/\eta}}\right)\right)^{\eta}\right)^{1/\eta}} \end{array} \right)$$

$$= \left(1 - e^{-\left(\Phi\left(\left(\sum_{j=1}^{\vartheta} \frac{T_j}{\sum_{j=1}^{\vartheta} T_j}\left(-\ln\left(1-\gamma_{\beta_j}\right)\right)^{\eta}\right)\right)\right)^{1/\eta}}, e^{-\left(\Phi\left(\left(\sum_{j=1}^{\vartheta} \frac{T_j}{\sum_{j=1}^{\vartheta} T_j}\left(-\ln\left(\delta_{\beta_j}\right)\right)^{\eta}\right)\right)\right)^{1/\eta}} \right)$$

Hence:

$$IFPAAA(\Phi\beta_1, \Phi\beta_2, \ldots, \Phi\beta_\vartheta) = \Phi IFPAAA(\beta_1, \beta_2, \ldots, \beta_\vartheta)$$

□

Theorem 7. *Let* $\beta_j = \left(\gamma_{\beta_j}, \delta_{\beta_j}\right)$ *be a collection of IFVs, and* $T_j = \prod_{k=1}^{j-1} S\ (\beta_k)(j = 2, \ldots \vartheta)$, $T_1 = 1$*, and* $S\ (\beta_k)$ *is the score of IFVs* β_k*, if* $\Phi > 0$, $\alpha = (\gamma_\alpha, \delta_\alpha)$ *is a IFVs on k. Then*

$$IFPAAA(\Phi\beta_1 \oplus \alpha, \Phi\beta_2 \oplus \alpha, \ldots, \Phi\beta_\vartheta \oplus \alpha) = \Phi IFPAAA(\beta_1, \beta_2, \ldots, \beta_\vartheta) \oplus \alpha$$

Proof.

$$IFPAAA(\Phi\beta_1 \oplus \alpha, \Phi\beta_2 \oplus \alpha, \ldots, \Phi\beta_\vartheta \oplus \alpha) = \Phi IFPAAA(\beta_1, \beta_2, \ldots, \beta_\vartheta) \oplus \alpha$$

$$IFPAAA(\beta_1, \beta_2, \ldots \beta_\vartheta) = \left(1 - e^{-\left(\sum_{j=1}^{\vartheta} \frac{T_j}{\sum_{j=1}^{\vartheta} T_j}(-ln(1-\gamma_{\beta_j}))^{\eta}\right)^{1/\eta}}, e^{-\left(\sum_{j=1}^{\vartheta} \frac{T_j}{\sum_{j=1}^{\vartheta} T_j}(-ln(\delta_{\beta_j}))^{\eta}\right)^{1/\eta}}\right)$$

$$\Phi IFPAAA(\beta_1, \beta_2, \ldots, \beta_\vartheta)$$

$$= \Phi\left(1 - e^{-\left(\sum_{j=1}^{\vartheta} \frac{T_j}{\sum_{j=1}^{\vartheta} T_j}(-ln(1-\gamma_{\beta_j}))^{\eta}\right)^{1/\eta}}, e^{-\left(\sum_{j=1}^{\vartheta} \frac{T_j}{\sum_{j=1}^{\vartheta} T_j}(-ln(\delta_{\beta_j}))^{\eta}\right)^{1/\eta}}\right)$$

$$\Phi IFPAAA(\beta_1, \beta_2, \ldots, \beta_\vartheta)$$

$$= \left(1 - e^{-\left(\Phi\left(\sum_{j=1}^{\vartheta} \frac{T_j}{\sum_{j=1}^{\vartheta} T_j}(-ln(1-\gamma_{\beta_j}))^{\eta}\right)\right)^{1/\eta}}, e^{-\left(\Phi\left(\sum_{j=1}^{\vartheta} \frac{T_j}{\sum_{j=1}^{\vartheta} T_j}(-ln(\delta_{\beta_j}))^{\eta}\right)\right)^{1/\eta}}\right)$$

$$\Phi IFPAAA(\beta_1, \beta_2, \ldots, \beta_\vartheta) \oplus \alpha$$

$$= \left(1 - e^{-\left(\Phi\left(\sum_{j=1}^{\vartheta} \frac{T_j}{\sum_{j=1}^{\vartheta} T_j}(-ln(1-\gamma_{\beta_j}))^{\eta}\right)\right)^{\frac{1}{\eta}}}, e^{-\left(\Phi\left(\sum_{j=1}^{\vartheta} \frac{T_j}{\sum_{j=1}^{\vartheta} T_j}(-ln(\delta_{\beta_j}))^{\eta}\right)\right)^{\frac{1}{\eta}}}\right) \oplus (\gamma_\alpha, \delta_\alpha)$$

$$\Phi IFPAAA(\beta_1, \beta_2, \ldots, \beta_\vartheta) \oplus \alpha = \begin{pmatrix} 1 - e^{-\left(\left(\Phi\left(\sum_{j=1}^{\vartheta} \frac{T_j}{\sum_{j=1}^{\vartheta} T_j}(-ln(1-\gamma_{\beta_j}))^{\eta}\right)\right) + (-ln(1-\gamma_\alpha))^{\eta}\right)^{\frac{1}{\eta}}}, \\ e^{-\left(\left(\left(\Phi\left(\sum_{j=1}^{\vartheta} \frac{T_j}{\sum_{j=1}^{\vartheta} T_j}(-ln(\delta_{\beta_j}))^{\eta}\right)\right)\right) + (-ln(\delta_\alpha))^{\eta}\right)^{1/\eta}} \end{pmatrix}$$

$$IFPAAA(\Phi\beta_1 \oplus \alpha, \Phi\beta_2 \oplus \alpha, \ldots, \Phi\beta_\vartheta \oplus \alpha)$$

$$\Phi\beta_j = \left(1 - e^{-\left(\Phi(-ln(1-\gamma_{\beta_j}))^{\eta}\right)^{1/\eta}}, e^{-\left(\Phi(-ln(\delta_{\beta_j}))^{\eta}\right)^{1/\eta}}\right)$$

$$\Phi\beta_j \oplus \alpha = \left(1 - e^{-\left(\Phi(-ln(1-\gamma_{\beta_j}))^{\eta}\right)^{1/\eta}}, e^{-\left(\Phi(-ln(\delta_{\beta_j}))^{\eta}\right)^{1/\eta}}\right) \oplus (\gamma_\alpha, \delta_\alpha)$$

$$\Phi\beta_j \oplus \alpha = \begin{pmatrix} 1 - e^{-\left(\left(-ln\left(1-\left(1-e^{-\left(\Phi(-ln(1-\gamma_{\beta_j}))^{\eta}\right)^{\frac{1}{\eta}}}\right)\right)\right)^{\eta} + (-ln(1-\gamma_\alpha))^{\eta}\right)^{\frac{1}{\eta}}}, \\ e^{-\left(\left(-ln\left(e^{-\left(\Phi(-ln(\delta_{\beta_j}))^{\eta}\right)^{1/\eta}}\right)\right)^{\eta} + (-ln(\delta_\alpha))^{\eta}\right)^{1/\eta}} \end{pmatrix}$$

$$= \begin{pmatrix} 1 - e^{-\left(\sum_{j=1}^{\vartheta} \frac{T_j}{\sum_{j=1}^{\vartheta} T_j}\left(-ln\left(1-\left(1-e^{-\left(\left(-ln\left(1-\left(1-e^{-\left(\Phi(-ln(1-\gamma_{\beta_j}))^{\eta}\right)^{\frac{1}{\eta}}}\right)\right)\right)^{\eta} + (-ln(1-\gamma_\alpha))^{\eta}\right)^{\frac{1}{\eta}}}\right)\right)\right)^{\eta}\right)^{\frac{1}{\eta}}}, \\ e^{-\left(\sum_{j=1}^{\vartheta} \frac{T_j}{\sum_{j=1}^{\vartheta} T_j}\left(-ln\left(e^{-\left(\left(-ln\left(e^{-\left(\Phi(-ln(\delta_{\beta_j}))^{\eta}\right)^{1/\eta}}\right)\right)^{\eta} + (-ln(\delta_\alpha))^{\eta}\right)^{1/\eta}}\right)\right)^{\eta}\right)^{1/\eta}} \end{pmatrix}$$

$$\begin{pmatrix} 1 - e^{-\left(\sum_{j=1}^{\vartheta} \frac{T_j}{\sum_{j=1}^{\vartheta} T_j}\left(\Phi\left((-ln(1-\gamma_{\beta_j}))^{\eta}\right)\right) + (-ln(1-\gamma_\alpha))^{\eta}\right)^{\frac{1}{\eta}}}, \\ e^{-\left(\sum_{j=1}^{\vartheta} \frac{T_j}{\sum_{j=1}^{\vartheta} T_j}\left(\left(\Phi\left((-ln(\delta_{\beta_j}))^{\eta}\right)\right)\right) + (-ln(\delta_\alpha))^{\eta}\right)^{1/\eta}} \end{pmatrix}$$

□

Theorem 8. *Let* $\beta_{j=}\left(\gamma_{\beta_j}, \delta_{\beta_j}\right)$ *and* $\alpha_{j=}\left(\gamma_{\alpha_j}, \delta_{\alpha_j}\right)$ *be two collections of IFVs, and* $T_{j=}\prod_{k=1}^{j-1} S\ (\beta_k)$ $(j = 2, \ldots \vartheta)$, $T_1 = 1$, *and* $S\ (\beta_k)$ *is the score of IFVs* β_k. *Then*

$$IFPAAA(\beta_1 \oplus \alpha_1, \beta_2 \oplus \alpha_2, \ldots, \beta_\vartheta \oplus \alpha_\vartheta) = IFPAAA(\beta_1, \beta_2, \ldots, \beta_\vartheta) \oplus\ IFPAAA(\alpha_1, \alpha_2, \ldots, \alpha_\vartheta)$$

Proof. According to Theorem 1, we have:

$$\beta_j \oplus \alpha_j = \left(1 - e^{-((-ln(1-\gamma_{\beta_j}))^{\eta} + (-ln(1-\gamma_{\alpha_j}))^{\eta})^{1/\eta}}, e^{-((-ln(\delta_{\beta_j}))^{\eta} + (-ln(\delta_{\alpha_j}))^{\eta})^{1/\eta}}\right)$$

$$IFPAAA(\beta_1, \beta_2, \ldots, \beta_\vartheta) = \left(1 - e^{-(\sum_{j=1}^{\vartheta} \frac{T_j}{\sum_{j=1}^{\vartheta} T_j}(-ln(1-\gamma_{\beta_j}))^{\eta})^{1/\eta}}, e^{-(\sum_{j=1}^{\vartheta} \frac{T_j}{\sum_{j=1}^{\vartheta} T_j}(-ln(\delta_{\beta_j}))^{\eta})^{1/\eta}}\right)$$

$$IFPAAA(\beta_1 \oplus \alpha_1, \beta_2 \oplus \alpha_2, \ldots, \beta_\vartheta \oplus \alpha_\vartheta) = \left(\begin{array}{c} 1 - e^{-(\sum_{j=1}^{\vartheta} \frac{T_j}{\sum_{j=1}^{\vartheta} T_j}(((-ln(1-\gamma_{\beta_j}))^{\eta} + (-ln(1-\gamma_{\alpha_j}))^{\eta})))^{\frac{1}{\eta}}}, \\ e^{-(\sum_{j=1}^{\vartheta} \frac{T_j}{\sum_{j=1}^{\vartheta} T_j}(((-ln(\delta_{\beta_j}))^{\eta} + (-ln(\delta_{\alpha_j}))^{\eta})))^{1/\eta}} \end{array}\right)$$

$$IFPAAA(\beta_1, \beta_2, \ldots, \beta_\vartheta) \oplus IFPAAA(\alpha_1, \alpha_2, \ldots, \alpha_\vartheta) = \left(\begin{array}{c} \left(1 - e^{-(\sum_{j=1}^{\vartheta} \frac{T_j}{\sum_{j=1}^{\vartheta} T_j}(-ln(1-\gamma_{\beta_j}))^{\eta})^{\frac{1}{\eta}}}, e^{-(\sum_{j=1}^{\vartheta} \frac{T_j}{\sum_{j=1}^{\vartheta} T_j}(-ln(\delta_{\beta_j}))^{\eta})^{\frac{1}{\eta}}}\right) \oplus \\ \left(1 - e^{-(\sum_{j=1}^{\vartheta} \frac{T_j}{\sum_{j=1}^{\vartheta} T_j}(-ln(1-\gamma_{\alpha_j}))^{\eta})^{1/\eta}}, e^{-(\sum_{j=1}^{\vartheta} \frac{T_j}{\sum_{j=1}^{\vartheta} T_j}(-ln(\delta_{\alpha_j}))^{\eta})^{1/\eta}}\right) \end{array}\right)$$

$$= \left(\begin{array}{c} 1 - e^{-((-ln(1-(1-e^{-(\sum_{j=1}^{\vartheta} \frac{T_j}{\sum_{j=1}^{\vartheta} T_j}(-ln(1-\gamma_{\beta_j}))^{\eta})^{\frac{1}{\eta}}})))^{\eta} + (-ln(1-(1-e^{-(\sum_{j=1}^{\vartheta} \frac{T_j}{\sum_{j=1}^{\vartheta} T_j}(-ln(1-\gamma_{\alpha_j}))^{\eta})^{\frac{1}{\eta}}})))^{\eta})^{\frac{1}{\eta}}}, \\ e^{-((-ln(e^{-(\sum_{j=1}^{\vartheta} \frac{T_j}{\sum_{j=1}^{\vartheta} T_j}(-ln(\delta_{\beta_j}))^{\eta})^{\frac{1}{\eta}}}))^{\eta} + (-ln(e^{-(\sum_{j=1}^{\vartheta} \frac{T_j}{\sum_{j=1}^{\vartheta} T_j}(-ln(\delta_{\alpha_j}))^{\eta})^{1/\eta}}))^{\eta})^{1/\eta}} \end{array}\right)$$

$$= \left(\begin{array}{c} 1 - e^{-(\sum_{j=1}^{\vartheta} \frac{T_j}{\sum_{j=1}^{\vartheta} T_j}((-ln(1-\gamma_{\beta_j}))^{\eta} + (-ln(1-\gamma_{\alpha_j}))^{\eta}))^{\frac{1}{\eta}}}, \\ e^{-(\sum_{j=1}^{\vartheta} \frac{T_j}{\sum_{j=1}^{\vartheta} T_j}(((-ln(\delta_{\beta_j}))^{\eta} + (-ln(\delta_{\alpha_j}))^{\eta})))^{1/\eta}} \end{array}\right)$$

□

Definition 8. *Let* $\beta_j = \left(\gamma_{\beta_j}, \delta_{\beta_j}\right)$ *be a collection of IFVs, and let IFPAAG:* $L^{*\vartheta} \to L^*$ *if:*

$$IFPAAG(\beta_1, \beta_2, \ldots \beta_\vartheta) = \otimes_{j=1}^{\vartheta} \beta_j^{\frac{T_j}{\sum_{j=1}^{\vartheta} T_j}}$$

Then the function IFPAAG is called an interval-valued IFPAAG operator, where $T_{j=} \prod_{k=1}^{j-1} S\ (\beta_k)$ $(j = 2, \ldots \vartheta)$, $T_1 = 1$, *and* $S\ (\beta_k)$ *is the score of IFVs* β_k.

Theorem 9. *Let* $\beta_j = \left(\gamma_{\beta_j}, \delta_{\beta_I}\right)$ *be a collection of IFVs. Then, the aggregated value using the IFPAAG operator is also an IFV, given by:*

$$IFPAAG(\beta_1, \beta_2, \ldots \beta_\vartheta) = \left(\begin{array}{c} , e^{-(\sum_{j=1}^{\vartheta} \frac{T_j}{\sum_{j=1}^{\vartheta} T_j}(-ln(\delta_{\beta_j}))^{\eta})^{\frac{1}{\eta}}}, \\ 1 - e^{-(\sum_{j=1}^{\vartheta} \frac{T_j}{\sum_{j=1}^{\vartheta} T_j}(-ln(1-\gamma_{\beta_j}))^{\eta})^{1/\eta}} \end{array}\right) \quad (4)$$

Proof. Theorem 9 can be demonstrated in the following way using the mathematical induction approach:

(I) For $\vartheta = 2$, using Aczel–Alsina operations of IFVs, we obtain

$$\beta_1^{\frac{T_1}{\sum_{j=1}^{\vartheta} T_j}} = \left(e^{-\left(\frac{T_1}{\sum_{j=1}^{\vartheta} T_j}\left(-ln\left(\delta_{\beta_1}\right)\right)^{\eta}\right)^{\frac{1}{\eta}}}, 1 - e^{-\left(\frac{T_1}{\sum_{j=1}^{\vartheta} T_j}\left(-ln\left(1-\gamma_{\beta_1}\right)\right)^{\eta}\right)^{\frac{1}{\eta}}} \right)$$

$$\beta_2^{\frac{T_2}{\sum_{j=1}^{\vartheta} T_j}} = \left(e^{-\left(\frac{T_2}{\sum_{j=1}^{\vartheta} T_j}\left(-ln\left(\delta_{\beta_2}\right)\right)^{\eta}\right)^{1/\eta}}, 1 - e^{-\left(\frac{T_2}{\sum_{j=1}^{\vartheta} T_j}\left(-ln\left(1-\gamma_{\beta_2}\right)\right)^{\eta}\right)^{1/\eta}} \right)$$

$$IFPAAG(\beta_1, \beta_2) = \beta_1^{\frac{T_1}{\sum_{j=1}^{\vartheta} T_j}} \otimes \beta_2^{\frac{T_2}{\sum_{j=1}^{\vartheta} T_j}}$$

$$= \left(e^{-\left(\frac{T_1}{\sum_{j=1}^{2} T_j}\left(-ln\left(\delta_{\beta_1}\right)\right)^{\eta}\right)^{1/\eta}}, 1 - e^{-\left(\frac{T_1}{\sum_{j=1}^{2} T_j}\left(-ln\left(1-\gamma_{\beta_1}\right)\right)^{\eta}\right)^{1/\eta}} \right) \otimes$$

$$\left(e^{-\left(\frac{T_2}{\sum_{j=1}^{2} T_j}\left(-ln\left(\delta_{\beta_2}\right)\right)^{\eta}\right)^{1/\eta}}, 1 - e^{-\left(\frac{T_2}{\sum_{j=1}^{2} T_j}\left(-ln\left(1-\gamma_{\beta_2}\right)\right)^{\eta}\right)^{1/\eta}} \right)$$

$$= \left(, e^{-\left(\frac{T_1}{\sum_{j=1}^{2} T_j}\left(-ln\left(\delta_{\beta_1}\right)\right)^{\eta} + \frac{T_2}{\sum_{j=1}^{2} T_j}\left(-ln\left(\delta_{\beta_2}\right)\right)^{\eta}\right)^{\frac{1}{\eta}}}, 1 - \right.$$

$$\left. e^{-\left(\frac{T_1}{\sum_{j=1}^{2} T_j}\left(-ln\left(1-\gamma_{\beta_1}\right)\right)^{\eta} + \frac{T_2}{\sum_{j=1}^{2} T_j}\left(-ln\left(1-\gamma_{\beta_2}\right)\right)^{\eta}\right)^{1/\eta}} \right)$$

$$= \left(, e^{-\left(\sum_{j=1}^{\vartheta} \frac{T_j}{\sum_{j=1}^{2} T_j}\left(-ln\left(\delta_{\beta_j}\right)\right)^{\eta}\right)^{1/\eta}}, 1 - e^{-\left(\sum_{j=1}^{\vartheta} \frac{T_j}{\sum_{j=1}^{2} T_j}\left(-ln\left(1-\gamma_{\beta_j}\right)\right)^{\eta}\right)^{1/\eta}}, \right)$$

Hence, Equation (4) is true for $\vartheta = 2$.

(II) If Equation (4) holds true for $\vartheta = k$, then we have

$$IFPAAG(\beta_1, \beta_2, \ldots \beta_k) = \otimes_{j=1}^{k} \beta_j^{\frac{T_j}{\sum_{j=1}^{k} T_j}} = \left(\begin{array}{c} , e^{-\left(\sum_{j=1}^{k} \frac{T_j}{\sum_{j=1}^{k} T_j}\left(-ln\left(\delta_{\beta_j}\right)\right)^{\eta}\right)^{\frac{1}{\eta}}}, \\ 1 - e^{-\left(\sum_{j=1}^{k} \frac{T_j}{\sum_{j=1}^{k} T_j}\left(-ln\left(1-\gamma_{\beta_j}\right)\right)^{\eta}\right)^{1/\eta}} \end{array} \right)$$

Now, for $\vartheta = k + 1$, we get

$$IFPAAG(\beta_1, \beta_2, \ldots \beta_{k+1}) = \otimes_{j=1}^{k} \beta_j^{\frac{T_j}{\sum_{j=1}^{k+1} T_j}} \otimes \beta_{k+1}^{\frac{T_{k+1}}{\sum_{j=1}^{k+1} T_j}}$$

$$\left(e^{-\left(\sum_{j=1}^{k} \frac{T_j}{\sum_{j=1}^{k+1} T_j}\left(-ln\left(\delta_{\beta_j}\right)\right)^{\eta}\right)^{\frac{1}{\eta}}}, 1 - e^{-\left(\sum_{j=1}^{k} \frac{T_j}{\sum_{j=1}^{k+1} T_j}\left(-ln\left(1-\gamma_{\beta_j}\right)\right)^{\eta}\right)^{\frac{1}{\eta}}} \right)$$

$$\otimes \left(e^{-\left(\frac{T_{k+1}}{\sum_{j=1}^{k+1} T_j}\left(-ln\left(1-\delta_{\beta_{k+1}}\right)\right)^{\eta}\right)^{1/\eta}}, 1 - e^{-\left(\frac{T_{k+1}}{\sum_{j=1}^{k+1} T_j}\left(-ln\left(1-\gamma_{\beta_{k+1}}\right)\right)^{\eta}\right)^{1/\eta}} \right)$$

$$\left(e^{-\left(\sum_{j=1}^{k+1} \frac{T_j}{\sum_{j=1}^{k+1} T_j}\left(-ln\left(\delta_{\beta_j}\right)\right)^{\eta}\right)^{1/\eta}}, 1 - e^{-\left(\sum_{j=1}^{k+1} \frac{T_j}{\sum_{j=1}^{k+1} T_j}\left(-ln\left(1-\gamma_{\beta_j}\right)\right)^{\eta}\right)^{1/\eta}} \right)$$

Equation (4) is therefore valid for $\vartheta = k + 1$.

We conclude that Equation (4) holds for any value of ϑ as a result of forms (I) and (II).

The following properties, given in Theorems 10, 11, and 12, are likely to satisfy using the IFPAAG operator. □

Theorem 10. *If all* $\beta_j = \left(\gamma_{\beta_j}, \delta_{\beta_j}\right)$ *is a collection of IFVs where* $T_j = \prod_{k=1}^{j-1} S\ (\beta_k)(j = 2, \ldots \vartheta)$, $T_1 = 1$, *and* $S\ (\beta_k)$ *is the score of IFVs* (β_k), *if all* $\beta_j = \beta$ *for all* j, *then* $IFPAAG(\beta_1, \beta_2, \ldots, \beta_\vartheta) = \beta$.

Proof. Since $\beta_j = \left(\gamma_{\beta_j}, \delta_{\beta_j}\right) = \beta = (\gamma_\beta, \delta_\beta)$, we then have, by Equation (4):

$$IFPAAG(\beta_1, \beta_2, \ldots \beta_\vartheta) = \left(, e^{-\left(\sum_{j=1}^{\vartheta} \frac{T_j}{\sum_{j=1}^{\vartheta} T_j} (-ln(\delta_{\beta_j}))^{\eta}\right)^{1/\eta}}, 1 - e^{-\left(\sum_{j=1}^{\vartheta} \frac{T_j}{\sum_{j=1}^{\vartheta} T_j} (-ln(1-\gamma_{\beta_j}))^{\eta}\right)^{1/\eta}} \right)$$

$$= \left(, e^{-\left((-ln(\delta_\beta))^{\eta}\right)^{1/\eta}}, 1 - e^{-\left((-ln(1-\gamma_\beta))^{\eta}\right)^{1/\eta}} \right)$$

$$= 1 - e^{-ln(1-\gamma_\beta)}, e^{ln\delta_\beta} = (\gamma_\beta, \delta_\beta) = \beta$$

Thus, $IFPAAG(\beta_1, \beta_2, \ldots, \beta_\varrho) = \beta$ holds. □

Theorem 11. *Let* $\beta_j = \left(\gamma_{\beta_j}, \delta_{\beta_j}\right)$ *be a collection of IFVs. Let* $\beta^- = min(\beta_1, \beta_2, \ldots, \beta_\vartheta)$ *and* $\beta^+ = max(\beta_1, \beta_2, \ldots, \beta_\vartheta)$. *Then* $\beta^- \leq IFPAAG(\beta_1, \beta_2, \ldots, \beta_\vartheta) \leq \beta^+$.

Proof. Let $\beta_j = \left(\gamma_{\beta_j}, \delta_{\beta_j}\right)$ be a collection of IFVs. Let $\beta^- = min(\beta_1, \beta_2, \ldots, \beta_\vartheta) = \left(\gamma_\beta^-, \delta_\beta^-\right)$ and $\beta^+ = max(\beta_1, \beta_2, \ldots, \beta_\vartheta) = \left(\gamma_\beta^+, \delta_\beta^+\right)$. Hence, there are the subsequent inequalities:

$$1 - e^{-\left(\sum_{j=1}^{\vartheta} \frac{T_j}{\sum_{j=1}^{\vartheta} T_j} (-ln(1-\gamma_\beta^-))^{\eta}\right)^{\frac{1}{\eta}}} \geq 1 - e^{-\left(\sum_{j=1}^{\vartheta} \frac{T_j}{\sum_{j=1}^{\vartheta} T_j} (-ln(1-\gamma_{\beta_j}))^{\eta}\right)^{\frac{1}{\eta}}}$$

$$\geq 1 - e^{-\left(\sum_{j=1} \frac{T_j}{\sum_{j=1}^{\vartheta} T_j} (-ln(1-\gamma_{\beta_j}))^{\eta}\right)^{1/\eta}}$$

$$e^{-\left(\sum_{j=1}^{\vartheta} \frac{T_j}{\sum_{j=1}^{\vartheta} T_j} (-ln(\delta_\beta^+))^{\eta}\right)^{1/\eta}} \leq e^{-\left(\sum_{j=1}^{\vartheta} \frac{T_j}{\sum_{j=1}^{\vartheta} T_j} (-ln(\delta_{\beta_j}))^{\eta}\right)^{1/\eta}} \leq e^{-\left(\sum_{j=1}^{\vartheta} \frac{T_j}{\sum_{j=1}^{\vartheta} T_j} (-ln(\delta_\beta^-))^{\eta}\right)^{1/\eta}}.$$

Therefore, $\beta^- \leq IFPAAG(\beta_1, \beta_2, \ldots, \beta_\vartheta \leq \beta^+)$. □

Theorem 12. *Let* $\beta_j = \left(\gamma_{\beta_j}, \delta_{\beta_j}\right)$ *be a collection of IFVs, where* $T_j = \prod_{k=1}^{j-1} S\ (\beta_k)(j = 2, \ldots \vartheta)$, $T_1 = 1$, *and* $S\ (\beta_k)$ *is the score of IFVs*(β_k). *If* $\alpha = (\gamma_\alpha, \delta_\alpha)$ *is IFVs on k, then:*

$$IFPAAG(\beta_1 \otimes \alpha, \beta_2 \otimes \alpha, \ldots, \beta_\vartheta \otimes \alpha) = IFPAAG(\beta_1, \beta_2, \ldots, \beta_\vartheta) \otimes \alpha$$

Proof. Theorem 5's proof can be used to prove Theorem 12 as well. □

Theorem 13. *Let* $\beta_j = \left(\gamma_{\beta_j}, \delta_{\beta_j}\right)$ *be a collection of IFVs, where* $T_j = \prod_{k=1}^{j-1} S\ (\beta_k)(j = 2, \ldots \vartheta)$, $T_1 = 1$, *and* $S\ (\beta_k)$ *is the score of IFVs* (β_k). *If* $r > 0$, *then:*

$$IFPAAG(\beta_1^r, \beta_2^r, \ldots, \beta_\vartheta^r) = IFPAAG(\beta_1, \beta_2, \ldots, \beta_\vartheta)^r$$

Proof. Theorem 6's proof can be used to prove Theorem 13 as well. □

Theorem 14. *Let* $\beta_j = \left(\gamma_{\beta_j}, \delta_{\beta_j}\right)$ *be a collection of IFVs, where* $T_{j=} \prod_{k=1}^{j-1} S\ (\beta_k)(j = 2, \ldots \vartheta)$, $T_1 = 1$ *, and* $S\ (\beta_k)$ *is the score of IFVs* (β_k)*. If* $r > 0, \alpha = (\gamma_\alpha, \delta_\alpha)$ *is IFV on k, then:*

$$IFPAAG(\beta_1^r \otimes \alpha, \beta_2^r \otimes \alpha, \ldots \beta_\vartheta^r \otimes \alpha) = IFPAAG(\beta_1, \beta_2, \ldots, \beta_\vartheta)^r \otimes \alpha$$

Proof. Theorem 7's proof can be used to prove Theorem 14 as well. □

Theorem 15. *Let* $\beta_{j=}\left(\gamma_{\beta_j}, \delta_{\beta_j}\right)$ *and* $\alpha_{j=}\left(\gamma_{\alpha_j}, \delta_{\alpha_j}\right)$ *be two collections of IFVs, and* $T_{j=} \prod_{k=1}^{j-1} S\ (\beta_k)$ $(j = 2, \ldots \vartheta)$, $T_1 = 1$, *and* $S\ (\beta_k)$ *be the score of IFVs* β_k*. Then*

$$IFPAAG(\beta_1 \otimes \alpha_1, \beta_2 \otimes \alpha_2, \ldots, \beta_\vartheta \otimes \alpha_\vartheta) = IFPAAG(\beta_1, \beta_2, \ldots, \beta_\vartheta) \otimes\ IFPAAG(\alpha_1, \alpha_2, \ldots, \alpha_\vartheta)$$

Proof. Theorem 8's proof can be used to prove Theorem 15 as well. □

4. MAGDM Methods Using Investigated Operators Based on IFVs

In this section, we will create an MADM methodology based on the proposed aggregation operators under IFVs to illustrate reliability and effectiveness. It is assumed that the set of alternatives in a group decision-making problem is $k = \{k_1, k_2, \ldots\ k_m\}$, and that the set of parameters in the problem is $A = \{a_1, a_2, \ldots, a_n\}$ and the parameters represented by the linear ordering are prioritized. $a_1 > a_2 > a_3, \ldots, a_n$ shows that the a_j criterion is more important than a_i if $j < i$. $E = \{e_1, e_2, \ldots, e_p\}$ is the set of decision makers; there is a prioritization among the decision makers indicated by linear ordering. $e_1 > e_2 >, \ldots, > e_p$ shows that the e_∂ criterion is more important than e_τ if $\partial < \tau$. Let $K^q = \left(K_{ij}^q\right)_{m \times n}$ be an IFV-based decision matrix and $K_{ij}^q = \left(\gamma_{ij}^q, \delta_{ij}^q\right)$ denote the attribute value provided by the decision maker e_q, which is expressed as IFVs, where $\left(\gamma_{ij}^q, \delta_{ij}^q\right)$ indicates the degree range that the alternative k_i satisfies. The attribute c_j expresses the decision maker e_q, such that $\left(\gamma_{ij}^q, \delta_{ij}^q\right) \subset (0,1)$, $\left(\gamma_{ij}^q + \delta_{ij}^q\right) \leq 1, i = 1, 2, \ldots m, j = 1, 2, \ldots n$.

If all the attributes $a_j (j = 1, 2, \ldots, n)$ are of the same type, then the attribute values do not need normalization. Otherwise, we normalize the decision-maker matrix $K^q = \left(K_{ij}^q\right)_{m \times n}$ into $R^q = \left(r_{ij}^q\right)_{m \times n}$, where:

$$r_{ij}^q = \begin{cases} k_{ij}^q, \ for\ benefit\ attribute\ a_j \\ k_{ij}^q, \ for\ \cos t\ attribute\ a_j \end{cases}$$

Then, we utilize the IFPAAA operator to develop an approach to multi-criteria decision-making under an interval-valued IF environment; the main steps are as follows:

Step 1: on the basis of the following equations, calculate the values of $T_{ij}^q, (q = 1, 2, \ldots p)$:

$$T_{j=} \prod_{k=1}^{j-1} S\left(r_{ij}^q\right)(q = 2, \ldots p),\ T_{ij}^1 = 1$$

Step 2: Utilize the IFPAAA operator given by:

$$r_{ij} = IFPAAA(\beta_{ij}{}^1, \beta_{ij}{}^2, \ldots, \beta_{ij}{}^p{}_\vartheta)$$
$$= \left(1 - e^{-\left(\sum_{j=1}^{\vartheta} \frac{T_j}{\sum_{j=1}^{\vartheta} T_j}^{(p)} (-ln(1-\gamma_{\beta_j}))^{\eta}\right)^{1/\eta}}, e^{-\left(\sum_{j=1}^{\vartheta} \frac{T_j}{\sum_{j=1}^{\vartheta} T_j}^{(p)} (-ln(\delta_{\beta_j}))^{\eta}\right)^{1/\eta}}\right)$$

or the IFPAAG operator:

$$r_{ij} = IFPAAG(\beta_{ij}{}^1, \beta_{ij}{}^2, \ldots \beta_{ij}{}^p{}_\vartheta)$$
$$= \left(,e^{-\left(\sum_{j=1}^{\vartheta} \frac{T_j}{\sum_{j=1}^{\vartheta} T_j}^{(p)} (-ln(\delta_{\beta_j}))^{\eta}\right)^{1/\eta}}, 1-e^{-\left(\sum_{j=1}^{\vartheta} \frac{T_j}{\sum_{j=1}^{\vartheta} T_j}^{(p)} (-ln(1-\gamma_{\beta_j}))^{\eta}\right)^{1/\eta}} \right)$$

to aggregate all the individual IF decision matrixes $R^q = \left(r_{ij}^q\right)_{m\times n}(q = 2,\ldots p)$ into the collective IF decision matrix $R = \left(r_{ij}\right)_{m\times n}$.

Step 3: Calculate the values of $T_{ij}, (i = 1,2,\ldots m,\ j = 1,2,\ldots n)$ based on the following equations:

$$T_j = \prod_{k=1}^{j-1} S\left(r_{ij}^q\right)(q = 2,\ldots p),\ T_{ij}^1 = 1$$

Step 4: Aggregate the IFVs r_{ij}:

$$IFPAAA(\beta_1, \beta_2, \ldots \beta_\vartheta) = \left(1-e^{-\left(\sum_{j=1}^{\vartheta} \frac{T_j}{\sum_{j=1}^{\vartheta} T_j}(-ln(1-\gamma_{\beta_j}))^{\eta}\right)^{1/\eta}}, e^{-\left(\sum_{j=1}^{\vartheta} \frac{T_j}{\sum_{j=1}^{\vartheta} T_j}(-ln(\delta_{\beta_j}))^{\eta}\right)^{1/\eta}}\right)$$

or

$$IFPAAG(\beta_1, \beta_2, \ldots \beta_\vartheta) = \left(, e^{-\left(\sum_{j=1}^{\vartheta} \frac{T_j}{\sum_{j=1}^{\vartheta} T_j}(-ln(\delta_{\beta_j}))^{\eta}\right)^{\frac{1}{\eta}}}, 1-e^{-\left(\sum_{j=1}^{\vartheta} \frac{T_j}{\sum_{j=1}^{\vartheta} T_j}(-ln(1-\gamma_{\beta_j}))^{\eta}\right)^{\frac{1}{\eta}}}\right)$$

Step 5: Rank all the alternatives by the score function described in Section 2:

$$Sco(\beta_i) = \gamma_{\beta_i} - \delta_{\beta_i}\ \ i = 1,2,\ldots m$$

then, the bigger the value of $S(r_i)$, the larger the overall IFVs (r_i), and thus the alternative $k_i(i = 1,2,\ldots m)$.

5. Practical Example

In this example, we take the selection of a doctor for a hospital. Suppose a hospital needs a doctor (medical specialist). There is a committee whose job is to select the most suitable candidate among a finite list of doctors. The committee consists of the president as e_1, the psychologist as e_2, and the medical specialist or dean as e_3. These experts are responsible for the whole induction process. They made a strict evaluation of five candidates $K_i(i = 1,2,\ldots,5)$ from four aspects, namely morality a_1, good communication skills a_2, competence a_3, and compassion a_4. The hospital president has absolute priority in decision-making, and the medical expert and psychologist come next. In addition, this introduction will be in strict accordance with the president combining ability with political integrity. Then, the prioritization relationship for the criteria is as below, $a_1 > a_2 > a_3,\ldots,a_n$. Three decision makers evaluate the candidates $K_i(i = 1,2,\ldots 5)$ with respect to the attributes $A_j(j = 1,2,\ldots 4)$ and construct the following three IF decision matrixes: $D^q = \left(d_{ij}^q\right)_{5\times 4}(q = 1,2,3)$. Since all the attributes $A_j(j = 1,2,\ldots,5)$ are of a beneficial type, we do not need normalization. The experts evaluated the candidates $K_i(i = 1,2,\ldots 5)$ with respect to the attributes $A_j(j = 1,2,\ldots 4)$ and constructed the following three IF decision matrixes $D^q = \left(d_{ij}^q\right)_{5\times 4}(q = 1,2,3)$ with all the attributes $A_j(j = 1,2,\ldots,5)$ given in Tables 1–3.

Table 1. IF decision matrix e_1.

	a_1		a_2		a_3		a_4	
k_1	0.4	0.3	0.5	0.3	0.3	0.1	0.6	0.2
k_2	0.6	0.2	0.6	0.3	0.2	0.1	0.7	0.1
k_3	0.4	0.3	0.5	0.4	0.6	0.22	0.6	0.22
k_4	0.4	0.3	0.3	0.2	0.2	0.1	0.3	0.1
k_5	0.6	0.1	0.7	0.2	0.5	0.1	0.4	0.2

Table 2. IF decision matrix e_2.

	a_1		a_2		a_3		a_4	
k_1	0.5	0.2	0.22	0.21	0.5	0.3	0.41	0.1
k_2	0.6	0.3	0.3	0.11	0.3	0.21	0.21	0.2
k_3	0.4	0.2	0.7	0.2	0.6	0.34	0.4	0.3
k_4	0.4	0.1	0.6	0.3	0.4	0.22	0.32	0.3
k_5	0.6	0.1	0.5	0.4	0.6	0.12	0.12	0.1

Table 3. IF decision matrix e_3.

	a_1		a_2		a_3		a_4	
k_1	0.5	0.3	0.6	0.4	0.4	0.2	0.3	0.2
k_2	0.4	0.3	0.3	0.1	0.6	0.1	0.3	0.1
k_3	0.3	0.1	0.3	0.1	0.4	0.3	0.41	0.4
k_4	0.6	0.1	0.2	0.1	0.4	0.3	0.6	0.2
k_5	0.5	0.2	0.3	0.21	0.4	0.1	0.1	0.1

Since the attribute values do not need to be normalized after modifying the type, the major stages are as follows when using the IFPAAA operator:

Step 1: Calculate the values of $T_{ij}^1, T_{ij}^2, T_{ij}^3$ based on

$$T_{ij}^1 = \begin{pmatrix} 1 & 1 & 1 & 1 \\ 1 & 1 & 1 & 1 \\ 1 & 1 & 1 & 1 \\ 1 & 1 & 1 & 1 \\ 1 & 1 & 1 & 1 \end{pmatrix}$$

$$T_{ij}^2 = \begin{pmatrix} 0.1 & 0.2 & 0.2 & 0.4 \\ 0.4 & 0.3 & 0.1 & 0.6 \\ 0.1 & 0.1 & 0.38 & 0.38 \\ 0.1 & 0.1 & 0.1 & 0.2 \\ 0.5 & 0.5 & 0.4 & 0.2 \end{pmatrix}$$

$$T_{ij}^3 = \begin{pmatrix} 0.03 & 0.002 & 0.04 & 0.124 \\ 0.12 & 0.057 & 0.009 & 0.006 \\ 0.02 & 0.05 & 0.0988 & 0.038 \\ 0.03 & 0.03 & 0.018 & 0.004 \\ 0.25 & 0.05 & 0.192 & 0.004 \end{pmatrix}$$

Step 2: Aggregate each individual IF decision matrix into the collective IF decision matrix $R = (r_{ij})_{5\times4}$ using the IFPAAA operator $R^q = \left(r_{ij}^q\right)_{4\times5} (q = 1,2,3)$ (Table 4).

Table 4. IF decision matrix R.

	a_1		a_2		a_3		a_4	
k_1	0.4124	0.2894	0.4618	0.2829	0.3403	0.1221	0.5364	0.1667
k_2	0.5870	0.2298	0.5365	0.2295	0.2140	0.1069	0.5679	0.1296
k_3	0.3984	0.2837	0.5147	0.3545	0.5890	0.2512	0.5494	0.2429
k_4	0.4064	0.2644	0.3315	0.2035	0.2239	0.1092	0.3046	0.1203
k_5	0.5870	0.1104	0.6365	0.2505	0.5168	0.1047	0.3597	0.1778

Step 3: Calculate the values of $T_{ij}, (i = 1,2,\ldots m,\ j = 1,2,\ldots n)$ based on

$$T_{ij} = \begin{pmatrix} 1 & 0.123 & 0.022015 & 0.004804 \\ 1 & 0.3572 & 0.109698 & 0.011747 \\ 1 & 0.1147 & 0.018376 & 0.006208 \\ 1 & 0.142 & 0.018168 & 0.002084 \\ 1 & 0.4766 & 0.183985 & 0.075814 \end{pmatrix}$$

Step 4: The IFPAAA operator can be used to combine all of the desired values $r_{ij}(i = 1,2,\ldots 5)$ on the ith line of R to obtain the overall preference values r_i. This information are given in Table 5.

Table 5. Result of decision matrix.

r_1=	0.4172	0.2833
r_2=	0.5544	0.2160
r_3=	0.4158	0.2893
r_4=	0.3950	0.2522
r_5=	0.5867	0.1404

Step 5: Determine each score for $r_i(1,2,\ldots 5)$ etc. as given in Table 6.

Table 6. Height priority.

s_1=	0.1339
s_2=	0.3384
s_3=	0.1265
s_4=	0.1428
s_5=	0.4463

Since

$$S_5 > S_2 > S_4 > S_1 > S_3$$

we have

$$k_5 > k_2 > k_4 > k_1 > k_3$$

Therefore, k_5 is the perfect selection.

The major steps are as follows based on the IFPAAG operator:

Step 1: Already performed.

Step 2: The individual IF decision matrix can be aggregated using the IVFPAAG operator $R^q = \left(r_{ij}^q\right)_{4\times 5}(q = 1,2,3)$ into the collective IF decision matrix $R^q = \left(r_{ij}^q\right)_{4\times 5}$ (see Table 7).

Table 7. IF decision matrix R.

	a_1		a_2		a_3		a_4	
k_1	0.4104	0.2917	0.436	0.2860	0.3288	0.1390	0.5131	0.1749
k_2	0.5811	0.2357	0.500	0.2540	0.2093	0.1105	0.4450	0.1387
k_3	0.3979	0.2884	0.504	0.3739	0.5840	0.2582	0.5328	0.2476
k_4	0.4043	0.2795	0.316	0.2069	0.2152	0.1150	0.3039	0.1371
k_5	0.5846	0.1150	0.611	0.2712	0.5095	0.1051	0.3260	0.1839

Step 3: Calculate the values of $T_{ij}, (i = 1,2,\ldots m,\ j = 1,2,\ldots n)$ based on

$$T_{ij} = \begin{pmatrix} 1 & 0.1187 & 0.017847 & 0.003386 \\ 1 & 0.3454 & 0.084959 & 0.008392 \\ 1 & 0.1095 & 0.014191 & 0.004623 \\ 1 & 0.1248 & 0.013564 & 0.001358 \\ 1 & 0.4695 & 0.159555 & 0.064536 \end{pmatrix}$$

Step 4: The IFPAAA operator can be used to combine all of the desired values $r_{ij}(i = 1,\ 2,\ldots 5)$ on the ith line of R to obtain the overall preference values r_i (see Table 8).

Table 8. Result of decision matrix.

r_1=	0.4119	0.2886
r_2=	0.5269	0.2328
r_3=	0.4096	0.2967
r_4=	0.3904	0.2699
r_5=	0.5713	0.1631

Step 5: Determine each score for $r_i(1,2,\ldots 5)$ etc. (see Table 9).

Table 9. Height priority.

s_1=	0.1233
s_2=	0.2941
s_3=	0.1129
s_4=	0.1205
s_5=	0.4082

The data given in Table 9 can be geometrically seen in Figure 1 below.

Therefore, k_5 is the optimal choice. The ranking of the alternatives is the same for the IFPAAA and IFPAAG operators. The proposed operators are simplified to the standard IF aggregation procedures if the criteria and the decision-makers have the same priority level. However, these four criteria and the three decision-makers have different degrees of significance. For instance, it is quite difficult to choose the candidate if the hospital president gave him a low assessment. From a different angle, a candidate cannot be chosen if they have poor moral character, despite how well they have performed in other areas such as integrity, communication skills, professionalism, and emotional stability. As a result, we need to think about how the criteria, or the decision makers are ranked in importance; the IFPAAG and IFPAAA operators are helpful tools for handling such circumstances. According to the analysis above, our operators have several advantages over conventional IF operators, including the ability to deal with the IF environment and the consideration of optimization between the criteria and the decision makers, which makes it more feasible and useful.

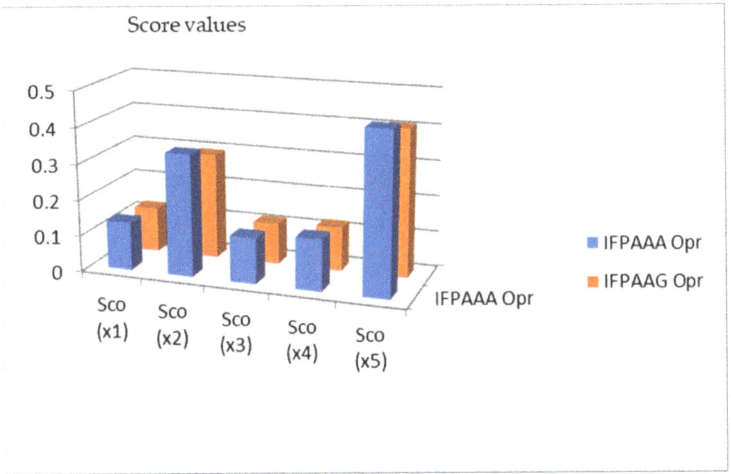

Figure 1. Graphical presentation of score values.

6. Comparative Study

This section compares the aggregated results obtained using the IFPAAA and IFPAAG operators with a variety of other AOs of IFVs. These AOs include the IFWA operator [9], IFDWA operator [44], IFFWA operator [13], and IFHWA operator [14]. We solved the problem studied earlier using these suggested AOs and display the results in Table 10 below.

Table 10. Comparative analysis of the proposed and existing operators using the information in Table 4.

Operator	Ranking
IFPAAA operator	$k5 > k2 > k1 > k4 > k3$
IFPAAG operator	$k5 > k2 > k1 > k4 > k3$
Seikh and Mandal [44]	$k5 > k2 > k4 > k1 > k3$
Seikh and Mandal [44]	$k5 > k2 > k1 > k4 > k3$
Huang [13]	$k5 > k2 > k1 > k4 > k3$
Huang [13]	$k5 > k2 > k1 > k4 > k3$
Zhang [14]	$k5 > k2 > k4 > k1 > k3$
Zhang [14]	$k5 > k2 > k1 > k4 > k3$
Xu [9]	$k5 > k2 > k1 > k4 > k3$
Xu and Yager [10]	$k5 > k2 > k1 > k4 > k3$

The IFPAAA and IFPAAG operators show that k_5 is the optimal option. Moreover, when we applied the AOs proposed by Xu [9], Xu and Yager [10], Huang [13], Zhang [14], and Seikh and Mandal [44], we obtained somewhat similar results. k_5 was proven to be the best alternative among them all. We claim that the results established by our proposed operators are better because our method considers the prioritization of attributes. Furthermore, in reference to Farahbod and Eftekhari [41], Aczel–Alsina t-norm-based aggregation is more reliable than other AOs. We can see that in the Dombi AOs proposed by Seikh and Mandal [44], where there is a slight change in the ranking results. The results obtained using Frank AOs by Zhang [14] also show a fluctuation in ranking order. However, the proposed results using the IFPAAA and IFPAAG operators give us a smooth ranking. A geometrical view of the comparative study is given in Figure 2.

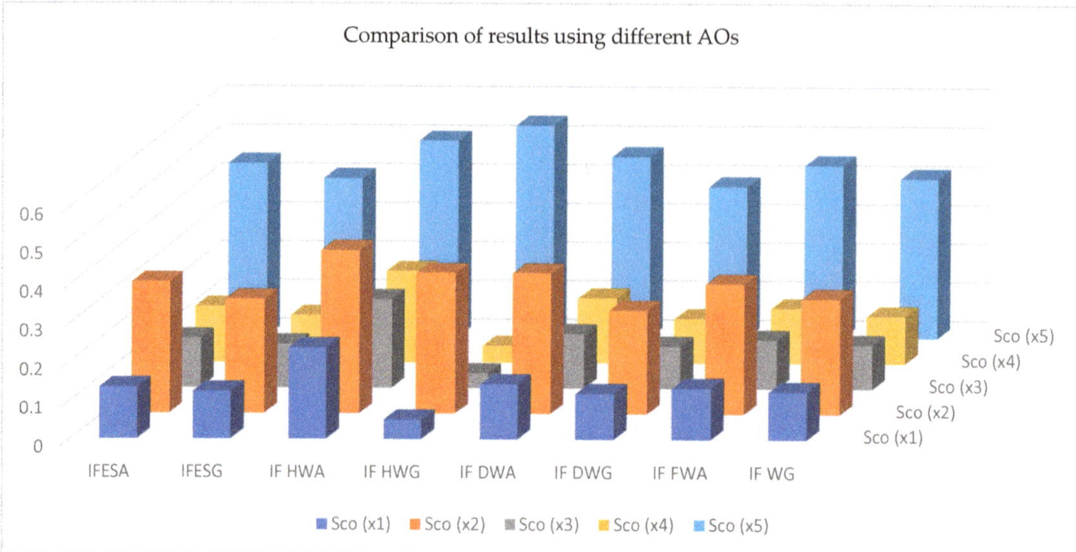

Figure 2. Results of the comparative study obtained in Table 10.

7. Conclusions

In this paper, we analyzed the Aczel–Alsina AOs of IFVs. We embedded the concept of prioritization in the Aczel–Alsina AOs of IFVs and proposed the IFPAAA and IFPAAG operators. The significance of the proposed prioritized AOs based on the Aczel–Alsina t-norm and t-conorm lies in the fact that in real-life decision-making problems, the attributes sometimes need prioritization, and in some cases the decision makers have a priority level. For this purpose, we proposed the IFPAAA and IFPAAG operators and studied their properties. We established several other results as well. To see the impact of the proposed IFPAAA and IFPAAG operators, we presented a numerical example where the selection of a doctor for a hospital was carried out using an MAGDM algorithm. The proposed MAGDM method considered the prioritization relationship among criteria and decision makers, which allowed our technique to have wide pragmatic application possibilities. Furthermore, we compared our results with other AOs with the concept of prioritization, and the results were analyzed. We found that the results were similar and compatible. The advantages of the proposed work include the inclusion of prioritization in aggregation for uncertain information where two aspects of human opinion are involved. On the other hand, the existing AOs do not improve the flexibility of data aggregation. Thus, our suggested AOs are more competent and accurate when making decisions using IF information. The proposed work has its limitations when the information expressing uncertainty has more characteristics and can be extended to the environment of interval-valued IFSs [45]. We also aim to extend this work to the frame of complex IFSs [46], complex Pythagorean fuzzy sets [47], complex q-rung orthopedic fuzzy sets [48], and T-spherical fuzzy sets (TSFSs) [49]. The proposed Aczel–Alsina AOs can also be associated with Maclaurin symmetric mean operators [24] and Bonferroni mean operators [50].

Author Contributions: Conceptualization, M.S., K.U. and M.A.; methodology, M.S., K.U., D.P. and D.B.; software, M.S., M.A., D.P. and D.B.; validation, K.U., M.A., D.P. and D.B.; formal analysis, D.P., and D.B.; investigation, M.S., K.U. and M.A.; resources, K.U., D.P. and D.B.; writing—original draft preparation, M.S., K.U., M.A., D.P. and D.B.; writing—review and editing, M.S., K.U., M.A., D.P. and D.B.; supervision, K.U., D.P. and D.B.; project administration, K.U., D.P. and D.B.; funding acquisition, D.P. and D.B. All authors have read and agreed to the published version of the manuscript.

Funding: This research received no external funding.

Institutional Review Board Statement: Not applicable.

Informed Consent Statement: Not Applicable.

Data Availability Statement: Not Applicable.

Conflicts of Interest: The authors have no conflict of interest regarding this paper.

References

1. Zadeh, L.A. Fuzzy Sets. *Inf. Control* **1965**, *8*, 338–353. [CrossRef]
2. Atanassov, K. Intuitionistic Fuzzy Sets. *Fuzzy Sets Syst.* **1986**, *20*, 87–96. [CrossRef]
3. Tang, Y.M.; Zhang, L.; Bao, G.Q.; Ren, F.J.; Pedrycz, W. Symmetric Implicational Algorithm Derived from Intuitionistic Fuzzy Entropy. *Iran. J. Fuzzy Syst.* **2022**, *19*, 27–44.
4. Reddy K., S.; Panwar, L.K.; Panigrahi, B.K.; Kumar, R. Computational Intelligence for Demand Response Exchange Considering Temporal Characteristics of Load Profile via Adaptive Fuzzy Inference System. *IEEE Trans. Emerg. Top. Comput. Intell.* **2018**, *2*, 235–245. [CrossRef]
5. Deschrijver, G.; Cornelis, C.; Kerre, E.E. On the Representation of Intuitionistic Fuzzy T-Norms and t-Conorms. *IEEE Trans. Fuzzy Syst.* **2004**, *12*, 45–61. [CrossRef]
6. Garg, H. Generalized Pythagorean Fuzzy Geometric Aggregation Operators Using Einstein T-Norm and t-Conorm for Multicriteria Decision-Making Process. *Int. J. Intell. Syst.* **2017**, *32*, 597–630. [CrossRef]
7. Gál, L.; Lovassy, R.; Rudas, I.J.; Kóczy, L.T. Learning the Optimal Parameter of the Hamacher T-Norm Applied for Fuzzy-Rule-Based Model Extraction. *Neural Comput. Applic* **2014**, *24*, 133–142. [CrossRef]
8. De Baets, B.; De Meyer, H.E. The Frank T-Norm Family in Fuzzy Similarity Measurement. In Proceedings of the EUSFLAT Conference, Leicester, UK, 5–7 September 2001; pp. 249–252.
9. Dombi, J. A General Class of Fuzzy Operators, the DeMorgan Class of Fuzzy Operators and Fuzziness Measures Induced by Fuzzy Operators. *Fuzzy Sets Syst.* **1982**, *8*, 149–163. [CrossRef]
10. Aczél, J.; Alsina, C. Characterizations of Some Classes of Quasilinear Functions with Applications to Triangular Norms and to Synthesizing Judgements. *Aequ. Math.* **1982**, *25*, 313–315. [CrossRef]
11. Xu, Z. Intuitionistic Fuzzy Aggregation Operators. *IEEE Trans. Fuzzy Syst.* **2007**, *15*, 1179–1187.
12. Xu, Z.; Yager, R.R. Some Geometric Aggregation Operators Based on Intuitionistic Fuzzy Sets. *Int. J. Gen. Syst.* **2006**, *35*, 417–433. [CrossRef]
13. Wang, W.; Liu, X. Intuitionistic Fuzzy Geometric Aggregation Operators Based on Einstein Operations. *Int. J. Intell. Syst.* **2011**, *26*, 1049–1075. [CrossRef]
14. Wang, W.; Liu, X. Intuitionistic Fuzzy Information Aggregation Using Einstein Operations. *IEEE Trans. Fuzzy Syst.* **2012**, *20*, 923–938. [CrossRef]
15. Huang, J.-Y. Intuitionistic Fuzzy Hamacher Aggregation Operators and Their Application to Multiple Attribute Decision Making. *J. Intell. Fuzzy Syst.* **2014**, *27*, 505–513. [CrossRef]
16. Zhang, X.; Liu, P.; Wang, Y. Multiple Attribute Group Decision Making Methods Based on Intuitionistic Fuzzy Frank Power Aggregation Operators. *J. Intell. Fuzzy Syst.* **2015**, *29*, 2235–2246. [CrossRef]
17. Senapati, T.; Chen, G.; Yager, R.R. Aczel–Alsina Aggregation Operators and Their Application to Intuitionistic Fuzzy Multiple Attribute Decision Making. *Int. J. Intell. Syst.* **2022**, *37*, 1529–1551. [CrossRef]
18. Hussain, A.; Ullah, K.; Alshahrani, M.N.; Yang, M.-S.; Pamucar, D. Novel Aczel–Alsina Operators for Pythagorean Fuzzy Sets with Application in Multi-Attribute Decision Making. *Symmetry* **2022**, *14*, 940. [CrossRef]
19. Khan, M.R.; Wang, H.; Ullah, K.; Karamti, H. Construction Material Selection by Using Multi-Attribute Decision Making Based on q-Rung Orthopair Fuzzy Aczel–Alsina Aggregation Operators. *Appl. Sci.* **2022**, *12*, 8537. [CrossRef]
20. Hussain, A.; Ullah, K.; Yang, M.-S.; Pamucar, D. Aczel-Alsina Aggregation Operators on T-Spherical Fuzzy (TSF) Information with Application to TSF Multi-Attribute Decision Making. *IEEE Access* **2022**, *10*, 26011–26023. [CrossRef]
21. Senapati, T. Approaches to Multi-Attribute Decision-Making Based on Picture Fuzzy Aczel–Alsina Average Aggregation Operators. *Comput. Appl. Math.* **2022**, *41*, 1–19. [CrossRef]
22. Senapati, T.; Chen, G.; Mesiar, R.; Yager, R.R. Novel Aczel–Alsina Operations-Based Interval-Valued Intuitionistic Fuzzy Aggregation Operators and Their Applications in Multiple Attribute Decision-Making Process. *Int. J. Intell. Syst.* **2021**, *37*, 5059–5081. [CrossRef]
23. Senapati, T.; Chen, G.; Mesiar, R.; Yager, R.R.; Saha, A. Novel Aczel–Alsina Operations-Based Hesitant Fuzzy Aggregation Operators and Their Applications in Cyclone Disaster Assessment. *Int. J. Gen. Syst.* **2022**, *51*, 511–546. [CrossRef]
24. Ullah, K. Picture Fuzzy Maclaurin Symmetric Mean Operators and Their Applications in Solving Multiattribute Decision-Making Problems. *Math. Probl. Eng.* **2021**, *2021*, 1098631. [CrossRef]
25. Khan, Q.; Mahmood, T.; Ullah, K. Applications of Improved Spherical Fuzzy Dombi Aggregation Operators in Decision Support System. *Soft Comput.* **2021**, *25*, 9097–9119. [CrossRef]
26. Yager, R.R. Prioritized Aggregation Operators. *Int. J. Approx. Reason.* **2008**, *48*, 263–274. [CrossRef]

27. Yager, R.R. Prioritized OWA Aggregation. *Fuzzy Optim. Decis. Mak.* **2009**, *8*, 245–262. [CrossRef]
28. Yan, H.-B.; Huynh, V.-N.; Nakamori, Y.; Murai, T. On Prioritized Weighted Aggregation in Multi-Criteria Decision Making. *Expert Syst. Appl.* **2011**, *38*, 812–823. [CrossRef]
29. Yu, X.; Xu, Z. Prioritized Intuitionistic Fuzzy Aggregation Operators. *Inf. Fusion* **2013**, *14*, 108–116. [CrossRef]
30. Ali, Z.; Mahmood, T.; Aslam, M.; Chinram, R. Another View of Complex Intuitionistic Fuzzy Soft Sets Based on Prioritized Aggregation Operators and Their Applications to Multiattribute Decision Making. *Mathematics* **2021**, *9*, 1922. [CrossRef]
31. Arora, R.; Garg, H. Group Decision-Making Method Based on Prioritized Linguistic Intuitionistic Fuzzy Aggregation Operators and Its Fundamental Properties. *Comp. Appl. Math.* **2019**, *38*, 36. [CrossRef]
32. Arora, R.; Garg, H. Prioritized Averaging/Geometric Aggregation Operators under the Intuitionistic Fuzzy Soft Set Environment. *Sci. Iran.* **2017**, *25*, 466–482. [CrossRef]
33. Chen, T.-Y. A Prioritized Aggregation Operator-Based Approach to Multiple Criteria Decision Making Using Interval-Valued Intuitionistic Fuzzy Sets: A Comparative Perspective. *Inf. Sci.* **2014**, *281*, 97–112. [CrossRef]
34. Gao, H. Pythagorean Fuzzy Hamacher Prioritized Aggregation Operators in Multiple Attribute Decision Making. *J. Intell. Fuzzy Syst.* **2018**, *35*, 2229–2245. [CrossRef]
35. Jana, C.; Pal, M.; Wang, J. Bipolar Fuzzy Dombi Prioritized Aggregation Operators in Multiple Attribute Decision Making. *Soft. Comput.* **2020**, *24*, 3631–3646. [CrossRef]
36. Riaz, M.; Pamucar, D.; Athar Farid, H.M.; Hashmi, M.R. Q-Rung Orthopair Fuzzy Prioritized Aggregation Operators and Their Application towards Green Supplier Chain Management. *Symmetry* **2020**, *12*, 976. [CrossRef]
37. Gao, H.; Wei, G.; Huang, Y. Dual Hesitant Bipolar Fuzzy Hamacher Prioritized Aggregation Operators in Multiple Attribute Decision Making. *IEEE Access* **2018**, *6*, 11508–11522. [CrossRef]
38. Liu, P.; Akram, M.; Sattar, A. Extensions of Prioritized Weighted Aggregation Operators for Decision-Making under Complex q-Rung Orthopair Fuzzy Information. *J. Intell. Fuzzy Syst.* **2020**, *39*, 7469–7493. [CrossRef]
39. Wei, G. Hesitant Fuzzy Prioritized Operators and Their Application to Multiple Attribute Decision Making. *Knowl.-Based Syst.* **2012**, *31*, 176–182. [CrossRef]
40. Mahmood, T.; Ali, Z. Prioritized Muirhead Mean Aggregation Operators under the Complex Single-Valued Neutrosophic Settings and Their Application in Multi-Attribute Decision Making. *J. Comput. Cogn. Eng.* **2022**, *1*, 104. [CrossRef]
41. Mahmood, T.; Warraich, M.S.; Ali, Z.; Pamucar, D. Generalized MULTIMOORA Method and Dombi Prioritized Weighted Aggregation Operators Based on T-Spherical Fuzzy Sets and Their Applications. *Int. J. Intell. Syst.* **2021**, *36*, 4659–4692. [CrossRef]
42. Mahmood, T. A Novel Approach towards Bipolar Soft Sets and Their Applications. *J. Math.* **2020**, *2020*, 4690808. [CrossRef]
43. Farahbod, F.; Eftekhari, M. Comparison of Different T-Norm Operators in Classification Problems. *Int. J. Fuzzy Log. Syst.* **2012**, *2*, 33–39. [CrossRef]
44. Seikh, M.R.; Mandal, U. Intuitionistic Fuzzy Dombi Aggregation Operators and Their Application to Multiple Attribute Decision-Making. *Granul. Comput.* **2021**, *6*, 473–488. [CrossRef]
45. Waqar, M.; Ullah, K.; Pamucar, D.; Jovanov, G.; Vranješ, Đ. An Approach for the Analysis of Energy Resource Selection Based on Attributes by Using Dombi T-Norm Based Aggregation Operators. *Energies* **2022**, *15*, 3939. [CrossRef]
46. Ali, Z.; Mahmood, T.; Ullah, K.; Pamucar, D.; Cirovic, G. Power Aggregation Operators Based on T-Norm and t-Conorm under the Complex Intuitionistic Fuzzy Soft Settings and Their Application in Multi-Attribute Decision Making. *Symmetry* **2021**, *13*, 1986. [CrossRef]
47. Wang, L.; Peng, X. An Approach to Decision Making with Interval-Valued Complex Pythagorean Fuzzy Model for Evaluating Personal Risk of Mental Patients. *J. Intell. Fuzzy Syst.* **2021**, *41*, 1461–1486. [CrossRef]
48. Liu, P.; Mahmood, T.; Ali, Z. Complex Q-Rung Orthopair Fuzzy Aggregation Operators and Their Applications in Multi-Attribute Group Decision Making. *Information* **2020**, *11*, 5. [CrossRef]
49. Mahmood, T.; Ullah, K.; Khan, Q.; Jan, N. An Approach toward Decision-Making and Medical Diagnosis Problems Using the Concept of Spherical Fuzzy Sets. *Neural Comput. Appl.* **2019**, *31*, 7041–7053. [CrossRef]
50. Akram, M.; Ullah, K.; Pamucar, D. Performance Evaluation of Solar Energy Cells Using the Interval-Valued T-Spherical Fuzzy Bonferroni Mean Operators. *Energies* **2022**, *15*, 292. [CrossRef]

symmetry MDPI

Article

Some Properties of Cubic Fuzzy Graphs with an Application

Xiaolong Shi [1], Maryam Akhoundi [2,*], Ali Asghar Talebi [3] and Seyed Hossein Sadati [3]

1 Institute of Computing Science and Technology, Guangzhou University, Guangzhou 510006, China
2 Clinical Research Development Unit of Rouhani Hospital, Babol University of Medical Sciences, Babol 47176-47745, Iran
3 Department of Mathematics, University of Mazandaran, Babolsar 47416-13534, Iran
* Correspondence: maryam.akhoundi@mubabol.ac.ir

Abstract: The advent of fuzzy sets, and consequently fuzzy graphs, has solved many problems in ambiguous and uncertain contexts. It is interesting and necessary to study the Wiener index in a cubic fuzzy graph that employs both fuzzy membership and interval-valued fuzzy membership at the same time. In this paper, the Wiener index in a cubic fuzzy graph is introduced as a cubic fuzzy number and some related results are described. The comparison between connectivity index and Wiener index, changes in Wiener index through deleting a node or an edge, and determining the Wiener index in some specific cubic fuzzy graphs have been the other topics studied in this research. In addition, the Wiener index is determined by mentioning concepts of the saturated cubic fuzzy cycle. In this review, the Wiener index is shown as a combination of classical and interval numbers. The results indicate that when some vertices are removed, the Wiener index may change. However, this change will not be exclusively related to both values. Finally, an application of the Wiener index is presented in the study of the properties of some monomer molecules.

Keywords: fuzzy graph; cubic fuzzy graph; connectivity index; Wiener index; saturated cubic fuzzy cycle

1. Introduction

The Wiener index is the first topological index based on the distance function. In fact, the Wiener index is the sum of the distances among all pairs of nodes in a connected graph. Topological indices are defined criteria of a graph that have theoretical and practical applications in areas such as mathematics, chemistry, physics, biology, cryptography, medicine, architecture and so on. Among these indices, the Wiener index has become one of the most widely used topological indices in chemistry. In general, a molecular graph is a graph that is attributed to a molecular structure. In this graph, each atom of a chemical molecule, as a node and bond between atoms, is called the edge of the graph. For example, in the drug design process, the aim is to make chemical compounds with certain properties that are not only dependent on the chemical formula, but also strongly hooked on the molecular structure. A Wiener index score is the encoding of all atom pairs in a molecule that includes the length of the shortest bond with the bond path and uses the shortest path algorithm. This is the fastest molecule screening method that calculates the molecular structure directly. This index was first named by Harold Wiener when studying the boiling point of paraffin in 1947 [1]. The creative results of the Wiener index were gradually published in the mid-1970s. After the introduction of the Wiener index, many generalizations were provided.

Today, there are many concepts that are associated with complexity, ambiguity and uncertainty, so that it is not possible to model them with ordinary graphs. These concepts, first popularized by Zadeh [2] with the introduction of fuzzy set (FS), marked the beginning of a revolution in the knowledge of the unknown. It was after the introduction of fuzzy graph (FG) by Rosenfeld [3] that vague and uncertain concepts were modeled and quickly analyzed by researchers. Next, researchers studied the types of FGs and their properties. Mordeson [4] defined some operations on FGs. Akram [5] generalized the concept of bipolar FGs in 2013 and explored some of their features. It was Atanasov [6] who generalized it to a new set named the intuitionistic fuzzy set (IFS) by considering the nonmembership values in FS. After this study, researchers generalize the various FS concepts in the IFS. Akram et al. [7–9] defined different concepts on IFG such as strong IFGs, balanced IFGs and intuitionistic fuzzy hypergraphs. Borzooei et al. [10] had many studies on vague graphs. Talebi et al. [11,12] investigated some new concepts of interval-valued intuitionistic fuzzy graph (IVIFG). Kosari et al. [13–18] examined some of the concepts in vague graphs. Shao et al. [19] introduced concepts of IFGs which were used in the water supplier systems. Some properties of complex fuzzy graphs, single-valued neutrosophic graph and interval-valued N-soft set were investigated by Ali et al. [20–22].

Jun et al. [23] presented the idea of a cubic fuzzy set (CFS) as a combination of FS and IVFS, which served as a more general tool for modeling uncertainty and ambiguity. By applying this concept, various problems that arise from uncertainties can be solved and the best choice can be made by using CFS in decision making. Jun et al. [24] combined the neutrosophic complex with CFS and presented the idea of neutrosophic CFS. They also studied some algebraic properties based on CFS [25–29]. A modified definition of a CFG is given by Muhiuddin et al. [30] along with concepts such as the strong edge, path, path strength, bridge and cut node. Rashmanlou et al. [31,32] explained some of the CFG concepts.

Connectivity is one of the basic and widely used concepts in graph theory. As a result, it did not take long for researchers to come to terms with uncertain issues. Matthew and Sunita [33] examined the node connectivity and the arc connectivity of an FG based on strong edges. They also introduced cyclic connectivity in FGs in 2013 [34]. Binu et al. [35–37] defined several indices such as the Wiener index, connectivity index and cyclic connectivity index in FGs and used them in different types of interconnection networks. Lee et al. [38] applied modifications to the Wiener index of FGs. Fang et al. [39] examined these indices in a fuzzy incidence graph. Poulik and Ghorai [40] described certain indices of graphs in a bipolar fuzzy environment. Mandal and Pal [41] investigated connectivity indices in an m-polar FG.

The Wiener index has already been studied in various fuzzy graph types that always have a fuzzy membership or an interval-valued fuzzy membership. The raised question here is whether it is possible to calculate this index when there are both fuzzy membership and interval-valued fuzzy membership. In this case, how will this index be expressed? A CFG with simultaneously assigned two membership values to each node is an interesting option in modeling problems where it is not possible to find two fuzzy or interval-valued memberships at the same time. Connectivity indices have a great influence on the interconnected networks analysis in a CFG. The existence of two different fuzzy memberships is effective in interpreting network connectivity. The limitations of previous definitions in this area have led us to redefine the Wiener index in a CFG. This definition is especially useful when faced with two different parameters for which an exact fuzzy value cannot be found.

This article is organized as follows: Section 2 includes an overview of some of the basic definitions and concepts used in this article. The Wiener index is represented in CFGs with different properties in Section 3. Moreover, by comparing the connectivity index and the Wiener index in CFGs, we examine the changes in the Wiener index if one node or one edge has been removed from the graph. In addition, the study of the Wiener index in some types of CFGs, such as the complete CFG and the saturated cubic fuzzy cycle, is another topic in this section. In Section 4, the application of the Wiener index is presented in some properties of monomer molecules in chemistry using a CFG. In Section 5, the conclusion of the research is stated.

2. Preliminaries

In this section, some basic concepts and definitions are provided to enter the main discussion.

In graph G, with the set of nodes and edges of V and E, the distance between the two nodes is defined as the minimum number of edges between the two nodes. The Wiener index $WI(G)$ of G is described as

$$WI(G) = \sum_{x,y \in V} d(x,y),$$

where $d(x,y)$ is the minimum distance between x and y.

Let U be a nonempty set. Then, $\theta : U \to [0,1]$ is named the fuzzy subset (FS) on U. A fuzzy graph (FG) is a pair of $F = (\theta, \eta)$, where θ is an FS on U and η is an FS on $U \times U$ so that $\eta(xy) \leq \theta(x) \wedge \theta(y)$, for all $x, y \in U$. In this definition, $\wedge$ means the minimum and η is assumed to be a reflective and symmetric fuzzy relation in θ.

$F^* = (\theta^*, \eta^*)$ is called the underlying graph of F whenever $\theta^* = \{x \in U | \theta(x) > 0\}$ and $\eta^* = \{xy \in U \times U | \eta(xy) > 0\}$. A sequence of different nodes of $x_0, x_1, \cdots, x_n$ where $\eta(x_{i-1}x_i) > 0$, for $i = 1, 2, \cdots, n$ is named a fuzzy path P with a length of n. The value of the fuzzy membership of the weakest edge in P is called the strength of a fuzzy path. A fuzzy path is named a fuzzy cycle if $x_0 = x_n$. The maximum strength of all fuzzy paths between x and y is named the strength of the connectivity between x and y and is shown by $CONN(x,y)$. For each $x, y \in \theta^*$, if $CONN(x,y) > 0$, then $F = (\theta, \eta)$ is named a connected FG. An edge xy in F is named strong if $\eta(xy) \geq CONN(x,y)$. A fuzzy path is named a strong fuzzy path if all of its edges are strong. xy is named a fuzzy bridge in F whenever the removal of xy reduces the strength of the connectivity between some pairs of nodes in F. If deleting the node x reduces the connectedness strength between some pairs of nodes in F, then, x is called a fuzzy cut node at F. A connected FG is named a fuzzy tree when the spanning fuzzy subgraph is a tree. F is named a complete FG whenever for all $x, y \in \theta^*$, $\eta(xy) = \theta(x) \wedge \theta(y)$ [42].

$[p, q]$ is called an interval-valued fuzzy number (IVFN) if p and q are fuzzy numbers so that $0 \leq p \leq q \leq 1$. For two IVFNs $[p_1, q_1]$ and $[p_2, q_2]$, we describe

$$\begin{aligned}
&[p_1, q_1] \wedge [p_2, q_2] = [p_1 \wedge p_2, q_1 \wedge q_2], \\
&[p_1, q_1] \vee [p_2, q_2] = [p_1 \vee p_2, q_1 \vee q_2], \\
&[p_1, q_1] \preccurlyeq [p_2, q_2] \Longleftrightarrow p_1 \leq p_2,\ q_1 \leq q_2.
\end{aligned}$$

An IVFS A in U is described as

$$A = \{[\alpha(z), \beta(z)] | z \in U\},$$

where α and β are FSs on U so that $\alpha(z) \leq \beta(z)$, for all $z \in U$. For two IVFSs A and B in U, we define

$$\begin{aligned}
A \cup B &= \{[\alpha_A(z) \vee \alpha_B(z), \beta_A(z) \vee \beta_B(z)] | z \in U\}, \\
A \cap B &= \{[\alpha_A(z) \wedge \alpha_B(z), \beta_A(z) \wedge \beta_B(z)] | z \in U\}.
\end{aligned}$$

Definition 1. *[23] A CFS in U is described as*

$$X = \{\langle [\alpha(z), \beta(z)], \gamma(z) \rangle | z \in U\},$$

where $[\alpha(z), \beta(z)]$ is named the IVF-membership value and $\gamma(z)$ is named the F-membership value of z, so that $\alpha, \beta, \gamma : U \in [0,1]$. X is named an interval CFS if $\gamma(z) \in [\alpha(z), \beta(z)]$ and an external CFS whenever $\gamma(z) \notin [\alpha(z), \beta(z)]$, for all $z \in U$.

Definition 2. *[30] A CFG over U is a pair $\mathcal{G} = (X, Y)$ where X is a CFS in U and Y is a CFS in $U \times U$, so that for all $zw \in Y$*

$$\begin{aligned} \alpha_Y(zw) &\leq \alpha_X(z) \wedge \alpha_X(w), \\ \beta_Y(zw) &\leq \beta_X(z) \wedge \beta_X(w), \\ \gamma_Y(zw) &\leq \gamma_X(z) \wedge \gamma_X(w). \end{aligned}$$

Definition 3. *[30] Let $\mathcal{G} = (X, Y)$ be a CFG over U. A cubic fuzzy path in $\mathcal{G}$ is a sequence of $P : z_1, z_2 \cdots, z_k$ of different nodes of U, so that*

$$\alpha_Y(z_{i-1}z_i) > 0, \ \ \beta_Y(z_{i-1}z_i) > 0, \ \ \gamma_Y(z_{i-1}z_i) > 0, \ \ for\ i = 1, 2, \cdots, k.$$

The strength of P is described as $S(P) = \langle [S_\alpha(P), S_\beta(P)], S\gamma(P) \rangle$ and is calculated by

$$S(P) = \left\langle \left[\bigwedge_{i=1}^{k} \alpha_Y(z_{i-1}z_i), \bigwedge_{i=1}^{k} \beta_Y(z_{i-1}z_i) \right], \bigwedge_{i=1}^{k} \gamma_Y(z_{i-1}z_i) \right\rangle.$$

Definition 4. *[30] The strength of the connectivity between z and w is shown by $C^\infty(z, w)$ and it is the maximum of the strengths of all cubic fuzzy paths between z and w.*

$$\begin{aligned} C^\infty(z, w) &= \langle [C_\alpha^\infty(z, w), C_\beta^\infty(z, w)], C_\gamma^\infty(z, w) \rangle \\ &= \langle [\max S_\alpha(P_i), \max S_\beta(P_i)], \max S_\gamma(P_i) \rangle. \end{aligned}$$

Definition 5. *[30] An edge zw in CFG $\mathcal{G}$ is called strong cubic fuzzy edge whenever*

$$\alpha_Y(zw) \geq C_\alpha^\infty(z, w), \ \beta_Y(zw) \geq C_\beta^\infty(z, w), \ \gamma_Y(zw) \geq C_\gamma^\infty(z, w).$$

Definition 6. *[30] $\mathcal{H} = (X', Y')$ is said to be the partial cubic fuzzy subgraph of CFG $\mathcal{G} = (X, Y)$ whenever*

$$\begin{aligned} &\alpha'_{X'} \subseteq \alpha_X, \ \beta'_{X'} \subseteq \beta_X, \ \gamma'_{X'} \subseteq \gamma_X, \\ &\alpha'_{Y'} \subseteq \alpha_Y, \ \beta'_{Y'} \subseteq \beta_Y, \ \gamma'_{Y'} \subseteq \gamma_Y. \end{aligned}$$

Definition 7. *A CFG $\mathcal{G} = (X, Y)$ is named a complete CFG whenever for $z, w \in U$*

$$\begin{aligned} \alpha_Y(zw) &= \alpha_X(z) \wedge \alpha_X(w), \\ \beta_Y(zw) &= \beta_X(z) \wedge \beta_X(w), \\ \gamma_Y(zw) &= \gamma_X(z) \wedge \gamma_X(w). \end{aligned}$$

3. A Description of the Wiener Index in a CFG

In this section, the Wiener index in a CFG is discussed and some of its results are studied.

Definition 8. *Let $\mathcal{G} = (X, Y)$ be a CFG on U. The Wiener index in $\mathcal{G}$ is described as*

$$WI(\mathcal{G}) = \langle [WI_\alpha(\mathcal{G}), WI_\beta(\mathcal{G})], WI_\gamma(\mathcal{G}) \rangle,$$

where for each $z, w \in U$,

$$\begin{aligned} WI_\alpha(\mathcal{G}) &= \sum_{z,w \in U} \alpha_X(z)\alpha_X(w)d_\alpha(z, w), \\ WI_\beta(\mathcal{G}) &= \sum_{z,w \in U} \beta_X(z)\beta_X(w)d_\beta(z, w), \\ WI_\gamma(\mathcal{G}) &= \sum_{z,w \in U} \gamma_X(z)\gamma_X(w)d_\gamma(z, w). \end{aligned}$$

In fact, the Wiener index is applied three times to the following values:

1. *The calculation of the Wiener index for the lower bounds of the membership intervals.*
2. *The calculation of the Wiener index for the upper bounds of the membership intervals.*
3. *The calculation of the Wiener index for fuzzy membership values.*

$[WI_\alpha(\mathcal{G}), WI_\beta(\mathcal{G})]$ *is named the interval-valued Wiener index and* $WI_\alpha(\mathcal{G})$ *is denoted the fuzzy Wiener index of* $\mathcal{G}$.

In this definition, $d_\alpha(z,w)$ and $d_\beta(z,w)$ are the minimum sum of the lower and upper boundaries weights of the IVF-membership, and $d_\gamma(z,w)$ is the minimum sum of weights of the F-membership of distances from z to w.

Example 1. *Consider a CFG* $\mathcal{G}$ *as shown in Figure 1.*

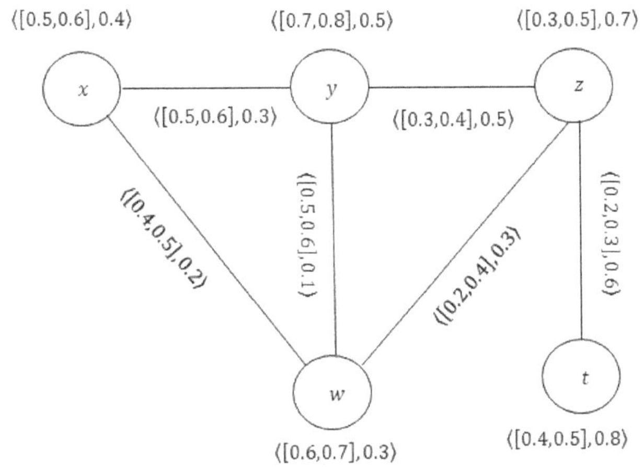

Figure 1. A CFG $\mathcal{G}$.

Here, the distance between the two nodes is as follows:

$$d(x,y) = \langle[0.5,0.6],0.3\rangle, \quad d(x,z) = \langle[0.8,1],0.8\rangle,$$
$$d(x,w) = \langle[0.4,0.5],0.2\rangle, \quad d(x,t) = \langle[0.8,1.2],1.1\rangle,$$
$$d(y,z) = \langle[0.3,0.4],0.5\rangle, \quad d(y,w) = \langle[0.5,0.6],0.1\rangle,$$
$$d(y,t) = \langle[0.5,0.7],1.1\rangle, \quad d(z,w) = \langle[0.2,0.4],0.3\rangle,$$
$$d(z,t) = \langle[0.2,0.3],0.6\rangle, \quad d(w,t) = \langle[0.4,0.7],0.9\rangle.$$

$$\begin{aligned} WI_\alpha(\mathcal{G}) &= 0.175 + 0.12 + 0.12 + 0.16 + 0.063 + 0.21 \\ &\quad + 0.14 + 0.036 + 0.024 + 0.096 = 1.144 \\ WI_\beta(\mathcal{G}) &= 0.288 + 0.3 + 0.21 + 0.36 + 0.16 + 0.336 \\ &\quad + 0.28 + 0.14 + 0.075 + 0.245 = 2.394 \\ WI_\gamma(\mathcal{G}) &= 0.06 + 0.224 + 0.024 + 0.352 + 0.175 + 0.015 \\ &\quad + 0.44 + 0.063 + 0.336 + 0.216 = 1.905. \end{aligned}$$

Therefore, $WI(\mathcal{G}) = \langle[1.144, 2.394], 1.905\rangle$.

The Wiener index value in a cubic fuzzy subgraph does not need to be less than or equal to the original Wiener index of a CFG. This point is described in the next example.

Example 2. *Consider the cubic fuzzy subgraph $\mathcal{H}$ from the CFG $\mathcal{G}$ drawn in Figure 1. We have*

$$WI(\mathcal{H}) = \langle [1.616, 3.138], 2.097 \rangle.$$

It is clear that

$$WI_{\alpha}(\mathcal{G}) < WI_{\alpha}(\mathcal{H}), \ \ WI_{\beta}(\mathcal{G}) < WI_{\beta}(\mathcal{H}), \ \ WI_{\gamma}(\mathcal{G}) < WI_{\gamma}(\mathcal{H}).$$

The cubic fuzzy subgraph $\mathcal{H}$ is drawn in Figure 2.

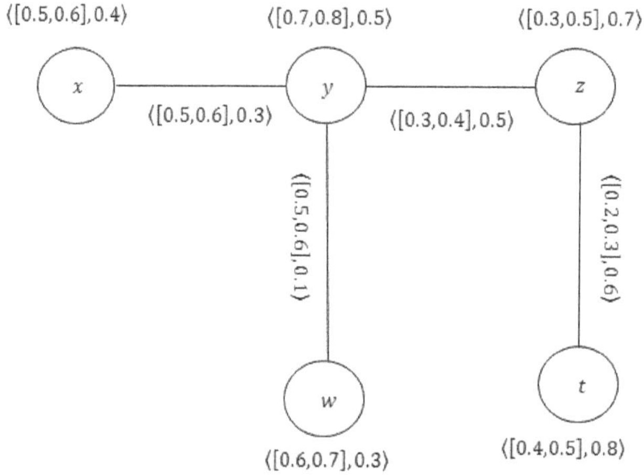

Figure 2. Cubic fuzzy subgraph $\mathcal{H}$ of $\mathcal{G}$.

It is also important to note that removing a node from a CFG also reduces the Wiener index. For example, in the CFG $\mathcal{G}$, by removing the node t, the Wiener index is obtained as follows:

$$WI(\mathcal{G} - t) = \langle [0.724, 1.434], 0.561 \rangle.$$

As can be seen, the Wiener index has decreased.

Theorem 1. *Let $\mathcal{G} = (X, Y)$ be a CFG with $\alpha_X(z) = \beta_X(z) = \gamma_X(z) = 1$ for all $z \in U$ and $|U| = n$. Let*

$$p = \min\{\alpha_Y(zw) | zw \in \alpha_Y^*, \alpha(zw) \geq C^{\infty}(z, w)\},$$
$$q = \min\{\beta_Y(zw) | zw \in \beta_Y^*, \beta(zw) \geq C^{\infty}(z, w)\},$$
$$r = \min\{\gamma_Y(zw) | zw \in \gamma_Y^*, \gamma(zw) \geq C^{\infty}(z, w)\}.$$

Then,

$$WI_{\alpha}(\mathcal{G}) \geq p[n(n-1) - |\alpha_Y^*|],$$
$$WI_{\beta}(\mathcal{G}) \geq q[n(n-1) - |\beta_Y^*|],$$
$$WI_{\gamma}(\mathcal{G}) \geq r[n(n-1) - |\gamma_Y^*|].$$

Proof. Assume that (z, w) is any arbitrary pair of U. If $z, w \in \alpha_Y^*$, then $d(z, w) \geq p$. Therefore, there are $|\alpha_Y^*|$ unordered pairs so that $d(z, w) \geq P$ and $\binom{n}{2} - |\alpha_Y^*|$ are unordered node pairs so that $d(z, w) \geq 2P$. Then,

$$
\begin{aligned}
WI_\alpha(\mathcal{G}) &= \sum d(z, w) \geq |\alpha_Y^*|p + (\binom{n}{2} - |\alpha_Y^*|)2P \\
&= P[|\alpha_Y^*| + 2\binom{n}{2} - 2|\alpha_Y^*|] = P[n(n-1) - |\alpha_Y^*|].
\end{aligned}
$$

Other inequalities similar to the above argument can be proved. □

Theorem 2. *If $\mathcal{G} = (X, Y)$ and $\mathcal{G}' = (X'.Y')$ are two isomorphic CFGs, then $WI(\mathcal{G}) = WI(\mathcal{G}')$.*

Proof. Consider $\mathcal{G}$ and $\mathcal{G}'$ to be two isomorphic CFGs. Thus, there is a bijective mapping $f : X \to X'$ so that, for every $z \in U$ and $zw \in U \times U$, we have

$$
\begin{aligned}
&\alpha_X(z) = \alpha'_{X'}(f(z)),\ \beta_X(z) = \beta'_{X'}(f(z)),\ \gamma_X(z) = \gamma'_{X'}(f(z)),\\
&\alpha_Y(zw) = \alpha'_{Y'}(f(z)f(w)),\ \beta_Y(zw) = \beta'_{Y'}(f(z)f(w)),\ \gamma_Y(zw) = \gamma'_{Y'}(f(z)f(w)).
\end{aligned}
$$

For all $z, w \in U$, suppose $P(z, w)$ is the cubic fuzzy path that belongs to $d(z, w)$. For each cubic fuzzy edge of $xy \in P(z, w)$, there exists a cubic fuzzy edge $f(x)f(y)$ in $\mathcal{G}'$ so that

$$
\alpha_Y(xy) = \alpha'_{Y'}(f(x)f(y)),\ \beta_Y(xy) = \beta'_{Y'}(f(x)f(y)),\ \gamma_Y(xy) = \gamma'_{Y'}(f(x)f(y)).
$$

Therefore, it can be directly said that corresponding to the cubic fuzzy path $P(z, w)$ in $\mathcal{G}$, there is a cubic fuzzy path $P(f(z), f(w))$ in $\mathcal{G}'$ so that the sum of the cubic fuzzy membership values of edges in $P(f(z), f(w))$ is the minimum among all shortest strong cubic fuzzy paths from $f(z)$ to $f(w)$. Thus,

$$
d(z, w) = d(f(z), f(w)).
$$

Then,

$$
\begin{aligned}
WI_\alpha(\mathcal{G}) &= \sum_{z,w \in X} \alpha_X(z)\alpha_X(w)d(z, w) \\
&= \sum_{f(z),f(w) \in X'} \alpha'_{X'}(f(z))\alpha'_{X'}(f(w))d(f(z), f(w)) \\
&= WI_{\alpha'}(\mathcal{G}').
\end{aligned}
$$

Likewise, $WI_\beta(\mathcal{G}) = WI_{\beta'}(\mathcal{G}')$ and $WI_\gamma(\mathcal{G}) = WI_{\gamma'}(\mathcal{G}')$. □

Corollary 1. *Let $\mathcal{G} = (X, Y)$ be a CFG so that $\mathcal{G}^*$ is a tree with $|U| = n$. Let $L_\alpha(z, w)$ be the sum of the lower boundaries of the interval-valued fuzzy membership at the cubic fuzzy edges of the cubic fuzzy path P, which connects z and w. If $\alpha_X(z) = \beta_X(z) = \gamma_X(z) = 1$, for all $z \in U$, then,*

$$
\begin{aligned}
WI_\alpha(\mathcal{G}) &= \sum_{z,w \in U, z \neq w} L_\alpha(z, w), \\
WI_\beta(\mathcal{G}) &= \sum_{z,w \in U, z \neq w} L_\beta(z, w), \\
WI_\gamma(\mathcal{G}) &= \sum_{z,w \in U, z \neq w} L_\gamma(z, w).
\end{aligned}
$$

This results in a CFG $\mathcal{G}$ where $\mathcal{G}^*$ is a star as follows

$$WI_\alpha(\mathcal{G}) = (n-1) \sum_{zw \in \alpha_Y^*} \alpha_Y(zw),$$
$$WI_\beta(\mathcal{G}) = (n-1) \sum_{zw \in \beta_Y^*} \beta_Y(zw),$$
$$WI_\gamma(\mathcal{G}) = (n-1) \sum_{zw \in \gamma_Y^*} \gamma_Y(zw).$$

In the following, we compare the Wiener index with the connectivity index. First, let us have a reminder of the connectivity index

Definition 9. *In the CFG $(\mathcal{G}) = (X, Y)$, $CI(\mathcal{G})$ in the following form is called the connectivity index whenever*

$$CI(\mathcal{G}) = \langle [CI_\alpha(\mathcal{G}), CI_\beta(\mathcal{G})], CI_\gamma(\mathcal{G}) \rangle$$
$$CI_\alpha(\mathcal{G}) = \sum_{z,w \in U} \alpha_X(z)\alpha_X(w) C_\alpha^\infty(z,w)$$
$$CI_\beta(\mathcal{G}) = \sum_{z,w \in U} \beta_X(z)\beta_X(w) C_\beta^\infty(z,w)$$
$$CI_\gamma(\mathcal{G}) = \sum_{z,w \in U} \gamma_X(z)\gamma_X(w) C_\gamma^\infty(z,w), \quad for\ all\ z,w \in U.$$

$[CI_\alpha(\mathcal{G}), CI_\beta(\mathcal{G})]$ is denoted as the interval-valued fuzzy connectivity index and $CI_\gamma(\mathcal{G})$ represents the fuzzy connectivity index of $\mathcal{G}$.

In the following example, we examine the comparison between the connectivity index and the Wiener index in a CFG.

Example 3. *Consider the CFG $\mathcal{G}$ drawn in Figure 3.*

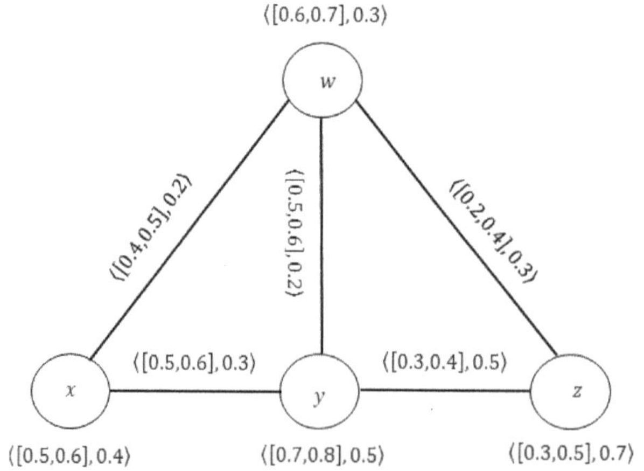

Figure 3. The comparison between $CI(\mathcal{G})$ and $WI(\mathcal{G})$ in a CFG $\mathcal{G}$.

$$C^{\infty}(x,y) = \langle [0.5, 0.6], 0.3 \rangle, \quad d(x,y) = \langle [0.5, 0.6], 0.3 \rangle,$$
$$C^{\infty}(x,z) = \langle [0.3, 0.4], 0.3 \rangle, \quad d(x,z) = \langle [0.6, 0.9], 0.5 \rangle,$$
$$C^{\infty}(x,w) = \langle [0.5, 0.6], 0.3 \rangle, \quad d(x,w) = \langle [0.4, 0.5], 0.2 \rangle,$$
$$C^{\infty}(y,z) = \langle [0.3, 0.4], 0.5 \rangle, \quad d(y,z) = \langle [0.3, 0.4], 0.5 \rangle,$$
$$C^{\infty}(y,w) = \langle [0.5, 0.6], 0.3 \rangle, \quad d(y,w) = \langle [0.5, 0.6], 0.2 \rangle,$$
$$C^{\infty}(z,w) = \langle [0.3, 0.4], 0.3 \rangle, \quad d(z,w) = \langle [0.2, 0.4], 0.3 \rangle.$$

After the calculations, we have

$$CI(\mathcal{G}) = \langle [0.697, 1.296], 0.463 \rangle,$$

and

$$WI(\mathcal{G}) = \langle [0.694, 1.404], 0.492 \rangle.$$

As observed, $CI_{\alpha}(\mathcal{G}) > WI_{\alpha}(\mathcal{G})$, $CI_{\beta}(\mathcal{G}) < WI_{\beta}(\mathcal{G})$ *and* $CI_{\gamma}(\mathcal{G}) < WI_{\gamma}(\mathcal{G})$.

The results show that the values of the connectivity and Wiener indices are higher in some components and lower in others.

Proposition 1. *If* $\mathcal{G} = (X, Y)$ *is a complete CFG, then*

$$CI(\mathcal{G}) = WI(\mathcal{G}).$$

Proof. Assume that $\mathcal{G} = (X, Y)$ is a complete CFG. Therefore, both nodes are connected by a cubic fuzzy edge in $\mathcal{G}$. Since all cubic fuzzy edges are strong, then $C^{\infty}(z,w) = d(z,w)$. Thus,

$$CI(\mathcal{G}) = WI(\mathcal{G}). \quad \square$$

The above proposition immediately gives the following result.

Corollary 2. *Let* $\mathcal{G} = (X, Y)$ *be a complete CFG. Let* $\alpha_X(z_i) = t_i$, $\beta_X(z_i) = s_i$ *and* $\gamma_X(z_i) = r_i$ *so that* $t_1 \leq t_2 \leq \cdots \leq t_n$, $s_1 \leq s_2 \leq \cdots \leq s_n$ *and* $r_1 \leq r_2 \leq \cdots \leq r_n$, *for all* $1 \leq i \leq n$. *Then,*

$$WI_{\alpha}(\mathcal{G}) = \sum_{i=1}^{n-1} t_i^2 \sum_{j=i+1}^{n} t_j,$$
$$WI_{\beta}(\mathcal{G}) = \sum_{i=1}^{n-1} s_i^2 \sum_{j=i+1}^{n} s_j,$$
$$WI_{\gamma}(\mathcal{G}) = \sum_{i=1}^{n-1} r_i^2 \sum_{j=i+1}^{n} r_j.$$

Proof. Suppose $\mathcal{G}$ is a complete CFG. Moreover, let $\alpha_X(z_1) = t_1$, $\beta_X(z_1) = s_1$ and $\gamma_X(z_1) = r_1$, for $z_1 \in U$. Since $\mathcal{G}$ is a complete CG, then

$$d_{\alpha}(z_1, z_j) = \alpha_X(z_1) = t_1,$$
$$d_{\beta}(z_1, z_j) = \beta_X(z_1) = s_1,$$
$$d_{\gamma}(z_1, z_j) = \gamma_X(z_1) = r_1, \text{ for all } j > 1.$$

According to the conditions, we have

$$\begin{aligned}\alpha_X(z_1) &\le \alpha_X(z_2) \le \cdots \le \alpha_X(z_n),\\ \beta_X(z_1) &\le \beta_X(z_2) \le \cdots \le \beta_X(z_n),\\ \gamma_X(z_1) &\le \gamma_X(z_2) \le \cdots \le \gamma_X(z_n).\end{aligned}$$

Therefore,

$$\begin{aligned}\alpha_X(z_1)\alpha_X(z_j)d_\alpha(z_1,z_j) &= t_1t_jt_1 = t_1^2t_j,\\ \beta_X(z_1)\beta_X(z_j)d_\beta(z_1,z_j) &= s_1s_js_1 = s_1^2s_j,\\ \gamma_X(z_1)\gamma_X(z_j)d_\gamma(z_1,z_j) &= r_1r_jr_1 = r_1^2r_j.\end{aligned}$$

$$\begin{aligned}\sum_{j=2}^{n}\alpha_X(z_1)\alpha_X(z_j)d_\alpha(z_1,z_j) &= \sum_{j=2}^{n}t_1^2t_j,\\ \sum_{j=2}^{n}\beta_X(z_1)\beta_X(z_j)d_\beta(z_1,z_j) &= \sum_{j=2}^{n}s_1^2s_j,\\ \sum_{j=2}^{n}\gamma_X(z_1)\gamma_X(z_j)d_\gamma(z_1,z_j) &= \sum_{j=2}^{n}r_1^2r_j.\end{aligned}$$

Thus,

$$\begin{aligned}WI_\alpha(\mathcal{G}) &= \sum_{i=1}^{n-1}t_i^2\sum_{j=i+1}^{n}t_j,\\ WI_\beta(\mathcal{G}) &= \sum_{i=1}^{n-1}s_i^2\sum_{j=i+1}^{n}s_j,\\ WI_\gamma(\mathcal{G}) &= \sum_{i=1}^{n-1}r_i^2\sum_{j=i+1}^{n}r_j. \quad \square\end{aligned}$$

Theorem 3. *If $\mathcal{G} = (X,Y)$ is a cubic fuzzy tree (CFT) with $|U| \ge 3$, then*

$$\begin{aligned}CI_\alpha(\mathcal{G}) &\le WI_\alpha(\mathcal{G}),\\ CI_\beta(\mathcal{G}) &\le WI_\beta(\mathcal{G}),\\ CI_\gamma(\mathcal{G}) &\le WI_\gamma(\mathcal{G}).\end{aligned}$$

Proof. Suppose $\mathcal{G} = (X,Y)$ to be a CFT. In a CFT, there is a unique strong cubic fuzzy path of P that connects each pair of nodes and is also the strongest unique cubic fuzzy path. For each $z,w \in U$, $d(z,w)$ is actually the sum of the membership values of all cubic fuzzy edges that is unique in the strongest strong cubic fuzzy path, where P connecting z and w and where $C^\infty(z,w)$ is the membership value of the weakest cubic fuzzy edge of P. Hence, $C_\alpha^\infty(z,w) \le d_\alpha(z,w)$, $C_\beta^\infty(z,w) \le d_\beta(z,w)$, $C_\gamma^\infty(z,w) \le d_\gamma(z,w)$. Therefore,

$$\sum_{z,w\in U}\alpha_X(z)\alpha_X(w)C_\alpha^\infty(z,w) \le \sum_{z,w\in U}\alpha_X(z)\alpha_X(w)d_\alpha(z,w).$$

Thus, $CI_\alpha(\mathcal{G}) \le WI_\alpha(\mathcal{G})$.
Similarly, $CI_\beta(\mathcal{G}) \le WI_\beta(\mathcal{G})$ and $CI_\gamma(\mathcal{G}) \le WI_\gamma(\mathcal{G})$. $\square$

In general, no direct relationship is found between the value of the Wiener index in a CFG and the value of the Wiener index after removing a node or an edge. The following example seeks further explanation.

Example 4. *Consider the CFG $\mathcal{G}$ drawn in Figure 3. The value of the Wiener index after removing the yw edge is as follows*

$$WI(\mathcal{G} - yw) = \langle [0.699, 1.516], 0.582 \rangle.$$

Therefore, we have

$$\begin{aligned} WI_\alpha(\mathcal{G} - yw) &= WI_\alpha(\mathcal{G}), \\ WI_\beta(\mathcal{G} - yw) &> WI_\beta(\mathcal{G}), \\ WI_\gamma(\mathcal{G} - yw) &> WI_\gamma(\mathcal{G}). \end{aligned}$$

While after deleting yz, the Wiener index is as follows

$$WI(\mathcal{G} - yz) = \langle [0.778, 1.644], 0.492 \rangle.$$

Therefore, we have

$$\begin{aligned} WI_\alpha(\mathcal{G} - yz) &> WI_\alpha(\mathcal{G}), \\ WI_\beta(\mathcal{G} - yz) &> WI_\beta(\mathcal{G}), \\ WI_\gamma(\mathcal{G} - yz) &= WI_\gamma(\mathcal{G}). \end{aligned}$$

On the other hand, after removing the node w, the Wiener index is $WI(\mathcal{G} - w) = \langle [0.358, 0.748], 0.459 \rangle$*, in which*

$$\begin{aligned} WI_\alpha(\mathcal{G} - w) &< WI_\alpha(\mathcal{G}), \\ WI_\beta(\mathcal{G} - w) &< WI_\beta(\mathcal{G}), \\ WI_\gamma(\mathcal{G} - w) &< WI_\gamma(\mathcal{G}). \end{aligned}$$

The following definitions are used in some of the results of the Wiener index.

Definition 10. *A cubic fuzzy edge zw of a CFG $\mathcal{G} = (X, Y)$ is named α-strong if*

$$\alpha_Y(zw) > C^{\infty}_{\mathcal{G}-zw}(z-w), \;\; \beta_Y(zw) > C^{\infty}_{\mathcal{G}-zw}(z-w), \;\; \gamma_Y(zw) > C^{\infty}_{\mathcal{G}-zw}(z-w).$$

zw is called β-strong if

$$\alpha_Y(zw) = C^{\infty}_{\mathcal{G}-zw}(z-w), \;\; \beta_Y(zw) = C^{\infty}_{\mathcal{G}-zw}(z-w), \;\; \gamma_Y(zw) = C^{\infty}_{\mathcal{G}-zw}(z-w),$$

and it is called δ-edge if

$$\alpha_Y(zw) < C^{\infty}_{\mathcal{G}-zw}(z-w), \;\; \beta_Y(zw) < C^{\infty}_{\mathcal{G}-zw}(z-w), \;\; \gamma_Y(zw) < C^{\infty}_{\mathcal{G}-zw}(z-w).$$

It is clear that a cubic fuzzy edge is strong if it is either α-strong or β-strong.

Definition 11. *Let $\mathcal{G}$ be a CFG. $\mathcal{G}$ is named α-saturated if at least one α-strong cubic fuzzy edge is incident at every node of $z \in U$. Moreover, $\mathcal{G}$ is named β-saturated if at least one β-strong cubic fuzzy edge occurs in each node.*

A CFG $\mathcal{G}$ is named saturated if it is both α-saturated and β-saturated.

Theorem 4. *Let $\mathcal{G}$ be a CFG. For $z, w \in U$, let $P(z, w)$ be the cubic fuzzy path that has the minimum sum of the membership values among the shortest strong cubic fuzzy paths between z and w.*

(i) If $st \in Y$ is a strong cubic fuzzy edge and st is not a part of any $P(z, w)$ with $\{z, w\} \neq \{s, t\}$, then $WI(\mathcal{G} - st) \neq WI(\mathcal{G})$.
(ii) If st is not a strong cubic fuzzy edge, then $WI(\mathcal{G} - st) = WI(\mathcal{G})$.

Proof. (*i*) Let $\mathcal{G} = (X, Y)$ be a CFG and $st \in Y$. Let st be a strong cubic fuzzy edge. Then, the shortest cubic fuzzy path that connects s and t is st and $d(s,t) = \langle[\alpha_Y(st), \beta_Y(st)], \gamma_Y(st)\rangle$. If there is no cubic fuzzy path to connect s and t in $\mathcal{G} - st$, then $d_{\mathcal{G}-st}(s,t) < d_{\mathcal{G}}(s,t)$. If s and t are connected in $\mathcal{G} - st$, then there is at least one cubic fuzzy path that connects s and t with a length of at least two. Assume that st is not part of any $P(z,w)$ where $z \neq s$, $w \neq t$. Therefore, $d_{\mathcal{G}-st}(s,t) > d_{\mathcal{G}}$ or $d_{\mathcal{G}-st}(s,t) < d_{\mathcal{G}}$ according to the path $P(s,t)$ in $\mathcal{G} - st$. Let $\{s,t\} \neq \{x,y\}$. By assuming st is not part of $P(x,y)$, then, $d_{\mathcal{G}-st}(a,b) = d_{\mathcal{G}}(a,b)$. Thus, either $WI(\mathcal{G} - st) < WI(\mathcal{G})$ or $WI(\mathcal{G} - st) > WI(\mathcal{G})$. This means $WI(\mathcal{G} - st) \neq WI(\mathcal{G})$.

(*ii*) If st is not a strong cubic fuzzy edge, then st is not part of any distance from z to w for any $z, w \in U$. Therefore, removing st from $\mathcal{G}$ does not change $d(z,w)$. Thus, $WI(\mathcal{G} - st) = WI(\mathcal{G})$. □

Corollary 3. *Let $\mathcal{G} = (X, Y)$ be a CFG so that each cubic fuzzy edge is strong. For $z, w \in U$, let $P(z,w)$ be the cubic fuzzy path that has at least the sum of the membership values among the shortest strong cubic fuzzy paths between z and w. Assume that st is not part of any $P(z,w)$ where $\{z,w\} \neq \{s,t\}$. Then,*

(*i*) *If $d_{\mathcal{G}-st}(s,t) \neq \langle[\alpha_Y(st), \beta_Y(st)], \gamma_Y(st)\rangle$, then $WI(\mathcal{G} - st) \neq WI(\mathcal{G})$.*
(*ii*) *If $d_{\mathcal{G}-st}(s,t) = \langle[\alpha_Y(st), \beta_Y(st)], \gamma_Y(st)\rangle$, then $WI(\mathcal{G} - st) = WI(\mathcal{G})$.*

Proof. (*i*) Since every edge in $\mathcal{G}$ is strong, so every edge in $\mathcal{G} - st$ is also strong. Therefore, $d_{\mathcal{G}}(s,t) = \langle[\alpha_Y(st), \beta_Y(st)], \gamma_Y(st)\rangle$. Assume that st is not part of any $P(a,b)$ with $\{a,b\} \neq \{s,t\}$. Then, $d_{\mathcal{G}-st}(a,b) = d_{\mathcal{G}}(a,b)$. Hence, we have

$$\begin{aligned} WI_\alpha(\mathcal{G} - st) &= \sum_{u,v \in U} \alpha_Y(u)\alpha_Y(v) d_\alpha^{\mathcal{G}-st}(u,v) \\ &= \sum_{u,v \in U} \alpha_Y(u)\alpha_Y(v) d_\alpha^{\mathcal{G}}(u,v) + (d_\alpha^{\mathcal{G}-st}(s,t) - d_\alpha^{\mathcal{G}}(s,t)) \\ &= WI_\alpha(\mathcal{G}) + d_\alpha^{\mathcal{G}-st}(s,t) - \alpha_Y(st). \end{aligned}$$

Therefore, if $d_\alpha^{\mathcal{G}-st}(s,t) > \alpha_Y(st)$, then $WI_\alpha(\mathcal{G} - st) > WI_\alpha(\mathcal{G})$. Similarly, $WI_\beta(\mathcal{G} - st) > WI_\beta(\mathcal{G})$ and $WI_\gamma(\mathcal{G} - st) > WI_\gamma(\mathcal{G})$. Thus, $WI(\mathcal{G} - st) > WI(\mathcal{G})$.

By the same way, it can be calculated that

$$WI(\mathcal{G} - st) < WI(\mathcal{G}).$$

Thus, $WI(\mathcal{G} - st) = WI(\mathcal{G})$.
(*ii*) is provable like (*i*). □

Theorem 5. *Let $\mathcal{G}$ be a cubic fuzzy cycle (CFC). Then, $\mathcal{G}$ is saturated CFC if and only if the following two conditions are satisfied.*

(*i*) *n is an even number.*
(*ii*) *α,β-strong cubic fuzzy edges appear consecutively on $\mathcal{G}$.*

Proof. Let $\mathcal{G}$ be a CFC. Therefore, $\mathcal{G}$ has no δ-strong cubic fuzzy edges. Suppose that $\mathcal{G}$ is a saturated CFC. Therefore, it is both α-saturated and β-saturated. This implies that the number of α-strong cubic fuzzy edges is equal to the number of β-strong cubic fuzzy edges. Therefore, n is an even number. Thus, each node is incident with both α,β-strong cubic fuzzy edges, which happens only when they appear consecutively on $\mathcal{G}$.

Conversely, assume that $\mathcal{G}$ is an even CFC and α,β-strong cubic fuzzy edges appear consecutively on $\mathcal{G}$. This means all the nodes are incident with exactly one α-strong and exactly with one β-strong cubic fuzzy edges. Therefore, $\mathcal{G}$ is both α-saturated and β-saturated. Then, G is a saturated CFC. □

Example 5. *Consider CFC $\mathcal{G}$ in Figure 4, where $\alpha(z) = \beta(z) = \gamma(z) = 1$, for all $z \in U$. All the cubic fuzzy edges appearing alternatively on $\mathcal{G}$ are α,β-strong. Then, $\mathcal{G}$ is a saturated CFC.*

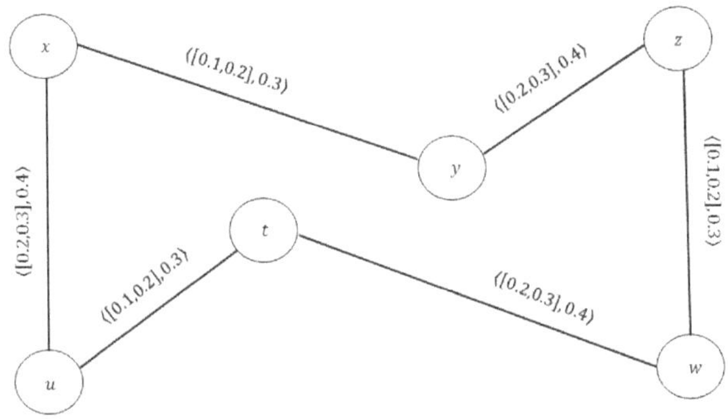

Figure 4. A saturated CFC.

Theorem 6. *Let $\mathcal{G} = (X, Y)$ be a saturated CFC with $\mathcal{G}^* = C_n$ of length n so that each α-strong cubic fuzzy edge has a strength of $\langle [s, t], r\rangle$ and that each β-strong cubic fuzzy edge is $\langle [s', t'], r'\rangle$. Moreover, $\alpha_X(z) = \beta_X(z) = \gamma_X(z) = 1$, for all $z \in U$. Then, for $m = 1, 2, \cdots$.*

$$WI_\alpha(\mathcal{G}) = \begin{cases} \frac{n^3}{16}(t+t') & n = 4m \\ \frac{n(n^2-4)}{16}t + \frac{n(n^2+4)}{16}t' & Otherwise \end{cases}$$

$$WI_\beta(\mathcal{G}) = \begin{cases} \frac{n^3}{16}(s+s') & n = 4m \\ \frac{n(n^2-4)}{16}s + \frac{n(n^2+4)}{16}s' & Otherwise \end{cases}$$

$$WI_\gamma(\mathcal{G}) = \begin{cases} \frac{n^3}{16}(r+r') & n = 4m \\ \frac{n(n^2-4)}{16}r + \frac{n(n^2+4)}{16}r' & Otherwise \end{cases}$$

Proof. Suppose $\mathcal{G}$ is a saturated CFC. Then, the cubic fuzzy edges that appear alternatively have a strength of $\langle [s, t], r\rangle$ and $\langle [s', t'], r'\rangle$, respectively. Considering the above theorem, n is an even number. Remember that each cubic fuzzy edge of a CFC is strong. The maximum length of the node z in C_n is $\frac{n}{2}$. For $k = 1, 2, \cdots, \frac{n}{2}$, we define

$$P_k = \{(z, w) \in X \times X |\ length\ of\ the\ distance\ between\ z\ and\ w\ is\ k.\}.$$

There are $\frac{n}{2}$ pairs of nodes (z, w) so that the length of the distance z and w is $\frac{n}{2}$. If $n = 4m$, for $m = 1, 2, \cdots$, then $d_\alpha(z, w) = \frac{n}{4}(t + t')$, for any $(z, w) \in P_{\frac{n}{2}}$, and $(\frac{n-2}{4})t + (\frac{n+2}{4})t'$, elsewhere. Therefore,

$$\sum_{z,w\in P_{\frac{n}{2}}} d_\alpha(z, w) = \begin{cases} \frac{n}{4}(t+t')\frac{n}{2} = \frac{n^2}{8}(t+t') & n = 4m \\ \frac{n}{2}((\frac{n-2}{4})t + (\frac{n+2}{4})t') & Otherwise. \end{cases}$$

For each node $z \in U$, there are exactly two nodes at a distance of k from z. Thus, there are $2n$ pairs of nodes. By avoiding repetition, there will be n pairs $(p, q) \in X \times X$ so that the length of the distance from p to q is k.

Let k be even and $1 \leq k < \frac{n}{2}$. There are $\frac{K}{2}$ number of α,β-strong cubic fuzzy edges in the distance of length k from z to w. Hence, $\sum_{z,w\in P_k} d_\alpha(z, w) = \frac{nk}{2}(t + t')$.

Let k be odd and $1 \leq k < \frac{n}{2}$. Consider $z \in U$ and x, y are two nodes at a distance k from z. One of the distances from z of length k contains $\frac{k+1}{2}$ α-strong cubic fuzzy edges and $\frac{k-1}{2}$ β-strong cubic fuzzy edges. The other one contain $\frac{k+1}{2}$ β-strong cubic fuzzy edges and $\frac{k-1}{2}$ α-strong cubic fuzzy edges. Therefore,

$$\begin{aligned}\sum_{z,w \in P_k} d_\alpha(z,w) &= \frac{n}{2}\left[\left(\frac{k+1}{2}\right)t + \left(\frac{k-1}{2}\right)t'\right] + \frac{n}{2}\left[\left(\frac{k+1}{2}\right)t' + \left(\frac{k-1}{2}\right)t\right] \\ &= \frac{n}{2}(kt + kt') = \frac{nk}{2}(t+t').\end{aligned}$$

Then, for $n = 4m$

$$\begin{aligned}WI_\alpha(\mathcal{G}) &= \frac{n^2}{8}(t+t') + \sum_{1 \leq k < \frac{n}{2}} \frac{nk}{2}(t+t') \\ &= (t+t')\frac{n}{2}\left(\frac{n}{4} + \sum_{1 \leq k < \frac{n}{2}-1} k\right) \\ &= \frac{n}{2}\left[\frac{n}{4} + \left(\frac{n}{2} - 1\right) \times \frac{1 + \frac{n}{2} - 1}{2}\right](t+t') \\ &= \frac{n}{2}\left[\frac{n}{4} + \left(\frac{n-2}{2}\right)\left(\frac{n}{4}\right)\right](t+t') \\ &= \frac{n}{2}\left[\frac{n}{4} + \frac{n^2 - 2n}{8}\right](t+t') \\ &= \frac{n}{2}\left[\frac{n^2}{8}\right](t+t') = \frac{n^3}{16}(t+t').\end{aligned}$$

where for n not a factor of 4,

$$\begin{aligned}WI_\alpha(\mathcal{G}) &= \frac{n}{2}\left[\left(\frac{n-2}{4}\right)t + \left(\frac{n+2}{4}\right)t'\right] + \sum_{1 \leq k < \frac{n}{2}} \frac{nk}{2}(t+t') \\ &= \frac{n}{2}\left[\left(\frac{n-2}{4}\right)t + \left(\frac{n+2}{4}\right)t'\right] + (t+t')\frac{n}{2}\left(\sum_{1 \leq k < \frac{n}{2}-1} k\right) \\ &= \frac{n}{2}\left[\left(\frac{n-2}{4}\right)t + \left(\frac{n+2}{4}\right)t'\right] + \frac{n}{2}\left[\left(\frac{n}{2} - 1\right) \times \frac{1 + \frac{n}{2} - 1}{2}\right](t+t') \\ &= \frac{n}{2}\left[\left(\frac{n-2}{4}\right)t + \left(\frac{n+2}{4}\right)t'\right] + \frac{n}{2}\left[\frac{n(n-2)}{8}\right](t+t') \\ &= \frac{n(n^2-4)}{16}t + \frac{n(n^2+4)}{16}t'.\end{aligned}$$

$WI_\beta(\mathcal{G})$ and $WI_\alpha(\mathcal{G})$ are also proved according to the above method. □

4. Application

Chemistry is concerned with how subatomic particles bond to form atoms. In addition, in chemistry, there is a focus on how atoms bond to form molecules. In a molecular graph, all atoms and chemical bonds are labeled. This labeled graph is used in the physical and chemical predictions of a compound, quantitatively and qualitatively describing the chemical structures, structural features and activities related to topological indices.

One of the characteristics of an atom that plays a very important role in the properties of compounds is the radius of the atom and its electronegative properties. Bond length and bond energy are also the important features of a bond. Electronegativity is the degree to which an atom in a molecule tends to attract a pair of bonding electrons to itself. The Pauling electronegative relative scale is the most common scale based on the experimental values of bond energies. The radius of an atom indicates its effective size, when measured in combination with other atoms. In fact, determining the atomic radius is difficult because there is uncertainty, so a constant atomic radius cannot be determined for an atom. The radius of a single atom is in the range of 30 to 300 pm or between 0.3 and 3 angstroms.

In molecular geometry, bond length or bond distance is defined as the average distance between two atoms bond in a molecule. The length of the bond depends on the order of the bond. When more electrons are present in a bond, we have a shorter bond. The length of the bond also inversely depends on the strength of the bond and the dissociation energy of the bond. The stronger the bond, the shorter it will be when all the factors are the same.

Until 1920, chemists did not think that molecules with a molecular weight greater than a thousand existed. Until a German chemist named Hermann Staudinger challenged this theory by studying the composition of substances such as rubber and cellulose. Contrary to popular belief, he suggested that these compounds were made up of macromolecules of 10,000 atoms or more. He formulated a polymer structure for rubber based on a repeated isoprene unit (called a monomer) and was awarded the 1953 Nobel Prize.

Monomers are actually the building blocks of polymer molecules. In simpler terms, one monomer is added to another to form a polymer chain. This process is called polymerization. Monomers are essential elements for many industries and have a variety of applications, from food packaging to coatings for vehicles and home appliances. Monomers provide selectivity, quality and compatibility, dispersion and emulsions for a variety of adhesives, coatings, inks, woven and nonwoven textiles, plastics and polymers and highly absorbent products

In this study, three monomers were examined, which included the molecules drawn in Figure 5.

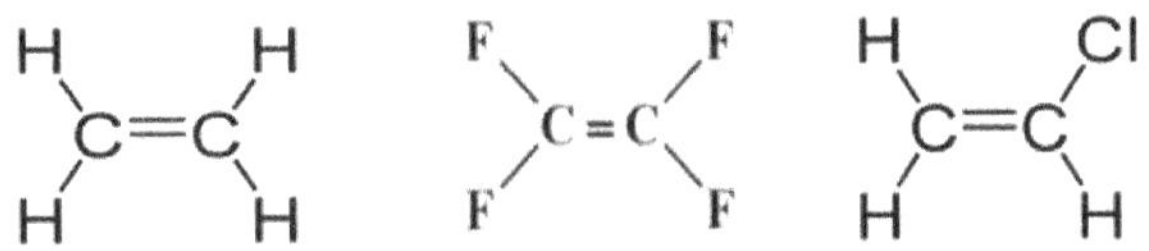

Ethene (C_2H_4) Tetrafluoroethylene (C_2F_4) Chloroethene (C_2H_3Cl)

Figure 5. Three types of monomers from the alkenes group.

A CFG can be useful in examining some properties of molecules. For this purpose, each of the above molecules was considered as a CFG. The atomic radius and electronegative number of some atoms along with their cubic fuzzy values are given in Table 1. In this table, the atomic radius with an interval-valued fuzzy number with a difference of 0.01 from the center of the interval and the electronegative number of each atom is shown with a fuzzy number, which is the ratio of the number of each atom to four. The values for the length and energy of some chemical bonds between atoms, along with the cubic fuzzy values for each of them, are presented in Table 2. In this table, the cubic fuzzy values of each bond are calculated in relation to a maximum of 300 and 1000 pm.

The Wiener index of each molecule is calculated in Table 3.

Looking at Table 3, it can be concluded that by substituting H atoms in ethene with F atoms, the bond energy increased tremendously because its fuzzy Wiener index increased more than that of other molecules. Polymers based on a C_2F_4 molecule seem to have a good level of strength. In addition, a decrease in the interval-valued Wiener index in C_2F_4 compared to C_2H_4 means a decrease in the bond length of this molecule and an increase in its melting point. The available data confirmed the results obtained.

Table 1. Cubic fuzzy values of atoms.

Atoms	Atomic Radius (pm)	Electronegative Number	Cubic Fuzzy Number
H	53	2.20	$\langle[0.16, 0.18], 0.13\rangle$
C	65	2.55	$\langle[0.20, 0.22], 0.63\rangle$
N	55	3.04	$\langle[0.17, 0.19], 0.76\rangle$
F	41	3.98	$\langle[0.12, 0.14], 0.99\rangle$
Cl	78	3.16	$\langle[0.25, 0.27], 0.79\rangle$

Table 2. Cubic fuzzy values of bonds.

Bonds	Length (pm)	Energy (kJ/mol)	Cubic Fuzzy Number
C–H	109	413	$\langle[0.35, 0.37], 0.41\rangle$
C–F	135	488	$\langle[0.44, 0.46], 0.48\rangle$
C–Cl	177	78	$\langle[0.58, 0.60], 0.07\rangle$
C=C	134	614	$\langle[0.43, 0.45], 0.61\rangle$
N–H	101	391	$\langle[0.32, 0.34], 0.39\rangle$
N=N	141	170	$\langle[0.46, 0.48], 0.17\rangle$

Table 3. The Wiener index values of molecules.

$WI(\mathcal{G})$	C_2H_4	C_2F_4	C_2H_3Cl
$WI_\alpha(\mathcal{G})$	0.313392	0.24376	0.426956
$WI_\beta(\mathcal{G})$	0.412452	0.334036	1.171176
$WI_\gamma(\mathcal{G})$	0.834961	12.195765	1.302109

The results for the C_2H_3Cl molecule were similar as those of C_2H_4, except for the fact that the interval-valued Wiener index in this molecule was higher than in the other two molecules, which provided a greater bond length between its atoms. It seems that by replacing Cl with H, we saw an increase in the length and energy of the bond in the molecule. The study of this issue in C_2HCl_3 molecule drawn in Figure 6 with Wiener index $\langle[0.70911, 0.87615], 2.775757\rangle$ confirmed this point.

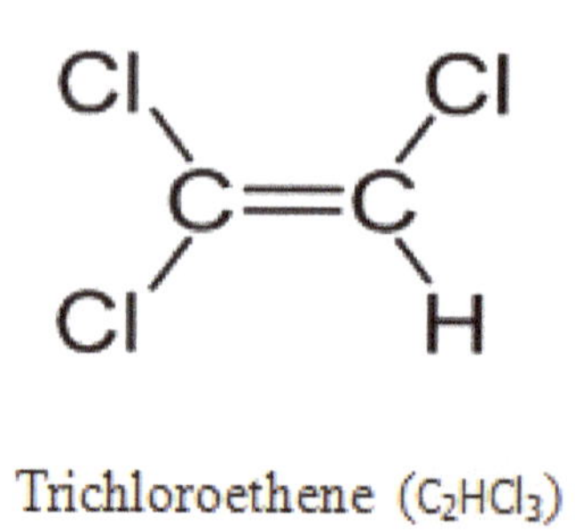

Figure 6. Molecular structure of trichloroethene.

A major part of the properties of these molecules depends on the two intermediate atoms. To confirm this, we calculated the Wiener index in N_2H_4 as shown in Figure 7.

Hydrazine (N_2H_4)

Figure 7. Molecular structure of hydrazine.

The Wiener index of this molecule was $\langle[0.273262, 0.364736], 0.565568\rangle$, which indicated a decrease for all components values compared to the above molecules.

5. Conclusions

A topological index is a real number based on the distance of nodes in a graph. Among these indices, the Wiener index was the first defined index to be used as a tool for modeling chemical, pharmacological and other molecular properties. The Wiener index is one of the defining criteria in fuzzy graphs, where we are faced with uncertain values. It is even more important to know that we are dealing with a fuzzy graph that has both fuzzy membership and interval-valued membership, that is, a CFG. Determining the Wiener index in a CFG is directly related to the bond strength between nodes. In this paper, by extending the Wiener index in fuzzy graphs to cubic graphs, we presented a new definition of the Wiener index with both numerical and interval values. Some of its basic properties were investigated, including determining the value of the Wiener index in certain CFGs, changing the Wiener index by removing one node or an edge of the CFG and the formula for the value of the Wiener index in a saturated CFC. The results showed that the value of the Wiener index was not always associated with a decrease or increase. In some cases, the value of the fuzzy Wiener index increased while the value of the interval-valued Wiener index decreased. Using the results obtained in determining the Wiener index of some monomer molecules, an application of this index in the study of the properties of polymer molecules was presented. Studying the properties of the connectivity index and the average connectivity index will be future work.

Author Contributions: X.S., A.A.T. and S.H.S.; methodology, X.S., M.A. and A.A.T.; formal analysis, X.S. and A.A.T.; investigation, X.S., M.A., A.A.T. and S.H.S.; data curation, X.S., M.A. and S.H.S.; writing—original draft preparation, X.S. and A.A.T.; writing—review and editing, X.S., M.A., A.A.T. and S.H.S.; visualization, X.S., M.A., A.A.T. and S.H.S.; funding acquisition, X.S. All authors have read and agreed to the published version of the manuscript.

Funding: This work was supported by the National Key R&D Program of China (grant 2019YFA0706 402), and the National Natural Science Foundation of China under grants 62172302, 62072129 and 61876047.

Institutional Review Board Statement: Not applicable.

Informed Consent Statement: Not applicable.

Data Availability Statement: Not applicable.

Conflicts of Interest: The authors declare no conflict of interest.

References

1. Wiener, H. Structural determination of paraffin boiling points. *J. Am. Chem. Soc.* **1947**, *69*, 17–20. [CrossRef]
2. Zadeh, L.A. Information and control. *Fuzzy Sets* **1965**, *8*, 338–353.
3. Rosenfeld, A. *Fuzzy Graphs, Fuzzy Sets and Their Applications*; Academic Press: New York, NY, USA, 1975; pp. 77–95.

4. Mordeson, J.N.; Chang-Shyh, P. Operations on fuzzy graphs. *Inf. Sci.* **1994**, *79*, 159–170. [CrossRef]
5. Akram, M. Bipolar fuzzy graphs with applications. *Knowl.-Based Syst.* **2013**, *39*, 1–8. [CrossRef]
6. Atanassov, K.T. Intuitionistic fuzzy sets. In *Physica;* Springer: Berlin/Heidelberg, Germany, 1999; pp. 1–137.
7. Akram, M.; Davvaz, B. Strong intuitionistic fuzzy graphs. *Filomat* **2012**, *26*, 177–196. [CrossRef]
8. Akram, M.; Karunambigai, M.G.; Palanivel, K.; Sivasankar, S. Balanced bipolar fuzzy graphs. *J. Adv. Res. Pure Math.* **2014**, *6*, 58–71.
9. Akram, M.; Dudek, W.A. Intuitionistic fuzzy hypergraphs with applications. *Inf. Sci.* **2013**, *218*, 182–193. [CrossRef]
10. Borzooei, R.A.; Rashmanlou, H. New concepts of vague graphs. *Int. J. Mach. Learn. Cybern.* **2016**, *8*, 1081–1092. [CrossRef]
11. Talebi, A.A.; Rashmanlou, H.; Sadati, S.H. New concepts on *m*-polar interval-valued intuitionistic fuzzy graph. *TWMS J. Appl. Eng. Math.* **2020**, *10*, 808-–816.
12. Talebi, A.A.; Rashmanlou, H.; Sadati, S.H. Interval-valued Intuitionistic Fuzzy Competition Graph. *J. Mult.-Valued Log. Soft Comput.* **2020**, *34*, 335–364.
13. Kosari, S.; Rao, Y.; Jiang, H.; Liu, X.; Wu, P.; Shao, Z. Vague graph structure with application in medical diagnosis. *Symmetry* **2020**, *12*, 15–82. [CrossRef]
14. Rao, Y.; Kosari, S.; Shao, Z. Certain properties of vague graphs with a novel application. *Mathematics* **2020**, *8*, 1647. [CrossRef]
15. Rao, Y.; Kosari, S.; Shao, Z.; Cai, R.; Xinyue, L. A study on domination in vague incidence graph and its application in medical sciences. *Symmetry* **2020**, *12*, 18–85. [CrossRef]
16. Shi, X.; Kosari, S. Certain Properties of Domination in Product Vague Graphs With Novel Application in Medicine. *Front. Phys.* **2021**, *9*, 3–85. [CrossRef]
17. Kou, Z.; Kosari, S.; Akhoundi, M. A Novel Description on Vague Graph with Application in Transportation Systems. *J. Math.* **2021**, *2021*, 4800499. [CrossRef]
18. Rao, Y.; Kosari, S.; Shao, Z.; Qiang, X.; Akhoundi, M.; Zhang, X. Equitable Domination in Vague Graphs With Application in Medical Sciences. *Front. Phys.* **2021**, *37*, 635642. [CrossRef]
19. Shao, Z.; Kosari, S.; Rashmanlou, H.; Shoaib, M. New concepts in intuitionistic fuzzy graph with application in water supplier systems. *Mathematics* **2020**, *8*, 12–41. [CrossRef]
20. Zeng, S.; Shoaib, M.; Ali, S.; Abbas, Q.; Nadeem, M.S. Complex vague graphs and their application in decision-making problems. *IEEE Access* **2020**, *8*, 174094–174104. [CrossRef]
21. Zeng, S.; Shoaib, M.; Ali, S.; Smarache, F.; Rashmanlou, H.; Mofidnakhaei, F. Certain properties of single-valued neutrosophic graph with application in food and agriculture organization. *Int. J. Comput. Intell. Syst.* **2021**, *14*, 1516–1540. [CrossRef]
22. Ali, S.; Kousar, M.; Xin, Q.; Pamučar, D.; Hameed, M.S.; Fayyaz, R. Belief and possibility belief interval-valued N-soft set and their applications in multi-attribute decision-making problems. *Entropy* **2021**, *23*, 1498. [CrossRef]
23. Jun, Y.B.; Kim, C.S.; Yang, K.O. Cubic sets. *Ann. Fuzzy Math. Inform.* **2012**, *4*, 83–98.
24. Jun, Y.B.; Smarache, F.; Kim, C.S. Neutrosophic cubic sets. *New Math. Nat. Comput.* **2017**, *13*, 41–54. [CrossRef]
25. Jun, Y.B.; Song, S.Z.; Kim, S.J. Cubic interval-valued intuitionistic fuzzy sets and their application in BCK/BCI-algebras. *Axioms* **2018**, *7*, 7. [CrossRef]
26. Jun, Y.B.; Lee, K.J.; Kang, M.S. Cubic structures applied to ideals of BCI-algebras. *Comput. Math. Appl.* **2011**, *62*, 3334–3342. [CrossRef]
27. Khan, M.; Jun, Y.B.; Gulistan, M.; Yaqoob, N. The generalized version of Jun's cubic sets in semigroups. *J. Intell. Fuzzy Syst.* **2015**, *28*, 947–960. [CrossRef]
28. Ali, A.; Jun, Y.B.; Khan, M.; Shi, F.G.; Anis, S. Generalized cubic soft sets and their applications to algebraic structures. *Ital. J. Pure Appl. Math.* **2015**, *35*, 393–414.
29. Senapati, T.; Jun, Y.B.; Muhiuddin, G.; Shum, K.P. Cubic intuitionistic structures applied to ideals of BCI-algebras. *Analele Stiintifice Ale Univ. Ovidius-Constanta-Ser. Mat.* **2019**, *27*, 213–232. [CrossRef]
30. Muhiuddin, G.; Takallo, M.M.; Jun, Y.B.; Borzooei, R.A. Cubic graphs and their application to a traffic flow problem. *Int. J. Comput. Intell. Syst.* **2020**, *13*, 1265–1280. [CrossRef]
31. Rashmanlou, H.; Muhiuddin, G.; Amanathulla, S.K.; Mofidnakhaei, F.; Pal, M. A study on cubic graphs with novel application. *J. Intell. Fuzzy Syst.* **2021**, *40*, 89–101. [CrossRef]
32. Jiang, H.; Talebi, A.A.; Shao, Z.; Sadati, S.H.; Rashmanlou, H. New Concepts of node Covering in Cubic Graphs with Its Applications. *Mathematics* **2022**, *10*, 307. [CrossRef]
33. Mathew, S.; Sunitha, M.S. Node connectivity and arc connectivity of a fuzzy graph. *Inf. Sci.* **2010**, *180*, 519–531. [CrossRef]
34. Mathew, S.; Sunitha, M.S. Cycle connectivity in fuzzy graphs. *J. Intell. Fuzzy Syst.* **2013**, *24*, 549–554. [CrossRef]
35. Binu, M.; Mathew, S.; Mordeson, J.N. Wiener index of a fuzzy graph and application to illegal immigration networks. *Fuzzy Set Syst.* **2019**, *384*, 132–147.
36. Binu, M.; Mathew, S.; Mordeson, J.N. Connectivity index of a fuzzy graph and its application to human trafficking. *Fuzzy Set Syst.* **2019**, *360*, 117–136.
37. Binu, M.; Mathew, S.; Mordeson, J.N. Cyclic connectivity index of fuzzy graphs. *IEEE Trans. Fuzzy Syst.* **2020**, *29*, 1340–1349. [CrossRef]
38. Lee, H.; Chen, X.G.; Sohn, M.Y. A Note on "Wiener Index of a Fuzzy Graph and Application to Illegal Immigration Networks". *Appl. Sci.* **2021**, *12*, 304. [CrossRef]

39. Fang, J.; Nazeer, I.; Rashid, T.; Liu, J.B. Connectivity and Wiener index of fuzzy incidence graphs. *Math. Probl. Eng.* **2021**, *2021*, 6682966. [CrossRef]
40. Poulik, S.; Ghorai, G. Certain indices of graphs under bipolar fuzzy environment with applications. *Soft Comput.* **2020**, *24*, 5119–5131. [CrossRef]
41. Mandal, S.; Pal, M. Connectivity Index of M-Polar Fuzzy Graph with Application. *Res. Sq.* **2021**. [CrossRef]
42. Mordeson, J.N.; Mathew, S.; Malik, D.S. *Fuzzy Graph Theory with Applications to Human Trafficking*; Springer: Berlin/Heidelberg, Germany, 2018; p. 365.

symmetry MDPI

Article

Bipolar Spherical Fuzzy Soft Topology with Applications to Multi-Criteria Group Decision-Making in Buildings Risk Assessment

Adem Yolcu

Department of Mathematics, Kafkas University, Kars 36100, Turkey; adem.yolcu@kafkas.edu.tr

Abstract: A generalized soft set model that is more accurate, useful, and realistic is the bipolar spherical fuzzy soft set (BSFSs). It is a more developed variant of current fuzzy soft set models that may be applied to characterize erroneous data in practical applications. Bipolar spherical fuzzy soft sets and bipolar spherical fuzzy soft topology are novel ideas that are intended to be introduced in this work. Bipolar spherical fuzzy soft intersection, bipolar spherical fuzzy soft null set, spherical fuzzy soft absolute set, and other operations on bipolar spherical fuzzy soft sets are some of the fundamental ideas defined in this work. The bipolar spherical fuzzy soft open set, the bipolar spherical fuzzy soft close set, the bipolar spherical fuzzy soft closure, and the spherical fuzzy soft interior are also defined. Additionally, the characteristics of this specified set are covered and described using pertinent instances. The innovative notion of BSFSs makes it easier to describe the symmetry of two or more objects. Moreover, a group decision-making algorithm based on the TOPSIS (Technique of Order Preference by Similarity to an Ideal Solution) approach to problem-solving is described. We analyze the symmetry of the optimal decision and ranking of feasible alternatives. A numerical example is used to show how the suggested approach may be used. The extensive benefits of the proposed work over the existing techniques have been listed.

Keywords: BSFS sets; BSFS topology; TOPSIS; decision-making

1. Introduction

The exponential rise of invention and evolving technologies that continuously redefine, restructure, and rebuild how the world is viewed and the instruments formerly used to address issues have become outmoded and inappropriate and are to blame for the complexity of human life today. There is no exception to this rule in any field of expertise. Due of the ambiguity and uncertainty it involves, the techniques frequently used in classical mathematics are not always effective. As mathematical models for dealing with uncertainty and variability, methods, such as fuzzy set theory (FS) [1], vague set theory (VS) [2], and interval mathematics [3], have been developed. However, these theories suffer from their inherent flaws and limitations to approach the problem at hand with greater objectivity. The fuzzy set theory developed by Zadeh was first widely applied. It is believed that fuzzy sets are an expanded form of classical sets, in which each component has a membership grade. In order to get around some of the restrictions placed on fuzzy sets, Atanassov [4] created the notion of intuitionistic fuzzy sets (IFS). There have been several further fuzzy set extensions proposed, such as interval-valued sets (IFS) [5], Pythagorean fuzzy sets (PyFS) [6], picture fuzzy sets (PFS) [7], and others. These sets were successfully used in a variety of fields, including economics, medicine, environmental science, and science and engineering [8–12]. The concepts of spherical fuzzy sets (SFS) and T-spherical fuzzy sets have recently been established by certain authors as an expansion of FS, IFS, and PFS in order to expand the latter due to its limitations [13]. Mahmood et al. [14] introduced the concept of the spherical fuzzy set (SFS) and T-spherical fuzzy set (T-SFS) as a generalization of FS, IFS, and PFS. The intricate spherical fuzzy model, which excels at conveying ambiguous information in two dimensions, was developed by Akram et al. [15]. There are several sectors where these sets are applied to tackle decision-making difficulties.

Bipolar-valued fuzzy sets are an extension of fuzzy sets with bipolarity, which Zhang [16] first proposed in 1994. For information including a property, as well as its opposite property, a bipolar fuzzy set is appropriate. Some fundamental bipolar-valued fuzzy set operations were covered by Lee [17]. A comparison of the interval-valued set, IFS, and bipolar fuzzy set (BFS) was put up by Lee and Cios in 2004 [18]. In order to evaluate both good and negative traits in human thinking, Bosc and Pivert [19] proposed that bipolarity offers the human mind the propensity to reason and draw conclusions that include both positive and negative parts.

Spherical fuzzy sets (SFS) were introduced by Kahraman and Gündogdu (2018) [20] as an extension of PFS. SFS intends to provide decision-makers with the ability to generalize various extensions of fuzzy sets by building a membership function on a spherical surface and individually assigning the parameters of that membership function with a broader domain. The SF aggregation operators were suggested by Ashraf et al. [21] to solve issues with decision-making. In addition, Ashraf et al. [22] established various operational rules and aggregation procedures based on Archimedean t-norm and t-conorm. They defined SFS as an extension of PFS. By Ashraf et al. [22], this work was expanded with some helpful operations, such as spherical fuzzy t′-norms and spherical fuzzy t-conorms. By taking into account the membership, hesitation, non-membership, and rejection grades in SFS, Rafiq et al. [23] examined the innovative similarity measures across SFS based on cosine function. The previously mentioned SFS and the application of the spherical fuzzy TOPSIS approach to the site selection of the solar power plant in this work were summarized by Gündoğdu [24]. Neutosophic TOPSIS and spherical fuzzy TOPSIS were both used by Boltürk [25], and the outcomes of each application were compared. By using hybrid SFS with concepts of covering the rough set, Zeng et al. [26] adopted a novel technique of covering-based spherical fuzzy rough set (CSFRS) models and proposed a TOPSIS approach using CSFRS models. Mathew et al. [27] eleborated a novel framework that combines AHP and TOPSIS with a spherical fuzzy set. Akram et al. [28] investigated presenting a decision-making strategy that takes use of the superior trends of the conventional TOPSIS method in a more expansive setting of complicated SFS (CSFSs). Khan et al. [29] developed some spherical logarithmic affregation operators and gave their application in decision support systems. Gundogdu and Kahraman [30] investigated a fuzzy TOPSIS method using emerging interval-valued SFS. Duleba et al. [31] presented an interval-valued spherical fuzzy AHP method to evaluate public transportation development. The topics and frequency of the published spherical fuzzy articles are shown in Figure 1 [32].

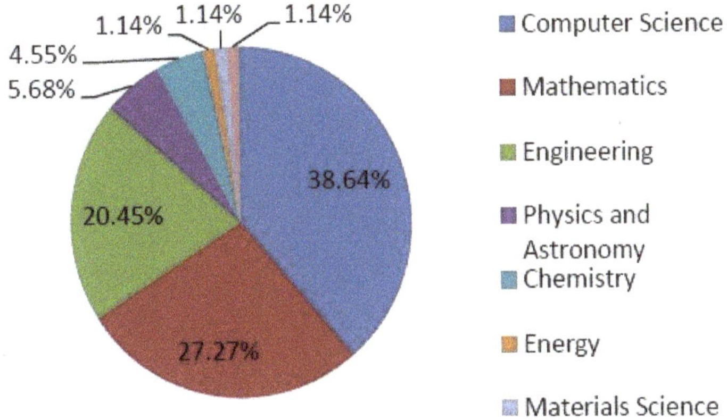

Figure 1. Ranking of alternatives.

Computer science and mathematics are the two fields that employ spherical fuzzy papers the most. To address ambiguity and uncertainty, Molodtsov [33] developed a new form of set in 1999 termed a soft set (SS). SS theory avoids the problem of defining the membership function that arises in fuzzy set theory, making the theory suitable to a variety of domains. After this, Maji et al. [34] conducted more research on SSs and proposed a decision-making issue as an application of SSs using Pawlak's crude mathematics [35]. Additionally, Maji et al. [36] created a hybrid structure combining SSs and FSs called fuzzy soft sets (FSS), which is a more potent mathematical model for dealing with many real-world scenarios. Numerous fuzzy set generalizations, including generalized FSS [37], group generalized FSS (GFSS) [38], intuitionistic fuzzy soft sets (IFSS) [39], Pythagorean fuzzy soft sets (PYFSS) [40], intuitionistic fuzzy hypersoft sets (IFHS) [41], fuzzy hypersoft sets (FHS) [42], and interval-valued picture fuzzy soft (IVPFSS) sets [43], were proposed as a result of the widespread interest in this idea. A more sophisticated type of FSS, called a spherical fuzzy soft set (SFSS), was recently developed by Perveen et al. [44]. Possibly the most realistic, useful, and accurate set is the one that has recently evolved. By combining soft sets, a new kind of image fuzzy soft set, known as SFSSs, was created. When tackling decision-making issues that arise in real-life situations, SFSS is more adept at representing ambiguity and uncertainty. The authors [45] implemented the suggested spherical fuzzy soft similarity measure in the field of medical science and created similarity measures of SFSS. These ideas have uses in topology and several other branches of mathematics. The idea of a fuzzy topological space was first put out by Chang [46] in 1968. Lowen [47] carried out a thorough investigation of the architecture of fuzzy topological spaces. An intuitionistic fuzzy topological space was first proposed by Coker [48] in 1995. Coker et al. [49,50] offered a number of other operations on intuitionistic fuzzy topological spaces. Olgun et al. [51], introduced the concept of Pythagorean fuzzy topological space. Topology and soft topology were addressed by Kiruthika and Thangavelu [52]. Dizman and Ozturk [53] defined fuzzy bipolar soft topological spaces. Ozturk [54,55] investigated bipolar soft point and bipolar soft topological spaces. Fuzzy soft topology was established by Tanay and Kandemir [56]. Additionally, they introduced FS subspace topology, FS basis, FS interior, and FS neighborhood. Fuzzy hypersoft topological spaces were introduced by Yolcu and Ozturk [57]. Intuitionistic fuzzy soft topological spaces were introduced by Osmanoglu and Tokat [58]. Pythagorean fuzzy soft topology was introduced by Riaz et al. [59] and is based on Pythagorean fuzzy soft sets. The TOPSIS approach is used for Pythagorean fuzzy soft topology in medical diagnostics. Many studies have been carried out recently on spherical fuzzy soft topological spaces. Table 1 shows some fuzzy models with existing limitations [60,61].

Table 1. Some fuzzy models with existing limitations.

Fuzzy Models	**Advantages**	**Limitations**
Fuzzy Set [1]	It can operate with imprecise data.	It cannot handle nonmembership values
Intuitionistic fuzzy set (IFS) [3]	It includes membership and nonmembership values.	An Intuitionistic fuzzy set assign the condition $0 \leq \rho + \psi \leq 1$
Pythagorean fuzzy set(PyFS) [6]	It is appropriate when the sum of membership and nonmembership grades exceeds one.	It will not work for the case $\rho^2 + \psi^2 > 1$
Picture Fuzzy Set (PFS) [7]	It is appropriate than IFS.This theory is used when we express the sum of membership, neutral and non-membership less than 1	It will not work for the case $\rho + \omega + \psi > 1$
Spherical Fuzzy Set [14,21,24]	It is efficient than PFS and PyFS. It works for the case $0 \leq \rho^2 + \omega^2 + \psi^2 \leq 1$	It will not work for the case $\rho^2 + \omega^2 + \psi^2 > 1$

Bipolarity of knowledge is an important factor to consider when developing a mathematical framework for most situations involving data analysis of various types. Bipolarity denotes the positive and negative aspects of a problem. The idea behind bipolarity is that bipolar subjective thoughts involve a wide range of human decision analysis. Happiness and grief, sweetness and sourness, effects and side-effects are all examples of different aspects of decision analysis. The balance and mutual coexistence of these two aspects is regarded as key to a healthy social environment. Therefore, in this study, the spherical fuzzy soft structure was generalized and the bipolar spherical fuzzy soft structure was defined. This study focused on two main themes. Firstly, the definition of bipolar spherical fuzzy soft set structure to define the concepts such as union, intersection, null set, and absolute set on this set structure. Secondly, presenting the idea of bipolar spherical fuzzy soft topology (BSFS-topology) on BSFS and explaining certain fundamental notions, such as BSFS-open set, BSFS- closed, BSFS-interior, and BSFS-closure. Additionally, in this research, we employed the SFS-topology in a TOPSIS-based group decision-making approach in a bipolar spherical fuzzy soft environment. Furthermore, we analyzed the symmetry of the optimal decision and ranking of feasible alternatives.

The rest of this paper is organized as follows across the remaining sections. In Section 2, some preliminary concepts are given. In Section 3, the structure of the bipolar spherical fuzzy soft set is defined, basic concepts, such as the empty set, absolute set, union, intersection, difference, and subset complement, are presented, and some important properties are examined. In Section 4, bipolar spherical fuzzy soft topology is defined, basic concepts, such as internal and closing operation on this structure, are presented, and some important features are examined. In Section 5, multi-criteria decision making application is given using bipolar spherical fuzzy soft topology (BSFS-topology) and topsis. In Section 6, the proposed method is compared with other methods, and in Section 7, the conclusions are presented.

2. Preliminaries

In this section, some basic concepts, such as FS, SS, and SFS, are presented.

Definition 1 ([1]). *Let Δ be a initial universe. A fuzzy set Λ in Δ, $\Lambda = \{(\kappa, \rho_\Lambda(\kappa)) : \kappa \in \Delta\}$, where $\rho_\Lambda : \Delta \to [0,1]$ is the membership function of the fuzzy set Λ; $\rho_\Lambda(\kappa) \in [0,1]$ is the membership $\kappa \in \Delta$ in Λ. The set of all fuzzy sets over Δ will be denoted by $FP(\Delta)$.*

Definition 2 ([24]). *Let Δ be a initial universe. A SFS S in Δ, $S = \{\rho_S(\kappa), \omega_S(\kappa), \psi_S(\kappa) : \kappa \in \Delta\}$, where $\rho_S, \omega_S, \psi_S : \Delta \to [0,1]$ is the positive, neutral and negative membership degrees of $\kappa \in \Delta$ respectively with the condition $0 \leq \rho_S^2(\kappa), \omega_S^2(\kappa), \psi_S^2(\kappa) \leq 1$.*

Definition 3 ([33]). *Let Δ be an universe and $\aleph$ be a set of parameters. A pair $(\Re, \aleph)$ is called a soft set over Δ, where $\Re$ is a mapping $\Re : \aleph \to \mathcal{P}(\Delta)$. In other words, the soft set is a parameterized family of subsets of the set Δ.*

Definition 4 ([44]). *Let $SFS(\Delta)$ be the set of all SFS over Δ. Spherical fuzzy soft set (SFSS) is a pair $(\Re, \aleph)$, where $\Re$ is a mapping from $\aleph$ to $SFS(\Delta)$. A spherical soft set $(\Re, \aleph)$ defined as*

$$(\Re, \aleph) = \left\{ \left(\varsigma, \left\langle \kappa, \left(\rho_{\Re(\varsigma)}(\kappa), \omega_{\Re(\varsigma)}(\kappa), \psi_{\Re(\varsigma)}(\kappa), \right) \right\rangle : \kappa \in \Delta \right) : \varsigma \in \aleph \right\}$$

where $\rho_{\Re(\varsigma)}(\kappa), \omega_{\Re(\varsigma)}(\kappa), \psi_{\Re(\varsigma)}(\kappa) \to [0,1]$ are membership degrees and hold the condition $0 \leq \rho^2_{\Re(\varsigma)}(\kappa), \omega^2_{\Re(\varsigma)}(\kappa), \psi^2_{\Re(\varsigma)}(\kappa) \leq 1$.

Definition 5 ([62]). *Let $SFS(\Delta, \aleph)$ be the family of all SFSS over Δ and $\tau \subset BSFS(\Delta, \aleph)$. Then τ is called to be a spherical fuzzy soft topology (SFS-topology) on Δ if*

1. $0_\varnothing$ *and* 1_Δ *belongs to* τ
2. *If* $(\Re_i, \aleph) \in \tau$ $\forall i \in I$, *an index set, then* $\cup_{i \in I}(\Re_i, \aleph) \in \tau$,
3. *If* $(\Re_1, \aleph)$, $(\Re_2, \aleph) \in \check{\tau}$, *then* $(\Re_1, \aleph) \sqcap (\Re_2, \aleph) \in \tau$.

Then $(\Delta, \tau, \aleph)$ is called to be a bipolar spherical fuzzy soft topological space over Δ.

Definition 6 ([63]). *Let Δ be a universe. A bipolar spherical fuzzy set $\mathfrak{R}$ in Δ is defined as:*

$$\mathfrak{R} = \{\langle \kappa, (\rho^+_{\mathfrak{R}}(\kappa), \omega^+_{\mathfrak{R}}(\kappa), \psi^+_{\mathfrak{R}}(\kappa), \rho^-_{\mathfrak{R}}(\kappa), \omega^-_{\mathfrak{R}}(\kappa), \psi^-_{\mathfrak{R}}(\kappa))\rangle : \kappa \in \Delta\}$$

where $\rho^+_{\mathfrak{R}}, \omega^+_{\mathfrak{R}}, \psi^+_{\mathfrak{R}} \rightarrow [0,1]$, $\rho^-_{\mathfrak{R}}, \omega^-_{\mathfrak{R}}, \psi^-_{\mathfrak{R}} \rightarrow [-1,0]$ *and* $0 \leq \left(\rho^+_{\mathfrak{R}(\varsigma)}(\kappa)\right)^2 + \left(\omega^+_{\mathfrak{R}(\varsigma)}(\kappa)\right)^2 + \left(\psi^+_{\mathfrak{R}(\varsigma)}(\kappa)\right)^2 \leq 1, -1 \leq -\left(\left(\rho^-_{\mathfrak{R}(\varsigma)}(\kappa)\right)^2 + \left(\omega^-_{\mathfrak{R}(\varsigma)}(\kappa)\right)^2 + \left(\psi^-_{\mathfrak{R}(\varsigma)}(\kappa)\right)^2\right) \leq 0$. *The positive memberships* $\rho^+_{\mathfrak{R}}(\kappa), \omega^+_{\mathfrak{R}}(\kappa), \psi^+_{\mathfrak{R}}(\kappa)$ *denote the membership functions of bipolar spherical fuzzy set* $\mathfrak{R}$ *and the negative memberships* $\rho^-_{\mathfrak{R}}(\kappa), \omega^-_{\mathfrak{R}}(\kappa), \psi^-_{\mathfrak{R}}(\kappa)$ *denote membership functions of an element* $\kappa \in \Delta$ *to some implicit mitigate corresponding to a bipolar spherical fuzzy set* $\mathfrak{R}$.

3. Bipolar Spherical Fuzzy Soft Sets

In this section, some basic operations are presented by defining the bipolar spherical fuzzy soft set structure.

Definition 7. *Let Δ be a universe and $\aleph$ be a set of parameters. A bipolar spherical fuzzy soft set* $(\mathfrak{R}, \aleph)$ *in Δ is defined as:*

$$(\mathfrak{R}, \aleph) = \left\{\left(\varsigma, \left\langle \kappa, \left(\rho^+_{\mathfrak{R}(\varsigma)}(\kappa), \omega^+_{\mathfrak{R}(\varsigma)}(\kappa), \psi^+_{\mathfrak{R}(\varsigma)}(\kappa), \rho^-_{\mathfrak{R}(\varsigma)}(\kappa), \omega^-_{\mathfrak{R}(\varsigma)}(\kappa), \psi^-_{\mathfrak{R}(\varsigma)}(\kappa)\right)\right\rangle : \kappa \in \Delta\right) : \varsigma \in \aleph\right\}$$

where $\rho^+_{\mathfrak{R}(\varsigma)}(\kappa), \omega^+_{\mathfrak{R}(\varsigma)}(\kappa), \psi^+_{\mathfrak{R}(\varsigma)}(\kappa) \rightarrow [0,1]$, $\rho^-_{\mathfrak{R}(\varsigma)}(\kappa), \omega^-_{\mathfrak{R}(\varsigma)}(\kappa), \psi^-_{\mathfrak{R}(\varsigma)}(\kappa) \rightarrow [-1,0]$ *and* $0 \leq \left(\rho^+_{\mathfrak{R}(\varsigma)}(\kappa)\right)^2 + \left(\omega^+_{\mathfrak{R}(\varsigma)}(\kappa)\right)^2 + \left(\psi^+_{\mathfrak{R}(\varsigma)}(\kappa)\right)^2 \leq 1, -1 \leq -\left(\left(\rho^-_{\mathfrak{R}(\varsigma)}(\kappa)\right)^2 + \left(\omega^-_{\mathfrak{R}(\varsigma)}(\kappa)\right)^2 + \left(\psi^-_{\mathfrak{R}(\varsigma)}(\kappa)\right)^2\right) \leq 0$. *The positive memberships* $\rho^+_{\mathfrak{R}(\varsigma)}(\kappa), \omega^+_{\mathfrak{R}(\varsigma)}(\kappa), \psi^+_{\mathfrak{R}(\varsigma)}(\kappa)$ *denote the membership functions of bipolar spherical fuzzy soft set* $(\mathfrak{R}, \aleph)$ *and the negative memberships* $\rho^-_{\mathfrak{R}(\varsigma)}(\kappa), \omega^-_{\mathfrak{R}(\varsigma)}(\kappa), \psi^-_{\mathfrak{R}(\varsigma)}(\kappa)$ *denote membership functions of an element* $\kappa \in \Delta$ *to some implicit mitigate corresponding to a bipolar spherical fuzzy soft set* $(\mathfrak{R}, \aleph)$.

Definition 8. *Let* $(\mathfrak{R}, \aleph)$ *be a bipolar spherical fuzzy soft set over Δ. Then, the complement of a bipolar spherical fuzzy soft set* $(\mathfrak{R}, \aleph)$ *is denoted by* $(\mathfrak{R}, \aleph)^c$ *and is defined as:*

$$(\mathfrak{R}, \aleph)^c = \left\{\left(\varsigma, \left\langle \kappa, \left(\begin{array}{c} \left(\rho^+_{\mathfrak{R}(\varsigma)}(\kappa)\right)^c, \left(\omega^+_{\mathfrak{R}(\varsigma)}(\kappa)\right)^c, \left(\psi^+_{\mathfrak{R}(\varsigma)}(\kappa)\right)^c, \\ \left(\rho^-_{\mathfrak{R}(\varsigma)}(\kappa)\right)^c, \left(\omega^-_{\mathfrak{R}(\varsigma)}(\kappa)\right)^c, \left(\psi^-_{\mathfrak{R}(\varsigma)}(\kappa)\right)^c \end{array}\right)\right\rangle : \kappa \in \Delta\right) : \varsigma \in \aleph\right\}$$

where

$$\begin{aligned}
\left(\rho^+_{\mathfrak{R}(\varsigma)}(\kappa)\right)^c &= \psi^+_{\mathfrak{R}(\varsigma)}(\kappa), \left(\rho^-_{\mathfrak{R}(\varsigma)}(\kappa)\right)^c = \psi^-_{\mathfrak{R}(\varsigma)}(\kappa) \\
\left(\omega^+_{\mathfrak{R}(\varsigma)}(\kappa)\right)^c &= \left\{\begin{array}{ll} \omega^+_{\mathfrak{R}(\varsigma)}(\kappa) & ; \text{ if } \left(\rho^+_{\mathfrak{R}(\varsigma)}(\kappa) \text{ or } \psi^+_{\mathfrak{R}(\varsigma)}(\kappa)\right) = 1 \\ 1 - \omega^+_{\mathfrak{R}(\varsigma)}(\kappa) & ; \quad \text{otherwise} \end{array}\right. \\
\left(\omega^-_{\mathfrak{R}(\varsigma)}(\kappa)\right)^c &= \left\{\begin{array}{ll} \omega^-_{\mathfrak{R}(\varsigma)}(\kappa) & ; \text{ if } \left(\rho^-_{\mathfrak{R}(\varsigma)}(\kappa) \text{ or } \psi^-_{\mathfrak{R}(\varsigma)}(\kappa)\right) = -1 \\ -1 - \omega^-_{\mathfrak{R}(\varsigma)}(\kappa) & ; \quad \text{otherwise} \end{array}\right. \\
\left(\psi^+_{\mathfrak{R}(\varsigma)}(\kappa)\right)^c &= \rho^+_{\mathfrak{R}(\varsigma)}(\kappa), \left(\psi^-_{\mathfrak{R}(\varsigma)}(\kappa)\right)^c = \rho^-_{\mathfrak{R}(\varsigma)}(\kappa).
\end{aligned}$$

Definition 9. *A null bipolar spherical fuzzy soft set $\eth_\emptyset$ over Δ is defined by:*

$$\eth_\emptyset = \{(\varsigma, \langle \kappa, (0,0,1,-1,0,0)\rangle : \kappa \in \Delta) : \varsigma \in \aleph\}.$$

An absolute bipolar spherical fuzzy soft set $\check{1}_{\Delta}$ over Δ is defined by:

$$\check{1}_{\Delta} = \{(\varsigma, \langle \kappa, (1, 0, 0, 0, 0, -1) \rangle : \kappa \in \Delta) : \varsigma \in \aleph\}.$$

Clearly, $\check{0}^c_{\emptyset} = \check{1}_{\Delta}$ and $\check{1}^c_{\Delta} = \check{0}_{\emptyset}$.

Definition 10. *Let $(\check{\Re}_1, \aleph)$ and $(\check{\Re}_2, \aleph)$ be two bipolar spherical fuzzy soft sets over Δ. $(\check{\Re}_1, \aleph)$ is a bipolar spherical fuzzy soft subset of $(\check{\Re}_2, \aleph)$ denoted by $(\check{\Re}_1, \aleph) \check{\sqsubseteq} (\check{\Re}_2, \aleph)$ if for all $(\varsigma, \kappa) \in \aleph \times \Delta$,*

$$\begin{cases} \rho^+_{\check{\Re}_1(\varsigma)}(\kappa) \le \rho^+_{\check{\Re}_2(\varsigma)}(\kappa), \omega^+_{\check{\Re}_1(\varsigma)}(\kappa) \le \omega^+_{\check{\Re}_2(\varsigma)}(\kappa), \psi^+_{\check{\Re}_1(\varsigma)}(\kappa) \ge \psi^+_{\check{\Re}_2(\varsigma)}(\kappa) & ; \text{if} \quad \rho^+_{\check{\Re}_2(\varsigma)}(\kappa) \ne 1 \\ \rho^+_{\check{\Re}_1(\varsigma)}(\kappa) \le \rho^+_{\check{\Re}_2(\varsigma)}(\kappa), \omega^+_{\check{\Re}_1(\varsigma)}(\kappa) \ge \omega^+_{\check{\Re}_2(\varsigma)}(\kappa), \psi^+_{\check{\Re}_1(\varsigma)}(\kappa) \ge \psi^+_{\check{\Re}_2(\varsigma)}(\kappa) & \text{otherwise} \end{cases}$$

and

$$\begin{cases} \rho^-_{\check{\Re}_1(\varsigma)}(\kappa) \le \rho^-_{\check{\Re}_2(\varsigma)}(\kappa), \omega^-_{\check{\Re}_1(\varsigma)}(\kappa) \le \omega^-_{\check{\Re}_2(\varsigma)}(\kappa), \psi^+_{\check{\Re}_1(\varsigma)}(\kappa) \ge \psi^-_{\check{\Re}_2(\varsigma)}(\kappa) & ; \text{if} \quad \rho^-_{\check{\Re}_2(\varsigma)}(\kappa) \ne -1 \\ \rho^-_{\check{\Re}_1(\varsigma)}(\kappa) \le \rho^-_{\check{\Re}_2(\varsigma)}(\kappa), \omega^-_{\check{\Re}_1(\varsigma)}(\kappa) \ge \omega^-_{\check{\Re}_2(\varsigma)}(\kappa), \psi^-_{\check{\Re}_1(\varsigma)}(\kappa) \ge \psi^-_{\check{\Re}_2(\varsigma)}(\kappa) & \text{otherwise} \end{cases}.$$

$(\check{\Re}_1, \aleph)$ is called to be bipolar spherical fuzzy soft equal to $(\check{\Re}_2, \aleph)$ if $(\check{\Re}_1, \aleph)$ is bipolar spherical fuzzy soft subset of $(\check{\Re}_2, \aleph)$ and $(\check{\Re}_2, \aleph)$ is bipolar spherical fuzzy soft subset of $(\check{\Re}_1, \aleph)$. It is denoted by $(\check{\Re}_1, \aleph) \check{=} (\check{\Re}_2, \aleph)$.

Example 1. *Let $\Delta = \{\kappa_1, \kappa_2\}$ and $\aleph = \{\varsigma_1, \varsigma_2\}$. If*

$$(\check{\Re}_1, \aleph) = \left\{ \begin{array}{l} (\varsigma_1, \langle \kappa_1, (0.2, 0.5, 0.3, -0.6, -0.4, -0.3) \rangle, \langle \kappa_2, (0.1, 0.5, 0.6, -0.3, -0.4, -0.3) \rangle), \\ (\varsigma_2, \langle \kappa_1, (0.5, 0.6, 0.3, -0.3, -0.2, -0.3) \rangle, \langle \kappa_2, (0.5, 0.6, 0.5, -0.3, -0.4, -0.2) \rangle) \end{array} \right\}$$

and

$$(\check{\Re}_2, \aleph) = \left\{ \begin{array}{l} (\varsigma_1, \langle \kappa_1, (0.3, 0.6, 0.1, -0.3, -0.2, -0.4) \rangle, \langle \kappa_2, (0.4, 0.6, 0.2, -0.2, -0.2, -0.5) \rangle), \\ (\varsigma_2, \langle \kappa_1, (0.4, 0.3, 0.4, -0.2, -0.1, -0.2) \rangle, \langle \kappa_2, (0.3, 0.3, 0.6, -0.2, -0.3, -0.4) \rangle) \end{array} \right\}$$

then, $(\check{\Re}_1, \aleph) \check{\sqsubseteq} (\check{\Re}_2, \aleph)$.

Definition 11. *Let $(\check{\Re}_i, \aleph) = \left\{ \left(\varsigma, \left\langle \kappa, \left(\begin{array}{c} \rho^+_{\check{\Re}_i(\varsigma)}(\kappa), \omega^+_{\check{\Re}_i(\varsigma)}(\kappa), \psi^+_{\check{\Re}_i(\varsigma)}(\kappa), \\ \rho^-_{\check{\Re}_i(\varsigma)}(\kappa), \omega^-_{\check{\Re}_i(\varsigma)}(\kappa), \psi^-_{\check{\Re}_i(\varsigma)}(\kappa) \end{array} \right) \right\rangle : \kappa \in \Delta \right) : \varsigma \in \aleph \right\}$ for $i = 1, 2$ be two bipolar spherical fuzzy soft sets over Δ. Then their union is denoted by $(\check{\Re}_1, \aleph) \check{\sqcup} (\check{\Re}_2, \aleph)$ and is defined as;*

$$\check{\bigsqcup_{i=1}^{2}} (\check{\Re}_i, \aleph) = \left\{ \left(\varsigma, \left\langle \kappa, \left(\begin{array}{c} \rho^+_{\check{\Re}(\varsigma)}(\kappa), \omega^+_{\check{\Re}(\varsigma)}(\kappa), \psi^+_{\check{\Re}(\varsigma)}(\kappa), \\ \rho^-_{\check{\Re}(\varsigma)}(\kappa), \omega^-_{\check{\Re}(\varsigma)}(\kappa), \psi^-_{\check{\Re}(\varsigma)}(\kappa) \end{array} \right) \right\rangle : \kappa \in \Delta \right) : \varsigma \in \aleph \right\}.$$

where

$$\rho^+_{\check{\Re}(\varsigma)}(\kappa) = \max\left\{ \rho^+_{\check{\Re}_1(\varsigma)}(\kappa), \rho^+_{\check{\Re}_2(\varsigma)}(\kappa) \right\}, \rho^-_{\check{\Re}(\varsigma)}(\kappa) = \max\left\{ \rho^-_{\check{\Re}_1(\varsigma)}(\kappa), \rho^-_{\check{\Re}_2(\varsigma)}(\kappa) \right\}$$

$$\omega^+_{\check{\Re}(\varsigma)}(\kappa) = \begin{cases} \max\left\{ \omega^+_{\check{\Re}_1(\varsigma)}(\kappa), \omega^+_{\check{\Re}_2(\varsigma)}(\kappa) \right\} ; & \begin{array}{c} \text{if} \left(\max\left\{ \rho^+_{\check{\Re}_1(\varsigma)}(\kappa), \rho^+_{\check{\Re}_2(\varsigma)}(\kappa) \right\} \right)^2 + \\ \left(\max\left\{ \omega^+_{\check{\Re}_1(\varsigma)}(\kappa), \omega^+_{\check{\Re}_2(\varsigma)}(\kappa) \right\} \right)^2 \\ + \left(\min\left\{ \psi^+_{\check{\Re}_1(\varsigma)}(\kappa), \psi^+_{\check{\Re}_2(\varsigma)}(\kappa) \right\} \right)^2 \le 1 \end{array} \\ \min\left\{ \omega^+_{\check{\Re}_1(\varsigma)}(\kappa), \omega^+_{\check{\Re}_2(\varsigma)}(\kappa) \right\} ; & \text{otherwise} \end{cases}$$

$$\omega^{-}_{\Re(\varsigma)}(\kappa) = \begin{cases} \max\left\{\omega^{-}_{\Re_1(\varsigma)}(\kappa), \omega^{-}_{\Re_2(\varsigma)}(\kappa)\right\} & ; \quad \begin{array}{c} if \left(\max\left\{\rho^{-}_{\Re_1(\varsigma)}(\kappa), \rho^{-}_{\Re_2(\varsigma)}(\kappa)\right\}\right)^2 + \\ \left(\max\left\{\omega^{-}_{\Re_1(\varsigma)}(\kappa), \omega^{-}_{\Re_2(\varsigma)}(\kappa)\right\}\right)^2 \\ + \left(\min\left\{\psi^{-}_{\Re_1(\varsigma)}(\kappa), \psi^{-}_{\Re_2(\varsigma)}(\kappa)\right\}\right)^2 \leq 1 \end{array} \\ \min\left\{\omega^{-}_{\Re_1(\varsigma)}(\kappa), \omega^{-}_{\Re_2(\varsigma)}(\kappa)\right\} & ; \quad otherwise \end{cases}$$

$$\psi^{+}_{\Re(\varsigma)}(\kappa) = \min\left\{\psi^{+}_{\Re_1(\varsigma)}(\kappa), \psi^{+}_{\Re_1(\varsigma)}(\kappa)\right\}, \psi^{-}_{\Re(\varsigma)}(\kappa) = \min\left\{\psi^{-}_{\Re_1(\varsigma)}(\kappa), \psi^{-}_{\Re_1(\varsigma)}(\kappa)\right\}$$

Definition 12. *Let* $(\Re_i, \aleph) = \left\{\left(\varsigma, \left\langle \kappa, \left(\begin{array}{c} \rho^{+}_{\Re_i(\varsigma)}(\kappa), \omega^{+}_{\Re_i(\varsigma)}(\kappa), \psi^{+}_{\Re_i(\varsigma)}(\kappa), \\ \rho^{-}_{\Re_i(\varsigma)}(\kappa), \omega^{-}_{\Re_i(\varsigma)}(\kappa), \psi^{-}_{\Re_i(\varsigma)}(\kappa) \end{array} \right) \right\rangle : \kappa \in \Delta \right) : \varsigma \in \aleph \right\}$ *for* $i = 1, 2$ *be two bipolar spherical fuzzy soft sets over* Δ*. Then their intersection is denoted by* $(\Re_1, \aleph) \sqcap (\Re_2, \aleph)$ *and is defined as:*

$$\mathop{\sqcap}_{i=1}^{2} (\Re_i, \aleph) = \left\{\left(\varsigma, \left\langle \kappa, \left(\begin{array}{c} \rho^{+}_{\Re(\varsigma)}(\kappa), \omega^{+}_{\Re(\varsigma)}(\kappa), \psi^{+}_{\Re(\varsigma)}(\kappa), \\ \rho^{-}_{\Re(\varsigma)}(\kappa), \omega^{-}_{\Re(\varsigma)}(\kappa), \psi^{-}_{\Re(\varsigma)}(\kappa) \end{array} \right) \right\rangle : \kappa \in \Delta \right) : \varsigma \in \aleph \right\}.$$

where

$$\rho^{+}_{\Re(\varsigma)}(\kappa) = \min\left\{\rho^{+}_{\Re_1(\varsigma)}(\kappa), \rho^{+}_{\Re_2(\varsigma)}(\kappa)\right\}, \rho^{-}_{\Re(\varsigma)}(\kappa) = \min\left\{\rho^{-}_{\Re_1(\varsigma)}(\kappa), \rho^{-}_{\Re_2(\varsigma)}(\kappa)\right\}$$

$$\omega^{+}_{\Re(\varsigma)}(\kappa) = \begin{cases} \max\left\{\omega^{+}_{\Re_1(\varsigma)}(\kappa), \omega^{+}_{\Re_2(\varsigma)}(\kappa)\right\} & ; \quad if \left(\rho^{+}_{\Re_1(\varsigma)}(\kappa) \text{ or } \rho^{+}_{\Re_2(\varsigma)}(\kappa)\right) = 1 \\ \min\left\{\omega^{+}_{\Re_1(\varsigma)}(\kappa), \omega^{+}_{\Re_2(\varsigma)}(\kappa)\right\} & ; \quad otherwise \end{cases}$$

$$\omega^{-}_{\Re(\varsigma)}(\kappa) = \begin{cases} \max\left\{\omega^{-}_{\Re_1(\varsigma)}(\kappa), \omega^{-}_{\Re_2(\varsigma)}(\kappa)\right\} & ; \quad if \left(\rho^{-}_{\Re_1(\varsigma)}(\kappa) \text{ or } \rho^{-}_{\Re_2(\varsigma)}(\kappa)\right) = -1 \\ \min\left\{\omega^{-}_{\Re_1(\varsigma)}(\kappa), \omega^{-}_{\Re_2(\varsigma)}(\kappa)\right\} & ; \quad otherwise \end{cases}$$

$$\psi^{+}_{\Re(\varsigma)}(\kappa) = \max\left\{\psi^{+}_{\Re_1(\varsigma)}(\kappa), \psi^{+}_{\Re_1(\varsigma)}(\kappa)\right\}, \psi^{-}_{\Re(\varsigma)}(\kappa) = \max\left\{\psi^{-}_{\Re_1(\varsigma)}(\kappa), \psi^{-}_{\Re_1(\varsigma)}(\kappa)\right\},$$

Definition 13. *Let* $(\Re_1, \aleph)$ *and* $(\Re_2, \aleph)$ *be two bipolar spherical fuzzy soft sets over* Δ*. Then "AND" operation on them is denoted by* $(\Re_1, \aleph) \wedge (\Re_2, \aleph) = (\Re_3, \aleph \times \aleph)$ *and is defined by:*

$$(\Re_3, \aleph \times \aleph) = \left\{\left((\varsigma_1, \varsigma_2), \left\langle \kappa, \left(\begin{array}{c} \rho^{+}_{\Re(\varsigma)}(\kappa), \omega^{+}_{\Re(\varsigma)}(\kappa), \psi^{+}_{\Re(\varsigma)}(\kappa), \\ \rho^{-}_{\Re(\varsigma)}(\kappa), \omega^{-}_{\Re(\varsigma)}(\kappa), \psi^{-}_{\Re(\varsigma)}(\kappa) \end{array} \right) \right\rangle : \kappa \in \Delta \right) : (\varsigma_1, \varsigma_2) \in \aleph \times \aleph \right\}$$

where

$$\rho^{+}_{\Re_3(\varsigma_1,\varsigma_2)}(\kappa) = \min\left\{\rho^{+}_{\Re_1(\varsigma_1)}(\kappa), \rho^{+}_{\Re_2(\varsigma_2)}(\kappa)\right\}, \rho^{-}_{\Re_3(\varsigma_1,\varsigma_2)}(\kappa) = \min\left\{\rho^{-}_{\Re_1(\varsigma_1)}(\kappa), \rho^{-}_{\Re_2(\varsigma_2)}(\kappa)\right\}$$

$$\omega^{+}_{\Re_3(\varsigma_1,\varsigma_2)}(\kappa) = \begin{cases} \max\left\{\omega^{+}_{\Re_1(\varsigma_1)}(\kappa), \omega^{+}_{\Re_2(\varsigma_2)}(\kappa)\right\} & ; \quad if \left(\rho^{+}_{\Re_1(\varsigma_1)}(\kappa) \text{ or } \rho^{+}_{\Re_2(\varsigma_2)}(\kappa)\right) = 1 \\ \min\left\{\omega^{+}_{\Re_1(\varsigma_1)}(\kappa), \omega^{+}_{\Re_2(\varsigma_2)}(\kappa)\right\} & ; \quad otherwise \end{cases}$$

$$\omega^{-}_{\Re_3(\varsigma_1,\varsigma_2)}(\kappa) = \begin{cases} \max\left\{\omega^{-}_{\Re_1(\varsigma_1)}(\kappa), \omega^{-}_{\Re_2(\varsigma_2)}(\kappa)\right\} & ; \quad if \left(\rho^{-}_{\Re_1(\varsigma_1)}(\kappa) \text{ or } \rho^{-}_{\Re_2(\varsigma_2)}(\kappa)\right) = -1 \\ \min\left\{\omega^{-}_{\Re_1(\varsigma_1)}(\kappa), \omega^{-}_{\Re_2(\varsigma_2)}(\kappa)\right\} & ; \quad otherwise \end{cases}$$

$$\psi^{+}_{\Re_3(\varsigma_1,\varsigma_2)}(\kappa) = \max\left\{\psi^{+}_{\Re_1(\varsigma_1)}(\kappa), \psi^{+}_{\Re_1(\varsigma_2)}(\kappa)\right\}, \psi^{-}_{\Re_3(\varsigma_1,\varsigma_2)}(\kappa) = \max\left\{\psi^{-}_{\Re_1(\varsigma_1)}(\kappa), \psi^{-}_{\Re_1(\varsigma_2)}(\kappa)\right\},$$

Definition 14. *Let* $(\Re_1, \aleph)$ *and* $(\Re_2, \aleph)$ *be two bipolar spherical fuzzy soft sets over* Δ*. Then "OR" operation on them is denoted by* $(\Re_1, \aleph) \vee (\Re_2, \aleph) = (\Re_3, \aleph \times \aleph)$ *and is defined by:*

$$(\Re_3, \aleph \times \aleph) = \left\{\left((\varsigma_1, \varsigma_2), \left\langle \kappa, \left(\begin{array}{c} \rho^{+}_{\Re(\varsigma)}(\kappa), \omega^{+}_{\Re(\varsigma)}(\kappa), \psi^{+}_{\Re(\varsigma)}(\kappa), \\ \rho^{-}_{\Re(\varsigma)}(\kappa), \omega^{-}_{\Re(\varsigma)}(\kappa), \psi^{-}_{\Re(\varsigma)}(\kappa) \end{array} \right) \right\rangle : \kappa \in \Delta \right) : (\varsigma_1, \varsigma_2) \in \aleph \times \aleph \right\}$$

where

$$
\begin{aligned}
\rho^{+}_{\mathfrak{R}_3(\varsigma_1,\varsigma_2)}(\kappa) &= \max\left\{\rho^{+}_{\mathfrak{R}_1(\varsigma_1)}(\kappa),\rho^{+}_{\mathfrak{R}_2(\varsigma_2)}(\kappa)\right\},\ \rho^{-}_{\mathfrak{R}_3(\varsigma_1,\varsigma_2)}(\kappa) = \max\left\{\rho^{-}_{\mathfrak{R}_1(\varsigma_1)}(\kappa),\rho^{-}_{\mathfrak{R}_2(\varsigma_2)}(\kappa)\right\} \\
\omega^{+}_{\mathfrak{R}_3(\varsigma_1,\varsigma_2)}(\kappa) &= \begin{cases} \max\left\{\omega^{+}_{\mathfrak{R}_1(\varsigma_1)}(\kappa),\omega^{+}_{\mathfrak{R}_2(\varsigma_2)}(\kappa)\right\} ; & \begin{array}{r} if\left(\max\left\{\rho^{+}_{\mathfrak{R}_1(\varsigma_1)}(\kappa),\rho^{+}_{\mathfrak{R}_2(\varsigma_2)}(\kappa)\right\}\right)^2+ \\ \left(\max\left\{\omega^{+}_{\mathfrak{R}_1(\varsigma_1)}(\kappa),\omega^{+}_{\mathfrak{R}_2(\varsigma_2)}(\kappa)\right\}\right)^2 \\ +\left(\min\left\{\psi^{+}_{\mathfrak{R}_1(\varsigma_1)}(\kappa),\psi^{+}_{\mathfrak{R}_1(\varsigma_2)}(\kappa)\right\}\right)^2 \leq 1 \end{array} \\ \min\left\{\omega^{+}_{\mathfrak{R}_1(\varsigma_1)}(\kappa),\omega^{+}_{\mathfrak{R}_2(\varsigma_2)}(\kappa)\right\} ; & otherwise \end{cases} \\
\omega^{-}_{\mathfrak{R}_3(\varsigma_1,\varsigma_2)}(\kappa) &= \begin{cases} \max\left\{\omega^{-}_{\mathfrak{R}_1(\varsigma_1)}(\kappa),\omega^{-}_{\mathfrak{R}_2(\varsigma_2)}(\kappa)\right\} ; & \begin{array}{r} if\left(\max\left\{\rho^{+}_{\mathfrak{R}_1(\varsigma_1)}(\kappa),\rho^{+}_{\mathfrak{R}_2(\varsigma_2)}(\kappa)\right\}\right)^2+ \\ \left(\max\left\{\omega^{+}_{\mathfrak{R}_1(\varsigma_1)}(\kappa),\omega^{+}_{\mathfrak{R}_2(\varsigma_2)}(\kappa)\right\}\right)^2 \\ +\left(\min\left\{\psi^{+}_{\mathfrak{R}_1(\varsigma_1)}(\kappa),\psi^{+}_{\mathfrak{R}_1(\varsigma_2)}(\kappa)\right\}\right)^2 \leq 1 \end{array} \\ \min\left\{\omega^{-}_{\mathfrak{R}_1(\varsigma_1)}(\kappa),\omega^{-}_{\mathfrak{R}_2(\varsigma_2)}(\kappa)\right\} ; & otherwise \end{cases} \\
\psi^{+}_{\mathfrak{R}_3(\varsigma_1,\varsigma_2)}(\kappa) &= \min\left\{\psi^{+}_{\mathfrak{R}_1(\varsigma_1)}(\kappa),\psi^{+}_{\mathfrak{R}_1(\varsigma_2)}(\kappa)\right\},\ \psi^{-}_{\mathfrak{R}_3(\varsigma_1,\varsigma_2)}(\kappa) = \min\left\{\psi^{-}_{\mathfrak{R}_1(\varsigma_1)}(\kappa),\psi^{-}_{\mathfrak{R}_1(\varsigma_2)}(\kappa)\right\},
\end{aligned}
$$

Proposition 1. *Let $\check{0}_{\emptyset}$ and $\check{1}_{\Delta}$ be the empty bipolar spherical fuzzy soft set and absolute bipolar spherical fuzzy soft set over Δ, respectively. Then,*

1. $\check{0}_{\emptyset}\check{\sqsubseteq}\check{1}_{\Delta}$,
2. $\check{0}_{\emptyset}\check{\sqcup}\check{1}_{\Delta} = \check{1}_{\Delta}$,
3. $\check{0}_{\emptyset}\check{\sqcap}\check{1}_{\Delta} = \check{0}_{\emptyset}$.

Proof. Straightforward. □

Example 2. *Let $\Delta = \{\kappa_1,\ \kappa_2\}$ and $\aleph = \{\varsigma_1,\ \varsigma_2\}$. If*

$$
\left(\mathfrak{R}_1,\aleph\right) = \left\{ \begin{array}{l} (\varsigma_1,\langle\kappa_1,(0.2,0.6,0.7,-0.3,-0.4,-0.6)\rangle,\langle\kappa_2,(0.5,0.2,0.2,-0.3,-0.2,-0.6)\rangle), \\ (\varsigma_2,\langle\kappa_1,(0.2,0.4,0.5,-0.4,-0.5,-0.3)\rangle,\langle\kappa_2,(0.3,0.6,0.5,-0.3,-0.5,-0.5)\rangle) \end{array} \right\}
$$

and

$$
\left(\mathfrak{R}_2,\aleph\right) = \left\{ \begin{array}{l} (\varsigma_1,\langle\kappa_1,(0.2,0.5,0.6,-0.4,-0.4,-0.6)\rangle,\langle\kappa_2,(0.4,0.3,0.2,-0.2,-0.3,-0.3)\rangle), \\ (\varsigma_2,\langle\kappa_1,(0.5,0.3,0.2,-0.3,-0.3,-0.7)\rangle,\langle\kappa_2,(0.4,0.6,0.3,-0.3,-0.4,-0.5)\rangle) \end{array} \right\}
$$

then

$$
\left(\mathfrak{R}_1,\aleph\right)\check{\sqcup}\left(\mathfrak{R}_2,\aleph\right) = \left\{ \begin{array}{l} (\varsigma_1,\langle\kappa_1,(0.2,0.6,0.6,-0.3,-0.4,-0.6)\rangle,\langle\kappa_2,(0.5,0.3,0.2,-0.2,-0.2,-0.6)\rangle), \\ (\varsigma_2,\langle\kappa_1,(0.5,0.4,0.2,-0.3,-0.3,-0.7)\rangle,\langle\kappa_2,(0.4,0.6,0.3,-0.3,-0.4,-0.5)\rangle) \end{array} \right\},
$$

$$
\left(\mathfrak{R}_1,\aleph\right)\check{\sqcap}\left(\mathfrak{R}_2,\aleph\right) = \left\{ \begin{array}{l} (\varsigma_1,\langle\kappa_1,(0.2,0.5,0.7,-0.4,-0.4,-0.6)\rangle,\langle\kappa_2,(0.4,0.2,0.2,-0.3,-0.3,-0.3)\rangle), \\ (\varsigma_2,\langle\kappa_1,(0.2,0.3,0.5,-0.4,-0.5,-0.3)\rangle,\langle\kappa_2,(0.3,0.6,0.5,-0.3,-0.5,-0.5)\rangle) \end{array} \right\},
$$

$$
\left(\mathfrak{R}_1,\aleph\right)\check{\vee}\left(\mathfrak{R}_2,\aleph\right) = \left\{ \begin{array}{l} ((\varsigma_1,\varsigma_1),\langle\kappa_1,(0.2,0.6,0.6,-0.3,-0.4,-0.6)\rangle,\langle\kappa_2,(0.5,0.3,0.2,-0.2,-0.2,-0.6)\rangle), \\ ((\varsigma_1,\varsigma_2),\langle\kappa_1,(0.5,0.6,0.2,-0.3,-0.3,-0.7)\rangle,\langle\kappa_2,(0.5,0.6,0.2,-0.3,-0.2,-0.6)\rangle), \\ ((\varsigma_2,\varsigma_1),\langle\kappa_1,(0.2,0.5,0.5,-0.4,-0.4,-0.6)\rangle,\langle\kappa_2,(0.4,0.6,0.2,-0.2,-0.3,-0.5)\rangle) \\ ((\varsigma_2,\varsigma_2),\langle\kappa_1,(0.5,0.4,0.2,-0.3,-0.3,-0.7)\rangle,\langle\kappa_2,(0.4,0.6,0.3,-0.3,-0.4,-0.5)\rangle) \end{array} \right\}
$$

$$
\left(\mathfrak{R}_1,\aleph\right)\check{\wedge}\left(\mathfrak{R}_2,\aleph\right) = \left\{ \begin{array}{l} ((\varsigma_1,\varsigma_1),\langle\kappa_1,(0.2,0.5,0.7,-0.4,-0.4,-0.6)\rangle,\langle\kappa_2,(0.4,0.2,0.2,-0.3,-0.3,-0.3)\rangle), \\ ((\varsigma_1,\varsigma_2),\langle\kappa_1,(0.2,0.3,0.7,-0.3,-0.4,-0.6)\rangle,\langle\kappa_2,(0.4,0.2,0.3,-0.3,-0.4,-0.5)\rangle), \\ ((\varsigma_2,\varsigma_1),\langle\kappa_1,(0.2,0.4,0.6,-0.4,-0.5,-0.3)\rangle,\langle\kappa_2,(0.3,0.3,0.5,-0.3,-0.5,-0.3)\rangle) \\ ((\varsigma_2,\varsigma_2),\langle\kappa_1,(0.2,0.3,0.5,-0.4,-0.5,-0.3)\rangle,\langle\kappa_2,(0.3,0.6,0.5,-0.3,-0.5,-0.5)\rangle) \end{array} \right\}
$$

Proposition 2. *Let $\left(\mathfrak{R}_1,\aleph\right)$, $\left(\mathfrak{R}_2,\aleph\right)$, and $\left(\mathfrak{R}_3,\aleph\right)$ be bipolar spherical fuzzy soft sets over Δ. Then,*

1. $\left(\breve{\Re}_1, \aleph\right) \breve{\sqcup} \left[\left(\breve{\Re}_2, \aleph\right) \breve{\sqcup} \left(\breve{\Re}_3, \aleph\right)\right] = \left[\left(\breve{\Re}_1, \aleph\right) \breve{\sqcup} \left(\breve{\Re}_2, \aleph\right)\right] \breve{\sqcup} \left(\breve{\Re}_3, \aleph\right)$ *and* $\left(\breve{\Re}_1, \aleph\right) \breve{\sqcap} \left[\left(\breve{\Re}_2, \aleph\right) \breve{\sqcap} \left(\breve{\Re}_3, \aleph\right)\right] = \left[\left(\breve{\Re}_1, \aleph\right) \breve{\sqcap} \left(\breve{\Re}_2, \aleph\right)\right] \breve{\sqcap} \left(\breve{\Re}_3, \aleph\right)$;
2. $\left(\breve{\Re}_1, \aleph\right) \breve{\sqcup} \left[\left(\breve{\Re}_2, \aleph\right) \breve{\sqcap} \left(\breve{\Re}_3, \aleph\right)\right] = \left[\left(\breve{\Re}_1, \aleph\right) \breve{\sqcup} \left(\breve{\Re}_2, \aleph\right)\right] \breve{\sqcap} \left[\left(\breve{\Re}_1, \aleph\right) \breve{\sqcup} \left(\breve{\Re}_3, \aleph\right)\right]$ *and* $\left(\breve{\Re}_1, \aleph\right) \breve{\sqcap} \left[\left(\breve{\Re}_2, \aleph\right) \breve{\sqcup} \left(\breve{\Re}_3, \aleph\right)\right] = \left[\left(\breve{\Re}_1, \aleph\right) \breve{\sqcap} \left(\breve{\Re}_2, \aleph\right)\right] \breve{\sqcup} \left[\left(\breve{\Re}_1, \aleph\right) \breve{\sqcap} \left(\breve{\Re}_3, \aleph\right)\right]$;
3. $\left(\breve{\Re}_1, \aleph\right) \breve{\sqcup} \breve{0}_\emptyset = \left(\breve{\Re}_1, \aleph\right)$ *and* $\left(\breve{\Re}_1, \aleph\right) \breve{\sqcap} \breve{0}_\emptyset = \breve{0}_\emptyset$;
4. $\left(\breve{\Re}_1, \aleph\right) \breve{\sqcup} \breve{1}_\Delta = \breve{1}_\Delta$ *and* $\left(\breve{\Re}_1, \aleph\right) \breve{\sqcap} \breve{1}_\Delta = \left(\breve{\Re}_1, \aleph\right)$;

Proof. Straightforward. □

Proposition 3. *Let* $\left(\breve{\Re}_1, \aleph\right)$ *and* $\left(\breve{\Re}_2, \aleph\right)$ *be two bipolar spherical fuzzy soft sets over* Δ. *Then,*

1. $\left[\left(\breve{\Re}_1, \aleph\right) \breve{\sqcup} \left(\breve{\Re}_2, \aleph\right)\right]^c = \left(\breve{\Re}_1, \aleph\right)^c \breve{\sqcap} \left(\breve{\Re}_2, \aleph\right)^c$;
2. $\left[\left(\breve{\Re}_1, \aleph\right) \breve{\sqcap} \left(\breve{\Re}_2, \aleph\right)\right]^c = \left(\breve{\Re}_1, \aleph\right)^c \breve{\sqcup} \left(\breve{\Re}_2, \aleph\right)^c$.

Proof. Straightforward. □

4. Bipolar Spherical Fuzzy Soft Topological Spaces

In this section, we defined BSFS-topology by the revised form of spherical fuzzy soft sets and we gave the basic structures of the bipolar spherical fuzzy soft topological spaces.

Definition 15. *Let* $BSFS(\Delta, \aleph)$ *be the family of all bipolar spherical fuzzy soft sets over* Δ *and* $\breve{\tau} \subset BSFS(\Delta, \aleph)$. *Then* $\breve{\tau}$ *is called to be a BSFS-topology on* Δ *if*

1. $\breve{0}_\emptyset$ *and* $\breve{1}_\Delta$ *belong to* $\breve{\tau}$
2. *If* $\left(\breve{\Re}_i, \aleph\right) \in \breve{\tau}$ $\forall i \in I$, *an index set, then* $\sqcup_{i \in I}\left(\breve{\Re}_i, \aleph\right) \in \breve{\tau}$,
3. *If* $\left(\breve{\Re}_1, \aleph\right), \left(\breve{\Re}_2, \aleph\right) \in \breve{\tau}$, *then* $\left(\breve{\Re}_1, \aleph\right) \breve{\sqcap} \left(\breve{\Re}_2, \aleph\right) \in \breve{\tau}$.

Then $(\Delta, \breve{\tau}, \aleph)$ *is called to be a bipolar spherical fuzzy soft topological space over* Δ. *Each member of* $\breve{\tau}$ *is called to be bipolar spherical fuzzy soft open set.* $\left(\breve{\Re}, \aleph\right)$ *is called to be bipolar spherical fuzzy soft closed set if its complement is a bipolar spherical fuzzy soft open set.*

Proposition 4. *Let* $(\Delta, \breve{\tau}, \aleph)$ *be a bipolar spherical fuzzy soft topological space over* Δ. *Then,*

1. $\breve{0}_\emptyset$ *and* $\breve{1}_\Delta$ *are bipolar spherical fuzzy soft closed sets over* Δ
2. *The intersection of any number of bipolar spherical fuzzy soft closed sets is a bipolar spherical fuzzy soft closed set over* Δ
3. *The union of finite number of bipolar spherical fuzzy soft closed sets is a bipolar spherical fuzzy soft closed set over* Δ.

Proof. It is easily obtained from the Definition bipolar spherical fuzzy soft topological space. □

Definition 16. *Let* $BSFS(\Delta, \aleph)$ *be the family of all bipolar spherical fuzzy soft sets over the universe set* Δ.

1. *If* $\breve{\tau} = \{\breve{0}_\emptyset, \breve{1}_\Delta\}$, *then* $\breve{\tau}$ *is called to be the bipolar spherical fuzzy soft indiscrete topology and* $(\Delta, \breve{\tau}, \aleph)$ *is called to be a bipolar spherical fuzzy soft indiscrete topological space over* Δ.
2. *If* $\breve{\tau} = BSFS(\Delta, \aleph)$, *then* $\breve{\tau}$ *is called to be the bipolar spherical fuzzy soft discrete topology and* $(\Delta, \breve{\tau}, \aleph)$ *is called to be a bipolar spherical fuzzy soft discrete topological space over* Δ.

Proposition 5. *Let $(\Delta, \check{\tau}, \aleph)$ and $(\Delta, \check{\tau}, \aleph)$ be two bipolar spherical fuzzy soft topological spaces over the same universe set Δ. Then $(\Delta, \check{\tau} \cap \check{\tau}, \aleph)$ is bipolar spherical fuzzy soft topological space over Δ.*

Proof. 1. Since $\check{0}_{\emptyset}, \check{1}_{\Delta} \in \check{\tau}$, and $\check{0}_{\emptyset}, \check{1}_{\Delta} \in \check{\tau}$, then $\check{0}_{\emptyset}, \check{1}_{\Delta} \in \check{\tau}\check{\sqcap}\check{\tau}$.

2. Suppose that $\left\{ \left(\check{\Re}_i, \aleph\right) \middle| i \in \omega \right\}$ is a family of bipolar spherical fuzzy soft sets in $\check{\tau} \cap \check{\tau}$. Then $\left(\check{\Re}_i, \aleph\right) \in \check{\tau}$ and $\left(\check{\Re}_i, \aleph\right) \in \check{\tau}$ for all $i \in \omega$, so $\underset{i\in\omega}{\sqcup}\left(\check{\Re}_i, \aleph\right) \in \check{\tau}$ and $\underset{i\in\omega}{\sqcup}\left(\check{\Re}_i, \aleph\right) \in \check{\tau}$. Thus $\underset{i\in\omega}{\sqcup}\left(\check{\Re}_i, \aleph\right) \in \check{\tau} \cap \check{\tau}$.

3. Let $\left\{ \left(\check{\Re}_i, \aleph\right) \middle| i = \overline{1,n} \right\}$ be a family of the finite number of bipolar spherical fuzzy soft sets in $\check{\tau} \cap \check{\tau}$. Then $\left(\check{\Re}_i, \aleph\right) \in \check{\tau}$ and $\left(\check{\Re}_i, \aleph\right) \in \check{\tau}$ for $i = \overline{1,n}$, so $\overset{n}{\underset{i=1}{\check{\sqcap}}}\left(\check{\Re}_i, \aleph\right) \in \check{\tau}$ and $\overset{n}{\underset{i=1}{\check{\sqcap}}}\left(\check{\Re}_i, \aleph\right) \in \check{\tau}$. Thus, $\overset{n}{\underset{i=1}{\check{\sqcap}}}\left(\check{\Re}_i, \aleph\right) \in \check{\tau}\check{\sqcap}\check{\tau}$.

□

Remark 1. *The union of two bipolar spherical fuzzy soft topologies over Δ may not be a BSFS-topology on Δ.*

Example 3. *Let $\Delta = \{\kappa_1, \kappa_2\}$ be an initial universe set, $\aleph = \{\varsigma_1, \varsigma_2\}$ be a set of parameters, and $\check{\tau}_1 = \left\{\check{0}_{\emptyset}, \check{1}_{\Delta}, \left(\check{\Re}_1, \aleph\right), \left(\check{\Re}_2, \aleph\right), \left(\check{\Re}_3, \aleph\right)\right\}$ and $\check{\tau}_2 = \left\{\check{0}_{\emptyset}, \check{1}_{\Delta}, \left(\check{\Re}_2, \aleph\right), \left(\check{\Re}_4, \aleph\right)\right\}$ be two bipolar spherical fuzzy soft topologies over Δ. Here, the bipolar spherical fuzzy soft sets $\left(\check{\Re}_1, \aleph\right)$, $\left(\check{\Re}_2, \aleph\right)$, $\left(\check{\Re}_3, \aleph\right)$ and $\left(\check{\Re}_4, \aleph\right)$ over Δ are defined as follows:*

$$\left(\check{\Re}_1, \aleph\right) = \left\{ \begin{array}{l} \varsigma_1, \langle \kappa_1, (0.6, 0.5, 0.3, -0.2, -0.5, -0.6) \rangle, \langle \kappa_2, (0.5, 0.7, 0.2, -0.1, -0.4, -0.7) \rangle \\ \varsigma_2, \langle \kappa_1, (0.5, 0.4, 0.1, -0.2, -0.2, -0,5) \rangle, \langle \kappa_2, (0.7, 0.6, 0.1, -0.2, -0.3, -0.6) \rangle \end{array} \right\},$$

$$\left(\check{\Re}_2, \aleph\right) = \left\{ \begin{array}{l} \varsigma_1, \langle \kappa_1, (0.5, 0.4, 0.4, -0.3, -0.6, -0.5) \rangle, \langle \kappa_2, (0.3, 0.6, 0.2, -0.2, -0.5, -0.5) \rangle \\ \varsigma_2, \langle \kappa_1, (0.4, 0.3, 0.2, -0.2, -0.3, -0.4) \rangle, \langle \kappa_2, (0.6, 0.5, 0.1, -0.3, -0.4, -0.6) \rangle \end{array} \right\},$$

$$\left(\check{\Re}_3, \aleph\right) = \left\{ \begin{array}{l} \varsigma_1, \langle \kappa_1, (0.4, 0.3, 0.5, -0.5, -0.6, -0.4) \rangle, \langle \kappa_2, (0.2, 0.5, 0.5, -0.3, -0.6, -0.1) \rangle \\ \varsigma_2, \langle \kappa_1, (0.2, 0.3, 0.3, -0.5, -0.6, -0.3) \rangle, \langle \kappa_2, (0.5, 0.4, 0.2, -0.4, -0.5, -0.5) \rangle \end{array} \right\},$$

$$\left(\check{\Re}_4, \aleph\right) = \left\{ \begin{array}{l} \varsigma_1, \langle \kappa_1, (0.6, 0.6, 0.3, -0.2, -0.5, -0.6) \rangle, \langle \kappa_2, (0.4, 0.8, 0.1, -0.1, -0.3, -0.6) \rangle \\ \varsigma_2, \langle \kappa_1, (0.5, 0.4, 0.1, -0.2, -0.3, -0.5) \rangle, \langle \kappa_2, (0.7, 0.7, 0.1, -0.2, -0.4, -0.7) \rangle \end{array} \right\}.$$

Since $\left(\check{\Re}_1, \aleph\right)\check{\sqcup}\left(\check{\Re}_4, \aleph\right) \notin \check{\tau}_1\check{\sqcup}\,\check{\tau}_2$, then $\check{\tau}_1\check{\sqcup}\,\check{\tau}_2$ is not a bipolar spherical fuzzy soft topology over Δ.

Proposition 6. *Let $(\Delta, \check{\tau}, \aleph)$ be a bipolar spherical fuzzy soft topological space over Δ and $\check{\tau} = \left\{\left(\check{\Re}_i, \aleph\right) : \left(\check{\Re}_i, \aleph\right) \in BSFS(\Delta, \aleph)\right\}$ where $\left(\check{\Re}_i, \aleph\right) = \left\{\left(\varsigma, \left\langle \kappa, \left(\rho^+_{\check{\Re}_i(\varsigma)}(\kappa), \omega^+_{\check{\Re}_i(\varsigma)}(\kappa), \psi^+_{\check{\Re}_i(\varsigma)}(\kappa), \rho^-_{\check{\Re}_i(\varsigma)}(\kappa), \omega^-_{\check{\Re}_i(\varsigma)}(\kappa), \psi^-_{\check{\Re}_i(\varsigma)}(\kappa)\right)\right\rangle : \kappa \in \Delta\right) : \varsigma \in \aleph\right\}$ for $i \in \omega$. Then*

$$\overset{NSS}{\tau} = \left\{\left(\check{\Re}^+_i, \aleph\right) = \left\{\left(\varsigma, \left\langle \kappa, \left(\rho^+_{\check{\Re}_i(\varsigma)}(\kappa), \omega^+_{\check{\Re}_i(\varsigma)}(\kappa), \psi^+_{\check{\Re}_i(\varsigma)}(\kappa)\right)\right\rangle : \kappa \in \Delta\right) : \varsigma \in \aleph\right\} : \left(\check{\Re}^+_i, \aleph\right) \in NSS(\Delta, \aleph)\right\}$$

define SFS-topology on Δ.

Proof. Straightforward. □

Definition 17. *Let $(\Delta, \check{\tau}, \aleph)$ be a bipolar spherical fuzzy soft topological space over Δ and $\left(\check{\Re}, \aleph\right) \in BSFS(\Delta, \aleph)$ be a bipolar spherical fuzzy soft set. Then, bipolar spherical fuzzy soft interior* *of* $\left(\breve{\mathfrak{R}},\aleph\right)$*, denoted* $\left(\breve{\mathfrak{R}},\aleph\right)^{\circ}$*, is defined as the bipolar spherical fuzzy soft union of all bipolar spherical fuzzy soft open subsets of* $\left(\breve{\mathfrak{R}},\aleph\right)$*.*

Clearly, $\left(\breve{\mathfrak{R}},\aleph\right)^{\circ}$ *is the biggest bipolar spherical fuzzy soft open set contained by* $\left(\breve{\mathfrak{R}},\aleph\right)$*.*

Example 4. *Let us consider the BSFS-topology* $\check{\mathfrak{t}}_1$ *given in Example 3. Suppose that any* $\left(\breve{\mathfrak{R}},\aleph\right) \in BSFS(\Delta,\aleph)$ *is defined as the following:*

$$\left(\breve{\mathfrak{R}},\aleph\right) = \left\{ \begin{array}{l} \varsigma_1, \langle \kappa_1, (0.6, 0.7, 0.3, -0.2, -0.6, -0.6)\rangle, \langle \kappa_2, (0.4, 0.7, 0.1, -0.2, -0.4, -0.6)\rangle \\ \varsigma_2, \langle \kappa_1, (0.6, 0.4, 0.3, -0.1, -0.3, -0.5)\rangle, \langle \kappa_2, (0.7, 0.6, 0.1, -0.2, -0.3, -0.7)\rangle \end{array} \right\}.$$

Then $\check{0}_{\varnothing}$, $\left(\breve{\mathfrak{R}}_2,\aleph\right)$, $\left(\breve{\mathfrak{R}}_3,\aleph\right) \sqsubseteq \left(\breve{\mathfrak{R}},\aleph\right)$*. Therefore,* $\left(\breve{\mathfrak{R}},\aleph\right)^{\circ} = \check{0}_{\varnothing} \breve{\sqcup} \left(\breve{\mathfrak{R}}_2,\aleph\right) \breve{\sqcup} \left(\breve{\mathfrak{R}}_3,\aleph\right) = \left(\breve{\mathfrak{R}}_2,\aleph\right)$*.*

Theorem 1. *Let* $(\Delta,\check{\mathfrak{t}},\aleph)$ *be a bipolar spherical fuzzy soft topological space over* Δ *and* $\left(\breve{\mathfrak{R}},\aleph\right) \in BSFS(\Delta,\aleph)$*.* $\left(\breve{\mathfrak{R}},\aleph\right)$ *is a bipolar spherical fuzzy soft open set iff* $\left(\breve{\mathfrak{R}},\aleph\right) = \left(\breve{\mathfrak{R}},\aleph\right)^{\circ}$*.*

Proof. Let $\left(\breve{\mathfrak{R}},\aleph\right)$ be a bipolar spherical fuzzy soft open set. Then the biggest bipolar spherical fuzzy soft open set that is contained by $\left(\breve{\mathfrak{R}},\aleph\right)$ is equal to $\left(\breve{\mathfrak{R}},\aleph\right)$. Hence, $\left(\breve{\mathfrak{R}},\aleph\right) = \left(\breve{\mathfrak{R}},\aleph\right)^{\circ}$.

Conversely, it is known that $\left(\breve{\mathfrak{R}},\aleph\right)^{\circ}$ is a bipolar spherical fuzzy soft open set, and if $\left(\breve{\mathfrak{R}},\aleph\right) = \left(\breve{\mathfrak{R}},\aleph\right)^{\circ}$, then $\left(\breve{\mathfrak{R}},\aleph\right)$ is a bipolar spherical fuzzy soft open set. □

Theorem 2. *Let* $(\Delta,\check{\mathfrak{t}},\aleph)$ *be a bipolar spherical fuzzy soft topological space over* Δ *and* $\left(\breve{\mathfrak{R}}_1,\aleph\right)$*,* $\left(\breve{\mathfrak{R}}_2,\aleph\right) \in BSFS(\Delta,\aleph)$*. Then,*

1. $\left[\left(\breve{\mathfrak{R}}_1,\aleph\right)^{\circ}\right]^{\circ} = \left(\breve{\mathfrak{R}}_1,\aleph\right)^{\circ}$,
2. $\check{0}_{\varnothing}^{\circ} = \check{0}_{\varnothing}$ *and* $\check{1}_{\Delta}^{\circ} = \check{1}_{\Delta}$,
3. $\left(\breve{\mathfrak{R}}_1,\aleph\right) \sqsubseteq \left(\breve{\mathfrak{R}}_2,\aleph\right) \Rightarrow \left(\breve{\mathfrak{R}}_1,\aleph\right)^{\circ} \sqsubseteq \left(\breve{\mathfrak{R}}_2,\aleph\right)^{\circ}$,
4. $\left[\left(\breve{\mathfrak{R}}_1,\aleph\right) \breve{\sqcap} \left(\breve{\mathfrak{R}}_2,\aleph\right)\right]^{\circ} = \left(\breve{\mathfrak{R}}_1,\aleph\right)^{\circ} \breve{\sqcap} \left(\breve{\mathfrak{R}}_2,\aleph\right)^{\circ}$,
5. $\left(\breve{\mathfrak{R}}_1,\aleph\right)^{\circ} \sqcup \left(\breve{\mathfrak{R}}_2,\aleph\right)^{\circ} \sqsubseteq \left[\left(\breve{\mathfrak{R}}_1,\aleph\right) \sqcup \left(\breve{\mathfrak{R}}_2,\aleph\right)\right]^{\circ}$.

Proof. 1. Let $\left(\breve{\mathfrak{R}}_1,\aleph\right)^{\circ} = \left(\breve{\mathfrak{R}}_2,\aleph\right)$. Then $\left(\breve{\mathfrak{R}}_2,\aleph\right) \in \check{\mathfrak{t}}$ iff $\left(\breve{\mathfrak{R}}_2,\aleph\right) = \left(\breve{\mathfrak{R}}_2,\aleph\right)^{\circ}$. So, $\left[\left(\breve{\mathfrak{R}}_1,\aleph\right)^{\circ}\right]^{\circ} = \left(\breve{\mathfrak{R}}_1,\aleph\right)^{\circ}$.

2. Straighforward.
3. It is known that $\left(\breve{\mathfrak{R}}_1,\aleph\right)^{\circ} \sqsubseteq \left(\breve{\mathfrak{R}}_1,\aleph\right) \sqsubseteq \left(\breve{\mathfrak{R}}_2,\aleph\right)$ and $\left(\breve{\mathfrak{R}}_2,\aleph\right)^{\circ} \sqsubseteq \left(\breve{\mathfrak{R}}_2,\aleph\right)$. Since $\left(\breve{\mathfrak{R}}_2,\aleph\right)^{\circ}$ is the biggest bipolar spherical fuzzy soft open set contained in $\left(\breve{\mathfrak{R}}_2,\aleph\right)$, then $\left(\breve{\mathfrak{R}}_1,\aleph\right)^{\circ} \sqsubseteq \left(\breve{\mathfrak{R}}_2,\aleph\right)^{\circ}$.
4. Since $\left(\breve{\mathfrak{R}}_1,\aleph\right) \breve{\sqcap} \left(\breve{\mathfrak{R}}_2,\aleph\right) \sqsubseteq \left(\breve{\mathfrak{R}}_1,\aleph\right)$ and $\left(\breve{\mathfrak{R}}_1,\aleph\right) \breve{\sqcap} \left(\breve{\mathfrak{R}}_2,\aleph\right) \sqsubseteq \left(\breve{\mathfrak{R}}_2,\aleph\right)$, then $\left[\left(\breve{\mathfrak{R}}_1,\aleph\right) \breve{\sqcap} \left(\breve{\mathfrak{R}}_2,\aleph\right)\right]^{\circ} \sqsubseteq \left(\breve{\mathfrak{R}}_1,\aleph\right)^{\circ}$ and $\left[\left(\breve{\mathfrak{R}}_1,\aleph\right) \breve{\sqcap} \left(\breve{\mathfrak{R}}_2,\aleph\right)\right]^{\circ} \sqsubseteq \left(\breve{\mathfrak{R}}_2,\aleph\right)^{\circ}$, and so, $\left[\left(\breve{\mathfrak{R}}_1,\aleph\right) \breve{\sqcap} \left(\breve{\mathfrak{R}}_2,\aleph\right)\right]^{\circ} \sqsubseteq \left(\breve{\mathfrak{R}}_1,\aleph\right)^{\circ} \breve{\sqcap} \left(\breve{\mathfrak{R}}_2,\aleph\right)^{\circ}$.

On the other hand, since $\left(\breve{\Re}_1,\aleph\right)^{\circ} \sqsubseteq \left(\breve{\Re}_1,\aleph\right)$ and $\left(\breve{\Re}_2,\aleph\right)^{\circ} \sqsubseteq \left(\breve{\Re}_2,\aleph\right)$, then $\left(\breve{\Re}_1,\aleph\right)^{\circ} \sqcap \left(\breve{\Re}_2,\aleph\right)^{\circ} \sqsubseteq \left(\breve{\Re}_1,\aleph\right) \sqcap \left(\breve{\Re}_2,\aleph\right)$. Furthermore, $\left[\left(\breve{\Re}_1,\aleph\right) \sqcap \left(\breve{\Re}_2,\aleph\right)\right]^{\circ} \sqsubseteq \left(\breve{\Re}_1,\aleph\right) \sqcap \left(\breve{\Re}_2,\aleph\right)$, and it is the biggest bipolar spherical fuzzy soft open set. Therefore, $\left(\breve{\Re}_1,\aleph\right)^{\circ} \sqcap \left(\breve{\Re}_2,\aleph\right)^{\circ} \sqsubseteq \left[\left(\breve{\Re}_1,\aleph\right) \sqcap \left(\breve{\Re}_2,\aleph\right)\right]^{\circ}$.
Thus, $\left[\left(\breve{\Re}_1,\aleph\right) \sqcap \left(\breve{\Re}_2,\aleph\right)\right]^{\circ} = \left(\breve{\Re}_1,\aleph\right)^{\circ} \sqcap \left(\breve{\Re}_2,\aleph\right)^{\circ}$.

5. Since $\left(\breve{\Re}_1,\aleph\right) \sqsubseteq \left(\breve{\Re}_1,\aleph\right) \sqcup \left(\breve{\Re}_2,\aleph\right)$ and $\left(\breve{\Re}_2,\aleph\right) \sqsubseteq \left(\breve{\Re}_1,\aleph\right) \sqcup \left(\breve{\Re}_2,\aleph\right)$, then $\left(\breve{\Re}_1,\aleph\right)^{\circ} \sqsubseteq \left[\left(\breve{\Re}_1,\aleph\right) \sqcup \left(\breve{\Re}_2,\aleph\right)\right]^{\circ}$ and $\left(\breve{\Re}_2,\aleph\right)^{\circ} \sqsubseteq \left[\left(\breve{\Re}_1,\aleph\right) \sqcup \left(\breve{\Re}_2,\aleph\right)\right]^{\circ}$. Therefore, $\left(\breve{\Re}_1,\aleph\right)^{\circ} \sqcup \left(\breve{\Re}_2,\aleph\right)^{\circ} \sqsubseteq \left[\left(\breve{\Re}_1,\aleph\right) \sqcup \left(\breve{\Re}_2,\aleph\right)\right]^{\circ}$.

□

Definition 18. *Let $(\Delta, \breve{\tau}, \aleph)$ be a bipolar spherical fuzzy soft topological space over Δ and $\left(\breve{\Re},\aleph\right) \in BSFS(\Delta,\aleph)$ be a bipolar spherical fuzzy soft set. Then, bipolar spherical fuzzy soft closure of $\left(\breve{\Re},\aleph\right)$, denoted $\overline{\left(\breve{\Re},\aleph\right)}$, is defined as the bipolar spherical fuzzy soft intersection of all bipolar spherical fuzzy soft closed supersets of $\left(\breve{\Re},\aleph\right)$.*

Clearly, $\overline{\left(\breve{\Re},\aleph\right)}$ is the smallest bipolar spherical fuzzy soft closed set that contains $\left(\breve{\Re},\aleph\right)$.

Example 5. *Let us consider the BSFS-topology $\breve{\tau}_1$ given in Example 3. Suppose that any $\left(\breve{\Re},\aleph\right) \in BSFS(\Delta,\aleph)$ is defined as the following:*

$$\left(\breve{\Re},\aleph\right) = \left\{ \begin{array}{l} \varsigma_1, \langle \kappa_1, (0.1,0.4,0.7,-0.7,-0.6,-0.1)\rangle, \langle \kappa_2, (0.2,0.2,0.6,-0.7,-0.7,-0.1)\rangle \\ \varsigma_2, \langle \kappa_1, (0.1,0.5,0.6,-0.5,-0.8,-0,1)\rangle, \langle \kappa_2, (0.1,0.3,0.8,-0.6,-0.7,-0.1)\rangle \end{array} \right\}.$$

It is then clear that $\breve{0}_{\varnothing}, \breve{1}_{\Delta}, \left(\breve{\Re}_1,\aleph\right)^c, \left(\breve{\Re}_2,\aleph\right)^c$, and $\left(\breve{\Re}_3,\aleph\right)^c$ are all bipolar spherical fuzzy soft closed sets over $(\Delta, \breve{\tau}, \aleph)$. They are given as following:

$$\begin{array}{rcl} \breve{0}_{\varnothing}^c & = & \breve{1}_{\Delta},\ (\breve{1}_{\Delta})^c = \breve{0}_{\varnothing} \\ \left(\breve{\Re}_1,\aleph\right)^c & = & \left\{ \begin{array}{l} \varsigma_1, \langle \kappa_1, (0.3,0.5,0.6,-0.6,-0.5,-0.2)\rangle, \langle \kappa_2, (0.2,0.3,0.5,-0.7,-0.6,-0.1)\rangle \\ \varsigma_2, \langle \kappa_1, (0.1,0.6,0.5,-0.5,-0.8,-0,2)\rangle, \langle \kappa_2, (0.1,0.4,0.7,-0.6,-0.7,-0.2)\rangle \end{array} \right\}, \\ \left(\breve{\Re}_2,\aleph\right)^c & = & \left\{ \begin{array}{l} \varsigma_1, \langle \kappa_1, (0.4,0.6,0.5,-0.5,-0.4,-0.3)\rangle, \langle \kappa_2, (0.2,0.4,0.3,-0.5,-0.5,-0.2)\rangle \\ \varsigma_2, \langle \kappa_1, (0.2,0.7,0.4,-0.4,-0.7,-0,2)\rangle, \langle \kappa_2, (0.1,0.5,0.6,-0.6,-0.6,-0.3)\rangle \end{array} \right\}, \\ \left(\breve{\Re}_3,\aleph\right)^c & = & \left\{ \begin{array}{l} \varsigma_1, \langle \kappa_1, (0.5,0.7,0.4,-0.4,-0.4,-0.5)\rangle, \langle \kappa_2, (0.5,0.5,0.2,-0.1,-0.4,-0.3)\rangle \\ \varsigma_2, \langle \kappa_1, (0.3,0.7,0.2,-0.3,-0.4,-0,5)\rangle, \langle \kappa_2, (0.2,0.6,0.5,-0.5,-0.5,-0.4)\rangle \end{array} \right\}. \end{array}$$

Then $(\breve{1}_{\Delta})^c, \left(\breve{\Re}_1,\aleph\right)^c, \left(\breve{\Re}_2,\aleph\right)^c, \left(\breve{\Re}_3,\aleph\right)^c \sqsupseteq \left(\breve{\Re},\aleph\right)$. Therefore, $\overline{\left(\breve{\Re},\aleph\right)} = (\breve{1}_{\Delta})^c \sqcap \left(\breve{\Re}_1,\aleph\right)^c \sqcap \left(\breve{\Re}_2,\aleph\right)^c \sqcap \left(\breve{\Re}_3,\aleph\right)^c = \left(\breve{\Re}_1,\aleph\right)^c$.

Theorem 3. *Let $(\Delta, \breve{\tau}, \aleph)$ be a bipolar spherical fuzzy soft topological space over Δ and $\left(\breve{\Re},\aleph\right) \in BSFS(\Delta,\aleph)$. $\left(\breve{\Re},\aleph\right)$ is bipolar spherical fuzzy soft closed set iff $\left(\breve{\Re},\aleph\right) = \overline{\left(\breve{\Re},\aleph\right)}$.*

Proof. Straightforward. □

Theorem 4. *Let $(\Delta, \breve{\tau}, \aleph)$ be a bipolar spherical fuzzy soft topological space over Δ and $\left(\breve{\Re}_1,\aleph\right)$, $\left(\breve{\Re}_2,\aleph\right) \in BSFS(\Delta,\aleph)$. Then,*

1. $\overline{\left[\overline{(\breve{\mathfrak{R}}_1,\aleph)}\right]} = \overline{(\breve{\mathfrak{R}}_1,\aleph)}$,
2. $\overline{\breve{0}_\varnothing} = \breve{0}_\varnothing$ *and* $\overline{\breve{1}_\Delta} = \breve{1}_\Delta$
3. $(\breve{\mathfrak{R}}_1,\aleph) \sqsubseteq (\breve{\mathfrak{R}}_2,\aleph) \Rightarrow \overline{(\breve{\mathfrak{R}}_1,\aleph)} \sqsubseteq \overline{(\breve{\mathfrak{R}}_2,\aleph)}$,
4. $\overline{\left[(\breve{\mathfrak{R}}_1,\aleph) \sqcup (\breve{\mathfrak{R}}_2,\aleph)\right]} = \overline{(\breve{\mathfrak{R}}_1,\aleph)} \sqcup \overline{(\breve{\mathfrak{R}}_2,\aleph)}$,
5. $\overline{\left[(\breve{\mathfrak{R}}_1,\aleph) \sqcap (\breve{\mathfrak{R}}_2,\aleph)\right]} \sqsubseteq \overline{(\breve{\mathfrak{R}}_1,\aleph)} \sqcap \overline{(\breve{\mathfrak{R}}_2,\aleph)}$.

Proof. 1. Let $\overline{(\breve{\mathfrak{R}}_1,\aleph)} = (\breve{\mathfrak{R}}_2,\aleph)$. Then, $(\breve{\mathfrak{R}}_2,\aleph)$ is a bipolar spherical fuzzy soft closed set. Hence, $(\breve{\mathfrak{R}}_2,\aleph)$ and $\overline{(\breve{\mathfrak{R}}_2,\aleph)}$ are equal. Therefore, $\overline{\left[\overline{(\breve{\mathfrak{R}}_1,\aleph)}\right]} = \overline{(\breve{\mathfrak{R}}_1,\aleph)}$.

2. Straightforward.

3. It is known that $(\breve{\mathfrak{R}}_1,\aleph) \sqsubseteq \overline{(\breve{\mathfrak{R}}_1,\aleph)}$ and $(\breve{\mathfrak{R}}_2,\aleph) \sqsubseteq \overline{(\breve{\mathfrak{R}}_2,\aleph)}$, and so, $(\breve{\mathfrak{R}}_1,\aleph) \sqsubseteq (\breve{\mathfrak{R}}_2,\aleph) \sqsubseteq \overline{(\breve{\mathfrak{R}}_2,\aleph)}$. Since $\overline{(\breve{\mathfrak{R}}_1,\aleph)}$ is the smallest bipolar spherical fuzzy soft closed set containing $(\breve{\mathfrak{R}}_1,\aleph)$, then $\overline{(\breve{\mathfrak{R}}_1,\aleph)} \sqsubseteq \overline{(\breve{\mathfrak{R}}_2,\aleph)}$.

4. Since $(\breve{\mathfrak{R}}_1,\aleph) \sqsubseteq (\breve{\mathfrak{R}}_1,\aleph) \sqcup (\breve{\mathfrak{R}}_2,\aleph)$ and $(\breve{\mathfrak{R}}_2,\aleph) \sqsubseteq (\breve{\mathfrak{R}}_1,\aleph) \sqcup (\breve{\mathfrak{R}}_2,\aleph)$, then $\overline{(\breve{\mathfrak{R}}_1,\aleph)} \sqsubseteq \overline{\left[(\breve{\mathfrak{R}}_1,\aleph) \sqcup (\breve{\mathfrak{R}}_2,\aleph)\right]}$ and $\overline{(\breve{\mathfrak{R}}_2,\aleph)} \sqsubseteq \overline{\left[(\breve{\mathfrak{R}}_1,\aleph) \sqcup (\breve{\mathfrak{R}}_2,\aleph)\right]}$, and so, $\overline{(\breve{\mathfrak{R}}_1,\aleph)} \sqcup \overline{(\breve{\mathfrak{R}}_2,\aleph)} \sqsubseteq \overline{\left[(\breve{\mathfrak{R}}_1,\aleph) \sqcup (\breve{\mathfrak{R}}_2,\aleph)\right]}$.

   Conversely, since $(\breve{\mathfrak{R}}_1,\aleph) \sqsubseteq \overline{(\breve{\mathfrak{R}}_1,\aleph)}$ and $(\breve{\mathfrak{R}}_2,\aleph) \sqsubseteq \overline{(\breve{\mathfrak{R}}_2,\aleph)}$, then $(\breve{\mathfrak{R}}_1,\aleph) \sqcup (\breve{\mathfrak{R}}_2,\aleph) \sqsubseteq \overline{(\breve{\mathfrak{R}}_1,\aleph)} \sqcup \overline{(\breve{\mathfrak{R}}_2,\aleph)}$. Furthermore, $\overline{\left[(\breve{\mathfrak{R}}_1,\aleph) \sqcup (\breve{\mathfrak{R}}_2,\aleph)\right]}$ is the smallest bipolar spherical fuzzy soft closed set that contains $(\breve{\mathfrak{R}}_1,\aleph) \sqcup (\breve{\mathfrak{R}}_2,\aleph)$. Therefore, $\overline{\left[(\breve{\mathfrak{R}}_1,\aleph) \sqcup (\breve{\mathfrak{R}}_2,\aleph)\right]} \sqsubseteq \overline{(\breve{\mathfrak{R}}_1,\aleph)} \sqcup \overline{(\breve{\mathfrak{R}}_2,\aleph)}$. Thus, $\overline{\left[(\breve{\mathfrak{R}}_1,\aleph) \sqcup (\breve{\mathfrak{R}}_2,\aleph)\right]} = \overline{(\breve{\mathfrak{R}}_1,\aleph)} \sqcup \overline{(\breve{\mathfrak{R}}_2,\aleph)}$.

5. Since $(\breve{\mathfrak{R}}_1,\aleph) \sqcap (\breve{\mathfrak{R}}_2,\aleph) \sqsubseteq \overline{(\breve{\mathfrak{R}}_1,\aleph)} \sqcap \overline{(\breve{\mathfrak{R}}_2,\aleph)}$ and $\overline{\left[(\breve{\mathfrak{R}}_1,\aleph) \sqcap (\breve{\mathfrak{R}}_2,\aleph)\right]}$ is the smallest bipolar spherical fuzzy soft closed set that containing $(\breve{\mathfrak{R}}_1,\aleph) \sqcap (\breve{\mathfrak{R}}_2,\aleph)$, then $\overline{\left[(\breve{\mathfrak{R}}_1,\aleph) \sqcap (\breve{\mathfrak{R}}_2,\aleph)\right]} \sqsubseteq \overline{(\breve{\mathfrak{R}}_1,\aleph)} \sqcap \overline{(\breve{\mathfrak{R}}_2,\aleph)}$.

□

Theorem 5. *Let* $(\Delta, \breve{\tau}, \aleph)$ *be a bipolar spherical fuzzy soft topological space over* Δ *and* $(\breve{\mathfrak{R}},\aleph) \in BSFS(\Delta,\aleph)$*. Then,*

1. $\left[\overline{(\breve{\mathfrak{R}},\aleph)}\right]^c = \left[(\breve{\mathfrak{R}},\aleph)^c\right]^\circ$,
2. $\left[(\breve{\mathfrak{R}},\aleph)^\circ\right]^c = \overline{\left[(\breve{\mathfrak{R}},\aleph)^c\right]}$.

Proof. 1. $\overline{(\breve{\mathfrak{R}},\aleph)} = \underset{i\in\omega}{\sqcap}\left\{(\breve{\mathfrak{R}}_i,\aleph) \in (\breve{\tau})^c : (\breve{\mathfrak{R}}_i,\aleph) \sqsupseteq (\breve{\mathfrak{R}},\aleph)\right\}$

$\Longrightarrow \left[\overline{(\breve{\mathfrak{R}},\aleph)}\right]^c = \left[\underset{i\in\omega}{\sqcap}\left\{(\breve{\mathfrak{R}}_i,\aleph) \in (\breve{\tau})^c : (\breve{\mathfrak{R}}_i,\aleph) \sqsupseteq (\breve{\mathfrak{R}},\aleph), \forall i \in \omega\right\}\right]^c =$
$\underset{i\in\omega}{\sqcup}\left\{(\breve{\mathfrak{R}}_i,\aleph)^c \in \overset{NSS}{\tau} : (\breve{\mathfrak{R}}_i,\aleph)^c \sqsubseteq (\breve{\mathfrak{R}},\aleph)^c\right\} = \left[(\breve{\mathfrak{R}},\aleph)^c\right]^\circ$.

2. $(\breve{\mathfrak{R}},\aleph)^\circ = \underset{i\in\omega}{\sqcup}\left\{(\breve{\mathfrak{R}}_i,\aleph) \in \breve{\tau} : (\breve{\mathfrak{R}}_i,\aleph) \sqsubseteq (\breve{\mathfrak{R}},\aleph)\right\}$

$$\Longrightarrow \left[\left(\breve{\Re},\aleph\right)^{\circ}\right]^{c} = \left[\bigsqcup_{i\in\omega}\left\{(\breve{\Re}_i,\aleph)\in \overset{NSS}{\tau} : (\breve{\Re}_i,\aleph)\sqsubseteq(\widetilde{\psi},\aleph)\right\}\right]^{c} =$$
$$\bigsqcap_{i\in\omega}\left\{(\breve{\Re}_i,\aleph)^{c}\in(\tau)^{c} : (\breve{\Re}_i,\aleph)^{c}\sqsupseteq\left(\breve{\Re},\aleph\right)^{c}\right\} = \overline{\left[\left(\breve{\Re},\aleph\right)^{c}\right]}.$$
□

5. Multi-Criteria Group Decision-Making Using Bipolar SFS-Topology

The operational procedure known as multi-criteria group decision-making (MCGDM) is used in commerce, industry, business, and other real-world settings. As part of the MCGDM branch of operation research, decision-makers assess several viable options in order to identify the best option and rate them from most to least preferred in order to determine which alternative is best.

5.1. BSFS-TOPSIS Method

Consider a GDM (group decision-making) procedure that includes a certain set of alternatives $T = \{t_1, t_2, \ldots, t_m\}$. Each alternative is evaluated under the set of parameters $\aleph = \{\alpha_1, \alpha_2, \ldots, \alpha_n\}$ by different experts $E = \{\Im_i : i = 1, \ldots, k\}$.

Step 1: Construct a weighted parameter matrix W by considering linguistic term from Table 2. That is

$$W = [\beta_{ij}]_{n\times m} = \begin{pmatrix} \beta_{11} & \beta_{12} & \beta_{13} & \cdots & \beta_{1m} \\ \beta_{21} & \beta_{22} & \beta_{23} & \cdots & \beta_{2m} \\ \vdots & \vdots & \vdots & \ddots & \vdots \\ \beta_{n1} & \beta_{n2} & \beta_{n3} & \cdots & \beta_{nm} \end{pmatrix} \tag{1}$$

Table 2. The Linguistic terms for alternatives.

Linguistic Terms	Weights
Most Risky (MR_1)	0.90
Medium Risky (MR_2)	0.80
Risky (R_1)	0.60
Low Risky (LR_1)	0.40
Least Risky (LR_2)	0.20
Riskless (R_2)	0.10

Step 2: Construct the wighted normalized matrix N as follows:

$$N = [\eta_{ij}]_{n\times m} = \begin{pmatrix} \eta_{11} & \eta_{12} & \eta_{13} & \cdots & \eta_{1m} \\ \eta_{21} & \eta_{22} & \eta_{23} & \cdots & \eta_{2m} \\ \vdots & \vdots & \vdots & \ddots & \vdots \\ \eta_{n1} & \eta_{n2} & \eta_{n3} & \cdots & \eta_{nm} \end{pmatrix} \tag{2}$$

where $\eta_{ij} = \beta_{ij}/\sqrt{\sum_{i=1}^{n}(\beta_{ij})^2}$.

Step 3: Compute the weight vector $P = \{\rho_1, \rho_2, \ldots, \rho_n\}$, where

$$\rho_i = \frac{\beta_i}{\sum\limits_{a=1}^{n}\beta_a}, \beta_i = \frac{1}{n}\sum_{i=1}^{n}\eta_{ij}. \tag{3}$$

Step 4: Construct BSFS decision matrices $\mathfrak{D}_i$ for each expert such that all $\mathfrak{D}_i$ make BSFS-topology and obtain an aggreating matris A.

$$\mathfrak{D}_i = [\theta^i_{jk}]_{l\times m} = \begin{pmatrix} \theta_{11} & \theta_{12} & \theta_{13} & \dots & \theta_{1m} \\ \theta_{21} & \theta_{22} & \theta_{23} & \dots & \theta_{2m} \\ \vdots & \vdots & \vdots & \ddots & \vdots \\ \theta_{l1} & \theta_{l2} & \theta_{l3} & \dots & \theta_{lm} \end{pmatrix} \tag{4}$$

where each θ_{jk} is a BSFS element. The aggregating matrix A can be obtained as follows:

$$A = \frac{1}{n}(\mathfrak{D}_1 + \mathfrak{D}_2 + \ldots + \mathfrak{D}_n) = [\theta_{jk}]_{l\times m} \tag{5}$$

where "+" is the matrix sum.

Step 5: Construct the weighted BSFS decision matrix $\mathfrak{B}$,

$$\mathfrak{B} = [\gamma_{jk}]_{l\times m} = \begin{pmatrix} \gamma_{11} & \gamma_{12} & \gamma_{13} & \dots & \gamma_{1m} \\ \gamma_{21} & \gamma_{22} & \gamma_{23} & \dots & \gamma_{2m} \\ \vdots & \vdots & \vdots & \ddots & \vdots \\ \gamma_{l1} & \gamma_{l2} & \gamma_{l3} & \dots & \gamma_{lm} \end{pmatrix} \tag{6}$$

where $\gamma_{jk} = \rho_i \cdot \theta_{jk}$ and each $\gamma_{jk} = \{\rho^+_{jk}, \omega^+_{jk}, \psi^+_{jk}, \rho^-_{jk}, \omega^-_{jk}, \psi^-_{jk}\}$.

Step 6: Obtain BSFS-valued positive ideal solution $(BSFS^+)$ and BSFS-valued negative ideal solution $(BSFS^-)$, where

$$\begin{aligned} BSFS^+ &= \{\overset{+}{\gamma}_1, \overset{+}{\gamma}_2, \ldots, \overset{+}{\gamma}_m\} \\ &= \{(\bigcup_j \gamma_{jk} : k \in \mathfrak{D}_1), (\bigcap_j \gamma_{jk} : k \in \mathfrak{D}_2; j \in l) \end{aligned} \tag{7}$$

$$\begin{aligned} BSFS^+ &= \{\bar{\gamma}_1, \bar{\gamma}_2, \ldots, \bar{\gamma}_m\} \\ &= \{(\bigcap_j \gamma_{jk} : k \in \mathfrak{D}_1), (\bigcup_j \gamma_{jk} : k \in \mathfrak{D}_2; j \in l) \end{aligned} \tag{8}$$

Step 7: Compute the BSFS separation measurement as follows:

$$d^+_j = \sqrt{\frac{1}{6l}\sum_{k=1}^{m}\begin{pmatrix} (\rho^+_{jk} - \overset{+}{\rho}{}^{+}_k)^2 + (\omega^+_{jk} - \overset{+}{\omega}{}^{+}_k)^2 + (\psi^+_{jk} - \overset{+}{\psi}{}^{+}_k)^2 + \\ (\rho^+_{jk} - \overset{+}{\rho}{}^{-}_k)^2 + (\omega^+_{jk} - \overset{+}{\omega}{}^{-}_k)^2 + (\psi^+_{jk} - \overset{+}{\psi}{}^{-}_k)^2 \end{pmatrix}} \tag{9}$$

$$d^-_j = \sqrt{\frac{1}{6l}\sum_{k=1}^{m}\begin{pmatrix} (\rho^+_{jk} - \bar{\rho}^{+}_k)^2 + (\omega^+_{jk} - \bar{\omega}^{+}_k)^2 + (\psi^+_{jk} - \bar{\psi}^{+}_k)^2 + \\ (\rho^+_{jk} - \bar{\rho}^{-}_k)^2 + (\omega^+_{jk} - \bar{\omega}^{-}_k)^2 + (\psi^+_{jk} - \bar{\psi}^{-}_k)^2 \end{pmatrix}} \tag{10}$$

Step 8: Compute the BSFS closeness coefficient of each alternative. Where

$$\mathfrak{C}_j = \frac{d^-_j}{d^+_j + d^-_j} \tag{11}$$

Step 9: Based on BSFS closeness coefficient and ranking of alternatives, the chosen order can be obtained by descending order.

Figure 2 shows a flow chart diagram of the proposed algorithm.

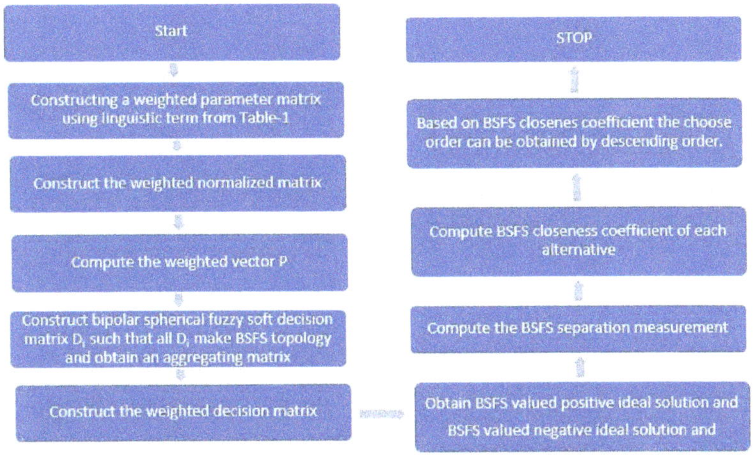

Figure 2. Flow chart diagram of proposed algorithm.

5.2. Illustrative Example

With the gear available today, an estimated 500,000 earthquakes are detected annually. One can detect about 100,000 of these. Nearly everywhere in the world, including California and Alaska in the United States, El Salvador, Mexico, Guatemala, Chile, Peru, Indonesia, the Philippines, Iran, Pakistan, the Azores in Portugal, Turkey, New Zealand, Greece, Italy, India, Nepal, and Japan, there are minor earthquakes happening on a regular basis. The ratio between magnitude and frequency of earthquakes is exponential; for instance, earthquakes of magnitude 4 occur around 10 times more frequently in a given time period than earthquakes of magnitude 5. For instance, it has been shown that the typical recurrences in the (low seismicity) United Kingdom are an earthquake measuring 3.7 to 4.6 every year, an earthquake measuring 4.7 to 5.5 every 10 years, and an earthquake measuring 5.6 or bigger every 100 years. The Gutenberg-Richter law may be seen in action here.

Buildings can be classified as soft-story, tilt-up, steel moment frame, or non-ductile concrete. Apartment complexes that include open parking on the bottom floor and residential units on the upper floors frequently have soft-story constructions. Other building types (retail, commercial) may have windows surrounding the soft story ground floor that do not give any structural support, making the structures incredibly susceptible to collapsing during a strong earthquake.

The construction of tilt-up structures involves pouring the building's walls on the spot and then levitating or "tilting" the panels into place. This technique was widely used in new commercial construction in California and across the country.

Prior to 1994, many tilt-up structures were designed with few or weak connections, which have been shown to fail after an earthquake, resulting in significant damage and/or collapse. Seismic retrofitting may readily fix these structural flaws.

Steel moment frame buildings employ a strong steel frame of beams joined to columns to support the various storeys of the building. At the welded connections between the beams and the columns, these constructions can withstand brittle fraying of the steel frames. The moment frames may be vulnerable to collapse in a significant earthquake is if they show fractures and fissures.

Concrete walls, columns, and/or frames support non-ductile concrete buildings' concrete floors and/or roofs. These buildings run the danger of collapsing during an earthquake due to their stiff design and insufficient ability to absorb the energy of significant ground shaking.

In this section, a risk analysis will be made in terms of different building alternatives by using parameters such as soft-story (α_1), tilt-up (α_2), steel moment frame (α_3), non-ductile concrete (α_4), and the proposed BSFS-topsis method. Suppose $T = \{t_1, t_2, t_3, t_4\}$ is the set of alternatives for risk assessment. Suppose $\aleph = \{\alpha_1, \alpha_2, \alpha_3, \alpha_4\}$ is the set of parameters or criterions and $E = \{\Im_1, \Im_2, \Im_3, \Im_4\}$ is the set of experts.

Step 1: Construct a weighted BFSF parameter matrix W by using (1),

$$W = [\beta_{ij}]_{4\times4} = \begin{pmatrix} 0.90 & 0.10 & 0.40 & 0.60 \\ 0.10 & 0.20 & 0.90 & 0.10 \\ 0.10 & 0.80 & 0.20 & 0.60 \\ 0.40 & 0.10 & 0.80 & 0.90 \end{pmatrix}$$

Step 2: The weighted normalized matrix N is constructed by using (2).

$$N = [\eta_{ij}]_{4\times4} = \begin{pmatrix} 0.90 & 0.12 & 0.31 & 0.48 \\ 0.10 & 0.24 & 0.70 & 0.08 \\ 0.10 & 0.96 & 0.16 & 0.48 \\ 0.40 & 0.12 & 0.62 & 0.73 \end{pmatrix}$$

Step 3: By using (3), the weight vector given parameters are computed as $P = \{0.19, 0.28, 0.26, 0.20\}$.

Step 4: The BSFS-decision matrix $\mathfrak{D}_i$ of each expert is provided, in which each row represents parameters and each column represents alternative buildings, and all $\mathfrak{D}_i$ make BNS-topology.

$$\mathfrak{D}_3 = \begin{Bmatrix} 0,0,1,-1,0,0 & 0,0,1,-1,0,0 & 0,0,1,-1,0,0 & 0,0,1,-1,0,0 \\ 0,0,1,-1,0,0 & 0,0,1,-1,0,0 & 0,0,1,-1,0,0 & 0,0,1,-1,0,0 \\ 0,0,1,-1,0,0 & 0,0,1,-1,0,0 & 0,0,1,-1,0,0 & 0,0,1,-1,0,0 \\ 0,0,1,-1,0,0 & 0,0,1,-1,0,0 & 0,0,1,-1,0,0 & 0,0,1,-1,0,0 \end{Bmatrix},$$

$$\mathfrak{D}_4 = \begin{Bmatrix} 1,0,0,0,0,-1 & 1,0,0,0,0,-1 & 1,0,0,0,0,-1 & 1,0,0,0,0,-1 \\ 1,0,0,0,0,-1 & 1,0,0,0,0,-1 & 1,0,0,0,0,-1 & 1,0,0,0,0,-1 \\ 1,0,0,0,0,-1 & 1,0,0,0,0,-1 & 1,0,0,0,0,-1 & 1,0,0,0,0,-1 \\ 1,0,0,0,0,-1 & 1,0,0,0,0,-1 & 1,0,0,0,0,-1 & 1,0,0,0,0,-1 \end{Bmatrix}$$

The aggregated matrix A is obtained by using (5).

$$\mathfrak{D}_1 = \left\{ \begin{array}{llll} 0.3, 0.2, 0.6, -0.1, -0.5, -0.7 & 0.4, 0.5, 0.6, -0.5, -0.4, -0.4 & 0, 3, 0.5, 0.6, -0.1, -0.4, -0.5 & 0.2, 0.7, 0.4, -0.3, -0.4, -0.3 \\ 0.6, 0.7, 0.2, -0.6, -0.4, -0.2 & 0.5, 0.3, 0.4, -0.3, -0.5, -0.6 & 0.4, 0.7, 0.3, -0.2, -0.6, -0.4 & 0.5, 0.2, 0.4, -0.2, -0.4, -0.2 \\ 0.3, 0.4, 0.7, -0.1, -0.5, -0.1 & 0.6, 0.1, 0.2, -0.5, -0.4, -0.2 & 0.8, 0.1, 0.2, -0.3, -0.1, -0.4 & 0.7, 0.2, 0.3, -0.5, -0.6, -0.1 \\ 0.2, 0.4, 0.6, -0.2, -0.3, -0.1 & 0.7, 0.3, 0.1, -0.2, -0.5, -0.3 & 0.9, 0.1, 0.2, -0.5, -0.3, -0.1 & 0.7, 0.2, 0.6, -0.6, -0.4, -0.7 \end{array} \right\},$$

$$\mathfrak{D}_2 = \left\{ \begin{array}{llll} 0.2, 0.1, 0.8, -0.4, -0.6, -0.4 & 0.3, 0.2, 0.4, -0.6, -0.5, -0.2 & 0.1, 0.3, 0.7, -0.4, -0.5, -0.2 & 0.1, 0.5, 0.6, -0.4, -0.5, -0.2 \\ 0.4, 0.4, 0.4, -0.7, -0.5, -0.1 & 0.4, 0.2, 0.5, -0.4, -0.6, -0.2 & 0.3, 0.6, 0.4, -0.4, -0.7, -0.1 & 0.3, 0.1, 0.6, -0.3, -0.6, -0.1 \\ 0.2, 0.2, 0.8, -0.6, -0.4, -0.1 & 0.4, 0.1, 0.5, -0.6, -0.5, -0.1 & 0.3, 0.1, 0.6, -0.5, -0.4, -0.2 & 0.5, 0.1, 0.5, -0.6, -0.6, -0.6 \\ 0.1, 0.3, 0.8, -0.4, -0.5, -0.1 & 0.6, 0.2, 0.6, -0.4, -0.7, -0.2 & 0.8, 0.1, 0.3, -0.6, -0.4, -0.1 & 0.6, 0.1, 0.7, -0.7, -0.5, -0.3 \end{array} \right\},$$

$$A = \left\{ \begin{array}{llll} 0.375, 0.075, 0.600, -0.375, -0.275, -0.525 & 0.425, 0.175, 0.500, -0.525, -0.225, -0.400 & 0.350, 0.200, 0.575, -0.375, -0.225, -0.425 & 0, 325, 0.300, 0.500, -0.425, -0.025, -0.225 \\ 0.500, 0.275, 0.400, -0.575, -0.225, -0.325 & 0.475, 0.125, 0.475, -0.425, -0.275, -0.350 & 0.425, 0.325, 0.425, -0.400, -0.325, -0.375 & 0.450, 0.075, 0.500, -0.375, -0, 250, -0.325 \\ 0.375, 0.150, 0, 625, -0.425, -0.225, -0.300 & 0.500, 0.050, 0.425, -0.525, -0.225, -0.325 & 0.525, 0.050, 0.450, -0.450, -0.125, -0.400 & 0.550, 0.075, 0.450, -0.525, -0, 300, -0.300 \\ 0.325, 0.175, 0, 600, -0.400, -0.200, -0.300 & 0.575, 0.125, 0.425, -0.400, -0.300, -0.375 & 0.675, 0.050, 0.375, -0.525, -0.175, -0.300 & 0.575, 0.075, 0.575, -0.575, -0, 225, -0.500 \end{array} \right\}$$

$$\mathfrak{B} = \left\{ \begin{array}{llll} 0.071, 0.014, 0.113, -0.071, -0.052, -0.099 & 0.117, 0.048, 0.138, -0.145, -0.062, -0.110 & 0.092, 0.053, 0.151, -0.099, -0.059, -0.112 & 0.065, 0.060, 0.101, -0.086, -0.005, -0.045 \\ 0.094, 0.052, 0.075, -0.108, -0.042, -0.061 & 0.131, 0.034, 0.131, -0.117, -0.076, -0.097 & 0.112, 0.086, 0.112, -0.105, -0.086, -0.099 & 0.091, 0.015, 0.101, -0.076, -0.050, -0.065 \\ 0.071, 0.028, 0.118, -0.080, -0.042, -0.057 & 0.138, 0.014, 0.117, -0.145, -0.062, -0.090 & 0.138, 0.013, 0.118, -0.118, -0.033, -0.105 & 0.111, 0.015, 0.091, -0.106, -0.060, -0.060 \\ 0.061, 0.033, 0.113, -0.075, -0.038, -0.057 & 0.159, 0.034, 0.117, -0.110, -0.083, -0.103 & 0.178, 0.013, 0.099, -0.138, -0.046, -0.079 & 0.116, 0.015, 0.116, -0.116, -0.045, -0.101 \end{array} \right\}$$

Step 5: Construct the weighted BSFS decision matrix $\mathfrak{B}$ by using (6).

Step 6: Obtain BSFS-valued positive ideal solution ($BSFS^+$) and BSFS-valued negative ideal solution ($BSFS^-$) by using (7) and (8) as

$$BSFS^+ = \left\{ \begin{array}{l} \langle 0.094, 0.052, 0.075, -0.071, -0.038, -0.099 \rangle, \langle 0.159, 0.048, 0.117, -0.110, -0.062, -0.110 \rangle \\ \langle 0.178, 0.086, 0.099, -0.099, -0.033, -0.112 \rangle, \langle 0.116, 0.060, 0.091, -0.076, -0.005, -0.101 \rangle \end{array} \right\}$$

$$BSFS^- = \left\{ \begin{array}{l} \langle 0.061, 0.014, 0.118, -0.108, -0.052, -0.057 \rangle, \langle 0.117, 0.014, 0.138, -0.145, -0.083, -0.090 \rangle \\ \langle 0.092, 0.013, 0.151, -0.138, -0.086, -0.079 \rangle, \langle 0.065, 0.015, 0.116, -0.116, -0.060, -0.045 \rangle \end{array} \right\}$$

Step 7: The BSFS separation measurements are computed as

$$\begin{array}{ll} d_1^+ = 0.062 & d_1^- = 0.051 \\ d_2^+ = 0.053 & d_2^- = 0.052 \\ d_3^+ = 0.061 & d_3^- = 0.043 \\ d_4^+ = 0.053 & d_4^- = 0.059 \end{array}$$

Step 8: Using Equation (11), compute the BSFS closeness coefficients of each alternatives,

$$\begin{array}{rcl} \mathfrak{C}_1 & = & 0.454 \\ \mathfrak{C}_2 & = & 0.496 \\ \mathfrak{C}_3 & = & 0.410 \\ \mathfrak{C}_4 & = & 0.525 \end{array}$$

Step 9: The rating order of given alternatives are shown as

$$\mathfrak{C}_3 < \mathfrak{C}_1 < \mathfrak{C}_2 < \mathfrak{C}_4$$

which corresponds to the alternatives $t_4 > t_2 > t_1 > t_3$. Therefore, as a result of the evaluation among the alternatives, the most risky structure is t_4. Figure 3 shows ranking of alternatives based on closeness coefficients.

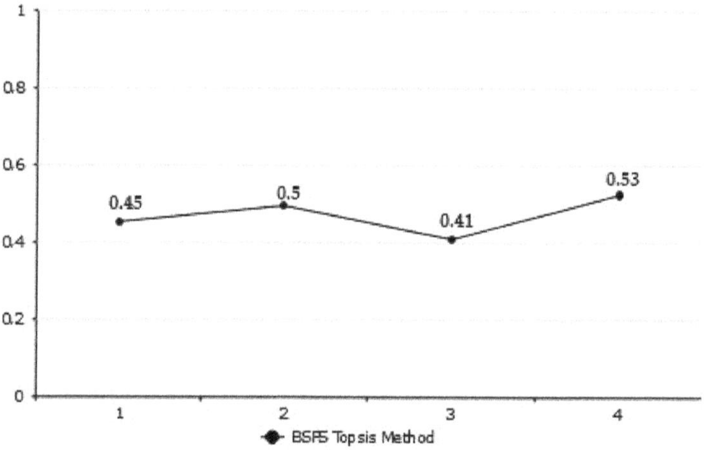

Figure 3. Ranking of alternatives.

6. Comparison of Proposed Method

In the context of the case studied in this paper, we found that the TOPSIS method is suitable for cautious decision-makers, whereas the other methods are suitable for situations in a which decision-maker would want to maximize profit, and the risk of decisions is less important for them. Experts, without a doubt, prefer discrete decisions. In buildings, the risk factor is the most important. Building similarities are important because of similarities in different construction methods. As a result, we conclude that the TOPSIS method is better suited to the problem at hand. Thus, in this paper, a revised discrete TOPSIS method is fostered in a bipolar spherical fuzzy soft topological environment. In this part, we compare the proposed TOPSIS technique to TOPSIS established on different extensions of fuzzy sets on the basis of sets. The TOPSIS defined on fuzzy soft set [64], intuitionistic fuzzy set [65], and spherical fuzzy set [62] comparative analysis is covered. We examine several things and we compare all of these TOPSIS methods. First off, these techniques fall short in capturing decision-making bipolarity, a crucial component of human thought and behaviour. Bipolar thinking is crucial for evaluating evidence throughout a certain time span in decision-making. Second, the process does not ensure agreement among the views of the decision-makers. The benefits of the suggested strategy are outlined below.

1. The suggested method takes truthness, falsehood, and indeterminacy into account while evaluating the positive and negative aspects of each particular characteristic (soft set parameters). This combination is more versatile and effective at handling issues with aggressive decision-making.
2. To obtain a sound choice, the topological structure fosters harmony among group decision-makers.
3. Topology introduction on BSFS appears to be crucial in both theoretical and real-world contexts.
4. To handle complicated decision-making situations, TOPSIS in conjunction with the aforementioned framework makes complete sense.

7. Conclusions

Following fuzzy set theory, bipolarity, spherical fuzzy, and soft set theory has emerged as a major theory to address the shortcomings of classical set theory. The spherical fuzzy soft set model is the most generalized of any extant fuzzy soft set model. This new notion is more exact, accurate, and reasonable, and the models may therefore solve a wide range of issues more effectively and realistically. In this study, firstly, the bipolar spherical fuzzy soft set structure and some basic concepts on this structure are defined. Topological structure on bipolar spherical fuzzy soft sets (BSFSs) offers a novel method to computational intelligence, data analysis, and fuzzy modeling. This paper covers a wide range of BSFS-topology-related issues. The concepts of BSFS union, BSFSS intersection, null BSFS, and absolute BSFS are used to build BSFS-topology. Meanwhile, several BSFS-topology elements, such as BSFS open sets, BSFS-closed sets, the BSFS interior, the BSFS closure, and so on, are described. A variety of relevant examples and proofs are provided to further explain the notion. BSFS-topology is a soft topology and image fuzzy topology extension. We illustrate two real-world MCGDM applications, employing BSFSs and BSFS topologies using the well-known and commonly used approach, TOPSIS. The proper algorithms and graphics are supplied to make the process easier to visualize. In this study, risk analysis of today's buildings against earthquakes was made by TOPSIS method according to various parameters. Although this paper concentrates on hybrid sets of fuzzy sets, it may be extended to other types of structures as well. Science and medical, information processing, machine learning, automation, signal processing, as well as industry, finance, and development studies are all conceivable application fields. Following the review of this research, it is predicted that further research on the issue will be conducted.

Funding: This research received no external funding.

Data Availability Statement: Not applicable.

Conflicts of Interest: The author declares no conflict of interest.

References

1. Zadeh, L.A. Fuzzy sets. *Inf. Control* **1965**, *8*, 338–353. [CrossRef]
2. Gau, W.L.; Buehrer, D.J. Vague sets. *IEEE Trans. Syst. Man Cybern. Syst.* **1993**, *23*, 610–614. [CrossRef]
3. Atanassov, K.T. Operators over interval valued intuitionistic fuzzy sets. *Fuzzy Sets Syst.* **1994**, *64*, 159–174. [CrossRef]

4. Atanassov, K.T. Intuitionistic fuzzy sets. *Fuzzy Sets Syst.* **1986**, *20*, 87–96. [CrossRef]
5. Atanassov, K.T.; Gargov, G. Interval valued intuitionistic fuzzy sets. *Fuzzy Sets Syst.* **1989**, *31*, 343–349. [CrossRef]
6. Yager, R.R. Pythagorean fuzzy subsets. In Proceedings of the IFSA World Congress and NAFIPS Annual Meeting (IFSA/NAFIPS), Edmonton, AL, Canada, 24–28 June 2013; pp. 57–61.
7. Cuong, B.C.; Kreinovich, V. Picture fuzzy sets-a new concept for computational intelligence problems. In Proceedings of the 2013 World Congress on Information and Communication Technologies (WICT 2013), Hanoi, Vietnam, 15–18 December 2013; pp. 1–6.
8. Ullah, K. Picture fuzzy maclaurin symmetric mean operators and their applications in solving multiattribute decision-making problems. *Math. Probl. Eng.* **2021**, *13*, 1098631. [CrossRef]
9. Gundogdu, F.K.; Duleba, S.; Moslem, S.; Aydın, S. Evaluating public transport service quality using picture fuzzy analytic hierarchy process and linear assignment model. *Appl. Soft Comput.* **2021**, *100*, 106920. [CrossRef]
10. Moslem, S.; Gul, M.; Farooq, D.; Celik, E.; Ghorbanzadeh, O.; Blaschke, T. An Integrated Approach of Best-Worst Method (BWM) and Triangular Fuzzy Sets for Evaluating Driver Behavior Factors Related to Road Safety. *Mathematics* **2020**, *8*, 414. [CrossRef]
11. Ortega, J.; Tóth, J.; Moslem, S.; Péter, T.; Duleba, S. An Integrated Approach of Analytic Hierarchy Process and Triangular Fuzzy Sets for Analyzing the Park-and-Ride Facility Location Problem. *Symmetry* **2020**, *12*, 1225. [CrossRef]
12. Moslem, S.; Ghorbanzadeh, O.; Blaschke, T.; Duleba, S. Analysing Stakeholder Consensus for a Sustainable Transport Development Decision by the Fuzzy AHP and Interval AHP. *Sustainability* **2019**, *11*, 3271. [CrossRef]
13. Ullah, K.; Mahmood, T.; Jan, N.; Ahmad, Z. Policy decision making based on some averaging aggregation operators of t-SFS; a multi-attribute decision making approach. *Ann. Optim. Theory Pract.* **2020**, *3*, 69–92.
14. Mahmood, T.; Ullah, K.; Khan, Q.; Jan, N. An approach toward decision-making and medical diagnosis problems using the concept of spherical fuzzy sets. *Neural Comput. Appl.* **2019**, *31*, 7041–7053. [CrossRef]
15. Akram, M.; Kahraman, C.; Zahid, K. Group decision making based on complex spherical fuzzy VIKOR approach. *Knowl. Based Syst.* **2021**, *216*, 106793. [CrossRef]
16. Zhang, W.R. Bipolar fuzzy sets and relations: A computational framework for cognitive modeling and multiagent decision analysis. In Proceedings of the IEEE Conference Fuzzy Information Processing Society Biannual Conference, San Antonio, TX, USA, 18–21 December 1994; pp. 305–309.
17. Lee, K.M. Bipolar-valued fuzzy sets and their basic operations. In Proceedings of the International Conference, Bangkok, Thailand, 9–13 October 2000; pp. 307–317.
18. Lee, K.M.; Lee, K.M.; Cios, K.J. Comparison of interval-valued fuzzy sets, intuitionistic fuzzy sets, and bipolar-valued fuzzy sets. *J. Fuzzy Logic Intell. Syst.* **2004**, *14*, 125–129.
19. Bosc, P.; Pivert, O. On a fuzzy bipolar relational algebra. *Inf. Sci.* **2013**, *219*, 1–16. [CrossRef]
20. Kahraman, C.; Gündogdu, F.K. From 1D to 3D membership: Spherical fuzzy sets. In Proceedings of the BOS/SOR2018 Conference, Warsaw, Poland, 24–26 September 2018.
21. Ashraf, S.; Abdullah, S.; Mahmood, T.; Ghani, F.; Mahmood, T.T. Spherical fuzzy sets and their applications in multi-attribute decision making problems. *J. Intell. Fuzzy Syst.* **2019**, *36*, 2829–2844. [CrossRef]
22. Ashraf, S.; Abdullah, S.; Aslam, M.; Qiyas, M.; Kutbi, M.A. Spherical fuzzy sets and its representation of spherical fuzzy t-norms and t-conorms. *J. Intell. Fuzzy. Syst.* **2019**, *36*, 6089–6102. [CrossRef]
23. Rafiq, M.; Ashraf, S.; Abdullah, S.; Mahmood, T.; Muhammad, S. The cosine similarity measuresof spherical fuzzy sets and their applications in decision making. *J. Intell. Fuzzy Syst.* **2019**, *36*, 6059–6073. [CrossRef]
24. Gündoğdu, F.K.; Kahraman, C. Spherical fuzzy sets and spherical fuzzy TOPSIS method. *J. Intell. Fuzzy Syst.* **2019**, *36*, 337–352. [CrossRef]
25. Boltürk, E. AS/RS Technology selection using spherical fuzzy TOPSIS and neutrosophic TOPSIS. In Proceedings of the International Conference on Intelligent and Fuzzy Systems, Istanbul, Turkey, 23–25 July 2019; pp. 969–976.
26. Zeng, S.; Hussain, A.; Mahmood, T.; Irfan Ali, M.; Ashraf, S.; Munir, M. Covering-Based Spherical Fuzzy Rough Set Model Hybrid with TOPSIS for Multi-Attribute Decision-Making. *Symmetry* **2019**, *11*, 547. [CrossRef]
27. Mathew, M.; Chakrabortty, R.K.; Ryan, M.J. A novel approach integrating AHP and TOPSIS under spherical fuzzy sets for advanced manufacturing system selection. *Eng. Appl. Artif. Intell.* **2020**, *96*, 103988. [CrossRef]
28. Akram, M.; Kahraman, C.; Zahid, K. Extension of TOPSIS model to the decision-making under complex spherical fuzzy information. *Soft Comput.* **2021**, *25*, 10771–10795. [CrossRef]
29. Khan, Q.; Mahmood, T.; Ullah, K. Applications of improved spherical fuzzy Dombi aggregation operators in decision support system. *Soft Comput.* **2021**, *25*, 9097–9119. [CrossRef]
30. Gundogdu, F.K.; Kahraman, C. A novel fuzzy TOPSIS method using emerging interval-valued spherical fuzzy sets. *Eng. Appl. Artif. Intell.* **2019**, *85*, 307–323. [CrossRef]
31. Duleba, S.; Kutlu Gündoğdu, F.; Moslem, S. Interval-valued spherical fuzzy analytic hierarchy process method to evaluate public transportation development. *Informatica* **2021**, *32*, 661–686. [CrossRef]
32. Kahraman, C.; Gundogdu, F.K. From Ordinary Fuzzy Sets to Spherical Fuzzy Sets. In *Decision Making with Spherical Fuzzy Sets*; Springer: Cham, Switzerland, 2021; pp. ix–xxvi. [CrossRef]
33. Molodtsov, D. Soft set theory-first results. *Comput. Math. Appl.* **1999**, *37*, 19–31. [CrossRef]
34. Maji, P.K.; Biswas, R.; Roy, A.R. An application of soft sets in a decision making problem. *Comput. Math. Appl.* **2022**, *44*, 1077–1083. [CrossRef]

35. Pawlak, Z. Rough sets. *Int. J. Inf. Comput. Sci.* **1982**, *11*, 341–356. [CrossRef]
36. Maji, P.K.; Biswas, R.; Roy, A.R. Fuzzy soft sets. *J. Fuzzy Math.* **2001**, *9*, 589–602.
37. Majumdar, P.; Samanta, S.K. Generalised fuzzy soft sets. *Comput. Math. Appl.* **2010**, *59*, 1425–1432. [CrossRef]
38. Garg, H.; Arora, R. Generalized and group-based generalized intuitionistic fuzzy soft sets with applications in decision-making. *Appl. Intell.* **2018**, *48*, 343–356. [CrossRef]
39. Maji, P.K.; Biswas, R.; Roy, A.R. Intuitionistic fuzzy soft sets. *J. Fuzzy Math.* **2001**, *9*, 677–692.
40. Yolcu, A.; Öztürk, T.Y. Some new results of pythagorean fuzzy soft topological spaces. *TWMS J. Appl. Eng. Math.* **2022**, *12*, 1107–1122.
41. Yolcu, A.; Smarandache, F.; Öztürk, T.Y. Intuitionistic fuzzy hypersoft sets. *Commun. Fac. Sci. Univ. Ank. Ser. A1 Math. Stat.* **2021**, *70*, 443–455. [CrossRef]
42. Yolcu, A.; Öztürk, T.Y. Fuzzy hypersoft sets and it's application to decision-making. In *Theory and Application of Hypersoft Set*; Pons Publishing House: Brussels, Belgium, 2021; pp. 50–64.
43. Khalil, A.M.; Li, S.G.; Garg, H.; Li, H.; Ma, S. New operations on interval-valued picture fuzzy set, interval-valued picture fuzzy soft set and their applications. *IEEE Access* **2019**, *7*, 51236–51253. [CrossRef]
44. Perveen, F.; Sunil, J.J.; Babitha, K.V.; Garg, H. Spherical fuzzy soft sets and its applications in decision-making problems. *J. Intell. Fuzzy Syst.* **2019**, *37*, 8237–8250. [CrossRef]
45. Perveen, P.A.; Sunil, J.J. A similarity measure of spherical fuzzy soft sets and its application. *Aip Conf. Proc.* **2021**, *2336*, 040009.
46. Chang, C.L. Fuzzy topological spaces. *J. Math. Anal. Appl.* **1968**, *24*, 182–190. [CrossRef]
47. Lowen, R. Fuzzy topological spaces and fuzzy compactness. *J. Math. Anal. Appl.* **1976**, *56*, 621–633. [CrossRef]
48. Çoker, D. An introduction to intuitionistic fuzzy topological spaces. *Fuzzy Sets Syst.* **1997**, *88*, 81–89. [CrossRef]
49. Çoker, D.; Haydar Es, A. On fuzzy compactness in intuitionistic fuzzy topological spaces. *J. Fuzzy Math.* **1995**, *3*, 899–910.
50. Çoker, D.; Turanli, N. Fuzzy connectedness in intuitionistic fuzzy topological spaces. *Fuzzy Sets Syst.* **2000**, *116*, 369–375.
51. Olgun, M.; Unver, M.; Yardimci, S. Pythagorean fuzzy topological spaces. *Complex Intell. Syst.* **2019**, *5*, 177–183. [CrossRef]
52. Kiruthika, M.; Angavelu, P. A link between topology and soft topology. *Hacet. J. Math. Stat.* **2019**, *48*, 800–804. [CrossRef]
53. Dizman, T.S.; Öztürk, T.Y. Fuzzy bipolar soft topological spaces. *TWMS J. Appl. Eng. Math.* **2021**, *11*, 151–159.
54. Öztürk, T.Y. On bipolar soft topological spaces. *J. New Theory* **2018**, *20*, 64–75.
55. Öztürk, T.Y. On bipolar soft points. *TWMS J. Appl. Eng. Math.* **2020**, *10*, 877–885.
56. Tanay, B.; Kandemir, M.B. Topological structure of fuzzy soft sets. *Comput. Math. Appl.* **2011**, *61*, 2952–2957. [CrossRef]
57. Yolcu, A.; Öztürk, T.Y. On fuzzy hypersoft topological spaces. *Caucasian J. Sci.* **2022**, *9*, 1–19. [CrossRef]
58. Osmanoglu, I.; Tokat, D. On intuitionistic Fuzzy soft topology. *Gen. Math. Notes* **2013**, *19*, 59–70.
59. Riaz, M.; Naeem, K.; Aslam, M.; Afzal, D.; Almahdi, F.A.A.; Jamal, S.S. Multi-criteria group decision making with Pythagorean fuzzy soft topology. *J. Intell. Fuzzy Syst.* **2020**, *39*, 6703–6720. [CrossRef]
60. Alshammari, I.; Parimala, M.; Ozel, C.; Riaz, M. Spherical Linear Diophantine Fuzzy TOPSIS Algorithm for Green Supply Chain Management System. *J. Funct. Spaces* **2022**, *12*, 3136462. [CrossRef]
61. Riaz, M.; Tanveer, S.; Pamucar, D.; Qin, D.S. Topological Data Analysis with Spherical Fuzzy Soft AHP-TOPSIS for Environmental Mitigation System. *Mathematics* **2022**, *10*, 1826. [CrossRef]
62. Garg, H.; Perveen, P.A.F.; John, S.J.; Perez-Dominguez, L. Spherical Fuzzy Soft Topology and Its Application in Group Decision-Making Problems. *Math. Probl. Eng.* **2022**, *2022*, 1007133. [CrossRef]
63. Princy, R.; Mohana, K. Spherical bipolar fuzzy sets and its application in multi criteria decision making problem. *J. New Theory* **2019**, *32*, 58–70.
64. Eraslan, F.; Karaasalan, F. A group decision making method based on TOPSIS under fuzzy soft environment. *J. New Theory* **2015**, *3*, 30–40.
65. Nan, J.; Wang, T.; An, J. Intuitionistic fuzzy distance based TOPSIS method and application to MADM. *Int. J. Fuzzy Syst. Appl.* **2016**, *5*, 43–56. [CrossRef]

MDPI AG
Grosspeteranlage 5
4052 Basel
Switzerland
Tel.: +41 61 683 77 34

Symmetry Editorial Office
E-mail: symmetry@mdpi.com
www.mdpi.com/journal/symmetry

www.ingramcontent.com/pod-product-compliance
Lightning Source LLC
Chambersburg PA
CBHW041935260926
51850CB00018B/182
* 9 7 8 3 7 2 5 8 5 3 3 1 1 *